PHILIP'S

ATLAS
OF THE
WORLD

PAPERBACK EDITION

Published in Great Britain in 1994
by George Philip Limited,
an imprint of Reed Consumer Books Limited,
Michelin House, 81 Fulham Road, London SW3 6RB,
and Auckland, Melbourne, Singapore and Toronto

Cartography by Philip's

Copyright © 1994 Reed International Books Limited

ISBN 0-540-05828-9

A CIP catalogue record for this book is available
from the British Library

Printed in China

PHILIP'S

ATLAS OF THE WORLD

PAPERBACK EDITION

CONTENTS

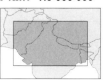

v

World Statistics: Countries

This alphabetical list includes the principal countries and territories of the world. If a territory is not completely independent, then the country it is associated with is named. The area figures give the total area of land, inland water and ice. Units for areas and populations are thousands. The annual income is the Gross National Product per capita in US dollars. The figures are the latest available, usually 1993.

Country/Territory	Area km² Thousands	Area miles² Thousands	Population Thousands	Capital	Annual Income US $
Afghanistan	648	250	19,062	Kabul	450
Albania	28.8	11.1	3,363	Tirana	1,000
Algeria	2,382	920	26,346	Algiers	1,980
American Samoa (US)	0.20	0.08	50	Pago Pago	6,000
Andorra	0.45	0.17	58	Andorra la Vella	–
Angola	1,247	481	10,609	Luanda	620
Anguilla (UK)	0.09	0.04	9	The Valley	–
Antigua & Barbuda	0.44	0.17	66	St John's	4,770
Argentina	2,767	1,068	33,101	Buenos Aires	2,790
Armenia	29.8	11.5	3,677	Yerevan	2,150
Aruba (Neths)	0.19	0.07	62	Oranjestad	6,000
Australia	7,687	2,968	17,529	Canberra	17,050
Austria	83.9	32.4	7,884	Vienna	20,140
Azerbaijan	86.6	33.4	7,398	Baku	1,670
Azores (Port.)	2.2	0.87	260	Ponta Delgada	–
Bahamas	13.9	5.4	262	Nassau	11,750
Bahrain	0.68	0.26	533	Manama	7,130
Bangladesh	144	56	119,288	Dacca	200
Barbados	0.43	0.17	259	Bridgetown	6,630
Belau (US)	0.46	0.18	16	Koror	–
Belgium	30.5	11.8	9,998	Brussels	18,950
Belize	23	8.9	198	Belmopan	2,010
Belorussia	207.6	80.1	10,297	Minsk	3,110
Benin	113	43	4,889	Porto-Novo	380
Bermuda (UK)	0.05	0.02	62	Hamilton	25,000
Bhutan	47	18.1	1,612	Thimphu	180
Bolivia	1,099	424	7,832	La Paz/Sucre	650
Bosnia-Herzegovina	51.2	19.8	4,366	Sarajevo	–
Botswana	582	225	1,373	Gaborone	2,590
Brazil	8,512	3,286	156,275	Brasilia	2,940
Brit. Antarctic Terr. (UK)	1,709	660	0.3	Stanley	–
Brit. Ind. Ocean Terr. (UK)	0.08	0.03	3	–	–
Brunei	5.8	2.2	270	Bandar Seri Begawan	6,000
Bulgaria	111	43	8,963	Sofia	1,840
Burkina Faso	274	106	9,490	Ouagadougou	290
Burma (Myanmar)	679	262	43,668	Rangoon	500
Burundi	27.8	10.7	5,786	Bujumbura	210
Cambodia	181	70	9,054	Phnom Penh	300
Cameroon	475	184	12,198	Yaoundé	850
Canada	9,976	3,852	27,562	Ottawa	20,440
Canary Is. (Spain)	7.3	2.8	1,700	Las Palmas/Santa Cruz	–
Cape Verde Is.	4	1.6	384	Praia	750
Cayman Is. (UK)	0.26	0.10	29	Georgetown	–
Central African Republic	623	241	3,173	Bangui	390
Chad	1,284	496	5,961	Ndjamena	220
Chile	757	292	13,599	Santiago	2,160
China	9,597	3,705	1,187,997	Beijing (Peking)	370
Colombia	1,139	440	33,424	Bogotá	1,260
Comoros	2.2	0.86	585	Moroni	500
Congo	342	132	2,368	Brazzaville	1,120
Costa Rica	51.1	19.7	3,099	San José	1,850
Croatia	56.5	21.8	4,764	Zagreb	1,800
Cuba	111	43	10,822	Havana	3,000
Cyprus	9.3	3.6	716	Nicosia	8,640
Czech Republic	78.9	30.4	10,299	Prague	2,370
Denmark	43.1	16.6	5,170	Copenhagen	23,700
Djibouti	23.2	9	467	Djibouti	1,000
Dominica	0.75	0.29	72	Roseau	2,440
Dominican Republic	48.7	18.8	7,471	Santo Domingo	950
Ecuador	284	109	10,741	Quito	1,020
Egypt	1,001	387	55,163	Cairo	620
El Salvador	21	8.1	5,396	San Salvador	1,070
Equatorial Guinea	28.1	10.8	369	Malabo	330
Eritrea	94	36	3,500	Asmera	–
Estonia	44.7	17.3	1,542	Tallinn	3,830
Ethiopia	1,128	436	55,117	Addis Ababa	120
Falkland Is. (UK)	12.2	4.7	2	Stanley	–
Faroe Is. (Den.)	1.4	0.54	47	Tórshavn	23,660
Fiji	18.3	7.1	739	Suva	1,930
Finland	338	131	5,042	Helsinki	23,980
France	552	213	57,372	Paris	20,380
French Guiana (Fr.)	90	34.7	104	Cayenne	2,500
French Polynesia (Fr.)	4	1.5	207	Papeete	6,000
Gabon	268	103	1,237	Libreville	3,780
Gambia, The	11.3	4.4	878	Banjul	360
Georgia	69.7	26.9	5,471	Tbilisi	1,640
Germany	357	138	80,569	Berlin	23,650
Ghana	239	92	15,400	Accra	400
Gibraltar (UK)	0.007	0.003	31	–	4,000
Greece	132	51	10,300	Athens	6,340
Greenland (Den.)	2,176	840	57	Godthåb	6,000
Grenada	0.34	0.13	91	St George's	2,180
Guadeloupe (Fr.)	1.7	0.66	400	Basse-Terre	7,000
Guam (US)	0.55	0.21	139	Agana	6,000
Guatemala	109	42	9,745	Guatemala City	930
Guinea	246	95	6,116	Conakry	450
Guinea-Bissau	36.1	13.9	1,006	Bissau	190
Guyana	215	83	808	Georgetown	430
Haiti	27.8	10.7	6,764	Port-au-Prince	370
Honduras	112	43	5,462	Tegucigalpa	570
Hong Kong (UK)	1.1	0.40	5,801	–	13,430
Hungary	93	35.9	10,313	Budapest	2,720
Iceland	103	40	260	Reykjavik	23,170
India	3,288	1,269	879,548	Delhi	330
Indonesia	1,905	735	191,170	Jakarta	610
Iran	1,648	636	56,964	Tehran	2,170
Iraq	438	169	19,290	Baghdad	2,000
Ireland	70.3	27.1	3,547	Dublin	11,120
Israel	27	10.3	4,946	Jerusalem	11,950
Italy	301	116	57,782	Rome	18,580
Ivory Coast	322	125	12,910	Abidjan	690
Jamaica	11	4.2	2,469	Kingston	1,480
Japan	378	146	124,336	Tokyo	26,920
Jordan	89.2	34.4	4,291	Amman	1,060
Kazakhstan	2,717	1,049	17,038	Alma Ata	7,570
Kenya	580	224	26,985	Nairobi	340
Kirghizia	198.5	76.6	4,472	Bishkek	4,000
Kiribati	0.72	0.28	74	Tarawa	750
Korea, North	121	47	22,618	Pyongyang	900
Korea, South	99	38.2	43,663	Seoul	6,340
Kuwait	17.8	6.9	1,970	Kuwait City	16,380
Laos	237	91	4,469	Vientiane	230
Latvia	65	25	2,632	Riga	3,410
Lebanon	10.4	4	2,838	Beirut	2,000
Lesotho	30.4	11.7	1,836	Maseru	580
Liberia	111	43	2,580	Monrovia	500
Libya	1,760	679	4,875	Tripoli	5,800
Liechtenstein	0.16	0.06	28	Vaduz	33,000
Lithuania	65.2	25.2	3,759	Vilnius	2,710
Luxembourg	2.6	1	390	Luxembourg	31,780
Macau (Port.)	0.02	0.006	374	–	2,000
Macedonia	25.3	9.8	2,174	Skopje	–
Madagascar	587	227	12,827	Antananarivo	210
Malawi	118	46	8,823	Lilongwe	230
Malaysia	330	127	18,181	Kuala Lumpur	2,520
Maldives	0.30	0.12	231	Malé	460
Mali	1,240	479	9,818	Bamako	280
Malta	0.32	0.12	359	Valletta	6,630
Martinique (Fr.)	1.1	0.42	368	Fort-de-France	4,000
Mauritania	1,025	396	2,143	Nouakchott	510
Mauritius	1.9	0.72	1,084	Port Louis	2,420
Mexico	1,958	756	89,538	Mexico City	3,030
Micronesia, Fed. States	0.70	0.27	110	Palikir	–
Moldavia	33.7	13	4,458	Kishinev	2,170
Monaco	0.002	0.0001	30	–	20,000
Mongolia	1,567	605	2,310	Ulan Bator	400
Montserrat (UK)	0.10	0.04	11	Plymouth	–
Morocco	447	172	26,318	Rabat	1,030
Mozambique	802	309	14,872	Maputo	80
Namibia	825	318	1,562	Windhoek	1,460
Nauru	0.02	0.008	10	Yaren	–
Nepal	141	54	20,577	Katmandu	180
Netherlands	41.5	16	15,178	Amsterdam	18,780
Neths Antilles (Neths)	0.99	0.38	175	Willemstad	6,000
New Caledonia (Fr.)	19	7.3	173	Nouméa	4,000
New Zealand	269	104	3,414	Wellington	12,350
Nicaragua	130	50	4,130	Managua	460
Niger	1,267	489	8,252	Niamey	300
Nigeria	924	357	88,515	Lagos/Abuja	340
Norway	324	125	4,286	Oslo	24,220
Oman	212	82	1,637	Muscat	6,120
Pakistan	796	307	115,520	Islamabad	400
Panama	77.1	29.8	2,515	Panama City	2,130
Papua New Guinea	463	179	4,056	Port Moresby	820
Paraguay	407	157	4,519	Asunción	1,270
Peru	1,285	496	22,454	Lima	1,070
Philippines	300	116	64,259	Manila	740
Poland	313	121	38,356	Warsaw	1,790
Portugal	92.4	35.7	9,846	Lisbon	5,930
Puerto Rico (US)	9	3.5	3,580	San Juan	6,470
Qatar	11	4.2	453	Doha	15,860
Réunion (Fr.)	2.5	0.97	624	St-Denis	4,000
Romania	238	92	23,185	Bucharest	1,390
Russia	17,075	6,592	149,527	Moscow	3,220
Rwanda	26.3	10.2	7,526	Kigali	260
St Christopher & Nevis	0.36	0.14	42	Basseterre	3,960
St Lucia	0.62	0.24	137	Castries	2,500
St Pierre & Miquelon (Fr.)	0.24	0.09	6	St-Pierre	–
St Vincent & Grenadines	0.39	0.15	109	Kingstown	1,730
San Marino	0.06	0.02	23	San Marino	–
São Tomé & Príncipe	0.96	0.37	124	São Tomé	350
Saudi Arabia	2,150	830	15,922	Riyadh	7,820
Senegal	197	76	7,736	Dakar	720
Seychelles	0.46	0.18	72	Victoria	5,110
Sierra Leone	71.7	27.7	4,376	Freetown	210
Singapore	0.62	0.24	2,812	Singapore	14,210
Slovak Republic	49	18.9	5,297	Bratislava	1,650
Slovenia	20.3	7.8	1,996	Ljubljana	–
Solomon Is.	28.9	11.2	342	Honiara	690
Somalia	638	246	9,204	Mogadishu	150
South Africa	1,219	471	39,790	Pretoria	2,560
Spain	505	195	39,085	Madrid	12,460
Sri Lanka	65.6	25.3	17,405	Colombo	500
Sudan	2,506	967	26,656	Khartoum	310
Surinam	163	63	438	Paramaribo	3,610
Swaziland	17.4	6.7	792	Mbabane	1,060
Sweden	450	174	8,678	Stockholm	25,110
Switzerland	41.3	15.9	6,905	Bern	33,610
Syria	185	71	12,958	Damascus	1,160
Taiwan	36	13.9	20,659	Taipei	6,600
Tajikistan	143.1	55.2	5,465	Dushanbe	2,980
Tanzania	945	365	27,829	Dar es Salaam	100
Thailand	513	198	57,760	Bangkok	1,580
Togo	56.8	21.9	3,763	Lomé	410
Tokelau (NZ)	0.01	0.005	2	Nukunonu	–
Tonga	0.75	0.29	97	Nuku'alofa	1,100
Trinidad & Tobago	5.1	2	1,265	Port of Spain	3,620
Tunisia	164	63	8,410	Tunis	1,510
Turkey	779	301	58,775	Ankara	1,820
Turkmenistan	488.1	188.5	3,714	Ashkhabad	1,700
Turks & Caicos Is. (UK)	0.43	0.17	13	Grand Turk	–
Tuvalu	0.03	0.01	12	Funafuti	600
Uganda	236	91	18,674	Kampala	160
Ukraine	603.7	233.1	52,200	Kiev	2,340
United Arab Emirates	83.6	32.3	1,629	Abu Dhabi	20,140
United Kingdom	243.3	94	57,848	London	16,550
United States of America	9,373	3,619	255,020	Washington	22,240
Uruguay	177	68	3,131	Montevideo	2,860
Uzbekistan	447.4	172.7	21,627	Tashkent	1,350
Vanuatu	12.2	4.7	157	Port Vila	1,120
Vatican City	0.0004	0.0002	1	–	–
Venezuela	912	352	20,249	Caracas	2,730
Vietnam	332	127	69,306	Hanoi	200
Virgin Is. (UK)	0.15	0.06	17	Road Town	–
Virgin Is. (US)	0.34	0.13	107	Charlotte Amalie	12,000
Western Sahara	266	103	250	El Aaiún	–
Western Samoa	2.8	1.1	161	Apia	960
Yemen	528	204	11,282	Sana	540
Yugoslavia	102.3	39.5	10,469	Belgrade	2,940
Zaire	2,345	906	39,882	Kinshasa	230
Zambia	753	291	8,638	Lusaka	460
Zimbabwe	391	151	10,583	Harare	650

World Statistics: Physical Dimensions

Each topic list is divided into continents and within a continent the items are listed in size order. The order of the continents is as in the atlas, Europe through to South America. The bottom part of many of the lists are selective. The world top ten are shown in square brackets; in the case of mountains this has not been done because the world top 30 are all in Asia. The figures are rounded as appropriate.

World, Continents, Oceans

	km^2	$miles^2$	%
The World	509,450,000	196,672,000	–
Land	149,450,000	57,688,000	29.3
Water	360,000,000	138,984,000	70.7
Asia	44,500,000	17,177,000	29.8
Africa	30,302,000	11,697,000	20.3
North America	24,241,000	9,357,000	16.2
South America	17,793,000	6,868,000	11.9
Antarctica	14,100,000	5,443,000	9.4
Europe	9,957,000	3,843,000	6.7
Australia & Oceania	8,557,000	3,303,000	5.7
Pacific Ocean	179,679,000	69,356,000	49.9
Atlantic Ocean	92,373,000	35,657,000	25.7
Indian Ocean	73,917,000	28,532,000	20.5
Arctic Ocean	14,090,000	5,439,000	3.9

Mountains

		m	ft
Europe			
Mont Blanc	*France/Italy*	4,807	15,771
Monte Rosa	*Italy/Switzerland*	4,634	15,203
Dom	*Switzerland*	4,545	14,911
Weisshorn	*Switzerland*	4,505	14,780
Matterhorn/Cervino	*Italy/Switzerland*	4,478	14,691
Mt Maudit	*France/Italy*	4,465	14,649
Finsteraarhorn	*Switzerland*	4,274	14,022
Aletschhorn	*Switzerland*	4,182	13,720
Jungfrau	*Switzerland*	4,158	13,642
Barre des Ecrins	*France*	4,103	13,461
Schreckhorn	*Switzerland*	4,078	13,380
Gran Paradiso	*Italy*	4,061	13,323
Piz Bernina	*Italy/Switzerland*	4,049	13,284
Ortles	*Italy*	3,899	12,792
Monte Viso	*Italy*	3,841	12,602
Grossglockner	*Austria*	3,797	12,457
Mulhacén	*Spain*	3,478	11,411
Pico de Aneto	*Spain*	3,404	11,168
Etna	*Italy*	3,340	10,958
Galdhöpiggen	*Norway*	2,469	8,100
Hvannadalshnúkur	*Iceland*	2,119	6,952
Ben Nevis	*UK*	1,343	4,406
Asia			
Everest	*China/Nepal*	8,848	29,029
Godwin Austen (K2)	*China/Kashmir*	8,611	28,251
Kanchenjunga	*India/Nepal*	8,598	28,208
Lhotse	*China/Nepal*	8,516	27,939
Makalu	*China/Nepal*	8,481	27,824
Cho Oyu	*China/Nepal*	8,201	26,906
Dhaulagiri	*Nepal*	8,172	26,811
Manaslu	*Nepal*	8,156	26,758
Nanga Parbat	*Kashmir*	8,126	26,660
Annapurna	*Nepal*	8,078	26,502
Gasherbrum	*China/Kashmir*	8,068	26,469
Broad Peak	*India*	8,051	26,414
Gosainthan	*China*	8,012	26,286
Disteghil Sar	*Kashmir*	7,885	25,869
Nuptse	*Nepal*	7,879	25,849
Elbrus	*Russia*	5,633	18,481
Fuji-san	*Japan*	3,776	12,388
Pidurutalagala	*Sri Lanka*	2,524	8,281
Africa			
Kilimanjaro	*Tanzania*	5,895	19,340
Mt Kenya	*Kenya*	5,199	17,057
Ruwenzori	*Uganda/Zaire*	5,109	16,762
Ras Dashan	*Ethiopia*	4,620	15,157
Meru	*Tanzania*	4,565	14,977
Karisimbi	*Rwanda/Zaïre*	4,507	14,787
Mt Elgon	*Kenya/Uganda*	4,321	14,176
Batu	*Ethiopia*	4,307	14,130
Guna	*Ethiopia*	4,231	13,882
Toubkal	*Morocco*	4,165	13,665
Oceania			
Puncak Jaya	*Indonesia*	5,029	16,499
Puncak Trikora	*Indonesia*	4,750	15,584
Puncak Mandala	*Indonesia*	4,702	15,427
Mt Wilhelm	*Papua New Guinea*	4,508	14,790
Mauna Kea	*USA (Hawaii)*	4,205	13,796
Mauna Loa	*USA (Hawaii)*	4,170	13,681
Mt Cook	*New Zealand*	3,753	12,313
Mt Kosciusko	*Australia*	2,237	7,339
North America			
Mt McKinley	*USA (Alaska)*	6,194	20,321
Mt Logan	*Canada*	5,959	19,551
Citlaltepetl	*Mexico*	5,700	18,701
Mt St Elias	*USA/Canada*	5,489	18,008
Popocatepetl	*Mexico*	5,452	17,887
Mt Foraker	*USA (Alaska)*	5,304	17,401
Ixtaccihuatl	*Mexico*	5,286	17,342
Lucania	*Canada*	5,227	17,149
Mt Steele	*Canada*	5,073	16,644
Mt Bona	*USA (Alaska)*	5,005	16,420
South America			
Aconcagua	*Argentina*	6,960	22,834
Illimani	*Bolivia*	6,882	22,578
Bonete	*Argentina*	6,872	22,546
Ojos del Salado	*Argentina/Chile*	6,863	22,516
Tupungato	*Argentina/Chile*	6,800	22,309
Pissis	*Argentina*	6,779	22,241
Mercedario	*Argentina/Chile*	6,770	22,211
Huascaran	*Peru*	6,768	22,204
Llullaillaco	*Argentina/Chile*	6,723	22,057
Nudo de Cachi	*Argentina*	6,720	22,047
Antarctica			
Vinson Massif		4,897	16,066

Ocean Depths

	m	ft
Atlantic Ocean		
Puerto Rico (Milwaukee) Deep [7]	9,220	30,249
Cayman Trench [10]	7,680	25,197
Gulf of Mexico	5,203	17,070
Mediterranean Sea	5,121	16,801
Black Sea	2,211	7,254
North Sea	660	2,165
Baltic Sea	463	1,519
Hudson Bay	258	846
Indian Ocean		
Java Trench	7,450	24,442
Red Sea	2,635	8,454
Persian Gulf	73	239
Pacific Ocean		
Mariana Trench [1]	11,022	36,161
Tonga Trench [2]	10,882	35,702
Japan Trench [3]	10,554	34,626
Kuril Trench [4]	10,542	34,587
Mindanao Trench [5]	10,497	34,439
Kermadec Trench [6]	10,047	32,962
Peru-Chile Trench [8]	8,050	26,410
Aleutian Trench [9]	7,822	25,662
Middle American Trench	6,662	21,857
Arctic Ocean		
Molloy Deep	5,608	18,399

Land Lows

		m	ft
Caspian Sea	*Europe*	–28	–92
Dead Sea	*Asia*	–400	–1,312
Lake Assal	*Africa*	–156	–512
Lake Eyre North	*Oceania*	–16	–52
Death Valley	*N. America*	–86	–282
Valdés Peninsula	*S. America*	–40	–131

Rivers

		km	miles
Europe			
Volga	*Caspian Sea*	3,700	2,300
Danube	*Black Sea*	2,850	1,770
Ural	*Caspian Sea*	2,535	1,574
Dnepr	*Volga*	2,285	1,420
Kama	*Volga*	2,030	1,260
Don	*Volga*	1,990	1,240
Petchora	*Arctic Ocean*	1,790	1,110
Dnestr	*Black Sea*	1,400	870
Rhine	*North Sea*	1,320	820
Elbe	*North Sea*	1,145	710
Vistula	*Baltic Sea*	1,090	675
Loire	*Atlantic Ocean*	1,020	635
W. Dvina	*Baltic Sea*	1,019	633
Asia			
Yangtze [3]	*Pacific Ocean*	6,380	3,960
Yenisey-Angara [5]	*Arctic Ocean*	5,550	3,445
Huang He [6]	*Pacific Ocean*	5,464	3,395
Ob-Irtysh [7]	*Arctic Ocean*	5,410	3,360
Mekong [9]	*Pacific Ocean*	4,500	2,795
Amur [10]	*Pacific Ocean*	4,400	2,730
Lena	*Arctic Ocean*	4,400	2,730
Irtysh	*Ob*	4,250	2,640
Yenisey	*Arctic Ocean*	4,090	2,540
Ob	*Arctic Ocean*	3,680	2,285
Indus	*Indian Ocean*	3,100	1,925
Brahmaputra	*Indian Ocean*	2,900	1,800
Syr Darya	*Aral Sea*	2,860	1,775
Salween	*Indian Ocean*	2,800	1,740
Euphrates	*Indian Ocean*	2,700	1,675
Vilyuy	*Lena*	2,650	1,645
Kolyma	*Arctic Ocean*	2,600	1,615
Amu Darya	*Aral Sea*	2,540	1,575
Ural	*Caspian Sea*	2,535	1,575
Ganges	*Indian Ocean*	2,510	1,560
Si Kiang	*Pacific Ocean*	2,100	1,305
Irrawaddy	*Indian Ocean*	2,010	1,250
Tigris	*Indian Ocean*	1,900	1,180
Africa			
Nile [1]	*Mediterranean Sea*	6,670	4,140
Zaïre/Congo [8]	*Atlantic Ocean*	4,670	2,900
Niger	*Atlantic Ocean*	4,180	2,595
Zambezi	*Indian Ocean*	3,540	2,200
Oubangi/Uele	*Zaïre*	2,250	1,400
Kasai	*Zaïre*	1,950	1,210
Shaballe	*Indian Ocean*	1,930	1,200
Orange	*Atlantic Ocean*	1,860	1,155
Australia			
Murray-Darling	*Indian Ocean*	3,750	2,330
Darling	*Murray*	3,070	1,905
Murray	*Indian Ocean*	2,575	1,600
Murrumbidgee	*Murray*	1,690	1,050
North America			
Mississippi-Missouri [4]	*Gulf of Mexico*	6,020	3,740
Mackenzie	*Arctic Ocean*	4,240	2,630
Mississippi	*Gulf of Mexico*	3,780	2,350
Missouri	*Mississippi*	3,780	2,350
Yukon	*Pacific Ocean*	3,185	1,980
Rio Grande	*Gulf of Mexico*	3,030	1,880
Arkansas	*Mississippi*	2,340	1,450
Colorado	*Pacific Ocean*	2,330	1,445
Red	*Mississippi*	2,040	1,270
Columbia	*Pacific Ocean*	1,950	1,210
Saskatchewan	*Lake Winnipeg*	1,940	1,205
Snake	*Columbia*	1,670	1,040
South America			
Amazon [2]	*Atlantic Ocean*	6,450	4,010
Paraná-Plate	*Atlantic Ocean*	4,500	2,800
Purus	*Amazon*	3,350	2,080
Madeira	*Amazon*	3,200	1,990
São Francisco	*Atlantic Ocean*	2,900	1,800
Paraná	*Plate*	2,800	1,740
Tocantins	*Atlantic Ocean*	2,750	1,710
Paraguay	*Paraná*	2,550	1,580
Orinoco	*Atlantic Ocean*	2,500	1,550
Pilcomayo	*Paraná*	2,500	1,550

Lakes

		km^2	$miles^2$
Europe			
Lake Ladoga	*Russia*	17,700	6,800
Lake Onega	*Russia*	9,700	3,700
Saimaa system	*Finland*	8,000	3,100
Asia			
Caspian Sea [1]	*Asia*	371,800	143,550
Aral Sea [6]	*Kazakh./Uzbek.*	36,000	13,900
Lake Baykal [9]	*Russia*	30,500	11,780
Tonlé Sap	*Cambodia*	20,000	7,700
Lake Balkhash	*Kazakhstan*	18,500	7,100
Africa			
Lake Victoria [3]	*E. Africa*	68,000	26,000
Lake Tanganyika [7]	*C. Africa*	33,000	13,000
Lake Malawi [10]	*E. Africa*	29,600	11,430
Lake Chad	*C. Africa*	25,000	9,700
Australia			
Lake Eyre	*Australia*	8,900	3,400
North America			
Lake Superior [2]	*Canada/USA*	82,350	31,800
Lake Huron [4]	*Canada/USA*	59,600	23,010
Lake Michigan [5]	*USA*	58,000	22,400
Great Bear Lake [8]	*Canada*	31,800	12,280
Great Slave Lake	*Canada*	28,500	11,000
Lake Erie	*Canada/USA*	25,700	9,900
Lake Winnipeg	*Canada*	24,400	9,400
Lake Ontario	*Canada/USA*	19,500	7,500
South America			
Lake Titicaca	*Bolivia/Peru*	8,300	3,200

Islands

		km^2	$miles^2$
Europe			
Great Britain [8]	*UK*	229,880	88,700
Iceland	*Atlantic Ocean*	103,000	39,800
Ireland	*Ireland/UK*	84,400	32,600
Asia			
Borneo [3]	*S. E. Asia*	744,360	287,400
Sumatra [6]	*Indonesia*	473,600	182,860
Honshu [7]	*Japan*	230,500	88,980
Celebes	*Indonesia*	189,000	73,000
Java	*Indonesia*	126,700	48,900
Luzon	*Philippines*	104,700	40,400
Mindanao	*Philippines*	101,500	39,200
Hokkaido	*Japan*	78,400	30,300
Sakhalin	*Russia*	74,060	28,600
Sri Lanka	*Indian Ocean*	65,600	25,300
Africa			
Madagascar [4]	*Indian Ocean*	587,040	226,660
Oceania			
New Guinea [2]	*Indonesia/Pap. NG*	821,030	317,000
New Zealand (S.)	*New Zealand*	150,500	58,100
New Zealand (N.)	*New Zealand*	114,700	44,300
Tasmania	*Australia*	67,800	26,200
North America			
Greenland [1]	*Greenland*	2,175,600	839,800
Baffin Is. [5]	*Canada*	508,000	196,100
Victoria Is. [9]	*Canada*	212,200	81,900
Ellesmere Is. [10]	*Canada*	212,000	81,800
Cuba	*Cuba*	110,860	42,800
Newfoundland	*Canada*	110,680	42,700
Hispaniola	*Atlantic Ocean*	76,200	29,400
South America			
Tierra del Fuego	*Argentina/Chile*	47,000	18,100

PHILIP'S WORLD MAPS

The reference maps which form the main body of this atlas have been prepared in accordance with the highest standards of international cartography to provide an accurate and detailed representation of the Earth. The scales and projections used have been carefully chosen to give balanced coverage of the world, while emphasizing the most densely populated and economically significant regions. A hallmark of Philip's mapping is the use of hill shading and relief colouring to create a graphic impression of landforms: this makes the maps exceptionally easy to read. However, knowledge of the key features employed in the construction and presentation of the maps will enable the reader to derive the fullest benefit from the atlas.

Map sequence

The atlas covers the Earth continent by continent: first Europe; then its land neighbour Asia (mapped north before south, in a clockwise sequence), then Africa, Australia and Oceania, North America and South America. This is the classic arrangement adopted by most cartographers since the 16th century. For each continent, there are maps at a variety of scales. First, physical relief and political maps of the whole continent; then a series of larger-scale maps of the regions within the continent, each followed, where required, by still larger-scale maps of the most important or densely populated areas. The governing principle is that by turning the pages of the atlas, the reader moves steadily from north to south through each continent, with each map overlapping its neighbours. A key map showing this sequence, and the area covered by each map, can be found on the endpapers of the atlas.

Map presentation

With very few exceptions (e.g. for the Arctic and Antarctic), the maps are drawn with north at the top, regardless of whether they are presented upright or sideways on the page. In the borders will be found the map title; a locator diagram showing the area covered and the page numbers for maps of adjacent areas; the scale; the projection used; the degrees of latitude and longitude; and the letters and figures used in the index for locating place names and geographical features. Physical relief maps also have a height reference panel identifying the colours used for each layer of contouring.

Map symbols

Each map contains a vast amount of detail which can only be conveyed clearly and accurately by the use of symbols. Points and circles of varying sizes locate and identify the relative importance of towns and cities; different styles of type are employed for administrative, geographical and

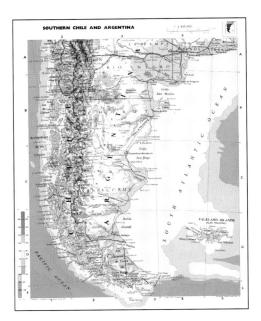

regional place names. A variety of pictorial symbols denote landscape features such as glaciers, marshes and reefs, and man-made structures including roads, railways, airports, canals and dams. International borders are shown by red lines. Where neighbouring countries are in dispute, for example in the Middle East, the maps show the *de facto* boundary between nations, regardless of the legal or historical situation. The symbols are explained on the first page of the World Maps section of the atlas.

Map scales

The scale of each map is given in the numerical form known as the 'representative fraction'. The first figure is always one, signifying one unit of distance on the map; the second figure, usually in millions, is the number by which the map unit must be multiplied to give the equivalent distance on the Earth's surface. Calculations can easily be made in centimetres and kilometres, by dividing the Earth units figure by 100 000 (i.e. deleting the last five 0s). Thus 1:1 000 000 means 1 cm = 10 km. The calculation for inches and miles is more laborious, but 1 000 000 divided by 63 360 (the number of inches in a mile) shows that 1:1 000 000 means approximately 1 inch = 16 miles. The table below provides distance equivalents for scales down to 1:50 000 000.

LARGE SCALE		
1:1 000 000	1 cm = 10 km	1 inch = 16 miles
1:2 500 000	1 cm = 25 km	1 inch = 39.5 miles
1:5 000 000	1 cm = 50 km	1 inch = 79 miles
1:6 000 000	1 cm = 60 km	1 inch = 95 miles
1:8 000 000	1 cm = 80 km	1 inch = 126 miles
1:10 000 000	1 cm = 100 km	1 inch = 158 miles
1:12 000 000	1 cm = 120 km	1 inch = 189 miles
1:15 000 000	1 cm = 150 km	1 inch = 237 miles
1:20 000 000	1 cm = 200 km	1 inch = 316 miles
1:50 000 000	1 cm = 500 km	1 inch = 790 miles
SMALL SCALE		

Measuring distances

Although each map is accompanied by a scale bar, distances cannot always be measured with confidence because of the distortions involved in portraying the curved surface of the Earth on a flat page. As a general rule, the larger the map scale (i.e. the lower the number of Earth units in the representative fraction), the more accurate and reliable will be the distance measured. On small-scale maps such as those of the world and of entire continents, measurement may only be accurate along the 'standard parallels', or central axes, and should not be attempted without first considering the map projection used.

Latitude and longitude

Accurate positioning of individual points on the Earth's surface is made possible by reference to the geometrical system of latitude and longitude. Latitude *parallels* are drawn west–east around the Earth and numbered by degrees north and south of the Equator, which is designated 0° of latitude. Longitude *meridians* are drawn north–south and numbered by degrees east and west of the *prime meridian*, 0° of longitude, which passes through Greenwich in England. By referring to these co-ordinates and their subdivisions of minutes (¹⁄₆₀th of a degree) and seconds (¹⁄₆₀th of a minute), any place on Earth can be located to within a few hundred yards. Latitude and longitude are indicated by blue lines on the maps; they are straight or curved according to the projection employed. Reference to these lines is the easiest way of determining the relative positions of places on different large-scale maps, and for plotting compass directions.

Name forms

For ease of reference, both English and local name forms appear in the atlas. Oceans, seas and countries are shown in English throughout the atlas; country names may be abbreviated to their commonly accepted form (e.g. Germany, not The Federal Republic of Germany). Conventional English forms are also used for place names on the smaller-scale maps of the continents. However, local name forms are used on all large-scale and regional maps, with the English form given in brackets only for important cities – the large-scale map of Eastern Europe and Turkey thus shows Moskva (Moscow). For countries which do not use a Roman script, place names have been transcribed according to the systems adopted by the British and US Geographic Names Authorities. For China, the Pin Yin system has been used, with some more widely known forms appearing in brackets, as with Beijing (Peking). Both English and local names appear in the index to the world maps.

INTRODUCTION TO WORLD GEOGRAPHY

PLANET EARTH

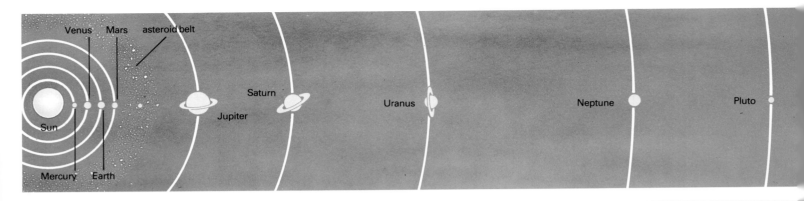

Venus Mars asteroid belt

Saturn

Uranus

Neptune

Pluto

Jupiter

Sun

Mercury Earth

THE SOLAR SYSTEM

A minute part of one of the billions of galaxies (collections of stars) that comprise the Universe, the Solar System lies some 27,000 light-years from the centre of our own galaxy, the 'Milky Way'. Thought to be over 4,700 million years old, it consists of a central sun with nine planets and their moons revolving around it, attracted by its gravitational pull. The planets orbit the Sun in the same direction – anti-clockwise when viewed from the Northern Heavens – and almost in the same plane. Their orbital paths, however, vary enormously.

The Sun's diameter is 109 times that of Earth, and the temperature at its core – caused by continuous thermonuclear fusions of hydrogen into helium – is estimated to be 15 million degrees Celsius. It is the Solar System's only source of light and heat.

PROFILE OF THE PLANETS

	Mean distance from Sun (million km)	Mass (Earth = 1)	Period of orbit	Period of rotation (in days)	Diameter (km)	Number of known satellites
Mercury	58.3	0.06	88 days	58.67	4,878	0
Venus	107.7	0.8	224.7 days	243.0	12,104	0
Earth	149.6	1.0	365.24 days	0.99	12,756	1
Mars	227.3	0.1	1.88 years	1.02	6,794	2
Jupiter	777.9	317.8	11.86 years	0.41	142,800	16
Saturn	1427.1	95.2	29.63 years	0.42	120,000	17
Uranus	2872.3	14.5	83.97 years	0.45	52,000	15
Neptune	4502.7	17.2	164.8 years	0.67	48,400	8
Pluto	5894.2	0.002	248.63 years	6.38	2,400	1

All planetary orbits are elliptical in form, but only Pluto and Mercury follow paths that deviate noticeably from a circular one. Near Perihelion – its closest approach to the Sun – Pluto actually passes inside the orbit of Neptune, an event that last occurred in 1983. Pluto will not regain its station as outermost planet until February 1999.

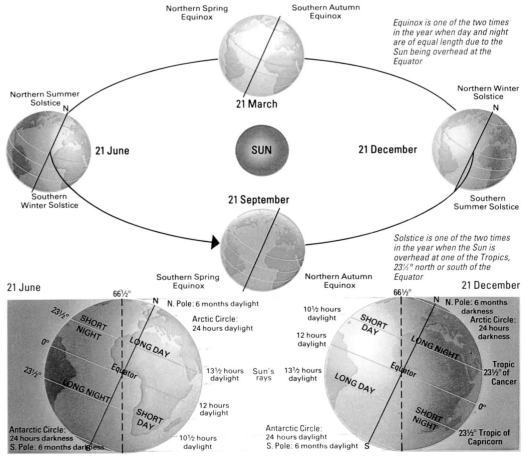

Northern Spring Equinox

Southern Autumn Equinox

Equinox is one of the two times in the year when day and night are of equal length due to the Sun being overhead at the Equator

21 March

Northern Summer Solstice N

Northern Winter Solstice N

21 June

SUN

21 December

Southern Winter Solstice

Southern Summer Solstice

21 September

Southern Spring Equinox

Northern Autumn Equinox

Solstice is one of the two times in the year when the Sun is overhead at one of the Tropics, 23½° north or south of the Equator

21 June

66½°

N. Pole: 6 months daylight
Arctic Circle: 24 hours daylight

23½° SHORT NIGHT

0° LONG DAY

Equator

23½° LONG NIGHT

13½ hours daylight

Sun's rays

12 hours daylight

SHORT DAY

Antarctic Circle: 24 hours darkness
S. Pole: 6 months darkness

10½ hours daylight

21 December

66½°

N. Pole: 6 months darkness
Arctic Circle: 24 hours darkness

10½ hours daylight

SHORT DAY

LONG NIGHT

12 hours daylight

Equator

13½ hours daylight

LONG DAY

SHORT NIGHT

Tropic 23½° of Cancer

0°

23½° Tropic of Capricorn

Antarctic Circle: 24 hours daylight
S. Pole: 6 months daylight

THE SEASONS

The Earth revolves around the Sun once a year in an 'anti-clockwise' direction, tilted at a constant angle 66½°. In June, the northern hemisphere is tilted towards the Sun: as a result it receives more hours of sunshine in a day and therefore has its warmest season, summer. By December, the Earth has rotated halfway round the Sun so that the southern hemisphere is tilted towards the Sun and has its summer; the hemisphere that is tilted away from the Sun has winter. On 21 June the Sun is directly overhead at the Tropic of Cancer (23½° N), and this is midsummer in the northern hemisphere. Midsummer in the southern hemisphere occurs on 21 December, when the Sun is overhead at the Tropic of Capricorn (23½° S).

DAY AND NIGHT

The Sun appears to rise in the east, reach its highest point at noon, and then set in the west, to be followed by night. In reality it is not the Sun that is moving but the Earth revolving from west to east. Due to the tilting of the Earth the length of day and night varies from place to place and month to month.

At the summer solstice in the northern hemisphere (21 June), the Arctic has total daylight and the Antarctic total darkness. The opposite occurs at the winter solstice (21 December). At the Equator, the length of day and night are almost equal all year, at latitude 30° the length of day varies from about 14 hours to 10 hours, and at latitude 50° from about 16 hours to about 8 hours.

TIME

Year: The time taken by the Earth to revolve around the Sun, or 365.24 days.

Month: The approximate time taken by the Moon to revolve around the Earth. The 12 months of the year in fact vary from 28 (29 in a Leap Year) to 31 days.

Week: An artificial period of 7 days, not based on astronomical time.

Day: The time taken by the Earth to complete one rotation on its axis.

Hour: 24 hours make one day. Usually the day is divided into hours AM (ante meridiem or before noon) and PM (post meridiem or after noon), although most timetables now use the 24-hour system, from midnight to midnight.

SUNRISE

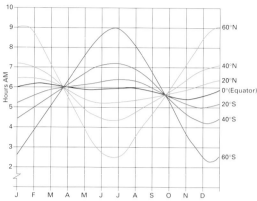

SUNSET

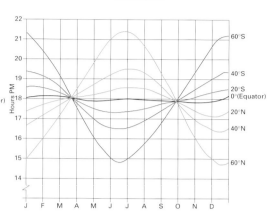

THE MOON

Distance from Earth: 356,410 km – 406,685 km; Mean diameter: 3,475.1 km;   Mass: approx. 1/81 that of Earth;
Surface gravity: one-sixth of Earth's; Daily range of temperature at lunar equator: 200°C; Average orbital speed: 3,683 km/h

PHASES OF THE MOON

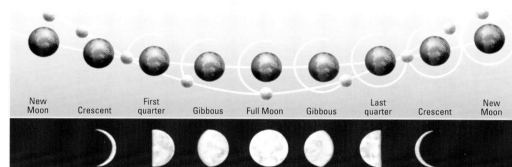

New Moon — Crescent — First quarter — Gibbous — Full Moon — Gibbous — Last quarter — Crescent — New Moon

The Moon rotates more slowly than the Earth, making one complete turn on its axis in just over 27 days. Since this corresponds to its period of revolution around the Earth, the Moon always presents the same hemisphere or face to us, and we never see 'the dark side'. The interval between one Full Moon and the next (and between New Moons) is about 29½ days – a lunar month. The apparent changes in the shape of the Moon are caused by its changing position in relation to the Earth; like the planets, it produces no light of its own and shines only by reflecting the rays of the Sun.

ECLIPSES

When the Moon passes between the Sun and the Earth it causes a partial eclipse of the Sun (1) if the Earth passes through the Moon's outer shadow (P), or a total eclipse (2) if the inner cone shadow crosses the Earth's surface. In a lunar eclipse, the Earth's shadow crosses the Moon and, again, provides either a partial or total eclipse. Eclipses of the Sun and the Moon do not occur every month because of the 5° difference between the plane of the Moon's orbit and the plane in which the Earth moves. In the 1990s only 14 lunar eclipses are possible, for example; seven partial and seven total; each is visible only from certain, and variable, parts of the world. The same period witnesses 13 solar eclipses – six partial (or annular) and seven total.

Partial eclipse (1)

P P P

Total eclipse (2)

Lunar eclipse

TIDES

The daily rise and fall of the ocean's tides are the result of the gravitational pull of the Moon and that of the Sun, though the effect of the latter is only 46.6% as strong as that of the Moon. This effect is greatest on the hemisphere facing the Moon and causes a tidal 'bulge'. When lunar and solar forces pull together, with Sun, Earth and Moon in line (near New and Full Moons), higher 'spring tides' (and lower low tides) occur; when lunar and solar forces are least coincident with the Sun and Moon at an angle (near the Moon's first and third quarters), 'neap tides' occur, which have a small tidal range.

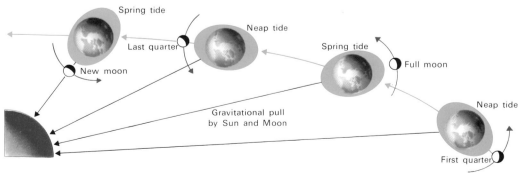

Spring tide

Neap tide

Last quarter

Spring tide

New moon

Full moon

Gravitational pull by Sun and Moon

Neap tide

First quarter

RESTLESS EARTH

THE EARTH'S STRUCTURE

Upper mantle
(c. 370 km)

Crust (average 5–50 km)

Transitional zone
(600 km)

Outer core (2,100 km)

Lower mantle
(1,700 km)

Inner core
(2,700 km)

CONTINENTAL DRIFT

About 200 million years ago the original Pangaea landmass began to split into two continental groups, which further separated over time to produce the present-day configuration.

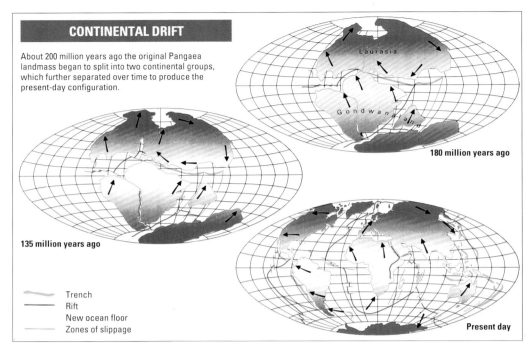

Laurasia

Gondwanaland

180 million years ago

135 million years ago

Present day

〰 Trench
— Rift
New ocean floor
Zones of slippage

EARTHQUAKES

Earthquake magnitude is usually rated according to either the Richter or the Modified Mercalli scale, both devised by seismologists in the 1930s. The Richter scale measures absolute earthquake power with mathematical precision: each step upwards represents a tenfold increase in shockwave amplitude. Theoretically, there is no upper limit, but the largest earthquakes measured have been rated at between 8.8 and 8.9. The 12–point Mercalli scale, based on observed effects, is often more meaningful, ranging from I (earthquakes noticed only by seismographs) to XII (total destruction); intermediate points include V (people awakened at night; unstable objects overturned), VII (collapse of ordinary buildings; chimneys and monuments fall) and IX (conspicuous cracks in ground; serious damage to reservoirs).

Epicentre — Normal fault

Shockwaves reach surface

Origin or focus

Shockwaves travel outwards

NOTABLE EARTHQUAKES SINCE 1900

Year	Location	Mag.	Deaths
1906	San Francisco, USA	8.3	503
1906	Valparaiso, Chile	8.6	22,000
1908	Messina, Italy	7.5	83,000
1915	Avezzano, Italy	7.5	30,000
1920	Gansu (Kansu), China	8.6	180,000
1923	Yokohama, Japan	8.3	143,000
1927	Nan Shan, China	8.3	200,000
1932	Gansu (Kansu), China	7.6	70,000
1934	Bihar, India/Nepal	8.4	10,700
1935	Quetta, India*	7.5	60,000
1939	Chillan, Chile	8.3	28,000
1939	Erzincan, Turkey	7.9	30,000
1960	Agadir, Morocco	5.8	12,000
1962	Khorasan, Iran	7.1	12,230
1963	Skopje, Yugoslavia**	6.0	1,000
1964	Anchorage, Alaska	8.4	131
1968	N.E. Iran	7.4	12,000
1970	N. Peru	7.7	66,794
1972	Managua, Nicaragua	6.2	5,000
1974	N. Pakistan	6.3	5,200
1976	Guatemala	7.5	22,778
1976	Tangshan, China	8.2	650,000
1978	Tabas, Iran	7.7	25,000
1980	El Asnam, Algeria	7.3	20,000
1980	S. Italy	7.2	4,800
1985	Mexico City, Mexico	8.1	4,200
1988	N.W. Armenia	6.8	55,000
1990	N. Iran	7.7	36,000
1993	Maharashtra, India	6.4	30,000

The highest magnitude recorded on the Richter scale was 8.9, in Japan on 2 March 1933 (2,990 deaths). The most devastating quake ever was in Shaanxi (Shensi) province, central China, on 24 January 1556, when an estimated 830,000 people were killed.

* now Pakistan   ** now Macedonia

DISTRIBUTION OF EARTHQUAKES

Major earthquake zones

Areas experiencing frequent earthquakes

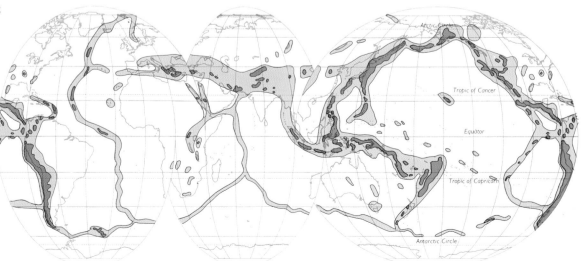

Arctic Circle

Tropic of Cancer

Equator

Tropic of Capricorn

Antarctic Circle

Earthquakes are a series of rapid vibrations originating from the slipping or faulting of parts of the Earth's crust when stresses within build up to breaking point. They usually happen at depths varying from 8 km to 30 km. Severe earthquakes cause extensive damage when they take place in populated areas, destroying structures and severing communications. Most initial loss of life occurs due to secondary causes such as falling masonry, fires and flooding.

PLATE TECTONICS

The drifting of the continents is a feature that is unique to Planet Earth. The complementary, almost jigsaw-puzzle fit of the coastlines on each side of the Atlantic Ocean inspired Alfred Wegener's theory of continental drift in 1915. The theory suggested that an ancient super-continent, which Wegener named Pangaea, incorporated all of the Earth's landmasses and gradually split up to form today's continents.

The original debate about continental drift was a prelude to a more radical idea: plate tectonics. The basic theory is that the Earth's crust is made up of a series of rigid plates which float on a soft layer of the mantle and are moved about by continental convection currents within the Earth's interior. These plates diverge and converge along margins marked by earthquakes, volcanoes and other seismic activity. Plates diverge from mid-ocean ridges where molten lava pushes upwards and forces the plates apart at a rate of up to 40 mm a year; converging plates form either a trench (where the oceanic plate sinks below the lighter continental rock) or mountain ranges (where two continents collide).

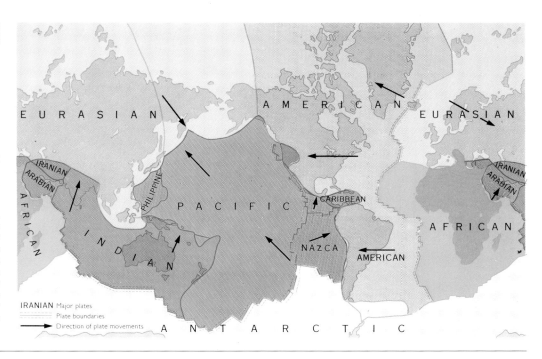

IRANIAN Major plates

Plate boundaries

→ Direction of plate movements

VOLCANOES

The word 'volcano' derives from the island of Vulcano off Sicily, in the Mediterranean Sea. In classical times the people of this area thought that Vulcano was the chimney of the forge of Vulcan, blacksmith of the Roman gods. Today

volcanoes might be the subject of scientific study but they remain both dramatic and unpredictable, if not exactly supernatural: in 1991 Mount Pinatubo, 100 kilometres north of the Philippines capital Manila, suddenly burst into life after more than six centuries of lying dormant.

Most of the world's active volcanoes occur in

a belt around the Pacific Ocean, on the edge of the Pacific plate, called the 'ring of fire'. Indonesia has the greatest concentration with 90 volcanoes, 12 of which are active. The most famous, Krakatau, erupted in 1883 with such force that the resulting tidal wave killed 36,000 people and tremors were felt as far away as Australia.

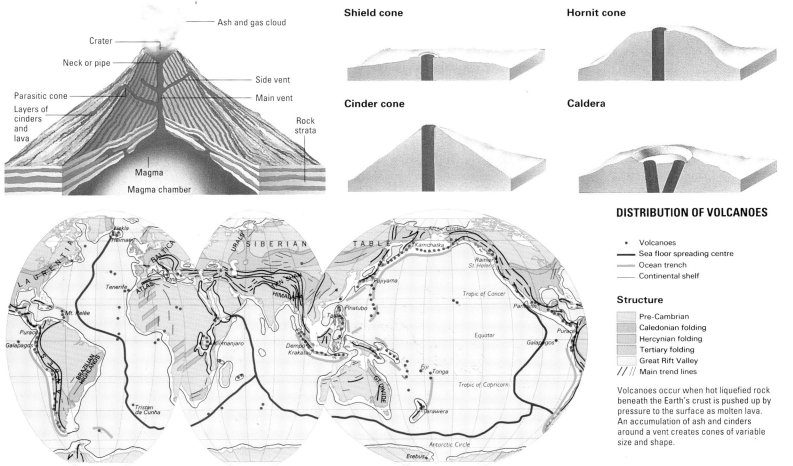

Shield cone

Hornit cone

Cinder cone

Caldera

DISTRIBUTION OF VOLCANOES

• Volcanoes

— Sea floor spreading centre

Ocean trench

Continental shelf

Structure

Pre-Cambrian
Caledonian folding
Hercynian folding
Tertiary folding
Great Rift Valley
/ // Main trend lines

Volcanoes occur when hot liquefied rock beneath the Earth's crust is pushed up by pressure to the surface as molten lava. An accumulation of ash and cinders around a vent creates cones of variable size and shape.

LANDSCAPE

Above and below the surface of the oceans, the features of the Earth's crust are constantly changing. The phenomenal forces generated by convection currents in the molten core of our planet carry the vast segments or 'plates' of the crust across the globe in an endless cycle of creation and destruction. A continent may travel little more than 25 millimetres [one inch] per year, yet in the vast span of geological time this process throws up giant mountain ranges and creates new land.

Destruction of the landscape, however, begins as soon as it is formed. Wind, water, ice and sea, the main agents of erosion, mount a constant assault that even the hardest rocks can

not withstand. Mountain peaks may dwindle by as little as a few millimetres each year, but if they are not uplifted by further movements of the crust they will eventually be reduced to rubble. Water is the most powerful destroyer – it has been estimated that 100 billion tonnes of rock is washed into the oceans every year.

Rivers and glaciers, like the sea itself, generate much of their effect through abrasion – pounding the landscape with the debris they carry with them. But as well as destroying they also create new landscapes, many of them spectacular: vast deltas like the Mississippi and the Nile, or the fjords cut by glaciers in British Columbia, Norway and New Zealand.

THE SPREADING EARTH

The vast ridges that divide the Earth's crust beneath each of the world's oceans mark the boundaries between tectonic plates which are moving gradually in opposite directions. As the plates shift apart, molten magma rises from the Earth's core to seal the rift and the sea floor slowly spreads towards the continental landmasses. The rate of spreading has been calculated by magnetic analysis of the rock at 40 mm [1.5 in] a year in the North Atlantic. Underwater volcanoes mark the line where the continental rise begins. As the plates meet, much of the denser ocean crust dips beneath the continental plate and melts back to the magma.

THE SPREADING EARTH

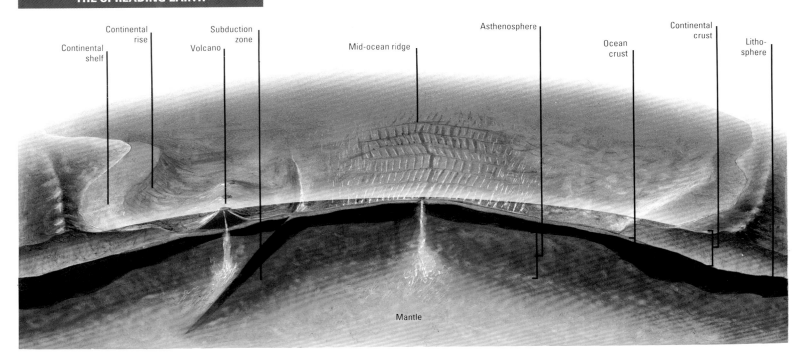

MOUNTAIN BUILDING

Mountains are formed when pressures on the Earth's crust caused by continental drift become so intense that the surface buckles or cracks. This happens most dramatically where two tectonic plates collide: the Rockies, Andes, Alps, Urals and Himalayas resulted from such impacts. These are all known as fold mountains, because they were formed by the compression of the rocks, forcing the surface to bend and fold like a crumpled rug.

The other main building process occurs when the crust fractures to create faults, allowing rock to be forced upwards in large blocks; or when the pressure of magma within the crust forces the surface to bulge into a dome, or erupts to form a volcano. Large mountain ranges may reveal a combination of those features; the Alps, for example, have been compressed so violently that the folds are fragmented by numerous faults and intrusions of molten rock.

Over millions of years, even the greatest mountain ranges can be reduced by erosion to a rugged landscape known as a peneplain.

Types of fold: Geographers give different names to the degrees of fold that result from continuing pressure on the rock strata. A simple fold may be symmetric, with even slopes on either side, but as the pressure builds up, one slope becomes steeper and the fold becomes asymmetric. Later, the ridge or 'anticline' at the top of the fold may slide over the lower ground or 'syncline' to form a recumbent fold. Eventually, the rock strata may break under the pressure to form an overthrust and finally a nappe fold.

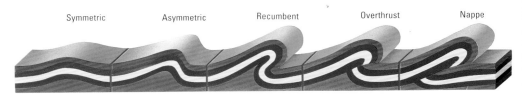

Types of faults: Faults are classified by the direction in which the blocks of rock have moved. A normal fault results when a vertical movement causes the surface to break apart; compression causes a reverse fault. Sideways movement causes shearing, known as a strike-slip fault. When the rock breaks in two places, the central block may be pushed up in a horst fault, or sink in a graben fault.

SHAPING FORCES: GLACIERS

Many of the world's most dramatic landscapes have been carved by glaciers. During the Ice Ages of the Pleistocene Epoch (over 10,000 years ago) up to a third of the land surface was glaciated; even today a tenth is covered in ice. Glaciers are formed from compressed snow, called *névé*, accumulating in a valley head or cirque. Slowly the glacier moves downhill scraping away debris from the mountains and valleys through which it passes. The debris, or moraine, adds to the abrasive power of the ice.

The rate of movement can vary from a few centimetres to several metres a day, but the end of the glacier may not reach the bottom of the valley – the position of the snout depends on the rate at which the ice melts. Glaciers create numerous distinctive landscape features from arête ridges and pyramidal peaks to ice-dammed lakes and truncated spurs, with the U-shape distinguishing a glacial valley from one cut by a river.

SHAPING FORCES: RIVERS

From their origins as upland rills and streams channelling rainfall, or as springs releasing water that has seeped into the ground, all rivers are incessantly at work cutting and shaping the landscape on their way to the sea. In highland regions their flow may be rapid, pounding rocks and boulders with enough violence to cut deep gorges and V-shaped valleys through softer rocks, or tumble as waterfalls over harder ones.

As they reach more gentle slopes, rivers release some of the pebbles they have carried downstream and flow more slowly, broadening out and raising levees or ridges along their banks by depositing mud and sand. In lowland plains, where the gradient is minimal, the river drifts into meanders, depositing deep layers of sediment especially on the inside of each bend, where the flow is weakest. Here farmers may dig drainage ditches and artificial levees to keep the floodplain dry.

As the river finally reaches the sea, it deposits all its remaining sediments, and estuaries are formed where the tidal currents are strong enough to remove them; if not, the debris creates a delta, through which the river cuts outlet streams known as distributaries.

SHAPING FORCES: THE SEA

Under the constant assault from tides and currents, wind and waves, coastlines change faster than most landscape features, both by erosion and by the build-up of sand and pebbles carried by the sea. In severe storms, giant waves pound the shoreline with rocks and boulders, and frequently destroy concrete coastal defences; but even in much quieter conditions, the sea steadily erodes cliffs and headlands, creating new land in the form of sand-dunes, spits and salt marshes.

Where the coastline is formed from soft rocks such as sandstones, debris may fall evenly and be carried away by currents from shelving beaches. In areas with harder rock, the waves may cut steep cliffs and form underwater platforms; eroded debris is deposited as a terrace. Bays are formed when sections of soft rock are carved away between headlands of harder rock. These are then battered by waves from both sides, until the headlands are eventually reduced to rock arches and stacks.

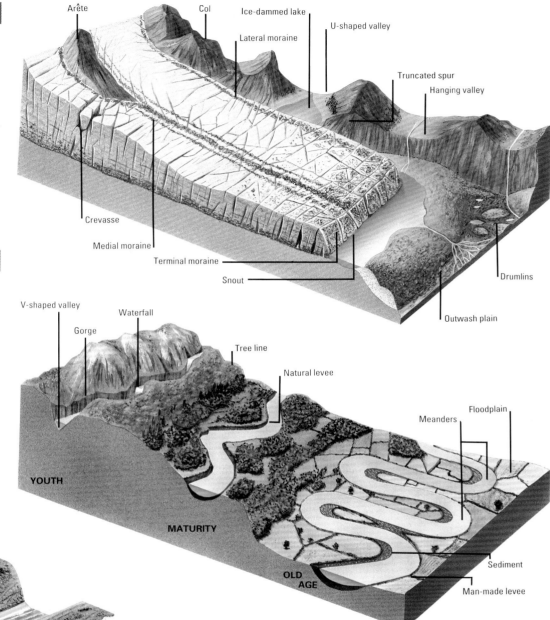

OCEANS

THE GREAT OCEANS

Relative sizes of the world's oceans

- Pacific
- Atlantic
- Indian
- Arctic

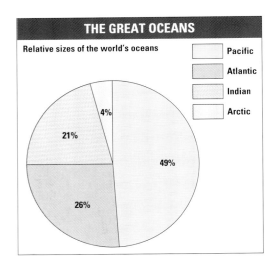

4%
21%
49%
26%

In a strict geographical sense there are only three true oceans – the Atlantic, Indian and Pacific. The legendary 'Seven Seas' would require these to be divided at the Equator and the addition of the Arctic Ocean – which accounts for less than 4% of the total sea area. The International Hydrographic Bureau does not recognize the Antarctic Ocean (even less the 'Southern Ocean') as a separate entity.

The Earth is a watery planet: more than 70% of its surface – over 360,000,000 square kilometres – is covered by the oceans and seas. The mighty Pacific alone accounts for nearly 36% of the total, and 49% of the sea area. Gravity holds in around 1,400 million cubic kilometres of water, of which over 97% is saline.

The vast underwater world starts in the shallows of the seaside and plunges to depths of more than 11,000 metres. The continental shelf, part of the landmass, drops gently to around 200 metres; here the seabed falls away suddenly at an angle of 3° to 6° – the continental slope. The third stage, called the continental rise, is more gradual with gradients varying from 1 in 100 to 1 in 700. At an average depth of 5,000 metres there begins the aptly-named abyssal plain – massive submarine depths where sunlight fails to penetrate and few creatures can survive.

From these plains rise volcanoes which, taken from base to top, rival and even surpass the biggest continental mountains in height. Mount Kea, on Hawaii, reaches a total of 10,203 metres, some 1,355 metres more than Mount Everest, though only 4,205 is visible above sea level.

In addition there are underwater mountain chains up to 1,000 kilometres across, whose peaks sometimes appear above sea level as islands such as Iceland and Tristan da Cunha.

THE OCEAN DEPTHS

Average and maximum depths of the world's great oceans, in metres

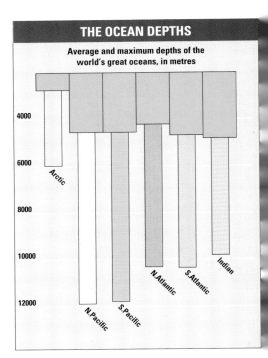

4000
6000
8000
10000
12000

Arctic
N.Pacific
S.Pacific
N.Atlantic
S.Atlantic
Indian

OCEAN CURRENTS

[Cold currents are shown in blue, warm currents in red]

WINTER IN NORTHERN HEMISPHERE

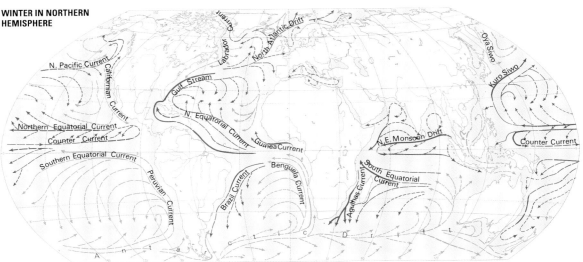

N. Pacific Current
Californian Current
Labrador Current
Gulf Stream
North Atlantic Drift
Oya Siwo
Kuro Siwo
Northern Equatorial Current
Counter Current
N. Equatorial Current
Guinea Current
N.E. Monsoon Drift
Counter Current
Southern Equatorial Current
Peruvian Current
Brazil Current
Benguela Current
Agulhas Current
South Equatorial Current
Antarctic

SUMMER IN NORTHERN HEMISPHERE

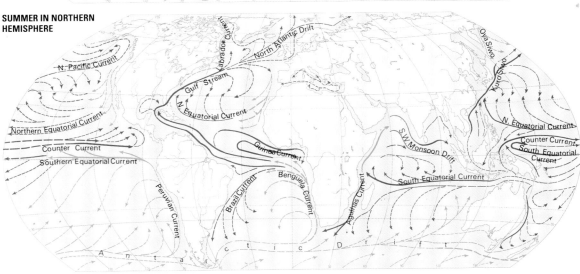

N. Pacific Current
Labrador Current
Gulf Stream
North Atlantic Drift
Oya Siwo
Kuro Siwo
Northern Equatorial Current
Counter Current
N. Equatorial Current
Guinea Current
S.W. Monsoon Drift
N. Equatorial Current
Counter Current
South Equatorial Current
Southern Equatorial Current
Brazil Current
Benguela Current
Peruvian Current
Agulhas Current
South Equatorial Current
Antarctic Drift

Moving immense quantities of energy as well as billions of tonnes of water every hour, the ocean currents are a vital part of the great heat engine that drives the Earth's climate. They themselves are produced by a twofold mechanism. At the surface, winds push huge masses of water before them; in the deep ocean, below an abrupt temperature gradient that separates the churning surface waters from the still depths, density variations cause slow vertical movements.

The pattern of circulation of the great surface currents is determined by the displacement known as the Coriolis effect. As the Earth turns beneath a moving object – whether it is a tennis ball or a vast mass of water – it appears to be deflected to one side. The deflection is most obvious near the Equator, where the Earth's surface is spinning eastwards at 1,700 km/h; currents moving polewards are curved clockwise in the northern hemisphere and anti-clockwise in the southern.

The result is a system of spinning circles known as gyres. The Coriolis effect piles up water on the left of each gyre, creating a narrow, fast-moving stream that is matched by a slower, broader returning current on the right. North and south of the Equator, the fastest currents are located in the west and in the east respectively. In each case, warm water moves from the Equator and cold water returns to it. Cold currents often bring an upwelling of nutrients with them, supporting the world's most economically important fisheries.

Depending on the prevailing winds, some currents on or near the Equator may reverse their direction in the course of the year – a seasonal variation on which Asian monsoon rains depend, and whose occasional failure can bring disaster to millions.

FISHING

Main commercial fishing areas

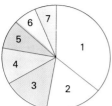

Percentage of world catch

1. North Pacific 36%
2. North Atlantic 17%
3. South Pacific 14%
4. Central Pacific 11%
5. Central Atlantic 9%
6. South Atlantic 7%
7. Indian 6%

Leading fishing nations

Japan 26.5% USSR 22.8% South Korea 8.3% North Korea 4.5% USA 3.3% China 3.1%

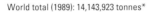

World total (1989): 14,143,923 tonnes*

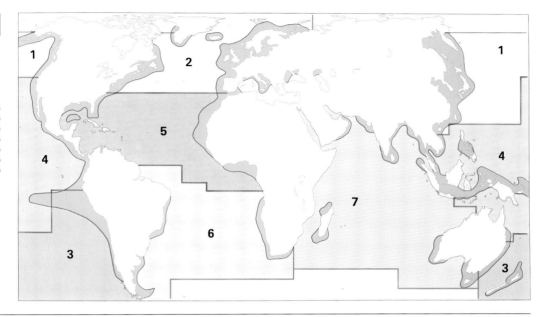

MARINE POLLUTION

Sources of marine oil pollution (1980s)

- Tanker operations — 22%
- Municipal wastes — 22%
- Tanker accidents — 12.5%
- Bilge and fuel oils — 9%
- Natural seeps — 7.5%
- Industrial waste — 6%
- Urban runoff — 3.5%
- Coastal oil refining — 3%
- Offshore oil rigs — 1.5%
- River runoffs — 12%
- Other — 1%

OIL SPILLS

Major oil spills from tankers and combined carriers

Year	Vessel	Location	Spill (barrels)**	Cause
1979	Atlantic Empress	West Indies	1,890,000	collision
1983	Castillo De Bellver	South Africa	1,760,000	fire
1978	Amoco Cadiz	France	1,628,000	grounding
1988	Odyssey	Canada	1,000,000	fire
1967	Torrey Canyon	UK	909,000	grounding
1972	Sea Star	Gulf of Oman	902,250	collision
1977	Hawaiian Patriot	Hawaiian Is.	742,500	fire
1979	Independenta	Turkey	696,350	collision
1976	Urquiola	Spain	670,000	grounding
1980	Irenes Serenade	Greece	600,000	fire
1989	Khark V	Morocco	560,000	fire

Other sources of major oil spills

Year	Vessel	Location	Spill (barrels)**	Cause
1983	Nowruz oilfield	Persian Gulf	4,250,000†	war
1979	Ixtoc 1 oilwell	Gulf of Mexico	4,200,000	blow-out
1991	Kuwait	Persian Gulf	2,500,000	war

** 1 barrel = 0.136 tonnes/159 lit./35 Imperial gal./42 US gal.   † estimated

RIVER POLLUTION

Sources of river pollution, USA (1987)

- Agriculture — 64%
- Mining — 9%
- Forestry — 9%
- Urban runoff — 6%
- Hydro-engineering — 5%
- Construction — 4%
- Land disposal — 9%
- Other — 2% / 1%

WATER POLLUTION

- ■ Severely polluted sea areas and lakes
- ■ Less polluted sea areas and lakes
- ■ Areas of frequent oil pollution by shipping
- ► Major oil tanker spills
- ▲ Major oil rig blow-outs
- ▼ Offshore dumpsites for industrial and municipal waste
- — Severely polluted rivers and estuaries

The most notorious tanker spillage of the 1980s occurred when the *Exxon Valdez* ran aground in Prince William Sound, Alaska, in 1989, spilling 267,000 barrels of crude oil close to shore in a sensitive ecological area. This rates as the world's 28th worst spill in terms of volume.

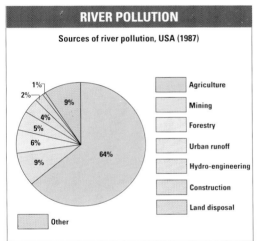

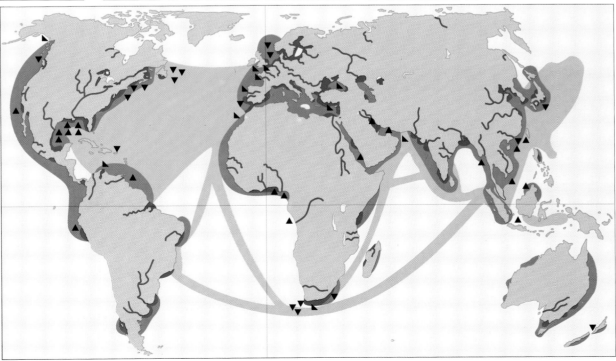

Statistics for the new republics of the former USSR, Czechoslovakia and Yugoslavia are not yet available.

CLIMATE

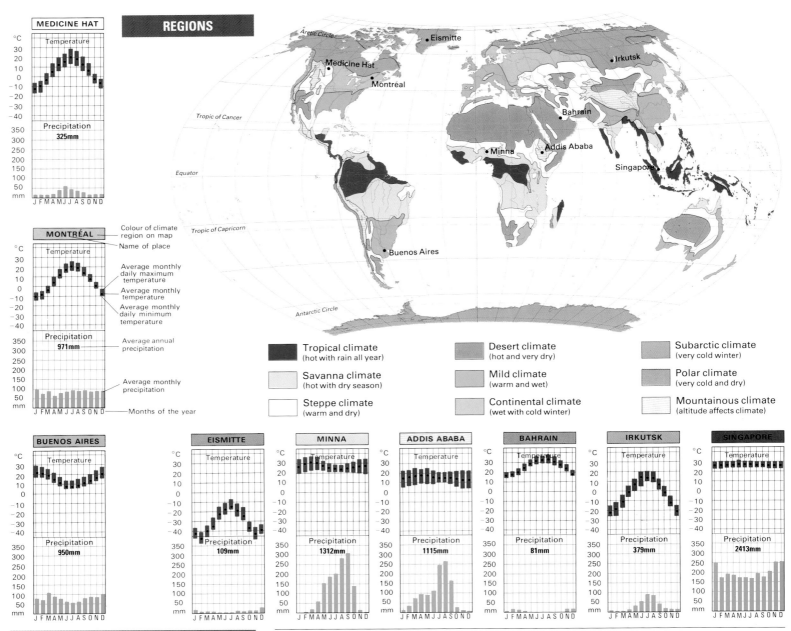

MEDICINE HAT
°C Temperature
30 20 10 0 -10 -20 -30 -40
Precipitation
325mm
350 300 250 200 150 100 50 mm
J F M A M J J A S O N D

MONTRÉAL
°C Temperature
30 20 10 0 -10 -20 -30 -40
— Colour of climate region on map
— Name of place
— Average monthly daily maximum temperature
— Average monthly temperature
— Average monthly daily minimum temperature
Precipitation
971mm
350 300 250 200 150 100 50 mm
— Average annual precipitation
— Average monthly precipitation
J F M A M J J A S O N D — Months of the year

Tropical climate (hot with rain all year)
Savanna climate (hot with dry season)
Steppe climate (warm and dry)

Desert climate (hot and very dry)
Mild climate (warm and wet)
Continental climate (wet with cold winter)

Subarctic climate (very cold winter)
Polar climate (very cold and dry)
Mountainous climate (altitude affects climate)

BUENOS AIRES
°C Temperature
30 20 10 0 -10 -20 -30 -40
Precipitation
950mm
350 300 250 200 150 100 50 mm
J F M A M J J A S O N D

EISMITTE
°C
30 20 10 0 -10 -20 -30 -40
Temperature
Precipitation
109mm
350 300 250 200 150 100 50 mm
J F M A M J J A S O N D

MINNA
°C Temperature
30 20 10 0 -10 -20 -30 -40
Precipitation
1312mm
350 300 250 200 150 100 50 mm
J F M A M J J A S O N D

ADDIS ABABA
°C Temperature
30 20 10 0 -10 -20 -30 -40
Precipitation
1115mm
350 300 250 200 150 100 50 mm
J F M A M J J A S O N D

BAHRAIN
°C Temperature
30 20 10 0 -10 -20 -30 -40
Precipitation
81mm
350 300 250 200 150 100 50 mm
J F M A M J J A S O N D

IRKUTSK
°C Temperature
30 20 10 0 -10 -20 -30 -40
Precipitation
379mm
350 300 250 200 150 100 50 mm
J F M A M J J A S O N D

SINGAPORE
°C Temperature
30 20 10 0 -10 -20 -30 -40
Precipitation
2413mm
350 300 250 200 150 100 50 mm
J F M A M J J A S O N D

CLIMATE RECORDS

Temperature

Highest recorded temperature: Al Aziziyah, Libya, 58°C [136.4°F], 13 September 1922.

Highest mean annual temperature: Dallol, Ethiopia, 34.4°C [94°F], 1960–66.

Longest heatwave: Marble Bar, W. Australia, 162 days over 38°C [100°F], 23 October 1923 to 7 April 1924.

Lowest recorded temperature (outside poles): Verkhoyansk, Siberia, -68°C [-90°F], 6 February 1933. Verkhoyansk also registered the greatest annual range of temperature: -70°C to 37°C [-94°F to 98°F].

Lowest mean annual temperature: Polus Nedostupnosti, Pole of Cold, Antarctica, -57.8°C [-72°F].

Precipitation

Driest place: Arica, N. Chile, 0.8mm [0.03 in] per year (60-year average).

Longest drought: Calama, N. Chile: no recorded rainfall in 400 years to 1971.

Wettest place (average): Tututendo, Colombia: mean annual rainfall 11,770 mm [463.4 in].

Wettest place (12 months): Cherrapunji, Meghalaya, N.E. India, 26,470 mm [1,040 in], August 1860 to August 1861. Cherrapunji also holds the record for rainfall in one month: 930 mm [37 in], July 1861.

Wettest place (24 hours): Cilaos, Réunion, Indian Ocean, 1,870 mm [73.6 in], 15–16 March 1952.

Heaviest hailstones: Gopalganj, Bangladesh, up to 1.02 kg [2.25 lb], 14 April 1986 (killed 92 people).

Heaviest snowfall (continuous): Bessans, Savoie, France, 1,730 mm [68 in] in 19 hours, 5–6 April 1969.

Heaviest snowfall (season/year): Paradise Ranger Station, Mt Rainier, Washington, USA, 31,102 mm [1,224.5 in], 19 February 1971 to 18 February 1972.

Pressure and winds

Highest barometric pressure: Agata, Siberia, 1,083.8 mb [32 in] at altitude 262 m [862 ft], 31 December 1968.

Lowest barometric pressure: Typhoon Tip, 480 km [300 mls] west of Guam, Pacific Ocean, 870 mb [25.69 in], 12 October 1979.

Highest recorded wind speed: Mt Washington, New Hampshire, USA, 371 km/h [231 mph], 12 April 1934. This is three times as strong as hurricane force on the Beaufort Scale.

Windiest place: Commonwealth Bay, George V Coast, Antarctica, where gales reach over 320 km/h [200 mph].

In sub-zero weather, even moderate winds significantly reduce effective temperatures. The chart below shows the windchill effect across a range of speeds. Figures in the pink zone are not dangerous to well-clad people; in the blue zone, the risk of serious frostbite is acute.

	Wind speed (km/h)				
	16	32	48	64	80
0°C	-8	-14	-17	-19	-20
-5°C	-14	-21	-25	-27	-28
-10°C	-20	-28	-33	-35	-36
-15°C	-26	-36	-40	-43	-44
-20°C	-32	-42	-48	-51	-52
-25°C	-38	-49	-56	-59	-60
-30°C	-44	-57	-63	-66	-68
-35°C	-51	-64	-72	-74	-76
-40°C	-57	-71	-78	-82	-84
-45°C	-63	-78	-86	-90	-92
-50°C	-69	-85	-94	-98	-100

BEAUFORT WIND SCALE

Named after the 19th-century British naval officer who devised it, the Beaufort Scale assesses wind speed according to its effects. It was originally designed as an aid for sailors, but has since been adapted for use on land.

Scale	Wind speed km/h	mph	Effect
0	0-1	0-1	Calm Smoke rises vertically
1	1-5	1-3	Light air Wind direction shown only by smoke drift
2	6-11	4-7	Light breeze Wind felt on face; leaves rustle; vanes moved by wind
3	12-19	8-12	Gentle breeze Leaves and small twigs in constant motion; wind extends small flag
4	20-28	13-18	Moderate Raises dust and loose paper; small branches move
5	29-38	19-24	Fresh Small trees in leaf sway; crested wavelets on inland waters
6	39-49	25-31	Strong Large branches move; difficult to use umbrellas; overhead wires whistle
7	50-61	32-38	Near gale Whole trees in motion; difficult to walk against wind
8	62-74	39-46	Gale Twigs break from trees; walking very difficult
9	75-88	47-54	Strong gale Slight structural damage
10	89-102	55-63	Storm Trees uprooted; serious structural damage
11	103-117	64-72	Violent storm Widespread damage
12	118+	73+	Hurricane

Conversions
°C = (°F −32) x 5/9;   °F = (°C x 9/5) + 32;   0°C = 32°F
1 in = 25.4 mm;   1 mm = 0.0394 in; 100 mm = 3.94 in

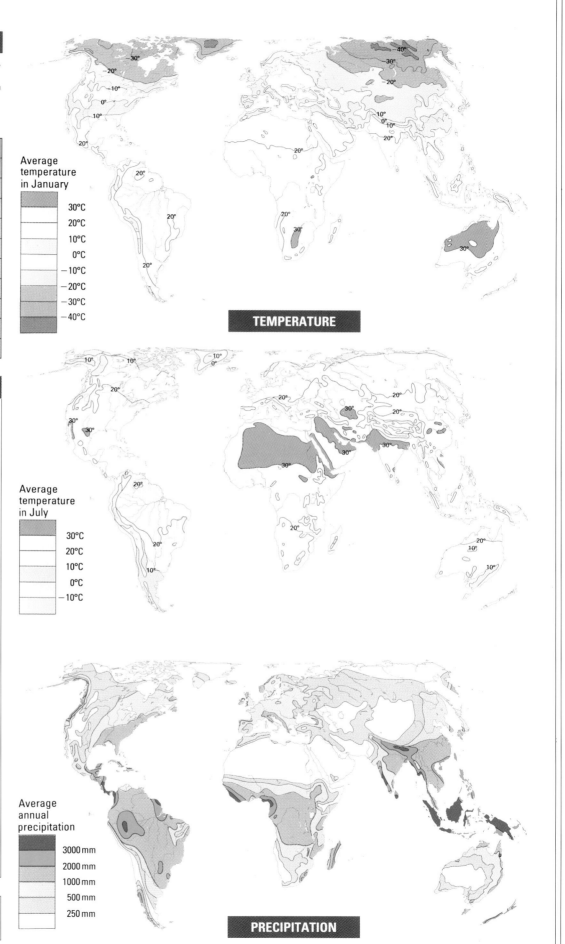

Average temperature in January

30°C
20°C
10°C
0°C
−10°C
−20°C
−30°C
−40°C

TEMPERATURE

Average temperature in July

30°C
20°C
10°C
0°C
−10°C

Average annual precipitation

3000 mm
2000 mm
1000 mm
500 mm
250 mm

PRECIPITATION

WATER

THE HYDROLOGICAL CYCLE

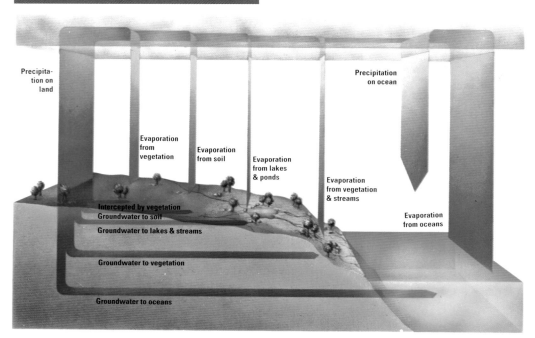

Precipitation on land

Precipitation on ocean

Evaporation from vegetation

Evaporation from soil

Evaporation from lakes & ponds

Evaporation from vegetation & streams

Evaporation from oceans

Intercepted by vegetation
Groundwater to soil
Groundwater to lakes & streams
Groundwater to vegetation
Groundwater to oceans

WATER DISTRIBUTION

The distribution of planetary water, by percentage. Oceans and ice-caps together account for more than 99% of the total; the breakdown of the remainder is estimated.

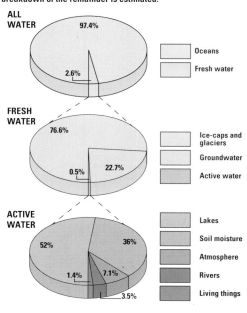

ALL WATER
97.4%
2.6%
- Oceans
- Fresh water

FRESH WATER
76.6%
0.5%
22.7%
- Ice-caps and glaciers
- Groundwater
- Active water

ACTIVE WATER
52%
36%
1.4%
7.1%
3.5%
- Lakes
- Soil moisture
- Atmosphere
- Rivers
- Living things

WATER RUNOFF

Annual freshwater runoff by continent in cubic kilometres

- Asia
- North America
- South America
- Australasia
- Europe
- Africa

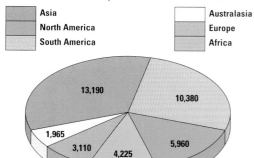

13,190
10,380
1,965
3,110
4,225
5,960

WATER UTILIZATION

The percentage breakdown of water usage by sector, selected countries (latest available year)*

- Domestic
- Industrial
- Agriculture

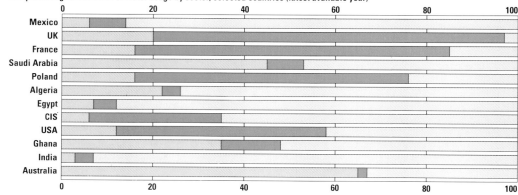

Mexico
UK
France
Saudi Arabia
Poland
Algeria
Egypt
CIS
USA
Ghana
India
Australia

0   20   40   60   80   100

WATER SUPPLY

Percentage of total population with access to safe drinking water (latest available year)*

- Over 90% with safe water
- 75 – 90% with safe water
- 60 – 75% with safe water
- 45 – 60% with safe water
- 30 – 45% with safe water
- Under 30% with safe water

Least well-provided countries

Country	%	Country	%
Cambodia	3%	Afghanistan	21%
Central Africa	12%	Congo	21%
Ethiopia	19%	Guinea-Bissau	21%
Uganda	20%	Sudan	21%

*Statistics for the new republics of the former USSR, Czechoslovakia and Yugoslavia are not yet available.
The map shows the statistics for the entire USSR, Czechoslovakia and Yugoslavia.

NATURAL VEGETATION

Regional variation in vegetation

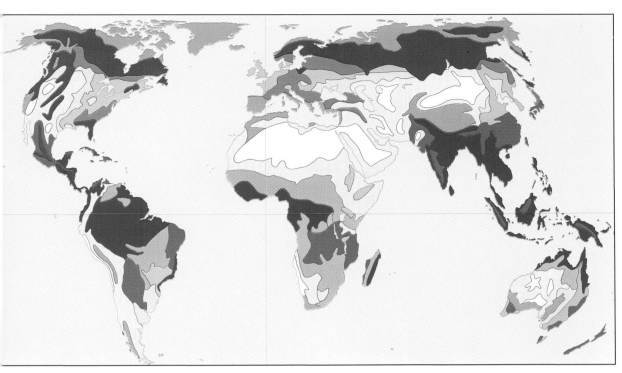

- Tundra and mountain vegetation
- Needleleaf evergreen forest
- Mixed needleleaf evergreen & broadleaf deciduous trees
- Broadleaf deciduous woodland
- Mid-latitude grassland
- Evergreen broadleaf and deciduous trees & shrubs
- Semi-desert scrub
- Desert
- Tropical grassland (savanna)
- Tropical broadleaf rainforest and monsoon forest
- Subtropical broadleaf and needleleaf forest

The map shows the natural 'climax vegetation' of regions, as dictated by climate and topography. In most cases, however, agricultural activity has drastically altered the vegetation pattern. Western Europe, for example, lost most of its broadleaf forest many centuries ago, while irrigation has turned some natural semi-desert into productive land.

LAND USE BY CONTINENT

- Forest
- Permanent pasture and rough grazing
- Permanent crops and plantations
- Arable
- Non-productive

NORTH AMERICA
32.2% · 37.6% · 17.3% · 12.6% · 0.3%

EUROPE
33.4% · 19.3% · 26.8% · 17.5% · 3%

ASIA
20.2% · 37.8% · 25% · 1.2% · 16%

SOUTH AMERICA
51.8% · 13.4% · 6.6% · 1.5% · 26.7%

AFRICA
23.2% · 44% · 26.6% · 0.6% · 5.6%

AUSTRALIA
23.5% · 18.5% · 5.7% · 0.1% · 52.2%

FORESTRY: PRODUCTION

	Forest & woodland (million hectares)	Annual production (1980s average, million cubic metres)	
		Fuelwood & charcoal	Industrial roundwood
World	*4,121.4*	*1,646.1*	*1,534.8*
USSR (1988)	928.6	85.6	284.9
S. America	867.1	217.0	91.7
N. America	806.6	154.4	538.7
Africa	705.3	384.7	53.4
Asia	497.2	739.1	245.7
Europe	159.1	56.5	292.1
Australasia	158.8	8.8	28.3

PAPER AND BOARD

Top producers (1988)**

USA	69,477
Japan	24,624
Canada	16,638
China	12,645
USSR	10,750

Top exporters (1988)**

Canada	11,420
Finland	7,185
Sweden	6,377
USA	4,294
Germany	3,780

** in thousand tonnes

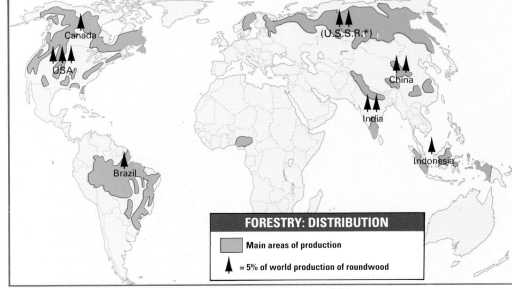

FORESTRY: DISTRIBUTION

- Main areas of production
- ▲ = 5% of world production of roundwood

Statistics for the new republics of the former USSR, Czechoslovakia and Yugoslavia are not yet available. The map shows the statistics for the entire USSR, Czechoslovakia and Yugoslavia.

ENVIRONMENT

Humans have always had a dramatic effect on their environment, at least since the invention of agriculture almost 10,000 years ago. Generally, the Earth has accepted human interference without obvious ill effects: the complex systems that regulate the global environment have been able to absorb substantial damage while maintaining a stable and comfortable home for the planet's trillions of lifeforms. But advancing human technology and the rapidly-expanding populations it supports are now threatening to overwhelm the Earth's ability to compensate.

Industrial wastes, acid rainfall, desertification and large-scale deforestation: all combine to create environmental change at a rate far faster than the slow cycles of planetary evolution can accommodate. Equipped with chain-saws and flamethrowers, humans can now destroy more forest in a day than their ancestors could in a century, upsetting the balance between plant and animal, carbon dioxide and oxygen, on which all life ultimately depends.

The fossil fuels that power industrial civilization have pumped enough carbon dioxide and other so-called greenhouse gases into the atmosphere to make climatic change a near-certainty. Chlorofluorocarbons – CFCs – and other man-made chemicals are rapidly eroding the ozone layer, the atmosphere's screen against ultra-violet radiation.

As a result, the Earth's average temperature has risen by approximately 0.5°C since the beginning of the 20th century, and is still rising.

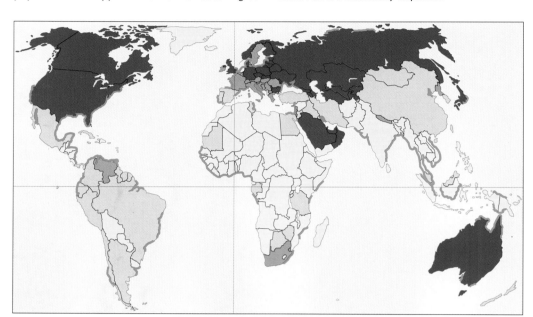

GLOBAL WARMING

Carbon dioxide emissions in tonnes per person per year (1980s)

High atmospheric concentrations of heat-absorbing gases, especially carbon dioxide, appear to be causing a steady rise in average temperatures worldwide – up to 1.5°C by the year 2020, according to some estimates. Global warming is likely to bring with it a rise in sea levels that may flood some of the Earth's most densely populated coastlines.

- Over 10 tonnes of CO_2
- 5 – 10 tonnes of CO_2
- 1 – 5 tonnes of CO_2
- Under 1 tonne of CO_2

— Coastal areas in danger of flooding from rising sea levels caused by global warming

GREENHOUSE POWER

Relative contributions to the Greenhouse Effect by the major heat-absorbing gases in the atmosphere

The chart combines greenhouse potency and volume. Carbon dioxide has a greenhouse potential of only 1, but its concentration of 350 parts per million makes it predominate. CFC 12, with 25,000 times the absorption capacity of CO_2, is present only as 0.00044 ppm.

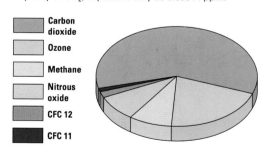

- Carbon dioxide
- Ozone
- Methane
- Nitrous oxide
- CFC 12
- CFC 11

CARBON DIOXIDE

Carbon dioxide released in millions of tonnes (1980s)

Although most of the net increase in atmospheric carbon dioxide comes from fossil fuel combustion, deforestation and changing land use also contribute.

- Fuel burning
- Deforestation

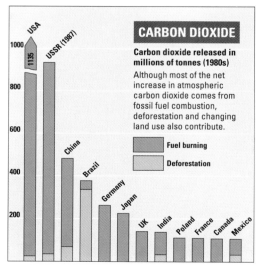

GLOBAL WARMING

The rise in average temperatures caused by carbon dioxide and other greenhouse gases (1960–2020)

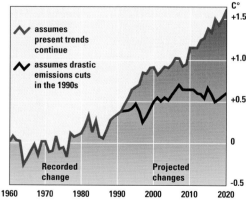

assumes present trends continue

assumes drastic emissions cuts in the 1990s

Recorded change

Projected changes

THE GREENHOUSE EFFECT

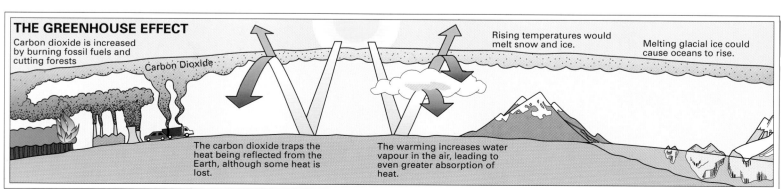

Carbon dioxide is increased by burning fossil fuels and cutting forests

Carbon Dioxide

Rising temperatures would melt snow and ice.

Melting glacial ice could cause oceans to rise.

The carbon dioxide traps the heat being reflected from the Earth, although some heat is lost.

The warming increases water vapour in the air, leading to even greater absorption of heat.

Statistics for the new republics of the former USSR, Czechoslovakia and Yugoslavia are not yet available.
The map shows the statistics for the entire USSR, Czechoslovakia and Yugoslavia.

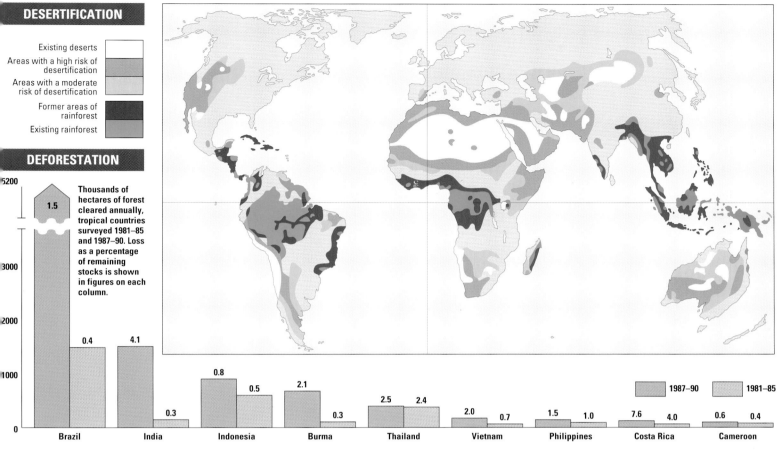

DESERTIFICATION

Existing deserts

Areas with a high risk of desertification

Areas with a moderate risk of desertification

Former areas of rainforest

Existing rainforest

DEFORESTATION

5200

1.5

Thousands of hectares of forest cleared annually, tropical countries surveyed 1981–85 and 1987–90. Loss as a percentage of remaining stocks is shown in figures on each column.

3000

2000

1000

0

1.5 / 0.4 — Brazil
4.1 / 0.3 — India
0.8 / 0.5 — Indonesia
2.1 / 0.3 — Burma
2.5 / 2.4 — Thailand
2.0 / 0.7 — Vietnam
1.5 / 1.0 — Philippines
7.6 / 4.0 — Costa Rica
0.6 / 0.4 — Cameroon

1987–90   1981–85

DESERTIFICATION

The result of overcultivation, overgrazing and overcutting of ground cover for firewood, desertification is also caused by faulty irrigation techniques that leave land too saline or alkaline to support viable crops. Changing rainfall patterns or prolonged droughts exacerbate the process. As much as 60% of the world's croplands and rangelands are in some danger, with 6 million hectares lost altogether every year and a further 21 million rendered agriculturally worthless. Africa is especially badly hit: in Mali, the Sahara advanced 350 kilometres southwards in only 20 years.

DEFORESTATION

The Earth's remaining forests are under attack from three directions: expanding agriculture, logging, and growing consumption of fuelwood, often in combination. Sometimes deforestation is the direct result of government policy, as in the efforts made to resettle the urban poor in some parts of Brazil; just as often, it comes about despite state attempts at conservation. Loggers, licensed or unlicensed, blaze a trail into virgin forest, often destroying twice as many trees as they harvest. Landless farmers follow, burning away most of what remains to plant their crops, completing the destruction.

ACID RAIN

Killing trees, poisoning lakes and rivers and eating away buildings, acid rain is mostly produced by sulphur dioxide emissions from industry, although the burning of savanna lands by African farmers has also caused acid downpours on tropical rainforests. By the late 1980s, acid rain had sterilized 4,000 or more of Sweden's lakes and left 45% of Switzerland's alpine conifers dead or dying, while the monuments of Greece were dissolving in Athens' smog. Prevailing wind patterns mean that the acids often fall many hundred kilometres from where the original pollutants were discharged.

ACID RAIN

Acid rainfall and sources of acidic emissions (1980s)

Acid rain is caused when sulphur and nitrogen oxides in the air combine with water vapour to form sulphuric, nitric and other acids.

Regions where sulphur and nitrogen oxides are released in high concentrations, mainly from fossil fuel combustion.

• Major cities with high levels of air pollution (including nitrogen and sulphur emissions)

Areas of heavy acid deposition

pH numbers indicate acidity, decreasing from a neutral 7. Normal rain, slightly acid from dissolved carbon dioxide, never exceeds a pH of 5.6.

pH less than 4.0 (most acidic)

pH 4.0 to 4.5

pH 4.5 to 5.0

Areas where acid rain is a potential problem

POPULATION

Developed nations such as the UK have populations evenly spread across age groups and, usually, a growing proportion of elderly people. Developing nations fall into a pattern somewhere between that of Kenya and the world model: the great majority of their people are in the younger age groups, about to enter their most fertile years. In time, even Kenya's population profile should resemble the world profile, but the transition will come about only after a few more generations of rapid population growth.

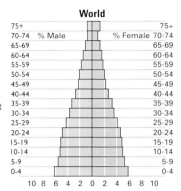

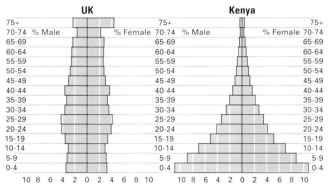

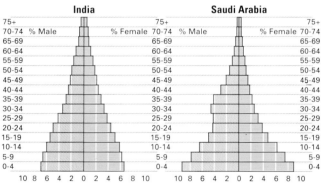

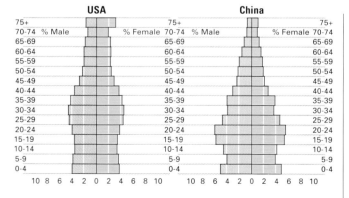

MOST POPULOUS NATIONS [in millions (1993)]

1.	China	1,187	9.	Pakistan	115	17.	Italy	57
2.	India	879	10.	Mexico	89	18.	Thailand	57
3.	USA	255	11.	Nigeria	88	19.	France	57
4.	Indonesia	191	12.	Germany	80	20.	Iran	56
5.	Brazil	156	13.	Vietnam	69	21.	Egypt	55
6.	Russia	149	14.	Philippines	64	22.	Ethiopia	55
7.	Japan	124	15.	Turkey	58	23.	Ukraine	52
8.	Bangladesh	119	16.	UK	57	24.	S. Korea	43

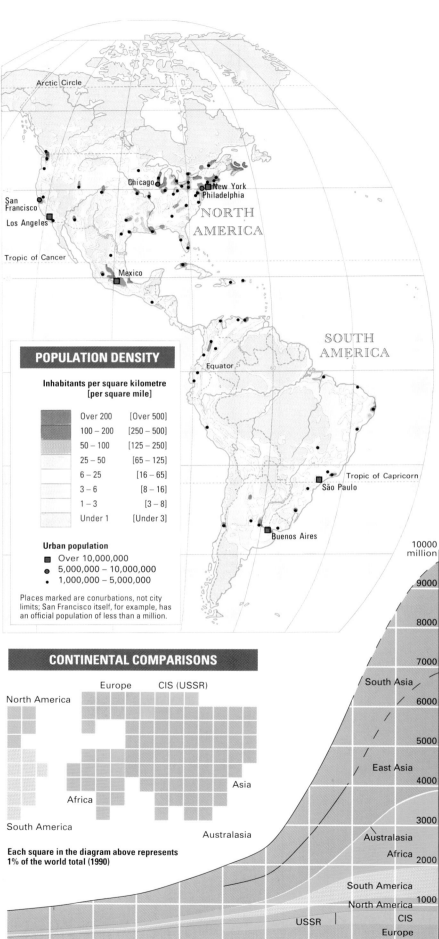

POPULATION DENSITY

Inhabitants per square kilometre [per square mile]

Over 200	[Over 500]
100 – 200	[250 – 500]
50 – 100	[125 – 250]
25 – 50	[65 – 125]
6 – 25	[16 – 65]
3 – 6	[8 – 16]
1 – 3	[3 – 8]
Under 1	[Under 3]

Urban population
- ■ Over 10,000,000
- ● 5,000,000 – 10,000,000
- • 1,000,000 – 5,000,000

Places marked are conurbations, not city limits; San Francisco itself, for example, has an official population of less than a million.

CONTINENTAL COMPARISONS

Each square in the diagram above represents 1% of the world total (1990)

CARTOGRAPHY BY PHILIP'S. COPYRIGHT REED INTERNATIONAL BOOKS LTD.

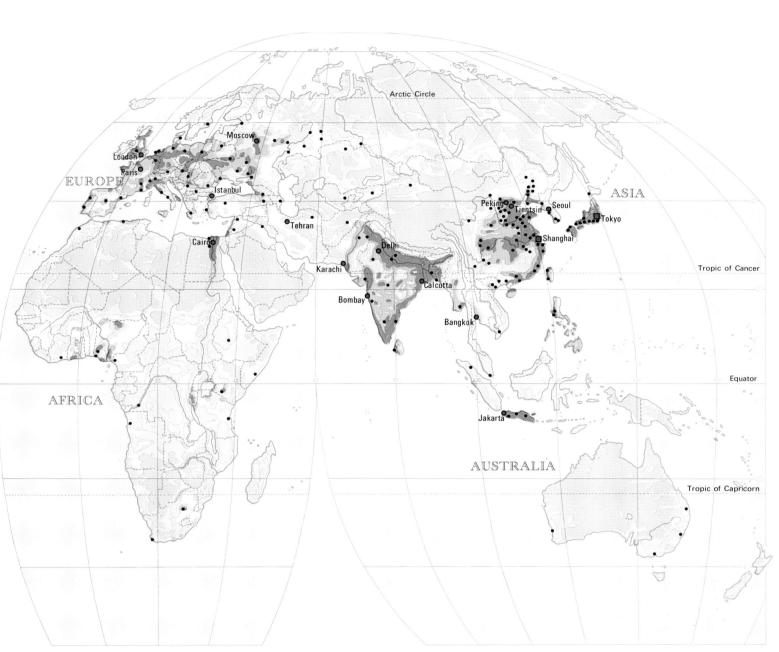

Arctic Circle

EUROPE

Moscow

London
Paris

Istanbul

Tehran

Cairo

AFRICA

ASIA

Peking Tientsin Seoul

Tokyo

Shanghai

Tropic of Cancer

Delhi

Karachi

Calcutta

Bombay

Bangkok

Equator

Jakarta

AUSTRALIA

Tropic of Capricorn

URBAN POPULATION

Percentage of total population living in towns and cities (1990)

Over 75%

50 – 75%

25 – 50%

10 – 25%

Under 10%

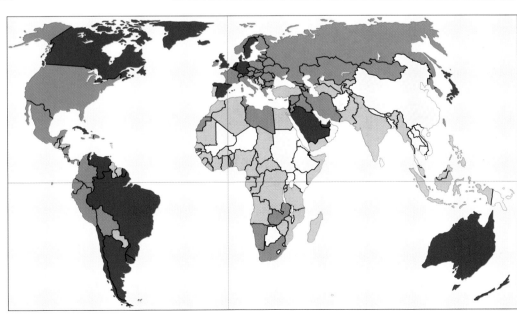

Most urbanized

Singapore	100%
Belgium	97%
Kuwait	96%
Hong Kong	93%
UK	93%

Least urbanized

Bhutan	5%
Burundi	7%
Rwanda	8%
Burkina Faso	9%
Nepal	10%

THE HUMAN FAMILY

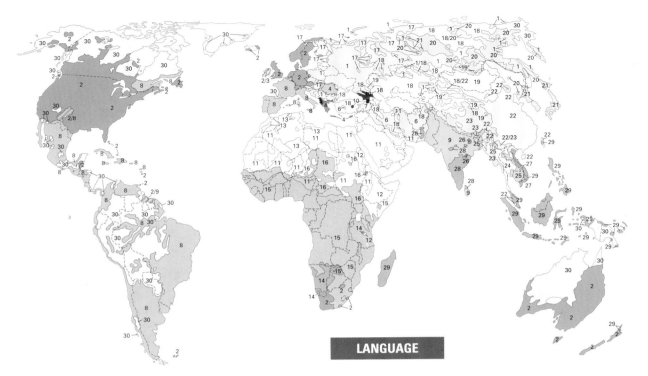

MOTHER TONGUES
Chinese 1,069 million (Mandarin 864), English 443, Hindi 352, Spanish 341, Russian 293, Arabic 197, Bengali 184, Portuguese 173, Malay-Indonesian 142, Japanese 125, French 121, German 118, Urdu 92, Punjabi 84, Korean 71.

OFFICIAL LANGUAGES
English 27% of world population, Chinese 19%, Hindi 13.5%, Spanish 5.4%, Russian 5.2%, French 4.2%, Arabic 3.3%, Portuguese 3%, Malay 3%, Bengali 2.9%, Japanese 2.3%

Language can be classified by ancestry and structure. For example, the Romance and Germanic groups are both derived from an Indo-European language believed to have been spoken 5,000 years ago.

LANGUAGE

INDO-EUROPEAN FAMILY

1	Balto-Slavic group (incl. Russian, Ukrainian)
2	Germanic group (incl. English, German)
3	Celtic group
4	Greek
5	Albanian
6	Iranian group
7	Armenian
8	Romance group (incl. Spanish, Portuguese, French, Italian)
9	Indo-Aryan group (incl. Hindi, Bengali, Urdu, Punjabi, Marathi)
10	CAUCASIAN FAMILY

AFRO-ASIATIC FAMILY

11	Semitic group (incl. Arabic)
12	Kushitic group
13	Berber group
14	KHOISAN FAMILY
15	NIGER-CONGO FAMILY
16	NILO-SAHARAN FAMILY
17	URALIC FAMILY

ALTAIC FAMILY

18	Turkic group
19	Mongolian group
20	Tungus-Manchu group
21	Japanese and Korean

SINO-TIBETAN FAMILY

22	Sinitic (Chinese) languages
23	Tibetic-Burmic languages
24	TAI FAMILY

AUSTRO-ASIATIC FAMILY

25	Mon-Khmer group
26	Munda group
27	Vietnamese
28	DRAVIDIAN FAMILY (incl. Telugu, Tamil)
29	AUSTRONESIAN FAMILY (incl. Malay-Indonesian)
30	OTHER LANGUAGES

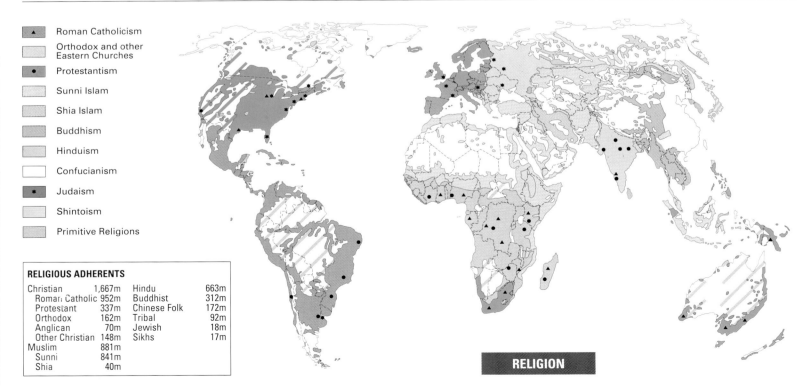

- ▲ Roman Catholicism
- Orthodox and other Eastern Churches
- ● Protestantism
- Sunni Islam
- Shia Islam
- Buddhism
- Hinduism
- Confucianism
- ✶ Judaism
- Shintoism
- Primitive Religions

RELIGION

RELIGIOUS ADHERENTS

Christian	1,667m	Hindu	663m
Roman Catholic	952m	Buddhist	312m
Protestant	337m	Chinese Folk	172m
Orthodox	162m	Tribal	92m
Anglican	70m	Jewish	18m
Other Christian	148m	Sikhs	17m
Muslim	881m		
Sunni	841m		
Shia	40m		

UNITED NATIONS

Created in 1945 to promote peace and co-operation and based in New York, the United Nations is the world's largest international organization, with 184 members and an annual budget of US $2.6 billion (1994–95). Each member of the General Assembly has one vote, while the permanent members of the 15-nation Security Council – USA, Russia, China, UK and France – hold a veto. The 54 members of the Economic and Social Council are responsible for economic, social, cultural, educational, health and related matters. The Secretariat is the UN's principal administrative arm; the only territory now administered by the Trusteeship Council is Belau (by the USA). The UN has 16 specialized agencies – based in Canada, France, Switzerland and Italy as well as the USA – which help members in fields such as education (UNESCO), agriculture (FAO), medicine (WHO) and finance (IFC).

[The International Court of Justice is based in The Hague]

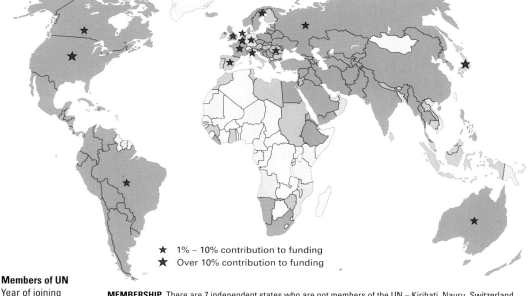

★ 1% – 10% contribution to funding
★ Over 10% contribution to funding

Members of UN
Year of joining

	1940s
	1950s
	1960s
	1970s
	1980s
	1990s
	Non-members

MEMBERSHIP There are 7 independent states who are not members of the UN – Kiribati, Nauru, Switzerland, Taiwan, Tonga, Tuvalu and Vatican City. By the end of 1992, all the successor states of the former USSR had joined. There were 51 members in 1945. Official languages are Chinese, English, French, Russian, Spanish and Arabic.

FUNDING The UN budget for 1994–95 is US $2.6 billion. Contributions are assessed by the members' ability to pay, with the maximum 25% of the total, the minimum 0.01%. Contributions for 1992–94 were: USA 25%, Japan 12.45%, Germany 8.93%, Russia 6.71%, France 6%, UK 5.02%, Italy 4.29%, Canada 3.11% (others 28.49%).

PEACEKEEPING The UN has been involved in 33 peacekeeping operations worldwide since 1948 and there are currently 17 areas of UN patrol. In July 1993 there were 80,146 'blue berets' from 74 countries.

EC As from December 1993 the European Union (EU) refers to matters of foreign policy, security and justice. The European Community (EC) refers to all other matters. The 12 members – Belgium, Denmark, France, Germany, Greece, Ireland, Italy, Luxembourg, Netherlands, Portugal, Spain and the UK – aim to integrate economies, co-ordinate social developments and bring about political union. These members of what is now the world's biggest market share agricultural and industrial policies and tariffs on trade.

EFTA European Free Trade Association (formed in 1960). Portugal left the 'Seven' in 1989 to join the EC.

ACP African-Caribbean-Pacific (1963).

NATO North Atlantic Treaty Organization (formed in 1949). It continues after 1991 despite the winding up of the Warsaw Pact.

OAS Organization of American States (1949). It aims to promote social and economic co-operation between developed countries of North America and developing nations of Latin America.

ASEAN Association of South-east Asian Nations (1967).

OAU Organization of African Unity (1963). Its 52 members represent over 90% of Africa's population.

LAIA Latin American Integration Association (1980).

OECD Organization for Economic Co-operation and Development (1961). The 24 major Western free-market economies. 'G7' is its 'inner group' of USA, Canada, Japan, UK, Germany, Italy and France.

COMMONWEALTH The Commonwealth of Nations evolved from the British Empire; it comprises 18 nations recognizing the British monarch as head of state and 32 with their own heads of state.

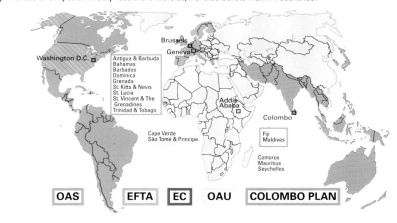

| OAS | EFTA | EC | OAU | COLOMBO PLAN |

OPEC Organization of Petroleum Exporting Countries (1960). It controls about three-quarters of the world's oil supply.

ARAB LEAGUE (1945) The League's aim is to promote economic, social, political and military co-operation.

COLOMBO PLAN (1951) Its 26 members aim to promote economic and social development in Asia and the Pacific.

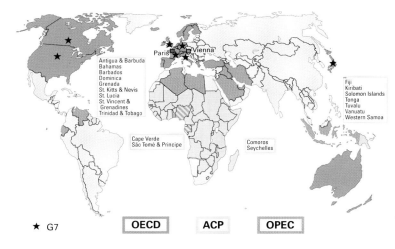

★ G7

| OECD | ACP | OPEC |

| NATO | LAIA | ARAB LEAGUE | COMMONWEALTH | ASEAN |

CARTOGRAPHY BY PHILIP'S. COPYRIGHT REED INTERNATIONAL BOOKS LTD

WEALTH

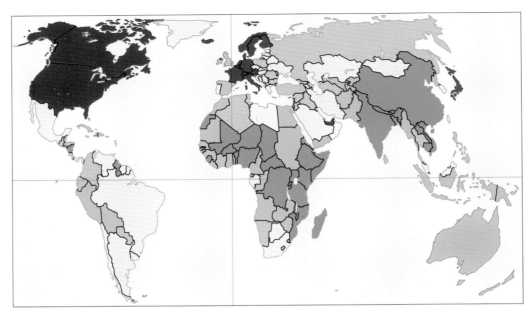

Gross National Product per capita: the value of total production divided by the population (1991)

Over 400% of world average

200 – 400% of world average

100 – 200% of world average

[World average wealth per person US $4,210]

50 – 100% of world average

25 – 50% of world average

10 – 25% of world average

Under 10% of world average

Richest countries		Poorest countries	
Switzerland	$33,510	Mozambique	$70
Luxembourg	$31,080	Tanzania	$100
Japan	$26,920	Ethiopia	$120
Sweden	$25,490	Somalia	$150

WEALTH CREATION

The Gross National Product (GNP) of the world's largest economies, US $ billion (1991)

1.	USA	5,686,038	21.	Austria	157,538
2.	Japan	3,337,191	22.	Iran	127,366
3.	Germany	1,516,785	23.	Finland	121,982
4.	France	1,167,749	24.	Denmark	121,695
5.	Italy	1,072,198	25.	Ukraine	121,458
6.	UK	963,696	26.	Indonesia	111,409
7.	Canada	568,765	27.	Saudi Arabia	105,133
8.	Spain	486,614	28.	Turkey	103,388
9.	Russia	479,546	29.	Norway	102,885
10.	Brazil	447,324	30.	Argentina	91,211
11.	China	424,012	31.	South Africa	90,953
12.	Australia	287,765	32.	Thailand	89,548
13.	India	284,668	33.	Hong Kong	77,302
14.	Netherlands	278,839	34.	Poland	70,640
15.	South Korea	274,464	35.	Greece	65,504
16.	Mexico	252,381	36.	Israel	59,128
17.	Switzerland	225,890	37.	Portugal	58,451
18.	Sweden	218,934	38.	Venezuela	52,775
19.	Belgium	192,370	39.	Algeria	52,239
20.	Taiwan	161,000	40.	Pakistan	46,725

THE WEALTH GAP

The world's richest and poorest countries, by Gross National Product per capita in US $ (1991)

1.	Switzerland	33,510	1.	Mozambique	70
2.	Liechtenstein	33,000	2.	Tanzania	100
3.	Luxembourg	31,080	3.	Ethiopia	120
4.	Japan	26,920	4.	Somalia	150
5.	Sweden	25,490	5.	Uganda	160
6.	Bermuda	25,000	6.	Bhutan	180
7.	Finland	24,400	7.	Nepal	180
8.	Norway	24,160	8.	Guinea-Bissau	190
9.	Denmark	23,660	9.	Cambodia	200
10.	Germany	23,650	10.	Burundi	210
11.	Iceland	22,580	11.	Madagascar	210
12.	USA	22,560	12.	Sierra Leone	210
13.	Canada	21,260	13.	Bangladesh	220
14.	France	20,600	14.	Chad	220
15.	Austria	20,380	15.	Zaire	220
16.	UAE	19,500	16.	Laos	230
17.	Belgium	19,300	17.	Malawi	230
18.	Italy	18,580	18.	Rwanda	260
19.	Netherlands	18,560	19.	Mali	280
20.	UK	16,750	20.	Guyana	290

GNP per capita is calculated by dividing a country's Gross National Product by its population.

CONTINENTAL SHARES

Shares of population and of wealth (GNP) by continent

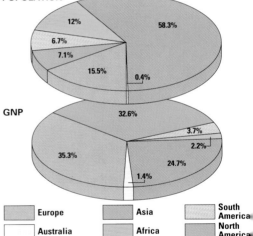

POPULATION

GNP

Europe	Asia	South America
Australia	Africa	North America

INFLATION

Average annual rate of inflation (1980–91)*

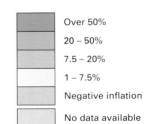

Over 50%

20 – 50%

7.5 – 20%

1 – 7.5%

Negative inflation

No data available

Highest average inflation		Lowest average inflation	
Nicaragua	584%	Oman	–3.1%
Argentina	417%	Kuwait	–2.7%
Brazil	328%	Saudi Arabia	–2.4%
Peru	287%	Equatorial Guinea	–0.9%
Bolivia	263%	Albania	–0.4%
Israel	89%	Bahrain	–0.3%
Mexico	66%	Libya	0.2%

*Statistics for the new republics of the former USSR, Czechoslovakia and Yugoslavia are not yet available.
The map shows the statistics for the entire USSR, Czechoslovakia and Yugoslavia.

Aid provided or received, divided by total population in US $ (1990)*

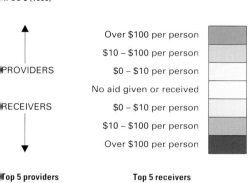

PROVIDERS
- Over $100 per person
- $10 – $100 per person
- $0 – $10 per person
- No aid given or received

RECEIVERS
- $0 – $10 per person
- $10 – $100 per person
- Over $100 per person

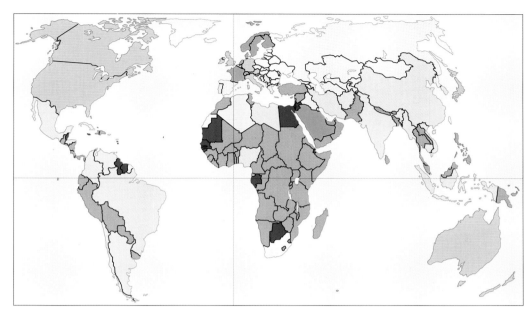

Top 5 providers
Kuwait	$793
UAE	$555
Norway	$287
Saudi Arabia	$248
Sweden	$234

Top 5 receivers
Israel	$295
Djibouti	$293
Jordan	$221
Dominica	$185
Surinam	$135

DEBT AND AID

International debtors and the aid they receive (1989)

Although aid grants make a vital contribution to many of the world's poorer countries, they are usually dwarfed by the burden of debt that developing economies are expected to repay. In the case of Mozambique, aid amounted to more than 70% of GNP. In 1990, the World Bank rated Mozambique as the world's poorest country; yet debt interest payments came to almost 75 times its entire export earnings.

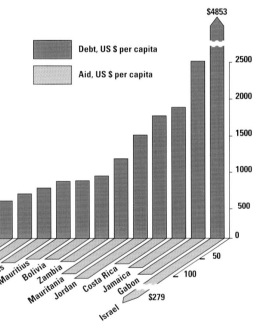

- Debt, US $ per capita
- Aid, US $ per capita

DISTRIBUTION OF SPENDING

Percentage share of household spending

- Food
- Clothing
- Energy & Housing
- Medicine & Education
- Transport
- Other

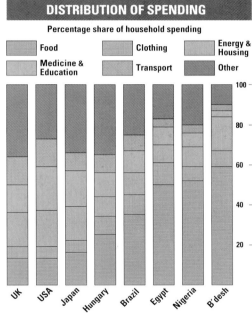

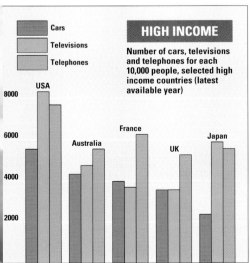

HIGH INCOME
- Cars
- Televisions
- Telephones

Number of cars, televisions and telephones for each 10,000 people, selected high income countries (latest available year)

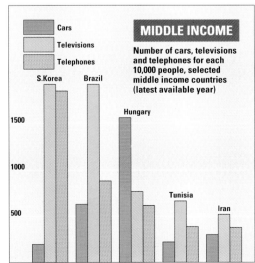

MIDDLE INCOME
- Cars
- Televisions
- Telephones

Number of cars, televisions and telephones for each 10,000 people, selected middle income countries (latest available year)

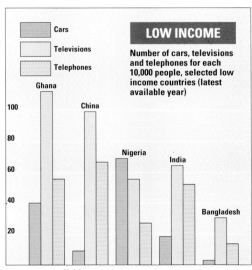

LOW INCOME
- Cars
- Televisions
- Telephones

Number of cars, televisions and telephones for each 10,000 people, selected low income countries (latest available year)

*Statistics for the new republics of the former USSR, Czechoslovakia and Yugoslavia are not yet available.
The map shows the statistics for the entire USSR, Czechoslovakia and Yugoslavia.*

QUALITY OF LIFE

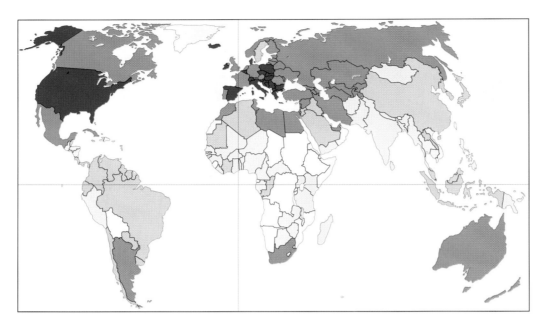

FOOD CONSUMPTION

Average daily food intake in calories per person (1989)*

- Over 3,500 calories per person
- 3,000 – 3,500 calories per person
- 2,500 – 3,000 calories per person
- 2,000 – 2,500 calories per person
- Under 2,000 calories per person
- No available data

Top 5 countries
Belgium	3,902 cal.
Greece	3,825 cal.
Ireland	3,778 cal.
Bulgaria	3,707 cal.
USA	3,650 cal.

Bottom 5 countries
Ethiopia	1,666 cal
Mozambique	1,679 cal
Chad	1,742 cal
Sierra Leone	1,799 cal
Angola	1,806 cal

[UK 3,148]

HOSPITAL CAPACITY

Hospital beds available for each 1,000 people (latest available year)

Highest capacity		Lowest capacity	
Finland	14.9	Bangladesh	0.2
Sweden	13.2	Nepal	0.2
France	12.9	Ethiopia	0.3
USSR	12.8	Mauritania	0.4
Netherlands	12.0	Mali	0.5
North Korea	11.7	Burkina Faso	0.6
Switzerland	11.3	Pakistan	0.6
Austria	10.4	Niger	0.7
Czechoslovakia	10.1	Haiti	0.8
Hungary	9.1	Chad	0.8

[USA 5.9] [UK 8]

Although the ratio of people to hospital beds gives a good approximation of a country's health provision, it is not an absolute indicator. Raw numbers may mask inefficiency and other weaknesses: the high availability of beds in North Korea, for example, has not prevented infant mortality rates almost three times as high as in the United Kingdom.

LIFE EXPECTANCY

Years of life expectancy at birth, selected countries (1988–89)

The chart shows combined data for both sexes. On average, women live longer than men worldwide, even in developing countries with high maternal mortality rates. Overall, life expectancy is steadily rising, though the difference between rich and poor nations remains dramatic.

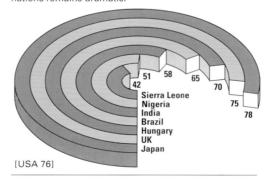

51 58 65
42   70
            75
              78

Sierra Leone
Nigeria
India
Brazil
Hungary
UK
Japan

[USA 76]

INFECTIOUS DISEASE

Deaths from infectious disease, per 100,000 people, selected countries (latest available year)

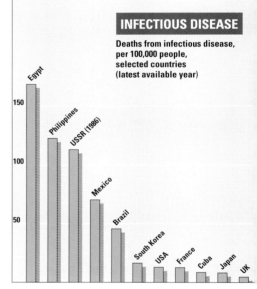

CHILD MORTALITY

Number of babies who will die before the age of one year, per 1,000 live births (average 1990–95)*

- Over 150 deaths per 1,000 births
- 100 – 150 deaths per 1,000 births
- 50 – 100 deaths per 1,000 births
- 20 – 50 deaths per 1,000 births
- 10 – 20 deaths per 1,000 births
- Under 10 deaths per 1,000 births

Highest child mortality		Lowest child mortality	
Afghanistan	162	Hong Kong	6
Mali	159	Denmark	6
Sierra Leone	143	Japan	5
Guinea-Bissau	140	Iceland	5
Malawi	138	Finland	5

[USA 9] [UK 8]

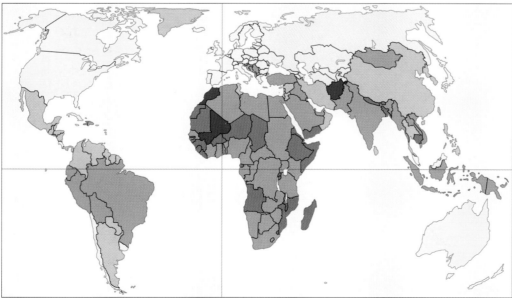

*Statistics for the new republics of the former USSR, Czechoslovakia and Yugoslavia are not yet available.
The map shows the statistics for the entire USSR, Czechoslovakia and Yugoslavia.

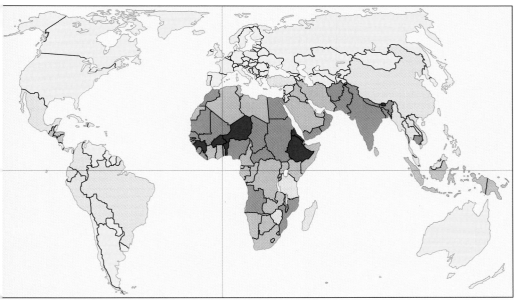

ILLITERACY

Percentage of the total population unable to read or write (latest available year)*

- Over 75% of population illiterate
- 50 – 75% of population illiterate
- 25 – 50% of population illiterate
- 10 – 15% of population illiterate
- Under 10% of population illiterate

Educational expenditure per person (latest available year)

Top 5 countries		Bottom 5 countries	
Sweden	$997	Chad	$2
Qatar	$989	Bangladesh	$3
Canada	$983	Ethiopia	$3
Norway	$971	Nepal	$4
Switzerland	$796	Somalia	$4

EDUCATION

Percentage of age group in secondary school, selected countries (latest available year)

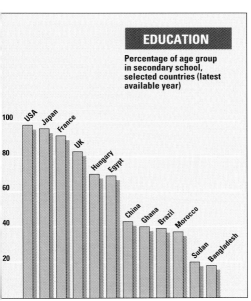

FERTILITY AND EDUCATION

Fertility rates compared with female education, selected countries (latest available year)

- Fertility rate: number of children borne by average woman
- Percentage of female age group in secondary education

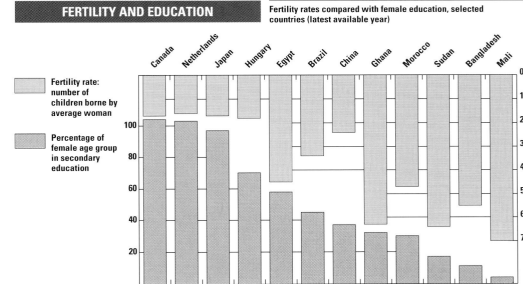

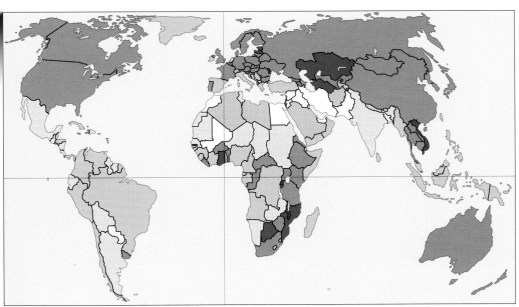

WOMEN IN THE WORKFORCE

Women in paid employment as a percentage of the total workforce (latest available year)

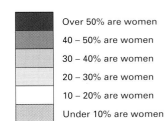

- Over 50% are women
- 40 – 50% are women
- 30 – 40% are women
- 20 – 30% are women
- 10 – 20% are women
- Under 10% are women

Most women in the workforce		Fewest women in the workforce	
Kazakhstan	54%	Guinea-Bissau	3%
Rwanda	54%	Oman	6%
Botswana	53%	Afghanistan	8%
Burundi	53%	Libya	8%
Mozambique	52%	Algeria	9%

*Statistics for the new republics of the former USSR, Czechoslovakia and Yugoslavia are not yet available.
The map shows the statistics for the entire USSR, Czechoslovakia and Yugoslavia.

ENERGY

PRODUCTION
[Each square represents 1% of world energy production]

CONSUMPTION
[Each square represents 1% of world energy consumption]

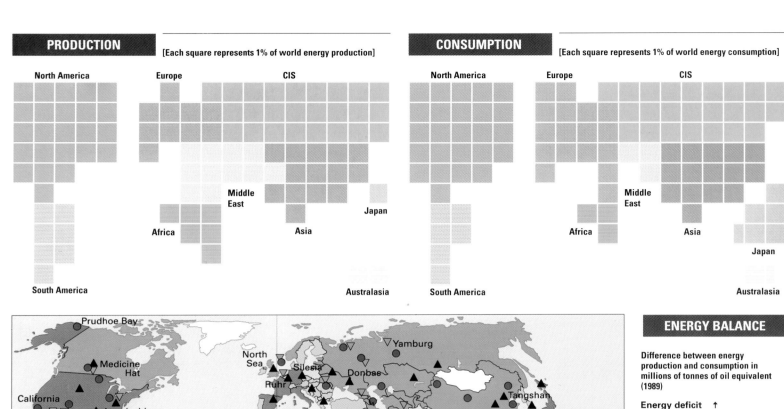

North America   Europe   CIS

Middle East

Japan

Africa   Asia

South America   Australasia

North America   Europe   CIS

Middle East

Africa   Asia

Japan

South America   Australasia

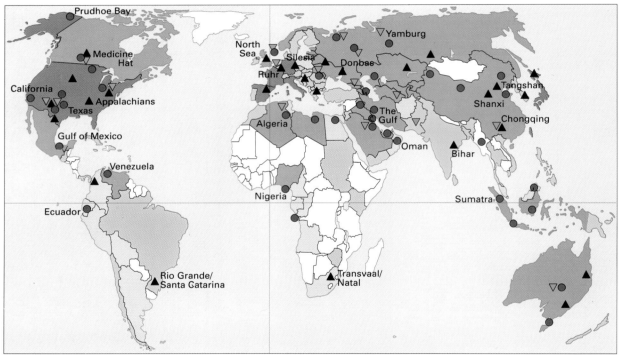

Prudhoe Bay
Medicine Hat
California
Appalachians
Texas
Gulf of Mexico
Venezuela
Ecuador
Rio Grande/ Santa Catarina

North Sea
Silesia
Ruhr
Donbas
Algeria
Nigeria
Transvaal/ Natal

Yamburg
The Gulf
Oman
Bihar
Tangshan
Shanxi
Chongqing
Sumatra

ENERGY BALANCE

Difference between energy production and consumption in millions of tonnes of oil equivalent (1989)

Energy deficit ↑

Over 35 MtOe

1 – 35 MtOe

Approx. balance

1 – 35 MtOe

Over 35 MtOe

Energy surplus ↓

●   Major oilfields

▽   Major gasfields

▲   Major coalfields

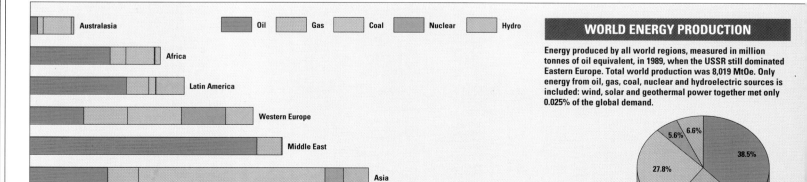

Australasia   ■ Oil   ▨ Gas   ▨ Coal   ▨ Nuclear   ▨ Hydro

Africa

Latin America

Western Europe

Middle East

Asia

North America

USSR & Eastern Europe

5   10   15   20

WORLD ENERGY PRODUCTION

Energy produced by all world regions, measured in million tonnes of oil equivalent, in 1989, when the USSR still dominated Eastern Europe. Total world production was 8,019 MtOe. Only energy from oil, gas, coal, nuclear and hydroelectric sources is included: wind, solar and geothermal power together met only 0.025% of the global demand.

6.6%
5.6%
38.5%
27.8%
21.5%

Statistics for the new republics of the former USSR, Czechoslovakia and Yugoslavia are not yet available.
The map shows the statistics for the entire USSR, Czechoslovakia and Yugoslavia.

NUCLEAR POWER

Percentage of electricity generated by nuclear power stations, leading nations (1988)

1.	France	70%	11.	Germany (W)	34%
2.	Belgium	66%	12.	Japan	28%
3.	Hungary	49%	13.	Czechoslovakia	27%
4.	South Korea	47%	14.	UK	18%
5.	Sweden	46%	15.	USA	17%
6.	Taiwan	41%	16.	Canada	16%
7.	Switzerland	37%	17.	Argentina	12%
8.	Finland	36%	18.	USSR (1989)	11%
9.	Spain	36%	19.	Yugoslavia	6%
10.	Bulgaria	36%	20.	Netherlands	5%

The decade 1980–90 was a bad time for the nuclear power industry. Major projects regularly ran vastly over-budget, and fears of long-term environmental damage were heavily reinforced by the 1986 Soviet disaster at Chernobyl. Although the number of reactors in service continued to increase throughout the period, orders for new plant shrank dramatically, and most countries cut back on their nuclear programmes.

HYDROELECTRICITY

Percentage of electricity generated by hydroelectrical power stations, leading nations (1988)

1.	Paraguay	99.9%	11.	Laos	95.5%
2.	Zambia	99.6%	12.	Nepal	95.2%
3.	Norway	99.5%	13.	Iceland	94.0%
4.	Congo	99.1%	14.	Uruguay	93.0%
5.	Costa Rica	98.3%	15.	Brazil	91.7%
6.	Uganda	98.3%	16.	Albania	87.2%
7.	Rwanda	97.7%	17.	Fiji	81.4%
8.	Malawi	97.6%	18.	Ecuador	80.7%
9.	Zaïre	97.4%	19.	C. African Rep.	80.4%
10.	Cameroon	97.2%	20.	Sri Lanka	80.4%

Countries heavily reliant on hydroelectricity are usually small and non-industrial: a high proportion of hydroelectric power more often reflects a modest energy budget than vast hydroelectric resources. The USA, for instance, produces only 8% of power requirements from hydroelectricity; yet that 8% amounts to more than three times the hydro-power generated by all of Africa.

ALTERNATIVE ENERGY SOURCES

Solar: Each year the sun bestows upon the Earth almost a million times as much energy as is locked up in all the planet's oil reserves, but only an insignificant fraction is trapped and used commercially. In some experimental installations, mirrors focus the sun's rays on to boilers, whose steam generates electricity by spinning conventional turbines. Solar cells turn sunlight into electricity directly. Efficiencies are still low, but advancing technology could make the sun a major electricity source by 2100.

Wind: Caused by the uneven heating of the spinning Earth, winds are themselves the product of solar energy. Traditional windmills turn wind power into mechanical work; recent models usually generate electricity. But efficient windmills are expensive to build, and suitable locations are few.

Tidal: The energy from tides is potentially enormous, although only a few installations have been built to exploit it. In theory, at least, waves and currents could also provide almost unimaginable power, and the thermal differences in the ocean depths are another huge well of potential energy.

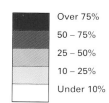

FUEL EXPORTS

Fuels as a percentage of total value of all exports (1986)

- Over 75%
- 50 – 75%
- 25 – 50%
- 10 – 25%
- Under 10%

Direction of trade

- Major movements of coal
- Major movements of oil

CONVERSIONS

For historical reasons, oil is still traded in 'barrels'. The weight and volume equivalents shown below are all based on average-density 'Arabian light' crude oil.

The energy equivalents given for a tonne of oil are also somewhat imprecise: oil and coal of different qualities will have varying energy contents, a fact usually reflected in their price on world markets.

1 barrel: 0.136 tonnes/159 litres/35 Imperial gallons/42 US gallons. **1 tonne:** 7.33 barrels/1,185 litres/256 Imperial gallons/261 US gallons. **1 tonne oil:** 1.5 tonnes hard coal/3.0 tonnes lignite/12,000 kWh.

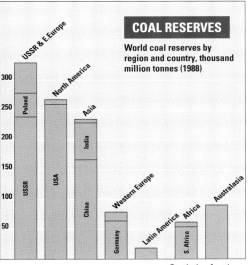

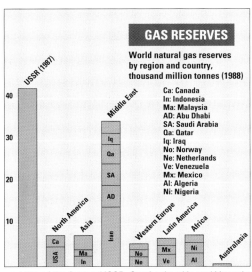

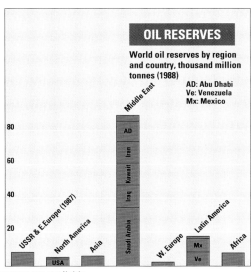

Statistics for the new republics of the former USSR, Czechoslovakia and Yugoslavia are not yet available.
The map shows the statistics for the entire USSR, Czechoslovakia and Yugoslavia.

PRODUCTION

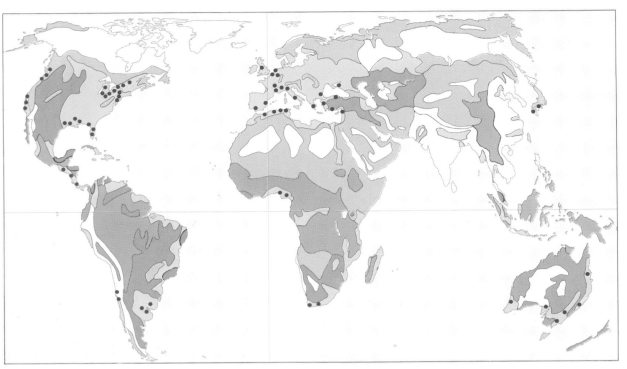

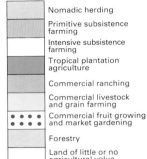

AGRICULTURE

- Nomadic herding
- Primitive subsistence farming
- Intensive subsistence farming
- Tropical plantation agriculture
- Commercial ranching
- Commercial livestock and grain farming
- • • • Commercial fruit growing and market gardening
- Forestry
- Land of little or no agricultural value

STAPLE CROPS

Separate figures for Russia, Ukraine and the other successors of the former USSR are not yet available

Wheat

China 16.9% | USSR 16.8% | USA 10.3% | India 10.0% | France 5.9% | Canada 4.5% | Turkey 2.9%

World total (1989): 538,056,000 tonnes

Rice

China 35.4% | India 21.2% | Indonesia 8.6% | Bangladesh 5.3% | Thailand 4.2% | Vietnam 3.6%

World total (1989): 506,291,000 tonnes

Maize

USA 40.7% | China 16.1% | Brazil 5.6% | USSR 3.6% | France 2.7%

World total (1989): 470,318,000 tonnes

Potatoes

USSR 26.0% | Poland 12.4% | China 10.9% | Germany 6.1% | USA 6.0% | India 5.2%

World total (1989): 276,740,000 tonnes

Millet

India 32.8% | China 18.7% | USSR 13.1% | Nigeria 11.5% | Niger 4.2%

World total (1989): 30,512,000 tonnes

Rye

USSR 53.9% | Poland 17.8% | Germany 11.2% | China 2.9% | Canada 2.4%

World total (1989): 34,893,000 tonnes

Soya

USA 48.9% | Brazil 22.4% | China 10.1% | Argentina 5.8%

World total (1989): 107,350,000 tonnes

Cassava

Thailand 15.9% | Brazil 15.8% | Indonesia 11.2% | Nigeria 11.9% | Zaire 11.1% | Tanzania 4.3% | India 3.6%

World total (1989): 147,500,000 tonnes

SUGARS

Sugar cane

Brazil 22.4% | India 19.7% | Cuba 7.3% | China 5.5% | Mexico 4.0% | Pakistan 3.7% | Thailand 3.6%

World total (1989): 1,007,184,000 tonne

Sugar beet

USSR 31.9% | Germany 8.8% | France 7.7% | Italy 7.6% | Poland 4.3% | Turkey 4.0%

World total (1989): 305,882,000 tonnes

BALANCE OF EMPLOYMENT

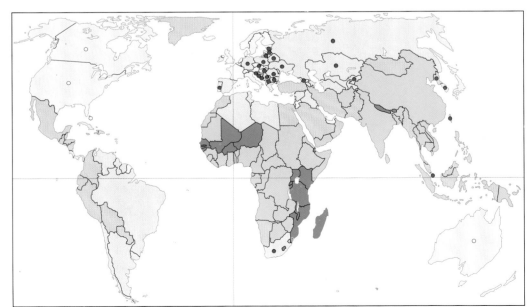

Percentage of total workforce employed in agriculture, including forestry and fishing (latest available year)*

- Over 75% in agriculture
- 50 – 75% in agriculture
- 25 – 50% in agriculture
- 10 – 25% in agriculture
- Under 10% in agriculture

- • Over 25% of total workforce employed in manufacturing

- ○ Over 75% of total workforce employed in service industries (work in offices, shops, tourism, transport, construction and government)

*Statistics for the new republics of the former USSR, Czechoslovakia and Yugoslavia are not yet available.
The map shows the statistics for the entire USSR, Czechoslovakia and Yugoslavia.

MINERAL PRODUCTION

Separate figures for Russia, Ukraine and the other successors of the former USSR are not yet available

Copper

Chile 17.7% | USA 16.5% | USSR 10.4% | Canada 8.1% | Zambia 5.5% | Zaire 4.8% | Poland 4.4% | China 4.2%
World total (1989): 9,100,000 tonnes

Iron
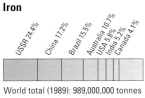
USSR 24.4% | China 17.2% | Brazil 15.5% | Australia 10.7% | USA 5.2% | India 5.2% | Canada 4.1%
World total (1989): 989,000,000 tonnes

Chromium
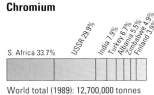
S. Africa 33.7% | USSR 29.9% | India 7.9% | Turkey 6.7% | Albania 5.5% | Zimbabwe 4.9% | Finland 3.9%
World total (1989): 12,700,000 tonnes

Gold

S. Africa 29.9% | USSR 14.1% | USA 13.1% | Australia 10.0% | Canada 7.9% | China 4.2% | Brazil 2.4%
World total (1989): 2,026,000 kilograms

Uranium
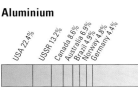
Canada 33.1% | USA 15.6% | Australia 10.8% | France 9.5% | Namibia 9.1% | Niger 8.8% | S. Africa 8.6%
World total (1989): 34,000 tonnes

Lead
USSR 14.7% | Australia 14.6% | USA 12.3% | China 10.1% | Canada 8.1% | Peru 5.7% | Mexico 4.8%
World total (1989): 3,400,000 tonnes

Tin
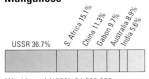
Brazil 22.5% | China 14.8% | Malaysia 14.4% | Indonesia 14.2% | Bolivia 7.1% | Thailand 6.6% | USSR 6.3%
World total (1989): 223,000 tonnes

Manganese

USSR 36.7% | S. Africa 15.1% | China 11.3% | Gabon 9.7% | Australia 8.9% | India 5.6%
World total (1989): 24,000,000 tonnes

Silver
Mexico 15.5% | USA 13.5% | Peru 12.4% | USSR 10.1% | Canada 8.6% | Australia 7.2% | Poland 6.7%
World total (1989): 14,896,000 kilograms

Aluminium
USA 22.4% | USSR 13.2% | Canada 8.6% | Australia 6.9% | Brazil 4.9% | Norway 4.8% | Germany 4.4%
World total (1989): 18,000,000 tonnes

Mercury
USSR 27.3% | China 18.2% | Spain 17.6% | Algeria 12.7% | USA 7.8% | Mexico 6.3% | Turkey 3.7%
World total (1989): 5,500,000 kilograms

Zinc
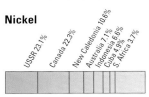
Canada 16.6% | USSR 12.9% | Australia 11.0% | China 8.5% | Peru 8.2% | USA 4.0% | Mexico 3.9%
World total (1989): 7,300,000 tonnes

Nickel
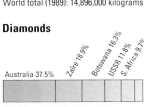
USSR 23.1% | Canada 22.3% | New Caledonia 10.6% | Australia 7.1% | Indonesia 6.6% | Cuba 4.9% | S. Africa 3.7%
World total (1989): 910,000 tonnes

Diamonds
Australia 37.5% | Zaïre 18.9% | Botswana 16.3% | USSR 11.8% | S. Africa 9.7%
World total (1989): 96,600,000 carats

MINERAL DISTRIBUTION

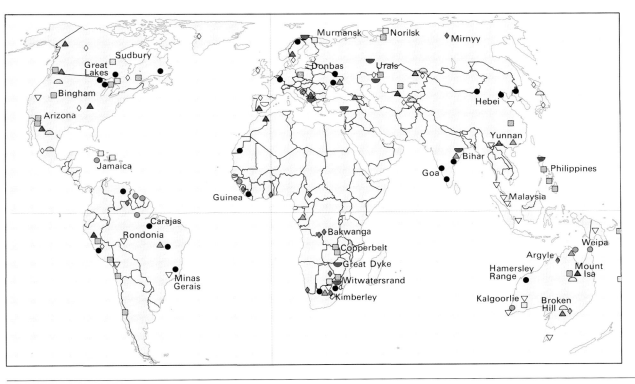

Murmansk, Norilsk, Mirnyy, Sudbury, Great Lakes, Donbas, Urals, Bingham, Arizona, Hebei, Jamaica, Yunnan, Bihar, Goa, Philippines, Guinea, Malaysia, Carajas, Rondonia, Bakwanga, Copperbelt, Great Dyke, Weipa, Argyle, Minas Gerais, Witwatersrand, Hamersley Range, Mount Isa, Kimberley, Kalgoorlie, Broken Hill

Light metals
- Bauxite

Base metals
- Copper
- Lead
- Mercury
- Tin
- Zinc

Iron and ferro-alloys
- Iron
- Chrome
- Manganese
- Nickel

Precious metals
- Gold
- Silver

Precious stones
- Diamonds

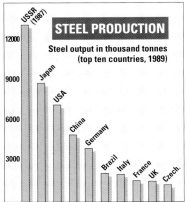

STEEL PRODUCTION
Steel output in thousand tonnes (top ten countries, 1989)

USSR (1987), Japan, USA, China, Germany, Brazil, Italy, France, UK, Czech.

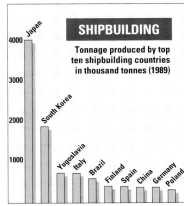

SHIPBUILDING
Tonnage produced by top ten shipbuilding countries in thousand tonnes (1989)

Japan, South Korea, Yugoslavia, Italy, Brazil, Finland, Spain, China, Germany, Poland

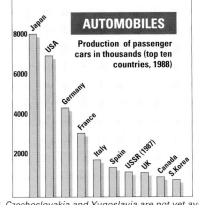

AUTOMOBILES
Production of passenger cars in thousands (top ten countries, 1988)

Japan, USA, Germany, France, Italy, Spain, USSR (1987), UK, Canada, S.Korea

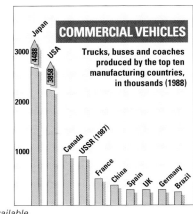

COMMERCIAL VEHICLES
Trucks, buses and coaches produced by the top ten manufacturing countries, in thousands (1988)

Japan 4488, USA 3858, Canada, USSR (1987), France, China, Spain, UK, Germany, Brazil

*Statistics for the new republics of the former USSR, Czechoslovakia and Yugoslavia are not yet available.
The map shows the statistics for the entire USSR, Czechoslovakia and Yugoslavia.

TRADE

SHARE OF WORLD TRADE

Percentage share of total world exports by value (1990)*

- Over 10% of world trade
- 5 – 10% of world trade
- 1 – 5% of world trade
- 0.5 – 1% of world trade
- 0.25 – 0.5% of world trade
- Under 0.25% of world trade

International trade is dominated by a handful of powerful maritime nations. The members of 'G7', the inner circle of OECD and the top seven countries listed in the diagram below, account for more than half the total. The majority of nations – including all but four in Africa – contribute less than one quarter of one per cent to the worldwide total of exports; the EC countries account for 40%, the Pacific Rim nations over 35%.

THE GREAT TRADING NATIONS

The imports and exports of the top ten trading nations as a percentage of world trade (latest available year). Each country's trade in manufactured goods is shown in orange.

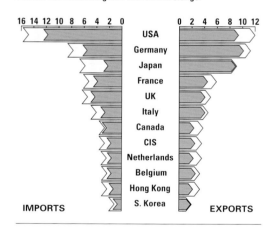

16 14 12 10 8 6 4 2 0   0 2 4 6 8 10 12

USA
Germany
Japan
France
UK
Italy
Canada
CIS
Netherlands
Belgium
Hong Kong
S. Korea

IMPORTS   EXPORTS

PATTERNS OF TRADE

Thriving international trade is the outward sign of a healthy world economy, the obvious indicator that some countries have goods to sell and others the wherewithal to buy them. Despite local fluctuations, trade throughout the 1980s grew consistently faster than output, increasing in value by almost 50% in the decade 1979–89. It remains dominated by the rich, industrialized countries of the Organization for Economic Development: between them, OECD members account for almost 75% of world imports and exports in most years. OECD dominance is just as marked in the trade in 'invisibles' – a column in the balance sheet that includes among other headings the export of services, interest payments on overseas investments, tourism and even remittances from migrant workers abroad. In the UK, invisibles account for more than half all trading income.

However, the size of these great trading economies means that imports and exports usually make up only a fraction of their total wealth: in the case of the famously export-conscious Japanese, trade in goods and services amounts to less than 18% of GDP. In poorer countries, trade – often in a single commodity – may amount to 50% GDP or more.

TRADED PRODUCTS

Top ten manufactures traded, by value in billions of US $ (latest available year)

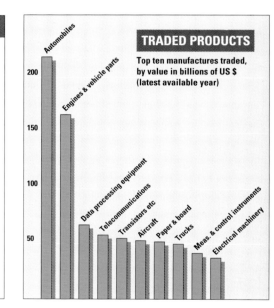

BALANCE OF TRADE

Value of exports in proportion to the value of imports (latest available year)

Exports exceed imports by:
- More than 40%
- 10 – 40%

10% either side

Imports exceed exports by:
- 10 – 40%
- More than 40%

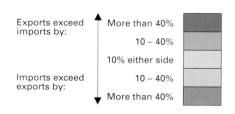

The total world trade balance should amount to zero, since exports must equal imports on a global scale. In practice, at least $100 billion in exports go unrecorded, leaving the world with an apparent deficit and many countries in a better position than public accounting reveals. However, a favourable trade balance is not necessarily a sign of prosperity: many poorer countries must maintain a high surplus in order to service debts, and do so by restricting imports below the levels needed to sustain successful economies.

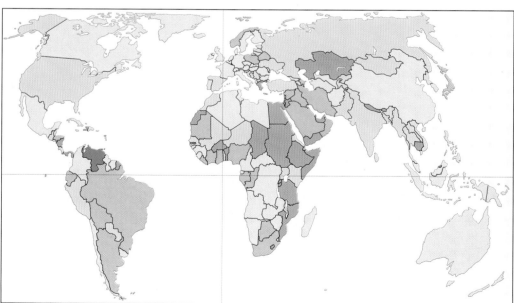

*Statistics for the new republics of the former USSR, Czechoslovakia and Yugoslavia are not yet available.
The map shows the statistics for the entire USSR, Czechoslovakia and Yugoslavia.

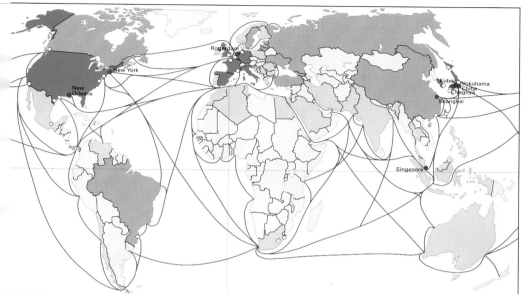

FREIGHT

Freight unloaded in millions of tonnes (latest available year)*

	Over 100
	50 – 100
	10 – 50
	5 – 10
	Under 5
	Landlocked countries

Major seaports

● Over 100 million tonnes per year

○ 50 – 100 million tonnes per year

CARGOES

Type of seaborne freight

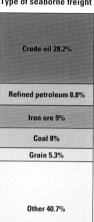

Crude oil 28.2%

Refined petroleum 8.8%

Iron ore 9%

Coal 8%

Grain 5.3%

Other 40.7%

MERCHANT FLEETS

National merchant fleets in thousand deadweight tonnes (1989). The chart records national ownership, not necessarily registry. The countries listed account for 83% of world shipping. The division of the former Soviet fleet among the USSR's successor republics was still incomplete in 1992.

France
Cyprus
Singapore
Iran
Taiwan
Denmark
India
Brazil
Italy
Germany
South Korea
China
UK
Hong Kong
USSR (1988)
Norway
USA
Japan
Greece

20,000   40,000   60,000   80,000

WORLD SHIPPING

World merchant fleet by type of vessel and deadweight tonnage (1989)

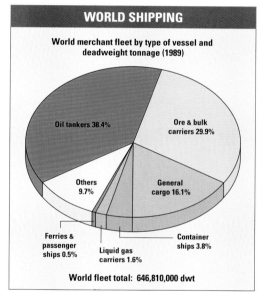

Oil tankers 38.4%

Ore & bulk carriers 29.9%

Others 9.7%

General cargo 16.1%

Ferries & passenger ships 0.5%

Liquid gas carriers 1.6%

Container ships 3.8%

World fleet total: 646,810,000 dwt

THE GREAT PORTS

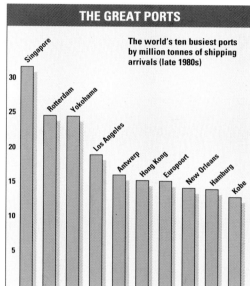

The world's ten busiest ports by million tonnes of shipping arrivals (late 1980s)

Singapore
Rotterdam
Yokohama
Los Angeles
Antwerp
Hong Kong
Europoort
New Orleans
Hamburg
Kobe

30
25
20
15
10
5

DEPENDENCE ON TRADE

Value of exports as a percentage of Gross Domestic Product (1991)

	Over 50% GDP
	40 – 50% GDP
	30 – 40% GDP
	20 – 30% GDP
	10 – 20% GDP
	Under 10% GDP

● Most dependent on industrial exports (over 75% of total exports)

● Most dependent on fuel exports (over 75% of total exports)

○ Most dependent on mineral and metal exports (over 75% of total exports)

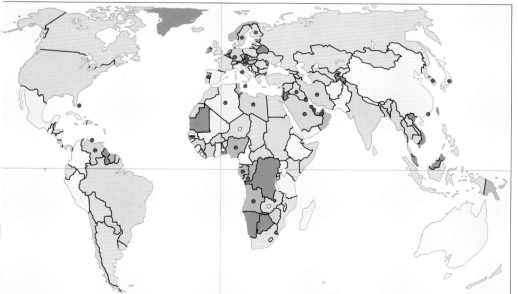

*Statistics for the new republics of the former USSR, Czechoslovakia and Yugoslavia are not yet available.
The map shows the statistics for the entire USSR, Czechoslovakia and Yugoslavia.

TRAVEL AND TOURISM

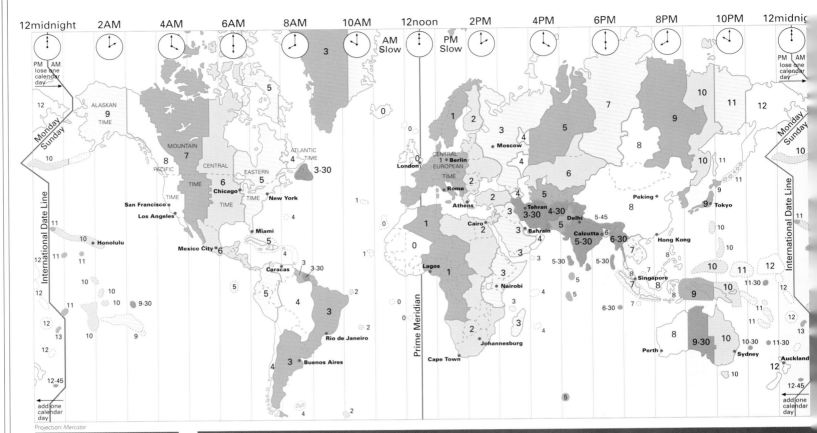

Projection: Mercator

TIME ZONES

Zones slow or fast of Greenwich Mean Time

Half-hour zones

The time when it is 12 noon at Greenwich

RAIL AND ROAD: THE LEADING NATIONS

Total rail network ('000 km)		Passenger km per head per year		Total road network ('000 km)		Vehicle km per head per year		Vehicle km per head per year per km road network	
1. USSR (1986)	247.2	Japan	2,745	1. USA	623.3	USA	12,505	Hong Kong	4,705.7
2. USA	225.4	Switzerland	1,523	2. Brazil	167.4	Luxembourg	7,989	Kuwait	3,433.4
3. Canada	65.8	Germany (E:'87)	1,353	3. USSR (1986)	158.6	Kuwait	7,251	Jordan	1,321.4
4. India	61.8	Czech'vakia	1,286	4. India	155.4	France	7,142	UK	929.6
5. China	52.6	Poland	1,282	5. Japan	110.4	Sweden	6,991	Italy	923.4
6. Germany	41.4	USSR	1,276	6. China	98.2	Germany	6,806	Germany	843.8
7. Australia	39.3	France	1,074	7. Australia	85.3	Denmark	6,764	Netherlands	761.4
8. France	34.6	Austria	971	8. Canada	84.4	Austria	6,518	Tunisia	726.4
9. Argentina	34.1	Denmark	937	9. France	80.5	Netherlands	5,984	Iraq	657.2
10. Poland	24.2	Hungary	906	10. Germany	49.4	UK	5,738	Luxembourg	581.3
11. South Africa	23.8	Bulgaria	897	11. Poland	36.1	Canada	5,493	Japan	497.0
12. Brazil	22.1	South Africa	873	12. UK	35.2	Italy	4,852	USA	494.2
13. Mexico	20.0	Italy	722	13. Turkey	32.1	Belgium	4,821	Denmark	491.0
14. Japan	19.9	Sweden	716	14. Spain	31.8	Japan	4,476	Austria	464.9
15. UK	16.6	Germany (W:'88)	640	15. Italy	30.2	South Africa	2,776	France	459.6

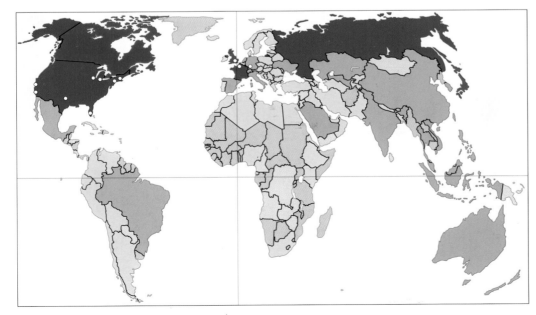

AIR TRAVEL

Passenger kilometres [the number of passengers, international and domestic, multiplied by the distance flown by each passenger from the airport of origin] (latest available year)

Over 100,000 million

50,000 – 100,000 million

10,000 – 50,000 million

1,000 – 10,000 million

500 – 1,000 million

Under 500 million

○ Major airports (handling over 20 million passengers in 1991)

World's busiest airports (total passengers)
1. Chicago (O'Hare)
2. Atlanta (Hatsfield)
3. Los Angeles (Intern'l)
4. Dallas (Dallas/Ft Worth)
5. London (Heathrow)

World's busiest airports (international passengers)
1. London (Heathrow)
2. London (Gatwick)
3. Frankfurt (International)
4. New York (Kennedy)
5. Paris (De Gaulle)

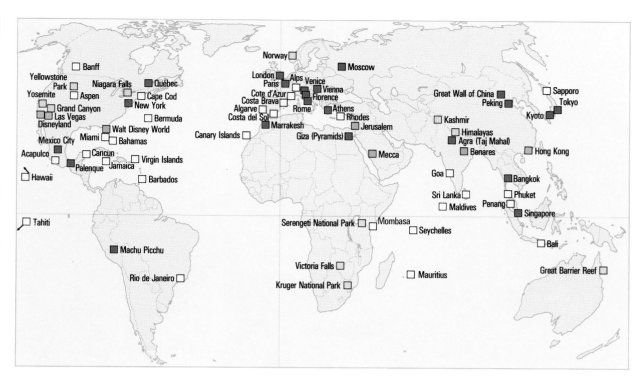

DESTINATIONS

- ■ Cultural & historical centres
- □ Coastal resorts
- □ Ski resorts
- ■ Centres of entertainment
- □ Places of pilgrimage
- □ Places of great natural beauty

VISITORS TO THE USA

International visitors spending in US $ million (1989)

1.	Japan	7,480
2.	Canada	6,020
3.	Mexico	4,170
4.	UK	4,130
5.	Germany	2,450
6.	France	1,290
7.	Australia	1,120
8.	All others	16,380

A record 38.3 million foreigners visited the US in 1989, about 70% of them on vacation. Between them they spent $43 billion.

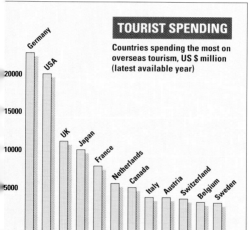

TOURIST SPENDING

Countries spending the most on overseas tourism, US $ million (latest available year)

Germany, USA, UK, Japan, France, Netherlands, Canada, Italy, Austria, Switzerland, Belgium, Sweden

IMPORTANCE OF TOURISM

		Arrivals from abroad (1987)	Receipts as % of GDP (1987)
1.	France	36,820,000	1.4%
2.	Spain	32,900,000	5.1%
3.	USA	28,790,000	0.4%
4.	Italy	25,750,000	1.6%
5.	Austria	15,760,000	6.5%
6.	UK	15,445,000	1.5%
7.	Canada	15,040,000	0.9%
8.	Germany	12,780,000	0.7%
9.	Hungary	11,830,000	3.2%
10.	Switzerland	11,600,000	3.1%
11.	China	10,760,000	0.7%
12.	Greece	7,564,000	4.7%

Small economies in attractive areas are often completely dominated by tourism: in some West Indian islands, tourist spending provides over 90% of total income. In cash terms the USA is the world leader: its 1987 earnings exceeded $15 billion, though that sum amounted to only 0.4% of GDP.

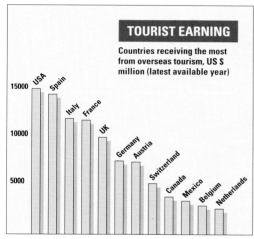

TOURIST EARNING

Countries receiving the most from overseas tourism, US $ million (latest available year)

USA, Spain, Italy, France, UK, Germany, Austria, Switzerland, Canada, Mexico, Belgium, Netherlands

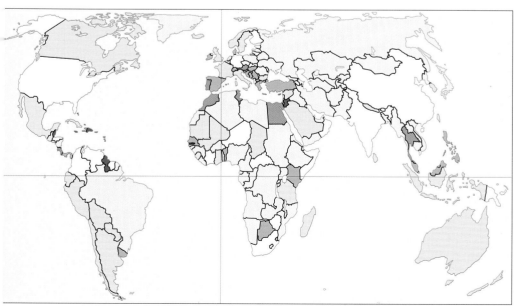

TOURISM

Receipts from tourism as a percentage of Gross National Product (1990)*

- ■ Over 10% of GNP from tourism
- ■ 5 – 10% of GNP from tourism
- ■ 2.5 – 5% of GNP from tourism
- □ 1 – 2.5% of GNP from tourism
- □ 0.5 – 1% of GNP from tourism
- □ Under 0.5% of GNP from tourism

Largest percentage share of total spending on tourism (1991)

USA	16%
Germany	13%
Japan	10%
UK	7%
Italy	6%

Largest percentage share of total world receipts from tourism (1991)

USA	16%
France	8%
Italy	8%
Spain	7%
UK	6%

*Statistics for the new republics of the former USSR, Czechoslovakia and Yugoslavia are not yet available. The map shows the statistics for the entire USSR, Czechoslovakia and Yugoslavia.

SUBJECT INDEX

WORLD MAPS

SETTLEMENTS

◻ PARIS · ▪ Berne · ◉ Livorno · ◉ Brugge · ◎ Algeciras · ○ Fréjus · ○ Oberammergau · ○ Thira

Settlement symbols and type styles vary according to the scale of each map and indicate the importance of towns on the map rather than specific population figures

∴ Ruins or Archæological Sites   ˅ Wells in Desert

ADMINISTRATION

_____ International Boundaries

_ _ _ International Boundaries (Undefined or Disputed)

.... Internal Boundaries

National Parks

Country Names

NICARAGUA

Administrative Area Names

KENT

CALABRIA

International boundaries show the *de facto* situation where there are rival claims to territory

COMMUNICATIONS

_____ Principal Roads

⌒ Other Roads

-.-.- Trails and Seasonal Roads

⤫ Passes

✿ Airfields

⌢ Principal Railroads

-.-.- Railroads Under Construction

⌒ Other Railroads

⌐---⌐ Railroad Tunnels

.... Principal Canals

PHYSICAL FEATURES

⌒ Perennial Streams

...... Intermittent Streams

◯ Perennial Lakes

⬭ Intermittent Lakes

Swamps and Marshes

Permanent Ice and Glaciers

▲ 8848 Elevations (m)

▾ 8050 Sea Depths (m)

1134 Height of Lake Surface Above Sea Level (m)

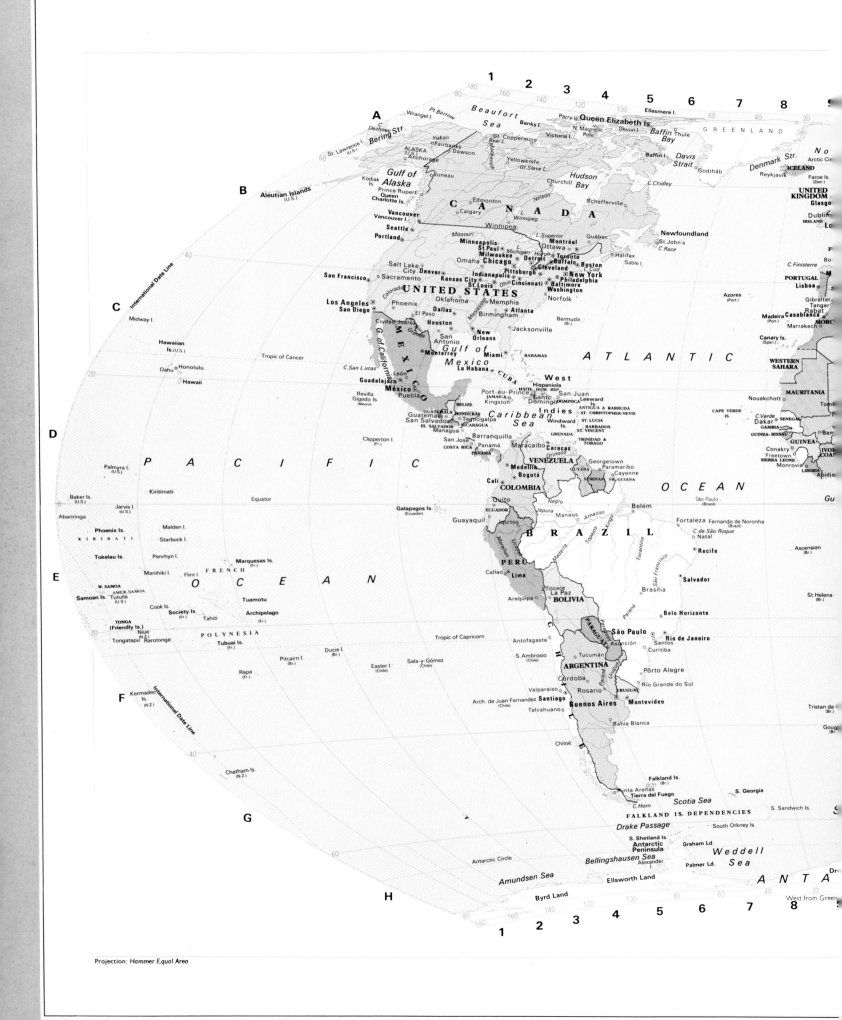

Projection: *Hammer Equal Area*

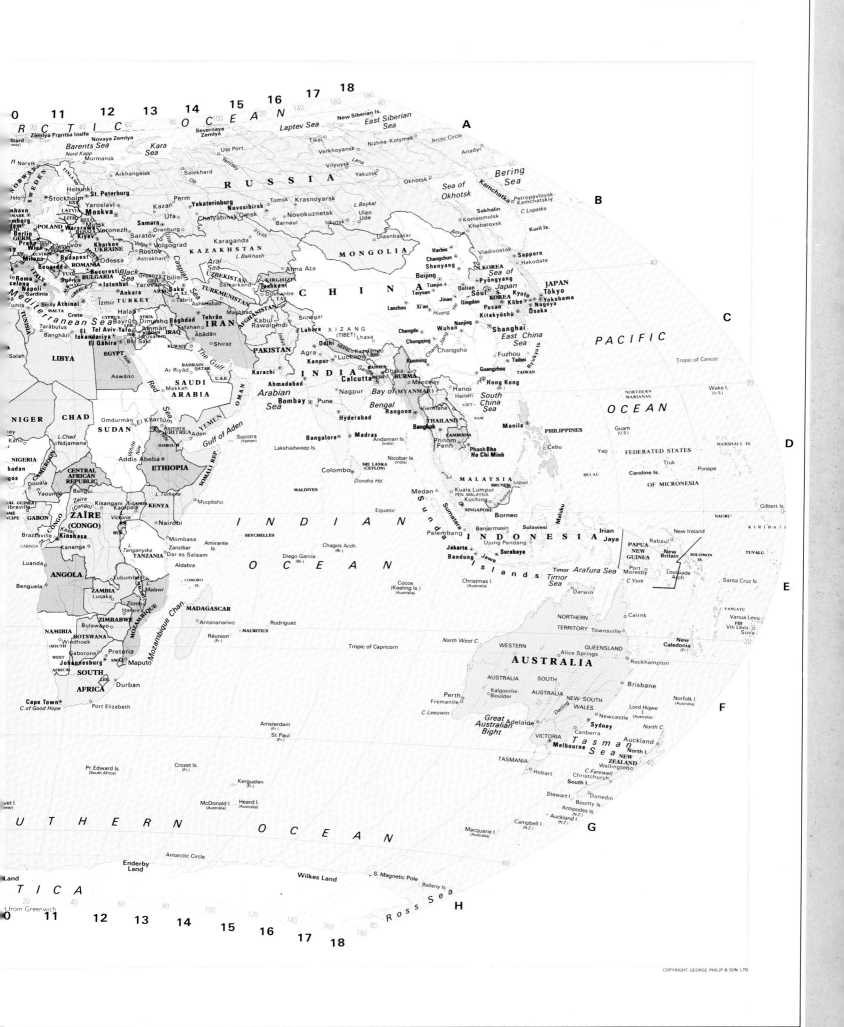

ARCTIC OCEAN

18
17
16
15
14
13
12
11
0

A

Laptev Sea
New Siberian Is.
East Siberian Sea

Severnaya Zemlya
Tiksi
Arctic Circle
Anadyr

Ibard
Zemlya Frantsa Iosifa
Novaya Zemlya
Kara Sea
Ust Port
Verkhoyansk
Nizhne-Kolymsk

Barents Sea
Salekhard
Yenisey
Lena
Yakutsk
Okhotsk
Bering Sea
B

Nord Kapp
Murmansk
Ob
Vilyuysk
Kamchatka
Petropavlovsk-Kamchatskiy

Narvik
Arkhangelsk
RUSSIA
Tomsk
Krasnoyarsk
L.Baykal
Sea of Okhotsk
C.Lopatka

NORWAY
FINLAND
Perm
Yekaterinburg
Novosibirsk
Omsk
Sakhalin
Kuril Is.

Helsinki
St.Peterburg
Kazan
Novokuznetsk
Komsomolsk
Khabarovsk

Oslo
Stockholm
Yaroslavl
Ufa
Chelyabinsk
Barnaul
Iskutsk
Ulan Ude
Amur
Vladivostok
Sapporo
Hakodate

DMARK
SWEDEN
LATVIA
Moskva
Samara
Orenburg
Karaganda
Ulaanbaatar
Harbin
Changchun
N.KOREA
Sea of Japan
Kyōto

POLAND
Warszawa
Minsk
Voronezh
Saratov
KAZAKHSTAN
L.Balkhash
MONGOLIA
Shenyang
Pyongyang
Tōkyō
JAPAN
Yokohama

Berlin
Kiyev
Volgograd
Rostov
Aral Sea
Alma Ata
Beijing
Tianjin
Dalian
Sŏul
S.KOREA
Kōbe
Nagoya

Praha
UKRAINE
Astrakhan
Caspian
UZBEKISTAN
Tashkent
KIRGHIZIA
Lanzhou
Xi'an
Jinan
Qingdao
Pusan
Ōsaka

Budapest
Odessa
Tbilisi
Samarkand
TURKMENISTAN
CHINA
Huang He
Kitakyūshū

ROMANIA
Black Sea
Grozny
Yerevan
Ashkhabad
TAJ.
Chengdu
Wuhan
Nanjing
Shanghai
East China Sea
C

BULGARIA
Istanbul
Ankara
AZ.
AFGHANISTAN
Kabul
XIZANG (TIBET)
Lhasa
Chongqing
Changsha

İzmir
TURKEY
Tabriz
Mashhad
Srinagar
Fuzhou

Sofiya
Athinai
CYPRUS
Halab
SYRIA
Tehrān
Rawalpindi
Lahore
Delhi
NEPAL
Kathmandu
Guangzhou
TAIWAN
Taibei

Crete
Dimashq
Baghdād
Esfahan
IRAN
PAKISTAN
Agra
Luckpow
Kunming
Hong Kong
Tropic of Cancer

Mediterranean Sea
Bayrūt
Ammān
IRAQ
Abādān
Shiraz
Karachi
Kanpur
Ganga
Dhaka
BURMA
Hanoi
Hainan
South China Sea
Wake I. (U.S)

Tarābulus
El Tel Aviv-Yafo
Jerusalem
KUWAIT
The Gulf
INDIA
Calcutta
Mandalay
(MYANMAR)

Banghāzī
Iskandariya
El Qāhira
BAHRAIN
QATAR
Ahmadabad
Nagpur
Bay of Bengal
Rangoon
Vientiane
NORTHERN MARIANAS
20

Salah
EGYPT
Ar Riyāḍ
U.A.E.
Bombay
Pune
Hyderabad
THAILAND
Manila
PHILIPPINES
Guam (U.S)
OCEAN

LIBYA
Aswān
Makkah
SAUDI ARABIA
OMAN
Arabian Sea
Bangalore
Madras
Andaman Is. (India)
Bangkok
CAMBODIA
Phnom Penh
Cebu
D

NIGER
CHAD
Omdurmān
El Khartūm
YEMEN
Aden
Gulf of Aden
Lakshadweep (India)
Nicobar Is. (India)
Phanh Bho Ho Chi Minh
Yap
FEDERATED STATES
Truk
Ponape
MARSHALL IS.

Kano
SUDAN
Asmera
ERITREA
DJIBOUTI
Colombo
SRI LANKA (CEYLON)
Medan
MALAYSIA
BRUNEI
SABAH
Caroline Is.
OF MICRONESIA

Ndjamena
Addis Abeba
ETHIOPIA
MALDIVES
Dondra Hd.
Kuala Lumpur
PEN. MALAYSIA
Kuching
BELAU

NIGERIA
CENTRAL AFRICAN REPUBLIC
Bangui
UGANDA
KENYA
Equator
SINGAPORE
Borneo
NAURU

Yaoundé
ZAIRE (CONGO)
Kisangani
Kampala
L.Turkana
Muqdisho
SEYCHELLES
Chagos Arch. (Br.)
Sumatera
INDONESIA
Irian Jaya
New Ireland
KIRIBATI
Gilbert Is.

GABON
Brazzaville
Kinshasa
Nairobi
Diego Garcia (Br.)
Palembang
Banjarmasin
Sulawesi
Rabaul
New Britain
SOLOMON IS.

Luanda
Kananga
TANZANIA
Mombasa
Zanzibar
Amirante Is.
Ujung Pandang
Jakarta
Surabaya
PAPUA NEW GUINEA
Port Moresby
Louisiade Arch.
TUVALU

ANGOLA
Lubumbashi
Dar es Salaam
Aldabra
Jawa
Bandung
Timor
Arafura Sea
C.York
Santa Cruz Is.
E

Benguela
ZAMBIA
Malawi
COMORO IS.
Cocos (Keeling Is.) (Australia)
Christmas I. (Australia)
Timor Sea
Darwin
VANUATU
Vanua Levu
FIJI

NAMIBIA
ZIMBABWE
MOZAMBIQUE
MADAGASCAR
Antananarivo
MAURITIUS
NORTHERN TERRITORY
Cairns
Townsville
New Caledonia (Fr.)
20

BOTSWANA
Harare
Mozambique Chan.
Rodriguez
Réunion (Fr.)
Tropic of Capricorn
North West C.
WESTERN AUSTRALIA
QUEENSLAND
Alice Springs
Rockhampton

Windhoek
Gaborone
Pretoria
Johannesburg
Maputo
AUSTRALIA
SOUTH AUSTRALIA
Brisbane

SOUTH AFRICA
Durban
Perth
Fremantle
NEW SOUTH WALES
Newcastle
Lord Howe (Australia)
Norfolk I. (Australia)
F

Cape Town
C.of Good Hope
Port Elizabeth
Amsterdam (Fr.)
St.Paul (Fr.)
C.Leeuwin
Great Australian Bight
Adelaide
Sydney
Darling
North C.

VICTORIA
Canberra
Melbourne
Tasman Sea
Auckland
North I.
NEW ZEALAND
Wellington

Pr.Edward Is. (South Africa)
Crozet Is. (Fr.)
Kerguelen (Fr.)
TASMANIA
Hobart
C.Farewell
Christchurch
South I.
40

McDonald I. (Australia)
Heard I. (Australia)
Stewart I.
Bounty Is. (N.Z.)
Antipodes Is. (N.Z.)
Auckland I. (N.Z.)
G

vet I.
SOUTHERN OCEAN
Macquarie I. (Australia)
Campbell I. (N.Z.)

Antarctic Circle

TICA
ot from Greenwich
Enderby Land
Wilkes Land
S. Magnetic Pole
Balleny Is.
Ross Sea
H

0
11
12
13
14
15
16
17
18

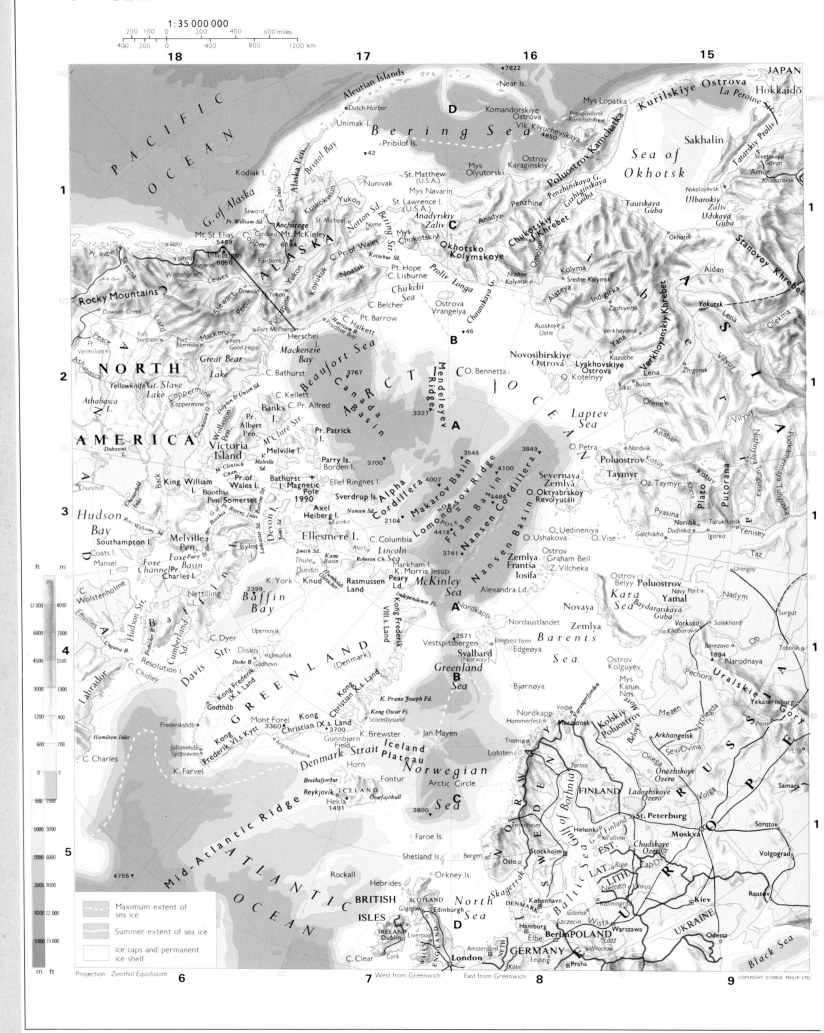

1 : 35 000 000

Projection: Zenithal Equidistant

West from Greenwich | East from Greenwich

COPYRIGHT GEORGE PHILIP LTD.

Maximum extent of sea ice

Summer extent of sea ice

Ice caps and permanent ice shelf

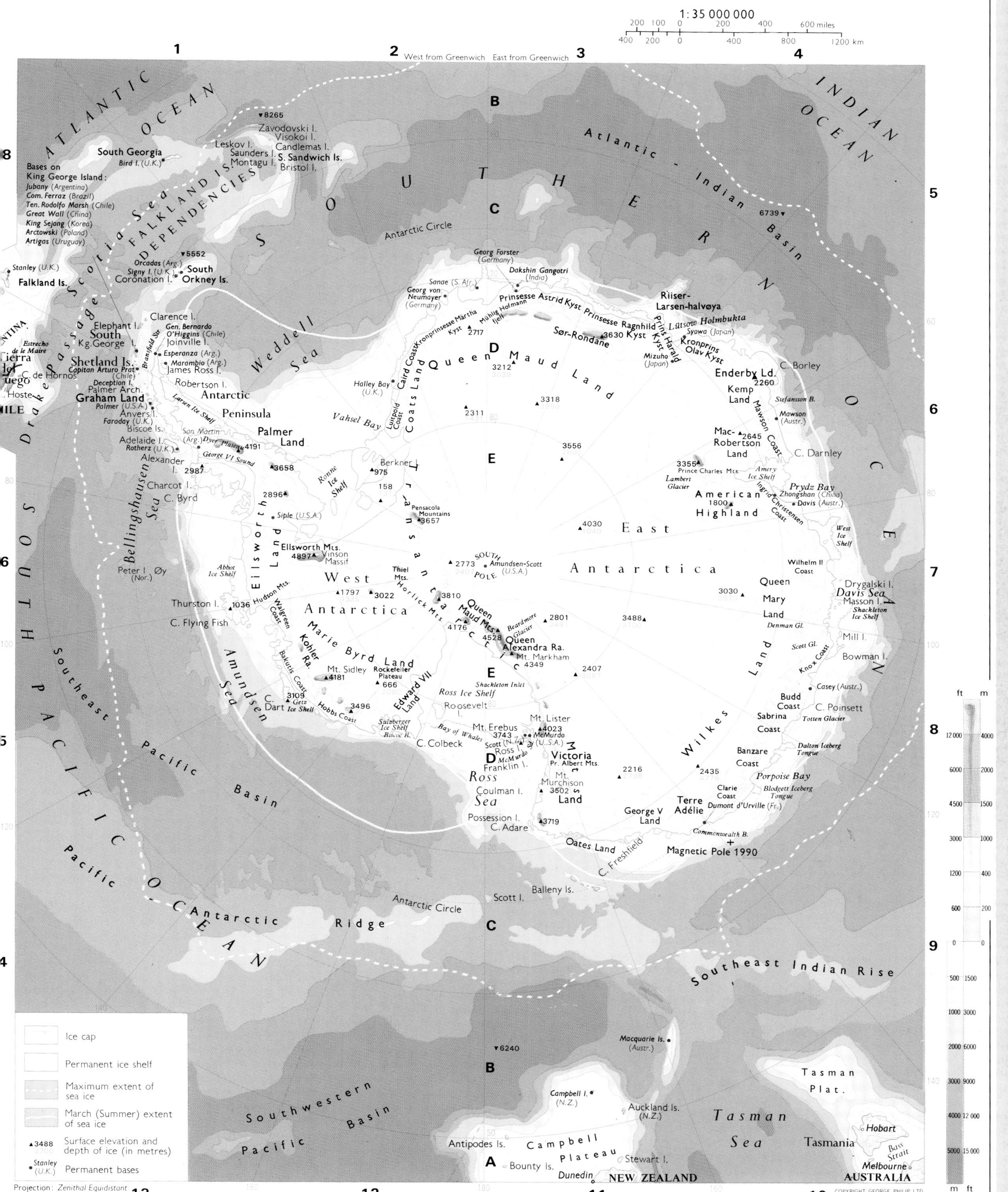

1 : 35 000 000

200 100 0 200 400 600 miles
400 200 0 400 800 1200 km

1 **2** West from Greenwich | East from Greenwich **3** **4**

ATLANTIC OCEAN

B

INDIAN OCEAN

▼8265

Zavodovski I.
Visokoi I.
Leskov I.
Saunders I. Candlemas I.
Montagu I. **S. Sandwich Is.**
Bristol I.

Atlantic – Indian Basin

South Georgia
Bird I. (U.K.)

Bases on
King George Island:
Jubany (Argentina)
Com. Ferraz (Brazil)
Ten. Rodolfo Marsh (Chile)
Great Wall (China)
King Sejong (Korea)
Arctowski (Poland)
Artigas (Uruguay)

S O U T H E R N

5

C

6739 ▼

Antarctic Circle

60

▼5552
Orcadas (Arg.)
Signy I. (U.K.) **South**
Coronation I. **Orkney Is.**

Georg Forster
(Germany)
Dakshin Gangotri
(India)

Sanae (S. Afr.)
Georg von
Neumayer
(Germany)

Prinsesse Astrid Kyst Prinsesse Ragnhild
Mühlig Hofmann fjell
Kyst 2717 3630 Kyst

Riiser-
Larsen-halvøya

Lützow Holmbukta

• Stanley (U.K.)
Falkland Is.

Sør-Rondane

Prins Harald Kyst

Syowa (Japan)

Kronprins
Olav Kyst

Mizuho
(Japan)

C. Borley

Clarence I.
Elephant I.
South Gen. Bernardo
Kg.George O'Higgins (Chile)
Joinville I.
Esperanza (Arg.)
Marambio (Arg.)
James Ross I.

Weddell
Sea

3212
3089

Queen Maud Land

Coats Land

Caird Coast Kronprinsesse Martha Kyst

3318

Enderby Ld. 2260
Kemp
Land

Stefansson B.

Mawson
(Austr.)

ARGENTINA
Estrecho
de le Maire
Tierra
del
Fuego
'Hoste
CHILE

Brønnøy Str.
Capitan Arturo Prat (Chile)
Deception I.
Palmer Arch.
Graham Land
Palmer (U.S.A.)
Anvers I.
Faraday (U.K.)
Biscoe Is.
Adelaide I.
Rotherz (U.K.)

Antarctic

Robertson I.

Halley Bay
(U.K.)

Luitpold
Coast

2311

3556

Mac-
Robertson 2645
Land

C. Darnley

6

Shetland Is.

Palmer
Land

Vahsel Bay

3355
Prince Charles Mts.
Lambert
Glacier

Amery
Ice Shelf

Peninsula

San Martin
(Arg.) Dyer Plateau 4191

Berkner
I. 975

Transantarctica

American
Highland 1800

Prydz Bay
Zhongshan (China)
Prinz-
Christensen
Coast

Davis (Austr.)

Drake Passage

Alexander
I. 2987

George VI Sound

Ronne
Ice
Shelf

158

2896

Pensacola
Mountains
3657

4030

East

West
Ice
Shelf

80

Charcot I.
C. Byrd

Siple (U.S.A.)

SOUTH
POLE 2773 Amundsen-Scott
(U.S.A.)

Antarctica

Wilhelm II
Coast

Peter I Øy
(Nor.)

Ellsworth Mts.
4897 Vinson
Massif

3030

Queen
Mary
Land

Drygalski I.
Davis Sea
Masson I.

7

Bellingshausen
Sea

Abbot
Ice Shelf

Thiel
Mts.

1797 3022

Horlick Mts.

West
Antarctica

3810

Queen
Maud Mts.
4176 4528

3488

Shackleton
Ice Shelf

Mill I.

Thurston I.
1036 Hudson Mts.

Walgreen
Coast

Bakutis Coast

Marie Byrd Land

Kohler
Ra.

Rockefeller
Plateau
• 666

4181

Beardmore
Glacier

Queen
Alexandra Ra.
Mt. Markham 4349

2801

Denman Gl.

Scott Gl.

Knox Coast

Bowman I.

100

C. Flying Fish

Mt. Sidley

3109
Dart Ice Shelf 3496

Sulzberger
Ice Shelf
Biscoe B.

Getz Ice Shelf
Hobbs Coast

Edward VII
Land

Shackleton Inlet

2407

Budd
Coast

Sabrina
Coast

Casey (Austr.)

C. Poinsett
Totten Glacier

8

Southeast

Amundsen
Sea

Pacific

Roosevelt
I.

Ross Ice Shelf

Mt. Lister
4023

Victoria

Banzare
Coast

Dalton Iceberg
Tongue

120

Bay of Whales

Mt. Erebus
3743

Pr. Albert Mts.

2216

Mt.
Murchison
3502

2435

Clarie
Coast
Terre
Adélie

Porpoise Bay

Blodgett Iceberg
Tongue

C. Colbeck

Scott (N.Z.)
Ross McMurdo (U.S.A.)
Franklin I.
D McMurdo

Land

George V
Land

Dumont d'Urville (Fr.)

Ross
Sea

Coulman I.

Possession I.
C. Adare 3719

Commonwealth B.
+ **Magnetic Pole 1990**

Oates Land

Wilkes

Land

Pacific

C. Freshfield

Scott I.

Balleny Is.

140

Antarctic Circle

C

Southeast Indian Rise

Basin

▼6240

Macquarie Is.
(Austr.)

Tasman
Plat.

B

Pacific

Southwestern

Basin

Campbell I.
(N.Z.)

Auckland Is.
(N.Z.)

Tasman

Sea

Hobart

Tasmania

Pacific
Ocean

Antipodes Is.
Bounty Is.

Campbell
Plateau

Stewart I.

Dunedin
NEW ZEALAND

Melbourne

AUSTRALIA

Bass
Strait

m ft

13 **12** **11** **10**

COPYRIGHT GEORGE PHILIP LTD.

Projection: Zenithal Equidistant

Legend:
- Ice cap
- Permanent ice shelf
- Maximum extent of sea ice
- March (Summer) extent of sea ice
- ▲3488 Surface elevation and depth of ice (in metres)
- • Stanley (U.K.) Permanent bases

	ft	m
	12 000	4000
	6000	
	4500	1500
	3000	1000
	1200	400
	600	200
	0	0
	500	1500
	1000	3000
	2000	6000
	3000	9000
	4000	12 000
	5000	15 000

The Antarctic Treaty was signed in Washington in 1959 so that scientific and technical research could continue unhampered by international politics.

All territorial claims covering land areas south of latitude 60°S have been suspended. Those claims were:

Norwegian claim	45°E – 20°W	
Australian claims	{ 45°E – 136°E	
	{ 142°E – 160°E	
French claim	136°E – 142°E	
New Zealand claim	160°E – 150°W	
Chilean claim	90°W – 53°W	
British claim	80°W – 20°W	
Argentine claim	74°W – 53°W	

1:20 000 000

100   0   100   200   300   400 miles
100   0   100 200 300 400 500 600 km

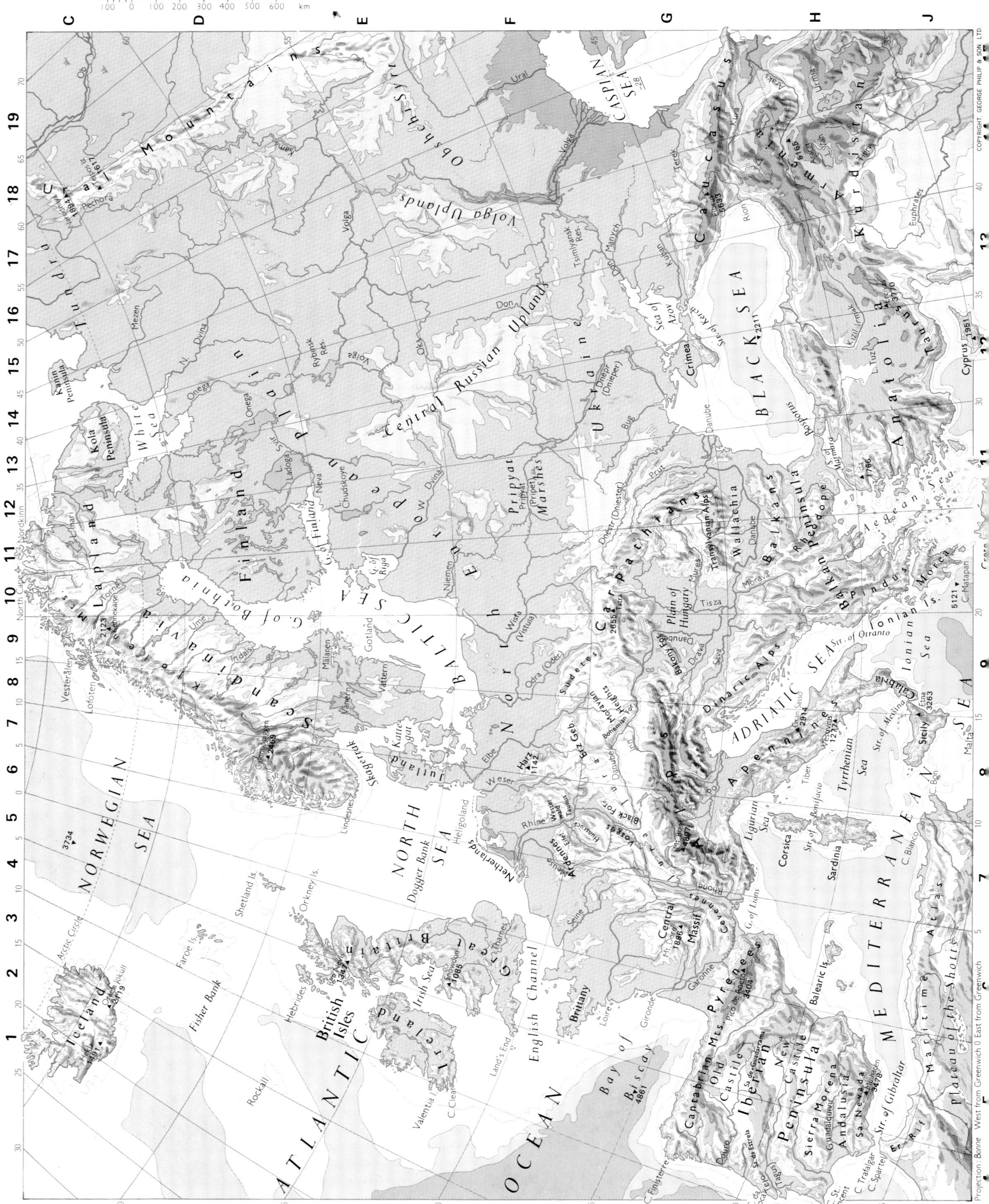

C   D   E   F   G   H   J

Ural Mountains
Ob
Pechora
Obshchi Syrt
Ural
CASPIAN SEA
Caucasus
Armenia
Kurdistan
Volga Uplands
Volga
Kuma
Terek
Kura
Rion
Tundra
Lapland
Kola Peninsula
Kanin Peninsula
White Sea
Mezen
N. Dvina
Onega
Pechora
Central Russian Uplands
Don
Sea of Azov
Crimea
BLACK SEA
Anatolia
Cyprus
Taurus
Finland
L. Ladoga
L. Onega
Rybinsk Res.
Volga
Tsimlyansk Res.
Don
Donets
Manych
Kuban
Str. of Kerch
Ukraine
Dnepr (Dnieper)
Bug
Danube
Pripyat Marshes
Pripyat (Pripet)
Dnestr (Dniester)
Prut
Carpathians
Transylvanian Alps
Wallachia
Balkans
Balkan Peninsula
Rodope
Aegean Sea
Pindus
Morea
C. Matapan
Ionian Is.
Ionian Sea
ADRIATIC SEA
Str. of Otranto
Dinaric Alps
Apennines
Tyrrhenian Sea
Sicily
Etna 3263
Str. of Messina
Malta
MEDITERRANEAN SEA
Vesuvius 1277
Sardinia
Corsica
Str. of Bonifacio
Ligurian Sea
C. Blanco
Balearic Is.
New Castile
Old Castile
Iberian Peninsula
Sierra Morena
Sierra Nevada
Andalusia
Str. of Gibraltar
C. Trafalgar
C. St. Vincent
C. Spartel
Plateau of the Shotts
Maritime Atlas
Tell Atlas
Cantabrian Mts.
Pyrenees
Pico de Aneto 3404
Douro
Tagus
Guadalquivir
Guadiana
Ebro
Sa. de Estrela
C. Finisterre
C. Ortegal
Bay of Biscay
Garonne
Gironde
Central Massif
Mt. Dore 1886
Cevennes
G. of Lions
Rhône
Saône
Loire
Brittany
Seine
English Channel
Land's End
Ireland
Great Britain
British Isles
Irish Sea
Thames
Snowdon 1085
Hebrides
Orkney Is.
Shetland Is.
Faroe Is.
Fisher Bank
Rockall
Valentia
C. Clear
ATLANTIC OCEAN
NORTH SEA
Dogger Bank
Heligoland
Netherlands
Rhine
Weser
Elbe
Ardennes
Vosges
Jura
Alps
Mt. Blanc 4807
Po
Lombardy
Black For.
Erz Geb.
Sudetes
Bohemian
Moravian
Odra (Oder)
Wisła (Vistula)
Niemen
G. of Riga
G. of Bothnia
BALTIC SEA
Gotland
Öland
Kattegat
Skagerrak
Jutland
Lindesnes
NORWEGIAN SEA
Scandinavia
Lofoten Is.
Vesterålen
North Cape
Nordkinn
Arctic Circle
Iceland
Vatnajökull
Hvannadalshnúkur 2119
Glittertind 2481
Hardangervidda
Kjölen
Galdhøpiggen 2468
Vänern
Vättern
Mälaren
Dal
Ume
Klar
Indals
Glåma
Gulf of Finland
L. Chudskoye
Neva
Harz 1142
Danube
Plain of Hungary
Tisza
Drava
Sava
Danube
Mur
Mraz
Morava

ft m
12 000 4000
6000 2000
3000 1000
1200 500
0
200 600 m ft
2000 6000
4000 12 000

Projection Bonne   West from Greenwich 0 East from Greenwich

1 : 20 000 000

100   0   100   200   300   400 miles
100   0   100   200   300   400   500   600 km

LONDON Capital Cities

Projection: Bonne   West from Greenwich   0   East from Greenwich

COPYRIGHT GEORGE PHILIP & SON, LTD.

ICELAND

ATLANTIC OCEAN

NORWAY

SWEDEN

FINLAND

DENMARK
COPENHAGEN

UNITED KINGDOM
IRELAND
Dublin
Glasgow
Edinburgh
SCOTLAND
ENGLAND
WALES
LONDON
Birmingham
Liverpool
Manchester

NETHERLANDS
Amsterdam
The Hague
Rotterdam
BELGIUM
BRUSSELS
LUXEMBOURG

FRANCE
PARIS

GERMANY
BERLIN
Hamburg
Bremen
Hanover
Cologne
Frankfurt
Munich
Stuttgart

SWITZERLAND
LIECH.
AUSTRIA
VIENNA

ITALY
Rome
Naples
Milan
Turin
Genoa
Venice
Florence

SPAIN
MADRID
Barcelona
Valencia

PORTUGAL
Lisbon
Oporto

POLAND
WARSAW
Łódź
Kraków

CZECH REP.
PRAGUE
SLOVAK REP.

HUNGARY
BUDAPEST

ROMANIA
BUCHAREST

BULGARIA
Sofia

YUGOSLAVIA
Belgrade
SERBIA
BOSNIA
CROATIA
MACEDONIA
ALBANIA

GREECE
ATHENS

ESTONIA
LATVIA
Riga
LITHUANIA
Vilnius
BELORUSSIA
Minsk
MOLDAVIA

R U S S I A
MOSCOW
St. Petersburg
Murmansk

UKRAINE
Kiev
Kharkov
Dnepropetrovsk
Donetsk
Odessa

GEORGIA
ARMENIA
Yerevan
AZERBAIJAN
Baku

TURKEY
Istanbul
Ankara

SYRIA
IRAQ
Baghdad
IRAN

CYPRUS
MALTA

MOROCCO
ALGERIA
Algiers
TUNISIA
Tunis

KAZAKHSTAN

CASPIAN SEA
BLACK SEA
MEDITERRANEAN SEA
ADRIATIC SEA
BALTIC SEA
NORTH SEA
BAY OF BISCAY
ARCTIC OCEAN
Arctic Circle

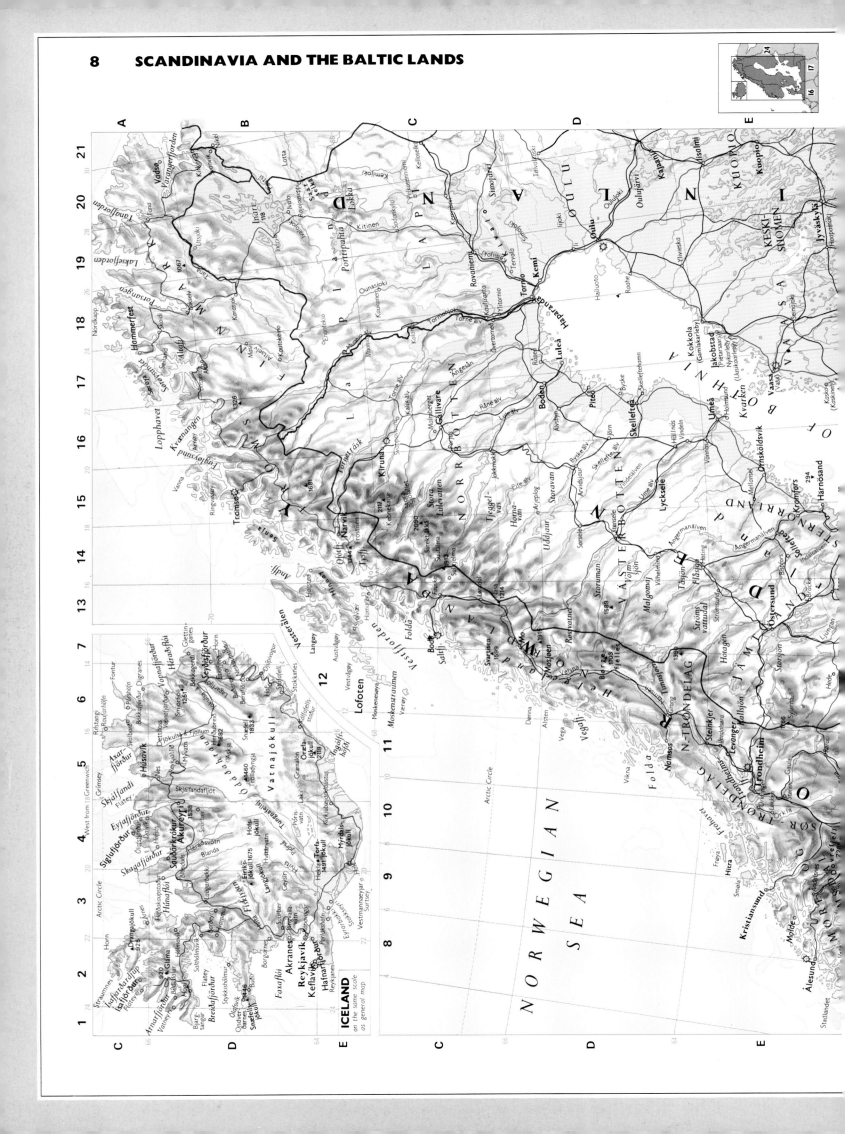

ICELAND
on the same scale
as general map

NORWEGIAN SEA

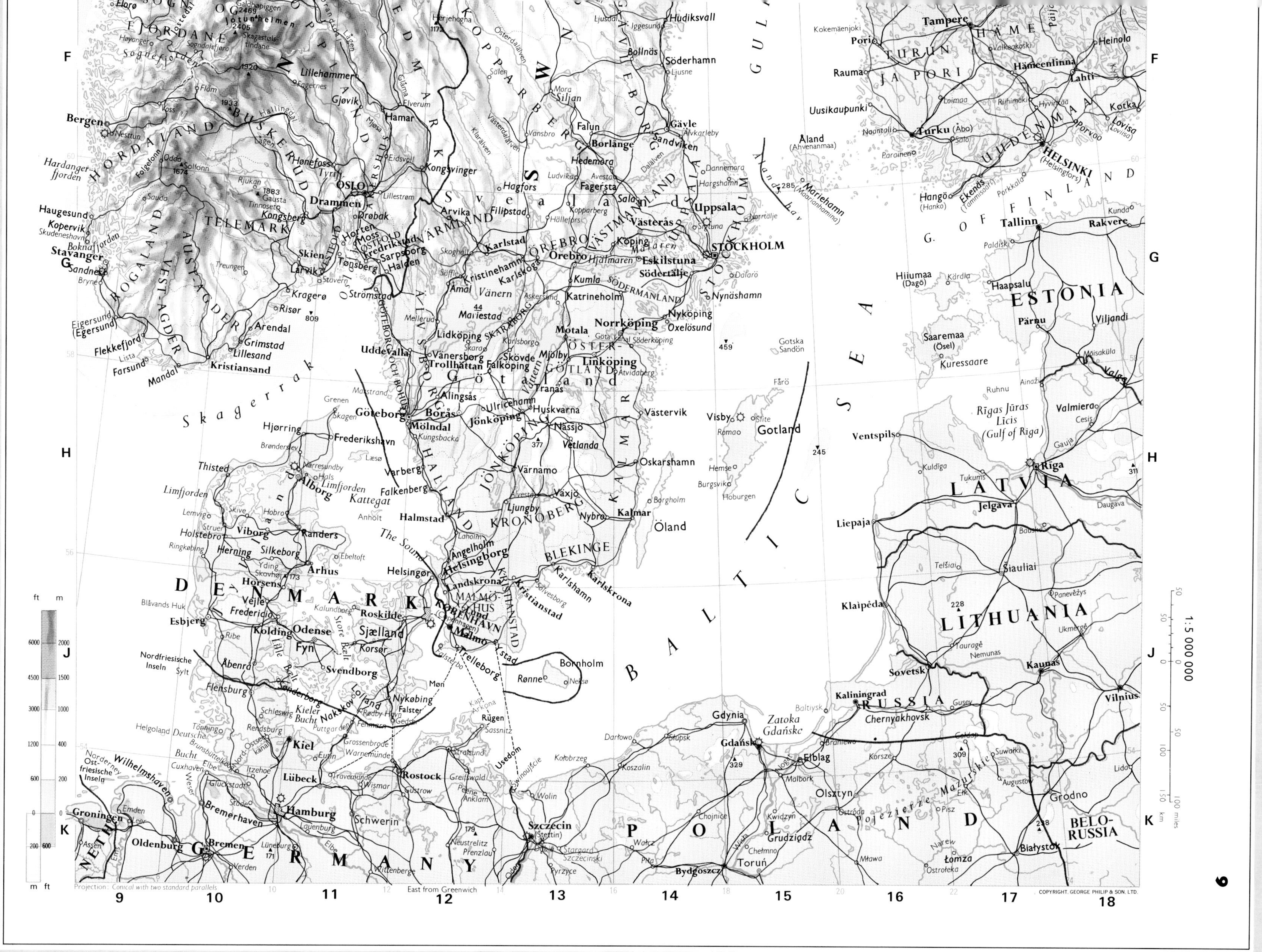

1 : 5 000 000

50   0   50   100 miles

50   0   50   100   150 km

COPYRIGHT GEORGE PHILIP & SON, LTD.

F   G   H   J   K

18

17

16

15

14

13

12

11

10

9

ESTONIA
LATVIA
LITHUANIA
RUSSIA
BELO-RUSSIA
POLAND
GERMANY
DENMARK
NETH.

FINLAND

BALTIC SEA

Helsinki (Helsingfors)
Tallinn
Tampere
Turku (Åbo)
Hämeenlinna
Heinola
Kotka
Lahti
Rakvere
Valmiera
Cēsis
Riga
Pärnu
Haapsalu
Viljandi
Valga
Hiiumaa (Dagö)
Saaremaa (Ösel)
Kuressaare
Ruhnu
Ventspils
Liepāja
Šiauliai
Jelgava
Klaipeda
Sovetsk
Kaliningrad
Chernyakhovsk
Panevėžys
Vilnius
Kaunas
Grodno
Białystok
Łomża
Ostrołęka
Olsztyn
Elbląg
Gdańsk
Gdynia
Grudziądz
Toruń
Bydgoszcz
Szczecin (Stettin)
Rostock
Schwerin
Lübeck
Hamburg
Kiel
Flensburg
Bremen
Bremerhaven
Wilhelmshaven
Oldenburg
Emden
Groningen

Gotland
Visby
Öland
Bornholm
Rügen
Rønne

Aland (Ahvenanmaa)
Mariehamn (Maarianhamina)

STOCKHOLM
Uppsala
Västerås
Eskilstuna
Södertälje
Nyköping
Oxelösund
Norrköping
Linköping
Motala
Örebro
Karlstad
Karlskoga
Falun
Borlänge
Gävle
Söderhamn
Hudiksvall
Bollnäs
Mora
Falköping
Jönköping
Nässjö
Växjö
Kalmar
Nybro
Vetlanda
Värnamo
Ljungby
Karlskrona
Karlshamn
Kristianstad
Halmstad
Varberg
Göteborg
Mölndal
Borås
Trollhättan
Vänersborg
Uddevalla
Strömstad
Lidköping
Mariestad
Åmål
Arvika
Filipstad
Ludvika
Hedemora
Sala
Katrineholm
Kumla
Nyköping
Västervik
Oskarshamn
Helsingborg
Landskrona
Malmö
Lund
Trelleborg
Ystad
Ängelholm

Göta Kanal
Vänern
Vättern
Mälaren
Hjälmaren
Siljan

Oslo
Drammen
Hamar
Lillehammer
Gjøvik
Kongsberg
Skien
Porsgrunn
Larvik
Tønsberg
Sarpsborg
Fredrikstad
Halden
Moss
Arendal
Grimstad
Lillesand
Kristiansand
Flekkefjord
Egersund (Egersund)
Stavanger
Sandnes
Haugesund
Bergen

København (Copenhagen)
Roskilde
Helsingør
Odense
Svendborg
Nykøbing
Nakskov
Randers
Århus
Silkeborg
Herning
Horsens
Vejle
Kolding
Fredericia
Esbjerg
Ribe
Åbenrå
Thisted
Viborg
Hjørring
Frederikshavn
Ålborg

Skagerrak
Kattegat
The Sound
Sjælland
Fyn

East from Greenwich

Projection-Conical with two standard parallels

m 2000 1500 1000 400 200 0 ft
ft 6000 4500 3000 1200 600 0 m

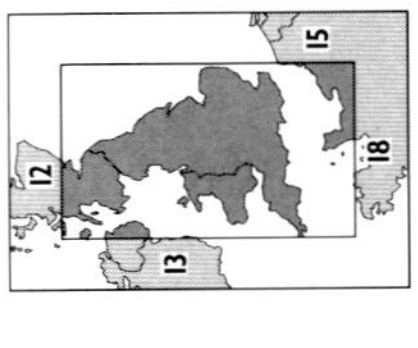

NORTH SEA

IRISH SEA

North Channel

SCOTLAND

Southern Uplands

Galloway

Pennines

CUMBRIA

Cumbrian Mts.

NORTHUMBERLAND

DURHAM

CLEVELAND

NORTH YORKSHIRE

WEST YORKSHIRE

SOUTH YORKSHIRE

HUMBERSIDE

LINCOLN

LANCASHIRE

MERSEYSIDE

CHESHIRE

DERBY

NOTTS

STAFFORD

GWYNEDD

CLWYD

N. York Moors

Holderness

Lincoln Wolds

Cheviot Hills

Forest of Bowland

Edinburgh **Glasgow** Paisley Greenock Port Glasgow Clydebank Dumbarton Rutherglen Hamilton Motherwell Wishaw Airdrie Coatbridge Falkirk Stirling Alloa Dunfermline Kirkcaldy Leith Musselburgh Kilmarnock Irvine Saltcoats Largs Ayr

Helensburgh Inveraray Campbeltown Gigha Arran Goat Fell 874

Fife Ness Anstruther Crail North Berwick Bass Rock Dunbar Eyemouth St. Abb's Hd. Holy I. Farne Is. Berwick-upon-Tweed Alnwick Coquet Morpeth Ashington Blyth Tynemouth North Shields South Shields Newcastle Gateshead Sunderland Houghton-le-Spring Peterlee Hartlepool Redcar Middlesbrough Stockton Billingham Darlington Bishop Auckland Durham Consett Hexham

Carlisle Gretna Green Longtown Annan Dumfries Kirkcudbright Dalbeattie Castle Douglas Newton Stewart Creetown Wigtown Whithorn Stranraer Portpatrick Luce Bay Mull of Galloway

Peebles Galashiels Selkirk Hawick Jedburgh Kelso Coldstream Moffat Sanquhar Leadhills Lanark Biggar Broad Law 840

ISLE OF MAN Ramsey Snaefell 620 Douglas Peel Port Erin Castletown Pt. of Ayre Calf of Man

Whitehaven Workington Maryport Cockermouth Keswick Skiddaw 931 Sca Fell 978 Ambleside Windermere Kendal Ulverston Barrow-in-Furness Morecambe Heysham Lancaster Fleetwood Blackpool Lytham St. Annes Southport Formby Pt. Preston Blackburn Burnley Nelson Colne Bradford Leeds Halifax Huddersfield Wakefield Barnsley Rotherham Sheffield Doncaster Scunthorpe Goole Selby York Harrogate Knaresborough Ripon Northallerton Thirsk Richmond Pen-y-Ghent 693 Settle Skipton

Liverpool Bootle Wallasey Birkenhead St. Helens Widnes Warrington Wigan Bolton Bury Rochdale Oldham Manchester Stockport Macclesfield Stoke-on-Trent Newcastle-under-Lyme Crewe Nantwich Northwich Buxton Chesterfield Matlock Alfreton Mansfield Sutton-in-Ashfield Nottingham Ilkeston Derby Burton-upon-Trent Uttoxeter Stafford

Holyhead Holy I. Anglesey Beaumaris Amlwch Menai Strait Caernarfon Bangor Conwy Llandudno Colwyn Bay Rhyl Denbigh Mold Wrexham Flint Llangollen Snowdon 1085 Blaenau Ffestiniog Harlech Pwllheli

Hull Beverley Bridlington Filey Scarborough Whitby Flamborough Hd. Hornsea Withernsea Spurn Hd. Grimsby Cleethorpes Immingham Barton-upon-Humber Gainsborough Lincoln Louth Mablethorpe Skegness Alford Horncastle Sleaford Grantham Newark Retford Worksop Boston Spalding Bourne Grantham

Kings Lynn Hunstanton Wells Sandringham Fakenham North Walsham Cromer The Wash The Broads

North York Moors Pickering Malton Pickering

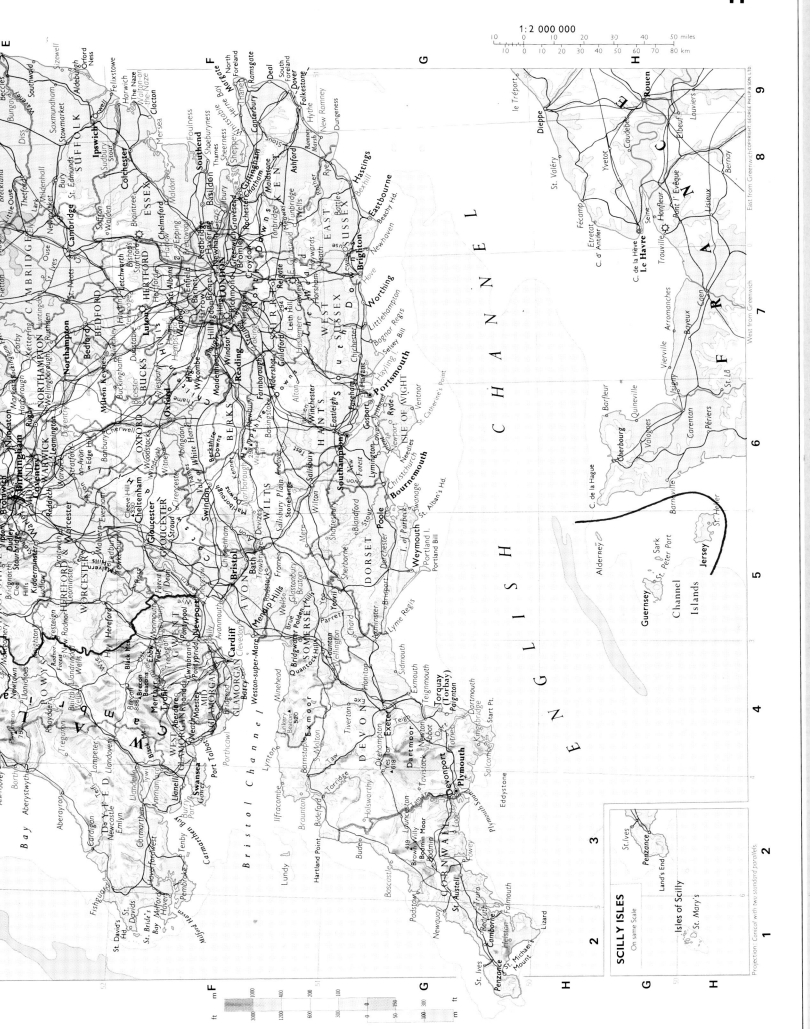

11

1:2 000 000

SCILLY ISLES
On same Scale
Isles of Scilly
Land's End
St. Ives
Penzance
St. Mary's

Projection: Conical with two standard parallels.

East from Greenwich COPYRIGHT GEORGE PHILIP & SON, LTD.

West from Greenwich

1:2 000 000

10   0   10   20   30   40   50 miles
10   0   10   20   30   40   50   60   70   80 km

1   2   3   4   5

ORKNEY IS.
On same scale

6

5

B

Westray
Rousay
Eday
Sanday
Stronsay
North Ronaldsay

Mainland
ORKNEY
Stromness
Shapinsay
Kirkwall

C

Hoy
Scapa Flow
South Ronaldsay

Pentland Firth
Dunnet Hd.
John O'Groats

6   7

C. Wrath
Durness
Strathy Pt.
Thurso
John O'Groats
Dounreay
Noss Hd.
Wick

Orkney Is.
Hoy
Scapa Flow
South Ronaldsay
Pentland Firth
Dunnet Hd.

Ben Hope 927
Tongue
Halladale
L. Loyal

Butt of Lewis

Flannan Is.
L. Roag
Stornoway
Broad Bay
Eye Pen

North Minch

Eddrachillis Bay
Lochinver
Enard Bay
L. Assynt
B. More Assynt
Loch Shin
Lairg
Brora
Helmsdale
Ord of Caithness
Helmsdale
Lybster

Lewis
Harris
Tarbert
Sound of Harris
North Uist
Lochmaddy

WESTERN ISLES

Outer Hebrides

Inner Minch

L. Seaforth

L. Lasford
Reay Forest

L. Broom
Ullapool
Oykell
Golspie
Dornoch
Dornoch Firth
Tarbat Ness
Tain
Moray Firth

Cullen
Portsoy
Banff
Macduff
Kinnaird's Head
Fraserburgh
Rattray Head
Peterhead
Buchan Ness

Monach Is.
Benbecula

South Uist
Ben More 620
Lochboisdale

Sound of Barra
Barra
Barra Hd.

Pt. of Ardnamurchan

Canna
Rhum
Eigg
Muck
Coll
Tiree
Staffa
Iona
Mull
Ben More 966

Tobermory
Morvern
Sound of Mull

Firth of Lorn

Colonsay

Rubh a' Mhail

Islay
Bowmore
Port Ellen

Gigha

Jura
Sound of Jura

Kintyre

Campbeltown
Mull of Kintyre

Rathlin
Fair Hd.
Ballycastle

NORTHERN IRELAND
Belfast
Ballymena
Larne
Belfast Lough
Bangor
Newtownards
Portpatrick

Monadhliath Mts.
Trotternish
Rubha Hunish
L. Gairloch
L. Ewe
L. Maree
Gairloch
Torridon
Rona
Raasay
Portree
Scalpay
Cuillin Hills
Cuillin Sound
Sound of Raasay
L. Bracadale

Garron
Stromeferry
Dornie
Kyle of Lochalsh
L. Hourn
Glen Affric
Glen Moriston
Fort Augustus
Glen Garry
L. Arkaig
Mallaig
L. Morar
Arisaig
Shiel
L. Eil
L. Moidart
L. Sunart
Loch Linnhe
Ardgour

NORTH WEST HIGHLANDS

B. Dearg 1081

Invergordon
Cromarty
Strathpeffer
Dingwall
Conon
Beauly
Fortrose
Nairn
Culloden Moor
INVERNESS
Findhorn
Forres
Elgin
Lossiemouth
Rothes
Keith
Dufftown
Huntly
Buckie
Deveron
Turriff
Elton
Ythan

GRAMPIAN

Ben Wyvis 1045

HIGHLAND

Glen More
Loch Ness
Grantown-on-Spey
Aviemore
Kingussie
Newtonmore
Cairn Gorm 1245
Cairn Toul 1293
Ben Macdhui 1311
Strath Spey
Tomintoul
Alford
Inverurie
Don
Aberdeen
Girdle Ness

Badenoch
Forest of Atholl
Blair Atholl
Pass of Killiecrankie
Pitlochry
Garry
Till
Braemar
Balmoral
Lochnagar 1154
Ballater
Aboyne
Dee
Banchory
Stonehaven

GRAMPIAN HIGHLANDS

Braes of Angus
N. Esk
Laurencekirk
Inverbervie

Fort William
Ben Nevis 1343
Glen Coe
Ballachulish
Rannoch Moor
Kinlochleven
Ben Cruachan 1124

Oban
Inveraray
L. Awe
L. Fyne

Ben More 1174
B. Vorlich 983
Crieff
L. Earn
Callander
Trossachs
Ben Ledi 974
L. Katrine
Dunblane
L. Lomond

Ben Lawers 1214
L. Tay
Aberfeldy
Killin
Breadalbane
Kenmore
L. Rannoch
L. Tummel
Tay
Dunkeld
Blairgowrie
Alyth
Kirriemuir
Forfar
Sidlaw Hills

Strathmore
Brechin
Montrose
Arbroath
Broughty Ferry
Dundee
Firth of Tay
Tayport
St. Andrews
Fife Ness
Anstruther

TAYSIDE
FIFE
Scone
PERTH
Earn
Kinross
Leven
Cupar
Ochil Hills
Cowdenbeath
Glenrothes
Lochgelly
Kirkcaldy
Buckhaven
Bass Rock
Alloa
Bannockburn
Dunfermline
Rosyth
Leith
North Berwick
Dunbar

CENTRAL
Stirling
Grangemouth
Falkirk
Linlithgow
EDINBURGH
Musselburgh
Haddington
Dalkeith
LOTHIAN
Penicuik
St. Abb's Hd.
Eyemouth

Lochgilphead
Crinan
Tarbert
Loch Fyne
Helensburgh
Dumbarton
Clydebank
Dunoon
Greenock
Port Glasgow
Renfrew
Paisley
Johnstone
GLASGOW
Rutherglen
Coatbridge
Airdrie
Cumbernauld
Kirkintilloch
Motherwell
Wishaw
Hamilton
E. Kilbride
Carstairs
Lanark
Biggar
Peebles
Moorfoot Hills
Galashiels
Melrose
Coldstream
Kelso
Flodden
Till
Holy I.
Berwick-upon-Tweed

STRATHCLYDE
Kilbride
Irvine
Kilmarnock
Troon
Prestwick
Ayr
Cumnock
Leadhills
Sanquhar
Moffat
Lammermuir Hills
Duns
Lauderdale
Tweed
Ettrick
Selkirk
Hawick
Jedburgh
Cheviot
The Cheviot 816
Coquet

Ardrossan
Saltcoats
Goat Fell 874
Arran
Brodick
Ailsa Craig
Girvan

Rothesay
Bute
Largs

Firth of Clyde

BORDERS
Broad Law 840
Yarrow
Southern Uplands
Cheviot Hills

Dalmellington
Doon
Merrick 843
Ken
L. Ryan
Stranraer
Newton Stewart
Wigtown
Whithorn
Luce Bay
Mull of Galloway
Wigtown Bay

DUMFRIES AND GALLOWAY
Dumfries
Annan
Gretna Green
Lockerbie
Langholm
Esk
N. Tyne
Hexham
HADRIAN'S WALL
Carlisle
ENGLAND

Galloway
Castle Douglas
Dalbeattie
Gatehouse of Fleet
Kirkcudbright
Solway Firth
Workington
Derwent
Skiddaw 931
Ullswater
Penrith
Cross Fell 893
Alston
Wear
S. Tyne
Tees
Barnard Castle

Cumbrian Mts.
CUMBRIAN MTS.

ATLANTIC OCEAN

NORTH SEA

North Channel

Firth of Clyde

West from Greenwich

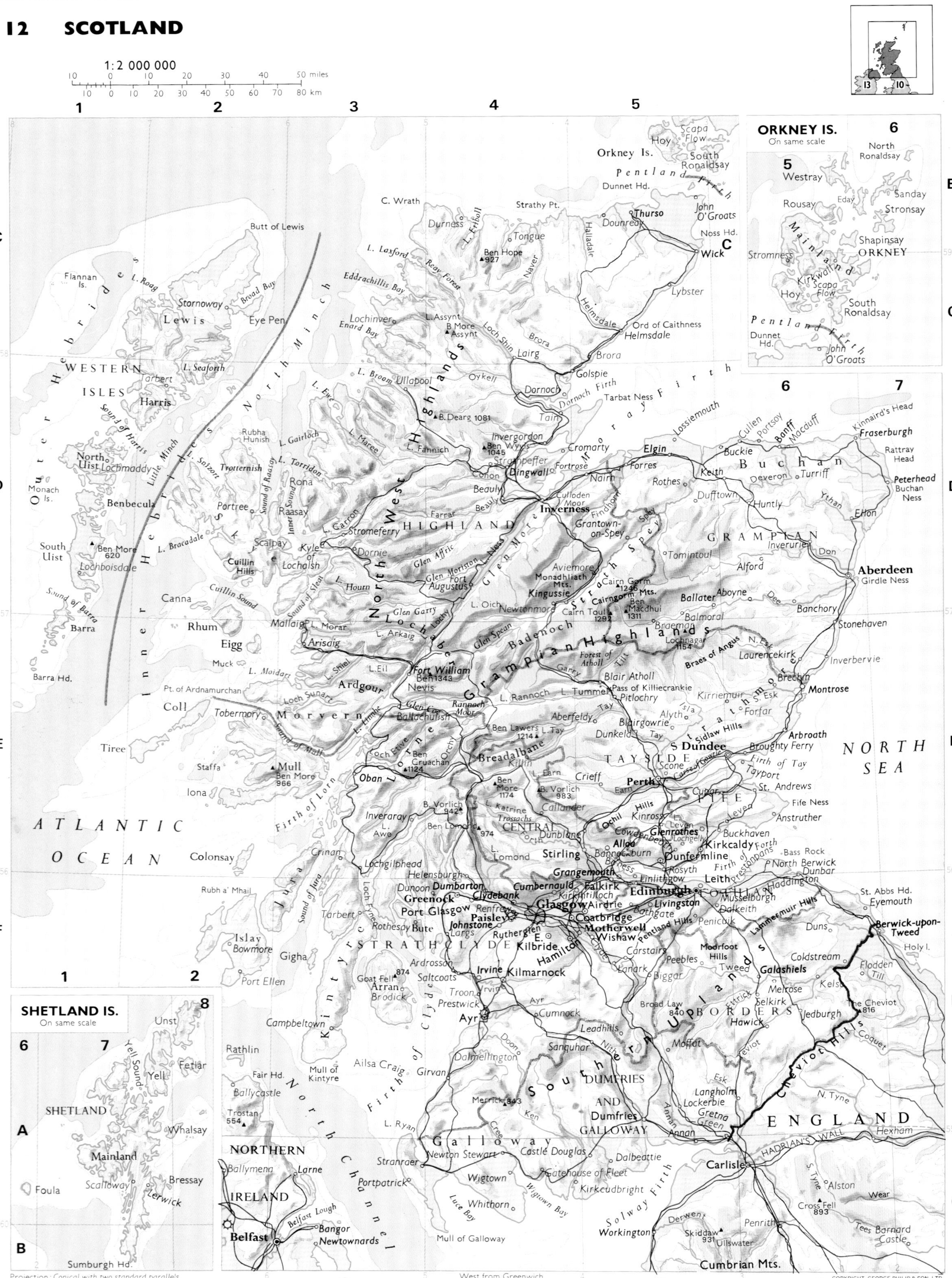

Projection: Conical with two standard parallels.

COPYRIGHT GEORGE PHILIP & SON LTD.

ft   m
3000   1000
1200   400
600   200
300   100
0   0
50   150
100   300
m   ft

SHETLAND IS.
On same scale

8

6   7

Unst
Fetlar
Yell
Yell Sound
Whalsay
SHETLAND
Mainland
Bressay
Scalloway
Lerwick
Foula
Sumburgh Hd.

A

B

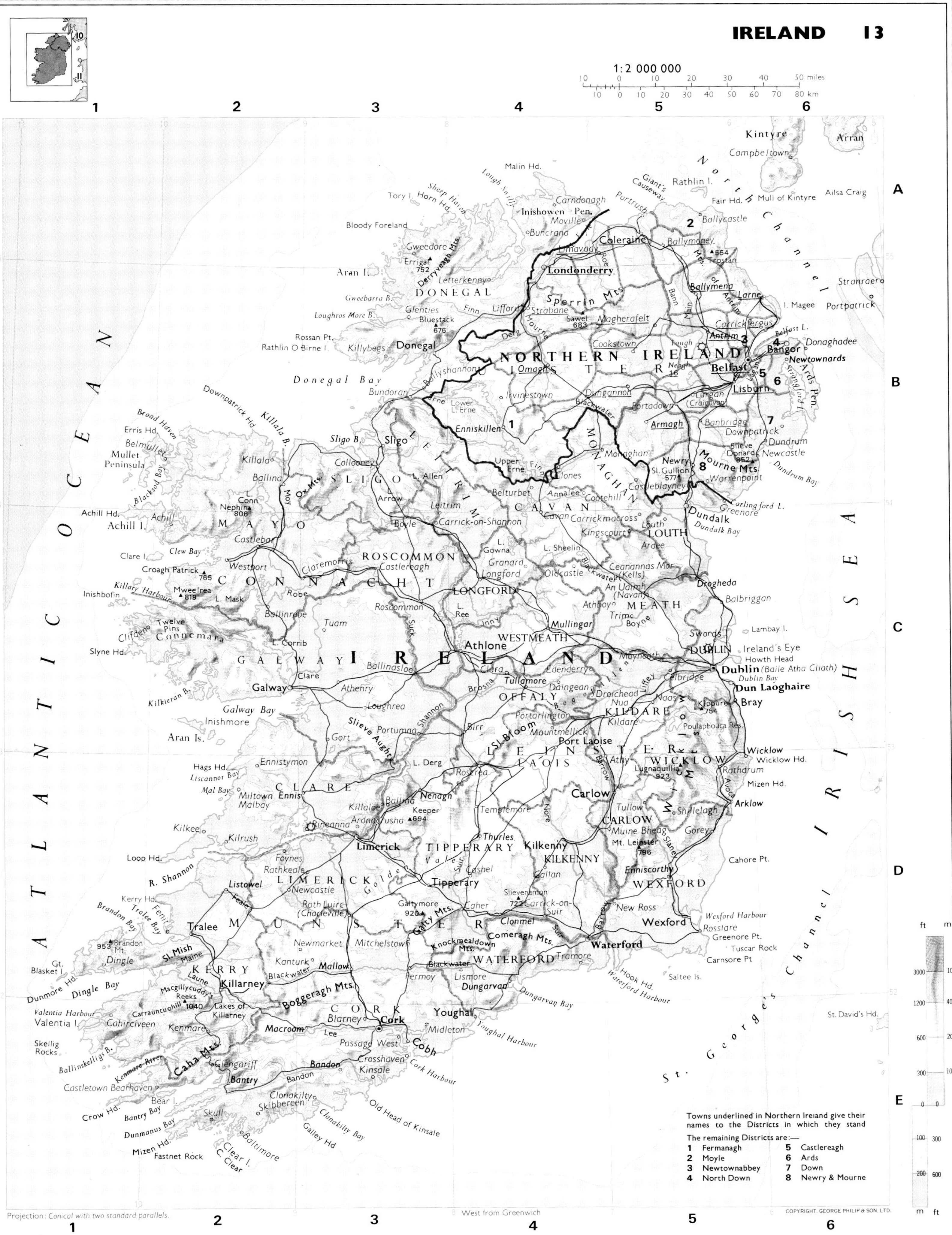

1:2 000 000

10 0 10 20 30 40 50 miles
10 0 10 20 30 40 50 60 70 80 km

ATLANTIC OCEAN

NORTHERN IRELAND

IRELAND

IRISH SEA

North Channel

St. George's Channel

Provinces / Regions
ULSTER · CONNACHT · LEINSTER · MUNSTER

Counties
DONEGAL · LEITRIM · SLIGO · MAYO · ROSCOMMON · LONGFORD · CAVAN · MONAGHAN · LOUTH · MEATH · WESTMEATH · GALWAY · OFFALY · KILDARE · WICKLOW · LAOIS · CARLOW · KILKENNY · WEXFORD · CLARE · TIPPERARY · LIMERICK · KERRY · CORK · WATERFORD

Selected place names
Kintyre · Campbeltown · Arran · Rathlin I. · Mull of Kintyre · Ailsa Craig · Malin Hd. · Giant's Causeway · Portrush · Fair Hd. · Stranraer · Portpatrick · Tory I. · Horn Hd. · Sheep Haven · Lough Swilly · Carndonagh · Inishowen Pen. · Moville · Ballycastle · Bloody Foreland · Buncrana · Coleraine · Ballymoney · Gweedore · Errigal 752 · Derryveagh Mts. · Limavady · Trostan 554 · Larne · Aran I. · Letterkenny · DONEGAL · Londonderry · Sperrin Mts. · Ballymena · Antrim · I. Magee · Gweebarra B. · Finn · Lifford · Strabane · Sawel 683 · Magherafelt · Carrickfergus · Belfast L. · Glenties · Bluestack 676 · Cookstown · Antrim · Bangor · Donaghadee · Rossan Pt. · Killybegs · Donegal · Omagh · Lough Neagh · Belfast · Newtownards · Rathlin O Birne I. · Dungannon · Lisburn · Ards Pen. · Donegal Bay · Bundoran · Ballyshannon · Lower L. Erne · Irvinestown · Blackwater · Lurgan (Craigavon) · Portadown · Armagh · Banbridge · Downpatrick · Dundrum · Downpatrick Hd. · Killala B. · Sligo B. · Sligo · LEITRIM · Enniskillen · Upper L. Erne · Finn · Clones · Slieve Donard 852 · Newcastle · Erris Hd. · Belmullet · Killala · Colloony · Allen · Leitrim · Newry · St. Gullion 577 · Mourne Mts. · Warrenpoint · Dundrum Bay · Mullet Peninsula · Blacksod Bay · Ballina · Moy · Arrow · Boyle · Carrick-on-Shannon · Belturbet · CAVAN · Annalee · Cootehill · Carrickmacross · Carlingford L. · Greenore · Achill Hd. · Achill I. · Clew Bay · L. Conn · Nephin 806 · Castlebar · Cavan · Kingscourts · Dundalk · Dundalk Bay · Clare I. · Croagh Patrick 765 · Westport · CONNACHT · ROSCOMMON · Castlereagh · L. Gowna · Granard · Oldcastle · Ceanannas Mor (Kells) · An Uaimh (Navan) · Drogheda · Balbriggan · Inishbofin · Killary Harbour · Mweelrea 819 · L. Mask · Ballinrobe · Robe · Roscommon · L. Ree · Athboy · Trim · Boyne · Swords · Lambay I. · Twelve Pins · Clifden · Connemara · L. Corrib · Tuam · Suck · Inny · MEATH · Slyne Hd. · GALWAY · Athlone · WESTMEATH · Mullingar · Maynooth · DUBLIN · Ireland's Eye · Howth Head · Galway · Clare · Ballinasloe · Clara · Edenderry · Dublin (Baile Atha Cliath) · Dublin Bay · Kilkieran B. · Athenry · Loughrea · Brosna · Tullamore · Daingean · Droichead Nua · Naas · Celbridge · Dun Laoghaire · Inishmore · Slieve Aughty · Portumna · Shannon · Birr · OFFALY · Bog · Portarlington · KILDARE · Kildare · Poulaphouca Res. · Bray · Aran Is. · Gort · L. Derg · Mountmellick · Kippure 754 · Hags Hd. · Ennistymon · Port Laoise · Athy · WICKLOW · Wicklow · Liscannor Bay · LAOIS · Barrow · Lugnaquillia 923 · Wicklow Hd. · Mal Bay · CLARE · Ennis · Roscrea · Nore · Rathdrum · Miltown Malbay · Killaloe · Ballina · Nenagh · Templemore · Carlow · Tullow · Mt. Leinster 796 · Shillelagh · Arklow · Kilkee · Kinvarra · Ardnacrusha · Keeper 694 · Thurles · CARLOW · Muine Bheag · Gorey · Kilrush · TIPPERARY · Kilkenny · KILKENNY · Cahore Pt. · Loop Hd. · Limerick · Cashel · Callan · Enniscorthy · WEXFORD · Foynes · LIMERICK · Golden · Tipperary · Slievenamon 722 · Carrick-on-Suir · New Ross · Rathkeale · Listowel · Newcastle · Rath Luirc (Charleville) · Galtymore 920 · Galty Mts. · Caher · Clonmel · Wexford · Wexford Harbour · Kerry Hd. · Feale · Fenit · Tralee Bay · Comeragh Mts. · Rosslare · Greenore Pt. · Tuscar Rock · Brandon Bay · Tralee · MUNSTER · Newmarket · Mitchelstown · Knockmealdown Mts. · Waterford · Tramore · Carnsore Pt. · Gt. Blasket I. · Brandon Mt. 953 · St. Mish · Maine · Kanturk · Blackwater · WATERFORD · Lismore · Dungarvan · Hook Hd. · Saltee Is. · St. David's Hd. · Dingle · KERRY · Killarney · Mallow · Fermoy · Dungarvan Bay · Waterford Harbour · Valentia Harbour · Macgillycuddy's Reeks · Lakes of Killarney · Boggeragh Mts. · Youghal · Youghal Harbour · Valentia I. · Carrauntuohill 1040 · CORK · Cork · Midleton · St. David's Hd. · Skellig Rocks · Kenmare · Lee · Blarney · Cobh · Cork Harbour · Caha Mts. · Passage West · Crosshaven · Castletown Bearhaven · Glengarriff · Bandon · Kinsale · Bear I. · Bantry · Bandon · Crow Hd. · Bantry Bay · Clonakilty · Skibbereen · Old Head of Kinsale · Dunmanus Bay · Skull · Clonakilty Bay · Galley Hd. · Mizen Hd. · Fastnet Rock · Baltimore · Clear I. · C. Clear

Legend
Towns underlined in Northern Ireland give their names to the Districts in which they stand

The remaining Districts are:—

1 Fermanagh   5 Castlereagh
2 Moyle   6 Ards
3 Newtownabbey   7 Down
4 North Down   8 Newry & Mourne

ft   m

3000 — 1000
1200 — 400
600 — 200
300 — 100
0 — 0
100 — 300
200 — 600

m   ft

1:4 000 000

The DISTRICTS of Northern Ireland have been numbered and can be identified by reference to this table.

1 Londonderry	14 Craigavon
2 Limavady	15 Armagh
3 Coleraine	16 Newry & Mourne
4 Ballymoney	17 Banbridge
5 Moyle	18 Down
6 Larne	19 Lisburn
7 Ballymena	20 Antrim
8 Magherafelt	21 Newtownabbey
9 Cookstown	22 Carrickfergus
10 Strabane	23 North Down
11 Omagh	24 Ards
12 Fermanagh	25 Castlereagh
13 Dungannon	26 Belfast

ORKNEY
HIGHLAND
Kirkwall

SHETLAND
Lerwick

○ Norwich — Administrative headquarters
MERSEYSIDE — Metropolitan counties
Antrim — Former Northern Ireland counties

West from Greenwich 0 East from Greenwich
COPYRIGHT GEORGE PHILIP & SON LTD.

1 : 2 500 000

Projection: Conical with two standard parallels

East from Greenwich

COPYRIGHT. GEORGE PHILIP & SON. LTD.

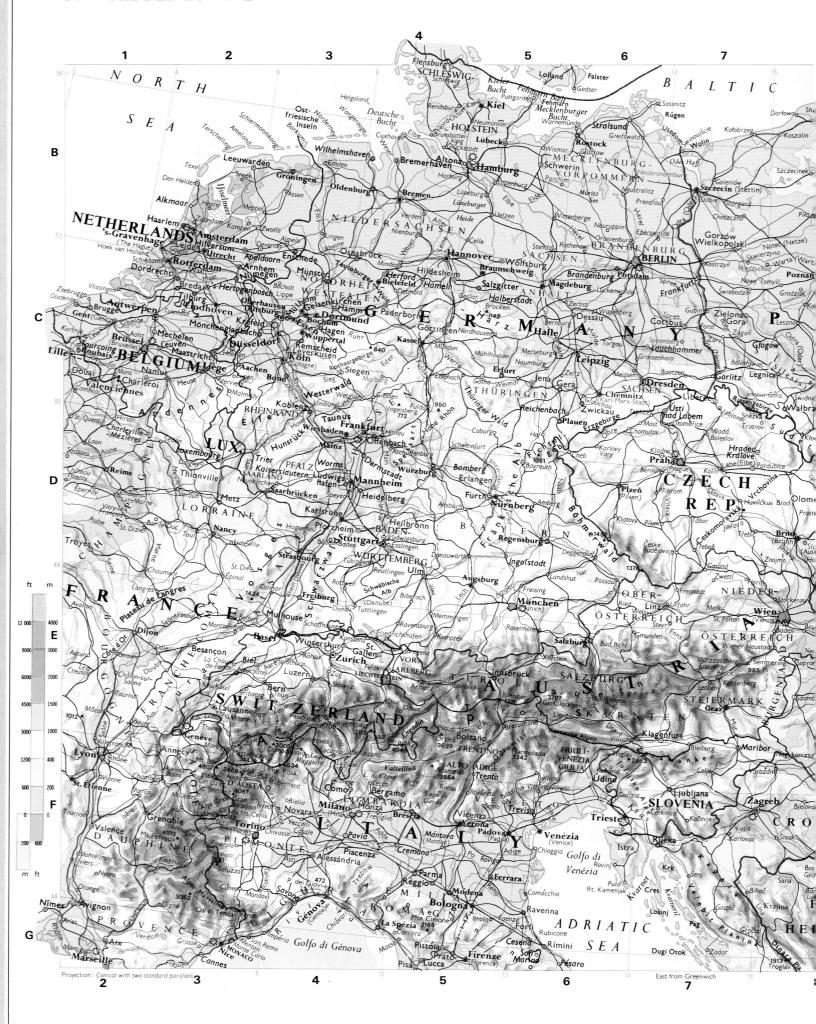

East from Greenwich

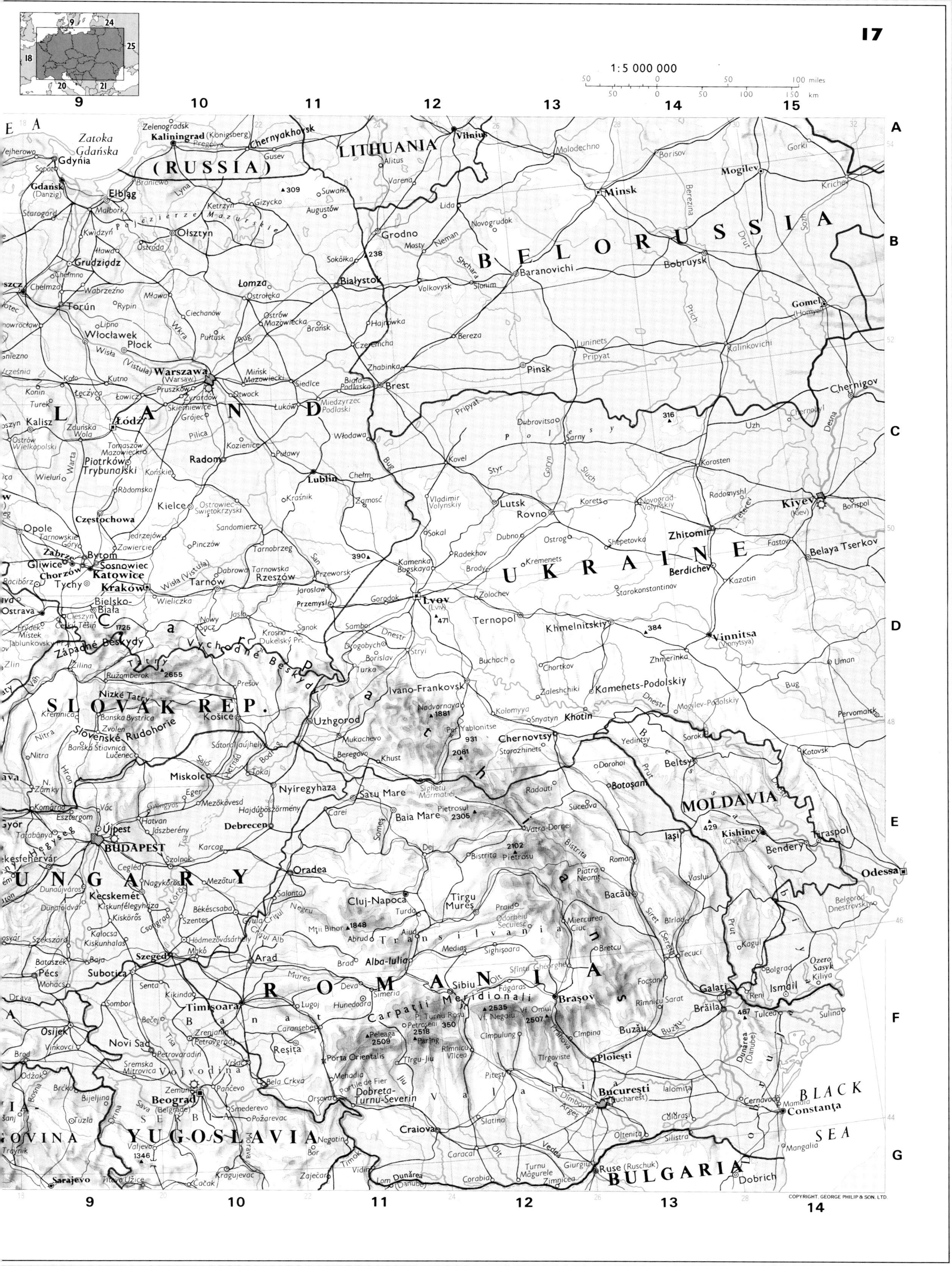

9 24
25
18
20 21
9

1:5 000 000
50 1:5 000 000 50 100 miles
50 0 50 100 150 km

9 10 11 12 13 14 15

E A
Zatoka Gdańska
Wejherowo
Sopot
Gdynia
Gdańsk (Danzig)
Starogard
Braniewo
Zelenogradsk
Kaliningrad (Königsberg)
Pregolya
Gusev
Chernyakhovsk
LITHUANIA
Alitus
Vilnius
Molodechno
Borisov
Gorki
A
Elbląg
Malbork
Kwidzyń
Iława
Ostróda
Olsztyn
Pojezierze Mazurskie
Lyna
Kętrzyn
Gizycko
309
Suwałki
Augustów
Varena
Lida
Novogrudok
Minsk
Berezina
Mogilev
Krichev
Sozh
B
Grudziądz
Chełmno
Wabrzeźno
Toruń
Rypin
Lipno
Mława
Ciechanów
Ostrów Mazowiecka
Brańsk
Grodno
Sokółka
238
Mosty
Neman
Shchara
Slonim
Volkovysk
Baranovichi
BELORUSSIA
Bobruysk
Drut
B
Włocławek
Płock
Wisła (Vistula)
Wkra
Pułtusk
Bug
Łomża
Białystok
Ostrołęka
Czeremcha
Bereza
Luninets
Pripyat
Kalinkovichi
Gomel (Homyel)
Gniezno
Września
Konin
Turek
Koło
Łęczyca
Kutno
Łowicz
Warszawa (Warsaw)
Pruszków
Mińsk Mazowiecki
Siedlce
Biała Podlaska
Brest
Pripyat
Pinsk
Zhabinka
Pitch
Chernigov
C
Kalisz
Zduńska Wola
Łódź
P O L A N D
Skierniewice
Grójec
Otwock
Łuków
Międzyrzec Podlaski
Włodawa
P o l y s y
Sarny
316
Uzh
Desna
C
Ostrów Wielkopolski
Wieluń
Piotrków Trybunalski
Radomsko
Tomaszów Mazowiecki
Pilica
Radom
Kozienice
Puławy
Lublin
Chełm
Bug
Kovel
Styr
Goryn
Sluch
Korosten
Radomyshl
Kiyev (Kiev)
Borispol
Opole
Częstochowa
Kielce
Ostrowiec Świętokrzyski
Kraśnik
Zamość
Vladimir Volynskiy
Lutsk
Rovno
Sokal
Dubno
Ostrog
Novograd-Volynskiy
Zhitomir
Fastov
Belaya Tserkov
Zabrze
Tarnowskie Góry
Bytom
Zawiercie
Jędrzejów
Sandomierz
Tarnobrzeg
390
San
Przeworsk
Radekhov
Brody
Kremenets
Berdichev
Kazatin
UKRAINE
Gliwice
Chorzów
Sosnowiec
Katowice
Kraków
Dąbrowa
Tarnowska
Wieliczka
Tarnów
Dabrowa
Jarosław
Gorodok
Lvov (Lviv)
471
Zolochev
Ternopol
Starokonstantinav
Khmelnitskiy
384
Vinnitsa (Vinnytsya)
D
Raciborz
Tychy
Bielsko-Biała
Cieszyn
Nowy Sącz
Jasło
Krosno
Dukelský Pr.
Sanok
Przemyśl
Sambor
Dnestr
Drogobych
Borislav
Turka
Stryi
Buchach
Chortkov
Zaleshchiki
Zhmerinka
Kamenets-Podolskiy
Uman
Pervomalsk
D
Ostrava
Frýdek Mistek
Jablunkovsky
1725
Západné Beskydy
Žilina
Ružomberok
2655
Vychodné Beskydy
Prešov
Ivano-Frankovsk
Nadvornaya
1881
Kolomyya
Snyatyn
Khotin
Dnestr
Mogilev-Podolskiy
Bug
Kremnica
Banská Bystrica
Zvolen
Slovenské Rudohorie
SLOVAK REP.
Košice
Uzhgorod
Mukachevo
931
Yablonitse
Chernovtsy
Storozhinets
Yedintsy
Sorok
Kotovsk
Beltsy
Nitra
Nitra
Banská Štiavnica
Lučeneč
Šalgótarján
Sátoraljaújhely
Beregovo
Khust
2061
Sighetu Marmatiei
Radauti
Dorohoi
Prut
MOLDAVIA
E
Zámky
Komárno
Miskolc
Eger
Mezőkövesd
Tokaj
Hernad
Nyiregyhaza
Satu Mare
Baia Mare
Pietrosul
2305
Vatra-Dornei
Suceava
Botoşani
Iaşi
429
Kishinev (Chişinău)
Bendery
Tiraspol
E
Győr
Tatabánya
Hatvan
Jászberény
Karcag
Debrecen
Hajdúböszörmény
Carei
Someş
Dej
2102
Bistrita
Pietrosu
Piatra Neamţ
Roman
Vaslui
Belgorod-Dnestrovskiy
Odessa
Budapest
Újpest
Vác
Esztergom
Cegléd
Szolnok
Oradea
Cluj-Napoca
Turda
Tirgu Mureş
Praid
Odorheiu Secuiesc
Miercurea Ciuc
Bretcu
Bacău
Bîrlad
Tecuci
Kagul
Kiliya
Ozero Sasyk
Reni
F
Kecskemét
Kiskunfélegyháza
Nagykőrös
Salonta
Negru
Mţii Bihor
1848
Aiud
Abrud
Transilvania
Sighişoara
Mediaş
Sfintu Gheorghe
Focşani
Siret
Galaţi
Ismail
Székesfehérvár
Dunaújváros
Dunaföldvár
Kalocsa
Kiskunhalas
Békéscsaba
Szentes
Hódmezővásárhely
Makó
Gyula
Crisul Alb
Brad
Deva
Alba-Iulia
Sibiu
Olt
Carpaţii Meridionali
2535
Vf. Negoiu
2507
Vf. Omu
Braşov
Rîmnicu Sarat
Brăila
467
Tulcea
Sulina
Dunărea (Danube)
F
Szekszárd
Pécs
Mohács
Subotica
Senta
Kikinda
Arad
Timişoara
Lugoj
Caransebeş
Hunedoara
Banat
Simeria
R O M A N I A
P. Turnu Roşu
Petroseni
2518
Paring
350
Cîmpina
Tîrgovişte
Ploieşti
Buzău
Buzău
Osijek
Sombor
Bečej
Zrenjanin (Petrovgrad)
Vršac
Reşiţa
2509
Peleaga
Porta Orientalis
Mehadia
Tirgu-Jiu
Rîmnicu Vîlcea
Cîmpulung
Piteşti
Bucureşti (Bucharest)
Ialomiţa
Cernavodă
BLACK
G
VOINA
Brod
Odžak
Brčko
Bijeljina
Tuzla
Novi Sad
Sremska Mitrovica
Zemun
Pančevo
Vojvodina
Bela Crkva
Orşova
Dobreta-Turnu-Severin
Jiu
V l a h i a
Dîmboviţa
Argeş
Călăraşi
Constanţa
Mamaia
SEA
Sava
Valjevo
1346
Beograd (Belgrade)
SERB
Smederevo
Požarevac
YUGOSLAVIA
Negotin
Timok
Vidin
Olt
Caracal
Slatina
Craiova
Oltenita
Silistra
Mangalia
Sarajevo
Titovo Užice
Čačak
Kragujevac
Zaječar
Lom
Dunărea (Danube)
Corabia
Turnu Măgurele
Zimnicea
Giurgiu
Ruse (Ruschuk)
Vedea
BULGARIA
Dobrich
G

9 10 11 12 13 14

18 FRANCE

1:5 000 000

50   0   50   100 miles
50   0   50   100   150 km.

FRENCH DEPARTMENTS

Abbr.	No.	Department
A.	01	Ain
Ai.	02	Aisne
Al.	03	Allier
A.H.P.	04	Alpes-de-Haute-Provence
H.A.	05	Hautes-Alpes
A.M.	06	Alpes-Maritimes
Ar.	07	Ardèche
	08	Ardennes
Ari.	09	Ariège
Aub.	10	Aube
Aud.	11	Aude
Av.	12	Aveyron
B.R.	13	Bouches-du-Rhône
	14	Calvados
C.	15	Cantal
Ch.	16	Charente
Ch.M.	17	Charente-Maritime
Che.	18	Cher
	19	Corrèze
Co.	20	a) Corse b) Corse du Sud
C.O.	21	Côte-d'Or
	22	Côtes-du-Nord
Cr.	23	Creuse
D.	24	Dordogne
Do.	25	Doubs
Dr.	26	Drôme
E.	27	Eure
E.L.	28	Eure-et-Loir
	29	Finistère
G.	30	Gard
H.G.	31	Haute-Garonne
Ge.	32	Gers
Gi.	33	Gironde
	34	Hérault
I.V.	35	Ille-et-Vilaine
I.	36	Indre
I.L.	37	Indre-et-Loire
Is.	38	Isère
J.	39	Jura
La.	40	Landes
L.C.	41	Loir-et-Cher
	42	Loire
H.L.	43	Haute-Loire
L.A.	44	Loire-Atlantique
Loi.	45	Loiret
Lot	46	Lot
L.G.	47	Lot-et-Garonne
Loz.	48	Lozère
M.	49	Maine-et-Loire
Ma.	50	Manche
M.	51	Marne
H.M.	52	Haute-Marne
May.	53	Mayenne
M.M.	54	Meurthe-et-Moselle
Meu.	55	Meuse
Mo.	56	Morbihan
Mos.	57	Moselle
Ni.	58	Nièvre
No.	59	Nord
O.	60	Oise
Or.	61	Orne
P.C.	62	Pas-de-Calais
P.D.	63	Puy-de-Dôme
P.A.	64	Pyrénées-Atlantiques
H.P.	65	Hautes-Pyrénées
P.O.	66	Pyrénées-Orientales
B.R.	67	Bas-Rhin
H.R.	68	Haut-Rhin
Rh.	69	Rhône
H.S.	70	Haute-Saône
S.L.	71	Saône-et-Loire
Sa.	72	Sarthe
Sav.	73	Savoie
H.Sa.	74	Haute-Savoie
	75	Paris
S.Me.	76	Seine-Maritime
S.M.	77	Seine-et-Marne
Y.	78	Yvelines
D.S.	79	Deux-Sèvres
So.	80	Somme
T.	81	Tarn
T.G.	82	Tarn-et-Garonne
Va.	83	Var
Vau.	84	Vaucluse
Ve.	85	Vendée
Vi.	86	Vienne
H.V.	87	Haute-Vienne
V.	88	Vosges
Y.	89	Yonne
B.	90	Belfort
Es.	91	Essonne
H.Se.	92	Hauts-de-Seine
S.S-D.	93	Seine-St-Denis
V.M.	94	Val-de-Marne
V.O.	95	Val-d'Oise

CORSICA On same scale

Corse — Haute-Corse — Corse du Sud

MEDITERRANEAN SEA

ENGLISH CHANNEL

BAY OF BISCAY

East from Greenwich / West from Greenwich

Projection: Conical with two standard parallels

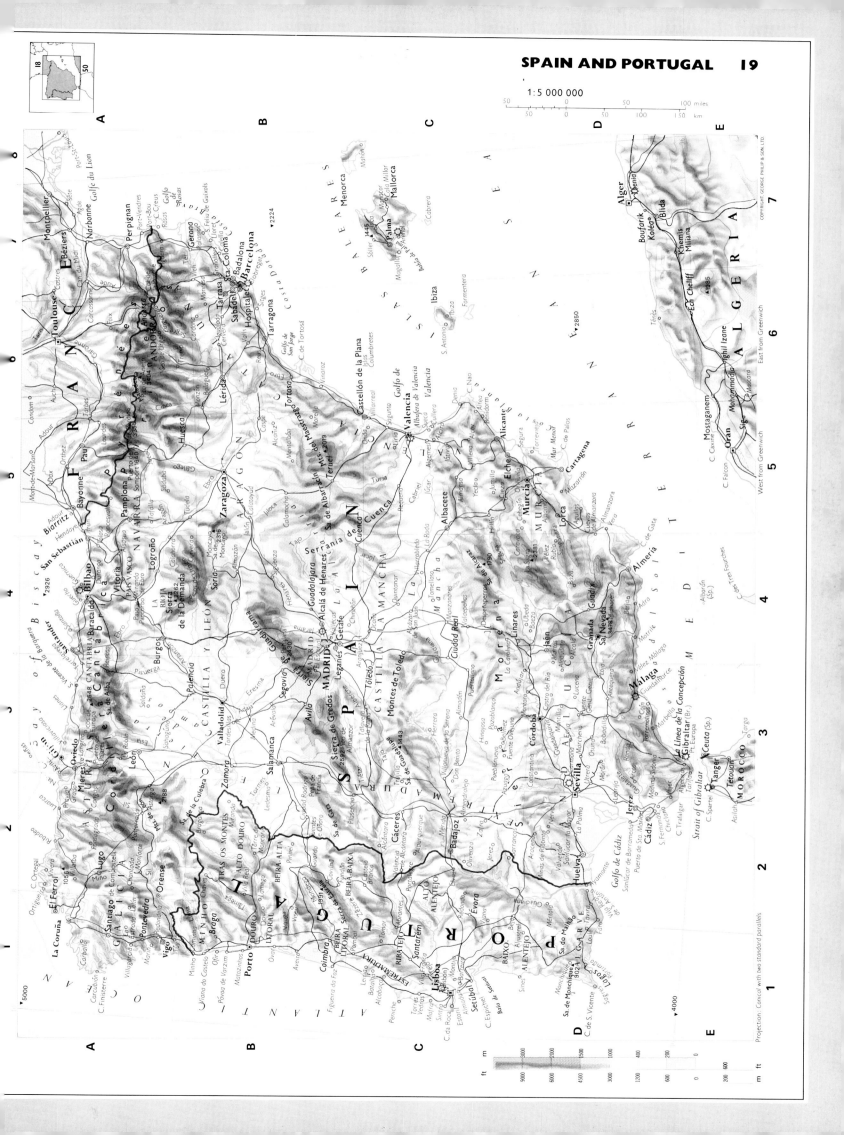

1 : 5 000 000

East from Greenwich

West from Greenwich

Projection: Conical with two standard parallels

Projection: Conical with two standard parallels

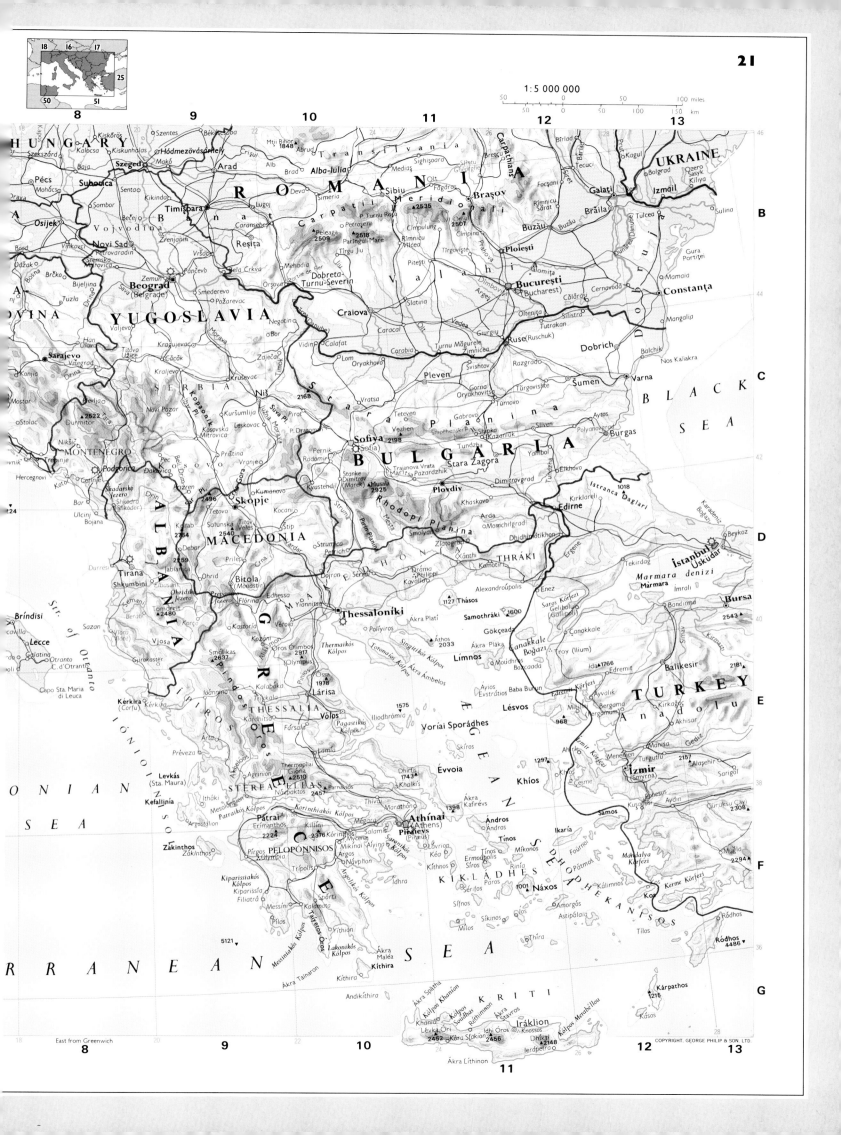

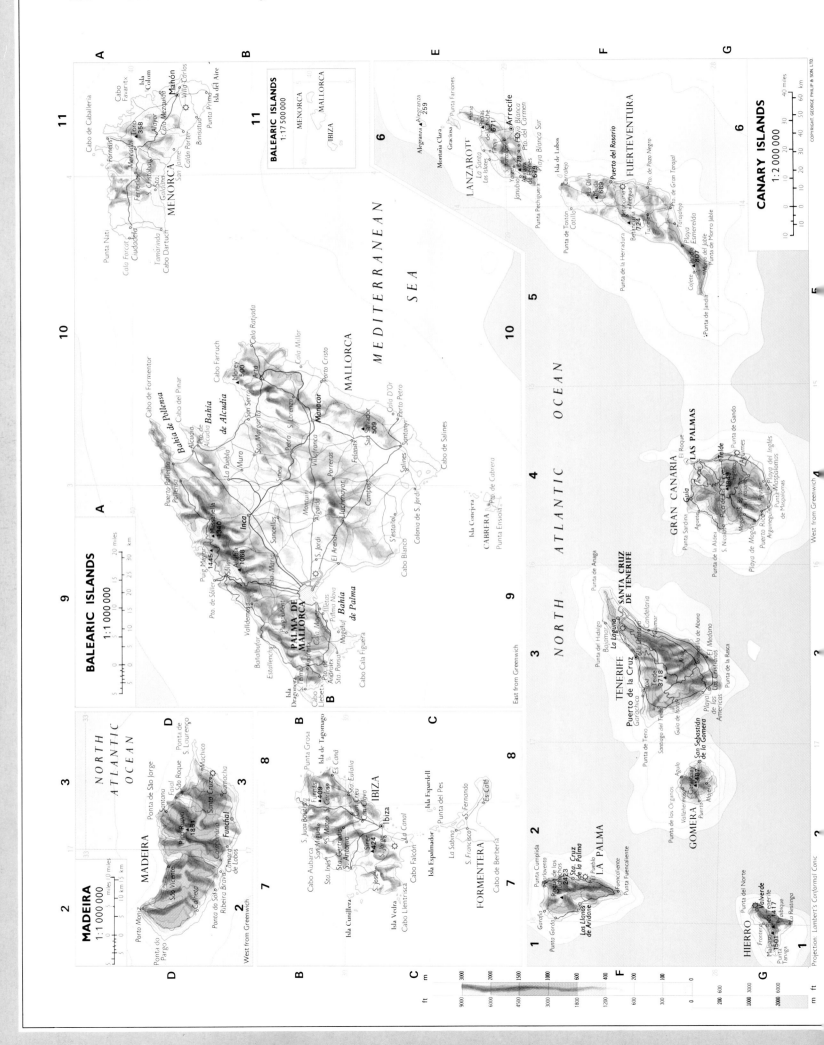

BALEARIC ISLANDS
1:17 500 000

MENORCA

MALLORCA

IBIZA

BALEARIC ISLANDS
1:1 000 000

MADEIRA
1:1 000 000

CANARY ISLANDS
1:2 000 000

MEDITERRANEAN SEA

NORTH ATLANTIC OCEAN

MENORCA

MALLORCA

CABRERA

IBIZA

FORMENTERA

MADEIRA

TENERIFE

GRAN CANARIA

LANZAROTE

FUERTEVENTURA

LA PALMA

GOMERA

HIERRO

West from Greenwich

East from Greenwich

Projection: Lambert's Conformal Conic

COPYRIGHT GEORGE PHILIP & SON LTD.

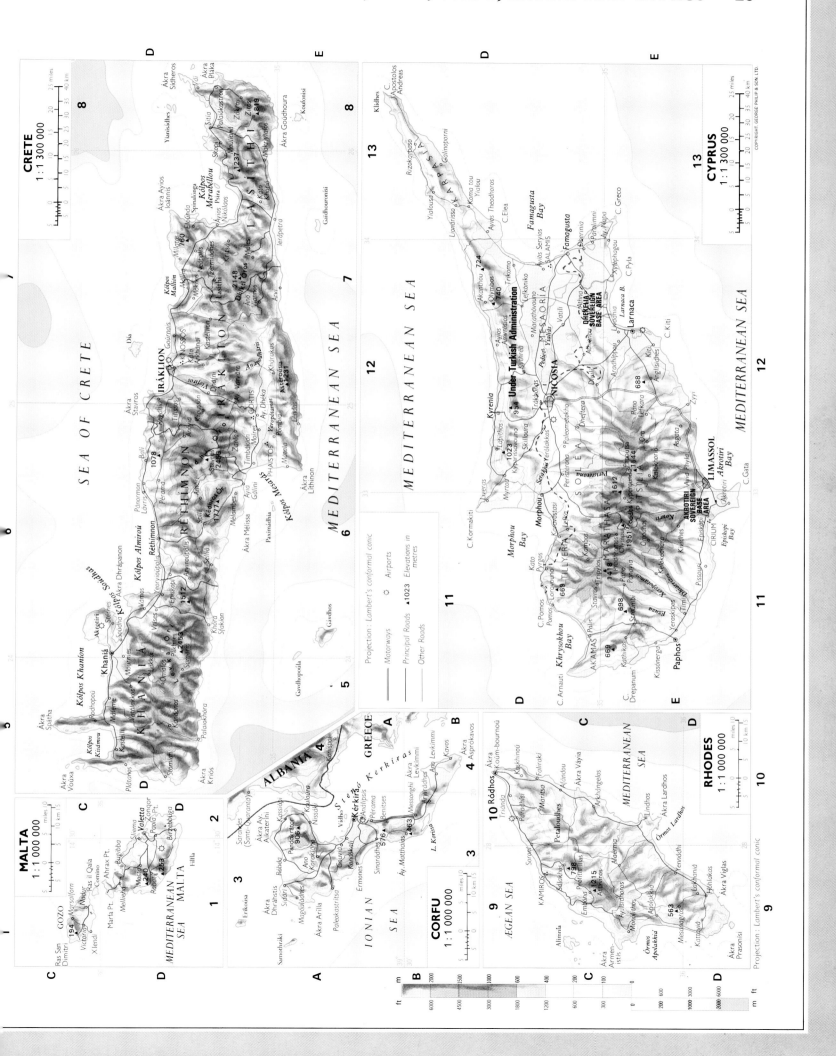

CRETE
1 : 1 300 000

MALTA
1 : 1 000 000

CORFU
1 : 1 000 000

RHODES
1 : 1 000 000

CYPRUS
1 : 1 300 000

Projection: Lambert's conformal conic

Motorways
Principal Roads
Other Roads
✈ Airports
▲1023 Elevations in metres

COPYRIGHT GEORGE PHILIP & SON LTD.

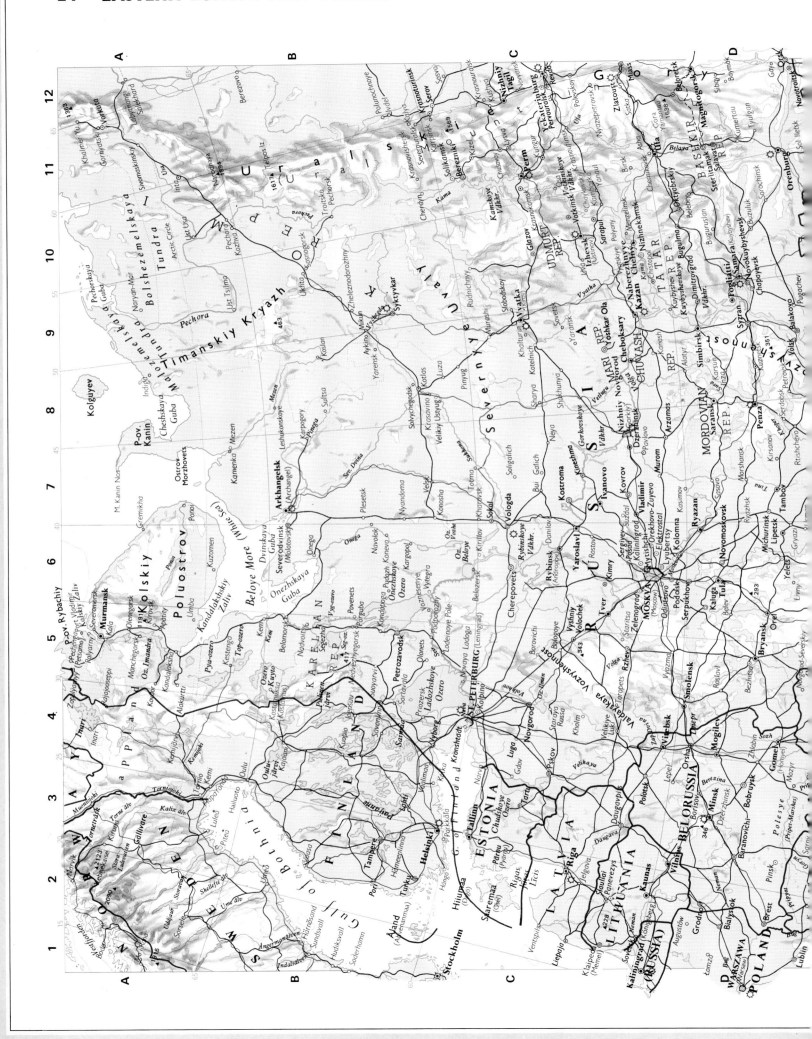

1:10 000 000

100 50 0 50 100 150 200 miles
100 0 100 200 300 km

Legend:
1 Kabardino-Balkar Rep.
2 North Ossetian Rep.
3 Nakhichevan Rep. (Azer.)
4 Checheno-Ingush Rep.

Karagiye Depression

East from Greenwich

------- Division between Greeks and Turks
in Cyprus: Turks to the North.

Projection: Conical with two standard parallels

Seas and water bodies:
CASPIAN SEA
BLACK SEA
Sea of Azov (Azovskoye More)
MEDITERRANEAN SEA
Levant
Zaliv Kara Bogaz Gol

Countries/regions:
KAZAKHSTAN
UKRAINE
ROMANIA
BULGARIA
MOLDAVIA
GEORGIA
ARMENIA
AZERBAIJAN
DAGESTAN REPUBLIC
KALMYK REP.
TURKEY
SYRIA
LEBANON
IRAQ
IRAN
CYPRUS
ABKHAZIA
Kirgiz Steppe
Pricaspiyskaya Nizmennost'
Yergeni Vozvyshennost'

Selected cities:
KYYEV, KHARKOV, Volgograd (Stalingrad), Astrakhan, Rostov, Tbilisi, Yerevan, BAKU, Ankara, İSTANBUL, TEHRAN, Baghdād, Dimashq (Damascus), Bayrūt (Beirut), Hamadān, Qom, Tabrīz, Kirkūk, Al Mawşil, Halab, Ḥamāh, Ḥims, Adana, Konya, İzmir (Smyrna), Bursa, BUCUREȘTI, Varna, Burgas, Sochi, Sukhumi, Batumi, Trabzon, Erzurum, Sevastopol, Simferopol, Odessa, Kherson, Nikolayev, Dnepropetrovsk, Donetsk, Makeyevka, Zaporozhye, Krasnodar, Stavropol, Groznyy, Vladikavkaz, Nalchik, Makhachkala, Derbent

Mountains/peaks:
Elbrus 5633
Kavkaz (Caucasus)
Aragats 4090
Ararat 5165
Anadolu Dağları
Kuzey Anadolu Dağları
Toros Dağları

Rivers:
Volga, Don, Ural, Dnepr, Dnestr, Kura, Araz, Nahr Dijlah (Tigris), Nahr al Furāt (Euphrates), Kızıl Irmak, Danube

Dhodhekanisos
Rhodos 1486
Ródhos

ft m
12 000 4000
6000 2000
3000 1000
1200 600
400 200
200 600
0

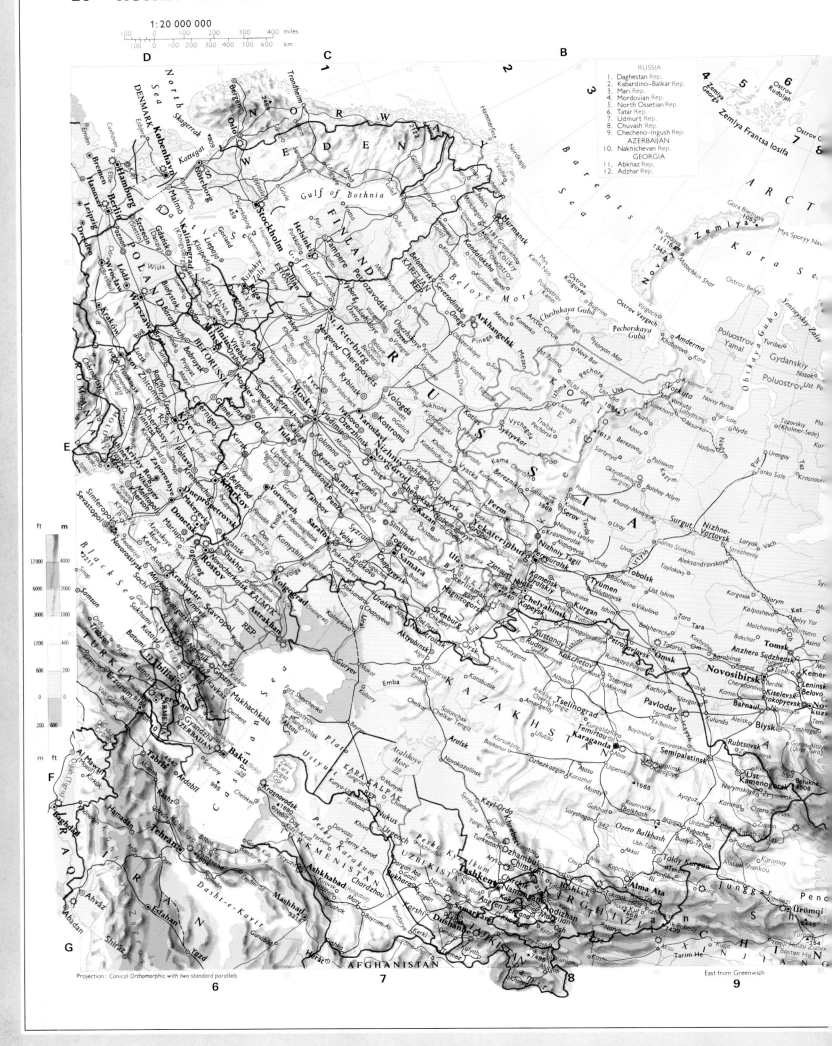

A   B   C

80 90 100 110 120 130 140 150 16 17 18 19

D

10 11

9 12

13

14 3800

15

Ostrov Shmidta
Mys Arkticheskiy
Ostrov Komsomolets
Ostrov Pioner
Ostrov Oktyabrskoy Revolyutsii
965
Severnaya Zemlya
Ostrov Bolshevik

Proliv Vilkutskogo

Ostrov Henrietta
Ostrov Jeanette
Ostrova Delong
Ostrov Zhokhova

Ostrov Bennetta
Ostrova

Ostrov Malyy Lyakhovskiy
Ostrov Bolshoy Lyakhovskiy
Ostrov Novaya Sibir
Ostrov Faddeyevskiy

Ostrov Vrangelya

Ostrova Medvezhi

OCEAN

L a p t e v   Novosibirskiye Ostrova

Sea

Ostrov Belkovskiy
Ostrov Kotelnyy
Ostrov Stolbovoy
Lyakhovskiye Ostrova
Proliv Dmitriya Lapteva

374

E a s t   S i b e r i a n   S e a

Chukotskoye More

Mys Dezhneva (East C.)

1863

Anadyrskiy Zaliv

St. Lawrence I. (U.S.A.)

Uelen
Lavrentiya
Providenya

Chukotskiy Khrebet

Pevek
Amguema
Ryrkaypiy
1863

Iultin
Egvekinot

Markovo

Korvakskiy Khrebet
2562

Poluostrov Kamchatka

Bering Sea

Komandorskiye Ostrova
Nikolskoye Ostrov

POLUOSTROV BYRRANGA

Gory Putorana
1701

Poluostrov Taymyr
Gory Byrranga Ostrov
1146

Oz. Taymyr

Nordvik

R U S S I A

Tiksi

Verkhoyansk
2389

Khrebet Cherskogo

Gora Chen
2682
Pobeda
3147

Srednekolymsk

Nizhne Kolymsk

Kolyma

Magadan
2359

Sredinnyy

Petropavlovsk-Kamchatskiy
3456

Okhotsk

Sea of Okhotsk

Ostrov Paramushir

Kurilskiye Ostrova

Verkhoyansk
Batagay
Lena
Vilyuysk
Yakutsk
Olekminsk

Y A K U T   R E P U B L I C

Aldan

1780

Sakhalin

Yuzhno-Sakhalinsk

Sovetskaya Gavan

Kirensk

Bratsk
Krasnoyarsk
Nizhneudinsk
Cheremkhovo
Usolye Sibirskoye
Angarsk
Irkutsk
Ulan Ude
Chita

BURYAT REP.
3491

Komsomolsk
2640

Khabarovsk

Birobidzhan

Blagoveshchensk

Amur

Stanovoy Khrebet

Jamusi

Khrebet Sikhote Alin

Vladivostok
Ussuriysk
Nakhodka

Hokkaidō
Sapporo
Hakodate

Muroran

MONGOLIA

Ulaanbaatar (Ulan Bator)
2800

Hangayn Nuruu

Hentiyn Nuruu

Har Nuur
Hyargas Nuur
Uvs Nuur

3957

Har Us Nuur

Edrengiyn Nuruu

Gaxun Nur

S E   R E P U B L I C

Hohhot
Baotou
Zhangjiakou
Beijing

Qiqihar
Harbin

Changchun
Jilin
Siping
1949

Dongbei

Shenyang
Fushun
Anshan
Yingkou
Dandong

NORTH KOREA

P'yongyang
Dalian
Chinnamp'o

Wŏnsan
Kansŏng

SOUTH KOREA
Sŏul
Inch'on
Taejon
Taegu
Pusan

Honshū
Niigata
JAPAN
Kanazawa
To-yama

Sea of Japan

Chongjin
2744

10 11 12 13 14

1:50 000 000

250   0   250   500   750   1000 miles
250   0   500   1000   1500   km

P A C I F I C   O C E A N

A R C T I C   O C E A N

I N D I A N   O C E A N

Aleutian Is.
7822
Bering Str.
C. Dezhnev
Kamchatka Peninsula
Klyuchevsk Vol. 4750
Sredinniy Ra.
Sea of Okhotsk
Gydan Ra. (Kolyma)
Wrangel I.
New Siberian Is.
Verkhoyansk Range
Indigirka
Kolyma
Lena
Oenek
Khatanga
Kotuy
Lower Tunguska
Taimyr Peninsula
Chelyuskin
Laptev Sea
Severnaya Zemlya
Central Siberian Plateau
Stanovoy Ra.
Yablonovy Ra.
Aldan
Amur
Sikhote Alin Ra.
Sakhalin
La Pérouse Str.
Hokkaido
8642
Kuril Is.
Sea of Japan
Korea Str.
Korea
Honshu
Kyushu
Shikoku
3776
9810
8554
Bonin Is.
10.022
Guam
Caroline Is.
Palau Is.
New Guinea
Cape Johnson Deep 10,497
Mindanao
Halmahera
Moluccas
Ceram
Celebes Sea
Celebes
Banda Sea
Arafura Sea
Timor
Flores
Java Sea
East Sea
Bali
Sunda Is.
Java
Sumatra
Str. of Malacca
Borneo
Sulu Sea
Palawan
Luzon
Philippine Is.
Formosa
Hainan
Tropic of Cancer
Ryukyu Is.
East China Sea
South China Sea
Yellow Sea
Po Hai
Hwang Ho
Great Plain of China
Si-kiang
G. of Tong-king (Hong) Kong
Red River
Mekong
Chao Phraya
G. of Thailand
Malay Peninsula
Salween
Irrawaddy
Bay of Bengal
Andaman Is.
Nicobar Is.
Ceylon
Polk Strait
Gulf of Mannar
C. Comorin
Laccadive Is.
Maldive Is.
Chagos Arch.
Seychelles
Amirantes
Equator
East from Greenwich
Australia

China
Manchurian Plain
Great Khingan Mts.
Sungari
Yenisei
Angara
Selenga
Sayan Mts.
Baikal
Plateau of Mongolia
Altai
Gobi
Koko Nor
Turfan Basin
Tarim
Takla Makan
Tarim Basin
Lop Nor
Kunlun Shan
Plateau of Tibet
Tsangpo
Everest 8848
Brahmaputra
Himalaya
Ganga
Yamuna
Narmada
Godavari
Krishna
Eastern Ghats
Western Ghats
India
Deccan
Thar
Sutlej
Sulaiman Ra.
Karakoram Ra. 8611
Tien Shan
Belukha 4506
West Siberian Plain
Ob
Irtysh
L. Balkhash
Ili
Chu
Pamir
Communism Pk. 7495
Hindu Kush
Amu Darya
Syr Darya
Aral Sea
Turanian Plain
Kizil Kum
Helmand
Plateau of Iran
Dasht-i-Lut
Great Salt Desert
Elburz Mts.
Demavend 5604
Caucasus 5633
Black Sea
Bosporus
Anatolia
Taurus Mts.
Cyprus
Mediterranean Sea
Adriatic Sea
Carpathians
Danube
Elbe
Öder
Vistula
North Sea
British Isles
Iceland
Greenland
Svalbard
Novaya Zemlya
Barents Sea
Kara Sea
Kolguyev I.
North Cape
White Sea
Kola Pen.
N. Dvina
Scandinavia
Finland
Baltic Sea
North European Plain
Central Russian Uplands
Volga
Ural
Ural Mountains 1640
Narodnaya 1894
Tobol
Don
Dnepr
Rhine
Steppes
Arctic Circle

Tigris
Euphrates
Mesopotamia
Syrian Desert
Dead Sea
Suez Canal
Suez Can.
Nile
Red Sea
Arabia
Al Rub' al Khali
The Gulf
G. of Oman
G. of Aden
Socotra
Ras Asir (C. Guardafui)
Somali Peninsula
Libyan Desert
Arabian Sea
Lake Victoria

COPYRIGHT GEORGE PHILIP & SON LTD

m   6000   4000   2000   1000   400   200   0   200   600   2000 6000   4000 8000
ft   18 000   12 000   6000   3000   1200   600   0   600   1800   6000 18 000   12 000 24 000   ft   m

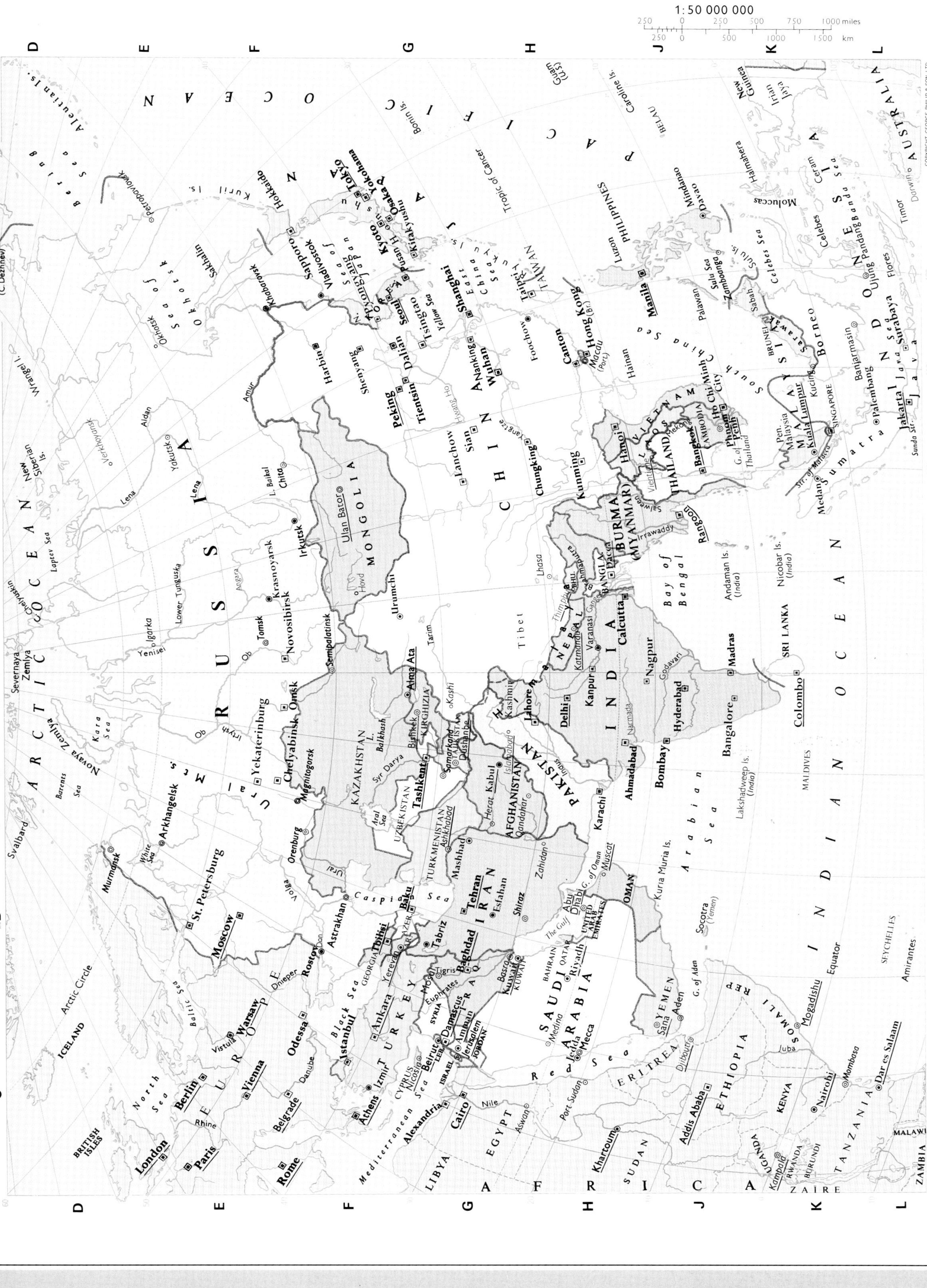

1:50 000 000

250   0   250   500   750   1000 miles
250   0   500   1000   1500   km

D   E   F   G   H   J   K   L

ARCTIC OCEAN

PACIFIC OCEAN

INDIAN OCEAN

U S S R

CHINA

MONGOLIA

INDIA

PAKISTAN

AFGHANISTAN

IRAN

IRAQ

SAUDI ARABIA

TURKEY

KAZAKHSTAN

UZBEKISTAN

TURKMENISTAN

KIRGHIZIA

JAPAN

KOREA

TAIWAN

PHILIPPINES

THAILAND

VIETNAM

LAOS

CAMBODIA

BURMA MYANMAR

MALAYSIA

INDONESIA

BRUNEI

NEPAL

BHUTAN

BANGLA DESH

SRI LANKA

MALDIVES

OMAN

YEMEN

EUROPE

AFRICA

AUSTRALIA

Moscow

Peking

Tokyo

Delhi

Tehran

Baghdad

Riyadh

Ankara

Damascus

Cairo

8 <u>Peking</u> Capital Cities

Projection: Bonne

East from Greenwich

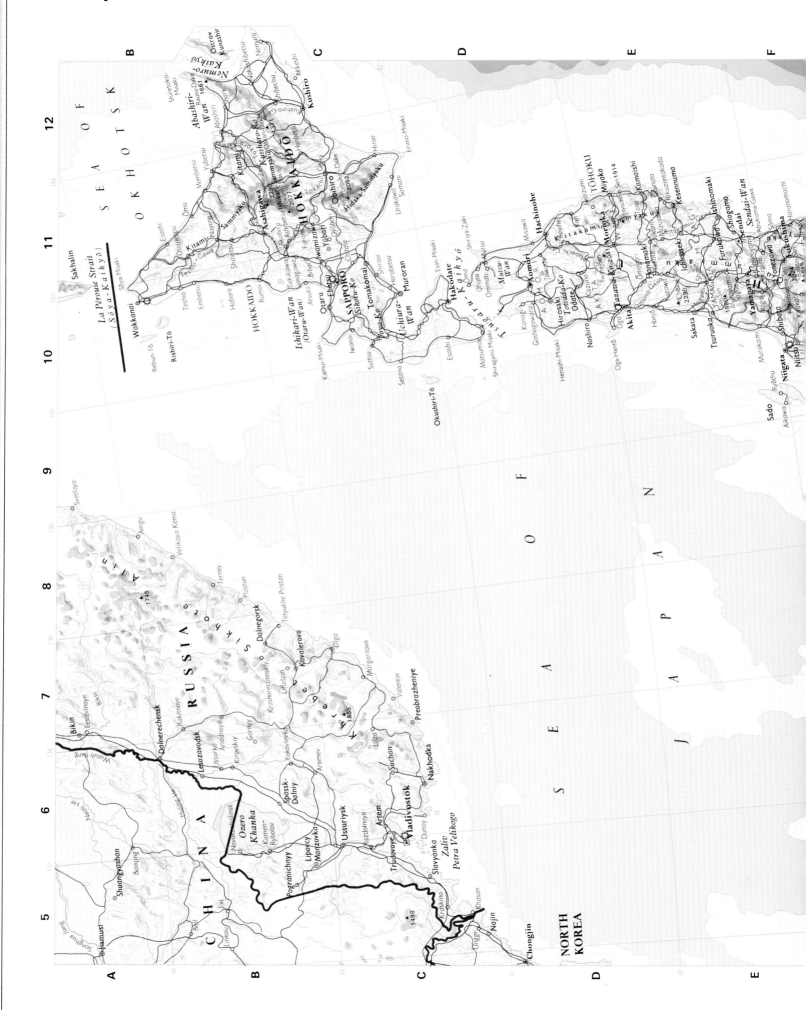

SEA OF OKHOTSK

HOKKAIDO

La Pérouse Strait
(Sōya-Kaikyō)

Nemuro-Kaikyō

Abashiri-Wan

Sapporo

Wakkanai

SEA OF JAPAN

RUSSIA

CHINA

NORTH
KOREA

Vladivostok

TŌHOKU

AOMORI

AKITA

Yamagata

Niigata

Sado

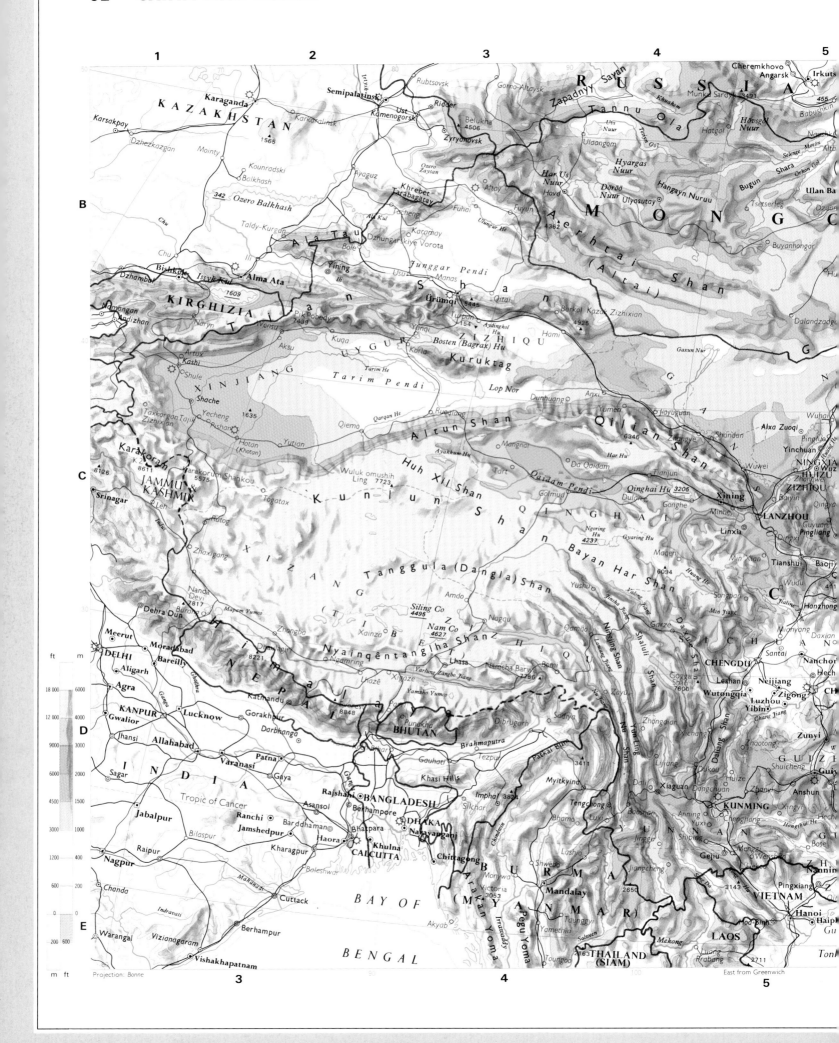

KAZAKHSTAN

Karaganda
Karsakpay
Dzhezkazgan
Mointy
Kounradski
Balkhash
Ozero Balkhash
Taldy-Kurgan

Semipalatinsk
Rubtsovsk
Ust Kamenogorsk
Ridder
Zyryanovsk
Belukha 4506
Khrebet Tarabagatay
Ayaguz
Ala Kul
Yacheng
Bole

RUSSIA
Gorno-Altaysk
Zapadnyy Sayan
Tannu Ola
Gornoye
Ulaangom
Har Us Nuur
Hovd
Ulyasutay

MONGOLIA
Aerhtai Shan (Altai)
Hangayn Nuruu
Bugun
Ulan Ba

Cheremkhovo
Angarsk
Irkuts
Munku Sardyk 3491
Hövsgöl Nuur
Hatgal

Bishkek
Dzhambul
Namangan
Andizhan
KIRGHIZIA
Issyk-Kul
Alma Ata
Ili
Naryn
Pik Pobedy 7439
Wensu

Yining
Dzhungarskiye Vorota
Usu
Manas

Junggar Pendi
Karamay
Ürümqi 5445
Qitai
Turpan
Aydingkol Hu 154

Barkol Kazak Zizhixian
Hami 4925

Dalandzadg

Artux
Kashi
Shule
Shache
XINJIANG

Aksu
Kuqa
Korla
Yanqi
Bosten (Bagrax) Hu
Kuruktag

ZIZHIQU

Gaxun Nur

Yutian
Pishan
Yecheng 1635
Hotan (Khotan)
Tarim He
Tarim Pendi
Qiemo
Qarqan He
Ruoqiang
Lop Nor
Dunhuang
Anxi
Yumen
Jiayuguan

Wuhai

Karakorah
K2 8611
Karakorum Shankou 5575
Taxkorgan Tajik Zizhixian

Altun Shan
Huh Xil Shan
Ayakkum Hu
Mangnai
Da Qaidam
Har Hu

Qilian Shan 6346
Zhangye
Shandan
Alxa Zuoqi
Yinchuan

NINGXIA HUIZU ZIZHIQU

8126
JAMMU & KASHMIR
Srinagar
Leh
Wuluk omushih Ling 7723
Togatax
Kun lun Shan
Qaidam Pendi
Golmud
Tian jun
Qinghai Hu 3205
Dulan
Gonghe

Xining
Minhe
Baiyin
Wuwei
LANZHOU
Linxia
Guyuan
Pingliang

Zhaxigang
XIZANG
Rutog
Ngoring Hu 4237
Gyaring Hu
Maqen
Bayan Har Shan 6094
Yushu
Huang He

Tianshui
Wudu
Baoji

Nanda Devi 7817
Buran
Mapam Yumco
Zhongba
Xainza
Siling Co 4495
Amdo
Nagqu
Nam Co 4627
Tanggula (Dangla) Shan
(TIBET)
Nyainqentanglha Shan
HIQU

Min Xian
Songpan
Maqen
Garze
Ganzi
Daxue Shan
Miunyang
Daxian
Santai

SICHUAN

Dehra Dun
Meerut
Moradabad
DELHI
Aligarh
Agra
Bareilly
Ghohra
HIMALAYA
Dibrugiri 8221
Ngamring
Lhaze
Xigaze
Yamaho Yumco
Lhasa
Yarlung Zangbo Jiang
Namcha Barwa 7756
Bomi

Nujiang
Zayu
Ninglang Shan
Shaluli Shan
Yun Ling
Zhongdian
Lijiang
Xichang
Gogg 7600
Leshan
Neijiang
CHENGDU
Wutongqiao
Luzhou
Yibin
Zigong

Nanchor
Hech

KANPUR
Gwalior
Jhansi
Lucknow
Gorakhpur
Darbhanga
Patna
NEPAL
Katmandu
Everest 8848
Punakha
BHUTAN
Bikar
Gauhati
Tezpur
Sadiya
Brahmaputra

Huize
Dukou
Dali
Xiaguan
Dongchuan

Zunyi
Zhaotong
GUIZH

Jabalpur
Sagar
Allahabad
Varanasi
Gaya
Rajshahi
INDIA
Tropic of Cancer
BANGLADESH
Berhampore
Khasi Hills
Silchar
Imphal 3824
Myitkyina
Bhamo
Tengchong
Luxi
Lashio
Shwebo

Anning
Chengjiang
Yuxi
Shiping
KUNMING
Xingyi
Anshun
Guiy

Raipur
Bilaspur
Ranchi
Jamshedpur
Barddhaman
Haora
Kharagpur
Asansol
DHAKA
Narayanganj
Bhatpara
Khulna
CALCUTTA
Chittagong

YUNNAN
Jiangcheng
Gejiu
Mengzi
Wenshan

Pingxiang
Nannin
VIETNAM

Nagpur
Chanda
Warangal
Vizianagaram
Berhampur
Cuttack
Baleshwar
Mahanadi

BAY OF

BURMA
(MYANMAR)
Arakan Yoma
Akyab
Pegu Yoma
Victoria 3053
Mandalay
Monywa
Taunggyi
Yamethin
Toungoo
Salween
2650
3143

Hanoi
Haiph
LAOS
Luang Prabang
Hoa Binh
Mekong
2711
Tonk

Warangal
Vishakhapatnam
BENGAL

THAILAND (SIAM)

East from Greenwich

ft m
18 000 6000
12 000 4000
9000 3000
6000 2000
4500 1500
3000 1000
1200 400
600 200
0 0
200 600
m ft

Projection: Bonne

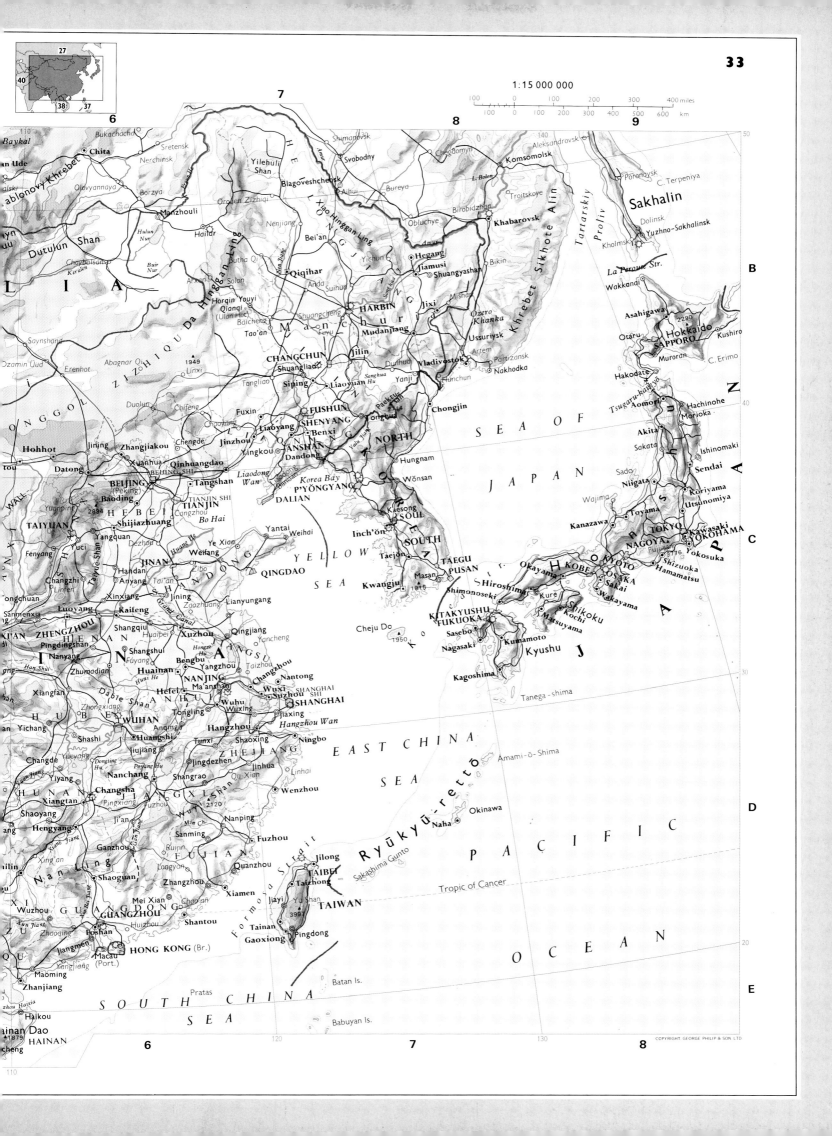

1:15 000 000

100   0   100   200   300   400 miles
100   0   100   200   300   400   500   600 km

Baykal
Bukachacha
Sretensk
Nerchinsk
Chita
Olovyannaya
Borzya
Manzhouli
Haildr
Hulun Nur
Buir Nur
Solon
Arxan
Shuangcheng

Shimanovsk
Svobodny
Blagoveshchensk
Aihui
Bureya
L. Bolon
Komsomolsk
C. Terpeniya
Poronaysk
Sakhalin
Troitskoye
Dolinsk
Khabarovsk
Yuzhno-Sakhalinsk
Kholmsk
La Perouse Str.
Wakkandi
Asahigawa
2290
Hokkaido
Otaru
SAPPORO
Kushiro
Muroran
C. Erimo

Ablonovy Khrebet
Nerchinsk
Olovyannaya
Borzya
Chaybalsansk
Kerulen

HEILONGJIANG
Yilehuli Shan
Xiao Hinggan Ling
Yichun
Hegang
Jiamusi
Shuangyashan
Bikin
Mishan
Jixi
Ozero Khanka
Ussuriysk
Artem
Khrebet Sikhote Alin
Tartarskiy Proliv

Nenjiang
Bei'an
Suihua
HARBIN
Mudanjiang
Fuyu
Vladivostok
Nakhodka
Partizansk
Hunchun
Chongjin
Tsugaru-kaikyō
Aomori
Hachinohe
Morioka
Akita
Ishinomaki
Sado
Sendai
Niigata
Koriyama
Utsunomiya
Wajima

CHANGCHUN
Jilin
Yanji
Paektu-san
2744
Hakodate

Shuangliao
Tangliao
Siping
Liaoyuan
Songhua Hu
Dunhua
Wōnsan

Fuxin
FUSHUN
SHENYANG
Benxi
NORTH
Hungnam
SEA   OF
JAPAN

Chengde
Jinzhou
Liaoyang
ANSHAN
Dandong
Yalu Jiang
Kanazawa
Toyama
TOKYO
Kawasaki
NAGOYA
YOKOHAMA
Yokosuka
3776
Shizuoka
Hamamatsu

Zhangjiakou
Xuanhua
Qinhuangdao
Lingkou
Liaodong Wan
Korea Bay
P'YŌNGYANG
DALIAN
SEOUL

BEIJING
(Peking)
BEIJING SHI
TIANJIN SHI
Tangshan
TIANJIN
Inch'ŏn
Kaesŏng
SŎUL

TAIYUAN
2894
Shijiazhuang
Cangzhou
Bo Hai
Yantai
Weihai
SOUTH
Okayama
KŌBE
OSAKA
OMOTO
Sakai
Wakayama

Yuanping
Baoding
Yangquan
Dezhou
Ye Xian
Weifang
Taejŏn
TAEGU
Hiroshima
Kure
Shikoku
Matsuyama
Kōchi

Fenyang
Yuci
JINAN
Zibo
QINGDAO
YELLOW
PUSAN
Masan
KITAKYUSHU
Shimonoseki
Fukuoka

Changzhi
Linfen
Handan
Anyang
Tai'an
Jining
Taiyue Shan
SEA
Kwangju
1915
Sasebo
Nagasaki
Kumamoto
Kyushu

Sanmenxia
Luoyang
Kaifeng
Zaozhuang
Lianyungang
Cheju Do
1950
Kagoshima

ZHENGZHOU
Shangqiu
Xuxhou
Qingjiang
Yancheng
Tanega-shima

HENAN
Pingdingshan
Shangshui
Hongze Hu
Bengbu
Yangzhou
Taizhou
JIANGSU
Nanyang
Huaibei
Huainan
Nantong

Zhumadian
Fuyang
NANJING
Changzhou
Wuxi
SUZHOU
Ma'anshan
SHANGHAI SHI

Xiangfan
HEFEI
Wuhu
Wuxing
SHANGHAI
Jiaxing

ANHUI
Tongling
Hangzhou
EAST   CHINA

Zhongxiang
Anqing
WUHAN
Huangshi
Tunxi
Shaoxing
Ningbo
Hangzhou Wan
SEA
Amami-ō-Shima

Shashi
Jiujiang
ZHEJIANG
Jingdezhen
Jinhua
Linhai

Changde
Yueyang
Dongting Hu
Poyang Hu
Shangrao
Qu Xian
Wenzhou

Yiyang
Nanchang
Shangrao

Changsha
JIANGXI
Wuyi Shan
2120
Nanping

Xiangtan
Pingxiang
Fuzhou
Ji'an
Min Ch.
FUJIAN
Fuzhou
RYŪKYŪ-rettō
Naha
Okinawa

Shaoyang
Hengyang
Sanming
TAIBEI
Jilong
Sakashima Gunto

Xing'an
Ganzhou
Ruijin
Longyan
Quanzhou
Taizhong
TAIWAN

Shaoguan
Zhangzhou
Xiamen
Jiayi
Yu Shan
3997
Tainan

Mei Xian
Chao'an
Shantou
Gaoxiong
Pingdong

GUANGDONG
GUANGZHOU
Huizhou

Zhaoqing
Foshan
HONG KONG (Br.)
Macau (Port.)
Batan Is.

Jiangmen
Yangjiang
PACIFIC
Tropic of Cancer

Maoming
Zhanjiang
SOUTH   CHINA
Pratas
Batan Is.

Haikou
Haixia
SEA
Babuyan Is.
OCEAN

Hainan Dao
1879
HAINAN
Formosa Strait

COPYRIGHT GEORGE PHILIP & SON LTD

110
6   7   8   9   120   7   130   8
50   B   Z   40   C   A   P   A   N   J   30   D   E   20

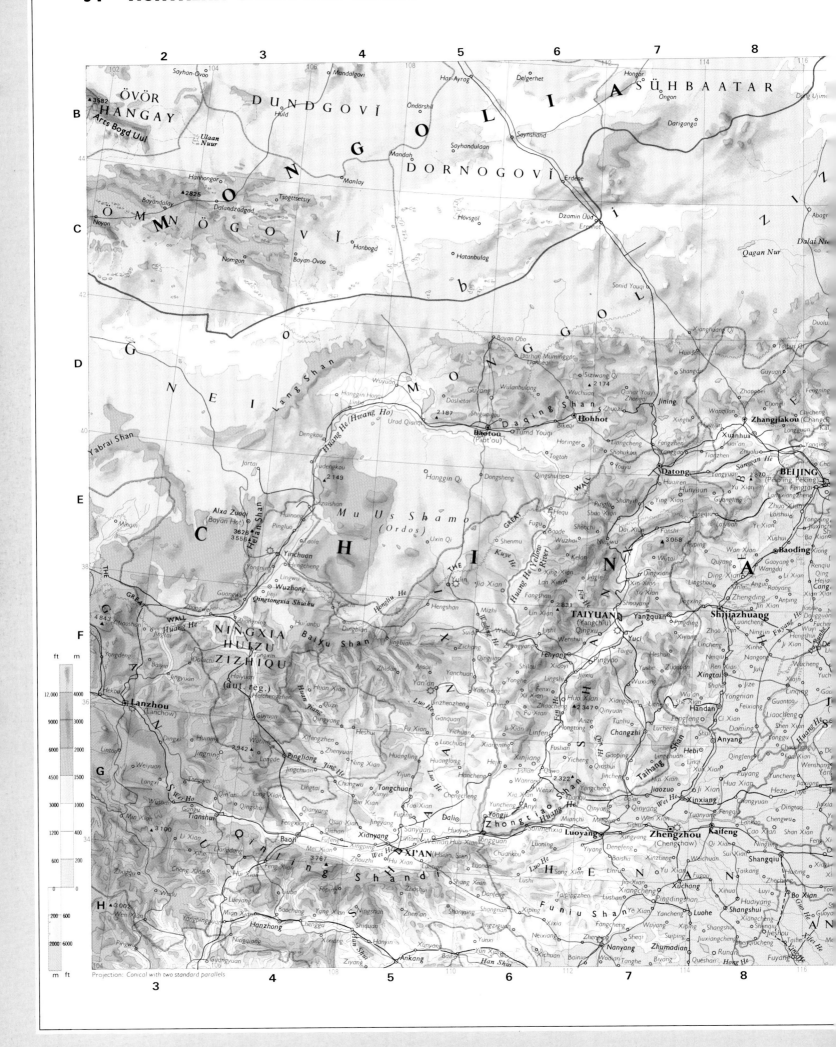

Projection: Conical with two standard parallels

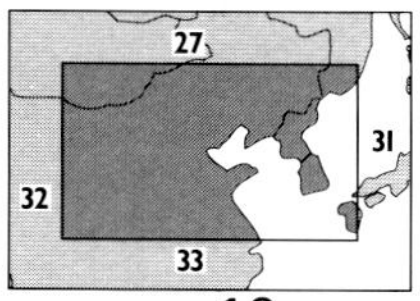

1:6 000 000

50   0   50   100   150 miles
50   0   50   100   150   200   km

9   10   11   12   13   14   15   16

27
31
32
33

East from Greenwich

COPYRIGHT. GEORGE PHILIP & SON. LTD.

B
C
D
E
F
G
H
I

44
42
40
38
36
34

118   120   122   124   126   128

HARBIN (Haerhpin)
Horqin Youyi Qianqi
Zhenlai
Nen Jiang
Maoxing Zhaoyuan
Baicheng
Songhua Jiang
Bin Xiano
Acheng
Yanshou
Jixi
Turiy He
HEILONGJIANG
RUSSIA
Hulin He
Tuquan
Tao'an
Da'an
Fuyu
Changchunling
Shangzhi
Yimianpo
Hailin
Maqiaohe
Ozero Khanka
Tarud Qi
Qian Gorlos
Shenjingzi
Koshan
Lalin He
Wuchang
Mudanjiang
Muling
Suiyang
Suifenhe
Pokrovka
1949
Tongyu
Nong'an
Dehui
Jiutai
Shulan
Ning'an
Wangqing
Dongning
Golenki
Ussuriysk (Voroshilov)
Changling
Zhangguangcailing
1690
Linxi
Beizhengzhen
Kailu
Shuangyang
 Yitong
Songhua Hu
Jiaohe
Emu
Chunyang
Razdolnoye
Artem
Bairin Zuoqi
JILIN
Changchun
Jilin (Kirin, Chilin)
Panshi
Huadian
Helong
Antu
Muren
Hunchun
Tavrichanka
Bairin Youqi
Hexigten Qi
Tongliao
Shuangliao
Huaide
Liaoyuan
Dongfeng
Huinan
Huifa
1677
(Manchuria)
Erdao Jiang
Yanji
Tumen
Hunchun
Vladivostok
Xinkai He
Kailu
Siping
Xifeng
Hailong
Jingyu
Fusong
Changbai Shan
Musan
Kyŏngsŏng
Slavyanka
Chifeng
Kangping
Hure Qi
Xiawa
WALL
Faku
Zhangwu
Xinmin
Kaiyuan
Shanchengzhen
Qingyuan
Linjiang
Paektu-san
Yupyongdong
2541
Nanam
Chuuronjang
Posyet
Xar Moron He
Laoha He
1885
Wutonghaolai
Fuxin
WILLOW
Liaoyang
Jinlun
Tieling
Tonghua
Chungang
Changbai
Hyesan
Hoeryong
Puryŏng
Chongjin
Paksikori
Ningcheng
Chaoyang
Beipiao
SHENYANG (Mukden)
Fushun
Xinbin
Huanren
Huadian
845
Manpojin
Inpundong
Kasan-dang
Irhyangdong
Hwadae
Ondaejin
Pugodong
2020
Ongniud Qi
THE
Liaozhong
Benxi
Qingchengzi
Huajiaozi
Hun Jiang
Hyesan
Pungsan
Hongwon
Simpungdong
Kimchaek (Songjin)
Musudan
Longhua
Chengde
Jinzhou
LIAONING
Anping
Kuandian
Yalu
Chosan
Kuup-tong
Koin-dong
2522
Pujon-chosuji
Kwanggaeri
Changjin
Hapsu
Pukchŏng
Sŏhori
Tanchŏn
Longhua
Shangbancheng
Daling
Yi Xian
Beizhen
Panshan
Goubangzi
Niuzhuang
Anshan
Lianshanguan
Xiuyan
Pyŏktong
Changjin-chosuji
Chongjin
Changbai
Sinhung
Pukchŏng
Hagaru-ri
anping
Pingquan
Jianchang
Xingcheng
Jinxi
Haicheng
Fengcheng
Cao He
Supung Sk.
Kuiup-tong
Hwanggye
Kasŏng-ni
Oro
Hamhung
Hongwon
Tongjosŏn Man
Kuancheng
Tianzhuangtai
Yingkou
Yongchang
Xuyan
Dandong
Sinŭiju
Pukchin
Hamhŭng
Hŭngnam
Shuangshanzi
Suizhong
Liaodong
Gai Xian
Xiongyuecheng
Wanfu
1131
Donggou
Yongampo
Kujang
Tŏkchŏn
Tŏkchŏn-ni
NORTH
Zunhua
Jianchangying
Yongkou
Wan.
Fengcheng
Yalu Jiang
Sŏnchŏn
Chŏngju
Anju
Yŏnghŭng
KOREA
Funing
Qinhuangdao
Changli
Leting
Fu Xian
Xiuyan
Zhuanghe
Sukchŏn
Unsan
Chŏngchŏn-gang
Kangdong
Munchon
Wŏnsan
Yŏngdŭgpo
Tongchon
Tangshan
Hangu
Fuxin
Jin Xian
Pikou
Cho-do
Sunan
Kangdong
Sŏngchŏn
Singye
Anbyŏn
Hoeyang
Kosŏng
TIENTSIN (TIANJIN) Tanggu
Dagu
Lüshun
DALIAN (Lüda)
P'YŎNGYANG
Chinnampo
Sunan
Chunghwa
Koksan
Sepo-ri
1638
Yangyang
Oikou
Bo Hai
Korea Bay
Sinmak
Nam-chŏn
Pyŏnggang
Kŭmhwa
Hwachŏn-chosuji
1578
Yangyang
(Gulf of Chihli)
Chinnampo
Sariwŏn
Suan
Chŏrwŏn
Cease Fire Line
Chunchŏn
Kangnŭng
Changyŏn
Chaeryŏng
Haeju
Kaesŏng
Panmunjom
Uijŏngbu
Hongchŏn
Samchŏk
SEA OF JAPAN
Paengnyong-do
Ongjin
Kanghwa
SEOUL (Seoul)
Hoengsŏng
Wŏnju
Yŏngwŏl
Ullung-do
Huang He
Penglai
Longkou
Huang Xian
Yantai
Weihai
INCH'ŎN
Suwŏn
Osan
P'yŏngt'aek
Chechŏn
Ulchin
Huimin
Kenli
Zhaoyuan
Fushan
Muping
Wendeng
Ichŏn
Chungju
Yŏngju
Laizhou Wan
Dongxindian
923
Qixia
SOUTH
Ch'ŏnan
Chochiwŏn
Chŏngju
Yechŏn
Andong
Yŏngdŏk
Zhanhua
Guangrao
Weifang
Pingdu
Laiyang
Rushan
Nanhuang
Shidao
KOREA
Sŏsan
Hongsŏng
Nonsan
Kongju
Sangju
Ŭisŏng
Chŏngha
Pohang
Boxing
Huantai
Shouguang
Changyi
Gaomi
Laixi
Haiyang
Anmyon-do
Taejŏn
Kimchŏn
Kyŏngju
Zibo Yidu
Linzi
Anqiu
Lancun
Chengyang
Taechŏn-ni
Yŏngdong
Waegwan
Ch'ŏngsong
Ulsan
SHANDONG
Laiwu
1108
Zhucheng
Jiao Xian
Kunsan
Chŏnju
Koryŏng
TAEGU
Xintai
Mengyin
Yishui
Wulian
Kimje
Kochang
Chinju
Masan
Tongnae
Mokpo
Pingyi
Fei Xian
Tangtou
QINGDAO (Ch'ingtao)
Sogwo-ri
Namwŏn
1915
Chinhae
PUSAN
Teng Xian
Zaozhuang
Ganyu
Sanchŏng-ni
Tamyang
Chinju
Samchŏnpo
Chungmu
Yi Xian
Rizhao
Sogcho
Kwangju
Pŏlgyo-ri
Yŏsu
Korea Strait
Sasuna
HUANG HAI (Yellow Sea)
Linyi
Haizhou Wan
Suncheon
Tsushima
Saka
Tancheng
Lianyungang
Chonghung
Najin
Posong
Kashima
Izuhara
Andongwei
Guanyun
Hagang
Xiangshui
Hdenam
JIANGSU
Lianyungang (Hsinhailien)
Tsushima-kaikyō
Iki
Karatsu
Imari
Guannan
Huaiyin
Funing
Cheju-do
JAPAN
Qingjiang
Huai'an
Baoying
Hongze Hu
Liuzhuang
Cheju
Hallim
1950
Onpyong-ni
Nakadóri-jima
Sasebo
Ōmura
Isahaya
Lingbi
Si Xian
Qingjiang
Yaowan
Suqian
Shuyang
Da Yunhe
Suining
Dongtai
Mosulpo
Sŏgwi-po
Fukue-jima
Nagasaki
Kuchinotsu
Bengbu
Fengyang
Gaoyou Hu
Xinghua

32 33
58
60 62

1 2 3 4 5

A

Letpadan · Madauk
Tharrawaddy
Insein
Yandoon
Maubin · RANGOON
Pyapon · G. of Moulmein
Martaban

Thaton
Thoeng
Uttaradit · Vientiane · Nong Khai
Nakhon Phanom · Ba Don
Phong · Dong Hoi
Phitsanulak · Loei · Udon Thani · Sakon
Nakhon · Thakhek · Quang Tri
Tak · Hue
2320 · Savannakhet
Khon Kaen · Dong Hene · Da Nang
(Tourane)
Phetchabun · Hoi An
2080 · Binh Son
Natkyizin · Nakhon · Chaiyaphum · Roi Et · Quang Ngai
Sawan · Mun · Saravane · Hoai Nhon (Bong Son)

THAILAND

B

Tavoy · Phra Nakhon Si Ayutthaya · Ubon Ratchathani · Pakse · 3280 · VIET-
Moscos Is. · Kanchanaburi · Buriram · Sisaket · Attopeu · Pleiku (Binh Dinh) · An Nhon
2075 · Nakhon Ratchasima (Khorat) · Srepok · Kontum · NAM · Qui Nhon
Mali Kyun · BANGKOK · Aranyaprathet · Koulen · Cheo Reo · Song Cau
Chachoengsao · Sisophon · Siem Reap · Stung-Treng · B. Me Thuat · Mui Varella
Kadan Kyun · Samut Prakan · Chon Buri · Battambang · Kg. Thom · 2405
Mergui · Phetchaburi · Si Racha · Tonlé Sap · Kompong Cham · Nha Trang
Hua Hin · CAMBODIA · Kg. Bang · Kratie
Tenasserim · Chanthaburi · Pursat · 1813 · Chhlong · 4424
Letsök-aw-Kyun · Ko Chang · Chhnang · Mekong · Bo Dúc
Lanbi Kyun · Prachuap Khiri Khan · Ko Kut · Phnom Penh · Prey Veng · Da Lat · Phan Rang
Bang Saphan · Kompong Som · Banam · Bien Hoa · Mui Ca Na
Bokpyin · Kho Khot Kra · Koh Kong · Takeo · Long · Go Cong · PHANH BHO HO CHI MINH (Saigon)
Kawthaung · Chhung Kg. Som · Xuyen · My Tho · Ba Ria · Vung Tau
Ranong · Phu Quoc · Rach Gia · Can Tho
Zadetkyi Kyun · Thailand · Hon Chong · Soc Trang
Ko Phangan · Sa Dec · Bac Lieu
Surat Thani · Ca Mau · Mui Bai Bung · Con Son

C

ANDAMAN SEA · 1786 · Nakhon Si Thammarat · Pak Phanang
Phangnga · Phatthalung · SOUTH CHINA SEA
Phuket · Trang · Songkhla (Singora) · Thale Luang
Ban Kantang · Pattani
Tarutao · Satun · Yala · Narathiwat · Spratly I.
Langkawi · Tumpat · Amboyna I.
We · Sabang (Kutaraja) · Alor Setar · Kota Baharu · Pasir Mas
Banda Aceh · Perhentian
Seulimeum · George Town · Kerai · Kuala Terengganu · MALAYSIA
Meureudu · Butterworth · Pinang · Tenggol
Sigli · Bireuen · Port Weld · Teiping · G. Tahan · Kuala Dungun · Islands (Philippines)

D

ft · m · Lhokseumawe · 2190 · Ipoh · Tapah · Cukai · C. Buliluyan
Calang · Takengon · Bukit Mertajam · Kuala Lipis · Kuantan · Kota Belud
ACEH · Langsa · Pangkalansusu · Jerantut · Kota Kinabalu (Jesselton) · 4101
Kualasimpang · Rangkalanbrandan · Temerloh · Kuala · Victoria · SABAH
Meulaboh · Leuser · 3466 · Belawan · Kuala Selangor · Gemas · Tioman · Kepulauan · Bandar Seri Begawan · BRUNEI
12 000 · 4000 · Binjai · MEDAN · Kelang · Segamat · Natuna · Pulau Labuan · 2438
Tapaktuan · Pematangsiantar · KUALA LUMPUR · Labis · Besar · Niah
Simeulue · Kisaran · Pelabuhan Kelang · Mersing · Telukbutun · Lutong · Miri
9000 · 3000 · Tanjungbalai · P. Dickson · Seremban · Natuna · Marudi
Sinabang · Sibolga · TARUTUNG · Bogasinambo · Kota Tinggi · Matak · Besar · 2938
Mursala · UTARA · Muar · Jemaya · Siantan · Oya · Mukah · SARAWAK
6000 · 2000 · Nias · Padang · Dumai · Rupat · Pahat · Kuala · Kepulauan · Subi · Kepulauan · Bintulu · Tubau · Banjaran
Laheva · Gunungsitoli · Sidempuan · Bengkalis · JOHOR BAHARU · Anambas · Midai · Natuna Selatan · Sibu · Kapit · Gunung Hose · Tanjungselor
Sungaipakning · SINGAPORE · Serasan · Kucing · 2988
Telukdalem · Pekanbaru · Siaksriindrapura · Bintan · Tg. Datu · Lundu · Simanggang · Betung · Putussibau · TIMUR
4500 · 1500 · Pipu · Lubuksikaping · Bongkinang · Kampar · Tanjungpinang · Singkawang · Niut · Serian · Lubok Antu · 2240 · Nameh
Kepulauan Batu · Bukittinggi · Kepulauan Riau · Kepulauan · 1701 · Sanggau · BARAT · 1758 · Muaratewe
Tanahbala · Payakumbuh · RIAU · Badas · Pontianak · Menote · Barito
3000 · 1000 · Padangpanjang · Solok · Lingga · Sambas · Sintang · Pegunungan · 2278
Siberut · PADANG · Muarabungo · Lingga · Tembelan · Nangapinoh · Schwaner · BORNEO · Muarakaman
Sabagalat · Kerinci · 3800 · Muaratembesi · Singkep · Sukadana · Nangatayap · KALIMANTAN · Tenggarong · Samarinda
Sipora · JAMBI (Telanaipura) · Berhala · Ketapang · TENGAH · Tanjung · Amuntai
1200 · 400 · Sungaipenuh · Hari · Selat · Karimata · Pangkalanbuun · Muaratewe · Kandangan · Barabai
Kepulauan Mentawai · Pulau Pagai Utara · Muntok · Selja Sigko · Kumai · Sampit · 1892 · SELATAN
Muaraenim · Sekayu · Pangkalpinang · Kepulauan · Palangkaraya · Kualakapuas · Kotabaru
Pulau Pagai Selatan · Bangka · Karimata · Kualajelai · BANJARMASIN
1800 · 600 · Lubuklinggau · Musi · Bangka · Kendawangan · Palaihari · Sebuku
Bengkulu · Lahat · Tebingtinggi · Sungaigerong · Tanjungpandan · Kotawaringin · Pangkalanbuun · Martapura · Pulau Laut
SELATAN · PALEMBANG · Pulau Belitung (Billiton) · Sukamara · Pagatan
600 · 200 · MUAREENIM · Kayuagung · Manggar · Teluk Sampit · Pelaihari · Sotui
BENGKULU · Baturaja · Tg. Lumut · Dendang · Tg. Puting · Karambu · Pulau Laut
3159 · Greater Sunda Islands · Tg. Selatan
0 · 0 · Menggala · JAVA SEA · Kepulauan · Laut Ketil

E

INDIAN · 6073 · Sukadana · Tanjungkarang · Kepulauan · Kepulauan Masalembo
200 · 600 · Enggano · LAMPUNG · Telukbetung · Karimunjawa · Bawean · Sangkapura
Kotaagung · Kalianda · Kepulauan Kangean
Pulau Rakata (Krakatau) · Serang · JAKARTA · Brebes · Semarang · Kudus
2000 · 6000 · OCEAN · Selat Sunda · Bogor · Cirebon · Pekalongan · Kendal · Bojonegoro · Tuban · Madura
Pelabuhan Ratu · Bandung · Tegal · Kendal · Rembang · Kepulauan (Kepulauan P.
4000 · 12 000 · Pengalengan · Sumedang · Slamet · Magelang · Semarang · Surabaya · Pasuruan · Probolinggo · Situbondo
6650 · Tasikmalaya · 3428 · TENGAH · 3265 · Madiun · TIMUR · Malang · Semeru · BALI · 3142
6000 · 18 000 · Cilacap · Purworejo · Yogyakarta · Surakarta · Kediri · Blitar · 3676 · Gunung Rinjani · 3726
Java Trench · J A V A (JAWA) · Tulungagung · Apecanang · NUSA TENGGARA · Lombok
8000 · 24 000 · Denpasar · Mataram
m · ft · Projection: Mercator · 1 · 2 · 3 · East from Greenwich · 115 · Singoraja

1 · 2 · 3 · 4

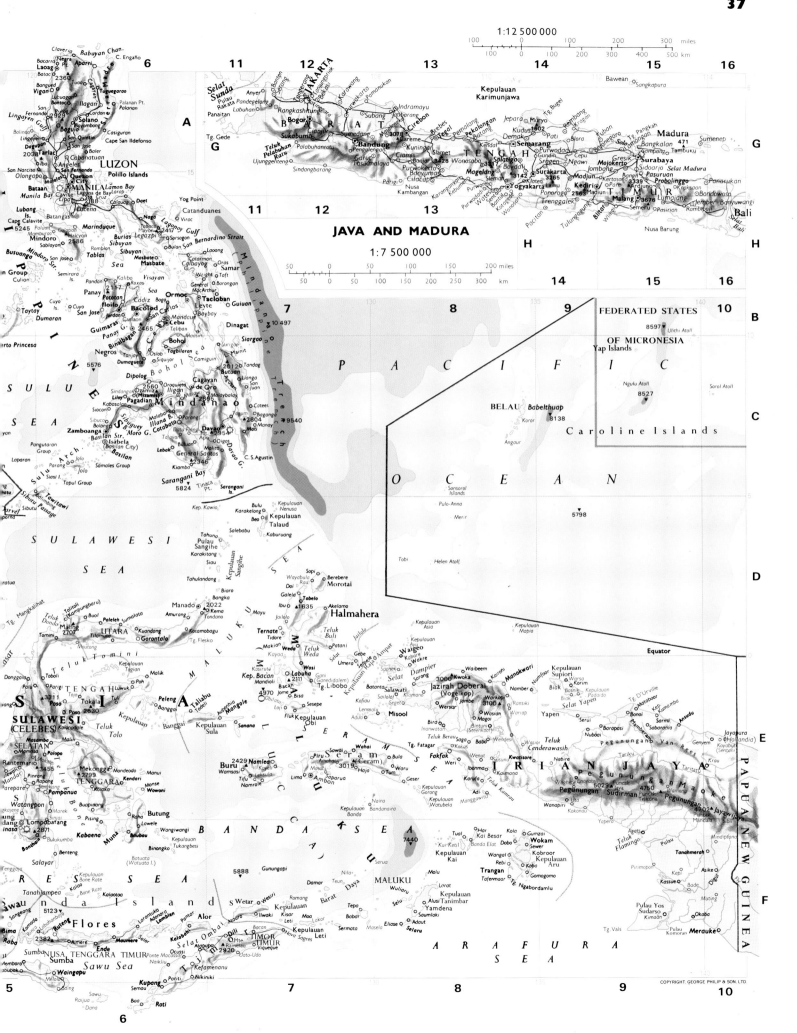

1:12 500 000

JAVA AND MADURA

1:7 500 000

FEDERATED STATES
OF MICRONESIA
Yap Islands

Caroline Islands

PACIFIC

OCEAN

Equator

LUZON

MANILA

Manila Bay

Mindoro

SULU
SEA

SULAWESI
SEA

SULAWESI
SEA

SULAWESI
(CELEBES)

Mindanao

Halmahera

BANDA SEA

Sunda Island

Flores

NUSA TENGGARA TIMUR

MALUKU

Kepulauan
Tanimbar
Yamdena

ARAFURA
SEA

IRIAN JAYA

PAPUA NEW GUINEA

Merauke

COPYRIGHT. GEORGE PHILIP & SON. LTD.

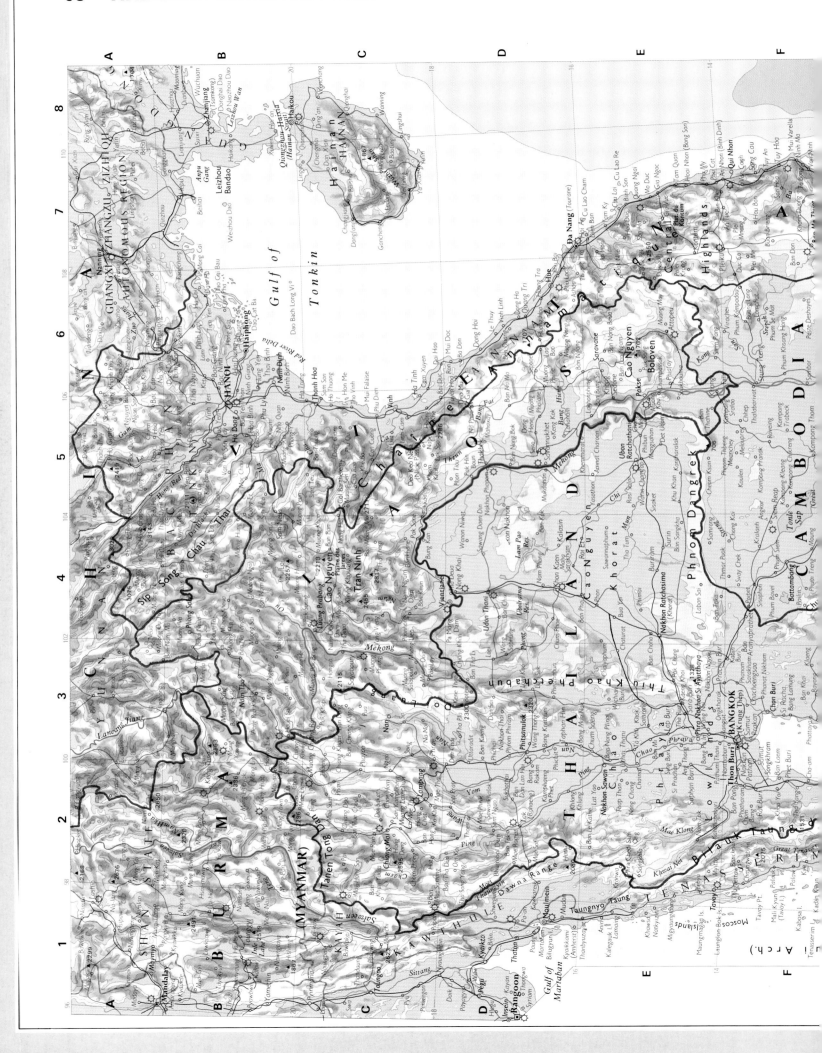

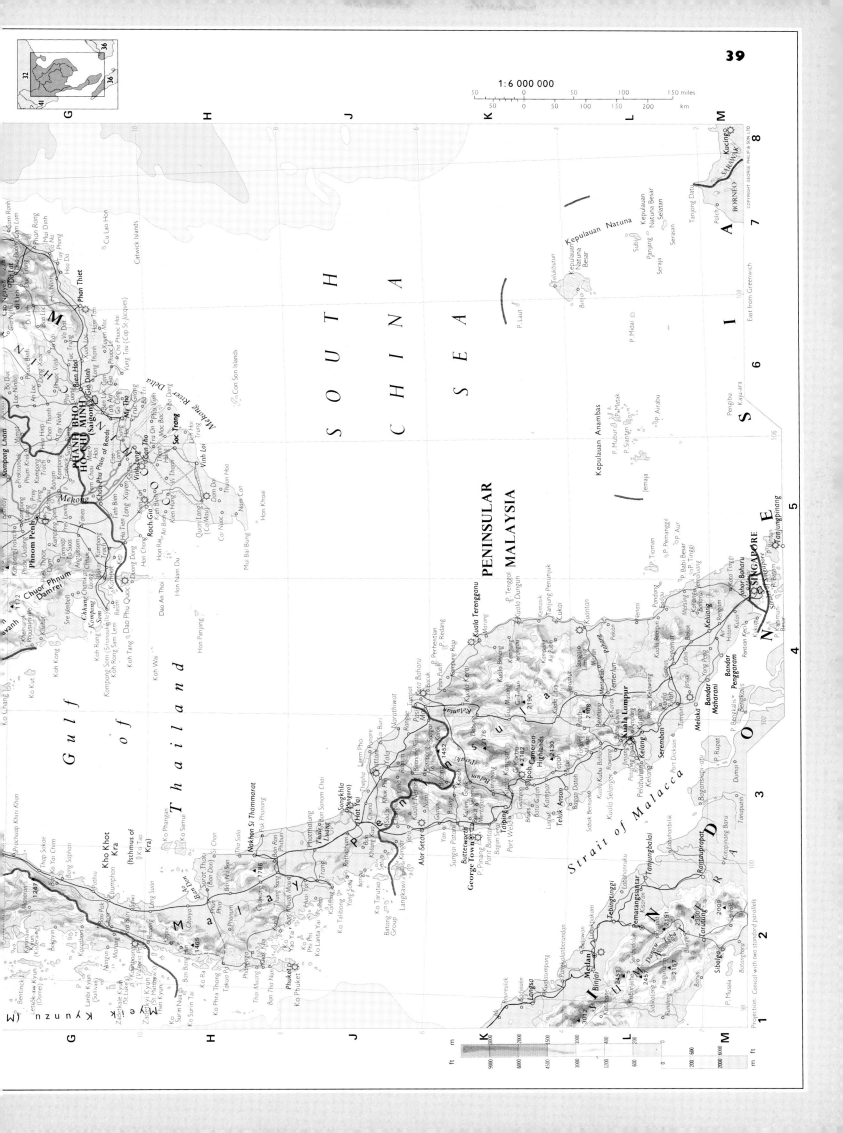

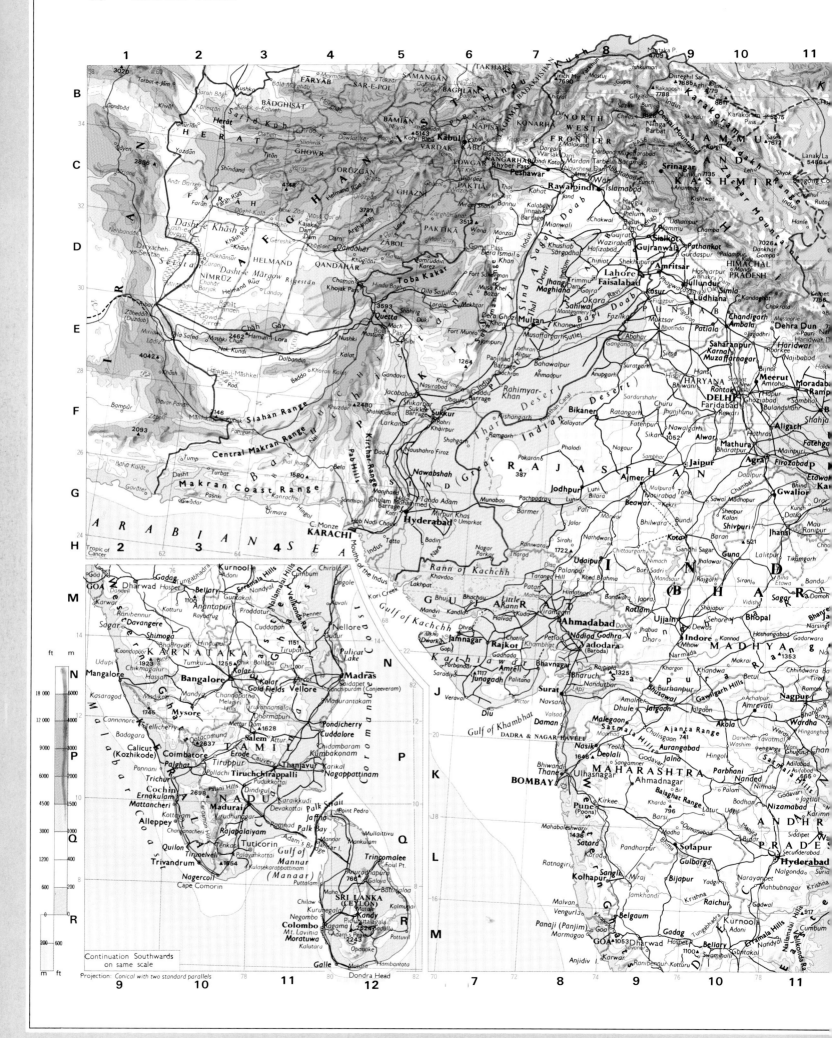

Continuation Southwards
on same scale

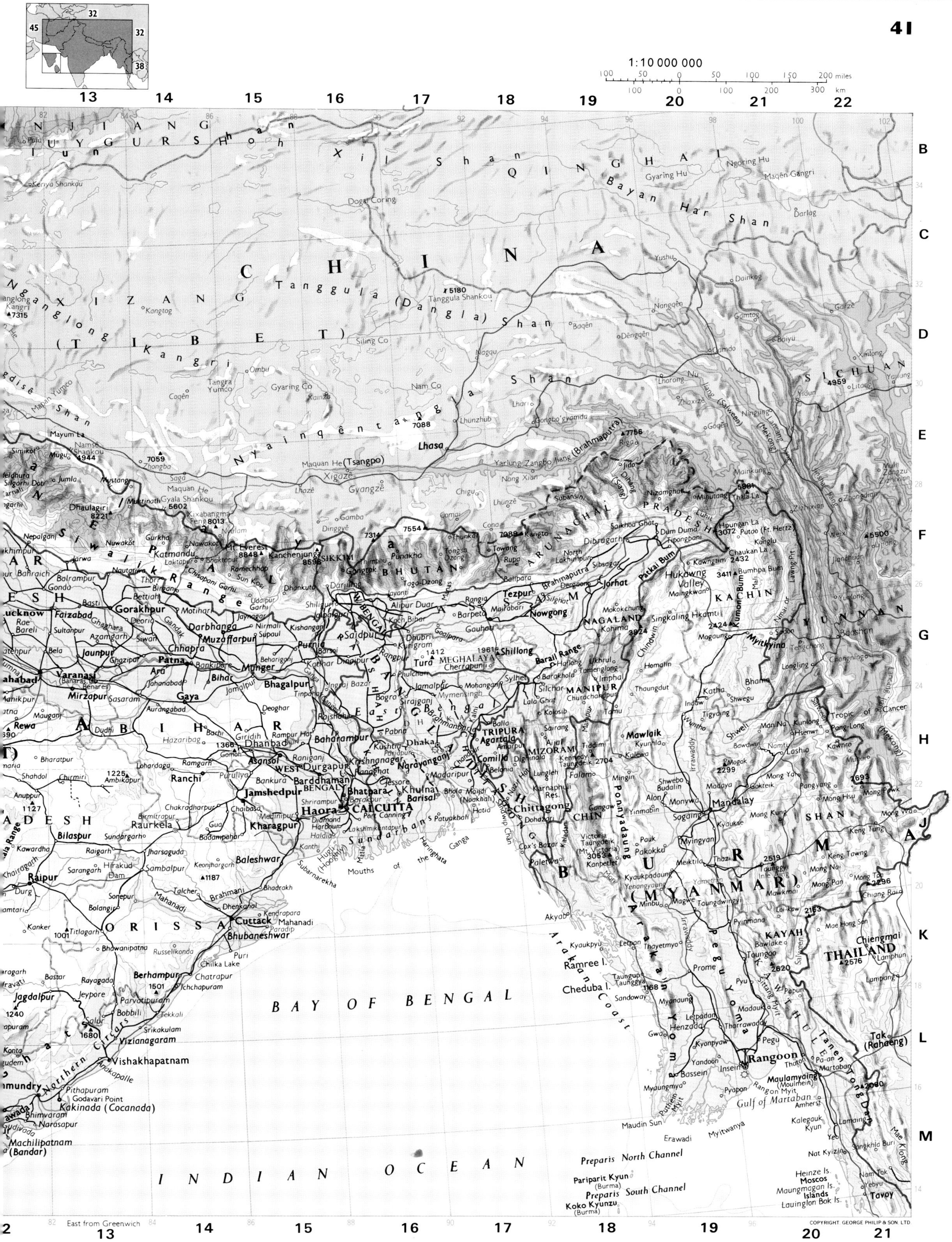

1:10 000 000

100   0   50   100   150   200 miles
100   0   100   200   300 km

B

C

CHINA

XIZANG

(TIBET)

Tanggula (Dangla) Shan

QINGHAI

Bayan Har Shan

SICHUAN

D

Nyainqêntanglha Shan

Lhasa

Yarlung Zangbo Jiang (Brahmaputra)

E

NEPAL

Dhaulagiri 8221

Mt. Everest 8848

Kanchenjunga 8598

SIKKIM

BHUTAN

ARUNACHAL PRADESH

YUNNAN

F

Katmandu

Gorakhpur

Darbhanga

Muzaffarpur

Patna

BIHAR

Gaya

Bhagalpur

Tezpur

Nowgong

Gauhati

NAGALAND

Kohima

MANIPUR

Imphal

KACHIN

Myitkyina

G

Varanasi (Banaras)

Mirzapur

WEST BENGAL

MEGHALAYA

Shillong

Cherrapunji

Barail Range

Silchar

Bhamo

H

Dhanbad

Asansol

Durgapur

Ranchi

Jamshedpur

Kharagpur

Haora

CALCUTTA

Barddhaman

BANGLADESH

Dhaka

TRIPURA

Agartala

MIZORAM

Comilla

CHIN

Chittagong

Mandalay

BURMA

(MYANMAR)

SHAN

J

Raurkela

Bilaspur

Raipur

Durg

ORISSA

Cuttack

Bhubaneshwar

Baleshwar

Khulna

Barisal

Cox's Bazar

Akyab

Arakan

KAYAH

THAILAND

Chiengmai

K

Berhampur

Ramree I.

Cheduba I.

BAY OF BENGAL

Pegu

Rangoon

L

Vizianagaram

Vishakhapatnam

Bassein

Insein

Maulamyaing (Moulmein)

Gulf of Martaban

M

Kakinada (Cocanada)

Machilipatnam (Bandar)

INDIAN OCEAN

Preparis North Channel

Pariparit Kyun (Burma)

Preparis South Channel

Koko Kyunzu (Burma)

Tavoy

East from Greenwich

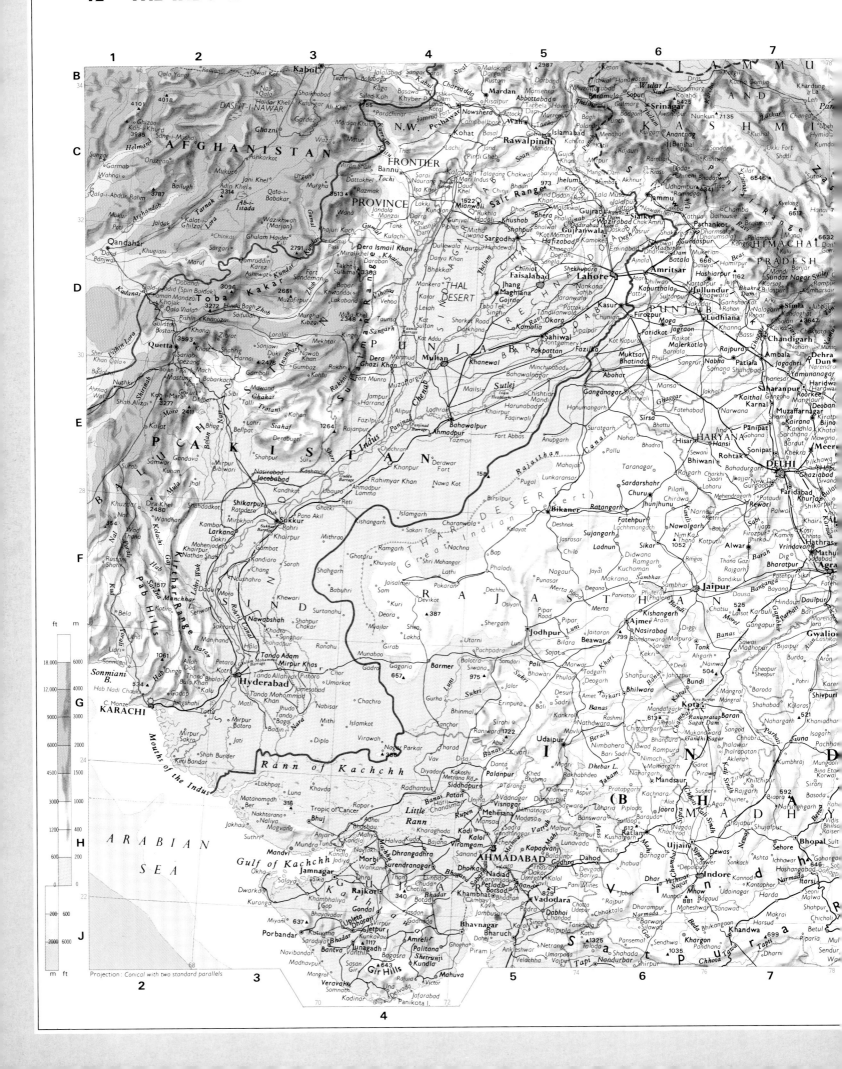

Projection: Conical with two standard parallels

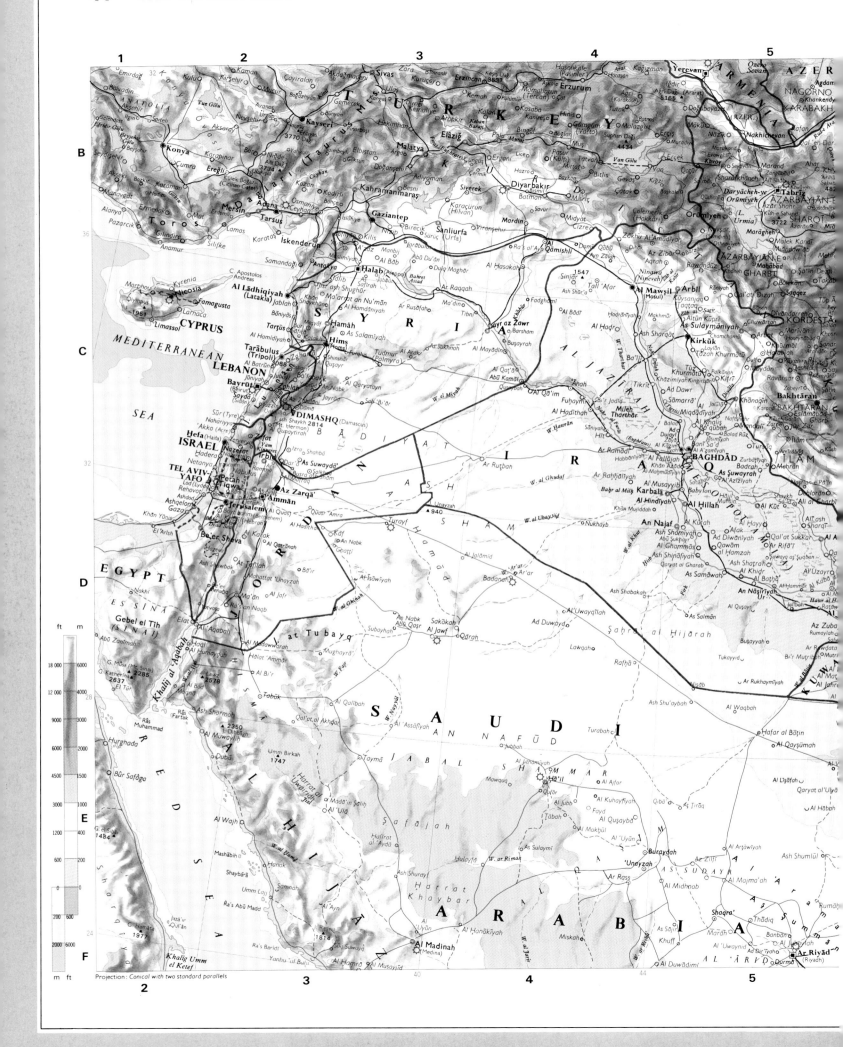

Projection : Conical with two standard parallels

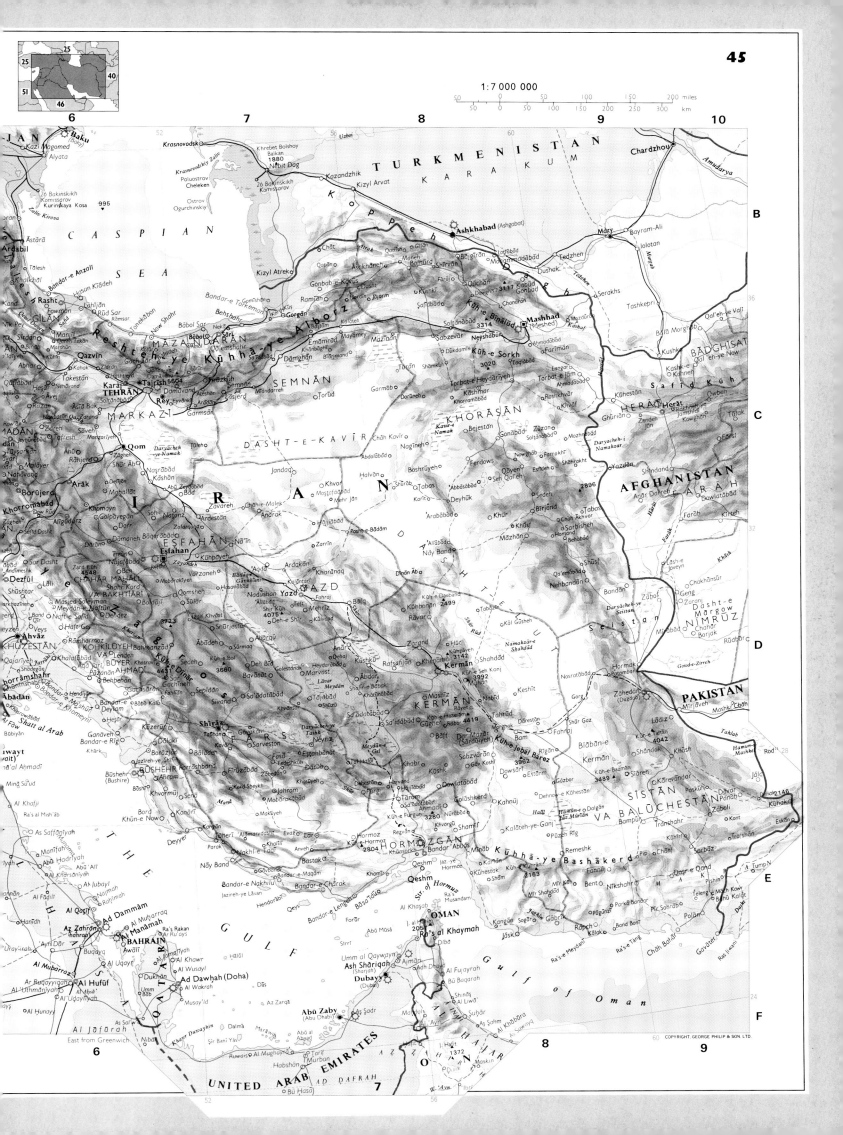

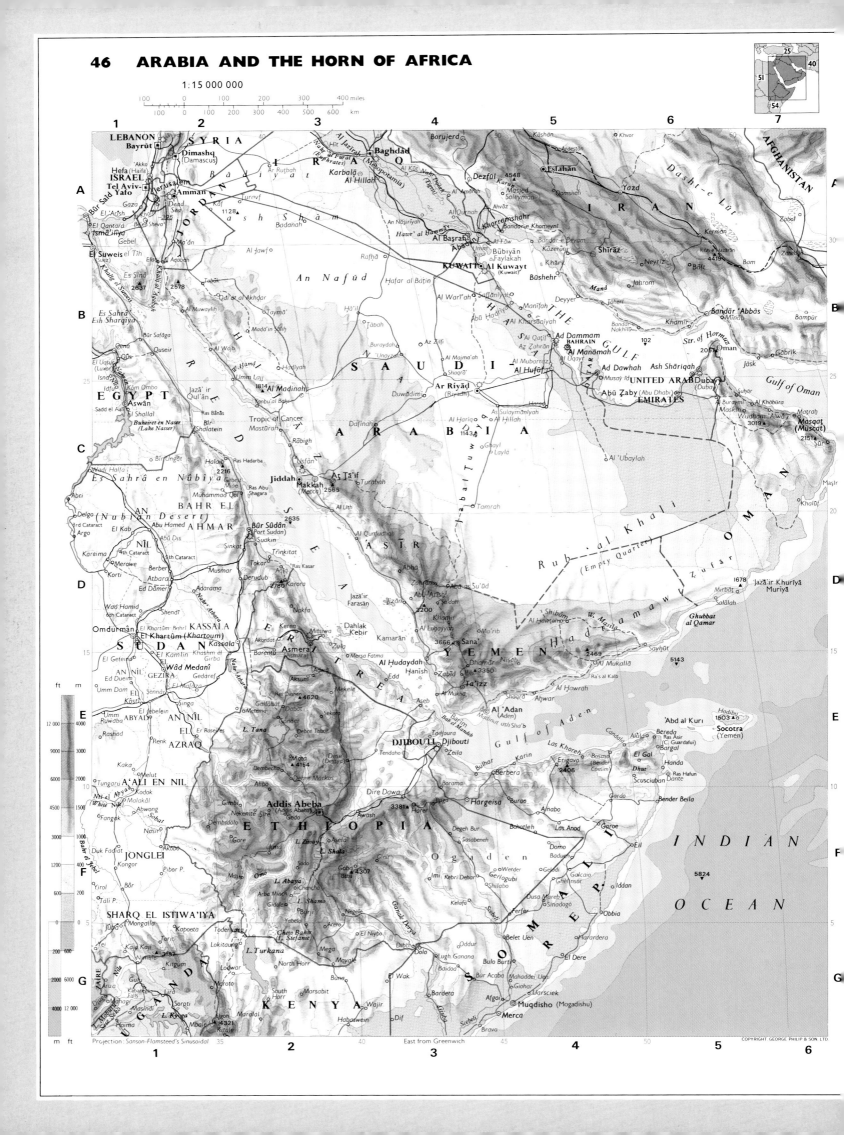

1:15 000 000

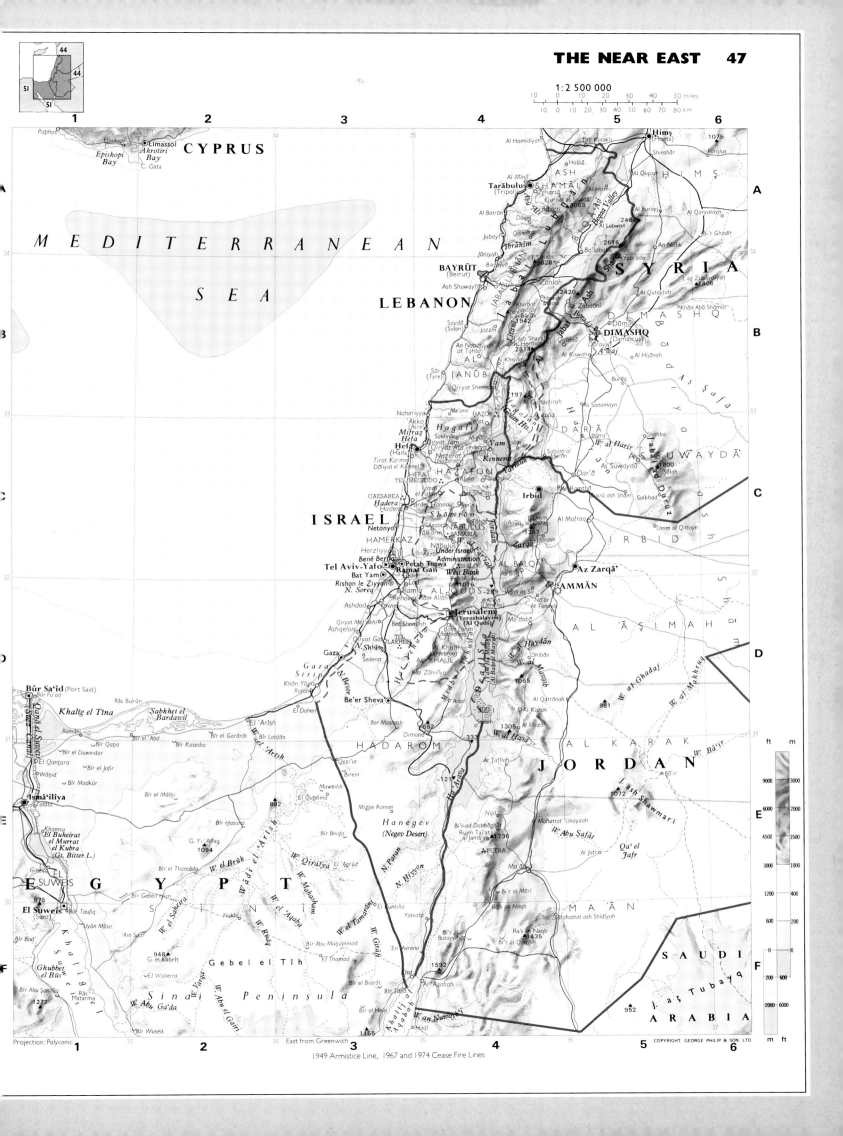

1:2 500 000

Projection: Polyconic

East from Greenwich

1949 Armistice Line, 1967 and 1974 Cease Fire Lines

CYPRUS

MEDITERRANEAN

SEA

LEBANON

SYRIA

BAYRŪT
(Beirut)

DIMASHQ
(Damascus)

ISRAEL

Tel Aviv-Yafo

Jerusalem
(Yerushalayim)
(Al Quds)

AMMĀN

JORDAN

EGYPT

Sinai Peninsula

Hanegev
(Negev Desert)

**SAUDI
ARABIA**

Khaliġ el Tīna

Bûr Sa'îd (Port Said)

Ismâ'ilîya

El Suweis
(Suez)

1:40 000 000

200   0   200   400   600   800   1000 miles
200   0   200 400 600 800 1200 1400 1600 km

A | B | C | D | E | F | G | H | J | K

1 | 2 | 3 | 4 | 5 | 6 | 7 | 8 | 9 | 10

British Isles

ATLANTIC

OCEAN

Bay of Biscay

Carpathians

Alps
Mt. Blanc 4807
Pyrenees
Apennines
Dinaric Alps
Adriatic Sea

Black Sea
Caucasus
Elbrus 5633
Caspian Sea
Aral Sea

Iberian
Peninsula
Corsica
Sardinia
Anatolia

6578

Str. of Gibraltar
High Plateaus
Saharan Atlas
Middle Atlas
High Atlas
Anti Atlas Toubkal
4165
Dra

Mediterranean Sea
C. Bon
Sicily
Malta
G. of Gabes
Chott Djerid
Crete
Cyprus
5121
Levant
Mesopotamia
Tigris
Syrian Desert
Euphrates

The Gulf
Bahrain

Madeira
Canary Is.
3718
Tenerife

Tripolitania
G. of Sidra
Cyrenaica

Libyan Desert
Egypt
Nile
Arabian Desert
Sinai
2642
Red Sea
Hejaz
Arabia

Tropic of Cancer

Ras Nouadhibou
El Djouf
Sahara
Tuat
Tasili Plateau
Fezzan
Hoggar
Air
Tibesti
3415
Adrar
Bilma
Kufra
El Kharga
Nubian Desert
Nubia
Rub' al Khali

Cape Verde Is.
C. Vert
Senegambia
Gambia
Fouta Djalon
Senegal
Niger (Joliba)
Volta
Niger
Sudan
L. Chad
Wadai
Darfur
Kordofan
White Nile
Atbara
Blue Nile
Ras Dashan
4620
L. Tana
Ethiopian Highlands
Perim
Bab el Mandeb
Gulf of Aden
Socotra
Ras Asir

Somali Peninsula

Guinea
Grain Coast
Gold Coast
Ivory Coast
C. Palmas
Slave Coast
Bight of Benin
6363
Bioko
Adamawa Highlands
Cameroon Peak
4070
Benue
Chari
Dar Banda
Bahr el Ghazal
Bahr el Ghazal
Bel Jebel
Uele

Bight of Bonny
Principe
São Tomé
C. Lopez
Gulf of Guinea
Ogoue
Oubangui
Congo
Zaire (Congo)
L. Mobutu Sese Seko
Chutes Boyoma
Ruwenzori
Turkana
Elgon
4321
Kenya
5199
Equator

Annobón
Basin
Zaire (Congo)
Kasai
Pool Malebo
Sankuru
Kasai
Lualaba
L. Kivu
L. Edward
L. Victoria
Kilimanjaro
5895

INDIAN OCEAN
Pemba
Zanzibar

Ascension

Cuanza
Cuango
Kasai
L. Tanganyika
Lukuga
Rungwe
2961
L. Nyasa
Ruvuma
C. Delgado
Aldabra Is.
Comoros Is.

L. Mweru
Shaba
L. Bangweulu
Luapula
Malawi
Zambezi

Bié Plateau
Cuando
Cubango
Zambezi
Mlanje
3000

ATLANTIC
St. Helena
OCEAN
C. Fria
Cunene
Victoria Falls

Namib Desert
Walvis Bay
Limpopo
Kalahari
Delagoa Bay

Tropic of Capricorn

Orange
Highveld
Compass B.
2505
Nieuveldberge
Gt. Karoo Swartberg
3482
Drakensberg
Orange

Madagascar
2643
Mozambique Channel
Réunion

C. of Good Hope
C. Agulhas
Agulhas Bank
Algoa Bay

ft m
12 000 4000
9000 3000
6000 2000
4500 1500
3000 1000
1200 400
600 200
0 0
200 500
2000 6000
4000 12 000
6000 18 000
m ft

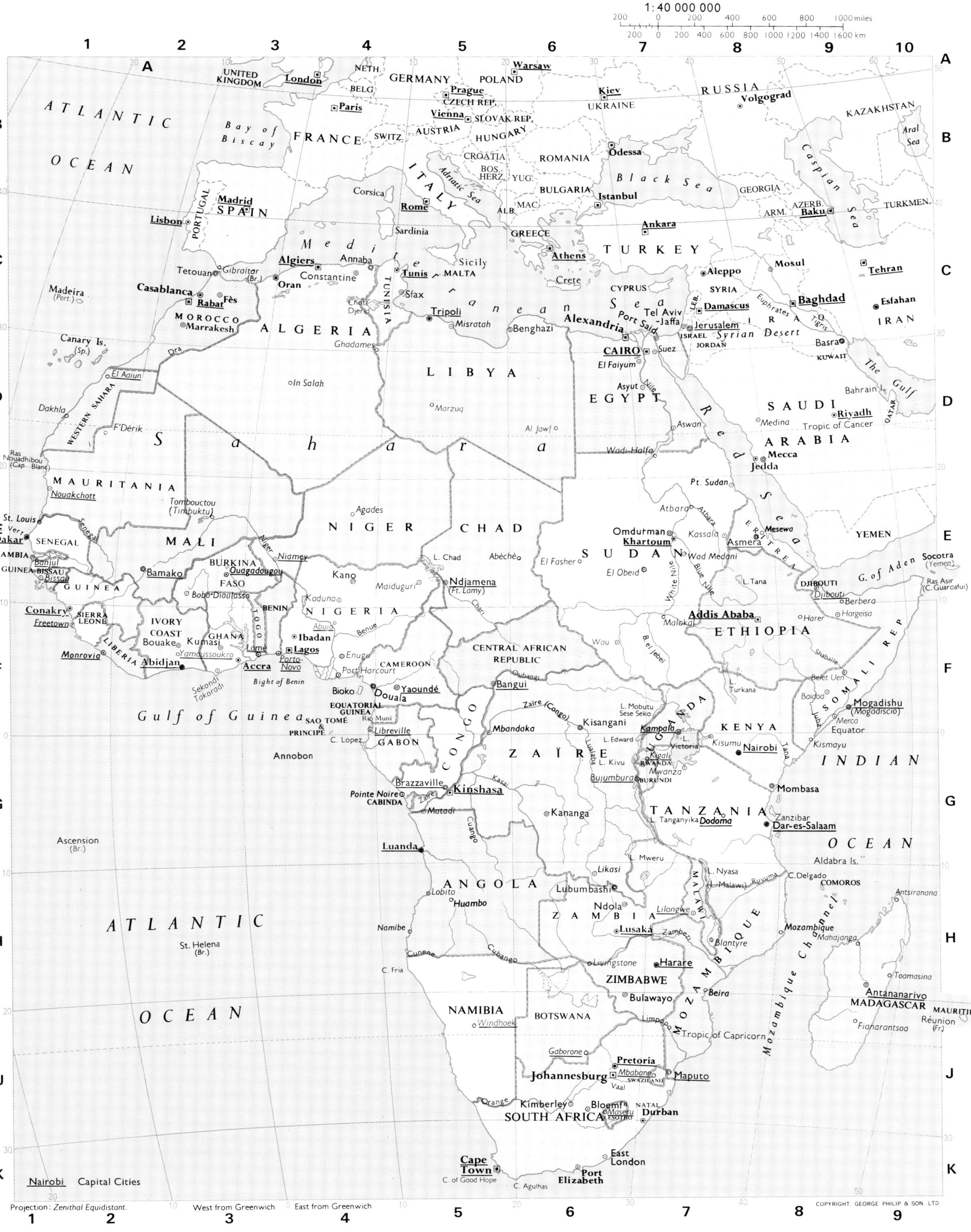

1:40 000 000

200 0 200 400 600 800 1000 miles
200 0 200 400 600 800 1000 1200 1400 1600 km

1   2   3   4   5   6   7   8   9   10

ATLANTIC OCEAN

UNITED KINGDOM   London   NETH.   GERMANY   POLAND   Warsaw
BELG.   Prague   CZECH REP.   Kiev   RUSSIA   Volgograd
Paris   Vienna   SLOVAK REP.   UKRAINE   KAZAKHSTAN
FRANCE   SWITZ.   AUSTRIA   HUNGARY   Aral Sea
Bay of Biscay   CROATIA   ROMANIA   Odessa   Caspian Sea
BOS. HERZ.   YUG.   Black Sea   GEORGIA
Corsica   ITALY   BULGARIA   Istanbul   AZERB.   Baku   TURKMEN.
Madrid   SPAIN   Rome   Sardinia   MAC.   ARM.
Lisbon   PORTUGAL   GREECE   Ankara   TURKEY
Algiers   Annaba   Sicily   Athens   Aleppo   Mosul   Tehran
Tetouan   Gibraltar (Br.)   Constantine   MALTA   CYPRUS   SYRIA   Damascus   Baghdad   Esfahan
Casablanca   Rabat   Fès   Oran   Tunis   Crete   Tel Aviv   Euphrates   Tigris   IRAN
MOROCCO   Marrakesh   TUNISIA   Sfax   Tripoli   Misratah   Benghazi   Alexandria   Port Said   Jaffa   Jerusalem   ISRAEL   Syrian Desert   Basra   KUWAIT
Canary Is. (Sp.)   Chott Djerid   Ghadames   CAIRO   JORDAN   Bahrain Is.   The Gulf   QATAR
Madeira (Port.)   ALGERIA   LIBYA   El Faiyum   Suez   SAUDI
Dakhla   In Salah   EGYPT   Asyut   Aswan   Medina   Riyadh   Tropic of Cancer
WESTERN SAHARA   F'Dérik   Marzuq   Al Jawf   Red Sea   ARABIA   Mecca
Ras Nouadhibou (Cap Blanc)   Sahara   Wadi Halfa   Jedda
MAURITANIA   Nouakchott   Tombouctou (Timbuktu)   Agades   Pt. Sudan   YEMEN
St. Louis   Senegal   MALI   NIGER   CHAD   Omdurman   Atbara   Atbara   Mesewa   Socotra (Yemen)
Dakar   SENEGAL   Niamey   Kano   L. Chad   Abéché   Khartoum   Kassala   Asmera   ERITREA   Ras Asir (C. Guardafui)
GAMBIA   Banjul   BURKINA   Ouagadougou   Maiduguri   Ndjamena (Ft. Lamy)   El Fasher   SUDAN   Wad Medani   G. of Aden   Berbera
GUINEA-BISSAU   Bissau   Bamako   FASO   Kaduna   El Obeid   White Nile   Blue Nile   DJIBOUTI   Djibouti
GUINEA   Conakry   SIERRA LEONE   Freetown   Bobo-Dioulasso   BENIN   NIGERIA   Abuja   Benue   CAMEROON   Malakal   L. Tana   Harer   Hargeisa
LIBERIA   Monrovia   IVORY COAST   Bouake   GHANA   Kumasi   TOGO   Ibadan   Lagos   Enugu   Wau   ETHIOPIA   Addis Ababa
Abidjan   Yamoussoukro   Accra   Porto-Novo   Port Harcourt   CENTRAL AFRICAN REPUBLIC   Bangui   Bel Jebel   Shabelle
Sekondi Takoradi   Bight of Benin   Bioko   Douala   Yaoundé   Ubangi   L. Turkana   SOMALI REP.   Baidoa   Belet Uen
Gulf of Guinea   EQUATORIAL GUINEA   SAO TOME   Rio Muni   Zaïre (Congo)   Kisangani   L. Mobutu Sese Seko   Mogadishu (Mogadiscio)
PRINCIPE   C. Lopez   GABON   Libreville   CONGO   Mbandaka   L. Edward   KENYA   Merca
Annobon   Brazzaville   ZAIRE   L. Kivu   Kigali   RWANDA   L. Victoria   Kisumu   Nairobi   Kismayu   INDIAN
Pointe Noire   CABINDA   Kinshasa   Bujumbura   BURUNDI   Mwanza   Mombasa
Matadi   Kanana   TANZANIA   L. Tanganyika   Dodoma   Zanzibar   Dar-es-Salaam   OCEAN
Luanda   Kasai   L. Mweru   Aldabra Is.
ATLANTIC   ANGOLA   Likasi   L. Nyasa   Ruvuma   C. Delgado   COMOROS   Antsiranana
Ascension (Br.)   Lubumbashi   Lilongwe   MALAWI   (L. Malawi)   Mozambique   Mahajanga
Lobito   Huambo   Ndola   ZAMBIA   Blantyre   Mozambique Channel
St. Helena (Br.)   Namibe   Lusaka   Zambezi   Beira
Cunene   Cubango   Livingstone   Harare   Bulawayo   ZIMBABWE   Antananarivo   MADAGASCAR   MAURITIUS
OCEAN   C. Fria   NAMIBIA   BOTSWANA   Limpopo   MOZAMBIQUE   Tropic of Capricorn   Réunion (Fr.)   Fianarantsoa   Toamasina
Windhoek   Gaborone   Pretoria   Mbabane   SWAZILAND   Maputo
Johannesburg   Vaal   Maseru   LESOTHO   NATAL   Durban
Orange   Kimberley   Bloemfontein   SOUTH AFRICA   East London
Cape Town   C. of Good Hope   C. Agulhas   Port Elizabeth

Nairobi   Capital Cities

Projection: Zenithal Equidistant.   West from Greenwich   East from Greenwich   COPYRIGHT. GEORGE PHILIP & SON. LTD.

1   2   3   4   5   6   7   8   9

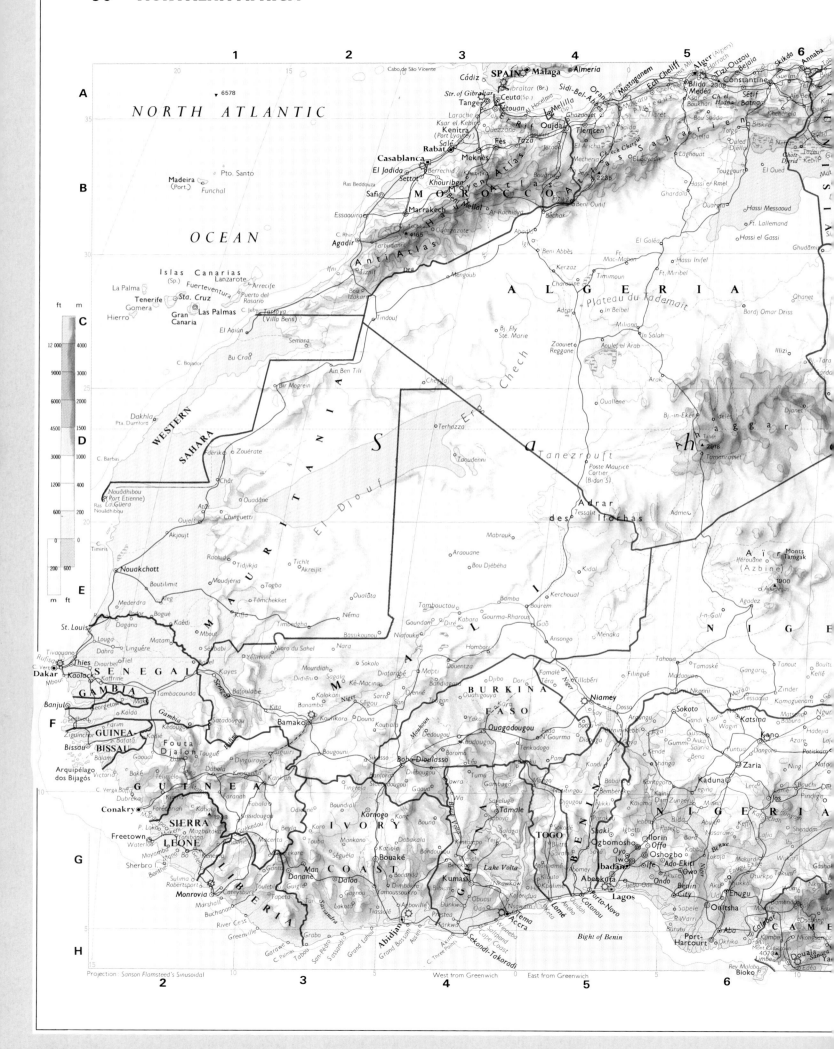

NORTH ATLANTIC

OCEAN

Projection: Sanson Flamsteed's Sinusoidal

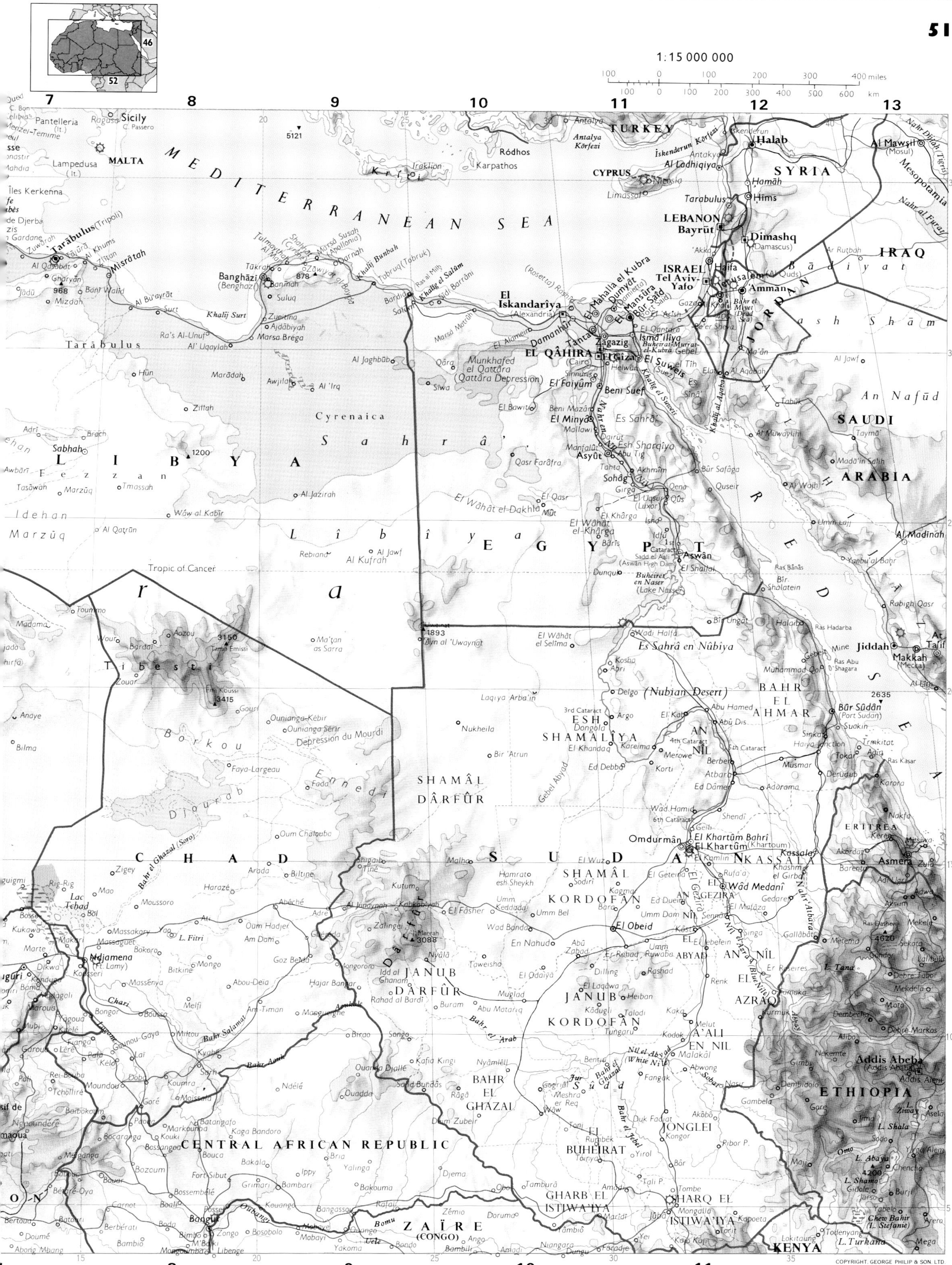

1:15 000 000

100   0   100   200   300   400 miles
100   0   100   200   300   400   500   600   km

46
52

7   8   9   10   11   12   13

MEDITERRANEAN SEA

Pantelleria (It.)
C. Bon
Menzel-Temime
Ragusa
Sicily
C. Passero
Lampedusa (It.)
MALTA
Îles Kerkenna
Île de Djerba
5121
Antalya
Antalya Körfezi
Ródhos
Karpathos
İskenderun Körfezi
İskenderun
TURKEY
Antakya
Halab
Al Mawşil (Mosul)
Nahr Dijlah (Tigris)
Iraklion
CYPRUS
Nicosia
Limassol
Al Lādhiqiya
SYRIA
Hamāh
Hims
IRAQ
Mesopotamia
Nahr al Furāt
Tarabulus
LEBANON
Bayrūt
Dimashq (Damascus)
Ar Rutbah
Bādiyat ash Shām

Tarābulus (Tripoli)
Al Khums
Misrātah
Al Qaḍāḥiḥ
Ghāryān
Bani Walid
968
Mizdah
Banghāzi (Benghazi)
Baninah
878
Zāwyt el Beida
Darnah
Khalīj Bunbah
Tobruq (Tobruk)
Ras al Milh
Bardīa
Sallum
El Alamein
Marsa Matruh
El Iskandariya (Alexandria)
Damanhûr
Haifa
ISRAEL
Tel Aviv-Yafo
Jerusalem (El Quds)
Gaza
Amman
JORDAN
Ma'ān
Al Jawf
An Nafūd
SAUDI
ARABIA
Taymā'

Khalīj Surt
Surt
Zueitina
Marsa Brega
Ra's Al-Unuf
Al 'Uqaylah
Ajdābiyah
Hûn
Marādah
Awjilah
Al 'Iraq
Qâra
Munkhafed el Qattâra (Qattâra Depression)
Siwa
El Alamein
Tanta
Zagazig
EL QÂHIRA (Cairo)
El Giza
Ismâ'iliya
Buheirat-Murrat-el-Kubra
El Suweis (Suez)
Sinâ
El 'Arish
Be'er Sheva
Al 'Aqabah
Țâbah

Tarābulus
Al Jaghbūb
Adri
Brach
Sabhâ
1200
LIBYA
Fezzan
Awbāri
Tasāwah
Marzūq
Tmassah
Al-Jazirah
Al Qatrūn
Wâw al Kabîr
Rebiana
Al Kufrah
Al Jawf
Al Qaṣr
El Wâhât el-Dâkhla
Mût
El Wâhât el-Khârga
Bâris
Siwa
El Bawîti
Beni Mazâr
El Faiyûm
Beni Suef
El Minya
Mallawi
Asyût
Qaṣr Farâfra
Girga
Sohâg
Akhmîm
Tanta
Qena
(Luxor)
Isnâ
El Khârga
Idfu
Qûs
Būr Safâga
Al Wajh
Umm Lajj
Al Madīnah

Idehan
Marzūq
Tibesti
Zouar
3150
Emi Koussi
3415
Tropic of Cancer
Toummo
Madama
Bardai
Aozou
Ma'tan as Sarra
'Ayn al 'Uwaynat
1893
El Wâhât el Selîma
Wadi Halfa
Es Sahrâ en Nûbiya
Bîr Shalatein
Ras Banâs
Dunqul
Buheirat en Naser (Lake Nasser)
Aswân
1st Cataract
Sadd el 'Ali (Aswan High Dam)
El Shallâl
Halaib
Ras Hadarba
Jiddah
Gebel Mine
Muhammad Qol
Bīr Shagara
Makkah (Mecca)
At Tâif
Al Ehb
Rabigh
Qasr

Andye
Bilma
Borkou
Ounianga-Kébir
Ounianga Serir
Depression du Mourdi
Faya-Largeau
Fada
Ennedi
Djourab
Nukheila
Bir 'Atrun
Laqiya Arba'in
3rd Cataract
Dongola
Argo
Abu Hamed
El Kâbo
Abû Dis
2635
Būr Sûdân (Port Sudan)
Suakin
BAHR
EL
AHMAR
Tokar
Trinkitat
Agig
Ras Kasar
(Nubian Desert)
Delgo
ESH
SHAMALÎYA
El Khandaq
Kareima
Merowe
4th Cataract
Berbero
Atbara
Adârma
Derudeb
Haiya Junction
Karora
Nakfa
ERITREA
Kerem
Asmera
Mitsiwa
Zula

Bilma
Zigey
Rig-Rig
Lac Tchad
Bol
Kukawa
Massakory
Ndjamena (Ft. Lamy)
Harazé
Biltine
Abéché
Adré
Am Dam
Oum Hadjer
Ati
Mongo
Moussoro
Bokoro
L. Fitri
Massaguet
Bitkine
Mongororo
Tiné
Kutum
Malha
Hamrat esh Sheikh
Sodiri
Umm Keddada
El Fasher
Wad Banda
Umm Bel
Ed Dueim
Wad Medanî
Gedaref
Gallabat
Metema
4620
ETHIOPIA
Addis Abeba (Addis Ababa)
Nekemte

CHAD
Mao
Massenya
Mongo
Melfi
Am-Timan
Goz Beïda
SHAMÂL
DÂRFÛR
SUDAN
KASSALA
Kassala
Khashm el Girba
AN
NIL
GEZIRA
El Matâna
Singa
Sennar
AN NÎL
EL
AZRAQ
Renk
Melut
Dembidolo
Gimbi
Gore

Marrah
3088
DÂRFÛR
JANUB
DÂRFÛR
Nyâlâ
Idd el Ganam
Buram
El Daien
Abû Zabad
En Nahud
El Obeid
SHAMÂL
KORDOFAN
Ed Dueim
Dilling
Rashad
Kâdugli
Talodi
JANUB
KORDOFAN
Heiban
El Debeiba
ABYAD
Renk
Malakal
A'ALI
EN NIL
Abwong
Sobat
Nasir
Gambela

CENTRAL AFRICAN REPUBLIC
Bossangoa
Bouca
Bakala
Bambari
Bria
Ippy
Yalinga
Djema
Ouanda Djallé
Kafia Kingi
Raga
Deim Zubeir
BAHR
EL
GHAZAL
Meshra er Req
Wâu
Tonj
Toni
EL
BUHEIRAT
Rumbek
Yirol
JONGLEI
Bor
Kongor
Duk Fadiat
Bentiu

Bangui
Zongo
Mobaye
Bomu
ZAÏRE
(CONGO)
Yakoma
Uele
Bangassou
Rafaï
Zémio
Dorumo
Dungu
Aba
GHARB EL
ISTIWA'IYA
Tambura
Yambio
Maridi
Tombe
Mongalla
SHARQ EL
ISTIWA'IYA
Juba
Kapoeta
KENYA
L. Turkana
Chew Bahir (L. Stefanie)
Mega

E   G   Y   P   T
Sahrâ' el Gharbîya
Cyrenaica
Sahrâ'
Lîbîya
RED SEA

COPYRIGHT, GEORGE PHILIP & SON, LTD.

15   8   9   20   10   25   30   11   35   12

CENTRAL AND SOUTHERN AFRICA

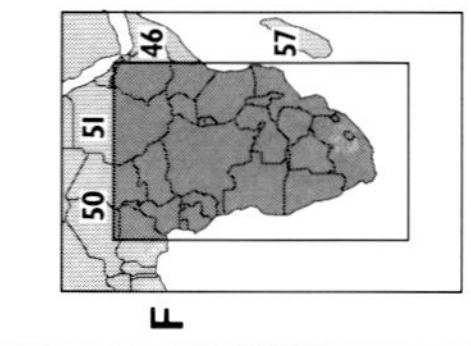

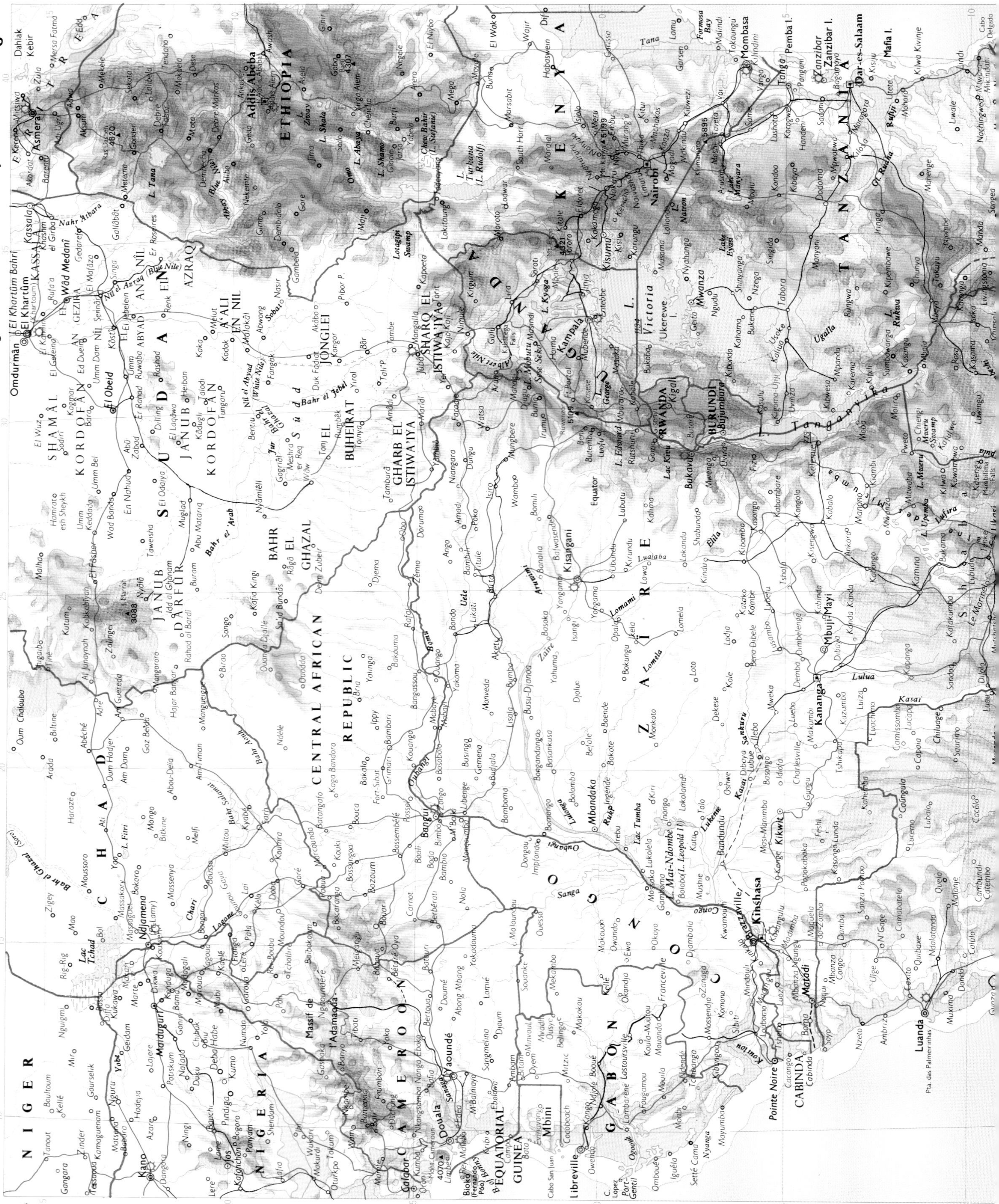

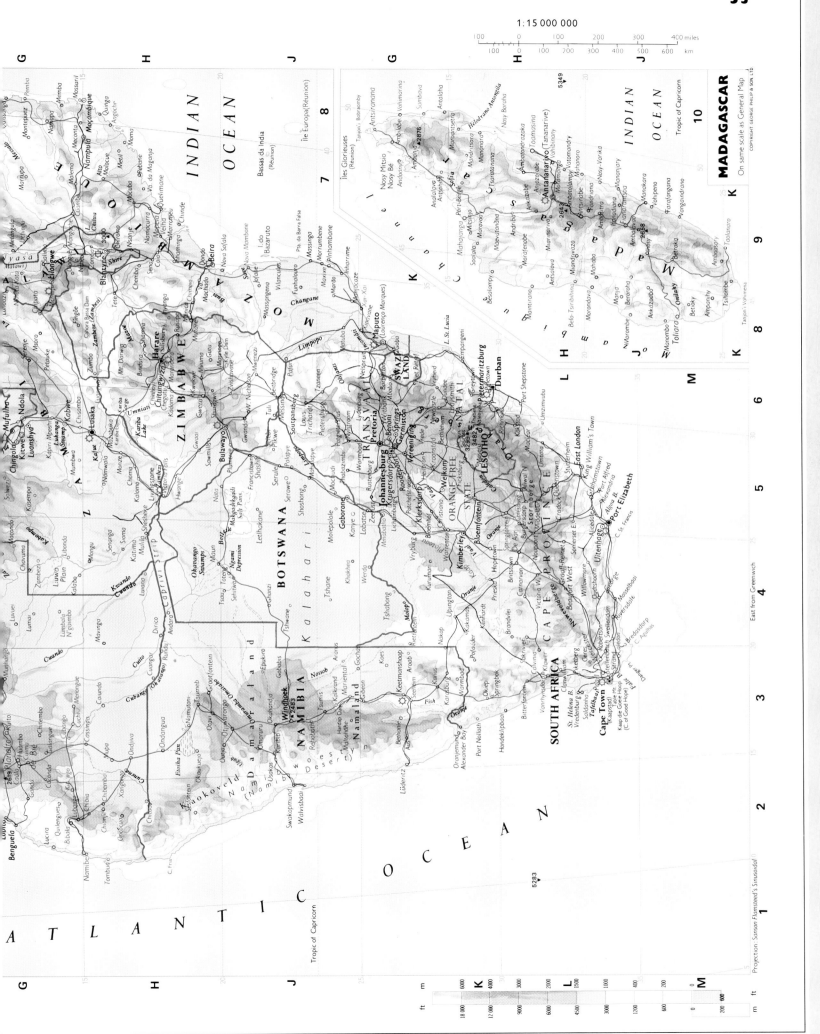

1:15 000 000

100   0   100   200   300   400 miles

100   0   100   200   300   400   500   600 km

MADAGASCAR

On same scale as General Map

COPYRIGHT GEORGE PHILIP & SON LTD

INDIAN OCEAN

ATLANTIC OCEAN

Tropic of Capricorn

East from Greenwich

Projection Sanson Flamsteed's Sinusoidal

ZIMBABWE

BOTSWANA

NAMIBIA

SOUTH AFRICA

CAPE PROVINCE

ORANGE FREE STATE

TRANSVAAL

NATAL

LESOTHO

SWAZILAND

Kalahari

Harare

Bulawayo

Gaborone

Windhoek

Johannesburg

Pretoria

Bloemfontein

Kimberley

Durban

Port Elizabeth

Cape Town

Lusaka

Ndola

Kitwe

Blantyre

Beira

Maputo

Pietermaritzburg

East London

m   ft

6000   18 000

4000   12 000

3000   9000

2000   6000

1500   4500

1000   3000

400   1200

200   600

0   0

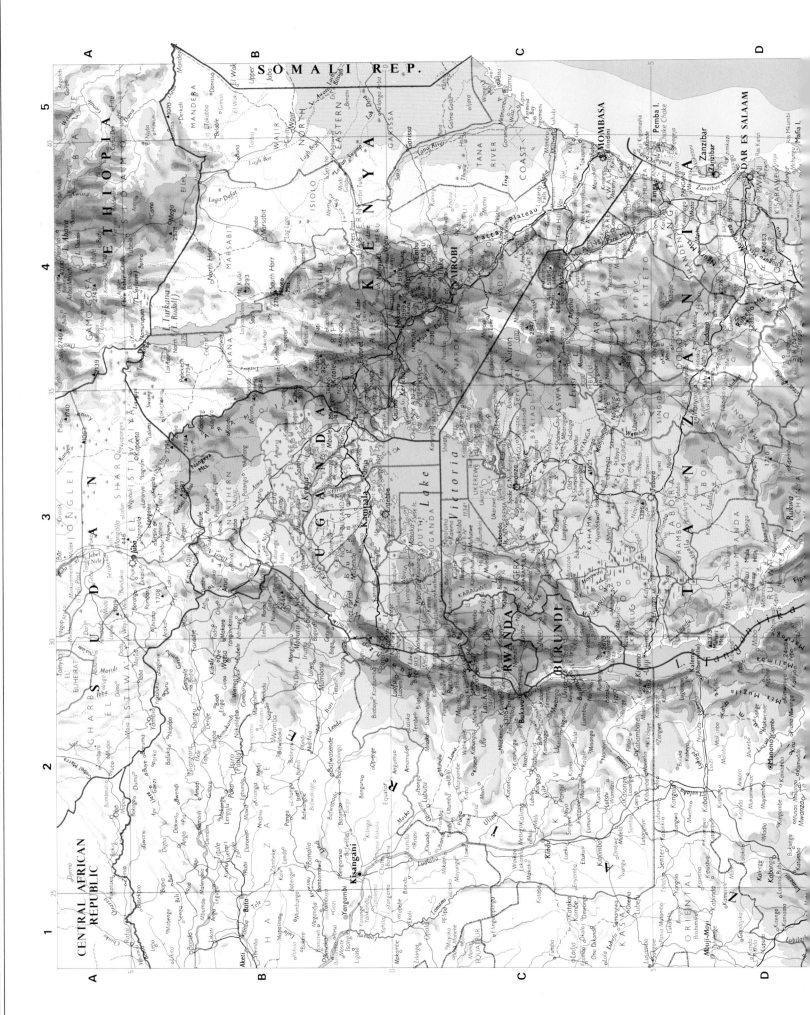

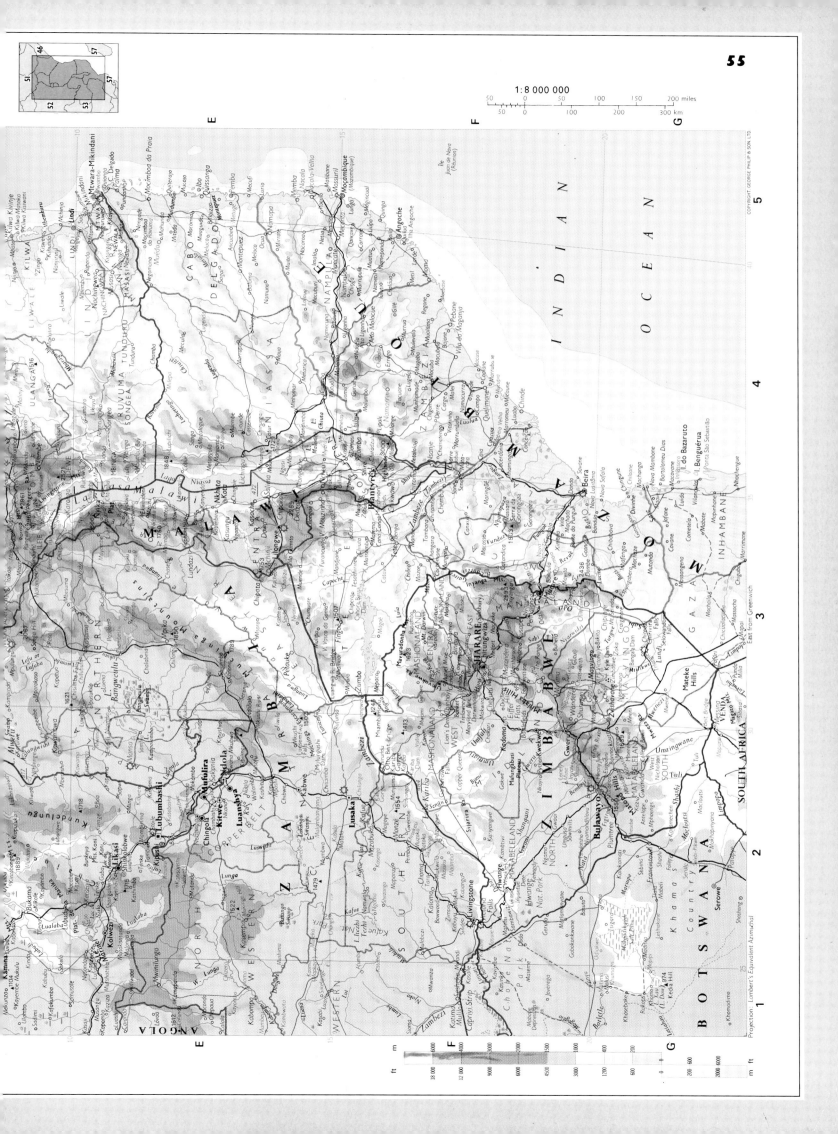

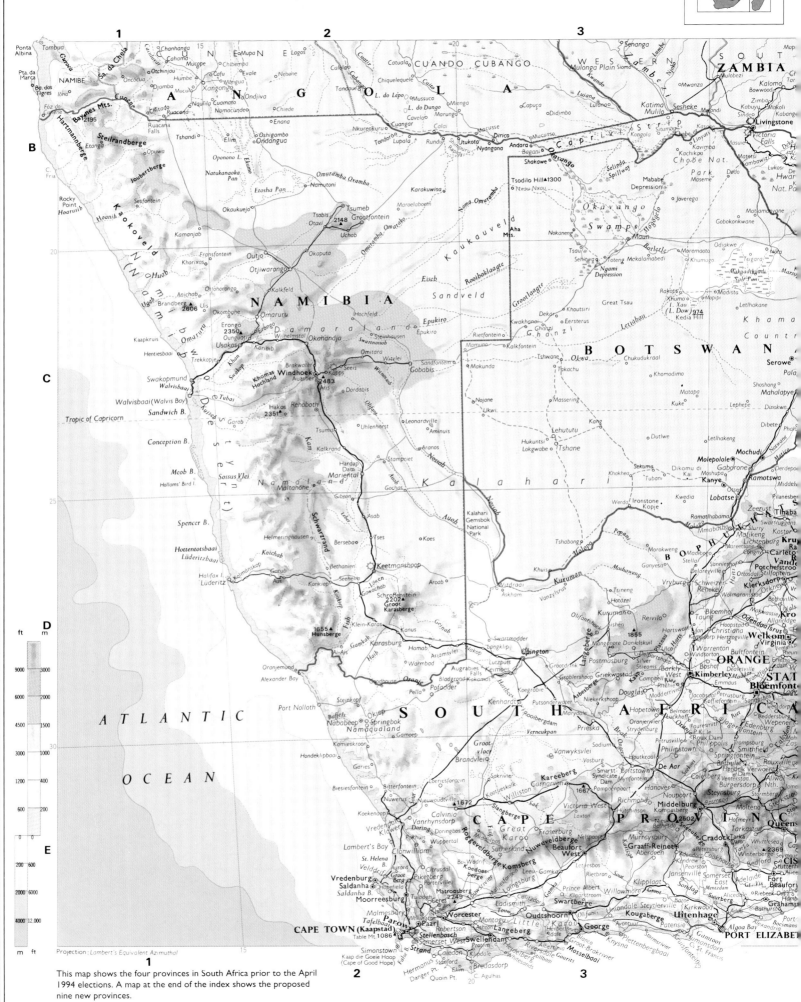

This map shows the four provinces in South Africa prior to the April 1994 elections. A map at the end of the index shows the proposed nine new provinces.

1 : 8 000 000

MOZAMBIQUE

CHANNEL

CHANNEL

MADAGASCAR

On same scale as General Map

East from Greenwich

COPYRIGHT GEORGE PHILIP & SON LTD.

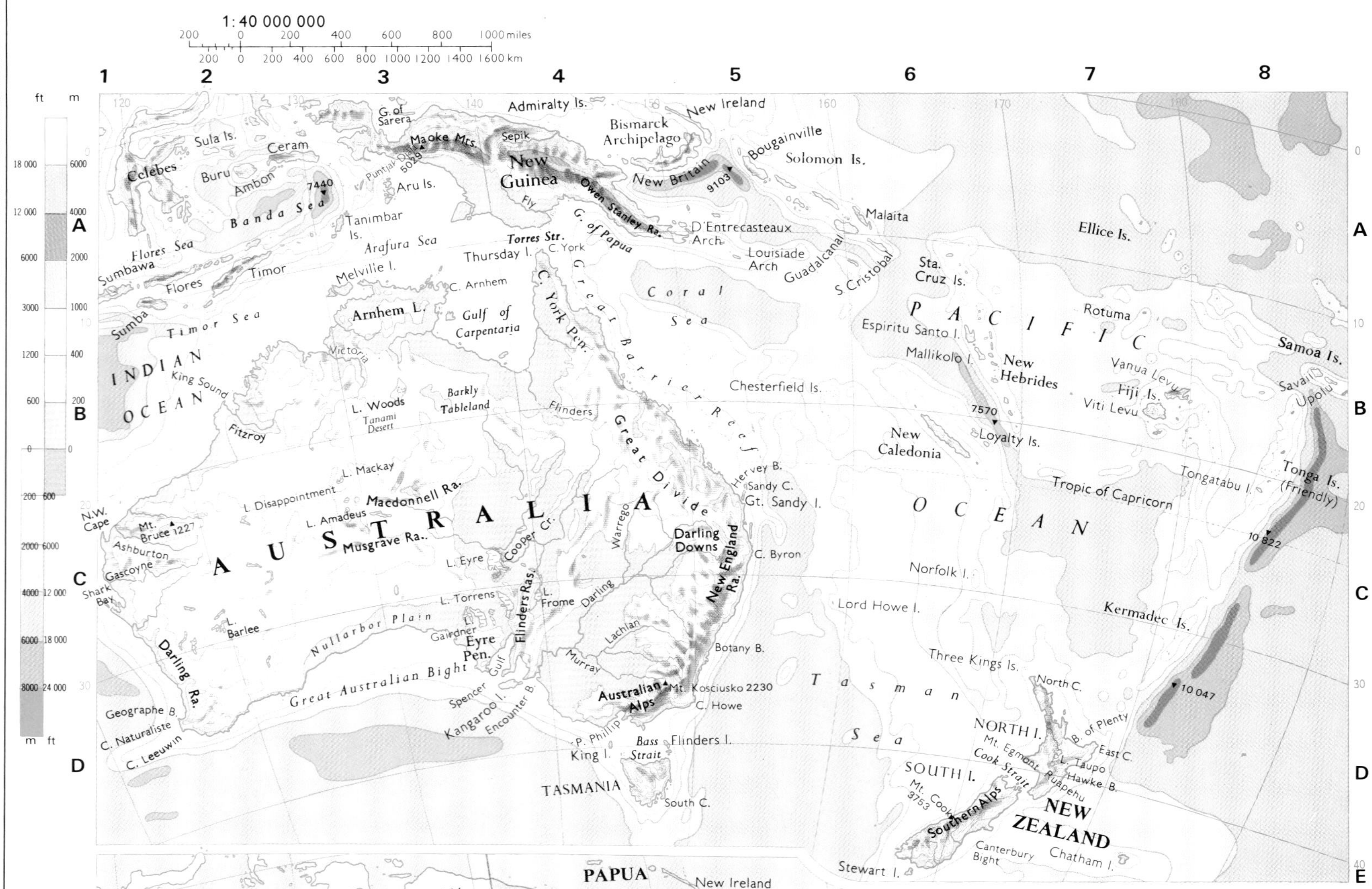

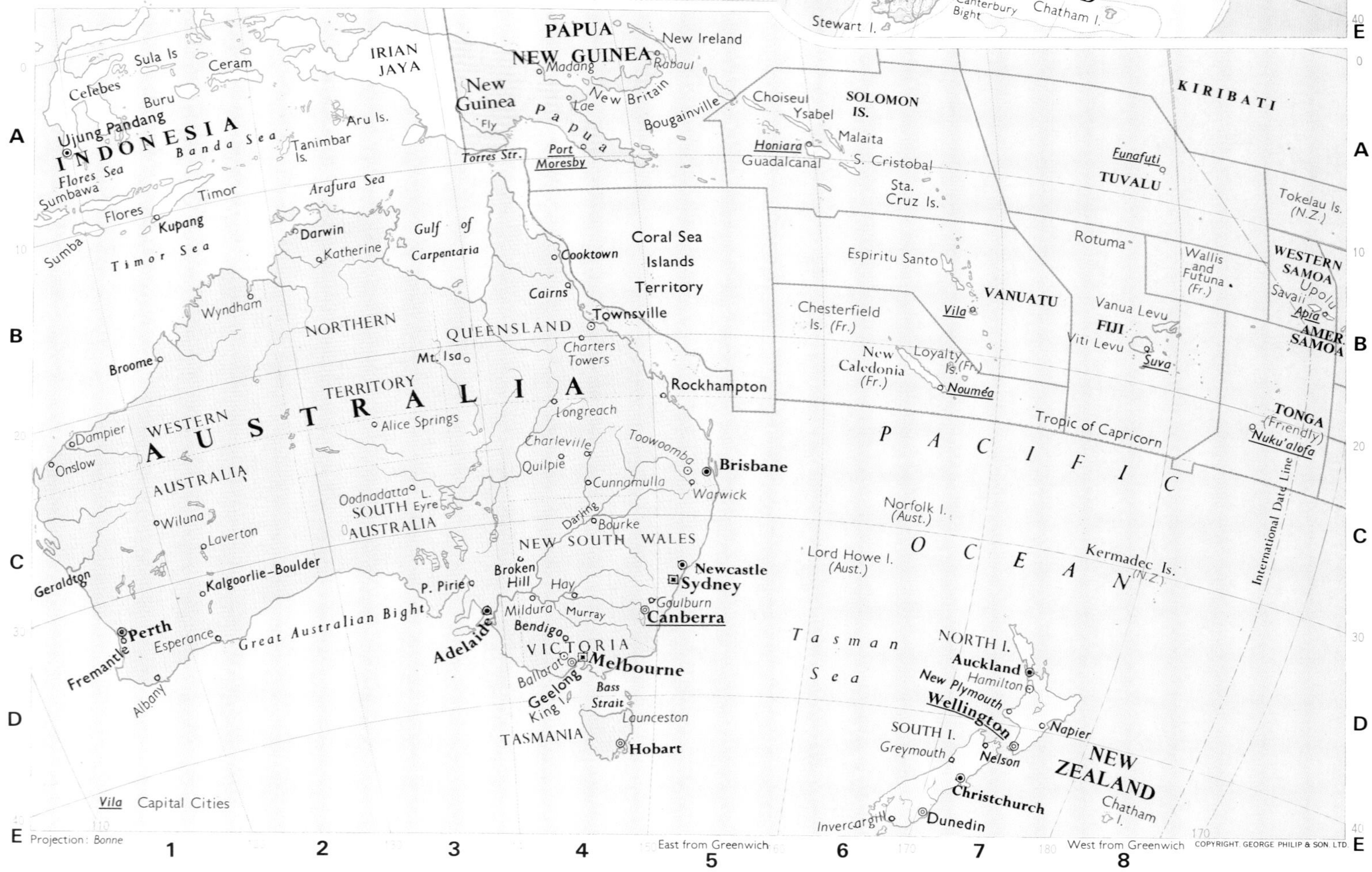

1:40 000 000

200 0 200 400 600 800 1000 miles
200 0 200 400 600 800 1000 1200 1400 1600 km

1 2 3 4 5 6 7 8

ft m
18 000 6000
12 000 4000
6000 2000
3000 1000
1200 400
600 200
0 0
200 600
2000 6000
4000 12 000
6000 18 000
8000 24 000
m ft

Top map (Physical):

120 130 140 150 160 170 180

Admiralty Is.
G. of Sarera
Maoke Mts. 5029
Sepik
New Ireland
Bismarck Archipelago
Bougainville
Solomon Is.
New Guinea
Owen Stanley Ra.
New Britain 9103
Malaita
Ellice Is.
Celebes
Sula Is.
Ceram
Buru
Ambon
Aru Is. 7440
Banda Sea
Puntjak
New Guinea
Fly
G. of Papua
D'Entrecasteaux Arch.
Louisiade Arch.
Guadalcanal
S. Cristobal
Sta. Cruz Is.
Rotuma
Samoa Is.
Flores Sea
Sumbawa
Flores
Timor
Tanimbar Is.
Arafura Sea
Thursday I.
C. York
Torres Str.
Coral Sea
Espiritu Santo I.
Mallikolo I.
New Hebrides
Vanua Levu
Fiji Is.
Viti Levu
Savai'i
Upolu
INDIAN OCEAN
Sumba
Timor Sea
Melville I.
C. Arnhem
Great Barrier Reef
Chesterfield Is.
7570
Loyalty Is.
Tonga Is. (Friendly)
Arnhem L.
Victoria
Gulf of Carpentaria
C. York Pen.
New Caledonia
Tropic of Capricorn
Tongatabu I.
King Sound
L. Woods
Tanami Desert
Barkly Tableland
Flinders
Great Divide
Hervey B.
Sandy C.
Gt. Sandy I.
Norfolk I.
10 822
Fitzroy
L. Mackay
Warrego
Darling Downs
New England Ra.
C. Byron
Lord Howe I.
Kermadec Is.
N.W. Cape
L. Disappointment
Macdonnell Ra.
L. Amadeus
Mt. Bruce 1227
Musgrave Ra.
L. Eyre
Cooper Cr.
PACIFIC OCEAN
Ashburton
Gascoyne
AUSTRALIA
Darling
Lachlan
Botany B.
Three Kings Is.
North C.
10 047
Shark Bay
Barlee
L. Torrens
L. Frome
Murray
Tasman Sea
Darling Ra.
Nullarbor Plain
Gairdner
Eyre Pen.
Flinders Ras.
Australian Alps
Mt. Kosciusko 2230
C. Howe
NORTH I.
Mt. Egmont
Ruapehu
B. of Plenty
East C.
Hawke B.
Geographe B.
C. Naturaliste
C. Leeuwin
Great Australian Bight
Spencer Gulf
Kangaroo I.
Encounter B.
P. Philip
King I.
Bass Strait
Flinders I.
South C.
TASMANIA
SOUTH I.
Mt. Cook 3753
Southern Alps
Canterbury Bight
Chatham I.
NEW ZEALAND
Stewart I.
Cook Strait
Taupo

Bottom map (Political):

PAPUA NEW GUINEA
New Ireland
IRIAN JAYA
Madang
Rabaul
New Britain
New Guinea
Lae
Papua
Bougainville
Choiseul
Ysabel
SOLOMON IS.
Malaita
KIRIBATI
Celebes
Sula Is.
Ceram
Buru
Aru Is.
Tanimbar Is.
Ujung Pandang
INDONESIA
Banda Sea
Torres Str.
Port Moresby
Honiara
Guadalcanal
S. Cristobal
Sta. Cruz Is.
Funafuti
TUVALU
Tokelau (N.Z.)
Flores Sea
Sumbawa
Flores
Timor
Kupang
Arafura Sea
Timor Sea
Darwin
Katherine
Gulf of Carpentaria
Cooktown
Coral Sea Islands Territory
Espiritu Santo
Rotuma
Wallis and Futuna (Fr.)
WESTERN SAMOA
Upolu
Savai'i
Sumba
Cairns
Townsville
Chesterfield Is. (Fr.)
Vila
VANUATU
Vanua Levu
Apia
AMER. SAMOA
Wyndham
NORTHERN TERRITORY
QUEENSLAND
Mt. Isa
Charters Towers
New Caledonia (Fr.)
Loyalty Is. (Fr.)
FIJI
Viti Levu
Suva
Broome
Rockhampton
Nouméa
Dampier
WESTERN AUSTRALIA
Alice Springs
Longreach
Toowoomba
Norfolk I. (Aust.)
PACIFIC OCEAN
TONGA (Friendly)
Nuku'alofa
Onslow
AUSTRALIA
Charleville
Quilpie
Cunnamulla
Warwick
Brisbane
Tropic of Capricorn
Wiluna
Oodnadatta
L. Eyre
SOUTH AUSTRALIA
Bourke
Darling
Lord Howe I. (Aust.)
Kermadec Is. (N.Z.)
Geraldton
Laverton
Kalgoorlie-Boulder
P. Pirie
Broken Hill
Hay
NEW SOUTH WALES
Newcastle
Sydney
International Date Line
Perth
Fremantle
Esperance
Great Australian Bight
Mildura
Murray
Goulburn
Canberra
Bendigo
VICTORIA
Melbourne
NORTH I.
Auckland
Hamilton
New Plymouth
Albany
Ballarat
Geelong
King I.
Bass Strait
Launceston
Tasman Sea
Wellington
Napier
Adelaide
SOUTH I.
Greymouth
Nelson
NEW ZEALAND
TASMANIA
Hobart
Christchurch
Chatham I.
Invercargill
Dunedin

Vila Capital Cities

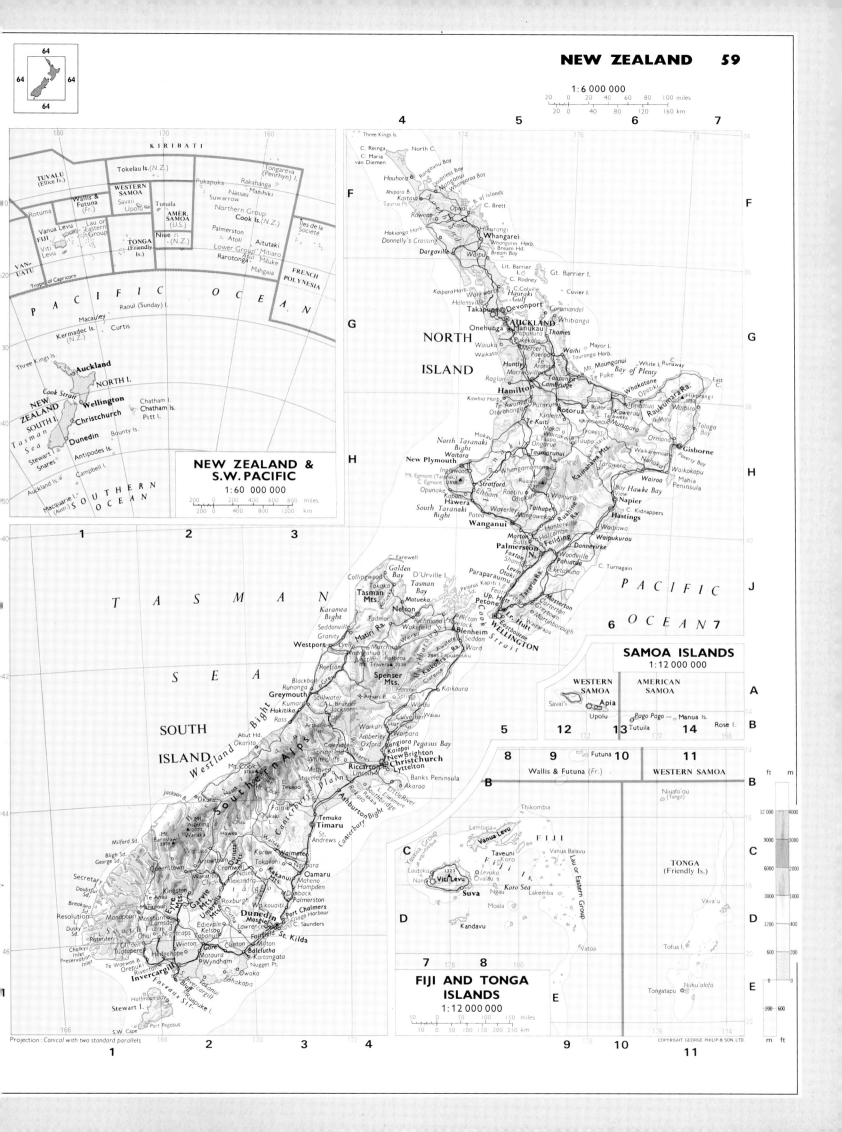

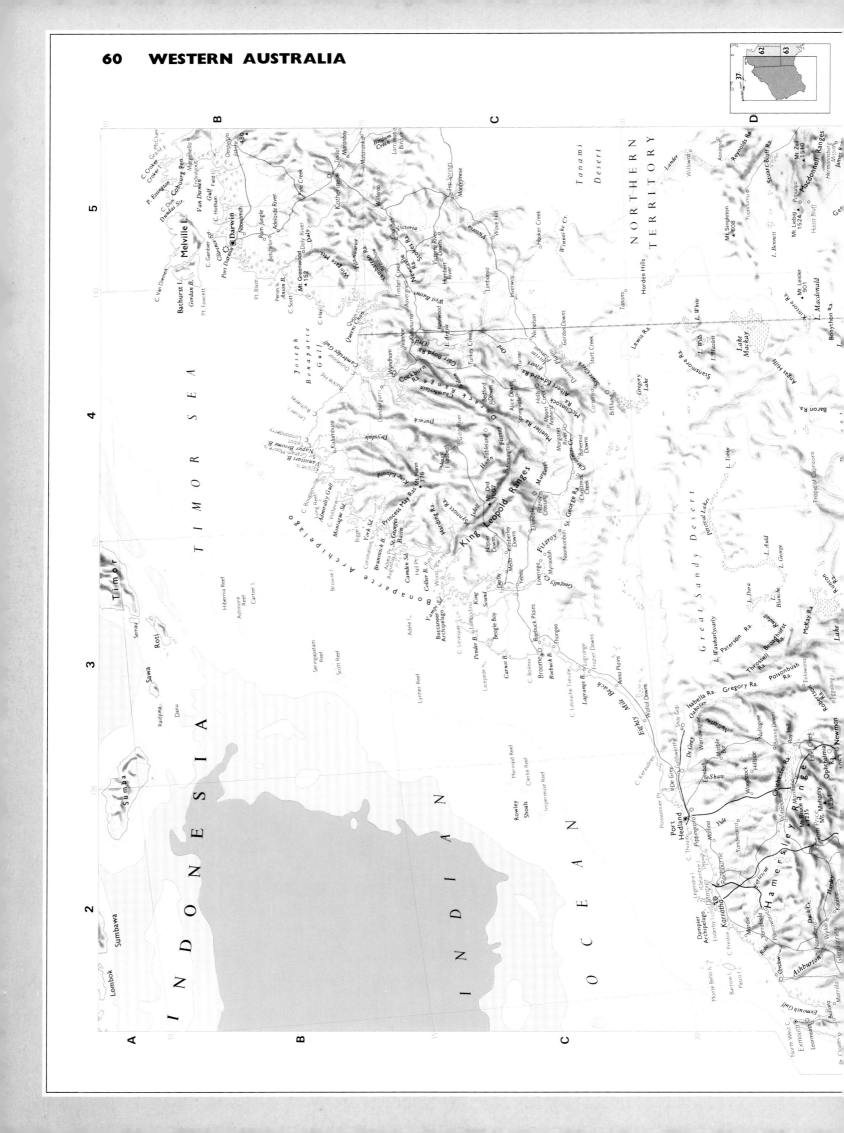

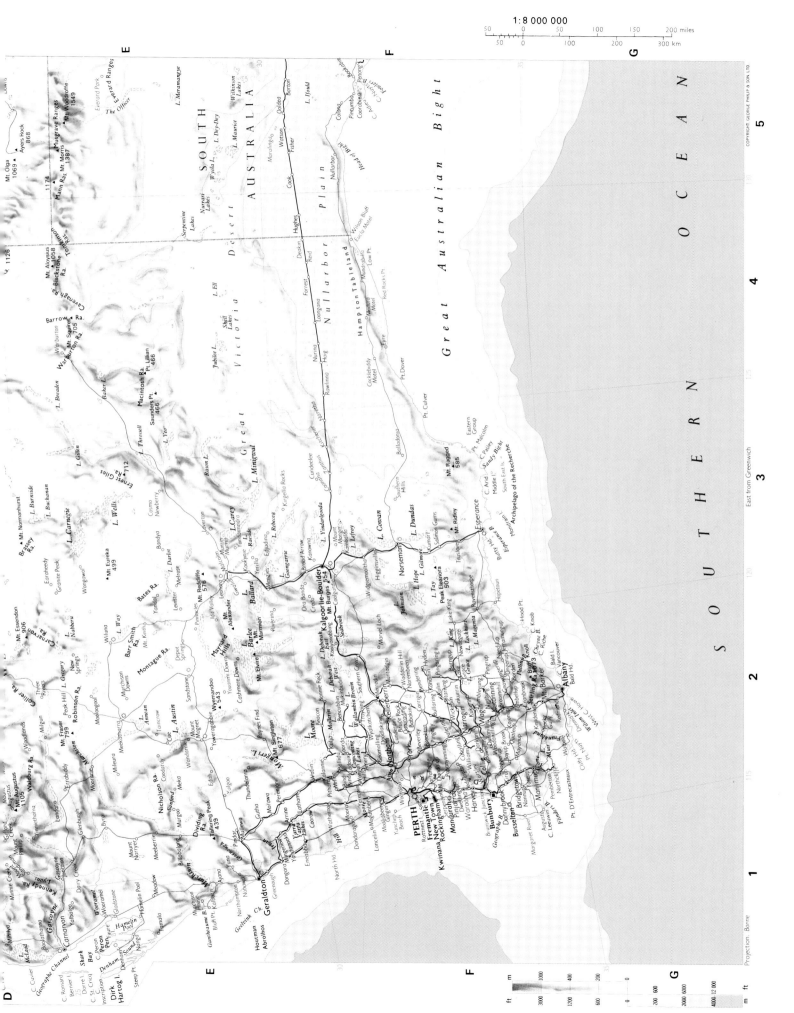

1 : 8 000 000

50   0   50   100   150   200 miles

50   0   50   100   200   300 km

D   E   F   G

SOUTH   AUSTRALIA

Great   Victoria   Desert

Nullarbor   Plain

Hampton   Tableland

Great   Australian   Bight

S   O   U   T   H   E   R   N   O   C   E   A   N

Ayers Rock
868
Mt. Olga
1069
Mt. Woodroffe
1549
Musgrave Ranges
Mann Ras. 1387
Mt. Morris 1058
Blackstone Ra.
Mt. Aloysius 1058
The Officer
L. Meramangye
Wilkinson
Lakes
L. Maurice
Ifould L.
L. Dey-Dey
Serpentine
Lakes
Nurrai
Lakes
Nullarbor
Coorabie
Penong
Fowler
Colona
Bookabie
Coorabie
Pintumba
Watson
Fisher
Cook
Hughes
Deakin
Reid
Forrest
Loongana
Nurina
Haig
Rawlinna
Kitchener
Naretha
Zanthus

Barrow Ra.
Mt. Squires Ra. 705
Warburton
Warburton Ra.
L. Breaden
Baker L.
L. Gillen
L. Throssell
L. Yeo
L. Lillian 466
Saunders Pt. 466
Macintosh Ra.
Ernest Giles Ra. 712

Mt. Normanhurst
L. Burnside
L. Buchanan
Brassey Ra.
Granite Peak
Ecrabeedy
L. Carnegie
Wongowol
Mt. Eureka 499
Wandya
Darlot
Melrose
L. Darlot

Jubilee L.
L. Rason
Shell
Lakes
L. Yindarlgooda
L. Minigwal
Great   Victoria

Collier Ra.
Three Rivers
Peak Hill
Robinson Ra.
Mt. Essendon 906
Carnarvon Ra.
L. Nabberu
Bates Ra.
Montague Ra.

Mt. Augustus 1105
Mount Gould
Dairy Creek
Kennedy Ra.
Mooloogool
Meekatharra
Murchison Downs
Wiluna
Barr Smith Ra.
Mt. Keith
Depot Springs
New Springs
Yakabindie

Mt. Redcliffe 576
Mt. Alexander
Pinnacles
Idd Valley
Lawlers
Leonora
Yundamindra

L. Carey
Laverton
Murrin
Yundamindra
Bandya
Edjudina
L. Raeside
Menzies
Kookynie
Niagara
Comet Vale
Goongarrie

Kalgoorlie-Boulder
Mt. Burges 554
Coolgardie
Kanowna
Broad Arrow
Bulla Bulla
Dora
Credo

Norseman
L. Cowan
L. Dundas
L. Hope
L. Tay
L. Johnston
Higginsville
Widgiemooltha
Kambalda
Mt. Monger

Mt. Ridley
Peak Eleanora 503
L. Gilmore
Salmon Gums
L. Magenta
Esperance
C. Arid
Cape Le Grand
Sandy Bight
C. Pasley
Mt. Ragged 585
Middle I.
Eastern Group
Archipelago of the Recherche

Geraldton
Houtman
Abrolhos
Greenough
Dongara
Mingenew
Three Springs
Carnamah
Coorow
Moora
Watheroo
Dalwallinu
Wongan Hills

Dirk Hartog I.
Shark Bay
Denham
Hamelin Pool
Nanga
Carnarvon
Gascoyne Junction

PERTH
Fremantle
Rottnest I.
Kwinana
Rockingham
Mandurah
Pinjarra
Waroona
Harvey
Bunbury
Busselton
Margaret River
Augusta
C. Leeuwin
Pt. D'Entrecasteaux
Manjimup
Pemberton
Bridgetown
Donnybrook
Collie
Darkan
Williams
Wagin
Katanning
Gnowangerup
Broomehill
Tambellup
Cranbrook
Mt. Barker
Stirling Ra.
Albany
King George Sd.
Denmark
Nornalup

Northam
York
Beverley
Brookton
Corrigin
Narrogin
Wickepin
Kondinin
Hyden
Kulin
Lake Grace
Newdegate
Ravensthorpe
Hopetoun
Jerramungup
Gairdner

Moora
Goomalling
Dowerin
Wyalkatchem
Kellerberrin
Merredin
Southern Cross
Bullfinch
Koolyanobbing
Bonnie Rock
Mukinbudin

Morawa
Perenjori
Latham
Dalwallinu
Wubin
Paynes Find

Mt. Singleton 677
Murgoo
Yalgoo
Mount Magnet
Sandstone
Wydgee
Youanmi

L. Moore
L. Austin
Cue
Lake Way

Mt. Jackson
Marvel Loch
Bencubbin
Nungarin
Trayning

Projection. Bonne

COPYRIGHT GEORGE PHILIP & SON, LTD.

East from Greenwich

1   2   3   4   5

ft   m
3000   1000
1200   400
600   200
0   0
200   600
2000   6000
4000 12000

m   ft

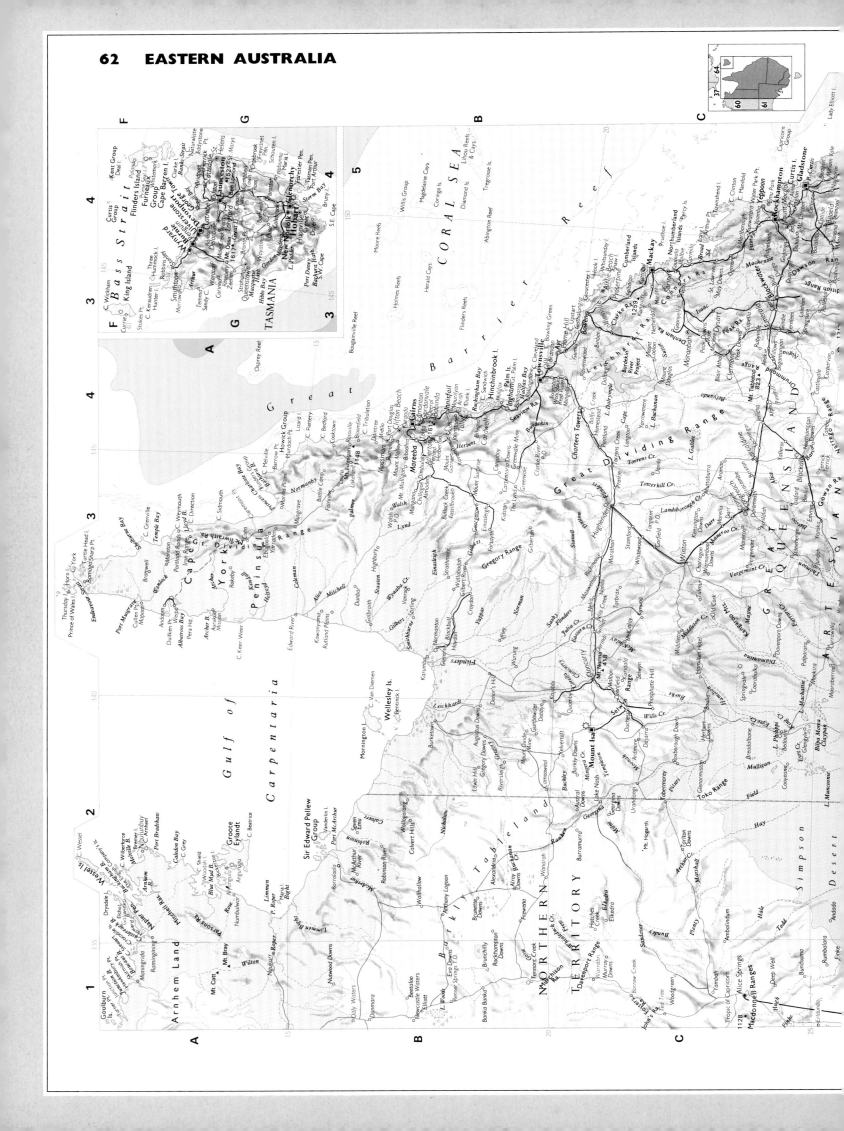

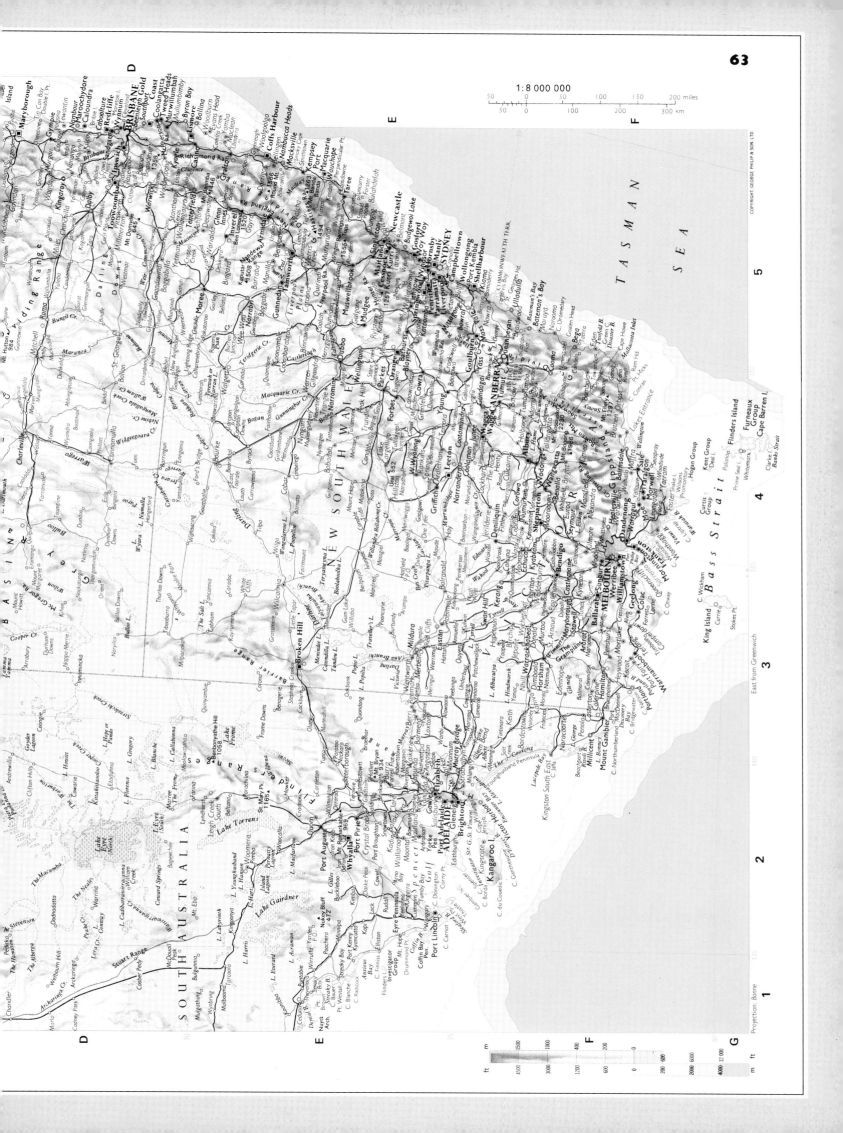

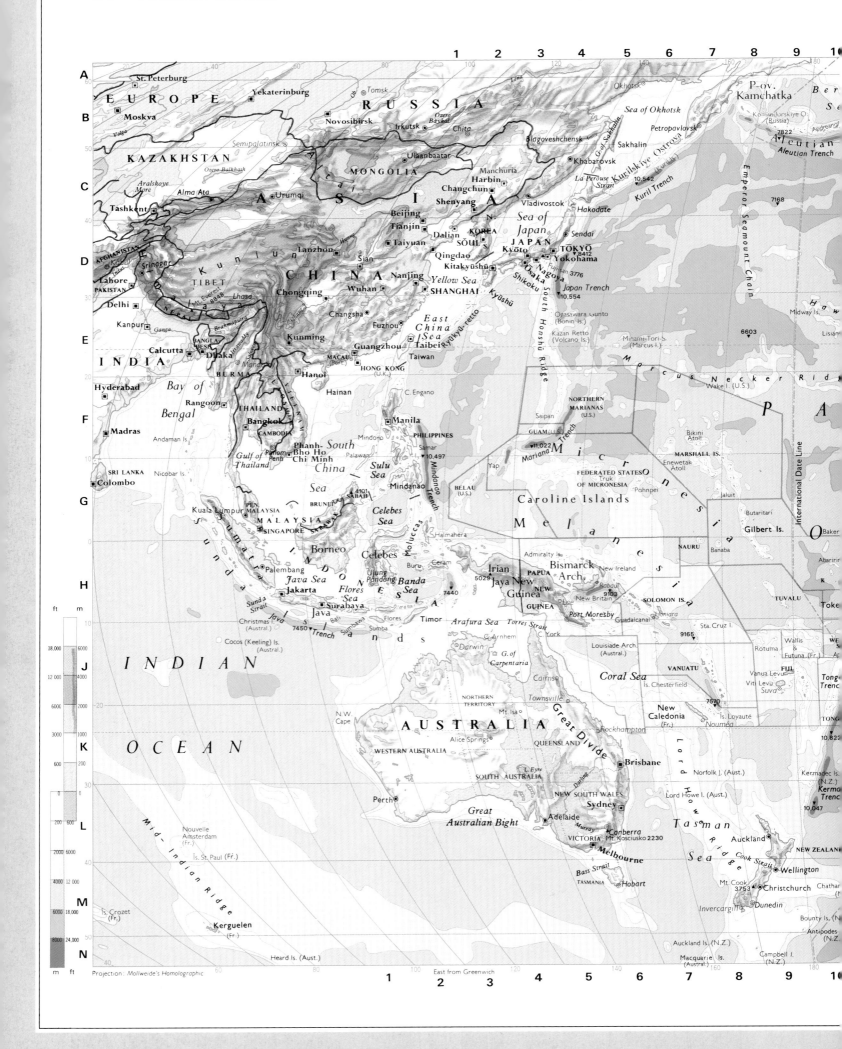

St. Peterburg
EUROPE
Moskva
Volga
Yekaterinburg
KAZAKHSTAN
Semipalatinsk
Aralskoye More
Ozero Balkhash
Tashkent
Alma Ata
Urumqi
AFGHANISTAN
Srinagar
Kabul
LAHORE
PAKISTAN
Delhi
Kanpur
Ganga
Kunlun
TIBET
Mt. Everest 8848
Lhasa
INDIA
Calcutta
BANGLA-DESH
Dhaka
Brahmaputra
Hyderabad
Bay of Bengal
Rangoon
Madras
BURMA
THAILAND
Bangkok
CAMBODIA
SRI LANKA
Colombo
Andaman Is.
Nicobar Is.
Gulf of Thailand
Phnom Penh
Phanh-Bho Ho Chi Minh
South China Sea
Kuala Lumpur
PEN. MALAYSIA
MALAYSIA
SINGAPORE
Sumatra
Palembang
Sunda Strait
Java
Jakarta
Java Sea
Surabaya
Bali
Borneo
INDONESIA
Celebes
Ujung Pandang
Flores Sea
Sumbawa
Flores
Banda Sea
Timor
Sumba
Christmas I. (Austral.)
7450 Java Trench
Cocos (Keeling) Is. (Austral.)

RUSSIA
Novosibirsk
Tomsk
Ob
Irkutsk
Ozero Baykal
Chita
MONGOLIA
Ulaanbaatar
Manchuria
Blagoveshchensk
Amur
Harbin
Changchun
Shenyang
Vladivostok
Beijing
Tianjin
Dalian
N. KOREA
SŌUL S. KOREA
Taiyuan
Lanzhou
Sian
Qingdao
Huang
CHINA
Nanjing
Wuhan
SHANGHAI
Chongqing
Changsha
Fuzhou
East China Sea
Kunming
Guangzhou
Taibei
MACAU (Port.)
HONG KONG (U.K.)
Taiwan
Hanoi
Hainan
VIETNAM
C. Engano
Mindoro
Manila
PHILIPPINES
Samar
Palawan
Mindanao
Sulu Sea
SABAH 4101
BRUNEI
Celebes Sea
Sarawak
Moluccas
Halmahera
Buru
Ceram
Irian Jaya
5029
New Guinea
PAPUA NEW GUINEA

Sea of Okhotsk
P-ov. Kamchatka
Okhotsk
Petropavlovsk
Sakhalin
Khabarovsk
La Pérouse Strait
Kuril'skiye Ostrova (Kurils)
10,542 Kuril Trench
Hakodate
Sea of Japan
Sendai
JAPAN
Kyōto TOKYO
Osaka Nagoya Yokohama
8412
Shikoku Honshū 3776
Kyūshū
South Honshū Ridge
Japan Trench 10,554
Ogasawara Gunto (Bonin Is.)
Kazan Retto (Volcano Is.)
Ryūkyū-retto
Tōkyō-retto

Kolmsundorskiye O. (Russia)
7822
Aleutian Is.
Aleutian Trench
7168
Emperor Seamount Chain
Midway Is.
Hawa
6603
Lisian

NORTHERN MARIANAS (U.S.)
Saipan
GUAM (U.S.)
11,022
Mariana Trench
10,497
Yap
BELAU (U.S.)
FEDERATED STATES OF MICRONESIA
Truk
Caroline Islands
Pohnpei
Micronesia
Melanesia
Mindanao Trench

Marcus Necker Ridge
Wake I. (U.S.)
Bikini Atoll
MARSHALL IS.
Enewetak Atoll
Jaluit
Butaritari
Gilbert Is.
NAURU
Banaba
Abariri
Baker

PACIFIC OCEAN
International Date Line

Bismarck Arch.
New Ireland
Admiralty Is.
Rabaul
NEW BRITAIN
9103
New Britain
Port Moresby
Guadalcanal
SOLOMON IS.
Honiara
7440
Arafura Sea
Torres Strait
C. York
Arnhem
Darwin
G. of Carpentaria
Cairns
NORTHERN TERRITORY
Mt. Isa
Townsville
N.W. Cape
AUSTRALIA
Alice Springs
WESTERN AUSTRALIA
QUEENSLAND
Rockhampton
Brisbane
Great Divide
SOUTH AUSTRALIA
L. Eyre
Darling
Perth
NEW SOUTH WALES
Sydney
Great Australian Bight
Adelaide
Murray
VICTORIA Canberra
Mt. Kosciusko 2230
Melbourne
Bass Strait
TASMANIA
Hobart

Sta. Cruz I.
9165
Louisiade Arch. (Austral.)
VANUATU
Is. Chesterfield
Coral Sea
Rotuma
Wallis & Futuna (Fr.)
Vanua Levu
FIJI
Viti Levu Suva
7570
New Caledonia (Fr.)
Nouméa
Is. Loyauté
Lord Howe I. (Aust.)
Norfolk I. (Aust.)
Tasman Sea
Lord Howe Ridge
Auckland
NEW ZEALAND
Cook Strait
Mt. Cook 3753
Christchurch
Invercargill
Dunedin
Wellington
WE
TU
TUVALU
Toke
Tong
Trenc
TONG
10,822
Kermadec Is. (N.Z.)
Kerma Trenc
10,047
Chatha
Bounty Is. (N
Antipodes (N.Z
Auckland Is. (N.Z.)
Campbell I. (N.Z.)

INDIAN
Mid-Indian Ridge
Nouvelle Amsterdam (Fr.)
Îs. St. Paul (Fr.)
OCEAN
Îs. Crozet (Fr.)
Kerguelen (Fr.)
Heard Is. (Aust.)
Macquarie Is. (Austral.)

ft m
18,000 6000
12,000 4000
6000 2000
3000 1000
600 200
0 0
200 600
2000 6000
4000 12,000
6000 18,000
8000 24,000
m ft

Projection: Mollweide's Homolographic
East from Greenwich

1:54 000 000

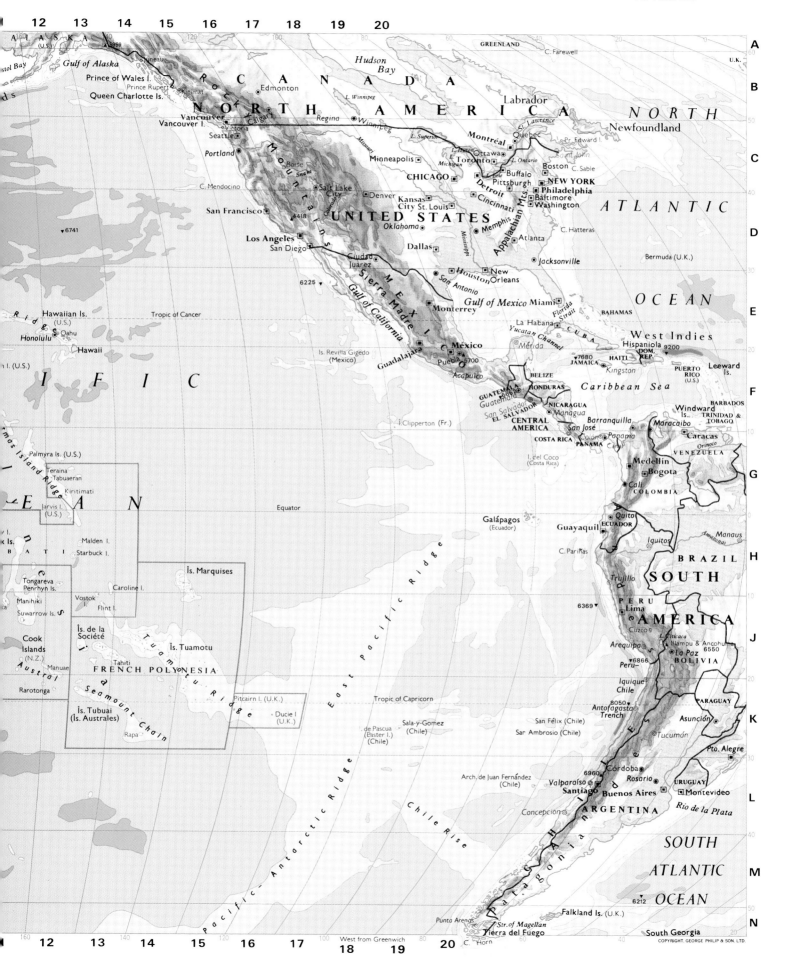

12 **13** **14** **15** **16** **17** **18** **19** **20**

A L A S K A (U.S.)

Gulf of Alaska
Juneau
Prince of Wales I.
Prince Rupert
Queen Charlotte Is.

GREENLAND
C. Farewell
U.K.

Hudson
Bay

C A N A D A

Edmonton
L. Winnipeg

Labrador
Newfoundland

NORTH AMERICA

NORTH

Vancouver
Vancouver I.
Victoria
Seattle

Calgary
Regina
Winnipeg
L. Superior
L. Huron
Montréal
Québec
Pr. Edward I.
Saint John

Portland

Minneapolis
L. Michigan
Ottawa
L. Ontario
Toronto
Detroit
Buffalo
Pittsburgh
Boston
C. Sable

NEW YORK
Philadelphia

ATLANTIC

C. Mendocino

CHICAGO
Cincinnati
Baltimore
Washington

San Francisco
Salt Lake City
Denver
Kansas City
St. Louis
Oklahoma
Memphis

UNITED STATES
Atlanta
C. Hatteras

4418

Los Angeles
San Diego
Dallas
Jacksonville
Bermuda (U.K.)

Ciudad Juárez
Mississippi
New Orleans
Houston
San Antonio
Gulf of Mexico
Miami
Florida
OCEAN

6741
6225

M E X I C O
Sierra Madre
Monterrey
BAHAMAS

Hawaiian Is. (U.S.)
Oahu
Honolulu
Hawaii

Tropic of Cancer

Gulf of California
Is. Revilla Gigedo (Mexico)
México
Puebla
5700
Guadalajara
Acapulco

La Habana
Yucatán Channel
Mérida
CUBA
Florida Strait
HAITI
Hispaniola
DOM. REP.
9200
West Indies

7680
JAMAICA
Kingston
PUERTO RICO (U.S.)
Leeward Is.

P A C I F I C

Palmyra Is. (U.S.)

GUATEMALA
Guatemala
6662
BELIZE
HONDURAS
Caribbean Sea
BARBADOS

San Salvador
EL SALVADOR
NICARAGUA
Managua
Barranquilla
Windward Is.
TRINIDAD & TOBAGO

CENTRAL AMERICA
San José
COSTA RICA
PANAMA
Panamá
Maracaibo
Caracas
VENEZUELA
Orinoco

I. Clipperton (Fr.)

I. del Coco (Costa Rica)

Medellín
Bogotá
Cali
COLOMBIA

Teraina
Tabuaeran
Kiritimati

Jarvis I. (U.S.)

Equator

Galápagos (Ecuador)
Guayaquil
Quito
ECUADOR
Manaus
Iquitos
Amazonas

Malden I.
Starbuck I.

C. Pariñas
Trujillo
BRAZIL
SOUTH

Îs. Marquises

Tongareva
Penrhyn Is.
Manihiki
Suwarrow Is.
Vostok
Caroline I.
Flint I.

6369
PERU
Lima

AMERICA

Cook Islands (N.Z.)
Îs. de la Société
Îs. Tuamotu
Manuae
Tahiti
FRENCH POLYNESIA
Cuzco
L. Titicaca
Arequipa
Illampu & Ancohuma
6550
La Paz
BOLIVIA

Rarotonga
Austral
6866
Perú
Iquique
Chile

Tropic of Capricorn

8050
Antofagasta
Trench
PARAGUAY

Îs. Tubuai (Îs. Australes)
Rapa

Pitcairn I. (U.K.)
Ducie I. (U.K.)
de Pascua (Easter I.) (Chile)
Sala-y-Gomez (Chile)
San Félix (Chile)
San Ambrosio (Chile)
Tucumán
Asunción
Pto. Alegre

East Pacific Ridge

Arch. de Juan Fernández (Chile)
Córdoba
Rosario
URUGUAY

Seamount Chain

6960
Valparaíso
Santiago
Buenos Aires
Montevideo
Río de la Plata

Chile Rise

Concepción
ARGENTINA

SOUTH

ATLANTIC

Pacific - Antarctic Ridge

6212

OCEAN

Punta Arenas
Str. of Magellan
Tierra del Fuego
C. Horn
Falkland Is. (U.K.)
South Georgia

12 **13** **14** **15** **16** **17** West from Greenwich **18** **19** **20**

COPYRIGHT. GEORGE PHILIP & SON. LTD.

1:35 000 000

200 0 200 400 600 800 miles
400 0 400 800 1200 km

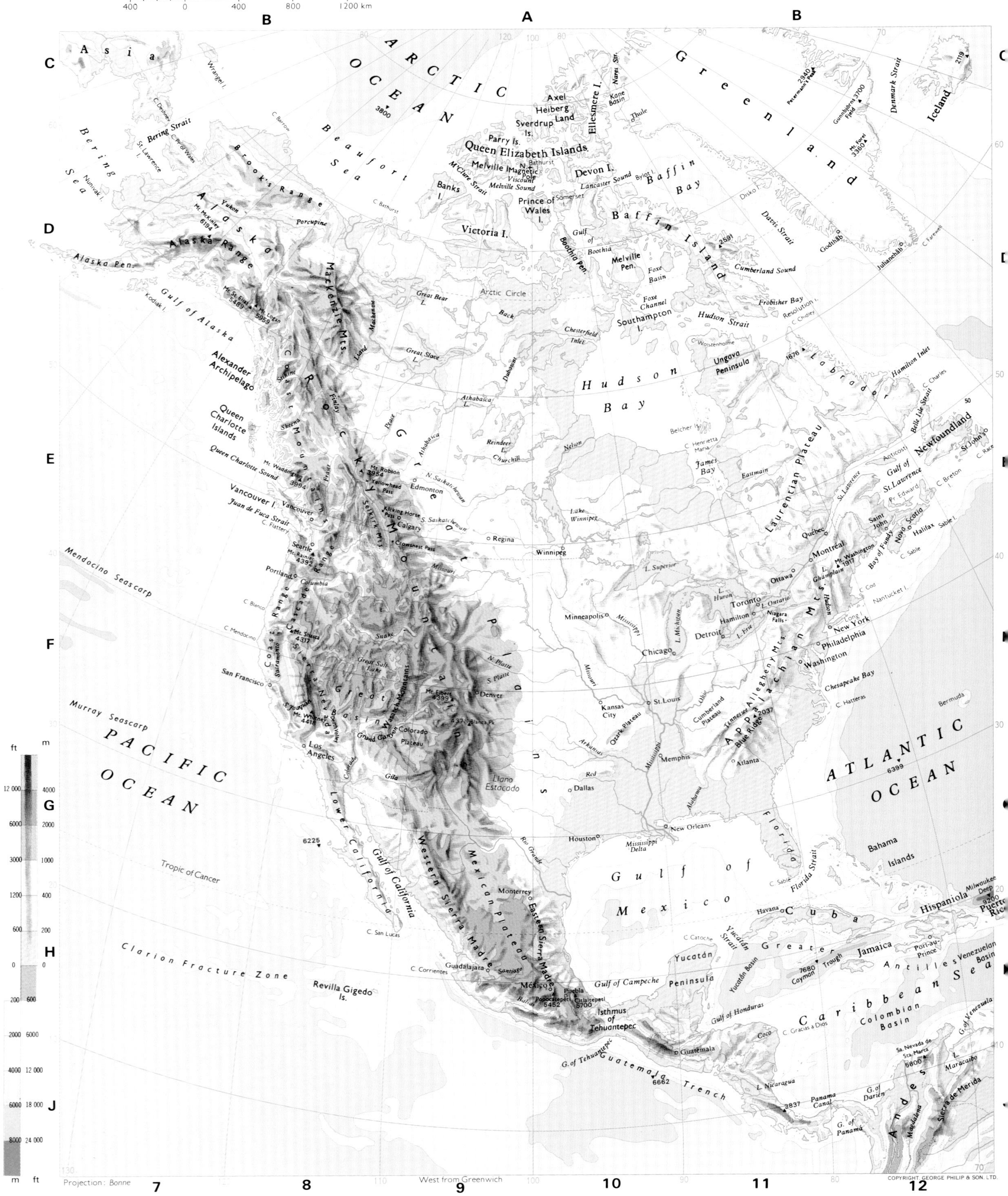

B A B

ARCTIC OCEAN

Asia

Greenland

Iceland

Wrangel I.
C. Dezhneva
Bering Strait
St. Lawrence I.
Cape of Wales
Nunivak I.
Bering Sea
C. Barrow
Brooks Range
Porcupine
Yukon
Alaska
Mt. McKinley 6194
Alaska Range
Alaska Pen.
Kodiak I.
Gulf of Alaska
Mt. St. Elias 5489
Logan 5959
Alexander Archipelago
Queen Charlotte Islands
Queen Charlotte Sound
Vancouver I. Vancouver
Juan de Fuca Strait
C. Flattery
Seattle
Portland
Columbia
Mt. Rainier 4391

Beaufort Sea
C. Bathurst
Banks I.
M'Clure Strait
Viscount Melville Sound
Victoria I.
Great Bear L.
Mackenzie
Mackenzie Mts.
Liard
Coast Mountains
Skeena
Fraser
Great Slave L.
Peace
Athabasca
Athabasca L.
Reindeer L.
Nelson
Churchill
Edmonton
N. Saskatchewan
Mt. Robson 3954
Yellowhead Pass
Kicking Horse Pass
Selkirk Mts.
Calgary
S. Saskatchewan
Crowsnest Pass
Regina

Axel Heiberg Land
Sverdrup Is.
Parry Is.
Queen Elizabeth Islands
Melville I.
Magnetic
Melville Sound
Bathurst
N.
Prince of Wales I.
Somerset I.
Gulf of Boothia
Boothia Pen.
Melville Pen.
Back
Chesterfield Inlet
Hudson Bay
James Bay
Eastmain

Ellesmere I.
Kane Basin
Nares Str.
Thule
Devon I.
Lancaster Sound
Bylot I.
Baffin Island
Baffin Bay
Cumberland Sound
2591
Foxe Basin
Foxe Channel
Southampton I.
Frobisher Bay
Resolution I.
C. Chidley
Hudson Strait
Wolstenholme
Ungava Peninsula
Belcher Is.
C. Henrietta Maria
1676
Labrador
Hamilton Inlet

2940 Petermann Peak
Gunnbjørns 3700 Fjeld
Mt. Forel 3360
Denmark Strait
2119
Godthåb
Julianehåb
C. Farewell
Davis Strait

Arctic Circle

Winnipeg
L. Winnipeg
Minneapolis
Minnesota
Chicago
L. Superior
L. Michigan
L. Huron
Detroit
L. Erie
Toronto
Hamilton
Niagara Falls
L. Ontario
Ottawa
Montreal
Quebec
St. Lawrence
L. Champlain
Mt. Washington 1917
Laurentian Plateau
Gulf of St. Lawrence
Newfoundland
Anticosti I.
C. Breton
Pr. Edward I.
Nova Scotia
Saint John
Bay of Fundy
Halifax
Sable I.
C. Sable
C. Race
St. John's

Mississippi
Missouri
Kansas City
St. Louis
Ozark Plateau
Arkansas
Memphis
Atlanta
Red
Dallas
Mississippi
New Orleans
Houston
Mississippi Delta

Cumberland Plateau
Tennessee
Appalachian Mts.
Allegheny Mts.
2037
Blue Ridge
Washington
Philadelphia
New York
Long I.
Chesapeake Bay
C. Hatteras
Nantucket I.
C. Cod

Bermuda
6399
ATLANTIC OCEAN

Rocky Mountains
Great Plains
Great Basin
Sierra Nevada
Mt. Whitney 4418
Yosemite
Death Valley
Mt. Shasta 4317
San Francisco
Los Angeles
Colorado
Grand Canyon
Colorado Plateau
Mt. Elbert 4397
Denver
Blanca Pk.
Snake
Great Salt Lake
N. Platte
S. Platte
Rio Grande
Gila
Llano Estacado

Mendocino Seascarp
C. Blanco
C. Mendocino
Murray Seascarp

PACIFIC OCEAN

Tropic of Cancer

Clarion Fracture Zone

6225

Gulf of California
Lower California
C. San Lucas
Revilla Gigedo Is.
C. Corrientes
Guadalajara
Santiago

Mexican Plateau
Western Sierra Madre
Eastern Sierra Madre
Monterrey
México
Puebla
Popocatépetl 5452
Orizaba 5700
Guadalajara
Colima
Isthmus of Tehuantepec
G. of Tehuantepec
Guatemala
6662
Guatemala Trench

Rio Grande
Gulf of Mexico
C. Catoche
Yucatán Strait
Yucatán Peninsula
Gulf of Campeche
Gulf of Honduras
Coco
C. Gracias a Dios
L. Nicaragua

Havana
Cuba
C. Sable
Florida
Florida Strait
Bahama Islands
Greater Antilles
Jamaica
Cayman Trough
7680
Yucatán Basin
Colombian Basin
Caribbean Sea
Hispaniola
Puerto Rico
Milwaukee Deep 9200
Port-au-Prince
Venezuela Basin
Venezuela
G. of Venezuela
Maracaibo
Sa. Nevada de Sta. Marta 5800
Panama Canal
3837
G. of Darién
G. of Panamá
Sierra de Mérida
Andes
Magdalena

ft m
12 000 4000
6000 2000
3000 1000
1200 400
600 200
0 0
200 600
2000 6000
4000 12 000
6000 18 000
8000 24 000
m ft

G
H
J

130
Projection: Bonne 7 8 West from Greenwich 9 10 11 12
70
COPYRIGHT GEORGE PHILIP & SON, LTD.

1:35 000 000

| 200 | 0 | 200 | 400 | 600 | 800 miles |
| 400 | 0 | 400 | 800 | 1200 km |

B   **A**   **B**

RUSSIA

ARCTIC OCEAN

C

GREENLAND (Denmark)

Denmark Strait

ICELAND
Reykjavik

Bering Strait

Bering Sea

ALASKA
Arctic Circle
Yukon
Fairbanks
Anchorage

Beaufort Sea

Queen Elizabeth Is.

Baffin Bay

60

D

Gulf of Alaska

Porcupine
INUVIK
YUKON TERRITORY
Whitehorse
Juneau

Victoria I.

KITIKMEOT

BAFFIN

Baffin I.

Godthaab

Davis Strait

Cape Farvel

BRITISH COLUMBIA
Skeena
Fraser
Peace

NORTHWEST TERRITORIES
FORT SMITH
Great Bear L.
Yellowknife
Great Slave L.
Back
Dubawnt

KEEWATIN

Hudson Strait

NEWFOUNDLAND

Labrador

50

E

Victoria
Vancouver
WASHINGTON
Olympia
Seattle
Portland
Columbia
Salem

ALBERTA
Edmonton
Calgary
N. Saskatchewan
Athabasca

SASKATCHEWAN
S. Saskatchewan
Regina

Churchill
Nelson

MANITOBA

L. Winnipeg
Winnipeg

ONTARIO

Hudson Bay

Eastmain

QUEBEC

St. Lawrence
Québec
Montréal

NEW BRUNSWICK
Fredericton
MAINE
Augusta

PR. EDWARD
Charlottetown
NOVA SCOTIA
Halifax
SPM
St. John's

40

F

PACIFIC OCEAN

Sacramento
San Francisco
San Jose
CALIFORNIA

OREGON
Helena
MONTANA
Missouri
IDAHO
Boise
Snake

WYOMING
Cheyenne

NORTH DAKOTA
Bismarck
SOUTH DAKOTA
Pierre

MINNESOTA
Minneapolis
St. Paul

WISCONSIN
Madison
Michigan
MICHIGAN
Lansing

L. Superior
L. Huron
Toronto
Detroit
Cleveland
L. Ontario
Ottawa
Buffalo
NEW YORK
VT.
N.H.
Concord
Albany
MASS.
Boston
Providence
R.I.
Hartford
NEW YORK
Trenton
Philadelphia

Carson City
NEVADA
Salt Lake City
UTAH

Denver
COLORADO
Arkansas

NEBRASKA
N. Platte
Lincoln
KANSAS
Topeka

IOWA
Des Moines
Chicago
ILLINOIS
Springfield
Indianapolis
INDIANA
Columbus
OHIO
Cincinnati
Frankfort
KENTUCKY

Pittsburgh
PENNSYLVANIA
Harrisburg
WEST VIRGINIA
Charleston
Washington
D.C.
Annapolis
Dover
VIRGINIA
Richmond

UNITED STATES

Las Vegas
LOS ANGELES
San Diego
Colorado
Gila

ARIZONA
Phoenix
Tucson

Santa Fe
Albuquerque
NEW MEXICO
El Paso
Red River

Oklahoma City
OKLAHOMA

Jefferson City
MISSOURI
St. Louis
Memphis
ARKANSAS
Little Rock
Nashville
TENNESSEE
Birmingham
MISSISSIPPI
ALABAMA
Montgomery
Jackson
GEORGIA
Atlanta
Columbia
SOUTH CAROLINA
NORTH CAROLINA
Raleigh

Bermuda (Br.)

ATLANTIC OCEAN

30

G

MEXICO

Dallas
TEXAS
Austin
Houston

LOUISIANA
Baton Rouge
New Orleans

Tampa
FLORIDA
Jacksonville

Tallahassee

C. Sable
Str. of Florida
Miami
Nassau
BAHAMAS

Turks & Caicos (Br.)

20

H

Tropic of Cancer

Monterrey

Gulf of Mexico

Havana
CUBA

Cayman Is. (Br.)
JAMAICA
Kingston

HAITI
Port-au-Prince
DOMINICAN REP.
Santo Domingo
San Juan
PUERTO RICO

Guadalajara

Revilla Gigedo Is. (Mexico)

MEXICO

Caribbean Sea

10

J

Belmopan
BELIZE

GUATEMALA
Guatemala
San Salvador
EL SALVADOR

HONDURAS
Tegucigalpa

NICARAGUA
Managua
L. Nicaragua

COSTA RICA
San José

PANAMA
Panamá

Maracaibo

Barranquilla
VENEZUELA

Medellín
COLOMBIA
Bogotá

SOUTH AMERICA

7

Washington Capital Cities

⊙ U.S. State Capitals and Canadian Provincial Capitals

C	CONNECTICUT	N.H.	NEW HAMPSHIRE
D.	DELAWARE	N.J.	NEW JERSEY
D.C.	DISTRICT OF COLUMBIA	R.I.	RHODE ISLAND
M.	MARYLAND	VER.	VERMONT
MASS.	MASSACHUSETTS	SPM	ST. PIERRE ET MIQUELON

Projection: Bonne

West from Greenwich

COPYRIGHT GEORGE PHILIP & SON. LTD.

8   **9**   **10**   **11**   **12**

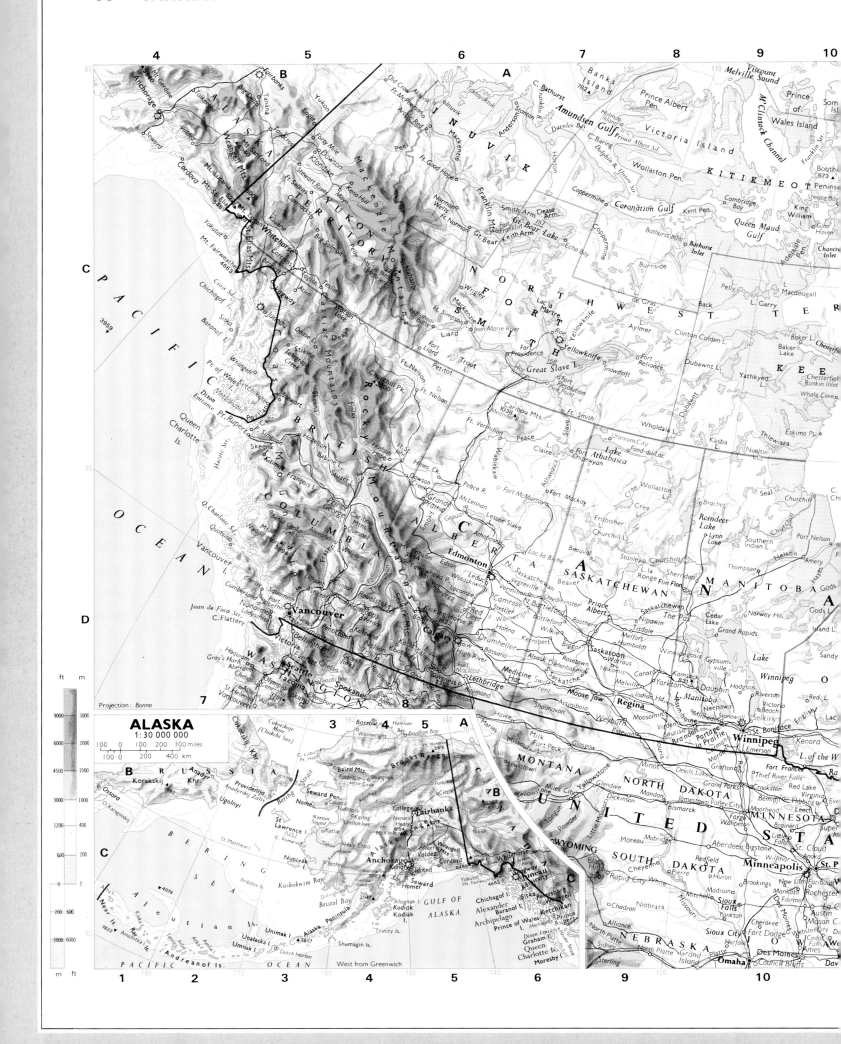

Projection: Bonne

ALASKA
1:30 000 000
100   0   100   200   300 miles
100   0   200   400 km

West from Greenwich

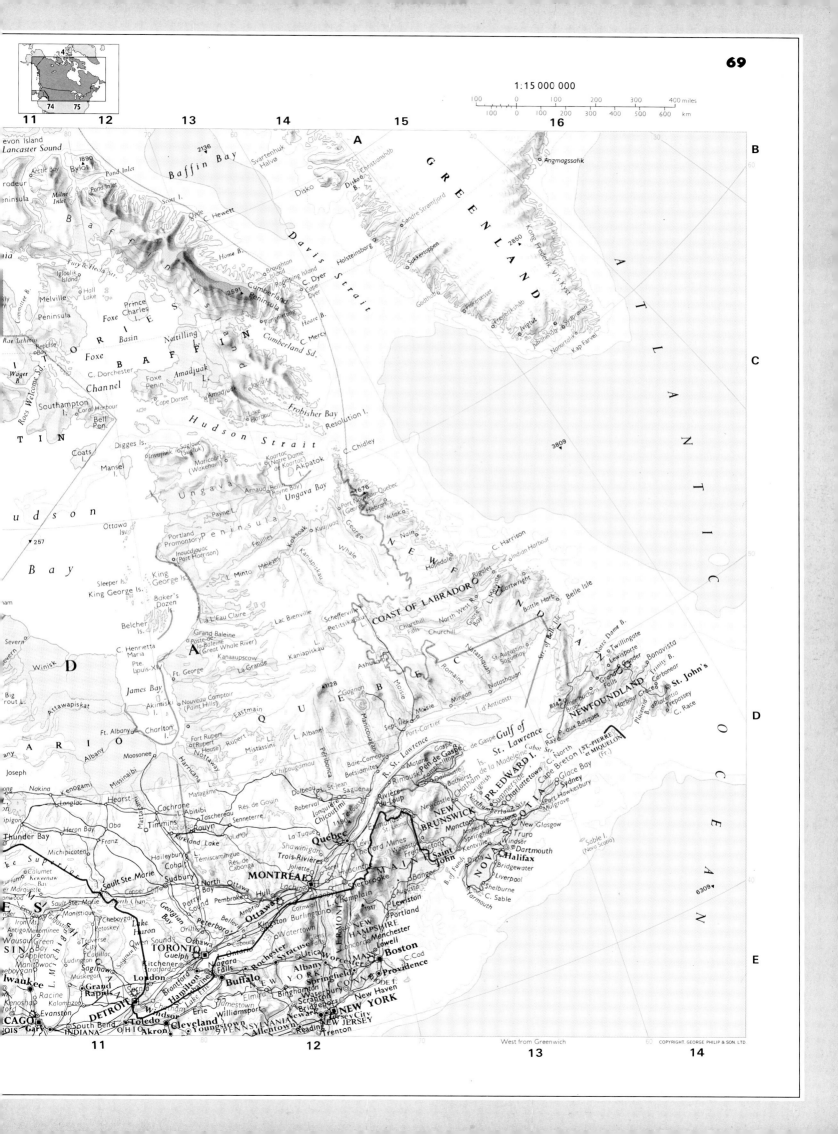

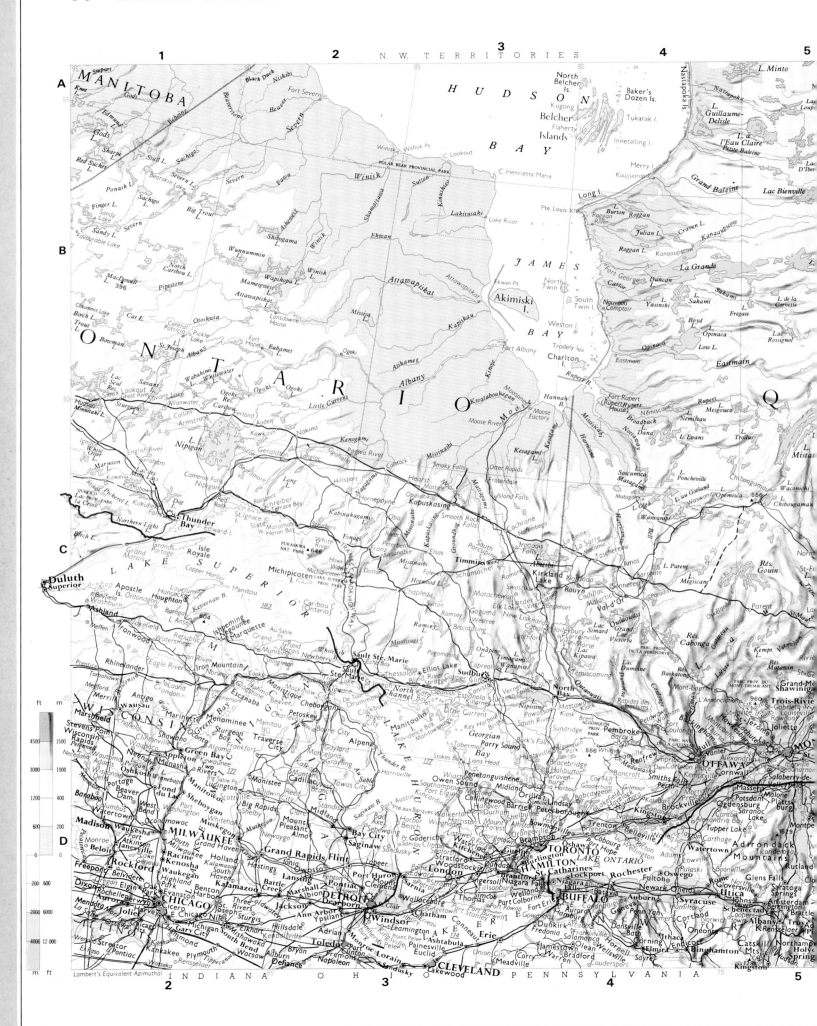

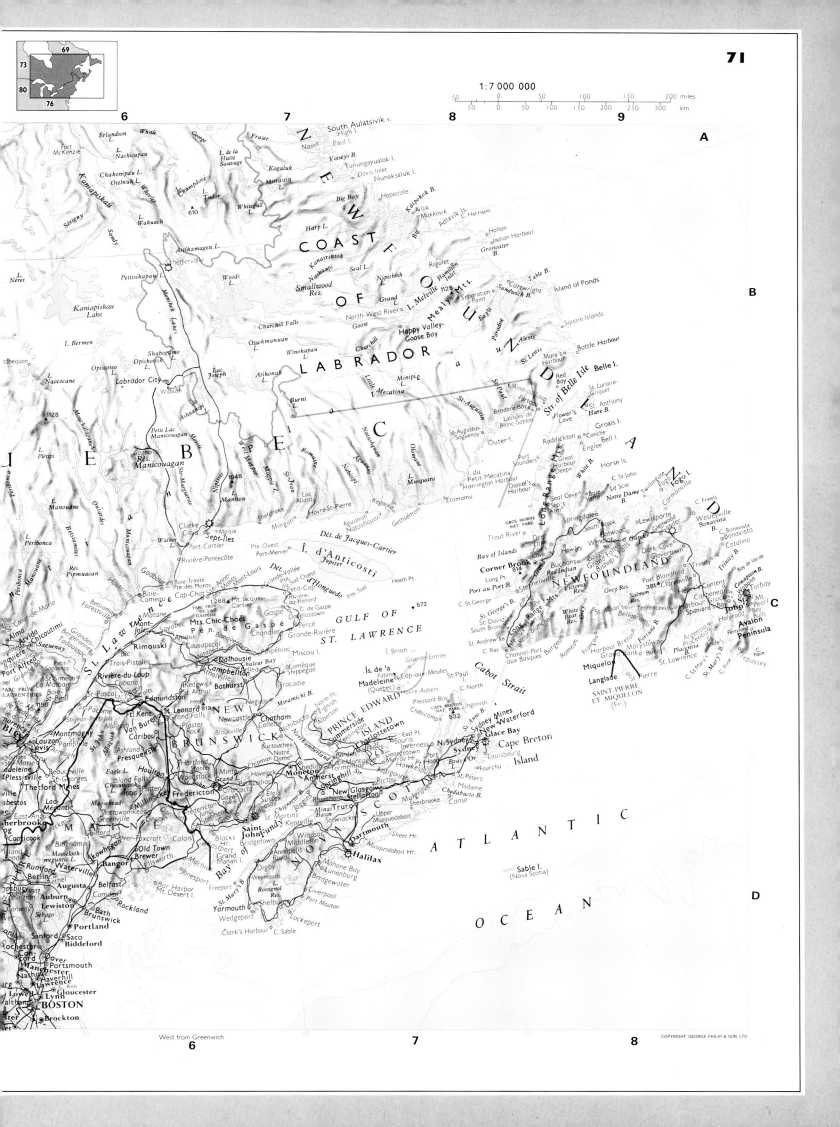

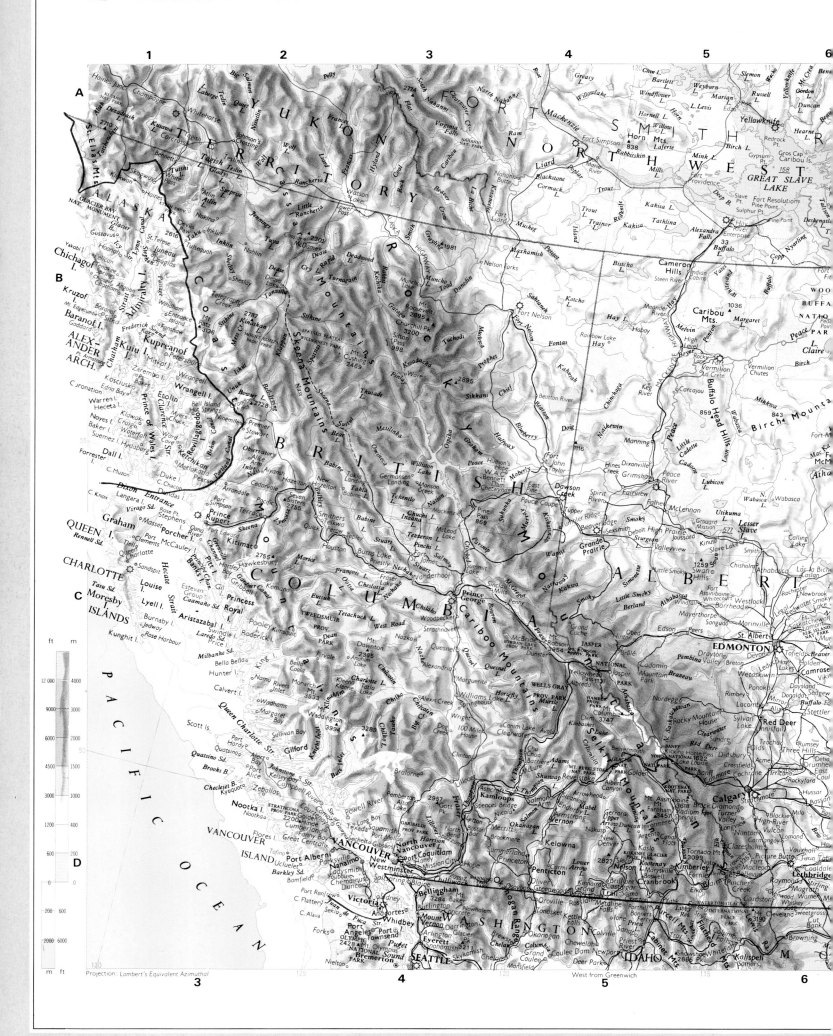

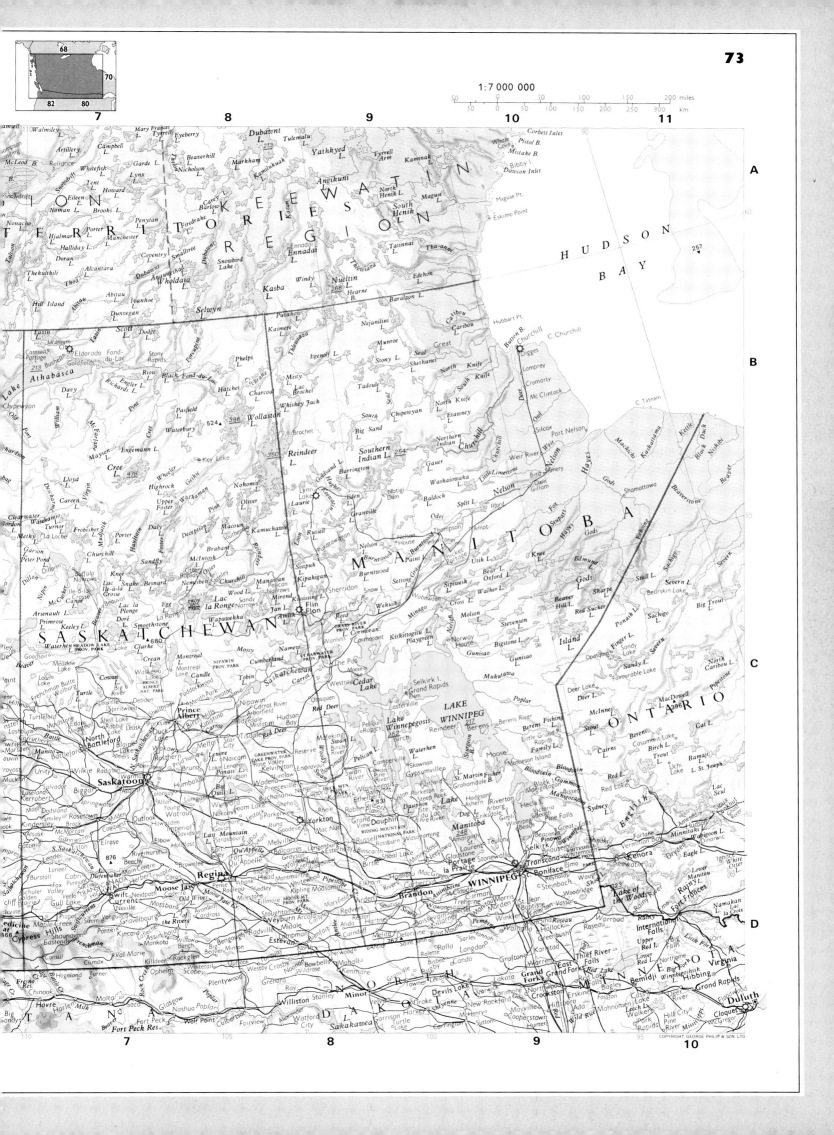

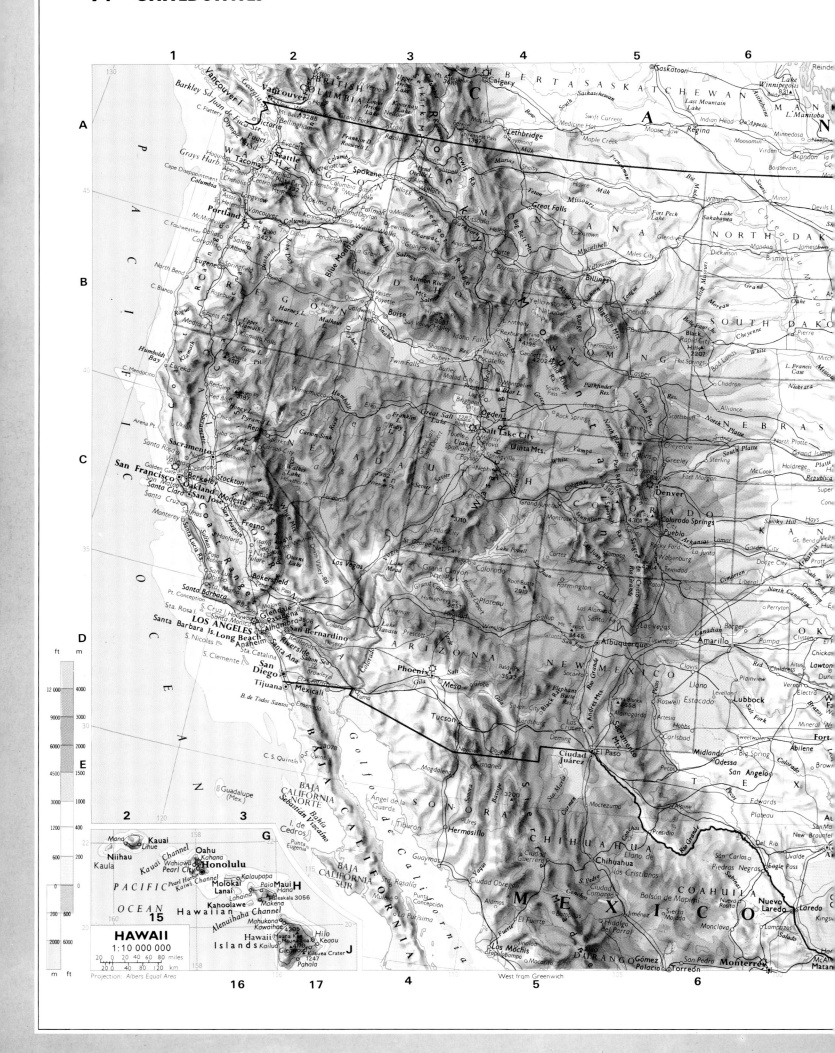

1 2 3 4 5 6

A
B
C
D
E
G
H
J

PACIFIC OCEAN

BRITISH COLUMBIA
ALBERTA SASKATCHEWAN MANITOBA
CANADA

Barkley Sd. Juan de Fuca St.
Vancouver I.
Vancouver
Victoria
Bellingham
Seattle
Tacoma
Olympia
Spokane

WASHINGTON
OREGON
Portland
Salem
Eugene

Saskatoon
Lake Winnipegosis
L. Manitoba
Regina
Moose Jaw
Calgary
Lethbridge
Medicine Hat
Great Falls

MONTANA
Helena
Butte
Billings

NORTH DAKOTA
Bismarck
SOUTH DAKOTA
Pierre

IDAHO
Boise
Idaho Falls
Pocatello
Twin Falls

WYOMING
Yellowstone National Park
Casper
Cheyenne

NEVADA
Reno
Carson City

UTAH
Salt Lake City
Ogden
Provo

Sacramento
San Francisco
Berkeley
Oakland
San Jose
Stockton
Modesto
Fresno

CALIFORNIA
Bakersfield
Santa Barbara
LOS ANGELES
Long Beach
Anaheim
San Bernardino
Riverside
San Diego
Tijuana
Mexicali

Las Vegas

ARIZONA
Phoenix
Mesa
Tucson
Yuma

COLORADO
Denver
Colorado Springs
Pueblo

NEBRASKA
North Platte

KANSAS
Dodge City

Grand Canyon Nat. Park

NEW MEXICO
Albuquerque
Santa Fe
Roswell

Amarillo
Lubbock

TEXAS
El Paso
Ciudad Juárez
Odessa
San Angelo
Midland

OKLAHOMA
Lawton

Abilene

BAJA CALIFORNIA NORTE
Ensenada

SONORA
Hermosillo
Guaymas

CHIHUAHUA
Chihuahua

COAHUILA
Monterrey
Nuevo Laredo
Torreón

DURANGO
Gómez Palacio

MEXICO

2 3

15 16 17 4 5 6

ft m

12 000 4000
9000 3000
6000 2000
4500 1500
3000 1000
1200 400
600 200
0 0
200 600
2000 6000
m ft

PACIFIC OCEAN
Hawaiian Islands

Kauai
Lihue
Niihau
Oahu
Wahiawa
Pearl City
Honolulu
Molokai
Lanai
Maui
Kahoolawe
Hawaii
Hilo

HAWAII
1:10 000 000
20 0 20 40 60 80 miles
20 0 40 80 120 km
Projection: Albers Equal Area

West from Greenwich

1:12 000 000

50   0   50   100   150   200   250   300 miles
50 0 50 100 150 200 250 300 350 400 450 km

68 69
86 87

8   9   10   11   12   13

A

B

C

D

E

F

CANADA

Lake Winnipeg   Trout Lake   L. St. Joseph   Moosonee

Winnipeg   Lake of the Woods   Kenora   Sioux Lookout   Nakina   Kenogami   Missinaibi   Longlac   Hearst

Thief River Falls   Rainy L.   Seine   Ignace   White River   Franz   L. au Goëland   L. Matagami   Rés. de Gouin   Roberval   Rivière-du-Loup   Edmundston   NEW BRUNSWICK

Red Lake   Virginia   Thunder Bay   Royale   Michipicoten I.   Michipicoten   Cobalt   Témiscamingue   Rés. de Baskatong   Trois-Rivières   Grand-Mère   St-Jean   Chicoutimi   Rimouski   Matane

Bemidji   Hibbing   Two Harbors   Laurium   Keweenaw Bay   Whitefish Bay   Sault Ste. Marie   Wawa   North Bay   Ottawa   Buckingham   Hull   Nicolet   Sorel   Québec   Sherbrooke   MAINE   Bangor   Bar Harbor

MINNESOTA   Duluth   Apostle Is.   Bessemer   Ironwood   Ishpeming   Marquette   Escanaba   Manistique   North Chan.   Manitoulin   Parry Sound   Gravenhurst   Huntsville   Pembroke   Arnprior   MONTREAL   Ottawa   St-Hyacinthe   St. Albans   Burlington   VERMONT   Rutland   Farmington   Waterville   Augusta   Penobscot Bay   Rockland

Superior   Ashland   Rhinelander   Antigo   Iron Mt.   Menominee   L. Nipissing   Georgian Bay   Orillia   Lindsay   Peterborough   Kingston   Watertown   Ogdensburg   Plattsburg   Glens Falls   Saratoga   NEW HAMPSHIRE   Concord   Manchester   Lawrence   Lowell   Lynn   C. Cod

Fergus Falls   Brainerd   St. Cloud   Eau Claire   Wausau   Stevens Point   Green Bay   Cadillac   Traverse City   Owen Sound   Barrie   L. Simcoe   Newmarket   Oshawa   TORONTO   Hamilton   Rochester   Auburn   Syracuse   Rome   Utica   Schenectady   Albany   Troy   Pittsfield   Springfield   Worcester   Providence   BOSTON   Brockton   Fall River   New Bedford   Martha's Vineyard

Willmar   Anoka   Minneapolis   St. Paul   Red Wing   Stillwater   Chippewa Falls   Wisconsin Rapids   Appleton   Sheboygan   Manitowoc   Ludington   Muskegon   Midland   Bay City   Saginaw   Flint   Pontiac   Sarnia   London   Brantford   St. Thomas   Niagara Falls   Buffalo   Jamestown   Hornell   Binghamton   Catskill   Poughkeepsie   Mts.   Hartford   Waterbury   New Haven   Bridgeport   Yonkers   NEW YORK   Jersey City

Mankato   New Ulm   Faribault   Rochester   Austin   WISCONSIN   Madison   Milwaukee   Racine   Kenosha   Grand Rapids   Lansing   Ann Arbor   Windsor   DETROIT   Erie   Warren   Youngstown   Oil City   Williamsport   Scranton   Wilkes Barre   Allentown   Reading   Newark   Paterson

Worthington   Mason City   Charles City   Waterloo   Janesville   Rockford   Kenosha   Evanston   CHICAGO   South Bend   Elkhart   Toledo   Sandusky   Lorain   Cleveland   Akron   Canton   Pittsburgh   Altoona   Harrisburg   Lancaster   York   Chester   PHILADELPHIA   Camden   Trenton   NEW JERSEY   Atlantic City

Cherokee   Fort Dodge   Ames   Marshalltown   Cedar Rapids   Clinton   Dixon   Aurora   Joliet   Gary   Ft. Wayne   Lima   Mansfield   Massillon   Wheeling   Johnstown   Cumberland   Hagerstown   Wilmington   Baltimore   DELAWARE   C. May   Delaware Bay

Des Moines   Newton   Iowa City   Davenport   Rock Island   Peoria   Bloomington   Kokomo   Marion   Muncie   Anderson   Dayton   Columbus   Zanesville   Parkersburg   Clarksburg   Fairmont   Frederick   WASHINGTON DC   Annapolis   Salisbury

Council Bluffs   Oskaloosa   Ottumwa   Burlington   Galesburg   Springfield   Decatur   Urbana   Danville   Indianapolis   Terre Haute   Richmond   Kettering   Chillicothe   Portsmouth   Ashland   Charleston   Staunton   Harrisonburg   Charlottesville   Fredericksburg

Red Oak   Shenandoah   Kirksville   Quincy   Hannibal   Jacksonville   ILLINOIS   INDIANA   Bloomington   Vincennes   New Albany   Covington   Cincinnati   Newport   Maysville   Huntington   WEST VIRGINIA   Lynchburg   Petersburg   Richmond   Newport News   Norfolk   Virginia Beach

Beatrice   Atchison   St. Joseph   Chillicothe   Columbia   Mexico   St. Charles   E. St. Louis   St. Louis   Alton   Belleville   Mt. Vernon   Evansville   Owensboro   Louisville   Frankfort   Lexington   Winchester   Somerset   Middlesboro   Bluefield   Roanoke   Danville   Elizabeth City   Albemarle Sd.

Leavenworth   Lawrence   Topeka   Ottawa   Kansas City   Sedalia   Jefferson City   MISSOURI   Rolla   Cape Girardeau   Cairo   Paducah   Hopkinsville   Bowling Green   Green River   KENTUCKY   Kentucky R.   Clarksville   Winston Salem   Greensboro   Durham   Raleigh   Henderson   Rocky Mount   Kinston   Washington   C. Hatteras   Pamlico

El Dorado   Fort Scott   Nevada   L. of the Ozarks   Lebanon   Springfield   Poplar Bluff   Dyersburg   Union City   Nashville   Knoxville   Oak Ridge   Asheville   Hickory   Salisbury   Charlotte   Raleigh   Goldsboro   New Bern   Pamlico Bay

Pittsburg   Parsons   Joplin   Carthage   OKLAHOMA   Fayetteville   Boston Mts.   Newport   Jonesboro   Blytheville   Jackson   Columbia   Chattanooga   TENNESSEE   Athens   Dalton   Greenville   Spartanburg   Union   Florence   Fayetteville   Wilmington   Cape Fear   Onslow Bay

Tulsa   Muskogee   Fort Smith   ARKANSAS   Little Rock   Russellville   Conway   White   Memphis   Florence   Huntsville   Gadsden   Anniston   Athens   Rome   Gainesville   Gastonia   Columbia   SOUTH CAROLINA   Georgetown   Long Bay

OKLAHOMA CITY   McAlester   Durant   Paris   Ouachita Mts.   Hot Springs   Pine Bluff   Clarksdale   Greenwood   Columbus   Tuscaloosa   Birmingham   Bessemer   Newnan   Atlanta   East Pt.   Decatur   Augusta   Aiken   Charleston   C. Royal

Sherman   Greenville   Texarkana   Hope   Camden   El Dorado   Minden   Monroe   Greenville   MISSISSIPPI   ALABAMA   Phenix   Columbus   Macon   Milledgeville   Dublin   Savannah

Dallas   Tyler   Nacogdoches   Marshall   Shreveport   Vicksburg   Jackson   Meridian   Selma   Montgomery   Troy   GEORGIA   Cordele   Waycross   Brunswick

Corsicana   Palestine   Lufkin   Alexandria   LOUISIANA   Natchez   Brookhaven   Laurel   Hattiesburg   Greenville   Andalusia   Dothan   Thomasville   Bainbridge   Valdosta   Jacksonville   St. Augustine

Bryan   Huntsville   Trinity   Neches   Lake Charles   Lafayette   Baton Rouge   Bogalusa   Mobile   Biloxi   Gulfport   Pensacola   Panama City   FLORIDA   Lake City   Gainesville   Palatka   Daytona Beach

Houston   Pasadena   Beaumont   Orange   Port Arthur   New Iberia   NEW ORLEANS   Pontchartrain   Chandeleur Is.   Choctawhatchee B.   Apalachicola   St. George's I.   Tallahassee   Ocala   L. George   Sanford   Orlando   C. Canaveral

Galveston   Freeport   Brazos   Breton Sd.   Delta of the Mississippi   Apalachee B.   St. Marks   Tampa   Clearwater   St. Petersburg   Tampa B.   Bradenton   Sarasota   Lakeland   Plant City   Ft. Pierce   West Palm Beach   Grand Bahama I.   Little Abaco   Gt. Abaco   Freeport

Matagorda I.   GULF OF MEXICO   Charlotte Harb.   Arcadia   L. Okeechobee   Ft. Myers   EVERGLADES   Fort Lauderdale   N.W. Providence Chan.   N.E. Providence Channel   BAHAMAS   Eleuthera I.

Aransas Pass   Rio Grande   C. Sable   Miami   Coral Gables   Florida Bay   Florida Keys   Key West   Andros I.   New Providence   Nassau   Exuma Sound   Cat I.   Long I.

Lake Superior   Lake Michigan   Lake Huron   Lake Erie   Lake Ontario   St. Lawrence   L. Champlain   Adirondack Mts.   ATLANTIC OCEAN

8   9   10   11   12

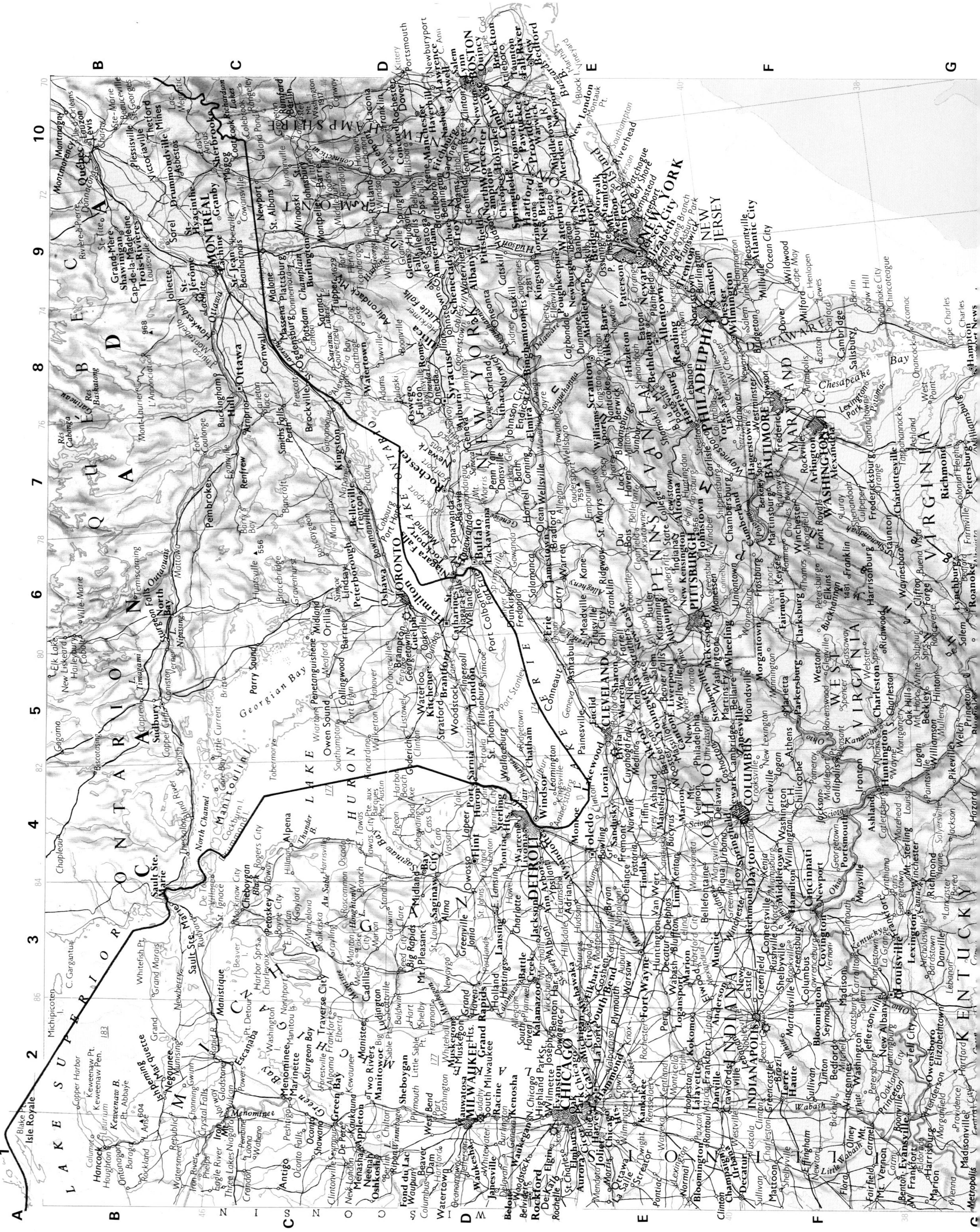
LAKE SUPERIOR
ONTARIO
QUEBEC
MICHIGAN
LAKE HURON
Georgian Bay
LAKE ONTARIO
LAKE ERIE
NEW YORK
PENNSYLVANIA
OHIO
INDIANA
ILLINOIS
WISCONSIN
KENTUCKY
WEST VIRGINIA
VIRGINIA
MARYLAND
DELAWARE
NEW JERSEY
NEW HAMPSHIRE
VERMONT
MASSACHUSETTS
CHICAGO
DETROIT
CLEVELAND
PITTSBURGH
PHILADELPHIA
NEW YORK
BOSTON
TORONTO
MONTREAL
BALTIMORE
WASHINGTON D.C.
MILWAUKEE
COLUMBUS
INDIANAPOLIS
Cincinnati
Buffalo
Rochester
Ottawa
Québec

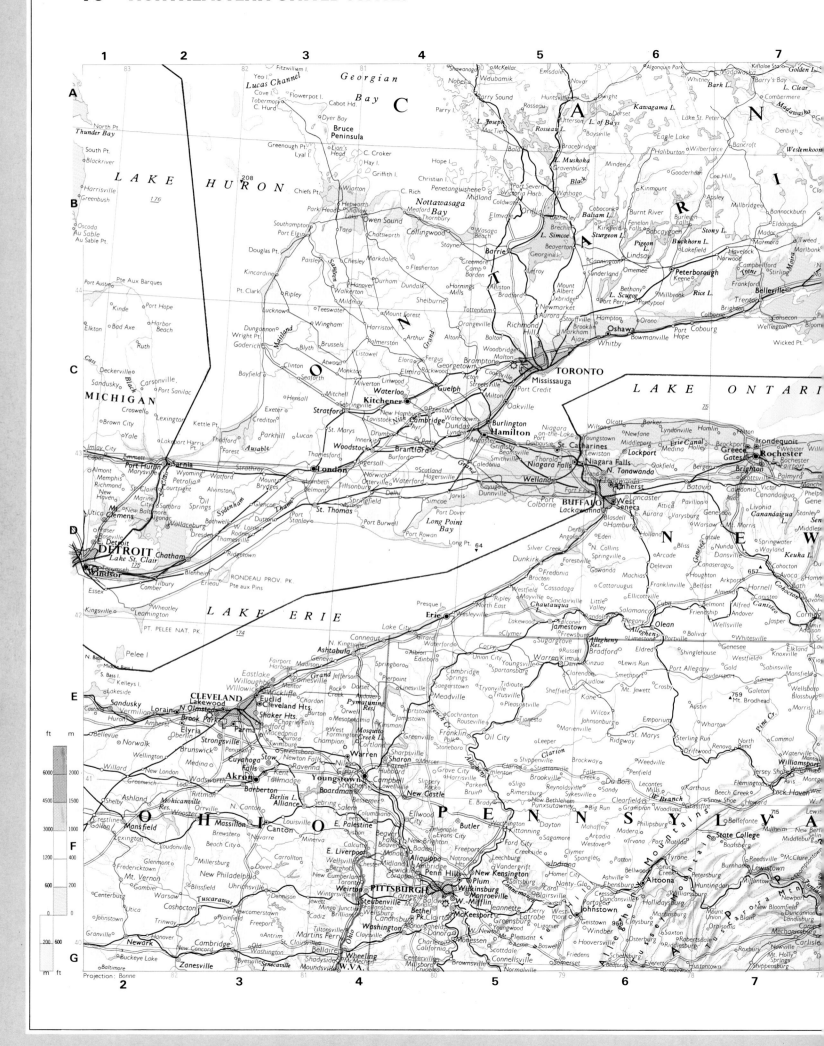

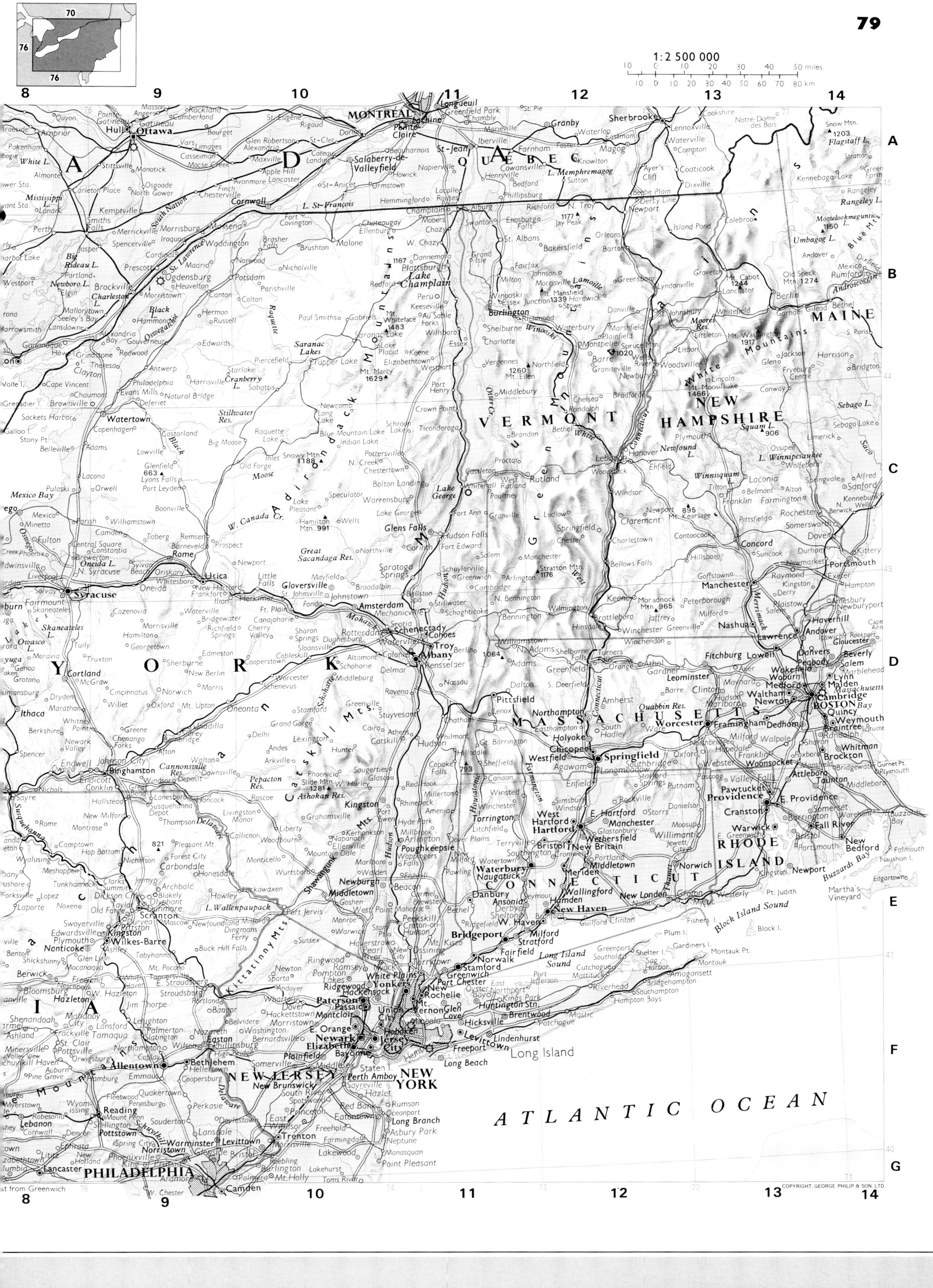

1:2 500 000

10 0 10 20 30 40 50 miles
10 0 10 20 30 40 50 60 70 80 km

ATLANTIC OCEAN

MONTREAL
OTTAWA Hull
QUEBEC
MAINE
VERMONT
NEW HAMPSHIRE
NEW YORK
MASSACHUSETTS
CONNECTICUT
RHODE ISLAND
NEW JERSEY
NEW YORK
PHILADELPHIA
Long Island

Lake Champlain
Cornwall
Watertown
Syracuse
Utica
Rome
Schenectady
Albany
Troy
Boston
Cambridge
Worcester
Springfield
Hartford
New Haven
Bridgeport
Providence
Concord
Manchester
Scranton
Wilkes-Barre
Allentown
Bethlehem
Reading
Lancaster
Trenton
Camden
Newark
Elizabeth
Paterson
Yonkers
Stamford

COPYRIGHT: GEORGE PHILIP & SON LTD.

West from Greenwich

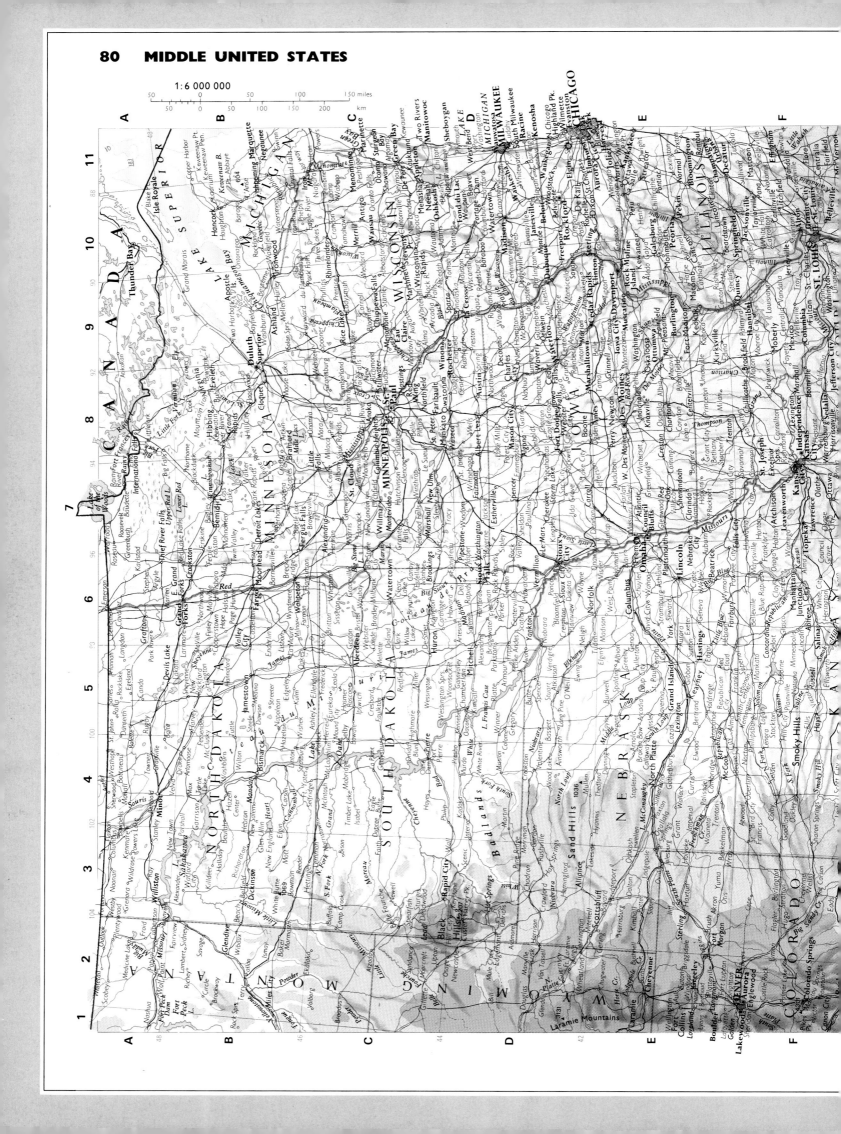

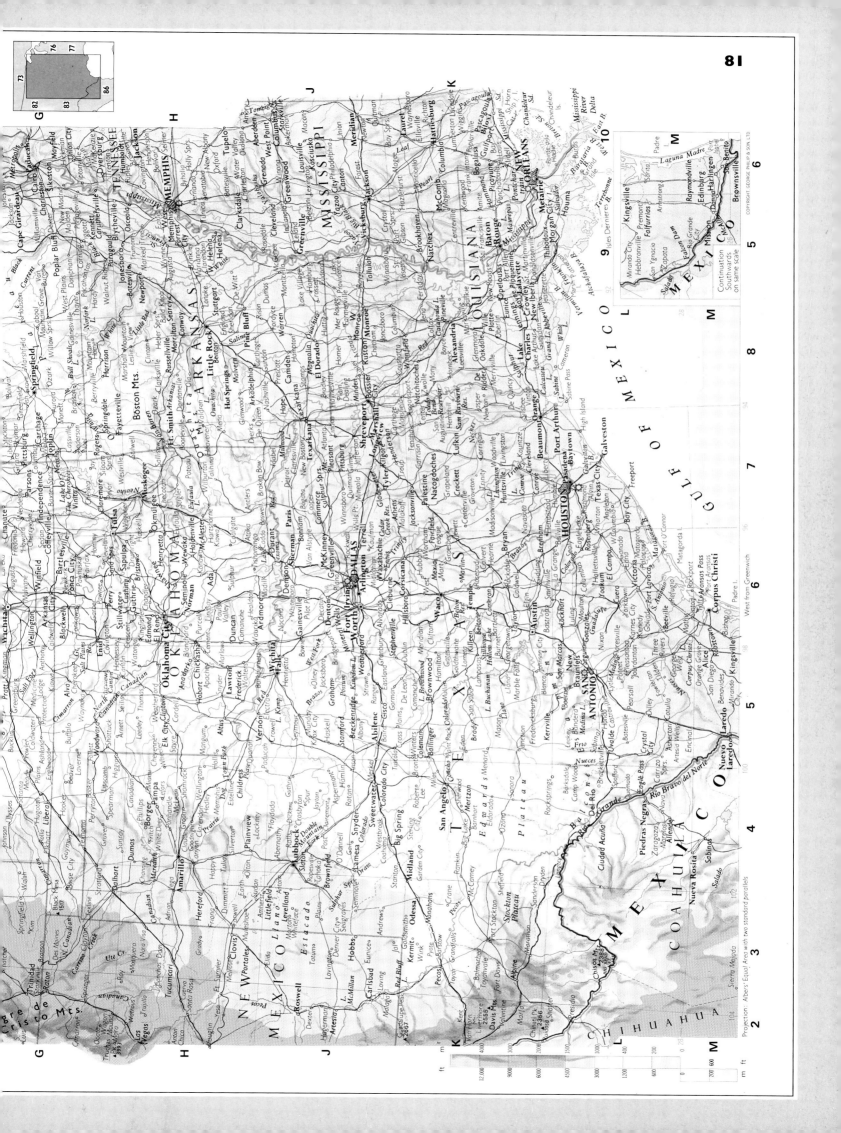

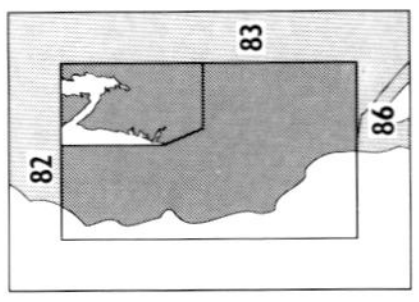

SEATTLE-PORTLAND REGION
On same scale

CANADA

Vancouver Island

Strait of Georgia

Juan de Fuca Strait

Olympic Mountains

WASHINGTON

SEATTLE
Everett
Bellevue
Renton
Kent
Auburn
Tacoma
Lakewood
Parkland
Bremerton

OREGON
PORTLAND
Vancouver
Columbia
Longview

PACIFIC OCEAN

Pahute Mesa

White Mts.

Inyo Mts.

Owens

Sparks
Reno

S i e r r a   N e v a d a

C A L I F O R N I A

Fresno
Clovis
Merced
Modesto
Stockton
Sacramento
Chico

Visalia
Tulare
Hanford

SAN FRANCISCO
Oakland
Berkeley
San Jose
Richmond
Daly City
Palo Alto
Santa Clara
Sunnyvale
Fremont
Hayward
San Mateo
Redwood City
Mountain View
Santa Cruz
Monterey Bay
Pacific Grove
Monterey
Seaside
Salinas

Santa Rosa
Napa
Vallejo
Concord
Walnut Creek
Fairfield
Livermore

Santa Lucia Range

Diablo Range

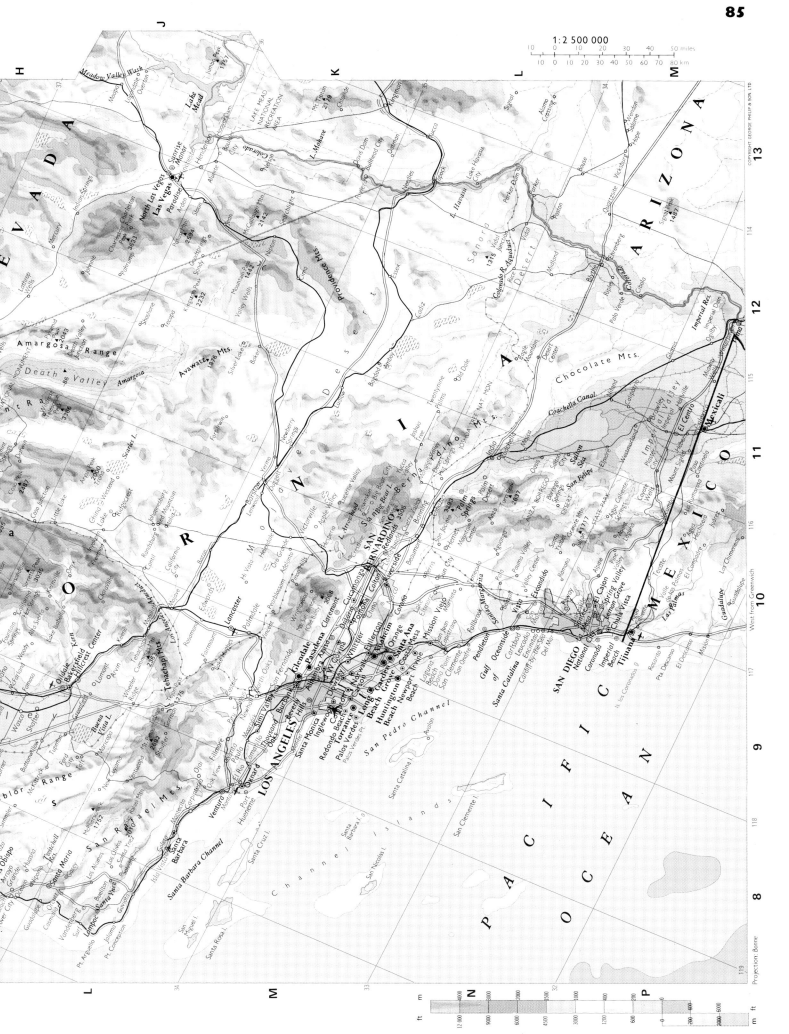

1 : 2 500 000

Projection Bonne

COPYRIGHT GEORGE PHILIP & SON LTD

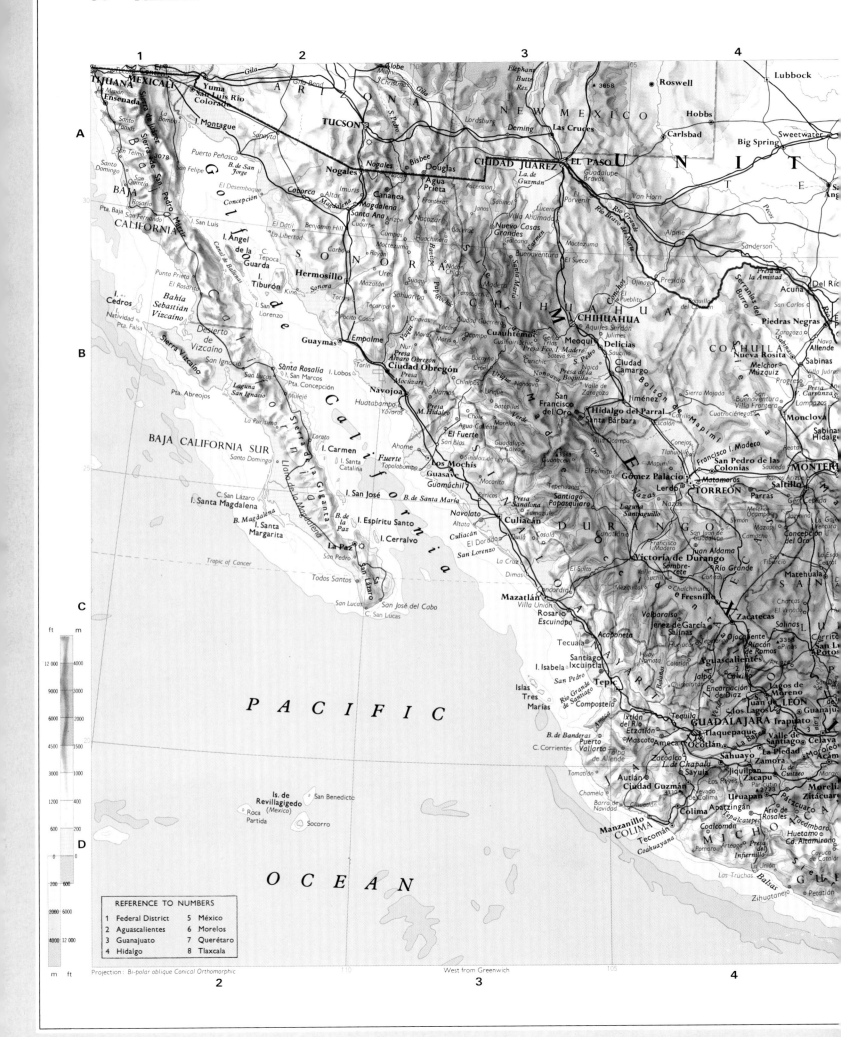

REFERENCE TO NUMBERS

1 Federal District   5 México
2 Aguascalientes   6 Morelos
3 Guanajuato   7 Querétaro
4 Hidalgo   8 Tlaxcala

Projection: Bi-polar oblique Conical Orthomorphic

West from Greenwich

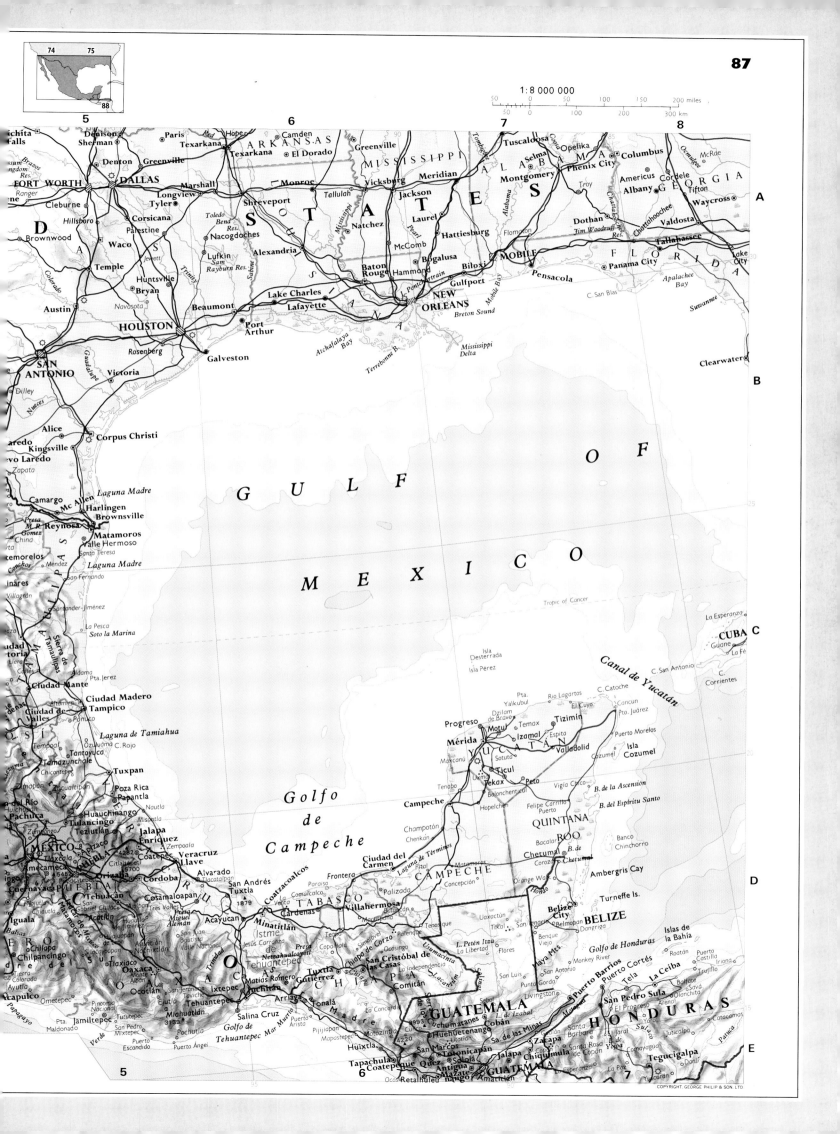

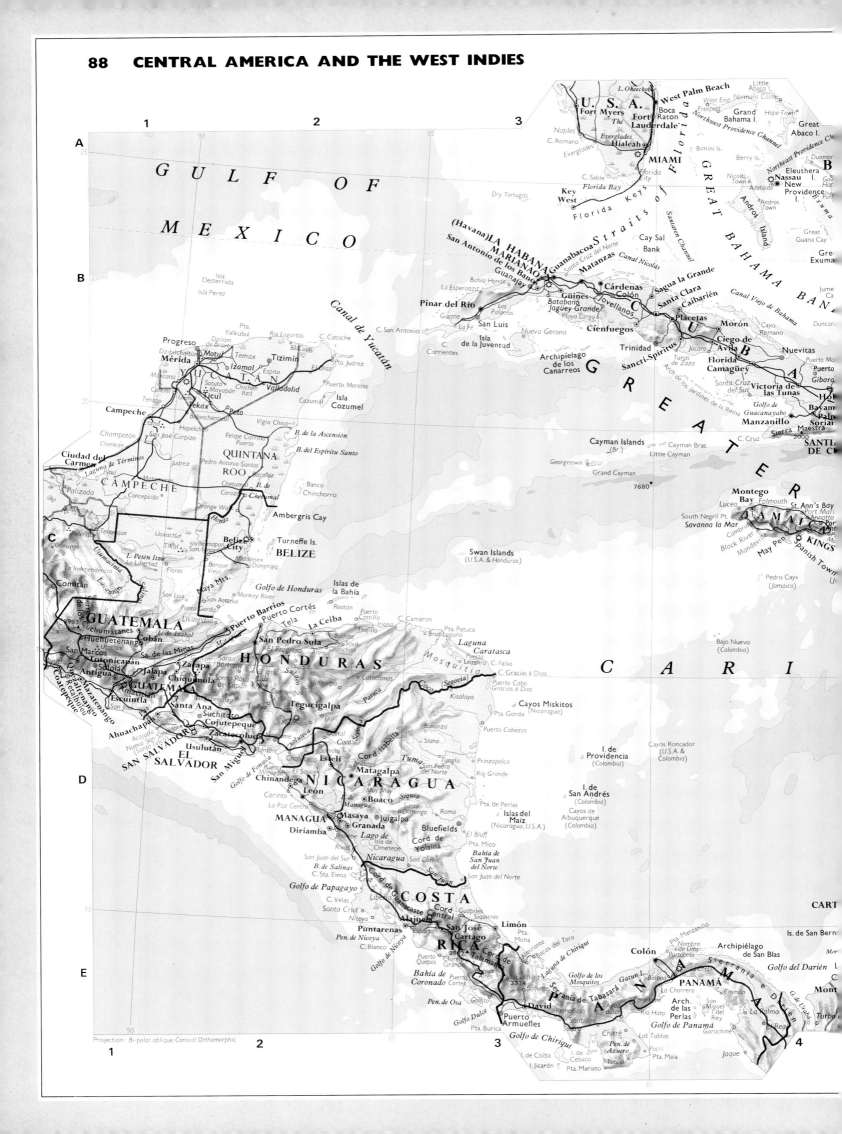

GULF OF MEXICO

U.S.A.

GREATER

CUBA

GREAT BAHAMA BANK

MIAMI

BELIZE

GUATEMALA

HONDURAS

NICARAGUA

EL SALVADOR

COSTA RICA

PANAMÁ

CARI

JAMAICA

Projection: Bi-polar oblique Conical Orthomorphic

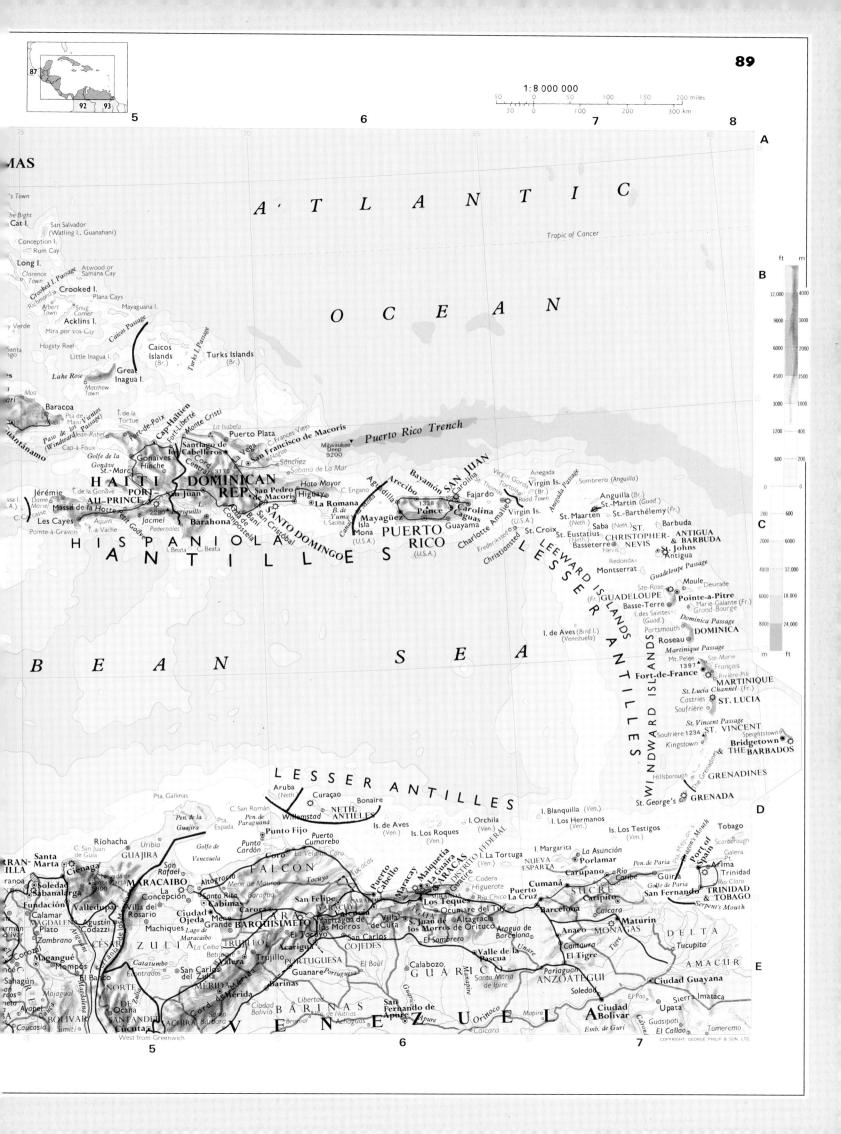

1:30 000 000

100 0 100 200 300 400 500 miles
100 0 200 400 600 800 km

1   2   3   4   5   6

A

Sa. Nevada de Santa Marta
Barranquilla
▲6800
Maracaibo
G. of Darién
Panama Canal
Margarita
Tobago I.
Caracas
Trinidad
ATLANTIC

L. Maracaibo
Cord. de Mérida
Orinoco
Georgetown
C. Orange
OCEAN
5994

B

Medellín
Cali
Bogotá
Cordillera Central
Cordillera Occidental
Cordillera Oriental
Magdalena
Guaviare
Meta
Llanos
Guiana Highlands
2810 ▲Roraima
Sierra Pacaraima
Caroní
Branco
Caquetá
Serra de Tumucumaque

C. de San Francisco
Quito
Cotopaxi ▲5897
Chimborazo ▲6267
Guayaquil
G. of Guayaquil
Pta. Pariñas
Pta. Aguja
Lobos Is.
Equator
Napo
Putumayo
Japurá
Negro
Amazon
Manaus
Marajó I.
Pará
Belém
Fortaleza
C. São Roque

C

Marañón
Juruá
Purus
Selvas
Madeira
Tapajós
Xingu
Tocantins
Araguaia
Aripuanã
Roosevelt
Teles Pires
Plateau of Borborema
C. Branco
Recife

PACIFIC
Huascarán ▲6768
Chile
Peru
Madre de Dios
Guaporé
Mamoré
Brazilian Highlands
São Francisco
Salvador

D

Lima
Chincha Is.
L. Titicaca
Ancohuma & Illampu ▲6550
La Paz
Bolivian Plateau
L. Poopó
Plateau of Mato Grosso
Brasília
Belo Horizonte
2890 ▲Pico da Bandeira
Serra da Mantiqueira
Abrolhos Bank

OCEAN
Trench

E

Tropic of Capricorn
8050
S. Félix
S. Ambrosio
Atacama Desert
Ojos del Salado ▲6863
Tucumán
Gran Chaco
Pilcomayo
Asunción
Paraguay
Iguaçu Falls
Paraná
São Paulo
Rio de Janeiro
C. Frio
Serra do Mar
Uruguay

ft m
18 000 6000
12 000 4000
9000 3000
6000 2000
3000 1000
1200 400
600 200
0 0

F

Salinas Grandes
Córdoba
Sierra de Córdoba
L. Mar Chiquita
Rosario
Entre Ríos
Paraná
Aconcagua ▲6960
Uspallata Pass
Santiago
Valparaíso
Arch. de Juan Fernández
Buenos Aires
La Plata
Montevideo
Rio de la Plata
Pta. Mogotes
Pórto Alegre
Lagoa dos Patos

SOUTH
ATLANTIC

-200 600
-2000 6000
-4000 12000

Colorado
Negro
Bahía Blanca
G. of San Matías
Valdés Peninsula
Argentine Basin

OCEAN

G

Chiloé I.
Chonos Archipelago
Taitao Peninsula
G. of Peñas
▲4058 S. Valentín
Patagonia
Chubut
G. of San Jorge
6212

-6000 18000
-8000 24000

Wellington
Madre de Dios I.
Magellan's Strait
Santa Inés
Cockburn Chan.
Beagle Chan.
C. Horn
West Falkland
Magellan's Strait
Falkland Islands
East Falkland
Tierra del Fuego
Staten I.

H

m ft

Chile Rise

1 : 30 000 000

100　0　100　200　300　400　500 miles
100　0　200　400　600　800 km

1　2　3　4　5　6

COSTA RICA
San José
PANAMA
Colón
Panamá
Golfo de Panamá
Golfo de Darién

Barranquilla
Cartagena
Maracaibo
Barquisimeto
Caracas
Valencia
Port of Spain
TRINIDAD AND TOBAGO

A

Cúcuta
San Cristóbal
Orinoco
Ciudad Guayana

Bucaramanga
VENEZUELA
Georgetown
Paramaribo
Cayenne
C. Orange

Medellín
Magdalena

Bogotá
GUYANA　SURINAM　FRENCH GUIANA

NORTH ATLANTIC OCEAN

B

Cali
COLOMBIA
Orinoco
Esequibo
Branco

C. de San Francisco
Caquetá

ECUADOR
Quito
Japurá
Negro
Amazon (Amazon)
Ilha de Marajó
Belém
Equator

Guayaquil
Napo
Putumayo
Manaus
Santarem
São Luís

G. de Guayaquil
Marañón
Iquitos
Juruá
Madeira
Tapajós
Teresina
Fortaleza (Ceará)

Pta. Aguja
Chiclayo
Purus
Tocantins
Xingu
Araguaia
Parnaíba
C. de São Roque
Natal

Trujillo
Ucayali
Pôrto Velho
Acre
São Francisco
João Pessoa
Recife (Pernambuco)

Chimbote

PERU
BRAZIL
Maceió
Aracaju

Callao
Lima
Cuzco
Madre de Dios
Guaporé
Mamoré
Salvador

Arequipa
L. Titicaca
BOLIVIA
Cuiabá
Brasília
Goiânia

La Paz
Cochabamba
Santa Cruz

D

Sucre
Campo Grande
Ribeirão Prêto
Belo Horizonte
Vitória

Iquique
Paraná
Juiz de Fora
Campos

Tropic of Capricorn
PARAGUAY
Londrina
Campinas
Niterói

Antofagasta
Pilcomayo
Paraguay
Asunción
São Paulo
Santos
RIO DE JANEIRO

Salta
Curitiba

Isla San Felix (Chile)
Isla San Ambrosio (Chile)
San Miguel de Tucumán
Resistencia
Corrientes
Uruguay

E

CHILE
Salado
Pôrto Alegre
Lagoa dos Patos

ARGENTINA
Córdoba
SOUTH

San Juan
Santa Fe
Paraná
Rosario
URUGUAY
Pelotas

Viña del Mar
Valparaíso
Mendoza
BUENOS AIRES
Montevideo
La Plata
Río de la Plata
ATLANTIC

Arch. de Juan Fernández (Chile)
Santiago

Talca
Concepción
Bahía Blanca
Mar del Plata

F

Valdivia
Colorado
Negro
OCEAN

Puerto Montt
Viedma

PACIFIC OCEAN

Chubut

G. de Penas
Golfo Comodoro Rivadavia
San Jorge

G

FALKLAND ISLANDS
West Falkland
(U.K.)
Stanley
East Falkland

Strait of Magellan
Punta Arenas
Tierra del Fuego
Cape Horn

H

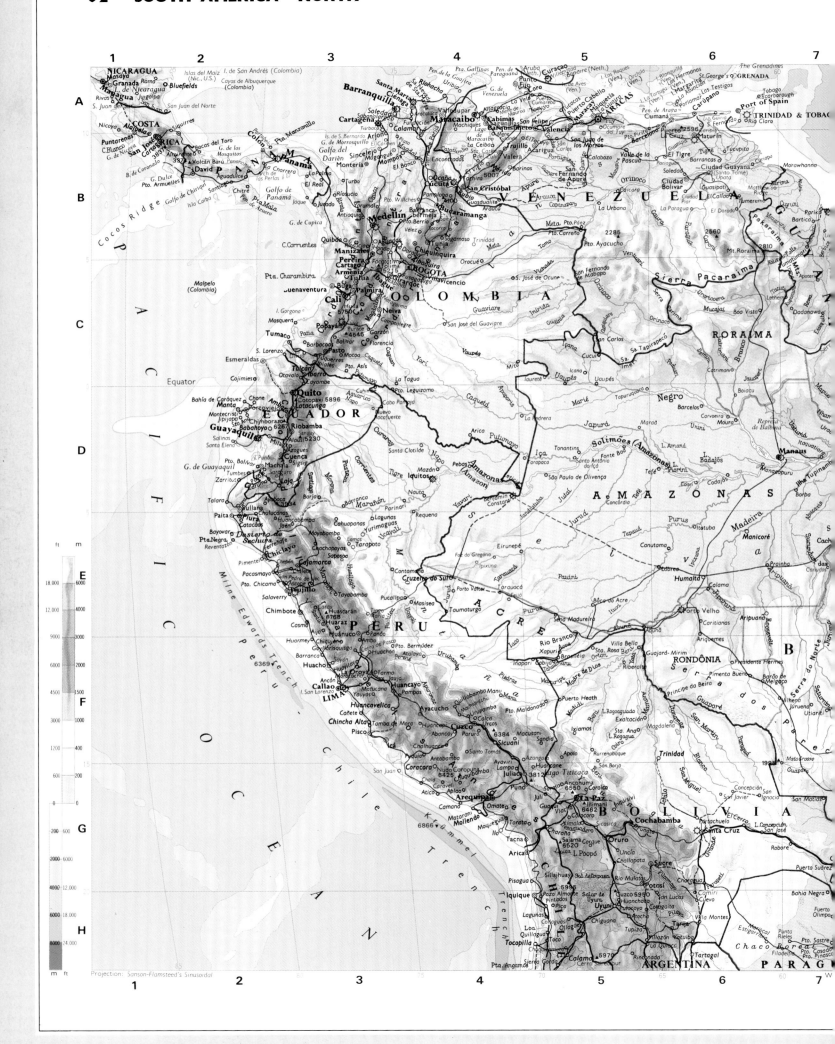

1:16 000 000

100 50 0   200   300 miles
100 0   100 200 300 400   km

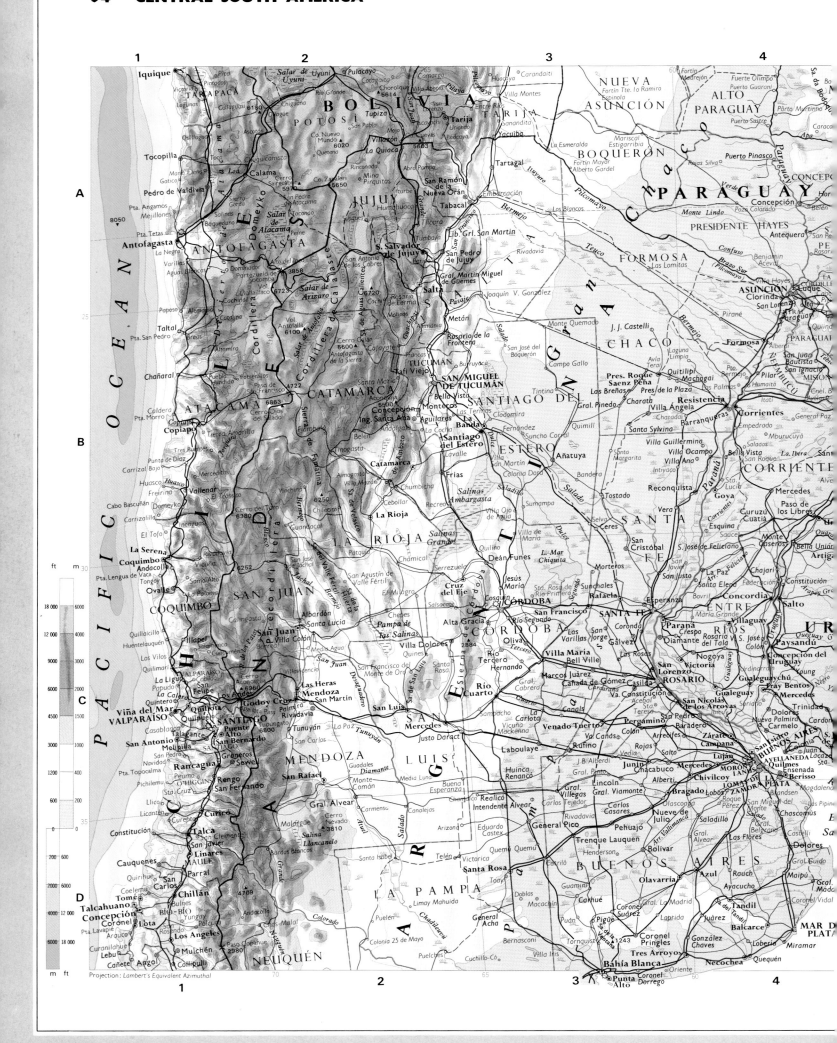

1:8 000 000

50 · 100 · 150 · 200 miles
50 · 100 · 200 · 300 km

BRAZIL

A T L A N T I C   O C E A N

Major cities and places:

BELO HORIZONTE, Vitória, Vila Velha, Guarapari, Itapemirim, Cachoeiro de Itapemirim, Campos, Macaé, Cabo Frio, RIO DE JANEIRO, NITERÓI, São Gonçalo, DUQUE DE CAXIAS, Nova Iguaçu, Petrópolis, Nova Friburgo, Barra do Piraí, Volta Redonda, Angra dos Reis, Mangaratiba, Além Paraíba, Três Rios, Leopoldina, Cataguases, Muriaé, Ubá, Ponte Nova, Ouro Prêto, Itabirito, Congonhas, Conselheiro Lafaiete, Barbacena, São João del Rei, Campo Belo, Oliveira, Lavras, Varginha, Alfenas, Três Corações, Pouso Alegre, Poços de Caldas, Guaxupé, Batatais, Passos, Ribeirão Prêto, Jaboticabal, Mococa, São Sebastião do Paraíso

São Paulo state: SÃO PAULO, SANTO ANDRÉ, São Bernardo del Campo, São Vicente, SANTOS, Mogi das Cruzes, Guarujá, Jundiaí, Sorocaba, Itapetininga, CAMPINAS, Americana, Piracicaba, Limeira, Rio Claro, Araras, Mogi-Mirim, Itu, Botucatu, Avaré, Tatuí, Bauru, Jaú, São Carlos, Araraquara, Catanduva, S. José do Rio Prêto, Mirassol, Olímpia, Bebedouro, Taquaritinga, Matão, Garça, Marília, Tupã, Lins, Penápolis, Birigui, Araçatuba, Andradina, Adamantina, Presidente Prudente, Martinópolis, Rancharia, Assis, Ourinhos, Jacarèzinho, Cornélio Procópio, Santa Cruz do Rio Pardo, Três Lagoas, Mirandópolis, Panorama, Pres. Epitácio, Guaratinguetá, Jacareí, S. J. dos Campos, Taubaté, Pindamonhangaba, Cruzeiro, Lorena

Paraná: CURITIBA, Ponta Grossa, Paranaguá, Antonina, Guaratuba, Irati, Palmeira, Castro, Prudentópolis, União da Vitória, Pato Branco, Guarapuava, Cascavel, Foz do Iguaçu, Guaíra, Umuarama, Cianorte, Paranavaí, Maringá, Londrina, Arapongas, Apucarana, Mandaguari, Jaguariaíva, Itararé, Apiaí, Registro, Iguape, Cananéia, Ilha Comprida, Ilha do Cardoso, Ilha de São Sebastião, Itanhaém

Santa Catarina: Florianópolis, Ilha de Santa Catarina, Itajaí, Brusque, Blumenau, Joinvile, São Francisco do Sul, Mafra, Rio Negro, Caçador, Rio do Sul, Lajes, Campos Novos, Joaçaba, Chapecó, Tubarão, Laguna, Criciúma, Araranguá

Rio Grande do Sul: PORTO ALEGRE, Canoas, São Leopoldo, Nôvo Hamburgo, Taquara, Viamão, Osório, Montenegro, Caxias do Sul, Bento Gonçalves, Guaporé, Vacaria, Passo Fundo, Caràzinho, Cruz Alta, Santa Maria, Santa Cruz do Sul, Cachoeira do Sul, Rio Pardo, São Gabriel, Santana do Livramento, Dom Pedrito, Bagé, Pelotas, Rio Grande, Lagoa dos Patos, Lagoa Mirim, Jaguarão, São Luís Gonzaga, Santo Ângelo, Santa Rosa, Erechim, Uruguaiana, Alegrete, Santiago, São Borja, Ijuí

Uruguay / Argentina border region: MONTEVIDEO, Maldonado, Rocha, Treinta y Tres, Melo, Minas, San Carlos, Aigua, José Batlle y Ordóñez, Santa Clara de Olimar, Río Branco, Rivera, Tacuarembó, Lascano

Misiones: Posadas, Encarnación, Obera, Leandro N. Alem, Apóstoles, San Javier, Eldorado, Bernardo de Irigoyen

Iguaçu Falls, Itaipú Dam, Paraná, Pedro Juan Caballero, Ponta Porã, Dourados, Maracaju

MATO GROSSO DO SUL

Tropic of Capricorn

5304

West from Greenwich

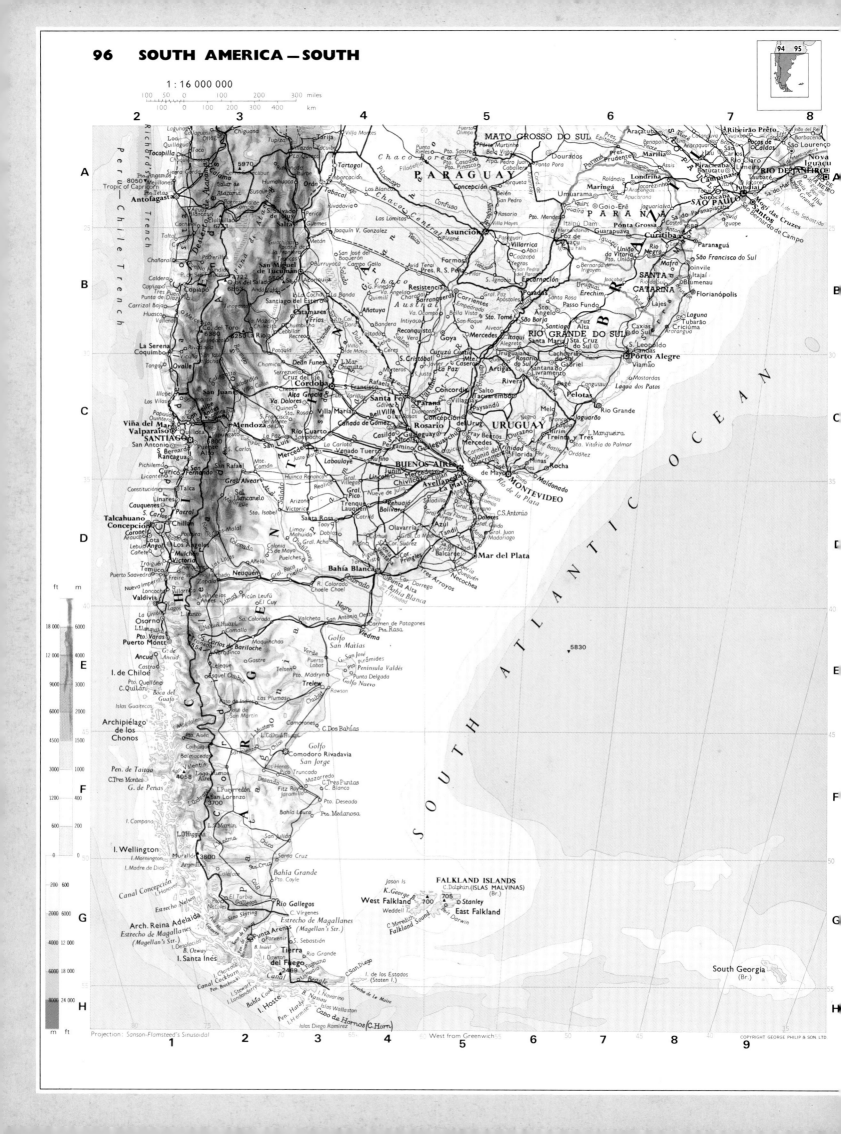

INDEX

The index contains the names of all the principal places and features shown on the World Maps. Each name is followed by an additional entry in italics giving the country or region within which it is located. The alphabetical order of names composed of two or more words is governed primarily by the first word and then by the second. This is an example of the rule:

Mīr Kūh, *Iran*	**45 E8**	26 22 N	58 55 E
Mīr Shahdād, *Iran*	**45 E8**	26 15 N	58 29 E
Miraj, *India*	**40 L9**	16 50 N	74 45 E
Miram Shah, *Pakistan*	**42 C4**	33 0 N	70 2 E
Miramar, *Mozam.*	**57 C6**	23 50 S	35 35 E

Physical features composed of a proper name (Erie) and a description (Lake) are positioned alphabetically by the proper name. The description is positioned after the proper name and is usually abbreviated:

Erie, L., *N. Amer.*	**78 D3**	42 15 N	81 0 W

Where a description forms part of a settlement or administrative name, however, it is always written in full and put in its true alphabetic position:

Mount Morris, *U.S.A.*	**78 D7**	42 44 N	77 52 W

Names beginning with M' and Mc are indexed as if they were spelled Mac. Names beginning St. are alphabetized under Saint, but Sankt, Sint, Sant', Santa and San are all spelled in full and are alphabetized accordingly. If the same place name occurs two or more times in the index and all are in the same country, each is followed by the name of the administrative subdivision in which it is located. The names are placed in the alphabetical order of the subdivisions. For example:

Jackson, *Ky., U.S.A.*	**76 G4**	37 33 N	83 23 W
Jackson, *Mich., U.S.A.*	**76 D3**	42 15 N	84 24 W
Jackson, *Minn., U.S.A.*	**80 D7**	43 37 N	95 1 W

The number in bold type which follows each name in the index refers to the number of the map page where that feature or place will be found. This is usually the largest scale at which the place or feature appears.

The letter and figure which are in bold type immediately after the page number give the grid square on the map page, within which the feature is situated. The letter represents the latitude and the figure the longitude.

In some cases the feature itself may fall within the specified square, while the name is outside. This is usually the case only with features which are larger than a grid square.

For a more precise location the geographical coordinates which follow the letter/figure references give the latitude and the longitude of each place. The first set of figures represent the latitude which is the distance north or south of the Equator measured as an angle at the centre of the Earth. The Equator is latitude 0°, the North Pole is 90°N, and the South Pole 90°S.

The second set of figures represent the longitude, which is the distance East or West of the prime meridian, which runs through Greenwich, England. Longitude is also measured as an angle at the centre of the earth and is given East or West of the prime meridian, from 0° to 180° in either direction.

The unit of measurement for latitude and longitude is the degree, which is subdivided into 60 minutes. Each index entry states the position of a place in degrees and minutes,
a space being left between the degrees and the minutes.

The latitude is followed by N(orth) or S(outh) and the longitude by E(ast) or W(est).

Rivers are indexed to their mouths or confluences, and carry the symbol → after their names. A solid square ■ follows the name of a country while, an open square □ refers to a first order administrative area.

Abbreviations used in the index

A.C.T. — Australian Capital Territory
Afghan. — Afghanistan
Ala. — Alabama
Alta. — Alberta
Amer. — America(n)
Arch. — Archipelago
Ariz. — Arizona
Ark. — Arkansas
Atl. Oc. — Atlantic Ocean
B. — Baie, Bahía, Bay, Bucht, Bugt
B.C. — British Columbia
Bangla. — Bangladesh
Barr. — Barrage
Bos. & H. — Bosnia and Herzegovina
C. — Cabo, Cap, Cape, Coast
C.A.R. — Central African Republic
C. Prov. — Cape Province
Calif. — California
Cent. — Central
Chan. — Channel
Colo. — Colorado
Conn. — Connecticut
Cord. — Cordillera
Cr. — Creek
D.C. — District of Columbia
Del. — Delaware
Dep. — Dependency
Des. — Desert
Dist. — District
Dj. — Djebel
Domin. — Dominica
Dom. Rep. — Dominican Republic
E. — East
El Salv. — El Salvador

Eq. Guin. — Equatorial Guinea
Fla. — Florida
Falk. Is. — Falkland Is.
G. — Golfe, Golfo, Gulf, Guba, Gebel
Ga. — Georgia
Gt. — Great, Greater
Guinea-Biss. — Guinea-Bissau
H.K. — Hong Kong
H.P. — Himachal Pradesh
Hants. — Hampshire
Harb. — Harbor, Harbour
Hd. — Head
Hts. — Heights
I.(s). — Île, Ilha, Insel, Isla, Island, Isle
Ill. — Illinois
Ind. — Indiana
Ind. Oc. — Indian Ocean
Ivory C. — Ivory Coast
J. — Jabal, Jebel, Jazira
Junc. — Junction
K. — Kap, Kapp
Kans. — Kansas
Kep. — Kepulauan
Ky. — Kentucky
L. — Lac, Lacul, Lago, Lagoa, Lake, Limni, Loch, Lough
La. — Louisiana
Liech. — Liechtenstein
Lux. — Luxembourg
Mad. P. — Madhya Pradesh
Madag. — Madagascar
Man. — Manitoba
Mass. — Massachusetts
Md. — Maryland

Me. — Maine
Medit. S. — Mediterranean Sea
Mich. — Michigan
Minn. — Minnesota
Miss. — Mississippi
Mo. — Missouri
Mont. — Montana
Mozam. — Mozambique
Mt.(e). — Mont, Monte, Monti, Montaña, Mountain
N. — Nord, Norte, North, Northern, Nouveau
N.B. — New Brunswick
N.C. — North Carolina
N. Cal. — New Caledonia
N. Dak. — North Dakota
N.H. — New Hampshire
N.I. — North Island
N.J. — New Jersey
N. Mex. — New Mexico
N.S. — Nova Scotia
N.S.W. — New South Wales
N.W.T. — North West Territory
N.Y. — New York
N.Z. — New Zealand
Nebr. — Nebraska
Neths. — Netherlands
Nev. — Nevada
Nfld. — Newfoundland
Nic. — Nicaragua
O. — Oued, Ouadi
Occ. — Occidentale
O.F.S. — Orange Free State
Okla. — Oklahoma
Ont. — Ontario
Or. — Orientale

Oreg. — Oregon
Os. — Ostrov
Oz. — Ozero
P. — Pass, Passo, Pasul, Pulau
P.E.I. — Prince Edward Island
Pa. — Pennsylvania
Pac. Oc. — Pacific Ocean
Papua N.G. — Papua New Guinea
Pass. — Passage
Pen. — Peninsula, Péninsule
Phil. — Philippines
Pk. — Park, Peak
Plat. — Plateau
P-ov. — Poluostrov
Prov. — Province, Provincial
Pt. — Point
Pta. — Ponta, Punta
Pte. — Pointe
Qué. — Québec
Queens. — Queensland
R. — Rio, River
R.I. — Rhode Island
Ra.(s). — Range(s)
Raj. — Rajasthan
Reg. — Region
Rep. — Republic
Res. — Reserve, Reservoir
S. — San, South, Sea
Si. Arabia — Saudi Arabia
S.C. — South Carolina
S. Dak. — South Dakota
S.I. — South Island
S. Leone — Sierra Leone
Sa. — Serra, Sierra
Sask. — Saskatchewan
Scot. — Scotland

Sd. — Sound
Sev. — Severnaya
Sib. — Siberia
Sprs. — Springs
St. — Saint, Sankt, Sint
Sta. — Santa, Station
Ste. — Sainte
Sto. — Santo
Str. — Strait, Stretto
Switz. — Switzerland
Tas. — Tasmania
Tenn. — Tennessee
Tex. — Texas
Tg. — Tanjung
Trin. & Tob. — Trinidad & Tobago
U.A.E. — United Arab Emirates
U.K. — United Kingdom
U.S.A. — United States of America
Ut. P. — Uttar Pradesh
Va. — Virginia
Vdkhr. — Vodokhranilishche
Vf. — Vîrful
Vic. — Victoria
Vol. — Volcano
Vt. — Vermont
W. — Wadi, West
W. Va. — West Virginia
Wash. — Washington
Wis. — Wisconsin
Wlkp. — Wielkopolski
Wyo. — Wyoming
Yorks. — Yorkshire

A Coruña

A

A Coruña = La Coruña, Spain 19 A1 43 20N 8 25W
Aachen, Germany 16 C3 50 47N 6 4 E
Aalborg = Ålborg, Denmark 9 H10 57 2N 9 54 E
A'âli en Nîl □, Sudan 51 G11 9 30N 31 30 E
Aalsmeer, Neths. 15 B4 52 17N 4 43 E
Aalst, Belgium 15 D4 50 56N 4 2 E
Aalten, Neths. 15 C6 51 56N 6 35 E
Aarau, Switz. 16 E4 47 23N 8 4 E
Aare →, Switz. 16 E4 47 33N 8 14 E
Aarhus = Århus, Denmark 9 H11 56 8N 10 11 E
Aarschot, Belgium 15 D4 50 59N 4 49 E
Aba, Nigeria 50 G6 5 10N 7 19 E
Aba, Zaïre 54 B3 3 58N 30 17 E
Ābādān, Iran 45 D6 30 22N 48 20 E
Ābādeh, Iran 45 D7 31 8N 52 40 E
Abadla, Algeria 50 B4 31 2N 2 45W
Abaetetuba, Brazil 93 D9 1 40S 48 50W
Abagnar Qi, China 34 C9 43 52N 116 2 E
Abai, Paraguay 95 B4 25 58S 55 54W
Abakan, Russia 27 D10 53 40N 91 10 E
Abancay, Peru 92 F4 13 35S 72 55W
Abariringa, Kiribati 64 H10 2 50S 171 40W
Abarqū, Iran 45 D7 31 10N 53 20 E
Abashiri, Japan 30 B12 44 0N 144 15 E
Abashiri-Wan, Japan 30 B12 44 0N 144 30 E
Abay, Kazakhstan 26 E8 49 38N 72 53 E
Abaya, L., Ethiopia 51 G12 6 30N 37 50 E
Abaza, Russia 26 D10 52 39N 90 6 E
'Abbāsābād, Iran 45 C8 33 34N 58 23 E
Abbay = Nîl el Azraq →, Sudan 51 E11 15 38N 32 31 E
Abbaye, Pt., U.S.A. 76 B1 46 58N 88 8W
Abbeville, France 18 A4 50 6N 1 49 E
Abbeville, La., U.S.A. 81 K8 29 58N 92 8W
Abbeville, S.C., U.S.A. 77 H4 34 11N 82 23W
Abbieglassie, Australia 63 D4 27 15S 147 28 E
Abbot Ice Shelf, Antarctica 5 D16 73 0S 92 0W
Abbotsford, Canada 72 D4 49 5N 122 20W
Abbotsford, U.S.A. 80 C9 44 57N 90 19W
Abbottabad, Pakistan 42 B5 34 10N 73 15 E
Abd al Kūrī, Ind. Oc. 46 E5 12 5N 52 20 E
Ābdar, Iran 45 D7 30 16N 55 19 E
'Abdolābād, Iran 45 C8 34 12N 56 30 E
Abéché, Chad 51 F9 13 50N 20 35 E
Åbenrå, Denmark 9 J10 55 3N 9 25 E
Abeokuta, Nigeria 50 G5 7 3N 3 19 E
Aber, Uganda 54 B3 2 12N 32 25 E
Aberaeron, U.K. 11 E3 52 15N 4 16W
Aberayron = Aberaeron, U.K. 11 E3 52 15N 4 16W
Abercorn = Mbala, Zambia 55 D3 8 46S 31 24 E
Abercorn, Australia 63 D5 25 12S 151 5 E
Aberdare, U.K. 11 F4 51 43N 3 27W
Aberdare Ra., Kenya 54 C4 0 15S 36 50 E
Aberdeen, Australia 63 E5 32 9S 150 56 E
Aberdeen, Canada 73 C7 52 20N 106 8W
Aberdeen, S. Africa 56 E3 32 28S 24 2 E
Aberdeen, U.K. 12 D6 57 9N 2 6W
Aberdeen, Ala., U.S.A. 77 J1 33 49N 88 33W
Aberdeen, Idaho, U.S.A. 82 E7 42 57N 112 50W
Aberdeen, S. Dak., U.S.A. 80 C5 45 28N 98 29W
Aberdeen, Wash., U.S.A. 84 D3 46 59N 123 50W
Aberdovey = Aberdyfi, U.K. 11 E3 52 33N 4 3W
Aberdyfi, U.K. 11 E3 52 33N 4 3W
Aberfeldy, U.K. 12 E5 56 37N 3 50W
Abergavenny, U.K. 11 F4 51 49N 3 1W
Abernathy, U.S.A. 81 J4 33 50N 101 51W
Abert, L., U.S.A. 82 E3 42 38N 120 14W
Aberystwyth, U.K. 11 E3 52 25N 4 6W
Abhar, Iran 45 B6 36 9N 49 13 E
Abhayapuri, India 43 F14 26 24N 90 38 E
Abidjan, Ivory C. 50 G4 5 26N 3 58W
Abilene, Kans., U.S.A. 80 F6 38 55N 97 13W
Abilene, Tex., U.S.A. 81 J5 32 28N 99 43W
Abingdon, U.K. 11 F6 51 40N 1 17W
Abingdon, Ill., U.S.A. 80 E9 40 48N 90 24W
Abingdon, Va., U.S.A. 77 G5 36 43N 81 59W
Abington Reef, Australia 62 B4 18 0S 149 35 E
Abitau →, Canada 73 B7 59 53N 109 3W
Abitau L., Canada 73 A7 60 27N 107 15W
Abitibi L., Canada 70 C4 48 40N 79 40W
Abkhaz Republic □, Georgia 25 F7 43 0N 41 0 E
Abkit, Russia 27 C16 64 10N 157 10 E
Abminga, Australia 63 D1 26 8S 134 51 E
Abohar, India 42 D6 30 10N 74 10 E
Abomey, Benin 50 G5 7 10N 2 5 E
Abong-Mbang, Cameroon 52 D2 4 0N 13 8 E
Abou-Deïa, Chad 51 F8 11 20N 19 20 E
Aboyne, U.K. 12 D6 57 4N 2 48W
Abra Pampa, Argentina 94 A2 22 43S 65 42W
Abrantes, Portugal 19 C1 39 24N 8 7W
Abreojos, Pta., Mexico 86 B2 26 50N 113 40W
Abri, Sudan 51 D11 20 50N 30 27 E
Abrolhos, Banka, Brazil 93 G11 18 0S 38 0W
Abrud, Romania 17 E11 46 19N 23 5 E
Abruzzi □, Italy 20 C5 42 15N 14 0 E
Absaroka Range, U.S.A. 82 D9 44 45N 109 50W
Abū al Khaşīb, Iraq 45 D6 30 25N 48 0 E
Abū 'Alī, Si. Arabia 45 E6 27 20N 49 27 E
Abū 'Alī →, Lebanon 47 A4 34 25N 35 50 E
Abu 'Arīsh, Si. Arabia 46 D3 16 53N 42 48 E
Abu Dhabi = Abū Ẓāby, U.A.E. 45 E7 24 28N 54 22 E
Abū Dis, Sudan 51 E11 19 12N 33 38 E
Abū Du'ān, Syria 44 B3 36 25N 38 15 E
Abu el Gairi, W. →, Egypt 47 F2 29 35N 33 30 E
Abu Ga'da, W. →, Egypt 47 F1 29 15N 32 53 E
Abū Ḩadrīyah, Si. Arabia 45 E6 27 20N 48 58 E
Abu Hamed, Sudan 51 E11 19 32N 33 13 E
Abū Kamāl, Syria 44 C4 34 30N 41 0 E
Abū Madd, Ra's, Si. Arabia 44 E3 24 50N 37 7 E
Abu Matariq, Sudan 51 F10 10 59N 26 9 E
Abu Şafāt, W. →, Jordan 47 E5 30 24N 36 7 E
Abū Şukhayr, Iraq 44 D5 31 54N 44 30 E
Abu Tig, Egypt 51 C11 27 4N 31 15 E
Abû Zabad, Sudan 51 F10 12 25N 29 10 E
Abū Ẓāby, U.A.E. 45 E7 24 28N 54 22 E
Abū Zeydābād, Iran 45 C6 33 54N 51 45 E
Abuja, Nigeria 50 G6 9 16N 7 2 E
Abukuma-Gawa →, Japan 30 E10 38 6N 140 52 E
Abukuma-Sammyaku, Japan 30 F10 37 30N 140 45 E
Abunã, Brazil 92 E5 9 40S 65 20W
Abunã →, Brazil 92 E5 9 41S 65 20W
Aburo, Zaïre 54 B3 2 4N 30 53 E
Abut Hd., N.Z. 59 K3 43 7S 170 15 E
Abwong, Sudan 51 G11 9 2N 32 14 E
Acajutla, El Salv. 88 D2 13 36N 89 50W
Acámbaro, Mexico 86 C4 20 0N 100 40W
Acaponeta, Mexico 86 C3 22 30N 105 20W
Acapulco, Mexico 87 D5 16 51N 99 56W
Acarigua, Venezuela 92 B5 9 33N 69 12W
Acatlán, Mexico 87 D5 18 10N 98 3W
Acayucan, Mexico 87 D6 17 59N 94 58W
Accomac, U.S.A. 76 G8 37 43N 75 40W
Accra, Ghana 50 G4 5 35N 0 6W
Accrington, U.K. 10 D5 53 46N 2 22W
Acebal, Argentina 94 C3 33 20S 60 50W
Aceh □, Indonesia 36 D1 4 15N 97 30 E
Achalpur, India 40 J10 21 22N 77 32 E
Acheng, China 35 B14 45 30N 126 58 E
Acher, India 42 H5 23 10N 72 32 E
Achill, Ireland 13 C2 53 56N 9 55W
Achill Hd., Ireland 13 C1 53 59N 10 15W
Achill I., Ireland 13 C1 53 58N 10 5W
Achill Sd., Ireland 13 C2 53 53N 9 55W
Achinsk, Russia 27 D10 56 20N 90 20 E
Ackerman, U.S.A. 81 J10 33 19N 89 11W
Acklins I., Bahamas 89 B5 22 30N 74 0W
Acme, Canada 72 C6 51 33N 113 30W
Aconcagua □, Chile 94 C1 32 15S 70 30W
Aconcagua, Cerro, Argentina 94 C2 32 39S 70 0W
Aconquija, Mt., Argentina 94 B2 27 0S 66 0W
Açores, Is. dos = Azores, Atl. Oc. 2 C8 38 44N 29 0W
Acraman, L., Australia 63 E2 32 2S 135 23 E
Acre = 'Akko, Israel 47 C4 32 55N 35 4 E
Acre □, Brazil 92 E4 9 1S 71 0W
Acre →, Brazil 92 E5 8 45S 67 22W
Acton, Canada 78 C4 43 38N 80 3W
Ad Dammām, Si. Arabia 45 E6 26 20N 50 5 E
Ad Dawhah, Qatar 45 E6 25 15N 51 35 E
Ad Dawr, Iraq 44 C4 34 27N 43 47 E
Ad Dir'īyah, Si. Arabia 44 E5 24 44N 46 35 E
Ad Dīwānīyah, Iraq 44 D5 32 0N 45 0 E
Ad Dujayl, Iraq 44 C5 33 51N 44 14 E
Ad Durūz, J., Jordan 47 C5 32 35N 36 40 E
Ada, Minn., U.S.A. 80 B6 47 18N 96 31W
Ada, Okla., U.S.A. 81 H6 34 46N 96 41W
Adaja →, Spain 19 B3 41 32N 4 52W
Adamaoua, Massif de l', Cameroon 51 G7 7 20N 12 20 E
Adamawa Highlands = Adamaoua, Massif de l', Cameroon 51 G7 7 20N 12 20 E
Adamello, Mt., Italy 20 A4 46 10N 10 34 E
Adaminaby, Australia 63 F4 36 0S 148 45 E
Adams, Mass., U.S.A. 79 D11 42 38N 73 7W
Adams, N.Y., U.S.A. 79 C8 43 49N 76 1W
Adams, Wis., U.S.A. 80 D10 43 57N 89 49W
Adam's Bridge, Sri Lanka 40 Q11 9 15N 79 40 E
Adams L., Canada 72 C5 51 10N 119 40W
Adams Mt., U.S.A. 84 D5 46 12N 121 30W
Adam's Peak, Sri Lanka 40 R12 6 48N 80 30 E
Adana, Turkey 25 G6 37 0N 35 16 E
Adapazarı, Turkey 25 F5 40 48N 30 25 E
Adarama, Sudan 51 E11 17 10N 34 52 E
Adare, C., Antarctica 5 D11 71 0S 171 0 E
Adaut, Indonesia 37 F8 8 8S 131 7 E
Adavale, Australia 63 D3 25 52S 144 32 E
Adda →, Italy 20 B3 45 8N 9 53 E
Addis Ababa = Addis Abeba, Ethiopia 51 G12 9 2N 38 42 E
Addis Abeba, Ethiopia 51 G12 9 2N 38 42 E
Addis Alem, Ethiopia 51 G12 9 0N 38 17 E
Addison, U.S.A. 78 D7 42 1N 77 14W
Addo, S. Africa 56 E4 33 32S 25 45 E
Ādeh, Iran 44 B5 37 42N 45 11 E
Adel, U.S.A. 77 K4 31 8N 83 25W
Adelaide, Australia 63 E2 34 52S 138 30 E
Adelaide, Bahamas 88 A4 25 4N 77 31W
Adelaide, S. Africa 56 E4 32 42S 26 20 E
Adelaide I., Antarctica 5 C17 67 15S 68 30W
Adelaide Pen., Canada 68 B10 68 15N 97 30W
Adelaide River, Australia 60 B5 13 15S 131 7 E
Adelanto, U.S.A. 85 L9 34 35N 117 22W
Adele I., Australia 60 C3 15 32S 123 9 E
Adélie, Terre, Antarctica 5 C10 68 0S 140 0 E
Adélie Land = Adélie, Terre, Antarctica 5 C10 68 0S 140 0 E
Aden = Al 'Adan, Yemen 46 E4 12 45N 45 0 E
Aden, G. of, Asia 46 E4 12 30N 47 30 E
Adendorp, S. Africa 56 E3 32 15S 24 30 E
Adh Dhayd, U.A.E. 45 E7 25 17N 55 53 E
Adhoi, India 42 H4 23 26N 70 32 E
Adi, Indonesia 37 E8 4 15S 133 30 E
Adi Ugri, Eritrea 51 F12 14 58N 38 48 E
Adieu, C., Australia 61 F5 32 0S 132 10 E
Adieu Pt., Australia 60 C3 15 14S 124 35 E
Adige →, Italy 20 B5 45 9N 12 20 E
Adilabad, India 40 K11 19 33N 78 20 E
Adin, U.S.A. 82 F3 41 12N 120 57W
Adin Khel, Afghan. 40 C6 32 45N 68 5 E
Adirondack Mts., U.S.A. 79 C10 44 0N 74 0W
Adjumani, Uganda 54 B3 3 20N 31 50 E
Adlavik Is., Canada 71 B8 55 2N 57 45W
Admer, Algeria 50 D6 20 21N 5 27 E
Admiralty G., Australia 60 B4 14 20S 125 55 E
Admiralty I., U.S.A. 68 C6 57 30N 134 30W
Admiralty Inlet, U.S.A. 82 C2 48 8N 122 58W
Admiralty Is., Papua N. G. 64 H6 2 0S 147 0 E
Ado Ekiti, Nigeria 50 G6 7 38N 5 12 E
Adonara, Indonesia 37 F6 8 15S 123 5 E
Adoni, India 40 M10 15 33N 77 18 E
Adour →, France 18 E3 43 32N 1 32W
Adra, India 43 H12 23 30N 86 42 E
Adra, Spain 19 D4 36 43N 3 3W
Adrano, Italy 20 F6 37 40N 14 49 E
Adrar, Algeria 50 C4 27 51N 0 11W
Adré, Chad 51 F9 13 40N 22 20 E
Adrī, Libya 51 C7 27 32N 13 2 E
Adrian, Mich., U.S.A. 76 E3 41 54N 84 2W
Adrian, Tex., U.S.A. 81 H3 35 16N 102 40W
Adriatic Sea, Europe 20 C6 43 0N 16 0 E
Adua, Indonesia 37 E7 1 45S 129 50 E
Adwa, Ethiopia 51 F12 14 15N 38 52 E
Adzhar Republic □, Georgia 25 F7 41 30N 42 0 E
Ægean Sea, Europe 21 E11 38 30N 25 0 E
Æolian Is. = Eólie, Is., Italy 20 E6 38 30N 14 50 E
Aerhtai Shan, Mongolia 32 B4 46 40N 92 45 E
'Afak, Iraq 44 C5 32 4N 45 15 E
Afándou, Greece 23 C10 36 18N 28 12 E
Afars & Issas, Terr. of = Djibouti ■, Africa 46 E3 12 0N 43 0 E
Afghanistan ■, Asia 40 C4 33 0N 65 0 E
Afgoi, Somali Rep. 46 G3 2 7N 44 59 E
Afognak I., U.S.A. 68 C4 58 15N 152 30W
Africa 48 E6 10 0N 20 0 E
'Afrīn, Syria 44 B3 36 32N 36 50 E
Afton, U.S.A. 79 D9 42 14N 75 32W
Afuá, Brazil 93 D8 0 15S 50 20W
Afula, Israel 47 C4 32 37N 35 17 E
Afyonkarahisar, Turkey 25 G5 38 45N 30 33 E
Agadès = Agadez, Niger 50 E6 16 58N 7 59 E
Agadez, Niger 50 E6 16 58N 7 59 E
Agadir, Morocco 50 B3 30 28N 9 55W
Agaete, Canary Is. 22 F4 28 6N 15 43W
Agapa, Russia 27 B9 71 27N 89 15 E
Agar, India 42 H7 23 40N 76 2 E
Agartala, India 41 H17 23 50N 91 23 E
Agassiz, Canada 72 D4 49 14N 121 46W
Agats, Indonesia 37 F9 5 33S 138 0 E
Agboville, Ivory C. 50 G4 5 55N 4 15W
Agde, France 18 E5 43 19N 3 28 E
Agen, France 18 D4 44 12N 0 38 E
Āgh Kand, Iran 45 B6 37 15N 48 4 E
Aginskoye, Russia 27 D12 51 6N 114 32 E
Agra, India 42 F7 27 17N 77 58 E
Agri →, Italy 20 D7 40 13N 16 44 E
Ağrı Dağı, Turkey 25 G7 39 50N 44 15 E
Ağrı Karakose, Turkey 25 G7 39 44N 43 3 E
Agrigento, Italy 20 F5 37 19N 13 33 E
Agrinion, Greece 21 E9 38 37N 21 27 E
Agua Caliente, Baja Calif. N., Mexico 85 N10 32 29N 116 59W
Agua Caliente, Sinaloa, Mexico 86 B3 26 30N 108 20W
Agua Caliente Springs, U.S.A. 85 N10 32 56N 116 19W
Água Clara, Brazil 93 H8 20 25S 52 45W
Agua Hechicero, Mexico 85 N10 32 26N 116 14W
Agua Prieta, Mexico 86 A3 31 20N 109 32W
Aguadas, Colombia 92 B3 5 40N 75 38W
Aguadilla, Puerto Rico 89 C6 18 26N 67 10W
Aguadulce, Panama 88 E3 8 15N 80 32W
Aguanga, U.S.A. 85 M10 33 27N 116 51W
Aguanish, Canada 71 B7 50 14N 62 2W
Aguanus →, Canada 71 B7 50 13N 62 5W
Aguapey →, Argentina 94 B4 29 7S 56 36W
Aguaray Guazú →, Paraguay 94 A4 24 47S 57 19W
Aguarico →, Ecuador 92 D3 0 59S 75 11W
Aguas Blancas, Chile 94 A2 24 15S 69 55W
Aguas Calientes, Sierra de, Argentina 94 B2 25 26S 66 40W
Aguascalientes, Mexico 86 C4 21 53N 102 12W
Aguascalientes □, Mexico 86 C4 22 0N 102 20W
Aguilares, Argentina 94 B2 27 26S 65 35W
Águilas, Spain 19 D5 37 23N 1 35W
Agüimes, Canary Is. 22 G4 27 58N 15 27W
Agulhas, C., S. Africa 56 E3 34 52S 20 0 E
Agulo, Canary Is. 22 F2 28 11N 17 12W
Agung, Indonesia 36 F5 8 20S 115 28 E
Agur, Uganda 54 B3 2 28N 32 55 E
Agusan →, Phil. 37 C7 9 0N 125 30 E
Aha Mts., Botswana 56 B3 19 45S 21 0 E
Ahaggar, Algeria 50 D6 23 0N 6 30 E
Ahar, Iran 44 B5 38 35N 47 0 E
Ahipara B., N.Z. 59 F4 35 5S 173 5 E
Ahiri, India 40 K12 19 30N 80 0 E
Ahmad Wal, Pakistan 42 E1 29 18N 65 58 E
Ahmadabad, India 42 H5 23 0N 72 40 E
Aḩmadābād, Khorāsān, Iran 45 C9 35 3N 60 50 E
Aḩmadābād, Khorāsān, Iran 45 C8 35 49N 59 42 E
Aḩmadī, Iran 45 E8 27 56N 56 42 E
Ahmadnagar, India 40 K9 19 7N 74 46 E
Ahmadpur, Pakistan 42 E4 29 12N 71 10 E
Ahmedabad = Ahmadabad, India 42 H5 23 0N 72 40 E
Ahmednagar = Ahmadnagar, India 40 K9 19 7N 74 46 E
Ahome, Mexico 86 B3 25 55N 109 11W
Ahram, Iran 45 D6 28 52N 51 16 E
Ahrax Pt., Malta 23 D1 35 59N 14 22 E
Āhū, Iran 45 C6 34 33N 50 2 E
Ahuachapán, El Salv. 88 D2 13 54N 89 52W
Ahvāz, Iran 45 D6 31 20N 48 40 E
Ahvenanmaa = Åland, Finland 9 F16 60 15N 20 0 E
Aḩwar, Yemen 46 E4 13 30N 46 40 E
Aichi □, Japan 31 G8 35 0N 137 15 E
Aigua, Uruguay 95 C5 34 13S 54 46W
Aigues-Mortes, France 18 E6 43 35N 4 12 E
Aihui, China 33 A7 50 10N 127 30 E
Aija, Peru 92 E3 9 50S 77 45W
Aikawa, Japan 30 E9 38 2N 138 15 E
Aiken, U.S.A. 77 J5 33 34N 81 43W
Aillik, Canada 71 A8 55 11N 59 18W
Ailsa Craig, U.K. 12 F3 55 15N 5 7W
'Ailūn, Jordan 47 C4 32 18N 35 47 E
Aim, Russia 27 D14 59 0N 133 55 E
Aimere, Indonesia 37 F6 8 45S 121 3 E
Aimogasta, Argentina 94 B2 28 33S 66 50W
Aimorés, Brazil 93 G10 19 30S 41 4W
Ain □, France 18 C6 46 5N 5 20 E
Aïn Beïda, Algeria 50 A6 35 50N 7 29 E
Aïn Ben Tili, Mauritania 50 C3 25 59N 9 27W
Aïn-Sefra, Algeria 50 B4 32 47N 0 37W
'Ain Sudr, Egypt 47 F2 29 50N 33 6 E
Ainabo, Somali Rep. 46 F4 9 0N 46 25 E
Ainsworth, U.S.A. 80 D5 42 33N 99 52W
Aïr, Niger 50 E6 18 30N 8 0 E
Air Hitam, Malaysia 39 M4 1 55N 103 11 E
Airdrie, U.K. 12 F5 55 53N 3 57W
Aire →, U.K. 10 D7 53 42N 0 55W
Aire, I. del, Spain 22 B11 39 48N 4 16 E
Airlie Beach, Australia 62 C4 20 16S 148 43 E
Aisne □, France 18 B5 49 42N 3 40 E
Aisne →, France 18 B5 49 26N 2 50 E
Aitkin, U.S.A. 80 B8 46 32N 93 42W
Aiud, Romania 17 E11 46 19N 23 44 E
Aix-en-Provence, France 18 E6 43 32N 5 27 E
Aix-la-Chapelle = Aachen, Germany 16 C3 50 47N 6 4 E
Aiyansh, Canada 72 B3 55 17N 129 2W
Aíyina, Greece 21 F10 37 45N 23 26 E
Aíyion, Greece 21 E10 38 15N 22 5 E
Aizawl, India 41 H18 23 40N 92 44 E
Aizuwakamatsu, Japan 30 F9 37 30N 139 56 E
Ajaccio, France 18 F8 41 55N 8 40 E
Ajalpan, Mexico 87 D5 18 22N 97 15W
Ajanta Ra., India 40 J9 20 28N 75 50 E
Ajari Rep. = Adzhar Republic □, Georgia 25 F7 41 30N 42 0 E
Ajax, Canada 78 C5 43 50N 79 1W
Ajdâbiyah, Libya 51 B9 30 54N 20 4 E
'Ajmān, U.A.E. 45 E7 25 25N 55 30 E
Ajmer, India 42 F6 26 28N 74 37 E
Ajo, U.S.A. 83 K7 32 22N 112 52W
Akabira, Japan 30 C11 43 33N 142 5 E
Akamas □, Cyprus 23 D11 35 3N 32 18 E
Akanthou, Cyprus 23 D12 35 22N 33 45 E
Akaroa, N.Z. 59 K4 43 49S 172 59 E
Akashi, Japan 31 G7 34 45N 134 58 E
Akelamo, Indonesia 37 D7 1 35N 129 40 E
Akershus fylke □, Norway 9 G11 60 0N 11 10 E
Aketi, Zaïre 52 D4 2 38N 23 47 E
Akhelóös →, Greece 21 E9 38 36N 21 14 E
Akhmîm, Egypt 51 C11 26 31N 31 47 E
Akhnur, India 43 C6 32 52N 74 45 E
Aki, Japan 31 H6 33 30N 133 54 E
Akimiski I., Canada 70 B3 52 50N 81 30W
Akita, Japan 30 E10 39 45N 140 7 E
Akita □, Japan 30 E10 39 40N 140 30 E
Akjoujt, Mauritania 50 E2 19 45N 14 15W
Akkeshi, Japan 30 C12 43 2N 144 51 E
'Akko, Israel 47 C4 32 55N 35 4 E
Akkol, Kazakhstan 26 E8 45 0N 75 39 E
Aklavik, Canada 68 B6 68 12N 135 0W
Akmolinsk = Tselinograd, Kazakhstan 26 D8 51 10N 71 30 E
Akō, Japan 31 G7 34 45N 134 24 E
Akobo →, Ethiopia 51 G11 7 48N 33 3 E
Akola, India 40 J10 20 42N 77 2 E
Akordat, Eritrea 51 E12 15 30N 37 40 E
Akpatok I., Canada 69 B13 60 25N 68 8W
Akranes, Iceland 8 D3 64 19N 22 5W
Akreïjit, Mauritania 50 E3 18 19N 9 11W
Akron, Colo., U.S.A. 80 E3 40 10N 103 13W
Akron, Ohio, U.S.A. 78 E3 41 5N 81 31W
Akrotiri, Cyprus 23 E11 34 36N 32 57 E
Akrotiri Bay, Cyprus 23 E12 34 35N 33 10 E
Aksai Chih, India 43 B8 35 15N 79 55 E
Aksarka, Russia 26 C7 66 31N 67 50 E
Aksay, Kazakhstan 24 D9 51 11N 53 0 E
Aksenovo Zilovskoye, Russia 27 D12 53 20N 117 40 E
Aksu, China 32 B3 41 5N 80 10 E
Aksum, Ethiopia 51 F12 14 5N 38 40 E
Aktogay, Kazakhstan 26 E8 46 57N 79 40 E
Aktyubinsk, Kazakhstan 25 D10 50 17N 57 10 E
Aku, Nigeria 50 G6 6 40N 7 18 E
Akure, Nigeria 50 G6 7 15N 5 5 E
Akureyri, Iceland 8 D4 65 40N 18 6W
Akuseki-Shima, Japan 31 K4 29 27N 129 37 E
Akyab = Sittwe, Burma 41 J18 20 18N 92 45 E
Al 'Adan, Yemen 46 E4 12 45N 45 0 E
Al Aḩsā, Si. Arabia 45 E6 25 50N 49 0 E
Al Ajfar, Si. Arabia 44 E4 27 26N 43 0 E
Al Amādīyah, Iraq 44 B4 37 5N 43 30 E
Al Amārah, Iraq 44 D5 31 55N 47 15 E
Al 'Aqabah, Jordan 47 F4 29 31N 35 0 E
Al Arak, Syria 44 C3 34 38N 38 35 E
Al 'Aramah, Si. Arabia 44 E5 25 30N 46 0 E
Al Arṭāwīyah, Si. Arabia 44 E5 26 31N 45 20 E
Al 'Āşimah □, Jordan 47 D5 31 40N 36 30 E
Al' Assāfīyah, Si. Arabia 44 D3 28 17N 38 59 E
Al 'Ayn, Oman 45 E7 24 15N 55 45 E
Al 'Ayn, Si. Arabia 44 E3 25 4N 38 6 E
Al A'ẓamīyah, Iraq 44 C5 33 22N 44 22 E
Al 'Azīzīyah, Iraq 44 C5 32 54N 45 4 E
Al Bāb, Syria 44 B3 36 23N 37 29 E
Al Bad', Si. Arabia 44 D2 28 28N 35 1 E
Al Bādī, Iraq 44 C4 35 56N 41 32 E
Al Baḩrah, Kuwait 44 D5 29 40N 47 52 E
Al Balqā' □, Jordan 47 C4 32 5N 35 45 E
Al Bārūk, J., Lebanon 47 B4 33 39N 35 40 E
Al Başrah, Iraq 44 D5 30 30N 47 50 E
Al Baṭḩā, Iraq 44 D5 31 6N 45 53 E
Al Batrūn, Lebanon 47 A4 34 15N 35 40 E
Al Bi'r, Si. Arabia 44 D3 28 51N 36 16 E
Al Bu'ayrāt, Libya 51 B8 31 24N 15 44 E
Al Burayj, Syria 47 A5 34 15N 36 46 E
Al Fallūjah, Iraq 44 C4 33 20N 43 55 E
Al Fāw, Iraq 45 D6 30 0N 48 30 E
Al Fujayrah, U.A.E. 45 E8 25 7N 56 18 E

Alvear

Al Ghadaf, W. →, Jordan 47 D5 31 26N 36 43 E
Al Ghammās, Iraq 44 D5 31 45N 44 37 E
Al Hābah, Si. Arabia 44 E5 27 10N 47 0 E
Al Ḩadīthah, Iraq 44 C4 34 0N 41 13 E
Al Ḩadīthah, Si. Arabia 44 D3 31 28N 37 8 E
Al Ḩājānah, Syria 47 B5 33 20N 36 33 E
Al Ḩāmad, Si. Arabia 44 D3 31 30N 39 30 E
Al Hamdānīyah, Syria 44 C3 35 25N 36 50 E
Al Ḩamīdīyah, Syria 47 A4 34 42N 35 57 E
Al Ḩammār, Iraq 44 D5 30 57N 46 51 E
Al Ḩarīr, W. →, Syria 47 C4 32 44N 35 59 E
Al Ḩasā, W. →, Jordan 47 D4 31 4N 35 29 E
Al Ḩasakah, Syria 44 B4 36 35N 40 45 E
Al Ḩawrah, Yemen 46 E4 13 50N 47 35 E
Al Ḩaydān, W. →, Jordan 47 D4 31 29N 35 34 E
Al Ḩayy, Iraq 44 C5 32 5N 46 5 E
Al Ḩijāz, Si. Arabia 46 B2 26 0N 37 30 E
Al Ḩillah, Iraq 44 C5 32 30N 44 25 E
Al Ḩillah, Si. Arabia 46 C4 23 35N 46 50 E
Al Hirmil, Lebanon 47 A5 34 26N 36 24 E
Al Hoceïma, Morocco 50 A4 35 8N 3 58W
Al Ḩudaydah, Yemen 46 E3 14 50N 43 0 E
Al Hufūf, Si. Arabia 45 E6 25 25N 49 45 E
Al Ḩumayḑah, Si. Arabia 44 D2 29 14N 34 56 E
Al Ḩunayy, Si. Arabia 45 E6 25 58N 48 45 E
Al Irq, Libya 51 C9 29 5N 21 35 E
Al Īsāwīyah, Si. Arabia 44 D3 30 43N 37 59 E
Al Ittihad = Madīnat ash Sha'b, Yemen 46 E3 12 50N 45 0 E
Al Jafr, Jordan 47 E5 30 18N 36 14 E
Al Jaghbūb, Libya 51 C9 29 42N 24 38 E
Al Jahrah, Kuwait 44 D5 29 25N 47 40 E
Al Jalāmīd, Si. Arabia 44 D3 31 20N 39 45 E
Al Jamalīyah, Qatar 45 E6 25 37N 51 5 E
Al Janūb □, Lebanon 47 B4 33 20N 35 20 E
Al Jawf, Libya 51 D9 24 10N 23 24 E
Al Jawf, Si. Arabia 44 D3 29 55N 39 40 E
Al Jazirah, Iraq 44 C5 33 30N 44 0 E
Al Jazirah, Libya 51 C9 26 10N 21 20 E
Al Jithāmīyah, Si. Arabia 44 E4 27 41N 41 43 E
Al Jubayl, Si. Arabia 45 E6 27 0N 49 50 E
Al Jubaylah, Si. Arabia 44 E5 24 55N 46 25 E
Al Jubb, Si. Arabia 44 E4 27 11N 42 17 E
Al Junaynah, Sudan 51 F9 13 27N 22 45 E
Al Kabā'ish, Iraq 44 D5 30 58N 47 0 E
Al Karak, Jordan 47 D4 31 11N 35 42 E
Al Karak □, Jordan 47 E5 31 0N 36 0 E
Al Kāzim Tyah, Iraq 44 C5 33 22N 44 12 E
Al Khalīl, Jordan 47 D4 31 32N 35 6 E
Al Khalīl □, Jordan 47 D4 31 35N 35 5 E
Al Khawr, Qatar 45 E6 25 41N 51 30 E
Al Khiḑr, Iraq 44 D5 31 12N 45 33 E
Al Khiyām, Lebanon 47 B4 33 20N 35 36 E
Al Kiswah, Syria 47 B5 33 23N 36 14 E
Al Kufrah, Libya 51 D9 24 17N 23 15 E
Al Kuhayfiyah, Si. Arabia 44 E4 27 12N 43 3 E
Al Kūt, Iraq 44 C5 32 30N 46 0 E
Al Kuwayt, Kuwait 44 D5 29 30N 48 0 E
Al Labwah, Lebanon 47 A5 34 11N 36 20 E
Al Lādhiqīyah, Syria 44 C2 35 30N 35 45 E
Al Liwā', Oman 45 E8 24 31N 56 36 E
Al Luḩayyah, Yemen 46 D3 15 45N 42 40 E
Al Madīnah, Iraq 44 D5 30 57N 47 16 E
Al Madīnah, Si. Arabia 46 C2 24 35N 39 52 E
Al-Mafraq, Jordan 47 C5 32 17N 36 14 E
Al Maḩmūdīyah, Iraq 44 C5 33 3N 44 21 E
Al Majma'ah, Si. Arabia 44 E5 25 57N 45 22 E
Al Makhruq, W. →, Jordan 47 D6 31 28N 37 0 E
Al Makḩūl, Si. Arabia 44 E4 26 37N 42 39 E
Al Manāmah, Bahrain 45 E6 26 10N 50 30 E
Al Maqwa', Kuwait 44 D5 29 10N 47 59 E
Al Marj, Libya 51 B9 32 25N 20 30 E
Al Maţlā, Kuwait 44 D5 29 24N 47 40 E
Al Mawjib, W. →, Jordan 47 D4 31 28N 35 36 E
Al Mawşil, Iraq 44 B4 36 15N 43 5 E
Al Mayādin, Syria 44 C4 35 1N 40 27 E
Al Mazār, Jordan 47 D4 31 4N 35 41 E
Al Midhnab, Si. Arabia 44 E5 25 50N 44 18 E
Al Minā', Lebanon 47 A4 34 24N 35 49 E
Al Miqdādīyah, Iraq 44 C5 34 0N 45 0 E
Al Mubarraz, Si. Arabia 45 E6 25 30N 49 40 E
Al Mughayrā', U.A.E. 45 E7 24 5N 53 32 E
Al Muḩarraq, Bahrain 45 E6 26 15N 50 40 E
Al Mukallā, Yemen 46 E4 14 33N 49 2 E
Al Mukhā, Yemen 46 E3 13 18N 43 15 E
Al Musayjīd, Si. Arabia 46 C2 24 5N 39 5 E
Al Musayyib, Iraq 44 C5 32 40N 44 25 E
Al Muwaylih, Si. Arabia 44 E2 27 40N 35 30 E
Al Qā'im, Iraq 44 C4 34 21N 41 7 E
Al Qalībah, Si. Arabia 44 D3 28 24N 37 42 E
Al Qaryatayn, Syria 47 A6 34 12N 37 13 E
Al Qaşabāt, Libya 51 B7 32 39N 14 1 E
Al Qaţ'ā, Syria 44 C4 34 40N 40 48 E
Al Qaţīf, Si. Arabia 45 E6 26 35N 50 0 E
Al Qatrānah, Jordan 47 D5 31 14N 36 26 E
Al Qaţrūn, Libya 51 D8 24 56N 15 3 E
Al Qayşūmah, Si. Arabia 44 D5 28 20N 46 7 E
Al Quds = Jerusalem, Israel 47 D4 31 47N 35 10 E
Al Quds □, Jordan 47 D4 31 50N 35 20 E
Al Qunaytirah, Syria 47 C4 32 55N 35 45 E
Al Qurnah, Iraq 44 D5 31 1N 47 25 E
Al Quşayr, Iraq 44 D5 30 39N 45 50 E
Al Quşayr, Syria 47 A5 34 31N 36 34 E
Al Qutayfah, Syria 47 B5 33 44N 36 36 E
Al' Uḑaylīyah, Si. Arabia 45 E6 25 8N 49 18 E
Al 'Ulā, Si. Arabia 44 E3 26 35N 38 0 E
Al Uqaylah ash Sharqigah, Libya 51 B8 30 12N 19 10 E
Al Uqayr, Si. Arabia 45 E6 25 40N 50 15 E
Al 'Uwaynid, Si. Arabia 44 E5 24 50N 46 0 E
Al' 'Uwayqīlah, Si. Arabia 44 D4 30 30N 42 10 E
Al 'Uyūn, Si. Arabia 44 E4 26 30N 43 50 E
Al 'Uyūn, Si. Arabia 44 E3 24 33N 39 35 E
Al Wajh, Si. Arabia 44 E3 26 10N 36 30 E
Al Wakrah, Qatar 45 E6 25 10N 51 40 E
Al Wannān, Si. Arabia 45 E6 26 55N 48 24 E
Al Waqbah, Si. Arabia 44 D5 28 48N 45 33 E
Al Wari'āh, Si. Arabia 44 E5 27 51N 47 25 E
Al Wusayl, Qatar 45 E6 25 29N 51 29 E
Ala Tau Shankou = Dzhungarskiye Vorota, Kazakhstan 32 B3 45 0N 82 0 E
Alabama □, U.S.A. 77 J2 33 0N 87 0W
Alabama →, U.S.A. 77 K2 31 8N 87 57W
Alaérma, Greece 23 C9 36 9N 27 57 E
Alagoa Grande, Brazil 93 E11 7 3S 35 35W
Alagoas □, Brazil 93 E11 9 0S 36 0W
Alagoinhas, Brazil 93 F11 12 7S 38 20W
Alajero, Canary Is. 22 F2 28 3N 17 13W
Alajuela, Costa Rica 88 D3 10 2N 84 8W
Alakamisy, Madag. 57 C8 21 19S 47 14 E
Alakurtti, Russia 24 A5 67 0N 30 30 E
Alameda, Calif., U.S.A. 84 H4 37 46N 122 15W
Alameda, N. Mex., U.S.A. 83 J10 35 11N 106 37W
Alamo, U.S.A. 85 J11 36 21N 115 10W
Alamo Crossing, U.S.A. 85 L13 34 16N 113 33W
Alamogordo, U.S.A. 83 K11 32 54N 105 57W
Alamos, Mexico 86 B3 27 0N 109 0W
Alamosa, U.S.A. 83 H11 37 28N 105 52W
Åland, Finland 9 F16 60 15N 20 0 E
Ålands hav, Sweden 9 G15 60 0N 19 30 E
Alandur, India 40 N12 13 0N 80 15 E
Alanya, Turkey 25 G5 36 38N 32 0 E
Alaotra, Farihin', Madag. 57 B8 17 30S 48 30 E
Alapayevsk, Russia 26 D7 57 52N 61 42 E
Alaşehir, Turkey 25 G4 38 23N 28 30 E
Alaska □, U.S.A. 68 B5 64 0N 154 0W
Alaska, G. of, Pac. Oc. 68 C5 58 0N 145 0W
Alaska Highway, Canada 72 B3 60 0N 130 0W
Alaska Peninsula, U.S.A. 68 C4 56 0N 159 0W
Alaska Range, U.S.A. 68 B4 62 50N 151 0W
Alatyr, Russia 24 D8 54 45N 46 35 E
Alausi, Ecuador 92 D3 2 0S 78 50W
Alava, C., U.S.A. 82 B1 48 10N 124 44W
Alawoona, Australia 63 E3 34 45S 140 30 E
'Alayh, Lebanon 47 B4 33 46N 35 33 E
Alayor, Spain 22 B11 39 57N 4 8 E
Alba, Italy 20 B3 44 41N 8 1 E
Alba Iulia, Romania 21 A10 46 8N 23 39 E
Albacete, Spain 19 C5 39 0N 1 50W
Albacutya, L., Australia 63 F3 35 45S 141 58 E
Albania ■, Europe 21 D9 41 0N 20 0 E
Albany, Australia 61 G2 35 1S 117 58 E
Albany, Ga., U.S.A. 77 K3 31 35N 84 10W
Albany, Minn., U.S.A. 80 C7 45 38N 94 34W
Albany, N.Y., U.S.A. 79 D11 42 39N 73 45W
Albany, Oreg., U.S.A. 82 D2 44 38N 123 6W
Albany, Tex., U.S.A. 81 J5 32 44N 99 18W
Albany →, Canada 70 B3 52 17N 81 31W
Albardón, Argentina 94 C2 31 20S 68 30W
Albarracín, Sierra de, Spain 19 B5 40 30N 1 30W
Albatross B., Australia 62 A3 12 45S 141 30 E
Albemarle, U.S.A. 77 H5 35 21N 80 11W
Albemarle Sd., U.S.A. 77 H7 36 5N 76 0W
Alberche →, Spain 19 C3 39 58N 4 46W
Alberdi, Paraguay 94 B4 26 14S 58 20W
Albert, L. = Mobutu Sese Seko, L., Africa 54 B3 1 30N 31 0 E
Albert, L., Australia 63 F2 35 30S 139 10 E
Albert Canyon, Canada 72 C5 51 8N 117 41W
Albert Edward Ra., Australia 60 C4 18 17S 127 57 E
Albert Lea, U.S.A. 80 D8 43 39N 93 22W
Albert Nile →, Uganda 54 B3 3 36N 32 2 E
Albert Town, Bahamas 89 B5 22 37N 74 33W
Alberta □, Canada 72 C6 54 40N 115 0W
Alberti, Argentina 94 D3 35 1S 60 16W
Albertinia, S. Africa 56 E3 34 11S 21 34 E
Alberton, Canada 71 C7 46 50N 64 0W
Albertville = Kalemie, Zaïre 54 D2 5 55S 29 9 E
Albi, France 18 E5 43 56N 2 9 E
Albia, U.S.A. 80 E8 41 2N 92 48W
Albina, Surinam 93 B8 5 37N 54 15W
Albina, Ponta, Angola 56 B1 15 52S 11 44 E
Albion, Idaho, U.S.A. 82 E7 42 25N 113 35W
Albion, Mich., U.S.A. 76 D3 42 15N 84 45W
Albion, Nebr., U.S.A. 80 E5 41 42N 98 0W
Albion, Pa., U.S.A. 78 E4 41 53N 80 22W
Ålborg, Denmark 9 H10 57 2N 9 54 E
Alborz, Reshteh-ye Kūhhā-ye, Iran 45 C7 36 0N 52 0 E
Albreda, Canada 72 C5 52 35N 119 10W
Albuquerque, U.S.A. 83 J10 35 5N 106 39W
Albuquerque, Cayos de, Caribbean 88 D3 12 10N 81 50W
Alburg, U.S.A. 79 B11 44 59N 73 18W
Alburquerque, Spain 19 C2 39 15N 6 59W
Albury, Australia 63 F4 36 3S 146 56 E
Alcalá de Henares, Spain 19 B4 40 28N 3 22W
Alcalá la Real, Spain 19 D4 37 27N 3 57W
Alcamo, Italy 20 F5 37 59N 12 55 E
Alcañiz, Spain 19 B5 41 2N 0 8W
Alcântara, Brazil 93 D10 2 20S 44 30W
Alcántara, Spain 19 C2 39 41N 6 57W
Alcantara L., Canada 73 A7 60 57N 108 9W
Alcaraz, Sierra de, Spain 19 C4 38 40N 2 20W
Alcaudete, Spain 19 D3 37 35N 4 5W
Alcázar de San Juan, Spain 19 C4 39 24N 3 12W
Alchevsk = Kommunarsk, Ukraine 25 E6 48 30N 38 45 E
Alcira, Spain 19 C5 39 9N 0 30W
Alcoa, U.S.A. 77 H4 35 48N 83 59W
Alcobaça, Portugal 19 C1 39 32N 9 0W
Alcova, U.S.A. 82 E10 42 34N 106 43W
Alcoy, Spain 19 C5 38 43N 0 30W
Alcudia, Spain 22 B10 39 51N 3 7 E
Alcudia, B. de, Spain 22 B10 39 47N 3 15 E
Aldabra Is., Seychelles 49 G8 9 22S 46 28 E
Aldama, Mexico 87 C5 23 0N 98 4W
Aldan, Russia 27 D13 58 40N 125 30 E
Aldan →, Russia 27 C13 63 28N 129 35 E
Aldea, Pta. de la, Canary Is. 22 G4 28 0N 15 50W
Aldeburgh, U.K. 11 E9 52 9N 1 35 E
Alder, U.S.A. 82 D7 45 19N 112 6W
Alder Pk., U.S.A. 84 K5 35 53N 121 22W
Alderney, Chan. Is. 11 H5 49 42N 2 12W
Aldershot, U.K. 11 F7 51 15N 0 43W
Aledo, U.S.A. 80 E9 41 12N 90 45W
Aleg, Mauritania 50 E2 17 3N 13 55W
Alegranza, Canary Is. 22 E6 29 23N 13 32W
Alegranza, I., Canary Is. 22 E6 29 23N 13 32W
Alegre, Brazil 95 A7 20 50S 41 30W
Alegrete, Brazil 95 B4 29 40S 56 0W
Aleisk, Russia 26 D9 52 40N 83 0 E
Aleksandrovsk-Sakhalinskiy, Russia 27 D15 50 50N 142 20 E
Aleksandrovskiy Zavod, Russia 27 D12 50 40N 117 50 E
Aleksandrovskoye, Russia 26 C8 60 35N 77 50 E
Além Paraíba, Brazil 95 A7 21 52S 42 41W
Alemania, Argentina 94 B2 25 40S 65 30W
Alemania, Chile 94 B2 25 10S 69 55W
Alençon, France 18 B4 48 27N 0 4 E
Alenuihaha Channel, U.S.A. 74 H17 20 30N 156 0W
Aleppo = Ḩalab, Syria 44 B3 36 10N 37 15 E
Aléria, France 20 C3 42 5N 9 26 E
Alert Bay, Canada 72 C3 50 30N 126 55W
Alès, France 18 D6 44 9N 4 5 E
Alessándria, Italy 20 B3 44 54N 8 37 E
Ålesund, Norway 8 E9 62 28N 6 12 E
Aleutian Is., Pac. Oc. 68 C2 52 0N 175 0W
Aleutian Trench, Pac. Oc. 64 B10 48 0N 180 0 E
Alexander, U.S.A. 80 B3 47 51N 103 39W
Alexander, Mt., Australia 61 E3 28 58S 120 16 E
Alexander Arch., U.S.A. 72 B2 56 0N 136 0W
Alexander B., S. Africa 56 D2 28 36S 16 33 E
Alexander Bay, S. Africa 56 D2 28 40S 16 30 E
Alexander City, U.S.A. 77 J3 32 56N 85 58W
Alexander I., Antarctica 5 C17 69 0S 70 0W
Alexandra, Australia 63 F4 37 8S 145 40 E
Alexandra, N.Z. 59 L2 45 14S 169 25 E
Alexandra Falls, Canada 72 A5 60 29N 116 18W
Alexandretta = İskenderun, Turkey 25 G6 36 32N 36 10 E
Alexandria = El Iskandarîya, Egypt 51 B10 31 0N 30 0 E
Alexandria, Australia 62 B2 19 5S 136 40 E
Alexandria, B.C., Canada 72 C4 52 35N 122 27W
Alexandria, Ont., Canada 70 C5 45 19N 74 38W
Alexandria, S. Africa 56 E4 33 38S 26 28 E
Alexandria, Ind., U.S.A. 76 E3 40 16N 85 41W
Alexandria, La., U.S.A. 81 K8 31 18N 92 27W
Alexandria, Minn., U.S.A. 80 C7 45 53N 95 22W
Alexandria, S. Dak., U.S.A. 80 D6 43 39N 97 47W
Alexandria, Va., U.S.A. 76 F7 38 48N 77 3W
Alexandria Bay, U.S.A. 79 B9 44 20N 75 55W
Alexandrina, L., Australia 63 F2 35 25S 139 10 E
Alexandroúpolis, Greece 21 D11 40 50N 25 54 E
Alexis →, Canada 71 B8 52 33N 56 8W
Alexis Creek, Canada 72 C4 52 10N 123 20W
Alfabia, Spain 22 B9 39 44N 2 44 E
Alfenas, Brazil 95 A6 21 20S 46 10W
Alford, U.K. 12 D6 57 13N 2 42W
Alfred, Maine, U.S.A. 79 C14 43 29N 70 43W
Alfred, N.Y., U.S.A. 78 D7 42 16N 77 48W
Alfreton, U.K. 10 D6 53 6N 1 22W
Alga, Kazakhstan 25 E10 49 53N 57 20 E
Algaida, Spain 22 B9 39 33N 2 53 E
Algarve, Portugal 19 D1 36 58N 8 20W
Algeciras, Spain 19 D3 36 9N 5 28W
Algemesí, Spain 19 C5 39 11N 0 27W
Alger, Algeria 50 A5 36 42N 3 8 E
Algeria ■, Africa 50 C5 28 30N 2 0 E
Alghero, Italy 20 D3 40 34N 8 20 E
Algiers = Alger, Algeria 50 A5 36 42N 3 8 E
Algoa B., S. Africa 56 E4 33 50S 25 45 E
Algoma, U.S.A. 76 C2 44 36N 87 26W
Algona, U.S.A. 80 D7 43 4N 94 14W
Algonac, U.S.A. 78 D2 42 37N 82 32W
Alhama de Murcia, Spain 19 D5 37 51N 1 25W
Alhambra, U.S.A. 85 L8 34 8N 118 6W
Alhucemas = Al Hoceïma, Morocco 50 A4 35 8N 3 58W
'Alī al Gharbī, Iraq 44 C5 32 30N 46 45 E
Alī ash Sharqī, Iraq 44 C5 32 7N 46 44 E
'Alī Khēl, Afghan. 42 C3 33 57N 69 43 E
Alī Shāh, Iran 44 B5 38 9N 45 50 E
'Alīābād, Khorāsān, Iran 45 C8 32 30N 57 30 E
Alīābād, Kordestān, Iran 44 C5 35 4N 46 58 E
'Alīābād, Yazd, Iran 45 D7 31 41N 53 49 E
Aliákmon →, Greece 21 D10 40 30N 22 36 E
Alibo, Ethiopia 51 G12 9 52N 37 5 E
Alicante, Spain 19 C5 38 23N 0 30W
Alice, S. Africa 56 E4 32 48S 26 55 E
Alice, U.S.A. 81 M5 27 45N 98 5W
Alice →, Queens., Australia 62 C3 24 2S 144 50 E
Alice →, Queens., Australia 62 B3 15 35S 142 20 E
Alice Arm, Canada 72 B3 55 29N 129 31W
Alice Downs, Australia 60 C4 17 45S 127 56 E
Alice Springs, Australia 62 C1 23 40S 133 50 E
Alicedale, S. Africa 56 E4 33 15S 26 4 E
Aliceville, U.S.A. 77 J1 33 8N 88 9W
Alick Cr. →, Australia 62 C3 20 55S 142 20 E
Alida, Canada 73 D8 49 25N 101 55W
Aligarh, Raj., India 42 G7 25 55N 76 15 E
Aligarh, Ut. P., India 42 F8 27 55N 78 10 E
Alīgūdarz, Iran 45 C6 33 25N 49 45 E
Alimnía, Greece 23 C9 36 16N 27 43 E
Alingsås, Sweden 9 H12 57 56N 12 31 E
Alipur, Pakistan 42 E4 29 25N 70 55 E
Alipur Duar, India 41 F16 26 30N 89 35 E
Aliquippa, U.S.A. 78 F4 40 37N 80 15W
Aliwal North, S. Africa 56 E4 30 45S 26 45 E
Alix, Canada 72 C6 52 24N 113 11W
Aljustrel, Portugal 19 D1 37 55N 8 10W
Alkmaar, Neths. 15 B4 52 37N 4 45 E
All American Canal, U.S.A. 83 K6 32 45N 115 15W
Allah Dad, Pakistan 42 G2 25 38N 67 34 E
Allahabad, India 43 G9 25 25N 81 58 E
Allakh-Yun, Russia 27 C14 60 50N 137 5 E
Allan, Canada 73 C7 51 53N 106 4W
Allanmyo, Burma 41 K19 19 30N 95 17 E
Allanridge, S. Africa 56 D4 27 45S 26 40 E
Allanwater, Canada 70 B1 50 14N 90 10W
Allegan, U.S.A. 76 D3 42 32N 85 51W
Allegany, U.S.A. 78 D6 42 6N 78 30W
Allegheny →, U.S.A. 78 F5 40 27N 80 1W
Allegheny Plateau, U.S.A. 76 G6 38 0N 80 0W
Allegheny Reservoir, U.S.A. 78 E6 41 50N 79 0W
Allen, Bog of, Ireland 13 C4 53 15N 7 0W
Allen, L., Ireland 13 B3 54 12N 8 5W
Allende, Mexico 86 B4 28 20N 100 50W
Allentown, U.S.A. 79 F9 40 37N 75 29W
Alleppey, India 40 Q10 9 30N 76 28 E
Alliance, Nebr., U.S.A. 80 D3 42 6N 102 52W
Alliance, Ohio, U.S.A. 78 F3 40 55N 81 6W
Allier □, France 18 C5 46 25N 2 40 E
Allier →, France 18 C5 46 57N 3 4 E
Alliston, Canada 70 D4 44 9N 79 52W
Alloa, U.K. 12 E5 56 7N 3 49W
Allora, Australia 63 D5 28 2S 152 0 E
Alluitsup Paa = Sydprøven, Greenland 4 C5 60 30N 45 35W
Alma, Canada 71 C5 48 35N 71 40W
Alma, Ga., U.S.A. 77 K4 31 33N 82 28W
Alma, Kans., U.S.A. 80 F6 39 1N 96 17W
Alma, Mich., U.S.A. 76 D3 43 23N 84 39W
Alma, Nebr., U.S.A. 80 E5 40 6N 99 22W
Alma, Wis., U.S.A. 80 C9 44 20N 91 55W
Alma Ata, Kazakhstan 26 E8 43 15N 76 57 E
Almada, Portugal 19 C1 38 40N 9 9W
Almaden, Australia 62 B3 17 22S 144 40 E
Almadén, Spain 19 C3 38 49N 4 52W
Almanor, L., U.S.A. 82 F3 40 14N 121 9W
Almansa, Spain 19 C5 38 51N 1 5W
Almanzor, Pico de, Spain 19 B3 40 15N 5 18W
Almanzora →, Spain 19 D5 37 14N 1 46W
Almaty = Alma Ata, Kazakhstan 26 E8 43 15N 76 57 E
Almazán, Spain 19 B4 41 30N 2 30W
Almeirim, Brazil 93 D8 1 30S 52 34W
Almelo, Neths. 15 B6 52 22N 6 42 E
Almendralejo, Spain 19 C2 38 41N 6 26W
Almería, Spain 19 D4 36 52N 2 27W
Almirante, Panama 88 E3 9 10N 82 30W
Almiroú, Kólpos, Greece 23 D6 35 23N 24 20 E
Almont, U.S.A. 78 D1 42 55N 83 3W
Almonte, Canada 79 A8 45 14N 76 12W
Almora, India 43 E8 29 38N 79 40 E
Alnwick, U.K. 10 B6 55 25N 1 42W
Aloi, Uganda 54 B3 2 16N 33 10 E
Alon, Burma 41 H19 22 12N 95 5 E
Alor, Indonesia 37 F6 8 15S 124 30 E
Alor Setar, Malaysia 39 J3 6 7N 100 22 E
Aloysius, Mt., Australia 61 E4 26 0S 128 38 E
Alpaugh, U.S.A. 84 K7 35 53N 119 29W
Alpena, U.S.A. 76 C4 45 4N 83 27W
Alpes-de-Haute-Provence □, France 18 D7 44 8N 6 10 E
Alpes-Maritimes □, France 18 E7 43 55N 7 10 E
Alpha, Australia 62 C4 23 39S 146 37 E
Alpine, Ariz., U.S.A. 83 K9 33 51N 109 9W
Alpine, Calif., U.S.A. 85 N10 32 50N 116 46W
Alpine, Tex., U.S.A. 81 K3 30 22N 103 40W
Alps, Europe 16 E4 46 30N 9 30 E
Alroy Downs, Australia 62 B2 19 20S 136 5 E
Alsace, France 18 B7 48 15N 7 25 E
Alsask, Canada 73 C7 51 21N 109 59W
Alsásua, Spain 19 A4 42 54N 2 10W
Alsten, Norway 8 D12 65 58N 12 40 E
Alta, Norway 8 B17 69 57N 23 10 E
Alta Gracia, Argentina 94 C3 31 40S 64 30W
Alta Lake, Canada 72 C4 50 10N 123 0W
Alta Sierra, U.S.A. 85 K8 35 42N 118 33W
Altaelva →, Norway 8 B17 69 46N 23 45 E
Altafjorden, Norway 8 A17 70 5N 23 5 E
Altagracia, Venezuela 92 A4 10 45N 71 30W
Altai = Aerhtai Shan, Mongolia 32 B4 46 40N 92 45 E
Altai = Aerhtai Shan, Mongolia 32 B4 46 40N 92 45 E
Altamaha →, U.S.A. 77 K5 31 20N 81 20W
Altamira, Brazil 93 D8 3 12S 52 10W
Altamira, Chile 94 B2 25 47S 69 51W
Altamira, Mexico 87 C5 22 24N 97 55W
Altamont, U.S.A. 79 D10 42 43N 74 3W
Altanbulag, Mongolia 32 A5 50 16N 106 30 E
Altar, Mexico 86 A2 30 40N 111 50W
Altata, Mexico 86 C3 24 30N 108 0W
Altavista, U.S.A. 76 G6 37 6N 79 17W
Altay, China 32 B3 47 48N 88 10 E
Alto Adige = Trentino-Alto Adige □, Italy 20 A4 46 30N 11 0 E
Alto-Alentejo, Portugal 19 C2 39 0N 7 40W
Alto Araguaia, Brazil 93 G8 17 15S 53 20W
Alto Cuchumatanes = Cuchumatanes, Sierra de los, Guatemala 88 C1 15 35N 91 25W
Alto del Inca, Chile 94 A2 24 10S 68 10W
Alto Ligonha, Mozam. 55 F4 15 30S 38 11 E
Alto Molocue, Mozam. 55 F4 15 50S 37 35 E
Alto Paraguay □, Paraguay 94 A4 21 0S 58 30W
Alto Paraná □, Paraguay 95 B5 25 30S 54 50W
Alton, Canada 78 C4 43 54N 80 5W
Alton, U.S.A. 80 F9 38 53N 90 11W
Alton Downs, Australia 63 D2 26 7S 138 57 E
Altoona, U.S.A. 78 F6 40 31N 78 24W
Altūn Kūprī, Iraq 44 C5 35 45N 44 9 E
Altun Shan, China 32 C3 38 30N 88 0 E
Alturas, U.S.A. 82 F3 41 29N 120 32W
Altus, U.S.A. 81 H5 34 38N 99 20W
Alùla, Somali Rep. 46 E5 11 50N 50 45 E
Alunite, U.S.A. 85 K12 35 59N 114 55W
Alusi, Indonesia 37 F8 7 35S 131 40 E
Al'Uzayr, Iraq 44 D5 31 19N 47 25 E
Alva, U.S.A. 81 G5 36 48N 98 40W
Alvarado, Mexico 87 D5 18 40N 95 50W
Alvarado, U.S.A. 81 J6 32 24N 97 13W
Alvaro Obregón, Presa, Mexico 86 B3 27 55N 109 52W
Alvear, Argentina 94 B4 29 5S 56 30W

Ashland

Antsiranana, *Madag.* **57 A8** 12 25S 49 20 E
Antsohihy, *Madag.* **57 A8** 14 50S 47 59 E
Antsohimbondrona Seranana, *Madag.* **57 A8** 13 7S 48 48 E
Antu, *China* **35 C15** 42 30N 128 20 E
Antwerp = Antwerpen, *Belgium* **15 C4** 51 13N 4 25 E
Antwerp, *U.S.A.* **79 B9** 44 12N 75 37W
Antwerpen, *Belgium* **15 C4** 51 13N 4 25 E
Antwerpen □, *Belgium* **15 C4** 51 15N 4 40 E
Anupgarh, *India* **42 E5** 29 10N 73 10 E
Anuradhapura, *Sri Lanka* **40 Q12** 8 22N 80 28 E
Anveh, *Iran* **45 E7** 27 23N 54 11 E
Anvers = Antwerpen, *Belgium* **15 C4** 51 13N 4 25 E
Anvers I., *Antarctica* **5 C17** 64 30S 63 40W
Anxi, *China* **32 B4** 40 30N 95 43 E
Anxious B., *Australia* **63 E1** 33 24S 134 45 E
Anyang, *China* **34 F8** 36 5N 114 21 E
Anyi, *China* **34 G6** 35 2N 111 2 E
Anza, *U.S.A.* **85 M10** 33 35N 116 39W
Anze, *China* **34 F7** 36 10N 112 12 E
Anzhero-Sudzhensk, *Russia* **26 D9** 56 10N 86 0 E
Ánzio, *Italy* **20 D5** 41 28N 12 37 E
Aoga-Shima, *Japan* **31 H9** 32 28N 139 46 E
Aomori, *Japan* **30 D10** 40 45N 140 45 E
Aomori □, *Japan* **30 D10** 40 45N 140 40 E
Aonla, *India* **43 E8** 28 16N 79 11 E
Aosta, *Italy* **20 B2** 45 43N 7 20 E
Aoudéras, *Niger* **50 E6** 17 45N 8 20 E
Aoulef el Arab, *Algeria* **50 C5** 26 55N 1 2 E
Apa →, *S. Amer.* **94 A4** 22 6S 58 2W
Apache, *U.S.A.* **81 H5** 34 54N 98 22W
Apalachee B., *U.S.A.* **77 L3** 30 0N 84 0W
Apalachicola, *U.S.A.* **77 L3** 29 43N 84 59W
Apalachicola →, *U.S.A.* **77 L3** 29 43N 84 58W
Apaporis →, *Colombia* **92 D5** 1 23S 69 25W
Aparri, *Phil.* **37 A6** 18 22N 121 38 E
Apàtity, *Russia* **24 A5** 67 34N 33 22 E
Apatzingán, *Mexico* **86 D4** 19 0N 102 20W
Apeldoorn, *Neths.* **15 B5** 52 13N 5 57 E
Apennines = Appennini, *Italy* **20 C4** 44 0N 10 0 E
Apia, *W. Samoa* **59 A13** 13 50S 171 50W
Apiacás, Serra dos, *Brazil* **92 E7** 9 50S 57 0W
Apizaco, *Mexico* **87 D5** 19 26N 98 9W
Aplao, *Peru* **92 G4** 16 0S 72 40W
Apo, Mt., *Phil.* **37 C7** 6 53N 125 14 E
Apolakkiá, *Greece* **23 C9** 36 5N 27 48 E
Apolakkiá, Órmos, *Greece* **23 C9** 36 5N 27 45 E
Apollonia = Marsá Susah, *Libya* **51 B9** 32 52N 21 59 E
Apolo, *Bolivia* **92 F5** 14 30S 68 30W
Apostle Is., *U.S.A.* **80 B9** 47 0N 90 40W
Apóstoles, *Argentina* **95 B4** 28 0S 56 0W
Apostolos Andreas, C., *Cyprus* **23 D13** 35 42N 34 35 E
Apoteri, *Guyana* **92 C7** 4 2N 58 32W
Appalachian Mts., *U.S.A.* **76 G6** 38 0N 80 0W
Appennini, *Italy* **20 C4** 44 0N 10 0 E
Apple Hill, *Canada* **79 A10** 45 13N 74 46W
Apple Valley, *U.S.A.* **85 L9** 34 32N 117 14W
Appleby, *U.K.* **10 C5** 54 35N 2 29W
Appleton, *U.S.A.* **76 C1** 44 16N 88 25W
Approuague, *Fr. Guiana* **93 C8** 4 20N 52 0W
Apucarana, *Brazil* **95 A5** 23 55S 51 33W
Apulia = Púglia □, *Italy* **20 D7** 41 0N 16 30 E
Apure →, *Venezuela* **92 B5** 7 37N 66 25W
Apurimac →, *Peru* **92 F4** 12 17S 73 56W
Aqabah = Al 'Aqabah, *Jordan* **47 F4** 29 31N 35 0 E
'Aqabah, Khalīj al, *Red Sea* **44 D2** 28 15N 33 20 E
'Aqdā, *Iran* **45 C7** 32 26N 53 37 E
Aqīq, *Sudan* **51 E12** 18 14N 38 12 E
Aqmola = Tselinograd, *Kazakhstan* **26 D8** 51 10N 71 30 E
Aqrah, *Iraq* **44 B4** 36 46N 43 45 E
Aqtöbe = Aktyubinsk, *Kazakhstan* **25 D10** 50 17N 57 10 E
Aquidauana, *Brazil* **93 H7** 20 30S 55 50W
Aquiles Serdán, *Mexico* **86 B3** 28 37N 105 54W
Aquin, *Haiti* **89 C5** 18 16N 73 24W
Ar Rachidiya, *Morocco* **50 B4** 31 58N 4 20W
Ar Rafid, *Syria* **47 C4** 32 57N 35 52 E
Ar Raḩḩālīyah, *Iraq* **44 C4** 32 44N 43 23 E
Ar Ramādī, *Iraq* **44 C4** 33 25N 43 20 E
Ar Ramthā, *Jordan* **47 C5** 32 34N 36 0 E
Ar Raqqah, *Syria* **44 C3** 36 0N 38 55 E
Ar Rass, *Si. Arabia* **44 E4** 25 50N 43 40 E
Ar Rifā'ī, *Si. Arabia* **44 D5** 31 50N 46 10 E
Ar Riyāḑ, *Si. Arabia* **46 C4** 24 41N 46 42 E
Ar Ru'ays, *Qatar* **45 E6** 26 8N 51 12 E
Ar Rukhaymīyah, *Iraq* **44 D5** 29 22N 45 38 E
Ar Ruqayyidah, *Si. Arabia* **45 E6** 25 21N 49 34 E
Ar Ruşāfah, *Syria* **44 C3** 35 52N 36 53 E
Ar Ruţbah, *Iraq* **44 C4** 33 0N 40 15 E
Ara, *India* **43 G11** 25 35N 84 32 E
'Arab, Bahr el →, *Sudan* **51 G10** 9 0N 29 30 E
'Arabābād, *Iran* **45 C8** 33 2N 57 41 E
Arabia, *Asia* **46 C4** 25 0N 45 0 E
Arabian Desert = Es Sahrâ' Esh Sharqîya, *Egypt* **51 C11** 27 30N 32 30 E
Arabian Gulf = Gulf, The, *Asia* **45 E6** 27 0N 50 0 E
Arabian Sea, *Ind. Oc.* **29 H10** 16 0N 65 0 E
Aracaju, *Brazil* **93 F11** 10 55S 37 4W
Aracataca, *Colombia* **92 A4** 10 38N 74 9W
Aracati, *Brazil* **93 D11** 4 30S 37 44W
Araçatuba, *Brazil* **95 A5** 21 10S 50 30W
Aracena, *Spain* **19 D2** 37 53N 6 38W
Araçuaí, *Brazil* **93 G10** 16 52S 42 4W
'Arad, *Israel* **47 D4** 31 15N 35 12 E
Arad, *Romania* **17 E10** 46 10N 21 20 E
Arada, *Chad* **51 F9** 15 0N 20 20 E
Aradhippou, *Cyprus* **23 E12** 34 57N 33 36 E
Arafura Sea, *E. Indies* **37 F8** 9 0S 135 0 E
Aragón □, *Spain* **19 B5** 41 25N 0 40W
Aragón →, *Spain* **19 A5** 42 13N 1 44W
Araguacema, *Brazil* **93 E9** 8 50S 49 20W
Araguaia →, *Brazil* **93 E9** 5 21S 48 41W
Araguari, *Brazil* **93 G9** 18 38S 48 11W
Araguari →, *Brazil* **93 C9** 1 15N 49 55W
Arak, *Algeria* **50 C5** 25 20N 3 45 E
Arāk, *Iran* **45 C6** 34 0N 49 40 E
Arakan Coast, *Burma* **41 K19** 19 0N 94 0 E
Arakan Yoma, *Burma* **41 K19** 20 0N 94 40 E
Araks = Aras, Rūd-e →, *Iran* **44 B5** 39 10N 47 10 E
Aral Sea = Aralskoye More, *Asia* **26 E7** 44 30N 60 0 E
Aralsk, *Kazakhstan* **26 E7** 46 50N 61 20 E
Aralskoye More, *Asia* **26 E7** 44 30N 60 0 E
Aramac, *Australia* **62 C4** 22 58S 145 14 E
Arambag, *India* **43 H12** 22 53N 87 48 E
Aran I., *Ireland* **13 B3** 55 0N 8 30W
Aran Is., *Ireland* **13 C2** 53 5N 9 42W
Arandān, *Iran* **44 C5** 35 23N 46 55 E
Aranjuez, *Spain* **19 B4** 40 1N 3 40W
Aranos, *Namibia* **56 C2** 24 9S 19 7 E
Aransas Pass, *U.S.A.* **81 M6** 27 55N 97 9W
Araouane, *Mali* **50 E4** 18 55N 3 30W
Arapahoe, *U.S.A.* **80 E5** 40 18N 99 54W
Arapey Grande →, *Uruguay* **94 C4** 30 55S 57 49W
Arapiraca, *Brazil* **93 E11** 9 45S 36 39W
Arapongas, *Brazil* **95 A5** 23 29S 51 28W
Ar'ar, *Si. Arabia* **44 D4** 30 59N 41 2 E
Araranguá, *Brazil* **95 B6** 29 0S 49 30W
Araraquara, *Brazil* **93 H9** 21 50S 48 0W
Ararás, Serra das, *Brazil* **95 B5** 25 0S 53 10W
Ararat, *Australia* **63 F3** 37 16S 143 0 E
Ararat, Mt. = Ağrı Dağı, *Turkey* **25 G7** 39 50N 44 15 E
Araria, *India* **43 F12** 26 9N 87 33 E
Araripe, Chapada do, *Brazil* **93 E11** 7 20S 40 0W
Araruama, L. de, *Brazil* **95 A7** 22 53S 42 12W
Aras, Rūd-e →, *Iran* **44 B5** 39 10N 47 10 E
Arauca, *Colombia* **92 B4** 7 0N 70 40W
Arauca →, *Venezuela* **92 B5** 7 24N 66 35W
Arauco, *Chile* **94 D1** 37 16S 73 25W
Arauco □, *Chile* **94 D1** 37 40S 73 25W
Araxá, *Brazil* **93 G9** 19 35S 46 55W
Araya, Pen. de, *Venezuela* **92 A6** 10 40N 64 0W
Arbat, *Iraq* **44 C5** 35 25N 45 35 E
Arbatax, *Italy* **20 E3** 39 57N 9 42 E
Arbaza, *Russia* **27 D10** 52 40N 92 30 E
Arbīl, *Iraq* **44 B5** 36 15N 44 5 E
Arborfield, *Canada* **73 C8** 53 6N 103 39W
Arborg, *Canada* **73 C9** 50 54N 97 13W
Arbroath, *U.K.* **12 E6** 56 34N 2 35W
Arbuckle, *U.S.A.* **84 F4** 39 1N 122 3W
Arcachon, *France* **18 D3** 44 40N 1 10W
Arcade, *U.S.A.* **78 D6** 42 32N 78 25W
Arcadia, *Fla., U.S.A.* **77 M5** 27 13N 81 52W
Arcadia, *La., U.S.A.* **81 J8** 32 33N 92 55W
Arcadia, *Nebr., U.S.A.* **80 E5** 41 25N 99 8W
Arcadia, *Pa., U.S.A.* **78 F6** 40 47N 78 51W
Arcadia, *Wis., U.S.A.* **80 C9** 44 15N 91 30W
Arcata, *U.S.A.* **82 F1** 40 52N 124 5W
Archangel = Arkhangelsk, *Russia* **24 B7** 64 40N 41 0 E
Archbald, *U.S.A.* **79 E9** 41 30N 75 32W
Archer →, *Australia* **62 A3** 13 28S 141 41 E
Archer B., *Australia* **62 A3** 13 20S 141 30 E
Archers Post, *Kenya* **54 B4** 0 35N 37 35 E
Arcila = Asilah, *Morocco* **50 A3** 35 29N 6 0W
Arckaringa, *Australia* **63 D1** 27 56S 134 45 E
Arckaringa Cr. →, *Australia* **63 D2** 28 10S 135 22 E
Arco, *U.S.A.* **82 E7** 43 38N 113 18W
Arcola, *Canada* **73 D8** 49 40N 102 30W
Arcos, *Spain* **19 B4** 41 12N 2 16W
Arcot, *India* **40 N11** 12 53N 79 20 E
Arcoverde, *Brazil* **93 E11** 8 25S 37 4W
Arctic Bay, *Canada* **69 A11** 73 1N 85 7W
Arctic Ocean, *Arctic* **4 B18** 78 0N 160 0W
Arctic Red River, *Canada* **68 B6** 67 15N 134 0W
Arda →, *Bulgaria* **21 D12** 41 40N 26 29 E
Ardabīl, *Iran* **45 B6** 38 15N 48 18 E
Ardakān = Sepīdān, *Iran* **45 D7** 30 20N 52 5 E
Ardèche □, *France* **18 D6** 44 42N 4 16 E
Ardee, *Ireland* **13 C5** 53 51N 6 32W
Arden, *Canada* **78 B8** 44 43N 76 56W
Arden, *Calif., U.S.A.* **84 G5** 38 36N 121 33W
Arden, *Nev., U.S.A.* **85 J11** 36 1N 115 14W
Ardenne, *Belgium* **15 E5** 49 50N 5 5 E
Ardennes = Ardenne, *Belgium* **15 E5** 49 50N 5 5 E
Ardennes □, *France* **18 B6** 49 35N 4 40 E
Ardestān, *Iran* **45 C7** 33 20N 52 25 E
Ardgour, *U.K.* **12 E3** 56 45N 5 25W
Ardlethan, *Australia* **63 E4** 34 22S 146 53 E
Ardmore, *Australia* **62 C2** 21 39S 139 11 E
Ardmore, *Okla., U.S.A.* **81 H6** 34 10N 97 8W
Ardmore, *Pa., U.S.A.* **79 G9** 39 58N 75 18W
Ardmore, *S. Dak., U.S.A.* **80 D3** 43 1N 103 40W
Ardnacrusha, *Ireland* **13 D3** 52 43N 8 38W
Ardnamurchan, Pt. of, *U.K.* **12 E2** 56 44N 6 14W
Ardrossan, *Australia* **63 E2** 34 26S 137 53 E
Ardrossan, *U.K.* **12 F4** 55 39N 4 50W
Ards □, *U.K.* **13 B6** 54 35N 5 30W
Ards Pen., *U.K.* **13 B6** 54 30N 5 25W
Arecibo, *Puerto Rico* **89 C6** 18 29N 66 43W
Areia Branca, *Brazil* **93 D11** 5 0S 37 0W
Arena, Pt., *U.S.A.* **84 G3** 38 57N 123 44W
Arendal, *Norway* **9 G10** 58 28N 8 46 E
Arequipa, *Peru* **92 G4** 16 20S 71 30W
Arero, *Ethiopia* **51 H12** 4 41N 38 50 E
Arévalo, *Spain* **19 B3** 41 3N 4 43W
Arezzo, *Italy* **20 C4** 43 28N 11 50 E
Argamakmur, *Indonesia* **36 E2** 3 35S 102 0 E
Argentário, Mte., *Italy* **20 C4** 42 23N 11 11 E
Argentia, *Canada* **71 C9** 47 18N 53 58W
Argentina ■, *S. Amer.* **96 D3** 35 0S 66 0W
Argentina Is., *Antarctica* **5 C17** 66 0S 64 0W
Argentino, L., *Argentina* **96 G2** 50 10S 73 0W
Argeş →, *Romania* **17 F13** 44 12N 26 14 E
Arghandab →, *Afghan.* **42 D1** 31 30N 64 15 E
Argo, *Sudan* **51 E11** 19 28N 30 30 E
Argolikós Kólpos, *Greece* **21 F10** 37 20N 22 52 E
Argonne, *France* **18 B6** 49 10N 5 0 E
Árgos, *Greece* **21 F10** 37 40N 22 43 E
Argostólion, *Greece* **21 E9** 38 12N 20 33 E
Arguello, Pt., *U.S.A.* **85 L6** 34 35N 120 39W
Arguineguín, *Canary Is.* **22 G4** 27 46N 15 41W
Argun →, *Russia* **27 D13** 53 20N 121 28 E
Argungu, *Nigeria* **50 F5** 12 40N 4 31 E
Argus Pk., *U.S.A.* **85 K9** 35 52N 117 26W
Argyle, *U.S.A.* **80 A6** 48 20N 96 49W
Argyle, L., *Australia* **60 C4** 16 20S 128 40 E
Århus, *Denmark* **9 H11** 56 8N 10 11 E
Ariadnoye, *Russia* **30 B7** 45 8N 134 25 E
Ariamsvlei, *Namibia* **56 D2** 28 9S 19 51 E
Arica, *Chile* **92 G4** 18 32S 70 20W
Arica, *Colombia* **92 D4** 2 0S 71 50W
Arico, *Canary Is.* **22 F3** 28 9N 16 29W
Arid, C., *Australia* **61 F3** 34 1S 123 10 E
Arida, *Japan* **31 G7** 34 5N 135 8 E
Ariège □, *France* **18 E4** 42 56N 1 30 E
Arīḩā, *Syria* **44 C3** 35 49N 36 35 E
Arílla, Ákra, *Greece* **23 A3** 39 43N 19 39 E
Arima, *Trin. & Tob.* **89 D7** 10 38N 61 17W
Arinos →, *Brazil* **92 F7** 10 25S 58 20W
Ario de Rosales, *Mexico* **86 D4** 19 12N 102 0W
Aripuanã, *Brazil* **92 E6** 9 25S 60 30W
Aripuanã →, *Brazil* **92 E6** 5 7S 60 25W
Ariquemes, *Brazil* **92 E6** 9 55S 63 6W
Arisaig, *U.K.* **12 E3** 56 55N 5 50W
Aristazabal I., *Canada* **72 C3** 52 40N 129 10W
Arivaca, *U.S.A.* **83 L8** 31 37N 111 25W
Arivonimamo, *Madag.* **57 B8** 19 1S 47 11 E
Arizaro, Salar de, *Argentina* **94 A2** 24 40S 67 50W
Arizona, *Argentina* **94 D2** 35 45S 65 25W
Arizona □, *U.S.A.* **83 J8** 34 0N 112 0W
Arizpe, *Mexico* **86 A2** 30 20N 110 11W
Arjeplog, *Sweden* **8 C15** 66 3N 18 2 E
Arjona, *Colombia* **92 A3** 10 14N 75 22W
Arjuno, *Indonesia* **37 G15** 7 49S 112 34 E
Arka, *Russia* **27 C15** 60 15N 142 0 E
Arkadelphia, *U.S.A.* **81 H8** 34 7N 93 4W
Arkaig, L., *U.K.* **12 E3** 56 58N 5 10W
Arkalyk, *Kazakhstan* **26 D7** 50 13N 66 50 E
Arkansas □, *U.S.A.* **81 H8** 35 0N 92 30W
Arkansas →, *U.S.A.* **81 J9** 33 47N 91 4W
Arkansas City, *U.S.A.* **81 G6** 37 4N 97 2W
Arkhángelos, *Greece* **23 C10** 36 13N 28 7 E
Arkhangelsk, *Russia* **24 B7** 64 40N 41 0 E
Arklow, *Ireland* **13 D5** 52 48N 6 10W
Arkticheskiy, Mys, *Russia* **27 A10** 81 10N 95 0 E
Arlanzón →, *Spain* **19 A3** 42 3N 4 17W
Arlberg Pass, *Austria* **16 E5** 47 9N 10 12 E
Arlee, *U.S.A.* **82 C6** 47 10N 114 5W
Arles, *France* **18 E6** 43 41N 4 40 E
Arlington, *S. Africa* **57 D4** 28 1S 27 53 E
Arlington, *Oreg., U.S.A.* **82 D3** 45 43N 120 12W
Arlington, *S. Dak., U.S.A.* **80 C6** 44 22N 97 8W
Arlington, *Va., U.S.A.* **76 F7** 38 53N 77 7W
Arlington, *Wash., U.S.A.* **84 B4** 48 12N 122 8W
Arlon, *Belgium* **15 E5** 49 42N 5 49 E
Armagh, *U.K.* **13 B5** 54 22N 6 40W
Armagh □, *U.K.* **13 B5** 54 18N 6 37W
Armagnac, *France* **18 E4** 43 50N 0 10 E
Armavir, *Russia* **25 E7** 45 2N 41 7 E
Armenia, *Colombia* **92 C3** 4 35N 75 45W
Armenia ■, *Asia* **25 F7** 40 20N 45 0 E
Armenistís, Ákra, *Greece* **23 C9** 36 8N 27 42 E
Armidale, *Australia* **63 E5** 30 30S 151 40 E
Armour, *U.S.A.* **80 D5** 43 19N 98 21W
Armstrong, *B.C., Canada* **72 C5** 50 25N 119 10W
Armstrong, *Ont., Canada* **70 B2** 50 18N 89 4W
Armstrong, *U.S.A.* **81 M6** 26 56N 97 47W
Armstrong →, *Australia* **60 C5** 16 35S 131 40 E
Arnarfjörður, *Iceland* **8 D2** 65 48N 23 40W
Arnaud →, *Canada* **69 B12** 60 0N 70 0W
Arnauti, C., *Cyprus* **23 D11** 35 6N 32 17 E
Árnes, *Iceland* **8 C3** 66 1N 21 31W
Arnett, *U.S.A.* **81 G5** 36 8N 99 46W
Arnhem, *Neths.* **15 C5** 51 58N 5 55 E
Arnhem, C., *Australia* **62 A2** 12 20S 137 30 E
Arnhem B., *Australia* **62 A2** 12 20S 136 10 E
Arnhem Land, *Australia* **62 A1** 13 10S 134 30 E
Arno →, *Italy* **20 C4** 43 41N 10 17 E
Arno Bay, *Australia* **63 E2** 33 54S 136 34 E
Arnold, *Calif., U.S.A.* **84 G6** 38 15N 120 20W
Arnold, *Nebr., U.S.A.* **80 E4** 41 26N 100 12W
Arnot, *Canada* **73 B9** 55 56N 96 41W
Arnøy, *Norway* **8 A16** 70 9N 20 40 E
Arnprior, *Canada* **70 C4** 45 26N 76 21W
Aroab, *Namibia* **56 D2** 26 41S 19 39 E
Arrabury, *Australia* **63 D3** 26 45S 141 0 E
Arrah = Ara, *India* **43 G11** 25 35N 84 32 E
Arran, *U.K.* **12 F3** 55 34N 5 12W
Arrandale, *Canada* **72 C3** 54 57N 130 0W
Arras, *France* **18 A5** 50 17N 2 46 E
Arrecife, *Canary Is.* **22 F6** 28 57N 13 37W
Arrecifes, *Argentina* **94 C3** 34 6S 60 9W
Arrée, Mts. d', *France* **18 B2** 48 26N 3 55W
Arriaga, *Chiapas, Mexico* **87 D6** 16 15N 93 52W
Arriaga, *San Luis Potosí, Mexico* **86 C4** 21 55N 101 23W
Arrilalah P.O., *Australia* **62 C3** 23 43S 143 54 E
Arrino, *Australia* **61 E2** 29 30S 115 40 E
Arrow, L., *Ireland* **13 B3** 54 3N 8 20W
Arrow Rock Res., *U.S.A.* **82 E6** 43 45N 115 50W
Arrowhead, *Canada* **72 C5** 50 40N 117 55W
Arrowhead, L., *U.S.A.* **85 L9** 34 16N 117 10W
Arrowtown, *N.Z.* **59 L2** 44 57S 168 50 E
Arroyo Grande, *U.S.A.* **85 K6** 35 7N 120 35W
Ars, *Iran* **44 B5** 37 9N 47 46 E
Arsenault L., *Canada* **73 B7** 55 6N 108 32W
Arsenev, *Russia* **30 B6** 44 10N 133 15 E
Árta, *Greece* **21 E9** 39 8N 21 2 E
Artá, *Spain* **22 B10** 39 41N 3 21 E
Arteaga, *Mexico* **86 D4** 18 50N 102 20W
Artem, *Russia* **30 C6** 43 22N 132 13 E
Artemovsk, *Russia* **27 D10** 54 45N 93 35 E
Artesia = Mosomane, *Botswana* **56 C4** 24 2S 26 19 E
Artesia, *U.S.A.* **81 J2** 32 51N 104 24W
Artesia Wells, *U.S.A.* **81 L5** 28 17N 99 17W
Artesian, *U.S.A.* **80 C6** 44 1N 97 55W
Arthur →, *Australia* **62 G3** 41 2S 144 40 E
Arthur Cr. →, *Australia* **62 C2** 22 30S 136 25 E
Arthur Pt., *Australia* **62 C5** 22 7S 150 3 E
Arthur's Pass, *N.Z.* **59 K3** 42 54S 171 35 E
Arthur's Town, *Bahamas* **89 B4** 24 38N 75 42W
Artigas, *Uruguay* **94 C4** 30 20S 56 30W
Artillery L., *Canada* **73 A7** 63 9N 107 52W
Artois, *France* **18 A5** 50 20N 2 30 E
Artvin, *Turkey* **25 F7** 41 14N 41 44 E
Aru, Kepulauan, *Indonesia* **37 F8** 6 0S 134 30 E
Aru Is. = Aru, Kepulauan, *Indonesia* **37 F8** 6 0S 134 30 E
Aru Meru □, *Tanzania* **54 C4** 3 20S 36 50 E
Arua, *Uganda* **54 B3** 3 1N 30 58 E
Aruanã, *Brazil* **93 F8** 14 54S 51 10W
Aruba ■, *W. Indies* **89 D6** 12 30N 70 0W
Arucas, *Canary Is.* **22 F4** 28 7N 15 32W
Arumpo, *Australia* **63 E3** 33 48S 142 55 E
Arun →, *Nepal* **43 F12** 26 55N 87 10 E
Arunachal Pradesh □, *India* **41 E19** 28 0N 95 0 E
Arusha, *Tanzania* **54 C4** 3 20S 36 40 E
Arusha □, *Tanzania* **54 C4** 4 0S 36 30 E
Arusha Chini, *Tanzania* **54 C4** 3 32S 37 20 E
Aruwimi →, *Zaïre* **54 B1** 1 13N 23 36 E
Arvada, *U.S.A.* **82 D10** 44 39N 106 8W
Árvi, *Greece* **23 E7** 34 59N 25 28 E
Arvida, *Canada* **71 C5** 48 25N 71 14W
Arvidsjaur, *Sweden* **8 D15** 65 35N 19 10 E
Arvika, *Sweden* **9 G12** 59 40N 12 36 E
Arvin, *U.S.A.* **85 K8** 35 12N 118 50W
Arxan, *China* **33 B6** 47 11N 119 57 E
Aryirádhes, *Greece* **23 B3** 39 27N 19 58 E
Aryiroúpolis, *Greece* **23 D6** 35 17N 24 20 E
Arys, *Kazakhstan* **26 E7** 42 26N 68 48 E
Arzamas, *Russia* **24 C7** 55 27N 43 55 E
Arzew, *Algeria* **50 A4** 35 50N 0 23W
Aş Şadr, *U.A.E.* **45 E7** 24 40N 54 41 E
Aş Şafā, *Syria* **47 B6** 33 10N 37 0 E
'As Saffānīyah, *Si. Arabia* **45 D6** 28 5N 48 50 E
As Safīrah, *Syria* **44 B3** 36 5N 37 21 E
Aş Şahm, *Oman* **45 E8** 24 10N 56 53 E
As Sājir, *Si. Arabia* **44 E5** 25 11N 44 36 E
As Salamīyah, *Syria* **44 C3** 35 1N 37 2 E
As Salt, *Jordan* **47 C4** 32 2N 35 43 E
As Sal'w'a, *Qatar* **45 E6** 24 23N 50 50 E
As Samāwah, *Iraq* **44 D5** 31 15N 45 15 E
As Sanamayn, *Syria* **47 B5** 33 3N 36 10 E
As Sukhnah, *Syria* **44 C3** 34 52N 38 52 E
As Sulaymānīyah, *Iraq* **44 C5** 35 35N 45 29 E
As Sulaymī, *Si. Arabia* **44 E4** 26 17N 41 21 E
As Summān, *Si. Arabia* **44 E5** 25 0N 47 0 E
As Suwaydā', *Syria* **47 C5** 32 40N 36 30 E
As Suwaydā' □, *Syria* **47 C5** 32 45N 36 45 E
Aş Şuwayrah, *Iraq* **44 C5** 32 55N 45 0 E
Asab, *Namibia* **56 D2** 25 30S 18 0 E
Asahi-Gawa →, *Japan* **31 G6** 34 36N 133 58 E
Asahigawa, *Japan* **30 C11** 43 46N 142 22 E
Asansol, *India* **43 H12** 23 40N 87 1 E
Asbesberge, *S. Africa* **56 D3** 29 0S 23 0 E
Asbestos, *Canada* **71 C5** 45 47N 71 58W
Asbury Park, *U.S.A.* **79 F10** 40 13N 74 1W
Ascensión, *Mexico* **86 A3** 31 6N 107 59W
Ascensión, B. de la, *Mexico* **87 D7** 19 50N 87 20W
Ascension I., *Atl. Oc.* **2 E9** 8 0S 14 15W
Aschaffenburg, *Germany* **16 D4** 49 58N 9 8 E
Áscoli Piceno, *Italy* **20 C5** 42 51N 13 34 E
Ascope, *Peru* **92 E3** 7 46S 79 8W
Ascotán, *Chile* **94 A2** 21 45S 68 17W
Aseb, *Eritrea* **46 E3** 13 0N 42 40 E
Asela, *Ethiopia* **51 G12** 8 0N 39 0 E
Asgata, *Cyprus* **23 E12** 34 46N 33 15 E
Ash Fork, *U.S.A.* **83 J7** 35 13N 112 29W
Ash Grove, *U.S.A.* **81 G8** 37 19N 93 35W
Ash Shamāl □, *Lebanon* **47 A5** 34 25N 36 0 E
Ash Shāmīyah, *Iraq* **44 D5** 31 55N 44 35 E
Ash Shāriqah, *U.A.E.* **45 E7** 25 23N 55 26 E
Ash Sharmah, *Si. Arabia* **44 D2** 28 1N 35 16 E
Ash Sharqāt, *Iraq* **44 C4** 35 27N 43 16 E
Ash Sharqi, Al Jabal, *Lebanon* **47 B5** 33 40N 36 10 E
Ash Shaţrah, *Iraq* **44 D5** 31 30N 46 10 E
Ash Shawbak, *Jordan* **44 D2** 30 32N 35 34 E
Ash Shawmari, J., *Jordan* **47 E5** 30 35N 36 35 E
Ash Shaykh, J., *Lebanon* **47 B4** 33 25N 35 50 E
Ash Shināfīyah, *Iraq* **44 D5** 31 35N 44 39 E
Ash Shu'aybah, *Si. Arabia* **44 E5** 27 53N 44 43 E
Ash Shumlūl, *Si. Arabia* **44 E5** 26 31N 47 20 E
Ash Shūr'a, *Iraq* **44 C4** 35 58N 43 13 E
Ash Shurayf, *Si. Arabia* **44 E3** 25 43N 39 14 E
Ash Shuwayfāt, *Lebanon* **47 B4** 33 45N 35 30 E
Asha, *Russia* **24 D10** 55 0N 57 16 E
Ashau, *Vietnam* **38 D6** 16 6N 107 22 E
Ashburn, *U.S.A.* **77 K4** 31 43N 83 39W
Ashburton, *N.Z.* **59 K3** 43 53S 171 48 E
Ashburton →, *Australia* **60 D1** 21 40S 114 56 E
Ashburton Downs, *Australia* **60 D2** 23 25S 117 4 E
Ashby de la Zouch, *U.K.* **10 E6** 52 45N 1 29W
Ashcroft, *Canada* **72 C4** 50 40N 121 20W
Ashdod, *Israel* **47 D3** 31 49N 34 35 E
Asheboro, *U.S.A.* **77 H6** 35 43N 79 49W
Asherton, *U.S.A.* **81 L5** 28 27N 99 46W
Asheville, *U.S.A.* **77 H4** 35 36N 82 33W
Asheweig →, *Canada* **70 B2** 54 17N 87 12W
Ashford, *Australia* **63 D5** 29 15S 151 3 E
Ashford, *U.K.* **11 F8** 51 8N 0 53 E
Ashford, *U.S.A.* **82 C2** 46 46N 122 2W
Ashgabat = Ashkhabad, *Turkmenistan* **26 F6** 38 0N 57 50 E
Ashibetsu, *Japan* **30 C11** 43 31N 142 11 E
Ashikaga, *Japan* **31 F9** 36 28N 139 29 E
Ashizuri-Zaki, *Japan* **31 H6** 32 44N 133 0 E
Ashkarkot, *Afghan.* **42 C2** 33 3N 67 58 E
Ashkhabad, *Turkmenistan* **26 F6** 38 0N 57 50 E
Ashland, *Kans., U.S.A.* **81 G5** 37 11N 99 46W
Ashland, *Ky., U.S.A.* **76 F4** 38 28N 82 38W
Ashland, *Maine, U.S.A.* **71 C6** 46 38N 68 24W

Ashland

Big Lake

Beizhengzhen, *China* . . . **35 B12** 44 31N 123 30 E
Beja, *Portugal* **19 C2** 38 2N 7 53W
Béja, *Tunisia* . . . . **50 A6** 36 43N 9 12 E
Bejaia, *Algeria* . . . . **50 A6** 36 42N 5 2 E
Bejestān, *Iran* . . . . **45 C8** 34 30N 58 5 E
Bekasi, *Indonesia* . . . . . . **37 G12** 6 14S 106 59 E
Békéscsaba, *Hungary* . . . **17 E10** 46 40N 21 5 E
Bekily, *Madag.* . . . . **57 C8** 24 13S 45 19 E
Bekok, *Malaysia* . . . . **39 L4** 2 20N 103 7 E
Bela, *India* . . . . **43 G9** 25 50N 82 0 E
Bela, *Pakistan* . . . . **42 F2** 26 12N 66 20 E
Bela Crkva, *Serbia, Yug.* **21 B9** 44 55N 21 27 E
Bela Vista, *Brazil* **94 A4** 22 12S 56 20W
Bela Vista, *Mozam.* . . . . **57 D5** 26 10S 32 44 E
Belarus = Belorussia ■, *Europe* . . . . **24 D4** 53 30N 27 0 E
Belau ■, *Pac. Oc.* . . . . . . **64 G5** 7 30N 134 30 E
Belavenona, *Madag.* . . . . **57 C8** 24 50S 47 4 E
Belawan, *Indonesia* . . . . **36 D1** 3 33N 98 32 E
Belaya →, *Russia* . . . . . **24 C9** 54 40N 56 0 E
Belaya Tserkov, *Ukraine* **25 E5** 49 45N 30 10 E
Belcher Is., *Canada* **69 C12** 56 15N 78 45W
Belden, *U.S.A.* **84 E5** 40 2N 121 17W
Belebey, *Russia* . . . . **24 D9** 54 7N 54 7 E
Belém, *Brazil* **93 D9** 1 20S 48 30W
Belén, *Argentina* **94 B2** 27 40S 67 5W
Belén, *Paraguay* **94 A4** 23 30S 57 6W
Belen, *U.S.A.* **83 J10** 34 40N 106 46W
Belet Uen, *Somali Rep.* . **46 G4** 4 30N 45 5 E
Belev, *Russia* . . . . **24 D6** 53 50N 36 5 E
Belfair, *U.S.A.* **84 C4** 47 27N 122 50W
Belfast, *S. Africa* . . . . . . **57 D5** 25 42S 30 2 E
Belfast, *U.K.* **13 B6** 54 35N 5 56W
Belfast, *Maine, U.S.A.* . . **71 D6** 44 26N 69 1W
Belfast, *N.Y., U.S.A.* **78 D6** 42 21N 78 7W
Belfast □, *U.K.* **13 B6** 54 35N 5 56W
Belfast L., *U.K.* **13 B6** 54 40N 5 50W
Belfield, *U.S.A.* **80 B3** 46 53N 103 12W
Belfort, *France* . . . . **18 C7** 47 38N 6 50 E
Belfort, Territoire de □, *France* . . . . **18 C7** 47 40N 6 55 E
Belfry, *U.S.A.* **82 D9** 45 9N 109 1W
Belgaum, *India* . . . . **40 M9** 15 55N 74 35 E
Belgium ■, *Europe* . . . . . **15 D5** 50 30N 5 0 E
Belgorod, *Russia* . . . . **25 D6** 50 35N 36 35 E
Belgorod-Dnestrovskiy, *Ukraine* . . . . **25 E5** 46 11N 30 23 E
Belgrade = Beograd, *Serbia, Yug.* . . . . **21 B9** 44 50N 20 37 E
Belgrade, *U.S.A.* **82 D8** 45 47N 111 11W
Belhaven, *U.S.A.* **77 H7** 35 33N 76 37W
Beli Drim →, *Europe* . . **21 C9** 42 6N 20 25 E
Belinga, *Gabon* . . . . **52 D2** 1 10N 13 2 E
Belinyu, *Indonesia* . . . . . **36 E3** 1 35S 105 50 E
Beliton Is. = Belitung, *Indonesia* . . . . **36 E3** 3 10S 107 50 E
Belitung, *Indonesia* . . . . **36 E3** 3 10S 107 50 E
Belize ■, *Cent. Amer.* . . **87 D7** 17 0N 88 30W
Belize City, *Belize* **87 D7** 17 25N 88 0W
Belkovskiy, Ostrov, *Russia* . . . . **27 B14** 75 32N 135 44 E
Bell →, *Canada* **70 C4** 49 48N 77 38W
Bell Bay, *Australia* . . . . . **62 G4** 41 6S 146 53 E
Bell I., *Canada* **71 B8** 50 46N 55 35W
Bell-Irving →, *Canada* . **72 B3** 56 12N 129 5W
Bell Peninsula, *Canada* . **69 B11** 63 50N 82 0W
Bell Ville, *Argentina* **94 C3** 32 40S 62 40W
Bella Bella, *Canada* **72 C3** 52 10N 128 10W
Bella Coola, *Canada* **72 C3** 52 25N 126 40W
Bella Unión, *Uruguay* . . . **94 C4** 30 15S 57 40W
Bella Vista, *Corrientes, Argentina* **94 B4** 28 33S 59 0W
Bella Vista, *Tucuman, Argentina* **94 B2** 27 10S 65 25W
Bellaire, *U.S.A.* **78 F4** 40 1N 80 45W
Bellary, *India* . . . . **40 M10** 15 10N 76 56 E
Bellata, *Australia* . . . . . . **63 D4** 29 53S 149 46 E
Belle Fourche, *U.S.A.* . . . **80 C3** 44 40N 103 51W
Belle Fourche →, *U.S.A.* **80 C3** 44 26N 102 18W
Belle Glade, *U.S.A.* **77 M5** 26 41N 80 40W
Belle-Ile, *France* **18 C2** 47 20N 3 10W
Belle Isle, *Canada* **71 B8** 51 57N 55 25W
Belle Isle, Str. of, *Canada* **71 B8** 51 30N 56 30W
Belle Plaine, *Iowa, U.S.A.* **80 E8** 41 54N 92 17W
Belle Plaine, *Minn., U.S.A.* **80 C8** 44 37N 93 46W
Belledune, *Canada* **71 C6** 47 55N 65 50W
Bellefontaine, *U.S.A.* **76 E4** 40 22N 83 46W
Bellefonte, *U.S.A.* **78 F7** 40 55N 77 47W
Belleoram, *Canada* **71 C8** 47 31N 55 25W
Belleville, *Canada* **70 D4** 44 10N 77 23W
Belleville, *Ill., U.S.A.* . . . **80 F10** 38 31N 89 59W
Belleville, *Kans., U.S.A.* . **80 F6** 39 50N 97 38W
Belleville, *N.Y., U.S.A.* . . **79 C8** 43 46N 76 10W
Bellevue, *Canada* **72 D6** 49 35N 114 22W
Bellevue, *Idaho, U.S.A.* . **82 E6** 43 28N 114 16W
Bellevue, *Ohio, U.S.A.* . . **78 E2** 41 17N 82 51W
Bellevue, *Wash., U.S.A.* . **84 C4** 47 37N 122 12W
Bellin, *Canada* **69 B13** 60 0N 70 0W
Bellingen, *Australia* . . . . **63 E5** 30 25S 152 50 E
Bellingham, *U.S.A.* **84 B4** 48 46N 122 29W
Bellingshausen Sea, *Antarctica* **5 C17** 66 0S 80 0W
Bellinzona, *Switz.* . . . . . . **16 E4** 46 11N 9 1 E
Bellows Falls, *U.S.A.* . . . **79 C12** 43 8N 72 27W
Bellpat, *Pakistan* . . . . **42 E3** 29 0N 68 5 E
Belluno, *Italy* . . . . **20 A5** 46 8N 12 13 E
Bellville, *U.S.A.* **81 L6** 29 57N 96 15W
Bellwood, *U.S.A.* **78 F6** 40 36N 78 20W
Bélmez, *Spain* **19 C3** 38 17N 5 17W
Belmont, *Australia* . . . . . **63 E5** 33 4S 151 42 E
Belmont, *Canada* **78 D3** 42 53N 81 5W
Belmont, *S. Africa* . . . . . **56 D3** 29 28S 24 22 E
Belmont, *U.S.A.* **78 D6** 42 14N 78 2W
Belmonte, *Brazil* **93 G11** 16 0S 39 0W
Belmopan, *Belize* **87 D7** 17 18N 88 30W
Belmullet, *Ireland* **13 B2** 54 13N 9 58W
Belo Horizonte, *Brazil* . . **93 G10** 19 55S 43 56W
Belo-sur-Mer, *Madag.* . . **57 C7** 20 42S 44 0 E
Belo-Tsiribihina, *Madag.* **57 B7** 19 40S 44 30 E
Belogorsk, *Russia* . . . . . . **27 D13** 51 0N 128 20 E
Beloha, *Madag.* . . . . **57 D8** 25 10S 45 3 E
Beloit, *Kans., U.S.A.* **80 F5** 39 28N 98 6W
Beloit, *Wis., U.S.A.* **80 D10** 42 31N 89 2W
Belomorsk, *Russia* . . . . . . **24 B5** 64 35N 34 30 E
Belonia, *India* . . . . **41 H17** 23 15N 91 30 E
Beloretsk, *Russia* . . . . . . **24 D10** 53 58N 58 24 E
Belorussia ■, *Europe* . . . **24 D4** 53 30N 27 0 E
Belovo, *Russia* . . . . **26 D9** 54 30N 86 0 E
Beloye, Oz., *Russia* . . . . . **24 B6** 60 10N 37 35 E
Beloye More, *Russia* . . . **24 A6** 66 30N 38 0 E
Belozersk, *Russia* . . . . . . **24 B6** 60 4N 37 30 E
Beltana, *Australia* . . . . . . **63 E2** 30 48S 138 25 E
Belterra, *Brazil* **93 D8** 2 45S 55 0W
Belton, *S.C., U.S.A.* **77 H4** 34 31N 82 30W
Belton, *Tex., U.S.A.* **81 K6** 31 3N 97 28W
Belton Res., *U.S.A.* **81 K6** 31 8N 97 32W
Beltsy, *Moldavia* . . . . **25 E4** 47 48N 28 0 E
Belturbet, *Ireland* **13 B4** 54 6N 7 28W
Belukha, *Russia* . . . . **26 E9** 49 50N 86 50 E
Beluran, *Malaysia* . . . . . . **36 C5** 5 48N 117 35 E
Belvidere, *Ill., U.S.A.* . . . **80 D10** 42 15N 88 50W
Belvidere, *N.J., U.S.A.* . . **79 F9** 40 50N 75 5W
Belyando →, *Australia* . **62 C4** 21 38S 146 50 E
Belyy, Ostrov, *Russia* . . . **26 B8** 73 30N 71 0 E
Belyy Yar, *Russia* . . . . . . **26 D9** 58 26N 84 39 E
Belzoni, *U.S.A.* **81 J9** 33 11N 90 29W
Bemaraha, Lembalemban' i, *Madag.* . . . . **57 B7** 18 40S 44 45 E
Bemarivo, *Madag.* . . . . . . **57 C7** 21 45S 44 45 E
Bemarivo →, *Madag.* . . . **57 B8** 15 27S 47 40 E
Bemavo, *Madag.* . . . . **57 C8** 21 33S 45 25 E
Bembéréke, *Benin* . . . . . . **50 F5** 10 11N 2 43 E
Bembesi, *Zimbabwe* . . . . **55 F2** 20 0S 28 58 E
Bembesi →, *Zimbabwe* . **55 F2** 18 57S 27 47 E
Bemidji, *U.S.A.* **80 B7** 47 28N 94 53W
Ben, *Iran* . . . . **45 C6** 32 32N 50 45 E
Ben Cruachan, *U.K.* **12 E3** 56 26N 5 8W
Ben Dearg, *U.K.* **12 D4** 57 47N 4 58W
Ben Gardane, *Tunisia* . . **51 B7** 33 11N 11 11 E
Ben Hope, *U.K.* **12 C4** 58 24N 4 36W
Ben Lawers, *U.K.* **12 E4** 56 33N 4 13W
Ben Lomond, *N.S.W., Australia* . . . . **63 E5** 30 1S 151 43 E
Ben Lomond, *Tas., Australia* . . . . **62 G4** 41 38S 147 42 E
Ben Lomond, *U.K.* **12 E4** 56 12N 4 39W
Ben Luc, *Vietnam* . . . . . . **39 G6** 10 39N 106 29 E
Ben Macdhui, *U.K.* **12 D5** 57 4N 3 40W
Ben Mhor, *U.K.* **12 D1** 57 16N 7 21W
Ben More, *Central, U.K.* . **12 E4** 56 23N 4 31W
Ben More, *Strath., U.K.* . **12 E2** 56 26N 6 2W
Ben More Assynt, *U.K.* . . **12 C4** 58 7N 4 51W
Ben Nevis, *U.K.* **12 E4** 56 48N 4 58W
Ben Quang, *Vietnam* . . . **38 D6** 17 3N 106 55 E
Ben Tre, *Vietnam* . . . . . . **39 G6** 10 3N 106 36 E
Ben Vorlich, *U.K.* **12 E4** 56 22N 4 15W
Ben Wyvis, *U.K.* **12 D4** 57 40N 4 35W
Bena, *Nigeria* . . . . **50 F6** 11 20N 5 50 E
Bena Dibele, *Zaïre* . . . . . **52 E4** 4 4S 22 50 E
Benagerie, *Australia* . . . . **63 E3** 31 25S 140 22 E
Benalla, *Australia* . . . . . . **63 F4** 36 30S 146 0 E
Benambra, Mt., *Australia* **63 F4** 36 31S 147 34 E
Benares = Varanasi, *India* **43 G10** 25 22N 83 0 E
Benavides, *U.S.A.* **81 M5** 27 36N 98 25W
Benbecula, *U.K.* **12 D1** 57 26N 7 21W
Benbonyathe, *Australia* . **63 E2** 30 25S 139 11 E
Bencubbin, *Australia* . . . **61 F2** 30 48S 117 52 E
Bend, *U.S.A.* **82 D3** 44 4N 121 19W
Bender Beila, *Somali Rep.* . . . . **46 F5** 9 30N 50 48 E
Bendering, *Australia* . . . . **61 F2** 32 23S 118 18 E
Bendery, *Moldavia* . . . . . . **25 E4** 46 50N 29 30 E
Bendigo, *Australia* . . . . . . **63 F3** 36 40S 144 15 E
Benē Beraq, *Israel* . . . . . **47 C3** 32 6N 34 51 E
Benenitra, *Madag.* . . . . . . **57 C8** 23 27S 45 5 E
Benevento, *Italy* . . . . **20 D6** 41 7N 14 45 E
Benga, *Mozam.* . . . . **55 F3** 16 11S 33 40 E
Bengal, Bay of, *Ind. Oc.* . **41 K16** 15 0N 90 0 E
Bengbu, *China* . . . . **35 H9** 32 58N 117 20 E
Benghazi = Banghāzī, *Libya* . . . . **51 B9** 32 11N 20 3 E
Bengkalis, *Indonesia* . . . . **36 D2** 1 30N 102 10 E
Bengkulu, *Indonesia* . . . . **36 E2** 3 50S 102 12 E
Bengkulu □, *Indonesia* . . **36 E2** 3 48S 102 16 E
Bengough, *Canada* **73 D7** 49 25N 105 10W
Benguela, *Angola* . . . . . . **53 G2** 12 37S 13 25 E
Benguérua, I., *Mozam.* . . **57 C6** 21 58S 35 28 E
Beni, *Zaïre* . . . . **54 B2** 0 30N 29 27 E
Beni →, *Bolivia* **92 F5** 10 23S 65 24W
Beni Abbès, *Algeria* **50 B4** 30 5N 2 5W
Beni Mazâr, *Egypt* . . . . . . **51 C11** 28 32N 30 44 E
Beni Mellal, *Morocco* **50 B3** 32 21N 6 21W
Beni Ounif, *Algeria* **50 B4** 32 0N 1 10W
Beni Suef, *Egypt* . . . . **51 C11** 29 5N 31 6 E
Beniah L., *Canada* **72 A6** 63 23N 112 17W
Benicia, *U.S.A.* **84 G4** 38 3N 122 9W
Benidorm, *Spain* **19 C5** 38 33N 0 9W
Benin ■, *Africa* . . . . **50 G5** 10 0N 2 0 E
Benin, Bight of, *W. Afr.* . **50 H5** 5 0N 3 0 E
Benin City, *Nigeria* . . . . . **50 G6** 6 20N 5 31 E
Benitses, *Greece* . . . . **23 A3** 39 32N 19 55 E
Benjamin Aceval, *Paraguay* **94 A4** 24 58S 57 34W
Benjamin Constant, *Brazil* **92 D4** 4 40S 70 15W
Benjamin Hill, *Mexico* . . **86 A2** 30 10N 111 10W
Benkelman, *U.S.A.* **80 E4** 40 3N 101 32W
Benlidi, *Australia* . . . . . . **62 C3** 24 35S 144 50 E
Bennett, *Canada* **72 B2** 59 56N 134 53W
Bennett, L., *Australia* . . . **60 D5** 22 50S 131 2 E
Bennett, Ostrov, *Russia* . **27 B15** 76 21N 148 56 E
Bennettsville, *U.S.A.* . . . **77 H6** 34 37N 79 41W
Bennington, *U.S.A.* **79 D11** 43 0N 71 55W
Benoni, *S. Africa* . . . . **57 D4** 26 11S 28 18 E
Benque Viejo, *Belize* **87 D7** 17 5N 89 8W
Benson, *U.S.A.* **83 L8** 31 58N 110 18W
Bent, *Iran* . . . . **45 E8** 26 20N 59 31 E
Benteng, *Indonesia* . . . . . **37 F6** 6 10S 120 30 E
Bentinck I., *Australia* . . . **62 B2** 17 3S 139 35 E
Bento Gonçalves, *Brazil* . **95 B5** 29 10S 51 31W
Benton, *Ark., U.S.A.* **81 H8** 34 34N 92 35W
Benton, *Calif., U.S.A.* . . . **84 H8** 37 48N 118 32W
Benton, *Ill., U.S.A.* **80 F10** 38 0N 88 55W
Benton Harbor, *U.S.A.* . . **76 D2** 42 6N 86 27W
Bentung, *Malaysia* . . . . . **39 L3** 3 31N 101 55 E
Benue →, *Nigeria* . . . . . **50 G6** 7 48N 6 46 E
Benxi, *China* . . . . **35 D12** 41 20N 123 48 E
Beo, *Indonesia* . . . . **37 D7** 4 25N 126 50 E
Beograd, *Serbia, Yug.* . . **21 B9** 44 50N 20 37 E
Beowawe, *U.S.A.* **82 F5** 40 35N 116 29W
Beppu, *Japan* . . . . **31 H5** 33 15N 131 30 E
Berau, Teluk, *Indonesia* . **37 E8** 2 30S 132 30 E
Berber, *Sudan* . . . . **51 E11** 18 0N 34 0 E
Berbera, *Somali Rep.* . . . **46 E4** 10 30N 45 2 E
Berbérati, *C.A.R.* . . . . **52 D3** 4 15N 15 40 E
Berberia, C. del, *Spain* . . **22 C7** 38 39N 1 24 E
Berbice →, *Guyana* **92 B7** 6 20N 57 32W
Berdichev, *Ukraine* . . . . . **25 E4** 49 57N 28 30 E
Berdsk, *Russia* . . . . **26 D9** 54 47N 83 2 E
Berdyansk, *Ukraine* . . . . . **25 E6** 46 45N 36 50 E
Berdychiv = Berdichev, *Ukraine* . . . . **25 E4** 49 57N 28 30 E
Berea, *U.S.A.* **76 G3** 37 34N 84 17W
Berebere, *Indonesia* . . . . **37 D7** 2 25N 128 45 E
Bereda, *Somali Rep.* . . . . **46 E5** 11 45N 51 0 E
Berekum, *Ghana* **50 G4** 7 29N 2 34W
Berens →, *Canada* **73 C9** 52 25N 97 2W
Berens I., *Canada* **73 C9** 52 18N 97 18W
Berens River, *Canada* . . **73 C9** 52 25N 97 0W
Berevo, *Mahajanga, Madag.* . . . . **57 B7** 17 14S 44 17 E
Berevo, *Toliara, Madag.* . **57 B7** 19 44S 44 58 E
Berezina →, *Belorussia* **24 D5** 52 33N 30 14 E
Berezniki, *Russia* . . . . . . **26 D6** 59 24N 56 46 E
Berezovo, *Russia* . . . . . . **24 B11** 64 0N 65 0 E
Bérgamo, *Italy* . . . . **20 B3** 45 42N 9 40 E
Bergen, *Neths.* . . . . **15 B4** 52 40N 4 43 E
Bergen, *Norway* . . . . **9 F8** 60 23N 5 20 E
Bergen, *U.S.A.* **78 C7** 43 5N 77 57W
Bergen-op-Zoom, *Neths.* **15 C4** 51 28N 4 18 E
Bergerac, *France* . . . . **18 D4** 44 51N 0 30 E
Bergum, *Neths.* . . . . **15 A5** 53 13N 5 59 E
Bergville, *S. Africa* . . . . . **57 D4** 28 52S 29 18 E
Berhala, Selat, *Indonesia* **36 E2** 1 0S 104 15 E
Berhampore = Baharampur, *India* . . . **43 G13** 24 2N 88 27 E
Berhampur, *India* . . . . . . **41 K14** 19 15N 84 54 E
Bering Sea, *Pac. Oc.* . . . . **68 C1** 58 0N 171 0 E
Bering Strait, *U.S.A.* **68 B3** 65 30N 169 0W
Beringen, *Belgium* . . . . . . **15 C5** 51 3N 5 14 E
Beringovskiy, *Russia* . . . **27 C18** 63 3N 179 19 E
Berisso, *Argentina* **94 C4** 34 56S 57 50W
Berja, *Spain* **19 D4** 36 50N 2 56W
Berkeley, *U.K.* **11 F5** 51 41N 2 28W
Berkeley, *U.S.A.* **84 H4** 37 52N 122 16W
Berkeley Springs, *U.S.A.* **76 F6** 39 38N 78 14W
Berkner I., *Antarctica* . . . **5 D18** 79 30S 50 0W
Berkshire □, *U.K.* **11 F6** 51 30N 1 20W
Berland →, *Canada* **72 C5** 54 0N 116 50W
Berlin, *Germany* . . . . **16 B6** 52 32N 13 24 E
Berlin, *Md., U.S.A.* **76 F8** 38 20N 75 13W
Berlin, *N.H., U.S.A.* **79 B13** 44 28N 71 11W
Berlin, *Wis., U.S.A.* **76 D1** 43 58N 88 57W
Bermejo →, *Formosa, Argentina* **94 B4** 26 51S 58 23W
Bermejo →, *San Juan, Argentina* **94 C2** 32 30S 67 30W
Bermuda ■, *Atl. Oc.* **2 C6** 32 45N 65 0W
Bern, *Switz.* . . . . **16 E3** 46 57N 7 28 E
Bernado, *U.S.A.* **83 J10** 34 30N 106 53W
Bernalillo, *U.S.A.* **83 J10** 35 18N 106 33W
Bernardo de Irigoyen, *Argentina* **95 B5** 26 15S 53 40W
Bernardo O'Higgins □, *Chile* **94 C1** 34 15S 70 45W
Bernasconi, *Argentina* . . **94 D3** 37 55S 63 44W
Bernburg, *Germany* . . . . **16 C5** 51 40N 11 42 E
Berne = Bern, *Switz.* . . . **16 E3** 46 57N 7 28 E
Bernier I., *Australia* . . . . **61 D1** 24 50S 113 12 E
Beroroha, *Madag.* . . . . . . **57 C8** 21 40S 45 10 E
Beroun, *Czech.* . . . . **16 D7** 49 57N 14 5 E
Berrechid, *Morocco* **50 B3** 33 18N 7 36W
Berri, *Australia* . . . . **63 E3** 34 14S 140 35 E
Berry, *Australia* . . . . **63 E5** 34 46S 150 43 E
Berry, *France* . . . . **18 C5** 46 50N 2 0 E
Berry Is., *Bahamas* **88 A4** 25 40N 77 50W
Berryessa L., *U.S.A.* **84 G4** 38 31N 122 6W
Berryville, *U.S.A.* **81 G8** 36 22N 93 34W
Berthold, *U.S.A.* **80 A4** 48 19N 101 44W
Berthoud, *U.S.A.* **80 E2** 40 19N 105 5W
Bertoua, *Cameroon* . . . . . **52 D2** 4 30N 13 45 E
Bertrand, *U.S.A.* **80 E5** 40 32N 99 38W
Berufjörður, *Iceland* **8 D6** 64 48N 14 29W
Berwick, *U.S.A.* **79 E8** 41 3N 76 14W
Berwick-upon-Tweed, *U.K.* **10 B5** 55 47N 2 0W
Berwyn Mts., *U.K.* **10 E4** 52 54N 3 26W
Besal, *Pakistan* . . . . **43 B5** 35 4N 73 56 E
Besalampy, *Madag.* . . . . . **57 B7** 16 43S 44 29 E
Besançon, *France* . . . . . . **18 C7** 47 15N 6 2 E
Besar, *Indonesia* . . . . **36 E5** 2 40S 116 0 E
Besnard L., *Canada* **73 B7** 55 25N 106 0W
Besor, N. →, *Egypt* . . . . **47 D3** 31 28N 34 22 E
Bessarabiya, *Moldavia* . . **17 E14** 47 0N 28 10 E
Bessemer, *Ala., U.S.A.* . . **77 J2** 33 24N 86 58W
Bessemer, *Mich., U.S.A.* . **80 B9** 46 29N 90 3W
Bet She'an, *Israel* . . . . . . **47 C4** 32 30N 35 30 E
Bet Shemesh, *Israel* . . . . **47 D3** 31 44N 35 0 E
Betafo, *Madag.* . . . . **57 B8** 19 50S 46 51 E
Betancuria, *Canary Is.* . . **22 F5** 28 25N 14 3W
Bétaré Oya, *Cameroon* . . **52 C2** 5 40N 14 5 E
Bethal, *S. Africa* . . . . **57 D4** 26 27S 29 28 E
Bethanien, *Namibia* . . . . . **56 D2** 26 31S 17 8 E
Bethany, *S. Africa* . . . . . . **56 D4** 29 34S 25 59 E
Bethany, *U.S.A.* **80 E7** 40 16N 94 2W
Bethel, *Alaska, U.S.A.* . . . **68 B3** 60 48N 161 45W
Bethel, *Vt., U.S.A.* **79 C12** 43 50N 72 38W
Bethel Park, *U.S.A.* **78 F4** 40 20N 80 1W
Bethlehem = Bayt Lahm, *Jordan* . . . . **47 D4** 31 43N 35 12 E
Bethlehem, *S. Africa* . . . . **57 D4** 28 14S 28 18 E
Bethlehem, *U.S.A.* **79 F9** 40 37N 75 23W
Bethulie, *S. Africa* . . . . . . **56 E4** 30 30S 25 59 E
Béthune, *France* . . . . **18 A5** 50 30N 2 38 E
Bethungra, *Australia* . . . . **63 E4** 34 45S 147 51 E
Betioky, *Madag.* . . . . **57 C7** 23 48S 44 20 E
Betong, *Thailand* . . . . **39 K3** 5 45N 101 5 E
Betoota, *Australia* . . . . . . **62 D3** 25 45S 140 42 E
Betroka, *Madag.* . . . . **57 C8** 23 16S 46 0 E
Betsiamites, *Canada* . . . **71 C6** 48 56N 68 40W
Betsiamites →, *Canada* **71 C6** 48 56N 68 38W
Betsiboka →, *Madag.* . . **57 B8** 16 3S 46 36 E
Betsjoeanaland, *S. Africa* **56 D3** 26 30S 22 30 E
Bettiah, *India* . . . . **43 F11** 26 48N 84 33 E
Betul, *India* . . . . **40 J10** 21 58N 77 59 E
Betung, *Malaysia* . . . . **36 D4** 1 24N 111 31 E
Beulah, *U.S.A.* **80 B4** 47 16N 101 47W
Beverley, *Australia* . . . . . **61 F2** 32 9S 116 56 E
Beverley, *U.K.* **10 D7** 53 52N 0 26W
Beverly, *Mass., U.S.A.* . . **79 D14** 42 33N 70 53W
Beverly, *Wash., U.S.A.* . . **82 C4** 46 50N 119 56W
Beverly Hills, *U.S.A.* **85 L8** 34 4N 118 25W
Beverwijk, *Neths.* . . . . . . **15 B4** 52 28N 4 38 E
Beyānlū, *Iran* . . . . **44 C5** 36 0N 47 51 E
Beyla, *Guinea* **50 G3** 8 30N 8 38W
Beyneu, *Kazakhstan* . . . . **25 E10** 45 10N 55 3 E
Beypazarı, *Turkey* . . . . . . **25 F5** 40 10N 31 56 E
Beyşehir Gölü, *Turkey* . . **25 G5** 37 40N 31 45 E
Bezhitsa, *Russia* . . . . **24 D5** 53 19N 34 17 E
Béziers, *France* . . . . **18 E5** 43 20N 3 12 E
Bezwada = Vijayawada, *India* . . . . **41 L12** 16 31N 80 39 E
Bhachau, *India* . . . . **40 H7** 23 20N 70 16 E
Bhadarwah, *India* . . . . . . **43 C6** 32 58N 75 46 E
Bhadrakh, *India* . . . . **41 J15** 21 10N 86 30 E
Bhadravati, *India* . . . . . . **40 N9** 13 49N 75 40 E
Bhagalpur, *India* . . . . **43 G12** 25 10N 87 0 E
Bhakkar, *Pakistan* . . . . . . **42 D4** 31 40N 71 5 E
Bhakra Dam, *India* . . . . . **42 D7** 31 30N 76 45 E
Bhamo, *Burma* . . . . **41 G20** 24 15N 97 15 E
Bhandara, *India* . . . . **40 J11** 21 5N 79 42 E
Bhanrer Ra., *India* . . . . . **42 H8** 23 40N 79 45 E
Bharat = India ■, *Asia* . **40 K11** 20 0N 78 0 E
Bharatpur, *India* . . . . **42 F7** 27 15N 77 30 E
Bhatinda, *India* . . . . **42 D6** 30 15N 74 57 E
Bhatpara, *India* . . . . **43 H13** 22 50N 88 25 E
Bhaun, *Pakistan* . . . . **42 C5** 32 55N 72 40 E
Bhaunagar = Bhavnagar, *India* . . . . **42 J5** 21 45N 72 10 E
Bhavnagar, *India* . . . . **42 J5** 21 45N 72 10 E
Bhawanipatna, *India* . . . . **41 K12** 19 55N 80 10 E
Bhera, *Pakistan* . . . . **42 C5** 32 29N 72 57 E
Bhilsa = Vidisha, *India* . . **42 H7** 23 28N 77 53 E
Bhilwara, *India* . . . . **42 G6** 25 25N 74 38 E
Bhima →, *India* . . . . **40 L10** 16 25N 77 17 E
Bhimavaram, *India* . . . . . **41 L12** 16 30N 81 30 E
Bhimbar, *Pakistan* . . . . . . **43 C6** 32 59N 74 3 E
Bhind, *India* . . . . **43 F8** 26 30N 78 46 E
Bhiwandi, *India* . . . . **40 K8** 19 20N 73 0 E
Bhiwani, *India* . . . . **42 E7** 28 50N 76 9 E
Bhola, *Bangla.* . . . . **41 H17** 22 45N 90 35 E
Bhopal, *India* . . . . **42 H7** 23 20N 77 30 E
Bhubaneshwar, *India* . . . **41 J14** 20 15N 85 50 E
Bhuj, *India* . . . . **42 H3** 23 15N 69 49 E
Bhumiphol Dam = Phumiphon, Khuan, *Thailand* . . . . **38 D2** 17 15N 98 58 E
Bhusaval, *India* . . . . **40 J9** 21 3N 75 46 E
Bhutan ■, *Asia* . . . . **41 F17** 27 25N 90 30 E
Biafra, B. of = Bonny, Bight of, *Africa* . . . . . . **52 D1** 3 30N 9 20 E
Biak, *Indonesia* . . . . **37 E9** 1 10S 136 6 E
Biała Podlaska, *Poland* . . **17 B11** 52 4N 23 6 E
Białystok, *Poland* . . . . . . **17 B11** 53 10N 23 10 E
Bīārjmand, *Iran* . . . . **45 B7** 36 6N 55 53 E
Biaro, *Indonesia* . . . . **37 D7** 2 5N 125 26 E
Biarritz, *France* **18 E3** 43 29N 1 33W
Bibai, *Japan* . . . . **30 C10** 43 19N 141 52 E
Bibala, *Angola* . . . . **53 G2** 14 44S 13 24 E
Bibby I., *Canada* **73 A10** 61 55N 93 0W
Biberach, *Germany* . . . . . **16 D4** 48 5N 9 49 E
Bibiani, *Ghana* **50 G4** 6 30N 2 8W
Biboohra, *Australia* . . . . . **62 B4** 16 56S 145 25 E
Bibungwa, *Zaïre* . . . . **54 C2** 2 40S 28 15 E
Bic, *Canada* **71 C6** 48 20N 68 41W
Bickerton I., *Australia* . . . **62 A2** 13 45S 136 10 E
Bicknell, *Ind., U.S.A.* **76 F2** 38 47N 87 19W
Bicknell, *Utah, U.S.A.* . . . **83 G8** 38 20N 111 33W
Bida, *Nigeria* . . . . **50 G6** 9 3N 5 58 E
Bidar, *India* . . . . **40 L10** 17 55N 77 35 E
Biddeford, *U.S.A.* **71 D5** 43 30N 70 28W
Bideford, *U.K.* **11 F3** 51 1N 4 13W
Bidon 5 = Poste Maurice Cortier, *Algeria* . . . . . . **50 D5** 22 14N 1 2 E
Bidor, *Malaysia* . . . . **39 K3** 4 6N 101 15 E
Bié, Planalto de, *Angola* . **53 G3** 12 0S 16 0 E
Bieber, *U.S.A.* **82 F3** 41 7N 121 8W
Biel, *Switz.* . . . . **16 E3** 47 8N 7 14 E
Bielé Karpaty, *Europe* . . **17 D8** 49 5N 18 0 E
Bielefeld, *Germany* . . . . . **16 B4** 52 2N 8 31 E
Biella, *Italy* . . . . **20 B3** 45 33N 8 3 E
Bielsko-Biała, *Poland* . . . **17 D9** 49 50N 19 2 E
Bien Hoa, *Vietnam* . . . . . . **39 G6** 10 57N 106 49 E
Bienfait, *Canada* **73 D8** 49 10N 102 50W
Bienne = Biel, *Switz.* . . . . **16 E3** 47 8N 7 14 E
Bienville, L., *Canada* **70 A5** 55 5N 72 40W
Biesiesfontein, *S. Africa* . **56 E2** 30 57S 17 58 E
Big →, *Canada* **71 B8** 54 50N 58 55W
Big B., *Canada* **71 A7** 55 43N 60 35W
Big Bear City, *U.S.A.* **85 L10** 34 16N 116 51W
Big Bear Lake, *U.S.A.* . . . **85 L10** 34 15N 116 56W
Big Beaver, *Canada* **73 D7** 49 10N 105 10W
Big Belt Mts., *U.S.A.* **82 C8** 46 30N 111 25W
Big Bend, *Swaziland* . . . . **57 D5** 26 50S 31 58 E
Big Bend National Park, *U.S.A.* **81 L3** 29 20N 103 5W
Big Black →, *U.S.A.* **81 J9** 32 3N 91 4W
Big Blue →, *U.S.A.* **80 F6** 39 35N 96 34W
Big Cr. →, *Canada* **72 C4** 51 42N 122 41W
Big Creek, *U.S.A.* **84 H7** 37 11N 119 14W
Big Cypress Swamp, *U.S.A.* **77 M5** 26 12N 81 10W
Big Falls, *U.S.A.* **80 A8** 48 12N 93 48W
Big Fork →, *U.S.A.* **80 A8** 48 31N 93 43W
Big Horn Mts. = Bighorn Mts., *U.S.A.* **82 D10** 44 30N 107 30W
Big Lake, *U.S.A.* **81 K4** 31 12N 101 28W

Big Moose

Bridgnorth

Bole, China 32 B3 45 11N 81 37 E
Bolesławiec, Poland 16 C7 51 17N 15 37 E
Bolinao C., Phil. 37 A5 16 23N 119 55 E
Bolívar, Argentina 94 D3 36 15S 60 53W
Bolívar, Colombia 92 C3 2 0N 77 0W
Bolivar, Mo., U.S.A. 81 G8 37 37N 93 25W
Bolivar, Tenn., U.S.A. 81 H10 35 12N 89 0W
Bolivia ■, S. Amer. 92 G6 17 6S 64 0W
Bolivian Plateau, S. Amer. 90 D3 20 0S 67 30W
Bollnäs, Sweden 9 F14 61 21N 16 24 E
Bollon, Australia 63 D4 28 2S 147 29 E
Bolobo, Zaïre 52 E3 2 6S 16 20 E
Bologna, Italy 20 B4 44 30N 11 20 E
Bologoye, Russia 24 C5 57 55N 34 5 E
Bolomba, Zaïre 52 D3 0 35N 19 0 E
Bolonchenticul, Mexico 87 D7 20 0N 89 49W
Bolong, Phil. 37 C6 7 6N 122 14 E
Boloven, Cao Nguyen, Laos 38 E6 15 10N 106 30 E
Bolpur, India 43 H12 23 40N 87 45 E
Bolsena, L. di, Italy 20 C4 42 35N 11 55 E
Bolshereche, Russia 26 D8 56 4N 74 45 E
Bolshevik, Ostrov, Russia 27 B11 78 30N 102 0 E
Bolshezemelskaya Tundra, Russia 24 A10 67 0N 56 0 E
Bolshoi Kavkas, Asia 25 F7 42 50N 44 0 E
Bolshoy Anyuy →, Russia 27 C17 68 30N 160 49 E
Bolshoy Atlym, Russia 26 C7 62 25N 66 50 E
Bolshoy Begichev, Ostrov, Russia 27 B12 74 20N 112 30 E
Bolshoy Lyakhovskiy, Ostrov, Russia 27 B15 73 35N 142 0 E
Bolsward, Neths. 15 A5 53 3N 5 32 E
Bolton, Canada 78 C5 43 54N 79 45W
Bolton, U.K. 10 D5 53 35N 2 26W
Bolu, Turkey 25 F5 40 45N 31 35 E
Bolvadin, Turkey 25 G5 38 45N 31 4 E
Bolzano, Italy 20 A4 46 30N 11 20 E
Bom Despacho, Brazil 93 G9 19 43S 45 15W
Bom Jesus da Lapa, Brazil 93 F10 13 15S 43 25W
Boma, Zaïre 52 F2 5 50S 13 4 E
Bomaderry, Australia 63 E5 34 52S 150 37 E
Bombala, Australia 63 F4 36 56S 149 15 E
Bombay, India 40 K8 18 55N 72 50 E
Bomboma, Zaïre 52 D3 2 25N 18 55 E
Bombombwa, Zaïre 54 B2 1 40N 25 40 E
Bomili, Zaïre 54 B2 1 45N 27 5 E
Bomokandi →, Zaïre 54 B2 3 39N 26 8 E
Bomongo, Zaïre 52 D3 1 27N 18 21 E
Bomu →, C.A.R. 52 D4 4 40N 22 30 E
Bon, C., Tunisia 51 A7 37 1N 11 2 E
Bon Sar Pa, Vietnam 38 F6 12 24N 107 35 E
Bonaire, Neth. Ant. 89 D6 12 10N 68 15W
Bonang, Australia 63 F4 37 11S 148 41 E
Bonanza, Nic. 88 D3 13 54N 84 35W
Bonaparte Arch., Australia 60 B3 14 0S 124 30 E
Bonaventure, Canada 71 C6 48 5N 65 32W
Bonavista, Canada 71 C9 48 40N 53 5W
Bonavista, C., Canada 71 C9 48 42N 53 5W
Bondo, Zaïre 54 B1 3 55N 23 53 E
Bondoukou, Ivory C. 50 G4 8 2N 2 47W
Bondowoso, Indonesia 37 G15 7 55S 113 49 E
Bone, Teluk, Indonesia 37 E6 4 10S 120 50 E
Bone Rate, Indonesia 37 F6 7 25S 121 5 E
Bone Rate, Kepulauan, Indonesia 37 F6 6 30S 121 10 E
Bo'ness, U.K. 12 E5 56 0N 3 38W
Bong Son = Hoai Nhon, Vietnam 38 E7 14 28N 109 1 E
Bongandanga, Zaïre 52 D4 1 24N 21 3 E
Bongor, Chad 51 F8 10 35N 15 20 E
Bonham, U.S.A. 81 J6 33 35N 96 11W
Bonifacio, France 18 F9 41 24N 9 10 E
Bonifacio, Bouches de, Medit. S. 20 D3 41 12N 9 15 E
Bonifacio, Str. of, Medit. S. 20 D3 41 12N 9 15 E
Bonin Is. = Ogasawara Gunto, Pac. Oc. 64 E6 27 0N 142 0 E
Bonn, Germany 16 C3 50 43N 7 6 E
Bonne Terre, U.S.A. 81 G9 37 55N 90 33W
Bonners Ferry, U.S.A. 82 B5 48 42N 116 19W
Bonney, L., Australia 63 F3 37 50S 140 20 E
Bonnie Downs, Australia 62 C3 22 7S 143 50 E
Bonnie Rock, Australia 61 F2 30 29S 118 22 E
Bonny, Bight of, Africa 52 D1 3 30N 9 20 E
Bonnyville, Canada 73 C6 54 20N 110 45W
Bonoi, Indonesia 37 E9 1 45S 137 41 E
Bonsall, U.S.A. 85 M9 33 16N 117 14W
Bontang, Indonesia 36 D5 0 10N 117 30 E
Bonthain, Indonesia 37 F5 5 34S 119 56 E
Bonthe, S. Leone 50 G2 7 30N 12 33W
Bontoc, Phil. 37 A6 17 7N 120 58 E
Bonython Ra., Australia 60 D4 23 40S 128 45 E
Bookabie, Australia 61 F5 31 50S 132 41 E
Booker, U.S.A. 81 G4 36 27N 100 32W
Boolaboolka L., Australia 63 E3 32 38S 143 10 E
Booligal, Australia 63 E3 33 58S 144 53 E
Boom, Belgium 15 C4 51 6N 4 20 E
Boonah, Australia 63 D5 27 58S 152 41 E
Boone, Iowa, U.S.A. 80 D8 42 4N 93 53W
Boone, N.C., U.S.A. 77 G5 36 13N 81 41W
Booneville, Ark., U.S.A. 81 H8 35 8N 93 55W
Booneville, Miss., U.S.A. 77 H1 34 39N 88 34W
Boonville, Calif., U.S.A. 84 F3 39 1N 123 22W
Boonville, Ind., U.S.A. 76 F2 38 3N 87 16W
Boonville, Mo., U.S.A. 80 F8 38 58N 92 44W
Boonville, N.Y., U.S.A. 79 C9 43 29N 75 20W
Boorindal, Australia 63 E4 30 22S 146 11 E
Boorowa, Australia 63 E4 34 28S 148 44 E
Boothia, Gulf of, Canada 69 A11 71 0N 90 0W
Boothia Pen., Canada 68 A10 71 0N 94 0W
Bootle, Cumb., U.K. 10 C4 54 17N 3 24W
Bootle, Mersey., U.K. 10 D4 53 28N 3 1W
Booué, Gabon 52 E2 0 5S 11 55 E
Bophuthatswana □, S. Africa 56 D4 25 49S 25 30 E
Boquete, Panama 88 E3 8 46N 82 27W
Boquilla, Presa de la, Mexico 86 B3 27 40N 105 30W
Boquillas del Carmen, Mexico 86 B4 29 17N 102 53W
Bor, Serbia, Yug. 21 B10 44 5N 22 7 E
Bôr, Sudan 51 G11 6 10N 31 40 E
Bor Mashash, Israel 47 D3 31 7N 34 50 E
Boradā →, Syria 47 B5 33 33N 36 34 E
Borah Peak, U.S.A. 82 D7 44 8N 113 47W
Borama, Somali Rep. 46 F3 9 55N 43 7 E
Borås, Sweden 9 H12 57 43N 12 56 E
Borāzjān, Iran 45 D6 29 22N 51 10 E
Borba, Brazil 92 D7 4 12S 59 34W
Bord Khūn-e Now, Iran 45 D6 28 3N 51 28 E
Borda, C., Australia 63 F2 35 45S 136 34 E
Bordeaux, France 18 D3 44 50N 0 36W
Borden, Australia 61 F2 34 3S 118 12 E
Borden, Canada 71 C7 46 18N 63 47W
Borden I., Canada 4 B2 78 30N 111 30W
Borders □, U.K. 12 F6 55 35N 2 50W
Bordertown, Australia 63 F3 36 19S 140 45 E
Borðeyri, Iceland 8 D3 65 12N 21 6W
Bordj Fly Ste. Marie, Algeria 50 C4 27 19N 2 32W
Bordj-in-Eker, Algeria 50 D6 24 9N 5 3 E
Bordj Omar Driss, Algeria 50 C6 28 10N 6 40 E
Bordj-Tarat, Algeria 50 C6 25 55N 9 3 E
Borgå, Finland 9 F18 60 24N 25 40 E
Borgarnes, Iceland 8 D3 64 32N 21 55W
Børgefjellet, Norway 8 D12 65 20N 13 45 E
Borger, Neths. 15 B6 52 54N 6 44 E
Borger, U.S.A. 81 H4 35 39N 101 24W
Borgholm, Sweden 9 H14 56 52N 16 39 E
Borikhane, Laos 38 C4 18 33N 103 43 E
Borisoglebsk, Russia 25 D7 51 27N 42 5 E
Borisov, Belorussia 24 D4 54 17N 28 28 E
Borja, Peru 92 D3 4 20S 77 40W
Borkou, Chad 51 E8 18 15N 18 50 E
Borkum, Germany 16 B3 53 36N 6 42 E
Borlänge, Sweden 9 F13 60 29N 15 26 E
Borley, C., Antarctica 5 C5 66 15S 52 30 E
Borneo, E. Indies 36 D5 1 0N 115 0 E
Bornholm, Denmark 9 J13 55 10N 15 0 E
Borobudur, Indonesia 37 G14 7 36S 110 13 E
Borogontsy, Russia 27 C14 62 42N 131 8 E
Boromo, Burkina Faso 50 F4 11 45N 2 58W
Boron, U.S.A. 85 L9 35 0N 117 39W
Borongan, Phil. 37 B7 11 37N 125 26 E
Bororen, Australia 62 C5 24 13S 151 33 E
Borovichi, Russia 24 C5 58 25N 33 55 E
Borrego Springs, U.S.A. 85 M10 33 15N 116 23W
Borroloola, Australia 62 B2 16 4S 136 17 E
Borth, U.K. 11 E3 52 29N 4 3W
Borujerd, Iran 45 C6 33 55N 48 50 E
Borzya, Russia 27 D12 50 24N 116 31 E
Bosa, Italy 20 D3 40 17N 8 32 E
Bosanska Gradiška, Bos.-H. 20 B7 45 10N 17 15 E
Bosaso, Somali Rep. 46 E4 11 12N 49 18 E
Boscastle, U.K. 11 G3 50 42N 4 42W
Boshan, China 35 F9 36 28N 117 49 E
Boshoek, S. Africa 56 D4 25 30S 27 9 E
Boshof, S. Africa 56 D4 28 31S 25 13 E
Boshrūyeh, Iran 45 C8 33 50N 57 30 E
Bosna →, Bos.-H. 21 B8 45 4N 18 29 E
Bosna i Hercegovina = Bosnia-Herzegovina ■, Europe 20 B7 44 0N 17 0 E
Bosnia-Herzegovina ■, Europe 20 B7 44 0N 17 0 E
Bosnik, Indonesia 37 E9 1 5S 136 10 E
Bosobolo, Zaïre 52 D3 4 15N 19 50 E
Bosporus = Karadeniz Boğazı, Turkey 21 D13 41 10N 29 10 E
Bossangoa, C.A.R. 51 G8 6 35N 17 30 E
Bossekop, Norway 8 B17 69 57N 23 15 E
Bossembélé, C.A.R. 51 G8 5 25N 17 40 E
Bossier City, U.S.A. 81 J8 32 31N 93 44W
Bosso, Niger 51 F7 13 43N 13 19 E
Bostānābād, Iran 44 B5 37 50N 46 50 E
Bosten Hu, China 32 B3 41 55N 87 40 E
Boston, U.K. 10 E7 52 59N 0 2W
Boston, U.S.A. 79 D13 42 22N 71 4W
Boston Bar, Canada 72 D4 49 52N 121 30W
Boswell, Canada 72 D5 49 28N 116 45W
Boswell, Okla., U.S.A. 81 H7 34 2N 95 52W
Boswell, Pa., U.S.A. 78 F5 40 10N 79 2W
Botad, India 42 H4 22 15N 71 40 E
Botany B., Australia 63 E5 34 0S 151 14 E
Botene, Laos 38 D3 17 35N 101 12 E
Bothaville, S. Africa 56 D4 27 23S 26 34 E
Bothnia, G. of, Europe 8 E16 63 0N 20 15 E
Bothwell, Australia 62 G4 42 20S 147 1 E
Bothwell, Canada 78 D3 42 38N 81 52W
Botletle →, Botswana 56 C3 20 10S 23 15 E
Botoşani, Romania 17 E13 47 42N 26 41 E
Botswana ■, Africa 56 C3 22 0S 24 0 E
Bottineau, U.S.A. 80 A4 48 50N 100 27W
Bottrop, Germany 15 C6 51 34N 6 59 E
Botucatu, Brazil 95 A6 22 55S 48 30W
Botwood, Canada 71 C8 49 6N 55 23W
Bou Djébéha, Mali 50 E4 18 25N 2 45W
Bou Izakarn, Morocco 50 C3 29 12N 9 46W
Bouaké, Ivory C. 50 G3 7 40N 5 2W
Bouar, C.A.R. 52 C3 6 0N 15 40 E
Bouârfa, Morocco 50 B4 32 32N 1 58W
Bouca, C.A.R. 51 G8 6 45N 18 25 E
Boucaut B., Australia 62 A1 12 0S 134 25 E
Bouches-du-Rhône □, France 18 E6 43 37N 5 2 E
Bougainville, C., Australia 60 B4 13 57S 126 4 E
Bougainville Reef, Australia 62 B4 15 30S 147 5 E
Bougie = Bejaia, Algeria 50 A6 36 42N 5 2 E
Bougouni, Mali 50 F3 11 30N 7 20W
Bouillon, Belgium 15 E5 49 44N 5 3 E
Boulder, Colo., U.S.A. 80 E2 40 1N 105 17W
Boulder, Mont., U.S.A. 82 C7 46 14N 112 7W
Boulder City, U.S.A. 85 K12 35 59N 114 50W
Boulder Creek, U.S.A. 84 H4 37 7N 122 7W
Boulder Dam = Hoover Dam, U.S.A. 85 K12 36 1N 114 44W
Boulia, Australia 62 C2 22 52S 139 51 E
Boulogne-sur-Mer, France 18 A4 50 42N 1 36 E
Boultoum, Niger 50 F7 14 45N 10 25 E
Boun Neua, Laos 38 B3 21 38N 101 54 E
Boun Tai, Laos 38 B3 21 23N 101 58 E
Bouna, Ivory C. 50 G4 9 10N 3 0W
Boundary Peak, U.S.A. 84 H8 37 51N 118 21W
Boundiali, Ivory C. 50 G3 9 30N 6 20W
Bountiful, U.S.A. 82 F8 40 53N 111 53W
Bounty Is., Pac. Oc. 64 M9 48 0S 178 30 E
Bourbonnais, France 18 C5 46 28N 3 0 E
Bourem, Mali 50 E4 17 0N 0 24W
Bourg-en-Bresse, France 18 C6 46 13N 5 12 E
Bourges, France 18 C5 47 9N 2 25 E
Bourget, Canada 79 A9 45 26N 75 9W
Bourgogne, France 18 C6 47 0N 4 50 E
Bourke, Australia 63 E4 30 8S 145 55 E
Bournemouth, U.K. 11 G6 50 43N 1 53W
Bouse, U.S.A. 85 M13 33 56N 114 0W
Bousso, Chad 51 F8 10 34N 16 52 E
Boutilimit, Mauritania 50 E2 17 45N 14 40W
Bouvet I. = Bouvetøya, Antarctica 3 G10 54 26S 3 24 E
Bouvetøya, Antarctica 3 G10 54 26S 3 24 E
Bovigny, Belgium 15 D5 50 12N 5 55 E
Bovill, U.S.A. 82 C5 46 51N 116 24W
Bow Island, Canada 72 D6 49 50N 111 23W
Bowbells, U.S.A. 80 A3 48 48N 102 15W
Bowdle, U.S.A. 80 C5 45 27N 99 39W
Bowelling, Australia 61 F2 33 25S 116 30 E
Bowen, Australia 62 C4 20 0S 148 16 E
Bowen Mts., Australia 63 F4 37 0S 147 50 E
Bowie, Ariz., U.S.A. 83 K9 32 19N 109 29W
Bowie, Tex., U.S.A. 81 J6 33 34N 97 51W
Bowkān, Iran 44 B5 36 31N 46 12 E
Bowland, Forest of, U.K. 10 D5 54 0N 2 30W
Bowling Green, Ky., U.S.A. 76 G2 36 59N 86 27W
Bowling Green, Ohio, U.S.A. 76 E4 41 23N 83 39W
Bowling Green, C., Australia 62 B4 19 19S 147 25 E
Bowman, U.S.A. 80 B3 46 11N 103 24W
Bowman I., Antarctica 5 C8 65 0S 104 0 E
Bowmans, Australia 63 E2 34 10S 138 17 E
Bowmanville, Canada 70 D4 43 55N 78 41W
Bowmore, U.K. 12 F2 55 45N 6 18W
Bowral, Australia 63 E5 34 26S 150 27 E
Bowraville, Australia 63 E5 30 37S 152 52 E
Bowron →, Canada 72 C4 54 3N 121 50W
Bowser L., Canada 72 B3 56 30N 129 30W
Bowsman, Canada 73 C8 52 14N 101 12W
Bowwood, Zambia 55 F2 17 5S 26 20 E
Boxtel, Neths. 15 C5 51 36N 5 20 E
Boyce, U.S.A. 81 K8 31 23N 92 40W
Boyer →, Canada 72 B5 58 27N 115 57W
Boyle, Ireland 13 C3 53 58N 8 19W
Boyne →, Ireland 13 C5 53 43N 6 15W
Boyne City, U.S.A. 76 C3 45 13N 85 1W
Boynton Beach, U.S.A. 77 M5 26 32N 80 4W
Boyoma, Chutes, Zaïre 54 B2 0 35N 25 23 E
Boyup Brook, Australia 61 F2 33 50S 116 23 E
Bozeman, U.S.A. 82 D8 45 41N 111 2W
Bozen = Bolzano, Italy 20 A4 46 30N 11 20 E
Bozoum, C.A.R. 51 G8 6 25N 16 35 E
Brabant □, Belgium 15 D4 50 46N 4 30 E
Brabant L., Canada 73 B8 55 58N 103 43W
Brač, Croatia 20 C7 43 20N 16 40 E
Bracadale, L., U.K. 12 D2 57 20N 6 30W
Bracciano, L. di, Italy 20 C5 42 8N 12 11 E
Bracebridge, Canada 70 C4 45 2N 79 19W
Brach, Libya 51 C7 27 31N 14 20 E
Bräcke, Sweden 8 E13 62 45N 15 26 E
Brackettville, U.S.A. 81 L4 29 19N 100 25W
Brad, Romania 17 E11 46 10N 22 50 E
Bradenton, U.S.A. 77 M4 27 30N 82 34W
Bradford, Canada 78 B5 44 7N 79 34W
Bradford, U.K. 10 D6 53 47N 1 45W
Bradford, Pa., U.S.A. 78 E6 41 58N 78 38W
Bradford, Vt., U.S.A. 79 C12 43 59N 72 9W
Bradley, Ark., U.S.A. 81 J8 33 6N 93 39W
Bradley, Calif., U.S.A. 84 K6 35 52N 120 48W
Bradley, S. Dak., U.S.A. 80 C6 45 5N 97 39W
Bradley Institute, Zimbabwe 55 F3 17 7S 31 25 E
Bradore Bay, Canada 71 B8 51 27N 57 18W
Bradshaw, Australia 60 C5 15 21S 130 16 E
Brady, U.S.A. 81 K5 31 9N 99 20W
Braemar, Australia 63 E2 33 12S 139 35 E
Braeside, Canada 79 A8 45 28N 76 24W
Braga, Portugal 19 B1 41 35N 8 25W
Bragado, Argentina 94 D3 35 2S 60 27W
Bragança, Brazil 93 D9 1 0S 47 2W
Bragança, Portugal 19 B2 41 48N 6 50W
Bragança Paulista, Brazil 95 A6 22 55S 46 32W
Brahmanbaria, Bangla. 41 H17 23 58N 91 15 E
Brahmani →, India 41 J15 20 39N 86 46 E
Brahmaputra →, India 43 G13 23 58N 89 50 E
Braich-y-pwll, U.K. 10 E3 52 47N 4 46W
Braidwood, Australia 63 F4 35 27S 149 49 E
Brăila, Romania 21 B12 45 19N 27 59 E
Brainerd, U.S.A. 80 B7 46 22N 94 12W
Braintree, U.K. 11 F8 51 53N 0 34 E
Braintree, U.S.A. 79 D14 42 13N 71 0W
Brak →, S. Africa 56 D3 29 35S 22 55 E
Brakwater, Namibia 56 C2 22 28S 17 3 E
Bralorne, Canada 72 C4 50 50N 122 50W
Brampton, Canada 70 D4 43 45N 79 45W
Bramwell, Australia 62 A3 12 8S 142 37 E
Branco →, Brazil 92 D6 1 20S 61 50W
Brandenburg = Neubrandenburg, Germany 16 B6 53 33N 13 17 E
Brandenburg, Germany 16 B6 52 24N 12 33 E
Brandfort, S. Africa 56 D4 28 40S 26 30 E
Brandon, Canada 73 D9 49 50N 99 57W
Brandon, U.S.A. 79 C11 43 48N 73 4W
Brandon B., Ireland 13 D1 52 17N 10 8W
Brandon Mt., Ireland 13 D1 52 15N 10 15W
Brandsen, Argentina 94 D4 35 10S 58 15W
Brandvlei, S. Africa 56 E3 30 25S 20 30 E
Branford, U.S.A. 79 E12 41 17N 72 49W
Braniewo, Poland 17 A9 54 25N 19 50 E
Bransfield Str., Antarctica 5 C18 63 0S 59 0W
Brańsk, Poland 17 B11 52 45N 22 50 E
Branson, Colo., U.S.A. 81 G3 37 1N 103 53W
Branson, Mo., U.S.A. 81 G8 36 39N 93 13W
Brantford, Canada 70 D3 43 10N 80 15W
Branxholme, Australia 63 F3 37 52S 141 49 E
Bras d'Or, L., Canada 71 C7 45 50N 60 50W
Brasil, Planalto, Brazil 93 G9 18 0S 46 30W
Brasiléia, Brazil 92 F5 11 0S 68 45W
Brasília, Brazil 93 G9 15 47S 47 55W
Braşov, Romania 21 B11 45 38N 25 35 E
Brasschaat, Belgium 15 C4 51 19N 4 27 E
Brassey, Banjaran, Malaysia 36 D5 5 0N 117 15 E
Brassey Ra., Australia 61 E3 25 8S 122 15 E
Brasstown Bald, U.S.A. 77 H4 34 53N 83 49W
Bratislava, Slovakia 16 D8 48 10N 17 7 E
Bratsk, Russia 27 D11 56 10N 101 30 E
Brattleboro, U.S.A. 79 D12 42 51N 72 34W
Braunschweig, Germany 16 B5 52 17N 10 28 E
Braunton, U.K. 11 F3 51 6N 4 9W
Brava, Somali Rep. 46 G3 1 20N 44 8 E
Bravo del Norte →, Mexico 86 B5 25 57N 97 9W
Brawley, U.S.A. 85 N11 32 59N 115 31W
Bray, Ireland 13 C5 53 12N 6 6W
Bray, Mt., Australia 62 A1 14 0S 134 30 E
Bray-sur-Seine, France 18 B5 48 25N 3 14 E
Brazeau →, Canada 72 C5 52 55N 115 14W
Brazil, U.S.A. 76 F2 39 32N 87 8W
Brazil ■, S. Amer. 93 F9 12 0S 50 0W
Brazilian Highlands = Brasil, Planalto, Brazil 93 G9 18 0S 46 30W
Brazo Sur →, S. Amer. 94 B4 25 21S 57 42W
Brazos →, U.S.A. 81 L7 28 53N 95 23W
Brazzaville, Congo 52 E3 4 9S 15 12 E
Brčko, Bos.-H. 21 B8 44 54N 18 46 E
Breadalbane, Australia 62 C2 23 50S 139 35 E
Breadalbane, U.K. 12 E4 56 30N 4 15W
Breaden, L., Australia 61 E4 25 51S 125 28 E
Breaksea Sd., N.Z. 59 L1 45 35S 166 35 E
Bream B., N.Z. 59 F5 35 56S 174 28 E
Bream Hd., N.Z. 59 F5 35 51S 174 36 E
Breas, Chile 94 B1 25 29S 70 24W
Brebes, Indonesia 37 G13 6 52S 109 3 E
Brechin, Canada 78 B5 44 32N 79 10W
Brechin, U.K. 12 E6 56 44N 2 40W
Breckenridge, Colo., U.S.A. 82 G10 39 29N 106 3W
Breckenridge, Minn., U.S.A. 80 B6 46 16N 96 35W
Breckenridge, Tex., U.S.A. 81 J5 32 45N 98 54W
Breckland, U.K. 11 E8 52 30N 0 40 E
Brecon, U.K. 11 F4 51 57N 3 23W
Brecon Beacons, U.K. 11 F4 51 53N 3 27W
Breda, Neths. 15 C4 51 35N 4 45 E
Bredasdorp, S. Africa 56 E3 34 33S 20 2 E
Bredbo, Australia 63 F4 35 58S 149 10 E
Bregenz, Austria 16 E4 47 30N 9 45 E
Breiðafjörður, Iceland 8 D2 65 15N 23 15W
Brejo, Brazil 93 D10 3 41S 42 47W
Bremen, Germany 16 B4 53 4N 8 47 E
Bremer I., Australia 62 A2 12 5S 136 45 E
Bremerhaven, Germany 16 B4 53 34N 8 35 E
Bremerton, U.S.A. 84 C4 47 34N 122 38W
Brenham, U.S.A. 81 K6 30 10N 96 24W
Brenner Pass, Austria 16 E5 47 2N 11 30 E
Brent, Canada 70 C4 46 2N 78 29W
Brent, U.K. 11 F7 51 33N 0 18W
Brentwood, U.K. 11 F8 51 37N 0 19 E
Brentwood, U.S.A. 79 F11 40 47N 73 15W
Bréscia, Italy 20 B4 45 33N 10 13 E
Breskens, Neths. 15 C3 51 23N 3 33 E
Breslau = Wrocław, Poland 16 C8 51 5N 17 5 E
Bressanone, Italy 20 A4 46 43N 11 40 E
Bressay, U.K. 12 A7 60 10N 1 5W
Bresse, France 18 C6 46 50N 5 10 E
Brest, Belorussia 24 D3 52 10N 23 40 E
Brest, France 18 B1 48 24N 4 31W
Brest-Litovsk = Brest, Belorussia 24 D3 52 10N 23 40 E
Bretagne, France 18 B2 48 10N 3 0W
Bretçu, Romania 17 E13 46 7N 26 18 E
Breton, Canada 72 C6 53 7N 114 28W
Breton Sd., U.S.A. 81 L10 29 35N 89 15W
Brett, C., N.Z. 59 F5 35 10S 174 20 E
Brevard, U.S.A. 77 H4 35 14N 82 44W
Brewarrina, Australia 63 D4 30 0S 146 51 E
Brewer, U.S.A. 71 D6 44 48N 68 46W
Brewer, Mt., U.S.A. 84 J8 36 44N 118 28W
Brewster, N.Y., U.S.A. 79 E11 41 23N 73 37W
Brewster, Wash., U.S.A. 82 B4 48 6N 119 47W
Brewster, Kap, Greenland 4 B6 70 7N 22 0W
Brewton, U.S.A. 77 K2 31 7N 87 4W
Breyten, S. Africa 57 D4 26 16S 30 0 E
Brezhnev = Naberezhnyye Chelny, Russia 26 D6 55 42N 52 19 E
Bria, C.A.R. 51 G9 6 30N 21 58 E
Briançon, France 18 D7 44 54N 6 39 E
Bribie I., Australia 63 D5 27 0S 153 10 E
Bridgehampton, U.S.A. 79 F12 40 56N 72 19W
Bridgend, U.K. 11 F4 51 30N 3 35W
Bridgeport, Calif., U.S.A. 83 G4 38 15N 119 14W
Bridgeport, Conn., U.S.A. 79 E11 41 11N 73 12W
Bridgeport, Nebr., U.S.A. 80 E3 41 40N 103 6W
Bridgeport, Tex., U.S.A. 81 J6 33 13N 97 45W
Bridger, U.S.A. 82 D9 45 18N 108 55W
Bridgeton, U.S.A. 76 F8 39 26N 75 14W
Bridgetown, Australia 61 F2 33 58S 116 7 E
Bridgetown, Barbados 89 D8 13 5N 59 30W
Bridgetown, Canada 71 D6 44 55N 65 18W
Bridgewater, Canada 71 D7 44 25N 64 31W
Bridgewater, Mass., U.S.A. 79 E14 41 59N 70 58W
Bridgewater, S. Dak., U.S.A. 80 D6 43 33N 97 30W
Bridgewater, C., Australia 63 F3 38 23S 141 23 E
Bridgnorth, U.K. 11 E5 52 33N 2 25W

Bridgton

Bridgton, U.S.A. 79 B14 44 3N 70 42W
Bridgwater, U.K. 11 F4 51 7N 3 0W
Bridlington, U.K. 10 C7 54 6N 0 11W
Bridport, Australia 62 G4 40 59S 147 23 E
Bridport, U.K. 11 G5 50 43N 2 45W
Brie, Plaine de la, France 18 B5 48 35N 3 10 E
Brig, Switz. 16 E3 46 18N 7 59 E
Brigg, U.K. 10 D7 53 33N 0 30W
Briggsdale, U.S.A. 80 E2 40 38N 104 20W
Brigham City, U.S.A. 82 F7 41 31N 112 1W
Bright, Australia 63 F4 36 42S 146 56 E
Brighton, Australia 63 F2 35 5S 138 30 E
Brighton, Canada 70 D4 44 2N 77 44W
Brighton, U.K. 11 G7 50 50N 0 9W
Brighton, U.S.A. 80 F2 39 59N 104 49W
Brilliant, Canada 72 D5 49 19N 117 38W
Brilliant, U.S.A. 78 F4 40 15N 80 39W
Bríndisi, Italy 21 D7 40 39N 17 55 E
Brinkley, U.S.A. 81 H9 34 53N 91 12W
Brinkworth, Australia 63 E2 33 42S 138 26 E
Brinnon, U.S.A. 84 C4 47 41N 122 54W
Brion, I., Canada 71 C7 47 46N 61 26W
Brisbane, Australia 63 D5 27 25S 153 2 E
Brisbane →, Australia 63 D5 27 24S 153 9 E
Bristol, U.K. 11 F5 51 26N 2 35W
Bristol, Conn., U.S.A. 79 E12 41 40N 72 57W
Bristol, Pa., U.S.A. 79 F10 40 6N 74 51W
Bristol, R.I., U.S.A. 79 E13 41 40N 71 16W
Bristol, S. Dak., U.S.A. 80 C6 45 21N 97 45W
Bristol, Tenn., U.S.A. 77 G4 36 36N 82 11W
Bristol B., U.S.A. 68 C4 58 0N 160 0W
Bristol Channel, U.K. 11 F3 51 18N 4 30W
Bristol I., Antarctica 5 B1 58 45S 28 0W
Bristol L., U.S.A. 83 J5 34 23N 116 50W
Bristow, U.S.A. 81 H6 35 50N 96 23W
British Columbia □, Canada 72 C3 55 0N 125 15W
British Guiana = Guyana ■, S. Amer. 92 C7 5 0N 59 0W
British Honduras = Belize ■, Cent. Amer. 87 D7 17 0N 88 30W
British Isles, Europe 6 E5 54 0N 4 0W
Brits, S. Africa 57 D4 25 37S 27 48 E
Britstown, S. Africa 56 E3 30 37S 23 30 E
Britt, Canada 70 C3 45 46N 80 34W
Brittany = Bretagne, France 18 B2 48 10N 3 0W
Britton, U.S.A. 80 C6 45 48N 97 45W
Brixton, Australia 62 C3 23 32S 144 57 E
Brlik, Kazakhstan 26 E8 43 40N 73 49 E
Brno, Czech. 16 D8 49 10N 16 35 E
Broad →, U.S.A. 77 J5 34 1N 81 4W
Broad Arrow, Australia 61 F3 30 23S 121 15 E
Broad B., U.K. 12 C2 58 14N 6 16W
Broad Haven, Ireland 13 B2 54 20N 9 55W
Broad Law, U.K. 12 F5 55 30N 3 22W
Broad Sd., Australia 62 C4 22 0S 149 45 E
Broadhurst Ra., Australia 60 D3 22 30S 122 30 E
Broads, The, U.K. 10 E9 52 45N 1 30 E
Broadus, U.S.A. 80 C2 45 27N 105 25W
Broadview, Canada 73 C8 50 22N 102 35W
Brochet, Canada 73 B8 57 53N 101 40W
Brochet, L., Canada 73 B8 58 36N 101 35W
Brock, Canada 73 C7 51 26N 108 43W
Brocken, Germany 16 C5 51 48N 10 40 E
Brockport, U.S.A. 78 C7 43 13N 77 56W
Brockton, U.S.A. 79 D13 42 5N 71 1W
Brockville, Canada 70 D4 44 35N 75 41W
Brockway, Mont., U.S.A. 80 B2 47 18N 105 45W
Brockway, Pa., U.S.A. 78 E6 41 15N 78 47W
Brocton, U.S.A. 78 D5 42 23N 79 26W
Brodeur Pen., Canada 69 A11 72 30N 88 10W
Brodick, U.K. 12 F3 55 34N 5 9W
Brogan, U.S.A. 82 D5 44 15N 117 31W
Broken Bow, Nebr., U.S.A. 80 E5 41 24N 99 38W
Broken Bow, Okla., U.S.A. 81 H7 34 2N 94 44W
Broken Hill = Kabwe, Zambia 55 E2 14 30S 28 29 E
Broken Hill, Australia 63 E3 31 58S 141 29 E
Bromfield, U.K. 11 E5 52 25N 2 45W
Bromley, U.K. 11 F8 51 20N 0 5 E
Brønderslev, Denmark 9 H10 57 16N 9 57 E
Bronkhorstspruit, S. Africa 57 D4 25 46S 28 45 E
Bronte, U.S.A. 81 K4 31 53N 100 18W
Bronte Park, Australia 62 G4 42 8S 146 30 E
Brook Park, U.S.A. 78 E4 41 24N 80 51W
Brookfield, U.S.A. 80 F8 39 47N 93 4W
Brookhaven, U.S.A. 81 K9 31 35N 90 26W
Brookings, Oreg., U.S.A. 82 E1 42 3N 124 17W
Brookings, S. Dak., U.S.A. 80 C6 44 19N 96 48W
Brooklin, Canada 78 C6 43 55N 78 55W
Brookmere, Canada 72 D4 49 52N 120 53W
Brooks, Canada 72 C6 50 35N 111 55W
Brooks B., Canada 72 C3 50 15N 127 55W
Brooks L., Canada 73 A7 61 55N 106 35W
Brooks Ra., U.S.A. 68 B5 68 40N 147 0W
Brooksville, U.S.A. 77 L4 28 33N 82 23W
Brookville, U.S.A. 76 F3 39 25N 85 1W
Brooloo, Australia 63 D5 26 30S 152 43 E
Broom, L., U.K. 12 D3 57 55N 5 15W
Broome, Australia 60 C3 18 0S 122 15 E
Broomehill, Australia 61 F2 33 51S 117 39 E
Brora, U.K. 12 C5 58 3N 3 50W
Brora →, U.K. 12 C5 58 4N 3 52W
Brosna →, Ireland 13 C4 53 8N 8 0W
Brothers, U.S.A. 82 E3 43 49N 120 36W
Brough, U.K. 10 C5 54 32N 2 19W
Broughton Island, Canada 69 B13 67 33N 63 0W
Broughty Ferry, U.K. 12 E6 56 29N 2 50W
Brouwershaven, Neths. 15 C3 51 45N 3 55 E
Browerville, U.S.A. 80 B7 46 5N 94 52W
Brown, Pt., Australia 63 E1 32 32S 133 50 E
Brown Willy, U.K. 11 G3 50 35N 4 34W
Brownfield, U.S.A. 81 J3 33 11N 102 17W
Browning, U.S.A. 82 B7 48 34N 113 1W
Brownlee, Canada 73 C7 50 43N 106 1W
Brownsville, Oreg., U.S.A. 82 D2 44 24N 122 59W
Brownsville, Tenn., U.S.A. 81 H10 35 36N 89 16W
Brownsville, Tex., U.S.A. 81 N6 25 54N 97 30W
Brownwood, U.S.A. 81 K5 31 43N 98 59W
Brownwood, L., U.S.A. 81 K5 31 51N 98 35W
Browse I., Australia 60 B3 14 7S 123 33 E
Bruas, Malaysia 39 K3 4 30N 100 47 E
Bruay-en-Artois, France 18 A5 50 29N 2 33 E
Bruce, Mt., Australia 60 D2 22 37S 118 8 E
Bruce Pen., Canada 78 A3 45 0N 81 30W
Bruce Rock, Australia 61 F2 31 52S 118 8 E
Bruck an der Leitha, Austria 16 D8 48 1N 16 47 E
Brue →, U.K. 11 F5 51 10N 2 59W
Bruges = Brugge, Belgium 15 C3 51 13N 3 13 E
Brugge, Belgium 15 C3 51 13N 3 13 E
Brûlé, Canada 72 C5 53 15N 117 58W
Brumado, Brazil 93 F10 14 14S 41 40W
Brunchilly, Australia 62 B1 18 50S 134 30 E
Brundidge, U.S.A. 77 K3 31 43N 85 49W
Bruneau, U.S.A. 82 E6 42 53N 115 48W
Bruneau →, U.S.A. 82 E6 42 56N 115 57W
Brunei = Bandar Seri Begawan, Brunei 36 C4 4 52N 115 0 E
Brunei ■, Asia 36 D4 4 50N 115 0 E
Brunette Downs, Australia 62 B2 18 40S 135 55 E
Brunner, L., N.Z. 59 K3 42 37S 171 27 E
Bruno, Canada 73 C7 52 20N 105 30W
Brunsbüttel, Germany 16 B4 53 52N 9 13 E
Brunswick = Braunschweig, Germany 16 B5 52 17N 10 28 E
Brunswick, Ga., U.S.A. 77 K5 31 10N 81 30W
Brunswick, Maine, U.S.A. 71 D6 43 55N 69 58W
Brunswick, Md., U.S.A. 76 F7 39 19N 77 38W
Brunswick, Mo., U.S.A. 80 F8 39 26N 93 8W
Brunswick, Ohio, U.S.A. 78 E3 41 14N 81 51W
Brunswick, Pen. de, Chile 96 G2 53 30S 71 30W
Brunswick B., Australia 60 C3 15 15S 124 50 E
Brunswick Junction, Australia 61 F2 33 15S 115 50 E
Bruny I., Australia 62 G4 43 20S 147 15 E
Brus Laguna, Honduras 88 C3 15 47N 84 35W
Brush, U.S.A. 80 E3 40 15N 103 37W
Brushton, U.S.A. 79 B10 44 50N 74 31W
Brusque, Brazil 95 B6 27 5S 49 0W
Brussel, Belgium 15 D4 50 51N 4 21 E
Brussels = Brussel, Belgium 15 D4 50 51N 4 21 E
Brussels, Canada 78 C3 43 44N 81 15W
Bruthen, Australia 63 F4 37 42S 147 50 E
Bruxelles = Brussel, Belgium 15 D4 50 51N 4 21 E
Bryan, Ohio, U.S.A. 76 E3 41 28N 84 33W
Bryan, Tex., U.S.A. 81 K6 30 40N 96 22W
Bryan, Mt., Australia 63 E2 33 30S 139 0 E
Bryansk, Russia 24 D5 53 13N 34 25 E
Bryant, U.S.A. 80 C6 44 35N 97 28W
Bryne, Norway 9 G8 58 44N 5 38 E
Bryson City, U.S.A. 77 H4 35 26N 83 27W
Bsharri, Lebanon 47 A5 34 15N 36 0 E
Bū Baqarah, U.A.E. 45 E8 25 35N 56 25 E
Bu Craa, W. Sahara 50 C2 26 45N 12 50W
Bū Ḥasā, U.A.E. 45 F7 23 30N 53 20 E
Bua Yai, Thailand 38 E4 15 33N 102 26 E
Buapinang, Indonesia 37 E6 4 40S 121 30 E
Buayan, Phil. 37 C7 6 3N 125 6 E
Bubanza, Burundi 54 C2 3 6S 29 23 E
Būbiyān, Kuwait 45 D6 29 45N 48 15 E
Bucaramanga, Colombia 92 B4 7 0N 73 0W
Buccaneer Arch., Australia 60 C3 16 7S 123 20 E
Buchan, U.K. 12 D6 57 32N 2 8W
Buchan Ness, U.K. 12 D7 57 29N 1 48W
Buchanan, Canada 73 C8 51 40N 102 45W
Buchanan, Liberia 50 G2 5 57N 10 2W
Buchanan, L., Queens., Australia 62 C4 21 35S 145 52 E
Buchanan, L., W. Austral., Australia 61 E3 25 33S 123 2 E
Buchanan, L., U.S.A. 81 K5 30 45N 98 25W
Buchanan Cr. →, Australia 62 B2 19 13S 136 33 E
Buchans, Canada 71 C8 48 50N 56 52W
Bucharest = Bucureşti, Romania 21 B12 44 27N 26 10 E
Buchon, Pt., U.S.A. 84 K6 35 15N 120 54W
Buckeye, U.S.A. 83 K7 33 22N 112 35W
Buckhannon, U.S.A. 76 F5 39 0N 80 8W
Buckhaven, U.K. 12 E5 56 10N 3 2W
Buckie, U.K. 12 D6 57 40N 2 58W
Buckingham, Canada 70 C4 45 37N 75 24W
Buckingham, U.K. 11 F7 52 0N 0 59W
Buckingham B., Australia 62 A2 12 10S 135 40 E
Buckinghamshire □, U.K. 11 F7 51 50N 0 55W
Buckle Hd., Australia 60 B4 14 26S 127 52 E
Buckleboo, Australia 63 E2 32 54S 136 12 E
Buckley, U.S.A. 82 C2 47 10N 122 2W
Buckley →, Australia 62 C2 20 10S 138 49 E
Bucklin, U.S.A. 81 G5 37 33N 99 38W
Bucks L., U.S.A. 84 F5 39 54N 121 12W
Buctouche, Canada 71 C7 46 30N 64 45W
Bucureşti, Romania 21 B12 44 27N 26 10 E
Bucyrus, U.S.A. 76 E4 40 48N 82 59W
Budalin, Burma 41 H19 22 20N 95 10 E
Budapest, Hungary 17 E9 47 29N 19 5 E
Budaun, India 43 E8 28 5N 79 10 E
Budd Coast, Antarctica 5 C8 68 0S 112 0 E
Bude, U.K. 11 G3 50 49N 4 33W
Budennovsk, Russia 25 F7 44 50N 44 10 E
Budge Budge = Baj Baj, India 43 H13 22 30N 88 5 E
Budgewoi, Australia 63 E5 33 13S 151 34 E
Búðareyri, Iceland 8 D6 65 2N 14 13W
Búðir, Iceland 8 D2 64 49N 23 23W
Budjala, Zaïre 52 D3 2 50N 19 40 E
Buellton, U.S.A. 85 L6 34 37N 120 12W
Buena Vista, Colo., U.S.A. 83 G10 38 51N 106 8W
Buena Vista, Va., U.S.A. 76 G6 37 44N 79 21W
Buena Vista L., U.S.A. 85 K7 35 12N 119 18W
Buenaventura, Colombia 92 C3 3 53N 77 4W
Buenaventura, Mexico 86 B3 29 50N 107 30W
Buenos Aires, Argentina 94 C4 34 30S 58 20W
Buenos Aires, Costa Rica 88 E3 9 10N 83 20W
Buenos Aires □, Argentina 94 D4 36 30S 60 0W
Buenos Aires, L., Chile 96 F2 46 35S 72 30W
Buffalo, Mo., U.S.A. 81 G8 37 39N 93 6W
Buffalo, N.Y., U.S.A. 78 D6 42 53N 78 53W
Buffalo, Okla., U.S.A. 81 G5 36 50N 99 38W
Buffalo, S. Dak., U.S.A. 80 C3 45 35N 103 33W
Buffalo, Wyo., U.S.A. 82 D10 44 21N 106 42W
Buffalo →, Canada 72 A5 60 5N 115 5W
Buffalo Head Hills, Canada 72 B5 57 25N 115 55W
Buffalo L., Canada 72 C6 52 27N 112 54W
Buffalo Narrows, Canada 73 B7 55 51N 108 29W
Buffels →, S. Africa 56 D2 29 36S 17 3 E
Buford, U.S.A. 77 H4 34 10N 84 0W
Bug →, Poland 17 B10 52 31N 21 5 E
Bug →, Ukraine 25 E5 46 59N 31 58 E
Buga, Colombia 92 C3 4 0N 76 15W
Buganda, Uganda 54 C3 0 0 31 30 E
Buganga, Uganda 54 C3 0 3S 32 0 E
Bugel, Tanjung, Indonesia 36 F4 6 26S 111 3 E
Bugibba, Malta 23 D1 35 57N 14 25 E
Bugsuk, Phil. 36 C5 8 15N 117 15 E
Bugulma, Russia 24 D9 54 33N 52 48 E
Bugun Shara, Mongolia 32 B5 49 0N 104 0 E
Bugun Shara, Mongolia 32 B5 49 0N 104 0 E
Buguruslan, Russia 24 D9 53 39N 52 26 E
Buheirat-Murrat-el-Kubra, Egypt 51 B11 30 15N 32 40 E
Buhl, Idaho, U.S.A. 82 E6 42 36N 114 46W
Buhl, Minn., U.S.A. 80 B8 47 30N 92 46W
Buick, U.S.A. 81 G9 37 38N 91 2W
Builth Wells, U.K. 11 E4 52 10N 3 26W
Buir Nur, Mongolia 33 B6 47 50N 117 42 E
Bujumbura, Burundi 54 C2 3 16S 29 18 E
Bukachacha, Russia 27 D12 52 55N 116 50 E
Bukama, Zaïre 55 D2 9 10S 25 50 E
Bukavu, Zaïre 54 C2 2 20S 28 52 E
Bukene, Tanzania 54 C3 4 15S 32 48 E
Bukhara, Uzbekistan 26 F7 39 48N 64 25 E
Bukhoro = Bukhara, Uzbekistan 26 F7 39 48N 64 25 E
Bukima, Tanzania 54 C3 1 50S 33 25 E
Bukit Mertajam, Malaysia 39 K3 5 22N 100 28 E
Bukittinggi, Indonesia 36 E2 0 20S 100 20 E
Bukoba, Tanzania 54 C3 1 20S 31 49 E
Bukoba □, Tanzania 54 C3 1 30S 32 0 E
Bukuya, Uganda 54 B3 0 40N 31 52 E
Bula, Indonesia 37 E8 3 6S 130 30 E
Bulahdelah, Australia 63 E5 32 23S 152 13 E
Bulan, Phil. 37 B6 12 40N 123 52 E
Bulandshahr, India 42 E7 28 28N 77 51 E
Bulawayo, Zimbabwe 55 G2 20 7S 28 32 E
Bulgaria ■, Europe 21 C11 42 35N 25 30 E
Bulgroo, Australia 63 D3 25 47S 143 58 E
Bulgunnia, Australia 63 E1 30 10S 134 53 E
Bulhar, Somali Rep. 46 E3 10 25N 44 30 E
Buli, Teluk, Indonesia 37 D7 1 5N 128 25 E
Buliluyan, C., Phil. 36 C5 8 20N 117 15 E
Bulkley →, Canada 72 B3 55 15N 127 40W
Bull Shoals L., U.S.A. 81 G8 36 22N 92 35W
Bullara, Australia 60 D1 22 40S 114 3 E
Bullaring, Australia 61 F2 32 30S 117 45 E
Bulli, Australia 63 E5 34 15S 150 57 E
Bullock Creek, Australia 62 B3 17 43S 144 31 E
Bulloo →, Australia 63 D3 28 43S 142 30 E
Bulloo Downs, Queens., Australia 63 D3 28 31S 142 57 E
Bulloo Downs, W. Austral., Australia 60 D2 24 0S 119 32 E
Bulloo L., Australia 63 D3 28 43S 142 25 E
Bulls, N.Z. 59 J5 40 10S 175 24 E
Bulnes, Chile 94 D1 36 42S 72 19W
Bulo Burti, Somali Rep. 46 G4 3 50N 45 33 E
Bulsar = Valsad, India 40 J8 20 40N 72 58 E
Bultfontein, S. Africa 56 D4 28 18S 26 10 E
Bulu Karakelong, Indonesia 37 D7 4 35N 126 50 E
Bulukumba, Indonesia 37 F6 5 33S 120 11 E
Bulun, Russia 27 B13 70 37N 127 30 E
Bumba, Zaïre 52 D4 2 13N 22 30 E
Bumbiri I., Tanzania 54 C3 1 40S 31 55 E
Bumhpa Bum, Burma 41 F20 26 51N 97 14 E
Bumi →, Zimbabwe 55 F2 17 0S 28 20 E
Buna, Kenya 54 B4 2 58N 39 30 E
Bunazi, Tanzania 54 C3 1 3S 31 23 E
Bunbah, Khalīj, Libya 51 B9 32 20N 23 15 E
Bunbury, Australia 61 F2 33 20S 115 35 E
Buncrana, Ireland 13 A4 55 8N 7 28W
Bundaberg, Australia 63 C5 24 54S 152 22 E
Bundey →, Australia 62 C2 21 46S 135 37 E
Bundi, India 42 G6 25 30N 75 35 E
Bundooma, Australia 62 C1 24 54S 134 16 E
Bundoran, Ireland 13 B3 54 24N 8 17W
Bung Kan, Thailand 38 C4 18 23N 103 37 E
Bungatakada, Japan 31 H5 33 35N 131 25 E
Bungil Cr. →, Australia 62 D4 27 5S 149 5 E
Bungo-Suidō, Japan 31 H6 33 0N 132 15 E
Bungoma, Kenya 54 B3 0 34N 34 34 E
Bungu, Tanzania 54 D4 7 35S 39 0 E
Bunia, Zaïre 54 B3 1 35N 30 20 E
Bunji, Pakistan 43 B6 35 45N 74 40 E
Bunkie, U.S.A. 81 K8 30 57N 92 11W
Bunnell, U.S.A. 77 L5 29 28N 81 16W
Buntok, Indonesia 36 E4 1 40S 114 58 E
Bunyu, Indonesia 36 D5 3 35N 117 50 E
Buol, Indonesia 37 D6 1 15N 121 32 E
Buon Brieng, Vietnam 38 F7 13 9N 108 12 E
Buon Me Thuot, Vietnam 38 F7 12 40N 108 3 E
Buong Long, Cambodia 38 F6 13 44N 106 59 E
Buorkhaya, Mys, Russia 27 B14 71 50N 132 40 E
Buqayq, Si. Arabia 45 E6 26 0N 49 45 E
Bur Acaba, Somali Rep. 46 G3 3 12N 44 20 E
Bûr Safâga, Egypt 51 C11 26 43N 33 57 E
Bûr Sa'îd, Egypt 51 B11 31 16N 32 18 E
Bûr Sûdân, Sudan 51 E12 19 32N 37 9 E
Bura, Kenya 54 C4 1 4S 39 58 E
Burao, Somali Rep. 46 F4 9 32N 45 32 E
Burāq, Syria 47 B5 33 11N 36 29 E
Buras, U.S.A. 81 L10 29 22N 89 32W
Buraydah, Si. Arabia 44 E5 26 20N 44 8 E
Burbank, U.S.A. 85 L8 34 11N 118 19W
Burcher, Australia 63 E4 33 30S 147 16 E
Burdekin →, Australia 62 B4 19 38S 147 25 E
Burdett, Canada 72 D6 49 50N 111 32W
Burdur, Turkey 25 G5 37 45N 30 17 E
Burdwan = Barddhaman, India 43 H12 23 14N 87 39 E
Bure →, U.K. 10 E9 52 38N 1 45 E
Bureya →, Russia 27 E13 49 27N 129 30 E
Burford, Canada 78 C4 43 7N 80 27W
Burgas, Bulgaria 21 C12 42 33N 27 29 E
Burgenland □, Austria 16 E8 47 20N 16 20 E
Burgeo, Canada 71 C8 47 37N 57 38W
Burgersdorp, S. Africa 56 E4 31 0S 26 20 E
Burges, Mt., Australia 61 F3 30 50S 121 5 E
Burgos, Spain 19 A4 42 21N 3 41W
Burgsvik, Sweden 9 H15 57 3N 18 19 E
Burgundy = Bourgogne, France 18 C6 47 0N 4 50 E
Burhanpur, India 40 J10 21 18N 76 14 E
Burias, Phil. 37 B6 12 55N 123 5 E
Burica, Pta., Costa Rica 88 E3 8 3N 82 51W
Burigi, L., Tanzania 54 C3 2 2S 31 22 E
Burin, Canada 71 C8 47 1N 55 14W
Buriram, Thailand 38 E4 15 0N 103 0 E
Burj Sāfitā, Syria 44 C3 34 48N 36 7 E
Burji, Ethiopia 51 G12 5 29N 37 51 E
Burkburnett, U.S.A. 81 H5 34 6N 98 34W
Burke, U.S.A. 82 C6 47 31N 115 49W
Burke →, Australia 62 C2 23 12S 139 33 E
Burketown, Australia 62 B2 17 45S 139 33 E
Burkina Faso ■, Africa 50 F4 12 0N 1 0W
Burk's Falls, Canada 70 C4 45 37N 79 24W
Burley, U.S.A. 82 E7 42 32N 113 48W
Burlingame, U.S.A. 84 H4 37 35N 122 21W
Burlington, Canada 78 C5 43 18N 79 45W
Burlington, Colo., U.S.A. 80 F3 39 18N 102 16W
Burlington, Iowa, U.S.A. 80 E9 40 49N 91 14W
Burlington, Kans., U.S.A. 80 F7 38 12N 95 45W
Burlington, N.C., U.S.A. 77 G6 36 6N 79 26W
Burlington, N.J., U.S.A. 79 F10 40 4N 74 51W
Burlington, Vt., U.S.A. 79 B11 44 29N 73 12W
Burlington, Wash., U.S.A. 84 B4 48 28N 122 20W
Burlington, Wis., U.S.A. 76 D1 42 41N 88 17W
Burlyu-Tyube, Kazakhstan 26 E8 46 30N 79 10 E
Burma ■, Asia 41 J20 21 0N 96 30 E
Burnaby I., Canada 72 C2 52 25N 131 19W
Burnet, U.S.A. 81 K5 30 45N 98 14W
Burney, U.S.A. 82 F3 40 53N 121 40W
Burngup, Australia 61 F2 33 2S 118 42 E
Burnham, U.S.A. 78 F7 40 38N 77 34W
Burnie, Australia 62 G4 41 4S 145 56 E
Burnley, U.K. 10 D5 53 47N 2 15W
Burns, Oreg., U.S.A. 82 E4 43 35N 119 3W
Burns, Wyo., U.S.A. 80 E2 41 12N 104 21W
Burns Lake, Canada 72 C3 54 20N 125 45W
Burnside →, Canada 68 B9 66 51N 108 4W
Burnside, L., Australia 61 E3 25 22S 123 0 E
Burnt River, Canada 78 B6 44 41N 78 42W
Burntwood →, Canada 73 B9 56 8N 96 34W
Burntwood L., Canada 73 B8 55 22N 100 26W
Burqān, Kuwait 44 D5 29 0N 47 57 E
Burra, Australia 63 E2 33 40S 138 55 E
Burramurra, Australia 62 C2 20 25S 137 15 E
Burren Junction, Australia 63 E4 30 7S 148 59 E
Burrendong Dam, Australia 63 E4 32 39S 149 6 E
Burrinjuck Res., Australia 63 F4 35 0S 148 36 E
Burro, Serranías del, Mexico 86 B4 29 0N 102 0W
Burruyacú, Argentina 94 B3 26 30S 64 40W
Burry Port, U.K. 11 F3 51 41N 4 17W
Bursa, Turkey 25 F4 40 15N 29 5 E
Burstall, Canada 73 C7 50 39N 109 54W
Burton L., Canada 70 B4 54 45N 78 20W
Burton upon Trent, U.K. 10 E6 52 48N 1 39W
Burtundy, Australia 63 E3 33 45S 142 15 E
Buru, Indonesia 37 E7 3 30S 126 30 E
Burûn, Râs, Egypt 47 D2 31 14N 33 7 E
Burundi ■, Africa 54 C3 3 15S 30 0 E
Bururi, Burundi 54 C2 3 57S 29 37 E
Burutu, Nigeria 50 G6 5 20N 5 29 E
Burwell, U.S.A. 80 E5 41 47N 99 8W
Bury, U.K. 10 D5 53 36N 2 19W
Bury St. Edmunds, U.K. 11 E8 52 15N 0 42 E
Buryat Republic □, Russia 27 D11 53 0N 110 0 E
Busango Swamp, Zambia 55 E2 14 15S 25 45 E
Buşayrah, Syria 44 C4 35 9N 40 26 E
Buşayyah, Iraq 44 D5 30 0N 46 10 E
Būshehr, Iran 45 D6 28 55N 50 55 E
Būshehr □, Iran 45 D6 28 20N 51 45 E
Bushell, Canada 73 B7 59 31N 108 45W
Bushenyi, Uganda 54 C3 0 35S 30 10 E
Bushire = Būshehr, Iran 45 D6 28 55N 50 55 E
Bushnell, Ill., U.S.A. 80 E9 40 33N 90 31W
Bushnell, Nebr., U.S.A. 80 E3 41 14N 103 54W
Busia □, Kenya 54 B3 0 25N 34 6 E
Businga, Zaïre 52 D4 3 16N 20 59 E
Buskerud fylke □, Norway 9 F10 60 13N 9 0 E
Busoga □, Uganda 54 B3 0 5N 33 30 E
Busra ash Shām, Syria 47 C5 32 30N 36 25 E
Busselton, Australia 61 F2 33 42S 115 15 E
Bussum, Neths. 15 B5 52 16N 5 10 E
Busto Arsizio, Italy 20 B3 45 40N 8 50 E
Busu-Djanoa, Zaïre 52 D4 1 43N 21 23 E
Busuanga, Phil. 37 B5 12 10N 120 0 E
Buta, Zaïre 54 B1 2 50N 24 53 E
Butare, Rwanda 54 C2 2 31S 29 52 E
Butaritari, Kiribati 64 G9 3 30N 174 0 E
Bute, U.K. 12 F3 55 48N 5 2W
Bute Inlet, Canada 72 C4 50 40N 124 53W
Butemba, Uganda 54 B3 1 9N 31 37 E
Butembo, Zaïre 54 B2 0 9N 29 18 E
Butha Qi, China 33 B7 48 0N 122 32 E
Butiaba, Uganda 54 B3 1 50N 31 20 E
Butler, Mo., U.S.A. 80 F7 38 16N 94 20W
Butler, Pa., U.S.A. 78 F5 40 52N 79 54W
Butte, Mont., U.S.A. 82 C7 46 0N 112 32W

Canton L.

Butte, *Nebr., U.S.A.* **80 D5** 42 58N 98 51W
Butte Creek →, *U.S.A.* **84 F5** 39 12N 121 56W
Butterworth = Gcuwa, *S. Africa* **57 E4** 32 20S 28 11 E
Butterworth, *Malaysia* **39 K3** 5 24N 100 23 E
Buttfield, Mt., *Australia* **61 D4** 24 45S 128 9 E
Button B., *Canada* **73 B10** 58 45N 94 23W
Buttonwillow, *U.S.A.* **85 K7** 35 24N 119 28W
Butty Hd., *Australia* **61 F3** 33 54S 121 39 E
Butuan, *Phil.* **37 C7** 8 57N 125 33 E
Butung, *Indonesia* **37 E6** 5 0S 122 45 E
Buturlinovka, *Russia* **25 D7** 50 50N 40 35 E
Buxar, *India* **43 G10** 25 34N 83 58 E
Buxton, *S. Africa* **56 D3** 27 38S 24 42 E
Buxton, *U.K.* **10 D6** 53 16N 1 54W
Buy, *Russia* **24 C7** 58 28N 41 28 E
Buyaga, *Russia* **27 D13** 59 50N 127 0 E
Buzău, *Romania* **21 B12** 45 10N 26 50 E
Buzău →, *Romania* **17 F13** 45 26N 27 44 E
Buzen, *Japan* **31 H5** 33 35N 131 5 E
Buzi →, *Mozam.* **55 F3** 19 50S 34 43 E
Buzuluk, *Russia* **24 D9** 52 48N 52 12 E
Buzzards Bay, *U.S.A.* **79 E14** 41 45N 70 37W
Bwana Mkubwe, *Zaïre* **55 E2** 13 8S 28 38 E
Bydgoszcz, *Poland* **17 B8** 53 10N 18 0 E
Byelarus = Belorussia ■, *Europe* **24 D4** 53 30N 27 0 E
Byelorussia = Belorussia ■, *Europe* **24 D4** 53 30N 27 0 E
Byers, *U.S.A.* **80 F2** 39 43N 104 14W
Byesville, *U.S.A.* **78 G3** 39 58N 81 32W
Byhalia, *U.S.A.* **81 H10** 34 52N 89 41W
Bylas, *U.S.A.* **83 K8** 33 8N 110 7W
Bylot I., *Canada* **69 A12** 73 13N 78 34W
Byrd, C., *Antarctica* **5 C17** 69 38S 76 7W
Byro, *Australia* **61 E2** 26 5S 116 11 E
Byrock, *Australia* **63 E4** 30 40S 146 27 E
Byron Bay, *Australia* **63 D5** 28 43S 153 37 E
Byrranga, Gory, *Russia* **27 B11** 75 0N 100 0 E
Byrranga Mts. = Byrranga, Gory, *Russia* **27 B11** 75 0N 100 0 E
Byske, *Sweden* **8 D16** 64 57N 21 11 E
Byske älv →, *Sweden* **8 D16** 64 57N 21 13 E
Bytom, *Poland* **17 C9** 50 25N 18 54 E
Byumba, *Rwanda* **54 C3** 1 35S 30 4 E

C

C.I.S. = Commonwealth of Independent States ■, *Eurasia* **27 D11** 60 0N 100 0 E
Ca →, *Vietnam* **38 C5** 18 45N 105 45 E
Ca Mau = Quan Long, *Vietnam* **39 H5** 9 7N 105 8 E
Ca Mau, Mui = Bai Bung, Mui, *Vietnam* **39 H5** 8 38N 104 44 E
Ca Na, *Vietnam* **39 G7** 11 20N 108 54 E
Caacupé, *Paraguay* **94 B4** 25 23S 57 5W
Caála, *Angola* **53 G3** 12 46S 15 30 E
Caamano Sd., *Canada* **72 C3** 52 55N 129 25W
Caazapá, *Paraguay* **94 B4** 26 8S 56 19W
Caazapá □, *Paraguay* **95 B4** 26 10S 56 0W
Caballeria, C. de, *Spain* **22 A11** 40 5N 4 5 E
Cabanatuan, *Phil.* **37 A6** 15 30N 120 58 E
Cabano, *Canada* **71 C6** 47 40N 68 56W
Cabazon, *U.S.A.* **85 M10** 33 55N 116 47W
Cabedelo, *Brazil* **93 E12** 7 0S 34 50W
Cabildo, *Chile* **94 C1** 32 30S 71 5W
Cabimas, *Venezuela* **92 A4** 10 23N 71 25W
Cabinda, *Angola* **52 F2** 5 33S 12 11 E
Cabinda □, *Angola* **52 F2** 5 0S 12 30 E
Cabinet Mts., *U.S.A.* **82 C6** 48 0N 115 30W
Cabo Blanco, *Argentina* **96 F3** 47 15S 65 47W
Cabo Frio, *Brazil* **95 A7** 22 51S 42 3W
Cabo Pantoja, *Peru* **92 D3** 1 0S 75 10W
Cabonga, Réservoir, *Canada* **70 C4** 47 20N 76 40W
Cabool, *U.S.A.* **81 G8** 37 7N 92 6W
Caboolture, *Australia* **63 D5** 27 5S 152 58 E
Cabora Bassa Dam = Cahora Bassa Dam, *Mozam.* **55 F3** 15 20S 32 50 E
Caborca, *Mexico* **86 A2** 30 40N 112 10W
Cabot, Mt., *U.S.A.* **79 B13** 44 30N 71 25W
Cabot Str., *Canada* **71 C8** 47 15N 59 40W
Cabrera, I., *Spain* **22 B9** 39 8N 2 57 E
Cabri, *Canada* **73 C7** 50 35N 108 25W
Cabriel →, *Spain* **19 C5** 39 14N 1 3W
Čačak, *Serbia, Yug.* **21 C9** 43 54N 20 20 E
Cáceres, *Brazil* **92 G7** 16 5S 57 40W
Cáceres, *Spain* **19 C2** 39 26N 6 23W
Cache Bay, *Canada* **70 C4** 46 22N 80 0W
Cache Cr. →, *U.S.A.* **84 G5** 38 42N 121 42W
Cachi, *Argentina* **94 B2** 25 5S 66 10W
Cachimbo, Serra do, *Brazil* **93 E7** 9 30S 55 30W
Cachoeira, *Brazil* **93 F11** 12 30S 39 0W
Cachoeira de Itapemirim, *Brazil* **95 A7** 20 51S 41 7W
Cachoeira do Sul, *Brazil* **95 C5** 30 3S 52 53W
Cacólo, *Angola* **52 G3** 10 9S 19 21 E
Caconda, *Angola* **53 G3** 13 48S 15 8 E
Cacongo, *Angola* **52 F2** 5 11S 12 5 E
Caddo, *U.S.A.* **81 H6** 34 7N 96 16W
Cadell Cr. →, *Australia* **62 C3** 22 35S 141 51 E
Cader Idris, *U.K.* **10 E4** 52 43N 3 56W
Cadibarrawirracanna, L., *Australia* **63 D2** 28 52S 135 27 E
Cadillac, *Canada* **70 C4** 48 14N 78 23W
Cadillac, *U.S.A.* **76 C3** 44 15N 85 24W
Cadiz, *Phil.* **37 B6** 10 57N 123 15 E
Cádiz, *Spain* **19 D2** 36 30N 6 20W
Cadiz, *U.S.A.* **78 F4** 40 22N 81 0W
Cádiz, G. de, *Spain* **19 D2** 36 40N 7 0W
Cadney Park, *Australia* **63 D1** 27 55S 134 3 E
Cadomin, *Canada* **72 C5** 53 2N 117 20W
Cadotte →, *Canada* **72 B5** 56 43N 117 10W
Cadoux, *Australia* **61 F2** 30 46S 117 7 E
Caen, *France* **18 B3** 49 10N 0 22W
Caernarfon, *U.K.* **10 D3** 53 8N 4 17W
Caernarfon B., *U.K.* **10 D3** 53 4N 4 40W
Caernarvon = Caernarfon, *U.K.* **10 D3** 53 8N 4 17W
Caerphilly, *U.K.* **11 F4** 51 34N 3 13W
Caesarea, *Israel* **47 C3** 32 30N 34 53 E
Caeté, *Brazil* **93 G10** 19 55S 43 40W
Caetité, *Brazil* **93 F10** 13 50S 42 32W
Cafayate, *Argentina* **94 B2** 26 2S 66 0W
Cafu, *Angola* **56 B2** 16 30S 15 8 E
Cagayan →, *Phil.* **37 A6** 18 25N 121 42 E
Cagayan de Oro, *Phil.* **37 C6** 8 30N 124 40 E
Cágliari, *Italy* **20 E3** 39 15N 9 6 E
Cágliari, G. di, *Italy* **20 E3** 39 8N 9 10 E
Caguas, *Puerto Rico* **89 C6** 18 14N 66 2W
Caha Mts., *Ireland* **13 E2** 51 45N 9 40W
Cahama, *Angola* **56 B1** 16 17S 14 19 E
Caher, *Ireland* **13 D4** 52 23N 7 56W
Cahersiveen, *Ireland* **13 E1** 51 57N 10 13W
Cahora Bassa Dam, *Mozam.* **55 F3** 15 20S 32 50 E
Cahore Pt., *Ireland* **13 D5** 52 34N 6 11W
Cahors, *France* **18 D4** 44 27N 1 27 E
Cahuapanas, *Peru* **92 E3** 5 15S 77 0W
Cai Bau, Dao, *Vietnam* **38 B6** 21 10N 107 27 E
Cai Nuoc, *Vietnam* **39 H5** 8 56N 105 1 E
Caia, *Mozam.* **55 F4** 17 51S 35 24 E
Caianda, *Angola* **55 E1** 11 2S 23 31 E
Caibarién, *Cuba* **88 B4** 22 30N 79 30W
Caicara, *Venezuela* **92 B5** 7 38N 66 10W
Caicó, *Brazil* **93 E11** 6 20S 37 0W
Caicos Is., *W. Indies* **89 B5** 21 40N 71 40W
Caicos Passage, *W. Indies* **89 B5** 22 45N 72 45W
Caird Coast, *Antarctica* **5 D1** 75 0S 25 0W
Cairn Gorm, *U.K.* **12 D5** 57 7N 3 40W
Cairn Toul, *U.K.* **12 D5** 57 3N 3 44W
Cairngorm Mts., *U.K.* **12 D5** 57 6N 3 42W
Cairns, *Australia* **62 B4** 16 57S 145 45 E
Cairo = El Qâhira, *Egypt* **51 B11** 30 1N 31 14 E
Cairo, *Ga., U.S.A.* **77 K3** 30 52N 84 13W
Cairo, *Ill., U.S.A.* **81 G10** 37 0N 89 11W
Caithness, Ord of, *U.K.* **12 C5** 58 9N 3 37W
Caiundo, *Angola* **53 H3** 15 50S 17 28 E
Caiza, *Bolivia* **92 H5** 20 2S 65 40W
Cajamarca, *Peru* **92 E3** 7 5S 78 28W
Cajàzeiras, *Brazil* **93 E11** 6 52S 38 30W
Cala d'Or, *Spain* **22 B10** 39 23N 3 14 E
Cala Figuera, C., *Spain* **22 B9** 39 27N 2 31 E
Cala Forcat, *Spain* **22 A10** 40 0N 3 47 E
Cala Mayor, *Spain* **22 B9** 39 33N 2 37 E
Cala Mezquida, *Spain* **22 B11** 39 55N 4 16 E
Cala Millor, *Spain* **22 B10** 39 35N 3 22 E
Cala Ratjada, *Spain* **22 B10** 39 43N 3 27 E
Calabar, *Nigeria* **50 H6** 4 57N 8 20 E
Calábria □, *Italy* **20 E7** 39 24N 16 30 E
Calafate, *Argentina* **96 G2** 50 19S 72 15W
Calahorra, *Spain* **19 A5** 42 18N 1 59W
Calais, *France* **18 A4** 50 57N 1 56 E
Calais, *U.S.A.* **71 C6** 45 11N 67 17W
Calalaste, Cord. de, *Argentina* **94 B2** 25 0S 67 0W
Calama, *Brazil* **92 E6** 8 0S 62 50W
Calama, *Chile* **94 A2** 22 30S 68 55W
Calamar, *Bolívar, Colombia* **92 A4** 10 15N 74 55W
Calamar, *Vaupés, Colombia* **92 C4** 1 58N 72 32W
Calamian Group, *Phil.* **37 B5** 11 50N 119 55 E
Calamocha, *Spain* **19 B5** 40 50N 1 17W
Calán Porter, *Spain* **22 B11** 39 52N 4 8 E
Calang, *Indonesia* **36 D1** 4 37N 95 37 E
Calapan, *Phil.* **37 B6** 13 25N 121 7 E
Calatayud, *Spain* **19 B5** 41 20N 1 40W
Calauag, *Phil.* **37 B6** 13 55N 122 15 E
Calavite, C., *Phil.* **37 B6** 13 26N 120 20 E
Calbayog, *Phil.* **37 B6** 12 4N 124 38 E
Calca, *Peru* **92 F4** 13 22S 72 0W
Calcasieu L., *U.S.A.* **81 L8** 29 55N 93 18W
Calcutta, *India* **43 H13** 22 36N 88 24 E
Calder →, *U.K.* **10 D6** 53 44N 1 21W
Caldera, *Chile* **94 B1** 27 5S 70 55W
Caldwell, *Idaho, U.S.A.* **82 E5** 43 40N 116 41W
Caldwell, *Kans., U.S.A.* **81 G6** 37 2N 97 37W
Caldwell, *Tex., U.S.A.* **81 K6** 30 32N 96 42W
Caledon, *S. Africa* **56 E2** 34 14S 19 26 E
Caledon →, *S. Africa* **56 E4** 30 31S 26 5 E
Caledon B., *Australia* **62 A2** 12 45S 137 0 E
Caledonia, *Canada* **78 C5** 43 7N 79 58W
Caledonia, *U.S.A.* **78 D7** 42 58N 77 51W
Calella, *Spain* **19 B7** 41 37N 2 40 E
Calemba, *Angola* **56 B2** 16 0S 15 44 E
Calexico, *U.S.A.* **85 N11** 32 40N 115 30W
Calf of Man, *U.K.* **10 C3** 54 3N 4 49W
Calgary, *Canada* **72 C6** 51 0N 114 10W
Calheta, *Madeira* **22 D2** 32 44N 17 11W
Calhoun, *U.S.A.* **77 H3** 34 30N 84 57W
Cali, *Colombia* **92 C3** 3 25N 76 35W
Calicut, *India* **40 P9** 11 15N 75 43 E
Caliente, *U.S.A.* **83 H6** 37 37N 114 31W
California, *Mo., U.S.A.* **80 F8** 38 38N 92 34W
California, *Pa., U.S.A.* **78 F5** 40 4N 79 54W
California □, *U.S.A.* **83 H4** 37 30N 119 30W
California, Baja, *Mexico* **86 A1** 32 10N 115 12W
California, Baja, T.N. □, *Mexico* **86 B2** 30 0N 115 0W
California, Baja, T.S. □, *Mexico* **86 B2** 25 50N 111 50W
California, G. de, *Mexico* **86 B2** 27 0N 111 0W
California City, *U.S.A.* **85 K9** 35 10N 117 55W
California Hot Springs, *U.S.A.* **85 K8** 35 51N 118 41W
Calingasta, *Argentina* **94 C2** 31 15S 69 30W
Calipatria, *U.S.A.* **85 M11** 33 8N 115 31W
Calistoga, *U.S.A.* **84 G4** 38 35N 122 35W
Calitzdorp, *S. Africa* **56 E3** 33 33S 21 42 E
Callabonna, L., *Australia* **63 D3** 29 40S 140 5 E
Callan, *Ireland* **13 D4** 52 33N 7 25W
Callander, *U.K.* **12 E4** 56 15N 4 14W
Callao, *Peru* **92 F3** 12 0S 77 0W
Callaway, *U.S.A.* **80 E5** 41 18N 99 56W
Calles, *Mexico* **87 C5** 23 2N 98 42W
Callide, *Australia* **62 C5** 24 18S 150 28 E
Calling Lake, *Canada* **72 B6** 55 15N 113 12W
Calliope, *Australia* **62 C5** 24 0S 151 16 E
Calola, *Angola* **56 B2** 16 25S 17 48 E
Caloundra, *Australia* **63 D5** 26 45S 153 10 E
Calpella, *U.S.A.* **84 F3** 39 14N 123 12W
Calpine, *U.S.A.* **84 F6** 39 40N 120 27W
Calstock, *Canada* **70 C3** 49 47N 84 9W
Caltagirone, *Italy* **20 F6** 37 13N 14 30 E
Caltanissetta, *Italy* **20 F6** 37 30N 14 3 E
Calulo, *Angola* **52 G2** 10 1S 14 56 E
Calumet, *U.S.A.* **76 B1** 47 14N 88 27W
Calunda, *Angola* **53 G4** 12 7S 23 36 E
Calvados □, *France* **18 B3** 49 5N 0 15W
Calvert, *U.S.A.* **81 K6** 30 59N 96 40W
Calvert →, *Australia* **62 B2** 16 17S 137 44 E
Calvert Hills, *Australia* **62 B2** 17 15S 137 20 E
Calvert I., *Canada* **72 C3** 51 30N 128 0W
Calvert Ra., *Australia* **60 D3** 24 0S 122 30 E
Calvi, *France* **18 E8** 42 34N 8 45 E
Calvillo, *Mexico* **86 C4** 21 51N 102 43W
Calvinia, *S. Africa* **56 E2** 31 28S 19 45 E
Calwa, *U.S.A.* **84 J7** 36 42N 119 46W
Cam →, *U.K.* **11 E8** 52 21N 0 16 E
Cam Lam, *Vietnam* **39 G7** 11 54N 109 10 E
Cam Pha, *Vietnam* **38 B6** 21 7N 107 18 E
Cam Ranh, *Vietnam* **39 G7** 11 54N 109 12 E
Cam Xuyen, *Vietnam* **38 C6** 18 15N 106 0 E
Camabatela, *Angola* **52 F3** 8 20S 15 26 E
Camacha, *Madeira* **22 D3** 32 41N 16 49W
Camacho, *Mexico* **86 C4** 24 25N 102 18W
Camacupa, *Angola* **53 G3** 11 58S 17 22 E
Camagüey, *Cuba* **88 B4** 21 20N 78 0W
Camaná, *Peru* **92 G4** 16 30S 72 50W
Camanche Reservoir, *U.S.A.* **84 G6** 38 14N 121 1W
Camaquã →, *Brazil* **95 C5** 31 17S 51 47W
Câmara de Lobos, *Madeira* **22 D3** 32 39N 16 59W
Camaret, *France* **18 B1** 48 16N 4 37W
Camargo, *Bolivia* **92 H5** 20 38S 65 15W
Camarillo, *U.S.A.* **85 L7** 34 13N 119 2W
Camarón, C., *Honduras* **88 C2** 16 0N 85 5W
Camarones, *Argentina* **96 E3** 44 50S 65 40W
Camas, *U.S.A.* **84 E4** 45 35N 122 24W
Camas Valley, *U.S.A.* **82 E2** 43 2N 123 40W
Cambará, *Brazil* **95 A5** 23 2S 50 5W
Cambay = Khambhat, *India* **42 H5** 22 23N 72 33 E
Cambay, G. of = Khambhat, G. of, *India* **42 J5** 20 45N 72 30 E
Cambodia ■, *Asia* **38 F5** 12 15N 105 0 E
Camborne, *U.K.* **11 G2** 50 13N 5 18W
Cambrai, *France* **18 A5** 50 11N 3 14 E
Cambria, *U.S.A.* **83 J3** 35 34N 121 5W
Cambrian Mts., *U.K.* **11 E4** 52 25N 3 52W
Cambridge, *Canada* **70 D3** 43 23N 80 15W
Cambridge, *Jamaica* **88 C4** 18 18N 77 54W
Cambridge, *N.Z.* **59 G5** 37 54S 175 29 E
Cambridge, *U.K.* **11 E8** 52 13N 0 8 E
Cambridge, *Idaho, U.S.A.* **82 D5** 44 34N 116 41W
Cambridge, *Mass., U.S.A.* **79 D13** 42 22N 71 6W
Cambridge, *Md., U.S.A.* **76 F7** 38 34N 76 5W
Cambridge, *Minn., U.S.A.* **80 C8** 45 34N 93 13W
Cambridge, *N.Y., U.S.A.* **79 C11** 43 2N 73 22W
Cambridge, *Nebr., U.S.A.* **80 E4** 40 17N 100 10W
Cambridge, *Ohio, U.S.A.* **78 F3** 40 2N 81 35W
Cambridge Bay, *Canada* **68 B9** 69 10N 105 0W
Cambridge G., *Australia* **60 B4** 14 55S 128 15 E
Cambridge Springs, *U.S.A.* **78 E4** 41 48N 80 4W
Cambridgeshire □, *U.K.* **11 E8** 52 12N 0 7 E
Cambuci, *Brazil* **95 A7** 21 35S 41 55W
Cambundi-Catembo, *Angola* **52 G3** 10 10S 17 35 E
Camden, *Ala., U.S.A.* **77 K2** 31 59N 87 17W
Camden, *Ark., U.S.A.* **81 J8** 33 35N 92 50W
Camden, *Maine, U.S.A.* **71 D6** 44 13N 69 4W
Camden, *N.J., U.S.A.* **79 G9** 39 56N 75 7W
Camden, *S.C., U.S.A.* **77 H5** 34 16N 80 36W
Camden Sd., *Australia* **60 C3** 15 27S 124 25 E
Camdenton, *U.S.A.* **81 F8** 38 1N 92 45W
Cameron, *Ariz., U.S.A.* **83 J8** 35 53N 111 25W
Cameron, *La., U.S.A.* **81 L8** 29 48N 93 20W
Cameron, *Mo., U.S.A.* **80 F7** 39 44N 94 14W
Cameron, *Tex., U.S.A.* **81 K6** 30 51N 96 59W
Cameron Falls, *Canada* **70 C2** 49 8N 88 19W
Cameron Highlands, *Malaysia* **39 K3** 4 27N 101 22 E
Cameron Hills, *Canada* **72 B5** 59 48N 118 0W
Cameroon ■, *Africa* **51 G7** 6 0N 12 30 E
Cameroun, Mt., *Cameroon* **50 H6** 4 13N 9 10 E
Cametá, *Brazil* **93 D9** 2 12S 49 30W
Caminha, *Portugal* **19 B1** 41 50N 8 50W
Camino, *U.S.A.* **84 G6** 38 44N 120 41W
Camira Creek, *Australia* **63 D5** 29 15S 152 58 E
Camissombo, *Angola* **52 F4** 8 7S 20 38 E
Cammal, *U.S.A.* **78 E7** 41 24N 77 28W
Camocim, *Brazil* **93 D10** 2 55S 40 50W
Camooweal, *Australia* **62 B2** 19 56S 138 7 E
Camopi →, *Fr. Guiana* **93 C8** 3 10N 52 20W
Camp Crook, *U.S.A.* **80 C3** 45 33N 103 59W
Camp Nelson, *U.S.A.* **85 J8** 36 8N 118 39W
Camp Wood, *U.S.A.* **81 L4** 29 40N 100 1W
Campana, *Argentina* **94 C4** 34 10S 58 55W
Campana, I., *Chile* **96 F1** 48 20S 75 20W
Campanário, *Madeira* **22 D2** 32 39N 17 2W
Campania □, *Italy* **20 D6** 40 50N 14 45 E
Campbell, *S. Africa* **56 D3** 28 48S 23 44 E
Campbell, *Calif., U.S.A.* **84 H5** 37 17N 121 57W
Campbell, *Ohio, U.S.A.* **78 E4** 41 5N 80 37W
Campbell I., *Pac. Oc.* **64 N8** 52 30S 169 0 E
Campbell L., *Canada* **73 A7** 63 14N 106 55W
Campbell River, *Canada* **72 C3** 50 5N 125 20W
Campbell Town, *Australia* **62 G4** 41 52S 147 30 E
Campbellford, *Canada* **78 B7** 44 18N 77 48W
Campbellpur, *Pakistan* **42 C5** 33 46N 72 26 E
Campbellsville, *U.S.A.* **76 G3** 37 21N 85 20W
Campbellton, *Canada* **71 C6** 47 57N 66 43W
Campbelltown, *Australia* **63 E5** 34 4S 150 49 E
Campbeltown, *U.K.* **12 F3** 55 25N 5 36W
Campeche, *Mexico* **87 D6** 19 50N 90 32W
Campeche □, *Mexico* **87 D6** 19 50N 90 32W
Campeche, B. de, *Mexico* **87 D6** 19 30N 93 0W
Camperdown, *Australia* **63 F3** 38 14S 143 9 E
Camperville, *Canada* **73 C8** 51 59N 100 9W
Campina Grande, *Brazil* **93 E11** 7 20S 35 47W
Campinas, *Brazil* **95 A6** 22 50S 47 0W
Campo, *Cameroon* **52 D1** 2 22N 9 50 E
Campo Belo, *Brazil* **93 H9** 20 52S 45 16W
Campo Formoso, *Brazil* **93 F10** 10 30S 40 20W
Campo Grande, *Brazil* **93 H8** 20 25S 54 40W
Campo Maíor, *Brazil* **93 D10** 4 50S 42 12W
Campo Mourão, *Brazil* **95 A5** 24 3S 52 22W
Campoalegre, *Colombia* **92 C3** 2 41N 75 20W
Campobasso, *Italy* **20 D6** 41 34N 14 40 E
Campos, *Brazil* **95 A7** 21 50S 41 20W
Campos Belos, *Brazil* **93 F9** 13 10S 47 3W
Campos del Puerto, *Spain* **22 B10** 39 26N 3 1 E
Campos Novos, *Brazil* **95 B5** 27 21S 51 50W
Camptonville, *U.S.A.* **84 F5** 39 27N 121 3W
Campuya →, *Peru* **92 D4** 1 40S 73 30W
Camrose, *Canada* **72 C6** 53 0N 112 50W
Camsell Portage, *Canada* **73 B7** 59 37N 109 15W
Can Clavo, *Spain* **22 C7** 38 57N 1 27 E
Can Creu, *Spain* **22 C7** 38 58N 1 28 E
Can Gio, *Vietnam* **39 G6** 10 25N 106 58 E
Can Tho, *Vietnam* **39 G5** 10 2N 105 46 E
Canaan, *U.S.A.* **79 D11** 42 2N 73 20W
Canada ■, *N. Amer.* **68 C10** 60 0N 100 0W
Cañada de Gómez, *Argentina* **94 C3** 32 40S 61 30W
Canadian, *U.S.A.* **81 H4** 35 55N 100 23W
Canadian →, *U.S.A.* **81 H7** 35 28N 95 3W
Canadian Shield, *Canada* **69 C10** 53 0N 75 0W
Çanakkale, *Turkey* **25 F4** 40 8N 26 24 E
Çanakkale Boğazı, *Turkey* **21 D12** 40 17N 26 32 E
Canal Flats, *Canada* **72 C5** 50 10N 115 48W
Canalejas, *Argentina* **94 D2** 35 15S 66 34W
Canals, *Argentina* **94 C3** 33 35S 62 53W
Canandaigua, *U.S.A.* **78 D7** 42 54N 77 17W
Cananea, *Mexico* **86 A2** 31 0N 110 20W
Canarias, Is., *Atl. Oc.* **22 F4** 28 30N 16 0W
Canarreos, Arch. de los, *Cuba* **88 B3** 21 35N 81 40W
Canary Is. = Canarias, Is., *Atl. Oc.* **22 F4** 28 30N 16 0W
Canatlán, *Mexico* **86 C4** 24 31N 104 47W
Canaveral, C., *U.S.A.* **77 L5** 28 27N 80 32W
Canavieiras, *Brazil* **93 G11** 15 39S 39 0W
Canbelego, *Australia* **63 E4** 31 32S 146 18 E
Canberra, *Australia* **63 F4** 35 15S 149 8 E
Canby, *Calif., U.S.A.* **82 F3** 41 27N 120 52W
Canby, *Minn., U.S.A.* **80 C6** 44 43N 96 16W
Canby, *Oreg., U.S.A.* **84 E4** 45 16N 122 42W
Cancún, *Mexico* **87 C7** 21 8N 86 44W
Candala, *Somali Rep.* **46 E4** 11 30N 49 58 E
Candelaria, *Argentina* **95 B4** 27 29S 55 44W
Candelaria, *Canary Is.* **22 F3** 28 22N 16 22W
Candelo, *Australia* **63 F4** 36 47S 149 43 E
Candia = Iráklion, *Greece* **23 D7** 35 20N 25 12 E
Candle L., *Canada* **73 C7** 53 50N 105 18W
Candlemas I., *Antarctica* **5 B1** 57 3S 26 40W
Cando, *U.S.A.* **80 A5** 48 32N 99 12W
Canea = Khaniá, *Greece* **23 D6** 35 30N 24 4 E
Canelones, *Uruguay* **95 C4** 34 32S 56 17W
Cañete, *Chile* **94 D1** 37 50S 73 30W
Cañete, *Peru* **92 F3** 13 8S 76 30W
Cangas, *Spain* **19 A1** 42 16N 8 47W
Canguaretama, *Brazil* **93 E11** 6 20S 35 5W
Canguçu, *Brazil* **95 C5** 31 22S 52 43W
Cangzhou, *China* **34 E9** 38 19N 116 52 E
Canim Lake, *Canada* **72 C4** 51 47N 120 54W
Canindeyu □, *Paraguay* **95 A4** 24 10S 55 0W
Canipaan, *Phil.* **36 C5** 8 33N 117 15 E
Canisteo, *U.S.A.* **78 D7** 42 16N 77 36W
Canisteo →, *U.S.A.* **78 D7** 42 7N 77 8W
Cañitas, *Mexico* **86 C4** 23 36N 102 43W
Çankırı, *Turkey* **25 F5** 40 40N 33 37 E
Cankuzo, *Burundi* **54 C3** 3 10S 30 31 E
Canmore, *Canada* **72 C5** 51 7N 115 18W
Cann River, *Australia* **63 F4** 37 35S 149 7 E
Canna, *U.K.* **12 D2** 57 3N 6 33W
Cannanore, *India* **40 P9** 11 53N 75 27 E
Cannes, *France* **18 E7** 43 32N 7 1 E
Canning Town = Port Canning, *India* **43 H13** 22 23N 88 40 E
Cannington, *Canada* **78 B5** 44 20N 79 2W
Cannock, *U.K.* **10 E5** 52 42N 2 2W
Cannon Ball →, *U.S.A.* **80 B4** 46 20N 100 38W
Cannondale Mt., *Australia* **62 D4** 25 13S 148 57 E
Canoas, *Brazil* **95 B5** 29 56S 51 11W
Canoe L., *Canada* **73 B7** 55 10N 108 15W
Canon City, *U.S.A.* **80 F2** 38 27N 105 14W
Canora, *Canada* **73 C8** 51 40N 102 30W
Canowindra, *Australia* **63 E4** 33 35S 148 38 E
Canso, *Canada* **71 C7** 45 20N 61 0W
Cantabria □, *Spain* **19 A4** 43 10N 4 0W
Cantabrian Mts. = Cantábrica, Cordillera, *Spain* **19 A3** 43 0N 5 10W
Cantábrica, Cordillera, *Spain* **19 A3** 43 0N 5 10W
Cantal □, *France* **18 D5** 45 5N 2 45 E
Canterbury, *Australia* **62 D3** 25 23S 141 53 E
Canterbury, *U.K.* **11 F9** 51 17N 1 5 E
Canterbury □, *N.Z.* **59 K3** 43 45S 171 19 E
Canterbury Bight, *N.Z.* **59 L3** 44 16S 171 55 E
Canterbury Plains, *N.Z.* **59 K3** 43 55S 171 22 E
Cantil, *U.S.A.* **85 K9** 35 18N 117 58W
Canton = Guangzhou, *Guangdong, China* **33 D6** 23 5N 113 10 E
Canton = Guangzhou, *Guangdong, China* **33 D6** 23 5N 113 10 E
Canton, *Ga., U.S.A.* **77 H3** 34 14N 84 29W
Canton, *Ill., U.S.A.* **80 E9** 40 33N 90 2W
Canton, *Miss., U.S.A.* **81 J9** 32 37N 90 2W
Canton, *Mo., U.S.A.* **80 E9** 40 8N 91 32W
Canton, *N.Y., U.S.A.* **79 B9** 44 36N 75 10W
Canton, *Ohio, U.S.A.* **78 F3** 40 48N 81 23W
Canton, *Okla., U.S.A.* **81 G5** 36 3N 98 35W
Canton, *S. Dak., U.S.A.* **80 D6** 43 18N 96 35W
Canton L., *U.S.A.* **81 G5** 36 6N 98 35W

Canudos

Chichagof I.

Chichagof I., *U.S.A.* 72 B1 57 30N 135 30W
Chicheng, *China* 34 D8 40 55N 115 55 E
Chichester, *U.K.* 11 G7 50 50N 0 47W
Chichibu, *Japan* 31 F9 36 5N 139 10 E
Ch'ich'ihaerh = Qiqihar, *China* 27 E13 47 26N 124 0 E
Chickasha, *U.S.A.* 81 H5 35 3N 97 58W
Chiclana de la Frontera, *Spain* 19 D2 36 26N 6 9W
Chiclayo, *Peru* 92 E3 6 42S 79 50W
Chico, *U.S.A.* 84 F5 39 44N 121 50W
Chico →, *Chubut, Argentina* 96 E3 44 0S 67 0W
Chico →, *Santa Cruz, Argentina* 96 G3 50 0S 68 30W
Chicomo, *Mozam.* 57 C5 24 31S 34 6 E
Chicontepec, *Mexico* 87 C5 20 58N 98 10W
Chicopee, *U.S.A.* 79 D12 42 9N 72 37W
Chicoutimi, *Canada* 71 C5 48 28N 71 5W
Chicualacuala, *Mozam.* 57 C5 22 6S 31 42 E
Chidambaram, *India* 40 P11 11 20N 79 45 E
Chidenguele, *Mozam.* 57 C5 24 55S 34 11 E
Chidley, C., *Canada* 69 B13 60 23N 64 26W
Chiede, *Angola* 56 B2 17 15S 16 22 E
Chiefs Pt., *Canada* 78 B3 44 41N 81 18W
Chiem Hoa, *Vietnam* 38 A5 22 12N 105 17 E
Chiengi, *Zambia* 55 D2 8 45S 29 10 E
Chiengmai = Chiang Mai, *Thailand* 38 C2 18 47N 98 59 E
Chiese →, *Italy* 20 B4 45 8N 10 25 E
Chieti, *Italy* 20 C6 42 22N 14 10 E
Chifeng, *China* 35 C10 42 18N 118 58 E
Chignecto B., *Canada* 71 C7 45 30N 64 40W
Chiguana, *Bolivia* 94 A2 21 0S 67 58W
Chiha-ri, *N. Korea* 35 E14 38 40N 126 30 E
Chihli, G. of = Bo Hai, *China* 35 E10 39 0N 119 0 E
Chihuahua, *Mexico* 86 B3 28 40N 106 3W
Chihuahua □, *Mexico* 86 B3 28 40N 106 3W
Chiili, *Kazakhstan* 26 E7 44 20N 66 15 E
Chik Bollapur, *India* 40 N10 13 25N 77 45 E
Chikmagalur, *India* 40 N9 13 15N 75 45 E
Chikwawa, *Malawi* 55 F3 16 2S 34 50 E
Chilac, *Mexico* 87 D5 18 20N 97 24W
Chilako →, *Canada* 72 C4 53 53N 122 57W
Chilam Chavki, *Pakistan* 43 B6 35 5N 75 5 E
Chilanga, *Zambia* 55 F2 15 33S 28 16 E
Chilapa, *Mexico* 87 D5 17 40N 99 11W
Chilas, *Pakistan* 43 B6 35 25N 74 5 E
Chilaw, *Sri Lanka* 40 R11 7 30N 79 50 E
Chilcotin →, *Canada* 72 C4 51 44N 122 23W
Childers, *Australia* 63 D5 25 15S 152 17 E
Childress, *U.S.A.* 81 H4 34 25N 100 13W
Chile ■, *S. Amer.* 96 D2 35 0S 72 0W
Chile Rise, *Pac. Oc.* 65 L18 38 0S 92 0W
Chilecito, *Argentina* 94 B2 29 10S 67 30W
Chilete, *Peru* 92 E3 7 10S 78 50W
Chililabombwe, *Zambia* 55 E2 12 18S 27 43 E
Chilin = Jilin, *China* 35 C14 43 44N 126 30 E
Chilka L., *India* 41 K14 19 40N 85 25 E
Chilko →, *Canada* 72 C4 52 0N 123 40W
Chilko, L., *Canada* 72 C4 51 20N 124 10W
Chillagoe, *Australia* 62 B3 17 7S 144 33 E
Chillán, *Chile* 94 D1 36 40S 72 10W
Chillicothe, *Ill., U.S.A.* 80 E10 40 55N 89 29W
Chillicothe, *Mo., U.S.A.* 80 F8 39 48N 93 33W
Chillicothe, *Ohio, U.S.A.* 76 F4 39 20N 82 59W
Chilliwack, *Canada* 72 D4 49 10N 121 54W
Chilo, *India* 42 F5 27 25N 73 32 E
Chiloane, I., *Mozam.* 57 C5 20 40S 34 55 E
Chiloé, I. de, *Chile* 96 E2 42 30S 73 50W
Chilpancingo, *Mexico* 87 D5 17 30N 99 30W
Chiltern Hills, *U.K.* 11 F7 51 44N 0 42W
Chilton, *U.S.A.* 76 C1 44 2N 88 10W
Chiluage, *Angola* 52 F4 9 30S 21 50 E
Chilubi, *Zambia* 55 E2 11 5S 29 58 E
Chilubula, *Zambia* 55 E3 10 14S 30 51 E
Chilumba, *Malawi* 55 E3 10 28S 34 12 E
Chilung, *Taiwan* 33 D7 25 3N 121 45 E
Chilwa, L., *Malawi* 55 F4 15 15S 35 40 E
Chimaltitán, *Mexico* 86 C4 21 46N 103 50W
Chimán, *Panama* 88 E4 8 45N 78 40W
Chimay, *Belgium* 15 D4 50 3N 4 20 E
Chimbay, *Uzbekistan* 26 E6 42 57N 59 47 E
Chimborazo, *Ecuador* 92 D3 1 29S 78 55W
Chimbote, *Peru* 92 E3 9 0S 78 35W
Chimkent, *Kazakhstan* 26 E7 42 18N 69 36 E
Chimoio, *Mozam.* 55 F3 19 4S 33 30 E
Chimpembe, *Zambia* 55 D2 9 31S 29 33 E
Chin □, *Burma* 41 J18 22 0N 93 0 E
Chin Ling Shan = Qinling Shandi, *China* 34 H5 33 50N 108 10 E
China, *Mexico* 87 B5 25 40N 99 20W
China ■, *Asia* 34 E3 30 0N 110 0 E
China Lake, *U.S.A.* 85 K9 35 44N 117 37W
Chinan = Jinan, *China* 34 F9 36 38N 117 1 E
Chinandega, *Nic.* 88 D2 12 35N 87 12W
Chinati Peak, *U.S.A.* 81 K2 29 57N 104 29W
Chincha Alta, *Peru* 92 F3 13 25S 76 7W
Chinchilla, *Australia* 63 D5 26 45S 150 38 E
Chinchón, *Spain* 19 B4 40 9N 3 26W
Chinchorro, Banco, *Mexico* 87 D7 18 35N 87 20W
Chinchou = Jinzhou, *China* 35 D11 41 5N 121 3 E
Chincoteague, *U.S.A.* 76 G8 37 56N 75 23W
Chinde, *Mozam.* 55 F4 18 35S 36 30 E
Chindo, *S. Korea* 35 G14 34 28N 126 15 E
Chindwin →, *Burma* 41 J19 21 26N 95 15 E
Chineni, *India* 43 C6 33 2N 75 15 E
Chinga, *Mozam.* 55 F4 15 13S 38 35 E
Chingola, *Zambia* 55 E2 12 31S 27 53 E
Chingole, *Malawi* 55 E3 13 4S 34 17 E
Ch'ingtao = Qingdao, *China* 35 F11 36 5N 120 20 E
Chinguetti, *Mauritania* 50 D2 20 25N 12 24W
Chingune, *Mozam.* 57 C5 20 33S 34 58 E
Chinhae, *S. Korea* 35 G15 35 9N 128 47 E
Chinhanguanine, *Mozam.* 57 D5 25 21S 32 30 E
Chinhoyi, *Zimbabwe* 55 F3 17 20S 30 8 E
Chiniot, *Pakistan* 42 D5 31 45N 73 0 E
Chínipas, *Mexico* 86 B3 27 22N 108 32W
Chinju, *S. Korea* 35 G15 35 12N 128 2 E
Chinle, *U.S.A.* 83 H9 36 9N 109 33W
Chinnampo, *N. Korea* 35 E13 38 52N 125 10 E
Chino, *Japan* 31 G9 35 59N 138 9 E
Chino, *U.S.A.* 85 L9 34 1N 117 41W
Chino Valley, *U.S.A.* 83 J7 34 45N 112 27W
Chinon, *France* 18 C4 47 10N 0 15 E
Chinook, *Canada* 73 C6 51 28N 110 59W
Chinook, *U.S.A.* 82 B9 48 35N 109 14W
Chinsali, *Zambia* 55 E3 10 30S 32 2 E
Chióggia, *Italy* 20 B5 45 13N 12 15 E
Chíos = Khíos, *Greece* 21 E12 38 27N 26 9 E
Chipata, *Zambia* 55 E3 13 38S 32 28 E
Chipewyan L., *Canada* 73 B9 58 0N 98 27W
Chipinge, *Zimbabwe* 55 G3 20 13S 32 28 E
Chipley, *U.S.A.* 77 K3 30 47N 85 32W
Chipman, *Canada* 71 C6 46 6N 65 53W
Chipoka, *Malawi* 55 E3 13 57S 34 28 E
Chippenham, *U.K.* 11 F5 51 27N 2 7W
Chippewa →, *U.S.A.* 80 C8 44 25N 92 5W
Chippewa Falls, *U.S.A.* 80 C9 44 56N 91 24W
Chiquián, *Peru* 92 F3 10 10S 77 0W
Chiquimula, *Guatemala* 88 D2 14 51N 89 37W
Chiquinquira, *Colombia* 92 B4 5 37N 73 50W
Chirala, *India* 40 M12 15 50N 80 26 E
Chiramba, *Mozam.* 55 F3 16 55S 34 39 E
Chirawa, *India* 42 E6 28 14N 75 42 E
Chirchik, *Uzbekistan* 26 E7 41 29N 69 35 E
Chiricahua Peak, *U.S.A.* 83 L9 31 51N 109 18W
Chiriquí, G. de, *Panama* 88 E3 8 0N 82 10W
Chiriquí, L. de, *Panama* 88 E3 9 10N 82 0W
Chirivira Falls, *Zimbabwe* 55 G3 21 10S 32 12 E
Chirmiri, *India* 41 H13 23 15N 82 20 E
Chiromo, *Malawi* 53 H7 16 30S 35 7 E
Chirripó Grande, Cerro, *Costa Rica* 88 E3 9 29N 83 29W
Chisamba, *Zambia* 55 E2 14 55S 28 20 E
Chisapani Garhi, *Nepal* 41 F14 27 30N 84 2 E
Chisholm, *Canada* 72 C6 54 55N 114 10W
Chishtian Mandi, *Pakistan* 42 E5 29 50N 72 55 E
Chisimba Falls, *Zambia* 55 E3 10 12S 30 56 E
Chişinău = Kishinev, *Moldavia* 25 E4 47 0N 28 50 E
Chisos Mts., *U.S.A.* 81 L3 29 5N 103 15W
Chistopol, *Russia* 24 C9 55 25N 50 38 E
Chita, *Russia* 27 D12 52 0N 113 35 E
Chitado, *Angola* 53 H2 17 10S 14 8 E
Chitembo, *Angola* 53 G3 13 30S 16 50 E
Chitipa, *Malawi* 55 D3 9 41S 33 19 E
Chitose, *Japan* 30 C10 42 49N 141 39 E
Chitral, *Pakistan* 40 B7 35 50N 71 56 E
Chitré, *Panama* 88 E3 7 59N 80 27W
Chittagong, *Bangla.* 41 H17 22 19N 91 48 E
Chittagong □, *Bangla.* 41 G17 24 5N 91 0 E
Chittaurgarh, *India* 42 G6 24 52N 74 38 E
Chittoor, *India* 40 N11 13 15N 79 5 E
Chitungwiza, *Zimbabwe* 55 F3 18 0S 31 6 E
Chiusi, *Italy* 20 C4 43 1N 11 58 E
Chivasso, *Italy* 20 B2 45 10N 7 52 E
Chivhu, *Zimbabwe* 55 F3 19 2S 30 52 E
Chivilcoy, *Argentina* 94 C4 34 55S 60 0W
Chiwanda, *Tanzania* 55 E3 11 23S 34 55 E
Chizera, *Zambia* 55 E1 13 10S 25 0 E
Chkalov = Orenburg, *Russia* 24 D10 51 45N 55 6 E
Chloride, *U.S.A.* 85 K12 35 25N 114 12W
Cho Bo, *Vietnam* 38 B5 20 46N 105 10 E
Cho-do, *N. Korea* 35 E13 38 30N 124 40 E
Cho Phuoc Hai, *Vietnam* 39 G6 10 26N 107 18 E
Choba, *Kenya* 54 B4 2 30N 38 5 E
Chobe National Park, *Botswana* 56 B3 18 0S 25 0 E
Chochiwŏn, *S. Korea* 35 F14 36 37N 127 18 E
Choctawhatchee B., *U.S.A.* 75 D9 30 20N 86 20W
Choele Choel, *Argentina* 96 D3 39 11S 65 40W
Choix, *Mexico* 86 B3 26 40N 108 23W
Chojnice, *Poland* 17 B8 53 42N 17 32 E
Chōkai-San, *Japan* 30 E10 39 6N 140 3 E
Chokurdakh, *Russia* 27 B15 70 38N 147 55 E
Cholame, *U.S.A.* 84 K6 35 44N 120 18W
Cholet, *France* 18 C3 47 4N 0 52W
Choluteca, *Honduras* 88 D2 13 20N 87 14W
Choluteca →, *Honduras* 88 D2 13 0N 87 20W
Chom Bung, *Thailand* 38 F2 13 37N 99 36 E
Chom Thong, *Thailand* 38 C2 18 25N 98 41 E
Choma, *Zambia* 55 F2 16 48S 26 59 E
Chomun, *India* 42 F6 27 15N 75 40 E
Chomutov, *Czech.* 16 C6 50 28N 13 23 E
Chon Buri, *Thailand* 38 F3 13 21N 101 1 E
Chon Thanh, *Vietnam* 39 G6 11 24N 106 36 E
Chonan, *S. Korea* 35 F14 36 48N 127 9 E
Chone, *Ecuador* 92 D2 0 40S 80 0W
Chong Kai, *Cambodia* 38 F4 13 57N 103 35 E
Chong Mek, *Thailand* 38 E5 15 10N 105 27 E
Chŏngdo, *S. Korea* 35 G15 35 38N 128 42 E
Chŏngha, *S. Korea* 35 F15 36 12N 129 21 E
Chŏngjin, *N. Korea* 35 D15 41 47N 129 50 E
Chŏngju, *N. Korea* 35 E13 39 40N 125 5 E
Chŏngju, *S. Korea* 35 F14 36 39N 127 27 E
Chongli, *China* 34 D8 40 58N 115 15 E
Chongqing, *China* 32 D5 29 35N 106 25 E
Chŏngŭp, *S. Korea* 35 G14 35 35N 126 50 E
Chŏnju, *S. Korea* 35 G14 35 50N 127 4 E
Chonos, Arch. de los, *Chile* 96 F2 45 0S 75 0W
Chopim →, *Brazil* 95 B5 25 35S 53 5W
Chorbat La, *India* 43 B7 34 42N 76 37 E
Chorley, *U.K.* 10 D5 53 39N 2 39W
Chorolque, Cerro, *Bolivia* 94 A2 20 59S 66 5W
Chorregon, *Australia* 62 C3 22 40S 143 32 E
Chŏrwŏn, *S. Korea* 35 E14 38 15N 127 10 E
Chorzów, *Poland* 17 C9 50 18N 18 57 E
Chos-Malal, *Argentina* 94 D1 37 20S 70 15W
Chosan, *N. Korea* 35 D13 40 50N 125 47 E
Choszczno, *Poland* 16 B7 53 7N 15 25 E
Choteau, *U.S.A.* 82 C7 47 49N 112 11W
Chotila, *India* 42 H4 22 23N 71 15 E
Chowchilla, *U.S.A.* 83 H3 37 7N 120 16W
Choybalsan, *Mongolia* 33 B6 48 4N 114 30 E
Christchurch, *N.Z.* 59 K4 43 33S 172 47 E
Christchurch, *U.K.* 11 G6 50 44N 1 45W
Christian I., *Canada* 78 B4 44 50N 80 12W
Christiana, *S. Africa* 56 D4 27 52S 25 8 E
Christiansted, *Virgin Is.* 89 C7 17 45N 64 42W
Christie B., *Canada* 73 A6 62 32N 111 10W
Christina →, *Canada* 73 B6 56 40N 111 3W
Christmas Cr. →, *Australia* 60 C4 18 29S 125 23 E
Christmas Creek, *Australia* 60 C4 18 29S 125 23 E
Christmas I. = Kiritimati, *Kiribati* 65 G12 1 58N 157 27W
Christmas I., *Ind. Oc.* 64 J2 10 30S 105 40 E
Christopher L., *Australia* 61 D4 24 49S 127 42 E
Chtimba, *Malawi* 55 E3 10 35S 34 13 E
Chu, *Kazakhstan* 26 E8 43 36N 73 42 E
Chu →, *Vietnam* 38 C5 19 53N 105 45 E
Chu Chua, *Canada* 72 C4 51 22N 120 10W
Chu Lai, *Vietnam* 38 E7 15 28N 108 45 E
Ch'uanchou = Quanzhou, *China* 33 D6 24 55N 118 34 E
Chuankou, *China* 34 G6 34 20N 110 59 E
Chūbu □, *Japan* 31 F8 36 45N 137 30 E
Chubut →, *Argentina* 96 E3 43 20S 65 5W
Chuchi L., *Canada* 72 B4 55 12N 124 30W
Chudskoye, Oz., *Estonia* 24 C4 58 13N 27 30 E
Chūgoku □, *Japan* 31 G6 35 0N 133 0 E
Chūgoku-Sanchi, *Japan* 31 G6 35 0N 133 0 E
Chugwater, *U.S.A.* 80 E2 41 46N 104 50W
Chukotskiy Khrebet, *Russia* 27 C18 68 0N 175 0 E
Chukotskoye More, *Russia* 27 C19 68 0N 175 0W
Chula Vista, *U.S.A.* 85 N9 32 39N 117 5W
Chulman, *Russia* 27 D13 56 52N 124 52 E
Chulucanas, *Peru* 92 E2 5 8S 80 10W
Chulym →, *Russia* 26 D9 57 43N 83 51 E
Chum Phae, *Thailand* 38 D4 16 40N 102 6 E
Chum Saeng, *Thailand* 38 E3 15 55N 100 15 E
Chumar, *India* 43 C8 32 40N 78 35 E
Chumbicha, *Argentina* 94 B2 29 0S 66 10W
Chumikan, *Russia* 27 D14 54 40N 135 10 E
Chumphon, *Thailand* 39 G2 10 35N 99 14 E
Chumuare, *Mozam.* 55 E3 14 31S 31 50 E
Chumunjin, *S. Korea* 35 F15 37 55N 128 54 E
Chuna →, *Russia* 27 D10 57 47N 94 37 E
Chunchŏn, *S. Korea* 35 F14 37 58N 127 44 E
Chunchura, *India* 43 H13 22 53N 88 27 E
Chunga, *Zambia* 55 F2 15 0S 26 2 E
Chunggang-ŭp, *N. Korea* 35 D14 41 48N 126 48 E
Chunghwa, *N. Korea* 35 E13 38 52N 125 47 E
Chungju, *S. Korea* 35 F14 36 58N 127 58 E
Chungking = Chongqing, *China* 32 D5 29 35N 106 25 E
Chungmu, *S. Korea* 35 G15 34 50N 128 20 E
Chungt'iaoshan = Zhongtiao Shan, *China* 34 G6 35 0N 111 10 E
Chunian, *Pakistan* 42 D6 30 57N 74 0 E
Chunya, *Tanzania* 55 D3 8 30S 33 27 E
Chunya □, *Tanzania* 54 D3 7 48S 33 0 E
Chunyang, *China* 35 C15 43 38N 129 23 E
Chuquibamba, *Peru* 92 G4 15 47S 72 44W
Chuquicamata, *Chile* 94 A2 22 15S 69 0W
Chur, *Switz.* 16 E4 46 52N 9 32 E
Churachandpur, *India* 41 G18 24 20N 93 40 E
Churchill, *Canada* 73 B10 58 47N 94 11W
Churchill →, *Man., Canada* 73 B10 58 47N 94 12W
Churchill →, *Nfld., Canada* 71 B7 53 19N 60 10W
Churchill, C., *Canada* 73 B10 58 46N 93 12W
Churchill Falls, *Canada* 71 B7 53 36N 64 19W
Churchill L., *Canada* 73 B7 55 55N 108 20W
Churchill Pk., *Canada* 72 B3 58 10N 125 10W
Churu, *India* 42 E6 28 20N 74 50 E
Chushal, *India* 43 C8 33 40N 78 40 E
Chusovoy, *Russia* 24 C10 58 15N 57 40 E
Chuuronjang, *N. Korea* 35 D15 41 35N 129 40 E
Chuvash Republic □, *Russia* 24 C8 55 30N 47 0 E
Chuwārtah, *Iraq* 44 C5 35 43N 45 34 E
Ci Xian, *China* 34 F8 36 20N 114 25 E
Cianjur, *Indonesia* 37 G12 6 49S 107 8 E
Cibadok, *Indonesia* 37 G12 6 53S 106 47 E
Cibatu, *Indonesia* 37 G12 7 8S 107 59 E
Cibola, *U.S.A.* 85 M12 33 17N 114 42W
Cicero, *U.S.A.* 76 E2 41 48N 87 48W
Ciechanów, *Poland* 17 B10 52 52N 20 38 E
Ciego de Avila, *Cuba* 88 B4 21 50N 78 50W
Ciénaga, *Colombia* 92 A4 11 1N 74 15W
Cienfuegos, *Cuba* 88 B3 22 10N 80 30W
Cieszyn, *Poland* 17 D9 49 45N 18 35 E
Cieza, *Spain* 19 C5 38 17N 1 23W
Cihuatlán, *Mexico* 86 D4 19 14N 104 35W
Cijulang, *Indonesia* 37 G13 7 42S 108 27 E
Cikajang, *Indonesia* 37 G12 7 25S 107 48 E
Cikampek, *Indonesia* 37 G12 6 23S 107 28 E
Cilacap, *Indonesia* 37 G13 7 43S 109 0 E
Cima, *U.S.A.* 85 K11 35 14N 115 30W
Cimahi, *Indonesia* 37 G12 6 53S 107 33 E
Cimarron, *Kans., U.S.A.* 81 G4 37 48N 100 21W
Cimarron, *N. Mex., U.S.A.* 81 G2 36 31N 104 55W
Cimarron →, *U.S.A.* 81 G6 36 10N 96 17W
Cimone, Mte., *Italy* 20 B4 44 10N 10 40 E
Cimpina, *Romania* 17 F12 45 10N 25 45 E
Cimpulung, *Romania* 17 F12 45 17N 25 3 E
Cinca →, *Spain* 19 B6 41 26N 0 21 E
Cincinnati, *U.S.A.* 76 F3 39 6N 84 31W
Ciney, *Belgium* 15 D5 50 18N 5 5 E
Cinto, Mte., *France* 18 E8 42 24N 8 54 E
Circle, *Alaska, U.S.A.* 68 B5 65 50N 144 4W
Circle, *Mont., U.S.A.* 80 B2 47 25N 105 35W
Circleville, *Ohio, U.S.A.* 76 F4 39 36N 82 57W
Circleville, *Utah, U.S.A.* 83 G7 38 10N 112 16W
Cirebon, *Indonesia* 37 G13 6 45S 108 32 E
Cirencester, *U.K.* 11 F6 51 43N 1 59W
Cirium, *Cyprus* 23 E11 34 40N 32 53 E
Cisco, *U.S.A.* 81 J5 32 23N 98 59W
Ciskei □, *S. Africa* 57 E4 33 0S 27 0 E
Citlaltépetl, *Mexico* 87 D5 19 0N 97 20W
Citrus Heights, *U.S.A.* 84 G5 38 42N 121 17W
Citrusdal, *S. Africa* 56 E2 32 35S 19 0 E
Ciudad Altamirano, *Mexico* 86 D4 18 20N 100 40W
Ciudad Bolívar, *Venezuela* 92 B6 8 5N 63 36W
Ciudad Camargo, *Mexico* 86 B3 27 41N 105 10W
Ciudad Chetumal, *Mexico* 87 D7 18 30N 88 20W
Ciudad de Valles, *Mexico* 87 C5 22 0N 99 0W
Ciudad del Carmen, *Mexico* 87 D6 18 38N 91 50W
Ciudad Delicias = Delicias, *Mexico* 86 B3 28 10N 105 30W
Ciudad Guayana, *Venezuela* 92 B6 8 0N 62 30W
Ciudad Guerrero, *Mexico* 86 B3 28 33N 107 28W
Ciudad Guzmán, *Mexico* 86 D4 19 40N 103 30W
Ciudad Juárez, *Mexico* 86 A3 31 40N 106 28W
Ciudad Madero, *Mexico* 87 C5 22 19N 97 50W
Ciudad Mante, *Mexico* 87 C5 22 50N 99 0W
Ciudad Obregón, *Mexico* 86 B3 27 28N 109 59W
Ciudad Real, *Spain* 19 C4 38 59N 3 55W
Ciudad Rodrigo, *Spain* 19 B2 40 35N 6 32W
Ciudad Trujillo = Santo Domingo, *Dom. Rep.* 89 C6 18 30N 69 59W
Ciudad Victoria, *Mexico* 87 C5 23 41N 99 9W
Ciudadela, *Spain* 22 B10 40 0N 3 50 E
Civitanova Marche, *Italy* 20 C5 43 18N 13 41 E
Civitavécchia, *Italy* 20 C4 42 6N 11 46 E
Cizre, *Turkey* 25 G7 37 19N 42 10 E
Clacton-on-Sea, *U.K.* 11 F9 51 47N 1 10 E
Claire, L., *Canada* 72 B6 58 35N 112 5W
Clairemont, *U.S.A.* 81 J4 33 9N 100 44W
Clairton, *U.S.A.* 78 F5 40 18N 79 53W
Clallam Bay, *U.S.A.* 84 B2 48 15N 124 16W
Clanton, *U.S.A.* 77 J2 32 51N 86 38W
Clanwilliam, *S. Africa* 56 E2 32 11S 18 52 E
Clara, *Ireland* 13 C4 53 20N 7 38W
Clara →, *Australia* 62 B3 19 8S 142 30 E
Claraville, *U.S.A.* 85 K8 35 24N 118 20W
Clare, *Australia* 63 E2 33 50S 138 37 E
Clare, *U.S.A.* 76 D3 43 49N 84 46W
Clare □, *Ireland* 13 D3 52 45N 9 0W
Clare →, *Ireland* 13 C2 53 22N 9 5W
Clare I., *Ireland* 13 C2 53 48N 10 0W
Claremont, *Calif., U.S.A.* 85 L9 34 6N 117 43W
Claremont, *N.H., U.S.A.* 79 C12 43 23N 72 20W
Claremont Pt., *Australia* 62 A3 14 1S 143 41 E
Claremore, *U.S.A.* 81 G7 36 19N 95 36W
Claremorris, *Ireland* 13 C3 53 45N 9 0W
Clarence →, *Australia* 63 D5 29 25S 153 22 E
Clarence →, *N.Z.* 59 K4 42 10S 173 56 E
Clarence, I., *Chile* 96 G2 54 0S 72 0W
Clarence I., *Antarctica* 5 C18 61 10S 54 0W
Clarence Str., *Australia* 60 B5 12 0S 131 0 E
Clarence Str., *U.S.A.* 72 B2 55 40N 132 10W
Clarence Town, *Bahamas* 89 B5 23 6N 74 59W
Clarendon, *Ark., U.S.A.* 81 H9 34 42N 91 19W
Clarendon, *Tex., U.S.A.* 81 H4 34 56N 100 53W
Clarenville, *Canada* 71 C9 48 10N 54 1W
Claresholm, *Canada* 72 C6 50 0N 113 33W
Clarie Coast, *Antarctica* 5 C9 68 0S 135 0 E
Clarinda, *U.S.A.* 80 E7 40 44N 95 2W
Clarion, *Iowa, U.S.A.* 80 D8 42 44N 93 44W
Clarion, *Pa., U.S.A.* 78 E5 41 13N 79 23W
Clarion →, *U.S.A.* 78 E5 41 7N 79 41W
Clark, *U.S.A.* 80 C6 44 53N 97 44W
Clark, Pt., *Canada* 78 B3 44 4N 81 45W
Clark Fork, *U.S.A.* 82 B5 48 9N 116 11W
Clark Fork →, *U.S.A.* 82 B5 48 9N 116 15W
Clark Hill Res., *U.S.A.* 77 J4 33 45N 82 20W
Clarkdale, *U.S.A.* 83 J7 34 46N 112 3W
Clarke City, *Canada* 71 B6 50 12N 66 38W
Clarke I., *Australia* 62 G4 40 32S 148 10 E
Clarke L., *Canada* 73 C7 54 24N 106 54W
Clarke Ra., *Australia* 62 C4 20 40S 148 30 E
Clark's Fork →, *U.S.A.* 82 D9 45 39N 108 43W
Clark's Harbour, *Canada* 71 D6 43 25N 65 38W
Clarks Summit, *U.S.A.* 79 E9 41 30N 75 42W
Clarksburg, *U.S.A.* 76 F5 39 17N 80 30W
Clarksdale, *U.S.A.* 81 H9 34 12N 90 35W
Clarkston, *U.S.A.* 82 C5 46 25N 117 3W
Clarksville, *Ark., U.S.A.* 81 H8 35 28N 93 28W
Clarksville, *Tenn., U.S.A.* 77 G2 36 32N 87 21W
Clarksville, *Tex., U.S.A.* 81 J7 33 37N 95 3W
Clatskanie, *U.S.A.* 84 D3 46 6N 123 12W
Claude, *U.S.A.* 81 H4 35 7N 101 22W
Claveria, *Phil.* 37 A6 18 37N 121 4 E
Clay, *U.S.A.* 84 G5 38 17N 121 10W
Clay Center, *U.S.A.* 80 F6 39 23N 97 8W
Claypool, *U.S.A.* 83 K8 33 25N 110 51W
Claysville, *U.S.A.* 78 F4 40 7N 80 25W
Clayton, *Idaho, U.S.A.* 82 D6 44 16N 114 24W
Clayton, *N. Mex., U.S.A.* 81 G3 36 27N 103 11W
Cle Elum, *U.S.A.* 82 C3 47 12N 120 56W
Clear, C., *Ireland* 13 E2 51 26N 9 30W
Clear I., *Ireland* 13 E2 51 26N 9 30W
Clear L., *U.S.A.* 84 F4 39 2N 122 47W
Clear Lake, *S. Dak., U.S.A.* 80 C6 44 45N 96 41W
Clear Lake, *Wash., U.S.A.* 82 B2 48 27N 122 15W
Clear Lake Reservoir, *U.S.A.* 82 F3 41 56N 121 5W
Clearfield, *Pa., U.S.A.* 76 E6 41 2N 78 27W
Clearfield, *Utah, U.S.A.* 82 F7 41 7N 112 2W
Clearlake Highlands, *U.S.A.* 84 G4 38 57N 122 38W
Clearmont, *U.S.A.* 82 D10 44 38N 106 23W
Clearwater, *Canada* 72 C4 51 38N 120 2W
Clearwater, *U.S.A.* 77 M4 27 58N 82 48W
Clearwater →, *Alta., Canada* 72 C6 52 22N 114 57W
Clearwater →, *Alta., Canada* 73 B6 56 44N 111 23W
Clearwater Cr. →, *Canada* 72 A3 61 36N 125 30W
Clearwater Mts., *U.S.A.* 82 C6 46 5N 115 20W
Clearwater Prov. Park, *Canada* 73 C8 54 0N 101 0W
Cleburne, *U.S.A.* 81 J6 32 21N 97 23W
Cleethorpes, *U.K.* 10 D7 53 33N 0 2W
Cleeve Hill, *U.K.* 11 F6 51 54N 2 0W
Clerke Reef, *Australia* 60 C2 17 22S 119 20 E
Clermont, *Australia* 62 C4 22 49S 147 39 E

Cooper Cr.

Clermont-Ferrand, France 18 D5 45 46N 3 4 E
Clervaux, Lux. 15 D6 50 4N 6 2 E
Cleveland, Australia 63 D5 27 30S 153 15 E
Cleveland, Miss., U.S.A. 81 J9 33 45N 90 43W
Cleveland, Ohio, U.S.A. 78 E3 41 30N 81 42W
Cleveland, Okla., U.S.A. 81 G6 36 19N 96 28W
Cleveland, Tenn., U.S.A. 77 H3 35 10N 84 53W
Cleveland, Tex., U.S.A. 81 K7 30 21N 95 5W
Cleveland □, U.K. 10 C9 54 35N 1 8 E
Cleveland, C., Australia 62 B4 19 11S 147 1 E
Cleveland Heights, U.S.A. 78 E3 41 30N 81 34W
Clevelândia, Brazil 95 B5 26 24S 52 23W
Clew B., Ireland 13 C2 53 54N 9 50W
Clewiston, U.S.A. 77 M5 26 45N 80 56W
Clifden, Ireland 13 C1 53 30N 10 2W
Clifden, N.Z. 59 M1 46 1S 167 42 E
Cliffdell, U.S.A. 84 D5 46 56N 121 5W
Clifton, Australia 63 D5 27 59S 151 53 E
Clifton, Ariz., U.S.A. 83 K9 33 3N 109 18W
Clifton, Tex., U.S.A. 81 K6 31 47N 97 35W
Clifton Beach, Australia 62 B4 16 46S 145 39 E
Clifton Forge, U.S.A. 76 G6 37 49N 79 50W
Clifton Hills, Australia 63 D2 27 1S 138 54 E
Climax, Canada 73 D7 49 10N 108 20W
Clinch →, U.S.A. 77 H3 35 53N 84 29W
Clingmans Dome, U.S.A. 77 H4 35 34N 83 30W
Clint, U.S.A. 83 L10 31 35N 106 14W
Clinton, B.C., Canada 72 C4 51 6N 121 35W
Clinton, Ont., Canada 70 D3 43 37N 81 32W
Clinton, N.Z. 59 M2 46 12S 169 23 E
Clinton, Ark., U.S.A. 81 H8 35 36N 92 28W
Clinton, Ill., U.S.A. 80 E10 40 9N 88 57W
Clinton, Ind., U.S.A. 76 F2 39 40N 87 24W
Clinton, Iowa, U.S.A. 80 E9 41 51N 90 12W
Clinton, Mass., U.S.A. 79 D13 42 25N 71 41W
Clinton, Mo., U.S.A. 80 F8 38 22N 93 46W
Clinton, N.C., U.S.A. 77 H6 35 0N 78 22W
Clinton, Okla., U.S.A. 81 H5 35 31N 98 58W
Clinton, S.C., U.S.A. 77 H5 34 29N 81 53W
Clinton, Tenn., U.S.A. 77 G3 36 6N 84 8W
Clinton, Wash., U.S.A. 84 C4 47 59N 122 21W
Clinton C., Australia 62 C5 22 30S 150 45 E
Clinton Colden L., Canada 68 B9 63 58N 107 27W
Clintonville, U.S.A. 80 C10 44 37N 88 46W
Clipperton, I., Pac. Oc. 65 F17 10 18N 109 13W
Clive L., Canada 72 A5 63 13N 118 54W
Cloates, Pt., Australia 60 D1 22 43S 113 40 E
Clocolan, S. Africa 57 D4 28 55S 27 34 E
Clodomira, Argentina 94 B3 27 35S 64 14W
Clonakilty, Ireland 13 E3 51 37N 8 53W
Clonakilty B., Ireland 13 E3 51 33N 8 50W
Cloncurry, Australia 62 C3 20 40S 140 28 E
Cloncurry →, Australia 62 B3 18 37S 140 40 E
Clones, Ireland 13 B4 54 10N 7 13W
Clonmel, Ireland 13 D4 52 22N 7 42W
Cloquet, U.S.A. 80 B8 46 43N 92 28W
Clorinda, Argentina 94 B4 25 16S 57 45W
Cloud Peak, U.S.A. 82 D10 44 23N 107 11W
Cloudcroft, U.S.A. 83 K11 32 58N 105 45W
Cloverdale, U.S.A. 84 G4 38 48N 123 1W
Clovis, Calif., U.S.A. 83 H4 36 49N 119 42W
Clovis, N. Mex., U.S.A. 81 H3 34 24N 103 12W
Cluj-Napoca, Romania 17 E11 46 47N 23 38 E
Clunes, Australia 63 F3 37 20S 143 45 E
Cluny, France 18 C6 46 26N 4 38 E
Clutha →, N.Z. 59 M2 46 20S 169 49 E
Clwyd □, U.K. 10 D4 53 5N 3 20W
Clwyd →, U.K. 10 D4 53 20N 3 30W
Clyde, N.Z. 59 L2 45 12S 169 20 E
Clyde, U.S.A. 78 C8 43 5N 76 52W
Clyde →, U.K. 12 F4 55 56N 4 29W
Clyde, Firth of, U.K. 12 F4 55 20N 5 0W
Clyde River, Canada 69 A13 70 30N 68 30W
Clydebank, U.K. 12 F4 55 54N 4 25W
Clymer, U.S.A. 78 D5 40 40N 79 1W
Coachella, U.S.A. 85 M10 33 41N 116 10W
Coachella Canal, U.S.A. 85 N12 32 43N 114 57W
Coahoma, U.S.A. 81 J4 32 18N 101 18W
Coahuayana →, Mexico 86 D4 18 41N 103 45W
Coahuayutla, Mexico 86 D4 18 19N 101 42W
Coahuila □, Mexico 86 B4 27 0N 103 0W
Coal →, Canada 72 B3 59 39N 126 57W
Coalane, Mozam. 55 F4 17 48S 37 2 E
Coalcomán, Mexico 86 D4 18 40N 103 10W
Coaldale, Canada 72 D6 49 45N 112 35W
Coalgate, U.S.A. 81 H6 34 32N 96 13W
Coalinga, U.S.A. 83 H3 36 9N 120 21W
Coalville, U.K. 10 E6 52 43N 1 21W
Coalville, U.S.A. 82 F8 40 55N 111 24W
Coari, Brazil 92 D6 4 8S 63 7W
Coast □, Kenya 54 C4 2 40S 39 45 E
Coast Mts., Canada 72 C3 55 0N 129 20W
Coast Ranges, U.S.A. 84 E4 41 0N 123 0W
Coatbridge, U.K. 12 F4 55 52N 4 2W
Coatepec, Mexico 87 D5 19 27N 96 58W
Coatepeque, Guatemala 88 D1 14 46N 91 55W
Coatesville, U.S.A. 76 F8 39 59N 75 50W
Coaticook, Canada 71 C5 45 10N 71 46W
Coats I., Canada 69 B11 62 30N 83 0W
Coats Land, Antarctica 5 D1 77 0S 25 0W
Coatzacoalcos, Mexico 87 D6 18 7N 94 25W
Cobalt, Canada 70 C4 47 25N 79 42W
Cobán, Guatemala 88 C1 15 30N 90 21W
Cobar, Australia 63 E4 31 27S 145 48 E
Cóbh, Ireland 13 E3 51 50N 8 18W
Cobham, Australia 63 E3 30 18S 142 7 E
Cobija, Bolivia 92 F5 11 0S 68 50W
Cobleskill, U.S.A. 79 D10 42 41N 74 29W
Coboconk, Canada 78 B6 44 39N 78 48W
Cobourg, Canada 70 D4 43 58N 78 10W
Cobourg Pen., Australia 60 B5 11 20S 132 15 E
Cobram, Australia 63 F4 35 54S 145 40 E
Cobre, U.S.A. 82 F6 41 7N 114 24W
Cóbué, Mozam. 55 E3 12 0S 34 58 E
Coburg, Germany 16 C5 50 15N 10 58 E
Cocanada = Kakinada, India 41 L13 16 57N 82 11 E
Cochabamba, Bolivia 92 G5 17 26S 66 10W
Cochemane, Mozam. 55 F3 17 0S 32 54 E
Cochin, India 40 Q10 9 59N 76 22 E
Cochin China = Nam-Phan, Vietnam 39 G6 10 30N 106 0 E
Cochise, U.S.A. 83 K9 32 7N 109 55W
Cochran, U.S.A. 77 J4 32 23N 83 21W
Cochrane, Alta., Canada 72 C6 51 11N 114 30W
Cochrane, Ont., Canada 70 C3 49 0N 81 0W
Cochrane →, Canada 73 B8 59 0N 103 40W
Cochrane, L., Chile 96 F2 47 10S 72 0W
Cockburn, Australia 63 E3 32 5S 141 0 E
Cockburn, Canal, Chile 96 G2 54 30S 72 0W
Cockburn I., Canada 70 C3 45 55N 83 22W
Cockburn Ra., Australia 60 C4 15 46S 128 0 E
Cocklebiddy Motel, Australia 61 F4 32 0S 126 3 E
Coco →, Cent. Amer. 88 D3 15 0N 83 8W
Cocoa, U.S.A. 77 L5 28 21N 80 44W
Cocobeach, Gabon 52 D1 0 59N 9 34 E
Cocos, I. del, Pac. Oc. 65 G19 5 25N 87 55W
Cocos Is., Ind. Oc. 64 J1 12 10S 96 55 E
Cod, C., U.S.A. 75 B13 42 5N 70 10W
Codajás, Brazil 92 D6 3 55S 62 0W
Coderre, Canada 73 C7 50 11N 106 31W
Codó, Brazil 93 D10 4 30S 43 55W
Cody, U.S.A. 82 D9 44 32N 109 3W
Coe Hill, Canada 70 D4 44 52N 77 50W
Coelemu, Chile 94 D1 36 30S 72 48W
Coen, Australia 62 A3 13 52S 143 12 E
Cœur d'Alene, U.S.A. 82 C5 47 45N 116 51W
Cœur d'Alene L., U.S.A. 82 C5 47 32N 116 48W
Coevorden, Neths. 15 B6 52 40N 6 44 E
Cofete, Canary Is. 22 F5 28 6N 14 23W
Coffeyville, U.S.A. 81 G7 37 2N 95 37W
Coffin B., Australia 63 E2 34 38S 135 28 E
Coffin Bay Peninsula, Australia 63 E2 34 32S 135 15 E
Coffs Harbour, Australia 63 E5 30 16S 153 5 E
Coghinas →, Italy 20 D3 40 55N 8 48 E
Cognac, France 18 D3 45 41N 0 20W
Cohagen, U.S.A. 82 C10 47 3N 106 37W
Cohoes, U.S.A. 79 D11 42 46N 73 42W
Cohuna, Australia 63 F3 35 45S 144 15 E
Coiba, I., Panama 88 E3 7 30N 81 40W
Coig →, Argentina 96 G3 51 0S 69 10W
Coihaique, Chile 96 F2 45 30S 71 45W
Coimbatore, India 40 P10 11 2N 76 59 E
Coimbra, Brazil 92 G7 19 55S 57 48W
Coimbra, Portugal 19 B1 40 15N 8 27W
Coín, Spain 19 D3 36 40N 4 48W
Cojimies, Ecuador 92 C2 0 20N 80 0W
Cojutepequé, El Salv. 88 D2 13 41N 88 54W
Cokeville, U.S.A. 82 E8 42 5N 110 57W
Colac, Australia 63 F3 38 21S 143 35 E
Colatina, Brazil 93 G10 19 32S 40 37W
Colbeck, C., Antarctica 5 D13 77 6S 157 48W
Colbinabbin, Australia 63 F3 36 38S 144 48 E
Colborne, Canada 78 B7 44 0N 77 53W
Colby, U.S.A. 80 F4 39 24N 101 3W
Colchagua □, Chile 94 C1 34 30S 71 0W
Colchester, U.K. 11 F8 51 54N 0 55 E
Coldstream, U.K. 12 F6 55 39N 2 14W
Coldwater, Canada 78 B5 44 42N 79 40W
Coldwater, U.S.A. 81 G5 37 16N 99 20W
Colebrook, Australia 62 G4 42 31S 147 21 E
Colebrook, U.S.A. 79 B13 44 54N 71 30W
Coleman, Canada 72 D6 49 40N 114 30W
Coleman, U.S.A. 81 K5 31 50N 99 26W
Coleman →, Australia 62 B3 15 6S 141 38 E
Colenso, S. Africa 57 D4 28 44S 29 50 E
Coleraine, Australia 63 F3 37 36S 141 40 E
Coleraine, U.K. 13 A5 55 8N 6 40W
Coleraine □, U.K. 13 A5 55 8N 6 40W
Coleridge, L., N.Z. 59 K3 43 17S 171 30 E
Colesberg, S. Africa 56 E4 30 45S 25 5 E
Coleville, U.S.A. 84 G7 38 34N 119 30W
Colfax, Calif., U.S.A. 84 F6 39 6N 120 57W
Colfax, La., U.S.A. 81 K8 31 31N 92 42W
Colfax, Wash., U.S.A. 82 C5 46 53N 117 22W
Colhué Huapi, L., Argentina 96 F3 45 30S 69 0W
Coligny, S. Africa 57 D4 26 17S 26 15 E
Colima, Mexico 86 D4 19 10N 103 40W
Colima □, Mexico 86 D4 19 10N 103 40W
Colima, Nevado de, Mexico 86 D4 19 35N 103 45W
Colina, Chile 94 C1 33 13S 70 45W
Colinas, Brazil 93 E10 6 0S 44 10W
Coll, U.K. 12 E2 56 40N 6 35W
Collaguasi, Chile 94 A2 21 5S 68 45W
Collarenebri, Australia 63 D4 29 33S 148 34 E
Collbran, U.S.A. 83 G10 39 14N 107 58W
Colleen Bawn, Zimbabwe 55 G2 21 0S 29 12 E
College Park, U.S.A. 77 J3 33 40N 84 27W
Collette, Canada 71 C6 46 40N 65 30W
Collie, Australia 61 F2 33 22S 116 8 E
Collier B., Australia 60 C3 16 10S 124 15 E
Collier Ra., Australia 60 D2 24 45S 119 10 E
Collingwood, Canada 78 B4 44 29N 80 13W
Collingwood, N.Z. 59 J4 40 41S 172 40 E
Collins, Canada 70 B2 50 17N 89 27W
Collinsville, Australia 62 C4 20 30S 147 56 E
Collipulli, Chile 94 D1 37 55S 72 30W
Collooney, Ireland 13 B3 54 11N 8 28W
Colmar, France 18 B7 48 5N 7 20 E
Colne, U.K. 10 D5 53 51N 2 11W
Colo →, Australia 63 E5 33 25S 150 52 E
Cologne = Köln, Germany 16 C3 50 56N 6 58 E
Colom, I., Spain 22 B11 39 58N 4 16 E
Coloma, U.S.A. 84 G6 38 48N 120 53W
Colomb-Béchar = Béchar, Algeria 50 B4 31 38N 2 18W
Colômbia, Brazil 93 H9 20 10S 48 40W
Colombia ■, S. Amer. 92 C4 3 45N 73 0W
Colombo, Sri Lanka 40 R11 6 56N 79 58 E
Colome, U.S.A. 80 D5 43 16N 99 43W
Colón, Argentina 94 C4 32 12S 58 10W
Colón, Cuba 88 B3 22 42N 80 54W
Colón, Panama 88 E4 9 20N 79 54W
Colona, Australia 61 F5 31 38S 132 4 E
Colonia, Uruguay 94 C4 34 25S 57 50W
Colonia de San Jordi, Spain 22 B9 39 19N 2 59 E
Colonia Dora, Argentina 94 B3 28 34S 62 59W
Colonial Heights, U.S.A. 76 G7 37 15N 77 25W
Colonsay, Canada 73 C7 51 59N 105 52W
Colonsay, U.K. 12 E2 56 4N 6 12W
Colorado □, U.S.A. 83 G10 39 30N 105 30W
Colorado →, Argentina 96 D4 39 50S 62 8W
Colorado →, N. Amer. 83 L6 31 45N 114 40W
Colorado →, U.S.A. 81 L7 28 36N 95 59W
Colorado City, U.S.A. 81 J4 32 24N 100 52W
Colorado Desert, U.S.A. 74 D3 34 20N 116 0W
Colorado Plateau, U.S.A. 83 H8 37 0N 111 0W
Colorado River Aqueduct, U.S.A. 85 L12 34 17N 114 10W
Colorado Springs, U.S.A. 80 F2 38 50N 104 49W
Colotlán, Mexico 86 C4 22 6N 103 16W
Colton, Calif., U.S.A. 85 L9 34 4N 117 20W
Colton, N.Y., U.S.A. 79 B10 44 33N 74 56W
Colton, Wash., U.S.A. 82 C5 46 34N 117 8W
Columbia, La., U.S.A. 81 J8 32 6N 92 5W
Columbia, Miss., U.S.A. 81 K10 31 15N 89 50W
Columbia, Mo., U.S.A. 80 F8 38 57N 92 20W
Columbia, Pa., U.S.A. 79 F8 40 2N 76 30W
Columbia, S.C., U.S.A. 77 H5 34 0N 81 2W
Columbia, Tenn., U.S.A. 77 H2 35 37N 87 2W
Columbia →, U.S.A. 82 C1 46 15N 124 5W
Columbia, C., Canada 4 A4 83 0N 70 0W
Columbia, District of □, U.S.A. 76 F7 38 55N 77 0W
Columbia, Mt., Canada 72 C5 52 8N 117 20W
Columbia Basin, U.S.A. 82 C4 46 45N 119 5W
Columbia Falls, U.S.A. 82 B6 48 23N 114 11W
Columbia Heights, U.S.A. 80 C8 45 3N 93 15W
Columbiana, U.S.A. 78 F4 40 53N 80 42W
Columbretes, Is., Spain 19 C6 39 50N 0 50 E
Columbus, Ga., U.S.A. 77 J3 32 28N 84 59W
Columbus, Ind., U.S.A. 76 F3 39 13N 85 55W
Columbus, Kans., U.S.A. 81 G7 37 10N 94 50W
Columbus, Miss., U.S.A. 77 J1 33 30N 88 25W
Columbus, Mont., U.S.A. 82 D9 45 38N 109 15W
Columbus, N. Dak., U.S.A. 80 A3 48 54N 102 47W
Columbus, N. Mex., U.S.A. 83 L10 31 50N 107 38W
Columbus, Nebr., U.S.A. 80 E6 41 26N 97 22W
Columbus, Ohio, U.S.A. 76 F4 39 58N 83 0W
Columbus, Tex., U.S.A. 81 L6 29 42N 96 33W
Columbus, Wis., U.S.A. 80 D10 43 21N 89 1W
Colusa, U.S.A. 84 F4 39 13N 122 1W
Colville, U.S.A. 82 B5 48 33N 117 54W
Colville →, U.S.A. 68 A4 70 25N 150 30W
Colville, C., N.Z. 59 G5 36 29S 175 21 E
Colwyn Bay, U.K. 10 D4 53 17N 3 44W
Comácchio, Italy 20 B5 44 41N 12 10 E
Comalcalco, Mexico 87 D6 18 16N 93 13W
Comallo, Argentina 96 E2 41 0S 70 5W
Comanche, Okla., U.S.A. 81 H6 34 22N 97 58W
Comanche, Tex., U.S.A. 81 K5 31 54N 98 36W
Comayagua, Honduras 88 D2 14 25N 87 37W
Combahee →, U.S.A. 77 J5 32 30N 80 31W
Comber, Canada 78 D2 42 14N 82 33W
Comblain-au-Pont, Belgium 15 D5 50 29N 5 35 E
Comeragh Mts., Ireland 13 D4 52 17N 7 35W
Comet, Australia 62 C4 23 36S 148 38 E
Comilla, Bangla. 41 H17 23 28N 91 10 E
Comino, Malta 23 C1 36 2N 14 20 E
Comitán, Mexico 87 D6 16 18N 92 9W
Commerce, Ga., U.S.A. 77 H4 34 12N 83 28W
Commerce, Tex., U.S.A. 81 J7 33 15N 95 54W
Committee B., Canada 69 B11 68 30N 86 30W
Commonwealth B., Antarctica 5 C10 67 0S 144 0 E
Commonwealth of Independent States ■, Eurasia 27 D11 60 0N 100 0 E
Commoron Cr. →, Australia 63 D5 28 22S 150 8 E
Communism Pk. = Kommunizma, Pik, Tajikistan 26 F8 39 0N 72 2 E
Como, Italy 20 B3 45 48N 9 5 E
Como, L. di, Italy 20 A3 46 5N 9 17 E
Comodoro Rivadavia, Argentina 96 F3 45 50S 67 40W
Comorin, C., India 40 Q10 8 3N 77 40 E
Comoro Is. = Comoros ■, Ind. Oc. 49 H8 12 10S 44 15 E
Comoros ■, Ind. Oc. 49 H8 12 10S 44 15 E
Comox, Canada 72 D4 49 42N 124 55W
Compiègne, France 18 B5 49 24N 2 50 E
Compostela, Mexico 86 C4 21 15N 104 53W
Comprida, I., Brazil 95 A6 24 50S 47 42W
Compton, U.S.A. 85 M8 33 54N 118 13W
Compton Downs, Australia 63 E4 30 28S 146 30 E
Con Cuong, Vietnam 38 C5 19 2N 104 54 E
Con Son, Is., Vietnam 39 H6 8 41N 106 37 E
Conakry, Guinea 50 G2 9 29N 13 49W
Conara Junction, Australia 62 G4 41 50S 147 26 E
Concarneau, France 18 C2 47 52N 3 56W
Conceição, Mozam. 55 F4 18 47S 36 7 E
Conceição da Barra, Brazil 93 G11 18 35S 39 45W
Conceição do Araguaia, Brazil 93 E9 8 0S 49 2W
Concepción, Argentina 94 B2 27 20S 65 35W
Concepción, Bolivia 92 G6 16 15S 62 8W
Concepción, Chile 94 D1 36 50S 73 0W
Concepción, Mexico 87 D6 18 15N 90 5W
Concepción, Paraguay 94 A4 23 22S 57 26W
Concepción □, Chile 94 D1 37 0S 72 30W
Concepción →, Mexico 86 A2 30 32N 113 2W
Concepción, L., Bolivia 92 G6 17 20S 61 20W
Concepción, Punta, Mexico 86 B2 26 55N 111 59W
Concepción del Oro, Mexico 86 C4 24 40N 101 30W
Concepción del Uruguay, Argentina 94 C4 32 35S 58 20W
Conception, Pt., U.S.A. 85 L6 34 27N 120 28W
Conception B., Namibia 56 C1 23 55S 14 22 E
Conception I., Bahamas 89 B4 23 52N 75 9W
Concession, Zimbabwe 55 F3 17 27S 30 56 E
Conchas Dam, U.S.A. 81 H2 35 22N 104 11W
Conche, Canada 71 B8 50 55N 55 58W
Concho, U.S.A. 83 J9 34 28N 109 36W
Concho →, U.S.A. 81 K5 31 34N 99 43W
Conchos →, Chihuahua, Mexico 86 B4 29 32N 105 0W
Conchos →, Tamaulipas, Mexico 87 B5 25 9N 98 35W
Concord, Calif., U.S.A. 84 H4 37 59N 122 2W
Concord, N.C., U.S.A. 77 H5 35 25N 80 35W
Concord, N.H., U.S.A. 79 C13 43 12N 71 32W
Concordia, Argentina 94 C4 31 20S 58 2W
Concórdia, Brazil 92 D5 4 36S 66 36W
Concordia, Mexico 86 C3 23 18N 106 2W
Concordia, U.S.A. 80 F6 39 34N 97 40W
Concrete, U.S.A. 82 B3 48 32N 121 45W
Condamine, Australia 63 D5 26 56S 150 9 E
Conde, U.S.A. 80 C5 45 9N 98 6W
Condeúba, Brazil 93 F10 14 52S 42 0W
Condobolin, Australia 63 E4 33 4S 147 6 E
Condon, U.S.A. 82 D3 45 14N 120 11W
Conejera, I., Spain 22 B9 39 11N 2 58 E
Conejos, Mexico 86 B4 26 14N 103 53W
Confuso →, Paraguay 94 B4 25 9S 57 34W
Congleton, U.K. 10 D5 53 10N 2 12W
Congo = Zaïre →, Africa 52 F2 6 4S 12 24 E
Congo (Kinshasa) = Zaïre ■, Africa 52 E4 3 0S 23 0 E
Congo ■, Africa 52 E3 1 0S 16 0 E
Congo Basin, Africa 48 G6 0 10S 24 30 E
Congonhas, Brazil 95 A7 20 30S 43 52W
Congress, U.S.A. 83 J7 34 9N 112 51W
Coniston, Canada 70 C3 46 29N 80 51W
Conjeeveram = Kanchipuram, India 40 N11 12 52N 79 45 E
Conjuboy, Australia 62 B3 18 35S 144 35 E
Conklin, Canada 73 B6 55 38N 111 5W
Conlea, Australia 63 E3 30 7S 144 35 E
Conn, L., Ireland 13 B2 54 3N 9 15W
Connacht, Ireland 13 C3 53 23N 8 40W
Conneaut, U.S.A. 78 E4 41 57N 80 34W
Connecticut □, U.S.A. 79 E12 41 30N 72 45W
Connecticut →, U.S.A. 79 E12 41 16N 72 20W
Connell, U.S.A. 82 C4 46 40N 118 52W
Connellsville, U.S.A. 78 F5 40 1N 79 35W
Connemara, Ireland 13 C2 53 29N 9 45W
Connemaugh →, U.S.A. 78 F5 40 28N 79 19W
Connersville, U.S.A. 76 F3 39 39N 85 8W
Connors Ra., Australia 62 C4 21 40S 149 10 E
Conoble, Australia 63 E3 32 55S 144 33 E
Cononaco →, Ecuador 92 D3 1 32S 75 35W
Cononbridge, U.K. 12 D4 57 32N 4 30W
Conquest, Canada 73 C7 51 32N 107 14W
Conrad, U.S.A. 82 B8 48 10N 111 57W
Conran, C., Australia 63 F4 37 49S 148 44 E
Conroe, U.S.A. 81 K7 30 19N 95 27W
Conselheiro Lafaiete, Brazil 95 A7 20 40S 43 48W
Consort, Canada 73 C6 52 1N 110 46W
Constance = Konstanz, Germany 16 E4 47 39N 9 10 E
Constance, L. = Bodensee, Europe 16 E4 47 35N 9 25 E
Constanța, Romania 21 B13 44 14N 28 38 E
Constantina, Spain 19 D3 37 51N 5 40W
Constantine, Algeria 50 A6 36 25N 6 42 E
Constitución, Chile 94 D1 35 20S 72 30W
Constitución, Uruguay 94 C4 31 0S 57 50W
Consul, Canada 73 D7 49 20N 109 30W
Contact, U.S.A. 82 F6 41 46N 114 45W
Contai, India 43 J12 21 54N 87 46 E
Contamana, Peru 92 E4 7 19S 74 55W
Contas →, Brazil 93 F11 14 17S 39 1W
Contoocook, U.S.A. 79 C13 43 13N 71 45W
Contra Costa, Mozam. 57 D5 25 9S 33 30 E
Conway = Conwy, U.K. 10 D4 53 17N 3 50W
Conway = Conwy →, U.K. 10 D4 53 18N 3 50W
Conway, Ark., U.S.A. 81 H8 35 5N 92 26W
Conway, N.H., U.S.A. 79 C13 43 59N 71 7W
Conway, S.C., U.S.A. 77 J6 33 51N 79 3W
Conway, L., Australia 63 D2 28 17S 135 35 E
Conwy, U.K. 10 D4 53 17N 3 50W
Conwy →, U.K. 10 D4 53 18N 3 50W
Coober Pedy, Australia 63 D1 29 1S 134 43 E
Cooch Behar = Koch Bihar, India 41 F16 26 22N 89 29 E
Coodardy, Australia 51 E2 27 15S 117 39 E
Cook, Australia 61 F5 30 37S 130 25 E
Cook, U.S.A. 80 B8 47 49N 92 39W
Cook, B., Chile 96 H3 55 10S 70 0W
Cook, Mt., N.Z. 59 K3 43 36S 170 9 E
Cook Inlet, U.S.A. 68 C4 60 0N 152 0W
Cook Is., Pac. Oc. 65 J11 17 0S 160 0W
Cook Strait, N.Z. 59 J5 41 15S 174 29 E
Cookeville, U.S.A. 77 G3 36 10N 85 30W
Cookhouse, S. Africa 56 E4 32 44S 25 47 E
Cookshire, Canada 79 A13 45 25N 71 38W
Cookstown, U.K. 13 B5 54 40N 6 43W
Cookstown □, U.K. 13 B5 54 40N 6 43W
Cooksville, Canada 78 C5 43 36N 79 35W
Cooktown, Australia 62 B4 15 30S 145 16 E
Coolabah, Australia 63 E4 31 1S 146 43 E
Cooladdi, Australia 63 D4 26 37S 145 23 E
Coolah, Australia 63 E4 31 48S 149 41 E
Coolamon, Australia 63 E4 34 46S 147 8 E
Coolangatta, Australia 63 D5 28 11S 153 29 E
Coolgardie, Australia 61 F3 30 55S 121 8 E
Coolibah, Australia 60 C5 15 33S 130 56 E
Coolidge, U.S.A. 83 K8 32 59N 111 31W
Coolidge Dam, U.S.A. 83 K8 33 0N 110 20W
Cooma, Australia 63 F4 36 12S 149 8 E
Coonabarabran, Australia 63 E4 31 14S 149 18 E
Coonamble, Australia 63 E4 30 56S 148 27 E
Coonana, Australia 61 F3 31 0S 123 0 E
Coondapoor, India 40 N9 13 42N 74 40 E
Coongie, Australia 63 D3 27 9S 140 8 E
Coongoola, Australia 63 D4 27 43S 145 51 E
Cooninie, L., Australia 63 D2 26 4S 139 59 E
Cooper, U.S.A. 81 J7 33 23N 95 42W
Cooper →, U.S.A. 77 J6 32 50N 79 56W
Cooper Cr. →, Australia 63 D2 28 29S 137 46 E

Cooperstown

Cooperstown, N. Dak., U.S.A. **80 B5** 47 27N 98 8W
Cooperstown, N.Y., U.S.A. **79 D10** 42 42N 74 56W
Coorabie, Australia **61 F5** 31 54S 132 18 E
Coorabulka, Australia **62 C3** 23 41S 140 20 E
Coorow, Australia **61 E2** 29 53S 116 2 E
Cooroy, Australia **63 D5** 26 22S 152 54 E
Coos Bay, U.S.A. **82 E1** 43 22N 124 13W
Cootamundra, Australia **63 E4** 34 36S 148 1 E
Cootehill, Ireland **13 B4** 54 5N 7 5W
Cooyar, Australia **63 D5** 26 59S 151 51 E
Cooyeana, Australia **62 C2** 24 29S 138 45 E
Copahue Paso, Argentina **94 D1** 37 49S 71 8W
Copainalá, Mexico **87 D6** 17 8N 93 11W
Copán, Honduras **88 D2** 14 50N 89 9W
Cope, U.S.A. **80 F3** 39 40N 102 51W
Copenhagen = København, Denmark **9 J12** 55 41N 12 34 E
Copiapó, Chile **94 B1** 27 30S 70 20W
Copiapó →, Chile **94 B1** 27 19S 70 56W
Copley, Australia **63 E2** 30 36S 138 26 E
Copp L., Canada **72 A6** 60 14N 114 40W
Copper Center, U.S.A. **68 B5** 61 58N 145 18W
Copper Cliff, Canada **70 C3** 46 28N 81 4W
Copper Harbor, U.S.A. **76 B2** 47 28N 87 53W
Copper Queen, Zimbabwe **55 F2** 17 29S 29 18 E
Copperbelt □, Zambia **55 E2** 13 15S 27 30 E
Coppermine, Canada **68 B8** 67 50N 115 5W
Coppermine →, Canada **68 B8** 67 49N 116 4W
Copperopolis, U.S.A. **84 H6** 37 58N 120 38W
Coquet →, U.K. **10 B6** 55 18N 1 45W
Coquilhatville = Mbandaka, Zaïre **52 D3** 0 1N 18 18 E
Coquille, U.S.A. **82 E1** 43 11N 124 11W
Coquimbo, Chile **94 B1** 30 0S 71 20W
Coquimbo □, Chile **94 C1** 31 0S 71 0W
Corabia, Romania **17 G12** 43 48N 24 30 E
Coracora, Peru **92 G4** 15 5S 73 45W
Coral Gables, U.S.A. **77 N5** 25 45N 80 16W
Coral Harbour, Canada **69 B11** 64 8N 83 10W
Coral Sea, Pac. Oc. **64 J7** 15 0S 150 0 E
Coraopolis, U.S.A. **78 F4** 40 31N 80 10W
Corato, Italy **20 D7** 41 12N 16 22 E
Corbin, U.S.A. **76 G3** 36 57N 84 6W
Corby, U.K. **11 E7** 52 29N 0 41W
Corby Glen, U.K. **11 E7** 52 49N 0 31W
Corcoran, U.S.A. **83 H4** 36 6N 119 33W
Corcubión, Spain **19 A1** 42 56N 9 12W
Cordele, U.S.A. **77 K4** 31 58N 83 47W
Cordell, U.S.A. **81 H5** 35 17N 98 59W
Córdoba, Argentina **94 C3** 31 20S 64 10W
Córdoba, Mexico **87 D5** 18 50N 97 0W
Córdoba, Spain **19 D3** 37 50N 4 50W
Córdoba □, Argentina **94 C3** 31 22S 64 15W
Córdoba, Sierra de, Argentina **94 C3** 31 10S 64 25W
Cordon, Phil. **37 A6** 16 42N 121 32 E
Cordova, Ala., U.S.A. **77 J2** 33 46N 87 11W
Cordova, Alaska, U.S.A. **68 B5** 60 33N 145 45W
Corella →, Australia **62 B3** 19 34S 140 47 E
Corfield, Australia **62 C3** 21 40S 143 21 E
Corfu = Kérkira, Greece **23 A3** 39 38N 19 50 E
Corfu, Str of, Greece **23 A4** 39 34N 20 0 E
Corigliano Cálabro, Italy **20 E7** 39 36N 16 31 E
Coringa Is., Australia **62 B4** 16 58S 149 58 E
Corinna, Australia **62 G4** 41 35S 145 10 E
Corinth = Kórinthos, Greece **21 F10** 37 56N 22 55 E
Corinth, Miss., U.S.A. **77 H1** 34 56N 88 31W
Corinth, N.Y., U.S.A. **79 C11** 43 15N 73 49W
Corinth, G. of = Korinthiakós Kólpos, Greece **21 E10** 38 16N 22 30 E
Corinto, Brazil **93 G10** 18 20S 44 30W
Corinto, Nic. **88 D2** 12 30N 87 10W
Cork, Ireland **13 E3** 51 54N 8 30W
Cork □, Ireland **13 E3** 51 50N 8 50W
Cork Harbour, Ireland **13 E3** 51 46N 8 16W
Cormack L., Canada **72 A4** 60 56N 121 37W
Cormorant, Canada **73 C8** 54 14N 100 35W
Cormorant L., Canada **73 C8** 54 15N 100 50W
Corn Is. = Maiz, Is. del, Nic. **88 D3** 12 15N 83 4W
Cornélio Procópio, Brazil **95 A5** 23 7S 50 40W
Cornell, U.S.A. **80 C9** 45 10N 91 9W
Corner Brook, Canada **71 C8** 48 57N 57 58W
Corning, Ark., U.S.A. **81 G9** 36 25N 90 35W
Corning, Calif., U.S.A. **82 G2** 39 56N 122 11W
Corning, Iowa, U.S.A. **80 E7** 40 59N 94 44W
Corning, N.Y., U.S.A. **78 D7** 42 9N 77 3W
Cornwall, Canada **70 C5** 45 2N 74 44W
Cornwall □, U.K. **11 G3** 50 26N 4 40W
Corny Pt., Australia **63 E2** 34 55S 137 0 E
Coro, Venezuela **92 A5** 11 25N 69 41W
Coroatá, Brazil **93 D10** 4 8S 44 0W
Corocoro, Bolivia **92 G5** 17 15S 68 28W
Coroico, Bolivia **92 G5** 16 0S 67 50W
Coromandel, N.Z. **59 G5** 36 45S 175 31 E
Coromandel Coast, India **40 N12** 12 30N 81 0 E
Corona, Australia **63 E3** 31 16S 141 24 E
Corona, Calif., U.S.A. **85 M9** 33 53N 117 34W
Corona, N. Mex., U.S.A. **83 J11** 34 15N 105 36W
Coronado, U.S.A. **85 N9** 32 41N 117 11W
Coronado, B. de, Costa Rica **88 E3** 9 0N 83 40W
Coronados, Is. los, U.S.A. **85 N9** 32 25N 117 15W
Coronation, Canada **72 C6** 52 5N 111 27W
Coronation Gulf, Canada **68 B8** 68 25N 110 0W
Coronation I., Antarctica **5 C18** 60 45S 46 0W
Coronation I., U.S.A. **72 B2** 55 52N 134 20W
Coronation Is., Australia **60 B3** 14 57S 124 55 E
Coronda, Argentina **94 C3** 31 58S 60 56W
Coronel, Chile **94 D1** 37 0S 73 10W
Coronel Bogado, Paraguay **94 B4** 27 11S 56 18W
Coronel Dorrego, Argentina **94 D3** 38 40S 61 10W
Coronel Oviedo, Paraguay **94 B4** 25 24S 56 30W
Coronel Pringles, Argentina **94 D3** 38 0S 61 30W
Coronel Suárez, Argentina **94 D3** 37 30S 61 52W
Coronel Vidal, Argentina **94 D4** 37 28S 57 45W
Corowa, Australia **63 F4** 35 58S 146 21 E
Corozal, Belize **87 D7** 18 23N 88 23W
Corpus, Argentina **95 B4** 27 10S 55 30W
Corpus Christi, U.S.A. **81 M6** 27 47N 97 24W
Corpus Christi, L., U.S.A. **81 L6** 28 2N 97 52W
Corque, Bolivia **92 G5** 18 20S 67 41W
Corralejo, Canary Is. **22 F6** 28 43N 13 53W
Correntes, C. das, Mozam. **57 C6** 24 6S 35 34 E
Corrèze □, France **18 D4** 45 20N 1 45 E
Corrib, L., Ireland **13 C2** 53 5N 9 10W
Corrientes, Argentina **94 B4** 27 30S 58 45W
Corrientes □, Argentina **94 B4** 28 0S 57 0W
Corrientes →, Argentina **94 C4** 30 42S 59 38W
Corrientes →, Peru **92 D4** 3 43S 74 35W
Corrientes, C., Colombia **92 B3** 5 30N 77 34W
Corrientes, C., Cuba **88 B3** 21 43N 84 30W
Corrientes, C., Mexico **86 C3** 20 25N 105 42W
Corrigan, U.S.A. **81 K7** 31 0N 94 52W
Corrigin, Australia **61 F2** 32 20S 117 53 E
Corry, U.S.A. **78 E5** 41 55N 79 39W
Corse, France **18 F9** 42 0N 9 0 E
Corse, C., France **20 C3** 43 1N 9 25 E
Corse-du-Sud □, France **18 F9** 41 45N 9 0 E
Corsica = Corse, France **18 F9** 42 0N 9 0 E
Corsicana, U.S.A. **81 J6** 32 6N 96 28W
Cortez, U.S.A. **83 H9** 37 21N 108 35W
Cortland, U.S.A. **79 D8** 42 36N 76 11W
Cortona, Italy **20 C4** 43 16N 12 0 E
Çorum, Turkey **25 F5** 40 30N 34 57 E
Corumbá, Brazil **92 G7** 19 0S 57 30W
Corumbá de Goiás, Brazil **93 G9** 16 0S 48 50W
Corunna = La Coruña, Spain **19 A1** 43 20N 8 25W
Corvallis, U.S.A. **82 D2** 44 34N 123 16W
Corvette, L. de la, Canada **70 B5** 53 25N 74 3W
Corydon, U.S.A. **80 E8** 40 46N 93 19W
Cosalá, Mexico **86 C3** 24 28N 106 40W
Cosamaloapan, Mexico **87 D5** 18 23N 95 50W
Cosenza, Italy **20 E7** 39 17N 16 14 E
Coshocton, U.S.A. **78 F3** 40 16N 81 51W
Cosmo Newberry, Australia **61 E3** 28 0S 122 54 E
Coso Junction, U.S.A. **85 J9** 36 3N 117 57W
Coso Pk., U.S.A. **85 J9** 36 13N 117 44W
Cosquín, Argentina **94 C3** 31 15S 64 30W
Costa Blanca, Spain **19 C5** 38 25N 0 10W
Costa Brava, Spain **19 B7** 41 30N 3 0 E
Costa del Sol, Spain **19 D3** 36 30N 4 30W
Costa Dorada, Spain **19 B6** 40 45N 1 15 E
Costa Mesa, U.S.A. **85 M9** 33 38N 117 55W
Costa Rica ■, Cent. Amer. **88 D3** 10 0N 84 0W
Costilla, U.S.A. **83 H11** 36 59N 105 32W
Cosumnes →, U.S.A. **84 G5** 38 16N 121 26W
Cotabato, Phil. **37 C6** 7 14N 124 15 E
Cotagaita, Bolivia **94 A2** 20 45S 65 40W
Côte-d'Ivoire ■ = Ivory Coast ■, Africa **50 G3** 7 30N 5 0W
Côte-d'Or □, France **18 C6** 47 30N 4 50 E
Coteau des Prairies, U.S.A. **80 C6** 45 20N 97 50W
Coteau du Missouri, U.S.A. **80 B4** 47 0N 100 0W
Coteau Landing, Canada **79 A10** 45 15N 74 13W
Cotentin, France **18 B3** 49 15N 1 30W
Côtes-d'Armor □, France **18 B2** 48 25N 2 40W
Côtes-du-Nord = Côtes-d'Armor □, France **18 B2** 48 25N 2 40W
Cotillo, Canary Is. **22 F5** 28 41N 14 1W
Cotonou, Benin **50 G5** 6 20N 2 25 E
Cotopaxi, Ecuador **92 D3** 0 40S 78 30W
Cotswold Hills, U.K. **11 F5** 51 42N 2 10W
Cottage Grove, U.S.A. **82 E2** 43 48N 123 3W
Cottbus, Germany **16 C7** 51 44N 14 20 E
Cottingham, U.K. **10 C5** 53 47N 0 23W
Cottonwood, U.S.A. **83 J7** 34 45N 112 1W
Cotulla, U.S.A. **81 L5** 28 26N 99 14W
Coudersport, U.S.A. **78 E6** 41 46N 78 1W
Couedic, C. du, Australia **63 F2** 36 5S 136 40 E
Coulee City, U.S.A. **82 C4** 47 37N 119 17W
Coulman I., Antarctica **5 D11** 73 35S 170 0 E
Coulonge →, Canada **70 C4** 45 52N 76 46W
Coulterville, U.S.A. **84 H6** 37 43N 120 12W
Council, Alaska, U.S.A. **68 B3** 64 55N 163 45W
Council, Idaho, U.S.A. **82 D5** 44 44N 116 26W
Council Bluffs, U.S.A. **80 E7** 41 16N 95 52W
Council Grove, U.S.A. **80 F6** 38 40N 96 29W
Coupeville, U.S.A. **84 B4** 48 13N 122 41W
Courantyne →, S. Amer. **92 B7** 5 55N 57 5W
Courtenay, Canada **72 D3** 49 45N 125 0W
Courtland, U.S.A. **84 G5** 38 20N 121 34W
Courtrai = Kortrijk, Belgium **15 D3** 50 50N 3 17 E
Courtright, Canada **78 D2** 42 49N 82 28W
Coushatta, U.S.A. **81 J8** 32 1N 93 21W
Coutts, Canada **72 D6** 49 0N 111 57W
Coventry, U.K. **11 E6** 52 25N 1 31W
Coventry L., Canada **73 A7** 61 15N 106 15W
Covilhã, Portugal **19 B2** 40 17N 7 31W
Covington, Ga., U.S.A. **77 J4** 33 36N 83 51W
Covington, Ky., U.S.A. **76 F3** 39 5N 84 31W
Covington, Okla., U.S.A. **81 G6** 36 18N 97 35W
Covington, Tenn., U.S.A. **81 H10** 35 34N 89 39W
Cowal, L., Australia **63 E4** 33 40S 147 25 E
Cowan, Canada **73 C8** 52 5N 100 45W
Cowan, L., Australia **61 F3** 31 45S 121 45 E
Cowan L., Canada **73 C7** 54 0N 107 15W
Cowangie, Australia **63 F3** 35 12S 141 26 E
Cowansville, Canada **79 A12** 45 14N 72 46W
Cowarie, Australia **63 D2** 27 45S 138 15 E
Cowcowing Lakes, Australia **61 F2** 30 55S 117 20 E
Cowdenbeath, U.K. **12 E5** 56 7N 3 20W
Cowell, Australia **63 E2** 33 39S 136 56 E
Cowes, U.K. **11 G6** 50 45N 1 18W
Cowlitz →, U.S.A. **84 D4** 46 6N 122 55W
Cowra, Australia **63 E4** 33 49S 148 42 E
Coxilha Grande, Brazil **95 B5** 28 18S 51 30W
Coxim, Brazil **93 G8** 18 30S 54 55W
Cox's Bazar, Bangla. **41 J17** 21 26N 91 59 E
Cox's Cove, Canada **71 C8** 49 7N 58 5W
Coyame, Mexico **86 B3** 29 28N 105 6W
Coyote Wells, U.S.A. **85 N11** 32 44N 115 58W
Coyuca de Benítez, Mexico **87 D4** 17 1N 100 8W
Coyuca de Catalan, Mexico **86 D4** 18 18N 100 41W
Cozad, U.S.A. **80 E5** 40 52N 99 59W
Cozumel, Mexico **87 C7** 20 31N 86 55W
Cozumel, I. de, Mexico **87 C7** 20 30N 86 40W
Craboon, Australia **63 E4** 32 3S 149 30 E
Cracow = Kraków, Poland **17 C9** 50 4N 19 57 E
Cracow, Australia **63 D5** 25 17S 150 17 E
Cradock, S. Africa **56 E4** 32 8S 25 36 E
Craig, Alaska, U.S.A. **72 B2** 55 29N 133 9W
Craig, Colo., U.S.A. **82 F10** 40 31N 107 33W
Craigavon = Lurgan, U.K. **13 B5** 54 28N 6 20W
Craigmore, Zimbabwe **55 G3** 20 28S 32 50 E
Craiova, Romania **21 B10** 44 21N 23 48 E
Cramsie, Australia **62 C3** 23 20S 144 15 E
Cranberry Portage, Canada **73 C8** 54 35N 101 23W
Cranbrook, Tas., Australia **62 G4** 42 0S 148 5 E
Cranbrook, W. Austral., Australia **61 F2** 34 18S 117 33 E
Cranbrook, Canada **72 D5** 49 30N 115 46W
Crandon, U.S.A. **80 C10** 45 34N 88 54W
Crane, Oreg., U.S.A. **82 E4** 43 25N 118 35W
Crane, Tex., U.S.A. **81 K3** 31 24N 102 21W
Cranston, U.S.A. **79 E13** 41 47N 71 26W
Crater L., U.S.A. **82 E2** 42 56N 122 6W
Crateús, Brazil **93 E10** 5 10S 40 39W
Crato, Brazil **93 E11** 7 10S 39 25W
Crawford, U.S.A. **80 D3** 42 41N 103 25W
Crawfordsville, U.S.A. **76 E2** 40 2N 86 54W
Crawley, U.K. **11 F7** 51 7N 0 10W
Crazy Mts., U.S.A. **82 C8** 46 12N 110 20W
Crean L., Canada **73 C7** 54 5N 106 9W
Crécy-en-Ponthieu, France **18 A4** 50 15N 1 53 E
Crediton, Canada **78 C3** 43 17N 81 33W
Credo, Australia **61 F3** 30 28S 120 45 E
Cree →, Canada **73 B7** 58 57N 105 47W
Cree →, U.K. **12 G4** 54 51N 4 24W
Cree L., Canada **73 B7** 57 30N 106 30W
Creede, U.S.A. **83 H10** 37 51N 106 56W
Creel, Mexico **86 B3** 27 45N 107 38W
Creighton, U.S.A. **80 D6** 42 28N 97 54W
Cremona, Italy **20 B4** 45 8N 10 2 E
Cres, Croatia **20 B6** 44 58N 14 25 E
Cresbard, U.S.A. **80 C5** 45 10N 98 57W
Crescent, Okla., U.S.A. **81 H6** 35 57N 97 36W
Crescent, Oreg., U.S.A. **82 E3** 43 28N 121 42W
Crescent City, U.S.A. **82 F1** 41 45N 124 12W
Crespo, Argentina **94 C3** 32 2S 60 19W
Cressy, Australia **63 F3** 38 2S 143 40 E
Crested Butte, U.S.A. **83 G10** 38 52N 106 59W
Crestline, Calif., U.S.A. **85 L9** 34 14N 117 18W
Crestline, Ohio, U.S.A. **78 F2** 40 47N 82 44W
Creston, Canada **72 D5** 49 10N 116 31W
Creston, Calif., U.S.A. **84 K6** 35 32N 120 33W
Creston, Iowa, U.S.A. **80 E7** 41 4N 94 22W
Creston, Wash., U.S.A. **82 C4** 47 46N 118 31W
Crestview, Calif., U.S.A. **84 H8** 37 46N 118 58W
Crestview, Fla., U.S.A. **77 K2** 30 46N 86 34W
Crete = Kríti, Greece **23 D7** 35 15N 25 0 E
Crete, U.S.A. **80 E6** 40 38N 96 58W
Creus, C., Spain **19 A7** 42 20N 3 19 E
Creuse □, France **18 C5** 46 10N 2 0 E
Creuse →, France **18 C4** 47 0N 0 34 E
Crewe, U.K. **10 D5** 53 6N 2 28W
Criciúma, Brazil **95 B6** 28 40S 49 23W
Crieff, U.K. **12 E5** 56 22N 3 50W
Crimea = Krymskiy Poluostrov, Ukraine **25 E5** 45 0N 34 0 E
Crişul Alb →, Romania **17 E10** 46 42N 21 17 E
Crişul Negru →, Romania **17 E10** 46 42N 21 16 E
Crna Gora = Montenegro □, Montenegro, Yug. **21 C8** 42 40N 19 20 E
Crna Gora, Serbia **21 C9** 42 10N 21 30 E
Crna Reka →, Macedonia **21 D9** 41 33N 21 59 E
Croagh Patrick, Ireland **13 C2** 53 46N 9 40W
Croatia ■, Europe **20 B7** 45 20N 16 0 E
Crocker, Banjaran, Malaysia **36 C5** 5 40N 116 30 E
Crockett, U.S.A. **81 K7** 31 19N 95 27W
Crocodile = Krokodil →, Mozam. **57 D5** 25 14S 32 18 E
Crocodile Is., Australia **62 A1** 12 3S 134 58 E
Croix, L. La, Canada **70 C1** 48 20N 92 15W
Croker, C., Australia **60 B5** 10 58S 132 35 E
Croker I., Australia **60 B5** 11 12S 132 32 E
Cromarty, Canada **73 B10** 58 3N 94 9W
Cromarty, U.K. **12 D4** 57 40N 4 2W
Cromer, U.K. **10 E9** 52 56N 1 18 E
Cromwell, N.Z. **59 L2** 45 3S 169 14 E
Cronulla, Australia **63 E5** 34 3S 151 8 E
Crooked →, Canada **72 C4** 54 50N 122 54W
Crooked →, U.S.A. **82 D3** 44 32N 121 16W
Crooked I., Bahamas **89 B5** 22 50N 74 10W
Crooked Island Passage, Bahamas **89 B5** 23 0N 74 30W
Crookston, Minn., U.S.A. **80 B6** 47 47N 96 37W
Crookston, Nebr., U.S.A. **80 D4** 42 56N 100 45W
Crooksville, U.S.A. **76 F4** 39 46N 82 6W
Crookwell, Australia **63 E4** 34 28S 149 24 E
Crosby, Minn., U.S.A. **80 B8** 46 29N 93 58W
Crosby, N. Dak., U.S.A. **73 D8** 48 55N 103 18W
Crosby, Pa., U.S.A. **78 E6** 41 45N 78 23W
Crosbyton, U.S.A. **81 J4** 33 40N 101 14W
Cross City, U.S.A. **77 L4** 29 38N 83 7W
Cross Fell, U.K. **10 C5** 54 44N 2 29W
Cross L., Canada **73 C9** 54 45N 97 30W
Cross Plains, U.S.A. **81 J5** 32 8N 99 11W
Cross Sound, U.S.A. **68 C6** 58 0N 135 0W
Crossett, U.S.A. **81 J9** 33 8N 91 58W
Crossfield, Canada **72 C6** 51 25N 114 0W
Crosshaven, Ireland **13 E3** 51 48N 8 19W
Croton-on-Hudson, U.S.A. **79 E11** 41 12N 73 55W
Crotone, Italy **20 E7** 39 5N 17 6 E
Crow →, Canada **72 B4** 59 41N 124 20W
Crow Agency, U.S.A. **82 D10** 45 36N 107 28W
Crow Hd., Ireland **13 E1** 51 34N 10 9W
Crowell, U.S.A. **81 J5** 33 59N 99 43W
Crowley, U.S.A. **81 K8** 30 13N 92 22W
Crowley, L., U.S.A. **84 H8** 37 35N 118 42W
Crown Point, U.S.A. **76 E2** 41 25N 87 22W
Crows Landing, U.S.A. **84 H5** 37 23N 121 6W
Crows Nest, Australia **63 D5** 27 16S 152 4 E
Crowsnest Pass, Canada **72 D6** 49 40N 114 40W
Croydon, Australia **62 B3** 18 13S 142 14 E
Croydon, U.K. **11 F7** 51 18N 0 5W
Crozet Is., Ind. Oc. **3 G12** 46 27S 52 0 E
Cruz, C., Cuba **88 C4** 19 50N 77 50W
Cruz Alta, Brazil **95 B5** 28 45S 53 40W
Cruz del Eje, Argentina **94 C3** 30 45S 64 50W
Cruzeiro, Brazil **95 A7** 22 33S 45 0W
Cruzeiro do Oeste, Brazil **95 A5** 23 46S 53 4W
Cruzeiro do Sul, Brazil **92 E4** 7 35S 72 35W
Cry L., Canada **72 B3** 58 45N 129 0W
Crystal Bay, U.S.A. **84 F7** 39 15N 120 0W
Crystal Brook, Australia **63 E2** 33 21S 138 12 E
Crystal City, Mo., U.S.A. **80 F9** 38 13N 90 23W
Crystal City, Tex., U.S.A. **81 L5** 28 41N 99 50W
Crystal Falls, U.S.A. **76 B1** 46 5N 88 20W
Crystal River, U.S.A. **77 L4** 28 54N 82 35W
Crystal Springs, U.S.A. **81 K9** 31 59N 90 21W
Csongrád, Hungary **17 E10** 46 43N 20 12 E
Cu Lao Hon, Vietnam **39 G7** 10 54N 108 18 E
Cua Rao, Vietnam **38 C5** 19 16N 104 27 E
Cuácua →, Mozam. **55 F4** 17 54S 37 0 E
Cuamato, Angola **56 B2** 17 2S 15 7 E
Cuamba, Mozam. **55 E4** 14 45S 36 22 E
Cuando →, Angola **53 H4** 17 30S 23 15 E
Cuando Cubango □, Angola **56 B3** 16 25S 20 0 E
Cuangar, Angola **56 B2** 17 36S 18 39 E
Cuanza →, Angola **48 G5** 9 2S 13 30 E
Cuarto →, Argentina **94 C3** 33 25S 63 2W
Cuatrociénegas, Mexico **86 B4** 26 59N 102 5W
Cuauhtémoc, Mexico **86 B3** 28 25N 106 52W
Cuba, N. Mex., U.S.A. **83 J10** 36 1N 107 4W
Cuba, N.Y., U.S.A. **78 D6** 42 13N 78 17W
Cuba ■, W. Indies **88 B4** 22 0N 79 0W
Cuballing, Australia **61 F2** 32 50S 117 10 E
Cubango →, Africa **56 B3** 18 50S 22 25 E
Cucamonga, U.S.A. **85 L9** 34 10N 117 30W
Cuchi, Angola **53 G3** 14 37S 16 58 E
Cuchumatanes, Sierra de los, Guatemala **88 C1** 15 35N 91 25W
Cucurpe, Mexico **86 A2** 30 20N 110 43W
Cúcuta, Colombia **92 B4** 7 54N 72 31W
Cudahy, U.S.A. **76 D2** 42 58N 87 52W
Cuddalore, India **40 P11** 11 46N 79 45 E
Cuddapah, India **40 M11** 14 30N 78 47 E
Cuddapan, L., Australia **62 D3** 25 45S 141 26 E
Cudgewa, Australia **63 F4** 36 10S 147 42 E
Cue, Australia **61 E2** 27 25S 117 54 E
Cuenca, Ecuador **92 D3** 2 50S 79 9W
Cuenca, Spain **19 B4** 40 5N 2 10W
Cuenca, Serranía de, Spain **19 C5** 39 55N 1 50W
Cuernavaca, Mexico **87 D5** 18 50N 99 20W
Cuero, U.S.A. **81 L6** 29 6N 97 17W
Cuervo, U.S.A. **81 H2** 35 2N 104 25W
Cuevas del Almanzora, Spain **19 D5** 37 18N 1 58W
Cuevo, Bolivia **92 H6** 20 15S 63 30W
Cuiabá, Brazil **93 G7** 15 30S 56 0W
Cuiabá →, Brazil **93 G7** 17 5S 56 36W
Cuilco, Guatemala **88 C1** 15 24N 91 58W
Cuillin Hills, U.K. **12 D2** 57 14N 6 15W
Cuillin Sd., U.K. **12 D2** 57 4N 6 20W
Cuima, Angola **53 G3** 13 25S 15 45 E
Cuito →, Angola **56 B3** 18 1S 20 48 E
Cuitzeo, L. de, Mexico **86 D4** 19 55N 101 5W
Cukai, Malaysia **39 K4** 4 13N 103 25 E
Culbertson, U.S.A. **80 A2** 48 9N 104 31W
Culcairn, Australia **63 F4** 35 41S 147 3 E
Culebra, Sierra de la, Spain **19 B2** 41 55N 6 20W
Culgoa →, Australia **63 D4** 29 56S 146 20 E
Culiacán, Mexico **86 C3** 24 50N 107 23W
Culiacán →, Mexico **86 C3** 24 30N 107 42W
Culion, Phil. **37 B6** 11 54N 120 1 E
Cullarin Ra., Australia **63 E4** 34 30S 149 30 E
Cullen, U.K. **12 D6** 57 45N 2 50W
Cullen Pt., Australia **62 A3** 11 57S 141 54 E
Cullera, Spain **19 C5** 39 9N 0 17W
Cullman, U.S.A. **77 H2** 34 11N 86 51W
Culloden Moor, U.K. **12 D4** 57 29N 4 7W
Culpeper, U.S.A. **76 F7** 38 30N 78 0W
Culuene →, Brazil **93 F8** 12 56S 52 51W
Culver, Pt., Australia **61 F3** 32 54S 124 43 E
Culverden, N.Z. **59 K4** 42 47S 172 49 E
Cumaná, Venezuela **92 A6** 10 30N 64 5W
Cumberland, Canada **72 D3** 49 40N 125 0W
Cumberland, Md., U.S.A. **76 F6** 39 39N 78 46W
Cumberland, Wis., U.S.A. **80 C8** 45 32N 92 1W
Cumberland →, U.S.A. **77 G2** 36 15N 87 0W
Cumberland I., U.S.A. **77 K5** 30 50N 81 25W
Cumberland Is., Australia **62 C4** 20 35S 149 10 E
Cumberland L., Canada **73 C8** 54 3N 102 18W
Cumberland Pen., Canada **69 B13** 67 0N 64 0W
Cumberland Plateau, U.S.A. **77 H3** 36 0N 85 0W
Cumberland Sd., Canada **69 B13** 65 30N 66 0W
Cumborah, Australia **63 D4** 29 40S 147 45 E
Cumbria □, U.K. **10 C5** 54 35N 2 55W
Cumbrian Mts., U.K. **10 C4** 54 30N 3 0W
Cumbum, India **40 M11** 15 40N 79 10 E
Cummings Mt., U.S.A. **85 K8** 35 2N 118 34W
Cummins, Australia **63 E2** 34 16S 135 43 E
Cumnock, Australia **63 E4** 32 59S 148 46 E
Cumnock, U.K. **12 F4** 55 27N 4 18W
Cumpas, Mexico **86 A3** 30 0N 109 48W

Delaware

Cumplida, Pta., *Canary Is.* **22 F2** 28 50N 17 48W
Cuncumén, *Chile* **94 C1** 31 53S 70 38W
Cundeelee, *Australia* **61 F3** 30 43S 123 26 E
Cunderdin, *Australia* **61 F2** 31 37S 117 12 E
Cunene →, *Angola* **56 B1** 17 20S 11 50 E
Cúneo, *Italy* **20 B2** 44 23N 7 31 E
Cunillera, I., *Spain* **22 C7** 38 59N 1 13 E
Cunnamulla, *Australia* **63 D4** 28 2S 145 38 E
Cupar, *Canada* **73 C8** 50 57N 104 10W
Cupar, *U.K.* **12 E5** 56 20N 3 3W
Cupica, G. de, *Colombia* **92 B3** 6 25N 77 30W
Curaçao, *Neth. Ant.* **89 D6** 12 10N 69 0W
Curanilahue, *Chile* **94 D1** 37 29S 73 28W
Curaray →, *Peru* **92 D4** 2 20S 74 5W
Curepto, *Chile* **94 D1** 35 8S 72 1W
Curiapo, *Venezuela* **92 B6** 8 33N 61 5W
Curicó, *Chile* **94 C1** 34 55S 71 20W
Curicó □, *Chile* **94 C1** 34 50S 71 15W
Curitiba, *Brazil* **95 B6** 25 20S 49 10W
Currabubula, *Australia* **63 E5** 31 16S 150 44 E
Currais Novos, *Brazil* **93 E11** 6 13S 36 30W
Curralinho, *Brazil* **93 D9** 1 45S 49 46W
Currant, *U.S.A.* **82 G6** 38 51N 115 32W
Curraweena, *Australia* **63 E4** 30 47S 145 54 E
Currawilla, *Australia* **62 D3** 25 10S 141 20 E
Current →, *U.S.A.* **81 G9** 36 15N 90 55W
Currie, *Australia* **62 F3** 39 56S 143 53 E
Currie, *U.S.A.* **82 F6** 40 16N 114 45W
Currie, Mt., *S. Africa* **57 E4** 30 29S 29 21 E
Currituck Sd., *U.S.A.* **77 G8** 36 20N 75 52W
Curtis, *U.S.A.* **80 E4** 40 38N 100 31W
Curtis Group, *Australia* **62 F4** 39 30S 146 37 E
Curtis I., *Australia* **62 C5** 23 35S 151 10 E
Curuápanema →, *Brazil* **93 D7** 2 25S 55 2W
Curuçá, *Brazil* **93 D9** 0 43S 47 50W
Curuguaty, *Paraguay* **95 A4** 24 31S 55 42W
Çürüksu Çayi →, *Turkey* **25 G4** 37 27N 27 11 E
Curup, *Indonesia* **36 E2** 4 26S 102 13 E
Cururupu, *Brazil* **93 D10** 1 50S 44 50W
Curuzú Cuatiá, *Argentina* **94 B4** 29 50S 58 5W
Cushing, *U.S.A.* **81 H6** 35 59N 96 46W
Cushing, Mt., *Canada* **72 B3** 57 35N 126 57W
Cusihuiriáchic, *Mexico* **86 B3** 28 10N 106 50W
Custer, *U.S.A.* **80 D3** 43 46N 103 36W
Cut Bank, *U.S.A.* **82 B7** 48 38N 112 20W
Cuthbert, *U.S.A.* **77 K3** 31 46N 84 48W
Cutler, *U.S.A.* **84 J7** 36 31N 119 17W
Cuttaburra →, *Australia* **63 D3** 29 43S 144 22 E
Cuttack, *India* **41 J14** 20 25N 85 57 E
Cuvier, C., *Australia* **61 D1** 23 14S 113 22 E
Cuvier I., *N.Z.* **59 G5** 36 27S 175 50 E
Cuxhaven, *Germany* **16 B5** 53 51N 8 41 E
Cuyahoga Falls, *U.S.A.* **78 E3** 41 8N 81 29W
Cuyo, *Phil.* **37 B6** 10 50N 121 5 E
Cuzco, *Bolivia* **92 H5** 20 0S 66 50W
Cuzco, *Peru* **92 F4** 13 32S 72 0W
Cwmbran, *U.K.* **11 F4** 51 39N 3 3W
Cyangugu, *Rwanda* **54 C2** 2 29S 28 54 E
Cyclades = Kikládhes, *Greece* **21 F11** 37 20N 24 30 E
Cygnet, *Australia* **62 G4** 43 8S 147 1 E
Cynthiana, *U.S.A.* **76 F3** 38 23N 84 18W
Cypress Hills, *Canada* **73 D7** 49 40N 109 30W
Cyprus ■, *Asia* **23 E12** 35 0N 33 0 E
Cyrenaica, *Libya* **51 C9** 27 0N 23 0 E
Cyrene = Shaḥḥāt, *Libya* **51 B9** 32 48N 21 54 E
Czar, *Canada* **73 C6** 52 27N 110 50W
Czech Rep. ■, *Europe* **16 D7** 50 0N 15 0 E
Czeremcha, *Poland* **17 B11** 52 31N 23 21 E
Częstochowa, *Poland* **17 C9** 50 49N 19 7 E

D

Da →, *Vietnam* **38 B5** 21 15N 105 20 E
Da Hinggan Ling, *China* **33 B7** 48 0N 121 0 E
Da Lat, *Vietnam* **39 G7** 11 56N 108 25 E
Da Nang, *Vietnam* **38 D7** 16 4N 108 13 E
Da Qaidam, *China* **32 C4** 37 50N 95 15 E
Da Yunhe →, *China* **35 G11** 34 25N 120 5 E
Da'an, *China* **35 B13** 45 30N 124 7 E
Daba Shan, *China* **33 C5** 32 0N 109 0 E
Dabakala, *Ivory C.* **50 G4** 8 15N 4 20W
Dabhoi, *India* **42 H5** 22 10N 73 20 E
Dąbie, *Poland* **16 B7** 53 27N 14 45 E
Dabo, *Indonesia* **36 E2** 0 30S 104 33 E
Dabola, *Guinea* **50 F2** 10 50N 11 5W
Daboya, *Ghana* **50 G4** 9 30N 1 20W
Dabrowa Tarnówska, *Poland* **17 C10** 50 10N 20 59 E
Dabung, *Malaysia* **39 K4** 5 23N 102 1 E
Dacca = Dhaka, *Bangla.* **43 H14** 23 43N 90 26 E
Dacca = Dhaka □, *Bangla.* **43 G14** 24 25N 90 25 E
Dadanawa, *Guyana* **92 C7** 2 50N 59 30W
Dade City, *U.S.A.* **77 L4** 28 22N 82 11W
Dadra and Nagar Haveli □, *India* **40 J8** 20 5N 73 0 E
Dadri = Charkhi Dadri, *India* **42 E7** 28 37N 76 17 E
Dadu, *Pakistan* **42 F2** 26 45N 67 45 E
Daet, *Phil.* **37 B6** 14 2N 122 55 E
Dagana, *Senegal* **50 E1** 16 30N 15 35W
Daggett, *U.S.A.* **85 L10** 34 52N 116 52W
Daghestan Republic □, *Russia* **25 F8** 42 30N 47 0 E
Dagö = Hiiumaa, *Estonia* **24 C3** 58 50N 22 45 E
Dagu, *China* **35 E9** 38 59N 117 40 E
Dagupan, *Phil.* **37 A6** 16 3N 120 20 E
Dahlak Kebir, *Eritrea* **46 D3** 15 50N 40 10 E
Dahlonega, *U.S.A.* **77 H4** 34 32N 83 59W
Dahod, *India* **42 H6** 22 50N 74 15 E
Dahomey = Benin ■, *Africa* **50 G5** 10 0N 2 0 E
Dahra, *Senegal* **50 E1** 15 22N 15 30W
Dai Hao, *Vietnam* **38 C6** 18 1N 106 25 E
Dai-Sen, *Japan* **31 G6** 35 22N 133 32 E
Dai Xian, *China* **34 E7** 39 4N 112 58 E
Daicheng, *China* **34 E9** 38 42N 116 38 E
Daingean, *Ireland* **13 C4** 53 18N 7 15W
Daintree, *Australia* **62 B4** 16 20S 145 20 E
Daiō-Misaki, *Japan* **31 G8** 34 15N 136 45 E
Dairût, *Egypt* **51 C11** 27 34N 30 43 E
Daisetsu-Zan, *Japan* **30 C11** 43 30N 142 57 E
Dajarra, *Australia* **62 C2** 21 42S 139 30 E
Dak Dam, *Cambodia* **38 F6** 12 20N 107 21 E
Dak Nhe, *Vietnam* **38 E6** 15 28N 107 48 E
Dak Pek, *Vietnam* **38 E6** 15 4N 107 44 E
Dak Song, *Vietnam* **39 F6** 12 19N 107 35 E
Dak Sui, *Vietnam* **38 E6** 14 55N 107 43 E
Dakar, *Senegal* **50 F1** 14 34N 17 29W
Dakhla, *W. Sahara* **50 D1** 23 50N 15 53W
Dakhla, El Wâhât el-, *Egypt* **51 C10** 25 30N 28 50 E
Dakhovskaya, *Russia* **25 F7** 44 13N 40 13 E
Dakor, *India* **42 H5** 22 45N 73 11 E
Dakota City, *U.S.A.* **80 D6** 42 25N 96 25W
Đakovica, *Serbia* **21 C9** 42 22N 20 26 E
Dalachi, *China* **34 F3** 36 48N 105 0 E
Dalai Nur, *China* **34 C9** 43 20N 116 45 E
Dālakī, *Iran* **45 D6** 29 26N 51 17 E
Dalälven, *Sweden* **9 F14** 60 12N 16 43 E
Dalandzadgad, *Mongolia* **34 C3** 43 27N 104 30 E
Dalarö, *Sweden* **9 G15** 59 8N 18 24 E
Dālbandīn, *Pakistan* **40 E4** 29 0N 64 23 E
Dalbeattie, *U.K.* **12 G5** 54 55N 3 50W
Dalby, *Australia* **63 D5** 27 10S 151 17 E
Dalgān, *Iran* **45 E8** 27 31N 59 19 E
Dalhart, *U.S.A.* **81 G3** 36 4N 102 31W
Dalhousie, *Canada* **71 C6** 48 5N 66 26W
Dalhousie, *India* **42 C6** 32 38N 75 58 E
Dali, *Shaanxi, China* **34 G5** 34 48N 109 58 E
Dali, *Yunnan, China* **32 D5** 25 40N 100 10 E
Dalian, *China* **35 E11** 38 50N 121 40 E
Daliang Shan, *China* **32 D5** 28 0N 102 45 E
Daling He →, *China* **35 D11** 40 55N 121 40 E
Dāliyat el Karmel, *Israel* **47 C4** 32 43N 35 2 E
Dalkeith, *U.K.* **12 F5** 55 54N 3 5W
Dall I., *U.S.A.* **72 C2** 54 59N 133 25W
Dallarnil, *Australia* **63 D5** 25 19S 152 2 E
Dallas, *Oreg., U.S.A.* **82 D2** 44 55N 123 19W
Dallas, *Tex., U.S.A.* **81 J6** 32 47N 96 49W
Dalmacija = Dalmatia □, *Croatia* **20 C7** 43 20N 17 0 E
Dalmatia □, *Croatia* **20 C7** 43 20N 17 0 E
Dalmellington, *U.K.* **12 F4** 55 20N 4 25W
Dalnegorsk, *Russia* **27 E14** 44 32N 135 33 E
Dalnerechensk, *Russia* **27 E14** 45 50N 133 40 E
Daloa, *Ivory C.* **50 G3** 7 0N 6 30W
Daltenganj, *India* **43 G11** 24 0N 84 4 E
Dalton, *Canada* **70 C3** 48 11N 84 1W
Dalton, *Ga., U.S.A.* **77 H3** 34 46N 84 58W
Dalton, *Mass., U.S.A.* **79 D11** 42 28N 73 11W
Dalton, *Nebr., U.S.A.* **80 E3** 41 25N 102 58W
Dalton Iceberg Tongue, *Antarctica* **5 C9** 66 15S 121 30 E
Dalvík, *Iceland* **8 D4** 65 58N 18 32W
Daly →, *Australia* **60 B5** 13 35S 130 19 E
Daly City, *U.S.A.* **84 H4** 37 42N 122 28W
Daly L., *Canada* **73 B7** 56 32N 105 39W
Daly Waters, *Australia* **62 B1** 16 15S 133 24 E
Dam Doi, *Vietnam* **39 H5** 8 50N 105 12 E
Dam Ha, *Vietnam* **38 B6** 21 21N 107 36 E
Daman, *India* **40 J8** 20 25N 72 57 E
Dāmaneh, *Iran* **45 C6** 33 1N 50 29 E
Damanhûr, *Egypt* **51 B11** 31 0N 30 30 E
Damanzhuang, *China* **34 E9** 38 5N 116 35 E
Damar, *Indonesia* **37 F7** 7 7S 128 40 E
Damaraland, *Namibia* **56 C2** 21 0S 17 0 E
Damascus = Dimashq, *Syria* **47 B5** 33 30N 36 18 E
Damāvand, *Iran* **45 C7** 35 47N 52 0 E
Damāvand, Qolleh-ye, *Iran* **45 C7** 35 56N 52 10 E
Damba, *Angola* **52 F3** 6 44S 15 20 E
Dame Marie, *Haiti* **89 C5** 18 36N 74 26W
Dāmghān, *Iran* **45 B7** 36 10N 54 17 E
Damietta = Dumyât, *Egypt* **51 B11** 31 24N 31 48 E
Daming, *China* **34 F8** 36 15N 115 6 E
Damīr Qābū, *Syria* **44 B4** 36 58N 41 51 E
Dammam = Ad Dammām, *Si. Arabia* **45 E6** 26 20N 50 5 E
Damodar →, *India* **43 H12** 23 17N 87 35 E
Damoh, *India* **43 H8** 23 50N 79 28 E
Dampier, *Australia* **60 D2** 20 41S 116 42 E
Dampier, Selat, *Indonesia* **37 E8** 0 40S 131 0 E
Dampier Arch., *Australia* **60 D2** 20 38S 116 32 E
Damrei, Chuor Phnum, *Cambodia* **39 G4** 11 30N 103 0 E
Dana, *Indonesia* **37 F6** 11 0S 122 52 E
Dana, L., *Canada* **70 B4** 50 53N 77 20W
Dana, Mt., *U.S.A.* **84 H7** 37 54N 119 12W
Danbury, *U.S.A.* **79 E11** 41 24N 73 28W
Danby L., *U.S.A.* **83 J6** 34 13N 115 5W
Dand, *Afghan.* **42 D1** 31 28N 65 32 E
Dandaragan, *Australia* **61 F2** 30 40S 115 40 E
Dandeldhura, *Nepal* **43 E9** 29 20N 80 35 E
Dandeli, *India* **40 M9** 15 5N 74 30 E
Dandenong, *Australia* **63 F4** 38 0S 145 15 E
Dandong, *China* **35 D13** 40 10N 124 20 E
Danfeng, *China* **34 H6** 33 45N 110 25 E
Danforth, *U.S.A.* **71 C6** 45 40N 67 52W
Danger Is. = Pukapuka, *Cook Is.* **65 J11** 10 53S 165 49W
Danger Pt., *S. Africa* **56 E2** 34 40S 19 17 E
Dangora, *Nigeria* **50 F6** 11 30N 8 7 E
Dangrek, Phnom, *Thailand* **38 E5** 14 15N 105 0 E
Dangriga, *Belize* **87 D7** 17 0N 88 13W
Dangshan, *China* **34 G9** 34 27N 116 22 E
Daniel, *U.S.A.* **82 E8** 42 52N 110 4W
Daniel's Harbour, *Canada* **71 B8** 50 13N 57 35W
Danielskuil, *S. Africa* **56 D3** 28 11S 23 33 E
Danielson, *U.S.A.* **79 E13** 41 48N 71 53W
Danilov, *Russia* **24 C7** 58 16N 40 13 E
Daning, *China* **34 F6** 36 28N 110 45 E
Danissa, *Kenya* **54 B5** 3 15N 40 58 E
Dankhar Gompa, *India* **40 C11** 32 10N 78 10 E
Danlí, *Honduras* **88 D2** 14 4N 86 35W
Dannemora, *Sweden* **9 F14** 60 12N 17 51 E
Dannemora, *U.S.A.* **79 B11** 44 43N 73 44W
Dannevirke, *N.Z.* **59 J6** 40 12S 176 8 E
Dannhauser, *S. Africa* **57 D5** 28 0S 30 3 E
Dansville, *U.S.A.* **78 D7** 42 34N 77 42W
Dantan, *India* **43 J12** 21 57N 87 20 E
Dante, *Somali Rep.* **46 E5** 10 25N 51 16 E
Danube →, *Europe* **21 B13** 45 20N 29 40 E
Danvers, *U.S.A.* **79 D14** 42 34N 70 56W
Danville, *Ill., U.S.A.* **76 E2** 40 8N 87 37W
Danville, *Ky., U.S.A.* **76 G3** 37 39N 84 46W
Danville, *Va., U.S.A.* **77 G6** 36 36N 79 23W
Danzig = Gdańsk, *Poland* **17 A9** 54 22N 18 40 E
Dao, *Phil.* **37 B6** 10 30N 121 57 E
Daoud = Aïn Beïda, *Algeria* **50 A6** 35 50N 7 29 E
Daqing Shan, *China* **34 D6** 40 40N 111 0 E
Dar es Salaam, *Tanzania* **54 D4** 6 50S 39 12 E
Dar Mazār, *Iran* **45 D8** 29 14N 57 20 E
Dar'ā, *Syria* **47 C5** 32 36N 36 7 E
Dar'ā □, *Syria* **47 C5** 32 55N 36 10 E
Dārāb, *Iran* **45 D7** 28 50N 54 30 E
Daraj, *Libya* **50 B7** 30 10N 10 28 E
Dārān, *Iran* **45 C6** 32 59N 50 24 E
Dārayyā, *Syria* **47 B5** 33 28N 36 15 E
Darband, *Pakistan* **42 B5** 34 20N 72 50 E
Darband, Kūh-e, *Iran* **45 D8** 31 34N 57 8 E
Darbhanga, *India* **43 F11** 26 15N 85 55 E
Darby, *U.S.A.* **82 C6** 46 1N 114 11W
Dardanelle, *Ark., U.S.A.* **81 H8** 35 13N 93 9W
Dardanelle, *Calif., U.S.A.* **84 G7** 38 20N 119 50W
Dardanelles = Çanakkale Boğazı, *Turkey* **21 D12** 40 17N 26 32 E
Dārestān, *Iran* **45 D8** 29 9N 58 42 E
Dârfûr, *Sudan* **51 F9** 13 40N 24 0 E
Dargai, *Pakistan* **42 B4** 34 25N 71 55 E
Dargan Ata, *Uzbekistan* **26 E7** 40 29N 62 10 E
Dargaville, *N.Z.* **59 F4** 35 57S 173 52 E
Darhan Muminggan Lianheqi, *China* **34 D6** 41 40N 110 28 E
Darién, G. del, *Colombia* **92 B3** 9 0N 77 0W
Dariganga, *Mongolia* **34 B7** 45 21N 113 45 E
Darjeeling = Darjiling, *India* **43 F13** 27 3N 88 18 E
Darjiling, *India* **43 F13** 27 3N 88 18 E
Dark Cove, *Canada* **71 C9** 48 47N 54 13W
Darkan, *Australia* **61 F2** 33 20S 116 43 E
Darkhazīneh, *Iran* **45 D6** 31 54N 48 39 E
Darkot Pass, *Pakistan* **43 A5** 36 45N 73 26 E
Darling →, *Australia* **63 E3** 34 4S 141 54 E
Darling Downs, *Australia* **63 D5** 27 30S 150 30 E
Darling Ra., *Australia* **61 F2** 32 30S 116 0 E
Darlington, *U.K.* **10 C6** 54 33N 1 33W
Darlington, *S.C., U.S.A.* **77 H6** 34 18N 79 52W
Darlington, *Wis., U.S.A.* **80 D9** 42 41N 90 7W
Darlot, L., *Australia* **61 E3** 27 48S 121 35 E
Darłowo, *Poland* **16 A8** 54 25N 16 25 E
Darmstadt, *Germany* **16 D4** 49 51N 8 40 E
Darnah, *Libya* **51 B9** 32 40N 22 35 E
Darnall, *S. Africa* **57 D5** 29 23S 31 18 E
Darnley, C., *Antarctica* **5 C6** 68 0S 69 0 E
Darnley B., *Canada* **68 B7** 69 30N 123 30W
Darr, *Australia* **62 C3** 23 13S 144 7 E
Darr →, *Australia* **62 C3** 23 39S 143 50 E
Darrington, *U.S.A.* **82 B3** 48 15N 121 36W
Dart →, *U.K.* **11 G4** 50 24N 3 36W
Dart, C., *Antarctica* **5 D14** 73 6S 126 20W
Dartmoor, *U.K.* **11 G4** 50 36N 4 0W
Dartmouth, *Australia* **62 C3** 23 31S 144 44 E
Dartmouth, *Canada* **71 D7** 44 40N 63 30W
Dartmouth, *U.K.* **11 G4** 50 21N 3 35W
Dartmouth, L., *Australia* **63 D4** 26 4S 145 18 E
Dartuch, C., *Spain* **22 B10** 39 55N 3 49 E
Darvaza, *Turkmenistan* **26 E6** 40 11N 58 24 E
Darvel, Teluk, *Malaysia* **37 D5** 4 50N 118 20 E
Darwha, *India* **40 J10** 20 15N 77 45 E
Darwin, *Australia* **60 B5** 12 25S 130 51 E
Darwin, *U.S.A.* **85 J9** 36 15N 117 35W
Darwin River, *Australia* **60 B5** 12 50S 130 58 E
Daryoi Amu = Amudarya →, *Uzbekistan* **26 E6** 43 40N 59 0 E
Dās, *U.A.E.* **45 E7** 25 20N 53 30 E
Dashetai, *China* **34 D5** 41 0N 109 5 E
Dasht, *Iran* **45 B8** 37 17N 56 7 E
Dasht →, *Pakistan* **40 G2** 25 10N 61 40 E
Dasht-e Mārgow, *Afghan.* **40 D3** 30 40N 62 30 E
Dasht-i-Nawar, *Afghan.* **42 C3** 33 52N 68 0 E
Daska, *Pakistan* **42 C6** 32 20N 74 20 E
Dasseneiland, *S. Africa* **56 E2** 33 25S 18 3 E
Datia, *India* **43 G8** 25 39N 78 27 E
Datong, *China* **34 D7** 40 6N 113 18 E
Datu, Tanjung, *Indonesia* **36 D3** 2 5N 109 39 E
Datu Piang, *Phil.* **37 C6** 7 2N 124 30 E
Daugava →, *Latvia* **24 C3** 57 4N 24 3 E
Daugavpils, *Latvia* **24 C4** 55 53N 26 32 E
Daulpur, *India* **42 F7** 26 45N 77 59 E
Dauphin, *Canada* **73 C8** 51 9N 100 5W
Dauphin I., *U.S.A.* **77 K1** 30 15N 88 11W
Dauphin L., *Canada* **73 C9** 51 20N 99 45W
Dauphiné, *France* **18 D6** 45 15N 5 25 E
Dausa, *India* **42 F7** 26 52N 76 20 E
Davangere, *India* **40 M9** 14 25N 75 55 E
Davao, *Phil.* **37 C7** 7 0N 125 40 E
Davao, G. of, *Phil.* **37 C7** 6 30N 125 48 E
Dāvar Panāh, *Iran* **45 E9** 27 25N 62 15 E
Davenport, *Calif., U.S.A.* **84 H4** 37 1N 122 12W
Davenport, *Iowa, U.S.A.* **80 E9** 41 32N 90 35W
Davenport, *Wash., U.S.A.* **82 C4** 47 39N 118 9W
Davenport Downs, *Australia* **62 C3** 24 8S 141 7 E
Davenport Ra., *Australia* **62 C1** 20 28S 134 0 E
David, *Panama* **88 E3** 8 30N 82 30W
David City, *U.S.A.* **80 E6** 41 15N 97 8W
Davidson, *Canada* **73 C7** 51 16N 105 59W
Davis, *U.S.A.* **84 G5** 38 33N 121 44W
Davis Dam, *U.S.A.* **85 K12** 35 11N 114 34W
Davis Inlet, *Canada* **71 A7** 55 50N 60 59W
Davis Mts., *U.S.A.* **81 K2** 30 50N 103 55W
Davis Sea, *Antarctica* **5 C7** 66 0S 92 0 E
Davis Str., *N. Amer.* **69 B14** 65 0N 58 0W
Davos, *Switz.* **16 E4** 46 48N 9 49 E
Davy L., *Canada* **73 B7** 58 53N 108 18W
Dawes Ra., *Australia* **62 C5** 24 40S 150 40 E
Dawson, *Canada* **68 B6** 64 10N 139 30W
Dawson, *Ga., U.S.A.* **77 K3** 31 46N 84 27W
Dawson, *N. Dak., U.S.A.* **80 B5** 46 52N 99 45W
Dawson, I., *Chile* **96 G2** 53 50S 70 50W
Dawson Creek, *Canada* **72 B4** 55 45N 120 15W
Dawson Inlet, *Canada* **73 A10** 61 50N 93 25W
Dawson Ra., *Australia* **62 C4** 24 30S 149 48 E
Daxian, *China* **32 C5** 31 15N 107 23 E
Daxindian, *China* **35 F11** 37 30N 120 50 E
Daxinggou, *China* **35 C15** 43 25N 129 40 E
Daxue Shan, *China* **32 C5** 30 30N 101 30 E
Daylesford, *Australia* **63 F3** 37 21S 144 9 E
Dayr az Zawr, *Syria* **44 C4** 35 20N 40 5 E
Daysland, *Canada* **72 C6** 52 50N 112 20W
Dayton, *Nev., U.S.A.* **84 F7** 39 14N 119 36W
Dayton, *Ohio, U.S.A.* **76 F3** 39 45N 84 12W
Dayton, *Pa., U.S.A.* **78 F5** 40 53N 79 15W
Dayton, *Tenn., U.S.A.* **77 H3** 35 30N 85 1W
Dayton, *Wash., U.S.A.* **82 C4** 46 19N 117 59W
Daytona Beach, *U.S.A.* **77 L5** 29 13N 81 1W
Dayville, *U.S.A.* **82 D4** 44 28N 119 32W
De Aar, *S. Africa* **56 E3** 30 39S 24 0 E
De Funiak Springs, *U.S.A.* **77 K2** 30 43N 86 7W
De Grey, *Australia* **60 D2** 20 12S 119 12 E
De Grey →, *Australia* **60 D2** 20 12S 119 13 E
De Kalb, *U.S.A.* **80 E10** 41 56N 88 46W
De Land, *U.S.A.* **77 L5** 29 2N 81 18W
De Leon, *U.S.A.* **81 J5** 32 7N 98 32W
De Pere, *U.S.A.* **76 C1** 44 27N 88 4W
De Queen, *U.S.A.* **81 H7** 34 2N 94 21W
De Quincy, *U.S.A.* **81 K8** 30 27N 93 26W
De Ridder, *U.S.A.* **81 K8** 30 51N 93 17W
De Smet, *U.S.A.* **80 C6** 44 23N 97 33W
De Soto, *U.S.A.* **80 F9** 38 8N 90 34W
De Tour Village, *U.S.A.* **76 C4** 46 0N 83 56W
De Witt, *U.S.A.* **81 H9** 34 18N 91 20W
Dead Sea, *Asia* **47 D4** 31 30N 35 30 E
Deadwood, *U.S.A.* **80 C3** 44 23N 103 44W
Deadwood L., *Canada* **72 B3** 59 10N 128 30W
Deakin, *Australia* **61 F4** 30 46S 128 58 E
Deal, *U.K.* **11 F9** 51 13N 1 25 E
Deal I., *Australia* **62 F4** 39 30S 147 20 E
Dealesville, *S. Africa* **56 D4** 28 41S 25 44 E
Dean, Forest of, *U.K.* **11 F5** 51 50N 2 35W
Deán Funes, *Argentina* **94 C3** 30 20S 64 20W
Dearborn, *U.S.A.* **70 D3** 42 19N 83 11W
Dease →, *Canada* **72 B3** 59 56N 128 32W
Dease L., *Canada* **72 B2** 58 40N 130 5W
Dease Lake, *Canada* **72 B2** 58 25N 130 6W
Death Valley, *U.S.A.* **85 J10** 36 15N 116 50W
Death Valley Junction, *U.S.A.* **85 J10** 36 20N 116 25W
Death Valley National Monument, *U.S.A.* **85 J10** 36 45N 117 15W
Deba Habe, *Nigeria* **50 F7** 10 14N 11 20 E
Debar, *Macedonia* **21 D9** 41 31N 20 30 E
Debden, *Canada* **73 C7** 53 30N 106 50W
Debolt, *Canada* **72 B5** 55 12N 118 1W
Deborah East, L., *Australia* **61 F2** 30 45S 119 0 E
Deborah West, L., *Australia* **61 F2** 30 45S 118 50 E
Debre Markos, *Ethiopia* **51 F12** 10 20N 37 40 E
Debre Tabor, *Ethiopia* **51 F12** 11 50N 38 26 E
Debrecen, *Hungary* **17 E10** 47 33N 21 42 E
Decatur, *Ala., U.S.A.* **77 H2** 34 36N 86 59W
Decatur, *Ga., U.S.A.* **77 J3** 33 47N 84 18W
Decatur, *Ill., U.S.A.* **80 F10** 39 51N 88 57W
Decatur, *Ind., U.S.A.* **76 E3** 40 50N 84 56W
Decatur, *Tex., U.S.A.* **81 J6** 33 14N 97 35W
Deccan, *India* **40 M10** 18 0N 79 0 E
Deception L., *Canada* **73 B8** 56 33N 104 13W
Deckerville, *U.S.A.* **78 C2** 43 32N 82 44W
Decorah, *U.S.A.* **80 D9** 43 18N 91 48W
Dedéagach = Alexandroúpolis, *Greece* **21 D11** 40 50N 25 54 E
Dedham, *U.S.A.* **79 D13** 42 15N 71 10W
Dédougou, *Burkina Faso* **50 F4** 12 30N 3 25W
Dedza, *Malawi* **55 E3** 14 20S 34 20 E
Dee →, *Clwyd, U.K.* **10 D4** 53 15N 3 7W
Dee →, *Gramp., U.K.* **12 D6** 57 4N 2 7W
Deep B., *Canada* **72 A5** 61 15N 116 35W
Deep Well, *Australia* **62 C1** 24 20S 134 0 E
Deepwater, *Australia* **63 D5** 29 25S 151 51 E
Deer →, *Canada* **73 B10** 58 23N 94 13W
Deer Lake, *Nfld., Canada* **71 C8** 49 11N 57 27W
Deer Lake, *Ont., Canada* **73 C10** 52 36N 94 20W
Deer Lodge, *U.S.A.* **82 C7** 46 24N 112 44W
Deer Park, *U.S.A.* **82 C5** 47 57N 117 28W
Deer River, *U.S.A.* **80 B8** 47 20N 93 48W
Deeral, *Australia* **62 B4** 17 14S 145 55 E
Deerdepoort, *S. Africa* **56 C4** 24 37S 26 27 E
Deferiet, *U.S.A.* **79 B9** 44 2N 75 41W
Defiance, *U.S.A.* **76 E3** 41 17N 84 22W
Degeh Bur, *Ethiopia* **46 F3** 8 11N 43 31 E
Deggendorf, *Germany* **16 D6** 48 49N 12 59 E
Deh Bīd, *Iran* **45 D7** 30 39N 53 11 E
Deh-e Shīr, *Iran* **45 D7** 31 29N 53 45 E
Dehaj, *Iran* **45 D7** 30 42N 54 53 E
Dehdez, *Iran* **45 D6** 31 43N 50 17 E
Dehestān, *Iran* **45 D7** 28 30N 55 35 E
Dehgolān, *Iran* **44 C5** 35 17N 47 25 E
Dehi Titan, *Afghan.* **40 C3** 33 45N 63 50 E
Dehibat, *Tunisia* **50 B7** 32 0N 10 47 E
Dehlorān, *Iran* **44 C5** 32 41N 47 16 E
Dehnow-e Kūhestān, *Iran* **45 E8** 27 58N 58 32 E
Dehra Dun, *India* **42 D8** 30 20N 78 4 E
Dehri, *India* **43 G11** 24 50N 84 15 E
Dehui, *China* **35 B13** 44 30N 125 40 E
Deinze, *Belgium* **15 D3** 50 59N 3 32 E
Dej, *Romania* **17 E11** 47 10N 23 52 E
Dekese, *Zaire* **52 E4** 3 24S 21 24 E
Del Mar, *U.S.A.* **85 N9** 32 58N 117 16W
Del Norte, *U.S.A.* **83 H10** 37 41N 106 21W
Del Rio, *U.S.A.* **81 L4** 29 22N 100 54W
Delano, *U.S.A.* **85 K7** 35 46N 119 15W
Delareyville, *S. Africa* **56 D4** 26 41S 25 26 E
Delavan, *U.S.A.* **80 D10** 42 38N 88 39W
Delaware, *U.S.A.* **76 E4** 40 18N 83 4W
Delaware □, *U.S.A.* **76 F8** 39 0N 75 30W
Delaware →, *U.S.A.* **76 F8** 39 15N 75 20W

Delaware B.

East C.

Don →, S. Yorks., U.K. 10 D7 53 41N 0 51W
Don, C., Australia 60 B5 11 18S 131 46 E
Don Benito, Spain 19 C3 38 53N 5 51W
Don Duong, Vietnam 39 G7 11 51N 108 35 E
Don Martín, Presa de, Mexico 86 B4 27 30N 100 50W
Dona Ana = Nhamaabué, Mozam. 55 F4 17 25S 35 5 E
Donaghadee, U.K. 13 B6 54 38N 5 32W
Donald, Australia 63 F3 36 23S 143 0 E
Donalda, Canada 72 C6 52 35N 112 34W
Donaldsonville, U.S.A. 81 K9 30 6N 90 59W
Donalsonville, U.S.A. 77 K3 31 3N 84 53W
Donau →, Austria 16 D8 48 10N 17 0 E
Donauwörth, Germany 16 D5 48 42N 10 47 E
Doncaster, U.K. 10 D6 53 31N 1 9W
Dondo, Angola 52 F2 9 45S 14 25 E
Dondo, Mozam. 55 F3 19 33S 34 46 E
Dondo, Teluk, Indonesia 37 D6 0 29N 120 30 E
Dondra Head, Sri Lanka 40 S12 5 55N 80 40 E
Donegal, Ireland 13 B3 54 39N 8 8W
Donegal □, Ireland 13 B4 54 53N 8 0W
Donegal B., Ireland 13 B3 54 30N 8 35W
Donets →, Russia 25 E7 47 33N 40 55 E
Donetsk, Ukraine 25 E6 48 0N 37 45 E
Dong Ba Thin, Vietnam 39 F7 12 8N 109 13 E
Dong Dang, Vietnam 38 B6 21 54N 106 42 E
Dong Giam, Vietnam 38 C5 19 25N 105 31 E
Dong Ha, Vietnam 38 D6 16 55N 107 8 E
Dong Hene, Laos 38 D5 16 40N 105 18 E
Dong Hoi, Vietnam 38 D6 17 29N 106 36 E
Dong Khe, Vietnam 38 A6 22 26N 106 27 E
Dong Ujimqin Qi, China 34 B9 45 32N 116 55 E
Dong Van, Vietnam 38 A5 23 16N 105 22 E
Dong Xoai, Vietnam 39 G6 11 32N 106 55 E
Dongara, Australia 61 E1 29 14S 114 57 E
Dongbei, China 35 D13 42 0N 125 0 E
Dongchuan, China 32 D5 26 8N 103 1 E
Dongfang, China 38 C7 18 50N 108 33 E
Dongfeng, China 35 C13 42 40N 125 34 E
Donggala, Indonesia 37 E5 0 30S 119 40 E
Donggou, China 35 E13 39 52N 124 10 E
Dongguang, China 34 F9 37 50N 116 30 E
Dongjingcheng, China 35 B15 44 5N 129 10 E
Dongning, China 35 B16 44 2N 131 5 E
Dongola, Sudan 51 E11 19 9N 30 22 E
Dongou, Congo 52 D3 2 0N 18 5 E
Dongping, China 34 G9 35 55N 116 20 E
Dongsheng, China 34 E6 39 50N 110 0 E
Dongtai, China 35 H11 32 51N 120 21 E
Dongting Hu, China 33 D6 29 18N 112 45 E
Donington, C., Australia 63 E2 34 45S 136 0 E
Doniphan, U.S.A. 81 G9 36 37N 90 50W
Dønna, Norway 8 C12 66 6N 12 30 E
Donna, U.S.A. 81 M5 26 9N 98 4W
Donnaconna, Canada 71 C5 46 41N 71 41W
Donnelly's Crossing, N.Z. 59 F4 35 42S 173 38 E
Donnybrook, Australia 61 F2 33 34S 115 48 E
Donnybrook, S. Africa 57 D4 29 59S 29 48 E
Donora, U.S.A. 78 F5 40 11N 79 52W
Donor's Hill, Australia 62 B3 18 42S 140 33 E
Donostia = San Sebastián, Spain 19 A5 43 17N 1 58W
Doon →, U.K. 12 F4 55 26N 4 41W
Dora, L., Australia 60 D3 22 0S 123 0 E
Dora Báltea →, Italy 20 B3 45 11N 8 5 E
Doran L., Canada 73 A7 61 13N 108 6W
Dorchester, U.K. 11 G5 50 42N 2 28W
Dorchester, C., Canada 69 B12 65 27N 77 27W
Dordogne □, France 18 D4 45 5N 0 40 E
Dordogne →, France 18 D3 45 2N 0 36W
Dordrecht, Neths. 15 C4 51 48N 4 39 E
Dordrecht, S. Africa 56 E4 31 20S 27 3 E
Dore, Mts., France 18 D5 45 32N 2 50 E
Doré L., Canada 73 C7 54 46N 107 17W
Doré Lake, Canada 73 C7 54 38N 107 36W
Dori, Burkina Faso 50 F4 14 3N 0 2W
Doring →, S. Africa 56 E2 31 54S 18 39 E
Doringbos, S. Africa 56 E2 31 59S 19 16 E
Dorion, Canada 70 C5 45 23N 74 3W
Dornoch, U.K. 12 D4 57 52N 4 5W
Dornoch Firth, U.K. 12 D4 57 52N 4 0W
Dornogovĭ □, Mongolia 34 B6 44 0N 110 0 E
Dorohoi, Romania 17 E13 47 56N 26 30 E
Döröö Nuur, Mongolia 32 B4 48 0N 93 0 E
Dorr, Iran 45 C6 33 17N 50 38 E
Dorre I., Australia 61 E1 25 13S 113 12 E
Dorrigo, Australia 63 E5 30 20S 152 44 E
Dorris, U.S.A. 82 F3 41 58N 121 55W
Dorset, Canada 78 A6 45 14N 78 54W
Dorset, U.S.A. 78 E4 41 4N 80 40W
Dorset □, U.K. 11 G5 50 48N 2 25W
Dortmund, Germany 16 C3 51 32N 7 28 E
Doruma, Zaïre 54 B2 4 42N 27 33 E
Dorūneh, Iran 45 C8 35 10N 57 18 E
Dos Bahías, C., Argentina 96 E3 44 58S 65 32W
Dos Palos, U.S.A. 84 J6 36 59N 120 37W
Dosso, Niger 50 F5 13 0N 3 13 E
Dothan, U.S.A. 77 K3 31 13N 85 24W
Doty, U.S.A. 84 D3 46 38N 123 17W
Douai, France 18 A5 50 21N 3 4 E
Douala, Cameroon 50 H6 4 0N 9 45 E
Douarnenez, France 18 B1 48 6N 4 21W
Double Island Pt., Australia 63 D5 25 56S 153 11 E
Doubs □, France 18 C7 47 10N 6 20 E
Doubs →, France 18 C6 46 53N 5 1 E
Doubtful Sd., N.Z. 59 L1 45 20S 166 49 E
Doubtless B., N.Z. 59 F4 34 55S 173 26 E
Douentza, Mali 50 F4 14 58N 2 48W
Douglas, S. Africa 56 D3 29 4S 23 46 E
Douglas, U.K. 10 C3 54 9N 4 29W
Douglas, Alaska, U.S.A. 72 B2 58 17N 134 24W
Douglas, Ariz., U.S.A. 83 L9 31 21N 109 33W
Douglas, Ga., U.S.A. 77 K4 31 31N 82 51W
Douglas, Wyo., U.S.A. 80 D2 42 45N 105 24W
Douglastown, Canada 71 C7 48 46N 64 24W
Douglasville, U.S.A. 77 J3 33 45N 84 45W
Doumé, Cameroon 52 D2 4 15N 13 25 E
Dounreay, U.K. 12 C5 58 34N 3 44W
Dourados, Brazil 95 A5 22 9S 54 50W
Dourados →, Brazil 95 A5 21 58S 54 18W
Douro →, Europe 19 B1 41 8N 8 40W
Douro Litoral, Portugal 19 B1 41 10N 8 20W
Dove →, U.K. 10 E6 52 51N 1 36W
Dove Creek, U.S.A. 83 H9 37 46N 108 54W
Dover, Australia 62 G4 43 18S 147 2 E
Dover, U.K. 11 F9 51 7N 1 19 E
Dover, Del., U.S.A. 76 F8 39 10N 75 32W
Dover, N.H., U.S.A. 79 C14 43 12N 70 56W
Dover, N.J., U.S.A. 79 F10 40 53N 74 34W
Dover, Ohio, U.S.A. 78 F3 40 32N 81 29W
Dover, Pt., Australia 61 F4 32 32S 125 32 E
Dover, Str. of, Europe 18 A4 51 0N 1 30 E
Dover-Foxcroft, U.S.A. 71 C6 45 11N 69 13W
Dover Plains, U.S.A. 79 E11 41 43N 73 35W
Dovey = Dyfi →, U.K. 11 E4 52 32N 4 0W
Dovrefjell, Norway 8 E10 62 15N 9 33 E
Dow Rūd, Iran 45 C6 33 28N 49 4 E
Dowa, Malawi 55 E3 13 38S 33 58 E
Dowagiac, U.S.A. 76 E2 41 59N 86 6W
Dowgha'i, Iran 45 B8 36 54N 58 32 E
Dowlatābād, Iran 45 D8 28 20N 56 40 E
Down □, U.K. 13 B6 54 20N 5 47W
Downey, Calif., U.S.A. 85 M8 33 56N 118 7W
Downey, Idaho, U.S.A. 82 E7 42 26N 112 7W
Downham Market, U.K. 11 E8 52 36N 0 22 E
Downieville, U.S.A. 84 F6 39 34N 120 50W
Downpatrick, U.K. 13 B6 54 20N 5 43W
Downpatrick Hd., Ireland 13 B2 54 20N 9 21W
Dowsārī, Iran 45 D8 28 25N 57 59 E
Doyle, U.S.A. 84 E6 40 2N 120 6W
Doylestown, U.S.A. 79 F9 40 21N 75 10W
Draa, Oued →, Morocco 50 C2 28 40N 11 10W
Drachten, Neths. 15 A6 53 7N 6 5 E
Dragoman, Prokhod, Bulgaria 21 C10 42 58N 22 53 E
Dragonera, I., Spain 22 B9 39 35N 2 19 E
Draguignan, France 18 E7 43 32N 6 27 E
Drain, U.S.A. 82 E2 43 40N 123 19W
Drake, Australia 63 D5 28 55S 152 25 E
Drake, U.S.A. 80 B4 47 55N 100 23W
Drake Passage, S. Ocean 5 B17 58 0S 68 0W
Drakensberg, S. Africa 57 E4 31 0S 28 0 E
Dráma, Greece 21 D11 41 9N 24 10 E
Drammen, Norway 9 G11 59 42N 10 12 E
Drangajökull, Iceland 8 C2 66 9N 22 15W
Dras, India 43 B6 34 25N 75 48 E
Drau = Drava →, Croatia 21 B8 45 33N 18 55 E
Drava →, Croatia 21 B8 45 33N 18 55 E
Drayton Valley, Canada 72 C6 53 12N 114 58W
Drenthe □, Neths. 15 B6 52 52N 6 40 E
Drepanum, C., Cyprus 23 E11 34 54N 32 19 E
Dresden, Canada 78 D2 42 35N 82 11W
Dresden, Germany 16 C6 51 2N 13 45 E
Dreux, France 18 B4 48 44N 1 23 E
Driffield = Great Driffield, U.K. 10 C7 54 0N 0 25W
Driftwood, U.S.A. 78 E6 41 20N 78 8W
Driggs, U.S.A. 82 E8 43 44N 111 6W
Drina →, Bos.-H. 21 B8 44 53N 19 21 E
Drøbak, Norway 9 G11 59 39N 10 39 E
Drogheda, Ireland 13 C5 53 45N 6 20W
Drogobych, Ukraine 25 E3 49 20N 23 30 E
Drohobych = Drogobych, Ukraine 25 E3 49 20N 23 30 E
Droichead Nua, Ireland 13 C5 53 11N 6 50W
Droitwich, U.K. 11 E5 52 16N 2 10W
Drôme □, France 18 D6 44 38N 5 15 E
Dromedary, C., Australia 63 F5 36 17S 150 10 E
Dronfield, Australia 62 C3 21 12S 140 3 E
Drumbo, Canada 78 C4 43 16N 80 35W
Drumheller, Canada 72 C6 51 25N 112 40W
Drummond, U.S.A. 82 C7 46 40N 113 9W
Drummond I., U.S.A. 70 C3 46 1N 83 39W
Drummond Pt., Australia 63 E2 34 9S 135 16 E
Drummond Ra., Australia 62 C4 23 45S 147 10 E
Drummondville, Canada 70 C5 45 55N 72 25W
Drumright, U.S.A. 81 H6 35 59N 96 36W
Druzhina, Russia 27 C15 68 14N 145 18 E
Dry Tortugas, U.S.A. 88 B3 24 38N 82 55W
Dryden, Canada 73 D10 49 47N 92 50W
Dryden, U.S.A. 81 K3 30 3N 102 7W
Drygalski I., Antarctica 5 C7 66 0S 92 0 E
Drysdale →, Australia 60 B4 13 59S 126 51 E
Drysdale I., Australia 62 A2 11 41S 136 0 E
Dschang, Cameroon 50 G7 5 32N 10 3 E
Du Bois, U.S.A. 78 E6 41 8N 78 46W
Du Quoin, U.S.A. 80 G10 38 1N 89 14W
Duanesburg, U.S.A. 79 D10 42 45N 74 11W
Duaringa, Australia 62 C4 23 42S 149 42 E
Dubā, Si. Arabia 44 E2 27 10N 35 40 E
Dubai = Dubayy, U.A.E. 45 E7 25 18N 55 20 E
Dubawnt →, Canada 73 A8 64 33N 100 6W
Dubawnt, L., Canada 73 A8 63 4N 101 42W
Dubayy, U.A.E. 45 E7 25 18N 55 20 E
Dubbo, Australia 63 E4 32 11S 148 35 E
Dubele, Zaïre 54 B2 2 56N 29 35 E
Dublin, Ireland 13 C5 53 20N 6 18W
Dublin, Ga., U.S.A. 77 J4 32 32N 82 54W
Dublin, Tex., U.S.A. 81 J5 32 5N 98 21W
Dublin □, Ireland 13 C5 53 24N 6 20W
Dublin B., Ireland 13 C5 53 18N 6 5W
Dubois, U.S.A. 82 D7 44 10N 112 14W
Dubovka, Russia 25 E7 49 5N 44 50 E
Dubrajpur, India 43 H12 23 48N 87 25 E
Dubréka, Guinea 50 G2 9 46N 13 31W
Dubrovnik, Croatia 21 C8 42 39N 18 6 E
Dubrovskoye, Russia 27 D12 58 55N 111 10 E
Dubuque, U.S.A. 80 D9 42 30N 90 41W
Duchesne, U.S.A. 82 F8 40 10N 110 24W
Duchess, Australia 62 C2 21 20S 139 50 E
Ducie I., Pac. Oc. 65 K15 24 40S 124 48W
Duck Cr. →, Australia 60 D2 22 37S 116 53 E
Duck Lake, Canada 73 C7 52 50N 106 16W
Duck Mountain Prov. Park, Canada 73 C8 51 45N 101 0W
Duckwall, Mt., U.S.A. 84 H6 37 58N 120 7W
Dudhi, India 41 G13 24 15N 83 10 E
Dudinka, Russia 27 C9 69 30N 86 13 E
Dudley, U.K. 11 E5 52 30N 2 5W
Duero = Douro →, Europe 19 B1 41 8N 8 40W
Dufftown, U.K. 12 D5 57 26N 3 9W
Dugi Otok, Croatia 20 B6 44 0N 15 3 E
Duifken Pt., Australia 62 A3 12 33S 141 38 E
Duisburg, Germany 16 C3 51 27N 6 42 E
Duiwelskloof, S. Africa 57 C5 23 42S 30 10 E
Dūkdamīn, Iran 45 C8 35 59N 57 43 E
Duke I., U.S.A. 72 C2 54 50N 131 20W
Dukhān, Qatar 45 E6 25 25N 50 50 E
Duki, Pakistan 40 D6 30 14N 68 25 E
Duku, Nigeria 50 F7 10 43N 10 43 E
Dulce →, Argentina 94 C3 30 32S 62 33W
Dulce, G., Costa Rica 88 E3 8 40N 83 20W
Dulf, Iraq 44 C5 35 7N 45 51 E
Dulit, Banjaran, Malaysia 36 D4 3 15N 114 30 E
Duliu, China 34 E9 39 2N 116 55 E
Dullewala, Pakistan 42 D4 31 50N 71 25 E
Dulq Maghār, Syria 44 B3 36 22N 38 39 E
Dululu, Australia 62 C5 23 48S 150 15 E
Duluth, U.S.A. 80 B8 46 47N 92 6W
Dum Dum, India 43 H13 22 39N 88 33 E
Dum Duma, India 41 F19 27 40N 95 40 E
Dum Hadjer, Chad 51 F8 13 18N 19 41 E
Dūmā, Lebanon 47 A4 34 12N 35 50 E
Dūmā, Syria 47 B5 33 34N 36 24 E
Dumaguete, Phil. 37 C6 9 17N 123 15 E
Dumai, Indonesia 36 D2 1 35N 101 28 E
Dumaran, Phil. 37 B5 10 33N 119 50 E
Dumas, Ark., U.S.A. 81 J9 33 53N 91 29W
Dumas, Tex., U.S.A. 81 H4 35 52N 101 58W
Dumbarton, U.K. 12 F4 55 58N 4 35W
Dumbleyung, Australia 61 F2 33 17S 117 42 E
Dumfries, U.K. 12 F5 55 4N 3 37W
Dumfries & Galloway □, U.K. 12 F5 55 5N 4 0W
Dumka, India 43 G12 24 12N 87 15 E
Dumoine →, Canada 70 C4 46 13N 77 51W
Dumoine L., Canada 70 C4 46 55N 77 55W
Dumraon, India 43 G11 25 33N 84 8 E
Dumyât, Egypt 51 B11 31 24N 31 48 E
Dun Laoghaire, Ireland 13 C5 53 17N 6 9W
Dunaföldvár, Hungary 17 E9 46 50N 18 57 E
Dunărea →, Romania 17 F14 45 20N 29 40 E
Dunay, Russia 30 C6 42 52N 132 22 E
Dunback, N.Z. 59 L3 45 23S 170 36 E
Dunbar, Australia 62 B3 16 0S 142 22 E
Dunbar, U.K. 12 E6 56 0N 2 32W
Dunblane, U.K. 12 E5 56 10N 3 58W
Duncan, Canada 72 D4 48 45N 123 40W
Duncan, Ariz., U.S.A. 83 K9 32 43N 109 6W
Duncan, Okla., U.S.A. 81 H6 34 30N 97 57W
Duncan, L., Canada 70 B4 53 29N 77 58W
Duncan L., Canada 72 A6 62 51N 113 58W
Duncan Town, Bahamas 88 B4 22 15N 75 45W
Duncannon, U.S.A. 78 F7 40 23N 77 2W
Dundalk, Canada 78 B4 44 10N 80 24W
Dundalk, Ireland 13 B5 54 1N 6 25W
Dundalk Bay, Ireland 13 C5 53 55N 6 15W
Dundas, Canada 70 D4 43 17N 79 59W
Dundas, L., Australia 61 F3 32 35S 121 50 E
Dundas I., Canada 72 C2 54 30N 130 50W
Dundas Str., Australia 60 B5 11 15S 131 35 E
Dundee, S. Africa 57 D5 28 11S 30 15 E
Dundee, U.K. 12 E6 56 29N 3 0W
Dundgovĭ □, Mongolia 34 B4 45 10N 106 0 E
Dundoo, Australia 63 D3 27 40S 144 37 E
Dundrum, U.K. 13 B6 54 17N 5 50W
Dundrum B., U.K. 13 B6 54 12N 5 40W
Dundwara, India 43 F8 27 48N 79 9 E
Dunedin, N.Z. 59 L3 45 50S 170 33 E
Dunedin, U.S.A. 77 L4 28 1N 82 47W
Dunedin →, Canada 72 B4 59 30N 124 5W
Dunfermline, U.K. 12 E5 56 5N 3 28W
Dungannon, Canada 78 C3 43 51N 81 36W
Dungannon, U.K. 13 B5 54 30N 6 47W
Dungannon □, U.K. 13 B5 54 30N 6 55W
Dungarpur, India 42 H5 23 52N 73 45 E
Dungarvan, Ireland 13 D4 52 6N 7 40W
Dungarvan Bay, Ireland 13 D4 52 5N 7 35W
Dungeness, U.K. 11 G8 50 54N 0 59 E
Dungo, L. do, Angola 56 B2 17 15S 19 0 E
Dungog, Australia 63 E5 32 22S 151 46 E
Dungu, Zaïre 54 B2 3 40N 28 32 E
Dunhua, China 35 C15 43 20N 128 14 E
Dunhuang, China 32 B4 40 8N 94 36 E
Dunk I., Australia 62 B4 17 59S 146 29 E
Dunkeld, U.K. 12 E5 56 34N 3 36W
Dunkerque, France 18 A5 51 2N 2 20 E
Dunkery Beacon, U.K. 11 F4 51 15N 3 37W
Dunkirk = Dunkerque, France 18 A5 51 2N 2 20 E
Dunkirk, U.S.A. 78 D5 42 29N 79 20W
Dunkwa, Ghana 50 G4 6 0N 1 47W
Dunlap, U.S.A. 80 E7 41 51N 95 36W
Dúnleary = Dun Laoghaire, Ireland 13 C5 53 17N 6 9W
Dunmanus B., Ireland 13 E2 51 31N 9 50W
Dunmara, Australia 62 B1 16 42S 133 25 E
Dunmore, U.S.A. 79 E9 41 25N 75 38W
Dunmore Hd., Ireland 13 D1 52 10N 10 35W
Dunmore Town, Bahamas 88 A4 25 30N 76 39W
Dunn, U.S.A. 77 H6 35 19N 78 37W
Dunnellon, U.S.A. 77 L4 29 3N 82 28W
Dunnet Hd., U.K. 12 C5 58 38N 3 22W
Dunning, U.S.A. 80 E4 41 50N 100 6W
Dunnville, Canada 78 D5 42 54N 79 36W
Dunolly, Australia 63 F3 36 51S 143 44 E
Dunoon, U.K. 12 F4 55 57N 4 56W
Dunqul, Egypt 51 D11 23 26N 31 37 E
Duns, U.K. 12 F6 55 47N 2 20W
Dunseith, U.S.A. 80 A4 48 50N 100 3W
Dunsmuir, U.S.A. 82 F2 41 13N 122 16W
Dunstable, U.K. 11 F7 51 53N 0 31W
Dunstan Mts., N.Z. 59 L2 44 53S 169 35 E
Dunster, Canada 72 C5 53 8N 119 50W
Dunvegan L., Canada 73 A7 60 8N 107 10W
Duolun, China 34 C9 42 12N 116 28 E
Duong Dong, Vietnam 39 G4 10 13N 103 58 E
Dupree, U.S.A. 80 C4 45 4N 101 35W
Dupuyer, U.S.A. 82 B7 48 13N 112 30W
Duque de Caxias, Brazil 95 A7 22 45S 43 19W
Durack →, Australia 60 C4 15 33S 127 52 E
Durack Ra., Australia 60 C4 16 50S 127 40 E
Durance →, France 18 E6 43 55N 4 45 E
Durand, U.S.A. 76 D4 42 55N 83 59W
Durango = Victoria de Durango, Mexico 86 C4 24 3N 104 39W
Durango, Spain 19 A4 43 13N 2 40W
Durango, U.S.A. 83 H10 37 16N 107 53W
Durango □, Mexico 86 C4 25 0N 105 0W
Duranillin, Australia 61 F2 33 30S 116 45 E
Durant, U.S.A. 81 J6 33 59N 96 25W
Durazno, Uruguay 94 C4 33 25S 56 31W
Durazzo = Durrësi, Albania 21 D8 41 19N 19 28 E
Durban, S. Africa 57 D5 29 49S 31 1 E
Durg, India 41 J12 21 15N 81 22 E
Durgapur, India 43 H12 23 30N 87 20 E
Durham, Canada 78 B4 44 10N 80 49W
Durham, U.K. 10 C6 54 47N 1 34W
Durham, Calif., U.S.A. 84 F5 39 39N 121 48W
Durham, N.C., U.S.A. 77 G6 35 59N 78 54W
Durham □, U.K. 10 C6 54 42N 1 45W
Durham Downs, Australia 63 D4 26 6S 149 5 E
Durmitor, Montenegro, Yug. 21 C8 43 10N 19 0 E
Durness, U.K. 12 C4 58 34N 4 45W
Durrësi, Albania 21 D8 41 19N 19 28 E
Durrie, Australia 62 D3 25 40S 140 15 E
Duru, Zaïre 54 B2 4 14N 28 50 E
D'Urville, Tanjung, Indonesia 37 E9 1 28S 137 54 E
D'Urville I., N.Z. 59 J4 40 50S 173 55 E
Duryea, U.S.A. 79 E9 41 20N 75 45W
Dusa Mareb, Somali Rep. 46 F4 5 30N 46 15 E
Dushak, Turkmenistan 26 F7 37 13N 60 1 E
Dushanbe, Tajikistan 26 F7 38 33N 68 48 E
Dusky Sd., N.Z. 59 L1 45 47S 166 30 E
Dussejour, C., Australia 60 B4 14 45S 128 13 E
Düsseldorf, Germany 16 C3 51 15N 6 46 E
Dutch Harbor, U.S.A. 68 C3 53 53N 166 32W
Dutlwe, Botswana 56 C3 23 58S 23 46 E
Dutton, Canada 78 D3 42 39N 81 30W
Dutton →, Australia 62 C3 20 44S 143 10 E
Duyun, China 32 D5 26 18N 107 29 E
Duzdab = Zāhedān, Iran 45 D9 29 30N 60 50 E
Dvina, Sev. →, Russia 24 B7 64 32N 40 30 E
Dvinsk = Daugavpils, Latvia 24 C4 55 53N 26 32 E
Dvinskaya Guba, Russia 24 B6 65 0N 39 0 E
Dwarka, India 42 H3 22 18N 69 8 E
Dwellingup, Australia 61 F2 32 43S 116 4 E
Dwight, Canada 78 A5 45 20N 79 1W
Dwight, U.S.A. 76 E1 41 5N 88 26W
Dyer, C., Canada 69 B13 66 40N 61 0W
Dyer Plateau, Antarctica 5 D17 70 45S 65 30W
Dyersburg, U.S.A. 81 G10 36 3N 89 23W
Dyfed □, U.K. 11 E3 52 0N 4 30W
Dyfi →, U.K. 11 E4 52 32N 4 0W
Dynevor Downs, Australia 63 D3 28 10S 144 20 E
Dysart, Canada 73 C8 50 57N 104 2W
Dzamin Üüd, Mongolia 34 C6 43 50N 111 58 E
Dzerzhinsk, Belorussia 24 D4 53 40N 27 1 E
Dzerzhinsk, Russia 24 C7 56 14N 43 30 E
Dzhalinda, Russia 27 D13 53 26N 124 0 E
Dzhambul, Kazakhstan 26 E8 42 54N 71 22 E
Dzhankoi, Ukraine 25 E5 45 40N 34 20 E
Dzhardzhan, Russia 27 C13 68 10N 124 10 E
Dzhelinde, Russia 27 C12 70 0N 114 20 E
Dzhetygara, Kazakhstan 26 D7 52 11N 61 12 E
Dzhezkazgan, Kazakhstan 26 E7 47 44N 67 40 E
Dzhikimde, Russia 27 D13 59 1N 121 47 E
Dzhizak, Uzbekistan 26 E7 40 6N 67 50 E
Dzhugdzur, Khrebet, Russia 27 D14 57 30N 138 0 E
Dzhungarskiye Vorota, Kazakhstan 32 B3 45 0N 82 0 E
Dzilam de Bravo, Mexico 87 C7 21 24N 88 53W
Dzungaria = Junggar Pendi, China 32 B3 44 30N 86 0 E
Dzungarian Gates = Dzhungarskiye Vorota, Kazakhstan 32 B3 45 0N 82 0 E
Dzuumod, Mongolia 32 B5 47 45N 106 58 E

E

Eabamet, L., Canada 70 B2 51 30N 87 46W
Eads, U.S.A. 80 F3 38 29N 102 47W
Eagle, U.S.A. 82 G10 39 39N 106 50W
Eagle →, Canada 71 B8 53 36N 57 26W
Eagle Butte, U.S.A. 80 C4 45 0N 101 10W
Eagle Grove, U.S.A. 80 D8 42 40N 93 54W
Eagle L., Calif., U.S.A. 82 F3 40 39N 120 45W
Eagle L., Maine, U.S.A. 71 C6 46 20N 69 22W
Eagle Lake, U.S.A. 81 L6 29 35N 96 20W
Eagle Mountain, U.S.A. 85 M11 33 49N 115 27W
Eagle Nest, U.S.A. 83 H11 36 33N 105 16W
Eagle Pass, U.S.A. 81 L4 28 43N 100 30W
Eagle Pk., U.S.A. 84 G7 38 10N 119 25W
Eagle Pt., Australia 60 C3 16 11S 124 23 E
Eagle River, U.S.A. 80 C10 45 55N 89 15W
Ealing, U.K. 11 F7 51 30N 0 19W
Earaheedy, Australia 61 E3 25 34S 121 29 E
Earl Grey, Canada 73 C8 50 57N 104 43W
Earle, U.S.A. 81 H9 35 16N 90 28W
Earlimart, U.S.A. 85 K7 35 53N 119 16W
Earn →, U.K. 12 E5 56 20N 3 19W
Earn, L., U.K. 12 E4 56 23N 4 14W
Earnslaw, Mt., N.Z. 59 L2 44 32S 168 27 E
Earth, U.S.A. 81 H3 34 14N 102 24W
Easley, U.S.A. 77 H4 34 50N 82 36W
East Angus, Canada 71 C5 45 30N 71 40W
East Aurora, U.S.A. 78 D6 42 46N 78 37W
East B., U.S.A. 81 L10 29 0N 89 15W
East Bengal, Bangla. 41 G17 24 0N 90 0 E
East Beskids = Vychodné Beskydy, Europe 17 D10 49 20N 22 0 E
East Brady, U.S.A. 78 F5 40 59N 79 36W
East C., N.Z. 59 G7 37 42S 178 35 E

Fannich, L.

Emporium, U.S.A. 78 E6 41 31N 78 14W
Empress, Canada 73 C6 50 57N 110 0W
Empty Quarter = Rub' al Khali, Si. Arabia 46 D4 18 0N 48 0 E
Ems →, Germany 16 B3 53 22N 7 15 E
Emsdale, Canada 78 A5 45 32N 79 19W
Emu, China 35 C15 43 40N 128 6 E
Emu Park, Australia 62 C5 23 13S 150 50 E
'En 'Avrona, Israel 47 F3 29 43N 35 0 E
En Nahud, Sudan 51 F10 12 45N 28 25 E
Ena, Japan 31 G8 35 25N 137 25 E
Enana, Namibia 56 B2 17 30S 16 23 E
Enaratoli, Indonesia 37 E9 3 55S 136 21 E
Enard B., U.K. 12 C3 58 5N 5 20W
Enare = Inarijärvi, Finland 8 B19 69 0N 28 0 E
Encantadas, Serra, Brazil 95 C5 30 40S 53 0W
Encanto, C., Phil. 37 A6 15 45N 121 38 E
Encarnación, Paraguay 95 B4 27 15S 55 50W
Encarnación de Diaz, Mexico 86 C4 21 30N 102 13W
Encinal, U.S.A. 81 L5 28 2N 99 21W
Encinitas, U.S.A. 85 M9 33 3N 117 17W
Encino, U.S.A. 83 J11 34 39N 105 28W
Encounter B., Australia 63 F2 35 45S 138 45 E
Ende, Indonesia 37 F6 8 45S 121 40 E
Endeavour, Canada 73 C8 52 10N 102 39W
Endeavour Str., Australia 62 A3 10 45S 142 0 E
Enderbury I., Kiribati 64 H10 3 8S 171 5W
Enderby, Canada 72 C5 50 35N 119 10W
Enderby I., Australia 60 D2 20 35S 116 30 E
Enderby Land, Antarctica 5 C5 66 0S 53 0 E
Enderlin, U.S.A. 80 B6 46 38N 97 36W
Endicott, N.Y., U.S.A. 79 D8 42 6N 76 4W
Endicott, Wash., U.S.A. 82 C5 46 56N 117 41W
Endyalgout I., Australia 60 B5 11 40S 132 35 E
Enewetak Atoll, Pac. Oc. 64 F8 11 30N 162 15 E
Enez, Turkey 21 D12 40 45N 26 5 E
Enfield, U.K. 11 F7 51 39N 0 4W
Engadin, Switz. 16 E5 46 45N 10 10 E
Engaño, C., Dom. Rep. 89 C6 18 30N 68 20W
Engaño, C., Phil. 37 A6 18 35N 122 23 E
Engcobo, S. Africa 57 E4 31 37S 28 0 E
Engels = Pokrovsk, Russia 24 D8 51 28N 46 6 E
Engemann L., Canada 73 B7 58 0N 106 55W
Enggano, Indonesia 36 F2 5 20S 102 40 E
Enghien, Belgium 15 D4 50 37N 4 2 E
Engkilili, Malaysia 36 D4 1 3N 111 42 E
England, U.S.A. 81 H9 34 33N 91 58W
England □, U.K. 7 E5 53 0N 2 0W
Englee, Canada 71 B8 50 45N 56 5W
Englehart, Canada 70 C4 47 49N 79 52W
Engler L., Canada 73 B7 59 8N 106 52W
Englewood, Colo., U.S.A. 80 F2 39 39N 104 59W
Englewood, Kans., U.S.A. 81 G5 37 2N 99 59W
English →, Canada 73 C10 50 35N 93 30W
English Bazar = Ingraj Bazar, India 43 G13 24 58N 88 10 E
English Channel, Europe 11 G6 50 0N 2 0W
English River, Canada 70 C1 49 14N 91 0W
Enid, U.S.A. 81 G6 36 24N 97 53W
Enkhuizen, Neths. 15 B5 52 42N 5 17 E
Enna, Italy 20 F6 37 34N 14 15 E
Ennadai, Canada 73 A8 61 8N 100 53W
Ennadai L., Canada 73 A8 61 0N 101 0W
Ennedi, Chad 51 E9 17 15N 22 0 E
Enngonia, Australia 63 D4 29 21S 145 50 E
Ennis, Ireland 13 D3 52 51N 8 59W
Ennis, Mont., U.S.A. 82 D8 45 21N 111 44W
Ennis, Tex., U.S.A. 81 J6 32 20N 96 38W
Enniscorthy, Ireland 13 D5 52 30N 6 35W
Enniskillen, U.K. 13 B4 54 20N 7 40W
Ennistimon, Ireland 13 D2 52 56N 9 18W
Enns →, Austria 16 D7 48 14N 14 32 E
Enontekiö, Finland 8 B17 68 23N 23 37 E
Enriquillo, L., Dom. Rep. 89 C5 18 20N 72 5W
Enschede, Neths. 15 B6 52 13N 6 53 E
Ensenada, Argentina 94 C4 34 55S 57 55W
Ensenada, Mexico 86 A1 31 50N 116 50W
Ensiola, Pta., Spain 22 B9 39 7N 2 55 E
Entebbe, Uganda 54 B3 0 4N 32 28 E
Enterprise, Canada 72 A5 60 47N 115 45W
Enterprise, Oreg., U.S.A. 82 D5 45 25N 117 17W
Enterprise, Utah, U.S.A. 83 H7 37 34N 113 43W
Entre Ríos, Bolivia 94 A3 21 30S 64 25W
Entre Ríos □, Argentina 94 C4 30 30S 58 30W
Enugu, Nigeria 50 G6 6 20N 7 30 E
Enugu Ezike, Nigeria 50 G6 7 0N 7 29 E
Enumclaw, U.S.A. 84 C5 47 12N 121 59W
Eólie, Is., Italy 20 E6 38 30N 14 50 E
Epe, Neths. 15 B5 52 21N 5 59 E
Épernay, France 18 B5 49 3N 3 56 E
Ephraim, U.S.A. 82 G8 39 22N 111 35W
Ephrata, U.S.A. 82 C4 47 19N 119 33W
Épinal, France 18 B7 48 10N 6 27 E
Episkopi, Cyprus 23 E11 34 40N 32 54 E
Episkopi, Greece 23 D6 35 20N 24 20 E
Episkopi Bay, Cyprus 23 E11 34 35N 32 50 E
Epping, U.K. 11 F8 51 42N 0 8 E
Epukiro, Namibia 56 C2 21 40S 19 9 E
Equatorial Guinea ■, Africa 52 D1 2 0N 8 0 E
Er Rahad, Sudan 51 F11 12 45N 30 32 E
Er Rif, Morocco 50 A4 35 1N 4 1W
Er Roseires, Sudan 51 F11 11 55N 34 30 E
Erāwadī Myit = Irrawaddy →, Burma 41 M19 15 50N 95 6 E
Erbil = Arbīl, Iraq 44 B5 36 15N 44 5 E
Ercha, Russia 27 C15 69 45N 147 20 E
Erciyaş Dağı, Turkey 25 G6 38 30N 35 30 E
Erdao Jiang →, China 35 C14 43 0N 127 0 E
Erdene, Mongolia 34 B6 44 13N 111 10 E
Erebus, Mt., Antarctica 5 D11 77 35S 167 0 E
Erechim, Brazil 95 B5 27 35S 52 15W
Ereğli, Konya, Turkey 25 G5 37 31N 34 4 E
Ereğli, Zonguldak, Turkey 25 F5 41 15N 31 24 E
Erenhot, China 34 C7 43 48N 112 2 E
Eresma →, Spain 19 B3 41 26N 4 45W
Erewadi Myitwanya, Burma 41 M19 15 30N 95 0 E
Erfenisdam, S. Africa 56 D4 28 30S 26 50 E
Erfurt, Germany 16 C5 50 58N 11 2 E
Ergene →, Turkey 21 D12 41 1N 26 22 E
Ergeni Vozvyshennost, Russia 25 E7 47 0N 44 0 E
Eriboll, L., U.K. 12 C4 58 28N 4 41W
Érice, Italy 20 E5 38 4N 12 34 E
Erie, U.S.A. 78 D4 42 8N 80 5W
Erie, L., N. Amer. 78 D3 42 15N 81 0W
Erie Canal, U.S.A. 78 C6 43 5N 78 43W
Erieau, Canada 78 D3 42 16N 81 57W
Erigavo, Somali Rep. 46 E4 10 35N 47 20 E
Erikoúsa, Greece 23 A3 39 53N 19 34 E
Eriksdale, Canada 73 C9 50 52N 98 7W
Erímanthos, Greece 21 F9 37 57N 21 50 E
Erimo-misaki, Japan 30 D11 41 50N 143 15 E
Eritrea ■, Africa 51 F12 14 0N 38 30 E
Erlangen, Germany 16 D5 49 35N 11 2 E
Erldunda, Australia 62 D1 25 14S 133 12 E
Ermelo, Neths. 15 B5 52 18N 5 35 E
Ermelo, S. Africa 57 D4 26 31S 29 59 E
Ermones, Greece 23 A3 39 37N 19 46 E
Ermoúpolis = Síros, Greece 21 F11 37 28N 24 57 E
Ernakulam = Cochin, India 40 Q10 9 59N 76 22 E
Erne →, Ireland 13 B3 54 30N 8 16W
Erne, Lower L., U.K. 13 B4 54 26N 7 46W
Erne, Upper L., U.K. 13 B4 54 14N 7 22W
Ernest Giles Ra., Australia 61 E3 27 0S 123 45 E
Erode, India 40 P10 11 24N 77 45 E
Eromanga, Australia 63 D3 26 40S 143 11 E
Erongo, Namibia 56 C2 21 39S 15 58 E
Errabiddy, Australia 61 E2 25 25S 117 5 E
Erramala Hills, India 40 M11 15 30N 78 15 E
Errigal, Ireland 13 A3 55 2N 8 8W
Erris Hd., Ireland 13 B1 54 19N 10 0W
Erskine, U.S.A. 80 B7 47 40N 96 0W
Ertis = Irtysh →, Russia 26 C7 61 4N 68 52 E
Erwin, U.S.A. 77 G4 36 9N 82 25W
Erzgebirge, Germany 16 C6 50 25N 13 0 E
Erzin, Russia 27 D10 50 15N 95 10 E
Erzincan, Turkey 25 G6 39 46N 39 30 E
Erzurum, Turkey 25 G7 39 57N 41 15 E
Es Caló, Spain 22 C8 38 40N 1 30 E
Es Caná, Spain 22 B8 39 2N 1 36 E
Es Sahrâ' Esh Sharqîya, Egypt 51 C11 27 30N 32 30 E
Es Sînâ', Egypt 51 C11 29 0N 34 0 E
Esambo, Zaïre 54 C1 3 48S 23 30 E
Esan-Misaki, Japan 30 D10 41 40N 141 10 E
Esashi, Hokkaidō, Japan 30 B11 44 56N 142 35 E
Esashi, Hokkaidō, Japan 30 D10 41 52N 140 7 E
Esbjerg, Denmark 9 J10 55 29N 8 29 E
Escalante, U.S.A. 83 H8 37 47N 111 36W
Escalante →, U.S.A. 83 H8 37 24N 110 57W
Escalón, Mexico 86 B4 26 46N 104 20W
Escambia →, U.S.A. 77 K2 30 32N 87 11W
Escanaba, U.S.A. 76 C2 45 45N 87 4W
Esch-sur-Alzette, Lux. 15 E6 49 32N 6 0 E
Escondido, U.S.A. 85 M9 33 7N 117 5W
Escuinapa, Mexico 86 C3 22 50N 105 50W
Escuintla, Guatemala 88 D1 14 20N 90 48W
Eşfahān, Iran 45 C6 33 0N 51 30 E
Esfideh, Iran 45 C8 33 39N 59 46 E
Esh Sham = Dimashq, Syria 47 B5 33 30N 36 18 E
Esh Shamâlîya □, Sudan 51 E10 19 0N 29 0 E
Eshowe, S. Africa 57 D5 28 50S 31 30 E
Esil = Ishim →, Russia 26 D8 57 45N 71 10 E
Esk →, Dumf. & Gall., U.K. 12 G5 54 58N 3 4W
Esk →, N. Yorks., U.K. 10 C7 54 27N 0 36W
Eskifjörður, Iceland 8 D7 65 3N 13 55W
Eskilstuna, Sweden 9 G14 59 22N 16 32 E
Eskimo Pt., Canada 73 A10 61 10N 94 15W
Eskişehir, Turkey 25 G5 39 50N 30 35 E
Esla →, Spain 19 B2 41 29N 6 3W
Eslāmābād-e Gharb, Iran 44 C5 34 10N 46 30 E
Esmeraldas, Ecuador 92 C3 1 0N 79 40W
Espalmador, I., Spain 22 C7 38 47N 1 26 E
Espanola, Canada 70 C3 46 15N 81 46W
Espardell, I. del, Spain 22 C7 38 48N 1 29 E
Esparta, Costa Rica 88 E3 9 59N 84 40W
Esperance, Australia 61 F3 33 45S 121 55 E
Esperance B., Australia 61 F3 33 48S 121 55 E
Esperanza, Argentina 94 C3 31 29S 61 3W
Espichel, C., Portugal 19 C1 38 22N 9 16W
Espigão, Serra do, Brazil 95 B5 26 35S 50 30W
Espinal, Colombia 92 C4 4 9N 74 53W
Espinazo, Sierra del = Espinhaço, Serra do, Brazil 93 G10 17 30S 43 30W
Espinhaço, Serra do, Brazil 93 G10 17 30S 43 30W
Espinilho, Serra do, Brazil 95 B5 28 30S 55 0W
Espírito Santo □, Brazil 93 G10 20 0S 40 45W
Espíritu Santo, B. del, Mexico 87 D7 19 15N 87 0W
Espíritu Santo, I., Mexico 86 C2 24 30N 110 23W
Espita, Mexico 87 C7 21 1N 88 19W
Espungabera, Mozam. 57 C5 20 29S 32 45 E
Esquel, Argentina 96 E2 42 55S 71 20W
Esquina, Argentina 94 B4 30 0S 59 30W
Essaouira, Morocco 50 B3 31 32N 9 42W
Essebie, Zaïre 54 B3 2 58N 30 40 E
Essen, Belgium 15 C4 51 28N 4 28 E
Essen, Germany 16 C3 51 28N 6 59 E
Essendon, Mt., Australia 61 E3 25 0S 120 29 E
Essequibo →, Guyana 92 B7 6 50N 58 30W
Essex, Canada 78 D2 42 10N 82 49W
Essex, Calif., U.S.A. 85 L11 34 44N 115 15W
Essex, N.Y., U.S.A. 79 B11 44 19N 73 21W
Essex □, U.K. 11 F8 51 48N 0 30 E
Esslingen, Germany 16 D4 48 43N 9 19 E
Essonne □, France 18 B5 48 30N 2 20 E
Estados, I. de Los, Argentina 96 G4 54 40S 64 30W
Eşţahbānāt, Iran 45 D7 29 8N 54 4 E
Estallenchs, Spain 22 B9 39 39N 2 29 E
Estância, Brazil 93 F11 11 16S 37 26W
Estancia, U.S.A. 83 J10 34 46N 106 4W
Estārm, Iran 45 D8 28 21N 58 21 E
Estcourt, S. Africa 57 D4 29 0S 29 53 E
Estelí, Nic. 88 D2 13 9N 86 22W
Estelline, S. Dak., U.S.A. 80 C6 44 35N 96 54W
Estelline, Tex., U.S.A. 81 H4 34 33N 100 26W
Esterhazy, Canada 73 C8 50 37N 102 5W
Estevan, Canada 73 D8 49 10N 102 59W
Estevan Group, Canada 72 C3 53 3N 129 38W
Estherville, U.S.A. 80 D7 43 24N 94 50W
Eston, Canada 73 C7 51 8N 108 40W
Estonia ■, Europe 24 C4 58 30N 25 30 E
Estoril, Portugal 19 C1 38 42N 9 23W
Estrêla, Serra da, Portugal 19 B2 40 10N 7 45W
Estremadura, Portugal 19 C1 39 0N 9 0W
Estrondo, Serra do, Brazil 93 E9 7 20S 48 0W
Esztergom, Hungary 17 E9 47 47N 18 44 E
Etadunna, Australia 63 D2 28 43S 138 38 E
Etah, India 43 F8 27 35N 78 40 E
Etamamu, Canada 71 B8 50 18N 59 59W
Etanga, Namibia 56 B1 17 55S 13 0 E
Etawah, India 43 F8 26 48N 79 6 E
Etawah →, U.S.A. 77 H3 34 20N 84 15W
Etawney L., Canada 73 B9 57 50N 96 50W
Ethel, U.S.A. 84 D4 46 32N 122 46W
Ethel Creek, Australia 60 D3 22 55S 120 11 E
Ethelbert, Canada 73 C8 51 32N 100 25W
Ethiopia ■, Africa 46 F3 8 0N 40 0 E
Ethiopian Highlands, Ethiopia 48 E7 10 0N 37 0 E
Etive, L., U.K. 12 E3 56 30N 5 12W
Etna, Italy 20 F6 37 45N 15 0 E
Etoile, Zaïre 55 E2 11 33S 27 30 E
Etolin I., U.S.A. 72 B2 56 5N 132 20W
Etosha Pan, Namibia 56 B2 18 40S 16 30 E
Etowah, U.S.A. 77 H3 35 20N 84 32W
Ettrick Water →, U.K. 12 F6 55 31N 2 55W
Etuku, Zaïre 54 C2 3 42S 25 45 E
Etzatlán, Mexico 86 C4 20 48N 104 5W
Euboea = Évvoia, Greece 21 E11 38 30N 24 0 E
Eucla Motel, Australia 61 F4 31 41S 128 52 E
Euclid, U.S.A. 78 E3 41 34N 81 32W
Eucumbene, L., Australia 63 F4 36 2S 148 40 E
Eudora, U.S.A. 81 J9 33 7N 91 16W
Eufaula, Ala., U.S.A. 77 K3 31 54N 85 9W
Eufaula, Okla., U.S.A. 81 H7 35 17N 95 35W
Eufaula L., U.S.A. 81 H7 35 18N 95 21W
Eugene, U.S.A. 82 E2 44 5N 123 4W
Eugowra, Australia 63 E4 33 22S 148 24 E
Eulo, Australia 63 D4 28 10S 145 3 E
Eunice, La., U.S.A. 81 K8 30 30N 92 25W
Eunice, N. Mex., U.S.A. 81 J3 32 26N 103 10W
Eupen, Belgium 15 D6 50 37N 6 3 E
Euphrates = Furāt, Nahr al →, Asia 44 D5 31 0N 47 25 E
Eure □, France 18 B4 49 10N 1 0 E
Eure-et-Loir □, France 18 B4 48 22N 1 30 E
Eureka, Canada 4 B3 80 0N 85 56W
Eureka, Calif., U.S.A. 82 F1 40 47N 124 9W
Eureka, Kans., U.S.A. 81 G6 37 49N 96 17W
Eureka, Mont., U.S.A. 82 B6 48 53N 115 3W
Eureka, Nev., U.S.A. 82 G5 39 31N 115 58W
Eureka, S. Dak., U.S.A. 80 C5 45 46N 99 38W
Eureka, Utah, U.S.A. 82 G7 39 58N 112 7W
Eureka, Mt., Australia 61 E3 26 35S 121 35 E
Euroa, Australia 63 F4 36 44S 145 35 E
Europa, Î., Ind. Oc. 53 J8 22 20S 40 22 E
Europa, Picos de, Spain 19 A3 43 10N 4 49W
Europa, Pta. de, Gib. 19 D3 36 3N 5 21W
Europa Pt. = Europa, Pta. de, Gib. 19 D3 36 3N 5 21W
Europe 6 F10 50 0N 20 0 E
Europoort, Neths. 15 C4 51 57N 4 10 E
Eustis, U.S.A. 77 L5 28 51N 81 41W
Eutsuk L., Canada 72 C3 53 20N 126 45W
Eva Downs, Australia 62 B1 18 1S 134 52 E
Evale, Angola 56 B2 16 33S 15 44 E
Evans, U.S.A. 80 E2 40 23N 104 41W
Evans Head, Australia 63 D5 29 7S 153 27 E
Evans L., Canada 70 B4 50 50N 77 0W
Evans Mills, U.S.A. 79 B9 44 6N 75 48W
Evanston, Ill., U.S.A. 76 D2 42 3N 87 41W
Evanston, Wyo., U.S.A. 82 F8 41 16N 110 58W
Evansville, Ind., U.S.A. 76 F2 37 58N 87 35W
Evansville, Wis., U.S.A. 80 D10 42 47N 89 18W
Evaz, Iran 45 E7 27 46N 53 59 E
Eveleth, U.S.A. 80 B8 47 28N 92 32W
Evensk, Russia 27 C16 62 12N 159 30 E
Everard, L., Australia 63 E1 31 30S 135 0 E
Everard Park, Australia 61 E5 27 5S 132 43 E
Everard Ras., Australia 61 E5 27 5S 132 28 E
Everest, Mt., Nepal 43 E12 28 5N 86 58 E
Everett, Pa., U.S.A. 78 F6 40 1N 78 23W
Everett, Wash., U.S.A. 84 C4 47 59N 122 12W
Everglades, The, U.S.A. 77 N5 25 50N 81 0W
Everglades City, U.S.A. 77 N5 25 52N 81 23W
Everglades National Park, U.S.A. 77 N5 25 30N 81 0W
Evergreen, U.S.A. 77 K2 31 26N 86 57W
Everson, U.S.A. 82 B2 48 57N 122 22W
Evesham, U.K. 11 E6 52 6N 1 57W
Evinayong, Eq. Guin. 52 D2 1 26N 10 35 E
Évora, Portugal 19 C2 38 33N 7 57W
Evowghlī, Iran 44 B5 38 43N 45 13 E
Évreux, France 18 B4 49 3N 1 8 E
Évvoia, Greece 21 E11 38 30N 24 0 E
Ewe, L., U.K. 12 D3 57 49N 5 38W
Ewing, U.S.A. 80 D5 42 16N 98 21W
Ewo, Congo 52 E2 0 48S 14 45 E
Exaltación, Bolivia 92 F5 13 10S 65 20W
Excelsior Springs, U.S.A. 80 F7 39 20N 94 13W
Exe →, U.K. 11 G4 50 38N 3 27W
Exeter, Canada 78 C3 43 21N 81 29W
Exeter, U.K. 11 G4 50 43N 3 31W
Exeter, Calif., U.S.A. 83 H4 36 18N 119 9W
Exeter, N.H., U.S.A. 79 D14 42 59N 70 57W
Exeter, Nebr., U.S.A. 80 E6 40 39N 97 27W
Exmoor, U.K. 11 F4 51 10N 3 59W
Exmouth, Australia 60 D1 21 54S 114 10 E
Exmouth, U.K. 11 G4 50 37N 3 26W
Exmouth G., Australia 60 D1 22 15S 114 15 E
Expedition Ra., Australia 62 C4 24 30S 149 12 E
Extremadura □, Spain 19 C2 39 30N 6 5W
Exuma Sound, Bahamas 88 B4 24 30N 76 20W
Eyasi, L., Tanzania 54 C4 3 30S 35 0 E
Eyeberry L., Canada 73 A8 63 8N 104 43W
Eyemouth, U.K. 12 F6 55 53N 2 5W
Eyjafjörður, Iceland 8 C4 66 15N 18 30W
Eyrarbakki, Iceland 8 E3 63 52N 21 9W
Eyre, Australia 61 F4 32 15S 126 18 E
Eyre (North), L., Australia 63 D2 28 30S 137 20 E
Eyre (South), L., Australia 63 D2 29 18S 137 25 E
Eyre Cr. →, Australia 63 D2 26 40S 139 0 E
Eyre Mts., N.Z. 59 L2 45 25S 168 25 E
Eyre Pen., Australia 63 E2 33 30S 136 17 E
Eyvānkī, Iran 45 C6 35 24N 51 56 E
Ezouza →, Cyprus 23 E11 34 44N 32 27 E

F

Fabens, U.S.A. 83 L10 31 30N 106 10W
Fabriano, Italy 20 C5 43 20N 12 52 E
Facatativá, Colombia 92 C4 4 49N 74 22W
Fachi, Niger 50 E7 18 6N 11 34 E
Fada, Chad 51 E9 17 13N 21 34 E
Fada-n-Gourma, Burkina Faso 50 F5 12 10N 0 30 E
Faddeyevskiy, Ostrov, Russia 27 B15 76 0N 144 0 E
Fadghāmī, Syria 44 C4 35 53N 40 52 E
Faenza, Italy 20 B4 44 17N 11 53 E
Făgăras, Romania 17 F12 45 48N 24 58 E
Fagernes, Norway 9 F10 60 59N 9 14 E
Fagersta, Sweden 9 F13 60 1N 15 46 E
Fagnano, L., Argentina 96 G3 54 30S 68 0W
Fahlīān, Iran 45 D6 30 11N 51 28 E
Fahraj, Kermān, Iran 45 D8 29 0N 59 0 E
Fahraj, Yazd, Iran 45 D7 31 46N 54 36 E
Faial, Madeira 22 D3 32 47N 16 53W
Fair Hd., U.K. 13 A5 55 14N 6 10W
Fair Oaks, U.S.A. 84 G5 38 39N 121 16W
Fairbank, U.S.A. 83 L8 31 43N 110 11W
Fairbanks, U.S.A. 68 B5 64 51N 147 43W
Fairbury, U.S.A. 80 E6 40 8N 97 11W
Fairfax, U.S.A. 81 G6 36 34N 96 42W
Fairfield, Ala., U.S.A. 77 J2 33 29N 86 55W
Fairfield, Calif., U.S.A. 84 G4 38 15N 122 3W
Fairfield, Conn., U.S.A. 79 E11 41 9N 73 16W
Fairfield, Idaho, U.S.A. 82 E6 43 21N 114 44W
Fairfield, Ill., U.S.A. 76 F1 38 23N 88 22W
Fairfield, Iowa, U.S.A. 80 E9 40 56N 91 57W
Fairfield, Mont., U.S.A. 82 C8 47 37N 111 59W
Fairfield, Tex., U.S.A. 81 K7 31 44N 96 10W
Fairford, Canada 73 C9 51 37N 98 38W
Fairhope, U.S.A. 77 K2 30 31N 87 54W
Fairlie, N.Z. 59 L3 44 5S 170 49 E
Fairmead, U.S.A. 84 H6 37 5N 120 10W
Fairmont, Minn., U.S.A. 80 D7 43 39N 94 28W
Fairmont, W. Va., U.S.A. 76 F5 39 29N 80 9W
Fairmount, U.S.A. 85 L8 34 45N 118 26W
Fairplay, U.S.A. 83 G11 39 15N 106 2W
Fairport, U.S.A. 78 C7 43 6N 77 27W
Fairport Harbor, U.S.A. 78 E3 41 45N 81 17W
Fairview, Australia 62 B3 15 31S 144 17 E
Fairview, Canada 72 B5 56 5N 118 25W
Fairview, Mont., U.S.A. 80 B2 47 51N 104 3W
Fairview, Okla., U.S.A. 81 G5 36 16N 98 29W
Fairview, Utah, U.S.A. 82 G8 39 50N 111 0W
Fairweather, Mt., U.S.A. 68 C6 58 55N 137 32W
Faisalabad, Pakistan 42 D5 31 30N 73 5 E
Faith, U.S.A. 80 C3 45 2N 102 2W
Faizabad, India 43 F10 26 45N 82 10 E
Fajardo, Puerto Rico 89 C6 18 20N 65 39W
Fakfak, Indonesia 37 E8 3 0S 132 15 E
Faku, China 35 C12 42 32N 123 21 E
Falaise, France 18 B3 48 54N 0 12W
Falaise, Mui, Vietnam 38 C5 19 6N 105 45 E
Falam, Burma 41 H18 23 0N 93 45 E
Falcón, C., Spain 22 C7 38 50N 1 23 E
Falcon Dam, U.S.A. 81 M5 26 50N 99 20W
Falconer, U.S.A. 78 D5 42 7N 79 13W
Falfurrias, U.S.A. 81 M5 27 14N 98 9W
Falher, Canada 72 B5 55 44N 117 15W
Faliraki, Greece 23 C10 36 22N 28 12 E
Falkenberg, Sweden 9 H12 56 54N 12 30 E
Falkirk, U.K. 12 F5 56 0N 3 47W
Falkland Is. ■, Atl. Oc. 96 G5 51 30S 59 0W
Falkland Is. Dependency □, Atl. Oc. 5 B1 57 0S 40 0W
Falkland Sd., Falk. Is. 96 G5 52 0S 60 0W
Falköping, Sweden 9 G12 58 12N 13 33 E
Fall River, U.S.A. 79 E13 41 43N 71 10W
Fall River Mills, U.S.A. 82 F3 41 3N 121 26W
Fallbrook, U.S.A. 83 K5 33 25N 117 12W
Fallbrook, Calif., U.S.A. 85 M9 33 23N 117 15W
Fallon, Mont., U.S.A. 80 B2 46 50N 105 8W
Fallon, Nev., U.S.A. 82 G4 39 28N 118 47W
Falls City, Nebr., U.S.A. 80 E7 40 3N 95 36W
Falls City, Oreg., U.S.A. 82 D2 44 52N 123 26W
Falls Creek, U.S.A. 78 E6 41 9N 78 48W
Falmouth, Jamaica 88 C4 18 30N 77 40W
Falmouth, U.K. 11 G2 50 9N 5 5W
Falmouth, U.S.A. 76 F3 38 41N 84 20W
False B., S. Africa 56 E2 34 15S 18 40 E
Falso, C., Honduras 88 C3 15 12N 83 21W
Falster, Denmark 9 J11 54 45N 11 55 E
Falsterbo, Sweden 9 J12 55 23N 12 50 E
Falun, Sweden 9 F13 60 37N 15 37 E
Famagusta, Cyprus 23 D12 35 8N 33 55 E
Famagusta Bay, Cyprus 23 D13 35 15N 34 0 E
Famatina, Sierra de, Argentina 94 B2 27 30S 68 0W
Family L., Canada 73 C9 51 54N 95 27W
Famoso, U.S.A. 85 K7 35 37N 119 12W
Fan Xian, China 34 G8 35 55N 115 38 E
Fandriana, Madag. 57 C8 20 14S 47 21 E
Fang, Thailand 38 C2 19 55N 99 13 E
Fangcheng, China 34 H7 33 18N 112 59 E
Fangshan, China 34 E6 38 3N 111 25 E
Fangzi, China 35 F10 36 33N 119 10 E
Fanjiatun, China 35 C13 43 40N 125 15 E
Fannich, L., U.K. 12 D4 57 40N 5 0W

Fannūj

Fannūj, *Iran* **45 E8** 26 35N 59 38 E
Fanny Bay, *Canada* **72 D4** 49 37N 124 48W
Fano, *Italy* **20 C5** 43 50N 13 0 E
Fanshaw, *U.S.A.* **72 B2** 57 11N 133 30W
Fanshi, *China* **34 E7** 39 12N 113 20 E
Fao = Al Fāw, *Iraq* **45 D6** 30 0N 48 30 E
Faqirwali, *Pakistan* **42 E5** 29 27N 73 0 E
Faradje, *Zaïre* **54 B2** 3 50N 29 45 E
Farafangana, *Madag.* **57 C8** 22 49S 47 50 E
Farāh, *Afghan.* **40 C3** 32 20N 62 7 E
Farāh □, *Afghan.* **40 C3** 32 25N 62 10 E
Farahalana, *Madag.* **57 A9** 14 26S 50 10 E
Faranah, *Guinea* **50 F2** 10 3N 10 45W
Farasān, Jazā'ir, *Si. Arabia* **46 D3** 16 45N 41 55 E
Farasan Is. = Farasān, Jazā'ir, *Si. Arabia* **46 D3** 16 45N 41 55 E
Faratsiho, *Madag.* **57 B8** 19 24S 46 57 E
Fareham, *U.K.* **11 G6** 50 52N 1 11W
Farewell, C., *N.Z.* **59 J4** 40 29S 172 43 E
Farewell C. = Farvel, Kap, *Greenland* **4 D5** 59 48N 43 55W
Farghona = Fergana, *Uzbekistan* **26 E8** 40 23N 71 19 E
Fargo, *U.S.A.* **80 B6** 46 53N 96 48W
Fari'a →, *Jordan* **47 C4** 32 12N 35 27 E
Faribault, *U.S.A.* **80 C8** 44 18N 93 16W
Faridkot, *India* **42 D6** 30 44N 74 45 E
Faridpur, *Bangla.* **43 H13** 23 15N 89 55 E
Farim, *Guinea-Biss.* **50 F1** 12 27N 15 9W
Farīmān, *Iran* **45 C8** 35 40N 59 49 E
Farina, *Australia* **63 E2** 30 3S 138 15 E
Fariones, Pta., *Canary Is.* **22 E6** 29 13N 13 28W
Farmerville, *U.S.A.* **81 J8** 32 47N 92 24W
Farmington, *Calif., U.S.A.* **84 H6** 37 55N 120 59W
Farmington, *N.H., U.S.A.* **79 C13** 43 24N 71 4W
Farmington, *N. Mex., U.S.A.* **83 H9** 36 44N 108 12W
Farmington, *Utah, U.S.A.* **82 F8** 41 0N 111 12W
Farmington →, *U.S.A.* **79 E12** 41 51N 72 38W
Farmville, *U.S.A.* **76 G6** 37 18N 78 24W
Farnborough, *U.K.* **11 F7** 51 17N 0 46W
Farne Is., *U.K.* **10 B6** 55 38N 1 37W
Farnham, *Canada* **79 A12** 45 17N 72 59W
Faro, *Brazil* **93 D7** 2 10S 56 39W
Faro, *Portugal* **19 D2** 37 2N 7 55W
Fårö, *Sweden* **9 H15** 57 55N 19 5 E
Faroe Is. = Føroyar, *Atl. Oc.* **7 C4** 62 0N 7 0W
Farquhar, C., *Australia* **61 D1** 23 50S 113 36 E
Farrars Cr. →, *Australia* **62 D3** 25 35S 140 43 E
Farrāshband, *Iran* **45 D7** 28 57N 52 5 E
Farrell, *U.S.A.* **78 E4** 41 13N 80 30W
Farrell Flat, *Australia* **63 E2** 33 48S 138 48 E
Farrokhī, *Iran* **45 C8** 33 50N 59 31 E
Farruch, C., *Spain* **22 B10** 39 47N 3 21 E
Farrukhabad-cum-Fatehgarh, *India* **43 F8** 27 30N 79 32 E
Fārs □, *Iran* **45 D7** 29 30N 55 0 E
Fársala, *Greece* **21 E10** 39 17N 22 23 E
Farsund, *Norway* **9 G9** 58 5N 6 55 E
Fartak, Râs, *Si. Arabia* **44 D2** 28 5N 34 34 E
Fartura, Serra da, *Brazil* **95 B5** 26 21S 52 52W
Fārūj, *Iran* **45 B8** 37 14N 58 14 E
Farvel, Kap, *Greenland* **4 D5** 59 48N 43 55W
Farwell, *U.S.A.* **81 H3** 34 23N 103 2W
Fasā, *Iran* **45 D7** 29 0N 53 39 E
Fastnet Rock, *Ireland* **13 E2** 51 22N 9 37W
Fatagar, Tanjung, *Indonesia* **37 E8** 2 46S 131 57 E
Fatehgarh, *India* **43 F8** 27 25N 79 35 E
Fatehpur, *Raj., India* **42 F6** 28 0N 74 40 E
Fatehpur, *Ut. P., India* **43 G9** 25 56N 81 13 E
Fatima, *Canada* **71 C7** 47 24N 61 53W
Faulkton, *U.S.A.* **80 C5** 45 2N 99 8W
Faure I., *Australia* **61 E1** 25 52S 113 50 E
Fauresmith, *S. Africa* **56 D4** 29 44S 25 17 E
Fauske, *Norway* **8 C13** 67 17N 15 25 E
Favara, *Italy* **20 F5** 37 19N 13 39 E
Favaritx, C., *Spain* **22 A11** 40 0N 4 15 E
Favignana, *Italy* **20 F5** 37 56N 12 18 E
Favourable Lake, *Canada* **70 B1** 52 50N 93 39W
Fawn →, *Canada* **70 A2** 55 20N 87 35W
Fawnskin, *U.S.A.* **85 L10** 34 16N 116 56W
Faxaflói, *Iceland* **8 D2** 64 29N 23 0W
Faya-Largeau, *Chad* **51 E8** 17 58N 19 6 E
Fayd, *Si. Arabia* **44 E4** 27 1N 42 52 E
Fayette, *Ala., U.S.A.* **77 J2** 33 41N 87 50W
Fayette, *Mo., U.S.A.* **80 F8** 39 9N 92 41W
Fayetteville, *Ark., U.S.A.* **81 G7** 36 4N 94 10W
Fayetteville, *N.C., U.S.A.* **77 H6** 35 3N 78 53W
Fayetteville, *Tenn., U.S.A.* **77 H2** 35 9N 86 34W
Fazilka, *India* **42 D6** 30 27N 74 2 E
Fazilpur, *Pakistan* **42 E4** 29 18N 70 29 E
Fdérik, *Mauritania* **50 D2** 22 40N 12 45W
Feale →, *Ireland* **13 D2** 52 26N 9 40W
Fear, C., *U.S.A.* **77 J7** 33 50N 77 58W
Feather →, *U.S.A.* **82 G3** 38 47N 121 36W
Feather Falls, *U.S.A.* **84 F5** 39 36N 121 16W
Featherston, *N.Z.* **59 J5** 41 6S 175 20 E
Featherstone, *Zimbabwe* **55 F3** 18 42S 30 55 E
Fécamp, *France* **18 B4** 49 45N 0 22 E
Federación, *Argentina* **94 C4** 31 0S 57 55W
Fedeshkūh, *Iran* **45 D7** 28 49N 53 50 E
Fehmarn, *Germany* **16 A5** 54 26N 11 10 E
Fehmarn Bælt, *Denmark* **16 A5** 54 35N 11 20 E
Fei Xian, *China* **35 G9** 35 18N 117 59 E
Feilding, *N.Z.* **59 J5** 40 13S 175 35 E
Feira de Santana, *Brazil* **93 F11** 12 15S 38 57W
Feixiang, *China* **34 F8** 36 30N 114 45 E
Felanitx, *Spain* **22 B10** 39 28N 3 9 E
Feldkirch, *Austria* **16 E4** 47 15N 9 37 E
Felipe Carrillo Puerto, *Mexico* **87 D7** 19 38N 88 3W
Felixstowe, *U.K.* **11 F9** 51 58N 1 22 E
Felton, *U.K.* **10 B6** 55 18N 1 42W
Felton, *U.S.A.* **84 H4** 37 3N 122 4W
Femunden, *Norway* **8 E11** 62 10N 11 53 E
Fen He →, *China* **34 G6** 35 36N 110 42 E
Fenelon Falls, *Canada* **78 B6** 44 32N 78 45W
Feng Xian, *Jiangsu, China* **34 G9** 34 43N 116 35 E
Feng Xian, *Shaanxi, China* **34 H4** 33 54N 106 40 E
Fengcheng, *China* **35 D13** 40 28N 124 5 E
Fengfeng, *China* **34 F8** 36 28N 114 8 E
Fengjie, *China* **33 C5** 31 5N 109 36 E
Fengning, *China* **34 D9** 41 10N 116 33 E
Fengqiu, *China* **34 G8** 35 2N 114 25 E
Fengrun, *China* **35 E10** 39 48N 118 8 E
Fengtai, *China* **34 E9** 39 50N 116 18 E
Fengxiang, *China* **34 G4** 34 29N 107 25 E
Fengyang, *China* **35 H9** 32 51N 117 29 E
Fengzhen, *China* **34 D7** 40 25N 113 2 E
Fenit, *Ireland* **13 D2** 52 17N 9 51W
Fennimore, *U.S.A.* **80 D9** 42 59N 90 39W
Fenoarivo Afovoany, *Madag.* **57 B8** 18 26S 46 34 E
Fenoarivo Atsinanana, *Madag.* **57 B8** 17 22S 49 25 E
Fens, The, *U.K.* **10 E8** 52 45N 0 2 E
Fenton, *U.S.A.* **76 D4** 42 48N 83 42W
Fenxi, *China* **34 F6** 36 40N 111 31 E
Fenyang, *China* **33 C6** 37 19N 111 46 E
Fenyang, *Shanxi, China* **34 F6** 37 18N 111 48 E
Feodosiya, *Ukraine* **25 E6** 45 2N 35 16 E
Ferdows, *Iran* **45 C8** 33 58N 58 2 E
Ferfer, *Somali Rep.* **46 F4** 5 4N 45 9 E
Fergana, *Uzbekistan* **26 E8** 40 23N 71 19 E
Fergus, *Canada* **70 D3** 43 43N 80 24W
Fergus Falls, *U.S.A.* **80 B6** 46 17N 96 4W
Ferland, *Canada* **70 B2** 50 19N 88 27W
Fermanagh □, *U.K.* **13 B4** 54 21N 7 40W
Fermoy, *Ireland* **13 D3** 52 4N 8 18W
Fernández, *Argentina* **94 B3** 27 55S 63 50W
Fernandina Beach, *U.S.A.* **77 K5** 30 40N 81 27W
Fernando de Noronha, *Brazil* **93 D12** 4 0S 33 10W
Fernando Póo = Bioko, *Eq. Guin.* **50 H6** 3 30N 8 40 E
Ferndale, *Calif., U.S.A.* **82 F1** 40 35N 124 16W
Ferndale, *Wash., U.S.A.* **84 B4** 48 51N 122 36W
Fernie, *Canada* **72 D5** 49 30N 115 5W
Fernlees, *Australia* **62 C4** 23 51S 148 7 E
Fernley, *U.S.A.* **82 G4** 39 36N 119 15W
Ferozepore = Firozpur, *India* **42 D6** 30 55N 74 40 E
Ferrara, *Italy* **20 B4** 44 50N 11 36 E
Ferreñafe, *Peru* **92 E3** 6 42S 79 50W
Ferrerías, *Spain* **22 B11** 39 59N 4 1 E
Ferriday, *U.S.A.* **81 K9** 31 38N 91 33W
Ferrol = El Ferrol, *Spain* **19 A1** 43 29N 8 15W
Ferron, *U.S.A.* **83 G8** 39 5N 111 8W
Ferryland, *Canada* **71 C9** 47 2N 52 53W
Fertile, *U.S.A.* **80 B6** 47 32N 96 17W
Fès, *Morocco* **50 B4** 34 0N 5 0W
Feshi, *Zaïre* **52 F3** 6 8S 18 10 E
Fessenden, *U.S.A.* **80 B5** 47 39N 99 38W
Fetlar, *U.K.* **12 A8** 60 36N 0 52W
Feuilles →, *Canada* **69 C12** 58 47N 70 4W
Fezzan, *Libya* **51 C8** 27 0N 15 0 E
Ffestiniog, *U.K.* **10 E4** 52 58N 3 56W
Fiambalá, *Argentina* **94 B2** 27 45S 67 37W
Fianarantsoa, *Madag.* **57 C8** 21 26S 47 5 E
Fianarantsoa □, *Madag.* **57 B8** 19 30S 47 0 E
Fianga, *Cameroon* **51 G8** 9 55N 15 9 E
Fichtelgebirge, *Germany* **16 C6** 50 10N 12 0 E
Ficksburg, *S. Africa* **57 D4** 28 51S 27 53 E
Field, *Canada* **70 C3** 46 31N 80 1W
Field →, *Australia* **62 C2** 23 48S 138 0 E
Field I., *Australia* **60 B5** 12 5S 132 23 E
Fife □, *U.K.* **12 E5** 56 13N 3 2W
Fife Ness, *U.K.* **12 E6** 56 17N 2 35W
Figeac, *France* **18 D5** 44 37N 2 2 E
Figtree, *Zimbabwe* **55 G2** 20 22S 28 20 E
Figueira da Foz, *Portugal* **19 B1** 40 7N 8 54W
Figueras, *Spain* **19 A7** 42 18N 2 58 E
Figuig, *Morocco* **50 B4** 32 5N 1 11W
Fihaonana, *Madag.* **57 B8** 18 36S 47 12 E
Fiherenana, *Madag.* **57 B8** 18 29S 48 24 E
Fiherenana →, *Madag.* **57 C7** 23 19S 43 37 E
Fiji ■, *Pac. Oc.* **59 C8** 17 20S 179 0 E
Filer, *U.S.A.* **82 E6** 42 34N 114 37W
Filey, *U.K.* **10 C7** 54 13N 0 18W
Filfla, *Malta* **23 D1** 35 47N 14 24 E
Filiatrá, *Greece* **21 F9** 37 9N 21 35 E
Filipstad, *Sweden* **9 G13** 59 43N 14 9 E
Fillmore, *Canada* **73 D8** 49 50N 103 25W
Fillmore, *Calif., U.S.A.* **85 L8** 34 24N 118 55W
Fillmore, *Utah, U.S.A.* **83 G7** 38 58N 112 20W
Finch, *Canada* **79 A9** 45 11N 75 7W
Findhorn →, *U.K.* **12 D5** 57 38N 3 38W
Findlay, *U.S.A.* **76 E4** 41 2N 83 39W
Finger L., *Canada* **73 C10** 53 33N 93 30W
Fingõe, *Mozam.* **55 E3** 14 55S 31 50 E
Finistère □, *France* **18 B2** 48 20N 4 0W
Finisterre, C., *Spain* **19 A1** 42 50N 9 19W
Finke, *Australia* **62 D1** 25 34S 134 35 E
Finke →, *Australia* **63 D2** 27 0S 136 10 E
Finland ■, *Europe* **9 E19** 63 0N 27 0 E
Finland, G. of, *Europe* **9 G19** 60 0N 26 0 E
Finlay →, *Canada* **72 B3** 57 0N 125 10W
Finley, *Australia* **63 F4** 35 38S 145 35 E
Finley, *U.S.A.* **80 B6** 47 31N 97 50W
Finn →, *Ireland* **13 B4** 54 50N 7 55W
Finnigan, Mt., *Australia* **62 B4** 15 49S 145 17 E
Finniss, C., *Australia* **63 E1** 33 8S 134 51 E
Finnmark fylke □, *Norway* **8 B18** 69 30N 25 0 E
Fiora →, *Italy* **20 C4** 42 20N 11 35 E
Fiq, *Syria* **47 C4** 32 46N 35 41 E
Firat = Furāt, Nahr al →, *Asia* **44 D5** 31 0N 47 25 E
Fire River, *Canada* **70 C3** 48 47N 83 21W
Firebag →, *Canada* **73 B6** 57 45N 111 21W
Firebaugh, *U.S.A.* **84 J6** 36 52N 120 27W
Firedrake L., *Canada* **73 A8** 61 25N 104 30W
Firenze, *Italy* **20 C4** 43 47N 11 15 E
Firk →, *Iraq* **44 D5** 30 59N 44 34 E
Firozabad, *India* **43 F8** 27 10N 78 25 E
Firozpur, *India* **42 D6** 30 55N 74 40 E
Fīrūzābād, *Iran* **45 D7** 28 52N 52 35 E
Fīrūzkūh, *Iran* **45 C7** 35 50N 52 50 E
Firvale, *Canada* **72 C3** 52 27N 126 13W
Fish →, *Namibia* **56 D2** 28 7S 17 10 E
Fish →, *S. Africa* **56 E3** 31 30S 20 16 E
Fisher, *Australia* **61 F5** 30 30S 131 0 E
Fisher B., *Canada* **73 C9** 51 35N 97 13W
Fishguard, *U.K.* **11 F3** 51 59N 4 59W
Fishing L., *Canada* **73 C9** 52 10N 95 24W
Fitchburg, *U.S.A.* **79 D13** 42 35N 71 48W
Fitri, L., *Chad* **51 F8** 12 50N 17 28 E
Fitz Roy, *Argentina* **96 F3** 47 0S 67 0W
Fitzgerald, *Canada* **72 B6** 59 51N 111 36W
Fitzgerald, *U.S.A.* **77 K4** 31 43N 83 15W
Fitzmaurice →, *Australia* **60 B5** 14 45S 130 5 E
Fitzroy →, *Queens., Australia* **62 C5** 23 32S 150 52 E
Fitzroy →, *W. Austral., Australia* **60 C3** 17 31S 123 35 E
Fitzroy Crossing, *Australia* **60 C4** 18 9S 125 38 E
Fitzwilliam I., *Canada* **78 A3** 45 30N 81 45W
Fiume = Rijeka, *Croatia* **20 B6** 45 20N 14 21 E
Five Points, *U.S.A.* **84 J6** 36 26N 120 6W
Fizi, *Zaïre* **54 C2** 4 17S 28 55 E
Flagler, *U.S.A.* **80 F3** 39 18N 103 4W
Flagstaff, *U.S.A.* **83 J8** 35 12N 111 39W
Flaherty I., *Canada* **70 A4** 56 15N 79 15W
Flåm, *Norway* **9 F9** 60 50N 7 7 E
Flambeau →, *U.S.A.* **80 C9** 45 18N 91 14W
Flamborough Hd., *U.K.* **10 C7** 54 8N 0 4W
Flaming Gorge Dam, *U.S.A.* **82 F9** 40 55N 109 25W
Flaming Gorge Reservoir, *U.S.A.* **82 F9** 41 10N 109 25W
Flamingo, Teluk, *Indonesia* **37 F9** 5 30S 138 0 E
Flanders = West-Vlaanderen □, *Belgium* **15 D3** 51 0N 3 0 E
Flanders = West-Vlaanderen □, *Belgium* **15 D3** 51 0N 3 0 E
Flandre Occidentale = West-Vlaanderen □, *Belgium* **15 D3** 51 0N 3 0 E
Flandre Orientale = Oost-Vlaanderen □, *Belgium* **15 C3** 51 5N 3 50 E
Flandreau, *U.S.A.* **80 C6** 44 3N 96 36W
Flanigan, *U.S.A.* **84 E7** 40 10N 119 53W
Flannan Is., *U.K.* **12 C1** 58 9N 7 52W
Flåsjön, *Sweden* **8 D13** 64 5N 15 40 E
Flat →, *Canada* **72 A3** 61 33N 125 18W
Flat River, *U.S.A.* **81 G9** 37 51N 90 31W
Flatey, *Barðastrandarsýsla, Iceland* **8 C5** 66 10N 17 52W
Flatey, *Suður-þingeyjarsýsla, Iceland* **8 D2** 65 22N 22 56W
Flathead L., *U.S.A.* **82 C6** 47 51N 114 8W
Flattery, C., *U.S.A.* **84 B2** 48 23N 124 29W
Flattery, C., *Australia* **62 A4** 14 58S 145 21 E
Flaxton, *U.S.A.* **80 A3** 48 54N 102 24W
Fleetwood, *U.K.* **10 D4** 53 55N 3 1W
Flekkefjord, *Norway* **9 G9** 58 18N 6 39 E
Flemington, *U.S.A.* **78 E7** 41 7N 77 28W
Flensburg, *Germany* **16 A4** 54 46N 9 28 E
Flesherton, *Canada* **78 B4** 44 16N 80 33W
Flesko, Tanjung, *Indonesia* **37 D6** 0 29N 124 30 E
Flevoland □, *Neths.* **15 B5** 52 30N 5 30 E
Flin Flon, *Canada* **73 C8** 54 46N 101 53W
Flinders →, *Australia* **62 B3** 17 36S 140 36 E
Flinders B., *Australia* **61 F2** 34 19S 115 19 E
Flinders Group, *Australia* **62 A3** 14 11S 144 15 E
Flinders I., *Australia* **62 F4** 40 0S 148 0 E
Flinders Ras., *Australia* **63 E2** 31 30S 138 30 E
Flinders Reefs, *Australia* **62 B4** 17 37S 148 31 E
Flint, *U.K.* **10 D4** 53 15N 3 7W
Flint, *U.S.A.* **76 D4** 43 1N 83 41W
Flint →, *U.S.A.* **77 K3** 30 57N 84 34W
Flint I., *Kiribati* **65 J12** 11 26S 151 48W
Flinton, *Australia* **63 D4** 27 55S 149 32 E
Flodden, *U.K.* **10 B5** 55 37N 2 8W
Floodwood, *U.S.A.* **80 B8** 46 55N 92 55W
Flora, *U.S.A.* **76 F1** 38 40N 88 29W
Florala, *U.S.A.* **77 K2** 31 0N 86 20W
Florence = Firenze, *Italy* **20 C4** 43 47N 11 15 E
Florence, *Ala., U.S.A.* **77 H2** 34 48N 87 41W
Florence, *Ariz., U.S.A.* **83 K8** 33 2N 111 23W
Florence, *Colo., U.S.A.* **80 F2** 38 23N 105 8W
Florence, *Oreg., U.S.A.* **82 E1** 43 58N 124 7W
Florence, *S.C., U.S.A.* **77 H6** 34 12N 79 46W
Florence, L., *Australia* **63 D2** 28 53S 138 9 E
Florennes, *Belgium* **15 D4** 50 15N 4 35 E
Florenville, *Belgium* **15 E5** 49 40N 5 19 E
Flores, *Guatemala* **88 C2** 16 59N 89 50W
Flores, *Indonesia* **37 F6** 8 35S 121 0 E
Flores I., *Canada* **72 D3** 49 20N 126 10W
Flores Sea, *Indonesia* **37 F6** 6 30S 120 0 E
Floresville, *U.S.A.* **81 L5** 29 8N 98 10W
Floriano, *Brazil* **93 E10** 6 50S 43 0W
Florianópolis, *Brazil* **95 B6** 27 30S 48 30W
Florida, *Cuba* **88 B4** 21 32N 78 14W
Florida, *Uruguay* **95 C4** 34 7S 56 10W
Florida □, *U.S.A.* **77 L5** 28 0N 82 0W
Florida, Straits of, *U.S.A.* **88 B3** 25 0N 80 0W
Florida B., *U.S.A.* **88 A3** 25 0N 80 45W
Florida Keys, *U.S.A.* **75 F10** 24 40N 81 0W
Florø, *Norway* **9 F8** 61 35N 5 1 E
Flower Station, *Canada* **79 A8** 45 10N 76 41W
Flower's Cove, *Canada* **71 B8** 51 14N 56 46W
Floydada, *U.S.A.* **81 J4** 33 59N 101 20W
Fluk, *Indonesia* **37 E7** 1 42S 127 44 E
Flushing = Vlissingen, *Neths.* **15 C3** 51 26N 3 34 E
Flying Fish, C., *Antarctica* **5 D15** 72 6S 102 29W
Foam Lake, *Canada* **73 C8** 51 40N 103 32W
Fóggia, *Italy* **20 D6** 41 28N 15 31 E
Fogo, *Canada* **71 C9** 49 43N 54 17W
Fogo I., *Canada* **71 C9** 49 40N 54 5W
Foix, *France* **18 E4** 42 58N 1 38 E
Folda, *Nord-Trøndelag, Norway* **8 D11** 64 41N 10 50 E
Folda, *Nordland, Norway* **8 C13** 67 38N 14 50 E
Foleyet, *Canada* **70 C3** 48 15N 82 25W
Folgefonn, *Norway* **9 F9** 60 3N 6 23 E
Folkestone, *U.K.* **11 F9** 51 5N 1 11 E
Folkston, *U.S.A.* **77 K5** 30 50N 82 0W
Follett, *U.S.A.* **81 G4** 36 26N 100 8W
Folsom Res., *U.S.A.* **84 G5** 38 42N 121 9W
Fond-du-Lac, *Canada* **73 B7** 59 19N 107 12W
Fond du Lac, *U.S.A.* **80 D10** 43 47N 88 27W
Fond-du-Lac →, *Canada* **73 B7** 59 17N 106 0W
Fonda, *U.S.A.* **79 D10** 42 57N 74 22W
Fonseca, G. de, *Cent. Amer.* **88 D2** 13 10N 87 40W
Fontainebleau, *France* **18 B5** 48 24N 2 40 E
Fontas →, *Canada* **72 B4** 58 14N 121 48W
Fonte Boa, *Brazil* **92 D5** 2 33S 66 0W
Fontenay-le-Comte, *France* **18 C3** 46 28N 0 48W
Fontur, *Iceland* **8 C6** 66 23N 14 32W
Foochow = Fuzhou, *China* **33 D6** 26 5N 119 16 E
Foping, *China* **34 H4** 33 41N 108 0 E
Forbes, *Australia* **63 E4** 33 22S 148 0 E
Forbesganj, *India* **43 F12** 26 17N 87 18 E
Ford City, *Calif., U.S.A.* **85 K7** 35 9N 119 27W
Ford City, *Pa., U.S.A.* **78 F5** 40 46N 79 32W
Ford's Bridge, *Australia* **63 D4** 29 41S 145 29 E
Fordyce, *U.S.A.* **81 J8** 33 49N 92 25W
Forécariah, *Guinea* **50 G2** 9 28N 13 10W
Forel, Mt., *Greenland* **4 C6** 66 52N 36 55W
Foremost, *Canada* **72 D6** 49 26N 111 34W
Forest, *Canada* **78 C3** 43 6N 82 0W
Forest, *U.S.A.* **81 J10** 32 22N 89 29W
Forest City, *Iowa, U.S.A.* **80 D8** 43 16N 93 39W
Forest City, *N.C., U.S.A.* **77 H5** 35 20N 81 52W
Forest City, *Pa., U.S.A.* **79 E9** 41 39N 75 28W
Forest Grove, *U.S.A.* **84 E3** 45 31N 123 7W
Forestburg, *Canada* **72 C6** 52 35N 112 1W
Foresthill, *U.S.A.* **84 F6** 39 1N 120 49W
Forestier Pen., *Australia* **62 G4** 43 0S 148 0 E
Forestville, *Canada* **71 C6** 48 48N 69 2W
Forestville, *Calif., U.S.A.* **84 G4** 38 28N 122 54W
Forestville, *Wis., U.S.A.* **76 C2** 44 41N 87 29W
Forez, Mts. du, *France* **18 D5** 45 40N 3 50 E
Forfar, *U.K.* **12 E6** 56 40N 2 53W
Forks, *U.S.A.* **84 C2** 47 57N 124 23W
Forlì, *Italy* **20 B5** 44 14N 12 2 E
Forman, *U.S.A.* **80 B6** 46 7N 97 38W
Formby Pt., *U.K.* **10 D4** 53 33N 3 7W
Formentera, *Spain* **22 C7** 38 43N 1 27 E
Formentor, C. de, *Spain* **22 B10** 39 58N 3 13 E
Formosa = Taiwan ■, *Asia* **33 D7** 23 30N 121 0 E
Formosa, *Argentina* **94 B4** 26 15S 58 10W
Formosa □, *Argentina* **94 B3** 25 0S 60 0W
Formosa, Serra, *Brazil* **93 F8** 12 0S 55 0W
Formosa Bay, *Kenya* **54 C5** 2 40S 40 20 E
Fornells, *Spain* **22 A11** 40 3N 4 7 E
Føroyar, *Atl. Oc.* **7 C4** 62 0N 7 0W
Forres, *U.K.* **12 D5** 57 37N 3 38W
Forrest, *Vic., Australia* **63 F3** 38 33S 143 47 E
Forrest, *W. Austral., Australia* **61 F4** 30 51S 128 6 E
Forrest, Mt., *Australia* **61 D4** 24 48S 127 45 E
Forrest City, *U.S.A.* **81 H9** 35 1N 90 47W
Forsayth, *Australia* **62 B3** 18 33S 143 34 E
Forster, *Australia* **63 E5** 32 12S 152 31 E
Forsyth, *Ga., U.S.A.* **77 J4** 33 2N 83 56W
Forsyth, *Mont., U.S.A.* **82 C10** 46 16N 106 41W
Fort Albany, *Canada* **70 B3** 52 15N 81 35W
Fort Apache, *U.S.A.* **83 K9** 33 50N 110 0W
Fort Assiniboine, *Canada* **72 C6** 54 20N 114 45W
Fort Augustus, *U.K.* **12 D4** 57 9N 4 40W
Fort Beaufort, *S. Africa* **56 E4** 32 46S 26 40 E
Fort Benton, *U.S.A.* **82 C8** 47 49N 110 40W
Fort Bragg, *U.S.A.* **82 G2** 39 26N 123 48W
Fort Bridger, *U.S.A.* **82 F8** 41 19N 110 23W
Fort Chipewyan, *Canada* **73 B6** 58 42N 111 8W
Fort Collins, *U.S.A.* **80 E2** 40 35N 105 5W
Fort-Coulonge, *Canada* **70 C4** 45 50N 76 45W
Fort Davis, *U.S.A.* **81 K3** 30 35N 103 54W
Fort-de-France, *Martinique* **89 D7** 14 36N 61 2W
Fort de Possel = Possel, *C.A.R.* **52 C3** 5 5N 19 10 E
Fort Defiance, *U.S.A.* **83 J9** 35 45N 109 5W
Fort Dodge, *U.S.A.* **80 D7** 42 30N 94 11W
Fort Edward, *U.S.A.* **79 C11** 43 16N 73 35W
Fort Frances, *Canada* **73 D10** 48 36N 93 24W
Fort Franklin, *Canada* **68 B7** 65 10N 123 30W
Fort Garland, *U.S.A.* **83 H11** 37 26N 105 26W
Fort George, *Canada* **70 B4** 53 50N 79 0W
Fort Good-Hope, *Canada* **68 B7** 66 14N 128 40W
Fort Hancock, *U.S.A.* **83 L11** 31 18N 105 51W
Fort Hertz = Putao, *Burma* **41 F20** 27 28N 97 30 E
Fort Hope, *Canada* **70 B2** 51 30N 88 0W
Fort Irwin, *U.S.A.* **85 K10** 35 16N 116 34W
Fort Jameson = Chipata, *Zambia* **55 E3** 13 38S 32 28 E
Fort Kent, *U.S.A.* **71 C6** 47 15N 68 36W
Fort Klamath, *U.S.A.* **82 E3** 42 42N 122 0W
Fort Lallemand, *Algeria* **50 B6** 31 13N 6 17 E
Fort-Lamy = Ndjamena, *Chad* **51 F7** 12 10N 14 59 E
Fort Laramie, *U.S.A.* **80 D2** 42 13N 104 31W
Fort Lauderdale, *U.S.A.* **77 M5** 26 7N 80 8W
Fort Liard, *Canada* **72 A4** 60 14N 123 30W
Fort Liberté, *Haiti* **89 C5** 19 42N 71 51W
Fort Lupton, *U.S.A.* **80 E2** 40 5N 104 49W
Fort Mackay, *Canada* **72 B6** 57 12N 111 41W
Fort McKenzie, *Canada* **71 A6** 57 20N 69 0W
Fort Macleod, *Canada* **72 D6** 49 45N 113 30W
Fort MacMahon, *Algeria* **50 C5** 29 43N 1 45 E
Fort McMurray, *Canada* **72 B6** 56 44N 111 7W
Fort McPherson, *Canada* **68 B6** 67 30N 134 55W
Fort Madison, *U.S.A.* **80 E9** 40 38N 91 27W
Fort Meade, *U.S.A.* **77 M5** 27 45N 81 48W
Fort Miribel, *Algeria* **50 C5** 29 25N 2 55 E
Fort Morgan, *U.S.A.* **80 E3** 40 15N 103 48W
Fort Myers, *U.S.A.* **77 M5** 26 39N 81 52W
Fort Nelson, *Canada* **72 B4** 58 50N 122 44W
Fort Nelson →, *Canada* **72 B4** 59 32N 124 0W
Fort Norman, *Canada* **68 B7** 64 57N 125 30W

Gangoh

Fort Payne, U.S.A. 77 H3 34 26N 85 43W
Fort Peck, U.S.A. 82 B10 48 1N 106 27W
Fort Peck Dam, U.S.A. 82 C10 48 0N 106 26W
Fort Peck L., U.S.A. 82 C10 48 0N 106 26W
Fort Pierce, U.S.A. 77 M5 27 27N 80 20W
Fort Pierre, U.S.A. 80 C4 44 21N 100 22W
Fort Plain, U.S.A. 79 D10 42 56N 74 37W
Fort Portal, Uganda 54 B3 0 40N 30 20 E
Fort Providence, Canada 72 A5 61 3N 117 40W
Fort Qu'Appelle, Canada 73 C8 50 45N 103 50W
Fort Resolution, Canada 72 A6 61 10N 113 40W
Fort Rixon, Zimbabwe 55 G2 20 2S 29 17 E
Fort Rosebery = Mansa, Zambia 55 E2 11 13S 28 55 E
Fort Ross, U.S.A. 84 G3 38 32N 123 13W
Fort Rupert, Canada 70 B4 51 30N 78 40W
Fort St. James, Canada 72 C4 54 30N 124 10W
Fort St. John, Canada 72 B4 56 15N 120 50W
Fort Sandeman, Pakistan 42 D3 31 20N 69 31 E
Fort Saskatchewan, Canada 72 C6 53 40N 113 15W
Fort Scott, U.S.A. 81 G7 37 50N 94 42W
Fort Severn, Canada 70 A2 56 0N 87 40W
Fort Shevchenko, Kazakhstan 25 F9 43 40N 51 20 E
Fort-Sibut, C.A.R. 51 G8 5 46N 19 10 E
Fort Simpson, Canada 72 A4 61 45N 121 15W
Fort Smith, Canada 72 B6 60 0N 111 51W
Fort Smith, U.S.A. 81 H7 35 23N 94 25W
Fort Stanton, U.S.A. 83 K11 33 30N 105 31W
Fort Stockton, U.S.A. 81 K3 30 53N 102 53W
Fort Sumner, U.S.A. 81 H2 34 28N 104 15W
Fort Trinquet = Bir Mogrein, Mauritania 50 C2 25 10N 11 25W
Fort Valley, U.S.A. 77 J4 32 33N 83 53W
Fort Vermilion, Canada 72 B5 58 24N 116 0W
Fort Walton Beach, U.S.A. 77 K2 30 25N 86 36W
Fort Wayne, U.S.A. 76 E3 41 4N 85 9W
Fort William, U.K. 12 E3 56 48N 5 8W
Fort Worth, U.S.A. 81 J6 32 45N 97 18W
Fort Yates, U.S.A. 80 B4 46 5N 100 38W
Fort Yukon, U.S.A. 68 B5 66 34N 145 16W
Fortaleza, Brazil 93 D11 3 45S 38 35W
Forteau, Canada 71 B8 51 28N 56 58W
Forth →, U.K. 12 E5 56 9N 3 50W
Forth, Firth of, U.K. 12 E6 56 5N 2 55W
Fortrose, U.K. 12 D4 57 35N 4 10W
Fortuna, Calif., U.S.A. 82 F1 40 36N 124 9W
Fortuna, N. Dak., U.S.A. 80 A3 48 55N 103 47W
Fortune B., Canada 71 C8 47 30N 55 22W
Foshan, China 33 D6 23 4N 113 5 E
Fossil, U.S.A. 82 D3 45 0N 120 9W
Fossilbrook, Australia 62 B3 17 47S 144 29 E
Fosston, U.S.A. 80 B7 47 35N 95 45W
Foster, Canada 79 A12 45 17N 72 30W
Foster →, Canada 73 B7 55 47N 105 49W
Fosters Ra., Australia 62 C1 21 35S 133 48 E
Fostoria, U.S.A. 76 E4 41 10N 83 25W
Fougamou, Gabon 52 E2 1 16S 10 30 E
Fougères, France 18 B3 48 21N 1 14W
Foul Pt., Sri Lanka 40 Q12 8 35N 81 18 E
Foula, U.K. 12 A6 60 10N 2 5W
Foulness I., U.K. 11 F8 51 36N 0 55 E
Foulpointe, Madag. 57 B8 17 41S 49 31 E
Foumban, Cameroon 50 G7 5 45N 10 50 E
Fountain, Colo., U.S.A. 80 F2 38 41N 104 42W
Fountain, Utah, U.S.A. 82 G8 39 41N 111 37W
Fountain Springs, U.S.A. 85 K8 35 54N 118 51W
Fourchu, Canada 71 C7 45 43N 60 17W
Fouriesburg, S. Africa 56 D4 28 38S 28 14 E
Fouta Djalon, Guinea 50 F2 11 20N 12 10W
Foux, Cap-à-, Haiti 89 C5 19 43N 73 27W
Foveaux Str., N.Z. 59 M2 46 42S 168 10 E
Fowey, U.K. 11 G3 50 20N 4 39W
Fowler, Calif., U.S.A. 83 H4 36 38N 119 41W
Fowler, Colo., U.S.A. 80 F2 38 8N 104 2W
Fowler, Kans., U.S.A. 81 G4 37 23N 100 12W
Fowlers B., Australia 61 F5 31 59S 132 34 E
Fowlerton, U.S.A. 81 L5 28 28N 98 48W
Fox →, Canada 73 B10 56 3N 93 18W
Fox Valley, Canada 73 C7 50 30N 109 25W
Foxe Basin, Canada 69 B12 66 0N 77 0W
Foxe Chan., Canada 69 B11 65 0N 80 0W
Foxe Pen., Canada 69 B12 65 0N 76 0W
Foxpark, U.S.A. 82 F10 41 5N 106 9W
Foxton, N.Z. 59 J5 40 29S 175 18 E
Foyle, Lough, U.K. 13 A4 55 6N 7 8W
Foynes, Ireland 13 D2 52 37N 9 5W
Fóz do Cunene, Angola 56 B1 17 15S 11 48 E
Foz do Gregório, Brazil 92 E4 6 47S 70 44W
Foz do Iguaçu, Brazil 95 B5 25 30S 54 30W
Frackville, U.S.A. 79 F8 40 47N 76 14W
Framingham, U.S.A. 79 D13 42 17N 71 25W
Franca, Brazil 93 H9 20 33S 47 30W
Francavilla Fontana, Italy 21 D7 40 32N 17 35 E
France ■, Europe 18 C5 47 0N 3 0 E
Frances, Australia 63 F3 36 41S 140 55 E
Frances →, Canada 72 A3 60 16N 129 10W
Frances L., Canada 72 A3 61 23N 129 30W
Francés Viejo, C., Dom. Rep. 89 C6 19 40N 69 55W
Franceville, Gabon 52 E2 1 40S 13 32 E
Franche-Comté, France 18 C6 46 50N 5 55 E
Francisco I. Madero, Coahuila, Mexico 86 B4 25 48N 103 18W
Francisco I. Madero, Durango, Mexico 86 C4 24 32N 104 22W
Francistown, Botswana 57 C4 21 7S 27 33 E
François, Canada 71 C8 47 35N 56 45W
François L., Canada 72 C3 54 0N 125 30W
Franeker, Neths. 15 A5 53 12N 5 33 E
Frankfort, S. Africa 57 D4 27 17S 28 30 E
Frankfort, Ind., U.S.A. 76 E2 40 17N 86 31W
Frankfort, Kans., U.S.A. 80 F6 39 42N 96 25W
Frankfort, Ky., U.S.A. 76 F3 38 12N 84 52W
Frankfort, Mich., U.S.A. 76 C2 44 38N 86 14W
Frankfurt am Main, Germany 16 C4 50 7N 8 40 E
Frankfurt an der Oder, Germany 16 B7 52 20N 14 31 E
Fränkische Alb, Germany 16 D5 49 20N 11 30 E
Frankland →, Australia 61 G2 35 0S 116 48 E
Franklin, Ky., U.S.A. 77 G2 36 43N 86 35W
Franklin, La., U.S.A. 81 L9 29 48N 91 30W
Franklin, Mass., U.S.A. 79 D13 42 5N 71 24W
Franklin, N.H., U.S.A. 79 C13 43 27N 71 39W
Franklin, Nebr., U.S.A. 80 E5 40 6N 98 57W
Franklin, Pa., U.S.A. 78 E5 41 24N 79 50W
Franklin, Tenn., U.S.A. 77 H2 35 55N 86 52W
Franklin, Va., U.S.A. 77 G7 36 41N 76 56W
Franklin, W. Va., U.S.A. 76 F6 38 39N 79 20W
Franklin B., Canada 68 B7 69 45N 126 0W
Franklin D. Roosevelt L., U.S.A. 82 B4 48 18N 118 9W
Franklin I., Antarctica 5 D11 76 10S 168 30 E
Franklin L., U.S.A. 82 F6 40 25N 115 22W
Franklin Mts., Canada 68 B7 65 0N 125 0W
Franklin Str., Canada 68 A10 72 0N 96 0W
Franklinton, U.S.A. 81 K9 30 51N 90 9W
Franklinville, U.S.A. 78 D6 42 20N 78 27W
Franks Pk., U.S.A. 82 E9 43 58N 109 18W
Frankston, Australia 63 F4 38 8S 145 8 E
Frantsa Iosifa, Zemlya, Russia 26 A6 82 0N 55 0 E
Franz, Canada 70 C3 48 25N 84 30W
Franz Josef Land = Frantsa Iosifa, Zemlya, Russia 26 A6 82 0N 55 0 E
Fraser →, B.C., Canada 72 D4 49 7N 123 11W
Fraser →, Nfld., Canada 71 A7 56 39N 62 10W
Fraser, Mt., Australia 61 E2 25 35S 118 20 E
Fraser I., Australia 63 D5 25 15S 153 10 E
Fraser Lake, Canada 72 C4 54 0N 124 50W
Fraserburg, S. Africa 56 E3 31 55S 21 30 E
Fraserburgh, U.K. 12 D6 57 41N 2 3W
Fraserdale, Canada 70 C3 49 55N 81 37W
Fray Bentos, Uruguay 94 C4 33 10S 58 15W
Frazier Downs, Australia 60 C3 18 48S 121 42 E
Fredericia, Denmark 9 J10 55 34N 9 45 E
Frederick, Md., U.S.A. 76 F7 39 25N 77 25W
Frederick, Okla., U.S.A. 81 H5 34 23N 99 1W
Frederick, S. Dak., U.S.A. 80 C5 45 50N 98 31W
Frederick Sd., U.S.A. 72 B2 57 10N 134 0W
Fredericksburg, Tex., U.S.A. 81 K5 30 16N 98 52W
Fredericksburg, Va., U.S.A. 76 F7 38 18N 77 28W
Fredericktown, U.S.A. 81 G9 37 34N 90 18W
Frederico I. Madero, Presa, Mexico 86 B3 28 7N 105 40W
Fredericton, Canada 71 C6 45 57N 66 40W
Fredericton Junc., Canada 71 C6 45 41N 66 40W
Frederikshåb, Greenland 4 C5 62 0N 49 43W
Frederikshavn, Denmark 9 H11 57 28N 10 31 E
Frederiksted, Virgin Is. 89 C7 17 43N 64 53W
Fredonia, Ariz., U.S.A. 83 H7 36 57N 112 32W
Fredonia, Kans., U.S.A. 81 G7 37 32N 95 49W
Fredonia, N.Y., U.S.A. 78 D5 42 26N 79 20W
Fredrikstad, Norway 9 G11 59 13N 10 57 E
Freehold, U.S.A. 79 F10 40 16N 74 17W
Freel Peak, U.S.A. 84 G7 38 52N 119 54W
Freeland, U.S.A. 79 E9 41 1N 75 54W
Freels, C., Canada 71 C9 49 15N 53 30W
Freeman, Calif., U.S.A. 85 K9 35 35N 117 53W
Freeman, S. Dak., U.S.A. 80 D6 43 21N 97 26W
Freeport, Bahamas 88 A4 26 30N 78 47W
Freeport, Canada 71 D6 44 15N 66 20W
Freeport, Ill., U.S.A. 80 D10 42 17N 89 36W
Freeport, N.Y., U.S.A. 79 F11 40 39N 73 35W
Freeport, Tex., U.S.A. 81 L7 28 57N 95 21W
Freetown, S. Leone 50 G2 8 30N 13 17W
Frégate, L., Canada 70 B5 53 15N 74 45W
Freiburg, Germany 16 E3 48 0N 7 52 E
Freire, Chile 96 D2 38 54S 72 38W
Freirina, Chile 94 B1 28 30S 71 10W
Freising, Germany 16 D5 48 24N 11 47 E
Freistadt, Austria 16 D7 48 30N 14 30 E
Fréjus, France 18 E7 43 25N 6 44 E
Fremantle, Australia 61 F2 32 7S 115 47 E
Fremont, Calif., U.S.A. 83 H2 37 32N 121 57W
Fremont, Mich., U.S.A. 76 D3 43 28N 85 57W
Fremont, Nebr., U.S.A. 80 E6 41 26N 96 30W
Fremont, Ohio, U.S.A. 76 E4 41 21N 83 7W
Fremont →, U.S.A. 83 G8 38 24N 110 42W
Fremont L., U.S.A. 82 E9 42 57N 109 48W
French Camp, U.S.A. 84 H5 37 53N 121 16W
French Creek →, U.S.A. 78 E5 41 24N 79 50W
French Guiana ■, S. Amer. 93 C8 4 0N 53 0W
French Pass, N.Z. 59 J4 40 55S 173 55 E
French Polynesia ■, Pac. Oc. 65 J13 20 0S 145 0W
French Terr. of Afars & Issas = Djibouti ■, Africa 46 E3 12 0N 43 0 E
Frenchglen, U.S.A. 82 E4 42 50N 118 55W
Frenchman Butte, Canada 73 C7 53 35N 109 38W
Frenchman Cr. →, Mont., U.S.A. 82 B10 48 31N 107 10W
Frenchman Cr. →, Nebr., U.S.A. 80 E4 40 14N 100 50W
Fresco →, Brazil 93 E8 7 15S 51 30W
Freshfield, C., Antarctica 5 C10 68 25S 151 10 E
Fresnillo, Mexico 86 C4 23 10N 103 0W
Fresno, U.S.A. 83 H4 36 44N 119 47W
Fresno Reservoir, U.S.A. 82 B9 48 36N 109 57W
Frew →, Australia 62 C2 20 0S 135 38 E
Frewena, Australia 62 B2 19 25S 135 25 E
Freycinet Pen., Australia 62 G4 42 10S 148 25 E
Fria, C., Namibia 56 B1 18 0S 12 0 E
Friant, U.S.A. 84 J7 36 59N 119 43W
Frías, Argentina 94 B2 28 40S 65 5W
Friday Harbor, U.S.A. 84 B3 48 32N 123 1W
Friedrichshafen, Germany 16 E4 47 39N 9 29 E
Friendly Is. = Tonga ■, Pac. Oc. 59 D11 19 50S 174 30W
Friesland □, Neths. 15 A5 53 5N 5 50 E
Frio →, U.S.A. 81 L5 28 26N 98 11W
Friona, U.S.A. 81 H3 34 38N 102 43W
Fritch, U.S.A. 81 H4 35 38N 101 36W
Friuli-Venezia Giulia □, Italy 20 A5 46 0N 13 0 E
Frobisher B., Canada 69 B13 62 30N 66 0W
Frobisher Bay = Iqaluit, Canada 69 B13 63 44N 68 31W
Frobisher L., Canada 73 B7 56 20N 108 15W
Frohavet, Norway 8 E10 63 50N 9 35 E
Froid, U.S.A. 80 A2 48 20N 104 30W
Fromberg, U.S.A. 82 D9 45 24N 108 54W
Frome, U.K. 11 F5 51 16N 2 17W
Frome, L., Australia 63 E2 30 45S 139 45 E
Frome Downs, Australia 63 E2 31 13S 139 45 E
Front Range, U.S.A. 82 G11 40 25N 105 45W
Front Royal, U.S.A. 76 F6 38 55N 78 12W
Frontera, Canary Is. 22 G2 27 47N 17 59W
Frontera, Mexico 87 D6 18 30N 92 40W
Frosinone, Italy 20 D5 41 38N 13 20 E
Frostburg, U.S.A. 76 F6 39 39N 78 56W
Frostisen, Norway 8 B14 68 14N 17 10 E
Frøya, Norway 8 E10 63 43N 8 40 E
Frunze = Bishkek, Kirghizia 26 E8 42 54N 74 46 E
Frutal, Brazil 93 G9 20 0S 49 0W
Frýdek-Místek, Czech. 17 D9 49 40N 18 20 E
Fu Xian, Liaoning, China 35 E11 39 38N 121 58 E
Fu Xian, Shaanxi, China 34 F5 36 0N 109 20 E
Fucheng, China 34 F9 37 50N 116 10 E
Fuchou = Fuzhou, China 33 D6 26 5N 119 16 E
Fuchū, Japan 31 G6 34 34N 133 14 E
Fuencaliente, Canary Is. 22 F2 28 28N 17 50W
Fuencaliente, Pta., Canary Is. 22 F2 28 27N 17 51W
Fuente Ovejuna, Spain 19 C3 38 15N 5 25W
Fuentes de Oñoro, Spain 19 B2 40 33N 6 52W
Fuerte →, Mexico 86 B3 25 50N 109 25W
Fuerte Olimpo, Paraguay 94 A4 21 0S 57 51W
Fuerteventura, Canary Is. 22 F6 28 30N 14 0W
Fufeng, China 34 G4 34 22N 108 0 E
Fugløysund, Norway 8 A16 70 15N 20 20 E
Fugou, China 34 G8 34 3N 114 25 E
Fugu, China 34 E6 39 2N 111 3 E
Fuhai, China 32 B3 47 2N 87 25 E
Fuḥaymī, Iraq 44 C4 34 16N 42 10 E
Fuji, Japan 31 G9 35 9N 138 39 E
Fuji-San, Japan 31 G9 35 22N 138 44 E
Fuji-yoshida, Japan 31 G9 35 30N 138 46 E
Fujian □, China 33 D6 26 0N 118 0 E
Fujinomiya, Japan 31 G9 35 10N 138 40 E
Fujisawa, Japan 31 G9 35 22N 139 29 E
Fukien = Fujian □, China 33 D6 26 0N 118 0 E
Fukuchiyama, Japan 31 G7 35 19N 135 9 E
Fukue-Shima, Japan 31 H4 32 40N 128 45 E
Fukui, Japan 31 F8 36 5N 136 10 E
Fukui □, Japan 31 G8 36 0N 136 12 E
Fukuoka, Japan 31 H5 33 39N 130 21 E
Fukuoka □, Japan 31 H5 33 30N 131 0 E
Fukushima, Japan 30 F10 37 44N 140 28 E
Fukushima □, Japan 30 F10 37 30N 140 15 E
Fukuyama, Japan 31 G6 34 35N 133 20 E
Fulda, Germany 16 C4 50 32N 9 41 E
Fulda →, Germany 16 C4 51 27N 9 40 E
Fullerton, Calif., U.S.A. 85 M9 33 53N 117 56W
Fullerton, Nebr., U.S.A. 80 E5 41 22N 97 58W
Fulongquan, China 35 B13 44 20N 124 42 E
Fulton, Mo., U.S.A. 80 F9 38 52N 91 57W
Fulton, N.Y., U.S.A. 79 C8 43 19N 76 25W
Fulton, Tenn., U.S.A. 77 G1 36 31N 88 53W
Funabashi, Japan 31 G10 35 45N 140 0 E
Funchal, Madeira 22 D3 32 38N 16 54W
Fundación, Colombia 92 A4 10 31N 74 11W
Fundão, Portugal 19 B2 40 8N 7 30W
Fundy, B. of, Canada 71 D6 45 0N 66 0W
Funing, Hebei, China 35 E10 39 53N 119 12 E
Funing, Jiangsu, China 35 H10 33 45N 119 50 E
Funiu Shan, China 34 H7 33 30N 112 20 E
Funtua, Nigeria 50 F6 11 30N 7 18 E
Fuping, Hebei, China 34 E8 38 48N 114 12 E
Fuping, Shaanxi, China 34 G5 34 42N 109 10 E
Furano, Japan 30 C11 43 21N 142 23 E
Furāt, Nahr al →, Asia 44 D5 31 0N 47 25 E
Fūrg, Iran 45 D7 28 18N 55 13 E
Furnás, Spain 22 B8 39 3N 1 32 E
Furnas, Represa de, Brazil 95 A6 20 50S 45 30W
Furneaux Group, Australia 62 G4 40 10S 147 50 E
Furness, U.K. 10 C4 54 14N 3 8W
Furqlus, Syria 47 A6 34 36N 37 8 E
Fürth, Germany 16 D5 49 29N 11 0 E
Furukawa, Japan 30 E10 38 34N 140 58 E
Fury and Hecla Str., Canada 69 B11 69 56N 84 0W
Fusagasuga, Colombia 92 C4 4 21N 74 22W
Fushan, Shandong, China 35 F11 37 30N 121 15 E
Fushan, Shanxi, China 34 G6 35 58N 111 51 E
Fushun, China 35 D12 41 50N 123 56 E
Fusong, China 35 C14 42 20N 127 15 E
Futuna, Wall. & F. Is. 59 B8 14 25S 178 20 E
Fuxin, China 35 C11 42 5N 121 48 E
Fuyang, China 34 H8 33 0N 115 48 E
Fuyang He →, China 34 E9 38 12N 117 0 E
Fuyu, China 35 B13 45 12N 124 43 E
Fuzhou, China 33 D6 26 5N 119 16 E
Fylde, U.K. 10 D5 53 50N 2 58W
Fyn, Denmark 9 J11 55 20N 10 30 E
Fyne, L., U.K. 12 F3 56 0N 5 20W

G

Gabela, Angola 52 G2 11 0S 14 24 E
Gabès, Tunisia 50 B7 33 53N 10 2 E
Gabès, G. de, Tunisia 51 B7 34 0N 10 30 E
Gabon ■, Africa 52 E2 0 10S 10 0 E
Gaborone, Botswana 56 C4 24 45S 25 57 E
Gabriels, U.S.A. 79 B10 44 26N 74 12W
Gābrīk, Iran 45 E8 25 44N 58 28 E
Gabrovo, Bulgaria 21 C11 42 52N 25 19 E
Gāch Sār, Iran 45 B6 36 7N 51 19 E
Gachsārān, Iran 45 D6 30 15N 50 45 E
Gadag, India 40 M9 15 30N 75 45 E
Gadap, Pakistan 42 G2 25 5N 67 28 E
Gadarwara, India 43 H8 22 50N 78 50 E
Gadhada, India 42 J4 22 0N 71 35 E
Gadsden, Ala., U.S.A. 77 H2 34 1N 86 1W
Gadsden, Ariz., U.S.A. 83 K6 32 33N 114 47W
Gadwal, India 40 L10 16 10N 77 50 E
Gaffney, U.S.A. 77 H5 35 5N 81 39W
Gafsa, Tunisia 50 B6 34 24N 8 43 E
Gagetown, Canada 71 C6 45 46N 66 10W
Gagnoa, Ivory C. 50 G3 6 56N 5 16W
Gagnon, Canada 71 B6 51 50N 68 5W
Gagnon, L., Canada 73 A6 62 3N 110 27W
Gahini, Rwanda 54 C3 1 50S 30 30 E
Gahmar, India 43 G10 25 27N 83 49 E
Gai Xian, China 35 D12 40 22N 122 20 E
Gaïdhouronísi, Greece 23 E7 34 53N 25 41 E
Gail, U.S.A. 81 J4 32 46N 101 27W
Gaines, U.S.A. 78 E7 41 46N 77 35W
Gainesville, Fla., U.S.A. 77 L4 29 40N 82 20W
Gainesville, Ga., U.S.A. 77 H4 34 18N 83 50W
Gainesville, Mo., U.S.A. 81 G8 36 36N 92 26W
Gainesville, Tex., U.S.A. 81 J6 33 38N 97 8W
Gainsborough, U.K. 10 D7 53 23N 0 46W
Gairdner, L., Australia 63 E2 31 30S 136 0 E
Gairloch, L., U.K. 12 D3 57 43N 5 45W
Gakuch, Pakistan 43 A5 36 7N 73 45 E
Galán, Cerro, Argentina 94 B2 25 55S 66 52W
Galana →, Kenya 54 C5 3 9S 40 8 E
Galangue, Angola 53 G3 13 42S 16 9 E
Galápagos, Pac. Oc. 65 H18 0 0 91 0W
Galashiels, U.K. 12 F6 55 37N 2 50W
Galaţi, Romania 21 B13 45 27N 28 2 E
Galatina, Italy 21 D8 40 10N 18 10 E
Galax, U.S.A. 77 G5 36 40N 80 56W
Galbraith, Australia 62 B3 16 25S 141 30 E
Galcaio, Somali Rep. 46 F4 6 30N 47 30 E
Galdhøpiggen, Norway 9 F10 61 38N 8 18 E
Galeana, Mexico 86 C4 24 50N 100 4W
Galela, Indonesia 37 D7 1 50N 127 49 E
Galera Point, Trin. & Tob. 89 D7 10 8N 61 0W
Galesburg, U.S.A. 80 E9 40 57N 90 22W
Galeton, U.S.A. 78 E7 41 44N 77 39W
Galich, Russia 24 C7 58 23N 42 12 E
Galicia □, Spain 19 A2 42 43N 7 45W
Galilee = Hagalil, Israel 47 C4 32 53N 35 18 E
Galilee, L., Australia 62 C4 22 20S 145 50 E
Galilee, Sea of = Yam Kinneret, Israel 47 C4 32 45N 35 35 E
Galinoporni, Cyprus 23 D13 35 31N 34 18 E
Galion, U.S.A. 78 F2 40 44N 82 47W
Galiuro Mts., U.S.A. 83 K8 32 30N 110 20W
Gallabat, Sudan 51 F12 12 58N 36 11 E
Gallatin, U.S.A. 77 G2 36 24N 86 27W
Galle, Sri Lanka 40 R12 6 5N 80 10 E
Gállego →, Spain 19 B5 41 39N 0 51W
Gallegos →, Argentina 96 G3 51 35S 69 0W
Galley Hd., Ireland 13 E3 51 32N 8 56W
Gallinas, Pta., Colombia 92 A4 12 28N 71 40W
Gallipoli = Gelibolu, Turkey 21 D12 40 28N 26 43 E
Gallipoli, Italy 21 D8 40 8N 18 0 E
Gallipolis, U.S.A. 76 F4 38 49N 82 12W
Gällivare, Sweden 8 C16 67 9N 20 40 E
Galloway, U.K. 12 G4 55 0N 4 25W
Galloway, Mull of, U.K. 12 G4 54 38N 4 50W
Gallup, U.S.A. 83 J9 35 32N 108 45W
Galong, Australia 63 E4 34 37S 148 34 E
Galoya, Sri Lanka 40 Q12 8 10N 80 55 E
Galt, U.S.A. 84 G5 38 15N 121 18W
Galty Mts., Ireland 13 D3 52 22N 8 10W
Galtymore, Ireland 13 D3 52 22N 8 12W
Galva, U.S.A. 80 E9 41 10N 90 3W
Galveston, U.S.A. 81 L7 29 18N 94 48W
Galveston B., U.S.A. 81 L7 29 36N 94 50W
Gálvez, Argentina 94 C3 32 0S 61 14W
Galway, Ireland 13 C2 53 16N 9 4W
Galway □, Ireland 13 C2 53 16N 9 3W
Galway B., Ireland 13 C2 53 10N 9 20W
Gam →, Vietnam 38 B5 21 55N 105 12 E
Gamagori, Japan 31 G8 34 50N 137 14 E
Gambaga, Ghana 50 F4 10 30N 0 28W
Gambat, Pakistan 42 F3 27 17N 68 26 E
Gambela, Ethiopia 51 G11 8 14N 34 38 E
Gambia ■, W. Afr. 50 F1 13 25N 16 0W
Gambia →, W. Afr. 50 F1 13 28N 16 34W
Gambier, C., Australia 60 B5 11 56S 130 57 E
Gambier Is., Australia 63 F2 35 3S 136 30 E
Gamboli, Pakistan 42 E3 29 53N 68 24 E
Gamboma, Congo 52 E3 1 55S 15 52 E
Gamerco, U.S.A. 83 J9 35 34N 108 46W
Gamlakarleby = Kokkola, Finland 8 E17 63 50N 23 8 E
Gammon →, Canada 73 C9 51 24N 95 44W
Gan Jiang →, China 33 D6 29 15N 116 0 E
Ganado, Ariz., U.S.A. 83 J9 35 43N 109 33W
Ganado, Tex., U.S.A. 81 L6 29 2N 96 31W
Gananoque, Canada 70 D4 44 20N 76 10W
Ganaveh, Iran 45 D6 29 35N 50 35 E
Gäncä = Gyandzha, Azerbaijan 25 F8 40 45N 46 20 E
Gand = Gent, Belgium 15 C3 51 2N 3 42 E
Ganda, Angola 53 G2 13 3S 14 35 E
Gandak →, India 43 G11 25 39N 85 13 E
Gandava, Pakistan 42 E2 28 32N 67 32 E
Gander, Canada 71 C9 48 58N 54 35W
Gander L., Canada 71 C9 48 58N 54 35W
Ganderowe Falls, Zimbabwe 55 F2 17 20S 29 10 E
Gandhi Sagar, India 42 G6 24 40N 75 40 E
Gandi, Nigeria 50 F6 12 55N 5 49 E
Gando, Pta., Canary Is. 22 G4 27 55N 15 22W
Ganedidalem = Gani, Indonesia 37 E7 0 48S 128 14 E
Ganga →, India 43 H14 23 20N 90 30 E
Ganga, Mouths of the, India 43 J13 21 30N 90 0 E
Ganganagar, India 42 E5 29 56N 73 56 E
Gangapur, India 42 F7 26 32N 76 49 E
Gangara, Niger 50 F6 14 35N 8 29 E
Gangaw, Burma 41 H19 22 5N 94 5 E
Gangdisê Shan, China 41 D12 31 20N 81 0 E
Ganges = Ganga →, India 43 H14 23 20N 90 30 E
Gangoh, India 42 E7 29 46N 77 18 E

Great Artesian Basin

Great Artesian Basin, *Australia* **62 C3** 23 0S 144 0 E
Great Australian Bight, *Australia* **61 F5** 33 30S 130 0 E
Great Bahama Bank, *Bahamas* **88 B4** 23 15N 78 0W
Great Barrier I., *N.Z.* **59 G5** 36 11S 175 25 E
Great Barrier Reef, *Australia* **62 B4** 18 0S 146 50 E
Great Barrington, *U.S.A.* **79 D11** 42 12N 73 22W
Great Basin, *U.S.A.* **82 G5** 40 0N 117 0W
Great Bear →, *Canada* **68 B7** 65 0N 124 0W
Great Bear L., *Canada* **68 B7** 65 30N 120 0W
Great Belt = Store Bælt, *Denmark* **9 J11** 55 20N 11 0 E
Great Bend, *Kans., U.S.A.* **80 F5** 38 22N 98 46W
Great Bend, *Pa., U.S.A.* **79 E9** 41 58N 75 45W
Great Blasket I., *Ireland* **13 D1** 52 5N 10 30W
Great Britain, *Europe* **6 E5** 54 0N 2 15W
Great Central, *Canada* **72 D3** 49 20N 125 10W
Great Dividing Ra., *Australia* **62 C4** 23 0S 146 0 E
Great Driffield, *U.K.* **10 C7** 54 0N 0 25W
Great Exuma I., *Bahamas* **88 B4** 23 30N 75 50W
Great Falls, *Canada* **73 C9** 50 27N 96 1W
Great Falls, *U.S.A.* **82 C8** 47 30N 111 17W
Great Fish = Groot Vis →, *S. Africa* **56 E4** 33 28S 27 5 E
Great Guana Cay, *Bahamas* **88 B4** 24 0N 76 20W
Great Harbour Deep, *Canada* **71 B8** 50 25N 56 32W
Great Inagua I., *Bahamas* **89 B5** 21 0N 73 20W
Great Indian Desert = Thar Desert, *India* **42 F4** 28 0N 72 0 E
Great I., *Canada* **73 B9** 58 53N 96 35W
Great Karoo, *S. Africa* **56 E3** 31 55S 21 0 E
Great Lake, *Australia* **62 G4** 41 50S 146 40 E
Great Ormes Head, *U.K.* **10 D4** 53 20N 3 52W
Great Ouse →, *U.K.* **10 E8** 52 47N 0 22 E
Great Palm I., *Australia* **62 B4** 18 45S 146 40 E
Great Plains, *N. Amer.* **74 A6** 47 0N 105 0W
Great Ruaha →, *Tanzania* **54 D4** 7 56S 37 52 E
Great Saint Bernard P. = Grand St-Bernard, Col du, *Switz.* **16 F3** 45 50N 7 10 E
Great Salt L., *U.S.A.* **82 F7** 41 15N 112 40W
Great Salt Lake Desert, *U.S.A.* **82 F7** 40 50N 113 30W
Great Salt Plains L., *U.S.A.* **81 G5** 36 45N 98 8W
Great Sandy Desert, *Australia* **60 D3** 21 0S 124 0 E
Great Sangi = Sangihe, P., *Indonesia* **37 D7** 3 45N 125 30 E
Great Slave L., *Canada* **72 A5** 61 23N 115 38W
Great Smoky Mts. Nat. Pk., *U.S.A.* **77 H4** 35 40N 83 40W
Great Stour = Stour →, *U.K.* **11 F9** 51 15N 1 20 E
Great Victoria Desert, *Australia* **61 E4** 29 30S 126 30 E
Great Wall, *China* **34 E5** 38 30N 109 30 E
Great Whernside, *U.K.* **10 C6** 54 9N 1 59W
Great Yarmouth, *U.K.* **10 E9** 52 40N 1 45 E
Greater Antilles, *W. Indies* **89 C5** 17 40N 74 0W
Greater London □, *U.K.* **11 F7** 51 31N 0 6W
Greater Manchester □, *U.K.* **10 D5** 53 30N 2 15W
Greater Sunda Is., *Indonesia* **36 F4** 7 0S 112 0 E
Greco, C., *Cyprus* **23 E13** 34 57N 34 5 E
Gredos, Sierra de, *Spain* **19 B3** 40 20N 5 0W
Greece, *U.S.A.* **78 C7** 43 13N 77 41W
Greece ■, *Europe* **21 E10** 40 0N 23 0 E
Greeley, *Colo., U.S.A.* **80 E2** 40 25N 104 42W
Greeley, *Nebr., U.S.A.* **80 E5** 41 33N 98 32W
Green →, *Ky., U.S.A.* **76 G2** 37 54N 87 30W
Green →, *Utah, U.S.A.* **83 G9** 38 11N 109 53W
Green B., *U.S.A.* **76 C2** 45 0N 87 30W
Green Bay, *U.S.A.* **76 C2** 44 31N 88 0W
Green C., *Australia* **63 F5** 37 13S 150 1 E
Green Cove Springs, *U.S.A.* **77 L5** 29 59N 81 42W
Green River, *U.S.A.* **83 G8** 38 59N 110 10W
Greenbank, *U.S.A.* **84 B4** 48 6N 122 34W
Greenbush, *Mich., U.S.A.* **78 B1** 44 35N 83 19W
Greenbush, *Minn., U.S.A.* **80 A6** 48 42N 96 11W
Greencastle, *U.S.A.* **76 F2** 39 38N 86 52W
Greene, *U.S.A.* **79 D9** 42 20N 75 46W
Greenfield, *Calif., U.S.A.* **84 J5** 36 19N 121 15W
Greenfield, *Calif., U.S.A.* **85 K8** 35 15N 119 0W
Greenfield, *Ind., U.S.A.* **76 F3** 39 47N 85 46W
Greenfield, *Iowa, U.S.A.* **80 E7** 41 18N 94 28W
Greenfield, *Mass., U.S.A.* **79 D12** 42 35N 72 36W
Greenfield, *Mo., U.S.A.* **81 G8** 37 25N 93 51W
Greenfield Park, *Canada* **79 A11** 45 29N 73 29W
Greenland ■, *N. Amer.* **4 C5** 66 0N 45 0W
Greenland Sea, *Arctic* **4 B7** 73 0N 10 0W
Greenock, *U.K.* **12 F4** 55 57N 4 46W
Greenore, *Ireland* **13 B5** 54 2N 6 8W
Greenore Pt., *Ireland* **13 D5** 52 15N 6 20W
Greenough →, *Australia* **61 E1** 28 51S 114 38 E
Greenport, *U.S.A.* **79 E12** 41 6N 72 22W
Greensboro, *Ga., U.S.A.* **77 J4** 33 35N 83 11W
Greensboro, *N.C., U.S.A.* **77 G6** 36 4N 79 48W
Greensburg, *Ind., U.S.A.* **76 F3** 39 20N 85 29W
Greensburg, *Kans., U.S.A.* **81 G5** 37 36N 99 18W
Greensburg, *Pa., U.S.A.* **78 F5** 40 18N 79 33W
Greenville, *Liberia* **50 G3** 5 1N 9 6W
Greenville, *Ala., U.S.A.* **77 K2** 31 50N 86 38W
Greenville, *Calif., U.S.A.* **84 E6** 40 8N 120 57W
Greenville, *Ill., U.S.A.* **80 F10** 38 53N 89 25W
Greenville, *Maine, U.S.A.* **71 C6** 45 28N 69 35W
Greenville, *Mich., U.S.A.* **76 D3** 43 11N 85 15W
Greenville, *Miss., U.S.A.* **81 J9** 33 24N 91 4W
Greenville, *N.C., U.S.A.* **77 H7** 35 37N 77 23W
Greenville, *Ohio, U.S.A.* **76 E3** 40 6N 84 38W
Greenville, *Pa., U.S.A.* **78 E4** 41 24N 80 23W
Greenville, *S.C., U.S.A.* **77 H4** 34 51N 82 24W
Greenville, *Tenn., U.S.A.* **77 G4** 36 13N 82 51W
Greenville, *Tex., U.S.A.* **81 J6** 33 8N 96 7W
Greenwater Lake Prov. Park, *Canada* **73 C8** 52 32N 103 30W
Greenwich, *U.K.* **11 F8** 51 28N 0 0 E
Greenwich, *Conn., U.S.A.* **79 E11** 41 2N 73 38W
Greenwich, *N.Y., U.S.A.* **79 C11** 43 5N 73 30W
Greenwich, *Ohio, U.S.A.* **78 E2** 41 2N 82 31W
Greenwood, *Canada* **72 D5** 49 10N 118 40W
Greenwood, *Miss., U.S.A.* **81 J9** 33 31N 90 11W
Greenwood, *S.C., U.S.A.* **77 H4** 34 12N 82 10W
Greenwood, Mt., *Australia* **60 B5** 13 48S 130 4 E
Gregory, *U.S.A.* **80 D5** 43 14N 99 20W
Gregory →, *Australia* **62 B2** 17 53S 139 17 E
Gregory, L., *S. Austral., Australia* **63 D2** 28 55S 139 0 E
Gregory, L., *W. Austral., Australia* **61 E2** 25 38S 119 58 E
Gregory Downs, *Australia* **62 B2** 18 35S 138 45 E
Gregory L., *Australia* **60 D4** 20 0S 127 40 E
Gregory Ra., *Queens., Australia* **62 B3** 19 30S 143 40 E
Gregory Ra., *W. Austral., Australia* **60 D3** 21 20S 121 12 E
Greifswald, *Germany* **16 A6** 54 5N 13 23 E
Gremikha, *Russia* **24 A6** 67 50N 39 40 E
Grenada, *U.S.A.* **81 J10** 33 47N 89 49W
Grenada ■, *W. Indies* **89 D7** 12 10N 61 40W
Grenadines, *W. Indies* **89 D7** 12 40N 61 20W
Grenen, *Denmark* **9 H11** 57 44N 10 40 E
Grenfell, *Australia* **63 E4** 33 52S 148 8 E
Grenfell, *Canada* **73 C8** 50 30N 102 56W
Grenoble, *France* **18 D6** 45 12N 5 42 E
Grenora, *U.S.A.* **80 A3** 48 37N 103 56W
Grenville, C., *Australia* **62 A3** 12 0S 143 13 E
Grenville Chan., *Canada* **72 C3** 53 40N 129 46W
Gresham, *U.S.A.* **84 E4** 45 30N 122 26W
Gresik, *Indonesia* **37 G15** 7 13S 112 38 E
Gretna Green, *U.K.* **12 F5** 55 0N 3 3W
Grevenmacher, *Lux.* **15 E6** 49 41N 6 26 E
Grey →, *N.Z.* **59 K3** 42 27S 171 12 E
Grey, C., *Australia* **62 A2** 13 0S 136 35 E
Grey Ra., *Australia* **63 D3** 27 0S 143 30 E
Grey Res., *Canada* **71 C8** 48 20N 56 30W
Greybull, *U.S.A.* **82 D9** 44 30N 108 3W
Greymouth, *N.Z.* **59 K3** 42 29S 171 13 E
Greytown, *N.Z.* **59 J5** 41 5S 175 29 E
Greytown, *S. Africa* **57 D5** 29 1S 30 36 E
Gribbell I., *Canada* **72 C3** 53 23N 129 0W
Gridley, *U.S.A.* **84 F5** 39 22N 121 42W
Griekwastad, *S. Africa* **56 D3** 28 49S 23 15 E
Griffin, *U.S.A.* **77 J3** 33 15N 84 16W
Griffith, *Australia* **63 E4** 34 18S 146 2 E
Grimari, *C.A.R.* **51 G9** 5 43N 20 6 E
Grimes, *U.S.A.* **84 F5** 39 4N 121 54W
Grimsby, *Canada* **78 C5** 43 12N 79 34W
Grimsby, *U.K.* **10 D7** 53 35N 0 5W
Grímsey, *Iceland* **8 C5** 66 33N 17 58W
Grimshaw, *Canada* **72 B5** 56 10N 117 40W
Grimstad, *Norway* **9 G10** 58 22N 8 35 E
Grinnell, *U.S.A.* **80 E8** 41 45N 92 43W
Gris-Nez, C., *France* **18 A4** 50 52N 1 35 E
Groais I., *Canada* **71 B8** 50 55N 55 35W
Groblersdal, *S. Africa* **57 D4** 25 15S 29 25 E
Grodno, *Belorussia* **24 D3** 53 42N 23 52 E
Grodzisk Wielkopolski, *Poland* **16 B8** 52 15N 16 22 E
Groesbeck, *U.S.A.* **81 K6** 30 48N 96 31W
Grójec, *Poland* **17 C10** 51 50N 20 58 E
Grong, *Norway* **8 D12** 64 25N 12 8 E
Groningen, *Neths.* **15 A6** 53 15N 6 35 E
Groningen □, *Neths.* **15 A6** 53 16N 6 40 E
Groom, *U.S.A.* **81 H4** 35 12N 101 6W
Groot →, *S. Africa* **56 E3** 33 45S 24 36 E
Groot Berg →, *S. Africa* **56 E2** 32 47S 18 8 E
Groot-Brakrivier, *S. Africa* **56 E3** 34 2S 22 18 E
Groot-Kei →, *S. Africa* **57 E4** 32 41S 28 22 E
Groot Vis →, *S. Africa* **56 E4** 33 28S 27 5 E
Groote Eylandt, *Australia* **62 A2** 14 0S 136 40 E
Grootfontein, *Namibia* **56 B2** 19 31S 18 6 E
Grootlaagte →, *Africa* **56 C3** 20 55S 21 27 E
Grootvloer, *S. Africa* **56 E3** 30 0S 20 40 E
Gros C., *Canada* **72 A6** 61 59N 113 32W
Grosa, Pta., *Spain* **22 B8** 39 6N 1 36 E
Gross Glockner, *Austria* **16 E6** 47 5N 12 40 E
Grossenhain, *Germany* **16 C6** 51 17N 13 32 E
Grosseto, *Italy* **20 C4** 42 45N 11 7 E
Groswater B., *Canada* **71 B8** 54 20N 57 40W
Groton, *Conn., U.S.A.* **79 E12** 41 21N 72 5W
Groton, *S. Dak., U.S.A.* **80 C5** 45 27N 98 6W
Grouard Mission, *Canada* **72 B5** 55 33N 116 9W
Groundhog →, *Canada* **70 C3** 48 45N 82 58W
Grouse Creek, *U.S.A.* **82 F7** 41 42N 113 53W
Grove City, *U.S.A.* **78 E4** 41 10N 80 5W
Groveland, *U.S.A.* **84 H6** 37 50N 120 14W
Grover City, *U.S.A.* **85 K6** 35 7N 120 37W
Groveton, *N.H., U.S.A.* **79 B13** 44 36N 71 31W
Groveton, *Tex., U.S.A.* **81 K7** 31 4N 95 8W
Groznyy, *Russia* **25 F8** 43 20N 45 45 E
Grudziądz, *Poland* **17 B9** 53 30N 18 47 E
Grundy Center, *U.S.A.* **80 D8** 42 22N 92 47W
Gruver, *U.S.A.* **81 G4** 36 16N 101 24W
Gryazi, *Russia* **24 D6** 52 30N 39 58 E
Gryazovets, *Russia* **26 D5** 58 50N 40 10 E
Gua, *India* **41 H14** 22 18N 85 20 E
Gua Musang, *Malaysia* **39 K3** 4 53N 101 58 E
Guacanayabo, G. de, *Cuba* **88 B4** 20 40N 77 20W
Guachípas →, *Argentina* **94 B2** 25 40S 65 30W
Guadalajara, *Mexico* **86 C4** 20 40N 103 20W
Guadalajara, *Spain* **19 B4** 40 37N 3 12W
Guadalcanal, *Solomon Is.* **64 H8** 9 32S 160 12 E
Guadales, *Argentina* **94 C2** 34 30S 67 55W
Guadalete →, *Spain* **19 D2** 36 35N 6 13W
Guadalhorce →, *Spain* **19 D3** 36 41N 4 27W
Guadalquivir →, *Spain* **19 D2** 36 47N 6 22W
Guadalupe = Guadeloupe ■, *W. Indies* **89 C7** 16 20N 61 40W
Guadalupe, *Mexico* **85 N10** 32 4N 116 32W
Guadalupe, *U.S.A.* **85 L6** 34 59N 120 33W
Guadalupe →, *Mexico* **85 N10** 32 6N 116 51W
Guadalupe →, *U.S.A.* **81 L6** 28 27N 96 47W
Guadalupe, Sierra de, *Spain* **19 C3** 39 28N 5 30W
Guadalupe Bravos, *Mexico* **86 A3** 31 20N 106 10W
Guadalupe Peak, *U.S.A.* **83 L11** 31 50N 104 52W
Guadalupe y Calvo, *Mexico* **86 B3** 26 6N 106 58W
Guadarrama, Sierra de, *Spain* **19 B4** 41 0N 4 0W
Guadeloupe ■, *W. Indies* **89 C7** 16 20N 61 40W
Guadeloupe Passage, *W. Indies* **89 C7** 16 50N 62 15W
Guadiana →, *Portugal* **19 D2** 37 14N 7 22W
Guadix, *Spain* **19 D4** 37 18N 3 11W
Guafo, Boca del, *Chile* **96 E2** 43 35S 74 0W
Guaira, *Brazil* **95 A5** 24 5S 54 10W
Guaitecas, Is., *Chile* **96 E2** 44 0S 74 30W
Guajará-Mirim, *Brazil* **92 F5** 10 50S 65 20W
Guajira, Pen. de la, *Colombia* **92 A4** 12 0N 72 0W
Gualán, *Guatemala* **88 C2** 15 8N 89 22W
Gualeguay, *Argentina* **94 C4** 33 10S 59 14W
Gualeguaychú, *Argentina* **94 C4** 33 3S 59 31W
Guam ■, *Pac. Oc.* **64 F6** 13 27N 144 45 E
Guaminí, *Argentina* **94 D3** 37 1S 62 28W
Guamúchil, *Mexico* **86 B3** 25 25N 108 3W
Guanabacoa, *Cuba* **88 B3** 23 8N 82 18W
Guanacaste, Cordillera del, *Costa Rica* **88 D2** 10 40N 85 4W
Guanaceví, *Mexico* **86 B3** 25 40N 106 0W
Guanahani = San Salvador, *Bahamas* **89 B5** 24 0N 74 40W
Guanajay, *Cuba* **88 B3** 22 56N 82 42W
Guanajuato, *Mexico* **86 C4** 21 0N 101 20W
Guanajuato □, *Mexico* **86 C4** 20 40N 101 20W
Guandacol, *Argentina* **94 B2** 29 30S 68 40W
Guane, *Cuba* **88 B3** 22 10N 84 7W
Guangdong □, *China* **33 D6** 23 0N 113 0 E
Guangling, *China* **34 E8** 39 47N 114 22 E
Guangrao, *China* **35 F10** 37 5N 118 25 E
Guangwu, *China* **34 F3** 37 48N 105 57 E
Guangxi Zhuangzu Zizhiqu □, *China* **33 D5** 24 0N 109 0 E
Guangzhou, *China* **33 D6** 23 5N 113 10 E
Guanipa →, *Venezuela* **92 B6** 9 56N 62 26W
Guannan, *China* **35 G10** 34 8N 119 21 E
Guantánamo, *Cuba* **89 B4** 20 10N 75 14W
Guantao, *China* **34 F8** 36 42N 115 25 E
Guanyun, *China* **35 G10** 34 20N 119 18 E
Guápiles, *Costa Rica* **88 D3** 10 10N 83 46W
Guaporé →, *Brazil* **92 F5** 11 55S 65 4W
Guaqui, *Bolivia* **92 G5** 16 41S 68 54W
Guarapari, *Brazil* **95 A7** 20 40S 40 30W
Guarapuava, *Brazil* **95 B5** 25 20S 51 30W
Guaratinguetá, *Brazil* **95 A6** 22 49S 45 9W
Guaratuba, *Brazil* **95 B6** 25 53S 48 38W
Guarda, *Portugal* **19 B2** 40 32N 7 20W
Guardafui, C. = Asir, Ras, *Somali Rep.* **46 E5** 11 55N 51 10 E
Guaria □, *Paraguay* **94 B4** 25 45S 56 30W
Guarujá, *Brazil* **95 A6** 24 2S 46 25W
Guarus, *Brazil* **95 A7** 21 44S 41 20W
Guasave, *Mexico* **86 B3** 25 34N 108 27W
Guasdualito, *Venezuela* **92 B4** 7 15N 70 44W
Guasipati, *Venezuela* **92 B6** 7 28N 61 54W
Guatemala, *Guatemala* **88 D1** 14 40N 90 22W
Guatemala ■, *Cent. Amer.* **88 C1** 15 40N 90 30W
Guatire, *Venezuela* **92 A5** 10 28N 66 32W
Guaviare □, *Colombia* **92 C4** 2 0N 72 30W
Guaviare →, *Colombia* **92 C5** 4 3N 67 44W
Guaxupé, *Brazil* **95 A6** 21 10S 47 5W
Guayama, *Puerto Rico* **89 C6** 17 59N 66 7W
Guayaquil, *Ecuador* **92 D3** 2 15S 79 52W
Guayaquil, G. de, *Ecuador* **92 D2** 3 10S 81 0W
Guaymas, *Mexico* **86 B2** 27 59N 110 54W
Guba, *Zaïre* **55 E2** 10 38S 26 27 E
Gudbrandsdalen, *Norway* **9 F10** 61 33N 9 55 E
Guddu Barrage, *Pakistan* **40 E6** 28 30N 69 50 E
Gudivada, *India* **41 L12** 16 30N 81 3 E
Gudur, *India* **40 M11** 14 12N 79 55 E
Guecho, *Spain* **19 A4** 43 21N 2 59W
Guékédou, *Guinea* **50 G2** 8 40N 10 5W
Guelma, *Algeria* **50 A6** 36 25N 7 29 E
Guelph, *Canada* **70 D3** 43 35N 80 20W
Guéréda, *Chad* **51 F9** 14 31N 22 5 E
Guéret, *France* **18 C4** 46 11N 1 51 E
Guerneville, *U.S.A.* **84 G4** 38 30N 123 0W
Guernica, *Spain* **19 A4** 43 19N 2 40W
Guernsey, *U.K.* **11 H5** 49 30N 2 35W
Guernsey, *U.S.A.* **80 D2** 42 19N 104 45W
Guerrero □, *Mexico* **87 D5** 17 30N 100 0W
Gueydan, *U.S.A.* **81 K8** 30 2N 92 31W
Gügher, *Iran* **45 D8** 29 28N 56 27 E
Guia, *Canary Is.* **22 F4** 28 8N 15 38W
Guia de Isora, *Canary Is.* **22 F3** 28 12N 16 46W
Guia Lopes da Laguna, *Brazil* **95 A4** 21 26S 56 7W
Guiglo, *Ivory C.* **50 G3** 6 45N 7 30W
Guijá, *Mozam.* **57 C5** 24 27S 33 0 E
Guildford, *U.K.* **11 F7** 51 14N 0 34W
Guilford, *U.S.A.* **71 C6** 45 10N 69 23W
Guilin, *China* **33 D6** 25 18N 110 15 E
Guilvinec, *France* **18 C1** 47 48N 4 17W
Güimar, *Canary Is.* **22 F3** 28 18N 16 24W
Guimarães, *Brazil* **93 D10** 2 9S 44 42W
Guimaras, *Phil.* **37 B6** 10 35N 122 37 E
Guinda, *U.S.A.* **84 G4** 38 50N 122 12W
Guinea ■, *W. Afr.* **50 F2** 10 20N 11 30W
Guinea, Gulf of, *Atl. Oc.* **48 F3** 3 0N 2 30 E
Guinea-Bissau ■, *Africa* **50 F2** 12 0N 15 0W
Güines, *Cuba* **88 B3** 22 50N 82 0W
Guingamp, *France* **18 B2** 48 34N 3 10W
Güiria, *Venezuela* **92 A6** 10 32N 62 18W
Guiuan, *Phil.* **37 B7** 11 5N 125 55 E
Guiyang, *China* **32 D5** 26 32N 106 40 E
Guizhou □, *China* **32 D5** 27 0N 107 0 E
Gujarat □, *India* **42 H4** 23 20N 71 0 E
Gujranwala, *Pakistan* **42 C6** 32 10N 74 12 E
Gujrat, *Pakistan* **42 C6** 32 40N 74 2 E
Gulbarga, *India* **40 L10** 17 20N 76 50 E
Gulf, The, *Asia* **45 E6** 27 0N 50 0 E
Gulfport, *U.S.A.* **81 K10** 30 22N 89 6W
Gulgong, *Australia* **63 E4** 32 20S 149 49 E
Gulistan, *Pakistan* **42 D2** 30 30N 66 35 E
Gull Lake, *Canada* **73 C7** 50 10N 108 29W
Gulmarg, *India* **43 B6** 34 3N 74 25 E
Gulshad, *Kazakhstan* **26 E8** 46 45N 74 25 E
Gulu, *Uganda* **54 B3** 2 48N 32 17 E
Gulwe, *Tanzania* **54 D4** 6 30S 36 25 E
Gum Lake, *Australia* **63 E3** 32 42S 143 9 E
Gumal →, *Pakistan* **42 D4** 31 40N 71 50 E
Gumbaz, *Pakistan* **42 D3** 30 2N 69 0 E
Gumlu, *Australia* **62 B4** 19 53S 147 41 E
Gumma □, *Japan* **31 F9** 36 30N 138 20 E
Gummi, *Nigeria* **50 F6** 12 4N 5 9 E
Gumzai, *Indonesia* **37 F8** 5 28S 134 42 E
Guna, *India* **42 G7** 24 40N 77 19 E
Gundagai, *Australia* **63 F4** 35 3S 148 6 E
Gundih, *Indonesia* **37 G14** 7 10S 110 56 E
Gungu, *Zaïre* **52 F3** 5 43S 19 20 E
Gunisao →, *Canada* **73 C9** 53 56N 97 53W
Gunisao L., *Canada* **73 C9** 53 33N 96 15W
Gunnbjørn Fjeld, *Greenland* **4 C6** 68 55N 29 47W
Gunnedah, *Australia* **63 E5** 30 59S 150 15 E
Gunningbar Cr. →, *Australia* **63 E4** 31 14S 147 6 E
Gunnison, *Colo., U.S.A.* **83 G10** 38 33N 106 56W
Gunnison, *Utah, U.S.A.* **82 G8** 39 9N 111 49W
Gunnison →, *U.S.A.* **83 G9** 39 4N 108 35W
Gunpowder, *Australia* **62 B2** 19 42S 139 22 E
Guntakal, *India* **40 M10** 15 11N 77 27 E
Guntersville, *U.S.A.* **77 H2** 34 21N 86 18W
Guntong, *Malaysia* **39 K3** 4 36N 101 3 E
Guntur, *India* **41 L12** 16 23N 80 30 E
Gunungapi, *Indonesia* **37 F7** 6 45S 126 30 E
Gunungsitoli, *Indonesia* **36 D1** 1 15N 97 30 E
Gunza, *Angola* **52 G2** 10 50S 13 50 E
Guo He →, *China* **35 H9** 32 59N 117 10 E
Guoyang, *China* **34 H9** 33 32N 116 12 E
Gupis, *Pakistan* **43 A5** 36 15N 73 20 E
Gurdaspur, *India* **42 C6** 32 5N 75 31 E
Gurdon, *U.S.A.* **81 J8** 33 55N 93 9W
Gurgaon, *India* **42 E7** 28 27N 77 1 E
Gurha, *India* **42 G4** 25 12N 71 39 E
Gurkha, *Nepal* **43 E11** 28 5N 84 40 E
Gurley, *Australia* **63 D4** 29 45S 149 48 E
Gurué, *Mozam.* **55 F4** 15 25S 36 58 E
Gurun, *Malaysia* **39 K3** 5 49N 100 27 E
Gurupá, *Brazil* **93 D8** 1 25S 51 35W
Gurupá, I. Grande de, *Brazil* **93 D8** 1 25S 51 45W
Gurupi →, *Brazil* **93 D9** 1 13S 46 6W
Guryev = Atyrau, *Kazakhstan* **25 E9** 47 5N 52 0 E
Gusau, *Nigeria* **50 F6** 12 12N 6 40 E
Gushan, *China* **35 E12** 39 50N 123 35 E
Gusinoozersk, *Russia* **27 D11** 51 16N 106 27 E
Gustine, *U.S.A.* **83 H3** 37 16N 121 0W
Güstrow, *Germany* **16 B6** 53 47N 12 12 E
Gutha, *Australia* **61 E2** 28 58S 115 55 E
Guthalongra, *Australia* **62 B4** 19 52S 147 50 E
Guthrie, *U.S.A.* **81 H6** 35 53N 97 25W
Guttenberg, *U.S.A.* **80 D9** 42 47N 91 6W
Guyana ■, *S. Amer.* **92 C7** 5 0N 59 0W
Guyane française = French Guiana ■, *S. Amer.* **93 C8** 4 0N 53 0W
Guyang, *China* **34 D6** 41 0N 110 5 E
Guyenne, *France* **18 D4** 44 30N 0 40 E
Guymon, *U.S.A.* **81 G4** 36 41N 101 29W
Guyra, *Australia* **63 E5** 30 15S 151 40 E
Guyuan, *Hebei, China* **34 D8** 41 37N 115 40 E
Guyuan, *Ningxia Huizu, China* **34 F4** 36 0N 106 20 E
Guzhen, *China* **35 H9** 33 22N 117 18 E
Guzmán, L. de, *Mexico* **86 A3** 31 25N 107 25W
Gwa, *Burma* **41 L19** 17 36N 94 34 E
Gwaai, *Zimbabwe* **55 F2** 19 15S 27 45 E
Gwabegar, *Australia* **63 E4** 30 31S 149 0 E
Gwādar, *Pakistan* **40 G3** 25 10N 62 18 E
Gwalia, *Australia* **61 E3** 28 54S 121 20 E
Gwalior, *India* **42 F8** 26 12N 78 10 E
Gwanda, *Zimbabwe* **55 G2** 20 55S 29 0 E
Gwane, *Zaïre* **54 B2** 4 45N 25 48 E
Gweebarra B., *Ireland* **13 B3** 54 52N 8 21W
Gweedore, *Ireland* **13 A3** 55 4N 8 15W
Gwent □, *U.K.* **11 F5** 51 45N 2 55W
Gweru, *Zimbabwe* **55 F2** 19 28S 29 45 E
Gwinn, *U.S.A.* **76 B2** 46 19N 87 27W
Gwydir →, *Australia* **63 D4** 29 27S 149 48 E
Gwynedd □, *U.K.* **10 E4** 53 0N 4 0W
Gyandzha, *Azerbaijan* **25 F8** 40 45N 46 20 E
Gyaring Hu, *China* **32 C4** 34 50N 97 40 E
Gydanskiy P-ov., *Russia* **26 C8** 70 0N 78 0 E
Gympie, *Australia* **63 D5** 26 11S 152 38 E
Gyöngyös, *Hungary* **17 E9** 47 48N 19 56 E
Györ, *Hungary* **17 E8** 47 41N 17 40 E
Gypsum Pt., *Canada* **72 A6** 61 53N 114 35W
Gypsumville, *Canada* **73 C9** 51 45N 98 40W
Gyumri = Kumayri, *Armenia* **25 F7** 40 47N 43 50 E

H

Ha 'Arava →, *Israel* **47 E4** 30 50N 35 20 E
Ha Coi, *Vietnam* **38 B6** 21 26N 107 46 E
Ha Dong, *Vietnam* **38 B5** 20 58N 105 46 E
Ha Giang, *Vietnam* **38 A5** 22 50N 104 59 E
Ha Tien, *Vietnam* **39 G5** 10 23N 104 29 E
Ha Tinh, *Vietnam* **38 C5** 18 20N 105 54 E
Ha Trung, *Vietnam* **38 C5** 19 58N 105 50 E
Haapamäki, *Finland* **8 E18** 62 18N 24 28 E
Haarlem, *Neths.* **15 B4** 52 23N 4 39 E
Haast →, *N.Z.* **59 K2** 43 50S 169 2 E
Haast Bluff, *Australia* **60 D5** 23 22S 132 0 E

Hab Nadi Chauki, *Pakistan* **42 G2** 25 0N 66 50 E
Habaswein, *Kenya* **54 B4** 1 2N 39 30 E
Habay, *Canada* **72 B5** 58 50N 118 44W
Habbānīyah, *Iraq* **44 C4** 33 17N 43 29 E
Haboro, *Japan* **30 B10** 44 22N 141 42 E
Hachijō-Jima, *Japan* **31 H9** 33 5N 139 45 E
Hachinohe, *Japan* **30 D10** 40 30N 141 29 E
Hachiōji, *Japan* **31 G9** 35 40N 139 20 E
Hachŏn, *N. Korea* **35 D15** 41 29N 129 2 E
Hackensack, *U.S.A.* **79 F10** 40 53N 74 3W
Hadali, *Pakistan* **42 C5** 32 16N 72 11 E
Hadarba, Ras, *Sudan* **51 D12** 22 4N 36 51 E
Hadarom □, *Israel* **47 E3** 31 0N 35 0 E
Haddington, *U.K.* **12 F6** 55 57N 2 48W
Hadejia, *Nigeria* **50 F7** 12 30N 10 5 E
Haden, *Australia* **63 D5** 27 13S 151 54 E
Hadera, *Israel* **47 C3** 32 27N 34 55 E
Hadera, N. —▸, *Israel* **47 C3** 32 28N 34 52 E
Hadhramaut = Haḍramawt, *Yemen* **46 D4** 15 30N 49 30 E
Hadong, *S. Korea* **35 G14** 35 5N 127 44 E
Haḍramawt, *Yemen* **46 D4** 15 30N 49 30 E
Ḥadrānīyah, *Iraq* **44 C4** 35 38N 43 14 E
Hadrian's Wall, *U.K.* **10 C5** 55 0N 2 30W
Haeju, *N. Korea* **35 E13** 38 3N 125 45 E
Haenam, *S. Korea* **35 G14** 34 34N 126 35 E
Haerhpin = Harbin, *China* **35 B14** 45 48N 126 40 E
Hafar al Bāṭin, *Si. Arabia* **44 D5** 28 25N 46 0 E
Ḥafīrat al 'Aydā, *Si. Arabia* **44 E3** 26 26N 39 12 E
Hafizabad, *Pakistan* **42 C5** 32 5N 73 40 E
Haflong, *India* **41 G18** 25 10N 93 5 E
Hafnarfjörður, *Iceland* **8 D3** 64 4N 21 57W
Hafun, Ras, *Somali Rep.* **46 E5** 10 29N 51 30 E
Hagalil, *Israel* **47 C4** 32 53N 35 18 E
Hagen, *Germany* **16 C3** 51 21N 7 29 E
Hagerman, *U.S.A.* **81 J2** 33 7N 104 20W
Hagerstown, *U.S.A.* **76 F7** 39 39N 77 43W
Hagfors, *Sweden* **9 F12** 60 3N 13 45 E
Hagi, *Iceland* **8 D2** 65 28N 23 25W
Hagi, *Japan* **31 G5** 34 30N 131 22 E
Hagolan, *Syria* **47 B4** 33 0N 35 45 E
Hagondange-Briey, *France* **18 B7** 49 16N 6 11 E
Hags Hd., *Ireland* **13 D2** 52 57N 9 30W
Hague, C. de la, *France* **18 B3** 49 44N 1 56W
Hague, The = 's-Gravenhage, *Neths.* **15 B4** 52 7N 4 17 E
Haguenau, *France* **18 B7** 48 49N 7 47 E
Hai □, *Tanzania* **54 C4** 3 10S 37 10 E
Hai Duong, *Vietnam* **38 B6** 20 56N 106 19 E
Haicheng, *China* **35 D12** 40 50N 122 45 E
Haidar Khel, *Afghan.* **42 C3** 33 58N 68 38 E
Haifa = Ḥefa, *Israel* **47 C3** 32 46N 35 0 E
Haig, *Australia* **61 F4** 30 55S 126 10 E
Haikou, *China* **33 D6** 20 1N 110 16 E
Ḥā'il, *Si. Arabia* **44 E4** 27 28N 41 45 E
Hailar, *China* **33 B6** 49 10N 119 38 E
Hailey, *U.S.A.* **82 E6** 43 31N 114 19W
Haileybury, *Canada* **70 C4** 47 30N 79 38W
Hailin, *China* **35 B15** 44 37N 129 30 E
Hailong, *China* **35 C13** 42 32N 125 40 E
Hailuoto, *Finland* **8 D18** 65 3N 24 45 E
Hainan □, *China* **33 E5** 19 0N 109 30 E
Hainaut □, *Belgium* **15 D4** 50 30N 4 0 E
Haines, *U.S.A.* **82 D5** 44 55N 117 56W
Haines City, *U.S.A.* **77 L5** 28 7N 81 38W
Haines Junction, *Canada* **72 A1** 60 45N 137 30W
Haiphong, *Vietnam* **32 D5** 20 47N 106 41 E
Haiti ■, *W. Indies* **89 C5** 19 0N 72 30W
Haiya Junction, *Sudan* **51 E12** 18 20N 36 21 E
Haiyang, *China* **35 F11** 36 47N 121 9 E
Haiyuan, *China* **34 F3** 36 35N 105 52 E
Haizhou, *China* **35 G10** 34 37N 119 7 E
Haizhou Wan, *China* **35 G10** 34 50N 119 20 E
Haja, *Indonesia* **37 E7** 3 19S 129 37 E
Hajar Bangar, *Sudan* **51 F9** 10 40N 22 45 E
Hajdúböszörmény, *Hungary* **17 E10** 47 40N 21 30 E
Hajipur, *India* **43 G11** 25 45N 85 13 E
Ḥājjī Muḥsin, *Iraq* **44 C5** 32 35N 45 29 E
Ḥājjīābād, *Eşfahan, Iran* **45 C7** 33 41N 54 50 E
Ḥājjīābād, *Hormozgān, Iran* **45 D7** 28 19N 55 55 E
Hajnówka, *Poland* **17 B11** 52 47N 23 35 E
Hakansson, Mts., *Zaïre* **55 D2** 8 40S 25 45 E
Hakken-Zan, *Japan* **31 G7** 34 10N 135 54 E
Hakodate, *Japan* **30 D10** 41 45N 140 44 E
Haku-San, *Japan* **31 F8** 36 9N 136 46 E
Hakui, *Japan* **31 F8** 36 53N 136 47 E
Hala, *Pakistan* **40 G6** 25 43N 68 20 E
Ḥalab, *Syria* **44 B3** 36 10N 37 15 E
Ḥalabjah, *Iraq* **44 C5** 35 10N 45 58 E
Halaib, *Sudan* **51 D12** 22 12N 36 30 E
Hālat' Ammār, *Si. Arabia* **44 D3** 29 10N 36 4 E
Halbā, *Lebanon* **47 A5** 34 34N 36 6 E
Halberstadt, *Germany* **16 C5** 51 53N 11 2 E
Halcombe, *N.Z.* **59 J5** 40 8S 175 30 E
Halcon, Mt., *Phil.* **37 B6** 13 0N 121 30 E
Halden, *Norway* **9 G11** 59 9N 11 23 E
Haldia, *India* **41 H16** 22 5N 88 3 E
Haldwani, *India* **43 E8** 29 31N 79 30 E
Hale —▸, *Australia* **62 C2** 24 56S 135 53 E
Haleakala Crater, *U.S.A.* **74 H16** 20 43N 156 16W
Haleyville, *U.S.A.* **77 H2** 34 14N 87 37W
Halfway —▸, *Canada* **72 B4** 56 12N 121 32W
Haliburton, *Canada* **70 C4** 45 3N 78 30W
Halifax, *Australia* **62 B4** 18 32S 146 22 E
Halifax, *Canada* **71 D7** 44 38N 63 35W
Halifax, *U.K.* **10 D6** 53 43N 1 51W
Halifax B., *Australia* **62 B4** 18 50S 147 0 E
Halifax I., *Namibia* **56 D2** 26 38S 15 4 E
Halīl —▸, *Iran* **45 E8** 27 40N 58 30 E
Hall Beach, *Canada* **69 B11** 68 46N 81 12W
Hall Pt., *Australia* **60 C3** 15 40S 124 23 E
Hallands län □, *Sweden* **9 H12** 56 50N 12 50 E
Halle, *Belgium* **15 D4** 50 44N 4 13 E
Halle, *Germany* **16 C5** 51 29N 12 0 E
Hällefors, *Sweden* **9 G13** 59 47N 14 31 E
Hallett, *Australia* **63 E2** 33 25S 138 55 E
Hallettsville, *U.S.A.* **81 L6** 29 27N 96 57W
Halliday, *U.S.A.* **80 B3** 47 21N 102 20W
Halliday L., *Canada* **73 A7** 61 21N 108 56W
Hallim, *S. Korea* **35 H14** 33 24N 126 15 E
Hallingdal —▸, *Norway* **9 F10** 60 34N 9 12 E
Hällnäs, *Sweden* **8 D15** 64 19N 19 36 E
Hallock, *U.S.A.* **73 D9** 48 47N 96 57W
Halls Creek, *Australia* **60 C4** 18 16S 127 38 E
Hallstead, *U.S.A.* **79 E9** 41 58N 75 45W
Halmahera, *Indonesia* **37 D7** 0 40N 128 0 E
Halmstad, *Sweden* **9 H12** 56 41N 12 52 E
Halq el Oued, *Tunisia* **51 A7** 36 53N 10 18 E
Hals, *Denmark* **9 H11** 56 59N 10 18 E
Hälsingborg = Helsingborg, *Sweden* **9 H12** 56 3N 12 42 E
Halstad, *U.S.A.* **80 B6** 47 21N 96 50W
Halul, *Qatar* **45 E7** 25 40N 52 40 E
Ḥalvān, *Iran* **45 C8** 33 57N 56 15 E
Ham Tan, *Vietnam* **39 G6** 10 40N 107 45 E
Ham Yen, *Vietnam* **38 A5** 22 4N 105 3 E
Hamab, *Namibia* **56 D2** 28 7S 19 16 E
Hamada, *Japan* **31 G6** 34 56N 132 4 E
Hamadān, *Iran* **45 C6** 34 52N 48 32 E
Hamadān □, *Iran* **45 C6** 35 0N 49 0 E
Hamāh, *Syria* **44 C3** 35 5N 36 40 E
Hamamatsu, *Japan* **31 G8** 34 45N 137 45 E
Hamar, *Norway* **9 F11** 60 48N 11 7 E
Hamarøy, *Norway* **8 B13** 68 5N 15 38 E
Hambantota, *Sri Lanka* **40 R12** 6 10N 81 10 E
Hamber Prov. Park, *Canada* **72 C5** 52 20N 118 0W
Hamburg, *Germany* **16 B4** 53 32N 9 59 E
Hamburg, *Ark., U.S.A.* **81 J9** 33 14N 91 48W
Hamburg, *Iowa, U.S.A.* **80 E7** 40 36N 95 39W
Hamburg, *N.Y., U.S.A.* **78 D6** 42 43N 78 50W
Hamburg, *Pa., U.S.A.* **79 F9** 40 33N 75 59W
Ḥamḍ, W. al —▸, *Si. Arabia* **44 E3** 24 55N 36 20 E
Hamden, *U.S.A.* **79 E12** 41 23N 72 54W
Hame □ = Hämeen lääni □, *Finland* **9 F18** 61 30N 24 0 E
Hämeen lääni □, *Finland* **9 F18** 61 30N 24 0 E
Hämeenlinna, *Finland* **9 F18** 61 0N 24 28 E
Hamelin Pool, *Australia* **61 E1** 26 22S 114 20 E
Hameln, *Germany* **16 B4** 52 7N 9 24 E
Hamerkaz □, *Israel* **47 C3** 32 15N 34 55 E
Hamersley Ra., *Australia* **60 D2** 22 0S 117 45 E
Hamhung, *N. Korea* **35 E14** 39 54N 127 30 E
Hami, *China* **32 B4** 42 55N 93 25 E
Hamilton, *Australia* **63 F3** 37 45S 142 2 E
Hamilton, *Canada* **70 D4** 43 15N 79 50W
Hamilton, *N.Z.* **59 G5** 37 47S 175 19 E
Hamilton, *U.K.* **12 F4** 55 47N 4 2W
Hamilton, *Mo., U.S.A.* **80 F8** 39 45N 93 59W
Hamilton, *Mont., U.S.A.* **82 C6** 46 15N 114 10W
Hamilton, *N.Y., U.S.A.* **79 D9** 42 50N 75 33W
Hamilton, *Ohio, U.S.A.* **76 F3** 39 24N 84 34W
Hamilton, *Tex., U.S.A.* **81 K5** 31 42N 98 7W
Hamilton —▸, *Australia* **62 C2** 23 30S 139 47 E
Hamilton City, *U.S.A.* **84 F4** 39 45N 122 1W
Hamilton Hotel, *Australia* **62 C3** 22 45S 140 40 E
Hamilton Inlet, *Canada* **71 B8** 54 0N 57 30W
Hamiota, *Canada* **73 C8** 50 11N 100 38W
Hamlet, *U.S.A.* **77 H6** 34 53N 79 42W
Hamley Bridge, *Australia* **63 E2** 34 17S 138 35 E
Hamlin = Hameln, *Germany* **16 B4** 52 7N 9 24 E
Hamlin, *N.Y., U.S.A.* **78 C7** 43 17N 77 55W
Hamlin, *Tex., U.S.A.* **81 J4** 32 53N 100 8W
Hamm, *Germany* **16 C3** 51 40N 7 49 E
Hammerfest, *Norway* **8 A17** 70 39N 23 41 E
Hammond, *Ind., U.S.A.* **76 E2** 41 38N 87 30W
Hammond, *La., U.S.A.* **81 K9** 30 30N 90 28W
Hammonton, *U.S.A.* **76 F8** 39 39N 74 48W
Hampden, *N.Z.* **59 L3** 45 18S 170 50 E
Hampshire □, *U.K.* **11 F6** 51 3N 1 20W
Hampshire Downs, *U.K.* **11 F6** 51 10N 1 10W
Hampton, *Ark., U.S.A.* **81 J8** 33 32N 92 28W
Hampton, *Iowa, U.S.A.* **80 D8** 42 45N 93 13W
Hampton, *N.H., U.S.A.* **79 D14** 42 57N 70 50W
Hampton, *S.C., U.S.A.* **77 J5** 32 52N 81 7W
Hampton, *Va., U.S.A.* **76 G7** 37 2N 76 21W
Hampton Tableland, *Australia* **61 F4** 32 0S 127 0 E
Hamrat esh Sheykh, *Sudan* **51 F10** 14 38N 27 55 E
Hamyang, *S. Korea* **35 G14** 35 32N 127 42 E
Ḥana, *U.S.A.* **74 H17** 20 45N 155 59W
Ḥanak, *Si. Arabia* **44 E3** 25 32N 37 0 E
Hanamaki, *Japan* **30 E10** 39 23N 141 7 E
Hanang, *Tanzania* **54 C4** 4 30S 35 25 E
Hanau, *Germany* **16 C4** 50 8N 8 56 E
Hanbogd, *Mongolia* **34 C4** 43 11N 107 10 E
Hancheng, *China* **34 G6** 35 31N 110 25 E
Hancock, *Mich., U.S.A.* **80 B10** 47 8N 88 35W
Hancock, *Minn., U.S.A.* **80 C7** 45 30N 95 48W
Hancock, *N.Y., U.S.A.* **79 E9** 41 57N 75 17W
Handa, *Japan* **31 G8** 34 53N 136 55 E
Handa, *Somali Rep.* **46 E5** 10 37N 51 2 E
Handan, *China* **34 F8** 36 35N 114 28 E
Handeni, *Tanzania* **54 D4** 5 25S 38 2 E
Handeni □, *Tanzania* **54 D4** 5 30S 38 0 E
Handwara, *India* **43 B6** 34 21N 74 20 E
Hanegev, *Israel* **47 E3** 30 50N 35 0 E
Haney, *Canada* **72 D4** 49 12N 122 40W
Hanford, *U.S.A.* **83 H4** 36 20N 119 39W
Hang Chat, *Thailand* **38 C2** 18 20N 99 21 E
Hang Dong, *Thailand* **38 C2** 18 41N 98 55 E
Hangang —▸, *S. Korea* **35 F14** 37 50N 126 30 E
Hangayn Nuruu, *Mongolia* **32 B4** 47 30N 99 0 E
Hangchou = Hangzhou, *China* **33 C7** 30 18N 120 11 E
Hanggin Houqi, *China* **34 D4** 40 58N 107 4 E
Hanggin Qi, *China* **34 E5** 39 52N 108 50 E
Hangö, *Finland* **9 G17** 59 50N 22 57 E
Hangu, *China* **35 E9** 39 18N 117 53 E
Hangzhou, *China* **33 C7** 30 18N 120 11 E
Hangzhou Wan, *China* **33 C7** 30 15N 120 45 E
Hanhongor, *Mongolia* **34 C3** 43 55N 104 28 E
Ḥanīdh, *Si. Arabia* **45 E6** 26 35N 48 38 E
Ḥanīsh, *Yemen* **46 E3** 13 45N 42 46 E
Hankinson, *U.S.A.* **80 B6** 46 4N 96 54W
Hanko = Hangö, *Finland* **9 G17** 59 50N 22 57 E
Hanko, *Finland* **9 G17** 59 50N 22 57 E
Hanksville, *U.S.A.* **83 G8** 38 22N 110 43W
Hanle, *India* **43 C8** 32 42N 79 4 E
Hanmer Springs, *N.Z.* **59 K4** 42 32S 172 50 E
Hann —▸, *Australia* **60 C4** 17 26S 126 17 E
Hann, Mt., *Australia* **60 C4** 15 45S 126 0 E
Hanna, *Canada* **72 C6** 51 40N 111 54W
Hannaford, *U.S.A.* **80 B5** 47 19N 98 11W
Hannah, *U.S.A.* **80 A5** 48 58N 98 42W
Hannah B., *Canada* **70 B4** 51 40N 80 0W
Hannibal, *U.S.A.* **80 F9** 39 42N 91 22W
Hannover, *Germany* **16 B4** 52 23N 9 43 E
Hanoi, *Vietnam* **32 D5** 21 5N 105 55 E
Hanover = Hannover, *Germany* **16 B4** 52 23N 9 43 E
Hanover, *Canada* **78 B3** 44 9N 81 2W
Hanover, *S. Africa* **56 E3** 31 4S 24 29 E
Hanover, *N.H., U.S.A.* **79 C12** 43 42N 72 17W
Hanover, *Ohio, U.S.A.* **78 F2** 40 4N 82 16W
Hanover, *Pa., U.S.A.* **76 F7** 39 48N 76 59W
Hanover, I., *Chile* **96 G2** 51 0S 74 50W
Hansi, *India* **42 E6** 29 10N 75 57 E
Hanson, L., *Australia* **63 E2** 31 0S 136 15 E
Hanzhong, *China* **34 H4** 33 10N 107 1 E
Hanzhuang, *China* **35 G9** 34 33N 117 23 E
Haora, *India* **43 H13** 22 37N 88 20 E
Haparanda, *Sweden* **8 D18** 65 52N 24 8 E
Happy, *U.S.A.* **81 H4** 34 45N 101 52W
Happy Camp, *U.S.A.* **82 F2** 41 48N 123 23W
Happy Valley-Goose Bay, *Canada* **71 B7** 53 15N 60 20W
Hapsu, *N. Korea* **35 D15** 41 13N 128 51 E
Hapur, *India* **42 E7** 28 45N 77 45 E
Ḥaql, *Si. Arabia* **47 F3** 29 10N 34 58 E
Har, *Indonesia* **37 F8** 5 16S 133 14 E
Har-Ayrag, *Mongolia* **34 B5** 45 47N 109 16 E
Har Hu, *China* **32 C4** 38 20N 97 38 E
Har Us Nuur, *Mongolia* **32 B4** 48 0N 92 0 E
Har Yehuda, *Israel* **47 D3** 31 35N 34 57 E
Ḥaraḍ, *Si. Arabia* **46 C4** 24 22N 49 0 E
Haranomachi, *Japan* **30 F10** 37 38N 140 58 E
Harardera, *Somali Rep.* **46 G4** 4 33N 47 38 E
Harare, *Zimbabwe* **55 F3** 17 43S 31 2 E
Harazé, *Chad* **51 F8** 14 20N 19 12 E
Harbin, *China* **35 B14** 45 48N 126 40 E
Harbor Beach, *U.S.A.* **76 D4** 43 51N 82 39W
Harbor Springs, *U.S.A.* **76 C3** 45 26N 85 0W
Harbour Breton, *Canada* **71 C8** 47 29N 55 50W
Harbour Grace, *Canada* **71 C9** 47 40N 53 22W
Harburg, *Germany* **16 B4** 53 27N 9 58 E
Harda, *India* **42 H7** 22 27N 77 5 E
Hardangerfjorden, *Norway* **9 F8** 60 15N 6 0 E
Hardap Dam, *Namibia* **56 C2** 24 32S 17 50 E
Hardenberg, *Neths.* **15 B6** 52 34N 6 37 E
Harderwijk, *Neths.* **15 B5** 52 21N 5 38 E
Hardey —▸, *Australia* **60 D2** 22 45S 116 8 E
Hardin, *U.S.A.* **82 D10** 45 44N 107 37W
Harding, *S. Africa* **57 E4** 30 35S 29 55 E
Harding Ra., *Australia* **60 C3** 16 17S 124 55 E
Hardisty, *Canada* **72 C6** 52 40N 111 18W
Hardman, *U.S.A.* **82 D4** 45 10N 119 41W
Hardoi, *India* **43 F9** 27 26N 80 6 E
Hardwar = Haridwar, *India* **42 E8** 29 58N 78 9 E
Hardwick, *U.S.A.* **79 B12** 44 30N 72 22W
Hardy, *U.S.A.* **81 G9** 36 19N 91 29W
Hardy, Pen., *Chile* **96 H3** 55 30S 68 20W
Hare B., *Canada* **71 B8** 51 15N 55 45W
Harer, *Ethiopia* **46 F3** 9 20N 42 8 E
Hargeisa, *Somali Rep.* **46 F3** 9 30N 44 2 E
Hargshamn, *Sweden* **9 F15** 60 12N 18 30 E
Hari —▸, *Indonesia* **36 E2** 1 16S 104 5 E
Haria, *Canary Is.* **22 E6** 29 8N 13 32W
Haridwar, *India* **42 E8** 29 58N 78 9 E
Haringhata —▸, *Bangla.* **41 J16** 22 0N 89 58 E
Harīrūd —▸, *Asia* **40 A2** 37 24N 60 38 E
Harlan, *Iowa, U.S.A.* **80 E7** 41 39N 95 19W
Harlan, *Ky., U.S.A.* **77 G4** 36 51N 83 19W
Harlech, *U.K.* **10 E3** 52 52N 4 7W
Harlem, *U.S.A.* **82 B9** 48 32N 108 47W
Harlingen, *Neths.* **15 A5** 53 11N 5 25 E
Harlingen, *U.S.A.* **81 M6** 26 12N 97 42W
Harlowton, *U.S.A.* **82 C9** 46 26N 109 50W
Harney Basin, *U.S.A.* **82 E4** 43 30N 119 0W
Harney L., *U.S.A.* **82 E4** 43 14N 119 8W
Harney Peak, *U.S.A.* **80 D3** 43 52N 103 32W
Härnösand, *Sweden* **8 E14** 62 38N 17 55 E
Harp L., *Canada* **71 A7** 55 5N 61 50W
Harrand, *Pakistan* **42 E4** 29 28N 70 3 E
Harriman, *U.S.A.* **77 H3** 35 56N 84 33W
Harrington Harbour, *Canada* **71 B8** 50 31N 59 30W
Harris, *U.K.* **12 D2** 57 50N 6 55W
Harris, Sd. of, *U.K.* **12 D1** 57 44N 7 6W
Harris L., *Australia* **63 E2** 31 10S 135 10 E
Harrisburg, *Ill., U.S.A.* **81 G10** 37 44N 88 32W
Harrisburg, *Nebr., U.S.A.* **80 E3** 41 33N 103 44W
Harrisburg, *Oreg., U.S.A.* **82 D2** 44 16N 123 10W
Harrisburg, *Pa., U.S.A.* **78 F8** 40 16N 76 53W
Harrismith, *S. Africa* **57 D4** 28 15S 29 8 E
Harrison, *Ark., U.S.A.* **81 G8** 36 14N 93 7W
Harrison, *Idaho, U.S.A.* **82 C5** 47 27N 116 47W
Harrison, *Nebr., U.S.A.* **80 D3** 42 41N 103 53W
Harrison, C., *Canada* **71 B8** 54 55N 57 55W
Harrison Bay, *U.S.A.* **68 A4** 70 40N 151 0W
Harrison L., *Canada* **72 D4** 49 33N 121 50W
Harrisonburg, *U.S.A.* **76 F6** 38 27N 78 52W
Harrisonville, *U.S.A.* **80 F7** 38 39N 94 21W
Harriston, *Canada* **70 D3** 43 57N 80 53W
Harrisville, *U.S.A.* **78 B1** 44 39N 83 17W
Harrogate, *U.K.* **10 D6** 53 59N 1 32W
Harrow, *U.K.* **11 F7** 51 35N 0 15W
Harsīn, *Iran* **44 C5** 35 12N 46 34 E
Harstad, *Norway* **8 B14** 68 48N 16 30 E
Hart, *U.S.A.* **76 D2** 43 42N 86 22W
Hart, L., *Australia* **63 E2** 31 10S 136 25 E
Hartbees —▸, *S. Africa* **56 D3** 28 45S 20 32 E
Hartford, *Conn., U.S.A.* **79 E12** 41 46N 72 41W
Hartford, *Ky., U.S.A.* **76 G2** 37 27N 86 55W
Hartford, *S. Dak., U.S.A.* **80 D6** 43 38N 96 57W
Hartford, *Wis., U.S.A.* **80 D10** 43 19N 88 22W
Hartford City, *U.S.A.* **76 E3** 40 27N 85 22W
Hartland, *Canada* **71 C6** 46 20N 67 32W
Hartland Pt., *U.K.* **11 F3** 51 2N 4 32W
Hartlepool, *U.K.* **10 C6** 54 42N 1 11W
Hartley Bay, *Canada* **72 C3** 53 25N 129 15W
Hartmannberge, *Namibia* **56 B1** 17 0S 13 0 E
Hartney, *Canada* **73 D8** 49 30N 100 35W
Harts —▸, *S. Africa* **56 D3** 28 24S 24 17 E
Hartselle, *U.S.A.* **77 H2** 34 27N 86 56W
Hartshorne, *U.S.A.* **81 H7** 34 51N 95 34W
Hartsville, *U.S.A.* **77 H5** 34 23N 80 4W
Hartwell, *U.S.A.* **77 H4** 34 21N 82 56W
Harunabad, *Pakistan* **42 E5** 29 35N 73 8 E
Harvand, *Iran* **45 D7** 28 25N 55 43 E
Harvey, *Australia* **61 F2** 33 5S 115 54 E
Harvey, *Ill., U.S.A.* **76 E2** 41 36N 87 50W
Harvey, *N. Dak., U.S.A.* **80 B5** 47 47N 99 56W
Harwich, *U.K.* **11 F9** 51 56N 1 18 E
Haryana □, *India* **42 E7** 29 0N 76 10 E
Harz, *Germany* **16 C5** 51 40N 10 40 E
Hasan Kīādeh, *Iran* **45 B6** 37 24N 49 58 E
Ḥasanābād, *Iran* **45 C7** 32 8N 52 44 E
Hasanpur, *India* **42 E8** 28 43N 78 17 E
Hashimoto, *Japan* **31 G7** 34 19N 135 37 E
Hashtjerd, *Iran* **45 C6** 35 52N 50 40 E
Haskell, *Okla., U.S.A.* **81 H7** 35 50N 95 40W
Haskell, *Tex., U.S.A.* **81 J5** 33 10N 99 44W
Hasselt, *Belgium* **15 D5** 50 56N 5 21 E
Hassi Inifel, *Algeria* **50 C5** 29 50N 3 41 E
Hassi Messaoud, *Algeria* **50 B6** 31 43N 6 8 E
Hastings, *N.Z.* **59 H6** 39 39S 176 52 E
Hastings, *U.K.* **11 G8** 50 51N 0 36 E
Hastings, *Mich., U.S.A.* **76 D3** 42 39N 85 17W
Hastings, *Minn., U.S.A.* **80 C8** 44 44N 92 51W
Hastings, *Nebr., U.S.A.* **80 E5** 40 35N 98 23W
Hastings Ra., *Australia* **63 E5** 31 15S 152 14 E
Hat Yai, *Thailand* **39 J3** 7 1N 100 27 E
Hatanbulag, *Mongolia* **34 C5** 43 8N 109 5 E
Hatay = Antalya, *Turkey* **25 G5** 36 52N 30 45 E
Hatch, *U.S.A.* **83 K10** 32 40N 107 9W
Hatches Creek, *Australia* **62 C2** 20 56S 135 12 E
Hatchet L., *Canada* **73 B8** 58 36N 103 40W
Hateruma-Shima, *Japan* **31 M1** 24 3N 123 47 E
Hatfield P.O., *Australia* **63 E3** 33 54S 143 49 E
Hatgal, *Mongolia* **32 A5** 50 26N 100 9 E
Hathras, *India* **42 F8** 27 36N 78 6 E
Hatia, *Bangla.* **41 H17** 22 30N 91 5 E
Hato Mayor, *Dom. Rep.* **89 C6** 18 46N 69 15W
Hattah, *Australia* **63 E3** 34 48S 142 17 E
Hatteras, C., *U.S.A.* **77 H8** 35 14N 75 32W
Hattiesburg, *U.S.A.* **81 K10** 31 20N 89 17W
Hatvan, *Hungary* **17 E9** 47 40N 19 45 E
Hau Bon = Cheo Reo, *Vietnam* **38 F7** 13 25N 108 28 E
Hau Duc, *Vietnam* **38 E7** 15 20N 108 13 E
Haugesund, *Norway* **9 G8** 59 23N 5 13 E
Haultain —▸, *Canada* **73 B7** 55 51N 106 46W
Hauraki G., *N.Z.* **59 G5** 36 35S 175 5 E
Haut Atlas, *Morocco* **50 B3** 32 30N 5 0W
Haut-Rhin □, *France* **18 C7** 48 0N 7 15 E
Haut Zaïre □, *Zaïre* **54 B2** 2 20N 26 0 E
Haute-Corse □, *France* **18 E9** 42 30N 9 30 E
Haute-Garonne □, *France* **18 E4** 43 30N 1 30 E
Haute-Loire □, *France* **18 D5** 45 5N 3 50 E
Haute-Marne □, *France* **18 B6** 48 10N 5 20 E
Haute-Saône □, *France* **18 C7** 47 45N 6 10 E
Haute-Savoie □, *France* **18 C7** 46 0N 6 20 E
Haute-Vienne □, *France* **18 D4** 45 50N 1 10 E
Hauterive, *Canada* **71 C6** 49 10N 68 16W
Hautes-Alpes □, *France* **18 D7** 44 42N 6 20 E
Hautes Fagnes = Hohe Venn, *Belgium* **15 D6** 50 30N 6 5 E
Hautes-Pyrénées □, *France* **18 E4** 43 0N 0 10 E
Hauts-de-Seine □, *France* **18 B5** 48 52N 2 15 E
Hauts Plateaux, *Algeria* **50 A5** 35 0N 1 0 E
Havana = La Habana, *Cuba* **88 B3** 23 8N 82 22W
Havana, *U.S.A.* **80 E9** 40 18N 90 4W
Havant, *U.K.* **11 G7** 50 51N 0 59W
Havasu, L., *U.S.A.* **85 L12** 34 18N 114 28W
Havel —▸, *Germany* **16 B6** 52 40N 12 1 E
Havelange, *Belgium* **15 D5** 50 23N 5 15 E
Havelian, *Pakistan* **42 B5** 34 2N 73 10 E
Havelock, *N.B., Canada* **71 C6** 46 2N 65 24W
Havelock, *Ont., Canada* **70 D4** 44 26N 77 53W
Havelock, *N.Z.* **59 J4** 41 17S 173 48 E
Haverfordwest, *U.K.* **11 F3** 51 48N 4 59W
Haverhill, *U.S.A.* **79 D13** 42 47N 71 5W
Havering, *U.K.* **11 F8** 51 33N 0 20 E
Haverstraw, *U.S.A.* **79 E11** 41 12N 73 58W
Havlíčkův Brod, *Czech.* **16 D7** 49 36N 15 33 E
Havre, *U.S.A.* **82 B9** 48 33N 109 41W
Havre-Aubert, *Canada* **71 C7** 47 12N 61 56W
Havre-St.-Pierre, *Canada* **71 B7** 50 18N 63 33W
Haw —▸, *U.S.A.* **77 H6** 35 36N 79 3W
Hawaii □, *U.S.A.* **74 H16** 19 30N 156 30W
Hawaii I., *Pac. Oc.* **74 J17** 20 0N 155 0W
Hawaiian Is., *Pac. Oc.* **74 H17** 20 30N 156 0W
Hawaiian Ridge, *Pac. Oc.* **65 E11** 24 0N 165 0W
Hawarden, *Canada* **73 C7** 51 25N 106 36W
Hawarden, *U.S.A.* **80 D6** 43 0N 96 29W
Hawea, L., *N.Z.* **59 L2** 44 28S 169 19 E
Hawera, *N.Z.* **59 H5** 39 35S 174 19 E
Hawick, *U.K.* **12 F6** 55 25N 2 48W
Hawk Junction, *Canada* **70 C3** 48 5N 84 38W
Hawke B., *N.Z.* **59 H6** 39 25S 177 20 E
Hawker, *Australia* **63 E2** 31 59S 138 22 E
Hawkesbury, *Canada* **70 C5** 45 37N 74 37W
Hawkesbury I., *Canada* **72 C3** 53 37N 129 3W
Hawkesbury Pt., *Australia* **62 A1** 11 55S 134 5 E
Hawkinsville, *U.S.A.* **77 J4** 32 17N 83 28W
Hawkwood, *Australia* **63 D5** 25 45S 150 50 E
Hawley, *U.S.A.* **80 B6** 46 53N 96 19W
Ḥawrān, *Syria* **47 C5** 32 45N 36 15 E
Hawsh Mūssá, *Lebanon* **47 B4** 33 45N 35 55 E
Hawthorne, *U.S.A.* **82 G4** 38 32N 118 38W
Haxtun, *U.S.A.* **80 E3** 40 39N 102 38W
Hay, *Australia* **63 E3** 34 30S 144 51 E
Hay —▸, *Australia* **62 C2** 24 50S 138 0 E
Hay —▸, *Canada* **72 A5** 60 50N 116 26W

Ichihara

Ichihara, *Japan* **31 G10** 35 28N 140 5 E
Ichikawa, *Japan* **31 G9** 35 44N 139 55 E
Ichilo →, *Bolivia* **92 G6** 15 57S 64 50W
Ichinohe, *Japan* **30 D10** 40 13N 141 17 E
Ichinomiya, *Japan* **31 G8** 35 18N 136 48 E
Ichinoseki, *Japan* **30 E10** 38 55N 141 8 E
Ichŏn, *S. Korea* **35 F14** 37 17N 127 27 E
Icod, *Canary Is.* **22 F3** 28 22N 16 43W
Icy Str., *U.S.A.* **72 B1** 58 20N 135 30W
Ida Grove, *U.S.A.* **80 D7** 42 21N 95 28W
Ida Valley, *Australia* **61 E3** 28 42S 120 29 E
Idabel, *U.S.A.* **81 J7** 33 54N 94 50W
Idaho □, *U.S.A.* **82 D6** 45 0N 115 0W
Idaho City, *U.S.A.* **82 E6** 43 50N 115 50W
Idaho Falls, *U.S.A.* **82 E7** 43 30N 112 2W
Idaho Springs, *U.S.A.* **82 G11** 39 45N 105 31W
Idd el Ghanam, *Sudan* **51 F9** 11 30N 24 19 E
Iddan, *Somali Rep.* **46 F4** 6 10N 48 55 E
Idehan, *Libya* **51 C7** 27 10N 11 30 E
Idehan Marzūq, *Libya* **51 D7** 24 50N 13 51 E
Idelès, *Algeria* **50 D6** 23 50N 5 53 E
Idfû, *Egypt* **51 D11** 24 55N 32 49 E
Ídhi Óros, *Greece* **23 D6** 35 15N 24 45 E
Ídhra, *Greece* **21 F10** 37 20N 23 28 E
Idi, *Indonesia* **36 C1** 5 2N 97 37 E
Idiofa, *Zaïre* **52 E3** 4 55S 19 42 E
Idlib, *Syria* **44 C3** 35 55N 36 36 E
Idria, *U.S.A.* **84 J6** 36 25N 120 41W
Idutywa, *S. Africa* **57 E4** 32 8S 28 18 E
Ieper, *Belgium* **15 D2** 50 51N 2 53 E
Ierápetra, *Greece* **23 E7** 35 0N 25 44 E
Ierzu, *Italy* **20 E3** 39 48N 9 32 E
'Ifâl, W. al →, *Si. Arabia* **44 D2** 28 7N 35 3 E
Ifanadiana, *Madag.* **57 C8** 21 19S 47 39 E
Ife, *Nigeria* **50 G5** 7 30N 4 31 E
Iffley, *Australia* **62 B3** 18 53S 141 12 E
Ifni, *Morocco* **50 C2** 29 29N 10 12W
Iforas, Adrar des, *Mali* **50 E5** 19 40N 1 40 E
Ifould, L., *Australia* **61 F5** 30 52S 132 6 E
Iganga, *Uganda* **54 B3** 0 37N 33 28 E
Igarapava, *Brazil* **93 H9** 20 3S 47 47W
Igarapé Açu, *Brazil* **93 D9** 1 4S 47 33W
Igarka, *Russia* **26 C9** 67 30N 86 33 E
Igatimi, *Paraguay* **95 A4** 24 5S 55 40W
Igbetti, *Nigeria* **50 G5** 8 44N 4 8 E
Iggesund, *Sweden* **9 F14** 61 39N 17 10 E
Iglésias, *Italy* **20 E3** 39 19N 8 27 E
Igli, *Algeria* **50 B4** 30 25N 2 19W
Igloolik, *Canada* **69 B11** 69 20N 81 49W
Ignace, *Canada* **70 C1** 49 30N 91 40W
Iguaçu →, *Brazil* **95 B5** 25 36S 54 36W
Iguaçu, Cat. del, *Brazil* **95 B5** 25 41S 54 26W
Iguaçu Falls = Iguaçu, Cat. del, *Brazil* **95 B5** 25 41S 54 26W
Iguala, *Mexico* **87 D5** 18 20N 99 40W
Igualada, *Spain* **19 B6** 41 37N 1 37 E
Iguassu = Iguaçu →, *Brazil* **95 B5** 25 36S 54 36W
Iguatu, *Brazil* **93 E11** 6 20S 39 18W
Iguéla, *Gabon* **52 E1** 2 0S 9 16 E
Igunga □, *Tanzania* **54 C3** 4 20S 33 45 E
Iheya-Shima, *Japan* **31 L3** 27 4N 127 58 E
Ihosy, *Madag.* **57 C8** 22 24S 46 8 E
Ihotry, L., *Madag.* **57 C7** 21 56S 43 41 E
Ii, *Finland* **8 D18** 65 19N 25 22 E
Ii-Shima, *Japan* **31 L3** 26 43N 127 47 E
Iida, *Japan* **31 G8** 35 35N 137 50 E
Iijoki →, *Finland* **8 D18** 65 20N 25 20 E
Iisalmi, *Finland* **8 E19** 63 32N 27 10 E
Iiyama, *Japan* **31 F9** 36 51N 138 22 E
Iizuka, *Japan* **31 H5** 33 38N 130 42 E
Ijebu-Ode, *Nigeria* **50 G5** 6 47N 3 58 E
IJmuiden, *Neths.* **15 B4** 52 28N 4 35 E
IJssel →, *Neths.* **15 B5** 52 35N 5 50 E
IJsselmeer, *Neths.* **15 B5** 52 45N 5 20 E
Ijuí →, *Brazil* **95 B4** 27 58S 55 20W
Ikaría, *Greece* **21 F12** 37 35N 26 10 E
Ikeda, *Japan* **31 G6** 34 1N 133 48 E
Ikela, *Zaïre* **52 E4** 1 6S 23 6 E
Iki, *Japan* **31 H4** 33 45N 129 42 E
Ikimba L., *Tanzania* **54 C3** 1 30S 31 20 E
Ikopa →, *Madag.* **57 B8** 16 45S 46 40 E
Ikungu, *Tanzania* **54 C3** 1 33S 33 42 E
Ilagan, *Phil.* **37 A6** 17 7N 121 53 E
Īlām, *Iran* **44 C5** 33 0N 46 0 E
Ilam, *Nepal* **43 F12** 26 58N 87 58 E
Ilanskiy, *Russia* **27 D10** 56 14N 96 3 E
Ilbilbie, *Australia* **62 C4** 21 45S 149 20 E
Ile-à-la-Crosse, *Canada* **73 B7** 55 27N 107 53W
Ile-à-la-Crosse, Lac, *Canada* **73 B7** 55 40N 107 45W
Île-de-France, *France* **18 B5** 49 0N 2 20 E
Ilebo, *Zaïre* **52 E4** 4 17S 20 55 E
Ileje □, *Tanzania* **55 D3** 9 30S 33 25 E
Ilek, *Russia* **26 D6** 51 32N 53 21 E
Ilek →, *Russia* **24 D9** 51 30N 53 22 E
Ilford, *Canada* **73 B9** 56 4N 95 35W
Ilfracombe, *Australia* **62 C3** 23 30S 144 30 E
Ilfracombe, *U.K.* **11 F3** 51 13N 4 8W
Ilhéus, *Brazil* **93 F11** 14 49S 39 2W
Ili →, *Kazakhstan* **26 E8** 45 53N 77 10 E
Ilich, *Kazakhstan* **26 E7** 40 50N 68 27 E
Iliff, *U.S.A.* **80 E3** 40 45N 103 4W
Iligan, *Phil.* **37 C6** 8 12N 124 13 E
Iliodhrómia, *Greece* **21 E10** 39 12N 23 50 E
Ilion, *U.S.A.* **79 D9** 43 1N 75 2W
Ilkeston, *U.K.* **10 E6** 52 59N 1 19W
Illampu = Ancohuma, Nevada, *Bolivia* **92 G5** 16 0S 68 50W
Illana B., *Phil.* **37 C6** 7 35N 123 45 E
Illapel, *Chile* **94 C1** 32 0S 71 10W
Ille-et-Vilaine □, *France* **18 B3** 48 10N 1 30W
Iller →, *Germany* **16 D4** 48 23N 9 58 E
Illetas, *Spain* **22 B9** 39 32N 2 35 E
Illimani, *Bolivia* **92 G5** 16 30S 67 50W
Illinois □, *U.S.A.* **75 C9** 40 15N 89 30W
Illinois →, *U.S.A.* **75 C8** 38 58N 90 28W
Ilmen, Oz., *Russia* **24 C5** 58 15N 31 10 E
Ilo, *Peru* **92 G4** 17 40S 71 20W
Iloilo, *Phil.* **37 B6** 10 45N 122 33 E
Ilorin, *Nigeria* **50 G5** 8 30N 4 35 E
Ilwaco, *U.S.A.* **84 D2** 46 19N 124 3W
Ilwaki, *Indonesia* **37 F7** 7 55S 126 30 E
Imabari, *Japan* **31 G6** 34 4N 133 0 E
Imaloto →, *Madag.* **57 C8** 23 27S 45 13 E
Imandra, Oz., *Russia* **24 A5** 67 30N 33 0 E
Imari, *Japan* **31 H4** 33 15N 129 52 E
Imbler, *U.S.A.* **82 D5** 45 28N 117 58W
imeni 26 Bakinskikh Komissarov, *Azerbaijan* **25 G8** 39 19N 49 12 E
imeni 26 Bakinskikh Komissarov, *Turkmenistan* **25 G9** 39 22N 54 10 E
Imeni Poliny Osipenko, *Russia* **27 D14** 52 30N 136 29 E
Imeri, Serra, *Brazil* **92 C5** 0 50N 65 25W
Imerimandroso, *Madag.* **57 B8** 17 26S 48 35 E
Imi, *Ethiopia* **46 F3** 6 28N 42 10 E
Imlay, *U.S.A.* **82 F4** 40 40N 118 9W
Imlay City, *U.S.A.* **78 C1** 43 2N 83 5W
Immingham, *U.K.* **10 D7** 53 37N 0 12W
Immokalee, *U.S.A.* **77 M5** 26 25N 81 25W
Imola, *Italy* **20 B4** 44 20N 11 42 E
Imperatriz, *Brazil* **93 E9** 5 30S 47 29W
Impéria, *Italy* **20 C3** 43 52N 8 3 E
Imperial, *Canada* **73 C7** 51 21N 105 28W
Imperial, *Calif., U.S.A.* **85 N11** 32 51N 115 34W
Imperial, *Nebr., U.S.A.* **80 E4** 40 31N 101 39W
Imperial Beach, *U.S.A.* **85 N9** 32 35N 117 8W
Imperial Dam, *U.S.A.* **85 N12** 32 55N 114 25W
Imperial Reservoir, *U.S.A.* **85 N12** 32 53N 114 28W
Imperial Valley, *U.S.A.* **85 N11** 33 0N 115 30W
Imperieuse Reef, *Australia* **60 C2** 17 36S 118 50 E
Impfondo, *Congo* **52 D3** 1 40N 18 0 E
Imphal, *India* **41 G18** 24 48N 93 56 E
Imuruan B., *Phil.* **37 B5** 10 40N 119 10 E
In Belbel, *Algeria* **50 C5** 27 55N 1 12 E
In Salah, *Algeria* **50 C5** 27 10N 2 32 E
Ina, *Japan* **31 G8** 35 50N 137 55 E
Inangahua Junction, *N.Z.* **59 J3** 41 52S 171 59 E
Inanwatan, *Indonesia* **37 E8** 2 10S 132 14 E
Iñapari, *Peru* **92 F5** 11 0S 69 40W
Inari, *Finland* **8 B19** 68 54N 27 5 E
Inarijärvi, *Finland* **8 B19** 69 0N 28 0 E
Inawashiro-Ko, *Japan* **30 F10** 37 29N 140 6 E
Inca, *Spain* **22 B9** 39 43N 2 54 E
Incaguasi, *Chile* **94 B1** 29 12S 71 5W
İnce-Burnu, *Turkey* **25 F5** 42 7N 34 56 E
Inchon, *S. Korea* **35 F14** 37 27N 126 40 E
Incomáti →, *Mozam.* **57 D5** 25 46S 32 43 E
Indalsälven →, *Sweden* **8 E14** 62 36N 17 30 E
Indaw, *Burma* **41 G20** 24 15N 96 5 E
Independence, *Calif., U.S.A.* **83 H4** 36 48N 118 12W
Independence, *Iowa, U.S.A.* **80 D9** 42 28N 91 54W
Independence, *Kans., U.S.A.* **81 G7** 37 14N 95 42W
Independence, *Mo., U.S.A.* **80 F7** 39 6N 94 25W
Independence, *Oreg., U.S.A.* **82 D2** 44 51N 123 11W
Independence Fjord, *Greenland* **4 A6** 82 10N 29 0W
Independence Mts., *U.S.A.* **82 F5** 41 20N 116 0W
Index, *U.S.A.* **84 C5** 47 50N 121 33W
India ■, *Asia* **40 K11** 20 0N 78 0 E
Indian →, *U.S.A.* **77 M5** 27 59N 80 34W
Indian Cabins, *Canada* **72 B5** 59 52N 117 40W
Indian Harbour, *Canada* **71 B8** 54 27N 57 13W
Indian Head, *Canada* **73 C8** 50 30N 103 41W
Indian Ocean **28 K11** 5 0S 75 0 E
Indian Springs, *U.S.A.* **85 J11** 36 35N 115 40W
Indiana, *U.S.A.* **78 F5** 40 37N 79 9W
Indiana □, *U.S.A.* **76 E3** 40 0N 86 0W
Indianapolis, *U.S.A.* **76 F2** 39 46N 86 9W
Indianola, *Iowa, U.S.A.* **80 E8** 41 22N 93 34W
Indianola, *Miss., U.S.A.* **81 J9** 33 27N 90 39W
Indiga, *Russia* **24 A8** 67 50N 48 50 E
Indigirka →, *Russia* **27 B15** 70 48N 148 54 E
Indio, *U.S.A.* **85 M10** 33 43N 116 13W
Indonesia ■, *Asia* **36 F5** 5 0S 115 0 E
Indore, *India* **42 H6** 22 42N 75 53 E
Indramayu, *Indonesia* **37 G13** 6 20S 108 19 E
Indravati →, *India* **41 K12** 19 20N 80 20 E
Indre □, *France* **18 C4** 46 50N 1 39 E
Indre-et-Loire □, *France* **18 C4** 47 20N 0 40 E
Indus →, *Pakistan* **42 G2** 24 20N 67 47 E
Indus, Mouth of the, *Pakistan* **42 H2** 24 0N 68 0 E
İnebolu, *Turkey* **25 F5** 41 55N 33 40 E
Infiernillo, Presa del, *Mexico* **86 D4** 18 9N 102 0W
Ingende, *Zaïre* **52 E3** 0 12S 18 57 E
Ingenio, *Canary Is.* **22 G4** 27 55N 15 26W
Ingenio Santa Ana, *Argentina* **94 B2** 27 25S 65 40W
Ingersoll, *Canada* **78 C4** 43 4N 80 55W
Ingham, *Australia* **62 B4** 18 43S 146 10 E
Ingleborough, *U.K.* **10 C5** 54 11N 2 23W
Inglewood, *Queens., Australia* **63 D5** 28 25S 151 2 E
Inglewood, *Vic., Australia* **63 F3** 36 29S 143 53 E
Inglewood, *N.Z.* **59 H5** 39 9S 174 14 E
Inglewood, *U.S.A.* **85 M8** 33 58N 118 21W
Ingólfshöfði, *Iceland* **8 E5** 63 48N 16 39W
Ingolstadt, *Germany* **16 D5** 48 45N 11 26 E
Ingomar, *U.S.A.* **82 C10** 46 35N 107 23W
Ingonish, *Canada* **71 C7** 46 42N 60 18W
Ingraj Bazar, *India* **43 G13** 24 58N 88 10 E
Ingrid Christensen Coast, *Antarctica* **5 C6** 69 30S 76 0 E
Ingulec, *Ukraine* **25 E5** 47 42N 33 14 E
Ingwavuma, *S. Africa* **57 D5** 27 9S 31 59 E
Inhaca, I., *Mozam.* **57 D5** 26 1S 32 57 E
Inhafenga, *Mozam.* **57 C5** 20 36S 33 53 E
Inhambane, *Mozam.* **57 C6** 23 54S 35 30 E
Inhambane □, *Mozam.* **57 C5** 22 30S 34 20 E
Inhaminga, *Mozam.* **55 F4** 18 26S 35 0 E
Inharrime, *Mozam.* **57 C6** 24 30S 35 0 E
Inharrime →, *Mozam.* **57 C6** 24 30S 35 0 E
Ining = Yining, *China* **26 E9** 43 58N 81 10 E
Inirida →, *Colombia* **92 C5** 3 55N 67 52W
Inishbofin, *Ireland* **13 C1** 53 35N 10 12W
Inishmore, *Ireland* **13 C2** 53 8N 9 45W
Inishowen, *Ireland* **13 A4** 55 14N 7 15W
Injune, *Australia* **63 D4** 25 53S 148 32 E
Inklin, *Canada* **72 B2** 58 56N 133 5W
Inklin →, *Canada* **72 B2** 58 50N 133 10W
Inkom, *U.S.A.* **82 E7** 42 48N 112 15W
Inle L., *Burma* **41 J20** 20 30N 96 58 E
Inn →, *Austria* **16 D6** 48 35N 13 28 E
Innamincka, *Australia* **63 D3** 27 44S 140 46 E
Inner Hebrides, *U.K.* **12 D2** 57 0N 6 30W
Inner Mongolia = Nei Monggol Zizhiqu □, *China* **34 C6** 42 0N 112 0 E
Inner Sound, *U.K.* **12 D3** 57 30N 5 55W
Innerkip, *Canada* **78 C4** 43 13N 80 42W
Innetalling I., *Canada* **70 A4** 56 0N 79 0W
Innisfail, *Australia* **62 B4** 17 33S 146 5 E
Innisfail, *Canada* **72 C6** 52 0N 113 57W
In'no-shima, *Japan* **31 G6** 34 19N 133 10 E
Innsbruck, *Austria* **16 E5** 47 16N 11 23 E
Inny →, *Ireland* **13 C4** 53 30N 7 50W
Inongo, *Zaïre* **52 E3** 1 55S 18 30 E
Inoucdjouac, *Canada* **69 C12** 58 25N 78 15W
Inowrocław, *Poland* **17 B9** 52 50N 18 12 E
Inpundong, *N. Korea* **35 D14** 41 25N 126 34 E
Inquisivi, *Bolivia* **92 G5** 16 50S 67 10W
Inscription, C., *Australia* **61 E1** 25 29S 112 59 E
Insein, *Burma* **41 L20** 16 50N 96 5 E
Inta, *Russia* **24 A11** 66 5N 60 8 E
Intendente Alvear, *Argentina* **94 D3** 35 12S 63 32W
Interior, *U.S.A.* **80 D4** 43 44N 101 59W
Interlaken, *Switz.* **16 E3** 46 41N 7 50 E
International Falls, *U.S.A.* **80 A8** 48 36N 93 25W
Intiyaco, *Argentina* **94 B3** 28 43S 60 5W
Inútil, B., *Chile* **96 G2** 53 30S 70 15W
Inuvik, *Canada* **68 B6** 68 16N 133 40W
Inveraray, *U.K.* **12 E3** 56 13N 5 5W
Inverbervie, *U.K.* **12 E6** 56 50N 2 17W
Invercargill, *N.Z.* **59 M2** 46 24S 168 24 E
Inverell, *Australia* **63 D5** 29 45S 151 8 E
Invergordon, *U.K.* **12 D4** 57 41N 4 10W
Invermere, *Canada* **72 C5** 50 30N 116 2W
Inverness, *Canada* **71 C7** 46 15N 61 19W
Inverness, *U.K.* **12 D4** 57 29N 4 12W
Inverness, *U.S.A.* **77 L4** 28 50N 82 20W
Inverurie, *U.K.* **12 D6** 57 15N 2 21W
Inverway, *Australia* **60 C4** 17 50S 129 38 E
Investigator Group, *Australia* **63 E1** 34 45S 134 20 E
Investigator Str., *Australia* **63 F2** 35 30S 137 0 E
Inya, *Russia* **26 D9** 50 28N 86 37 E
Inyanga, *Zimbabwe* **55 F3** 18 12S 32 40 E
Inyangani, *Zimbabwe* **55 F3** 18 5S 32 50 E
Inyantue, *Zimbabwe* **55 F2** 18 30S 26 40 E
Inyo Mts., *U.S.A.* **83 H5** 36 40N 118 0W
Inyokern, *U.S.A.* **85 K9** 35 39N 117 49W
Inza, *Russia* **24 D8** 53 55N 46 25 E
Iō-Jima, *Japan* **31 J5** 30 48N 130 18 E
Iola, *U.S.A.* **81 G7** 37 55N 95 24W
Iona, *U.K.* **12 E2** 56 20N 6 25W
Ione, *Calif., U.S.A.* **84 G6** 38 21N 120 56W
Ione, *Wash., U.S.A.* **82 B5** 48 45N 117 25W
Ionia, *U.S.A.* **76 D3** 42 59N 85 4W
Ionian Is. = Iónioi Nísoi, *Greece* **21 E9** 38 40N 20 0 E
Ionian Sea, *Europe* **21 E7** 37 30N 17 30 E
Iónioi Nísoi, *Greece* **21 E9** 38 40N 20 0 E
Íos, *Greece* **21 F11** 36 41N 25 20 E
Iowa □, *U.S.A.* **80 D8** 42 18N 93 30W
Iowa City, *U.S.A.* **80 E9** 41 40N 91 32W
Iowa Falls, *U.S.A.* **80 D8** 42 31N 93 16W
Ipala, *Tanzania* **54 C3** 4 30S 32 52 E
Ipameri, *Brazil* **93 G9** 17 44S 48 9W
Ipatinga, *Brazil* **93 G10** 19 32S 42 30W
Ipiales, *Colombia* **92 C3** 0 50N 77 37W
Ipin = Yibin, *China* **32 D5** 28 45N 104 32 E
Ípiros □, *Greece* **21 E9** 39 30N 20 30 E
Ipixuna, *Brazil* **92 E4** 7 0S 71 40W
Ipoh, *Malaysia* **39 K3** 4 35N 101 5 E
Ippy, *C.A.R.* **51 G9** 6 5N 21 7 E
Ipswich, *Australia* **63 D5** 27 35S 152 40 E
Ipswich, *U.K.* **11 E9** 52 4N 1 9 E
Ipswich, *Mass., U.S.A.* **79 D14** 42 41N 70 50W
Ipswich, *S. Dak., U.S.A.* **80 C5** 45 27N 99 2W
Ipu, *Brazil* **93 D10** 4 23S 40 44W
Iqaluit, *Canada* **69 B13** 63 44N 68 31W
Iquique, *Chile* **92 H4** 20 19S 70 5W
Iquitos, *Peru* **92 D4** 3 45S 73 10W
Irabu-Jima, *Japan* **31 M2** 24 50N 125 10 E
Iracoubo, *Fr. Guiana* **93 B8** 5 30N 53 10W
Īrafshān, *Iran* **45 E9** 26 42N 61 56 E
Iráklion, *Greece* **23 D7** 35 20N 25 12 E
Iráklion □, *Greece* **23 D7** 35 10N 25 10 E
Irala, *Paraguay* **95 B5** 25 55S 54 35W
Iramba □, *Tanzania* **54 C3** 4 30S 34 30 E
Iran ■, *Asia* **45 C7** 33 0N 53 0 E
Iran, Gunung-Gunung, *Malaysia* **36 D4** 2 20N 114 50 E
Iran Ra. = Iran, Gunung-Gunung, *Malaysia* **36 D4** 2 20N 114 50 E
Īrānshahr, *Iran* **45 E9** 27 15N 60 40 E
Irapuato, *Mexico* **86 C4** 20 40N 101 30W
Iraq ■, *Asia* **44 C5** 33 0N 44 0 E
Irati, *Brazil* **95 B5** 25 25S 50 38W
Irbid, *Jordan* **47 C4** 32 35N 35 48 E
Irbid □, *Jordan* **47 C5** 32 15N 36 35 E
Irebu, *Zaïre* **52 E3** 0 40S 17 46 E
Ireland ■, *Europe* **13 D4** 53 0N 8 0W
Ireland's Eye, *Ireland* **13 C5** 53 25N 6 4W
Iret, *Russia* **27 C16** 60 3N 154 20 E
Irhyangdong, *N. Korea* **35 D15** 41 15N 129 30 E
Iri, *S. Korea* **35 G14** 35 59N 127 0 E
Irian Jaya □, *Indonesia* **37 E9** 4 0S 137 0 E
Iringa, *Tanzania* **54 D4** 7 48S 35 43 E
Iringa □, *Tanzania* **54 D4** 7 48S 35 43 E
Iriomote-Jima, *Japan* **31 M1** 24 19N 123 48 E
Iriona, *Honduras* **88 C2** 15 57N 85 11W
Iriri →, *Brazil* **93 D8** 3 52S 52 37W
Irish Republic ■, *Europe* **13 D4** 53 0N 8 0W
Irish Sea, *Europe* **10 D3** 54 0N 5 0W
Irkineyeva, *Russia* **27 D10** 58 30N 96 49 E
Irkutsk, *Russia* **27 D11** 52 18N 104 20 E
Irma, *Canada* **73 C6** 52 55N 111 14W
Irō-Zaki, *Japan* **31 G9** 34 36N 138 51 E
Iron Baron, *Australia* **63 E2** 32 58S 137 11 E
Iron Gate = Portile de Fier, *Europe* **17 F11** 44 42N 22 30 E
Iron Knob, *Australia* **63 E2** 32 46S 137 8 E
Iron Mountain, *U.S.A.* **76 C1** 45 49N 88 4W
Iron Ra., *Australia* **62 A3** 12 46S 143 16 E
Iron River, *U.S.A.* **80 B10** 46 6N 88 39W
Ironbridge, *U.K.* **11 E5** 52 38N 2 29W
Irondequoit, *U.S.A.* **78 C7** 43 13N 77 35W
Ironstone Kopje, *Botswana* **56 D3** 25 17S 24 5 E
Ironton, *Mo., U.S.A.* **81 G9** 37 36N 90 38W
Ironton, *Ohio, U.S.A.* **76 F4** 38 32N 82 41W
Ironwood, *U.S.A.* **80 B9** 46 27N 90 9W
Iroquois Falls, *Canada* **70 C3** 48 46N 80 41W
Irrara Cr. →, *Australia* **63 D4** 29 35S 145 31 E
Irrawaddy □, *Burma* **41 L19** 17 0N 95 0 E
Irrawaddy →, *Burma* **41 M19** 15 50N 95 6 E
Irtysh →, *Russia* **26 C7** 61 4N 68 52 E
Irumu, *Zaïre* **54 B2** 1 32N 29 53 E
Irún, *Spain* **19 A5** 43 20N 1 52W
Irunea = Pamplona, *Spain* **19 A5** 42 48N 1 38W
Irvine, *Canada* **73 D6** 49 57N 110 16W
Irvine, *U.K.* **12 F4** 55 37N 4 40W
Irvine, *Calif., U.S.A.* **85 M9** 33 41N 117 46W
Irvine, *Ky., U.S.A.* **76 G4** 37 42N 83 58W
Irvinestown, *U.K.* **13 B4** 54 28N 7 38W
Irving, *U.S.A.* **81 J6** 32 49N 96 56W
Irvona, *U.S.A.* **78 F6** 40 46N 78 33W
Irwin →, *Australia* **61 E1** 29 15S 114 54 E
Irymple, *Australia* **63 E3** 34 14S 142 8 E
Isaac →, *Australia* **62 C4** 22 55S 149 20 E
Isabel, *U.S.A.* **80 C4** 45 24N 101 26W
Isabela, I., *Mexico* **86 C3** 21 51N 105 55W
Isabela, *Phil.* **37 C6** 6 40N 122 10 E
Isabella, Cord., *Nic.* **88 D2** 13 30N 85 25W
Isabella Ra., *Australia* **60 D3** 21 0S 121 4 E
Ísafjarðardjúp, *Iceland* **8 C2** 66 10N 23 0W
Ísafjörður, *Iceland* **8 C2** 66 5N 23 9W
Isagarh, *India* **42 G7** 24 48N 77 51 E
Isahaya, *Japan* **31 H5** 32 52N 130 2 E
Isaka, *Tanzania* **54 C3** 3 56S 32 59 E
Isangi, *Zaïre* **52 D4** 0 52N 24 10 E
Isar →, *Germany* **16 D6** 48 49N 12 58 E
Íschia, *Italy* **20 D5** 40 45N 13 51 E
Isdell →, *Australia* **60 C3** 16 27S 124 51 E
Ise, *Japan* **31 G8** 34 25N 136 45 E
Ise-Wan, *Japan* **31 G8** 34 43N 136 43 E
Iseramagazi, *Tanzania* **54 C3** 4 37S 32 10 E
Isère □, *France* **18 D6** 45 15N 5 40 E
Isère →, *France* **18 D6** 44 59N 4 51 E
Ishigaki-Shima, *Japan* **31 M2** 24 20N 124 10 E
Ishikari-Gawa →, *Japan* **30 C10** 43 15N 141 23 E
Ishikari-Sammyaku, *Japan* **30 C11** 43 30N 143 0 E
Ishikari-Wan, *Japan* **30 C10** 43 25N 141 1 E
Ishikawa □, *Japan* **31 F8** 36 30N 136 30 E
Ishim, *Russia* **26 D7** 56 10N 69 30 E
Ishim →, *Russia* **26 D8** 57 45N 71 10 E
Ishinomaki, *Japan* **30 E10** 38 32N 141 20 E
Ishioka, *Japan* **31 F10** 36 11N 140 16 E
Ishkuman, *Pakistan* **43 A5** 36 30N 73 50 E
Ishpeming, *U.S.A.* **76 B2** 46 29N 87 40W
Isil Kul, *Russia* **26 D8** 54 55N 71 16 E
Isiolo, *Kenya* **54 B4** 0 24N 37 33 E
Isiolo □, *Kenya* **54 B4** 2 30N 37 30 E
Isipingo Beach, *S. Africa* **57 E5** 30 0S 30 57 E
Isiro, *Zaïre* **54 B2** 2 53N 27 40 E
Isisford, *Australia* **62 C3** 24 15S 144 21 E
İskenderun, *Turkey* **25 G6** 36 32N 36 10 E
İskenderun Körfezi, *Turkey* **25 G6** 36 40N 35 50 E
Iskut →, *Canada* **72 B2** 56 45N 131 49W
Isla →, *U.K.* **12 E5** 56 32N 3 20W
Isla Vista, *U.S.A.* **85 L7** 34 25N 119 53W
Islamabad, *Pakistan* **42 C5** 33 40N 73 10 E
Islamkot, *Pakistan* **42 G4** 24 42N 70 13 E
Island →, *Canada* **72 A4** 60 25N 121 12W
Island Falls, *Canada* **70 C3** 49 35N 81 20W
Island Falls, *U.S.A.* **71 C6** 46 1N 68 16W
Island L., *Canada* **73 C10** 53 47N 94 25W
Island Lagoon, *Australia* **63 E2** 31 30S 136 40 E
Island Pond, *U.S.A.* **79 B13** 44 49N 71 53W
Islands, B. of, *Canada* **71 C8** 49 11N 58 15W
Islay, *U.K.* **12 F2** 55 46N 6 10W
Isle aux Morts, *Canada* **71 C8** 47 35N 59 0W
Isle of Wight □, *U.K.* **11 G6** 50 40N 1 20W
Isle Royale, *U.S.A.* **80 A10** 48 0N 88 54W
Isleta, *U.S.A.* **83 J10** 34 55N 106 42W
Isleton, *U.S.A.* **84 G5** 38 10N 121 37W
Ismail, *Ukraine* **25 E4** 45 22N 28 46 E
Ismâ'ilîya, *Egypt* **51 B11** 30 37N 32 18 E
Ismay, *U.S.A.* **80 B2** 46 30N 104 48W
Isna, *Egypt* **51 C11** 25 17N 32 30 E
Isogstalo, *India* **43 B8** 34 15N 78 46 E
Isparta, *Turkey* **25 G5** 37 47N 30 30 E
Íspica, *Italy* **20 F6** 36 47N 14 53 E
Israel ■, *Asia* **47 D3** 32 0N 34 50 E
Issyk-Kul, Ozero, *Kirghizia* **26 E8** 42 25N 77 15 E
Istaihah, *U.A.E.* **45 F7** 23 19N 54 4 E
İstanbul, *Turkey* **21 D13** 41 0N 29 0 E
Istokpoga, L., *U.S.A.* **77 M5** 27 23N 81 17W
Istra, *Croatia* **20 B5** 45 10N 14 0 E
Istria = Istra, *Croatia* **20 B5** 45 10N 14 0 E
Itá, *Paraguay* **94 B4** 25 29S 57 21W
Itabaiana, *Brazil* **93 E11** 7 18S 35 19W
Itaberaba, *Brazil* **93 F10** 12 32S 40 18W
Itabira, *Brazil* **93 G10** 19 37S 43 13W
Itabirito, *Brazil* **95 A7** 20 15S 43 48W
Itabuna, *Brazil* **93 F11** 14 48S 39 16W
Itaipu Dam, *Brazil* **95 B5** 25 30S 54 30W
Itaituba, *Brazil* **93 D7** 4 10S 55 50W
Itajaí, *Brazil* **95 B6** 27 50S 48 39W
Itajubá, *Brazil* **95 A6** 22 24S 45 30W
Itaka, *Tanzania* **55 D3** 8 50S 32 49 E

129

Kelloselkä

Kampot, *Cambodia* **39 G5** 10 36N 104 10 E
Kampuchea = Cambodia ■, *Asia* **38 F5** 12 15N 105 0 E
Kampung →, *Indonesia* **37 F9** 5 44S 138 24 E
Kampung Air Putih, *Malaysia* **39 K4** 4 15N 103 10 E
Kampung Jerangau, *Malaysia* **39 K4** 4 50N 103 10 E
Kampung Raja, *Malaysia* **39 K4** 5 45N 102 35 E
Kampungbaru = Tolitoli, *Indonesia* **37 D6** 1 5N 120 50 E
Kamrau, Teluk, *Indonesia* **37 E8** 3 30S 133 36 E
Kamsack, *Canada* **73 C8** 51 34N 101 54W
Kamskoye Vdkhr., *Russia* **24 C10** 58 0N 56 0 E
Kamuchawie L., *Canada* **73 B8** 56 18N 101 59W
Kamui-Misaki, *Japan* **30 C10** 43 20N 140 21 E
Kamyanets-Podilskyy = Kamenets-Podolskiy, *Ukraine* **25 E4** 48 45N 26 40 E
Kāmyārān, *Iran* **44 C5** 34 47N 46 56 E
Kamyshin, *Russia* **25 D8** 50 10N 45 24 E
Kanaaupscow, *Canada* **70 B4** 54 2N 76 30W
Kanab, *U.S.A.* **83 H7** 37 3N 112 32W
Kanab →, *U.S.A.* **83 H7** 36 24N 112 38W
Kanagi, *Japan* **30 D10** 40 54N 140 27 E
Kanairiktok →, *Canada* **71 A7** 55 2N 60 18W
Kananga, *Zaïre* **52 F4** 5 55S 22 18 E
Kanarraville, *U.S.A.* **83 H7** 37 32N 113 11W
Kanash, *Russia* **24 C8** 55 30N 47 32 E
Kanaskat, *U.S.A.* **84 C5** 47 19N 121 54W
Kanawha →, *U.S.A.* **76 F4** 38 50N 82 9W
Kanazawa, *Japan* **31 F8** 36 30N 136 38 E
Kanchanaburi, *Thailand* **38 E2** 14 2N 99 31 E
Kanchenjunga, *Nepal* **43 F13** 27 50N 88 10 E
Kanchipuram, *India* **40 N11** 12 52N 79 45 E
Kanda Kanda, *Zaïre* **52 F4** 6 52S 23 48 E
Kandahar = Qandahār, *Afghan.* **40 D4** 31 32N 65 30 E
Kandalaksha, *Russia* **24 A5** 67 9N 32 30 E
Kandalakshkiy Zaliv, *Russia* **24 A5** 66 0N 35 0 E
Kandalu, *Afghan.* **40 E3** 29 55N 63 20 E
Kandangan, *Indonesia* **36 E5** 2 50S 115 20 E
Kandanos, *Greece* **23 D5** 35 20N 23 45 E
Kandhkot, *Pakistan* **42 E3** 28 16N 69 8 E
Kandhla, *India* **42 E7** 29 18N 77 19 E
Kandi, *Benin* **50 F5** 11 7N 2 55 E
Kandi, *India* **43 H13** 23 58N 88 5 E
Kandla, *India* **42 H4** 23 0N 70 10 E
Kandos, *Australia* **63 E4** 32 45S 149 58 E
Kandy, *Sri Lanka* **40 R12** 7 18N 80 43 E
Kane, *U.S.A.* **78 E6** 41 40N 78 49W
Kane Basin, *Greenland* **4 B4** 79 1N 70 0W
Kangān, *Fārs, Iran* **45 E7** 27 50N 52 3 E
Kangān, *Hormozgān, Iran* **45 E8** 25 48N 57 28 E
Kangar, *Malaysia* **39 J3** 6 27N 100 12 E
Kangaroo I., *Australia* **63 F2** 35 45S 137 0 E
Kangavar, *Iran* **45 C6** 34 40N 48 0 E
Kāngdong, *N. Korea* **35 E14** 39 9N 126 5 E
Kangean, Kepulauan, *Indonesia* **36 F5** 6 55S 115 23 E
Kangean Is. = Kangean, Kepulauan, *Indonesia* **36 F5** 6 55S 115 23 E
Kanggye, *N. Korea* **35 D14** 41 0N 126 35 E
Kanggyŏng, *S. Korea* **35 F14** 36 10N 127 0 E
Kanghwa, *S. Korea* **35 F14** 37 45N 126 30 E
Kangnŭng, *S. Korea* **35 F15** 37 45N 128 54 E
Kango, *Gabon* **52 D2** 0 11N 10 5 E
Kangping, *China* **35 C12** 42 43N 123 18 E
Kangto, *India* **41 F18** 27 50N 92 35 E
Kaniama, *Zaïre* **54 D1** 7 30S 24 12 E
Kaniapiskau →, *Canada* **71 A6** 56 40N 69 30W
Kaniapiskau L., *Canada* **71 B6** 54 10N 69 55W
Kanin, P-ov., *Russia* **24 A8** 68 0N 45 0 E
Kanin Nos, Mys, *Russia* **24 A7** 68 45N 43 20 E
Kanin Pen. = Kanin, P-ov., *Russia* **24 A8** 68 0N 45 0 E
Kaniva, *Australia* **63 F3** 36 22S 141 18 E
Kanjut Sar, *Pakistan* **43 A6** 36 7N 75 25 E
Kankakee, *U.S.A.* **76 E2** 41 7N 87 52W
Kankakee →, *U.S.A.* **76 E1** 41 23N 88 15W
Kankan, *Guinea* **50 F3** 10 23N 9 15W
Kanker, *India* **41 J12** 20 10N 81 40 E
Kankunskiy, *Russia* **27 D13** 57 37N 126 8 E
Kannapolis, *U.S.A.* **77 H5** 35 30N 80 37W
Kannauj, *India* **43 F8** 27 3N 79 56 E
Kannod, *India* **40 H10** 22 45N 76 40 E
Kano, *Nigeria* **50 F6** 12 2N 8 30 E
Kan'onji, *Japan* **31 G6** 34 7N 133 39 E
Kanowit, *Malaysia* **36 D4** 2 14N 112 20 E
Kanowna, *Australia* **61 F3** 30 32S 121 31 E
Kanoya, *Japan* **31 J5** 31 25N 130 50 E
Kanpetlet, *Burma* **41 J18** 21 10N 93 59 E
Kanpur, *India* **43 F9** 26 28N 80 20 E
Kansas □, *U.S.A.* **80 F6** 38 30N 99 0W
Kansas →, *U.S.A.* **80 F7** 39 7N 94 37W
Kansas City, *Kans., U.S.A.* **80 F7** 39 7N 94 38W
Kansas City, *Mo., U.S.A.* **80 F7** 39 6N 94 35W
Kansenia, *Zaïre* **55 E2** 10 20S 26 0 E
Kansk, *Russia* **27 D10** 56 20N 95 37 E
Kansŏng, *S. Korea* **35 E15** 38 24N 128 30 E
Kansu = Gansu □, *China* **34 G3** 36 0N 104 0 E
Kantang, *Thailand* **39 J2** 7 25N 99 31 E
Kantharalak, *Thailand* **38 E5** 14 39N 104 39 E
Kantō □, *Japan* **31 F9** 36 15N 139 30 E
Kantō-Sanchi, *Japan* **31 G9** 35 59N 138 50 E
Kanturk, *Ireland* **13 D3** 52 10N 8 55W
Kanuma, *Japan* **31 F9** 36 34N 139 42 E
Kanus, *Namibia* **56 D2** 27 50S 18 39 E
Kanye, *Botswana* **56 C4** 24 55S 25 28 E
Kanzenze, *Zaïre* **55 E2** 10 30S 25 12 E
Kanzi, Ras, *Tanzania* **54 D4** 7 1S 39 33 E
Kaohsiung = Gaoxiong, *Taiwan* **33 D7** 22 38N 120 18 E
Kaohsiung, *Taiwan* **33 D7** 22 35N 120 16 E
Kaokoveld, *Namibia* **56 B1** 19 15S 14 30 E
Kaolack, *Senegal* **50 F1** 14 5N 16 8W
Kaoshan, *China* **35 B13** 44 38N 124 50 E
Kapadvanj, *India* **42 H5** 23 5N 73 0 E
Kapanga, *Zaïre* **52 F4** 8 30S 22 40 E
Kapchagai, *Kazakhstan* **26 E8** 43 51N 77 14 E
Kapela, *Croatia* **20 B6** 44 40N 15 40 E
Kapema, *Zaïre* **55 E2** 10 45S 28 22 E
Kapfenberg, *Austria* **16 E7** 47 26N 15 18 E
Kapiri Mposhi, *Zambia* **55 E2** 13 59S 28 43 E
Kapiskau →, *Canada* **70 B3** 52 47N 81 55W
Kapit, *Malaysia* **36 D4** 2 0N 112 55 E
Kapiti I., *N.Z.* **59 J5** 40 50S 174 56 E
Kapoe, *Thailand* **39 H2** 9 34N 98 32 E
Kapoeta, *Sudan* **51 H11** 4 50N 33 35 E
Kaposvár, *Hungary* **17 E8** 46 25N 17 47 E
Kapowsin, *U.S.A.* **84 D4** 46 59N 122 13W
Kapps, *Namibia* **56 C2** 22 32S 17 18 E
Kapsan, *N. Korea* **35 D15** 41 4N 128 19 E
Kapuas →, *Indonesia* **36 E3** 0 25S 109 20 E
Kapuas Hulu, Pegunungan, *Malaysia* **36 D4** 1 30N 113 30 E
Kapuas Hulu Ra. = Kapuas Hulu, Pegunungan, *Malaysia* **36 D4** 1 30N 113 30 E
Kapulo, *Zaïre* **55 D2** 8 18S 29 15 E
Kapunda, *Australia* **63 E2** 34 20S 138 56 E
Kapuni, *N.Z.* **59 H5** 39 29S 174 8 E
Kapurthala, *India* **42 D6** 31 23N 75 25 E
Kapuskasing, *Canada* **70 C3** 49 25N 82 30W
Kapuskasing →, *Canada* **70 C3** 49 49N 82 0W
Kaputar, *Australia* **63 E5** 30 15S 150 10 E
Kaputir, *Kenya* **54 B4** 2 5N 35 28 E
Kara, *Russia* **26 C7** 69 10N 65 0 E
Kara Bogaz Gol, Zaliv, *Turkmenistan* **25 F9** 41 0N 53 30 E
Kara Kalpak Republic □, *Uzbekistan* **26 E6** 43 0N 58 0 E
Kara Kum = Karakum, Peski, *Turkmenistan* **26 F6** 39 30N 60 0 E
Kara Sea, *Russia* **26 B7** 75 0N 70 0 E
Karabutak, *Kazakhstan* **26 E7** 49 59N 60 14 E
Karachi, *Pakistan* **42 G2** 24 53N 67 0 E
Karad, *India* **40 L9** 17 15N 74 10 E
Karadeniz Boğazı, *Turkey* **21 D13** 41 10N 29 10 E
Karaganda, *Kazakhstan* **26 E8** 49 50N 73 10 E
Karagayly, *Kazakhstan* **26 E8** 49 26N 76 0 E
Karaginskiy, Ostrov, *Russia* **27 D17** 58 45N 164 0 E
Karagiye Depression, *Kazakhstan* **25 F9** 43 27N 51 45 E
Karagwe □, *Tanzania* **54 C3** 2 0S 31 0 E
Karaikal, *India* **40 P11** 10 59N 79 50 E
Karaikkudi, *India* **40 P11** 10 5N 78 45 E
Karaj, *Iran* **45 C6** 35 48N 51 0 E
Karak, *Malaysia* **39 L4** 3 25N 102 2 E
Karakas, *Kazakhstan* **26 E9** 48 20N 83 30 E
Karakitang, *Indonesia* **37 D7** 3 14N 125 28 E
Karaklis, *Armenia* **25 F7** 40 48N 44 30 E
Karakoram Pass, *Pakistan* **43 B7** 35 33N 77 50 E
Karakoram Ra., *Pakistan* **43 B7** 35 30N 77 0 E
Karakum, Peski, *Turkmenistan* **26 F6** 39 30N 60 0 E
Karalon, *Russia* **27 D12** 57 5N 115 50 E
Karaman, *Turkey* **25 G5** 37 14N 33 13 E
Karamay, *China* **32 B3** 45 30N 84 58 E
Karambu, *Indonesia* **36 E5** 3 53S 116 6 E
Karamea Bight, *N.Z.* **59 J3** 41 22S 171 40 E
Karamoja □, *Uganda* **54 B3** 3 0N 34 15 E
Karamsad, *India* **42 H5** 22 35N 72 50 E
Karand, *Iran* **44 C5** 34 16N 46 15 E
Karanganyar, *Indonesia* **37 G13** 7 38S 109 37 E
Karasburg, *Namibia* **56 D2** 28 0S 18 44 E
Karasino, *Russia* **26 C9** 66 50N 86 50 E
Karasjok, *Norway* **8 B18** 69 27N 25 30 E
Karasuk, *Russia* **26 D8** 53 44N 78 2 E
Karasuyama, *Japan* **31 F10** 36 39N 140 9 E
Karatau, *Kazakhstan* **26 E8** 43 10N 70 28 E
Karatau, Khrebet, *Kazakhstan* **26 E7** 43 30N 69 30 E
Karauli, *India* **42 F7** 26 30N 77 4 E
Karavostasi, *Cyprus* **23 D11** 35 8N 32 50 E
Karawang, *Indonesia* **37 G12** 6 30S 107 15 E
Karawanken, *Europe* **20 A6** 46 30N 14 40 E
Karazhal, *Kazakhstan* **26 E8** 48 2N 70 49 E
Karbalā, *Iraq* **44 C5** 32 36N 44 3 E
Karcag, *Hungary* **17 E10** 47 19N 20 57 E
Karcha →, *Pakistan* **43 B7** 34 45N 76 10 E
Karda, *Russia* **27 D11** 55 0N 103 16 E
Kardhítsa, *Greece* **21 E9** 39 23N 21 54 E
Kareeberge, *S. Africa* **56 E3** 30 59S 21 50 E
Karelian Republic □, *Russia* **24 A5** 65 30N 32 30 E
Karevāndar, *Iran* **45 E9** 27 53N 60 44 E
Kargasok, *Russia* **26 D9** 59 3N 80 53 E
Kargat, *Russia* **26 D9** 55 10N 80 15 E
Kargil, *India* **43 B7** 34 32N 76 12 E
Kargopol, *Russia* **24 B6** 61 30N 38 58 E
Karīān, *Iran* **45 E8** 26 57N 57 14 E
Kariba, *Zimbabwe* **55 F2** 16 28S 28 50 E
Kariba, L., *Zimbabwe* **55 F2** 16 40S 28 25 E
Kariba Dam, *Zimbabwe* **55 F2** 16 30S 28 35 E
Kariba Gorge, *Zambia* **55 F2** 16 30S 28 50 E
Karibib, *Namibia* **56 C2** 22 0S 15 56 E
Karimata, Kepulauan, *Indonesia* **36 E3** 1 25S 109 0 E
Karimata, Selat, *Indonesia* **36 E3** 2 0S 108 40 E
Karimata Is. = Karimata, Kepulauan, *Indonesia* **36 E3** 1 25S 109 0 E
Karimnagar, *India* **40 K11** 18 26N 79 10 E
Karimunjawa, Kepulauan, *Indonesia* **36 F4** 5 50S 110 30 E
Karin, *Somali Rep.* **46 E4** 10 50N 45 52 E
Karīt, *Iran* **45 C8** 33 29N 56 55 E
Kariya, *Japan* **31 G8** 34 58N 137 1 E
Karkaralinsk, *Kazakhstan* **26 E8** 49 26N 75 30 E
Karkinitskiy Zaliv, *Ukraine* **25 E5** 45 56N 33 0 E
Karl-Marx-Stadt = Chemnitz, *Germany* **16 C6** 50 50N 12 55 E
Karlovac, *Croatia* **20 B6** 45 31N 15 36 E
Karlovy Vary, *Czech.* **16 C6** 50 13N 12 51 E
Karlsbad = Karlovy Vary, *Czech.* **16 C6** 50 13N 12 51 E
Karlsborg, *Sweden* **9 G13** 58 33N 14 33 E
Karlshamn, *Sweden* **9 H13** 56 10N 14 51 E
Karlskoga, *Sweden* **9 G13** 59 22N 14 33 E
Karlskrona, *Sweden* **9 H13** 56 10N 15 35 E
Karlsruhe, *Germany* **16 D4** 49 3N 8 23 E
Karlstad, *Sweden* **9 G12** 59 23N 13 30 E
Karlstad, *U.S.A.* **80 A6** 48 35N 96 31W
Karnal, *India* **42 E7** 29 42N 77 2 E
Karnali →, *Nepal* **43 E9** 28 45N 81 16 E
Karnaphuli Res., *Bangla.* **41 H18** 22 40N 92 20 E
Karnataka □, *India* **40 N10** 13 15N 77 0 E
Karnes City, *U.S.A.* **81 L6** 28 53N 97 54W
Karnische Alpen, *Europe* **20 A5** 46 36N 13 0 E
Kärnten □, *Austria* **16 E6** 46 52N 13 30 E
Karoi, *Zimbabwe* **55 F2** 16 48S 29 45 E
Karonga, *Malawi* **55 D3** 9 57S 33 55 E
Karoonda, *Australia* **63 F2** 35 1S 139 59 E
Karora, *Sudan* **51 E12** 17 44N 38 15 E
Karpasia □, *Cyprus* **23 D13** 35 32N 34 15 E
Kárpathos, *Greece* **21 G12** 35 37N 27 10 E
Karpinsk, *Russia* **24 C11** 59 45N 60 1 E
Karpogory, *Russia* **24 B7** 63 59N 44 27 E
Kars, *Turkey* **25 F7** 40 40N 43 5 E
Karsakpay, *Kazakhstan* **26 E7** 47 55N 66 40 E
Karshi, *Uzbekistan* **26 F7** 38 53N 65 48 E
Karsiyang, *India* **43 F13** 26 56N 88 18 E
Karsun, *Russia* **24 D8** 54 14N 46 57 E
Kartaly, *Russia* **26 D7** 53 3N 60 40 E
Kartapur, *India* **42 D6** 31 27N 75 32 E
Karthaus, *U.S.A.* **78 E6** 41 8N 78 9W
Karufa, *Indonesia* **37 E8** 3 50S 133 20 E
Karumba, *Australia* **62 B3** 17 31S 140 50 E
Karumo, *Tanzania* **54 C3** 2 25S 32 50 E
Karumwa, *Tanzania* **54 C3** 3 12S 32 38 E
Karungu, *Kenya* **54 C3** 0 50S 34 10 E
Karwar, *India* **40 M9** 14 55N 74 13 E
Karwi, *India* **43 G9** 25 12N 80 57 E
Kasache, *Malawi* **55 E3** 13 25S 34 20 E
Kasai →, *Zaïre* **52 E3** 3 30S 16 10 E
Kasai Oriental □, *Zaïre* **54 C1** 5 0S 24 30 E
Kasaji, *Zaïre* **55 E1** 10 25S 23 27 E
Kasama, *Zambia* **55 E3** 10 16S 31 9 E
Kasan-dong, *N. Korea* **35 D14** 41 18N 126 55 E
Kasane, *Namibia* **56 B3** 17 34S 24 50 E
Kasanga, *Tanzania* **55 D3** 8 30S 31 10 E
Kasangulu, *Zaïre* **52 E3** 4 33S 15 15 E
Kasaragod, *India* **40 N9** 12 30N 74 58 E
Kasba L., *Canada* **73 A8** 60 20N 102 10W
Kāseh Garān, *Iran* **44 C5** 34 5N 46 2 E
Kasempa, *Zambia* **55 E2** 13 30S 25 44 E
Kasenga, *Zaïre* **55 E2** 10 20S 28 45 E
Kasese, *Uganda* **54 B3** 0 13N 30 3 E
Kasewa, *Zambia* **55 E2** 14 28S 28 53 E
Kasganj, *India* **43 F8** 27 48N 78 42 E
Kashabowie, *Canada* **70 C1** 48 40N 90 26W
Kāshān, *Iran* **45 C6** 34 5N 51 30 E
Kashi, *China* **32 C2** 39 30N 76 2 E
Kashimbo, *Zaïre* **55 E2** 11 12S 26 19 E
Kashipur, *India* **43 E8** 29 15N 79 0 E
Kashiwazaki, *Japan* **31 F9** 37 22N 138 33 E
Kashk-e Kohneh, *Afghan.* **40 B3** 34 55N 62 30 E
Kāshmar, *Iran* **45 C8** 35 16N 58 26 E
Kashmir, *Asia* **43 C7** 34 0N 76 0 E
Kashmor, *Pakistan* **42 E3** 28 28N 69 32 E
Kashun Noerh = Gaxun Nur, *China* **32 B5** 42 22N 100 30 E
Kasimov, *Russia* **24 D7** 54 55N 41 20 E
Kasinge, *Zaïre* **54 D2** 6 15S 26 58 E
Kasiruta, *Indonesia* **37 E7** 0 25S 127 12 E
Kaskaskia →, *U.S.A.* **80 G10** 37 58N 89 57W
Kaskattama →, *Canada* **73 B10** 57 3N 90 4W
Kaskinen, *Finland* **8 E16** 62 22N 21 15 E
Kaskö, *Finland* **8 E16** 62 22N 21 15 E
Kaslo, *Canada* **72 D5** 49 55N 116 55W
Kasmere L., *Canada* **73 B8** 59 34N 101 10W
Kasongo, *Zaïre* **54 C2** 4 30S 26 33 E
Kasongo Lunda, *Zaïre* **52 F3** 6 35S 16 49 E
Kásos, *Greece* **21 G12** 35 20N 26 55 E
Kassala, *Sudan* **51 E12** 15 30N 36 0 E
Kassalâ □, *Sudan* **51 E12** 15 20N 36 26 E
Kassel, *Germany* **16 C4** 51 19N 9 32 E
Kassiópi, *Greece* **23 A3** 39 48N 19 53 E
Kassue, *Indonesia* **37 F9** 6 58S 139 21 E
Kastamonu, *Turkey* **25 F5** 41 25N 33 43 E
Kastélli, *Greece* **23 D5** 35 29N 23 38 E
Kastéllion, *Greece* **23 D7** 35 12N 25 20 E
Kastoría, *Greece* **21 D9** 40 30N 21 19 E
Kasulu, *Tanzania* **54 C3** 4 37S 30 5 E
Kasulu □, *Tanzania* **54 C3** 4 37S 30 5 E
Kasumi, *Japan* **31 G7** 35 38N 134 38 E
Kasungu, *Malawi* **55 E3** 13 0S 33 29 E
Kasur, *Pakistan* **42 D6** 31 5N 74 25 E
Kata, *Russia* **27 D11** 58 46N 102 40 E
Kataba, *Zambia* **55 F2** 16 5S 25 10 E
Katako Kombe, *Zaïre* **54 C1** 3 25S 24 20 E
Katale, *Tanzania* **54 C3** 4 52S 31 7 E
Katamatite, *Australia* **63 F4** 36 6S 145 41 E
Katanda, *Kivu, Zaïre* **54 C2** 0 55S 29 21 E
Katanda, *Shaba, Zaïre* **54 D1** 7 52S 24 13 E
Katangi, *India* **40 J11** 21 56N 79 50 E
Katangli, *Russia* **27 D15** 51 42N 143 14 E
Katavi Swamp, *Tanzania* **54 D3** 6 50S 31 10 E
Katha, *Burma* **41 G20** 24 10N 96 30 E
Katherine, *Australia* **60 B5** 14 27S 132 20 E
Kathiawar, *India* **42 H4** 22 20N 71 0 E
Kathikas, *Cyprus* **23 E11** 34 55N 32 25 E
Katihar, *India* **43 G12** 25 34N 87 36 E
Katima Mulilo, *Zambia* **56 B3** 17 28S 24 13 E
Katimbira, *Malawi* **55 E3** 12 40S 34 0 E
Katingan = Mendawai →, *Indonesia* **36 E4** 3 30S 113 0 E
Katiola, *Ivory C.* **50 G3** 8 10N 5 10W
Katmandu, *Nepal* **43 F11** 27 45N 85 20 E
Káto Arkhánai, *Greece* **23 D7** 35 15N 25 10 E
Káto Khorió, *Greece* **23 D7** 35 3N 25 47 E
Kato Pyrgos, *Cyprus* **23 D11** 35 11N 32 41 E
Katompe, *Zaïre* **54 D2** 6 2S 26 23 E
Katonga →, *Uganda* **54 B3** 0 34N 31 50 E
Katoomba, *Australia* **63 E5** 33 41S 150 19 E
Katowice, *Poland* **17 C9** 50 17N 19 5 E
Katrine, L., *U.K.* **12 E4** 56 15N 4 30W
Katrineholm, *Sweden* **9 G14** 59 9N 16 12 E
Katsepe, *Madag.* **57 B8** 15 45S 46 15 E
Katsina, *Nigeria* **50 F6** 13 0N 7 32 E
Katsumoto, *Japan* **31 H4** 33 51N 129 42 E
Katsuura, *Japan* **31 G10** 35 10N 140 20 E
Katsuyama, *Japan* **31 F8** 36 3N 136 30 E
Kattaviá, *Greece* **23 D9** 35 57N 27 46 E
Kattegatt, *Denmark* **9 H11** 57 0N 11 20 E
Katumba, *Zaïre* **54 D2** 7 40S 25 17 E
Katungu, *Kenya* **54 C5** 2 55S 40 3 E
Katwa, *India* **43 H13** 23 30N 88 5 E
Katwijk-aan-Zee, *Neths.* **15 B4** 52 12N 4 24 E
Kauai, *U.S.A.* **74 H15** 22 3N 159 30W
Kauai Channel, *U.S.A.* **74 H15** 21 45N 158 50W
Kaufman, *U.S.A.* **81 J6** 32 35N 96 19W
Kaukauna, *U.S.A.* **76 C1** 44 17N 88 17W
Kaukauveld, *Namibia* **56 C3** 20 0S 20 15 E
Kaukonen, *Finland* **8 C18** 67 31N 24 53 E
Kauliranta, *Finland* **8 C17** 66 27N 23 41 E
Kaunas, *Lithuania* **24 D3** 54 54N 23 54 E
Kaura Namoda, *Nigeria* **50 F6** 12 37N 6 33 E
Kautokeino, *Norway* **8 B17** 69 0N 23 4 E
Kavacha, *Russia* **27 C17** 60 16N 169 51 E
Kavalerovo, *Russia* **30 B7** 44 15N 135 4 E
Kavali, *India* **40 M12** 14 55N 80 1 E
Kaválla, *Greece* **21 D11** 40 57N 24 28 E
Kavār, *Iran* **45 D7** 29 11N 52 44 E
Kavos, *Greece* **23 B4** 39 23N 20 3 E
Kaw, *Fr. Guiana* **93 C8** 4 30N 52 15W
Kawagama L., *Canada* **78 A6** 45 18N 78 45W
Kawagoe, *Japan* **31 G9** 35 55N 139 29 E
Kawaguchi, *Japan* **31 G9** 35 52N 139 45 E
Kawaihae, *U.S.A.* **74 H17** 20 3N 155 50W
Kawambwa, *Zambia* **55 D2** 9 48S 29 3 E
Kawanoe, *Japan* **31 G6** 34 1N 133 34 E
Kawardha, *India* **43 J9** 22 0N 81 17 E
Kawasaki, *Japan* **31 G9** 35 35N 139 42 E
Kawene, *Canada* **70 C1** 48 45N 91 15W
Kawerau, *N.Z.* **59 H6** 38 7S 176 42 E
Kawhia Harbour, *N.Z.* **59 H5** 38 5S 174 51 E
Kawio, Kepulauan, *Indonesia* **37 D7** 4 30N 125 30 E
Kawnro, *Burma* **41 H21** 22 48N 99 8 E
Kawthoolei = Kawthule □, *Burma* **41 L20** 18 0N 97 30 E
Kawthule □, *Burma* **41 L20** 18 0N 97 30 E
Kaya, *Burkina Faso* **50 F4** 13 4N 1 10W
Kayah □, *Burma* **41 K20** 19 15N 97 15 E
Kayan →, *Indonesia* **36 D5** 2 55N 117 35 E
Kaycee, *U.S.A.* **82 E10** 43 43N 106 38W
Kayeli, *Indonesia* **37 E7** 3 20S 127 10 E
Kayenta, *U.S.A.* **83 H8** 36 44N 110 15W
Kayes, *Mali* **50 F2** 14 25N 11 30W
Kayoa, *Indonesia* **37 D7** 0 1N 127 28 E
Kayomba, *Zambia* **55 E1** 13 11S 24 2 E
Kayrunnera, *Australia* **63 E3** 30 40S 142 30 E
Kayseri, *Turkey* **25 G6** 38 45N 35 30 E
Kaysville, *U.S.A.* **82 F8** 41 2N 111 56W
Kayuagung, *Indonesia* **36 E2** 3 24S 104 50 E
Kazachinskoye, *Russia* **27 D11** 56 16N 107 36 E
Kazachye, *Russia* **27 B14** 70 52N 135 58 E
Kazakhstan ■, *Asia* **26 E7** 50 0N 70 0 E
Kazan, *Russia* **24 C8** 55 48N 49 3 E
Kazan-Rettō, *Pac. Oc.* **64 E6** 25 0N 141 0 E
Kazanlŭk, *Bulgaria* **21 C11** 42 38N 25 20 E
Kāzerūn, *Iran* **45 D6** 29 38N 51 40 E
Kazumba, *Zaïre* **52 F4** 6 25S 22 5 E
Kazuno, *Japan* **30 D10** 40 10N 140 45 E
Kazym →, *Russia* **26 C7** 63 54N 65 50 E
Ké-Macina, *Mali* **50 F3** 13 58N 5 22W
Kéa, *Greece* **21 F11** 37 35N 24 22 E
Keams Canyon, *U.S.A.* **83 J8** 35 49N 110 12W
Kearney, *U.S.A.* **80 E5** 40 42N 99 5W
Keban, *Turkey* **25 G6** 38 50N 38 50 E
Kebnekaise, *Sweden* **8 C15** 67 53N 18 33 E
Kebri Dehar, *Ethiopia* **46 F3** 6 45N 44 17 E
Kebumen, *Indonesia* **37 G13** 7 42S 109 40 E
Kechika →, *Canada* **72 B3** 59 41N 127 12W
Kecskemét, *Hungary* **17 E9** 46 57N 19 42 E
Kedgwick, *Canada* **71 C6** 47 40N 67 20W
Kédhros Óros, *Greece* **23 D6** 35 11N 24 37 E
Kedia Hill, *Botswana* **56 C3** 21 28S 24 37 E
Kediri, *Indonesia* **37 G15** 7 51S 112 1 E
Kédougou, *Senegal* **50 F2** 12 35N 12 10W
Keeler, *U.S.A.* **84 J9** 36 29N 117 52W
Keeley L., *Canada* **73 C7** 54 54N 108 8W
Keeling Is. = Cocos Is., *Ind. Oc.* **64 J1** 12 10S 96 55 E
Keelung = Chilung, *Taiwan* **33 D7** 25 3N 121 45 E
Keene, *Calif., U.S.A.* **85 K8** 35 13N 118 33W
Keene, *N.H., U.S.A.* **79 D12** 42 56N 72 17W
Keeper Hill, *Ireland* **13 D3** 52 46N 8 17W
Keer-Weer, C., *Australia* **62 A3** 14 0S 141 32 E
Keeseville, *U.S.A.* **79 B11** 44 29N 73 30W
Keetmanshoop, *Namibia* **56 D2** 26 35S 18 8 E
Keewatin, *U.S.A.* **80 B8** 47 24N 93 5W
Keewatin □, *Canada* **73 A9** 63 20N 95 0W
Keewatin →, *Canada* **73 B8** 56 29N 100 46W
Kefallinía, *Greece* **21 E9** 38 20N 20 30 E
Kefamenanu, *Indonesia* **37 F6** 9 28S 124 29 E
Keffi, *Nigeria* **50 G6** 8 55N 7 43 E
Keflavík, *Iceland* **8 D2** 64 2N 22 35W
Keg River, *Canada* **72 B5** 57 54N 117 55W
Kegaska, *Canada* **71 B7** 50 9N 61 18W
Keighley, *U.K.* **10 D6** 53 52N 1 54W
Keimoes, *S. Africa* **56 D3** 28 41S 20 59 E
Keith, *Australia* **63 F3** 36 6S 140 20 E
Keith, *U.K.* **12 D6** 57 33N 2 58W
Keith Arm, *Canada* **68 B7** 64 20N 122 15W
Kejser Franz Joseph Fjord = Kong Franz Joseph Fd., *Greenland* **4 B6** 73 30N 24 30W
Kekri, *India* **42 G6** 26 0N 75 10 E
Kël, *Russia* **27 C13** 69 30N 124 10 E
Kelan, *China* **34 E6** 38 43N 111 31 E
Kelang, *Malaysia* **39 L3** 3 2N 101 26 E
Kelantan →, *Malaysia* **39 J4** 6 13N 102 14 E
Kelibia, *Tunisia* **51 A7** 36 50N 11 3 E
Kellé, *Congo* **52 E2** 0 8S 14 38 E
Keller, *U.S.A.* **82 B4** 48 5N 118 41W
Kellerberrin, *Australia* **61 F2** 31 36S 117 38 E
Kellett, C., *Canada* **4 B1** 72 0N 126 0W
Kelleys I., *U.S.A.* **78 E2** 41 36N 82 42W
Kellogg, *U.S.A.* **82 C5** 47 32N 116 7W
Kelloselkä, *Finland* **8 C20** 66 56N 28 53 E

Kells

Kontum, Plateau du

Kontum, Plateau du, *Vietnam* **38 E7** 14 30N 108 30 E
Konya, *Turkey* **25 G5** 37 52N 32 35 E
Konza, *Kenya* **54 C4** 1 45S 37 7 E
Kookynie, *Australia* **61 E3** 29 17S 121 22 E
Kooline, *Australia* **60 D2** 22 57S 116 20 E
Kooloonong, *Australia* **63 E3** 34 48S 143 10 E
Koolyanobbing, *Australia* **61 F2** 30 48S 119 36 E
Koondrook, *Australia* **63 F3** 35 33S 144 8 E
Koonibba, *Australia* **63 E1** 31 54S 133 25 E
Koorawatha, *Australia* **63 E4** 34 2S 148 33 E
Koorda, *Australia* **61 F2** 30 48S 117 35 E
Kooskia, *U.S.A.* **82 C6** 46 9N 115 59W
Kootenai →, *Canada* **82 B5** 49 15N 117 39W
Kootenay L., *Canada* **72 D5** 49 45N 116 50W
Kootenay Nat. Park, *Canada* **72 C5** 51 0N 116 0W
Kootjieskolk, *S. Africa* **56 E3** 31 15S 20 21 E
Kopaonik, *Serbia, Yug.* **21 C9** 43 10N 20 50 E
Kópavogur, *Iceland* **8 D3** 64 6N 21 55W
Koper, *Slovenia* **20 B5** 45 31N 13 44 E
Kopervik, *Norway* **9 G8** 59 17N 5 17 E
Kopeysk, *Russia* **26 D7** 55 7N 61 37 E
Kopi, *Australia* **63 E2** 33 24S 135 40 E
Köping, *Sweden* **9 G14** 59 31N 16 3 E
Kopparberg, *Sweden* **9 G13** 59 52N 15 0 E
Kopparbergs län □, *Sweden* **9 F13** 61 20N 14 15 E
Koppies, *S. Africa* **57 D4** 27 20S 27 30 E
Korab, *Macedonia* **21 D9** 41 44N 20 40 E
Korakiána, *Greece* **23 A3** 39 42N 19 45 E
Korba, *India* **43 H10** 22 20N 82 45 E
Korbu, G., *Malaysia* **39 K3** 4 41N 101 18 E
Korça, *Albania* **21 D9** 40 37N 20 50 E
Korce = Korça, *Albania* **21 D9** 40 37N 20 50 E
Korčula, *Croatia* **20 C7** 42 57N 17 8 E
Kord Kūy, *Iran* **45 B7** 36 48N 54 7 E
Kord Sheykh, *Iran* **45 D7** 28 31N 52 53 E
Kordestān □, *Iran* **44 C5** 36 0N 47 0 E
Korea, North ■, *Asia* **35 E14** 40 0N 127 0 E
Korea, South ■, *Asia* **35 F15** 36 0N 128 0 E
Korea Bay, *Korea* **35 E13** 39 0N 124 0 E
Korea Strait, *Asia* **35 G15** 34 0N 129 30 E
Korhogo, *Ivory C.* **50 G3** 9 29N 5 28W
Korim, *Indonesia* **37 E9** 0 58S 136 10 E
Korinthiakós Kólpos, *Greece* **21 E10** 38 16N 22 30 E
Kórinthos, *Greece* **21 F10** 37 56N 22 55 E
Korissa, Límni, *Greece* **23 B3** 39 27N 19 53 E
Kōriyama, *Japan* **30 F10** 37 24N 140 23 E
Korla, *China* **32 B3** 41 45N 86 4 E
Kormakiti, C., *Cyprus* **23 D11** 35 23N 32 56 E
Koro, *Fiji* **59 C8** 17 19S 179 23 E
Koro, *Ivory C.* **50 G3** 8 32N 7 30W
Koro, *Mali* **50 F4** 14 1N 2 58W
Koro Sea, *Fiji* **59 C9** 17 30S 179 45W
Korogwe, *Tanzania* **54 D4** 5 5S 38 25 E
Korogwe □, *Tanzania* **54 D4** 5 0S 38 20 E
Koroit, *Australia* **63 F3** 38 18S 142 24 E
Koror, *Pac. Oc.* **37 C8** 7 20N 134 28 E
Körös →, *Hungary* **17 E10** 46 43N 20 12 E
Korraraika, Helodranon' i, *Madag.* **57 B7** 17 45S 43 57 E
Korsakov, *Russia* **27 E15** 46 36N 142 42 E
Korshunovo, *Russia* **27 D12** 58 37N 110 10 E
Korsør, *Denmark* **9 J11** 55 20N 11 9 E
Korti, *Sudan* **51 E11** 18 6N 31 33 E
Kortrijk, *Belgium* **15 D3** 50 50N 3 17 E
Korwai, *India* **42 G8** 24 7N 78 5 E
Koryakskiy Khrebet, *Russia* **27 C18** 61 0N 171 0 E
Koryŏng, *S. Korea* **35 G15** 35 44N 128 15 E
Kos, *Greece* **21 F12** 36 50N 27 15 E
Koschagyl, *Kazakhstan* **25 E9** 46 40N 54 0 E
Kościan, *Poland* **16 B8** 52 5N 16 40 E
Kosciusko, *U.S.A.* **81 J10** 33 4N 89 35W
Kosciusko, Mt., *Australia* **63 F4** 36 27S 148 16 E
Kosciusko I., *U.S.A.* **72 B2** 56 0N 133 40W
Kosha, *Sudan* **51 D11** 20 50N 30 30 E
Kōshetau = Kokchetav, *Kazakhstan* **26 D7** 53 20N 69 25 E
K'oshih = Kashi, *China* **32 C2** 39 30N 76 2 E
Koshiki-Rettō, *Japan* **31 J4** 31 45N 129 49 E
Kosi, *India* **42 F7** 27 48N 77 29 E
Kosi-meer, *S. Africa* **57 D5** 27 0S 32 50 E
Košice, *Slovakia* **17 D10** 48 42N 21 15 E
Koskhinoú, *Greece* **23 C10** 36 23N 28 13 E
Koslan, *Russia* **24 B8** 63 28N 48 52 E
Kosŏng, *N. Korea* **35 E15** 38 40N 128 22 E
Kosovska-Mitrovica, *Serbia, Yug.* **21 C9** 42 54N 20 52 E
Kostamuksa, *Russia* **24 B5** 62 34N 32 44 E
Koster, *S. Africa* **56 D4** 25 52S 26 54 E
Kôstî, *Sudan* **51 F11** 13 8N 32 43 E
Kostroma, *Russia* **24 C7** 57 50N 40 58 E
Koszalin, *Poland* **16 A8** 54 11N 16 8 E
Kot Addu, *Pakistan* **42 D4** 30 30N 71 0 E
Kot Moman, *Pakistan* **42 C5** 32 13N 73 0 E
Kota, *India* **42 G6** 25 14N 75 49 E
Kota Baharu, *Malaysia* **39 J4** 6 7N 102 14 E
Kota Belud, *Malaysia* **36 C5** 6 21N 116 26 E
Kota Kinabalu, *Malaysia* **36 C5** 6 0N 116 4 E
Kota Tinggi, *Malaysia* **39 M4** 1 44N 103 53 E
Kotaagung, *Indonesia* **36 F2** 5 38S 104 29 E
Kotabaru, *Indonesia* **36 E5** 3 20S 116 20 E
Kotabumi, *Indonesia* **36 E2** 4 49S 104 54 E
Kotagede, *Indonesia* **37 G14** 7 54S 110 26 E
Kotamobagu, *Indonesia* **37 D6** 0 57N 124 31 E
Kotaneelee →, *Canada* **72 A4** 60 11N 123 42W
Kotawaringin, *Indonesia* **36 E4** 2 28S 111 27 E
Kotcho L., *Canada* **72 B4** 59 7N 121 12W
Kotelnich, *Russia* **24 C8** 58 20N 48 10 E
Kotelnikovo, *Russia* **25 E7** 47 38N 43 8 E
Kotelnyy, Ostrov, *Russia* **27 B14** 75 10N 139 0 E
Kothi, *India* **43 G9** 24 45N 80 40 E
Kotiro, *Pakistan* **42 F2** 26 17N 67 13 E
Kotka, *Finland* **9 F19** 60 28N 26 58 E
Kotlas, *Russia* **24 B8** 61 15N 47 0 E
Kotli, *Pakistan* **42 C5** 33 30N 73 55 E
Kotmul, *Pakistan* **43 B6** 35 32N 75 10 E
Kotor, *Montenegro, Yug.* **21 C8** 42 25N 18 47 E
Kotputli, *India* **42 F7** 27 43N 76 12 E
Kotri, *Pakistan* **42 G3** 25 22N 68 22 E
Kottayam, *India* **40 Q10** 9 35N 76 33 E
Kotturu, *India* **40 M10** 14 45N 76 10 E
Kotuy →, *Russia* **27 B11** 71 54N 102 6 E
Kotzebue, *U.S.A.* **68 B3** 66 53N 162 39W
Kouango, *C.A.R.* **52 C4** 5 0N 20 10 E
Koudougou, *Burkina Faso* **50 F4** 12 10N 2 20W
Koufonisi, *Greece* **23 E8** 34 56N 26 8 E
Kougaberge, *S. Africa* **56 E3** 33 48S 23 50 E
Kouilou →, *Congo* **52 E2** 4 10S 12 5 E
Kouki, *C.A.R.* **52 C3** 7 22N 17 3 E
Koula Moutou, *Gabon* **52 E2** 1 15S 12 25 E
Koulen, *Cambodia* **38 F5** 13 50N 104 40 E
Koulikoro, *Mali* **50 F3** 12 40N 7 50W
Kouloúra, *Greece* **23 A3** 39 42N 19 54 E
Koúm-bournoú, Ákra, *Greece* **23 C10** 36 15N 28 11 E
Koumala, *Australia* **62 C4** 21 38S 149 15 E
Koumra, *Chad* **51 G8** 8 50N 17 35 E
Kounradskiy, *Kazakhstan* **26 E8** 46 59N 75 0 E
Kountze, *U.S.A.* **81 K7** 30 22N 94 19W
Kouris →, *Cyprus* **23 E11** 34 38N 32 54 E
Kouroussa, *Guinea* **50 F3** 10 45N 9 45W
Kousseri, *Cameroon* **51 F7** 12 0N 14 55 E
Koutiala, *Mali* **50 F3** 12 25N 5 23W
Kovdor, *Russia* **24 A5** 67 34N 30 24 E
Kovel, *Ukraine* **24 D3** 51 10N 24 20 E
Kovrov, *Russia* **24 C7** 56 25N 41 25 E
Kowanyama, *Australia* **62 B3** 15 29S 141 44 E
Kowkash, *Canada* **70 B2** 50 20N 87 12W
Kowŏn, *N. Korea* **35 E14** 39 26N 127 14 E
Koyabuti, *Indonesia* **37 E10** 2 36S 140 37 E
Koyuk, *U.S.A.* **68 B3** 64 56N 161 9W
Koyukuk →, *U.S.A.* **68 B4** 64 55N 157 32W
Koza, *Japan* **31 L3** 26 19N 127 46 E
Kozáni, *Greece* **21 D9** 40 19N 21 47 E
Kozhikode = Calicut, *India* **40 P9** 11 15N 75 43 E
Kozhva, *Russia* **24 A10** 65 10N 57 0 E
Kpalimé, *Togo* **50 G5** 6 57N 0 44 E
Kra, Isthmus of = Kra, Kho Khot, *Thailand* **39 G2** 10 15N 99 30 E
Kra, Kho Khot, *Thailand* **39 G2** 10 15N 99 30 E
Kra Buri, *Thailand* **39 G2** 10 22N 98 46 E
Krabi, *Thailand* **39 H2** 8 4N 98 55 E
Kragan, *Indonesia* **37 G14** 6 43S 111 38 E
Kragerø, *Norway* **9 G10** 58 52N 9 25 E
Kragujevac, *Serbia, Yug.* **21 B9** 44 2N 20 56 E
Krakatau = Rakata, Pulau, *Indonesia* **36 F3** 6 10S 105 20 E
Krakor, *Cambodia* **38 F5** 12 32N 104 12 E
Kraków, *Poland* **17 C9** 50 4N 19 57 E
Kraksaan, *Indonesia* **37 G15** 7 43S 113 23 E
Kralanh, *Cambodia* **38 F4** 13 35N 103 25 E
Kraljevo, *Serbia, Yug.* **21 C9** 43 44N 20 41 E
Kramatorsk, *Ukraine* **25 E6** 48 50N 37 30 E
Kramfors, *Sweden* **8 E14** 62 55N 17 48 E
Krankskop, *S. Africa* **57 D5** 28 0S 30 47 E
Krasavino, *Russia* **24 B8** 60 58N 46 29 E
Kraskino, *Russia* **27 E14** 42 44N 130 48 E
Kraśnik, *Poland* **17 C11** 50 55N 22 5 E
Krasnoarmeysk, *Russia* **26 D5** 51 0N 45 42 E
Krasnodar, *Russia* **25 E6** 45 5N 39 0 E
Krasnokamsk, *Russia* **24 C10** 58 4N 55 48 E
Krasnoperekopsk, *Ukraine* **25 E5** 46 0N 33 54 E
Krasnorechenskiy, *Russia* **30 B7** 44 41N 135 14 E
Krasnoselkupsk, *Russia* **26 C9** 65 20N 82 10 E
Krasnoturinsk, *Russia* **24 C11** 59 46N 60 12 E
Krasnoufimsk, *Russia* **24 C10** 56 57N 57 46 E
Krasnouralsk, *Russia* **24 C11** 58 21N 60 3 E
Krasnovishersk, *Russia* **24 B10** 60 23N 57 3 E
Krasnovodsk, *Turkmenistan* **25 F9** 40 0N 52 52 E
Krasnoyarsk, *Russia* **27 D10** 56 8N 93 0 E
Krasnyy Luch, *Ukraine* **25 E6** 48 13N 39 0 E
Krasnyy Yar, *Russia* **25 E8** 46 43N 48 23 E
Kratie, *Cambodia* **38 F6** 12 32N 106 10 E
Krau, *Indonesia* **37 E10** 3 19S 140 5 E
Kravanh, Chuor Phnum, *Cambodia* **39 G4** 12 0N 103 32 E
Krefeld, *Germany* **16 C3** 51 20N 6 32 E
Kremenchug, *Ukraine* **25 E5** 49 5N 33 25 E
Kremenchugskoye Vdkhr., *Ukraine* **25 E5** 49 20N 32 30 E
Kremenchuk = Kremenchug, *Ukraine* **25 E5** 49 5N 33 25 E
Kremmling, *U.S.A.* **82 F10** 40 4N 106 24W
Kremnica, *Slovakia* **17 D9** 48 45N 18 50 E
Kribi, *Cameroon* **52 D1** 2 57N 9 56 E
Kriós, Ákra, *Greece* **23 D5** 35 13N 23 34 E
Krishna →, *India* **41 M12** 15 57N 80 59 E
Krishnanagar, *India* **43 H13** 23 24N 88 33 E
Kristiansand, *Norway* **9 G10** 58 9N 8 1 E
Kristianstad, *Sweden* **9 H13** 56 2N 14 9 E
Kristianstads län □, *Sweden* **9 H13** 56 15N 14 0 E
Kristiansund, *Norway* **8 E9** 63 7N 7 45 E
Kristiinankaupunki, *Finland* **8 E16** 62 16N 21 21 E
Kristinehamn, *Sweden* **9 G13** 59 18N 14 13 E
Kristinestad, *Finland* **8 E16** 62 16N 21 21 E
Kriti, *Greece* **23 D7** 35 15N 25 0 E
Kritsá, *Greece* **23 D7** 35 10N 25 41 E
Krivoy Rog, *Ukraine* **25 E5** 47 51N 33 20 E
Krk, *Croatia* **20 B6** 45 8N 14 40 E
Krokodil →, *Mozam.* **57 D5** 25 14S 32 18 E
Kronobergs län □, *Sweden* **9 H13** 56 45N 14 30 E
Kronprins Olav Kyst, *Antarctica* **5 C5** 69 0S 42 0 E
Kronshtadt, *Russia* **24 B4** 60 5N 29 45 E
Kroonstad, *S. Africa* **56 D4** 27 43S 27 19 E
Kropotkin, *Russia* **25 E7** 45 28N 40 28 E
Kropotkin, *Russia* **27 D12** 59 0N 115 30 E
Krosno, *Poland* **17 D10** 49 42N 21 46 E
Krotoszyn, *Poland* **17 C8** 51 42N 17 23 E
Kroussón, *Greece* **23 D6** 35 13N 24 59 E
Kruger Nat. Park, *S. Africa* **57 C5** 23 30S 31 40 E
Krugersdorp, *S. Africa* **57 D4** 26 5S 27 46 E
Kruisfontein, *S. Africa* **56 E3** 33 59S 24 43 E
Krung Thep = Bangkok, *Thailand* **38 F3** 13 45N 100 35 E
Kruševac, *Serbia, Yug.* **21 C9** 43 35N 21 28 E
Kruzof I., *U.S.A.* **72 B1** 57 10N 135 40W
Krymskiy Poluostrov, *Ukraine* **25 E5** 45 0N 34 0 E
Kryvyy Rih = Krivoy Rog, *Ukraine* **25 E5** 47 51N 33 20 E
Ksar el Boukhari, *Algeria* **50 A5** 35 51N 2 52 E
Ksar el Kebir, *Morocco* **50 B3** 35 0N 6 0W
Ksar es Souk = Ar Rachidiya, *Morocco* **50 B4** 31 58N 4 20W
Kuala, *Indonesia* **36 D3** 2 55N 105 47 E
Kuala Berang, *Malaysia* **39 K4** 5 5N 103 1 E
Kuala Dungun, *Malaysia* **39 K4** 4 45N 103 25 E
Kuala Kangsar, *Malaysia* **39 K3** 4 46N 100 56 E
Kuala Kelawang, *Malaysia* **39 L4** 2 56N 102 5 E
Kuala Kerai, *Malaysia* **39 K4** 5 30N 102 12 E
Kuala Kubu Baharu, *Malaysia* **39 L3** 3 34N 101 39 E
Kuala Lipis, *Malaysia* **39 K4** 4 10N 102 3 E
Kuala Lumpur, *Malaysia* **39 L3** 3 9N 101 41 E
Kuala Nerang, *Malaysia* **39 J3** 6 16N 100 37 E
Kuala Pilah, *Malaysia* **39 L4** 2 45N 102 15 E
Kuala Rompin, *Malaysia* **39 L4** 2 49N 103 29 E
Kuala Selangor, *Malaysia* **39 L3** 3 20N 101 15 E
Kuala Terengganu, *Malaysia* **39 K4** 5 20N 103 8 E
Kualajelai, *Indonesia* **36 E4** 2 58S 110 46 E
Kualakapuas, *Indonesia* **36 E4** 2 55S 114 20 E
Kualakurun, *Indonesia* **36 E4** 1 10S 113 50 E
Kualapembuang, *Indonesia* **36 E4** 3 14S 112 38 E
Kualasimpang, *Indonesia* **36 D1** 4 17N 98 3 E
Kuancheng, *China* **35 D10** 40 37N 118 30 E
Kuandang, *Indonesia* **37 D6** 0 56N 123 1 E
Kuandian, *China* **35 D13** 40 45N 124 45 E
Kuangchou = Guangzhou, *China* **33 D6** 23 5N 113 10 E
Kuantan, *Malaysia* **39 L4** 3 49N 103 20 E
Kuba, *Azerbaijan* **25 F8** 41 21N 48 32 E
Kuban →, *Russia* **25 E6** 45 20N 37 30 E
Kubokawa, *Japan* **31 H6** 33 12N 133 8 E
Kucha Gompa, *India* **43 B7** 34 25N 76 56 E
Kuchaman, *India* **42 F6** 27 13N 74 47 E
Kuchino-eruba-Jima, *Japan* **31 J5** 30 28N 130 12 E
Kuchino-Shima, *Japan* **31 K4** 29 57N 129 55 E
Kuchinotsu, *Japan* **31 H5** 32 36N 130 11 E
Kucing, *Malaysia* **36 D4** 1 33N 110 25 E
Kud →, *Pakistan* **42 F2** 26 5N 66 20 E
Kuda, *India* **40 H7** 23 10N 71 15 E
Kudat, *Malaysia* **36 C5** 6 55N 116 55 E
Kudus, *Indonesia* **37 G14** 6 48S 110 51 E
Kudymkar, *Russia* **26 D6** 59 1N 54 39 E
Kueiyang = Guiyang, *China* **32 D5** 26 32N 106 40 E
Kufstein, *Austria* **16 E6** 47 35N 12 11 E
Kugong I., *Canada* **70 A4** 56 18N 79 50W
Kūh-e Dīnār, *Iran* **45 D6** 30 40N 51 0 E
Kūh-e-Hazārām, *Iran* **45 D8** 29 35N 57 20 E
Kūhak, *Iran* **40 F3** 27 12N 63 10 E
Kūhbonān, *Iran* **45 D8** 31 23N 56 19 E
Kūhestak, *Iran* **45 E8** 26 47N 57 2 E
Kūhīn, *Iran* **45 C6** 35 13N 48 25 E
Kūhīrī, *Iran* **45 E9** 26 55N 61 2 E
Kūhpāyeh, *Eşfahan, Iran* **45 C7** 32 44N 52 20 E
Kūhpāyeh, *Kermān, Iran* **45 D8** 30 35N 57 15 E
Kui Buri, *Thailand* **39 F2** 12 3N 99 52 E
Kuito, *Angola* **53 G3** 12 22S 16 55 E
Kujang, *N. Korea* **35 E14** 39 57N 126 1 E
Kuji, *Japan* **30 D10** 40 11N 141 46 E
Kujū-San, *Japan* **31 H5** 33 5N 131 15 E
Kukawa, *Nigeria* **51 F7** 12 58N 13 27 E
Kukerin, *Australia* **61 F2** 33 13S 118 0 E
Kukup, *Malaysia* **39 M4** 1 20N 103 27 E
Kulai, *Malaysia* **39 M4** 1 44N 103 35 E
Kulal, Mt., *Kenya* **54 B4** 2 42N 36 57 E
Kulasekarappattinam, *India* **40 Q11** 8 20N 78 5 E
Kuldja = Yining, *China* **26 E9** 43 58N 81 10 E
Kulgam, *India* **43 C6** 33 36N 75 2 E
Kulim, *Malaysia* **39 K3** 5 22N 100 34 E
Kulin, *Australia* **61 F2** 32 40S 118 2 E
Kulja, *Australia* **61 F2** 30 28S 117 18 E
Kulm, *U.S.A.* **80 B5** 46 18N 98 57W
Kulsary, *Kazakhstan* **25 E9** 46 59N 54 1 E
Kulti, *India* **43 H12** 23 43N 86 50 E
Kulumbura, *Australia* **60 B4** 13 55S 126 35 E
Kulunda, *Russia* **26 D8** 52 35N 78 57 E
Kulungar, *Afghan.* **42 C3** 34 0N 69 2 E
Kūlvand, *Iran* **45 D7** 31 21N 54 35 E
Kulwin, *Australia* **63 F3** 35 0S 142 42 E
Kulyab, *Tajikistan* **26 F7** 37 55N 69 50 E
Kum Tekei, *Kazakhstan* **26 E8** 43 10N 79 30 E
Kuma →, *Russia* **25 F8** 44 55N 47 0 E
Kumagaya, *Japan* **31 F9** 36 9N 139 22 E
Kumai, *Indonesia* **36 E4** 2 44S 111 43 E
Kumamba, Kepulauan, *Indonesia* **37 E9** 1 36S 138 45 E
Kumamoto, *Japan* **31 H5** 32 45N 130 45 E
Kumamoto □, *Japan* **31 H5** 32 55N 130 55 E
Kumanovo, *Macedonia* **21 C9** 42 9N 21 42 E
Kumara, *N.Z.* **59 K3** 42 37S 171 12 E
Kumarl, *Australia* **61 F3** 32 47S 121 33 E
Kumasi, *Ghana* **50 G4** 6 41N 1 38W
Kumayri, *Armenia* **25 F7** 40 47N 43 50 E
Kumba, *Cameroon* **50 H6** 4 36N 9 24 E
Kumbakonam, *India* **40 P11** 10 58N 79 25 E
Kumbarilla, *Australia* **63 D5** 27 15S 150 55 E
Kŭmchŏn, *N. Korea* **35 E14** 38 10N 126 29 E
Kumdok, *India* **43 C8** 33 32N 78 10 E
Kume-Shima, *Japan* **31 L3** 26 20N 126 47 E
Kumertau, *Russia* **24 D10** 52 46N 55 47 E
Kŭmhwa, *S. Korea* **35 E14** 38 17N 127 28 E
Kumi, *Uganda* **54 B3** 1 30N 33 58 E
Kumla, *Sweden* **9 G13** 59 8N 15 10 E
Kumo, *Nigeria* **50 F7** 10 1N 11 12 E
Kumon Bum, *Burma* **41 F20** 26 30N 97 15 E
Kunama, *Australia* **63 F4** 35 35S 148 4 E
Kunashir, Ostrov, *Russia* **27 E15** 44 0N 146 0 E
Kundla, *India* **42 J4** 21 21N 71 25 E
Kungala, *Australia* **63 D5** 29 58S 153 7 E
Kunghit I., *Canada* **72 C2** 52 6N 131 3W
Kungrad, *Uzbekistan* **26 E6** 43 6N 58 54 E
Kungsbacka, *Sweden* **9 H12** 57 30N 12 5 E
Kungur, *Russia* **24 C10** 57 25N 56 57 E
Kungurri, *Australia* **62 C4** 21 3S 148 46 E
Kunhar →, *Pakistan* **43 B5** 34 20N 73 30 E
Kuningan, *Indonesia* **37 G13** 6 59S 108 29 E
Kunlong, *Burma* **41 H21** 23 20N 98 50 E
Kunlun Shan, *Asia* **32 C3** 36 0N 86 30 E
Kunming, *China* **32 D5** 25 1N 102 41 E
Kunsan, *S. Korea* **35 G14** 35 59N 126 45 E
Kununurra, *Australia* **60 C4** 15 40S 128 50 E
Kunwarara, *Australia* **62 C5** 22 55S 150 9 E
Kunya-Urgench, *Turkmenistan* **26 E6** 42 19N 59 10 E
Kuopio, *Finland* **8 E19** 62 53N 27 35 E
Kuopion lääni □, *Finland* **8 E19** 63 25N 27 10 E
Kupa →, *Croatia* **20 B7** 45 28N 16 24 E
Kupang, *Indonesia* **37 F6** 10 19S 123 39 E
Kupyansk, *Ukraine* **26 E4** 49 52N 37 35 E
Kuqa, *China* **32 B3** 41 35N 82 30 E
Kura →, *Azerbaijan* **25 G8** 39 50N 49 20 E
Kuranda, *Australia* **62 B4** 16 48S 145 35 E
Kurashiki, *Japan* **31 G6** 34 40N 133 50 E
Kurayoshi, *Japan* **31 G6** 35 26N 133 50 E
Kure, *Japan* **31 G6** 34 14N 132 32 E
Kurgaldzhino, *Kazakhstan* **26 D8** 50 35N 70 20 E
Kurgan, *Russia* **26 D7** 55 26N 65 18 E
Kuria Maria Is. = Khūriyā Mūrīyā, Jazā 'ir, *Oman* **46 D6** 17 30N 55 58 E
Kuridala, *Australia* **62 C3** 21 16S 140 29 E
Kurigram, *Bangla.* **41 G16** 25 49N 89 39 E
Kuril Is. = Kurilskiye Ostrova, *Russia* **27 E15** 45 0N 150 0 E
Kuril Trench, *Pac. Oc.* **64 C7** 44 0N 153 0 E
Kurilsk, *Russia* **27 E15** 45 14N 147 53 E
Kurilskiye Ostrova, *Russia* **27 E15** 45 0N 150 0 E
Kurino, *Japan* **31 J5** 31 57N 130 43 E
Kurmuk, *Sudan* **51 F11** 10 33N 34 21 E
Kurnool, *India* **40 M10** 15 45N 78 0 E
Kuro-Shima, *Kagoshima, Japan* **31 J4** 30 50N 129 57 E
Kuro-Shima, *Okinawa, Japan* **31 M2** 24 14N 124 1 E
Kurow, *N.Z.* **59 L3** 44 44S 170 29 E
Kurrajong, *Australia* **63 E5** 33 33S 150 42 E
Kurram →, *Pakistan* **42 C4** 32 36N 71 20 E
Kurri Kurri, *Australia* **63 E5** 32 50S 151 28 E
Kursk, *Russia* **24 D6** 51 42N 36 11 E
Kuršumlija, *Serbia, Yug.* **21 C9** 43 9N 21 19 E
Kuruktag, *China* **32 B3** 41 0N 89 0 E
Kuruman, *S. Africa* **56 D3** 27 28S 23 28 E
Kuruman →, *S. Africa* **56 D3** 26 56S 20 39 E
Kurume, *Japan* **31 H5** 33 15N 130 30 E
Kurunegala, *Sri Lanka* **40 R12** 7 30N 80 23 E
Kurya, *Russia* **27 C11** 61 15N 108 10 E
Kusatsu, *Japan* **31 F9** 36 37N 138 36 E
Kusawa L., *Canada* **72 A1** 60 20N 136 13W
Kushikino, *Japan* **31 J5** 31 44N 130 16 E
Kushima, *Japan* **31 J5** 31 29N 131 14 E
Kushimoto, *Japan* **31 H7** 33 28N 135 47 E
Kushiro, *Japan* **30 C12** 43 0N 144 25 E
Kushiro →, *Japan* **30 C12** 42 59N 144 23 E
Kūshk, *Iran* **45 D8** 28 46N 56 51 E
Kushka, *Turkmenistan* **26 F7** 35 20N 62 18 E
Kūshki, *Īlām, Iran* **44 C5** 33 31N 47 13 E
Kūshki, *Khorāsān, Iran* **45 B8** 37 2N 57 26 E
Kūshkū, *Iran* **45 E7** 27 19N 53 28 E
Kushol, *India* **43 C7** 33 40N 76 36 E
Kushtia, *Bangla.* **41 H16** 23 55N 89 5 E
Kushva, *Russia* **24 C10** 58 18N 59 45 E
Kuskokwim →, *U.S.A.* **68 B3** 60 5N 162 25W
Kuskokwim B., *U.S.A.* **68 C3** 59 45N 162 25W
Kussharo-Ko, *Japan* **30 C12** 43 38N 144 21 E
Kustanay, *Kazakhstan* **26 D7** 53 10N 63 35 E
Kut, Ko, *Thailand* **39 G4** 11 40N 102 35 E
Kütahya, *Turkey* **25 G5** 39 30N 30 2 E
Kutaisi, *Georgia* **25 F7** 42 19N 42 40 E
Kutaraja = Banda Aceh, *Indonesia* **36 C1** 5 35N 95 20 E
Kutch, Gulf of = Kachchh, Gulf of, *India* **42 H3** 22 50N 69 15 E
Kutch, Rann of = Kachchh, Rann of, *India* **42 G4** 24 0N 70 0 E
Kutiyana, *India* **42 J4** 21 36N 70 2 E
Kutno, *Poland* **17 B9** 52 15N 19 23 E
Kuttabul, *Australia* **62 C4** 21 5S 148 48 E
Kutu, *Zaire* **52 E3** 2 40S 18 11 E
Kutum, *Sudan* **51 F9** 14 10N 24 40 E
Kuujjuaq, *Canada* **69 C13** 58 6N 68 15W
Kuŭp-tong, *N. Korea* **35 D14** 40 45N 126 1 E
Kuwait = Al Kuwayt, *Kuwait* **44 D5** 29 30N 48 0 E
Kuwait ■, *Asia* **44 D5** 29 30N 47 30 E
Kuwana, *Japan* **31 G8** 35 5N 136 43 E
Kuybyshev = Samara, *Russia* **24 D9** 53 8N 50 6 E
Kuybyshev, *Russia* **26 D8** 55 27N 78 19 E
Kuybyshevskoye Vdkhr., *Russia* **24 C8** 55 2N 49 30 E
Kuye He →, *China* **34 E6** 38 23N 110 46 E
Kūyeh, *Iran* **44 B5** 38 45N 47 57 E
Kūysanjaq, *Iraq* **44 B5** 36 5N 44 38 E
Kuyto, Oz., *Russia* **24 B5** 64 40N 31 0 E
Kuyumba, *Russia* **27 C10** 60 58N 96 59 E
Kuzey Anadolu Dağlari, *Turkey* **25 F6** 41 30N 35 0 E
Kuznetsk, *Russia* **24 D8** 53 12N 46 40 E
Kuzomen, *Russia* **24 A6** 66 22N 36 50 E
Kvænangen, *Norway* **8 A16** 70 5N 21 15 E
Kvarner, *Croatia* **20 B6** 44 50N 14 10 E
Kvarnerič, *Croatia* **20 B6** 44 43N 14 37 E
Kwabhaca, *S. Africa* **57 E4** 30 51S 29 0 E
Kwadacha →, *Canada* **72 B3** 57 28N 125 38W
Kwakhanai, *Botswana* **56 C3** 21 39S 21 16 E
Kwakoegron, *Surinam* **93 B7** 5 12N 55 25W
Kwale, *Kenya* **54 C4** 4 15S 39 31 E
Kwale □, *Kenya* **54 C4** 4 15S 39 10 E
KwaMashu, *S. Africa* **57 D5** 29 45S 30 58 E

L'Annonciation

Malita

McDouall Peak, Australia 63 D1 29 51S 134 55 E
Macdougall L., Canada 68 B10 66 0N 98 27W
MacDowell L., Canada 70 B1 52 15N 92 45W
Macduff, U.K. 12 D6 57 40N 2 30W
Macedonia = Makedhonía □, Greece 21 D10 40 39N 22 0 E
Macedonia ■, Europe 21 D9 41 53N 21 40 E
Maceió, Brazil 93 E11 9 40S 35 41W
Macenta, Guinea 50 G3 8 35N 9 32W
Macerata, Italy 20 C5 43 19N 13 28 E
McFarland, U.S.A. 85 K7 35 41N 119 14W
McFarlane →, Canada 73 B7 59 12N 107 58W
Macfarlane, L., Australia 63 E2 32 0S 136 40 E
McGehee, U.S.A. 81 J9 33 38N 91 24W
McGill, U.S.A. 82 G6 39 23N 114 47W
Macgillycuddy's Reeks, Ireland 13 D2 52 2N 9 45W
MacGregor, Canada 73 D9 49 57N 98 48W
McGregor, U.S.A. 80 D9 43 1N 91 11W
McGregor →, Canada 72 B4 55 10N 122 0W
McGregor Ra., Australia 63 D3 27 0S 142 45 E
Mach, Pakistan 40 E5 29 50N 67 20 E
Māch Kowr, Iran 45 E9 25 48N 61 28 E
Machado = Jiparaná →, Brazil 92 E6 8 3S 62 52W
Machagai, Argentina 94 B3 26 56S 60 2W
Machakos, Kenya 54 C4 1 30S 37 15 E
Machakos □, Kenya 54 C4 1 30S 37 15 E
Machala, Ecuador 92 D3 3 20S 79 57W
Machanga, Mozam. 57 C6 20 59S 35 0 E
Machattie, L., Australia 62 C2 24 50S 139 48 E
Machava, Mozam. 57 D5 25 54S 32 28 E
Machece, Mozam. 55 F4 19 15S 35 32 E
Machevna, Russia 27 C18 61 20N 172 20 E
Machias, U.S.A. 71 D6 44 43N 67 28W
Machichi →, Canada 73 B10 57 3N 92 6W
Machico, Madeira 22 D3 32 43N 16 44W
Machilipatnam, India 41 L12 16 12N 81 8 E
Machiques, Venezuela 92 A4 10 4N 72 34W
Machupicchu, Peru 92 F4 13 8S 72 30W
Machynlleth, U.K. 11 E4 52 36N 3 51W
McIlwraith Ra., Australia 62 A3 13 50S 143 20 E
McIntosh, U.S.A. 80 C4 45 55N 101 21W
McIntosh L., Canada 73 B8 55 45N 105 0W
Macintosh Ra., Australia 61 E4 27 39S 125 32 E
Macintyre →, Australia 63 D5 28 37S 150 47 E
Mackay, Australia 62 C4 21 8S 149 11 E
Mackay, U.S.A. 82 E7 43 55N 113 37W
MacKay →, Canada 72 B6 57 10N 111 38W
Mackay, L., Australia 60 D4 22 30S 129 0 E
McKay Ra., Australia 60 D3 23 0S 122 30 E
McKeesport, U.S.A. 78 F5 40 21N 79 52W
McKenna, U.S.A. 84 D4 46 56N 122 33W
Mackenzie, Canada 72 B4 55 20N 123 5W
McKenzie, U.S.A. 77 G1 36 8N 88 31W
Mackenzie →, Australia 62 C4 23 38S 149 46 E
Mackenzie →, Canada 68 B6 69 10N 134 20W
McKenzie →, U.S.A. 82 D2 44 7N 123 6W
Mackenzie Bay, Canada 4 B1 69 0N 137 30W
Mackenzie City = Linden, Guyana 92 B7 6 0N 58 10W
Mackenzie Highway, Canada 72 B5 58 0N 117 15W
Mackenzie Mts., Canada 68 B6 64 0N 130 0W
Mackinaw City, U.S.A. 76 C3 45 47N 84 44W
McKinlay, Australia 62 C3 21 16S 141 18 E
McKinlay →, Australia 62 C3 20 50S 141 28 E
McKinley, Mt., U.S.A. 68 B4 63 4N 151 0W
McKinley Sea, Arctic 4 A7 84 0N 10 0W
McKinney, U.S.A. 81 J6 33 12N 96 37W
Mackinnon Road, Kenya 54 C4 3 40S 39 1 E
Macksville, Australia 63 E5 30 40S 152 56 E
McLaughlin, U.S.A. 80 C4 45 49N 100 49W
Maclean, Australia 63 D5 29 26S 153 16 E
McLean, U.S.A. 81 H4 35 14N 100 36W
McLeansboro, U.S.A. 80 F10 38 6N 88 32W
Maclear, S. Africa 57 E4 31 2S 28 23 E
Macleay →, Australia 63 E5 30 56S 153 0 E
McLennan, Canada 72 B5 55 42N 116 50W
MacLeod, B., Canada 73 A7 62 53N 110 0W
McLeod, L., Australia 61 D1 24 9S 113 47 E
MacLeod Lake, Canada 72 C4 54 58N 123 0W
M'Clintock Chan., Canada 68 A9 72 0N 102 0W
McLoughlin, Mt., U.S.A. 82 E2 42 27N 122 19W
McLure, Canada 72 C4 51 2N 120 13W
McMechen, U.S.A. 78 G4 39 57N 80 44W
McMillan, L., U.S.A. 81 J2 32 36N 104 21W
McMinnville, Oreg., U.S.A. 82 D2 45 13N 123 12W
McMinnville, Tenn., U.S.A. 77 H3 35 41N 85 46W
McMorran, Canada 73 C7 51 19N 108 42W
McMurdo Sd., Antarctica 5 D11 77 0S 170 0 E
McMurray = Fort McMurray, Canada 72 B6 56 44N 111 7W
McMurray, U.S.A. 84 B4 48 19N 122 14W
McNary, U.S.A. 83 J9 34 4N 109 51W
MacNutt, Canada 73 C8 51 5N 101 36W
Macodoene, Mozam. 57 C6 23 32S 35 5 E
Macomb, U.S.A. 80 E9 40 27N 90 40W
Mâcon, France 18 C6 46 19N 4 50 E
Macon, Ga., U.S.A. 77 J4 32 51N 83 38W
Macon, Miss., U.S.A. 77 J1 33 7N 88 34W
Macon, Mo., U.S.A. 80 F8 39 44N 92 28W
Macondo, Angola 53 G4 12 37S 23 46 E
Macossa, Mozam. 55 F3 17 55S 33 56 E
Macoun L., Canada 73 B8 56 32N 103 40W
Macovane, Mozam. 57 C6 21 30S 35 2 E
McPherson, U.S.A. 80 F6 38 22N 97 40W
McPherson Pk., U.S.A. 85 L7 34 53N 119 53W
McPherson Ra., Australia 63 D5 28 15S 153 15 E
Macquarie Harbour, Australia 62 G4 42 15S 145 23 E
Macquarie Is., Pac. Oc. 64 N7 54 36S 158 55 E
MacRobertson Land, Antarctica 5 D6 71 0S 64 0 E
Macroom, Ireland 13 E3 51 54N 8 57W
Macroy, Australia 60 D2 20 53S 118 2 E
MacTier, Canada 78 A5 45 9N 79 46W
Macubela, Mozam. 55 F4 16 53S 37 49 E
Macuiza, Mozam. 55 F3 18 7S 34 29 E
Macuse, Mozam. 55 F4 17 45S 37 10 E
Macuspana, Mexico 87 D6 17 46N 92 36W
Macusse, Angola 56 B3 17 48S 20 23 E
McVille, U.S.A. 80 B5 47 46N 98 11W
Madadeni, S. Africa 57 D5 27 43S 30 3 E
Madagali, Nigeria 51 F7 10 56N 13 33 E
Madagascar ■, Africa 57 C8 20 0S 47 0 E
Madā'in Sālih, Si. Arabia 44 E3 26 46N 37 57 E
Madama, Niger 51 D7 22 0N 13 40 E
Madame I., Canada 71 C7 45 30N 60 58W
Madaoua, Niger 50 F6 14 5N 6 27 E
Madaripur, Bangla. 41 H17 23 19N 90 15 E
Madauk, Burma 41 L20 17 56N 96 52 E
Madawaska, Canada 78 A7 45 30N 78 0W
Madawaska →, Canada 78 A8 45 27N 76 21W
Madaya, Burma 41 H20 22 12N 96 10 E
Madeira, Atl. Oc. 22 D3 32 50N 17 0W
Madeira →, Brazil 92 D7 3 22S 58 45W
Madeleine, Is. de la, Canada 71 C7 47 30N 61 40W
Madera, U.S.A. 83 H3 36 57N 120 3W
Madha, India 40 L9 18 0N 75 30 E
Madhubani, India 43 F12 26 21N 86 7 E
Madhya Pradesh □, India 42 J7 21 50N 78 0 E
Madikeri, India 40 N9 12 30N 75 45 E
Madill, U.S.A. 81 H6 34 6N 96 46W
Madimba, Zaïre 52 E3 4 58S 15 5 E
Ma'din, Syria 44 C3 35 45N 39 36 E
Madīnat ash Sha'b, Yemen 46 E3 12 50N 45 0 E
Madingou, Congo 52 E2 4 10S 13 33 E
Madirovalo, Madag. 57 B8 16 26S 46 32 E
Madison, Calif., U.S.A. 84 G5 38 41N 121 59W
Madison, Fla., U.S.A. 77 K4 30 28N 83 25W
Madison, Ind., U.S.A. 76 F3 38 44N 85 23W
Madison, Nebr., U.S.A. 80 E6 41 50N 97 27W
Madison, Ohio, U.S.A. 78 E3 41 46N 81 3W
Madison, S. Dak., U.S.A. 80 D6 44 0N 97 7W
Madison, Wis., U.S.A. 80 D10 43 4N 89 24W
Madison →, U.S.A. 82 D8 45 56N 111 31W
Madisonville, Ky., U.S.A. 76 G2 37 20N 87 30W
Madisonville, Tex., U.S.A. 81 K7 30 57N 95 55W
Madista, Botswana 56 C4 21 15S 25 6 E
Madiun, Indonesia 37 G14 7 38S 111 32 E
Madley, U.K. 11 E5 52 3N 2 51W
Madras = Tamil Nadu □, India 40 P10 11 0N 77 0 E
Madras, India 40 N12 13 8N 80 19 E
Madras, U.S.A. 82 D3 44 38N 121 8W
Madre, L., Mexico 87 B5 25 0N 97 30W
Madre, Laguna, U.S.A. 81 M6 27 0N 97 30W
Madre, Sierra, Phil. 37 A6 17 0N 122 0 E
Madre de Dios →, Bolivia 92 F5 10 59S 66 8W
Madre de Dios, I., Chile 96 G1 50 20S 75 10W
Madre del Sur, Sierra, Mexico 87 D5 17 30N 100 0W
Madre Occidental, Sierra, Mexico 86 B3 27 0N 107 0W
Madre Oriental, Sierra, Mexico 86 C4 25 0N 100 0W
Madri, India 42 G5 24 16N 73 32 E
Madrid, Spain 19 B4 40 25N 3 45W
Madura, Selat, Indonesia 37 G15 7 30S 113 20 E
Madura Motel, Australia 61 F4 31 55S 127 0 E
Madurai, India 40 Q11 9 55N 78 10 E
Madurantakam, India 40 N11 12 30N 79 50 E
Mae Chan, Thailand 38 B2 20 9N 99 52 E
Mae Hong Son, Thailand 38 C2 19 16N 98 1 E
Mae Khlong →, Thailand 38 F3 13 24N 100 0 E
Mae Phrik, Thailand 38 D2 17 27N 99 7 E
Mae Ramat, Thailand 38 D2 16 58N 98 31 E
Mae Rim, Thailand 38 C2 18 54N 98 57 E
Mae Sot, Thailand 38 D2 16 43N 98 34 E
Mae Suai, Thailand 38 C2 19 39N 99 33 E
Mae Tha, Thailand 38 C2 18 28N 99 8 E
Maebashi, Japan 31 F9 36 24N 139 4 E
Maesteg, U.K. 11 F4 51 36N 3 40W
Maestra, Sierra, Cuba 88 B4 20 15N 77 0W
Maestrazgo, Mts. del, Spain 19 B5 40 30N 0 25W
Maevatanana, Madag. 57 B8 16 56S 46 49 E
Mafeking = Mafikeng, S. Africa 56 D4 25 50S 25 38 E
Mafeking, Canada 73 C8 52 40N 101 10W
Mafeteng, Lesotho 56 D4 29 51S 27 15 E
Maffra, Australia 63 F4 37 53S 146 58 E
Mafia I., Tanzania 54 D4 7 45S 39 50 E
Mafikeng, S. Africa 56 D4 25 50S 25 38 E
Mafra, Brazil 95 B6 26 10S 49 55W
Mafra, Portugal 19 C1 38 55N 9 20W
Mafungabusi Plateau, Zimbabwe 55 F2 18 30S 29 8 E
Magadan, Russia 27 D16 59 38N 150 50 E
Magadi, Kenya 54 C4 1 54S 36 19 E
Magadi, L., Kenya 54 C4 1 54S 36 19 E
Magaliesburg, S. Africa 57 D4 26 0S 27 32 E
Magallanes, Estrecho de, Chile 96 G2 52 30S 75 0W
Magangué, Colombia 92 B4 9 14N 74 45W
Magburaka, S. Leone 50 G2 8 47N 12 0W
Magdalen Is. = Madeleine, Is. de la, Canada 71 C7 47 30N 61 40W
Magdalena, Argentina 94 D4 35 5S 57 30W
Magdalena, Bolivia 92 F6 13 13S 63 57W
Magdalena, Malaysia 36 D5 4 25N 117 55 E
Magdalena, Mexico 86 A2 30 50N 112 0W
Magdalena, U.S.A. 83 J10 34 7N 107 15W
Magdalena →, Colombia 92 A4 11 6N 74 51W
Magdalena →, Mexico 86 A2 30 40N 112 25W
Magdalena, B., Mexico 86 C2 24 30N 112 10W
Magdalena, Llano de la, Mexico 86 C2 25 0N 111 30W
Magdeburg, Germany 16 B5 52 8N 11 36 E
Magdelaine Cays, Australia 62 B5 16 33S 150 18 E
Magee, U.S.A. 81 K10 31 52N 89 44W
Magee, I., U.K. 13 B6 54 48N 5 44W
Magelang, Indonesia 37 G14 7 29S 110 13 E
Magellan's Str. = Magallanes, Estrecho de, Chile 96 G2 52 30S 75 0W
Magenta, L., Australia 61 F2 33 30S 119 2 E
Maggiore, L., Italy 20 A3 46 0N 8 35 E
Magherafelt, U.K. 13 B5 54 44N 6 37W
Magnetic Pole (North) = North Magnetic Pole, Canada 4 B2 77 58N 102 8W
Magnetic Pole (South) = South Magnetic Pole, Antarctica 5 C9 64 8S 138 8 E
Magnitogorsk, Russia 24 D10 53 27N 59 4 E
Magnolia, Ark., U.S.A. 81 J8 33 16N 93 14W
Magnolia, Miss., U.S.A. 81 K9 31 9N 90 28W
Magog, Canada 71 C5 45 18N 72 9W
Magoro, Uganda 54 B3 1 45N 34 12 E
Magosa = Famagusta, Cyprus 23 D12 35 8N 33 55 E
Magouládhes, Greece 23 A3 39 45N 19 42 E
Magoye, Zambia 55 F2 16 1S 27 30 E
Magpie L., Canada 71 B7 51 0N 64 41W
Magrath, Canada 72 D6 49 25N 112 50W
Magu □, Tanzania 54 C3 2 31S 33 28 E
Maguarinho, C., Brazil 93 D9 0 15S 48 30W
Maguse L., Canada 73 A9 61 40N 95 10W
Maguse Pt., Canada 73 A10 61 20N 93 50W
Magwe, Burma 41 J19 20 10N 95 0 E
Maha Sarakham, Thailand 38 D4 16 12N 103 16 E
Mahābād, Iran 44 B5 36 50N 45 45 E
Mahabharat Lekh, Nepal 43 E9 28 30N 82 0 E
Mahabo, Madag. 57 C7 20 23S 44 40 E
Mahadeo Hills, India 42 H8 22 20N 78 30 E
Mahagi, Zaïre 54 B3 2 20N 31 0 E
Mahajamba →, Madag. 57 B8 15 33S 47 8 E
Mahajamba, Helodranon' i, Madag. 57 B8 15 24S 47 5 E
Mahajan, India 42 E5 28 48N 73 56 E
Mahajanga, Madag. 57 B8 15 40S 46 25 E
Mahajanga □, Madag. 57 B8 17 0S 47 0 E
Mahajilo →, Madag. 57 B8 19 42S 45 22 E
Mahakam →, Indonesia 36 E5 0 35S 117 17 E
Mahalapye, Botswana 56 C4 23 1S 26 51 E
Maḩallāt, Iran 45 C6 33 55N 50 30 E
Māhān, Iran 45 D8 30 5N 57 18 E
Mahanadi →, India 41 J15 20 20N 86 25 E
Mahanoro, Madag. 57 B8 19 54S 48 48 E
Mahanoy City, U.S.A. 79 F8 40 49N 76 9W
Maharashtra □, India 40 J9 20 30N 75 30 E
Mahari Mts., Tanzania 54 D2 6 20S 30 0 E
Mahasham, W. →, Egypt 47 E3 30 15N 34 10 E
Mahasolo, Madag. 57 B8 19 7S 46 22 E
Mahattat ash Shīdiyah, Jordan 47 F4 29 55N 35 55 E
Mahattat 'Unayzah, Jordan 47 E4 30 30N 35 47 E
Mahaxay, Laos 38 D5 17 22N 105 12 E
Mahbubnagar, India 40 L10 16 45N 77 59 E
Maḩḑah, Oman 45 E7 24 24N 55 59 E
Mahdia, Tunisia 51 A7 35 28N 11 0 E
Mahe, India 43 C8 33 10N 78 32 E
Mahenge, Tanzania 55 D4 8 45S 36 41 E
Maheno, N.Z. 59 L3 45 10S 170 50 E
Mahesana, India 42 H5 23 39N 72 26 E
Mahia Pen., N.Z. 59 H6 39 9S 177 55 E
Mahilyow = Mogilev, Belorussia 24 D5 53 55N 30 18 E
Mahmud Kot, Pakistan 42 D4 30 16N 71 0 E
Mahnomen, U.S.A. 80 B7 47 19N 95 58W
Mahoba, India 43 G8 25 15N 79 55 E
Mahón, Spain 22 B11 39 53N 4 16 E
Mahone Bay, Canada 71 D7 44 30N 64 20W
Mai-Ndombe, L., Zaïre 52 E3 2 0S 18 20 E
Mai-Sai, Thailand 38 B2 20 20N 99 55 E
Maicurú →, Brazil 93 D8 2 14S 54 17W
Maidan Khula, Afghan. 42 C3 33 36N 69 50 E
Maidenhead, U.K. 11 F7 51 31N 0 42W
Maidstone, Canada 73 C7 53 5N 109 20W
Maidstone, U.K. 11 F8 51 16N 0 31 E
Maiduguri, Nigeria 51 F7 12 0N 13 20 E
Maijdi, Bangla. 41 H17 22 48N 91 10 E
Maikala Ra., India 41 J12 22 0N 81 0 E
Mailsi, Pakistan 42 E5 29 48N 72 15 E
Main →, Germany 16 D4 50 0N 8 18 E
Main →, U.K. 13 B5 54 49N 6 20W
Main Centre, Canada 73 C7 50 35N 107 21W
Maine, France 18 C3 47 55N 0 25W
Maine □, U.S.A. 71 C6 45 20N 69 0W
Maine →, Ireland 13 D2 52 10N 9 40W
Maine-et-Loire □, France 18 C3 47 31N 0 30W
Maingkwan, Burma 41 F20 26 15N 96 37 E
Mainit, L., Phil. 37 C7 9 31N 125 30 E
Mainland, Orkney, U.K. 12 C5 59 0N 3 10W
Mainland, Shet., U.K. 12 A7 60 15N 1 22W
Mainpuri, India 43 F8 27 18N 79 4 E
Maintirano, Madag. 57 B7 18 3S 44 1 E
Mainz, Germany 16 D4 50 0N 8 17 E
Maipú, Argentina 94 D4 36 52S 57 50W
Maiquetía, Venezuela 92 A5 10 36N 66 57W
Mairabari, India 41 F18 26 30N 92 22 E
Maisí, Cuba 89 B5 20 17N 74 9W
Maisi, Pta. de, Cuba 89 B5 20 10N 74 10W
Maitland, N.S.W., Australia 63 E5 32 33S 151 36 E
Maitland, S. Austral., Australia 63 E2 34 23S 137 40 E
Maitland →, Canada 78 C3 43 45N 81 43W
Maiz, Is. del, Nic. 88 D3 12 15N 83 4W
Maizuru, Japan 31 G7 35 25N 135 22 E
Majalengka, Indonesia 37 G13 6 50S 108 13 E
Majene, Indonesia 37 E5 3 38S 118 57 E
Maji, Ethiopia 51 G12 6 12N 35 30 E
Major, Canada 73 C7 51 52N 109 37W
Majorca = Mallorca, Spain 22 B10 39 30N 3 0 E
Maka, Senegal 50 F2 13 40N 14 10W
Makale, Indonesia 37 E5 3 6S 119 51 E
Makamba, Burundi 54 C2 4 8S 29 49 E
Makari, Cameroon 52 B2 12 35N 14 28 E
Makarikari = Makgadikgadi Salt Pans, Botswana 56 C4 20 40S 25 45 E
Makarovo, Russia 27 D11 57 40N 107 45 E
Makasar = Ujung Pandang, Indonesia 37 F5 5 10S 119 20 E
Makasar, Selat, Indonesia 37 E5 1 0S 118 20 E
Makasar, Str. of = Makasar, Selat, Indonesia 37 E5 1 0S 118 20 E
Makat, Kazakhstan 25 E9 47 39N 53 19 E
Makedhonía □, Greece 21 D10 40 39N 22 0 E
Makedonija = Macedonia ■, Europe 21 D9 41 53N 21 40 E
Makena, U.S.A. 74 H16 20 39N 156 27W
Makeni, S. Leone 50 G2 8 55N 12 5W
Makeyevka, Ukraine 25 E6 48 0N 38 0 E
Makgadikgadi Salt Pans, Botswana 56 C4 20 40S 25 45 E
Makhachkala, Russia 25 F8 43 0N 47 30 E
Makhmūr, Iraq 44 C4 35 46N 43 35 E
Makian, Indonesia 37 D7 0 20N 127 20 E
Makindu, Kenya 54 C4 2 18S 37 50 E
Makinsk, Kazakhstan 26 D8 52 37N 70 26 E
Makiyivka = Makeyevka, Ukraine 25 E6 48 0N 38 0 E
Makkah, Si. Arabia 46 C2 21 30N 39 54 E
Makkovik, Canada 71 A8 55 10N 59 10W
Makó, Hungary 17 E10 46 14N 20 33 E
Makokou, Gabon 52 D2 0 40N 12 50 E
Makongo, Zaïre 54 B2 3 25N 26 17 E
Makoro, Zaïre 54 B2 3 10N 29 59 E
Makoua, Congo 52 E3 0 5S 15 50 E
Makrai, India 40 H10 22 2N 77 0 E
Makran Coast Range, Pakistan 40 G4 25 40N 64 0 E
Makrana, India 42 F6 27 2N 74 46 E
Makriyialos, Greece 23 D7 35 2N 25 59 E
Maksimkin Yar, Russia 26 D9 58 42N 86 50 E
Mākū, Iran 44 B5 39 15N 44 31 E
Makumbi, Zaïre 52 F4 5 50S 20 43 E
Makunda, Botswana 56 C3 22 30S 20 7 E
Makurazaki, Japan 31 J5 31 15N 130 20 E
Makurdi, Nigeria 50 G6 7 43N 8 35 E
Makūyeh, Iran 45 D7 28 7N 53 9 E
Makwassie, S. Africa 56 D4 27 17S 26 0 E
Mal B., Ireland 13 D2 52 50N 9 30W
Mala, Pta., Panama 88 E3 7 28N 80 2W
Malabang, Phil. 37 C6 7 36N 124 3 E
Malabar Coast, India 40 P9 11 0N 75 0 E
Malabo = Rey Malabo, Eq. Guin. 50 H6 3 45N 8 50 E
Malacca, Str. of, Indonesia 39 L3 3 0N 101 0 E
Malad City, U.S.A. 82 E7 42 12N 112 15W
Málaga, Spain 19 D3 36 43N 4 23W
Malaga, U.S.A. 81 J2 32 14N 104 4W
Málaga □, Spain 19 D3 36 38N 4 58W
Malagarasi, Tanzania 54 D3 5 5S 30 50 E
Malagarasi →, Tanzania 54 D2 5 12S 29 47 E
Malaimbandy, Madag. 57 C8 20 20S 45 36 E
Malakâl, Sudan 51 G11 9 33N 31 40 E
Malakand, Pakistan 42 B4 34 40N 71 55 E
Malakoff, U.S.A. 81 J7 32 10N 96 1W
Malamyzh, Russia 27 E14 49 50N 136 50 E
Malang, Indonesia 37 G15 7 59S 112 45 E
Malanje, Angola 52 F3 9 36S 16 17 E
Mälaren, Sweden 9 G14 59 30N 17 10 E
Malargüe, Argentina 94 D2 35 32S 69 30W
Malartic, Canada 70 C4 48 9N 78 9W
Malatya, Turkey 25 G6 38 25N 38 20 E
Malawi ■, Africa 55 E3 11 55S 34 0 E
Malawi, L., Africa 55 E3 12 30S 34 30 E
Malay Pen., Asia 39 J3 7 25N 100 0 E
Malaybalay, Phil. 37 C7 8 5N 125 7 E
Malāyer, Iran 45 C6 34 19N 48 51 E
Malaysia ■, Asia 36 D4 5 0N 110 0 E
Malazgirt, Turkey 25 G7 39 10N 42 33 E
Malbon, Australia 62 C3 21 5S 140 17 E
Malbooma, Australia 63 E1 30 41S 134 11 E
Malbork, Poland 17 A9 54 3N 19 1 E
Malcolm, Australia 61 E3 28 51S 121 25 E
Malcolm, Pt., Australia 61 F3 33 48S 123 45 E
Maldegem, Belgium 15 C3 51 14N 3 26 E
Malden, Mass., U.S.A. 79 D13 42 26N 71 4W
Malden, Mo., U.S.A. 81 G10 36 34N 89 57W
Malden I., Kiribati 65 H12 4 3S 155 1W
Maldives ■, Ind. Oc. 29 J11 5 0N 73 0 E
Maldonado, Uruguay 95 C5 34 59S 55 0W
Maldonado, Punta, Mexico 87 D5 16 19N 98 35W
Malé Karpaty, Slovakia 16 D8 48 30N 17 20 E
Maléa, Ákra, Greece 21 F10 36 28N 23 7 E
Malebo, Pool, Africa 48 G5 4 17S 15 20 E
Malegaon, India 40 J9 20 30N 74 38 E
Malei, Mozam. 55 F4 17 12S 36 58 E
Malek Kandī, Iran 44 B5 37 9N 46 6 E
Malela, Zaïre 54 C2 4 22S 26 8 E
Malema, Mozam. 55 E4 14 57S 37 20 E
Máleme, Greece 23 D5 35 31N 23 49 E
Malerkotla, India 42 D6 30 32N 75 58 E
Máles, Greece 23 D7 35 6N 25 35 E
Malgomaj, Sweden 8 D14 64 40N 16 30 E
Malha, Sudan 51 E10 15 8N 25 10 E
Malhão, Sa. do, Portugal 19 D1 37 25N 8 0W
Malheur →, U.S.A. 82 D5 44 4N 116 59W
Malheur L., U.S.A. 82 E4 43 20N 118 48W
Mali ■, Africa 50 E4 17 0N 3 0W
Mali →, Burma 41 G20 25 40N 97 40 E
Malibu, U.S.A. 85 L8 34 2N 118 41W
Malik, Indonesia 37 E6 0 39S 123 16 E
Malili, Indonesia 37 E6 2 42S 121 6 E
Malimba, Mts., Zaïre 54 D2 7 30S 29 30 E
Malin Hd., Ireland 13 A4 55 18N 7 24W
Malindi, Kenya 54 C5 3 12S 40 5 E
Malines = Mechelen, Belgium 15 C4 51 2N 4 29 E
Maling, Indonesia 37 D6 1 0N 121 0 E
Malinyi, Tanzania 55 D4 8 56S 36 0 E
Malita, Phil. 37 C7 6 19N 125 39 E

Mallacoota

140

Medicine Bow Ra.

Markazī □, Iran **45 C6** 35 0N 49 30 E
Markdale, Canada **78 B4** 44 19N 80 39W
Marked Tree, U.S.A. **81 H9** 35 32N 90 25W
Marken, Neths. **15 B5** 52 26N 5 12 E
Market Drayton, U.K. **10 E5** 52 55N 2 30W
Market Harborough, U.K. **11 E7** 52 29N 0 55W
Markham, Canada **78 C5** 43 52N 79 16W
Markham, Mt., Antarctica **5 E11** 83 0S 164 0 E
Markham L., Canada **73 A8** 62 30N 102 35W
Markleeville, U.S.A. **84 G7** 38 42N 119 47W
Markovo, Russia **27 C17** 64 40N 169 40 E
Marks, Russia **24 D8** 51 45N 46 50 E
Marksville, U.S.A. **81 K8** 31 8N 92 4W
Marla, Australia **63 D1** 27 19S 133 33 E
Marlboro, U.S.A. **79 D13** 42 19N 71 33W
Marlborough, Australia **62 C4** 22 46S 149 52 E
Marlborough Downs, U.K. **11 F6** 51 25N 1 55W
Marlin, U.S.A. **81 K6** 31 18N 96 54W
Marlow, U.S.A. **81 H6** 34 39N 97 58W
Marmagao, India **40 M8** 15 25N 73 56 E
Marmara, Turkey **21 D12** 40 35N 27 38 E
Marmara, Sea of = Marmara Denizi, Turkey **21 D13** 40 45N 28 15 E
Marmara Denizi, Turkey **21 D13** 40 45N 28 15 E
Marmarth, U.S.A. **80 B3** 46 18N 103 54W
Marmion, Mt., Australia **61 E2** 29 16S 119 50 E
Marmion L., Canada **70 C1** 48 55N 91 20W
Marmolada, Mte., Italy **20 A4** 46 25N 11 55 E
Marmora, Canada **70 D4** 44 28N 77 41W
Marne □, France **18 B6** 48 50N 4 10 E
Marne →, France **18 B5** 48 48N 2 24 E
Maroala, Madag. **57 B8** 15 23S 47 59 E
Maroantsetra, Madag. **57 B8** 15 26S 49 44 E
Maromandia, Madag. **57 A8** 14 13S 48 5 E
Marondera, Zimbabwe **55 F3** 18 5S 31 42 E
Maroni →, Fr. Guiana **93 B8** 5 30N 54 0W
Maroochydore, Australia **63 D5** 26 29S 153 5 E
Maroona, Australia **63 F3** 37 27S 142 54 E
Marosakoa, Madag. **57 B8** 15 26S 46 38 E
Maroua, Cameroon **51 F7** 10 40N 14 20 E
Marovoay, Madag. **57 B8** 16 6S 46 39 E
Marquard, S. Africa **56 D4** 28 40S 27 28 E
Marquesas Is. = Marquises, Is., Pac. Oc. **65 H14** 9 30S 140 0W
Marquette, U.S.A. **76 B2** 46 33N 87 24W
Marquises, Is., Pac. Oc. **65 H14** 9 30S 140 0W
Marracuene, Mozam. **57 D5** 25 45S 32 35 E
Marrakech, Morocco **50 B3** 31 9N 8 0W
Marrawah, Australia **62 G3** 40 55S 144 42 E
Marree, Australia **63 D2** 29 39S 138 1 E
Marrilla, Australia **60 D1** 22 31S 114 25 E
Marrimane, Mozam. **57 C5** 22 58S 33 34 E
Marromeu, Mozam. **57 B6** 18 15S 36 25 E
Marrowie Cr. →, Australia **63 E4** 33 23S 145 40 E
Marrubane, Mozam. **55 F4** 18 0S 37 0 E
Marrupa, Mozam. **55 E4** 13 8S 37 30 E
Marsá Matrûh, Egypt **51 B10** 31 19N 27 9 E
Marsá Susah, Libya **51 B9** 32 52N 21 59 E
Marsabit, Kenya **54 B4** 2 18N 38 0 E
Marsabit □, Kenya **54 B4** 2 45N 37 45 E
Marsala, Italy **20 F5** 37 48N 12 25 E
Marsalforn, Malta **23 C1** 36 4N 14 15 E
Marsden, Australia **63 E4** 33 47S 147 32 E
Marseille, France **18 E6** 43 18N 5 23 E
Marseilles = Marseille, France **18 E6** 43 18N 5 23 E
Marsh I., U.S.A. **81 L9** 29 34N 91 53W
Marsh L., U.S.A. **80 C6** 45 5N 96 0W
Marshall, Liberia **50 G2** 6 8N 10 22W
Marshall, Ark., U.S.A. **81 H8** 35 55N 92 38W
Marshall, Mich., U.S.A. **76 D3** 42 16N 84 58W
Marshall, Minn., U.S.A. **80 C7** 44 25N 95 45W
Marshall, Mo., U.S.A. **80 F8** 39 7N 93 12W
Marshall, Tex., U.S.A. **81 J7** 32 33N 94 23W
Marshall →, Australia **62 C2** 22 59S 136 59 E
Marshall Is. ■, Pac. Oc. **64 G9** 9 0N 171 0 E
Marshalltown, U.S.A. **80 D8** 42 3N 92 55W
Marshfield, Mo., U.S.A. **81 G8** 37 15N 92 54W
Marshfield, Wis., U.S.A. **80 C9** 44 40N 90 10W
Marshūn, Iran **45 B6** 36 19N 49 23 E
Marstrand, Sweden **9 H11** 57 53N 11 35 E
Mart, U.S.A. **81 K6** 31 33N 96 50W
Martaban, Burma **41 L20** 16 30N 97 35 E
Martaban, G. of, Burma **41 L20** 16 5N 96 30 E
Martapura, Kalimantan, Indonesia **36 E4** 3 22S 114 47 E
Martapura, Sumatera, Indonesia **36 E2** 4 19S 104 22 E
Marte, Nigeria **51 F7** 12 23N 13 46 E
Martelange, Belgium **15 E5** 49 49N 5 43 E
Martha's Vineyard, U.S.A. **79 E14** 41 25N 70 38W
Martin, S. Dak., U.S.A. **80 D4** 43 11N 101 44W
Martin, Tenn., U.S.A. **81 G10** 36 21N 88 51W
Martin L., U.S.A. **77 J3** 32 41N 85 55W
Martinborough, N.Z. **59 J5** 41 14S 175 29 E
Martinez, U.S.A. **84 G4** 38 1N 122 8W
Martinique ■, W. Indies **89 D7** 14 40N 61 0W
Martinique Passage, W. Indies **89 C7** 15 15N 61 0W
Martinópolis, Brazil **95 A5** 22 11S 51 12W
Martins Ferry, U.S.A. **78 F4** 40 6N 80 44W
Martinsburg, Pa., U.S.A. **78 F6** 40 19N 78 20W
Martinsburg, W. Va., U.S.A. **76 F7** 39 27N 77 58W
Martinsville, Ind., U.S.A. **76 F2** 39 26N 86 25W
Martinsville, Va., U.S.A. **77 G6** 36 41N 79 52W
Marton, N.Z. **59 J5** 40 4S 175 23 E
Martos, Spain **19 D4** 37 44N 3 58W
Marudi, Malaysia **36 D4** 4 11N 114 19 E
Ma'ruf, Afghan. **40 D5** 31 30N 67 6 E
Marugame, Japan **31 G6** 34 15N 133 40 E
Marulan, Australia **63 E5** 34 43S 150 3 E
Marunga, Angola **56 B3** 17 28S 20 2 E
Marungu, Mts., Zaïre **54 D2** 7 30S 30 0 E
Marvast, Iran **45 D7** 30 30N 54 15 E
Marwar, India **42 G5** 25 43N 73 45 E
Mary, Turkmenistan **26 F7** 37 40N 61 50 E
Mary Frances L., Canada **73 A7** 63 19N 106 13W
Mary Kathleen, Australia **62 C2** 20 44S 139 48 E
Maryborough = Port Laoise, Ireland **13 C4** 53 2N 7 20W
Maryborough, Queens., Australia **63 D5** 25 31S 152 37 E
Maryborough, Vic., Australia **63 F3** 37 0S 143 44 E
Maryfield, Canada **73 D8** 49 50N 101 35W
Maryland □, U.S.A. **76 F7** 39 0N 76 30W
Maryland Junction, Zimbabwe **55 F3** 17 45S 30 31 E
Maryport, U.K. **10 C4** 54 43N 3 30W
Mary's Harbour, Canada **71 B8** 52 18N 55 51W
Marystown, Canada **71 C8** 47 10N 55 10W
Marysvale, U.S.A. **83 G7** 38 27N 112 14W
Marysville, Canada **72 D5** 49 35N 116 0W
Marysville, Calif., U.S.A. **84 F5** 39 9N 121 35W
Marysville, Kans., U.S.A. **80 F6** 39 51N 96 39W
Marysville, Mich., U.S.A. **78 D2** 42 54N 82 29W
Marysville, Ohio, U.S.A. **76 E4** 40 14N 83 22W
Marysville, Wash., U.S.A. **84 B4** 48 3N 122 11W
Maryvale, Australia **63 D5** 28 4S 152 12 E
Maryville, U.S.A. **77 H4** 35 46N 83 58W
Marzūq, Libya **51 C7** 25 53N 13 57 E
Masahunga, Tanzania **54 C3** 2 6S 33 18 E
Masai, Malaysia **39 M4** 1 29N 103 55 E
Masai Steppe, Tanzania **54 C4** 4 30S 36 30 E
Masaka, Uganda **54 C3** 0 21S 31 45 E
Masalembo, Kepulauan, Indonesia **36 F4** 5 35S 114 30 E
Masalima, Kepulauan, Indonesia **36 F5** 5 4S 117 5 E
Masamba, Indonesia **37 E6** 2 30S 120 15 E
Masan, S. Korea **35 G15** 35 11N 128 32 E
Masasi, Tanzania **55 E4** 10 45S 38 52 E
Masasi □, Tanzania **55 E4** 10 45S 38 50 E
Masaya, Nic. **88 D2** 12 0N 86 7W
Masbate, Phil. **37 B6** 12 21N 123 36 E
Mascara, Algeria **50 A5** 35 26N 0 6 E
Mascota, Mexico **86 C4** 20 30N 104 50W
Masela, Indonesia **37 F7** 8 9S 129 51 E
Maseru, Lesotho **56 D4** 29 18S 27 30 E
Mashaba, Zimbabwe **55 G3** 20 2S 30 29 E
Mashābih, Si. Arabia **44 E3** 25 35N 36 30 E
Masherbrum, Pakistan **43 B7** 35 38N 76 18 E
Mashhad, Iran **45 B8** 36 20N 59 35 E
Mashīz, Iran **45 D8** 29 56N 56 37 E
Mashkel, Hamun-i-, Pakistan **40 E3** 28 30N 63 0 E
Mashki Chāh, Pakistan **40 E3** 29 5N 62 30 E
Mashonaland Central □, Zimbabwe **57 B5** 17 30S 31 0 E
Mashonaland East □, Zimbabwe **57 B5** 18 0S 32 0 E
Mashonaland West □, Zimbabwe **57 B4** 17 30S 29 30 E
Masi, Norway **8 B17** 69 26N 23 40 E
Masi Manimba, Zaïre **52 E3** 4 40S 17 54 E
Masindi, Uganda **54 B3** 1 40N 31 43 E
Masindi Port, Uganda **54 B3** 1 43N 32 2 E
Masisea, Peru **92 E4** 8 35S 74 22W
Masisi, Zaïre **54 C2** 1 23S 28 49 E
Masjed Soleyman, Iran **45 D6** 31 55N 49 18 E
Mask, L., Ireland **13 C2** 53 36N 9 24W
Masoala, Tanjon' i, Madag. **57 B9** 15 59S 50 13 E
Masoarivo, Madag. **57 B7** 19 3S 44 19 E
Masohi, Indonesia **37 E7** 3 20S 128 55 E
Masomeloka, Madag. **57 C8** 20 17S 48 37 E
Mason, Nev., U.S.A. **84 G7** 38 56N 119 8W
Mason, Tex., U.S.A. **81 K5** 30 45N 99 14W
Mason City, U.S.A. **80 D8** 43 9N 93 12W
Maspalomas, Canary Is. **22 G4** 27 46N 15 35W
Maspalomas, Pta., Canary Is. **22 G4** 27 43N 15 36W
Masqat, Oman **46 C6** 23 37N 58 36 E
Massa, Italy **20 B4** 44 2N 10 7 E
Massachusetts □, U.S.A. **79 D12** 42 30N 72 0W
Massachusetts B., U.S.A. **79 D14** 42 20N 70 50W
Massaguet, Chad **51 F8** 12 28N 15 26 E
Massakory, Chad **51 F8** 13 0N 15 49 E
Massanella, Spain **22 B9** 39 48N 2 51 E
Massangena, Mozam. **57 C5** 21 34S 33 0 E
Massawa = Mitsiwa, Eritrea **51 E12** 15 35N 39 25 E
Massena, U.S.A. **79 B10** 44 56N 74 54W
Massénya, Chad **51 F8** 11 21N 16 9 E
Masset, Canada **72 C2** 54 2N 132 10W
Massif Central, France **18 D5** 44 55N 3 0 E
Massillon, U.S.A. **78 F3** 40 48N 81 32W
Massinga, Mozam. **57 C6** 23 15S 35 22 E
Masson, Canada **79 A9** 45 32N 75 25W
Masson I., Antarctica **5 C7** 66 10S 93 20 E
Masterton, N.Z. **59 J5** 40 56S 175 39 E
Mastuj, Pakistan **43 A5** 36 20N 72 36 E
Mastung, Pakistan **40 E5** 29 50N 66 56 E
Masuda, Japan **31 G5** 34 40N 131 51 E
Masvingo, Zimbabwe **55 G3** 20 8S 30 49 E
Masvingo □, Zimbabwe **55 G3** 21 0S 31 30 E
Maswa □, Tanzania **54 C3** 3 30S 34 0 E
Maşyāf, Syria **44 C3** 35 4N 36 20 E
Matabeleland North □, Zimbabwe **55 F2** 19 0S 28 0 E
Matabeleland South □, Zimbabwe **55 G2** 21 0S 29 0 E
Mataboor, Indonesia **37 E9** 1 41S 138 3 E
Matachewan, Canada **70 C3** 47 56N 80 39W
Matadi, Zaïre **52 F2** 5 52S 13 31 E
Matagalpa, Nic. **88 D2** 13 0N 85 58W
Matagami, Canada **70 C4** 49 45N 77 34W
Matagami, L., Canada **70 C4** 49 50N 77 40W
Matagorda, U.S.A. **81 L7** 28 42N 95 58W
Matagorda B., U.S.A. **81 L6** 28 40N 96 0W
Matagorda I., U.S.A. **81 L6** 28 15N 96 30W
Matak, P., Indonesia **39 L6** 3 18N 106 16 E
Matakana, Australia **63 E4** 32 59S 145 54 E
Mátala, Greece **23 E6** 34 59N 24 45 E
Matam, Senegal **50 E2** 15 34N 13 17W
Matamoros, Campeche, Mexico **87 D6** 18 50N 90 50W
Matamoros, Coahuila, Mexico **86 B4** 25 33N 103 15W
Matamoros, Puebla, Mexico **87 D5** 18 2N 98 17W
Matamoros, Tamaulipas, Mexico **87 B5** 25 50N 97 30W
Ma'ţan as Sarra, Libya **51 D9** 21 45N 22 0 E
Matandu →, Tanzania **55 D3** 8 45S 34 19 E
Matane, Canada **71 C6** 48 50N 67 33W
Matanzas, Cuba **88 B3** 23 0N 81 40W
Matapan, C. = Taínaron, Ákra, Greece **21 F10** 36 22N 22 27 E
Matapédia, Canada **71 C6** 48 0N 66 59W
Matara, Sri Lanka **40 S12** 5 58N 80 30 E
Mataram, Indonesia **36 F5** 8 41S 116 10 E
Matarani, Peru **92 G4** 17 0S 72 10W
Mataranka, Australia **60 B5** 14 55S 133 4 E
Matarma, Râs, Egypt **47 E1** 30 27N 32 44 E
Matatiele, S. Africa **57 E4** 30 20S 28 49 E
Mataura, N.Z. **59 M2** 46 11S 168 51 E
Matehuala, Mexico **86 C4** 23 40N 100 40W
Mateke Hills, Zimbabwe **55 G3** 21 48S 31 0 E
Matera, Italy **20 D7** 40 40N 16 37 E
Matetsi, Zimbabwe **55 F2** 18 12S 26 0 E
Matheson Island, Canada **73 C9** 51 45N 96 56W
Mathis, U.S.A. **81 L6** 28 6N 97 50W
Mathura, India **42 F7** 27 30N 77 40 E
Mati, Phil. **37 C7** 6 55N 126 15 E
Matías Romero, Mexico **87 D5** 16 53N 95 2W
Matibane, Mozam. **55 E5** 14 49S 40 45 E
Matima, Botswana **56 C3** 20 15S 24 26 E
Matiri Ra., N.Z. **59 J4** 41 38S 172 20 E
Matlock, U.K. **10 D6** 53 8N 1 32W
Matmata, Tunisia **50 B6** 33 37N 9 59 E
Mato Grosso □, Brazil **93 F8** 14 0S 55 0W
Mato Grosso, Planalto do, Brazil **93 G8** 15 0S 55 0W
Mato Grosso do Sul □, Brazil **93 G8** 18 0S 55 0W
Matochkin Shar, Russia **26 B6** 73 10N 56 40 E
Matopo Hills, Zimbabwe **55 G2** 20 36S 28 20 E
Matopos, Zimbabwe **55 G2** 20 20S 28 29 E
Matosinhos, Portugal **19 B1** 41 11N 8 42W
Matsue, Japan **31 G6** 35 25N 133 10 E
Matsumae, Japan **30 D10** 41 26N 140 7 E
Matsumoto, Japan **31 F9** 36 15N 138 0 E
Matsusaka, Japan **31 G8** 34 34N 136 32 E
Matsuura, Japan **31 H4** 33 20N 129 49 E
Matsuyama, Japan **31 H6** 33 45N 132 45 E
Mattagami →, Canada **70 B3** 50 43N 81 29W
Mattancheri, India **40 Q10** 9 50N 76 15 E
Mattawa, Canada **70 C4** 46 20N 78 45W
Mattawamkeag, U.S.A. **71 C6** 45 32N 68 21W
Matterhorn, Switz. **16 F3** 45 58N 7 39 E
Matthew Town, Bahamas **89 B5** 20 57N 73 40W
Matthew's Ridge, Guyana **92 B6** 7 37N 60 10W
Mattice, Canada **70 C3** 49 40N 83 20W
Mattituck, U.S.A. **79 F12** 40 59N 72 32W
Matuba, Mozam. **57 C5** 24 28S 32 49 E
Matucana, Peru **92 F3** 11 55S 76 25W
Matun, Afghan. **42 C3** 33 22N 69 58 E
Maturín, Venezuela **92 B6** 9 45N 63 11W
Mau, India **43 G10** 25 56N 83 33 E
Mau Escarpment, Kenya **54 C4** 0 40S 36 0 E
Mau Ranipur, India **43 G8** 25 16N 79 8 E
Maud, Pt., Australia **60 D1** 23 6S 113 45 E
Maude, Australia **63 E3** 34 29S 144 18 E
Maudin Sun, Burma **41 M19** 16 0N 94 30 E
Maués, Brazil **92 D7** 3 20S 57 45W
Mauganj, India **41 G12** 24 50N 81 55 E
Maui, U.S.A. **74 H16** 20 48N 156 20W
Maulamyaing = Moulmein, Burma **41 L20** 16 30N 97 40 E
Maule □, Chile **94 D1** 36 5S 72 30W
Maumee, U.S.A. **76 E4** 41 34N 83 39W
Maumee →, U.S.A. **76 E4** 41 42N 83 28W
Maumere, Indonesia **37 F6** 8 38S 122 13 E
Maun, Botswana **56 B3** 20 0S 23 26 E
Mauna Kea, U.S.A. **74 J17** 19 50N 155 28W
Mauna Loa, U.S.A. **74 J17** 19 30N 155 35W
Maungmagan Kyunzu, Burma **41 M20** 14 0N 97 48 E
Maupin, U.S.A. **82 D3** 45 11N 121 5W
Maurepas, L., U.S.A. **81 K9** 30 15N 90 30W
Maures, France **18 E7** 43 15N 6 15 E
Maurice, L., Australia **61 E5** 29 30S 131 0 E
Mauritania ■, Africa **50 D3** 20 50N 10 0W
Mauritius ■, Ind. Oc. **49 J9** 20 0S 57 0 E
Mauston, U.S.A. **80 D9** 43 48N 90 5W
Mavinga, Angola **53 H4** 15 50S 20 21 E
Mavli, India **42 G5** 24 45N 73 55 E
Mavuradonha Mts., Zimbabwe **55 F3** 16 30S 31 30 E
Mawa, Zaïre **54 B2** 2 45N 26 40 E
Mawana, India **42 E7** 29 6N 77 58 E
Mawand, Pakistan **42 E3** 29 33N 68 38 E
Mawk Mai, Burma **41 J20** 20 14N 97 37 E
Mawlaik, Burma **41 H19** 23 40N 94 26 E
Mawqiq, Si. Arabia **44 E4** 27 25N 41 8 E
Mawson Coast, Antarctica **5 C6** 68 30S 63 0 E
Max, U.S.A. **80 B4** 47 49N 101 18W
Maxcanú, Mexico **87 C6** 20 40N 92 0W
Maxesibeni, S. Africa **57 E4** 30 49S 29 23 E
Maxhamish L., Canada **72 B4** 59 50N 123 17W
Maxixe, Mozam. **57 C6** 23 54S 35 17 E
Maxville, Canada **79 A10** 45 17N 74 51W
Maxwell, U.S.A. **84 F4** 39 17N 122 11W
Maxwelton, Australia **62 C3** 20 43S 142 41 E
May Downs, Australia **62 C4** 22 38S 148 55 E
May Pen, Jamaica **88 C4** 17 58N 77 15W
Maya →, Russia **27 D14** 60 28N 134 28 E
Maya Mts., Belize **87 D7** 16 30N 89 0W
Mayaguana, Bahamas **89 B5** 22 30N 72 44W
Mayagüez, Puerto Rico **89 C6** 18 12N 67 9W
Mayāmey, Iran **45 B7** 36 24N 55 42 E
Mayarí, Cuba **89 B4** 20 40N 75 41W
Maybell, U.S.A. **82 F9** 40 31N 108 5W
Maydān, Iraq **44 C5** 34 55N 45 37 E
Maydena, Australia **62 G4** 42 45S 146 30 E
Mayenne, France **18 B3** 48 20N 0 38W
Mayenne □, France **18 B3** 48 10N 0 40W
Mayer, U.S.A. **83 J7** 34 24N 112 14W
Mayerthorpe, Canada **72 C5** 53 57N 115 8W
Mayfield, U.S.A. **77 G1** 36 44N 88 38W
Mayhill, U.S.A. **83 K11** 32 53N 105 29W
Maykop, Russia **25 F7** 44 35N 40 10 E
Maymyo, Burma **38 A1** 22 2N 96 28 E
Maynard, U.S.A. **84 C4** 47 59N 122 55W
Maynard Hills, Australia **61 E2** 28 28S 119 49 E
Mayne →, Australia **62 C3** 23 40S 141 55 E
Maynooth, Ireland **13 C5** 53 22N 6 38W
Mayo, Canada **68 B6** 63 38N 135 57W
Mayo □, Ireland **13 C2** 53 47N 9 7W
Mayo L., Canada **68 B6** 63 45N 135 0W
Mayon Volcano, Phil. **37 B6** 13 15N 123 41 E
Mayor I., N.Z. **59 G6** 37 16S 176 17 E
Mayson L., Canada **73 B7** 57 55N 107 10W
Maysville, U.S.A. **76 F4** 38 39N 83 46W
Mayu, Indonesia **37 D7** 1 30N 126 30 E
Mayville, N. Dak., U.S.A. **80 B6** 47 30N 97 20W
Mayville, N.Y., U.S.A. **78 D5** 42 15N 79 30W
Mayya, Russia **27 C14** 61 44N 130 18 E
Mazabuka, Zambia **55 F2** 15 52S 27 44 E
Mazagán = El Jadida, Morocco **50 B3** 33 11N 8 17W
Mazagão, Brazil **93 D8** 0 7S 51 16W
Mazán, Peru **92 D4** 3 30S 73 0W
Māzandarān □, Iran **45 B7** 36 30N 52 0 E
Mazapil, Mexico **86 C4** 24 38N 101 34W
Mazarredo, Argentina **96 F3** 47 10S 66 50W
Mazarrón, Spain **19 D5** 37 38N 1 19W
Mazaruni →, Guyana **92 B7** 6 25N 58 35W
Mazatán, Mexico **86 B2** 29 0N 110 8W
Mazatenango, Guatemala **88 D1** 14 35N 91 30W
Mazatlán, Mexico **86 C3** 23 10N 106 30W
Māzhān, Iran **45 C8** 32 30N 59 0 E
Mazīnān, Iran **45 B8** 36 19N 56 56 E
Mazoe, Mozam. **55 F3** 16 42S 33 7 E
Mazoe →, Mozam. **55 F3** 16 20S 33 30 E
Mazowe, Zimbabwe **55 F3** 17 28S 30 58 E
Mazurian Lakes = Mazurski, Pojezierze, Poland **17 B10** 53 50N 21 0 E
Mazurski, Pojezierze, Poland **17 B10** 53 50N 21 0 E
Mbabane, Swaziland **57 D5** 26 18S 31 6 E
Mbaïki, C.A.R. **52 D3** 3 53N 18 1 E
Mbala, Zambia **55 D3** 8 46S 31 24 E
Mbale, Uganda **54 B3** 1 8N 34 12 E
Mbalmayo, Cameroon **52 D2** 3 33N 11 33 E
Mbamba Bay, Tanzania **55 E3** 11 13S 34 49 E
Mbandaka, Zaïre **52 D3** 0 1N 18 18 E
Mbanza Congo, Angola **52 F2** 6 18S 14 16 E
Mbanza Ngungu, Zaïre **52 F2** 5 12S 14 53 E
Mbarara, Uganda **54 C3** 0 35S 30 40 E
Mbashe →, S. Africa **57 E4** 32 15S 28 54 E
Mbenkuru →, Tanzania **55 D4** 9 25S 39 50 E
Mberengwa, Zimbabwe **55 G2** 20 29S 29 57 E
Mberengwa, Mt., Zimbabwe **55 G2** 20 37S 29 55 E
Mbesuma, Zambia **55 D3** 10 0S 32 2 E
Mbeya, Tanzania **55 D3** 8 54S 33 29 E
Mbeya □, Tanzania **54 D3** 8 15S 33 30 E
Mbinga, Tanzania **55 E4** 10 50S 35 0 E
Mbinga □, Tanzania **55 E3** 10 50S 35 0 E
Mbini □, Eq. Guin. **52 D2** 1 30N 10 0 E
Mbour, Senegal **50 F1** 14 22N 16 54W
Mbout, Mauritania **50 E2** 16 1N 12 38W
Mbozi □, Tanzania **55 D3** 9 0S 32 50 E
Mbuji-Mayi, Zaïre **54 D1** 6 9S 23 40 E
Mbulu, Tanzania **54 C4** 3 45S 35 30 E
Mbulu □, Tanzania **54 C4** 3 52S 35 33 E
Mburucuyá, Argentina **94 B4** 28 1S 58 14W
Mchinja, Tanzania **55 D4** 9 44S 39 45 E
Mchinji, Malawi **55 E3** 13 47S 32 58 E
Mead, L., U.S.A. **85 J12** 36 1N 114 44W
Meade, U.S.A. **81 G4** 37 17N 100 20W
Meadow, Australia **61 E1** 26 35S 114 40 E
Meadow Lake, Canada **73 C7** 54 10N 108 26W
Meadow Lake Prov. Park, Canada **73 C7** 54 27N 109 0W
Meadow Valley Wash →, U.S.A. **85 J12** 36 40N 114 34W
Meadville, U.S.A. **78 E4** 41 39N 80 9W
Meaford, Canada **70 D3** 44 36N 80 35W
Mealy Mts., Canada **71 B8** 53 10N 58 0W
Meander River, Canada **72 B5** 59 2N 117 42W
Meares, C., U.S.A. **82 D2** 45 37N 124 0W
Mearim →, Brazil **93 D10** 3 4S 44 35W
Meath □, Ireland **13 C5** 53 32N 6 40W
Meath Park, Canada **73 C7** 53 27N 105 22W
Meaux, France **18 B5** 48 58N 2 50 E
Mebechi-Gawa →, Japan **30 D10** 40 31N 141 31 E
Mecanhelas, Mozam. **55 F4** 15 12S 35 54 E
Mecca = Makkah, Si. Arabia **46 C2** 21 30N 39 54 E
Mecca, U.S.A. **85 M10** 33 34N 116 5W
Mechanicsburg, U.S.A. **78 F8** 40 13N 77 1W
Mechanicville, U.S.A. **79 D11** 42 54N 73 41W
Mechelen, Belgium **15 C4** 51 2N 4 29 E
Mecheria, Algeria **50 B4** 33 35N 0 18W
Mecklenburger Bucht, Germany **16 A5** 54 20N 11 40 E
Meconta, Mozam. **55 E4** 14 59S 39 50 E
Meda, Australia **60 C3** 17 22S 123 59 E
Medan, Indonesia **36 D1** 3 40N 98 38 E
Medanosa, Pta., Argentina **96 F3** 48 8S 66 0W
Medéa, Algeria **50 A5** 36 12N 2 50 E
Medellín, Colombia **92 B3** 6 15N 75 35W
Medemblik, Neths. **15 B5** 52 46N 5 8 E
Mederdra, Mauritania **50 E1** 17 0N 15 38W
Medford, Mass., U.S.A. **79 D13** 42 25N 71 7W
Medford, Oreg., U.S.A. **82 E2** 42 19N 122 52W
Medford, Wis., U.S.A. **80 C9** 45 9N 90 20W
Media Agua, Argentina **94 C2** 31 58S 68 25W
Media Luna, Argentina **94 C2** 34 45S 66 44W
Mediaş, Romania **17 E12** 46 9N 24 22 E
Medical Lake, U.S.A. **82 C5** 47 34N 117 41W
Medicine Bow, U.S.A. **82 F10** 41 54N 106 12W
Medicine Bow Pk., U.S.A. **82 F10** 41 21N 106 19W
Medicine Bow Ra., U.S.A. **82 F10** 41 10N 106 25W

Medicine Hat

Monterey B.

Minas Basin, Canada 71 C7 45 20N 64 12W
Minas de Rio Tinto, Spain 19 D2 37 42N 6 35W
Minas Gerais □, Brazil 93 G9 18 50S 46 0W
Minatitlán, Mexico 87 D6 17 58N 94 35W
Minbu, Burma 41 J19 20 10N 94 52 E
Mindanao, Phil. 37 C6 8 0N 125 0 E
Mindanao Sea = Bohol Sea, Phil. 37 C6 9 0N 124 0 E
Mindanao Trench, Pac. Oc. 37 B7 12 0N 126 6 E
Minden, Canada 78 B6 44 55N 78 43W
Minden, Germany 16 B4 52 18N 8 45 E
Minden, La., U.S.A. 81 J8 32 37N 93 17W
Minden, Nev., U.S.A. 84 G7 38 57N 119 46W
Mindiptana, Indonesia 37 F10 5 55S 140 22 E
Mindoro, Phil. 37 B6 13 0N 121 0 E
Mindoro Str., Phil. 37 B6 12 30N 120 30 E
Mindouli, Congo 52 E2 4 12S 14 28 E
Mine, Japan 31 G5 34 12N 131 7 E
Minehead, U.K. 11 F4 51 12N 3 29W
Mineola, U.S.A. 81 J7 32 40N 95 29W
Mineral King, U.S.A. 84 J8 36 27N 118 36W
Mineral Wells, U.S.A. 81 J5 32 48N 98 7W
Minersville, Pa., U.S.A. 79 F8 40 41N 76 16W
Minersville, Utah, U.S.A. 83 G7 38 13N 112 56W
Minerva, U.S.A. 78 F3 40 44N 81 6W
Minetto, U.S.A. 79 C8 43 24N 76 28W
Mingan, Canada 71 B7 50 20N 64 0W
Mingechaurskoye Vdkhr., Azerbaijan 25 F8 40 56N 47 20 E
Mingela, Australia 62 B4 19 52S 146 38 E
Mingenew, Australia 61 E2 29 12S 115 21 E
Mingera Cr. →, Australia 62 C2 20 38S 137 45 E
Mingin, Burma 41 H19 22 50N 94 30 E
Mingt'iehkaitafan = Mintaka Pass, Pakistan 43 A6 37 0N 74 58 E
Mingyuegue, China 35 C15 43 2N 128 50 E
Minho, Portugal 19 B1 41 25N 8 20W
Minho →, Spain 19 B1 41 58N 8 40W
Minidoka, U.S.A. 82 E7 42 45N 113 29W
Minigwal, L., Australia 61 E3 29 31S 123 14 E
Minilya, Australia 61 D1 23 55S 114 0 E
Minilya →, Australia 61 D1 23 45S 114 0 E
Minipi, L., Canada 71 B7 52 25N 60 45W
Mink L., Canada 72 A5 61 54N 117 40W
Minna, Nigeria 50 G6 9 37N 6 30 E
Minneapolis, Kans., U.S.A. 80 F6 39 8N 97 42W
Minneapolis, Minn., U.S.A. 80 C8 44 59N 93 16W
Minnedosa, Canada 73 C9 50 14N 99 50W
Minnesota □, U.S.A. 80 B7 46 0N 94 15W
Minnie Creek, Australia 61 D2 24 3S 115 42 E
Minnipa, Australia 63 E2 32 51S 135 9 E
Minnitaki L., Canada 70 C1 49 57N 92 10W
Mino, Japan 31 G8 35 32N 136 55 E
Miño →, Spain 19 B1 41 52N 8 40W
Minorca = Menorca, Spain 22 B11 40 0N 4 0 E
Minore, Australia 63 E4 32 14S 148 27 E
Minot, U.S.A. 80 A4 48 14N 101 18W
Minqin, China 34 E2 38 38N 103 20 E
Minsk, Belorussia 24 D4 53 52N 27 30 E
Mińsk Mazowiecki, Poland 17 B10 52 10N 21 33 E
Mintaka Pass, Pakistan 43 A6 37 0N 74 58 E
Minto, U.S.A. 68 B5 64 53N 149 11W
Minton, Canada 73 D8 49 10N 104 35W
Minturn, U.S.A. 82 G10 39 35N 106 26W
Minusinsk, Russia 27 D10 53 50N 91 20 E
Minutang, India 41 E20 28 15N 96 30 E
Minvoul, Gabon 52 D2 2 9N 12 8 E
Mir, Niger 51 F7 14 5N 11 59 E
Mīr Kūh, Iran 45 E8 26 22N 58 55 E
Mīr Shahdād, Iran 45 E8 26 15N 58 29 E
Mira por vos Cay, Bahamas 89 B5 22 9N 74 30W
Miraj, India 40 L9 16 50N 74 45 E
Miram Shah, Pakistan 42 C4 33 0N 70 2 E
Miramar, Argentina 94 D4 38 15S 57 50W
Miramar, Mozam. 57 C6 23 50S 35 35 E
Miramichi B., Canada 71 C7 47 15N 65 0W
Miranda, Brazil 93 H7 20 10S 56 15W
Miranda de Ebro, Spain 19 A4 42 41N 2 57W
Mirando City, U.S.A. 81 M5 27 26N 99 0W
Mirandópolis, Brazil 95 A5 21 9S 51 6W
Mirango, Malawi 55 E3 13 32S 34 58 E
Mirani, Australia 62 C4 21 9S 148 53 E
Mirassol, Brazil 95 A6 20 46S 49 28W
Mirbāţ, Oman 46 D5 17 0N 54 45 E
Miri, Malaysia 36 D4 4 23N 113 59 E
Miriam Vale, Australia 62 C5 24 20S 151 33 E
Mirim, L., S. Amer. 95 C5 32 45S 52 50W
Mirnyy, Russia 27 C12 62 33N 113 53 E
Mirond L., Canada 73 B8 55 6N 102 47W
Mirpur, Pakistan 43 C5 33 32N 73 56 E
Mirpur Bibiwari, Pakistan 42 E2 28 33N 67 44 E
Mirpur Khas, Pakistan 42 G3 25 30N 69 0 E
Mirpur Sakro, Pakistan 42 G2 24 33N 67 41 E
Mirror, Canada 72 C6 52 30N 113 7W
Miryang, S. Korea 35 G15 35 31N 128 44 E
Mirzapur, India 43 G10 25 10N 82 34 E
Mirzapur-cum-Vindhyachal = Mirzapur, India 43 G10 25 10N 82 34 E
Misantla, Mexico 87 D5 19 56N 96 50W
Misawa, Japan 30 D10 40 41N 141 24 E
Miscou I., Canada 71 C7 47 57N 64 31W
Mish'āb, Ra'as al, Si. Arabia 45 D6 28 15N 48 43 E
Mishan, China 33 B8 45 37N 131 48 E
Mishawaka, U.S.A. 76 E2 41 40N 86 11W
Mishima, Japan 31 G9 35 10N 138 52 E
Misión, Mexico 85 N10 32 6N 116 53W
Misiones □, Argentina 95 B5 27 0S 55 0W
Misiones □, Paraguay 94 B4 27 0S 56 0W
Miskah, Si. Arabia 44 E4 24 49N 42 56 E
Miskitos, Cayos, Nic. 88 D3 14 26N 82 50W
Miskolc, Hungary 17 D10 48 7N 20 50 E
Misoke, Zaïre 54 C2 0 42S 28 2 E
Misool, Indonesia 37 E8 1 52S 130 10 E
Misrātah, Libya 51 B8 32 24N 15 3 E
Missanabie, Canada 70 C3 48 20N 84 6W
Missinaibi →, Canada 70 B3 50 43N 81 29W
Missinaibi L., Canada 70 C3 48 23N 83 40W
Mission, S. Dak., U.S.A. 80 D4 43 18N 100 39W
Mission, Tex., U.S.A. 81 M5 26 13N 98 20W
Mission City, Canada 72 D4 49 10N 122 15W
Mission Viejo, U.S.A. 85 M9 33 36N 117 40W
Missisa L., Canada 70 B2 52 20N 85 7W
Mississagi →, Canada 70 C3 46 15N 83 9W
Mississippi □, U.S.A. 81 J10 33 0N 90 0W
Mississippi →, U.S.A. 81 L10 29 9N 89 15W
Mississippi L., Canada 79 A8 45 5N 76 10W
Mississippi River Delta, U.S.A. 81 L9 29 10N 89 15W
Mississippi Sd., U.S.A. 81 K10 30 20N 89 0W
Missoula, U.S.A. 82 C6 46 52N 114 1W
Missouri □, U.S.A. 80 F8 38 25N 92 30W
Missouri →, U.S.A. 80 F9 38 49N 90 7W
Missouri Valley, U.S.A. 80 E7 41 34N 95 53W
Mist, U.S.A. 84 E3 45 59N 123 15W
Mistake B., Canada 73 A10 62 8N 93 0W
Mistassini →, Canada 71 C5 48 42N 72 20W
Mistassini L., Canada 70 B5 51 0N 73 30W
Mistastin L., Canada 71 A7 55 57N 63 20W
Mistatim, Canada 73 C8 52 52N 103 22W
Mistretta, Italy 20 F6 37 56N 14 20 E
Misty L., Canada 73 B8 58 53N 101 40W
Misurata = Misrātah, Libya 51 B8 32 24N 15 3 E
Mitchell, Australia 63 D4 26 29S 147 58 E
Mitchell, Canada 78 C3 43 28N 81 12W
Mitchell, Ind., U.S.A. 76 F2 38 44N 86 28W
Mitchell, Nebr., U.S.A. 80 E3 41 57N 103 49W
Mitchell, Oreg., U.S.A. 82 D3 44 34N 120 9W
Mitchell, S. Dak., U.S.A. 80 D5 43 43N 98 2W
Mitchell →, Australia 62 B3 15 12S 141 35 E
Mitchell, Mt., U.S.A. 77 H4 35 46N 82 16W
Mitchell Ras., Australia 62 A2 12 49S 135 36 E
Mitchelstown, Ireland 13 D3 52 16N 8 18W
Mitha Tiwana, Pakistan 42 C5 32 13N 72 6 E
Mito, Japan 31 F10 36 20N 140 30 E
Mitsinjo, Madag. 57 B8 16 1S 45 52 E
Mitsiwa, Eritrea 51 E12 15 35N 39 25 E
Mitsukaidō, Japan 31 F9 36 1N 139 59 E
Mittagong, Australia 63 E5 34 28S 150 29 E
Mitú, Colombia 92 C4 1 8N 70 3W
Mitumba, Tanzania 54 D3 7 8S 31 2 E
Mitumba, Chaîne des, Zaïre 54 D2 7 0S 27 30 E
Mitumba Mts. = Mitumba, Chaîne des, Zaïre 54 D2 7 0S 27 30 E
Mitwaba, Zaïre 55 D2 8 2S 27 17 E
Mityana, Uganda 54 B3 0 23N 32 2 E
Mitzic, Gabon 52 D2 0 45N 11 40 E
Mixteco →, Mexico 87 D5 18 11N 98 30W
Miyagi □, Japan 30 E10 38 15N 140 45 E
Miyah, W. el →, Syria 44 C3 34 44N 39 57 E
Miyake-Jima, Japan 31 G9 34 5N 139 30 E
Miyako, Japan 30 E10 39 40N 141 59 E
Miyako-Jima, Japan 31 M2 24 45N 125 20 E
Miyako-Rettō, Japan 31 M2 24 24N 125 0 E
Miyakonojō, Japan 31 J5 31 40N 131 5 E
Miyanoura-Dake, Japan 31 J5 30 20N 130 31 E
Miyazaki, Japan 31 J5 31 56N 131 30 E
Miyazaki □, Japan 31 H5 32 30N 131 30 E
Miyazu, Japan 31 G7 35 35N 135 10 E
Miyet, Bahr el = Dead Sea, Asia 47 D4 31 30N 35 30 E
Miyoshi, Japan 31 G6 34 48N 132 51 E
Miyun, China 34 D9 40 28N 116 50 E
Miyun Shuiku, China 35 D9 40 30N 117 0 E
Mizamis = Ozamiz, Phil. 37 C6 8 15N 123 50 E
Mizdah, Libya 51 B7 31 30N 13 0 E
Mizen Hd., Cork, Ireland 13 E2 51 27N 9 50W
Mizen Hd., Wick., Ireland 13 D5 52 52N 6 4W
Mizhi, China 34 F6 37 47N 110 12 E
Mizoram □, India 41 H18 23 30N 92 40 E
Mizpe Ramon, Israel 47 E3 30 34N 34 49 E
Mizusawa, Japan 30 E10 39 8N 141 8 E
Mjölby, Sweden 9 G13 58 20N 15 10 E
Mjøsa, Norway 9 F11 60 48N 11 0 E
Mkata, Tanzania 54 D4 5 45S 38 20 E
Mkokotoni, Tanzania 54 D4 5 55S 39 15 E
Mkomazi, Tanzania 54 C4 4 40S 38 7 E
Mkomazi →, S. Africa 57 E5 30 12S 30 50 E
Mkulwe, Tanzania 55 D3 8 37S 32 20 E
Mkumbi, Ras, Tanzania 54 D4 7 38S 39 55 E
Mkushi, Zambia 55 E2 14 25S 29 15 E
Mkushi River, Zambia 55 E2 13 32S 29 45 E
Mkuze, S. Africa 57 D5 27 10S 32 0 E
Mkuze →, S. Africa 57 D5 27 45S 32 30 E
Mladá Boleslav, Czech. 16 C7 50 27N 14 53 E
Mlala Hills, Tanzania 54 D3 6 50S 31 40 E
Mlange, Malawi 55 F4 16 2S 35 33 E
Mława, Poland 17 B10 53 9N 20 25 E
Mmabatho, S. Africa 56 D4 25 49S 25 30 E
Mo i Rana, Norway 8 C13 66 15N 14 7 E
Moa, Indonesia 37 F7 8 0S 128 0 E
Moab, U.S.A. 83 G9 38 35N 109 33W
Moabi, Gabon 52 E2 2 24S 10 59 E
Moala, Fiji 59 D8 18 36S 179 53 E
Moalie Park, Australia 63 D3 29 42S 143 3 E
Moba, Zaïre 54 D2 7 0S 29 48 E
Mobārakābād, Iran 45 D7 28 24N 53 20 E
Mobārakīyeh, Iran 45 C6 35 5N 51 47 E
Mobaye, C.A.R. 52 D4 4 25N 21 5 E
Mobayi, Zaïre 52 D4 4 15N 21 8 E
Moberly, U.S.A. 80 F8 39 25N 92 26W
Moberly →, Canada 72 B4 56 12N 120 55W
Mobile, U.S.A. 77 K1 30 41N 88 3W
Mobile B., U.S.A. 77 K2 30 30N 88 0W
Mobridge, U.S.A. 80 C4 45 32N 100 26W
Mobutu Sese Seko, L., Africa 54 B3 1 30N 31 0 E
Moc Chau, Vietnam 38 B5 20 50N 104 38 E
Moc Hoa, Vietnam 39 G5 10 46N 105 56 E
Mocabe Kasari, Zaïre 55 D2 9 58S 26 12 E
Moçambique, Mozam. 55 F5 15 3S 40 42 E
Moçâmedes = Namibe, Angola 53 H2 15 7S 12 11 E
Mochudi, Botswana 56 C4 24 27S 26 7 E
Mocimboa da Praia, Mozam. 55 E5 11 25S 40 20 E
Moclips, U.S.A. 84 C2 47 14N 124 13W
Mocoa, Colombia 92 C3 1 7N 76 35W
Mococa, Brazil 95 A6 21 28S 47 0W
Mocorito, Mexico 86 B3 25 30N 107 53W
Moctezuma, Mexico 86 B3 29 50N 109 0W
Moctezuma →, Mexico 87 C5 21 59N 98 34W
Mocuba, Mozam. 55 F4 16 54S 36 57 E
Mocúzari, Presa, Mexico 86 B3 27 10N 109 10W
Modane, France 18 D7 45 12N 6 40 E
Modasa, India 42 H5 23 30N 73 21 E
Modder →, S. Africa 56 D3 29 2S 24 37 E
Modderrivier, S. Africa 56 D3 29 2S 24 38 E
Módena, Italy 20 B4 44 39N 10 55 E
Modena, U.S.A. 83 H7 37 48N 113 56W
Modesto, U.S.A. 83 H3 37 39N 121 0W
Módica, Italy 20 F6 36 52N 14 45 E
Moe, Australia 63 F4 38 12S 146 19 E
Moebase, Mozam. 55 F4 17 3S 38 41 E
Moengo, Surinam 93 B8 5 45N 54 20W
Moffat, U.K. 12 F5 55 20N 3 27W
Moga, India 42 D6 30 48N 75 8 E
Mogadishu = Muqdisho, Somali Rep. 46 G4 2 2N 45 25 E
Mogador = Essaouira, Morocco 50 B3 31 32N 9 42W
Mogalakwena →, S. Africa 57 C4 22 38S 28 40 E
Mogami →, Japan 30 E10 38 45N 140 0 E
Mogán, Canary Is. 22 G4 27 53N 15 43W
Mogaung, Burma 41 G20 25 20N 97 0 E
Mogi das Cruzes, Brazil 95 A6 23 31S 46 11W
Mogi-Guaçu →, Brazil 95 A6 20 53S 48 10W
Mogi-Mirim, Brazil 95 A6 22 29S 47 0W
Mogilev, Belorussia 24 D5 53 55N 30 18 E
Mogilev-Podolskiy, Moldavia 25 E4 48 20N 27 40 E
Mogincual, Mozam. 55 F5 15 35S 40 25 E
Mogocha, Russia 27 D12 53 40N 119 50 E
Mogoi, Indonesia 37 E8 1 55S 133 10 E
Mogok, Burma 41 H20 23 0N 96 40 E
Mogumber, Australia 61 F2 31 2S 116 3 E
Mohács, Hungary 17 F9 45 58N 18 41 E
Mohales Hoek, Lesotho 56 E4 30 7S 27 26 E
Mohall, U.S.A. 80 A4 48 46N 101 31W
Moḩammadābād, Iran 45 B8 37 52N 59 5 E
Mohave, L., U.S.A. 85 K12 35 12N 114 34W
Mohawk →, U.S.A. 79 D11 42 47N 73 41W
Mohoro, Tanzania 54 D4 8 6S 39 8 E
Moidart, L., U.K. 12 E3 56 47N 5 40W
Mointy, Kazakhstan 26 E8 47 10N 73 18 E
Moires, Greece 23 D6 35 4N 24 56 E
Moisie, Canada 71 B6 50 12N 66 1W
Moisie →, Canada 71 B6 50 14N 66 5W
Moïssala, Chad 51 G8 8 21N 17 46 E
Mojave, U.S.A. 85 K8 35 3N 118 10W
Mojave Desert, U.S.A. 85 L10 35 0N 116 30W
Mojo, Bolivia 94 A2 21 48S 65 33W
Mojokerto, Indonesia 37 G15 7 28S 112 26 E
Mokai, N.Z. 59 H5 38 32S 175 56 E
Mokambo, Zaïre 55 E2 12 25S 28 20 E
Mokameh, India 43 G11 25 24N 85 55 E
Mokelumne →, U.S.A. 84 G5 38 13N 121 28W
Mokelumne Hill, U.S.A. 84 G6 38 18N 120 43W
Mokhós, Greece 23 D7 35 16N 25 27 E
Mokhotlong, Lesotho 57 D4 29 22S 29 2 E
Mokokchung, India 41 F19 26 15N 94 30 E
Mol, Belgium 15 C5 51 11N 5 5 E
Molchanovo, Russia 26 D9 57 40N 83 50 E
Mold, U.K. 10 D4 53 10N 3 10W
Moldavia ■, Europe 25 E4 47 0N 28 0 E
Molde, Norway 8 E9 62 45N 7 9 E
Moldova ■ = Moldavia ■, Europe 25 E4 47 0N 28 0 E
Molepolole, Botswana 56 C4 24 28S 25 28 E
Molfetta, Italy 20 D7 41 12N 16 35 E
Moline, U.S.A. 80 E9 41 30N 90 31W
Molinos, Argentina 94 B2 25 28S 66 15W
Moliro, Zaïre 54 D3 8 12S 30 30 E
Molise □, Italy 20 D6 41 45N 14 30 E
Mollahat, Bangla. 43 H13 22 56N 89 48 E
Mollendo, Peru 92 G4 17 0S 72 0W
Mollerin, L., Australia 61 F2 30 30S 117 35 E
Mölndal, Sweden 9 H12 57 40N 12 3 E
Molokai, U.S.A. 74 H16 21 8N 157 0W
Molong, Australia 63 E4 33 5S 148 54 E
Molopo →, Africa 56 D3 27 30S 20 13 E
Molotov = Perm, Russia 24 C10 58 0N 56 10 E
Moloundou, Cameroon 52 D3 2 8N 15 15 E
Molson L., Canada 73 C9 54 22N 96 40W
Molteno, S. Africa 56 E4 31 22S 26 22 E
Molu, Indonesia 37 F8 6 45S 131 40 E
Molucca Sea = Maluku Sea, Indonesia 37 E6 2 0S 124 0 E
Moluccas = Maluku, Indonesia 37 E7 1 0S 127 0 E
Moma, Mozam. 55 F4 16 47S 39 4 E
Moma, Zaïre 54 C1 1 35S 23 52 E
Mombasa, Kenya 54 C4 4 2S 39 43 E
Mombetsu, Japan 30 B11 44 21N 143 22 E
Momi, Zaïre 54 C2 1 42S 27 0 E
Mompós, Colombia 92 B4 9 14N 74 26W
Møn, Denmark 9 J12 54 57N 12 15 E
Mon →, Burma 41 J19 20 25N 94 30 E
Mona, Canal de la, W. Indies 89 C6 18 30N 67 45W
Mona, Isla, Puerto Rico 89 C6 18 5N 67 54W
Mona, Pta., Costa Rica 88 E3 9 37N 82 36W
Monach Is., U.K. 12 D1 57 32N 7 40W
Monaco ■, Europe 18 E7 43 46N 7 23 E
Monadhliath Mts., U.K. 12 D4 57 10N 4 4W
Monaghan, Ireland 13 B5 54 15N 6 58W
Monaghan □, Ireland 13 B5 54 15N 7 0W
Monahans, U.S.A. 81 K3 31 36N 102 54W
Monapo, Mozam. 55 E5 14 56S 40 19 E
Monarch Mt., Canada 72 C3 51 55N 125 57W
Monastir = Bitola, Macedonia 21 D9 41 5N 21 10 E
Monastir, Tunisia 51 A7 35 50N 10 49 E
Moncayo, Sierra del, Spain 19 B5 41 48N 1 50W
Mönchengladbach, Germany 16 C3 51 12N 6 23 E
Monchique, Portugal 19 D1 37 19N 8 38W
Monchique, Sa. de, Portugal 19 D1 37 18N 8 39W
Monclova, Mexico 86 B4 26 50N 101 30W
Moncton, Canada 71 C7 46 7N 64 51W
Mondego →, Portugal 19 B1 40 9N 8 52W
Mondeodo, Indonesia 37 E6 3 34S 122 9 E
Mondovì, Italy 20 B2 44 23N 7 49 E
Mondovi, U.S.A. 80 C9 44 34N 91 40W
Mondrain I., Australia 61 F3 34 9S 122 14 E
Monduli □, Tanzania 54 C4 3 0S 36 0 E
Monessen, U.S.A. 78 F5 40 9N 79 54W
Monett, U.S.A. 81 G8 36 55N 93 55W
Monforte, Portugal 19 C2 39 6N 7 25W
Mong Hsu, Burma 41 J21 21 54N 98 30 E
Mong Kung, Burma 41 J20 21 35N 97 35 E
Mong Nai, Burma 41 J20 20 32N 97 46 E
Mong Pawk, Burma 41 H21 22 4N 99 16 E
Mong Ton, Burma 41 J21 20 17N 98 45 E
Mong Wa, Burma 41 J22 21 26N 100 27 E
Mong Yai, Burma 41 H21 22 21N 98 3 E
Mongalla, Sudan 51 G11 5 8N 31 42 E
Mongers, L., Australia 61 E2 29 25S 117 5 E
Monghyr = Munger, India 43 G12 25 23N 86 30 E
Mongo, Chad 51 F8 12 14N 18 43 E
Mongolia ■, Asia 27 E10 47 0N 103 0 E
Mongororo, Chad 51 F9 12 3N 22 26 E
Mongu, Zambia 53 H4 15 16S 23 12 E
Mônguà, Angola 56 B2 16 43S 15 20 E
Monkey Bay, Malawi 55 E4 14 7S 35 1 E
Monkey River, Belize 87 D7 16 22N 88 29W
Monkira, Australia 62 C3 24 46S 140 30 E
Monkoto, Zaïre 52 E4 1 38S 20 35 E
Monmouth, U.K. 11 F5 51 48N 2 43W
Monmouth, U.S.A. 80 E9 40 55N 90 39W
Mono L., U.S.A. 83 H4 38 1N 119 1W
Monolith, U.S.A. 85 K8 35 7N 118 22W
Monólithos, Greece 23 C9 36 7N 27 45 E
Monongahela, U.S.A. 78 F5 40 12N 79 56W
Monópoli, Italy 20 D7 40 57N 17 18 E
Monqoumba, C.A.R. 52 D3 3 33N 18 40 E
Monroe, Ga., U.S.A. 77 J4 33 47N 83 43W
Monroe, La., U.S.A. 81 J8 32 30N 92 7W
Monroe, Mich., U.S.A. 76 E4 41 55N 83 24W
Monroe, N.C., U.S.A. 77 H5 34 59N 80 33W
Monroe, N.Y., U.S.A. 79 E10 41 20N 74 11W
Monroe, Utah, U.S.A. 83 G7 38 38N 112 7W
Monroe, Wash., U.S.A. 84 C5 47 51N 121 58W
Monroe, Wis., U.S.A. 80 D10 42 36N 89 38W
Monroe City, U.S.A. 80 F9 39 39N 91 44W
Monroeville, Ala., U.S.A. 77 K2 31 31N 87 20W
Monroeville, Pa., U.S.A. 78 F5 40 26N 79 45W
Monrovia, Liberia 50 G2 6 18N 10 47W
Monrovia, U.S.A. 83 J4 34 7N 118 1W
Mons, Belgium 15 D3 50 27N 3 58 E
Monse, Indonesia 37 E6 4 0S 123 10 E
Mont-de-Marsan, France 18 E3 43 54N 0 31W
Mont-Joli, Canada 71 C6 48 37N 68 10W
Mont-Laurier, Canada 70 C4 46 35N 75 30W
Mont-St.-Michel, Le = Le Mont-St.-Michel, France 18 B3 48 40N 1 30W
Mont Tremblant Prov. Park, Canada 70 C5 46 30N 74 30W
Montagu, S. Africa 56 E3 33 45S 20 8 E
Montagu I., Antarctica 5 B1 58 25S 26 20W
Montague, Canada 71 C7 46 10N 62 39W
Montague, U.S.A. 82 F2 41 44N 122 32W
Montague, I., Mexico 86 A2 31 40N 114 56W
Montague Ra., Australia 61 E2 27 15S 119 30 E
Montague Sd., Australia 60 B4 14 28S 125 20 E
Montalbán, Spain 19 B5 40 50N 0 45W
Montalvo, U.S.A. 85 L7 34 15N 119 12W
Montaña, Peru 92 E4 6 0S 73 0W
Montana □, U.S.A. 82 C9 47 0N 110 0W
Montaña Clara, I., Canary Is. 22 E6 29 17N 13 33W
Montargis, France 18 C5 47 59N 2 43 E
Montauban, France 18 D4 44 2N 1 21 E
Montauk, U.S.A. 79 E13 41 3N 71 57W
Montauk Pt., U.S.A. 79 E13 41 4N 71 52W
Montbéliard, France 18 C7 47 31N 6 48 E
Montclair, U.S.A. 79 F10 40 49N 74 13W
Monte Albán, Mexico 87 D5 17 2N 96 45W
Monte Alegre, Brazil 93 D8 2 0S 54 0W
Monte Azul, Brazil 93 G10 15 9S 42 53W
Monte Bello Is., Australia 60 D2 20 30S 115 45 E
Monte-Carlo, Monaco 18 E7 43 46N 7 23 E
Monte Caseros, Argentina 94 C4 30 10S 57 50W
Monte Comán, Argentina 94 C2 34 40S 67 53W
Monte Cristi, Dom. Rep. 89 C5 19 52N 71 39W
Monte Lindo →, Paraguay 94 A4 23 56S 57 12W
Monte Quemado, Argentina 94 B3 25 53S 62 41W
Monte Rio, U.S.A. 84 G4 38 28N 123 0W
Monte Sant' Ángelo, Italy 20 D6 41 42N 15 59 E
Monte Santu, C. di, Italy 20 D3 40 5N 9 42 E
Monte Vista, U.S.A. 83 H10 37 35N 106 9W
Monteagudo, Argentina 95 B5 27 14S 54 8W
Montebello, Canada 70 C5 45 40N 74 55W
Montecito, U.S.A. 85 L7 34 26N 119 40W
Montecristi, Ecuador 92 D2 1 0S 80 40W
Montego Bay, Jamaica 88 C4 18 30N 78 0W
Montejinnie, Australia 60 C5 16 40S 131 38 E
Montélimar, France 18 D6 44 33N 4 45 E
Montello, U.S.A. 80 D10 43 48N 89 20W
Montemorelos, Mexico 87 B5 25 11N 99 42W
Montenegro, Brazil 95 B5 29 39S 51 29W
Montenegro □, Montenegro 21 C8 42 40N 19 20 E
Montepuez, Mozam. 55 E4 13 8S 38 59 E
Montepuez →, Mozam. 55 E5 12 32S 40 27 E
Monterey, U.S.A. 83 H3 36 37N 121 55W
Monterey B., U.S.A. 84 J5 36 45N 122 0W

Nakuru

Mubi, *Nigeria* **51 F7** 10 18N 13 16 E
Mubur, P., *Indonesia* **39 L6** 3 20N 106 12 E
Muchachos, Roque de los, *Canary Is.* **22 F2** 28 44N 17 52W
Muchinga Mts., *Zambia* **55 E3** 11 30S 31 30 E
Muck, *U.K.* **12 E2** 56 50N 6 15W
Muckadilla, *Australia* **63 D4** 26 35S 148 23 E
Muconda, *Angola* **52 G4** 10 31S 21 15 E
Mucuri, *Brazil* **93 G11** 18 0S 39 36W
Mucusso, *Angola* **56 B3** 18 1S 21 25 E
Muda, *Canary Is.* **22 F6** 28 34N 13 57W
Mudan Jiang →, *China* **35 A15** 46 20N 129 30 E
Mudanjiang, *China* **35 B15** 44 38N 129 30 E
Muddy Cr. →, *U.S.A.* **83 H8** 38 24N 110 42W
Mudgee, *Australia* **63 E4** 32 32S 149 31 E
Mudjatik →, *Canada* **73 B7** 56 1N 107 36W
Muecate, *Mozam.* **55 E4** 14 55S 39 40 E
Muêda, *Mozam.* **55 E4** 11 36S 39 28 E
Mueller Ra., *Australia* **60 C4** 18 18S 126 46 E
Muende, *Mozam.* **55 E3** 14 28S 33 0 E
Muerto, Mar, *Mexico* **87 D6** 16 10N 94 10W
Mufindi □, *Tanzania* **55 D4** 8 30S 35 20 E
Mufulira, *Zambia* **55 E2** 12 32S 28 15 E
Mufumbiro Range, *Africa* **54 C2** 1 25S 29 30 E
Mughayrā', *Si. Arabia* **44 D3** 29 17N 37 41 E
Mugi, *Japan* **31 H7** 33 40N 134 25 E
Mugila, Mts., *Zaïre* **54 D2** 7 0S 28 50 E
Muğla, *Turkey* **25 G4** 37 15N 28 22 E
Mugu, *Nepal* **43 E10** 29 45N 82 30 E
Muhammad Qol, *Sudan* **51 D12** 20 53N 37 9 E
Muhammadabad, *India* **43 F10** 26 4N 83 25 E
Muhesi →, *Tanzania* **54 D4** 7 0S 35 20 E
Muheza □, *Tanzania* **54 C4** 5 0S 39 0 E
Mühlig Hofmann fjella, *Antarctica* **5 D3** 72 30S 5 0 E
Muhutwe, *Tanzania* **54 C3** 1 35S 31 45 E
Muikamachi, *Japan* **31 F9** 37 15N 138 50 E
Muine Bheag, *Ireland* **13 D5** 52 42N 6 57W
Muir, L., *Australia* **61 F2** 34 30S 116 40 E
Mukah, *Malaysia* **36 D4** 2 55N 112 5 E
Mukdahan, *Thailand* **38 D5** 16 32N 104 43 E
Mukden = Shenyang, *China* **35 D12** 41 48N 123 27 E
Mukhtuya = Lensk, *Russia* **27 C12** 60 48N 114 55 E
Mukinbudin, *Australia* **61 F2** 30 55S 118 5 E
Mukishi, *Zaïre* **55 D1** 8 30S 24 44 E
Mukomuko, *Indonesia* **36 E2** 2 30S 101 10 E
Mukomwenze, *Zaïre* **54 D2** 6 49S 27 15 E
Muktsar, *India* **42 D6** 30 30N 74 30 E
Mukur, *Afghan.* **42 C2** 32 50N 67 42 E
Mukutawa →, *Canada* **73 C9** 53 10N 97 24W
Mukwela, *Zambia* **55 F2** 17 0S 26 40 E
Mulange, *Zaïre* **54 C2** 3 40S 27 10 E
Mulchén, *Chile* **94 D1** 37 45S 72 20W
Mulde →, *Germany* **16 C6** 51 53N 12 15 E
Mule Creek, *U.S.A.* **80 D2** 43 19N 104 8W
Muleba, *Tanzania* **54 C3** 1 50S 31 37 E
Muleba □, *Tanzania* **54 C3** 2 0S 31 30 E
Muleshoe, *U.S.A.* **81 H3** 34 13N 102 43W
Mulgathing, *Australia* **63 E1** 30 15S 134 8 E
Mulgrave, *Canada* **71 C7** 45 38N 61 31W
Mulhacén, *Spain* **19 D4** 37 4N 3 20W
Mülheim, *Germany* **16 C3** 51 26N 6 53 E
Mulhouse, *France* **18 C7** 47 40N 7 20 E
Muling, *China* **35 B16** 44 35N 130 10 E
Mull, *U.K.* **12 E3** 56 27N 6 0W
Mullaittvu, *Sri Lanka* **40 Q12** 9 15N 80 49 E
Mullen, *U.S.A.* **80 D4** 42 3N 101 1W
Mullengudgery, *Australia* **63 E4** 31 43S 147 23 E
Mullens, *U.S.A.* **76 G5** 37 35N 81 23W
Muller, Pegunungan, *Indonesia* **36 D4** 0 30N 113 30 E
Mullet Pen., *Ireland* **13 B1** 54 10N 10 2W
Mullewa, *Australia* **61 E2** 28 29S 115 30 E
Mulligan →, *Australia* **62 C2** 25 0S 139 0 E
Mullin, *U.S.A.* **81 K5** 31 33N 98 40W
Mullingar, *Ireland* **13 C4** 53 31N 7 20W
Mullins, *U.S.A.* **77 H6** 34 12N 79 15W
Mullumbimby, *Australia* **63 D5** 28 30S 153 30 E
Mulobezi, *Zambia* **55 F2** 16 45S 25 7 E
Multan, *Pakistan* **42 D4** 30 15N 71 36 E
Mulumbe, Mts., *Zaïre* **55 D2** 8 40S 27 30 E
Mulungushi Dam, *Zambia* **55 E2** 14 48S 28 48 E
Mulvane, *U.S.A.* **81 G6** 37 29N 97 15W
Mulwala, *Australia* **63 F4** 35 59S 146 0 E
Mumbwa, *Zambia* **55 E2** 15 0S 27 0 E
Mun →, *Thailand* **38 E5** 15 19N 105 30 E
Muna, *Indonesia* **37 F6** 5 0S 122 30 E
München, *Germany* **16 D5** 48 8N 11 33 E
Munchen-Gladbach = Mönchengladbach, *Germany* **16 C3** 51 12N 6 23 E
Muncho Lake, *Canada* **72 B3** 59 0N 125 50W
Munchŏn, *N. Korea* **35 E14** 39 14N 127 19 E
Muncie, *U.S.A.* **76 E3** 40 12N 85 23W
Muncoonie, L., *Australia* **62 D2** 25 12S 138 40 E
Mundala, *Indonesia* **37 E10** 4 30S 141 0 E
Mundare, *Canada* **72 C6** 53 35N 112 20W
Munday, *U.S.A.* **81 J5** 33 27N 99 38W
Münden, *Germany* **16 C4** 51 25N 9 42 E
Mundiwindi, *Australia* **60 D3** 23 47S 120 9 E
Mundo Novo, *Brazil* **93 F10** 11 50S 40 29W
Mundra, *India* **42 H3** 22 54N 69 48 E
Mundrabilla, *Australia* **61 F4** 31 52S 127 51 E
Mungallala, *Australia* **63 D4** 26 28S 147 34 E
Mungallala Cr. →, *Australia* **63 D4** 28 53S 147 5 E
Mungana, *Australia* **62 B3** 17 8S 144 27 E
Mungaoli, *India* **42 G8** 24 24N 78 7 E
Mungari, *Mozam.* **55 F3** 17 12S 33 30 E
Mungbere, *Zaïre* **54 B2** 2 36N 28 28 E
Munger, *India* **43 G12** 25 23N 86 30 E
Mungindi, *Australia* **63 D4** 28 58S 149 1 E
Munhango, *Angola* **53 G3** 12 10S 18 38 E
Munich = München, *Germany* **16 D5** 48 8N 11 33 E
Munising, *U.S.A.* **76 B2** 46 25N 86 40W
Munku-Sardyk, *Russia* **27 D11** 51 45N 100 20 E
Muñoz Gamero, Pen., *Chile* **96 G2** 52 30S 73 5W
Munroe L., *Canada* **73 B9** 59 13N 98 35W
Munsan, *S. Korea* **35 F14** 37 51N 126 48 E
Münster, *Germany* **16 C3** 51 58N 7 37 E
Munster □, *Ireland* **13 D3** 52 20N 8 40W
Muntadgin, *Australia* **61 F2** 31 45S 118 33 E
Muntok, *Indonesia* **36 E3** 2 5S 105 10 E
Munyak, *Uzbekistan* **26 E6** 43 30N 59 15 E
Munyama, *Zambia* **55 F2** 16 5S 28 31 E
Muong Beng, *Laos* **38 B3** 20 23N 101 46 E
Muong Boum, *Vietnam* **38 A4** 22 24N 102 49 E
Muong Et, *Laos* **38 B5** 20 49N 104 1 E
Muong Hai, *Laos* **38 B3** 21 3N 101 49 E
Muong Hiem, *Laos* **38 B4** 20 5N 103 22 E
Muong Houn, *Laos* **38 B3** 20 8N 101 23 E
Muong Hung, *Vietnam* **38 B4** 20 56N 103 53 E
Muong Kau, *Laos* **38 E5** 15 6N 105 47 E
Muong Khao, *Laos* **38 C4** 19 38N 103 32 E
Muong Khoua, *Laos* **38 B4** 21 5N 102 31 E
Muong Liep, *Laos* **38 C3** 18 29N 101 40 E
Muong May, *Laos* **38 E6** 14 49N 106 56 E
Muong Ngeun, *Laos* **38 B3** 20 36N 101 3 E
Muong Ngoi, *Laos* **38 B4** 20 43N 102 41 E
Muong Nhie, *Vietnam* **38 A4** 22 12N 102 28 E
Muong Nong, *Laos* **38 D6** 16 22N 106 30 E
Muong Ou Tay, *Laos* **38 A3** 22 7N 101 48 E
Muong Oua, *Laos* **38 C3** 18 18N 101 20 E
Muong Peun, *Laos* **38 B4** 20 13N 103 52 E
Muong Phalane, *Laos* **38 D5** 16 39N 105 34 E
Muong Phieng, *Laos* **38 C3** 19 6N 101 32 E
Muong Phine, *Laos* **38 D6** 16 32N 106 2 E
Muong Sai, *Laos* **38 B3** 20 42N 101 59 E
Muong Saiapoun, *Laos* **38 C3** 18 24N 101 31 E
Muong Sen, *Vietnam* **38 C5** 19 24N 104 8 E
Muong Sing, *Laos* **38 B3** 21 11N 101 9 E
Muong Son, *Laos* **38 B4** 20 27N 103 19 E
Muong Soui, *Laos* **38 C4** 19 33N 102 52 E
Muong Va, *Laos* **38 B4** 21 53N 102 19 E
Muong Xia, *Vietnam* **38 B5** 20 19N 104 50 E
Muonio, *Finland* **8 C17** 67 57N 23 40 E
Mupa, *Angola* **53 H3** 16 5S 15 50 E
Muping, *China* **35 F11** 37 22N 121 36 E
Muqdisho, *Somali Rep.* **46 G4** 2 2N 45 25 E
Mur →, *Austria* **16 E8** 46 35N 16 3 E
Murakami, *Japan* **30 E9** 38 14N 139 29 E
Murallón, Cuerro, *Chile* **96 F2** 49 48S 73 30W
Muranda, *Rwanda* **54 C2** 1 52S 29 20 E
Murang'a, *Kenya* **54 C4** 0 45S 37 9 E
Murashi, *Russia* **24 C8** 59 30N 49 0 E
Murayama, *Japan* **30 E10** 38 30N 140 25 E
Murban, *U.A.E.* **45 F7** 23 50N 53 45 E
Murchison →, *Australia* **61 E1** 27 45S 114 0 E
Murchison, Mt., *Antarctica* **5 D11** 73 0S 168 0 E
Murchison Falls = Kabarega Falls, *Uganda* **54 B3** 2 15N 31 30 E
Murchison House, *Australia* **61 E1** 27 39S 114 14 E
Murchison Ra., *Australia* **62 C1** 20 0S 134 10 E
Murchison Rapids, *Malawi* **55 F3** 15 55S 34 35 E
Murcia, *Spain* **19 C5** 38 5N 1 10W
Murcia □, *Spain* **19 D5** 37 50N 1 30W
Murdo, *U.S.A.* **80 D4** 43 53N 100 43W
Murdoch Pt., *Australia* **62 A3** 14 37S 144 55 E
Mureş →, *Romania* **17 E10** 46 15N 20 13 E
Mureşul = Mureş →, *Romania* **17 E10** 46 15N 20 13 E
Murfreesboro, *U.S.A.* **77 H2** 35 51N 86 24W
Murgab, *Tajikistan* **26 F8** 38 10N 74 2 E
Murgon, *Australia* **63 D5** 26 15S 151 54 E
Murgoo, *Australia* **61 E2** 27 24S 116 28 E
Muria, *Indonesia* **37 G14** 6 36S 110 53 E
Muriaé, *Brazil* **95 A7** 21 8S 42 23W
Muriel Mine, *Zimbabwe* **55 F3** 17 14S 30 40 E
Müritz See, *Germany* **16 B6** 53 25N 12 40 E
Murka, *Kenya* **54 C4** 3 27S 38 0 E
Murmansk, *Russia* **24 A5** 68 57N 33 10 E
Muro, *Spain* **22 B10** 39 44N 3 3 E
Murom, *Russia* **24 C7** 55 35N 42 3 E
Muroran, *Japan* **30 C10** 42 25N 141 0 E
Muroto, *Japan* **31 H7** 33 18N 134 9 E
Muroto-Misaki, *Japan* **31 H7** 33 15N 134 10 E
Murphy, *U.S.A.* **82 E5** 43 13N 116 33W
Murphys, *U.S.A.* **84 G6** 38 8N 120 28W
Murphysboro, *U.S.A.* **81 G10** 37 46N 89 20W
Murray, *Ky., U.S.A.* **77 G1** 36 37N 88 19W
Murray, *Utah, U.S.A.* **82 F8** 40 40N 111 53W
Murray →, *Australia* **63 F2** 35 20S 139 22 E
Murray →, *Canada* **72 B4** 56 11N 120 45W
Murray, L., *U.S.A.* **77 H5** 34 3N 81 13W
Murray Bridge, *Australia* **63 F2** 35 6S 139 14 E
Murray Downs, *Australia* **62 C1** 21 4S 134 40 E
Murray Harbour, *Canada* **71 C7** 46 0N 62 28W
Murraysburg, *S. Africa* **56 E3** 31 58S 23 47 E
Murree, *Pakistan* **42 C5** 33 56N 73 28 E
Murrieta, *U.S.A.* **85 M9** 33 33N 117 13W
Murrin Murrin, *Australia* **61 E3** 28 58S 121 33 E
Murrumbidgee →, *Australia* **63 E3** 34 43S 143 12 E
Murrumburrah, *Australia* **63 E4** 34 32S 148 22 E
Murrurundi, *Australia* **63 E5** 31 42S 150 51 E
Mursala, *Indonesia* **36 D1** 1 41N 98 28 E
Murshidabad, *India* **43 G13** 24 11N 88 19 E
Murtle L., *Canada* **72 C5** 52 8N 119 38W
Murtoa, *Australia* **63 F3** 36 35S 142 28 E
Murungu, *Tanzania* **54 C3** 4 12S 31 10 E
Murwara, *India* **43 H9** 23 46N 80 28 E
Murwillumbah, *Australia* **63 D5** 28 18S 153 27 E
Mürzzuschlag, *Austria* **16 E7** 47 36N 15 41 E
Muş, *Turkey* **25 G7** 38 45N 41 30 E
Mûsa, G., *Egypt* **51 C11** 28 33N 33 59 E
Musa Khel, *Pakistan* **42 D3** 30 59N 69 52 E
Mūsá Qal'eh, *Afghan.* **40 C4** 32 20N 64 50 E
Musaffargarh, *Pakistan* **40 D7** 30 10N 71 10 E
Musala, *Bulgaria* **21 C10** 42 13N 23 37 E
Musan, *N. Korea* **35 C15** 42 12N 129 12 E
Musangu, *Zaïre* **55 E1** 10 28S 23 55 E
Musasa, *Tanzania* **54 C3** 3 25S 31 30 E
Musay'īd, *Qatar* **45 E6** 25 0N 51 33 E
Muscat = Masqat, *Oman* **46 C6** 23 37N 58 36 E
Muscat & Oman = Oman ■, *Asia* **46 C6** 23 0N 58 0 E
Muscatine, *U.S.A.* **80 E9** 41 25N 91 3W
Musgrave, *Australia* **62 A3** 14 47S 143 30 E
Musgrave Ras., *Australia* **61 E5** 26 0S 132 0 E
Mushie, *Zaïre* **52 E3** 2 56S 16 55 E
Musi →, *Indonesia* **36 E2** 2 20S 104 56 E
Muskeg →, *Canada* **72 A4** 60 20N 123 20W
Muskegon, *U.S.A.* **76 D2** 43 14N 86 16W
Muskegon →, *U.S.A.* **76 D2** 43 14N 86 21W
Muskegon Heights, *U.S.A.* **76 D2** 43 12N 86 16W
Muskogee, *U.S.A.* **81 H7** 35 45N 95 22W
Muskwa →, *Canada* **72 B4** 58 47N 122 48W
Muslīmiyah, *Syria* **44 B3** 36 19N 37 12 E
Musmar, *Sudan* **51 E12** 18 13N 35 40 E
Musofu, *Zambia* **55 E2** 13 30S 29 0 E
Musoma, *Tanzania* **54 C3** 1 30S 33 48 E
Musoma □, *Tanzania* **54 C3** 1 50S 34 30 E
Musquaro, L., *Canada* **71 B7** 50 38N 61 5W
Musquodoboit Harbour, *Canada* **71 D7** 44 50N 63 9W
Musselburgh, *U.K.* **12 F5** 55 57N 3 3W
Musselshell →, *U.S.A.* **82 C10** 47 21N 107 57W
Mussoorie, *India* **42 D8** 30 27N 78 6 E
Mussuco, *Angola* **56 B2** 17 2S 19 3 E
Mustang, *Nepal* **43 E10** 29 10N 83 55 E
Musters, L., *Argentina* **96 F3** 45 20S 69 25W
Musudan, *N. Korea* **35 D15** 40 50N 129 43 E
Muswellbrook, *Australia* **63 E5** 32 16S 150 56 E
Mût, *Egypt* **51 C10** 25 28N 28 58 E
Mutanda, *Mozam.* **57 C5** 21 0S 33 34 E
Mutanda, *Zambia* **55 E2** 12 24S 26 13 E
Mutaray, *Russia* **27 C11** 60 56N 101 0 E
Mutare, *Zimbabwe* **55 F3** 18 58S 32 38 E
Muting, *Indonesia* **37 F10** 7 23S 140 20 E
Mutshatsha, *Zaïre* **55 E1** 10 35S 24 20 E
Mutsu, *Japan* **30 D10** 41 5N 140 55 E
Mutsu-Wan, *Japan* **30 D10** 41 5N 140 55 E
Muttaburra, *Australia* **62 C3** 22 38S 144 29 E
Mutuáli, *Mozam.* **55 E4** 14 55S 37 0 E
Muweilih, *Egypt* **47 E3** 30 42N 34 19 E
Muxima, *Angola* **52 F2** 9 33S 13 58 E
Muy Muy, *Nic.* **88 D2** 12 39N 85 36W
Muya, *Russia* **27 D12** 56 27N 115 50 E
Muyinga, *Burundi* **54 C3** 3 14S 30 33 E
Muzaffarabad, *Pakistan* **43 B5** 34 25N 73 30 E
Muzaffargarh, *Pakistan* **42 D4** 30 5N 71 14 E
Muzaffarnagar, *India* **42 E7** 29 26N 77 40 E
Muzaffarpur, *India* **43 F11** 26 7N 85 23 E
Muzhi, *Russia* **26 C7** 65 25N 64 40 E
Muzon, C., *U.S.A.* **72 C2** 54 40N 132 42W
Mvuma, *Zimbabwe* **55 F3** 19 16S 30 30 E
Mvurwi, *Zimbabwe* **55 F3** 17 0S 30 57 E
Mwadui, *Tanzania* **54 C3** 3 26S 33 32 E
Mwambo, *Tanzania* **55 E5** 10 30S 40 22 E
Mwandi, *Zambia* **55 F1** 17 30S 24 51 E
Mwanza, *Tanzania* **54 C3** 2 30S 32 58 E
Mwanza, *Zaïre* **54 D2** 7 55S 26 43 E
Mwanza, *Zambia* **55 F1** 16 58S 24 28 E
Mwanza □, *Tanzania* **54 C3** 2 0S 33 0 E
Mwaya, *Tanzania* **55 D3** 9 32S 33 55 E
Mweelrea, *Ireland* **13 C2** 53 37N 9 48W
Mweka, *Zaïre* **52 E4** 4 50S 21 34 E
Mwenezi, *Zimbabwe* **55 G3** 21 15S 30 48 E
Mwenezi →, *Mozam.* **55 G3** 22 40S 31 50 E
Mwenga, *Zaïre* **54 C2** 3 1S 28 28 E
Mweru, L., *Zambia* **55 D2** 9 0S 28 40 E
Mweza Range, *Zimbabwe* **55 G3** 21 0S 30 0 E
Mwilambwe, *Zaïre* **54 D5** 8 7S 25 5 E
Mwimbi, *Tanzania* **55 D3** 8 38S 31 39 E
Mwinilunga, *Zambia* **55 E1** 11 43S 24 25 E
My Tho, *Vietnam* **39 G6** 10 29N 106 23 E
Myajlar, *India* **42 F4** 26 15N 70 20 E
Myanaung, *Burma* **41 K19** 18 18N 95 22 E
Myanmar = Burma ■, *Asia* **41 J20** 21 0N 96 30 E
Myaungmya, *Burma* **41 L19** 16 30N 94 40 E
Mycenae = Mikínai, *Greece* **21 F10** 37 43N 22 46 E
Myeik Kyunzu, *Burma* **39 G1** 11 30N 97 30 E
Myerstown, *U.S.A.* **79 F8** 40 22N 76 19W
Myingyan, *Burma* **41 J19** 21 30N 95 20 E
Myitkyina, *Burma* **41 G20** 25 24N 97 26 E
Mykolayiv = Nikolayev, *Ukraine* **25 E5** 46 58N 32 0 E
Mymensingh, *Bangla.* **41 G17** 24 45N 90 24 E
Mynydd Du, *U.K.* **11 F4** 51 45N 3 45W
Mýrdalsjökull, *Iceland* **8 E4** 63 40N 19 6W
Myroodah, *Australia* **60 C3** 18 7S 124 16 E
Myrtle Beach, *U.S.A.* **77 J6** 33 42N 78 53W
Myrtle Creek, *U.S.A.* **82 E2** 43 1N 123 17W
Myrtle Point, *U.S.A.* **82 E1** 43 4N 124 8W
Myrtou, *Cyprus* **23 D12** 35 18N 33 4 E
Mysore = Karnataka □, *India* **40 N10** 13 15N 77 0 E
Mysore, *India* **40 N10** 12 17N 76 41 E
Mystic, *U.S.A.* **79 E13** 41 21N 71 58W
Mytishchi, *Russia* **24 C6** 55 50N 37 50 E
Myton, *U.S.A.* **82 F8** 40 12N 110 4W
Mývatn, *Iceland* **8 D5** 65 36N 17 0W
Mzimba, *Malawi* **55 E3** 11 55S 33 39 E
Mzimkulu →, *S. Africa* **57 E5** 30 44S 30 28 E
Mzimvubu →, *S. Africa* **57 E4** 31 38S 29 33 E
Mzuzu, *Malawi* **55 E3** 11 30S 33 55 E

N

Na Noi, *Thailand* **38 C3** 18 19N 100 43 E
Na Phao, *Laos* **38 D5** 17 35N 105 44 E
Na Sam, *Vietnam* **38 A6** 22 3N 106 37 E
Na San, *Vietnam* **38 B5** 21 12N 104 2 E
Naab →, *Germany* **16 D6** 49 1N 12 2 E
Naantali, *Finland* **9 F17** 60 29N 22 2 E
Naas, *Ireland* **13 C5** 53 12N 6 40W
Nababiep, *S. Africa* **56 D2** 29 36S 17 46 E
Nabadwip = Navadwip, *India* **43 H13** 23 34N 88 20 E
Nabari, *Japan* **31 G8** 34 37N 136 5 E
Nabawa, *Australia* **61 E1** 28 30S 114 48 E
Nabberu, L., *Australia* **61 E3** 25 50S 120 30 E
Naberezhnyye Chelny, *Russia* **26 D6** 55 42N 52 19 E
Nabeul, *Tunisia* **51 A7** 36 30N 10 44 E
Nabha, *India* **42 D7** 30 26N 76 14 E
Nabīd, *Iran* **45 D8** 29 40N 57 38 E
Nabire, *Indonesia* **37 E9** 3 15S 135 26 E
Nabisar, *Pakistan* **42 G3** 25 8N 69 40 E
Nabisipi →, *Canada* **71 B7** 50 14N 62 13W
Nabiswera, *Uganda* **54 B3** 1 27N 32 15 E
Nablus = Nābulus, *Jordan* **47 C4** 32 14N 35 15 E
Naboomspruit, *S. Africa* **57 C4** 24 32S 28 40 E
Nābulus, *Jordan* **47 C4** 32 14N 35 15 E
Nābulus □, *Jordan* **47 C4** 32 20N 35 20 E
Nacala, *Mozam.* **55 E5** 14 31S 40 34 E
Nacala-Velha, *Mozam.* **55 E5** 14 32S 40 34 E
Nacaome, *Honduras* **88 D2** 13 31N 87 30W
Nacaroa, *Mozam.* **55 E4** 14 22S 39 56 E
Naches, *U.S.A.* **82 C3** 46 44N 120 42W
Naches →, *U.S.A.* **84 D6** 46 38N 120 31W
Nachingwea, *Tanzania* **55 E4** 10 23S 38 49 E
Nachingwea □, *Tanzania* **55 E4** 10 30S 38 30 E
Nachna, *India* **42 F4** 27 34N 71 41 E
Nacimiento Reservoir, *U.S.A.* **84 K6** 35 46N 120 53W
Nackara, *Australia* **63 E2** 32 48S 139 12 E
Naco, *Mexico* **86 A3** 31 20N 109 56W
Naco, *U.S.A.* **83 L9** 31 20N 109 57W
Nacogdoches, *U.S.A.* **81 K7** 31 36N 94 39W
Nácori Chico, *Mexico* **86 B3** 29 39N 109 1W
Nacozari, *Mexico* **86 A3** 30 24N 109 39W
Nadiad, *India* **42 H5** 22 41N 72 56 E
Nadur, *Malta* **23 C1** 36 2N 14 17 E
Nadūshan, *Iran* **45 C7** 32 2N 53 35 E
Nadvoitsy, *Russia* **24 B5** 63 52N 34 14 E
Nadym, *Russia* **26 C8** 65 35N 72 42 E
Nadym →, *Russia* **26 C8** 66 12N 72 0 E
Nafada, *Nigeria* **50 F7** 11 8N 11 20 E
Naftshahr, *Iran* **44 C5** 34 0N 45 30 E
Nafud Desert = An Nafūd, *Si. Arabia* **44 D4** 28 15N 41 0 E
Naga, *Phil.* **37 B6** 13 38N 123 15 E
Nagagami →, *Canada* **70 C3** 49 40N 84 40W
Nagahama, *Japan* **31 G8** 35 23N 136 16 E
Nagai, *Japan* **30 E10** 38 6N 140 2 E
Nagaland □, *India* **41 F19** 26 0N 94 30 E
Nagano, *Japan* **31 F9** 36 40N 138 10 E
Nagano □, *Japan* **31 F9** 36 15N 138 0 E
Nagaoka, *Japan* **31 F9** 37 27N 138 51 E
Nagappattinam, *India* **40 P11** 10 46N 79 51 E
Nagar Parkar, *Pakistan* **42 G4** 24 28N 70 46 E
Nagasaki, *Japan* **31 H4** 32 47N 129 50 E
Nagasaki □, *Japan* **31 H4** 32 50N 129 40 E
Nagato, *Japan* **31 G5** 34 19N 131 5 E
Nagaur, *India* **42 F5** 27 15N 73 45 E
Nagercoil, *India* **40 Q10** 8 12N 77 26 E
Nagina, *India* **43 E8** 29 30N 78 30 E
Nagīneh, *Iran* **45 C8** 34 20N 57 15 E
Nagir, *Pakistan* **43 A6** 36 12N 74 42 E
Nagoorin, *Australia* **62 C5** 24 17S 151 15 E
Nagornyy, *Russia* **27 D13** 55 58N 124 57 E
Nagoya, *Japan* **31 G8** 35 10N 136 50 E
Nagpur, *India* **40 J11** 21 8N 79 10 E
Nagua, *Dom. Rep.* **89 C6** 19 23N 69 50W
Nagykanizsa, *Hungary* **16 E8** 46 28N 17 0 E
Nagykörös, *Hungary* **17 E9** 47 5N 19 48 E
Naha, *Japan* **31 L3** 26 13N 127 42 E
Nahanni Butte, *Canada* **72 A4** 61 2N 123 31W
Nahanni Nat. Park, *Canada* **72 A3** 61 15N 125 0W
Nahariyya, *Israel* **44 C2** 33 1N 35 5 E
Nahāvand, *Iran* **45 C6** 34 10N 48 22 E
Nahlin, *Canada* **72 B2** 58 55N 131 38W
Naicá, *Mexico* **86 B3** 27 53N 105 31W
Naicam, *Canada* **73 C8** 52 30N 104 30W
Nā'ifah, *Si. Arabia* **46 D5** 19 59N 50 46 E
Nain, *Canada* **71 A7** 56 34N 61 40W
Nā'īn, *Iran* **45 C7** 32 54N 53 0 E
Naini Tal, *India* **43 E8** 29 30N 79 30 E
Nainpur, *India* **40 H12** 22 30N 80 10 E
Naira, *Indonesia* **37 E7** 4 28S 130 0 E
Nairn, *U.K.* **12 D5** 57 35N 3 54W
Nairobi, *Kenya* **54 C4** 1 17S 36 48 E
Naivasha, *Kenya* **54 C4** 0 40S 36 30 E
Naivasha, L., *Kenya* **54 C4** 0 48S 36 20 E
Najafābād, *Iran* **45 C6** 32 40N 51 15 E
Najibabad, *India* **42 E8** 29 40N 78 20 E
Najin, *N. Korea* **35 C16** 42 12N 130 15 E
Najmah, *Si. Arabia* **45 E6** 26 42N 50 6 E
Naju, *S. Korea* **35 G14** 35 3N 126 43 E
Nakadōri-Shima, *Japan* **31 H4** 32 57N 129 4 E
Nakalagba, *Zaïre* **54 B2** 2 50N 27 58 E
Nakaminato, *Japan* **31 F10** 36 21N 140 36 E
Nakamura, *Japan* **31 H6** 32 59N 132 56 E
Nakano, *Japan* **31 F9** 36 45N 138 22 E
Nakano-Shima, *Japan* **31 K4** 29 51N 129 52 E
Nakashibetsu, *Japan* **30 C12** 43 33N 144 59 E
Nakfa, *Eritrea* **51 E12** 16 40N 38 32 E
Nakhichevan, *Azerbaijan* **25 G8** 39 12N 45 15 E
Nakhichevan Republic □, *Azerbaijan* **25 G8** 39 14N 45 30 E
Nakhl, *Egypt* **47 F2** 29 55N 33 43 E
Nakhl-e Taqī, *Iran* **45 E7** 27 28N 52 36 E
Nakhodka, *Russia* **27 E14** 42 53N 132 54 E
Nakhon Nayok, *Thailand* **38 E3** 14 12N 101 13 E
Nakhon Pathom, *Thailand* **38 F3** 13 49N 100 3 E
Nakhon Phanom, *Thailand* **38 D5** 17 23N 104 43 E
Nakhon Ratchasima, *Thailand* **38 E4** 14 59N 102 12 E
Nakhon Sawan, *Thailand* **38 E3** 15 35N 100 10 E
Nakhon Si Thammarat, *Thailand* **39 H3** 8 29N 100 0 E
Nakhon Thai, *Thailand* **38 D3** 17 5N 100 44 E
Nakina, *B.C., Canada* **72 B2** 59 12N 132 52W
Nakina, *Ont., Canada* **70 B2** 50 10N 86 40W
Nakodar, *India* **42 D6** 31 8N 75 31 E
Nakskov, *Denmark* **9 J11** 54 50N 11 8 E
Naktong →, *S. Korea* **35 G15** 35 7N 128 57 E
Nakuru, *Kenya* **54 C4** 0 15S 36 4 E

Nakuru

Normanhurst, Mt.

New Caledonia, Pac. Oc. 64 K8 21 0S 165 0 E
New Castile = Castilla La Mancha □, Spain 19 C4 39 30N 3 30W
New Castle, Ind., U.S.A. 76 F3 39 55N 85 22W
New Castle, Pa., U.S.A. 78 E4 41 0N 80 21W
New City, U.S.A. 79 E11 41 9N 73 59W
New Cumberland, U.S.A. 78 F4 40 30N 80 36W
New Cuyama, U.S.A. 85 L7 34 57N 119 38W
New Delhi, India 42 E7 28 37N 77 13 E
New Denver, Canada 72 D5 50 0N 117 25W
New Don Pedro Reservoir, U.S.A. 84 H6 37 43N 120 24W
New England, U.S.A. 80 B3 46 32N 102 52W
New England Ra., Australia 63 E5 30 20S 151 45 E
New Forest, U.K. 11 G6 50 53N 1 40W
New Glasgow, Canada 71 C7 45 35N 62 36W
New Guinea, Oceania 64 H5 4 0S 136 0 E
New Hamburg, Canada 78 C4 43 23N 80 42W
New Hampshire □, U.S.A. 79 C13 44 0N 71 30W
New Hampton, U.S.A. 80 D8 43 3N 92 19W
New Hanover, S. Africa 57 D5 29 22S 30 31 E
New Haven, Conn., U.S.A. 79 E12 41 18N 72 55W
New Haven, Mich., U.S.A. 78 D2 42 44N 82 48W
New Hazelton, Canada 72 B3 55 20N 127 30W
New Hebrides = Vanuatu ■, Pac. Oc. 64 J8 15 0S 168 0 E
New Iberia, U.S.A. 81 K9 30 1N 91 49W
New Ireland, Papua N. G. 64 H7 3 20S 151 50 E
New Jersey □, U.S.A. 79 F10 40 0N 74 30W
New Kensington, U.S.A. 78 F5 40 34N 79 46W
New Lexington, U.S.A. 76 F4 39 43N 82 13W
New Liskeard, Canada 70 C4 47 31N 79 41W
New London, Conn., U.S.A. 79 E12 41 22N 72 6W
New London, Minn., U.S.A. 80 C7 45 18N 94 56W
New London, Ohio, U.S.A. 78 E2 41 5N 82 24W
New London, Wis., U.S.A. 80 C10 44 23N 88 45W
New Madrid, U.S.A. 81 G10 36 36N 89 32W
New Meadows, U.S.A. 82 D5 44 58N 116 18W
New Melones L., U.S.A. 84 H6 37 57N 120 31W
New Mexico □, U.S.A. 83 J10 34 30N 106 0W
New Milford, Conn., U.S.A. 79 E11 41 35N 73 25W
New Milford, Pa., U.S.A. 79 E9 41 52N 75 44W
New Norcia, Australia 61 F2 30 57S 116 13 E
New Norfolk, Australia 62 G4 42 46S 147 2 E
New Orleans, U.S.A. 81 K9 29 58N 90 4W
New Philadelphia, U.S.A. 78 F3 40 30N 81 27W
New Plymouth, N.Z. 59 H5 39 4S 174 5 E
New Plymouth, U.S.A. 82 E5 43 58N 116 49W
New Providence, Bahamas 88 A4 25 25N 78 35W
New Radnor, U.K. 11 E4 52 15N 3 10W
New Richmond, U.S.A. 80 C8 45 7N 92 32W
New Roads, U.S.A. 81 K9 30 42N 91 26W
New Rochelle, U.S.A. 79 F11 40 55N 73 47W
New Rockford, U.S.A. 80 B5 47 41N 99 8W
New Ross, Ireland 13 D5 52 24N 6 58W
New Salem, U.S.A. 80 B4 46 51N 101 25W
New Scone, U.K. 12 E5 56 25N 3 26W
New Siberian I. = Novaya Sibir, Ostrov, Russia 27 B16 75 10N 150 0 E
New Siberian Is. = Novosibirskiye Ostrova, Russia 27 B15 75 0N 142 0 E
New Smyrna Beach, U.S.A. 77 L5 29 1N 80 56W
New South Wales □, Australia 63 E4 33 0S 146 0 E
New Springs, Australia 61 E3 25 49S 120 1 E
New Town, U.S.A. 80 A3 47 59N 102 30W
New Ulm, U.S.A. 80 C7 44 19N 94 28W
New Waterford, Canada 71 C7 46 13N 60 4W
New Westminster, Canada 72 D4 49 13N 122 55W
New York □, U.S.A. 79 D9 43 0N 75 0W
New York City, U.S.A. 79 F11 40 45N 74 0W
New Zealand ■, Oceania 59 J5 40 0S 176 0 E
Newala, Tanzania 55 E4 10 58S 39 18 E
Newala □, Tanzania 55 E4 10 46S 39 20 E
Newark, Del., U.S.A. 76 F8 39 41N 75 46W
Newark, N.J., U.S.A. 79 F10 40 44N 74 10W
Newark, N.Y., U.S.A. 78 C7 43 3N 77 6W
Newark, Ohio, U.S.A. 78 F2 40 3N 82 24W
Newark-on-Trent, U.K. 10 D7 53 6N 0 48W
Newaygo, U.S.A. 76 D3 43 25N 85 48W
Newberg, U.S.A. 82 D2 45 18N 122 58W
Newberry, Mich., U.S.A. 76 B3 46 21N 85 30W
Newberry, S.C., U.S.A. 77 H5 34 17N 81 37W
Newberry Springs, U.S.A. 85 L10 34 50N 116 41W
Newbrook, Canada 72 C6 54 24N 112 57W
Newburgh, U.S.A. 79 E10 41 30N 74 1W
Newbury, U.K. 11 F6 51 24N 1 19W
Newbury, U.S.A. 79 B12 43 19N 72 3W
Newburyport, U.S.A. 79 D14 42 49N 70 53W
Newcastle, Australia 63 E5 33 0S 151 46 E
Newcastle, Canada 71 C6 47 1N 65 38W
Newcastle, S. Africa 57 D4 27 45S 29 58 E
Newcastle, U.K. 13 B6 54 13N 5 54W
Newcastle, Calif., U.S.A. 84 G5 38 53N 121 8W
Newcastle, Wyo., U.S.A. 80 D2 43 50N 104 11W
Newcastle Emlyn, U.K. 11 E3 52 2N 4 29W
Newcastle Ra., Australia 60 C5 15 45S 130 15 E
Newcastle-under-Lyme, U.K. 10 D5 53 2N 2 15W
Newcastle-upon-Tyne, U.K. 10 C6 54 59N 1 37W
Newcastle Waters, Australia 62 B1 17 30S 133 28 E
Newdegate, Australia 61 F2 33 6S 119 0 E
Newell, U.S.A. 80 C3 44 43N 103 25W
Newfoundland □, Canada 71 B8 53 0N 58 0W
Newhalem, U.S.A. 72 D4 48 40N 121 15W
Newhall, U.S.A. 85 L8 34 23N 118 32W
Newham, U.K. 11 F8 51 31N 0 2 E
Newhaven, U.K. 11 G8 50 47N 0 4 E
Newkirk, U.S.A. 81 G6 36 53N 97 3W
Newman, Australia 60 D2 23 18S 119 45 E
Newman, U.S.A. 84 H5 37 19N 121 1W
Newmarket, Canada 78 B5 44 3N 79 28W
Newmarket, Ireland 13 D3 52 13N 9 0W
Newmarket, U.K. 11 E8 52 15N 0 23 E
Newmarket, U.S.A. 79 C14 43 5N 70 56W
Newnan, U.S.A. 77 J3 33 23N 84 48W
Newport, Gwent, U.K. 11 F5 51 35N 3 0W
Newport, I. of W., U.K. 11 G6 50 42N 1 18W
Newport, Shrops., U.K. 11 E5 52 47N 2 22W
Newport, Ark., U.S.A. 81 H9 35 37N 91 16W
Newport, Ky., U.S.A. 76 F3 39 5N 84 30W
Newport, N.H., U.S.A. 79 C12 43 22N 72 10W
Newport, Oreg., U.S.A. 82 D1 44 39N 124 3W
Newport, Pa., U.S.A. 78 F7 40 29N 77 8W
Newport, R.I., U.S.A. 79 E13 41 29N 71 19W
Newport, Tenn., U.S.A. 77 H4 35 58N 83 11W
Newport, Vt., U.S.A. 79 B12 44 56N 72 13W
Newport, Wash., U.S.A. 82 B5 48 11N 117 3W
Newport Beach, U.S.A. 85 M9 33 37N 117 56W
Newport News, U.S.A. 76 G7 36 59N 76 25W
Newquay, U.K. 11 G2 50 24N 5 6W
Newry, U.K. 13 B5 54 10N 6 20W
Newry & Mourne □, U.K. 13 B5 54 10N 6 15W
Newton, Iowa, U.S.A. 80 E8 41 42N 93 3W
Newton, Mass., U.S.A. 79 D13 42 21N 71 12W
Newton, Miss., U.S.A. 81 J10 32 19N 89 10W
Newton, N.C., U.S.A. 77 H5 35 40N 81 13W
Newton, N.J., U.S.A. 79 E10 41 3N 74 45W
Newton, Tex., U.S.A. 81 K8 30 51N 93 46W
Newton Abbot, U.K. 11 G4 50 32N 3 37W
Newton Boyd, Australia 63 D5 29 45S 152 16 E
Newton Stewart, U.K. 12 G4 54 57N 4 30W
Newtonmore, U.K. 12 D4 57 4N 4 7W
Newtown, U.K. 11 E4 52 31N 3 19W
Newtownabbey □, U.K. 13 B6 54 45N 6 0W
Newtownards, U.K. 13 B6 54 37N 5 40W
Newville, U.S.A. 78 F7 40 10N 77 24W
Neya, Russia 24 C7 58 21N 43 49 E
Neyriz, Iran 45 D7 29 15N 54 19 E
Neyshābūr, Iran 45 B8 36 10N 58 50 E
Nezhin, Ukraine 25 D5 51 5N 31 55 E
Nezperce, U.S.A. 82 C5 46 14N 116 14W
Ngabang, Indonesia 36 D3 0 23N 109 55 E
Ngabordamlu, Tanjung, Indonesia 37 F8 6 56S 134 11 E
Ngami Depression, Botswana 56 C3 20 30S 22 46 E
Ngamo, Zimbabwe 55 F2 19 3S 27 32 E
Nganglong Kangri, China 41 C12 33 0N 81 0 E
Nganjuk, Indonesia 37 G14 7 32S 111 55 E
Ngao, Thailand 38 C2 18 46N 99 59 E
Ngaoundéré, Cameroon 52 C2 7 15N 13 35 E
Ngapara, N.Z. 59 L3 44 57S 170 46 E
Ngara, Tanzania 54 C3 2 29S 30 40 E
Ngara □, Tanzania 54 C3 2 29S 30 40 E
Ngawi, Indonesia 37 G14 7 24S 111 26 E
Nghia Lo, Vietnam 38 B5 21 33N 104 28 E
Ngoma, Malawi 55 E3 13 8S 33 45 E
Ngomahura, Zimbabwe 55 G3 20 26S 30 43 E
Ngomba, Tanzania 55 D3 8 20S 32 53 E
Ngoring Hu, China 32 C4 34 55N 97 5 E
Ngorongoro, Tanzania 54 C4 3 11S 35 32 E
Ngozi, Burundi 54 C2 2 54S 29 50 E
Ngudu, Tanzania 54 C3 2 58S 33 25 E
Nguigmi, Niger 51 F7 14 20N 13 20 E
Ngukurr, Australia 62 A1 14 44S 134 44 E
Ngunga, Tanzania 54 C3 3 37S 33 37 E
Nguru, Nigeria 50 F7 12 56N 10 29 E
Nguru Mts., Tanzania 54 D4 6 0S 37 30 E
Nguyen Binh, Vietnam 38 A5 22 39N 105 56 E
Nha Trang, Vietnam 39 F7 12 16N 109 10 E
Nhacoongo, Mozam. 57 C6 24 18S 35 14 E
Nhamaabué, Mozam. 55 F4 17 25S 35 5 E
Nhangutazi, L., Mozam. 57 C5 24 0S 34 30 E
Nhill, Australia 63 F3 36 18S 141 40 E
Nho Quan, Vietnam 38 B5 20 18N 105 45 E
Nhulunbuy, Australia 62 A2 12 10S 137 20 E
Nia-nia, Zaire 54 B2 1 30N 27 40 E
Niafounké, Mali 50 E4 16 0N 4 5W
Niagara, U.S.A. 76 C1 45 45N 88 0W
Niagara Falls, Canada 70 D4 43 7N 79 5W
Niagara Falls, U.S.A. 78 C6 43 5N 79 4W
Niagara-on-the-Lake, Canada 78 C5 43 15N 79 4W
Niah, Malaysia 36 D4 3 58N 113 46 E
Niamey, Niger 50 F5 13 27N 2 6 E
Niangara, Zaire 54 B2 3 42N 27 50 E
Nias, Indonesia 36 D1 1 0N 97 30 E
Niassa □, Mozam. 55 E4 13 30S 36 0 E
Nicaragua ■, Cent. Amer. 88 D2 11 40N 85 30W
Nicaragua, L. de, Nic. 88 D2 12 0N 85 30W
Nicastro, Italy 20 E7 38 58N 16 18 E
Nice, France 18 E7 43 42N 7 14 E
Niceville, U.S.A. 77 K2 30 31N 86 30W
Nichinan, Japan 31 J5 31 38N 131 23 E
Nicholás, Canal, W. Indies 88 B3 23 30N 80 5W
Nicholasville, U.S.A. 76 G3 37 53N 84 34W
Nichols, U.S.A. 79 D8 42 1N 76 22W
Nicholson, Australia 60 C4 18 2S 128 54 E
Nicholson, U.S.A. 79 E9 41 37N 75 47W
Nicholson →, Australia 62 B2 17 31S 139 36 E
Nicholson Ra., Australia 61 E2 27 15S 116 45 E
Nicobar Is., Ind. Oc. 28 J13 9 0N 93 0 E
Nicola, Canada 72 C4 50 12N 120 40W
Nicolet, Canada 70 C5 46 17N 72 35W
Nicolls Town, Bahamas 88 A4 25 8N 78 0W
Nicosia, Cyprus 23 D12 35 10N 33 25 E
Nicoya, Costa Rica 88 D2 10 9N 85 27W
Nicoya, G. de, Costa Rica 88 E3 10 0N 85 0W
Nicoya, Pen. de, Costa Rica 88 E2 9 45N 85 40W
Nidd →, U.K. 10 C6 54 1N 1 32W
Niekerkshoop, S. Africa 56 D3 29 19S 22 51 E
Niemba, Zaire 54 D2 5 58S 28 24 E
Niemen = Neman →, Lithuania 24 C3 55 25N 21 10 E
Nienburg, Germany 16 B4 52 38N 9 15 E
Nieu Bethesda, S. Africa 56 E3 31 51S 24 34 E
Nieuw Amsterdam, Surinam 93 B7 5 53N 55 5W
Nieuw Nickerie, Surinam 93 B7 6 0N 56 59W
Nieuwoudtville, S. Africa 56 E2 31 23S 19 7 E
Nieuwpoort, Belgium 15 C2 51 8N 2 45 E
Nieves, Pico de las, Canary Is. 22 G4 27 57N 15 35W
Nièvre □, France 18 C5 47 10N 3 40 E
Niğde, Turkey 25 G5 37 58N 34 40 E
Nigel, S. Africa 57 D4 26 27S 28 25 E
Niger ■, W. Afr. 50 E6 17 30N 10 0 E
Niger →, W. Afr. 50 G6 5 33N 6 33 E
Nigeria ■, W. Afr. 50 G6 8 30N 8 0 E
Nightcaps, N.Z. 59 L2 45 57S 168 2 E
Nihtaur, India 43 E8 29 20N 78 23 E
Nii-Jima, Japan 31 G9 34 20N 139 15 E
Niigata, Japan 30 F9 37 58N 139 0 E
Niigata □, Japan 31 F9 37 15N 138 45 E
Niihama, Japan 31 H6 33 55N 133 16 E
Niihau, U.S.A. 74 H14 21 54N 160 9W
Niimi, Japan 31 G6 34 59N 133 28 E
Niitsu, Japan 30 F9 37 48N 139 7 E
Nijil, Jordan 47 E4 30 32N 35 33 E
Nijkerk, Neths. 15 B5 52 13N 5 30 E
Nijmegen, Neths. 15 C5 51 50N 5 52 E
Nijverdal, Neths. 15 B6 52 22N 6 28 E
Nīk Pey, Iran 45 B6 36 50N 48 10 E
Nikel, Russia 8 B21 69 24N 30 12 E
Nikiniki, Indonesia 37 F6 9 49S 124 30 E
Nikki, Benin 50 G5 9 58N 3 12 E
Nikkō, Japan 31 F9 36 45N 139 35 E
Nikolayev, Ukraine 25 E5 46 58N 32 0 E
Nikolayevsk, Russia 25 D8 50 0N 45 35 E
Nikolayevsk-na-Amur, Russia 27 D15 53 8N 140 44 E
Nikolskoye, Russia 27 D17 55 12N 166 0 E
Nikopol, Ukraine 25 E5 47 35N 34 25 E
Nīkshahr, Iran 45 E9 26 15N 60 10 E
Nîl, Nahr en →, Africa 51 B11 30 10N 31 6 E
Nîl el Abyad →, Sudan 51 E11 15 38N 32 31 E
Nîl el Azraq →, Sudan 51 E11 15 38N 32 31 E
Niland, U.S.A. 85 M11 33 14N 115 31W
Nile = Nîl, Nahr en →, Africa 51 B11 30 10N 31 6 E
Nile □, Uganda 54 B3 2 0N 31 30 E
Niles, U.S.A. 78 E4 41 11N 80 46W
Nimach, India 42 G6 24 30N 74 56 E
Nimbahera, India 42 G6 24 37N 74 45 E
Nîmes, France 18 E6 43 50N 4 23 E
Nimmitabel, Australia 63 F4 36 29S 149 15 E
Nimneryskiy, Russia 27 D13 57 50N 125 10 E
Nimule, Sudan 52 D6 3 32N 32 3 E
Ninawá, Iraq 44 B4 36 25N 43 10 E
Nindigully, Australia 63 D4 28 21S 148 50 E
Ninemile, U.S.A. 72 B2 56 0N 130 7W
Nineveh = Ninawá, Iraq 44 B4 36 25N 43 10 E
Ning Xian, China 34 G4 35 30N 107 58 E
Ningaloo, Australia 60 D1 22 41S 113 41 E
Ning'an, China 35 B15 44 22N 129 20 E
Ningbo, China 33 D7 29 51N 121 28 E
Ningcheng, China 35 D10 41 32N 119 53 E
Ningjin, China 34 F8 37 35N 114 57 E
Ningjing Shan, China 32 C4 30 0N 98 20 E
Ningling, China 34 G8 34 25N 115 22 E
Ningpo = Ningbo, China 33 D7 29 51N 121 28 E
Ningqiang, China 34 H4 32 47N 106 15 E
Ningshan, China 34 H5 33 21N 108 21 E
Ningsia Hui A.R. = Ningxia Huizu Zizhiqu □, China 34 E3 38 0N 106 0 E
Ningwu, China 34 E7 39 0N 112 18 E
Ningxia Huizu Zizhiqu □, China 34 E3 38 0N 106 0 E
Ningyang, China 34 G9 35 47N 116 45 E
Ninh Binh, Vietnam 38 B5 20 15N 105 55 E
Ninh Giang, Vietnam 38 B6 20 44N 106 24 E
Ninh Hoa, Vietnam 38 F7 12 30N 109 7 E
Ninh Ma, Vietnam 38 F7 12 48N 109 21 E
Ninove, Belgium 15 D4 50 51N 4 2 E
Nioaque, Brazil 95 A4 21 5S 55 50W
Niobrara, U.S.A. 80 D6 42 45N 98 2W
Niobrara →, U.S.A. 80 D6 42 46N 98 3W
Nioro du Sahel, Mali 50 E3 15 15N 9 30W
Niort, France 18 C3 46 19N 0 29W
Nipawin, Canada 73 C8 53 20N 104 0W
Nipawin Prov. Park, Canada 73 C8 54 0N 104 37W
Nipigon, Canada 70 C2 49 0N 88 17W
Nipigon, L., Canada 70 C2 49 50N 88 30W
Nipin →, Canada 73 B7 55 46N 108 35W
Nipishish L., Canada 71 B7 54 12N 60 45W
Nipissing L., Canada 70 C4 46 20N 80 0W
Nipomo, U.S.A. 85 K6 35 3N 120 29W
Nipton, U.S.A. 85 K11 35 28N 115 16W
Niquelândia, Brazil 93 F9 14 33S 48 23W
Nīr, Iran 44 B5 38 2N 47 59 E
Nirasaki, Japan 31 G9 35 42N 138 27 E
Nirmal, India 40 K11 19 3N 78 20 E
Nirmali, India 43 F12 26 20N 86 35 E
Niš, Serbia, Yug. 21 C9 43 19N 21 58 E
Nişāb, Yemen 46 E4 14 25N 46 29 E
Nishinomiya, Japan 31 G7 34 45N 135 20 E
Nishin'omote, Japan 31 J5 30 43N 130 59 E
Nishiwaki, Japan 31 G7 34 59N 134 58 E
Niskibi →, Canada 70 A2 56 29N 88 9W
Nisqually →, U.S.A. 84 C4 47 6N 122 42W
Nissáki, Greece 23 A3 39 43N 19 52 E
Nisutlin →, Canada 72 A2 60 14N 132 34W
Nitchequon, Canada 71 B5 53 10N 70 58W
Niterói, Brazil 95 A7 22 52S 43 0W
Nith →, U.K. 12 F5 55 20N 3 5W
Nitra, Slovakia 17 D9 48 19N 18 4 E
Nitra →, Slovakia 17 E9 47 46N 18 10 E
Niuafo'ou, Tonga 59 B11 15 30S 175 58W
Niue, Cook Is. 65 J11 19 2S 169 54W
Niut, Indonesia 36 D4 0 55N 110 6 E
Niuzhuang, China 35 D12 40 58N 122 28 E
Nivelles, Belgium 15 D4 50 35N 4 20 E
Nivernais, France 18 C5 47 15N 3 30 E
Nixon, U.S.A. 81 L6 29 16N 97 46W
Nizamabad, India 40 K11 18 45N 78 7 E
Nizamghat, India 41 E19 28 20N 95 45 E
Nizhne Kolymsk, Russia 27 C17 68 34N 160 55 E
Nizhne-Vartovsk, Russia 26 C8 60 56N 76 38 E
Nizhneangarsk, Russia 27 D11 55 47N 109 30 E
Nizhnekamsk, Russia 24 C9 55 38N 51 49 E
Nizhneudinsk, Russia 27 D10 54 54N 99 3 E
Nizhneyansk, Russia 27 B14 71 26N 136 4 E
Nizhniy Novgorod, Russia 24 C7 56 20N 44 0 E
Nizhniy Tagil, Russia 24 C10 57 55N 59 57 E
Nizké Tatry, Slovakia 17 D9 48 55N 19 30 E
Njakwa, Malawi 55 E3 11 1S 33 56 E
Njanji, Zambia 55 E3 14 25S 31 46 E
Njinjo, Tanzania 55 D4 8 48S 38 54 E
Njombe, Tanzania 55 D3 9 20S 34 50 E
Njombe □, Tanzania 55 D3 9 20S 34 49 E
Njombe →, Tanzania 54 D4 6 56S 35 6 E
Nkambe, Cameroon 50 G7 6 35N 10 40 E
Nkana, Zambia 55 E2 12 50S 28 8 E
Nkawkaw, Ghana 50 G4 6 36N 0 49W
Nkayi, Zimbabwe 55 F2 19 41S 29 20 E
Nkhata Bay, Malawi 52 G6 11 33S 34 16 E
Nkhota Kota, Malawi 55 E3 12 56S 34 15 E
Nkongsamba, Cameroon 50 H6 4 55N 9 55 E
Nkurenkuru, Namibia 56 B2 17 42S 18 32 E
Nmai →, Burma 41 G20 25 30N 97 25 E
Noakhali = Maijdi, Bangla. 41 H17 22 48N 91 10 E
Noatak, U.S.A. 68 B3 67 34N 162 58W
Nobel, Canada 78 A4 45 25N 80 6W
Nobeoka, Japan 31 H5 32 36N 131 41 E
Noblesville, U.S.A. 76 E3 40 3N 86 1W
Nocera Inferiore, Italy 20 D6 40 45N 14 37 E
Nockatunga, Australia 63 D3 27 42S 142 42 E
Nocona, U.S.A. 81 J6 33 47N 97 44W
Noda, Japan 31 G9 35 56N 139 52 E
Noel, U.S.A. 81 G7 36 33N 94 29W
Nogales, Mexico 86 A2 31 20N 110 56W
Nogales, U.S.A. 83 L8 31 20N 110 56W
Nōgata, Japan 31 H5 33 48N 130 44 E
Noggerup, Australia 61 F2 33 32S 116 5 E
Noginsk, Russia 27 C10 64 30N 90 50 E
Nogoa →, Australia 62 C4 23 40S 147 55 E
Nogoyá, Argentina 94 C4 32 24S 59 48W
Nohar, India 42 E6 29 11N 74 49 E
Noirmoutier, I. de, France 18 C2 46 58N 2 10W
Nojane, Botswana 56 C3 23 15S 20 14 E
Nojima-Zaki, Japan 31 G9 34 54N 139 53 E
Nok Kundi, Pakistan 40 E3 28 50N 62 45 E
Nokaneng, Botswana 56 B3 19 40S 22 17 E
Nokhtuysk, Russia 27 C12 60 0N 117 45 E
Nokomis, Canada 73 C8 51 35N 105 0W
Nokomis L., Canada 73 B8 57 0N 103 0W
Nola, C.A.R. 52 D3 3 35N 16 4 E
Noma Omuramba →, Namibia 56 B3 18 52S 20 53 E
Noman L., Canada 73 A7 62 15N 108 55W
Nombre de Dios, Panama 88 E4 9 34N 79 28W
Nome, U.S.A. 68 B3 64 30N 165 25W
Nomo-Zaki, Japan 31 H4 32 35N 129 44 E
Nonacho L., Canada 73 A7 61 42N 109 40W
Nonda, Australia 62 C3 20 40S 142 28 E
Nong Chang, Thailand 38 E2 15 23N 99 51 E
Nong Het, Laos 38 C4 19 29N 103 59 E
Nong Khai, Thailand 38 D4 17 50N 102 46 E
Nong'an, China 35 B13 44 25N 125 5 E
Nongoma, S. Africa 57 D5 27 58S 31 35 E
Nonoava, Mexico 86 B3 27 28N 106 44W
Nonthaburi, Thailand 38 F3 13 51N 100 34 E
Noonamah, Australia 60 B5 12 40S 131 4 E
Noonan, U.S.A. 80 A3 48 54N 103 1W
Noondoo, Australia 63 D4 28 35S 148 30 E
Noonkanbah, Australia 60 C3 18 30S 124 50 E
Noord Brabant □, Neths. 15 C5 51 40N 5 0 E
Noord Holland □, Neths. 15 B4 52 30N 4 45 E
Noordbeveland, Neths. 15 C3 51 35N 3 50 E
Noordoostpolder, Neths. 15 B5 52 45N 5 45 E
Noordwijk aan Zee, Neths. 15 B4 52 14N 4 26 E
Nootka, Canada 72 D3 49 38N 126 38W
Nootka I., Canada 72 D3 49 32N 126 42W
Nóqui, Angola 52 F2 5 55S 13 30 E
Noranda, Canada 70 C4 48 20N 79 0W
Norco, U.S.A. 85 M9 33 56N 117 33W
Nord □, France 18 A5 50 15N 3 30 E
Nord-Ostsee Kanal, Germany 16 A4 54 15N 9 40 E
Nord-Trøndelag fylke □, Norway 8 D12 64 20N 12 10 E
Nordaustlandet, Svalbard 4 B9 79 14N 23 0 E
Nordegg, Canada 72 C5 52 29N 116 5W
Nordhausen, Germany 16 C5 51 29N 10 47 E
Nordkapp, Norway 8 A18 71 10N 25 44 E
Nordkapp, Svalbard 4 A9 80 31N 20 0 E
Nordkinn = Kinnarodden, Norway 6 A11 71 8N 27 40 E
Nordland fylke □, Norway 8 D12 65 40N 13 0 E
Nordrhein-Westfalen □, Germany 16 C3 51 45N 7 30 E
Nordvik, Russia 27 B12 74 2N 111 32 E
Norembega, Canada 70 C3 48 59N 80 43W
Norfolk, Nebr., U.S.A. 80 D6 42 2N 97 25W
Norfolk, Va., U.S.A. 76 G7 36 51N 76 17W
Norfolk □, U.K. 10 E9 52 39N 1 0 E
Norfolk Broads, U.K. 10 E9 52 30N 1 15 E
Norfolk I., Pac. Oc. 64 K8 28 58S 168 3 E
Norfork Res., U.S.A. 81 G8 36 13N 92 15W
Norilsk, Russia 27 C9 69 20N 88 6 E
Norley, Australia 63 D3 27 45S 143 48 E
Norma, Mt., Australia 62 C3 20 55S 140 42 E
Normal, U.S.A. 80 E10 40 31N 88 59W
Norman, U.S.A. 81 H6 35 13N 97 26W
Norman →, Australia 62 B3 19 18S 141 51 E
Norman Wells, Canada 68 B7 65 17N 126 51W
Normanby →, Australia 62 A3 14 23S 144 10 E
Normandie, France 18 B4 48 45N 0 10 E
Normandin, Canada 70 C5 48 49N 72 31W
Normandy = Normandie, France 18 B4 48 45N 0 10 E
Normanhurst, Mt., Australia 61 E3 25 4S 122 30 E

Oromocto

Obskaya Guba, Russia 26 C8 69 0N 73 0 E
Obuasi, Ghana 50 G4 6 17N 1 40W
Ocala, U.S.A. 77 L4 29 11N 82 8W
Ocampo, Mexico 86 B3 28 9N 108 24W
Ocaña, Spain 19 C4 39 55N 3 30W
Ocanomowoc, U.S.A. 80 D10 43 7N 88 30W
Ocate, U.S.A. 81 G2 36 11N 105 3W
Occidental, Cordillera, Colombia 92 C3 5 0N 76 0W
Ocean City, N.J., U.S.A. 76 F8 39 17N 74 35W
Ocean City, Wash., U.S.A. 84 C2 47 4N 124 10W
Ocean I. = Banaba, Kiribati 64 H8 0 45S 169 50 E
Ocean Park, U.S.A. 84 D2 46 30N 124 3W
Oceano, U.S.A. 85 K6 35 6N 120 37W
Oceanport, U.S.A. 79 F10 40 19N 74 3W
Oceanside, U.S.A. 85 M9 33 12N 117 23W
Ochil Hills, U.K. 12 E5 56 14N 3 40W
Ochre River, Canada 73 C9 51 4N 99 47W
Ocilla, U.S.A. 77 K4 31 36N 83 15W
Ocmulgee →, U.S.A. 77 K4 31 58N 82 33W
Oconee →, U.S.A. 77 K4 31 58N 82 33W
Oconto, U.S.A. 76 C2 44 53N 87 52W
Oconto Falls, U.S.A. 76 C1 44 52N 88 9W
Ocosingo, Mexico 87 D6 17 10N 92 15W
Ocotal, Nic. 88 D2 13 41N 86 31W
Ocotlán, Mexico 86 C4 20 21N 102 42W
Octave, U.S.A. 83 J7 34 10N 112 43W
Ocumare del Tuy, Venezuela 92 A5 10 7N 66 46W
Ōda, Japan 31 G6 35 11N 132 30 E
Ódáðahraun, Iceland 8 D5 65 5N 17 0W
Odate, Japan 30 D10 40 16N 140 34 E
Odawara, Japan 31 G9 35 20N 139 6 E
Odda, Norway 9 F9 60 3N 6 35 E
Oddur, Somali Rep. 46 G3 4 11N 43 52 E
Odei →, Canada 73 B9 56 6N 96 54W
Odendaalsrus, S. Africa 56 D4 27 48S 26 45 E
Odense, Denmark 9 J11 55 22N 10 23 E
Oder →, Germany 16 B7 53 33N 14 38 E
Odesa = Odessa, Ukraine 25 E5 46 30N 30 45 E
Odessa, Canada 79 B8 44 17N 76 43W
Odessa, Ukraine 25 E5 46 30N 30 45 E
Odessa, Tex., U.S.A. 81 K3 31 52N 102 23W
Odessa, Wash., U.S.A. 82 C4 47 20N 118 41W
Odiakwe, Botswana 56 C4 20 12S 25 17 E
Odienné, Ivory C. 50 G3 9 30N 7 34W
Odintsovo, Russia 24 C6 55 39N 37 15 E
O'Donnell, U.S.A. 81 J4 32 58N 101 50W
Odorheiu Secuiesc, Romania 17 E12 46 21N 25 21 E
Odra →, Poland 16 B7 53 33N 14 38 E
Odžak, Bos.-H. 21 B8 45 3N 18 18 E
Odzi, Zimbabwe 57 B5 19 0S 32 20 E
Oeiras, Brazil 93 E10 7 0S 42 8W
Oelrichs, U.S.A. 80 D3 43 11N 103 14W
Oelwein, U.S.A. 80 D9 42 41N 91 55W
Oenpelli, Australia 60 B5 12 20S 133 4 E
Ofanto →, Italy 20 D7 41 22N 16 13 E
Offa, Nigeria 50 G5 8 13N 4 42 E
Offaly □, Ireland 13 C4 53 15N 7 30W
Offenbach, Germany 16 C4 50 6N 8 46 E
Ofotfjorden, Norway 8 B14 68 27N 16 40 E
Ōfunato, Japan 30 E10 39 4N 141 43 E
Oga, Japan 30 E9 39 55N 139 50 E
Oga-Hantō, Japan 30 E9 39 58N 139 47 E
Ogahalla, Canada 70 B2 50 6N 85 51W
Ōgaki, Japan 31 G8 35 21N 136 37 E
Ogallala, U.S.A. 80 E4 41 8N 101 43W
Ogasawara Gunto, Pac. Oc. 64 E6 27 0N 142 0 E
Ogbomosho, Nigeria 50 G5 8 1N 4 11 E
Ogden, Iowa, U.S.A. 80 D8 42 2N 94 2W
Ogden, Utah, U.S.A. 82 F7 41 13N 111 58W
Ogdensburg, U.S.A. 79 B9 44 42N 75 30W
Ogeechee →, U.S.A. 77 K5 31 50N 81 3W
Ogilby, U.S.A. 85 N12 32 49N 114 50W
Oglio →, Italy 20 B4 45 2N 10 39 E
Ogmore, Australia 62 C4 22 37S 149 35 E
Ogoki →, Canada 70 B2 51 38N 85 57W
Ogoki L., Canada 70 B2 50 50N 87 10W
Ogoki Res., Canada 70 B2 50 45N 88 15W
Ogooué →, Gabon 52 E1 1 0S 9 0 E
Ogowe = Ogooué →, Gabon 52 E1 1 0S 9 0 E
Ohai, N.Z. 59 L2 45 55S 168 0 E
Ohakune, N.Z. 59 H5 39 24S 175 24 E
Ohanet, Algeria 50 C6 28 44N 8 46 E
Ohata, Japan 30 D10 41 24N 141 10 E
Ohau, L., N.Z. 59 L2 44 15S 169 53 E
Ohey, Belgium 15 D5 50 26N 5 8 E
Ohio □, U.S.A. 76 E3 40 15N 82 45W
Ohio →, U.S.A. 76 G1 36 59N 89 8W
Ohre →, Czech. 16 C7 50 30N 14 10 E
Ohridsko, Jezero, Macedonia 21 D9 41 8N 20 52 E
Ohrigstad, S. Africa 57 C5 24 39S 30 36 E
Oikou, China 35 E9 38 35N 117 42 E
Oil City, U.S.A. 78 E5 41 26N 79 42W
Oildale, U.S.A. 85 K7 35 25N 119 1W
Oise □, France 18 B5 49 28N 2 30 E
Ōita, Japan 31 H5 33 14N 131 36 E
Ōita □, Japan 31 H5 33 15N 131 30 E
Oiticica, Brazil 93 E10 5 3S 41 5W
Ojai, U.S.A. 85 L7 34 27N 119 15W
Ojinaga, Mexico 86 B4 29 34N 104 25W
Ojiya, Japan 31 F9 37 18N 138 48 E
Ojos del Salado, Cerro, Argentina 94 B2 27 0S 68 40W
Oka →, Russia 26 D5 56 20N 43 59 E
Okaba, Indonesia 37 F9 8 6S 139 42 E
Okahandja, Namibia 56 C2 22 0S 16 59 E
Okahukura, N.Z. 59 H5 38 48S 175 14 E
Okanagan L., Canada 72 C5 50 0N 119 30W
Okandja, Gabon 52 E2 0 35S 13 45 E
Okanogan, U.S.A. 82 B4 48 22N 119 35W
Okanogan →, U.S.A. 82 B4 48 6N 119 44W
Okaputa, Namibia 56 C2 20 5S 17 0 E
Okara, Pakistan 42 D5 30 50N 73 31 E
Okarito, N.Z. 59 K3 43 15S 170 9 E
Okaukuejo, Namibia 56 B2 19 10S 16 0 E
Okavango Swamps, Botswana 56 B3 18 45S 22 45 E
Okaya, Japan 31 F9 36 5N 138 10 E
Okayama, Japan 31 G6 34 40N 133 54 E
Okayama □, Japan 31 G6 35 0N 133 50 E
Okazaki, Japan 31 G8 34 57N 137 10 E
Okeechobee, U.S.A. 77 M5 27 15N 80 50W
Okeechobee, L., U.S.A. 77 M5 27 0N 80 50W
Okefenokee Swamp, U.S.A. 77 K4 30 40N 82 20W
Okehampton, U.K. 11 G3 50 44N 4 1W
Okha, Russia 27 D15 53 40N 143 0 E
Okhotsk, Russia 27 D15 59 20N 143 10 E
Okhotsk, Sea of, Asia 27 D15 55 0N 145 0 E
Okhotskiy Perevoz, Russia 27 C14 61 52N 135 35 E
Okhotsko Kolymskoye, Russia 27 C16 63 0N 157 0 E
Oki-Shotō, Japan 31 F6 36 5N 133 15 E
Okiep, S. Africa 56 D2 29 39S 17 53 E
Okinawa □, Japan 31 L3 26 40N 128 0 E
Okinawa-Guntō, Japan 31 L3 26 40N 128 0 E
Okinawa-Jima, Japan 31 L4 26 32N 128 0 E
Okino-erabu-Shima, Japan 31 L4 27 21N 128 33 E
Oklahoma □, U.S.A. 81 H6 35 20N 97 30W
Oklahoma City, U.S.A. 81 H6 35 30N 97 30W
Okmulgee, U.S.A. 81 H7 35 37N 95 58W
Okolo, Uganda 54 B3 2 37N 31 8 E
Okolona, U.S.A. 81 H10 34 0N 88 45W
Okrika, Nigeria 50 H6 4 40N 7 10 E
Oktabrsk, Kazakhstan 25 E10 49 28N 57 25 E
Oktyabrskiy, Russia 24 D9 54 28N 53 28 E
Oktyabrskoy Revolyutsii, Os., Russia 27 B10 79 30N 97 0 E
Oktyabrskoye, Russia 26 C7 62 28N 66 3 E
Okuru, N.Z. 59 K2 43 55S 168 55 E
Okushiri-Tō, Japan 30 C9 42 15N 139 30 E
Okwa →, Botswana 56 C3 22 30S 23 0 E
Ola, U.S.A. 81 H8 35 2N 93 13W
Ólafsfjörður, Iceland 8 C4 66 4N 18 39W
Ólafsvík, Iceland 8 D2 64 53N 23 43W
Olancha, U.S.A. 85 J8 36 17N 118 1W
Olancha Pk., U.S.A. 85 J8 36 15N 118 7W
Olanchito, Honduras 88 C2 15 30N 86 30W
Öland, Sweden 9 H14 56 45N 16 38 E
Olary, Australia 63 E3 32 18S 140 19 E
Olascoaga, Argentina 94 D3 35 15S 60 39W
Olathe, U.S.A. 80 F7 38 53N 94 49W
Olavarría, Argentina 94 D3 36 55S 60 20W
Ólbia, Italy 20 D3 40 55N 9 30 E
Old Bahama Chan. = Bahama, Canal Viejo de, W. Indies 88 B4 22 10N 77 30W
Old Baldy Pk. = San Antonio, Mt., U.S.A. 85 L9 34 17N 117 38W
Old Castile = Castilla y Leon □, Spain 19 B3 42 0N 5 0W
Old Castle, Ireland 13 C4 53 46N 7 10W
Old Cork, Australia 62 C3 22 57S 141 52 E
Old Crow, Canada 68 B6 67 30N 139 55W
Old Dale, U.S.A. 85 L11 34 8N 115 47W
Old Fletton, U.K. 11 E7 52 34N 0 13W
Old Forge, N.Y., U.S.A. 79 C10 43 43N 74 58W
Old Forge, Pa., U.S.A. 79 E9 41 22N 75 45W
Old Fort →, Canada 73 B6 58 36N 110 24W
Old Shinyanga, Tanzania 54 C3 3 33S 33 27 E
Old Speck Mt., U.S.A. 79 B14 44 34N 70 57W
Old Town, U.S.A. 71 D6 44 56N 68 39W
Old Wives L., Canada 73 C7 50 5N 106 0W
Oldbury, U.K. 11 F5 51 38N 2 30W
Oldeani, Tanzania 54 C4 3 22S 35 35 E
Oldenburg, Germany 16 B4 53 10N 8 10 E
Oldenzaal, Neths. 15 B6 52 19N 6 53 E
Oldham, U.K. 10 D5 53 33N 2 8W
Oldman →, Canada 72 D6 49 57N 111 42W
Olds, Canada 72 C6 51 50N 114 10W
Olean, U.S.A. 78 D6 42 5N 78 26W
Olekma →, Russia 27 C13 60 22N 120 42 E
Olekminsk, Russia 27 C13 60 25N 120 30 E
Olema, U.S.A. 84 G4 38 3N 122 47W
Olenegorsk, Russia 24 A5 68 9N 33 18 E
Olenek, Russia 27 C12 68 28N 112 18 E
Olenek →, Russia 27 B13 73 0N 120 10 E
Oléron, I. d', France 18 D3 45 55N 1 15W
Oleśnica, Poland 17 C8 51 13N 17 22 E
Olga, Russia 27 E14 43 50N 135 14 E
Olga, L., Canada 70 C4 49 47N 77 15W
Olga, Mt., Australia 61 E5 25 20S 130 50 E
Olifants →, Africa 57 C5 23 57S 31 58 E
Olifantshoek, S. Africa 56 D3 27 57S 22 42 E
Ólimbos, Óros, Greece 21 D10 40 6N 22 23 E
Olímpia, Brazil 95 A6 20 44S 48 54W
Olinda, Brazil 93 E12 8 1S 34 51W
Oliva, Argentina 94 C3 32 0S 63 38W
Olivehurst, U.S.A. 84 F5 39 6N 121 34W
Oliveira, Brazil 93 H10 20 39S 44 50W
Olivenza, Spain 19 C2 38 41N 7 9W
Oliver, Canada 72 D5 49 13N 119 37W
Oliver L., Canada 73 B8 56 56N 103 22W
Ollagüe, Chile 94 A2 21 15S 68 10W
Olney, Ill., U.S.A. 76 F1 38 44N 88 5W
Olney, Tex., U.S.A. 81 J5 33 22N 98 45W
Olomane →, Canada 71 B7 50 14N 60 37W
Olomouc, Czech. 16 D8 49 38N 17 12 E
Olonets, Russia 24 B5 61 10N 33 0 E
Olongapo, Phil. 37 B6 14 50N 120 18 E
Olovo, Bos.-H. 21 B8 44 8N 18 35 E
Olovo, Yugoslavia 21 B8 44 30N 19 0 E
Olovyannaya, Russia 27 D12 50 58N 115 35 E
Oloy →, Russia 27 C16 66 29N 159 29 E
Olsztyn, Poland 17 B10 53 48N 20 29 E
Olt →, Romania 21 C11 43 43N 24 51 E
Olteniţa, Romania 17 F13 44 7N 26 42 E
Olton, U.S.A. 81 H3 34 11N 102 8W
Olymbos, Cyprus 23 D12 35 21N 33 45 E
Olympia, Greece 21 F9 37 39N 21 39 E
Olympia, U.S.A. 84 D4 47 3N 122 53W
Olympic Mts., U.S.A. 84 C3 47 55N 123 45W
Olympic Nat. Park, U.S.A. 84 C3 47 48N 123 30W
Olympus, Cyprus 23 E11 34 56N 32 52 E
Olympus, Mt. = Ólimbos, Óros, Greece 21 D10 40 6N 22 23 E
Olympus, Mt., U.S.A. 84 C3 47 48N 123 43W
Olyphant, U.S.A. 79 E9 41 27N 75 36W
Om →, Russia 26 D8 54 59N 73 22 E
Om Koi, Thailand 38 D2 17 48N 98 22 E
Ōma, Japan 30 D10 41 45N 141 5 E
Ōmachi, Japan 31 F8 36 30N 137 50 E
Omae-Zaki, Japan 31 G9 34 36N 138 14 E
Ōmagari, Japan 30 E10 39 27N 140 29 E
Omagh, U.K. 13 B4 54 36N 7 20W
Omagh □, U.K. 13 B4 54 35N 7 15W
Omaha, U.S.A. 80 E7 41 17N 95 58W
Omak, U.S.A. 82 B4 48 25N 119 31W
Omalos, Greece 23 D5 35 19N 23 55 E
Oman ■, Asia 46 C6 23 0N 58 0 E
Oman, G. of, Asia 45 E8 24 30N 58 30 E
Omaruru, Namibia 56 C2 21 26S 16 0 E
Omaruru →, Namibia 56 C1 22 7S 14 15 E
Omate, Peru 92 G4 16 45S 71 0W
Ombai, Selat, Indonesia 37 F6 8 30S 124 50 E
Omboué, Gabon 52 E1 1 35S 9 15 E
Ombrone →, Italy 20 C4 42 39N 11 0 E
Omdurmân, Sudan 51 E11 15 40N 32 28 E
Omeonga, Zaïre 54 C1 3 40S 24 22 E
Ometepe, I. de, Nic. 88 D2 11 32N 85 35W
Ometepec, Mexico 87 D5 16 39N 98 23W
Ominato, Japan 30 D10 41 17N 141 10 E
Omineca →, Canada 72 B4 56 3N 124 16W
Omitara, Namibia 56 C2 22 16S 18 2 E
Ōmiya, Japan 31 G9 35 54N 139 38 E
Ommen, Neths. 15 B6 52 31N 6 26 E
Ömnögovĭ □, Mongolia 34 C3 43 15N 104 0 E
Omo →, Ethiopia 51 G12 6 25N 36 10 E
Omodhos, Cyprus 23 E11 34 51N 32 48 E
Omolon →, Russia 27 C16 68 42N 158 36 E
Omono-Gawa →, Japan 30 E10 39 46N 140 3 E
Omsk, Russia 26 D8 55 0N 73 12 E
Omsukchan, Russia 27 C16 62 32N 155 48 E
Ōmu, Japan 30 B11 44 34N 142 58 E
Omul, Vf., Romania 17 F12 45 27N 25 29 E
Ōmura, Japan 31 H4 32 56N 129 57 E
Omuramba Omatako →, Namibia 53 H4 17 45S 20 25 E
Ōmuta, Japan 31 H5 33 5N 130 26 E
Onaga, U.S.A. 80 F6 39 29N 96 10W
Onalaska, U.S.A. 80 D9 43 53N 91 14W
Onamia, U.S.A. 80 B8 46 4N 93 40W
Onancock, U.S.A. 76 G8 37 43N 75 45W
Onang, Indonesia 37 E5 3 2S 118 49 E
Onaping L., Canada 70 C3 47 3N 81 30W
Onavas, Mexico 86 B3 28 28N 109 30W
Onawa, U.S.A. 80 D6 42 2N 96 6W
Onaway, U.S.A. 76 C3 45 21N 84 14W
Oncócua, Angola 56 B1 16 30S 13 25 E
Onda, Spain 19 C5 39 55N 0 17W
Ondaejin, N. Korea 35 D15 41 34N 129 40 E
Ondangua, Namibia 56 B2 17 57S 16 4 E
Ondjiva, Angola 56 B2 16 48S 15 50 E
Ondo, Nigeria 50 G5 7 4N 4 47 E
Öndörshil, Mongolia 34 B5 45 13N 108 5 E
Öndverðarnes, Iceland 8 D1 64 52N 24 0W
Onega, Russia 24 B6 64 0N 38 10 E
Onega →, Russia 24 B6 63 58N 37 55 E
Onega, G. of = Onezhskaya Guba, Russia 24 B6 64 30N 37 0 E
Onega, L. = Onezhskoye Ozero, Russia 24 B6 62 0N 35 30 E
Onehunga, N.Z. 59 G5 36 55S 174 48 E
Oneida, U.S.A. 79 C9 43 6N 75 39W
Oneida L., U.S.A. 79 C9 43 12N 75 54W
O'Neill, U.S.A. 80 D5 42 27N 98 39W
Onekotan, Ostrov, Russia 27 E16 49 25N 154 45 E
Onema, Zaïre 54 C1 4 35S 24 30 E
Oneonta, Ala., U.S.A. 77 J2 33 57N 86 28W
Oneonta, N.Y., U.S.A. 79 D9 42 27N 75 4W
Onezhskaya Guba, Russia 24 B6 64 30N 37 0 E
Onezhskoye Ozero, Russia 24 B6 62 0N 35 30 E
Ongarue, N.Z. 59 H5 38 42S 175 19 E
Ongerup, Australia 61 F2 33 58S 118 28 E
Ongjin, N. Korea 35 F13 37 56N 125 21 E
Ongkharak, Thailand 38 E3 14 8N 101 1 E
Ongniud Qi, China 35 C10 43 0N 118 38 E
Ongoka, Zaïre 54 C2 1 20S 26 0 E
Ongole, India 40 M12 15 33N 80 2 E
Ongon, Mongolia 34 B7 45 41N 113 5 E
Onguren, Russia 27 D11 53 38N 107 36 E
Onida, U.S.A. 80 C4 44 42N 100 4W
Onilahy →, Madag. 57 C7 23 34S 43 45 E
Onitsha, Nigeria 50 G6 6 6N 6 42 E
Onoda, Japan 31 G5 34 2N 131 25 E
Onpyŏng-ni, S. Korea 35 H14 33 25N 126 55 E
Onslow, Australia 60 D2 21 40S 115 12 E
Onslow B., U.S.A. 77 H7 34 20N 77 15W
Onstwedde, Neths. 15 A7 53 2N 7 4 E
Ontake-San, Japan 31 G8 35 53N 137 29 E
Ontario, Calif., U.S.A. 85 L9 34 4N 117 39W
Ontario, Oreg., U.S.A. 82 D5 44 2N 116 58W
Ontario □, Canada 70 B2 48 0N 83 0W
Ontario, L., U.S.A. 70 D4 43 20N 78 0W
Ontonagon, U.S.A. 80 B10 46 52N 89 19W
Onyx, U.S.A. 85 K8 35 41N 118 14W
Oodnadatta, Australia 63 D2 27 33S 135 30 E
Ooldea, Australia 61 F5 30 27S 131 50 E
Oombulgurri, Australia 60 C4 15 15S 127 45 E
Oona River, Canada 72 C2 53 57N 130 16W
Oorindi, Australia 62 C3 20 40S 141 1 E
Oost-Vlaanderen □, Belgium 15 C3 51 5N 3 50 E
Oostende, Belgium 15 C2 51 15N 2 54 E
Oosterhout, Neths. 15 C4 51 39N 4 47 E
Oosterschelde, Neths. 15 C4 51 33N 4 0 E
Ootacamund, India 40 P10 11 30N 76 44 E
Ootsa L., Canada 72 C3 53 50N 126 2W
Opala, Russia 27 D16 51 58N 156 30 E
Opala, Zaïre 54 C1 0 40S 24 20 E
Opanake, Sri Lanka 40 R12 6 35N 80 40 E
Opasatika, Canada 70 C3 49 30N 82 50W
Opasquia, Canada 73 C10 53 16N 93 34W
Opava, Czech. 17 D8 49 57N 17 58 E
Opelousas, U.S.A. 81 K8 30 32N 92 5W
Opémisca, L., Canada 70 C5 49 56N 74 52W
Opheim, U.S.A. 82 B10 48 51N 106 24W
Ophthalmia Ra., Australia 60 D2 23 15S 119 30 E
Opinaca →, Canada 70 B4 52 15N 78 2W
Opinaca L., Canada 70 B4 52 39N 76 20W
Opiskotish, L., Canada 71 B6 53 10N 67 50W
Opole, Poland 17 C8 50 42N 17 58 E
Oporto = Porto, Portugal 19 B1 41 8N 8 40W
Opotiki, N.Z. 59 H6 38 1S 177 19 E
Opp, U.S.A. 77 K2 31 17N 86 16W
Oppland fylke □, Norway 9 F10 61 15N 9 40 E
Opua, N.Z. 59 F5 35 19S 174 9 E
Opunake, N.Z. 59 H4 39 26S 173 52 E
Ora, Cyprus 23 E12 34 51N 33 12 E
Ora Banda, Australia 61 F3 30 20S 121 0 E
Oracle, U.S.A. 83 K8 32 37N 110 46W
Oradea, Romania 17 E10 47 2N 21 58 E
Öræfajökull, Iceland 8 D5 64 2N 16 39W
Orai, India 43 G8 25 58N 79 30 E
Oral = Ural →, Kazakhstan 25 E9 47 0N 51 48 E
Oral = Uralsk, Kazakhstan 24 D9 51 20N 51 20 E
Oran, Algeria 50 A4 35 45N 0 39W
Oran, Argentina 94 A3 23 10S 64 20W
Orange = Oranje →, S. Africa 56 D2 28 41S 16 28 E
Orange, Australia 63 E4 33 15S 149 7 E
Orange, France 18 D6 44 8N 4 47 E
Orange, Calif., U.S.A. 85 M9 33 47N 117 51W
Orange, Mass., U.S.A. 79 D12 42 35N 72 19W
Orange, Tex., U.S.A. 81 K8 30 6N 93 44W
Orange, Va., U.S.A. 76 F6 38 15N 78 7W
Orange, C., Brazil 93 C8 4 20N 51 30W
Orange Cove, U.S.A. 84 J7 36 38N 119 19W
Orange Free State □, S. Africa 56 D4 28 30S 27 0 E
Orange Grove, U.S.A. 81 M6 27 58N 97 56W
Orange Walk, Belize 87 D7 18 6N 88 33W
Orangeburg, U.S.A. 77 J5 33 30N 80 52W
Orangeville, Canada 70 D3 43 55N 80 5W
Oranienburg, Germany 16 B6 52 45N 13 15 E
Oranje →, S. Africa 56 D2 28 41S 16 28 E
Oranje Vrystaat = Orange Free State □, S. Africa 56 D4 28 30S 27 0 E
Oranjemund, Namibia 56 D2 28 38S 16 29 E
Oranjerivier, S. Africa 56 D3 29 40S 24 12 E
Oras, Phil. 37 B7 12 9N 125 28 E
Oraşul Stalin = Braşov, Romania 21 B11 45 38N 25 35 E
Orbetello, Italy 20 C4 42 26N 11 11 E
Orbost, Australia 63 F4 37 40S 148 29 E
Orchila, I., Venezuela 92 A5 11 48N 66 10W
Orcutt, U.S.A. 85 L6 34 52N 120 27W
Ord →, Australia 60 C4 15 33S 128 15 E
Ord, Mt., Australia 60 C4 17 20S 125 34 E
Orderville, U.S.A. 83 H7 37 17N 112 38W
Ordos = Mu Us Shamo, Nei Mongol Zizhiqu, China 34 E5 39 0N 109 0 E
Ordos = Mu Us Shamo, Nei Mongol Zizhiqu, China 34 E5 39 0N 109 0 E
Ordway, U.S.A. 80 F3 38 13N 103 46W
Ordzhonikidze = Vladikavkaz, Russia 25 F7 43 0N 44 35 E
Ore, Zaïre 54 B2 3 17N 29 30 E
Ore Mts. = Erzgebirge, Germany 16 C6 50 25N 13 0 E
Örebro, Sweden 9 G13 59 20N 15 18 E
Örebro län □, Sweden 9 G13 59 27N 15 0 E
Oregon, U.S.A. 80 D10 42 1N 89 20W
Oregon □, U.S.A. 82 E3 44 0N 121 0W
Oregon City, U.S.A. 84 E4 45 21N 122 36W
Orekhovo-Zuyevo, Russia 24 C6 55 50N 38 55 E
Orel, Russia 24 D6 52 57N 36 3 E
Orem, U.S.A. 82 F8 40 19N 111 42W
Orenburg, Russia 24 D10 51 45N 55 6 E
Orense, Spain 19 A2 42 19N 7 55W
Orepuki, N.Z. 59 M1 46 19S 167 46 E
Øresund, Europe 9 H12 55 45N 12 45 E
Orford Ness, U.K. 11 E9 52 6N 1 31 E
Organos, Pta. de los, Canary Is. 22 F2 28 12N 17 17W
Orhon Gol →, Mongolia 32 A5 50 21N 106 0 E
Orient, Australia 63 D3 28 7S 142 50 E
Oriental, Cordillera, Colombia 92 B4 6 0N 73 0W
Oriente, Argentina 94 D3 38 44S 60 37W
Orihuela, Spain 19 C5 38 7N 0 55W
Orinoco →, Venezuela 92 B6 9 15N 61 30W
Orissa □, India 41 K14 20 0N 84 0 E
Oristano, Italy 20 E3 39 54N 8 35 E
Oristano, G. di, Italy 20 E3 39 50N 8 22 E
Orizaba, Mexico 87 D5 18 50N 97 10W
Orkanger, Norway 8 E10 63 18N 9 52 E
Orkla →, Norway 8 E10 63 18N 9 51 E
Orkney, S. Africa 56 D4 26 58S 26 40 E
Orkney □, U.K. 12 C6 59 0N 3 0W
Orkney Is., U.K. 12 C6 59 0N 3 0W
Orland, U.S.A. 84 F4 39 45N 122 12W
Orlando, U.S.A. 77 L5 28 33N 81 23W
Orléanais, France 18 C4 48 0N 2 0 E
Orléans, France 18 C4 47 54N 1 52 E
Orleans, U.S.A. 79 B12 44 49N 72 12W
Orléans, I. d', Canada 71 C5 46 54N 70 58W
Ormara, Pakistan 40 G4 25 16N 64 33 E
Ormoc, Phil. 37 B6 11 0N 124 37 E
Ormond, N.Z. 59 H6 38 33S 177 56 E
Ormond Beach, U.S.A. 77 L5 29 17N 81 3W
Ormstown, Canada 79 A11 45 8N 74 0W
Orne □, France 18 B4 48 40N 0 5 E
Örnsköldsvik, Sweden 8 E15 63 17N 18 40 E
Oro, N. Korea 35 D14 40 1N 127 27 E
Oro →, Mexico 86 B3 25 35N 105 2W
Oro Grande, U.S.A. 85 L9 34 36N 117 20W
Orocué, Colombia 92 C4 4 48N 71 20W
Orogrande, U.S.A. 83 K10 32 24N 106 5W
Oromocto, Canada 71 C6 45 54N 66 29W

Orono

Orono, Canada 78 C6 43 59N 78 37W
Oroqen Zizhiqi, China 33 A7 50 34N 123 43 E
Oroquieta, Phil. 37 C6 8 32N 123 44 E
Orós, Brazil 93 E11 6 15S 38 55W
Orotukan, Russia 27 C16 62 16N 151 42 E
Oroville, Calif., U.S.A. 84 F5 39 31N 121 33W
Oroville, Wash., U.S.A. 82 B4 48 56N 119 26W
Oroville, L., U.S.A. 84 F5 39 33N 121 29W
Orroroo, Australia 63 E2 32 43S 138 38 E
Orrville, U.S.A. 78 F3 40 50N 81 46W
Orsha, Belorussia 24 D5 54 30N 30 25 E
Orsk, Russia 24 D10 51 12N 58 34 E
Orşova, Romania 17 F11 44 41N 22 25 E
Ortegal, C., Spain 19 A2 43 43N 7 52W
Orthez, France 18 E3 43 29N 0 48W
Ortigueira, Spain 19 A2 43 40N 7 50W
Orting, U.S.A. 84 C4 47 6N 122 12W
Ortles, Italy 20 A4 46 31N 10 33 E
Ortón →, Bolivia 92 F5 10 50S 67 0W
Ortona, Italy 20 C6 42 21N 14 24 E
Orūmīyeh, Iran 44 B5 37 40N 45 0 E
Orūmīyeh, Daryācheh-ye, Iran 44 B5 37 50N 45 30 E
Oruro, Bolivia 92 G5 18 0S 67 9W
Orūzgān □, Afghan. 40 C5 33 30N 66 0 E
Orvieto, Italy 20 C5 42 43N 12 8 E
Orwell, U.S.A. 78 E4 41 32N 80 52W
Orwell →, U.K. 11 E9 52 2N 1 12 E
Oryakhovo, Bulgaria 21 C10 43 40N 23 57 E
Osa, Russia 24 C10 57 17N 55 26 E
Osa, Pen. de, Costa Rica 88 E3 8 0N 84 0W
Osage, Iowa, U.S.A. 80 D8 43 17N 92 49W
Osage, Wyo., U.S.A. 80 D2 43 59N 104 25W
Osage →, U.S.A. 80 F9 38 35N 91 57W
Osage City, U.S.A. 80 F7 38 38N 95 50W
Ōsaka, Japan 31 G7 34 40N 135 30 E
Osan, S. Korea 35 F14 37 11N 127 4 E
Osawatomie, U.S.A. 80 F7 38 31N 94 57W
Osborne, U.S.A. 80 F5 39 26N 98 42W
Osceola, Ark., U.S.A. 81 H10 35 42N 89 58W
Osceola, Iowa, U.S.A. 80 E8 41 2N 93 46W
Oscoda, U.S.A. 78 B1 44 26N 83 20W
Ösel = Saaremaa, Estonia 24 C3 58 30N 22 30 E
Osh, Kirghizia 26 E8 40 37N 72 49 E
Oshawa, Canada 70 D4 43 50N 78 50W
Oshkosh, Nebr., U.S.A. 80 E3 41 24N 102 21W
Oshkosh, Wis., U.S.A. 80 C10 44 1N 88 33W
Oshnovīyeh, Iran 44 B5 37 2N 45 6 E
Oshogbo, Nigeria 50 G5 7 48N 4 37 E
Oshtorīnān, Iran 45 C6 34 1N 48 38 E
Oshwe, Zaïre 52 E3 3 25S 19 28 E
Osijek, Croatia 21 B8 45 34N 18 41 E
Osipenko = Berdyansk, Ukraine 25 E6 46 45N 36 50 E
Osizweni, S. Africa 57 D5 27 49S 30 7 E
Oskaloosa, U.S.A. 80 E8 41 18N 92 39W
Oskarshamn, Sweden 9 H14 57 15N 16 27 E
Oskélanéo, Canada 70 C4 48 5N 75 15W
Öskemen = Ust-Kamenogorsk, Kazakhstan 26 E9 50 0N 82 36 E
Oslo, Norway 9 G11 59 55N 10 45 E
Oslob, Phil. 37 C6 9 31N 123 26 E
Oslofjorden, Norway 9 G11 59 20N 10 35 E
Osmanabad, India 40 K10 18 5N 76 10 E
Osmaniye, Turkey 25 G6 37 5N 36 10 E
Osnabrück, Germany 16 B4 52 16N 8 2 E
Osorio, Brazil 95 B5 29 53S 50 17W
Osorno, Chile 96 E2 40 25S 73 0W
Osoyoos, Canada 72 D5 49 0N 119 30W
Ospika →, Canada 72 B4 56 20N 124 0W
Osprey Reef, Australia 62 A4 13 52S 146 36 E
Oss, Neths. 15 C5 51 46N 5 32 E
Ossa, Mt., Australia 62 G4 41 52S 146 3 E
Óssa, Oros, Greece 21 E10 39 47N 22 42 E
Ossabaw I., U.S.A. 77 K5 31 50N 81 5W
Ossining, U.S.A. 79 E11 41 10N 73 55W
Ossipee, U.S.A. 79 C13 43 41N 71 7W
Ossokmanuan L., Canada 71 B7 53 25N 65 0W
Ossora, Russia 27 D17 59 20N 163 13 E
Ostend = Oostende, Belgium 15 C2 51 15N 2 54 E
Österdalälven →, Sweden 9 F12 61 30N 13 45 E
Östergötlands län □, Sweden 9 G13 58 35N 15 45 E
Östersund, Sweden 8 E13 63 10N 14 38 E
Østfold fylke □, Norway 9 G11 59 25N 11 25 E
Ostfriesische Inseln, Germany 16 B3 53 45N 7 15 E
Ostrava, Czech. 17 D9 49 51N 18 18 E
Ostróda, Poland 17 B9 53 42N 19 58 E
Ostrołęka, Poland 17 B10 53 4N 21 32 E
Ostrów Mazowiecka, Poland 17 B10 52 50N 21 51 E
Ostrów Wielkopolski, Poland 17 C8 51 36N 17 44 E
Ostrowiec-Świętokrzyski, Poland 17 C10 50 55N 21 22 E
Ōsumi-Kaikyō, Japan 31 J5 30 55N 131 0 E
Ōsumi-Shotō, Japan 31 J5 30 30N 130 0 E
Osuna, Spain 19 D3 37 14N 5 8W
Oswego, U.S.A. 79 C8 43 27N 76 31W
Oswestry, U.K. 10 E4 52 52N 3 3W
Otago □, N.Z. 59 L2 45 15S 170 0 E
Otago Harbour, N.Z. 59 L3 45 47S 170 42 E
Ōtake, Japan 31 G6 34 12N 132 13 E
Otaki, N.Z. 59 J5 40 45S 175 10 E
Otaru, Japan 30 C10 43 10N 141 0 E
Otaru-Wan = Ishikari-Wan, Japan 30 C10 43 25N 141 1 E
Otavalo, Ecuador 92 C3 0 13N 78 20W
Otavi, Namibia 56 B2 19 40S 17 24 E
Otchinjau, Angola 56 B1 16 30S 13 56 E
Othello, U.S.A. 82 C4 46 50N 119 10W
Otira Gorge, N.Z. 59 K3 42 53S 171 33 E
Otis, U.S.A. 80 E3 40 9N 102 58W
Otjiwarongo, Namibia 56 C2 20 30S 16 33 E
Otoineppu, Japan 30 B11 44 44N 142 16 E
Otorohanga, N.Z. 59 H5 38 12S 175 14 E
Otoskwin →, Canada 70 B2 52 13N 88 6W
Otosquen, Canada 73 C8 53 17N 102 1W
Otranto, Italy 21 D8 40 9N 18 28 E
Otranto, C. d', Italy 21 D8 40 7N 18 30 E
Otranto, Str. of, Italy 21 D8 40 15N 18 40 E
Otse, S. Africa 56 D4 25 2S 25 45 E
Ōtsu, Japan 31 G7 35 0N 135 50 E
Ōtsuki, Japan 31 G9 35 36N 138 57 E
Ottawa = Outaouais →, Canada 70 C5 45 27N 74 8W
Ottawa, Canada 70 C4 45 27N 75 42W
Ottawa, Ill., U.S.A. 80 E10 41 21N 88 51W
Ottawa, Kans., U.S.A. 80 F7 38 37N 95 16W
Ottawa Is., Canada 69 C11 59 35N 80 10W
Otter L., Canada 73 B8 55 35N 104 39W
Otter Rapids, Ont., Canada 70 B3 50 11N 81 39W
Otter Rapids, Sask., Canada 73 B8 55 38N 104 44W
Otterville, Canada 78 D4 42 55N 80 36W
Otto Beit Bridge, Zimbabwe 55 F2 15 59S 28 56 E
Ottosdal, S. Africa 56 D4 26 46S 25 59 E
Ottoshoop, S. Africa 56 D4 25 45S 25 58 E
Ottumwa, U.S.A. 80 E8 41 1N 92 25W
Oturkpo, Nigeria 50 G6 7 16N 8 8 E
Otway, B., Chile 96 G2 53 30S 74 0W
Otway, C., Australia 63 F3 38 52S 143 30 E
Otwock, Poland 17 B10 52 5N 21 20 E
Ou →, Laos 38 B4 20 4N 102 13 E
Ou Neua, Laos 38 A3 22 18N 101 48 E
Ou-Sammyaku, Japan 30 E10 39 20N 140 35 E
Ouachita →, U.S.A. 81 K9 31 38N 91 49W
Ouachita, L., U.S.A. 81 H8 34 34N 93 12W
Ouachita Mts., U.S.A. 81 H7 34 40N 94 25W
Ouadâne, Mauritania 50 D2 20 50N 11 40W
Ouadda, C.A.R. 51 G9 8 15N 22 20 E
Ouagadougou, Burkina Faso 50 F4 12 25N 1 30W
Ouahran = Oran, Algeria 50 A4 35 45N 0 39W
Ouallene, Algeria 50 D5 24 41N 1 11 E
Ouanda Djallé, C.A.R. 51 G9 8 55N 22 53 E
Ouango, C.A.R. 52 D4 4 19N 22 30 E
Ouargla, Algeria 50 B6 31 59N 5 16 E
Ouarzazate, Morocco 50 B3 30 55N 6 50W
Oubangi →, Zaïre 52 E3 0 30S 17 50 E
Ouddorp, Neths. 15 C3 51 50N 3 57 E
Oude Rijn →, Neths. 15 B4 52 12N 4 24 E
Oudenaarde, Belgium 15 D3 50 50N 3 37 E
Oudtshoorn, S. Africa 56 E3 33 35S 22 14 E
Ouessant, I. d', France 18 B1 48 28N 5 6W
Ouesso, Congo 52 D3 1 37N 16 5 E
Ouest, Pte., Canada 71 C7 49 52N 64 40W
Ouezzane, Morocco 50 B3 34 51N 5 35W
Ouidah, Benin 50 G5 6 25N 2 0 E
Oujda, Morocco 50 B4 34 41N 1 55W
Oujeft, Mauritania 50 D2 20 2N 13 0W
Ouled Djellal, Algeria 50 B6 34 28N 5 2 E
Oulu, Finland 8 D18 65 1N 25 29 E
Oulu □ = Oulun lääni □, Finland 8 D19 64 36N 27 20 E
Oulujärvi, Finland 8 D19 64 25N 27 15 E
Oulujoki →, Finland 8 D18 65 1N 25 30 E
Oulun lääni □, Finland 8 D19 64 36N 27 20 E
Oum Chalouba, Chad 51 E9 15 48N 20 46 E
Ounguati, Namibia 56 C2 22 0S 15 46 E
Ounianga-Kébir, Chad 51 E9 19 4N 20 29 E
Ounianga Sérir, Chad 51 E9 18 54N 20 51 E
Our →, Lux. 15 E6 49 55N 6 5 E
Ouray, U.S.A. 83 G10 38 1N 107 40W
Ourense = Orense, Spain 19 A2 42 19N 7 55W
Ouricuri, Brazil 93 E10 7 53S 40 5W
Ourinhos, Brazil 95 A6 23 0S 49 54W
Ouro Fino, Brazil 95 A6 22 16S 46 25W
Ouro Prêto, Brazil 95 A7 20 20S 43 30W
Ourthe →, Belgium 15 D5 50 29N 5 35 E
Ouse, Australia 62 G4 42 38S 146 42 E
Ouse →, E. Susx., U.K. 11 G8 50 43N 0 3 E
Ouse →, N. Yorks., U.K. 10 C8 54 3N 0 7 E
Outaouais →, Canada 70 C5 45 27N 74 8W
Outardes →, Canada 71 C6 49 24N 69 30W
Outer Hebrides, U.K. 12 D1 57 30N 7 40W
Outer I., Canada 71 B8 51 10N 58 35W
Outjo, Namibia 56 C2 20 5S 16 7 E
Outlook, Canada 73 C7 51 30N 107 0W
Outlook, U.S.A. 80 A2 48 53N 104 47W
Ouyen, Australia 63 F3 35 1S 142 22 E
Ovalau, Fiji 59 C8 17 40S 178 48 E
Ovalle, Chile 94 C1 30 33S 71 18W
Ovar, Portugal 19 B1 40 51N 8 40W
Overflakkee, Neths. 15 C4 51 44N 4 10 E
Overijssel □, Neths. 15 B6 52 25N 6 35 E
Overpelt, Belgium 15 C5 51 12N 5 20 E
Overton, U.S.A. 85 J12 36 33N 114 27W
Övertorneå, Sweden 8 C17 66 23N 23 38 E
Ovid, U.S.A. 80 E3 40 58N 102 23W
Oviedo, Spain 19 A3 43 25N 5 50W
Övör Hangay □, Mongolia 34 B2 45 0N 102 30 E
Ovruch, Ukraine 26 D3 51 25N 28 45 E
Owaka, N.Z. 59 M2 46 27S 169 40 E
Owase, Japan 31 G8 34 7N 136 12 E
Owatonna, U.S.A. 80 C8 44 5N 93 14W
Owbeh, Afghan. 40 B3 34 28N 63 10 E
Owego, U.S.A. 79 D8 42 6N 76 16W
Owen Falls, Uganda 54 B3 0 30N 33 5 E
Owen Sound, Canada 70 D3 44 35N 80 55W
Owendo, Gabon 52 D1 0 17N 9 30 E
Owens →, U.S.A. 84 J9 36 32N 117 59W
Owens L., U.S.A. 85 J9 36 26N 117 57W
Owensboro, U.S.A. 76 G2 37 46N 87 7W
Owensville, U.S.A. 80 F9 38 21N 91 30W
Owl →, Canada 73 B10 57 51N 92 44W
Owo, Nigeria 50 G6 7 10N 5 39 E
Owosso, U.S.A. 76 D3 43 0N 84 10W
Owyhee, U.S.A. 82 F5 41 57N 116 6W
Owyhee →, U.S.A. 82 E5 43 49N 117 2W
Owyhee, L., U.S.A. 82 E5 43 38N 117 14W
Ox Mts., Ireland 13 B3 54 6N 9 0W
Oxelösund, Sweden 9 G14 58 43N 17 15 E
Oxford, N.Z. 59 K4 43 18S 172 11 E
Oxford, U.K. 11 F6 51 45N 1 15W
Oxford, Miss., U.S.A. 81 H10 34 22N 89 31W
Oxford, N.C., U.S.A. 77 G6 36 19N 78 35W
Oxford, Ohio, U.S.A. 76 F3 39 31N 84 45W
Oxford L., Canada 73 C9 54 51N 95 37W
Oxfordshire □, U.K. 11 F6 51 45N 1 15W
Oxley, Australia 63 E3 34 11S 144 6 E
Oxnard, U.S.A. 85 L7 34 12N 119 11W
Oxus = Amudarya →, Uzbekistan 26 E6 43 40N 59 0 E
Oya, Malaysia 36 D4 2 55N 111 55 E
Oyama, Japan 31 F9 36 18N 139 48 E
Oyem, Gabon 52 D2 1 34N 11 31 E
Oyen, Canada 73 C6 51 22N 110 28W
Oykel →, U.K. 12 D4 57 55N 4 26W
Oymyakon, Russia 27 C15 63 25N 142 44 E
Oyo, Nigeria 50 G5 7 46N 3 56 E
Oyster Bay, U.S.A. 79 F11 40 52N 73 32W
Ōyūbari, Japan 30 C11 43 1N 142 5 E
Ozamiz, Phil. 37 C6 8 15N 123 50 E
Ozark, Ala., U.S.A. 77 K3 31 28N 85 39W
Ozark, Ark., U.S.A. 81 H8 35 29N 93 50W
Ozark, Mo., U.S.A. 81 G8 37 1N 93 12W
Ozark Plateau, U.S.A. 81 G9 37 20N 91 40W
Ozarks, L. of the, U.S.A. 80 F8 38 12N 92 38W
Ozette L., U.S.A. 84 B2 48 6N 124 38W
Ozona, U.S.A. 81 K4 30 43N 101 12W
Ozuluama, Mexico 87 C5 21 40N 97 50W

P

P.K. le Roux Dam, S. Africa 56 E3 30 4S 24 40 E
Pa-an, Burma 41 L20 16 51N 97 40 E
Pa Mong Dam, Thailand 38 D4 18 0N 102 22 E
Paamiut = Frederikshåb, Greenland 4 C5 62 0N 49 43W
Paarl, S. Africa 56 E2 33 45S 18 56 E
Paatsi →, Russia 8 B20 68 55N 29 0 E
Paauilo, U.S.A. 74 H17 20 2N 155 22W
Pab Hills, Pakistan 42 F2 26 30N 66 45 E
Pabna, Bangla. 41 G16 24 1N 89 18 E
Pabo, Uganda 54 B3 3 1N 32 10 E
Pacaja →, Brazil 93 D8 1 56S 50 50W
Pacaraima, Sierra, Venezuela 92 C6 4 0N 62 30W
Pacasmayo, Peru 92 E3 7 20S 79 35W
Pachhar, India 42 G7 24 40N 77 42 E
Pachpadra, India 40 G8 25 58N 72 10 E
Pachuca, Mexico 87 C5 20 10N 98 40W
Pacific, Canada 72 C3 54 48N 128 28W
Pacific-Antarctic Ridge, Pac. Oc. 65 M16 43 0S 115 0W
Pacific Grove, U.S.A. 83 H3 36 38N 121 56W
Pacific Ocean, Pac. Oc. 65 G14 10 0N 140 0W
Pacifica, U.S.A. 84 H4 37 36N 122 30W
Pacitan, Indonesia 37 H14 8 12S 111 7 E
Packwood, U.S.A. 84 D5 46 36N 121 40W
Padaido, Kepulauan, Indonesia 37 E9 1 5S 138 0 E
Padang, Indonesia 36 E2 1 0S 100 20 E
Padangpanjang, Indonesia 36 E2 0 40S 100 20 E
Padangsidempuan, Indonesia 36 D1 1 30N 99 15 E
Paddockwood, Canada 73 C7 53 30N 105 30W
Paderborn, Germany 16 C4 51 42N 8 44 E
Padloping Island, Canada 69 B13 67 0N 62 50W
Pádova, Italy 20 B4 45 24N 11 52 E
Padra, India 42 H5 22 15N 73 7 E
Padrauna, India 43 F10 26 54N 83 59 E
Padre I., U.S.A. 81 M6 27 10N 97 25W
Padstow, U.K. 11 G3 50 33N 4 57W
Padua = Pádova, Italy 20 B4 45 24N 11 52 E
Paducah, Ky., U.S.A. 76 G1 37 5N 88 37W
Paducah, Tex., U.S.A. 81 H4 34 1N 100 18W
Paengnyong-do, S. Korea 35 F13 37 57N 124 40 E
Paeroa, N.Z. 59 G5 37 23S 175 41 E
Pafúri, Mozam. 57 C5 22 28S 31 17 E
Pag, Croatia 20 B6 44 30N 14 50 E
Pagadian, Phil. 37 C6 7 55N 123 30 E
Pagai Selatan, P., Indonesia 36 E2 3 0S 100 15 E
Pagai Utara, Indonesia 36 E2 2 35S 100 0 E
Pagalu = Annobón, Atl. Oc. 49 G4 1 25S 5 36 E
Pagastikós Kólpos, Greece 21 E10 39 15N 23 0 E
Pagatan, Indonesia 36 E5 3 33S 115 59 E
Page, Ariz., U.S.A. 83 H8 36 57N 111 27W
Page, N. Dak., U.S.A. 80 B6 47 10N 97 34W
Pago Pago, Amer. Samoa 59 B13 14 16S 170 43W
Pagosa Springs, U.S.A. 83 H10 37 16N 107 1W
Pagwa River, Canada 70 B2 50 2N 85 14W
Pahala, U.S.A. 74 J17 19 12N 155 29W
Pahang →, Malaysia 39 L4 3 30N 103 9 E
Pahiatua, N.Z. 59 J5 40 27S 175 50 E
Pahokee, U.S.A. 77 M5 26 50N 80 40W
Pahrump, U.S.A. 85 J11 36 12N 115 59W
Pahute Mesa, U.S.A. 84 H10 37 20N 116 45W
Pai, Thailand 38 C2 19 19N 98 27 E
Paia, U.S.A. 74 H16 20 54N 156 22W
Paicines, U.S.A. 84 J5 36 44N 121 17W
Paignton, U.K. 11 G4 50 26N 3 33W
Päijänne, Finland 9 F18 61 30N 25 30 E
Painan, Indonesia 36 E2 1 21S 100 34 E
Painesville, U.S.A. 78 E3 41 43N 81 15W
Paint Hills = Nouveau Comptoir, Canada 70 B4 53 0N 78 49W
Paint L., Canada 73 B9 55 28N 97 57W
Paint Rock, U.S.A. 81 K5 31 31N 99 55W
Painted Desert, U.S.A. 83 J8 36 0N 111 0W
Paintsville, U.S.A. 76 G4 37 49N 82 48W
País Vasco □, Spain 19 A4 42 50N 2 45W
Paisley, Canada 78 B3 44 18N 81 16W
Paisley, U.K. 12 F4 55 51N 4 27W
Paisley, U.S.A. 82 E3 42 42N 120 32W
Paita, Peru 92 E2 5 11S 81 9W
Pak Lay, Laos 38 C3 18 15N 101 27 E
Pak Phanang, Thailand 39 H3 8 21N 100 12 E
Pak Sane, Laos 38 C4 18 22N 103 39 E
Pak Song, Laos 38 E6 15 11N 106 14 E
Pak Suong, Laos 38 C4 19 58N 102 15 E
Pakaraima Mts., Guyana 92 B6 6 0N 60 0W
Pákhnes, Greece 23 D6 35 16N 24 4 E
Pakistan ■, Asia 42 E3 30 0N 70 0 E
Pakistan, East = Bangladesh ■, Asia 41 H17 24 0N 90 0 E
Pakkading, Laos 38 C4 18 19N 103 59 E
Pakokku, Burma 41 J19 21 20N 95 0 E
Pakpattan, Pakistan 42 D5 30 25N 73 27 E
Pakse, Laos 38 E5 15 5N 105 52 E
Paktīā □, Afghan. 40 C6 33 0N 69 15 E
Pakwach, Uganda 54 B3 2 28N 31 27 E
Pala, Chad 51 G8 9 25N 15 5 E
Pala, U.S.A. 85 M9 33 22N 117 5W
Pala, Zaïre 54 D2 6 45S 29 30 E
Palabek, Uganda 54 B3 3 22N 32 33 E
Palacios, U.S.A. 81 L6 28 42N 96 13W
Palagruža, Croatia 20 C7 42 24N 16 15 E
Palaiókastron, Greece 23 D8 35 12N 26 15 E
Palaiokhóra, Greece 23 D5 35 16N 23 39 E
Palam, India 40 K10 19 0N 77 0 E
Palamós, Spain 19 B7 41 50N 3 10 E
Palampur, India 42 C7 32 10N 76 30 E
Palana, Australia 62 F4 39 45S 147 55 E
Palana, Russia 27 D16 59 10N 159 59 E
Palanan, Phil. 37 A6 17 8N 122 29 E
Palanan Pt., Phil. 37 A6 17 17N 122 30 E
Palandri, Pakistan 43 C5 33 42N 73 40 E
Palangkaraya, Indonesia 36 E4 2 16S 113 56 E
Palani Hills, India 40 P10 10 14N 77 33 E
Palanpur, India 42 G5 24 10N 72 25 E
Palapye, Botswana 56 C4 22 30S 27 7 E
Palas, Pakistan 43 B5 35 4N 73 14 E
Palatka, Russia 27 C16 60 6N 150 54 E
Palatka, U.S.A. 77 L5 29 39N 81 38W
Palau = Belau ■, Pac. Oc. 64 G5 7 30N 134 30 E
Palawan, Phil. 36 C5 9 30N 118 30 E
Palayankottai, India 40 Q10 8 45N 77 45 E
Paleleh, Indonesia 37 D6 1 10N 121 50 E
Palembang, Indonesia 36 E2 3 0S 104 50 E
Palencia, Spain 19 A3 42 1N 4 34W
Paleokastrítsa, Greece 23 A3 39 40N 19 41 E
Paleometokho, Cyprus 23 D12 35 7N 33 11 E
Palermo, Italy 20 E5 38 8N 13 20 E
Palermo, U.S.A. 82 G3 39 26N 121 33W
Palestine, Asia 47 D4 32 0N 35 0 E
Palestine, U.S.A. 81 K7 31 46N 95 38W
Paletwa, Burma 41 J18 21 10N 92 50 E
Palghat, India 40 P10 10 46N 76 42 E
Palgrave, Mt., Australia 60 D2 23 22S 115 58 E
Pali, India 42 G5 25 50N 73 20 E
Palisade, U.S.A. 80 E4 40 21N 101 7W
Palitana, India 42 J4 21 32N 71 49 E
Palizada, Mexico 87 D6 18 18N 92 8W
Palk Bay, Asia 40 Q11 9 30N 79 15 E
Palk Strait, Asia 40 Q11 10 0N 79 45 E
Palkānah, Iraq 44 C5 35 49N 44 26 E
Palla Road = Dinokwe, Botswana 56 C4 23 29S 26 37 E
Pallisa, Uganda 54 B3 1 12N 33 43 E
Pallu, India 42 E6 28 59N 74 14 E
Palm Beach, U.S.A. 77 M6 26 43N 80 2W
Palm Desert, U.S.A. 85 M10 33 43N 116 22W
Palm Is., Australia 62 B4 18 40S 146 35 E
Palm Springs, U.S.A. 85 M10 33 50N 116 33W
Palma, Mozam. 55 E5 10 46S 40 29 E
Palma →, Brazil 93 F9 12 33S 47 52W
Palma, B. de, Spain 22 B9 39 30N 2 39 E
Palma de Mallorca, Spain 22 B9 39 35N 2 39 E
Palma Soriano, Cuba 88 B4 20 15N 76 0W
Palmares, Brazil 93 E11 8 41S 35 28W
Palmas, Brazil 95 B5 26 29S 52 0W
Palmas, C., Liberia 50 H3 4 27N 7 46W
Pálmas, G. di, Italy 20 E3 39 0N 8 30 E
Palmdale, U.S.A. 85 L8 34 35N 118 7W
Palmeira dos Índios, Brazil 93 E11 9 25S 36 37W
Palmeirinhas, Pta. das, Angola 52 F2 9 2S 12 57 E
Palmer, U.S.A. 68 B5 61 36N 149 7W
Palmer →, Australia 62 B3 16 0S 142 26 E
Palmer Arch., Antarctica 5 C17 64 15S 65 0W
Palmer Lake, U.S.A. 80 F2 39 7N 104 55W
Palmer Land, Antarctica 5 D18 73 0S 63 0W
Palmerston, Canada 78 C4 43 50N 80 51W
Palmerston, N.Z. 59 L3 45 29S 170 43 E
Palmerston North, N.Z. 59 J5 40 21S 175 39 E
Palmerton, U.S.A. 79 F9 40 48N 75 37W
Palmetto, U.S.A. 77 M4 27 31N 82 34W
Palmi, Italy 20 E6 38 21N 15 51 E
Palmira, Argentina 94 C2 32 59S 68 34W
Palmira, Colombia 92 C3 3 32N 76 16W
Palmyra = Tudmur, Syria 44 C3 34 36N 38 15 E
Palmyra, Mo., U.S.A. 80 F9 39 48N 91 32W
Palmyra, N.Y., U.S.A. 78 C7 43 5N 77 18W
Palmyra Is., Pac. Oc. 65 G11 5 52N 162 5W
Palo Alto, U.S.A. 83 H2 37 27N 122 10W
Palo Verde, U.S.A. 85 M12 33 26N 114 44W
Palopo, Indonesia 37 E6 3 0S 120 16 E
Palos, C. de, Spain 19 D5 37 38N 0 40W
Palos Verdes, U.S.A. 85 M8 33 48N 118 23W
Palos Verdes, Pt., U.S.A. 85 M8 33 43N 118 26W
Palouse, U.S.A. 82 C5 46 55N 117 4W
Palparara, Australia 62 C3 24 47S 141 28 E
Palu, Indonesia 37 E5 1 0S 119 52 E
Palu, Turkey 25 G7 38 45N 40 0 E
Paluan, Phil. 37 B6 13 26N 120 29 E
Palwal, India 42 E7 28 8N 77 19 E
Pama, Burkina Faso 50 F5 11 19N 0 44 E
Pamanukan, Indonesia 37 G12 6 16S 107 49 E
Pamekasan, Indonesia 37 G15 7 10S 113 28 E
Pamirs, Tajikistan 26 F8 37 40N 73 0 E
Pamlico →, U.S.A. 77 H7 35 20N 76 28W
Pamlico Sd., U.S.A. 77 H8 35 20N 76 0W
Pampa, U.S.A. 81 H4 35 32N 100 58W
Pampa de las Salinas, Argentina 94 C2 32 1S 66 58W

151

Pôrto Esperança

Pôrto Esperança, Brazil 92 G7 19 37S 57 29W
Pôrto Franco, Brazil 93 E9 6 20S 47 24W
Porto Mendes, Brazil 95 A5 24 30S 54 15W
Porto Moniz, Madeira 22 D2 32 52N 17 11W
Pôrto Murtinho, Brazil 92 H7 21 45S 57 55W
Pôrto Nacional, Brazil 93 F9 10 40S 48 30W
Porto Novo, Benin 50 G5 6 23N 2 42 E
Porto Petro, Spain 22 B10 39 22N 3 13 E
Porto Santo, Madeira 50 B1 33 45N 16 25W
Pôrto São José, Brazil 95 A5 22 43S 53 10W
Pôrto Seguro, Brazil 93 G11 16 26S 39 5W
Porto Tórres, Italy 20 D3 40 50N 8 23 E
Pôrto União, Brazil 95 B5 26 10S 51 10W
Pôrto Válter, Brazil 92 E4 8 15S 72 40W
Porto-Vecchio, France 18 F9 41 35N 9 16 E
Pôrto Velho, Brazil 92 E6 8 46S 63 54W
Portobelo, Panama 88 E4 9 35N 79 42W
Portoferráio, Italy 20 C4 42 50N 10 20 E
Portola, U.S.A. 84 F6 39 49N 120 28W
Portoscuso, Italy 20 E3 39 12N 8 22 E
Portoviejo, Ecuador 92 D2 1 7S 80 28W
Portpatrick, U.K. 12 G3 54 50N 5 7W
Portree, U.K. 12 D2 57 25N 6 11W
Portrush, U.K. 13 A5 55 13N 6 40W
Portsmouth, Domin. 89 C7 15 34N 61 27W
Portsmouth, U.K. 11 G6 50 48N 1 6W
Portsmouth, N.H., U.S.A. 79 C14 43 5N 70 45W
Portsmouth, Ohio, U.S.A. 76 F4 38 44N 82 57W
Portsmouth, R.I., U.S.A. 79 E13 41 36N 71 15W
Portsmouth, Va., U.S.A. 76 G7 36 50N 76 18W
Portsoy, U.K. 12 D6 57 41N 2 41W
Porttipahta, Finland 8 B19 68 5N 26 40 E
Portugal ■, Europe 19 C2 40 0N 8 0W
Portuguese-Guinea = Guinea-Bissau ■, Africa 50 F2 12 0N 15 0W
Portumna, Ireland 13 C3 53 5N 8 12W
Portville, U.S.A. 78 D6 42 3N 78 20W
Porvenir, Chile 96 G2 53 10S 70 16W
Porvoo = Borgå, Finland 9 F18 60 24N 25 40 E
Posadas, Argentina 95 B4 27 30S 55 50W
Poshan = Boshan, China 35 F9 36 28N 117 49 E
Posht-e-Badam, Iran 45 C7 33 2N 55 23 E
Poso, Indonesia 37 E6 1 20S 120 55 E
Posong, S. Korea 35 G14 34 46N 127 5 E
Posse, Brazil 93 F9 14 4S 46 18W
Possel, C.A.R. 52 C3 5 5N 19 10 E
Possession I., Antarctica 5 D11 72 4S 172 0 E
Post, U.S.A. 81 J4 33 12N 101 23W
Post Falls, U.S.A. 82 C5 47 43N 116 57W
Poste Maurice Cortier, Algeria 50 D5 22 14N 1 2 E
Postmasburg, S. Africa 56 D3 28 18S 23 5 E
Postojna, Slovenia 20 B6 45 46N 14 12 E
Poston, U.S.A. 85 M12 34 0N 114 24W
Potchefstroom, S. Africa 56 D4 26 41S 27 7 E
Poteau, U.S.A. 81 H7 35 3N 94 37W
Poteet, U.S.A. 81 L5 29 2N 98 35W
Potenza, Italy 20 D6 40 40N 15 50 E
Poteriteri, L., N.Z. 59 M1 46 5S 167 10 E
Potgietersrus, S. Africa 57 C4 24 10S 28 55 E
Poti, Georgia 25 F7 42 10N 41 38 E
Potiskum, Nigeria 50 F7 11 39N 11 2 E
Potomac →, U.S.A. 76 F7 38 0N 76 23W
Potosí, Bolivia 92 G5 19 38S 65 50W
Potosi Mt., U.S.A. 85 K11 35 57N 115 29W
Pototan, Phil. 37 B6 10 54N 122 38 E
Potrerillos, Chile 94 B2 26 30S 69 30W
Potsdam, Germany 16 B6 52 23N 13 4 E
Potsdam, U.S.A. 79 B10 44 40N 74 59W
Potter, U.S.A. 80 E3 41 13N 103 19W
Pottstown, U.S.A. 79 F9 40 15N 75 39W
Pottsville, U.S.A. 79 F8 40 41N 76 12W
Pottuvil, Sri Lanka 40 R12 6 55N 81 50 E
Pouce Coupé, Canada 72 B4 55 40N 120 10W
Poughkeepsie, U.S.A. 79 E11 41 42N 73 56W
Poulaphouca Res., Ireland 13 C5 53 8N 6 30W
Poulsbo, U.S.A. 84 C4 47 44N 122 39W
Pouso Alegre, Mato Grosso, Brazil 93 F7 11 46S 57 16W
Pouso Alegre, Minas Gerais, Brazil 95 A6 22 14S 45 57W
Povenets, Russia 24 B5 62 50N 34 50 E
Poverty B., N.Z. 59 H7 38 43S 178 2 E
Póvoa de Varzim, Portugal 19 B1 41 25N 8 46W
Powassan, Canada 70 C4 46 5N 79 25W
Poway, U.S.A. 85 N9 32 58N 117 2W
Powder →, U.S.A. 80 B2 46 45N 105 26W
Powder River, U.S.A. 82 E10 43 2N 106 59W
Powell, U.S.A. 82 D9 44 45N 108 46W
Powell L., U.S.A. 83 H8 36 57N 111 29W
Powell River, Canada 72 D4 49 50N 124 35W
Powers, Mich., U.S.A. 76 C2 45 41N 87 32W
Powers, Oreg., U.S.A. 82 E1 42 53N 124 4W
Powers Lake, U.S.A. 80 A3 48 34N 102 39W
Powys □, U.K. 11 E4 52 20N 3 20W
Poyang Hu, China 33 D6 29 5N 116 20 E
Poyarkovo, Russia 27 E13 49 36N 128 41 E
Poza Rica, Mexico 87 C5 20 33N 97 27W
Požarevac, Serbia, Yug. 21 B9 44 35N 21 18 E
Poznań, Poland 16 B8 52 25N 16 55 E
Pozo, U.S.A. 85 K6 35 20N 120 24W
Pozo Almonte, Chile 92 H5 20 10S 69 50W
Pozo Colorado, Paraguay 94 A4 23 30S 58 45W
Pozo del Dátil, Mexico 86 B2 30 0N 112 15W
Pozoblanco, Spain 19 C3 38 23N 4 51W
Prachin Buri, Thailand 38 E3 14 0N 101 25 E
Prachuap Khiri Khan, Thailand 39 G2 11 49N 99 48 E
Prado, Brazil 93 G11 17 20S 39 13W
Prague = Praha, Czech. 16 C7 50 5N 14 22 E
Praha, Czech. 16 C7 50 5N 14 22 E
Praid, Romania 17 E12 46 32N 25 10 E
Prainha, Amazonas, Brazil 92 E6 7 10S 60 30W
Prainha, Pará, Brazil 93 D8 1 45S 53 30W
Prairie, Australia 62 C3 20 50S 144 35 E
Prairie →, U.S.A. 81 H5 34 30N 99 23W
Prairie City, U.S.A. 82 D4 44 28N 118 43W
Prairie du Chien, U.S.A. 80 D9 43 3N 91 9W
Prairies, Canada 68 C9 52 0N 108 0W
Pran Buri, Thailand 38 F2 12 23N 99 55 E
Prapat, Indonesia 36 D1 2 41N 98 58 E
Prasonísi, Ákra, Greece 23 D9 35 42N 27 46 E
Prata, Brazil 93 G9 19 25S 48 54W
Pratapgarh, India 42 G6 24 2N 74 40 E
Prato, Italy 20 C4 43 53N 11 5 E
Pratt, U.S.A. 81 G5 37 39N 98 44W
Prattville, U.S.A. 77 J2 32 28N 86 29W
Pravia, Spain 19 A2 43 30N 6 12W
Praya, Indonesia 36 F5 8 39S 116 17 E
Precordillera, Argentina 94 C2 30 0S 69 1W
Preeceville, Canada 73 C8 51 57N 102 40W
Prelate, Canada 73 C7 50 51N 109 24W
Premier, Canada 72 B3 56 4N 129 56W
Premont, U.S.A. 81 M5 27 22N 98 7W
Prentice, U.S.A. 80 C9 45 33N 90 17W
Prenzlau, Germany 16 B6 53 19N 13 51 E
Preobrazheniye, Russia 30 C6 42 54N 133 54 E
Prepansko Jezero, Macedonia 21 D9 40 55N 21 0 E
Preparis North Channel, Ind. Oc. 41 M18 15 12N 93 40 E
Preparis South Channel, Ind. Oc. 41 M18 14 36N 93 40 E
Přerov, Czech. 17 D8 49 28N 17 27 E
Prescott, Canada 70 D4 44 45N 75 30W
Prescott, Ariz., U.S.A. 83 J7 34 33N 112 28W
Prescott, Ark., U.S.A. 81 J8 33 48N 93 23W
Preservation Inlet, N.Z. 59 M1 46 8S 166 35 E
Presho, U.S.A. 80 D4 43 54N 100 3W
Presidencia de la Plaza, Argentina 94 B4 27 0S 59 50W
Presidencia Roque Saenz Peña, Argentina 94 B3 26 45S 60 30W
Presidente Epitácio, Brazil 93 H8 21 56S 52 6W
Presidente Hayes □, Paraguay 94 A4 24 0S 59 0W
Presidente Hermes, Brazil 92 F6 11 17S 61 55W
Presidente Prudente, Brazil 95 A5 22 5S 51 25W
Presidio, Mexico 86 B4 29 29N 104 23W
Presidio, U.S.A. 81 L2 29 34N 104 22W
Prespa, L. = Prepansko Jezero, Macedonia 21 D9 40 55N 21 0 E
Presque Isle, U.S.A. 71 C6 46 41N 68 1W
Prestbury, U.K. 11 F5 51 54N 2 2W
Presteigne, U.K. 11 E5 52 17N 3 0W
Preston, Canada 78 C4 43 23N 80 21W
Preston, U.K. 10 D5 53 46N 2 42W
Preston, Idaho, U.S.A. 82 E8 42 6N 111 53W
Preston, Minn., U.S.A. 80 D8 43 40N 92 5W
Preston, Nev., U.S.A. 82 G6 38 55N 115 4W
Preston, C., Australia 60 D2 20 51S 116 12 E
Prestonpans, U.K. 12 F6 55 58N 2 58W
Prestwick, U.K. 12 F4 55 30N 4 38W
Pretoria, S. Africa 57 D4 25 44S 28 12 E
Préveza, Greece 21 E9 38 57N 20 47 E
Pribilof Is., Bering S. 4 D17 56 0N 170 0W
Příbram, Czech. 16 D7 49 41N 14 2 E
Price, U.S.A. 82 G8 39 36N 110 49W
Price I., Canada 72 C3 52 23N 128 41W
Prichard, U.S.A. 77 K1 30 44N 88 5W
Prieska, S. Africa 56 D3 29 40S 22 42 E
Priest →, U.S.A. 82 B5 48 12N 116 54W
Priest L., U.S.A. 82 B5 48 35N 116 52W
Priest Valley, U.S.A. 84 J6 36 10N 120 39W
Priestly, Canada 72 C3 54 8N 125 20W
Prikaspiyskaya Nizmennost, Asia 25 E8 47 0N 48 0 E
Prilep, Macedonia 21 D9 41 21N 21 37 E
Priluki, Ukraine 25 D5 50 30N 32 24 E
Prime Seal I., Australia 62 G4 40 3S 147 43 E
Primrose L., Canada 73 C7 54 55N 109 45W
Prince Albert, Canada 73 C7 53 15N 105 50W
Prince Albert, S. Africa 56 E3 33 12S 22 2 E
Prince Albert Mts., Antarctica 5 D11 76 0S 161 30 E
Prince Albert Nat. Park, Canada 73 C7 54 0N 106 25W
Prince Albert Pen., Canada 68 A8 72 30N 116 0W
Prince Albert Sd., Canada 68 A8 70 25N 115 0W
Prince Alfred, C., Canada 4 B1 74 20N 124 40W
Prince Charles I., Canada 69 B12 67 47N 76 12W
Prince Charles Mts., Antarctica 5 D6 72 0S 67 0 E
Prince Edward I. □, Canada 71 C7 46 20N 63 20W
Prince Edward Is., Ind. Oc. 3 G11 46 35S 38 0 E
Prince George, Canada 72 C4 53 55N 122 50W
Prince of Wales, C., U.S.A. 66 C3 65 36N 168 5W
Prince of Wales I., Australia 62 A3 10 40S 142 10 E
Prince of Wales I., Canada 68 A10 73 0N 99 0W
Prince of Wales I., U.S.A. 72 B2 55 47N 132 50W
Prince Patrick I., Canada 4 B2 77 0N 120 0W
Prince Regent Inlet, Canada 4 B3 73 0N 90 0W
Prince Rupert, Canada 72 C2 54 20N 130 20W
Princess Charlotte B., Australia 62 A3 14 25S 144 0 E
Princess May Ras., Australia 60 C4 15 30S 125 30 E
Princess Royal I., Canada 72 C3 53 0N 128 40W
Princeton, Canada 72 D4 49 27N 120 30W
Princeton, Calif., U.S.A. 84 F4 39 24N 122 1W
Princeton, Ill., U.S.A. 80 E10 41 23N 89 28W
Princeton, Ind., U.S.A. 76 F2 38 21N 87 34W
Princeton, Ky., U.S.A. 76 G2 37 7N 87 53W
Princeton, Mo., U.S.A. 80 E8 40 24N 93 35W
Princeton, N.J., U.S.A. 79 F10 40 21N 74 39W
Princeton, W. Va., U.S.A. 76 G5 37 22N 81 6W
Principe, I. de, Atl. Oc. 48 F4 1 37N 7 27 E
Principe Chan., Canada 72 C2 53 28N 130 0W
Principe da Beira, Brazil 92 F6 12 20S 64 30W
Prineville, U.S.A. 82 D3 44 18N 120 51W
Prins Harald Kyst, Antarctica 5 D4 70 0S 35 1 E
Prinsesse Astrid Kyst, Antarctica 5 D3 70 45S 12 30 E
Prinsesse Ragnhild Kyst, Antarctica 5 D4 70 15S 27 30 E
Prinzapolca, Nic. 88 D3 13 20N 83 35W
Priozersk, Russia 24 B5 61 2N 30 7 E
Pripet = Pripyat →, Europe 24 D5 51 20N 30 15 E
Pripet Marshes = Polesye, Belorussia 24 D4 52 10N 28 10 E
Pripyat →, Europe 24 D5 51 20N 30 15 E
Pripyat Marshes = Polesye, Belorussia 24 D4 52 10N 28 10 E
Priština, Serbia, Yug. 21 C9 42 40N 21 13 E
Privas, France 18 D6 44 45N 4 37 E
Privolzhskaya Vozvyshennost, Russia 25 D8 51 0N 46 0 E
Prizren, Serbia, Yug. 21 C9 42 13N 20 45 E
Probolinggo, Indonesia 37 G15 7 46S 113 13 E
Proddatur, India 40 M11 14 45N 78 30 E
Prodhromos, Cyprus 23 E11 34 57N 32 50 E
Profítis Ilías, Greece 23 C9 36 17N 27 56 E
Progreso, Mexico 87 C7 21 20N 89 40W
Prokopyevsk, Russia 26 D9 54 0N 86 45 E
Prome = Pyè, Burma 41 K19 18 49N 95 13 E
Prophet →, Canada 72 B4 58 48N 122 40W
Propriá, Brazil 93 F11 10 13S 36 51W
Proserpine, Australia 62 C4 20 21S 148 36 E
Prosser, U.S.A. 82 C4 46 12N 119 46W
Prostějov, Czech. 16 D8 49 30N 17 9 E
Proston, Australia 63 D5 26 8S 151 32 E
Protection, U.S.A. 81 G5 37 12N 99 29W
Provence, France 18 E6 43 40N 5 46 E
Providence, Ky., U.S.A. 76 G2 37 24N 87 46W
Providence, R.I., U.S.A. 79 E13 41 49N 71 24W
Providence Bay, Canada 70 C3 45 41N 82 15W
Providence Mts., U.S.A. 83 J6 35 10N 115 15W
Providencia, I. de, Colombia 88 D3 13 25N 81 26W
Provideniya, Russia 27 C19 64 23N 173 18W
Provins, France 18 B5 48 33N 3 15 E
Provo, U.S.A. 82 F8 40 14N 111 39W
Provost, Canada 73 C6 52 25N 110 20W
Prud'homme, Canada 73 C7 52 20N 105 54W
Pruszków, Poland 17 B10 52 9N 20 49 E
Prut →, Romania 17 F14 45 28N 28 10 E
Prydz B., Antarctica 5 C6 69 0S 74 0 E
Pryluky = Priluki, Ukraine 25 D5 50 30N 32 24 E
Pryor, U.S.A. 81 G7 36 19N 95 19W
Przemysl, Poland 17 D11 49 50N 22 45 E
Przeworsk, Poland 17 C11 50 6N 22 32 E
Przhevalsk, Kirghizia 26 E8 42 30N 78 20 E
Psira, Greece 23 D7 35 12N 25 52 E
Pskov, Russia 24 C4 57 50N 28 25 E
Pu Xian, China 34 F6 36 24N 111 6 E
Pua, Thailand 38 C3 19 11N 100 55 E
Puán, Argentina 94 D3 37 30S 62 45W
Puan, S. Korea 35 G14 35 44N 126 44 E
Pucallpa, Peru 92 E4 8 25S 74 30W
Pudozh, Russia 24 B6 61 48N 36 32 E
Pudukkottai, India 40 P11 10 28N 78 47 E
Puebla, Mexico 87 D5 19 0N 98 10W
Puebla □, Mexico 87 D5 18 30N 98 0W
Pueblo, U.S.A. 80 F2 38 16N 104 37W
Pueblo Hundido, Chile 94 B1 26 20S 70 5W
Puelches, Argentina 94 D2 38 5S 65 51W
Puelén, Argentina 94 D2 37 32S 67 38W
Puente Alto, Chile 94 C1 33 32S 70 35W
Puente-Genil, Spain 19 D3 37 22N 4 47W
Puerco →, U.S.A. 83 J10 34 22N 107 50W
Puerto, Canary Is. 22 F2 28 5N 17 20W
Puerto Aisén, Chile 96 F2 45 27S 73 0W
Puerto Ángel, Mexico 87 D5 15 40N 96 29W
Puerto Arista, Mexico 87 D6 15 56N 93 48W
Puerto Armuelles, Panama 88 E3 8 20N 82 51W
Puerto Ayacucho, Venezuela 92 B5 5 40N 67 35W
Puerto Barrios, Guatemala 88 C2 15 40N 88 32W
Puerto Bermejo, Argentina 94 B4 26 55S 58 34W
Puerto Bermúdez, Peru 92 F4 10 20S 74 58W
Puerto Bolívar, Ecuador 92 D3 3 19S 79 55W
Puerto Cabello, Venezuela 92 A5 10 28N 68 1W
Puerto Cabezas, Nic. 88 D3 14 0N 83 30W
Puerto Cabo Gracias á Dios, Nic. 88 D3 15 0N 83 10W
Puerto Carreño, Colombia 92 B5 6 12N 67 22W
Puerto Castilla, Honduras 88 C2 16 0N 86 0W
Puerto Chicama, Peru 92 E3 7 45S 79 20W
Puerto Coig, Argentina 96 G3 50 54S 69 15W
Puerto Cortes, Costa Rica 88 E3 8 55N 84 0W
Puerto Cortés, Honduras 88 C2 15 51N 88 0W
Puerto Cumarebo, Venezuela 92 A5 11 29N 69 30W
Puerto de Alcudia, Spain 22 B10 39 50N 3 7 E
Puerto de Andraitx, Spain 22 B9 39 32N 2 23 E
Puerto de Cabrera, Spain 22 B9 39 8N 2 56 E
Puerto de Gran Tarajal, Canary Is. 22 F5 28 13N 14 1W
Puerto de la Cruz, Canary Is. 22 F3 28 24N 16 32W
Puerto de Pozo Negro, Canary Is. 22 F6 28 19N 13 55W
Puerto de Santa María, Spain 19 D2 36 36N 6 13W
Puerto de Sóller, Spain 22 B9 39 48N 2 42 E
Pto. del Carmen, Canary Is. 22 F6 28 55N 13 38W
Puerto del Rosario, Canary Is. 22 F6 28 30N 13 52W
Puerto Deseado, Argentina 96 F3 47 55S 66 0W
Puerto Heath, Bolivia 92 F5 12 34S 68 39W
Puerto Juárez, Mexico 87 C7 21 11N 86 49W
Puerto La Cruz, Venezuela 92 A6 10 13N 64 38W
Puerto Leguízamo, Colombia 92 D4 0 12S 74 46W
Puerto Lobos, Argentina 96 E3 42 0S 65 3W
Puerto Madryn, Argentina 96 E3 42 48S 65 4W
Puerto Maldonado, Peru 92 F5 12 30S 69 10W
Puerto Manotí, Cuba 88 B4 21 22N 76 50W
Puerto Montt, Chile 96 E2 41 28S 73 0W
Puerto Morelos, Mexico 87 C7 20 49N 86 52W
Puerto Natales, Chile 96 G2 51 45S 72 15W
Puerto Padre, Cuba 88 B4 21 13N 76 35W
Puerto Páez, Venezuela 92 B5 6 13N 67 28W
Puerto Peñasco, Mexico 86 A2 31 20N 113 33W
Puerto Pinasco, Paraguay 94 A4 22 36S 57 50W
Puerto Pirámides, Argentina 96 E4 42 35S 64 20W
Puerto Plata, Dom. Rep. 89 C5 19 48N 70 45W
Puerto Pollensa, Spain 22 B10 39 54N 3 4 E
Puerto Princesa, Phil. 37 C5 9 46N 118 45 E
Puerto Quellón, Chile 96 E2 43 7S 73 37W
Puerto Quepos, Costa Rica 88 E3 9 29N 84 6W
Puerto Rico, Canary Is. 22 G4 27 47N 15 42W
Puerto Rico ■, W. Indies 89 C6 18 15N 66 45W
Puerto Rico Trench, Atl. Oc. 89 C6 19 50N 66 0W
Puerto Sastre, Paraguay 94 A4 22 2S 57 55W
Puerto Suárez, Bolivia 92 G7 18 58S 57 52W
Puerto Vallarta, Mexico 86 C3 20 36N 105 15W
Puerto Wilches, Colombia 92 B4 7 21N 73 54W
Puertollano, Spain 19 C3 38 43N 4 7W
Pueyrredón, L., Argentina 96 F2 47 20S 72 0W
Pugachev, Kazakhstan 24 D8 52 0N 48 49 E
Puge, Tanzania 54 C3 4 45S 33 11 E
Puget Sound, U.S.A. 82 C2 47 50N 122 30W
Púglia □, Italy 20 D7 41 0N 16 30 E
Pugŏdong, N. Korea 35 C16 42 5N 130 0 E
Pugu, Tanzania 54 D4 6 55S 39 4 E
Pūgūnzī, Iran 45 E8 25 49N 59 10 E
Puig Mayor, Spain 22 B9 39 48N 2 47 E
Puigcerdá, Spain 19 A6 42 24N 1 50 E
Puigpuñent, Spain 22 B9 39 38N 2 32 E
Pujon-chosuji, N. Korea 35 D14 40 35N 127 35 E
Pukaki L., N.Z. 59 L3 44 4S 170 1 E
Pukapuka, Cook Is. 65 J11 10 53S 165 49W
Pukatawagan, Canada 73 B8 55 45N 101 20W
Pukchin, N. Korea 35 D13 40 12N 125 45 E
Pukchŏng, N. Korea 35 D15 40 14N 128 10 E
Pukekohe, N.Z. 59 G5 37 12S 174 55 E
Pulaski, N.Y., U.S.A. 79 C8 43 34N 76 8W
Pulaski, Tenn., U.S.A. 77 H2 35 12N 87 2W
Pulaski, Va., U.S.A. 76 G5 37 3N 80 47W
Pulga, U.S.A. 84 F5 39 48N 121 29W
Pulicat, L., India 40 N12 13 40N 80 15 E
Pullman, U.S.A. 82 C5 46 44N 117 10W
Pulog, Phil. 37 A6 16 40N 120 50 E
Pumlumon Fawr, U.K. 11 E4 52 29N 3 47W
Puna, Bolivia 92 G5 19 45S 65 28W
Puná, I., Ecuador 92 D2 2 55S 80 5W
Punakha, Bhutan 41 F16 27 42N 89 52 E
Punasar, India 42 F5 27 6N 73 6 E
Punata, Bolivia 92 G5 17 32S 65 50W
Punch, India 43 C6 33 48N 74 4 E
Pune, India 40 K8 18 29N 73 57 E
Pungsan, N. Korea 35 D15 40 50N 128 9 E
Pungue, Ponte de, Mozam. 55 F3 19 0S 34 0 E
Punjab □, India 42 D6 31 0N 76 0 E
Punjab □, Pakistan 42 E6 32 0N 74 30 E
Puno, Peru 92 G4 15 55S 70 3W
Punta Alta, Argentina 96 D4 38 53S 62 4W
Punta Arenas, Chile 96 G2 53 10S 71 0W
Punta de Díaz, Chile 94 B1 28 0S 70 45W
Punta Gorda, Belize 87 D7 16 10N 88 45W
Punta Gorda, U.S.A. 77 M5 26 56N 82 3W
Punta Prieta, Mexico 86 B2 28 58N 114 17W
Punta Prima, Spain 22 B11 39 48N 4 16 E
Puntabie, Australia 63 E1 32 12S 134 13 E
Puntarenas, Costa Rica 88 E3 10 0N 84 50W
Punto Fijo, Venezuela 92 A4 11 50N 70 13W
Punxsatawney, U.S.A. 78 F5 40 57N 78 59W
Puquio, Peru 92 F4 14 45S 74 10W
Pur →, Russia 26 C8 67 31N 77 55 E
Purace, Vol., Colombia 92 C3 2 21N 76 23W
Puralia = Puruliya, India 43 H12 23 17N 86 24 E
Purbeck, Isle of, U.K. 11 G5 50 40N 2 5W
Purcell, U.S.A. 81 H6 35 1N 97 22W
Puri, India 41 K14 19 50N 85 58 E
Purmerend, Neths. 15 B4 52 32N 4 58 E
Purnia, India 43 G12 25 45N 87 31 E
Purukcahu, Indonesia 36 E4 0 35S 114 35 E
Puruliya, India 43 H12 23 17N 86 24 E
Purus →, Brazil 92 D6 3 42S 61 28W
Purwakarta, Indonesia 37 G12 6 35S 107 29 E
Purwodadi, Jawa, Indonesia 37 G14 7 7S 110 55 E
Purwodadi, Jawa, Indonesia 37 G13 7 51S 110 0 E
Purwokerto, Indonesia 37 G13 7 25S 109 14 E
Purworejo, Indonesia 37 G14 7 43S 110 2 E
Puryŏng, N. Korea 35 C15 42 5N 129 43 E
Pusan, S. Korea 35 G15 35 5N 129 0 E
Pushchino, Russia 27 D16 54 10N 158 0 E
Pushkino, Russia 25 D8 51 16N 47 0 E
Putahow L., Canada 73 B8 59 54N 100 40W
Putao, Burma 41 F20 27 28N 97 30 E
Putaruru, N.Z. 59 H5 38 2S 175 50 E
Puthein Myit →, Burma 41 M19 15 56N 94 18 E
Putignano, Italy 20 D7 40 50N 17 5 E
Puting, Tanjung, Indonesia 36 E4 3 31S 111 46 E
Putnam, U.S.A. 79 E13 41 55N 71 55W
Putorana, Gory, Russia 27 C10 69 0N 95 0 E
Puttalam, Sri Lanka 40 Q11 8 1N 79 55 E
Putten, Neths. 15 B5 52 16N 5 36 E
Puttgarden, Germany 16 A5 54 28N 11 15 E
Putumayo →, S. Amer. 92 D5 3 7S 67 58W
Putussibau, Indonesia 36 D4 0 50N 112 56 E
Puy-de-Dôme, France 18 D5 45 46N 2 57 E
Puy-de-Dôme □, France 18 D5 45 40N 3 5 E
Puyallup, U.S.A. 84 C8 47 12N 122 18W
Puyang, China 34 G8 35 40N 115 1 E
Pūzeh Rīg, Iran 45 E8 27 20N 58 40 E
Pwani □, Tanzania 54 D4 7 0S 39 0 E

Ranobe, Helodranon' i

Pweto, *Zaïre* **55 D2** 8 25S 28 51 E
Pwllheli, *U.K.* **10 E3** 52 54N 4 26W
Pya-ozero, *Russia* **24 A5** 66 5N 30 58 E
Pyapon, *Burma* **41 L19** 16 20N 95 40 E
Pyasina →, *Russia* **27 B9** 73 30N 87 0 E
Pyatigorsk, *Russia* **25 F7** 44 2N 43 6 E
Pyè, *Burma* **41 K19** 18 49N 95 13 E
Pyinmana, *Burma* **41 K20** 19 45N 96 12 E
Pyla, C., *Cyprus* **23 E12** 34 56N 33 51 E
Pyŏktong, *N. Korea* **35 D13** 40 50N 125 50 E
Pyŏnggang, *N. Korea* **35 E14** 38 24N 127 17 E
Pyŏngtaek, *S. Korea* **35 F14** 37 1N 127 4 E
P'yŏngyang, *N. Korea* **35 E13** 39 0N 125 30 E
Pyote, *U.S.A.* **81 K3** 31 32N 103 8W
Pyramid L., *U.S.A.* **82 G4** 40 1N 119 35W
Pyramid Pk., *U.S.A.* **85 J10** 36 25N 116 37W
Pyrénées, *Europe* **18 E4** 42 45N 0 18 E
Pyrénées-Atlantiques □, *France* **18 E3** 43 10N 0 50W
Pyrénées-Orientales □, *France* **18 E5** 42 35N 2 26 E
Pyu, *Burma* **41 K20** 18 30N 96 28 E

Q

Qaanaaq = Thule, *Greenland* **4 B4** 77 40N 69 0W
Qachasnek, *S. Africa* **57 E4** 30 6S 28 42 E
Qādib, *Yemen* **46 E5** 12 37N 53 57 E
Qa'el Jafr, *Jordan* **47 E5** 30 20N 36 25 E
Qa'emābād, *Iran* **45 D9** 31 44N 60 2 E
Qā'emshahr, *Iran* **45 B7** 36 30N 52 53 E
Qagan Nur, *China* **34 C8** 43 30N 114 55 E
Qahar Youyi Zhongqi, *China* **34 D7** 41 12N 112 40 E
Qahremānshahr = Bākhtarān, *Iran* **44 C5** 34 23N 47 0 E
Qaidam Pendi, *China* **32 C4** 37 0N 95 0 E
Qajarīyeh, *Iran* **45 D6** 31 1N 48 22 E
Qala, Ras il, *Malta* **23 C1** 36 1N 14 20 E
Qala-i-Jadid, *Afghan.* **42 D2** 31 1N 66 25 E
Qala Yangi, *Afghan.* **42 B2** 34 20N 66 30 E
Qal'at al Akhḍar, *Si. Arabia* **44 E3** 28 0N 37 10 E
Qal'at Sukkar, *Iraq* **44 D5** 31 51N 46 5 E
Qal'eh Darreh, *Iran* **44 B5** 38 47N 47 2 E
Qal'eh Shaharak, *Afghan.* **40 B4** 34 10N 64 20 E
Qamar, Ghubbat al, *Yemen* **46 D5** 16 20N 52 30 E
Qamdo, *China* **32 C4** 31 15N 97 6 E
Qamruddin Karez, *Pakistan* **42 D3** 31 45N 68 20 E
Qandahār, *Afghan.* **40 D4** 31 32N 65 30 E
Qandahār □, *Afghan.* **40 D4** 31 0N 65 0 E
Qapān, *Iran* **45 B7** 37 40N 55 47 E
Qaqortoq = Julianehåb, *Greenland* **4 C5** 60 43N 46 0W
Qâra, *Egypt* **51 C10** 29 38N 26 30 E
Qara Qash →, *India* **43 B8** 35 0N 78 30 E
Qaraghandy = Karaganda, *Kazakhstan* **26 E8** 49 50N 73 10 E
Qārah, *Si. Arabia* **44 D4** 29 55N 40 3 E
Qareh →, *Iran* **44 B5** 39 25N 47 22 E
Qareh Tekān, *Iran* **45 B6** 36 38N 49 29 E
Qarqan He →, *China* **32 C3** 39 30N 88 30 E
Qarshi = Karshi, *Uzbekistan* **26 F7** 38 53N 65 48 E
Qartabā, *Lebanon* **47 A4** 34 4N 35 50 E
Qaryat al Gharab, *Iraq* **44 D5** 31 27N 44 48 E
Qaryat al 'Ulyā, *Si. Arabia* **44 E5** 27 33N 47 42 E
Qasr 'Amra, *Jordan* **44 D3** 31 48N 36 35 E
Qaṣr-e Qand, *Iran* **45 E9** 26 15N 60 45 E
Qasr Farâfra, *Egypt* **51 C10** 27 0N 28 1 E
Qatanā, *Syria* **47 B5** 33 26N 36 4 E
Qatar ■, *Asia* **45 E6** 25 30N 51 15 E
Qatlīsh, *Iran* **45 B8** 37 50N 57 19 E
Qattâra, Munkhafed el, *Egypt* **51 C10** 29 30N 27 30 E
Qattâra Depression = Qattâra, Munkhafed el, *Egypt* **51 C10** 29 30N 27 30 E
Qawām al Ḩamzah, *Iraq* **44 D5** 31 43N 44 58 E
Qāyen, *Iran* **45 C8** 33 40N 59 10 E
Qazaqstan = Kazakhstan ■, *Asia* **26 E7** 50 0N 70 0 E
Qazvin, *Iran* **45 B6** 36 15N 50 0 E
Qena, *Egypt* **51 C11** 26 10N 32 43 E
Qeqertarsuag = Disko, *Greenland* **4 C5** 69 45N 53 30W
Qeqertarsuaq = Godhavn, *Greenland* **4 C5** 69 15N 53 38W
Qeshlāq, *Iran* **44 C5** 34 55N 46 28 E
Qeshm, *Iran* **45 E8** 26 55N 56 10 E
Qezi'ot, *Israel* **47 E3** 30 52N 34 26 E
Qi Xian, *China* **34 G8** 34 40N 114 48 E
Qian Gorlos, *China* **35 B13** 45 5N 124 42 E
Qian Xian, *China* **34 G5** 34 31N 108 15 E
Qianyang, *China* **34 G4** 34 40N 107 8 E
Qibā', *Si. Arabia* **44 E5** 27 24N 44 20 E
Qila Safed, *Pakistan* **40 E2** 29 0N 61 30 E
Qila Saifullāh, *Pakistan* **42 D3** 30 45N 68 17 E
Qilian Shan, *China* **32 C4** 38 30N 96 0 E
Qin He →, *China* **34 G7** 35 1N 113 22 E
Qin Ling = Qinling Shandi, *China* **34 H5** 33 50N 108 10 E
Qin'an, *China* **34 G3** 34 48N 105 40 E
Qing Xian, *China* **34 E9** 38 35N 116 45 E
Qingcheng, *China* **35 F9** 37 15N 117 40 E
Qingdao, *China* **35 F11** 36 5N 120 20 E
Qingfeng, *China* **34 G8** 35 52N 115 8 E
Qinghai □, *China* **32 C4** 36 0N 98 0 E
Qinghai Hu, *China* **32 C5** 36 40N 100 10 E
Qinghecheng, *China* **35 D13** 41 15N 124 30 E
Qinghemen, *China* **35 D11** 41 48N 121 25 E
Qingjian, *China* **34 F6** 37 8N 110 8 E
Qingjiang, *China* **35 H10** 33 30N 119 2 E
Qingshui, *China* **34 G4** 34 48N 106 8 E
Qingshuihe, *China* **34 E6** 39 55N 111 35 E
Qingtongxia Shuiku, *China* **34 F3** 37 50N 105 58 E
Qingxu, *China* **34 F7** 37 34N 112 22 E
Qingyang, *China* **34 F4** 36 2N 107 55 E
Qingyuan, *China* **35 C13** 42 10N 124 55 E
Qingyun, *China* **35 F9** 37 45N 117 20 E
Qinhuangdao, *China* **35 E10** 39 56N 119 30 E
Qinling Shandi, *China* **34 H5** 33 50N 108 10 E
Qinshui, *China* **34 G7** 35 40N 112 8 E
Qinyang, *China* **34 G7** 35 7N 112 57 E
Qinyuan, *China* **34 F7** 36 29N 112 20 E
Qinzhou, *China* **32 D5** 21 58N 108 38 E
Qionghai, *China* **38 C8** 19 15N 110 26 E
Qiongshan, *China* **38 C8** 19 51N 110 26 E
Qiongzhou Haixia, *China* **38 B8** 20 10N 110 15 E
Qiqihar, *China* **27 E13** 47 26N 124 0 E
Qiraîya, W. →, *Egypt* **47 E3** 30 27N 34 0 E
Qiryat Ata, *Israel* **47 C4** 32 47N 35 6 E
Qiryat Gat, *Israel* **47 D3** 31 32N 34 46 E
Qiryat Mal'akhi, *Israel* **47 D3** 31 44N 34 44 E
Qiryat Shemona, *Israel* **47 B4** 33 13N 35 35 E
Qiryat Yam, *Israel* **47 C4** 32 51N 35 4 E
Qishan, *China* **34 G4** 34 25N 107 38 E
Qitai, *China* **32 B3** 44 2N 89 35 E
Qixia, *China* **35 F11** 37 17N 120 52 E
Qojūr, *Iran* **44 B5** 36 12N 47 55 E
Qom, *Iran* **45 C6** 34 40N 51 0 E
Qomsheh, *Iran* **45 D6** 32 0N 51 55 E
Qostanay = Kustanay, *Kazakhstan* **26 D7** 53 10N 63 35 E
Qu Xian, *China* **33 D6** 28 57N 118 54 E
Quairading, *Australia* **61 F2** 32 0S 117 21 E
Quakertown, *U.S.A.* **79 F9** 40 26N 75 21W
Qualeup, *Australia* **61 F2** 33 48S 116 48 E
Quambatook, *Australia* **63 F3** 35 49S 143 34 E
Quambone, *Australia* **63 E4** 30 57S 147 53 E
Quamby, *Australia* **62 C3** 20 22S 140 17 E
Quan Long, *Vietnam* **39 H5** 9 7N 105 8 E
Quanah, *U.S.A.* **81 H5** 34 18N 99 44W
Quandialla, *Australia* **63 E4** 34 1S 147 47 E
Quang Ngai, *Vietnam* **38 E7** 15 13N 108 58 E
Quang Yen, *Vietnam* **38 B6** 20 56N 106 52 E
Quantock Hills, *U.K.* **11 F4** 51 8N 3 10W
Quanzhou, *China* **33 D6** 24 55N 118 34 E
Quaraí, *Brazil* **94 C4** 30 15S 56 20W
Quartzsite, *U.S.A.* **85 M12** 33 40N 114 13W
Quatsino, *Canada* **72 C3** 50 30N 127 40W
Quatsino Sd., *Canada* **72 C3** 50 25N 127 58W
Qūchān, *Iran* **45 B8** 37 10N 58 27 E
Queanbeyan, *Australia* **63 F4** 35 17S 149 14 E
Québec, *Canada* **71 C5** 46 52N 71 13W
Québec □, *Canada* **71 B6** 48 0N 74 0W
Queen Alexandra Ra., *Antarctica* **5 E11** 85 0S 170 0 E
Queen Charlotte, *Canada* **72 C2** 53 15N 132 2W
Queen Charlotte Is., *Canada* **72 C2** 53 20N 132 10W
Queen Charlotte Str., *Canada* **72 C3** 51 0N 128 0W
Queen Elizabeth Is., *Canada* **66 B10** 76 0N 95 0W
Queen Elizabeth Nat. Park, *Uganda* **54 C3** 0 0 30 0 E
Queen Mary Land, *Antarctica* **5 D7** 70 0S 95 0 E
Queen Maud G., *Canada* **68 B9** 68 15N 102 30W
Queen Maud Land, *Antarctica* **5 D3** 72 30S 12 0 E
Queen Maud Mts., *Antarctica* **5 E13** 86 0S 160 0W
Queens Chan., *Australia* **60 C4** 15 0S 129 30 E
Queenscliff, *Australia* **63 F3** 38 16S 144 39 E
Queensland □, *Australia* **62 C3** 22 0S 142 0 E
Queenstown, *Australia* **62 G4** 42 4S 145 35 E
Queenstown, *N.Z.* **59 L2** 45 1S 168 40 E
Queenstown, *S. Africa* **56 E4** 31 52S 26 52 E
Queets, *U.S.A.* **84 C2** 47 32N 124 20W
Queguay Grande →, *Uruguay* **94 C4** 32 9S 58 9W
Queimadas, *Brazil* **93 F11** 11 0S 39 38W
Quela, *Angola* **52 F3** 9 10S 16 56 E
Quelimane, *Mozam.* **55 F4** 17 53S 36 58 E
Quelpart = Cheju Do, *S. Korea* **35 H14** 33 29N 126 34 E
Quemado, *N. Mex., U.S.A.* **83 J9** 34 20N 108 30W
Quemado, *Tex., U.S.A.* **81 L4** 28 58N 100 35W
Quemú-Quemú, *Argentina* **94 D3** 36 3S 63 36W
Quequén, *Argentina* **94 D4** 38 30S 58 30W
Querétaro, *Mexico* **86 C4** 20 40N 100 23W
Querétaro □, *Mexico* **86 C5** 20 30N 100 0W
Queshan, *China* **34 H8** 32 55N 114 2 E
Quesnel, *Canada* **72 C4** 53 0N 122 30W
Quesnel →, *Canada* **72 C4** 52 58N 122 29W
Quesnel L., *Canada* **72 C4** 52 30N 121 20W
Questa, *U.S.A.* **83 H11** 36 42N 105 36W
Quetico Prov. Park, *Canada* **70 C1** 48 30N 91 45W
Quetta, *Pakistan* **42 D2** 30 15N 66 55 E
Quezaltenango, *Guatemala* **88 D1** 14 50N 91 30W
Quezon City, *Phil.* **37 B6** 14 38N 121 0 E
Qufār, *Si. Arabia* **44 E4** 27 26N 41 37 E
Qui Nhon, *Vietnam* **38 F7** 13 40N 109 13 E
Quibaxe, *Angola* **52 F2** 8 24S 14 27 E
Quibdo, *Colombia* **92 B3** 5 42N 76 40W
Quiberon, *France* **18 C2** 47 29N 3 9W
Quick, *Canada* **72 C3** 54 36N 126 54W
Quiet L., *Canada* **72 A2** 61 5N 133 5W
Quiindy, *Paraguay* **94 B4** 25 58S 57 14W
Quila, *Mexico* **86 C3** 24 23N 107 13W
Quilán, C., *Chile* **96 E2** 43 15S 74 30W
Quilcene, *U.S.A.* **84 C4** 47 49N 122 53W
Quilengues, *Angola* **53 G2** 14 12S 14 12 E
Quilimarí, *Chile* **94 C1** 32 5S 71 30W
Quilino, *Argentina* **94 C3** 30 14S 64 29W
Quillabamba, *Peru* **92 F4** 12 50S 72 50W
Quillagua, *Chile* **94 A2** 21 40S 69 40W
Quillaicillo, *Chile* **94 C1** 31 17S 71 40W
Quillota, *Chile* **94 C1** 32 54S 71 16W
Quilmes, *Argentina* **94 C4** 34 43S 58 15W
Quilon, *India* **40 Q10** 8 50N 76 38 E
Quilpie, *Australia* **63 D3** 26 35S 144 11 E
Quilpué, *Chile* **94 C1** 33 5S 71 33W
Quilua, *Mozam.* **55 F4** 16 17S 39 54 E
Quimilí, *Argentina* **94 B3** 27 40S 62 30W
Quimper, *France* **18 B1** 48 0N 4 9W
Quimperlé, *France* **18 C2** 47 53N 3 33W
Quinault →, *U.S.A.* **84 C2** 47 21N 124 18W
Quincy, *Calif., U.S.A.* **84 F6** 39 56N 120 57W
Quincy, *Fla., U.S.A.* **77 K3** 30 35N 84 34W
Quincy, *Ill., U.S.A.* **80 F9** 39 56N 91 23W
Quincy, *Mass., U.S.A.* **79 D14** 42 15N 71 0W
Quincy, *Wash., U.S.A.* **82 C4** 47 22N 119 56W
Quines, *Argentina* **94 C2** 32 13S 65 48W
Quinga, *Mozam.* **55 F5** 15 49S 40 15 E
Quintana Roo □, *Mexico* **87 D7** 19 0N 88 0W
Quintanar de la Orden, *Spain* **19 C4** 39 36N 3 5W
Quintanar de la Sierra, *Spain* **19 B4** 41 57N 2 55W
Quintero, *Chile* **94 C1** 32 45S 71 30W
Quinyambie, *Australia* **63 E3** 30 15S 141 0 E
Quipungo, *Angola* **53 G2** 14 37S 14 40 E
Quirihue, *Chile* **94 D1** 36 15S 72 35W
Quirindi, *Australia* **63 E5** 31 28S 150 40 E
Quissanga, *Mozam.* **55 E5** 12 24S 40 28 E
Quitilipi, *Argentina* **94 B3** 26 50S 60 13W
Quitman, *Ga., U.S.A.* **77 K4** 30 47N 83 34W
Quitman, *Miss., U.S.A.* **77 J1** 32 2N 88 44W
Quitman, *Tex., U.S.A.* **81 J7** 32 48N 95 27W
Quito, *Ecuador* **92 D3** 0 15S 78 35W
Quixadá, *Brazil* **93 D11** 4 55S 39 0W
Quixaxe, *Mozam.* **55 F5** 15 17S 40 4 E
Qumbu, *S. Africa* **57 E4** 31 10S 28 48 E
Quneitra, *Syria* **47 B4** 33 7N 35 48 E
Quoin I., *Australia* **60 B4** 14 54S 129 32 E
Quoin Pt., *S. Africa* **56 E2** 34 46S 19 37 E
Quondong, *Australia* **63 E3** 33 6S 140 18 E
Quorn, *Australia* **63 E2** 32 25S 138 5 E
Quqon = Kokand, *Uzbekistan* **26 E8** 40 30N 70 57 E
Qurnat as Sawdā', *Lebanon* **47 A5** 34 18N 36 6 E
Qûs, *Egypt* **51 C11** 25 55N 32 50 E
Qusaybah, *Iraq* **44 C4** 34 24N 40 59 E
Quseir, *Egypt* **51 C11** 26 7N 34 16 E
Qūshchī, *Iran* **44 B5** 37 59N 45 3 E
Quthing, *Lesotho* **57 E4** 30 25S 27 36 E
Qūṭīābād, *Iran* **45 C6** 35 47N 48 30 E
Quwo, *China* **34 G6** 35 38N 111 25 E
Quyang, *China* **34 E8** 38 35N 114 40 E
Quynh Nhai, *Vietnam* **38 B4** 21 49N 103 33 E
Quzi, *China* **34 F4** 36 20N 107 20 E
Qyzylorda = Kzyl-Orda, *Kazakhstan* **26 E7** 44 48N 65 28 E

R

Ra, Ko, *Thailand* **39 H2** 9 13N 98 16 E
Raahe, *Finland* **8 D18** 64 40N 24 28 E
Raasay, *U.K.* **12 D2** 57 25N 6 4W
Raasay, Sd. of, *U.K.* **12 D2** 57 30N 6 8W
Raba, *Indonesia* **37 F5** 8 36S 118 55 E
Rabai, *Kenya* **54 C4** 3 50S 39 31 E
Rabat, *Malta* **23 D1** 35 53N 14 25 E
Rabat, *Morocco* **50 B3** 34 2N 6 48W
Rabaul, *Papua N. G.* **64 H7** 4 24S 152 18 E
Rabbit →, *Canada* **72 B3** 59 41N 127 12W
Rabbit Lake, *Canada* **73 C7** 53 8N 107 46W
Rabbitskin →, *Canada* **72 A4** 61 47N 120 42W
Rābor, *Iran* **45 D8** 29 17N 56 55 E
Race, C., *Canada* **71 C9** 46 40N 53 5W
Rach Gia, *Vietnam* **39 G5** 10 5N 105 5 E
Racine, *U.S.A.* **76 D2** 42 41N 87 51W
Rackerby, *U.S.A.* **84 F5** 39 26N 121 22W
Radama, Nosy, *Madag.* **57 A8** 14 0S 47 47 E
Radama, Saikanosy, *Madag.* **57 A8** 14 16S 47 53 E
Rădăuţi, *Romania* **17 E12** 47 50N 25 59 E
Radford, *U.S.A.* **76 G5** 37 8N 80 34W
Radhanpur, *India* **42 H4** 23 50N 71 38 E
Radisson, *Canada* **73 C7** 52 30N 107 20W
Radium Hot Springs, *Canada* **72 C5** 50 35N 116 2W
Radnor Forest, *U.K.* **11 E4** 52 17N 3 10W
Radom, *Poland* **17 C10** 51 23N 21 12 E
Radomir, *Bulgaria* **21 C10** 42 37N 23 4 E
Radomsko, *Poland* **17 C9** 51 5N 19 28 E
Radstock, *U.K.* **11 F5** 51 17N 2 25W
Radstock, C., *Australia* **63 E1** 33 12S 134 20 E
Radville, *Canada* **73 D8** 49 30N 104 15W
Rae, *Canada* **72 A5** 62 50N 116 3W
Rae Bareli, *India* **43 F9** 26 18N 81 20 E
Rae Isthmus, *Canada* **69 B11** 66 40N 87 30W
Raeren, *Belgium* **15 D6** 50 41N 6 7 E
Raeside, L., *Australia* **61 E3** 29 20S 122 0 E
Raetihi, *N.Z.* **59 H5** 39 25S 175 17 E
Rafaela, *Argentina* **94 C3** 31 10S 61 30W
Rafah, *Egypt* **47 D3** 31 18N 34 14 E
Rafai, *C.A.R.* **54 B1** 4 59N 23 58 E
Rafḩā, *Si. Arabia* **44 D4** 29 35N 43 35 E
Rafsanjān, *Iran* **45 D8** 30 30N 56 5 E
Raft Pt., *Australia* **60 C3** 16 4S 124 26 E
Ragama, *Sri Lanka* **40 R11** 7 0N 79 50 E
Ragged, Mt., *Australia* **61 F3** 33 27S 123 25 E
Raglan, *Australia* **62 C5** 23 42S 150 49 E
Raglan, *N.Z.* **59 G5** 37 55S 174 55 E
Ragusa, *Italy* **20 F6** 36 56N 14 42 E
Raha, *Indonesia* **37 E6** 4 55S 123 0 E
Rahad al Bardī, *Sudan* **51 F9** 11 20N 23 40 E
Rahaeng = Tak, *Thailand* **38 D2** 16 52N 99 8 E
Raḩīmah, *Si. Arabia* **45 E6** 26 42N 50 4 E
Rahimyar Khan, *Pakistan* **42 E4** 28 30N 70 25 E
Rāhjerd, *Iran* **45 C6** 34 22N 50 22 E
Raichur, *India* **40 L10** 16 10N 77 20 E
Raiganj, *India* **43 G13** 25 37N 88 10 E
Raigarh, *India* **41 J13** 21 56N 83 25 E
Raijua, *Indonesia* **37 F6** 10 37S 121 36 E
Railton, *Australia* **62 G4** 41 25S 146 28 E
Rainbow Lake, *Canada* **72 B5** 58 30N 119 23W
Rainier, *U.S.A.* **84 D4** 46 53N 122 41W
Rainier, Mt., *U.S.A.* **84 D5** 46 52N 121 46W
Rainy L., *Canada* **73 D10** 48 42N 93 10W
Rainy River, *Canada* **73 D10** 48 43N 94 29W
Raipur, *India* **41 J12** 21 17N 81 45 E
Raj Nandgaon, *India* **41 J12** 21 5N 81 5 E
Raja, Ujung, *Indonesia* **36 D1** 3 40N 96 25 E
Raja Ampat, Kepulauan, *Indonesia* **37 E7** 0 30S 130 0 E
Rajahmundry, *India* **41 L12** 17 1N 81 48 E
Rajajooseppi, *Finland* **8 B20** 68 28N 28 29 E
Rajang →, *Malaysia* **36 D4** 2 30N 112 0 E
Rajapalaiyam, *India* **40 Q10** 9 25N 77 35 E
Rajasthan □, *India* **42 F5** 26 45N 73 30 E
Rajasthan Canal, *India* **42 E5** 28 0N 72 0 E
Rajauri, *India* **43 C6** 33 25N 74 21 E
Rajgarh, *Mad. P., India* **42 G7** 24 2N 76 45 E
Rajgarh, *Raj., India* **42 E6** 28 40N 75 25 E
Rajkot, *India* **42 H4** 22 15N 70 56 E
Rajmahal Hills, *India* **43 G12** 24 30N 87 30 E
Rajpipla, *India* **40 J8** 21 50N 73 30 E
Rajpura, *India* **42 D7** 30 25N 76 32 E
Rajshahi, *Bangla.* **41 G16** 24 22N 88 39 E
Rajshahi □, *Bangla.* **43 G13** 25 0N 89 0 E
Rakaia, *N.Z.* **59 K4** 43 45S 172 1 E
Rakaia →, *N.Z.* **59 K4** 43 36S 172 15 E
Rakan, Ra's, *Qatar* **45 E6** 26 10N 51 20 E
Rakaposhi, *Pakistan* **43 A6** 36 10N 74 25 E
Rakata, Pulau, *Indonesia* **36 F3** 6 10S 105 20 E
Rakhni, *Pakistan* **42 D3** 30 4N 69 56 E
Rakitnoye, *Russia* **30 B7** 45 36N 134 17 E
Rakops, *Botswana* **56 C3** 21 1S 24 28 E
Raleigh, *U.S.A.* **77 H6** 35 47N 78 39W
Raleigh B., *U.S.A.* **77 H7** 34 50N 76 15W
Ralls, *U.S.A.* **81 J4** 33 41N 101 24W
Ram →, *Canada* **72 A4** 62 1N 123 41W
Rām Allāh, *Jordan* **47 D4** 31 55N 35 10 E
Ram Hd., *Australia* **63 F4** 37 47S 149 30 E
Rama, *Nic.* **88 D3** 12 9N 84 15W
Raman, *Thailand* **39 J3** 6 29N 101 18 E
Ramanathapuram, *India* **40 Q11** 9 25N 78 55 E
Ramanetaka, B. de, *Madag.* **57 A8** 14 13S 47 52 E
Ramat Gan, *Israel* **47 C3** 32 4N 34 48 E
Ramatlhabama, *S. Africa* **56 D4** 25 37S 25 33 E
Ramban, *India* **43 C6** 33 14N 75 12 E
Rambipuji, *Indonesia* **37 H15** 8 12S 113 37 E
Ramea, *Canada* **71 C8** 47 31N 57 23W
Ramechhap, *Nepal* **43 F12** 27 25N 86 10 E
Ramelau, *Indonesia* **37 F7** 8 55S 126 22 E
Ramgarh, *Bihar, India* **43 H11** 23 40N 85 35 E
Ramgarh, *Raj., India* **42 F6** 27 16N 75 14 E
Ramgarh, *Raj., India* **42 F4** 27 30N 70 36 E
Rāmhormoz, *Iran* **45 D6** 31 15N 49 35 E
Ramīān, *Iran* **45 B7** 37 3N 55 16 E
Ramingining, *Australia* **62 A2** 12 19S 135 3 E
Ramla, *Israel* **47 D3** 31 55N 34 52 E
Ramnad = Ramanathapuram, *India* **40 Q11** 9 25N 78 55 E
Ramnagar, *India* **43 C6** 32 47N 75 18 E
Ramona, *U.S.A.* **85 M10** 33 2N 116 52W
Ramore, *Canada* **70 C3** 48 30N 80 25W
Ramotswa, *Botswana* **56 C4** 24 50S 25 52 E
Rampur, *H.P., India* **42 D7** 31 26N 77 43 E
Rampur, *Mad. P., India* **42 H5** 23 25N 73 53 E
Rampur, *Ut. P., India* **43 E8** 28 50N 79 5 E
Rampur Hat, *India* **43 G12** 24 10N 87 50 E
Rampura, *India* **42 G6** 24 30N 75 27 E
Ramree I. = Ramree Kyun, *Burma* **41 K18** 19 0N 94 0 E
Ramree Kyun, *Burma* **41 K18** 19 0N 94 0 E
Rāmsar, *Iran* **45 B6** 36 53N 50 41 E
Ramsey, *Canada* **70 C3** 47 25N 82 20W
Ramsey, *U.K.* **10 C3** 54 20N 4 21W
Ramsgate, *U.K.* **11 F9** 51 20N 1 25 E
Ramtek, *India* **40 J11** 21 20N 79 15 E
Ranaghat, *India* **43 H13** 23 15N 88 35 E
Ranahu, *Pakistan* **42 G3** 25 55N 69 45 E
Ranau, *Malaysia* **36 C5** 6 2N 116 40 E
Rancagua, *Chile* **94 C1** 34 10S 70 50W
Rancheria →, *Canada* **72 A3** 60 13N 129 7W
Ranchester, *U.S.A.* **82 D10** 44 54N 107 10W
Ranchi, *India* **43 H11** 23 19N 85 27 E
Randers, *Denmark* **9 H11** 56 29N 10 1 E
Randfontein, *S. Africa* **57 D4** 26 8S 27 45 E
Randle, *U.S.A.* **84 D5** 46 32N 121 57W
Randolph, *Mass., U.S.A.* **79 D13** 42 10N 71 2W
Randolph, *N.Y., U.S.A.* **78 D6** 42 10N 78 59W
Randolph, *Utah, U.S.A.* **82 F8** 41 40N 111 11W
Randolph, *Vt., U.S.A.* **79 C12** 43 55N 72 40W
Råne älv →, *Sweden* **8 D17** 65 50N 22 20 E
Rangae, *Thailand* **39 J3** 6 19N 101 44 E
Rangaunu B., *N.Z.* **59 F4** 34 51S 173 15 E
Rangeley, *U.S.A.* **79 B14** 44 58N 70 39W
Rangely, *U.S.A.* **82 F9** 40 5N 108 48W
Ranger, *U.S.A.* **81 J5** 32 28N 98 41W
Rangia, *India* **41 F17** 26 28N 91 38 E
Rangiora, *N.Z.* **59 K4** 43 19S 172 36 E
Rangitaiki →, *N.Z.* **59 G6** 37 54S 176 49 E
Rangitata →, *N.Z.* **59 K3** 43 45S 171 15 E
Rangkasbitung, *Indonesia* **37 G12** 6 21S 106 15 E
Rangon →, *Burma* **41 L20** 16 28N 96 40 E
Rangoon, *Burma* **41 L20** 16 45N 96 20 E
Rangpur, *Bangla.* **41 G16** 25 42N 89 22 E
Rangsit, *Thailand* **38 F3** 13 59N 100 37 E
Ranibennur, *India* **40 M9** 14 35N 75 30 E
Raniganj, *India* **43 H12** 23 40N 87 5 E
Raniwara, *India* **40 G8** 24 50N 72 10 E
Rāniyah, *Iraq* **44 B5** 36 15N 44 53 E
Ranken →, *Australia* **62 C2** 20 31S 137 36 E
Rankin, *U.S.A.* **81 K4** 31 13N 101 56W
Rankin Inlet, *Canada* **68 B10** 62 30N 93 0W
Rankins Springs, *Australia* **63 E4** 33 49S 146 14 E
Rannoch, L., *U.K.* **12 E4** 56 41N 4 20W
Rannoch Moor, *U.K.* **12 E4** 56 38N 4 48W
Ranobe, Helodranon' i, *Madag.* **57 C7** 23 3S 43 33 E

Rutshuru

Rutshuru, Zaïre **54 C2** 1 13S 29 25 E
Ruurlo, Neths. **15 B6** 52 5N 6 24 E
Ruvu, Tanzania **54 D4** 6 49S 38 43 E
Ruvu →, Tanzania **54 D4** 6 23S 38 52 E
Ruvuma □, Tanzania **55 E4** 10 20S 36 0 E
Ruwais, U.A.E. **45 E7** 24 5N 52 50 E
Ruwenzori, Africa **54 B2** 0 30N 29 55 E
Ruyigi, Burundi **54 C3** 3 29S 30 15 E
Ružomberok, Slovakia **17 D9** 49 3N 19 17 E
Rwanda ■, Africa **54 C3** 2 0S 30 0 E
Ryan, L., U.K. **12 G3** 55 0N 5 2W
Ryazan, Russia **24 D6** 54 40N 39 40 E
Ryazhsk, Russia **24 D7** 53 45N 40 3 E
Rybache, Kazakhstan **26 E9** 46 40N 81 20 E
Rybachiy Poluostrov, Russia **24 A5** 69 43N 32 0 E
Rybinsk, Russia **24 C6** 58 5N 38 50 E
Rybinskoye Vdkhr., Russia **24 C6** 58 30N 38 25 E
Ryde, U.K. **11 G6** 50 44N 1 9W
Ryderwood, U.S.A. **84 D3** 46 23N 123 3W
Rye, U.K. **11 G8** 50 57N 0 46 E
Rye →, U.K. **10 C7** 54 12N 0 53W
Rye Patch Reservoir, U.S.A. **82 F4** 40 28N 118 19W
Ryegate, U.S.A. **82 C9** 46 18N 109 15W
Rylstone, Australia **63 E4** 32 46S 149 58 E
Ryōthu, Japan **30 E9** 38 5N 138 26 E
Rypin, Poland **17 B9** 53 3N 19 25 E
Ryūgasaki, Japan **31 G10** 35 54N 140 11 E
Ryūkyū Is. = Ryūkyū-rettō, Japan **31 M2** 26 0N 126 0 E
Ryūkyū-rettō, Japan **31 M2** 26 0N 126 0 E
Rzeszów, Poland **17 C10** 50 5N 21 58 E
Rzhev, Russia **24 C5** 56 20N 34 20 E

S

Sa, Thailand **38 C3** 18 34N 100 45 E
Sa Dec, Vietnam **39 G5** 10 20N 105 46 E
Sa'ādatābād, Fārs, Iran **45 D7** 30 10N 53 5 E
Sa'ādatābād, Kermān, Iran **45 D7** 28 3N 55 53 E
Saale →, Germany **16 C5** 51 57N 11 56 E
Saar →, Europe **16 D3** 49 41N 6 32 E
Saarbrücken, Germany **16 D3** 49 15N 6 58 E
Saaremaa, Estonia **24 C3** 58 30N 22 30 E
Saariselkä, Finland **8 B20** 68 16N 28 15 E
Saarland □, Germany **15 E7** 49 15N 7 0 E
Sab 'Bi'ār, Syria **44 C3** 33 46N 37 41 E
Saba, W. Indies **89 C7** 17 42N 63 26W
Sabadell, Spain **19 B7** 41 28N 2 7 E
Sabah □, Malaysia **36 C5** 6 0N 117 0 E
Sabak Bernam, Malaysia **39 L3** 3 46N 100 58 E
Sábana de la Mar, Dom. Rep. **89 C6** 19 7N 69 24W
Sábanalarga, Colombia **92 A4** 10 38N 74 55W
Sabang, Indonesia **36 C1** 5 50N 95 15 E
Sabará, Brazil **93 G10** 19 55S 43 46W
Sabarania, Indonesia **37 E9** 2 5S 138 18 E
Sabattis, U.S.A. **79 B10** 44 6N 74 40W
Sabáudia, Italy **20 D5** 41 17N 13 2 E
Sabhah, Libya **51 C7** 27 9N 14 29 E
Sabie, S. Africa **57 D5** 25 10S 30 48 E
Sabinal, Mexico **86 A3** 30 58N 107 25W
Sabinal, U.S.A. **81 L5** 29 19N 99 28W
Sabinas, Mexico **86 B4** 27 50N 101 10W
Sabinas →, Mexico **86 B4** 27 37N 100 42W
Sabinas Hidalgo, Mexico **86 B4** 26 33N 100 10W
Sabine →, U.S.A. **81 L8** 29 59N 93 47W
Sabine L., U.S.A. **81 L8** 29 53N 93 51W
Sabine Pass, U.S.A. **81 L8** 29 44N 93 54W
Sabkhet el Bardawîl, Egypt **47 D2** 31 10N 33 15 E
Sablayan, Phil. **37 B6** 12 50N 120 50 E
Sable, C., U.S.A. **75 E10** 25 9N 81 8W
Sable, C., Canada **71 D6** 43 29N 65 38W
Sable I., Canada **71 D8** 44 0N 60 0W
Sabolev, Russia **27 D16** 54 20N 155 30 E
Sabrina Coast, Antarctica **5 C9** 68 0S 120 0 E
Sabulubek, Indonesia **36 E1** 1 36S 98 40 E
Sabzevār, Iran **45 B8** 36 15N 57 40 E
Sabzvārān, Iran **45 D8** 28 45N 57 50 E
Sac City, U.S.A. **80 D7** 42 25N 95 0W
Sachigo →, Canada **70 A2** 55 6N 88 58W
Sachigo, L., Canada **70 B1** 53 50N 92 12W
Sackets Harbor, U.S.A. **79 C8** 43 57N 76 7W
Saco, Maine, U.S.A. **77 D10** 43 30N 70 27W
Saco, Mont., U.S.A. **82 B10** 48 28N 107 21W
Sacramento, U.S.A. **84 G5** 38 35N 121 29W
Sacramento →, U.S.A. **84 G5** 38 3N 121 56W
Sacramento Mts., U.S.A. **83 K11** 32 30N 105 30W
Sacramento Valley, U.S.A. **84 G5** 39 30N 122 0W
Sádaba, Spain **19 A5** 42 19N 1 12W
Sadani, Tanzania **54 D4** 5 58S 38 35 E
Sadao, Thailand **39 J3** 6 38N 100 26 E
Sadd el Aali, Egypt **51 D11** 23 54N 32 54 E
Saddle Mt., U.S.A. **84 E3** 45 58N 123 41W
Sadimi, Zaïre **55 D1** 9 25S 23 32 E
Sado, Japan **30 E9** 38 0N 138 25 E
Sadon, Burma **41 G20** 25 28N 97 55 E
Saegerstown, U.S.A. **78 E4** 41 43N 80 9W
Şafājah, Si. Arabia **44 E3** 26 25N 39 0 E
Säffle, Sweden **9 G12** 59 8N 12 55 E
Safford, U.S.A. **83 K9** 32 50N 109 43W
Saffron Walden, U.K. **11 E8** 52 2N 0 15 E
Safi, Morocco **50 B3** 32 18N 9 20W
Şafīābād, Iran **45 B8** 36 45N 57 58 E
Safīd Dasht, Iran **45 C6** 33 27N 48 11 E
Safīd Kūh, Afghan. **40 B3** 34 45N 63 0 E
Safwān, Iraq **44 D5** 30 7N 47 43 E
Sag Harbor, U.S.A. **79 F12** 41 0N 72 18W
Saga, Indonesia **37 E8** 2 40S 132 55 E
Saga, Japan **31 H5** 33 15N 130 16 E
Saga □, Japan **31 H5** 33 15N 130 20 E
Sagae, Japan **30 E10** 38 22N 140 17 E
Sagala, Mali **50 F3** 14 9N 6 38W
Sagar, India **40 M9** 14 14N 75 6 E
Sagara, L., Tanzania **54 D3** 5 20S 31 0 E
Saginaw, U.S.A. **76 D4** 43 26N 83 56W
Saginaw B., U.S.A. **76 D4** 43 50N 83 40W
Sagīr, Zab as →, Iraq **44 C4** 35 10N 43 20 E
Saglouc, Canada **69 B12** 62 14N 75 38W
Sagŏ-ri, S. Korea **35 G14** 35 25N 126 49 E
Sagres, Portugal **19 D1** 37 0N 8 58W
Sagua la Grande, Cuba **88 B3** 22 50N 80 10W
Saguache, U.S.A. **83 G10** 38 5N 106 8W
Saguenay →, Canada **71 C5** 48 22N 71 0W
Sagunto, Spain **19 C5** 39 42N 0 18W
Sahagún, Spain **19 A3** 42 18N 5 2W
Saḩam al Jawlān, Syria **47 C4** 32 45N 35 55 E
Sahand, Kūh-e, Iran **44 B5** 37 44N 46 27 E
Sahara, Africa **50 D5** 23 0N 5 0 E
Saharan Atlas = Saharien, Atlas, Algeria **50 B5** 33 30N 1 0 E
Saharanpur, India **42 E7** 29 58N 77 33 E
Saharien, Atlas, Algeria **50 B5** 33 30N 1 0 E
Sahasinaka, Madag. **57 C8** 21 49S 47 49 E
Sahaswan, India **43 E8** 28 5N 78 45 E
Sahibganj, India **43 G12** 25 12N 87 40 E
Sahiwal, Pakistan **42 D5** 30 45N 73 8 E
Şaḩneh, Iran **44 C5** 34 29N 47 41 E
Sahtaneh →, Canada **72 B4** 59 2N 122 28W
Sahuaripa, Mexico **86 B3** 29 0N 109 13W
Sahuarita, U.S.A. **83 L8** 31 57N 110 58W
Sahuayo, Mexico **86 C4** 20 4N 102 43W
Sai Buri, Thailand **39 J3** 6 43N 101 45 E
Sa'id Bundas, Sudan **51 G9** 8 24N 24 48 E
Saïda, Algeria **50 B5** 34 50N 0 11 E
Saīdābād, Kermān, Iran **45 D7** 29 30N 55 45 E
Sa'īdābād, Semnān, Iran **45 B7** 36 8N 54 11 E
Sa'īdīyeh, Iran **45 B6** 36 20N 48 55 E
Saidpur, Bangla. **41 G16** 25 48N 89 0 E
Saidu, Pakistan **43 B5** 34 43N 72 24 E
Saigon = Phanh Bho Ho Chi Minh, Vietnam **39 G6** 10 58N 106 40 E
Saijō, Japan **31 H6** 33 55N 133 11 E
Saikhoa Ghat, India **41 F19** 27 50N 95 40 E
Saiki, Japan **31 H5** 32 58N 131 51 E
Sailolof, Indonesia **37 E8** 1 7S 130 46 E
Şa'in Dezh, Iran **44 B5** 36 40N 46 25 E
St. Abb's Head, U.K. **12 F6** 55 55N 2 10W
St. Alban's, Canada **71 C8** 47 51N 55 50W
St. Albans, U.K. **11 F7** 51 44N 0 19W
St. Albans, Vt., U.S.A. **79 B11** 44 49N 73 5W
St. Albans, W. Va., U.S.A. **76 F5** 38 23N 81 50W
St. Alban's Head, U.K. **11 G5** 50 34N 2 3W
St. Albert, Canada **72 C6** 53 37N 113 32W
St. Andrew's, Canada **71 C8** 47 45N 59 15W
St. Andrews, U.K. **12 E6** 56 20N 2 48W
St-Anicet, Canada **79 A10** 45 8N 74 22W
St. Ann B., Canada **71 C7** 46 22N 60 25W
St. Ann's Bay, Jamaica **88 C4** 18 26N 77 15W
St. Anthony, Canada **71 B8** 51 22N 55 35W
St. Anthony, U.S.A. **82 E8** 43 58N 111 41W
St. Arnaud, Australia **63 F3** 36 40S 143 16 E
St. Arthur, Canada **71 C6** 47 33N 67 46W
St. Asaph, U.K. **10 D4** 53 15N 3 27W
St-Augustin-Saguenay, Canada **71 B8** 51 13N 58 38W
St. Augustine, U.S.A. **77 L5** 29 54N 81 19W
St. Austell, U.K. **11 G3** 50 20N 4 48W
St.-Barthélemy, I., W. Indies **89 C7** 17 50N 62 50W
St. Bee's Hd., U.K. **10 C4** 54 30N 3 38W
St. Boniface, Canada **73 D9** 49 53N 97 5W
St. Bride's, Canada **71 C9** 46 56N 54 10W
St. Brides B., U.K. **11 F2** 51 48N 5 15W
St-Brieuc, France **18 B2** 48 30N 2 46W
St. Catharines, Canada **70 D4** 43 10N 79 15W
St. Catherines I., U.S.A. **77 K5** 31 40N 81 10W
St. Catherine's Pt., U.K. **11 G6** 50 34N 1 18W
St. Charles, Ill., U.S.A. **76 E1** 41 54N 88 19W
St. Charles, Mo., U.S.A. **80 F9** 38 47N 90 29W
St. Christopher = St. Kitts, W. Indies **89 C7** 17 20N 62 40W
St. Christopher-Nevis ■, W. Indies **89 C7** 17 20N 62 40W
St. Clair, Mich., U.S.A. **78 D2** 42 50N 82 30W
St. Clair, Pa., U.S.A. **79 F8** 40 43N 76 12W
St. Clair, L., Canada **70 D3** 42 30N 82 45W
St. Clairsville, U.S.A. **78 F4** 40 5N 80 54W
St. Claude, Canada **73 D9** 49 40N 98 20W
St. Cloud, Fla., U.S.A. **77 L5** 28 15N 81 17W
St. Cloud, Minn., U.S.A. **80 C7** 45 34N 94 10W
St-Coeur de Marie, Canada **71 C5** 48 39N 71 43W
St. Cricq, C., Australia **61 E1** 25 17S 113 6 E
St. Croix, Virgin Is. **89 C7** 17 45N 64 45W
St. Croix →, U.S.A. **80 C8** 44 45N 92 48W
St. Croix Falls, U.S.A. **80 C8** 45 24N 92 38W
St. David's, Canada **71 C8** 48 12N 58 52W
St. David's, U.K. **11 F2** 51 54N 5 16W
St. David's Head, U.K. **11 F2** 51 55N 5 16W
St.-Denis, France **18 B5** 48 56N 2 22 E
St. Elias, Mt., U.S.A. **68 B5** 60 18N 140 56W
St. Elias Mts., Canada **72 A1** 60 33N 139 28W
St.-Étienne, France **18 D6** 45 27N 4 22 E
St. Eugène, Canada **79 A10** 45 30N 74 28W
St. Eustatius, W. Indies **89 C7** 17 20N 63 0W
St-Félicien, Canada **70 C5** 48 40N 72 25W
St.-Flour, France **18 D5** 45 2N 3 6 E
St. Francis, U.S.A. **80 F4** 39 47N 101 48W
St. Francis →, U.S.A. **81 H9** 34 38N 90 36W
St. Francis, C., S. Africa **56 E3** 34 14S 24 49 E
St. Francisville, U.S.A. **81 K9** 30 47N 91 23W
St-François, L., Canada **79 A10** 45 10N 74 22W
St-Gabriel-de-Brandon, Canada **70 C5** 46 17N 73 24W
St. Gallen = Sankt Gallen, Switz. **16 E4** 47 26N 9 22 E
St. George, Australia **63 D4** 28 1S 148 30 E
St. George, Canada **71 C6** 45 11N 66 50W
St. George, S.C., U.S.A. **77 J5** 33 11N 80 35W
St. George, Utah, U.S.A. **83 H7** 37 6N 113 35W
St. George, C., Canada **71 C8** 48 30N 59 16W
St. George, C., U.S.A. **77 L3** 29 40N 85 5W
St. George Ra., Australia **60 C4** 18 40S 125 0 E
St-Georges, Belgium **15 D5** 50 37N 5 20 E
St. George's, Canada **71 C8** 48 26N 58 31W
St-Georges, Canada **71 C5** 46 8N 70 40W
St.-Georges, Fr. Guiana **93 C8** 4 0N 52 0W
St. George's, Grenada **89 D7** 12 5N 61 43W
St. George's B., Canada **71 C8** 48 24N 58 53W
St. Georges Basin, Australia **60 C4** 15 23S 125 2 E
St. George's Channel, U.K. **13 E6** 52 0N 6 0W
St. Georges Hd., Australia **63 F5** 35 12S 150 42 E
St. Gotthard P. = San Gottardo, Paso del, Switz. **16 E4** 46 33N 8 33 E
St. Helena, U.S.A. **82 G2** 38 30N 122 28W
St. Helena ■, Atl. Oc. **2 E9** 15 55S 5 44W
St. Helena, Mt., U.S.A. **84 G4** 38 40N 122 36W
St. Helena B., S. Africa **56 E2** 32 40S 18 10 E
St. Helens, Australia **62 G4** 41 20S 148 15 E
St. Helens, U.K. **10 D5** 53 28N 2 44W
St. Helens, U.S.A. **84 E4** 45 52N 122 48W
St. Helens, Mt., U.S.A. **84 D4** 46 12N 122 12W
St. Helier, U.K. **11 H5** 49 11N 2 6W
St-Hubert, Belgium **15 D5** 50 2N 5 23 E
St-Hyacinthe, Canada **70 C5** 45 40N 72 58W
St. Ignace, U.S.A. **76 C3** 45 52N 84 44W
St. Ignace I., Canada **70 C2** 48 45N 88 0W
St. Ignatius, U.S.A. **82 C6** 47 19N 114 6W
St. Ives, Cambs., U.K. **11 E7** 52 20N 0 5W
St. Ives, Corn., U.K. **11 G2** 50 13N 5 29W
St. James, U.S.A. **80 D7** 43 59N 94 38W
St-Jean, Canada **70 C5** 45 20N 73 20W
St-Jean →, Canada **71 B7** 50 17N 64 20W
St-Jean, L., Canada **71 C5** 48 40N 72 0W
St. Jean Baptiste, Canada **73 D9** 49 15N 97 20W
St-Jean-Port-Joli, Canada **71 C5** 47 15N 70 13W
St-Jérôme, Qué., Canada **70 C5** 45 47N 74 0W
St-Jérôme, Qué., Canada **71 C5** 48 26N 71 53W
St. John, Canada **71 C6** 45 20N 66 8W
St. John, Kans., U.S.A. **81 G5** 38 0N 98 46W
St. John, N. Dak., U.S.A. **80 A5** 48 57N 99 43W
St. John →, U.S.A. **71 C6** 45 12N 66 5W
St. John, C., Canada **71 B8** 50 0N 55 32W
St. John's, Antigua **89 C7** 17 6N 61 51W
St. John's, Canada **71 C9** 47 35N 52 40W
St. Johns, Ariz., U.S.A. **83 J9** 34 30N 109 22W
St. Johns, Mich., U.S.A. **76 D3** 43 0N 84 33W
St. Johns →, U.S.A. **77 K5** 30 24N 81 24W
St. Johnsbury, U.S.A. **79 B12** 44 25N 72 1W
St. Johnsville, U.S.A. **79 C10** 43 0N 74 43W
St. Joseph, La., U.S.A. **81 K9** 31 55N 91 14W
St. Joseph, Mich., U.S.A. **76 D2** 42 6N 86 29W
St. Joseph, Mo., U.S.A. **80 F7** 39 46N 94 50W
St. Joseph →, U.S.A. **76 D2** 42 7N 86 29W
St. Joseph, I., Canada **70 C3** 46 12N 83 58W
St. Joseph, L., Canada **70 B1** 51 10N 90 35W
St-Jovite, Canada **70 C5** 46 8N 74 38W
St. Kilda, N.Z. **59 L3** 45 53S 170 31 E
St. Kitts, W. Indies **89 C7** 17 20N 62 40W
St. Kitts-Nevis = St. Christopher-Nevis ■, W. Indies **89 C7** 17 20N 62 40W
St. Laurent, Canada **73 C9** 50 25N 97 58W
St.-Laurent, Fr. Guiana **93 B8** 5 29N 54 3W
St. Lawrence, Australia **62 C4** 22 16S 149 31 E
St. Lawrence, Canada **71 C8** 46 54N 55 23W
St. Lawrence →, Canada **71 C6** 49 30N 66 0W
St. Lawrence, Gulf of, Canada **71 C7** 48 25N 62 0W
St. Lawrence I., U.S.A. **68 B3** 63 30N 170 30W
St. Leonard, Canada **71 C6** 47 12N 67 58W
St. Lewis →, Canada **71 B8** 52 26N 56 11W
St.-Lô, France **18 B3** 49 7N 1 5W
St-Louis, Senegal **50 E1** 16 8N 16 27W
St. Louis, Mich., U.S.A. **76 D3** 43 25N 84 36W
St. Louis, Mo., U.S.A. **80 F9** 38 37N 90 12W
St. Louis →, U.S.A. **80 B8** 47 15N 92 45W
St. Lucia ■, W. Indies **89 D7** 14 0N 60 50W
St. Lucia, L., S. Africa **57 D5** 28 5S 32 30 E
St. Lucia Channel, W. Indies **89 D7** 14 15N 61 0W
St. Lunaire-Griquet, Canada **71 B8** 51 31N 55 28W
St. Maarten, W. Indies **89 C7** 18 0N 63 5W
St.-Malo, France **18 B2** 48 39N 2 1W
St-Marc, Haiti **89 C5** 19 10N 72 41W
St. Maries, U.S.A. **82 C5** 47 19N 116 35W
St-Martin, W. Indies **89 C7** 18 0N 63 0W
St. Martin, L., Canada **73 C9** 51 40N 98 30W
St. Martins, Canada **71 C6** 45 22N 65 34W
St. Martinville, U.S.A. **81 K9** 30 7N 91 50W
St. Mary Pk., Australia **63 E2** 31 32S 138 34 E
St. Marys, Australia **62 G4** 41 35S 148 11 E
St. Marys, Canada **78 C3** 43 20N 81 10W
St. Mary's, U.K. **11 H1** 49 55N 6 18W
St. Marys, U.S.A. **78 E6** 41 26N 78 34W
St. Mary's, C., Canada **71 C9** 46 50N 54 12W
St. Mary's B., Canada **71 C9** 46 50N 53 50W
St. Marys Bay, Canada **71 D6** 44 25N 66 10W
St.-Mathieu, Pte., France **18 B1** 48 20N 4 45W
St. Matthews, I. = Zadetkyi Kyun, Burma **39 H2** 10 0N 98 25 E
St-Maurice →, Canada **70 C5** 46 21N 72 31W
St. Michael's Mount, U.K. **11 G2** 50 7N 5 30W
St.-Nazaire, France **18 C2** 47 17N 2 12W
St. Neots, U.K. **11 E7** 52 14N 0 16W
St. Niklass = Sint Niklaas, Belgium **15 C4** 51 10N 4 9 E
St.-Omer, France **18 A5** 50 45N 2 15 E
St-Pacome, Canada **71 C6** 47 24N 69 58W
St-Pamphile, Canada **71 C6** 46 58N 69 48W
St. Pascal, Canada **71 C6** 47 32N 69 48W
St. Paul, Canada **72 C6** 54 0N 111 17W
St. Paul, Minn., U.S.A. **80 C8** 44 57N 93 6W
St. Paul, Nebr., U.S.A. **80 E5** 41 13N 98 27W
St. Paul, I., Ind. Oc. **3 F13** 38 55S 77 34 E
St. Paul I., Canada **71 C7** 47 12N 60 9W
St. Peter, U.S.A. **80 C8** 44 20N 93 57W
St. Peter Port, Chan. Is. **11 H5** 49 27N 2 31W
St. Peters, N.S., Canada **71 C7** 45 40N 60 53W
St. Peters, P.E.I., Canada **71 C7** 46 25N 62 35W
St. Petersburg = Sankt-Peterburg, Russia **24 C5** 59 55N 30 20 E
St. Petersburg, U.S.A. **77 M4** 27 46N 82 39W
St.-Pierre, St- P. & M. **71 C8** 46 46N 56 12W
St-Pierre, L., Canada **70 C5** 46 12N 72 52W
St.-Pierre et Miquelon □, St- P. & M. **71 C8** 46 55N 56 10W
St.-Quentin, France **18 B5** 49 50N 3 16 E
St. Regis, U.S.A. **82 C6** 47 18N 115 6W
St. Sebastien, Tanjon' i, Madag. **57 A8** 12 26S 48 44 E
St-Siméon, Canada **71 C6** 47 51N 69 54W
St. Stephen, Canada **71 C6** 45 16N 67 17W
St. Thomas, Canada **70 D3** 42 45N 81 10W
St. Thomas I., Virgin Is. **89 C7** 18 20N 64 55W
St-Tite, Canada **70 C5** 46 45N 72 34W
St.-Tropez, France **18 E7** 43 17N 6 38 E
St. Troud = Sint Truiden, Belgium **15 D5** 50 48N 5 10 E
St.-Valéry-sur-Somme, France **18 A4** 50 11N 1 38 E
St. Vincent, W. Indies **89 D7** 13 10N 61 10W
St. Vincent, G., Australia **63 F2** 35 0S 138 0 E
St. Vincent & the Grenadines ■, W. Indies **89 D7** 13 0N 61 10W
St. Vincent Passage, W. Indies **89 D7** 13 30N 61 0W
St-Vith, Belgium **15 D6** 50 17N 6 9 E
Ste-Agathe-des-Monts, Canada **70 C5** 46 3N 74 17W
Ste-Anne de Beaupré, Canada **71 C5** 47 2N 70 58W
Ste-Anne-des-Monts, Canada **71 C6** 49 8N 66 30W
Ste. Genevieve, U.S.A. **80 G9** 37 59N 90 2W
Ste-Marguerite →, Canada **71 B6** 50 9N 66 36W
Ste.-Marie, Martinique **89 D7** 14 48N 61 1W
Ste-Marie de la Madeleine, Canada **71 C5** 46 26N 71 0W
Ste.-Rose, Guadeloupe **89 C7** 16 20N 61 45W
Ste. Rose du Lac, Canada **73 C9** 51 4N 99 30W
Saintes, France **18 D3** 45 45N 0 37W
Saintes, I. des, Guadeloupe **89 C7** 15 50N 61 35W
Saintonge, France **18 D3** 45 40N 0 50W
Saipan, Pac. Oc. **64 F6** 15 12N 145 45 E
Sairang, India **41 H18** 23 50N 92 45 E
Sairecábur, Cerro, Bolivia **94 A2** 22 43S 67 54W
Saitama □, Japan **31 F9** 36 25N 139 30 E
Sajama, Bolivia **92 G5** 18 7S 69 0W
Sajum, India **43 C8** 33 20N 79 0 E
Sak →, S. Africa **56 E3** 30 52S 20 25 E
Sakai, Japan **31 G7** 34 30N 135 30 E
Sakaide, Japan **31 G6** 34 15N 133 50 E
Sakaiminato, Japan **31 G6** 35 38N 133 11 E
Sakākah, Si. Arabia **44 D4** 30 0N 40 8 E
Sakakawea, L., U.S.A. **80 B3** 47 30N 101 25W
Sakami, L., Canada **70 B4** 53 15N 77 0W
Sakania, Zaïre **55 E2** 12 43S 28 30 E
Sakarya = Adapazan, Turkey **25 F5** 40 48N 30 25 E
Sakarya →, Turkey **25 F5** 41 7N 30 39 E
Sakashima-Guntō, Japan **31 M2** 24 46N 124 0 E
Sakata, Japan **30 E9** 38 55N 139 50 E
Sakchu, N. Korea **35 D13** 40 23N 125 2 E
Sakeny →, Madag. **57 C8** 20 0S 45 25 E
Sakha = Yakut Republic □, Russia **27 C13** 62 0N 130 0 E
Sakhalin, Russia **27 D15** 51 0N 143 0 E
Sakhalinskiy Zaliv, Russia **27 D15** 54 0N 141 0 E
Sakon Nakhon, Thailand **38 D5** 17 10N 104 9 E
Sakrand, Pakistan **42 F3** 26 10N 68 15 E
Sakrivier, S. Africa **56 E3** 30 54S 20 28 E
Sakuma, Japan **31 G8** 35 3N 137 49 E
Sakurai, Japan **31 G7** 34 30N 135 51 E
Sala, Sweden **9 G14** 59 58N 16 35 E
Sala-y-Gómez, Pac. Oc. **65 K17** 26 28S 105 28W
Salaberry-de-Valleyfield, Canada **70 C5** 45 15N 74 8W
Saladas, Argentina **94 B4** 28 15S 58 40W
Saladillo, Argentina **94 D4** 35 40S 59 55W
Salado →, Buenos Aires, Argentina **94 D4** 35 44S 57 22W
Salado →, La Pampa, Argentina **96 D3** 37 30S 67 0W
Salado →, Santa Fe, Argentina **94 C3** 31 40S 60 41W
Salado →, Mexico **86 B5** 26 52N 99 19W
Salaga, Ghana **50 G4** 8 31N 0 31W
Sālah, Syria **47 C5** 32 40N 36 45 E
Sálakhos, Greece **23 C9** 36 17N 27 57 E
Salālah, Oman **46 D5** 16 56N 53 59 E
Salamanca, Chile **94 C1** 31 46S 70 59W
Salamanca, Spain **19 B3** 40 58N 5 39W
Salamanca, U.S.A. **78 D6** 42 10N 78 43W
Salāmatābād, Iran **44 C5** 35 39N 47 50 E
Salamis, Cyprus **23 D12** 35 11N 33 54 E
Salamis, Greece **21 F10** 37 56N 23 30 E
Salar de Atacama, Chile **94 A2** 23 30S 68 25W
Salar de Uyuni, Bolivia **92 H5** 20 30S 67 45W
Salatiga, Indonesia **37 G14** 7 19S 110 30 E
Salavat, Russia **24 D10** 53 21N 55 55 E
Salaverry, Peru **92 E3** 8 15S 79 0W
Salawati, Indonesia **37 E8** 1 7S 130 52 E
Salayar, Indonesia **37 F6** 6 7S 120 30 E
Salcombe, U.K. **11 G4** 50 14N 3 47W
Saldaña, Spain **19 A3** 42 32N 4 48W
Saldanha, S. Africa **56 E2** 33 0S 17 58 E
Saldanha B., S. Africa **56 E2** 33 6S 18 0 E
Sale, Australia **63 F4** 38 6S 147 6 E
Salé, Morocco **50 B3** 34 3N 6 48W
Sale, U.K. **10 D5** 53 26N 2 19W
Salekhard, Russia **24 A12** 66 30N 66 35 E
Salem, India **40 P11** 11 40N 78 11 E
Salem, Ind., U.S.A. **76 F2** 38 36N 86 6W
Salem, Mass., U.S.A. **79 D14** 42 31N 70 53W
Salem, Mo., U.S.A. **81 G9** 37 39N 91 32W
Salem, N.J., U.S.A. **76 F8** 39 34N 75 28W

San Ramón de la Nueva Orán

Salem, Ohio, U.S.A. **78 F4** 40 54N 80 52W
Salem, Oreg., U.S.A. **82 D2** 44 56N 123 2W
Salem, S. Dak., U.S.A. **80 D6** 43 44N 97 23W
Salem, Va., U.S.A. **76 G5** 37 18N 80 3W
Salerno, Italy **20 D6** 40 40N 14 44 E
Salford, U.K. **10 D5** 53 30N 2 17W
Salida, U.S.A. **74 C5** 38 32N 106 0W
Salima, Malawi **53 G6** 13 47S 34 28 E
Salina, Italy **20 E6** 38 35N 14 50 E
Salina, U.S.A. **80 F6** 38 50N 97 37W
Salina Cruz, Mexico **87 D5** 16 10N 95 10W
Salinas, Brazil **93 G10** 16 10S 42 10W
Salinas, Chile **94 A2** 23 31S 69 29W
Salinas, Ecuador **92 D2** 2 10S 80 58W
Salinas, U.S.A. **83 H3** 36 40N 121 39W
Salinas →, Guatemala **87 D6** 16 28N 90 31W
Salinas →, U.S.A. **83 H3** 36 45N 121 48W
Salinas, B. de, Nic. **88 D2** 11 4N 85 45W
Salinas, C. de, Spain **22 B10** 39 16N 3 4 E
Salinas, Pampa de las, Argentina **94 C2** 31 58S 66 42W
Salinas Ambargasta, Argentina **94 B3** 29 0S 65 0W
Salinas de Hidalgo, Mexico **86 C4** 22 30N 101 40W
Salinas Grandes, Argentina **94 B2** 30 0S 65 0W
Saline →, Ark., U.S.A. **81 J8** 33 10N 92 8W
Saline →, Kans., U.S.A. **80 F6** 38 52N 97 30W
Salines, Spain **22 B10** 39 21N 3 3 E
Salinópolis, Brazil **93 D9** 0 40S 47 20W
Salisbury = Harare, Zimbabwe **55 F3** 17 43S 31 2 E
Salisbury, Australia **63 E2** 34 46S 138 40 E
Salisbury, U.K. **11 F6** 51 4N 1 48W
Salisbury, Md., U.S.A. **76 F8** 38 22N 75 36W
Salisbury, N.C., U.S.A. **77 H5** 35 40N 80 29W
Salisbury Plain, U.K. **11 F6** 51 13N 1 50W
Salkhad, Jordan **47 C5** 32 30N 36 43 E
Sallisaw, U.S.A. **81 H7** 35 28N 94 47W
Salmās, Iran **44 B5** 38 11N 44 47 E
Salmo, Canada **72 D5** 49 10N 117 20W
Salmon, U.S.A. **82 D7** 45 11N 113 54W
Salmon →, Canada **72 C4** 54 3N 122 40W
Salmon →, U.S.A. **82 D5** 45 51N 116 47W
Salmon Arm, Canada **72 C5** 50 40N 119 15W
Salmon Falls, U.S.A. **82 E6** 42 48N 114 59W
Salmon Gums, Australia **61 F3** 32 59S 121 38 E
Salmon Res., Canada **71 C8** 48 5N 56 0W
Salmon River Mts., U.S.A. **82 D6** 45 0N 114 30W
Salo, Finland **9 F17** 60 22N 23 10 E
Salome, U.S.A. **85 M13** 33 47N 113 37W
Salonica = Thessaloníki, Greece **21 D10** 40 38N 22 58 E
Salonta, Romania **17 E10** 46 49N 21 42 E
Salsacate, Argentina **94 C2** 31 20S 65 5W
Salsk, Russia **25 E7** 46 28N 41 30 E
Salso →, Italy **20 F5** 37 6N 13 55 E
Salt →, Canada **72 B6** 60 0N 112 25W
Salt →, U.S.A. **83 K7** 33 23N 112 19W
Salt Creek, Australia **63 F2** 36 8S 139 38 E
Salt Fork Arkansas →, U.S.A. **81 G6** 36 36N 97 3W
Salt Lake City, U.S.A. **82 F8** 40 45N 111 53W
Salt Range, Pakistan **42 C5** 32 30N 72 25 E
Salta, Argentina **94 A2** 24 57S 65 25W
Salta □, Argentina **94 A2** 24 48S 65 30W
Saltcoats, U.K. **12 F4** 55 38N 4 47W
Saltee Is., Ireland **13 D5** 52 7N 6 37W
Saltfjorden, Norway **8 C13** 67 15N 14 10 E
Salthólmavík, Iceland **8 D3** 65 24N 21 57W
Saltillo, Mexico **86 B4** 25 30N 100 57W
Salto, Argentina **94 C3** 34 20S 60 15W
Salto, Uruguay **94 C4** 31 27S 57 50W
Salton City, U.S.A. **85 M11** 33 29N 115 51W
Salton Sea, U.S.A. **85 M11** 33 15N 115 45W
Saltpond, Ghana **50 G4** 5 15N 1 3W
Saltville, U.S.A. **76 G5** 36 53N 81 46W
Saluda →, U.S.A. **77 H5** 34 1N 81 4W
Salûm, Egypt **51 B10** 31 31N 25 7 E
Salûm, Khâlig el, Egypt **51 B10** 31 30N 25 9 E
Salur, India **41 K13** 18 27N 83 18 E
Saluzzo, Italy **20 B2** 44 39N 7 29 E
Salvador, Brazil **93 F11** 13 0S 38 30W
Salvador, Canada **73 C7** 52 10N 109 32W
Salvador, L., U.S.A. **81 L9** 29 43N 90 15W
Salween →, Burma **41 L20** 16 31N 97 37 E
Salyany, Azerbaijan **25 G8** 39 10N 49 50 E
Salyersville, U.S.A. **76 G4** 37 45N 83 4W
Salzburg, Austria **16 E6** 47 48N 13 2 E
Salzburg □, Austria **16 E6** 47 15N 13 0 E
Salzgitter, Germany **16 B5** 52 13N 10 22 E
Sam Neua, Laos **38 B5** 20 29N 104 5 E
Sam Ngao, Thailand **38 D2** 17 18N 99 0 E
Sam Rayburn Reservoir, U.S.A. **81 K7** 31 4N 94 5W
Sam Son, Vietnam **38 C5** 19 44N 105 54 E
Sam Teu, Laos **38 C5** 19 59N 104 38 E
Sama, Russia **26 C7** 60 12N 60 22 E
Sama de Langreo, Spain **19 A3** 43 18N 5 40W
Samagaltai, Russia **27 D10** 50 36N 95 3 E
Samales Group, Phil. **37 C6** 6 0N 122 0 E
Samana, India **42 D7** 30 10N 76 13 E
Samana Cay, Bahamas **89 B5** 23 3N 73 45W
Samanga, Tanzania **55 D4** 8 20S 39 13 E
Samangwa, Zaïre **54 C1** 4 23S 24 10 E
Samani, Japan **30 C11** 42 7N 142 56 E
Samar, Phil. **37 B7** 12 0N 125 0 E
Samara, Russia **24 D9** 53 8N 50 6 E
Samaria = Shōmrōn, Jordan **47 C4** 32 15N 35 13 E
Samariá, Greece **23 D5** 35 17N 23 58 E
Samarinda, Indonesia **36 E5** 0 30S 117 9 E
Samarkand, Uzbekistan **26 F7** 39 40N 66 55 E
Samarqand = Samarkand, Uzbekistan **26 F7** 39 40N 66 55 E
Sāmarrā, Iraq **44 C4** 34 12N 43 52 E
Samastipur, India **43 G11** 25 50N 85 50 E
Samba, India **43 C6** 32 32N 75 10 E
Samba, Zaïre **54 C2** 4 38S 26 22 E
Sambalpur, India **41 J14** 21 28N 84 4 E
Sambar, Tanjung, Indonesia **36 E4** 2 59S 110 19 E
Sambas, Indonesia **36 D3** 1 20N 109 20 E
Sambava, Madag. **57 A9** 14 16S 50 10 E
Sambawizi, Zimbabwe **55 F2** 18 24S 26 13 E
Sambhal, India **43 E8** 28 35N 78 37 E
Sambhar, India **42 F6** 26 52N 75 6 E
Sambor, Cambodia **38 F6** 12 46N 106 0 E
Sambre →, Europe **15 D4** 50 27N 4 52 E
Samburu □, Kenya **54 B4** 1 10N 37 0 E
Samchŏk, S. Korea **35 F15** 37 30N 129 10 E
Samchonpo, S. Korea **35 G15** 35 0N 128 6 E
Same, Tanzania **54 C4** 4 2S 37 38 E
Samfya, Zambia **55 E2** 11 22S 29 31 E
Samnah, Si. Arabia **44 E3** 25 10N 37 15 E
Samo Alto, Chile **94 C1** 30 22S 71 0W
Samoorombón, B., Argentina **94 D4** 36 5S 57 20W
Sámos, Greece **21 F12** 37 45N 26 50 E
Samothráki, Évros, Greece **21 D11** 40 28N 25 28 E
Samothráki, Kérkira, Greece **23 A3** 39 48N 19 31 E
Sampacho, Argentina **94 C3** 33 20S 64 50W
Sampang, Indonesia **37 G15** 7 11S 113 13 E
Sampit, Indonesia **36 E4** 2 34S 113 0 E
Sampit, Teluk, Indonesia **36 E4** 3 5S 113 3 E
Samrong, Cambodia **38 E4** 14 15N 103 30 E
Samrong, Thailand **38 E3** 15 10N 100 40 E
Samsun, Turkey **25 F6** 41 15N 36 22 E
Samui, Ko, Thailand **39 H3** 9 30N 100 0 E
Samusole, Zaïre **55 E1** 10 2S 24 0 E
Samut Prakan, Thailand **38 F3** 13 32N 100 40 E
Samut Sakhon, Thailand **38 F3** 13 31N 100 13 E
Samut Songkhram →, Thailand **38 F3** 13 24N 100 1 E
Samwari, Pakistan **42 E2** 28 30N 66 46 E
San, Mali **50 F4** 13 15N 4 57W
San →, Cambodia **38 F5** 13 32N 105 57 E
San →, Poland **17 C10** 50 45N 21 51 E
San Agustin, C., Phil. **37 C7** 6 20N 126 13 E
San Agustín de Valle Fértil, Argentina **94 C2** 30 35S 67 30W
San Ambrosio, Pac. Oc. **65 K20** 26 28S 79 53W
San Andreas, U.S.A. **84 G6** 38 12N 120 41W
San Andrés, I. de, Caribbean **88 D3** 12 42N 81 46W
San Andres Mts., U.S.A. **83 K10** 33 0N 106 30W
San Andrés Tuxtla, Mexico **87 D5** 18 30N 95 20W
San Angelo, U.S.A. **81 K4** 31 28N 100 26W
San Anselmo, U.S.A. **84 H4** 37 59N 122 34W
San Antonio, Belize **87 D7** 16 15N 89 2W
San Antonio, Chile **94 C1** 33 40S 71 40W
San Antonio, N. Mex., U.S.A. **83 K10** 33 55N 106 52W
San Antonio, Tex., U.S.A. **81 L5** 29 25N 98 30W
San Antonio →, U.S.A. **81 L6** 28 30N 96 54W
San Antonio, C., Argentina **94 D4** 36 15S 56 40W
San Antonio, C., Cuba **88 B3** 21 50N 84 57W
San Antonio, Mt., U.S.A. **85 L9** 34 17N 117 38W
San Antonio Abad, Spain **22 C7** 38 59N 1 19 E
San Antonio de los Baños, Cuba **88 B3** 22 54N 82 31W
San Antonio de los Cobres, Argentina **94 A2** 24 10S 66 17W
San Antonio Oeste, Argentina **96 E4** 40 40S 65 0W
San Ardo, U.S.A. **84 J6** 36 1N 120 54W
San Augustín, Canary Is. **22 G4** 27 47N 15 32W
San Augustine, U.S.A. **81 K7** 31 30N 94 7W
San Bartolomé, Canary Is. **22 F6** 28 59N 13 37W
San Bartolomé de Tirajana, Canary Is. **22 G4** 27 54N 15 34W
San Benedicto, I., Mexico **86 D2** 19 18N 110 49W
San Benito, U.S.A. **81 M6** 26 8N 97 38W
San Benito →, U.S.A. **84 J5** 36 53N 121 34W
San Benito Mt., U.S.A. **84 J6** 36 22N 120 37W
San Bernardino, U.S.A. **85 L9** 34 7N 117 19W
San Bernardino Mts., U.S.A. **85 L10** 34 10N 116 45W
San Bernardino Str., Phil. **37 B6** 13 0N 125 0 E
San Bernardo, Chile **94 C1** 33 40S 70 50W
San Bernardo, I. de, Colombia **92 B3** 9 45N 75 50W
San Blas, Mexico **86 B3** 26 4N 108 46W
San Blas, Arch. de, Panama **88 E4** 9 50N 78 31W
San Blas, C., U.S.A. **77 L3** 29 40N 85 21W
San Borja, Bolivia **92 F5** 14 50S 66 52W
San Buenaventura, Mexico **86 B4** 27 5N 101 32W
San Carlos, Argentina **94 C2** 33 50S 69 0W
San Carlos, Chile **94 D1** 36 10S 72 0W
San Carlos, Mexico **86 B4** 29 0N 100 54W
San Carlos, Nic. **88 D3** 11 12N 84 50W
San Carlos, Phil. **37 B6** 10 29N 123 25 E
San Carlos, Spain **22 B8** 39 3N 1 34 E
San Carlos, Uruguay **95 C5** 34 46S 54 58W
San Carlos, U.S.A. **83 K8** 33 21N 110 27W
San Carlos, Amazonas, Venezuela **92 C5** 1 55N 67 4W
San Carlos, Cojedes, Venezuela **92 B5** 9 40N 68 36W
San Carlos de Bariloche, Argentina **96 E2** 41 10S 71 25W
San Carlos del Zulia, Venezuela **92 B4** 9 1N 71 55W
San Carlos L., U.S.A. **83 K8** 33 11N 110 32W
San Clemente, Chile **94 D1** 35 30S 71 29W
San Clemente, U.S.A. **85 M9** 33 26N 117 37W
San Clemente I., U.S.A. **85 N8** 32 53N 118 29W
San Cristóbal, Argentina **94 C3** 30 20S 61 10W
San Cristóbal, Dom. Rep. **89 C5** 18 25N 70 6W
San Cristóbal, Mexico **87 D6** 16 50N 92 33W
San Cristóbal, Spain **22 B11** 39 57N 4 3 E
San Cristóbal, Venezuela **92 B4** 7 46N 72 14W
San Diego, Calif., U.S.A. **85 N9** 32 43N 117 9W
San Diego, Tex., U.S.A. **81 M5** 27 46N 98 14W
San Diego, C., Argentina **96 G3** 54 40S 65 10W
San Diego de la Unión, Mexico **86 C4** 21 28N 100 52W
San Dimitri, Ras, Malta **23 C1** 36 4N 14 11 E
San Estanislao, Paraguay **94 A4** 24 39S 56 26W
San Felipe, Chile **94 C1** 32 43S 70 42W
San Felipe, Mexico **86 A2** 31 0N 114 52W
San Felipe, Venezuela **92 A5** 10 20N 68 44W
San Felipe →, U.S.A. **85 M11** 33 12N 115 49W
San Feliu de Guíxols, Spain **19 B7** 41 45N 3 1 E
San Félix, Pac. Oc. **65 K20** 26 23S 80 0W
San Fernando, Chile **94 C1** 34 30S 71 0W
San Fernando, Mexico **86 B1** 29 55N 115 10W
San Fernando, La Union, Phil. **37 A6** 16 40N 120 23 E
San Fernando, Pampanga, Phil. **37 A6** 15 5N 120 37 E
San Fernando, Baleares, Spain **22 C7** 38 42N 1 28 E
San Fernando, Cádiz, Spain **19 D2** 36 28N 6 17W
San Fernando, Trin. & Tob. **89 D7** 10 20N 61 30W
San Fernando, U.S.A. **85 L8** 34 17N 118 26W
San Fernando →, Mexico **86 C5** 24 55N 98 10W
San Fernando de Apure, Venezuela **92 B5** 7 54N 67 15W
San Fernando de Atabapo, Venezuela **92 C5** 4 3N 67 42W
San Francisco, Argentina **94 C3** 31 30S 62 5W
San Francisco, U.S.A. **83 H2** 37 47N 122 25W
San Francisco →, U.S.A. **83 K9** 32 59N 109 22W
San Francisco, Paso de, S. Amer. **94 B2** 27 0S 68 0W
San Francisco de Macorís, Dom. Rep. **89 C5** 19 19N 70 15W
San Francisco del Monte de Oro, Argentina **94 C2** 32 36S 66 8W
San Francisco del Oro, Mexico **86 B3** 26 52N 105 50W
San Francisco Javier, Spain **22 C7** 38 42N 1 26 E
San Gil, Colombia **92 B4** 6 33N 73 8W
San Gorgonio Mt., U.S.A. **85 L10** 34 7N 116 51W
San Gottardo, Paso del, Switz. **16 E4** 46 33N 8 33 E
San Gregorio, Uruguay **95 C4** 32 37S 55 40W
San Gregorio, U.S.A. **84 H4** 37 20N 122 23W
San Ignacio, Belize **87 D7** 17 10N 89 0W
San Ignacio, Bolivia **92 G6** 16 20S 60 55W
San Ignacio, Mexico **86 B2** 27 27N 113 0W
San Ignacio, Paraguay **94 B4** 26 52S 57 3W
San Ignacio, L., Mexico **86 B2** 26 50N 113 11W
San Ildefonso, C., Phil. **37 A6** 16 0N 122 1 E
San Isidro, Argentina **94 C4** 34 29S 58 31W
San Jacinto, U.S.A. **85 M10** 33 47N 116 57W
San Jaime, Spain **22 B11** 39 54N 4 4 E
San Javier, Misiones, Argentina **95 B4** 27 55S 55 5W
San Javier, Santa Fe, Argentina **94 C4** 30 40S 59 55W
San Javier, Bolivia **92 G6** 16 18S 62 30W
San Javier, Chile **94 D1** 35 40S 71 45W
San Jeronimo Taviche, Mexico **87 D5** 16 38N 96 32W
San Joaquin, U.S.A. **84 J6** 36 36N 120 11W
San Joaquin →, U.S.A. **83 G3** 38 4N 121 51W
San Joaquin Valley, U.S.A. **84 J6** 37 20N 121 0W
San Jordi, Spain **22 B9** 39 33N 2 46 E
San Jorge, Argentina **94 C3** 31 54S 61 50W
San Jorge, Spain **22 C7** 38 54N 1 24 E
San Jorge, B. de, Mexico **86 A2** 31 20N 113 20W
San Jorge, G., Argentina **96 F3** 46 0S 66 0W
San Jorge, G. de, Spain **19 B5** 40 50N 0 55W
San José, Bolivia **92 G6** 17 53S 60 50W
San José, Costa Rica **88 E3** 9 55N 84 2W
San José, Guatemala **88 D1** 14 0N 90 50W
San José, Mexico **86 C2** 25 0N 110 50W
San Jose, Phil. **37 A6** 15 45N 120 55 E
San José, Spain **22 C7** 38 55N 1 18 E
San Jose, U.S.A. **83 H3** 37 20N 121 53W
San Jose →, U.S.A. **83 J10** 34 25N 106 45W
San Jose de Buenovista, Phil. **37 B6** 12 27N 121 4 E
San José de Feliciano, Argentina **94 C4** 30 26S 58 46W
San José de Jáchal, Argentina **94 C2** 30 15S 68 46W
San José de Mayo, Uruguay **94 C4** 34 27S 56 40W
San José de Ocune, Colombia **92 C4** 4 15N 70 20W
San José del Cabo, Mexico **86 C3** 23 0N 109 40W
San José del Guaviare, Colombia **92 C4** 2 35N 72 38W
San Juan, Argentina **94 C2** 31 30S 68 30W
San Juan, Mexico **86 C4** 21 20N 102 50W
San Juan, Phil. **37 C7** 8 25N 126 20 E
San Juan, Puerto Rico **89 C6** 18 28N 66 7W
San Juan □, Argentina **94 C2** 31 9S 69 0W
San Juan →, Argentina **94 C2** 32 20S 67 25W
San Juan →, Nic. **88 D3** 10 56N 83 42W
San Juan →, U.S.A. **83 H8** 37 16N 110 26W
San Juan, C., Eq. Guin. **52 D1** 1 5N 9 20 E
San Juan Bautista, Paraguay **94 B4** 26 37S 57 6W
San Juan Bautista, Spain **22 B8** 39 5N 1 31 E
San Juan Bautista, U.S.A. **83 H3** 36 51N 121 32W
San Juan Bautista Valle Nacional, Mexico **87 D5** 17 47N 96 19W
San Juan Capistrano, U.S.A. **85 M9** 33 30N 117 40W
San Juan Cr. →, U.S.A. **84 J5** 35 40N 120 22W
San Juan de Guadalupe, Mexico **86 C4** 24 38N 102 44W
San Juan de los Morros, Venezuela **92 B5** 9 55N 67 21W
San Juan del Norte, Nic. **88 D3** 10 58N 83 40W
San Juan del Norte, B. de, Nic. **88 D3** 11 0N 83 40W
San Juan del Río, Mexico **87 C5** 20 25N 100 0W
San Juan del Sur, Nic. **88 D2** 11 20N 85 51W
San Juan I., U.S.A. **84 B3** 48 32N 123 5W
San Juan Mts., U.S.A. **83 H10** 37 30N 107 0W
San Julián, Argentina **96 F3** 49 15S 67 45W
San Justo, Argentina **94 C3** 30 47S 60 30W
San Kamphaeng, Thailand **38 C2** 18 45N 99 8 E
San Lázaro, C., Mexico **86 C2** 24 50N 112 18W
San Lázaro, Sa., Mexico **86 C3** 23 25N 110 0W
San Leandro, U.S.A. **83 H2** 37 44N 122 9W
San Lorenzo, Argentina **94 C3** 32 45S 60 45W
San Lorenzo, Ecuador **92 C3** 1 15N 78 50W
San Lorenzo, Paraguay **94 B4** 25 20S 57 32W
San Lorenzo, Spain **22 B10** 39 37N 3 17 E
San Lorenzo →, Mexico **86 C3** 24 15N 107 24W
San Lorenzo, I., Mexico **86 B2** 28 35N 112 50W
San Lorenzo, I., Peru **92 F3** 12 7S 77 15W
San Lorenzo, Mt., Argentina **96 F2** 47 40S 72 20W
San Lucas, Bolivia **92 H5** 20 5S 65 7W
San Lucas, Baja Calif. S., Mexico **86 C3** 22 53N 109 54W
San Lucas, Baja Calif. S., Mexico **86 B2** 27 10N 112 14W
San Lucas, U.S.A. **84 J5** 36 8N 121 1W
San Lucas, C., Mexico **86 C3** 22 50N 110 0W
San Luis, Argentina **94 C2** 33 20S 66 20W
San Luis, Cuba **88 B3** 22 17N 83 46W
San Luis, Guatemala **88 C2** 16 14N 89 27W
San Luis, U.S.A. **83 H11** 37 12N 105 25W
San Luis □, Argentina **94 C2** 34 0S 66 0W
San Luis, I., Mexico **86 B2** 29 58N 114 26W
San Luis, Sierra de, Argentina **94 C2** 32 30S 66 10W
San Luis de la Paz, Mexico **86 C4** 21 19N 100 32W
San Luis Obispo, U.S.A. **85 K6** 35 17N 120 40W
San Luis Potosí, Mexico **86 C4** 22 9N 100 59W
San Luis Potosí □, Mexico **86 C4** 22 10N 101 0W
San Luis Reservoir, U.S.A. **84 H5** 37 4N 121 5W
San Luis Río Colorado, Mexico **86 A2** 32 29N 114 58W
San Marcos, Guatemala **88 D1** 14 59N 91 52W
San Marcos, Mexico **86 B2** 27 13N 112 6W
San Marcos, U.S.A. **81 L6** 29 53N 97 56W
San Marino ■, Europe **20 C5** 43 56N 12 25 E
San Martín, Argentina **94 C2** 33 5S 68 28W
San Martín, L., Argentina **96 F2** 48 50S 72 50W
San Mateo, Spain **22 B7** 39 3N 1 23 E
San Mateo, U.S.A. **83 H2** 37 34N 122 19W
San Matías, Bolivia **92 G7** 16 25S 58 20W
San Matías, G., Argentina **96 E4** 41 30S 64 0W
San Miguel, El Salv. **88 D2** 13 30N 88 12W
San Miguel, Panama **88 E4** 8 27N 78 55W
San Miguel, Spain **22 B7** 39 3N 1 26 E
San Miguel, U.S.A. **83 J3** 35 45N 120 42W
San Miguel →, Bolivia **92 F6** 13 52S 63 56W
San Miguel de Tucumán, Argentina **94 B2** 26 50S 65 20W
San Miguel del Monte, Argentina **94 D4** 35 23S 58 50W
San Miguel I., U.S.A. **85 L6** 34 2N 120 23W
San Narciso, Phil. **37 A6** 15 2N 120 3 E
San Nicolás, Canary Is. **22 G4** 27 58N 15 47W
San Nicolás de los Arroyas, Argentina **94 C3** 33 25S 60 10W
San Nicolas I., U.S.A. **85 M7** 33 15N 119 30W
San Onofre, U.S.A. **85 M9** 33 22N 117 34W
San Pablo, Bolivia **94 A2** 21 43S 66 38W
San Pedro, Buenos Aires, Argentina **95 B5** 26 30S 54 10W
San Pedro, Jujuy, Argentina **94 A3** 24 12S 64 55W
San-Pédro, Ivory C. **50 H3** 4 50N 6 33W
San Pedro, Mexico **86 C2** 23 55N 110 17W
San Pedro □, Paraguay **94 A4** 24 0S 57 0W
San Pedro →, Chihuahua, Mexico **86 B3** 28 20N 106 10W
San Pedro →, Michoacan, Mexico **86 D4** 19 23N 103 51W
San Pedro →, Nayarit, Mexico **86 C3** 21 45N 105 30W
San Pedro →, U.S.A. **83 K8** 32 59N 110 47W
San Pedro, Pta., Chile **94 B1** 25 30S 70 38W
San Pedro Channel, U.S.A. **85 M8** 33 30N 118 25W
San Pedro de Atacama, Chile **94 A2** 22 55S 68 15W
San Pedro de Jujuy, Argentina **94 A3** 24 12S 64 55W
San Pedro de las Colonias, Mexico **86 B4** 25 50N 102 59W
San Pedro de Lloc, Peru **92 E3** 7 15S 79 28W
San Pedro de Macorís, Dom. Rep. **89 C6** 18 30N 69 18W
San Pedro del Norte, Nic. **88 D3** 13 4N 84 33W
San Pedro del Paraná, Paraguay **94 B4** 26 43S 56 13W
San Pedro Mártir, Sierra, Mexico **86 A1** 31 0N 115 30W
San Pedro Mixtepec, Mexico **87 D5** 16 2N 97 7W
San Pedro Ocampo = Melchor Ocampo, Mexico **86 C4** 24 52N 101 40W
San Pedro Sula, Honduras **88 C2** 15 30N 88 0W
San Quintín, Mexico **86 A1** 30 29N 115 57W
San Rafael, Argentina **94 C2** 34 40S 68 21W
San Rafael, Calif., U.S.A. **84 H4** 37 58N 122 32W
San Rafael, N. Mex., U.S.A. **83 J10** 35 7N 107 53W
San Rafael Mt., U.S.A. **85 L7** 34 41N 119 52W
San Rafael Mts., U.S.A. **85 L7** 34 40N 119 50W
San Ramón de la Nueva Orán, Argentina **94 A3** 23 10S 64 20W

Shackleton Inlet

Satna, *India* .... **43 G9** 24 35N 80 50 E
Sátoraljaújhely, *Hungary* **17 D10** 48 25N 21 41 E
Satpura Ra., *India* ...... **42 J7** 21 25N 76 10 E
Satsuna-Shotō, *Japan* .. **31 K5** 30 0N 130 0 E
Sattahip, *Thailand* ..... **38 F3** 12 41N 100 54 E
Satu Mare, *Romania* ... **17 E11** 47 46N 22 55 E
Satui, *Indonesia* .... **36 E5** 3 50S 115 27 E
Satun, *Thailand* .... **39 J3** 6 43N 100 2 E
Saturnina →, *Brazil* ... **92 F7** 12 15S 58 10W
Sauce, *Argentina* **94 C4** 30 5S 58 46W
Sauceda, *Mexico* **86 B4** 25 55N 101 18W
Saucillo, *Mexico* **86 B3** 28 1N 105 17W
Sauda, *Norway* .... **9 G9** 59 40N 6 20 E
Sauðarkrókur, *Iceland* .. **8 D4** 65 45N 19 40W
Saudi Arabia ■, *Asia* ... **46 B3** 26 0N 44 0 E
Sauer →, *Germany* .... **15 E6** 49 44N 6 31 E
Saugeen →, *Canada* .. **78 B3** 44 30N 81 22W
Saugerties, *U.S.A.* **79 D11** 42 5N 73 57W
Sauk Centre, *U.S.A.* **80 C7** 45 44N 94 57W
Sauk Rapids, *U.S.A.* **80 C7** 45 35N 94 10W
Sault Ste. Marie, *Canada* **70 C3** 46 30N 84 20W
Sault Ste. Marie, *U.S.A.* . **76 B3** 46 30N 84 21W
Saumlaki, *Indonesia* .... **37 F8** 7 55S 131 20 E
Saumur, *France* **18 C3** 47 15N 0 5W
Saunders C., *N.Z.* ...... **59 L3** 45 53S 170 45 E
Saunders I., *Antarctica* . **5 B1** 57 48S 26 28W
Saunders Point, *Australia* **61 E4** 27 52S 125 38 E
Saurbær,
Borgarfjarðarsýsla, Iceland **8 D3** 64 24N 21 35W
Saurbær,
Eyjafjarðarsýsla, Iceland **8 D4** 65 27N 18 13W
Sauri, *Nigeria* .... **50 F6** 11 42N 6 44 E
Saurimo, *Angola* .... **52 F4** 9 40S 20 12 E
Sausalito, *U.S.A.* **84 H4** 37 51N 122 29W
Savá, *Honduras* **88 C2** 15 32N 86 15W
Sava →, *Serbia, Yug.* . **21 B9** 44 50N 20 26 E
Savage, *U.S.A.* **80 B2** 47 27N 104 21W
Savage I. = Niue,
Cook Is. **65 J11** 19 2S 169 54W
Savai'i, *W. Samoa* **59 A12** 13 28S 172 24W
Savalou, *Benin* .... **50 G5** 7 57N 1 58 E
Savane, *Mozam.* .... **55 F4** 19 37S 35 8 E
Savanna, *U.S.A.* **80 D9** 42 5N 90 8W
Savanna la Mar, *Jamaica* **88 C4** 18 10N 78 10W
Savannah, *Ga., U.S.A.* .. **77 J5** 32 5N 81 6W
Savannah, *Mo., U.S.A.* . **80 F7** 39 56N 94 50W
Savannah, *Tenn., U.S.A.* **77 H1** 35 14N 88 15W
Savannah →, *U.S.A.* .. **77 J5** 32 2N 80 53W
Savannakhet, *Laos* ..... **38 D5** 16 30N 104 49 E
Savant L., *Canada* **70 B1** 50 16N 90 44W
Savant Lake, *Canada* ... **70 B1** 50 14N 90 40W
Savanur, *India* .... **40 M9** 14 59N 75 21 E
Savé, *Benin* .... **50 G5** 8 2N 2 29 E
Save →, *Mozam.* ..... **57 C5** 21 16S 34 0 E
Sāveh, *Iran* .... **45 C6** 35 2N 50 20 E
Savelugu, *Ghana* **50 G4** 9 38N 0 54W
Savoie □, *France* ...... **18 D7** 45 26N 6 25 E
Savona, *Italy* .... **20 B3** 44 19N 8 29 E
Savonlinna, *Finland* .... **24 B4** 61 52N 28 53 E
Sawahlunto, *Indonesia* . **36 E2** 0 40S 100 52 E
Sawai, *Indonesia* ...... **37 E7** 3 0S 129 5 E
Sawai Madhopur, *India* . **42 F7** 26 0N 76 25 E
Sawang Daen Din,
Thailand .... **38 D4** 17 28N 103 28 E
Sawankhalok, *Thailand* . **38 D2** 17 19N 99 50 E
Sawara, *Japan* .... **31 G10** 35 55N 140 30 E
Sawatch Mts., *U.S.A.* ... **83 G10** 38 30N 106 30W
Sawel, *U.K.* **13 B4** 54 48N 7 5W
Sawi, *Thailand* .... **39 G2** 10 14N 99 5 E
Sawmills, *Zimbabwe* .... **55 F2** 19 30S 28 2 E
Sawu, *Indonesia* .... **37 F6** 9 35S 121 50 E
Sawu Sea, *Indonesia* ... **37 F6** 9 30S 121 50 E
Saxby →, *Australia* ... **62 B3** 18 25S 140 53 E
Saxton, *U.S.A.* **78 F6** 40 13N 78 15W
Say, *Niger* .... **50 F5** 13 8N 2 22 E
Sayabec, *Canada* **71 C6** 48 35N 67 41W
Sayaboury, *Laos* .... **38 C3** 19 15N 101 45 E
Sayán, *Peru* **92 F3** 11 8S 77 12W
Sayan, Vostochnyy,
Russia .... **27 D10** 54 0N 96 0 E
Sayan, Zapadnyy, *Russia* **27 D10** 52 30N 94 0 E
Saydā, *Lebanon* .... **47 B4** 33 35N 35 25 E
Sayhan-Ovoo, *Mongolia* **34 B2** 45 27N 103 54 E
Sayhandulaan, *Mongolia* **34 B5** 44 40N 109 1 E
Sayḥut, *Yemen* .... **46 D5** 15 12N 51 10 E
Saynshand, *Mongolia* ... **34 B6** 44 55N 110 11 E
Sayre, *Okla., U.S.A.* **81 H5** 35 18N 99 38W
Sayre, *Pa., U.S.A.* **79 E8** 41 59N 76 32W
Sayula, *Mexico* **86 D4** 19 50N 103 40W
Sazan, *Albania* .... **21 D8** 40 30N 19 20 E
Sázava →, *Czech.* .... **16 D7** 49 53N 14 24 E
Sazin, *Pakistan* .... **43 B5** 35 35N 73 30 E
Scafell Pikes, *U.K.* **10 C4** 54 26N 3 14W
Scalpay, *U.K.* **12 D2** 57 51N 6 40W
Scandia, *Canada* **72 C6** 50 20N 112 0W
Scandinavia, *Europe* ... **8 E12** 64 0N 12 0 E
Scapa Flow, *U.K.* **12 C5** 58 52N 3 6W
Scappoose, *U.S.A.* **84 E4** 45 45N 122 53W
Scarborough,
Trin. & Tob. **89 D7** 11 11N 60 42W
Scarborough, *U.K.* **10 C7** 54 17N 0 24W
Scebeli, Wabi →,
Somali Rep. .... **46 G3** 2 0N 44 0 E
Scenic, *U.S.A.* **80 D3** 43 47N 102 33W
Schaffhausen, *Switz.* ... **16 E4** 47 42N 8 39 E
Schagen, *Neths.* .... **15 B4** 52 49N 4 48 E
Schefferville, *Canada* ... **71 B6** 54 48N 66 50W
Schelde →, *Belgium* ... **15 C4** 51 15N 4 16 E
Schell Creek Ra., *U.S.A.* **82 G6** 39 15N 114 30W
Schenectady, *U.S.A.* ... **79 D11** 42 49N 73 57W
Scheveningen, *Neths.* .. **15 B4** 52 6N 4 16 E
Schiedam, *Neths.* ...... **15 C4** 51 55N 4 25 E
Schiermonnikoog, *Neths.* **15 A6** 53 30N 6 15 E
Schio, *Italy* .... **20 B4** 45 42N 11 21 E
Schleswig, *Germany* ... **16 A4** 54 32N 9 34 E
Schleswig-Holstein □,
Germany .... **16 A4** 54 10N 9 40 E
Schofield, *U.S.A.* **80 C10** 44 54N 89 36W
Scholls, *U.S.A.* **84 E4** 45 24N 122 56W
Schouten I., *Australia* .. **62 G4** 42 20S 148 20 E
Schouten Is. = Supiori,
Kepulauan, *Indonesia* . **37 E9** 1 0S 136 0 E
Schouwen, *Neths.* ..... **15 C3** 51 43N 3 45 E
Schreiber, *Canada* **70 C2** 48 45N 87 20W
Schuler, *Canada* **73 C6** 50 20N 110 6W
Schumacher, *Canada* ... **70 C3** 48 30N 81 16W
Schurz, *U.S.A.* **82 G4** 38 57N 118 49W
Schuyler, *U.S.A.* **80 E6** 41 27N 97 4W
Schuylkill Haven, *U.S.A.* **79 F8** 40 37N 76 11W
Schwäbische Alb,
Germany .... **16 D4** 48 30N 9 30 E
Schwaner, Pegunungan,
Indonesia .... **36 E4** 1 0S 112 30 E
Schwarzwald, *Germany* . **16 E4** 48 0N 8 0 E
Schweinfurt, *Germany* .. **16 C5** 50 3N 10 12 E
Schweizer-Reneke,
S. Africa .... **56 D4** 27 11S 25 18 E
Schwerin, *Germany* .... **16 B5** 53 37N 11 22 E
Schwyz, *Switz.* .... **16 E4** 47 2N 8 39 E
Sciacca, *Italy* .... **20 F5** 37 30N 13 3 E
Scilla, *Italy* .... **20 E6** 38 18N 15 44 E
Scilly, Isles of, *U.K.* ... **11 H1** 49 55N 6 15W
Scioto →, *U.S.A.* **76 F4** 38 44N 83 1W
Scobey, *U.S.A.* **80 A2** 48 47N 105 25W
Scone, *Australia* ...... **63 E5** 32 5S 150 52 E
Scoresbysund, *Greenland* **4 B6** 70 20N 23 0W
Scotia, *Calif., U.S.A.* **82 F1** 40 29N 124 6W
Scotia, *N.Y., U.S.A.* **79 D11** 42 50N 73 58W
Scotia Sea, *Antarctica* .. **5 B18** 56 5S 56 0W
Scotland, *U.S.A.* **80 D6** 43 9N 97 43W
Scotland □, *U.K.* **12 E5** 57 0N 4 0W
Scotland Neck, *U.S.A.* .. **77 G7** 36 8N 77 25W
Scott, C., *Australia* .... **60 B4** 13 30S 129 49 E
Scott City, *U.S.A.* **80 F4** 38 29N 100 54W
Scott Glacier, *Antarctica* **5 C8** 66 15S 100 5 E
Scott I., *Antarctica* .... **5 C11** 67 0S 179 0 E
Scott Inlet, *Canada* **69 A12** 71 0N 71 0W
Scott Is., *Canada* **72 C3** 50 48N 128 40W
Scott L., *Canada* **73 B7** 59 55N 106 18W
Scott Reef, *Australia* ... **60 B3** 14 0S 121 50 E
Scottburgh, *S. Africa* ... **57 E5** 30 15S 30 47 E
Scottdale, *U.S.A.* **78 F5** 40 6N 79 35W
Scottsbluff, *U.S.A.* **80 E3** 41 52N 103 40W
Scottsboro, *U.S.A.* **77 H2** 34 40N 86 2W
Scottsburg, *U.S.A.* **76 F3** 38 41N 85 47W
Scottsdale, *Australia* ... **62 G4** 41 9S 147 31 E
Scottsville, *Ky., U.S.A.* .. **77 G2** 36 45N 86 11W
Scottsville, *N.Y., U.S.A.* . **78 C7** 43 2N 77 47W
Scottville, *U.S.A.* **76 D2** 43 58N 86 17W
Scranton, *U.S.A.* **79 E9** 41 25N 75 40W
Scugog, L., *Canada* **78 B6** 44 10N 78 55W
Scunthorpe, *U.K.* **10 D7** 53 35N 0 38W
Scusciuban, *Somali Rep.* **46 E5** 10 18N 50 12 E
Scutari = Üsküdar,
Turkey .... **21 D13** 41 0N 29 5 E
Seabrook, L., *Australia* . **61 F2** 30 55S 119 40 E
Seaford, *U.S.A.* **76 F8** 38 39N 75 37W
Seaforth, *Canada* **70 D3** 43 35N 81 25W
Seagraves, *U.S.A.* **81 J3** 32 57N 102 34W
Seal →, *Canada* **73 B10** 59 4N 94 48W
Seal Cove, *Canada* **71 C8** 49 57N 56 22W
Seal L., *Canada* **71 B7** 54 20N 61 30W
Sealy, *U.S.A.* **81 L6** 29 47N 96 9W
Searchlight, *U.S.A.* **85 K12** 35 28N 114 55W
Searcy, *U.S.A.* **81 H9** 35 15N 91 44W
Searles L., *U.S.A.* **85 K9** 35 44N 117 21W
Seaside, *Calif., U.S.A.* ... **84 J5** 36 37N 121 50W
Seaside, *Oreg., U.S.A.* .. **84 E3** 46 0N 123 56W
Seaspray, *Australia* .... **63 F4** 38 25S 147 15 E
Seattle, *U.S.A.* **84 C4** 47 36N 122 20W
Seaview Ra., *Australia* .. **62 B4** 18 40S 145 45 E
Sebastián Vizcaíno, B.,
Mexico **86 B2** 28 0N 114 30W
Sebastopol = Sevastopol,
Ukraine .... **25 F5** 44 35N 33 30 E
Sebastopol, *U.S.A.* **84 G4** 38 24N 122 49W
Sebewaing, *U.S.A.* **76 D4** 43 44N 83 27W
Sebha = Sabhah, *Libya* . **51 C7** 27 9N 14 29 E
Sebring, *Fla., U.S.A.* **77 M5** 27 30N 81 27W
Sebring, *Ohio, U.S.A.* ... **78 F3** 40 55N 81 2W
Sebringville, *Canada* ... **78 C3** 43 24N 81 4W
Sebta = Ceuta, *Morocco* **50 A3** 35 52N 5 18W
Sebuku, *Indonesia* ..... **36 E5** 3 30S 116 25 E
Sebuku, Teluk, *Malaysia* **36 D5** 4 0N 118 10 E
Sechelt, *Canada* **72 D4** 49 25N 123 42W
Sechura, Desierto de,
Peru **92 E2** 6 0S 80 30W
Secretary I., *N.Z.* ...... **59 L1** 45 15S 166 56 E
Secunderabad, *India* ... **40 L11** 17 28N 78 30 E
Sedalia, *U.S.A.* **80 F8** 38 42N 93 14W
Sedan, *Australia* ...... **63 E2** 34 34S 139 19 E
Sedan, *France* .... **18 B6** 49 43N 4 57 E
Sedan, *U.S.A.* **81 G6** 37 8N 96 11W
Seddon, *N.Z.* .... **59 J5** 41 40S 174 7 E
Seddonville, *N.Z.* ...... **59 J4** 41 33S 172 1 E
Sedeh, *Fārs, Iran* ...... **45 D7** 30 45N 52 11 E
Sedeh, *Khorāsān, Iran* .. **45 C8** 33 20N 59 14 E
Sederot, *Israel* .... **47 D3** 31 32N 34 37 E
Sedgewick, *Canada* **72 C6** 52 48N 111 41W
Sedhiou, *Senegal* **50 F1** 12 44N 15 30W
Sedley, *Canada* **73 C8** 50 10N 104 0W
Sedova, Pik, *Russia* .... **26 B6** 73 29N 54 58 E
Sedro-Woolley, *U.S.A.* .. **84 B4** 48 30N 122 14W
Seeheim, *Namibia* ..... **56 D2** 26 50S 17 45 E
Seekoei →, *S. Africa* .. **56 E4** 30 18S 25 1 E
Seg-ozero, *Russia* ..... **24 B5** 63 0N 33 10 E
Segamat, *Malaysia* .... **39 L4** 2 30N 102 50 E
Seget, *Indonesia* ...... **37 E8** 1 24S 130 58 E
Segezha, *Russia* ...... **24 B5** 63 44N 34 19 E
Ségou, *Mali* **50 F3** 13 30N 6 16W
Segovia = Coco →,
Cent. Amer. **88 D3** 15 0N 83 8W
Segovia, *Spain* **19 B3** 40 57N 4 10W
Segre →, *Spain* ...... **19 B6** 41 40N 0 43 E
Séguéla, *Ivory C.* **50 G3** 7 55N 6 40W
Seguin, *U.S.A.* **81 L6** 29 34N 97 58W
Segundo →, *Argentina* **94 C3** 30 53S 62 44W
Segura →, *Spain* **19 C5** 38 6N 0 54W
Seh Qal'eh, *Iran* .... **45 C8** 33 40N 58 24 E
Sehitwa, *Botswana* .... **56 C3** 20 30S 22 30 E
Sehore, *India* .... **42 H7** 23 10N 77 5 E
Sehwan, *Pakistan* ..... **42 F2** 26 28N 67 53 E
Seiland, *Norway* .... **8 A17** 70 25N 23 15 E
Seiling, *U.S.A.* **81 G5** 36 9N 98 56W
Seinäjoki →, *Finland* .. **8 E17** 62 40N 22 45 E
Seine →, *France* ..... **18 B4** 49 26N 0 26 E
Seine-et-Marne □, *France* **18 B5** 48 45N 3 0 E
Seine-Maritime □, *France* **18 B4** 49 40N 1 0 E
Seine-St.-Denis □, *France* **18 B5** 48 58N 2 24 E
Seistan, *Iran* .... **45 D9** 30 50N 61 0 E
Sekayu, *Indonesia* ..... **36 E2** 2 51S 103 51 E
Seke, *Tanzania* .... **54 C3** 3 20S 33 31 E
Sekenke, *Tanzania* ..... **54 C3** 4 18S 34 11 E
Sekondi-Takoradi, *Ghana* **50 H4** 4 58N 1 45W
Sekuma, *Botswana* .... **56 C3** 24 36S 23 50 E
Selah, *U.S.A.* **82 C3** 46 39N 120 32W
Selama, *Malaysia* ...... **39 K3** 5 12N 100 42 E
Selaru, *Indonesia* ...... **37 F8** 8 9S 131 0 E
Selby, *U.K.* **10 D6** 53 47N 1 5W
Selby, *U.S.A.* **80 C4** 45 31N 100 2W
Selden, *U.S.A.* **80 F4** 39 33N 100 34W
Sele →, *Italy* .... **20 D6** 40 27N 14 58 E
Selemdzha →, *Russia* . **27 D13** 51 42N 128 53 E
Selenga = Selenge
Mörön →, *Asia* ..... **32 A5** 52 16N 106 16 E
Selenge Mörön →, *Asia* **32 A5** 52 16N 106 16 E
Seletan, Tg., *Indonesia* . **36 E4** 4 10S 114 40 E
Selfridge, *U.S.A.* **80 B4** 46 2N 100 56W
Sélibabi, *Mauritania* **50 E2** 15 10N 12 15W
Seligman, *U.S.A.* **83 J7** 35 20N 112 53W
Selîma, El Wâhât el,
Sudan .... **51 D10** 21 22N 29 19 E
Selinda Spillway,
Botswana .... **56 B3** 18 35S 23 10 E
Selkirk, *Canada* **73 C9** 50 10N 96 55W
Selkirk, *U.K.* **12 F6** 55 33N 2 50W
Selkirk I., *Canada* **73 C9** 53 20N 99 6W
Selkirk Mts., *Canada* ... **72 C5** 51 15N 117 40W
Selliá, *Greece* .... **23 D6** 35 12N 24 23 E
Sells, *U.S.A.* **83 L8** 31 55N 111 53W
Selma, *Ala., U.S.A.* **77 J2** 32 25N 87 1W
Selma, *Calif., U.S.A.* **83 H4** 36 34N 119 37W
Selma, *N.C., U.S.A.* **77 H6** 35 32N 78 17W
Selmer, *U.S.A.* **77 H1** 35 10N 88 36W
Selowandoma Falls,
Zimbabwe .... **55 G3** 21 15S 31 50 E
Selpele, *Indonesia* ..... **37 E8** 0 1S 130 5 E
Selsey Bill, *U.K.* **11 G7** 50 44N 0 47W
Selu, *Indonesia* .... **37 F8** 7 32S 130 55 E
Selva, *Argentina* **94 B3** 29 50S 62 0W
Selvas, *Brazil* **92 E5** 6 30S 67 0W
Selwyn, *Australia* ...... **62 C3** 21 32S 140 30 E
Selwyn L., *Canada* **73 A8** 60 0N 104 30W
Selwyn Ra., *Australia* ... **62 C3** 21 10S 140 0 E
Seman →, *Albania* ..... **21 D8** 40 45N 19 50 E
Semarang, *Indonesia* ... **37 G14** 7 0S 110 26 E
Semau, *Indonesia* ..... **37 F6** 10 13S 123 22 E
Sembabule, *Uganda* .... **54 C3** 0 4S 31 25 E
Semeru, *Indonesia* ..... **37 H15** 8 4S 112 55 E
Semey = Semipalatinsk,
Kazakhstan .... **26 D9** 50 30N 80 10 E
Seminoe Reservoir,
U.S.A. **82 E10** 42 9N 106 55W
Seminole, *Okla., U.S.A.* . **81 H6** 35 14N 96 41W
Seminole, *Tex., U.S.A.* .. **81 J3** 32 43N 102 39W
Semiozernoye,
Kazakhstan .... **26 D7** 52 22N 64 8 E
Semipalatinsk,
Kazakhstan .... **26 D9** 50 30N 80 10 E
Semirara Is., *Phil.* ...... **37 B6** 12 0N 121 20 E
Semisopochnoi I., *U.S.A.* **68 C2** 51 55N 179 36 E
Semitau, *Indonesia* .... **36 D4** 0 29N 111 57 E
Semiyarskoye,
Kazakhstan .... **26 D8** 50 55N 78 23 E
Semmering Pass, *Austria* **16 E7** 47 41N 15 45 E
Semnān, *Iran* .... **45 C7** 35 55N 53 25 E
Semnān □, *Iran* .... **45 C7** 36 0N 54 0 E
Semois →, *Europe* .... **15 E4** 49 53N 4 44 E
Semporna, *Malaysia* ... **37 D5** 4 30N 118 33 E
Semuda, *Indonesia* .... **36 E4** 2 51S 112 58 E
Senā, *Iran* .... **45 D6** 28 27N 51 36 E
Sena, *Mozam.* .... **55 F3** 17 25S 35 0 E
Sena Madureira, *Brazil* . **92 E5** 9 5S 68 45W
Senador Pompeu, *Brazil* **93 E11** 5 40S 39 20W
Senaja, *Malaysia* ...... **36 C5** 6 45N 117 3 E
Senanga, *Zambia* ...... **56 B3** 16 2S 23 14 E
Senatobia, *U.S.A.* **81 H10** 34 37N 89 58W
Sendai, *Kagoshima, Japan* .... **31 J5** 31 50N 130 20 E
Sendai, *Miyagi, Japan* .. **30 E10** 38 15N 140 53 E
Sendai-Wan, *Japan* .... **30 E10** 38 15N 141 0 E
Seneca, *Oreg., U.S.A.* .. **82 D4** 44 8N 118 58W
Seneca, *S.C., U.S.A.* ... **77 H4** 34 41N 82 57W
Seneca Falls, *U.S.A.* ... **79 D8** 42 55N 76 48W
Seneca L., *U.S.A.* **78 D8** 42 40N 76 54W
Senegal ■, *W. Afr.* **50 F2** 14 30N 14 30W
Senegal →, *W. Afr.* ... **50 E1** 15 48N 16 32W
Senegambia, *Africa* **48 E2** 12 45N 12 0W
Senekal, *S. Africa* ..... **57 D4** 28 20S 27 36 E
Senga Hill, *Zambia* .... **55 D3** 9 19S 31 11 E
Senge Khambab =
Indus →, *Pakistan* ... **42 G2** 24 20N 67 47 E
Sengerema □, *Tanzania* **54 C3** 2 10S 32 20 E
Sengkang, *Indonesia* ... **37 E6** 4 8S 120 1 E
Sengua →, *Zimbabwe* . **55 F2** 17 7S 28 5 E
Senhor-do-Bonfim, *Brazil* **93 F10** 10 30S 40 10W
Senigállia, *Italy* .... **20 C5** 43 42N 13 12 E
Senj, *Croatia* .... **20 B6** 45 0N 14 58 E
Senja, *Norway* .... **8 B14** 69 25N 17 30 E
Senlis, *France* .... **18 B5** 49 13N 2 35 E
Senmonorom, *Cambodia* **38 F6** 12 27N 107 12 E
Sennâr, *Sudan* .... **51 F11** 13 30N 33 35 E
Senneterre, *Canada* **70 C4** 48 25N 77 15W
Seno, *Laos* .... **38 D5** 16 35N 104 50 E
Sens, *France* .... **18 B5** 48 11N 3 15 E
Senta, *Serbia, Yug.* ..... **21 B9** 45 55N 20 3 E
Sentery, *Zaire* .... **54 D2** 5 17S 25 42 E
Sentinel, *U.S.A.* **83 K7** 32 52N 113 13W
Sentolo, *Indonesia* ..... **37 G14** 7 55S 110 13 E
Seo de Urgel, *Spain* .... **19 A6** 42 22N 1 23 E
Seohara, *India* .... **43 E8** 29 15N 78 33 E
Seoni, *India* .... **43 H8** 22 5N 79 30 E
Seoul = Sŏul, *S. Korea* . **35 F14** 37 31N 126 58 E
Separation Point, *Canada* **71 B8** 53 37N 57 25W
Sepīdān, *Iran* .... **45 D7** 30 20N 52 5 E
Sepo-ri, *N. Korea* ...... **35 E14** 38 57N 127 25 E
Sepone, *Laos* .... **38 D6** 16 45N 106 13 E
Sept-Îles, *Canada* **71 B6** 50 13N 66 22W
Sequim, *U.S.A.* **84 B3** 48 5N 123 6W
Sequoia National Park,
U.S.A. **83 H4** 36 30N 118 30W
Seraing, *Belgium* ...... **15 D5** 50 35N 5 32 E
Seraja, *Indonesia* ...... **39 L7** 2 41N 108 35 E
Serakhis →, *Cyprus* ... **23 D11** 35 13N 32 55 E
Seram, *Indonesia* ...... **37 E7** 3 10S 129 0 E
Seram Laut, Kepulauan,
Indonesia .... **37 E8** 4 5S 131 25 E
Seram Sea, *Indonesia* .. **37 E7** 2 30S 128 30 E
Serang, *Indonesia* .... **37 G12** 6 8S 106 10 E
Serasan, *Indonesia* .... **39 L7** 2 29N 109 4 E
Serbia □, *Yugoslavia* ... **21 C9** 43 30N 21 0 E
Serdobsk, *Russia* ...... **24 D7** 52 28N 44 10 E
Seremban, *Malaysia* ... **39 L3** 2 43N 101 53 E
Serengeti □, *Tanzania* .. **54 C3** 2 0S 34 30 E
Serengeti Plain, *Tanzania* **54 C3** 2 40S 35 0 E
Serenje, *Zambia* .... **55 E3** 13 14S 30 15 E
Sereth = Siret →,
Romania .... **17 F14** 45 24N 28 1 E
Sergino, *Russia* .... **26 C7** 62 30N 65 38 E
Sergipe □, *Brazil* **93 F11** 10 30S 37 30W
Sergiyev Posad, *Russia* . **24 C6** 56 20N 38 10 E
Seria, *Brunei* .... **36 D4** 4 37N 114 23 E
Serian, *Malaysia* .... **36 D4** 1 10N 110 31 E
Seribu, Kepulauan,
Indonesia .... **36 F3** 5 36S 106 33 E
Seringapatam Reef,
Australia .... **60 B3** 13 38S 122 5 E
Sermata, *Indonesia* .... **37 F7** 8 15S 128 50 E
Serny Zavod,
Turkmenistan .... **26 F6** 39 59N 58 50 E
Serov, *Russia* .... **24 C11** 59 29N 60 35 E
Serowe, *Botswana* ..... **56 C4** 22 25S 26 43 E
Serpentine, *Australia* ... **61 F2** 32 23S 115 58 E
Serpentine Lakes,
Australia .... **61 E4** 28 30S 129 10 E
Serpukhov, *Russia* ..... **24 D6** 54 55N 37 28 E
Sérrai, *Greece* .... **21 D10** 41 5N 23 31 E
Serrezuela, *Argentina* .. **94 C2** 30 40S 65 20W
Serrinha, *Brazil* **93 F11** 11 39S 39 0W
Sertânia, *Brazil* **93 E11** 8 5S 37 20W
Sertanópolis, *Brazil* **95 A5** 23 4S 51 2W
Serua, *Indonesia* ...... **37 F8** 6 18S 130 1 E
Serui, *Indonesia* .... **37 E9** 1 53S 136 10 E
Serule, *Botswana* ...... **56 C4** 21 57S 27 20 E
Sese Is., *Uganda* ...... **54 C3** 0 20S 32 20 E
Sesepe, *Indonesia* ..... **37 E7** 1 30S 127 59 E
Sesfontein, *Namibia* ... **56 B1** 19 7S 13 39 E
Sesheke, *Zambia* ...... **56 B3** 17 29S 24 13 E
S'estañol, *Spain* ...... **22 B9** 39 22N 2 54 E
Setana, *Japan* .... **30 C9** 42 26N 139 51 E
Sète, *France* .... **18 E5** 43 25N 3 42 E
Sete Lagôas, *Brazil* **93 G10** 19 27S 44 16W
Sétif, *Algeria* .... **50 A6** 36 9N 5 26 E
Seto, *Japan* .... **31 G8** 35 14N 137 6 E
Setonaikai, *Japan* ...... **31 G6** 34 20N 133 30 E
Settat, *Morocco* **50 B3** 33 0N 7 40W
Setté-Cama, *Gabon* .... **52 E1** 2 32S 9 45 E
Setting L., *Canada* **73 B9** 55 0N 98 38W
Settle, *U.K.* **10 C5** 54 5N 2 18W
Settlement Pt., *Bahamas* **77 M6** 26 40N 79 0W
Setúbal, *Portugal* **19 C1** 38 30N 8 58W
Setúbal, B. de, *Portugal* . **19 C1** 38 40N 8 56W
Seulimeum, *Indonesia* .. **36 C1** 5 27N 95 15 E
Sevan, Ozero, *Armenia* . **25 F8** 40 30N 45 20 E
Sevastopol, *Ukraine* .... **25 F5** 44 35N 33 30 E
Seven Emu, *Australia* ... **62 B2** 16 20S 137 8 E
Seven Sisters, *Canada* .. **72 C3** 54 56N 128 10W
Severn →, *Canada* **70 A2** 56 2N 87 36W
Severn →, *U.K.* **11 F5** 51 35N 2 38W
Severn L., *Canada* **70 B1** 53 54N 90 48W
Severnaya Zemlya,
Russia .... **27 B10** 79 0N 100 0 E
Severnyye Uvaly, *Russia* **24 C8** 60 0N 50 0 E
Severo-Kurilsk, *Russia* .. **27 D16** 50 40N 156 8 E
Severo-Yeniseyskiy,
Russia .... **27 C10** 60 22N 93 1 E
Severodvinsk, *Russia* ... **24 B6** 64 27N 39 58 E
Severomorsk, *Russia* ... **24 A5** 69 5N 33 27 E
Severouralsk, *Russia* ... **24 B10** 60 9N 59 57 E
Sevier, *U.S.A.* **83 G7** 38 39N 112 11W
Sevier →, *U.S.A.* **83 G7** 39 4N 113 6W
Sevier L., *U.S.A.* **82 G7** 38 54N 113 9W
Sevilla, *Spain* **19 D3** 37 23N 6 0W
Seville = Sevilla, *Spain* . **19 D3** 37 23N 6 0W
Seward, *Alaska, U.S.A.* . **68 B5** 60 7N 149 27W
Seward, *Nebr., U.S.A.* .. **80 E6** 40 55N 97 6W
Seward Pen., *U.S.A.* ... **68 B3** 65 0N 164 0W
Sewell, *Chile* **94 C1** 34 10S 70 23W
Sewer, *Indonesia* ...... **37 F8** 5 53S 134 40 E
Sewickley, *U.S.A.* **78 F4** 40 32N 80 12W
Sexsmith, *Canada* **72 B5** 55 21N 118 47W
Seychelles ■, *Ind. Oc.* .. **29 K9** 5 0S 56 0 E
Seyðisfjörður, *Iceland* .. **8 D7** 65 16N 13 57W
Seydvān, *Iran* .... **44 B5** 38 34N 45 2 E
Seymchan, *Russia* ..... **27 C16** 62 54N 152 30 E
Seymour, *Australia* .... **63 F4** 37 0S 145 10 E
Seymour, *S. Africa* ..... **57 E4** 32 33S 26 46 E
Seymour, *Conn., U.S.A.* . **79 E11** 41 24N 73 4W
Seymour, *Ind., U.S.A.* .. **76 F3** 38 58N 85 53W
Seymour, *Tex., U.S.A.* .. **81 J5** 33 35N 99 16W
Seymour, *Wis., U.S.A.* .. **76 C1** 44 31N 88 20W
Sfax, *Tunisia* .... **51 B7** 34 49N 10 48 E
Sfîntu Gheorghe,
Romania .... **21 B11** 45 52N 25 48 E
Shaanxi □, *China* ...... **34 G5** 35 0N 109 0 E
Shaba □, *Zaïre* .... **54 D2** 8 0S 25 0 E
Shabunda, *Zaïre* ...... **54 C2** 2 40S 27 16 E
Shache, *China* .... **32 C2** 38 20N 77 10 E
Shackleton Ice Shelf,
Antarctica .... **5 C8** 66 0S 100 0 E
Shackleton Inlet,
Antarctica .... **5 E11** 83 0S 160 0 E

Somport, Puerto de

Siloam Springs, U.S.A. 81 G7 36 11N 94 32W
Silsbee, U.S.A. 81 K7 30 21N 94 11W
Silva Porto = Kuito, Angola 53 G3 12 22S 16 55 E
Silver City, N. Mex., U.S.A. 83 K9 32 46N 108 17W
Silver City, Nev., U.S.A. 82 G4 39 15N 119 48W
Silver Cr. ➝, U.S.A. 82 E4 43 16N 119 13W
Silver Creek, U.S.A. 78 D5 42 33N 79 10W
Silver L., U.S.A. 84 G6 38 39N 120 6W
Silver L., Calif., U.S.A. 85 K10 35 21N 116 7W
Silver Lake, U.S.A. 82 E3 43 8N 121 3W
Silver Streams, S. Africa 56 D3 28 20S 23 33 E
Silverton, Colo., U.S.A. 83 H10 37 49N 107 40W
Silverton, Tex., U.S.A. 81 H4 34 28N 101 19W
Silvies ➝, U.S.A. 82 E4 43 34N 119 2W
Simanggang, Malaysia 36 D4 1 15N 111 32 E
Simard, L., Canada 70 C4 47 40N 78 40W
Simba, Tanzania 54 C4 2 10S 37 36 E
Simbirsk, Russia 24 D8 54 20N 48 25 E
Simbo, Tanzania 54 C2 4 51S 29 41 E
Simcoe, Canada 70 D3 42 50N 80 20W
Simcoe, L., Canada 70 D4 44 25N 79 20W
Simenga, Russia 27 C11 62 42N 108 25 E
Simeulue, Indonesia 36 D1 2 45N 95 45 E
Simferopol, Ukraine 25 F5 44 55N 34 3 E
Simi Valley, U.S.A. 85 L8 34 16N 118 47W
Simikot, Nepal 43 E9 30 0N 81 50 E
Simla, India 42 D7 31 2N 77 9 E
Simmie, Canada 73 D7 49 56N 108 6W
Simmler, U.S.A. 85 K7 35 21N 119 59W
Simojärvi, Finland 8 C19 66 5N 27 3 E
Simojoki ➝, Finland 8 D18 65 35N 25 1 E
Simojovel, Mexico 87 D6 17 12N 92 38W
Simonette ➝, Canada 72 B5 55 9N 118 15W
Simonstown, S. Africa 56 E2 34 14S 18 26 E
Simplon Pass = Simplonpass, Switz. 16 E4 46 15N 8 3 E
Simplonpass, Switz. 16 E4 46 15N 8 3 E
Simpson Desert, Australia 62 D2 25 0S 137 0 E
Simpungdong, N. Korea 35 D15 40 56N 129 29 E
Simunjan, Malaysia 36 D4 1 25N 110 45 E
Simushir, Ostrov, Russia 27 E16 46 50N 152 30 E
Sinabang, Indonesia 36 D1 2 30N 96 24 E
Sinadogo, Somali Rep. 46 F4 5 50N 47 0 E
Sinai = Es Sînâ', Egypt 51 C11 29 0N 34 0 E
Sinai, Mt. = Mûsa, G., Egypt 51 C11 28 33N 33 59 E
Sinai Peninsula, Egypt 47 F2 29 30N 34 0 E
Sinaloa □, Mexico 86 C3 25 0N 107 30W
Sinaloa de Levya, Mexico 86 B3 25 50N 108 20W
Sinarádhes, Greece 23 A3 39 34N 19 51 E
Sīnāwan, Libya 50 B7 31 0N 10 37 E
Sincelejo, Colombia 92 B3 9 18N 75 24W
Sinchang, N. Korea 35 D15 40 7N 128 28 E
Sinchang-ni, N. Korea 35 E14 39 24N 126 8 E
Sinclair, U.S.A. 82 F10 41 47N 107 7W
Sinclair Mills, Canada 72 C4 54 5N 121 40W
Sincorá, Serra do, Brazil 93 F10 13 30S 41 0W
Sind, Pakistan 42 G3 26 0N 68 30 E
Sind □, Pakistan 42 F3 26 0N 69 0 E
Sind ➝, India 43 B6 34 18N 74 45 E
Sind Sagar Doab, Pakistan 42 D4 32 0N 71 30 E
Sindangan, Phil. 37 C6 8 10N 123 5 E
Sindangbarang, Indonesia 37 G12 7 27S 107 1 E
Sinde, Zambia 55 F2 17 28S 25 51 E
Sines, Portugal 19 D1 37 56N 8 51W
Sineu, Spain 22 B10 39 38N 3 1 E
Sing Buri, Thailand 38 E3 14 53N 100 25 E
Singa, Sudan 51 F11 13 10N 33 57 E
Singapore ■, Asia 39 M4 1 17N 103 51 E
Singapore, Straits of, Asia 39 M5 1 15N 104 0 E
Singaraja, Indonesia 36 F5 8 6S 115 10 E
Singida, Tanzania 54 C3 4 49S 34 48 E
Singida □, Tanzania 54 D3 6 0S 34 30 E
Singitikós Kólpos, Greece 21 D10 40 6N 24 0 E
Singkaling Hkamti, Burma 41 G19 26 0N 95 39 E
Singkawang, Indonesia 36 D3 1 0N 108 57 E
Singleton, Australia 63 E5 32 33S 151 0 E
Singleton, Mt., N. Terr., Australia 60 D5 22 0S 130 46 E
Singleton, Mt., W. Austral., Australia 61 E2 29 27S 117 15 E
Singoli, India 42 G6 25 0N 75 22 E
Singora = Songkhla, Thailand 39 J3 7 13N 100 37 E
Singosan, N. Korea 35 E14 38 52N 127 25 E
Sinhung, N. Korea 35 D14 40 11N 127 34 E
Sînî □, Egypt 47 F2 30 0N 34 0 E
Sinjai, Indonesia 37 F6 5 7S 120 20 E
Sinjār, Iraq 44 B4 36 19N 41 52 E
Sinkat, Sudan 51 E12 18 55N 36 49 E
Sinkiang Uighur = Xinjiang Uygur Zizhiqu □, China 32 B3 42 0N 86 0 E
Sinmak, N. Korea 35 E14 38 25N 126 14 E
Sinni ➝, Italy 20 D7 40 9N 16 42 E
Sinnuris, Egypt 51 C11 29 26N 30 31 E
Sinop, Turkey 25 F6 42 1N 35 11 E
Sinpo, N. Korea 35 E15 40 0N 128 13 E
Sinskoye, Russia 27 C13 61 8N 126 48 E
Sint Eustatius, I., Neth. Ant. 89 C7 17 30N 62 59W
Sint Maarten, I., W. Indies 89 C7 18 4N 63 4W
Sint Niklaas, Belgium 15 C4 51 10N 4 9 E
Sint Truiden, Belgium 15 D5 50 48N 5 10 E
Sintang, Indonesia 36 D4 0 5N 111 35 E
Sinton, U.S.A. 81 L6 28 2N 97 31W
Sintra, Portugal 19 C1 38 47N 9 25W
Sinŭiju, N. Korea 35 D13 40 5N 124 24 E
Siocon, Phil. 37 C6 7 40N 122 10 E
Sioma, Zambia 56 B3 16 25S 23 28 E
Sion, Switz. 16 E3 46 14N 7 20 E
Sioux City, U.S.A. 80 D6 42 30N 96 24W
Sioux Falls, U.S.A. 80 D6 43 33N 96 44W
Sioux Lookout, Canada 70 B1 50 10N 91 50W
Sip Song Chau Thai, Vietnam 38 B4 21 30N 103 30 E
Siping, China 35 C13 43 8N 124 21 E
Sipiwesk L., Canada 73 B9 55 5N 97 35W
Sipora, Indonesia 36 E1 2 18S 99 40 E
Siquia ➝, Nic. 88 D3 12 10N 84 20W
Siquijor, Phil. 37 C6 9 12N 123 35 E
Siquirres, Costa Rica 88 D3 10 6N 83 30W
Sir Edward Pellew Group, Australia 62 B2 15 40S 137 10 E
Sir Graham Moore Is., Australia 60 B4 13 53S 126 34 E
Siracusa, Italy 20 F6 37 4N 15 17 E
Sirajganj, Bangla. 43 G13 24 25N 89 47 E
Sirdān, Iran 45 B6 36 39N 49 12 E
Sirer, Spain 22 C7 38 56N 1 22 E
Siret ➝, Romania 17 F14 45 24N 28 1 E
Sirohi, India 42 G5 24 52N 72 53 E
Sironj, India 42 G7 24 5N 77 39 E
Síros, Greece 21 F11 37 28N 24 57 E
Sirretta Pk., U.S.A. 85 K8 35 56N 118 19W
Sirsa, India 42 E6 29 33N 75 4 E
Sisak, Croatia 20 B7 45 30N 16 21 E
Sisaket, Thailand 38 E5 15 8N 104 23 E
Sishen, S. Africa 56 D3 27 47S 22 59 E
Sishui, Henan, China 34 G7 34 48N 113 15 E
Sishui, Shandong, China 35 G9 35 42N 117 18 E
Sisipuk L., Canada 73 B8 55 45N 101 50W
Sisophon, Cambodia 38 F4 13 38N 102 59 E
Sisseton, U.S.A. 80 C6 45 40N 97 3W
Sīstān va Balūchestān □, Iran 45 E9 27 0N 62 0 E
Sisters, U.S.A. 82 D3 44 18N 121 33W
Sitamarhi, India 43 F11 26 37N 85 30 E
Sitapur, India 43 F9 27 38N 80 45 E
Siteki, Swaziland 57 D5 26 32S 31 58 E
Sitges, Spain 19 B6 41 17N 1 47 E
Sitia, Greece 23 D8 35 13N 26 6 E
Sitka, U.S.A. 68 C6 57 3N 135 20W
Sitoti, Botswana 56 C3 23 15S 23 40 E
Sittang Myit ➝, Burma 41 L20 17 20N 96 45 E
Sittard, Neths. 15 C5 51 0N 5 52 E
Sittwe, Burma 41 J18 20 18N 92 45 E
Siuna, Nic. 88 D3 13 37N 84 45W
Siuri, India 43 H12 23 50N 87 34 E
Sivana, India 42 E8 28 37N 78 6 E
Sivand, Iran 45 D7 30 5N 52 55 E
Sivas, Turkey 25 G6 39 43N 36 58 E
Sivomaskinskiy, Russia 24 A11 66 40N 62 35 E
Sivrihisar, Turkey 25 G5 39 30N 31 35 E
Sîwa, Egypt 51 C10 29 11N 25 31 E
Siwalik Range, Nepal 43 F10 28 0N 83 0 E
Siwan, India 43 F11 26 13N 84 21 E
Sizewell, U.K. 11 E9 52 13N 1 38 E
Siziwang Qi, China 34 D6 41 25N 111 40 E
Sjælland, Denmark 9 J11 55 30N 11 30 E
Sjumen = Šumen, Bulgaria 21 C12 43 18N 26 55 E
Skagafjörður, Iceland 8 D4 65 54N 19 35W
Skagastølstindane, Norway 9 F9 61 28N 7 52 E
Skagerrak, Denmark 9 H10 57 30N 9 0 E
Skagit ➝, U.S.A. 84 B4 48 23N 122 22W
Skagway, U.S.A. 72 B1 59 28N 135 19W
Skaidi, Norway 8 A18 70 26N 24 30 E
Skara, Sweden 9 G12 58 25N 13 30 E
Skaraborgs län □, Sweden 9 G12 58 20N 13 30 E
Skardu, Pakistan 43 B6 35 20N 75 44 E
Skeena ➝, Canada 72 C2 54 9N 130 5W
Skeena Mts., Canada 72 B3 56 40N 128 30W
Skegness, U.K. 10 D8 53 9N 0 20 E
Skeldon, Guyana 92 B7 5 55N 57 20W
Skellefte älv ➝, Sweden 8 D16 64 45N 21 10 E
Skellefteå, Sweden 8 D16 64 45N 20 50 E
Skelleftehamn, Sweden 8 D16 64 40N 20 59 E
Skerries, The, U.K. 10 D3 53 27N 4 40W
Skibbereen, Ireland 13 E2 51 33N 9 16W
Skiddaw, U.K. 10 C4 54 39N 3 9W
Skien, Norway 9 G10 59 12N 9 35 E
Skierniewice, Poland 17 C10 51 58N 20 10 E
Skikda, Algeria 50 A6 36 50N 6 58 E
Skilloura, Cyprus 23 D12 35 14N 33 10 E
Skipton, Australia 63 F3 37 39S 143 40 E
Skipton, U.K. 10 D5 53 57N 2 1W
Skirmish Pt., Australia 62 A1 11 59S 134 17 E
Skíros, Greece 21 E11 38 55N 24 34 E
Skive, Denmark 9 H10 56 33N 9 2 E
Skjálfandafljót ➝, Iceland 8 D5 65 59N 17 25W
Skjálfandi, Iceland 8 C5 66 5N 17 30W
Skoghall, Sweden 9 G12 59 20N 13 30 E
Skopí, Greece 23 D8 35 11N 26 2 E
Skopje, Macedonia 21 C9 42 1N 21 32 E
Skövde, Sweden 9 G12 58 24N 13 50 E
Skovorodino, Russia 27 D13 54 0N 124 0 E
Skowhegan, U.S.A. 71 D6 44 46N 69 43W
Skownan, Canada 73 C9 51 58N 99 35W
Skudeneshavn, Norway 9 G8 59 10N 5 10 E
Skull, Ireland 13 E2 51 32N 9 40W
Skunk ➝, U.S.A. 80 E9 40 42N 91 7W
Skwierzyna, Poland 16 B7 52 33N 15 30 E
Skye, U.K. 12 D2 57 15N 6 10W
Skykomish, U.S.A. 82 C3 47 42N 121 22W
Skyros = Skíros, Greece 21 E11 38 55N 24 34 E
Slamet, Indonesia 36 F3 7 16S 109 8 E
Slaney ➝, Ireland 13 D5 52 52N 6 45W
Śląsk, Poland 16 C8 51 0N 16 30 E
Slate Is., Canada 70 C2 48 40N 87 0W
Slatina, Romania 21 B11 44 28N 24 22 E
Slaton, U.S.A. 81 J4 33 26N 101 39W
Slave ➝, Canada 72 A6 61 18N 113 39W
Slave Coast, W. Afr. 48 F4 6 0N 2 30 E
Slave Lake, Canada 72 B6 55 17N 114 43W
Slave Pt., Canada 72 A5 61 11N 115 56W
Slavgorod, Russia 26 D8 53 1N 78 37 E
Slavkov, Czech. 16 D8 49 10N 16 52 E
Slavyanka, Russia 30 C5 42 53N 131 21 E
Slavyansk, Ukraine 25 E6 48 55N 37 36 E
Sleaford, U.K. 10 E7 53 0N 0 22W
Sleaford B., Australia 63 E2 34 55S 135 45 E
Sleat, Sd. of, U.K. 12 D3 57 5N 5 47W
Sleeper Is., Canada 69 C11 58 30N 81 0W
Sleepy Eye, U.S.A. 80 C7 44 18N 94 43W
Sleman, Indonesia 37 G14 7 40S 110 20 E
Slemon L., Canada 72 A5 63 13N 116 4W
Slidell, U.S.A. 81 K10 30 17N 89 47W
Sliedrecht, Neths. 15 C4 51 50N 4 45 E
Sliema, Malta 23 D2 35 54N 14 30 E
Slieve Aughty, Ireland 13 C3 53 4N 8 30W
Slieve Bloom, Ireland 13 C4 53 4N 7 40W
Slieve Donard, U.K. 13 B6 54 10N 5 57W
Slieve Gullion, U.K. 13 B5 54 8N 6 26W
Slieve Mish, Ireland 13 D2 52 12N 9 50W
Slievenamon, Ireland 13 D4 52 25N 7 37W
Sligo, Ireland 13 B3 54 17N 8 28W
Sligo □, Ireland 13 B3 54 10N 8 35W
Sligo B., Ireland 13 B3 54 20N 8 40W
Slite, Sweden 9 H15 57 42N 18 48 E
Sliven, Bulgaria 21 C12 42 42N 26 19 E
Sloan, U.S.A. 85 K11 35 57N 115 13W
Sloansville, U.S.A. 79 D10 42 45N 74 22W
Slobodskoy, Russia 24 C9 58 40N 50 6 E
Slocan, Canada 72 D5 49 48N 117 28W
Slochteren, Neths. 15 A6 53 12N 6 48 E
Slough, U.K. 11 F7 51 30N 0 35W
Sloughhouse, U.S.A. 84 G5 38 26N 121 12W
Slovak Rep. ■, Europe 17 D9 48 30N 20 0 E
Slovakian Ore Mts. = Slovenské Rudohorie, Slovakia 17 D9 48 45N 20 0 E
Slovenia ■, Europe 20 B6 45 58N 14 30 E
Slovenija = Slovenia ■, Europe 20 B6 45 58N 14 30 E
Slovenská Republika = Slovak Rep. ■, Europe 17 D9 48 30N 20 0 E
Slovenské Rudohorie, Slovakia 17 D9 48 45N 20 0 E
Slovyansk = Slavyansk, Ukraine 25 E6 48 55N 37 36 E
Sluis, Neths. 15 C3 51 18N 3 23 E
Slurry, S. Africa 56 D4 25 49S 25 42 E
Slyne Hd., Ireland 13 C1 53 25N 10 10W
Slyudyanka, Russia 27 D11 51 40N 103 40 E
Smalltree L., Canada 73 A7 61 0N 105 0W
Smara, Morocco 50 B3 32 9N 8 16W
Smartt Syndicate Dam, S. Africa 56 E3 30 45S 23 10 E
Smartville, U.S.A. 84 F5 39 13N 121 18W
Smeaton, Canada 73 C8 53 30N 104 49W
Smederevo, Serbia, Yug. 21 B9 44 40N 20 57 E
Smethport, U.S.A. 78 E6 41 49N 78 27W
Smidovich, Russia 27 E14 48 36N 133 49 E
Smiley, Canada 73 C7 51 38N 109 29W
Smith, Canada 72 B6 55 10N 114 0W
Smith ➝, Canada 72 B3 59 34N 126 30W
Smith Arm, Canada 68 B7 66 15N 123 0W
Smith Center, U.S.A. 80 F5 39 47N 98 47W
Smith Sund, Greenland 4 B4 78 30N 74 0W
Smithburne ➝, Australia 62 B3 17 3S 140 57 E
Smithers, Canada 72 C3 54 45N 127 10W
Smithfield, S. Africa 57 E4 30 9S 26 30 E
Smithfield, N.C., U.S.A. 77 H6 35 31N 78 21W
Smithfield, Utah, U.S.A. 82 F8 41 50N 111 50W
Smiths Falls, Canada 70 D4 44 55N 76 0W
Smithton, Australia 62 G4 40 53S 145 6 E
Smithtown, Australia 63 E5 30 58S 152 48 E
Smithville, Canada 78 C5 43 6N 79 33W
Smithville, U.S.A. 81 K6 30 1N 97 10W
Smoky ➝, Canada 72 B5 56 10N 117 21W
Smoky Bay, Australia 63 E1 32 22S 134 13 E
Smoky Falls, Canada 70 B3 50 4N 82 10W
Smoky Hill ➝, U.S.A. 80 F6 39 4N 96 48W
Smoky Lake, Canada 72 C6 54 10N 112 30W
Smøla, Norway 8 E10 63 23N 8 3 E
Smolensk, Russia 24 D5 54 45N 32 5 E
Smolikas, Óros, Greece 21 D9 40 9N 20 58 E
Smolyan, Bulgaria 21 D11 41 36N 24 38 E
Smooth Rock Falls, Canada 70 C3 49 17N 81 37W
Smoothstone L., Canada 73 C7 54 40N 106 50W
Smyrna = İzmir, Turkey 25 G4 38 25N 27 8 E
Snaefell, U.K. 10 C3 54 18N 4 26W
Snæfellsjökull, Iceland 8 D2 64 49N 23 46W
Snake ➝, U.S.A. 82 C4 46 12N 119 2W
Snake I., Australia 63 F4 38 47S 146 33 E
Snake L., Canada 73 B7 55 32N 106 35W
Snake Range, U.S.A. 82 G6 39 0N 114 20W
Snake River Plain, U.S.A. 82 E7 42 50N 114 0W
Sneek, Neths. 15 A5 53 2N 5 40 E
Sneeuberge, S. Africa 56 E3 31 46S 24 20 E
Snelling, U.S.A. 84 H6 37 31N 120 26W
Snizort, L., U.K. 12 D2 57 33N 6 28W
Snøhetta, Norway 8 E10 62 19N 9 16 E
Snohomish, U.S.A. 84 C4 47 55N 122 6W
Snoul, Cambodia 39 F6 12 4N 106 26 E
Snow Hill, U.S.A. 76 F8 38 11N 75 24W
Snow Lake, Canada 73 C8 54 52N 100 3W
Snow Mt., U.S.A. 84 F4 39 23N 122 45W
Snowbird L., Canada 73 A8 60 45N 103 0W
Snowdon, U.K. 10 D3 53 4N 4 8W
Snowdrift, Canada 73 A6 62 24N 110 44W
Snowdrift ➝, Canada 73 A6 62 24N 110 44W
Snowflake, U.S.A. 83 J8 34 30N 110 5W
Snowshoe Pk., U.S.A. 82 B6 48 13N 115 41W
Snowtown, Australia 63 E2 33 46S 138 14 E
Snowville, U.S.A. 82 F7 41 58N 112 43W
Snowy ➝, Australia 63 F4 37 46S 148 30 E
Snowy Mts., Australia 63 F4 36 30S 148 20 E
Snug Corner, Bahamas 89 B5 22 33N 73 52W
Snyder, Okla., U.S.A. 81 H5 34 40N 98 57W
Snyder, Tex., U.S.A. 81 J4 32 44N 100 55W
Soahanina, Madag. 57 B7 18 42S 44 13 E
Soalala, Madag. 57 B8 16 6S 45 20 E
Soan ➝, Pakistan 42 C4 33 1N 71 44 E
Soanierana-Ivongo, Madag. 57 B8 16 55S 49 35 E
Soap Lake, U.S.A. 82 C4 47 23N 119 29W
Sobat, Nahr ➝, Sudan 51 G11 9 22N 31 33 E
Sobhapur, India 42 H8 22 47N 78 17 E
Sobral, Brazil 93 D10 3 50S 40 20W
Soc Giang, Vietnam 38 A6 22 54N 106 1 E
Soc Trang, Vietnam 39 H5 9 37N 105 50 E
Soch'e = Shache, China 32 C2 38 20N 77 10 E
Sochi, Russia 25 F6 43 35N 39 40 E
Société, Is. de la, Pac. Oc. 65 J12 17 0S 151 0W
Society Is. = Société, Is. de la, Pac. Oc. 65 J12 17 0S 151 0W
Socompa, Portezuelo de, Chile 94 A2 24 27S 68 18W
Socorro, Colombia 92 B4 6 29N 73 16W
Socorro, U.S.A. 83 J10 34 4N 106 54W
Socorro, I., Mexico 86 D2 18 45N 110 58W
Socotra, Ind. Oc. 46 E5 12 30N 54 0 E
Soda L., U.S.A. 83 J5 35 10N 116 4W
Soda Plains, India 43 B8 35 30N 79 0 E
Soda Springs, U.S.A. 82 E8 42 39N 111 36W
Söderhamn, Sweden 9 F14 61 18N 17 10 E
Söderköping, Sweden 9 G14 58 31N 16 20 E
Södermanlands län □, Sweden 9 G14 59 10N 16 30 E
Södertälje, Sweden 9 G14 59 12N 17 39 E
Sodiri, Sudan 51 F10 14 27N 29 0 E
Sodo, Ethiopia 51 G12 7 0N 37 41 E
Sodus, U.S.A. 78 C7 43 14N 77 4W
Soekmekaar, S. Africa 57 C4 23 30S 29 55 E
Soest, Neths. 15 B5 52 9N 5 19 E
Sofia = Sofiya, Bulgaria 21 C10 42 45N 23 20 E
Sofia ➝, Madag. 57 B8 15 27S 47 23 E
Sofiiski, Russia 27 D14 52 15N 133 59 E
Sofiya, Bulgaria 21 C10 42 45N 23 20 E
Sōfu-Gan, Japan 31 K10 29 49N 140 21 E
Sogamoso, Colombia 92 B4 5 43N 72 56W
Sogār, Iran 45 E8 25 53N 58 6 E
Sogn og Fjordane fylke □, Norway 9 F9 61 40N 6 0 E
Sogndalsfjøra, Norway 9 F9 61 14N 7 5 E
Sognefjorden, Norway 9 F8 61 10N 5 50 E
Sŏgwi-po, S. Korea 35 H14 33 13N 126 34 E
Soh, Iran 45 C6 33 26N 51 27 E
Sohâg, Egypt 51 C11 26 33N 31 43 E
Sŏhori, N. Korea 35 D15 40 7N 128 23 E
Soignies, Belgium 15 D4 50 35N 4 5 E
Soissons, France 18 B5 49 25N 3 19 E
Sōja, Japan 31 G6 34 40N 133 45 E
Sojat, India 42 G5 25 55N 73 45 E
Sokelo, Zaïre 55 D1 9 55S 24 36 E
Sokhumi = Sukhumi, Georgia 25 F7 43 0N 41 0 E
Sokodé, Togo 50 G5 9 0N 1 11 E
Sokol, Russia 24 C7 59 30N 40 5 E
Sokółka, Poland 17 B11 53 25N 23 30 E
Sokolo, Mali 50 F3 14 53N 6 8W
Sokoto, Nigeria 50 F6 13 2N 5 16 E
Sol Iletsk, Russia 24 D10 51 10N 55 0 E
Solai, Kenya 54 B4 0 2N 36 12 E
Solano, Phil. 37 A6 16 31N 121 15 E
Solapur, India 40 L9 17 43N 75 56 E
Soléa □, Cyprus 23 D12 35 5N 33 4 E
Soledad, U.S.A. 83 H3 36 26N 121 20W
Soledad, Venezuela 92 B6 8 10N 63 34W
Solent, The, U.K. 11 G6 50 45N 1 25W
Solfonn, Norway 9 F9 60 2N 6 57 E
Soligalich, Russia 24 C7 59 5N 42 10 E
Solikamsk, Russia 24 C10 59 38N 56 50 E
Solila, Madag. 57 C8 21 25S 46 37 E
Solimões = Amazonas ➝, S. Amer. 93 C9 0 5S 50 0W
Solingen, Germany 15 C7 51 10N 7 4 E
Sollefteå, Sweden 8 E14 63 12N 17 20 E
Sóller, Spain 22 B9 39 46N 2 43 E
Sologne, France 18 C4 47 40N 1 45 E
Solok, Indonesia 36 E2 0 45S 100 40 E
Sololá, Guatemala 88 D1 14 49N 91 10W
Solomon, N. Fork ➝, U.S.A. 80 F5 39 29N 98 26W
Solomon, S. Fork ➝, U.S.A. 80 F5 39 25N 99 12W
Solomon Is. ■, Pac. Oc. 64 H7 6 0S 155 0 E
Solon, China 33 B7 46 32N 121 10 E
Solon Springs, U.S.A. 80 B9 46 22N 91 49W
Solor, Indonesia 37 F6 8 27S 123 0 E
Solothurn, Switz. 16 E3 47 13N 7 32 E
Solṭānābād, Khorāsān, Iran 45 C8 34 13N 59 58 E
Solṭānābād, Khorāsān, Iran 45 B8 36 29N 58 5 E
Solṭānābād, Markazī, Iran 45 C6 35 31N 51 10 E
Solunska Glava, Macedonia 21 D9 41 44N 21 31 E
Solvang, U.S.A. 85 L6 34 36N 120 8W
Solvay, U.S.A. 79 C8 43 3N 76 13W
Solvychegodsk, Russia 24 B8 61 21N 46 56 E
Solway Firth, U.K. 10 C4 54 45N 3 38W
Solwezi, Zambia 55 E2 12 11S 26 21 E
Sōma, Japan 30 F10 37 40N 140 50 E
Somali Rep. ■, Africa 46 F4 7 0N 47 0 E
Somalia ■ = Somali Rep. ■, Africa 46 F4 7 0N 47 0 E
Sombor, Serbia, Yug. 21 B8 45 46N 19 9 E
Sombra, Canada 78 D2 42 43N 82 29W
Sombrerete, Mexico 86 C4 23 40N 103 40W
Sombrero, Anguilla 89 C7 18 37N 63 30W
Somers, U.S.A. 82 B6 48 5N 114 13W
Somerset, Canada 73 D9 49 25N 98 39W
Somerset, Colo., U.S.A. 83 G10 38 56N 107 28W
Somerset, Ky., U.S.A. 76 G3 37 5N 84 36W
Somerset, Mass., U.S.A. 79 E13 41 47N 71 8W
Somerset, Pa., U.S.A. 78 F5 40 1N 79 5W
Somerset □, U.K. 11 F5 51 9N 3 0W
Somerset East, S. Africa 56 E4 32 42S 25 35 E
Somerset I., Canada 68 A10 73 30N 93 0W
Somerset West, S. Africa 56 E2 34 8S 18 50 E
Somerton, U.S.A. 83 K6 32 36N 114 43W
Somerville, U.S.A. 79 F10 40 35N 74 38W
Someş ➝, Romania 17 E11 47 49N 22 43 E
Sommariva, Australia 63 D4 26 24S 146 36 E
Somme □, France 18 B5 49 57N 2 20 E
Somoto, Nic. 88 D2 13 28N 86 37W
Somport, Puerto de, Spain 19 A5 42 48N 0 31W

Swainsboro

Swainsboro, *U.S.A.* **77 J4** 32 36N 82 20W
Swakopmund, *Namibia* **56 C1** 22 37S 14 30 E
Swale →, *U.K.* **10 C6** 54 5N 1 20W
Swan Hill, *Australia* **63 F3** 35 20S 143 33 E
Swan Hills, *Canada* **72 C5** 54 42N 115 24W
Swan Is., *W. Indies* **88 C3** 17 22N 83 57W
Swan L., *Canada* **73 C8** 52 30N 100 40W
Swan River, *Canada* **73 C8** 52 10N 101 16W
Swanage, *U.K.* **11 G6** 50 36N 1 59W
Swansea, *Australia* **63 E5** 33 3S 151 35 E
Swansea, *U.K.* **11 F4** 51 37N 3 57W
Swar →, *Pakistan* **43 B5** 34 40N 72 5 E
Swartberge, *S. Africa* **56 E3** 33 20S 22 0 E
Swartmodder, *S. Africa* **56 D3** 28 1S 20 32 E
Swartruggens, *S. Africa* **56 D4** 25 39S 26 42 E
Swastika, *Canada* **70 C3** 48 7N 80 6W
Swatow = Shantou, *China* **33 D6** 23 18N 116 40 E
Swaziland ■, *Africa* **57 D5** 26 30S 31 30 E
Sweden ■, *Europe* **9 H13** 57 0N 15 0 E
Sweet Home, *U.S.A.* **82 D2** 44 24N 122 44W
Sweetwater, *Nev., U.S.A.* **84 G7** 38 27N 119 9W
Sweetwater, *Tex., U.S.A.* **81 J4** 32 28N 100 25W
Sweetwater →, *U.S.A.* **82 E10** 42 31N 107 2W
Swellendam, *S. Africa* **56 E3** 34 1S 20 26 E
Świdnica, *Poland* **16 C8** 50 50N 16 30 E
Świebodzin, *Poland* **16 B7** 52 15N 15 31 E
Swift Current, *Canada* **73 C7** 50 20N 107 45W
Swiftcurrent →, *Canada* **73 C7** 50 38N 107 44W
Swilly, L., *Ireland* **13 A4** 55 12N 7 35W
Swindle, I., *Canada* **72 C3** 52 30N 128 35W
Swindon, *U.K.* **11 F6** 51 33N 1 47W
Swinemünde = Świnoujście, *Poland* **16 B7** 53 54N 14 16 E
Świnoujście, *Poland* **16 B7** 53 54N 14 16 E
Switzerland ■, *Europe* **16 E4** 46 30N 8 0 E
Swords, *Ireland* **13 C5** 53 27N 6 15W
Sydney, *Australia* **63 E5** 33 53S 151 10 E
Sydney, *Canada* **71 C7** 46 7N 60 7W
Sydney Mines, *Canada* **71 C7** 46 18N 60 15W
Sydprøven, *Greenland* **4 C5** 60 30N 45 35W
Sydra G. of = Surt, Khalīj, *Libya* **51 B8** 31 40N 18 30 E
Syktyvkar, *Russia* **24 B9** 61 45N 50 40 E
Sylacauga, *U.S.A.* **77 J2** 33 10N 86 15W
Sylarna, *Sweden* **8 E12** 63 2N 12 13 E
Sylhet, *Bangla.* **41 G17** 24 54N 91 52 E
Sylvan Lake, *Canada* **72 C6** 52 20N 114 3W
Sylvania, *U.S.A.* **77 J5** 32 45N 81 38W
Sylvester, *U.S.A.* **77 K4** 31 32N 83 50W
Sym, *Russia* **26 C9** 60 20N 88 18 E
Symón, *Mexico* **86 C4** 24 42N 102 35W
Synnott Ra., *Australia* **60 C4** 16 30S 125 20 E
Syracuse, *Kans., U.S.A.* **81 F4** 37 59N 101 45W
Syracuse, *N.Y., U.S.A.* **79 C8** 43 3N 76 9W
Syrdarya →, *Kazakhstan* **26 E7** 46 3N 61 0 E
Syria ■, *Asia* **44 C3** 35 0N 38 0 E
Syul'dzhyukyor, *Russia* **27 C12** 63 14N 113 32 E
Syzran, *Russia* **24 D8** 53 12N 48 30 E
Szczecin, *Poland* **16 B7** 53 27N 14 27 E
Szczecinek, *Poland* **16 B8** 53 43N 16 41 E
Szechwan = Sichuan □, *China* **32 C5** 31 0N 104 0 E
Szeged, *Hungary* **17 E10** 46 16N 20 10 E
Székesfehérvár, *Hungary* **17 E9** 47 15N 18 25 E
Szekszárd, *Hungary* **17 E9** 46 22N 18 42 E
Szentes, *Hungary* **17 E10** 46 39N 20 21 E
Szolnok, *Hungary* **17 E10** 47 10N 20 15 E
Szombathely, *Hungary* **16 E8** 47 14N 16 38 E

T

Ta Khli Khok, *Thailand* **38 E3** 15 18N 100 20 E
Ta Lai, *Vietnam* **39 G6** 11 24N 107 23 E
Tabacal, *Argentina* **94 A3** 23 15S 64 15W
Tabaco, *Phil.* **37 B6** 13 22N 123 44 E
Ṭābah, *Si. Arabia* **44 E4** 26 55N 42 38 E
Tabarka, *Tunisia* **50 A6** 36 56N 8 46 E
Ṭabas, *Khorāsān, Iran* **45 C9** 32 48N 60 12 E
Ṭabas, *Khorāsān, Iran* **45 C8** 33 35N 56 55 E
Tabasará, Serranía de, *Panama* **88 E3** 8 35N 81 40W
Tabasco □, *Mexico* **87 D6** 17 45N 93 30W
Tabatinga, Serra da, *Brazil* **93 F10** 10 30S 44 0W
Tabāzīn, *Iran* **45 D8** 31 12N 57 54 E
Taber, *Canada* **72 D6** 49 47N 112 8W
Tablas, *Phil.* **37 B6** 12 25N 122 2 E
Table B. = Tafelbaai, *S. Africa* **56 E2** 33 35S 18 25 E
Table B., *Canada* **71 B8** 53 40N 56 25W
Table Mt., *S. Africa* **56 E2** 34 0S 18 22 E
Tableland, *Australia* **60 C4** 17 16S 126 51 E
Tabletop, Mt., *Australia* **62 C4** 23 24S 147 11 E
Tábor, *Czech.* **16 D7** 49 25N 14 39 E
Tabora, *Tanzania* **54 D3** 5 2S 32 50 E
Tabora □, *Tanzania* **54 D3** 5 0S 33 0 E
Tabou, *Ivory C.* **50 H3** 4 30N 7 20W
Tabrīz, *Iran* **44 B5** 38 7N 46 20 E
Tabuaeran, *Pac. Oc.* **65 G12** 3 51N 159 22W
Tabūk, *Si. Arabia* **44 D3** 28 23N 36 36 E
Tacámbaro de Codallos, *Mexico* **86 D4** 19 14N 101 28W
Tacheng, *China* **32 B3** 46 40N 82 58 E
Tach'ing Shan = Daqing Shan, *China* **34 D6** 40 40N 111 0 E
Tacloban, *Phil.* **37 B6** 11 15N 124 58 E
Tacna, *Peru* **92 G4** 18 0S 70 20W
Tacoma, *U.S.A.* **84 C4** 47 14N 122 26W
Tacuarembó, *Uruguay* **95 C4** 31 45S 56 0W
Tademaït, Plateau du, *Algeria* **50 C5** 28 30N 2 30 E
Tadjoura, *Djibouti* **46 E3** 11 50N 42 55 E
Tadmor, *N.Z.* **59 J4** 41 27S 172 45 E
Tadoule, L., *Canada* **73 B9** 58 36N 98 20W
Tadoussac, *Canada* **71 C6** 48 11N 69 42W
Tadzhikistan = Tajikistan ■, *Asia* **26 F8** 38 30N 70 0 E
Taechŏn-ni, *S. Korea* **35 F14** 36 21N 126 36 E
Taegu, *S. Korea* **35 G15** 35 50N 128 37 E
Taegwan, *N. Korea* **35 D13** 40 13N 125 12 E
Taejŏn, *S. Korea* **35 F14** 36 20N 127 28 E
Tafalla, *Spain* **19 A5** 42 30N 1 41W
Tafelbaai, *S. Africa* **56 E2** 33 35S 18 25 E
Tafermaar, *Indonesia* **37 F8** 6 47S 134 10 E
Tafí Viejo, *Argentina* **94 B2** 26 43S 65 17W
Tafihān, *Iran* **45 D7** 29 25N 52 39 E
Taft, *Iran* **45 D7** 31 45N 54 14 E
Taft, *Phil.* **37 B7** 11 57N 125 30 E
Taft, *Calif., U.S.A.* **85 K7** 35 8N 119 28W
Taft, *Tex., U.S.A.* **81 M6** 27 59N 97 24W
Taga Dzong, *Bhutan* **41 F16** 27 5N 89 55 E
Taganrog, *Russia* **25 E6** 47 12N 38 50 E
Tagbilaran, *Phil.* **37 C6** 9 39N 123 51 E
Tagish, *Canada* **72 A2** 60 19N 134 16W
Tagish L., *Canada* **72 A2** 60 10N 134 20W
Tagliamento →, *Italy* **20 B5** 45 38N 13 5 E
Tagomago, I. de, *Spain* **22 B8** 39 2N 1 39 E
Taguatinga, *Brazil* **93 F10** 12 16S 42 26W
Tagum, *Phil.* **37 C7** 7 33N 125 53 E
Tagus = Tejo →, *Europe* **19 C1** 38 40N 9 24W
Tahakopa, *N.Z.* **59 M2** 46 30S 169 23 E
Tahan, Gunong, *Malaysia* **39 K4** 4 34N 102 17 E
Tahat, *Algeria* **50 D6** 23 18N 5 33 E
Tāherī, *Iran* **45 E7** 27 43N 52 20 E
Tahiti, *Pac. Oc.* **65 J13** 17 37S 149 27W
Tahoe, L., *U.S.A.* **84 G6** 39 6N 120 2W
Tahoe City, *U.S.A.* **84 F6** 39 10N 120 9W
Taholah, *U.S.A.* **84 C2** 47 21N 124 17W
Tahoua, *Niger* **50 F6** 14 57N 5 16 E
Tahta, *Egypt* **51 C11** 26 44N 31 32 E
Tahulandang, *Indonesia* **37 D7** 2 27N 125 23 E
Tahuna, *Indonesia* **37 D7** 3 38N 125 30 E
Taï, *Ivory C.* **50 G3** 5 55N 7 30W
Tai Shan, *China* **35 F9** 36 25N 117 20 E
Tai'an, *China* **35 F9** 36 12N 117 8 E
Taibei, *Taiwan* **33 D7** 25 4N 121 29 E
Taibique, *Canary Is.* **22 G2** 27 42N 17 58W
Taibus Qi, *China* **34 D8** 41 54N 115 22 E
T'aichung = Taizhong, *Taiwan* **33 D7** 24 12N 120 35 E
Taieri →, *N.Z.* **59 M3** 46 3S 170 12 E
Taigu, *China* **34 F7** 37 28N 112 30 E
Taihang Shan, *China* **34 G7** 36 0N 113 30 E
Taihape, *N.Z.* **59 H5** 39 41S 175 48 E
Taihe, *China* **34 H8** 33 20N 115 42 E
Taikang, *China* **34 G8** 34 5N 114 50 E
Tailem Bend, *Australia* **63 F2** 35 12S 139 29 E
Taimyr Peninsula = Taymyr, Poluostrov, *Russia* **27 B11** 75 0N 100 0 E
Tain, *U.K.* **12 D4** 57 49N 4 4W
Tainan, *Taiwan* **33 D7** 23 17N 120 18 E
Tainaron, Ákra, *Greece* **21 F10** 36 22N 22 27 E
T'aipei = Taibei, *Taiwan* **33 D7** 25 4N 121 29 E
T'aipei, *Taiwan* **33 D7** 25 2N 121 30 E
Taiping, *Malaysia* **39 K3** 4 51N 100 44 E
Taipingzhen, *China* **34 H6** 33 35N 111 42 E
Taita □, *Kenya* **54 C4** 4 0S 38 30 E
Taita Hills, *Kenya* **54 C4** 3 25S 38 15 E
Taitao, Pen. de, *Chile* **96 F2** 46 30S 75 0W
Taivalkoski, *Finland* **8 D20** 65 33N 28 12 E
Taiwan ■, *Asia* **33 D7** 23 30N 121 0 E
Taïyetos Óros, *Greece* **21 F10** 37 0N 22 23 E
Taiyiba, *Israel* **47 C4** 32 36N 35 27 E
Taiyuan, *China* **34 F7** 37 52N 112 33 E
Taizhong, *Taiwan* **33 D7** 24 12N 120 35 E
Ta'izz, *Yemen* **46 E3** 13 35N 44 2 E
Tājābād, *Iran* **45 D7** 30 2N 54 24 E
Tajikistan ■, *Asia* **26 F8** 38 30N 70 0 E
Tajima, *Japan* **31 F9** 37 12N 139 46 E
Tajo = Tejo →, *Europe* **19 C1** 38 40N 9 24W
Tajrīsh, *Iran* **45 C6** 35 48N 51 25 E
Tājūrā, *Libya* **51 B7** 32 51N 13 21 E
Tak, *Thailand* **38 D2** 16 52N 99 8 E
Takāb, *Iran* **44 B5** 36 24N 47 7 E
Takachiho, *Japan* **31 H5** 32 42N 131 18 E
Takada, *Japan* **31 F9** 37 7N 138 15 E
Takahagi, *Japan* **31 F10** 36 43N 140 45 E
Takaka, *N.Z.* **59 J4** 40 51S 172 50 E
Takamatsu, *Japan* **31 G7** 34 20N 134 5 E
Takaoka, *Japan* **31 F8** 36 47N 137 0 E
Takapuna, *N.Z.* **59 G5** 36 47S 174 47 E
Takasaki, *Japan* **31 F9** 36 20N 139 0 E
Takatsuki, *Japan* **31 G7** 34 51N 135 37 E
Takaungu, *Kenya* **54 C4** 3 38S 39 52 E
Takayama, *Japan* **31 F8** 36 18N 137 11 E
Take-Shima, *Japan* **31 J5** 30 49N 130 26 E
Takefu, *Japan* **31 G8** 35 50N 136 10 E
Takengon, *Indonesia* **36 D1** 4 45N 96 50 E
Takeo, *Cambodia* **39 G5** 10 59N 104 47 E
Takeo, *Japan* **31 H5** 33 12N 130 1 E
Tākestān, *Iran* **45 C6** 36 0N 49 40 E
Taketa, *Japan* **31 H5** 32 58N 131 24 E
Takh, *India* **43 C7** 33 6N 77 32 E
Takhman, *Cambodia* **39 G5** 11 29N 104 57 E
Takikawa, *Japan* **30 C10** 43 33N 141 54 E
Takla L., *Canada* **72 B3** 55 15N 125 45W
Takla Landing, *Canada* **72 B3** 55 30N 125 50W
Takla Makan = Taklamakan Shamo, *China* **28 F12** 38 0N 83 0 E
Taklamakan Shamo, *China* **28 F12** 38 0N 83 0 E
Taku →, *Canada* **72 B2** 58 30N 133 50W
Takum, *Nigeria* **50 G6** 7 18N 9 36 E
Tal Halāl, *Iran* **45 D7** 28 54N 55 1 E
Tala, *Uruguay* **95 C4** 34 21S 55 46W
Talagante, *Chile* **94 C1** 33 40S 70 50W
Talamanca, Cordillera de, *Cent. Amer.* **88 E3** 9 20N 83 20W
Talara, *Peru* **92 D2** 4 38S 81 18W
Talas, *Kirghizia* **26 E8** 42 30N 72 13 E
Talâta, *Egypt* **47 E1** 30 36N 32 20 E
Talaud, Kepulauan, *Indonesia* **37 D7** 4 30N 127 10 E
Talaud Is. = Talaud, Kepulauan, *Indonesia* **37 D7** 4 30N 127 10 E
Talavera de la Reina, *Spain* **19 C3** 39 55N 4 46W
Talawana, *Australia* **60 D3** 22 51S 121 9 E
Talayan, *Phil.* **37 C6** 6 52N 124 24 E
Talbot, C., *Australia* **60 B4** 13 48S 126 43 E
Talbragar →, *Australia* **63 E4** 32 12S 148 37 E
Talca, *Chile* **94 D1** 35 28S 71 40W
Talca □, *Chile* **94 D1** 35 20S 71 46W
Talcahuano, *Chile* **94 D1** 36 40S 73 10W
Talcher, *India* **41 J14** 21 0N 85 18 E
Taldy Kurgan, *Kazakhstan* **26 E8** 45 10N 78 45 E
Taldyqorghan = Taldy Kurgan, *Kazakhstan* **26 E8** 45 10N 78 45 E
Talesh, *Iran* **45 B6** 37 58N 48 58 E
Ṭalesh, Kūhhā-ye, *Iran* **45 B6** 39 0N 48 30 E
Tali Post, *Sudan* **51 G11** 5 55N 30 44 E
Taliabu, *Indonesia* **37 E6** 1 45S 124 55 E
Talibon, *Phil.* **37 B6** 10 9N 124 20 E
Talibong, Ko, *Thailand* **39 J2** 7 15N 99 23 E
Talihina, *U.S.A.* **81 H7** 34 45N 95 3W
Taliwang, *Indonesia* **36 F5** 8 50S 116 55 E
Tall 'Asūr, *Jordan* **47 D4** 31 59N 35 17 E
Tall Kalakh, *Syria* **47 A5** 34 41N 36 15 E
Talladega, *U.S.A.* **77 J2** 33 26N 86 6W
Tallahassee, *U.S.A.* **77 K3** 30 27N 84 17W
Tallangatta, *Australia* **63 F4** 36 15S 147 19 E
Tallarook, *Australia* **63 F4** 37 5S 145 6 E
Tallering Pk., *Australia* **61 E2** 28 6S 115 37 E
Tallinn, *Estonia* **24 C3** 59 22N 24 48 E
Tallulah, *U.S.A.* **81 J9** 32 25N 91 11W
Talodi, *Sudan* **51 F11** 10 35N 30 22 E
Talpa de Allende, *Mexico* **86 C4** 20 23N 104 51W
Taltal, *Chile* **94 B1** 25 23S 70 33W
Taltson →, *Canada* **72 A6** 61 24N 112 46W
Talwood, *Australia* **63 D4** 28 29S 149 29 E
Talyawalka Cr. →, *Australia* **63 E3** 32 28S 142 22 E
Tam Chau, *Vietnam* **39 G5** 10 48N 105 12 E
Tam Ky, *Vietnam* **38 E7** 15 34N 108 29 E
Tam Quan, *Vietnam* **38 E7** 14 35N 109 3 E
Tama, *U.S.A.* **80 E8** 41 58N 92 35W
Tamala, *Australia* **61 E1** 26 42S 113 47 E
Tamale, *Ghana* **50 G4** 9 22N 0 50W
Tamano, *Japan* **31 G6** 34 29N 133 59 E
Tamanrasset, *Algeria* **50 D6** 22 50N 5 30 E
Tamaqua, *U.S.A.* **79 F9** 40 48N 75 58W
Tamar →, *U.K.* **11 G3** 50 33N 4 15W
Tamarang, *Australia* **63 E5** 31 27S 150 5 E
Tamarinda, *Spain* **22 B10** 39 55N 3 49 E
Tamashima, *Japan* **31 G6** 34 32N 133 40 E
Tamaské, *Niger* **50 F6** 14 49N 5 43 E
Tamaulipas □, *Mexico* **87 C5** 24 0N 99 0W
Tamaulipas, Sierra de, *Mexico* **87 C5** 23 30N 98 20W
Tamazula, *Mexico* **86 C3** 24 55N 106 58W
Tamazunchale, *Mexico* **87 C5** 21 16N 98 47W
Tambacounda, *Senegal* **50 F2** 13 45N 13 40W
Tambelan, Kepulauan, *Indonesia* **36 D3** 1 0N 107 30 E
Tambellup, *Australia* **61 F2** 34 4S 117 37 E
Tambo, *Australia* **62 C4** 24 54S 146 14 E
Tambo de Mora, *Peru* **92 F3** 13 30S 76 8W
Tambohorano, *Madag.* **57 B7** 17 30S 43 58 E
Tambora, *Indonesia* **36 F5** 8 12S 118 5 E
Tambov, *Russia* **24 D7** 52 45N 41 28 E
Tambuku, *Indonesia* **37 G15** 7 8S 113 40 E
Tamburâ, *Sudan* **51 G10** 5 40N 27 25 E
Tâmchekket, *Mauritania* **50 E2** 17 25N 10 40W
Tamega →, *Portugal* **19 B1** 41 5N 8 21W
Tamenglong, *India* **41 G18** 25 0N 93 35 E
Tamgak, Mts., *Niger* **50 E6** 19 12N 8 35 E
Tamiahua, L. de, *Mexico* **87 C5** 21 30N 97 30W
Tamil Nadu □, *India* **40 P10** 11 0N 77 0 E
Tamluk, *India* **43 H12** 22 18N 87 58 E
Tammerfors = Tampere, *Finland* **9 F17** 61 30N 23 50 E
Tammisaari, *Finland* **9 F17** 60 0N 23 26 E
Tamo Abu, Pegunungan, *Malaysia* **36 D5** 3 10N 115 5 E
Tampa, *U.S.A.* **77 M4** 27 57N 82 27W
Tampa B., *U.S.A.* **77 M4** 27 50N 82 30W
Tampere, *Finland* **9 F17** 61 30N 23 50 E
Tampico, *Mexico* **87 C5** 22 20N 97 50W
Tampin, *Malaysia* **39 L4** 2 28N 102 13 E
Tamrida = Qādib, *Yemen* **46 E5** 12 37N 53 57 E
Tamu, *Burma* **41 G19** 24 13N 94 12 E
Tamworth, *Australia* **63 E5** 31 7S 150 58 E
Tamworth, *U.K.* **11 E6** 52 38N 1 41W
Tamyang, *S. Korea* **35 G14** 35 19N 126 59 E
Tan An, *Vietnam* **39 G6** 10 32N 106 25 E
Tana, *Norway* **8 A20** 70 26N 28 14 E
Tana →, *Kenya* **54 C5** 2 32S 40 31 E
Tana →, *Norway* **8 A20** 70 30N 28 23 E
Tana, L., *Ethiopia* **51 F12** 13 5N 37 30 E
Tana River, *Kenya* **54 C4** 2 0S 39 30 E
Tanabe, *Japan* **31 H7** 33 44N 135 22 E
Tanafjorden, *Norway* **8 A20** 70 45N 28 25 E
Tanaga, Pta., *Canary Is.* **22 G1** 27 42N 18 10W
Tanahbala, *Indonesia* **36 E1** 0 30S 98 30 E
Tanahgrogot, *Indonesia* **36 E5** 1 55S 116 15 E
Tanahjampea, *Indonesia* **37 F6** 7 10S 120 35 E
Tanahmasa, *Indonesia* **36 E1** 0 12S 98 39 E
Tanahmerah, *Indonesia* **37 F10** 6 5S 140 16 E
Tanakura, *Japan* **31 F10** 37 10N 140 20 E
Tanami, *Australia* **60 C4** 19 59S 129 43 E
Tanami Desert, *Australia* **60 C5** 18 50S 132 0 E
Tanana, *U.S.A.* **68 B4** 65 10N 152 4W
Tanana →, *U.S.A.* **68 B4** 65 10N 151 58W
Tananarive = Antananarivo, *Madag.* **57 B8** 18 55S 47 31 E
Tánaro →, *Italy* **20 B3** 45 1N 8 47 E
Tanbar, *Australia* **62 D3** 25 51S 141 55 E
Tancheng, *China* **35 G10** 34 25N 118 20 E
Tanchŏn, *N. Korea* **35 D15** 40 27N 128 54 E
Tanda, *Ut. P., India* **43 F10** 26 33N 82 35 E
Tanda, *Ut. P., India* **43 E8** 28 57N 78 56 E
Tandag, *Phil.* **37 C7** 9 4N 126 9 E
Tandaia, *Tanzania* **55 D3** 9 25S 34 15 E
Tandaué, *Angola* **56 B2** 16 58S 18 5 E
Tandil, *Argentina* **94 D4** 37 15S 59 6W
Tandil, Sa. del, *Argentina* **94 D4** 37 30S 59 0W
Tandlianwala, *Pakistan* **42 D5** 31 3N 73 9 E
Tando Adam, *Pakistan* **42 G3** 25 45N 68 40 E
Tandou L., *Australia* **63 E3** 32 40S 142 5 E
Tane-ga-Shima, *Japan* **31 J5** 30 30N 131 0 E
Taneatua, *N.Z.* **59 H6** 38 4S 177 1 E
Tanen Tong Dan, *Burma* **38 D2** 16 30N 98 30 E
Tanezrouft, *Algeria* **50 D5** 23 9N 0 11 E
Tang, Koh, *Cambodia* **39 G4** 10 16N 103 7 E
Tang Krasang, *Cambodia* **38 F5** 12 34N 105 3 E
Tanga, *Tanzania* **54 D4** 5 5S 39 2 E
Tanga □, *Tanzania* **54 D4** 5 20S 38 0 E
Tanganyika, L., *Africa* **54 D2** 6 40S 30 0 E
Tanger, *Morocco* **50 A3** 35 50N 5 49W
Tangerang, *Indonesia* **37 G12** 6 11S 106 37 E
Tanggu, *China* **35 E9** 39 2N 117 40 E
Tanggula Shan, *China* **32 C4** 32 40N 92 10 E
Tanghe, *China* **34 H7** 32 47N 112 50 E
Tangier = Tanger, *Morocco* **50 A3** 35 50N 5 49W
Tangorin P.O., *Australia* **62 C3** 21 47S 144 12 E
Tangshan, *China* **35 E10** 39 38N 118 10 E
Tangtou, *China* **35 G10** 35 28N 118 30 E
Tanimbar, Kepulauan, *Indonesia* **37 F8** 7 30S 131 30 E
Tanimbar Is. = Tanimbar, Kepulauan, *Indonesia* **37 F8** 7 30S 131 30 E
Tanjay, *Phil.* **37 C6** 9 30N 123 5 E
Tanjong Malim, *Malaysia* **39 L3** 3 42N 101 31 E
Tanjore = Thanjavur, *India* **40 P11** 10 48N 79 12 E
Tanjung, *Indonesia* **36 E5** 2 10S 115 25 E
Tanjungbalai, *Indonesia* **36 D1** 2 55N 99 44 E
Tanjungbatu, *Indonesia* **36 D5** 2 23N 118 3 E
Tanjungkarang Telukbetung, *Indonesia* **36 F3** 5 20S 105 10 E
Tanjungpandan, *Indonesia* **36 E3** 2 43S 107 38 E
Tanjungpinang, *Indonesia* **36 D2** 1 5N 104 30 E
Tanjungpriok, *Indonesia* **37 G12** 6 8S 106 55 E
Tanjungredeb, *Indonesia* **36 D5** 2 9N 117 29 E
Tanjungselor, *Indonesia* **36 D5** 2 55N 117 25 E
Tank, *Pakistan* **42 C4** 32 14N 70 25 E
Tannu-Ola, *Russia* **27 D10** 51 0N 94 0 E
Tanout, *Niger* **50 F6** 14 50N 8 55 E
Tanta, *Egypt* **51 B11** 30 45N 30 57 E
Tantoyuca, *Mexico* **87 C5** 21 21N 98 10W
Tantung = Dandong, *China* **35 D13** 40 10N 124 20 E
Tanunda, *Australia* **63 E2** 34 30S 139 0 E
Tanzania ■, *Africa* **54 D3** 6 0S 34 0 E
Tanzilla →, *Canada* **72 B2** 58 8N 130 43W
Tao Ko, *Thailand* **39 G2** 10 5N 99 52 E
Tao'an, *China* **35 B12** 45 22N 122 40 E
Tao'er He →, *China* **35 B13** 45 45N 124 5 E
Taolanaro, *Madag.* **57 D8** 25 2S 47 0 E
Taole, *China* **34 E4** 38 48N 106 40 E
Taos, *U.S.A.* **83 H11** 36 24N 105 35W
Taoudenni, *Mali* **50 D4** 22 40N 3 55W
Taourirt, *Morocco* **50 B4** 34 25N 2 53W
Tapa Shan = Daba Shan, *China* **33 C5** 32 0N 109 0 E
Tapachula, *Mexico* **87 E6** 14 54N 92 17W
Tapah, *Malaysia* **39 K3** 4 12N 101 15 E
Tapajós →, *Brazil* **93 D8** 2 24S 54 41W
Tapaktuan, *Indonesia* **36 D1** 3 15N 97 10 E
Tapanui, *N.Z.* **59 L2** 45 56S 169 18 E
Tapauá →, *Brazil* **92 E6** 5 40S 64 21W
Tapeta, *Liberia* **50 G3** 6 29N 8 52W
Taphan Hin, *Thailand* **38 D3** 16 13N 100 26 E
Tapi →, *India* **40 J8** 21 8N 72 41 E
Tapirapecó, Serra, *Venezuela* **92 C6** 1 10N 65 0W
Tappahannock, *U.S.A.* **76 G7** 37 56N 76 52W
Tapuaenuku, Mt., *N.Z.* **59 J4** 42 0S 173 39 E
Tapul Group, *Phil.* **37 C6** 5 35N 120 50 E
Taqīābād, *Iran* **45 C8** 35 33N 59 11 E
Ṭaqṭaq, *Iraq* **44 C5** 35 53N 44 35 E
Taquara, *Brazil* **95 B5** 29 36S 50 46W
Taquari →, *Brazil* **92 G7** 19 15S 57 17W
Tara, *Australia* **63 D5** 27 17S 150 31 E
Tara, *Canada* **78 B3** 44 28N 81 9W
Tara, *Russia* **26 D8** 56 55N 74 24 E
Tara, *Zambia* **55 F2** 16 58S 26 45 E
Tara →, *Montenegro, Yug.* **21 C8** 43 21N 18 51 E
Tara →, *Russia* **26 D8** 56 42N 74 36 E
Tarabagatay, Khrebet, *Kazakhstan* **26 E9** 48 0N 83 0 E
Tarābulus, *Lebanon* **47 A4** 34 31N 35 50 E
Tarābulus, *Libya* **51 B7** 32 49N 13 7 E
Tarajalejo, *Canary Is.* **22 F5** 28 12N 14 7W
Tarakan, *Indonesia* **36 D5** 3 20N 117 35 E
Tarakit, Mt., *Kenya* **54 B4** 2 2N 35 10 E
Taralga, *Australia* **63 E4** 34 26S 149 52 E
Tarama-Jima, *Japan* **31 M2** 24 39N 124 42 E
Taranagar, *India* **42 E6** 28 43N 74 50 E
Taranaki □, *N.Z.* **59 H5** 39 25S 174 30 E
Taranga, *India* **42 H5** 23 56N 72 43 E
Taranga Hill, *India* **42 H5** 24 0N 72 40 E
Táranto, *Italy* **20 D7** 40 30N 17 11 E
Táranto, G. di, *Italy* **20 D7** 40 0N 17 15 E
Tarapacá, *Colombia* **92 D5** 2 56S 69 46W
Tarapacá □, *Chile* **94 A2** 20 45S 69 30W
Tararua Ra., *N.Z.* **59 J5** 40 45S 175 25 E
Tarauacá, *Brazil* **92 E4** 8 6S 70 48W
Tarauacá →, *Brazil* **92 E5** 6 42S 69 48W
Tarawera, *N.Z.* **59 H6** 39 2S 176 36 E
Tarawera L., *N.Z.* **59 H6** 38 13S 176 27 E
Tarbat Ness, *U.K.* **12 D5** 57 52N 3 48W
Tarbela Dam, *Pakistan* **42 B5** 34 8N 72 52 E
Tarbert, *Strath., U.K.* **12 F3** 55 55N 5 25W
Tarbert, *W. Isles, U.K.* **12 D2** 57 54N 6 49W
Tarbes, *France* **18 E4** 43 15N 0 3 E
Tarboro, *U.S.A.* **77 H7** 35 54N 77 32W
Tarbrax, *Australia* **62 C3** 21 7S 142 26 E
Tarcoola, *Australia* **63 E1** 30 44S 134 36 E
Tarcoon, *Australia* **63 E4** 30 15S 146 43 E
Taree, *Australia* **63 E5** 31 50S 152 30 E
Tarentaise, *France* **18 D7** 45 30N 6 35 E
Tarfaya, *Morocco* **50 C2** 27 55N 12 55W
Tarifa, *Spain* **19 D3** 36 1N 5 36W

Thelon

Victoria I.

Ust-Kamenogorsk, *Kazakhstan* **26 E9** 50 0N 82 36 E
Ust-Karenga, *Russia* **27 D12** 54 25N 116 30 E
Ust Khayryuzova, *Russia* **27 D16** 57 15N 156 45 E
Ust-Kut, *Russia* **27 D11** 56 50N 105 42 E
Ust Kuyga, *Russia* **27 B14** 70 1N 135 43 E
Ust Maya, *Russia* **27 C14** 60 30N 134 28 E
Ust-Mil, *Russia* **27 D14** 59 40N 133 11 E
Ust-Nera, *Russia* **27 C15** 64 35N 143 15 E
Ust-Nyukzha, *Russia* **27 D13** 56 34N 121 37 E
Ust Olenek, *Russia* **27 B12** 73 0N 120 5 E
Ust-Omchug, *Russia* **27 C15** 61 9N 149 38 E
Ust Port, *Russia* **26 C9** 69 40N 84 26 E
Ust Tsilma, *Russia* **24 A9** 65 25N 52 0 E
Ust-Tungir, *Russia* **27 D13** 55 25N 120 36 E
Ust Urt = Ustyurt, Plato, *Kazakhstan* **26 E6** 44 0N 55 0 E
Ust Usa, *Russia* **24 A10** 66 0N 56 30 E
Ust Vorkuta, *Russia* **26 C7** 67 24N 64 0 E
Ústí nad Labem, *Czech.* **16 C7** 50 41N 14 3 E
Ustica, *Italy* **20 E5** 38 42N 13 10 E
Ustinov = Izhevsk, *Russia* **24 C9** 56 51N 53 14 E
Ustye, *Russia* **27 D10** 57 46N 94 37 E
Ustyurt, Plato, *Kazakhstan* **26 E6** 44 0N 55 0 E
Usu, *China* **32 B3** 44 27N 84 40 E
Usuki, *Japan* **31 H5** 33 8N 131 49 E
Usulután, *El Salv.* **88 D2** 13 25N 88 28W
Usumacinta →, *Mexico* **87 D6** 17 0N 91 0W
Usumbura = Bujumbura, *Burundi* **54 C2** 3 16S 29 18 E
Usure, *Tanzania* **54 C3** 4 40S 34 22 E
Uta, *Indonesia* **37 E9** 4 33S 136 0 E
Utah □, *U.S.A.* **82 G8** 39 20N 111 30W
Utah, L., *U.S.A.* **82 F8** 40 10N 111 58W
Ute Creek →, *U.S.A.* **81 H3** 35 21N 103 50W
Utete, *Tanzania* **54 D4** 8 0S 38 45 E
Uthai Thani, *Thailand* **38 E3** 15 22N 100 3 E
Uthal, *Pakistan* **42 G2** 25 44N 66 40 E
Utiariti, *Brazil* **92 F7** 13 0S 58 10W
Utica, *N.Y., U.S.A.* **79 C9** 43 6N 75 14W
Utica, *Ohio, U.S.A.* **78 F2** 40 14N 82 27W
Utik L., *Canada* **73 B9** 55 15N 96 0W
Utikuma L., *Canada* **72 B5** 55 50N 115 30W
Utrecht, *Neths.* **15 B5** 52 5N 5 8 E
Utrecht, *S. Africa* **57 D5** 27 38S 30 20 E
Utrecht □, *Neths.* **15 B5** 52 6N 5 7 E
Utrera, *Spain* **19 D3** 37 12N 5 48W
Utsjoki, *Finland* **8 B19** 69 51N 26 59 E
Utsunomiya, *Japan* **31 F9** 36 30N 139 50 E
Uttar Pradesh □, *India* **43 F9** 27 0N 80 0 E
Uttaradit, *Thailand* **38 D3** 17 36N 100 5 E
Uttoxeter, *U.K.* **10 E6** 52 53N 1 50W
Uudenmaan lääni □, *Finland* **9 F18** 60 25N 25 0 E
Uusikaarlepyy, *Finland* **8 E17** 63 32N 22 31 E
Uusikaupunki, *Finland* **9 F16** 60 47N 21 25 E
Uva, *Russia* **24 C9** 56 59N 52 13 E
Uvalde, *U.S.A.* **81 L5** 29 13N 99 47W
Uvat, *Russia* **26 D7** 59 5N 68 50 E
Uvinza, *Tanzania* **54 D3** 5 5S 30 24 E
Uvira, *Zaïre* **54 C2** 3 22S 29 3 E
Uvs Nuur, *Mongolia* **32 A4** 50 20N 92 30 E
Uwajima, *Japan* **31 H6** 33 10N 132 35 E
Uxbridge, *Canada* **78 B5** 44 6N 79 7W
Uxin Qi, *China* **34 E5** 38 50N 109 5 E
Uxmal, *Mexico* **87 C7** 20 22N 89 46W
Uyandi, *Russia* **27 C15** 69 19N 141 0 E
Uyuni, *Bolivia* **92 H5** 20 28S 66 47W
Uzbekistan ■, *Asia* **26 E7** 41 30N 65 0 E
Uzen, *Kazakhstan* **25 F9** 43 27N 53 10 E
Uzerche, *France* **18 D4** 45 25N 1 34 E

V

Vaal →, *S. Africa* **56 D3** 29 4S 23 38 E
Vaal Dam, *S. Africa* **57 D4** 27 0S 28 14 E
Vaalwater, *S. Africa* **57 C4** 24 15S 28 8 E
Vaasa, *Finland* **8 E16** 63 6N 21 38 E
Vaasan lääni □, *Finland* **8 E17** 63 2N 22 50 E
Vác, *Hungary* **17 E9** 47 49N 19 10 E
Vacaria, *Brazil* **95 B5** 28 31S 50 52W
Vacaville, *U.S.A.* **84 G5** 38 21N 121 59W
Vach →, *Russia* **26 C8** 60 45N 76 45 E
Vache, I.-à-, *Haiti* **89 C5** 18 2N 73 35W
Vadnagar, *India* **42 H5** 23 47N 72 40 E
Vadodara, *India* **42 H5** 22 20N 73 10 E
Vadsø, *Norway* **8 A20** 70 3N 29 50 E
Værøy, *Norway* **8 C12** 67 40N 12 40 E
Váh →, *Slovakia* **17 E9** 47 43N 18 7 E
Vahsel B., *Antarctica* **5 D1** 75 0S 35 0W
Vaï, *Greece* **23 D8** 35 15N 26 18 E
Vaigach, *Russia* **26 B6** 70 10N 59 0 E
Val-de-Marne □, *France* **18 B5** 48 45N 2 28 E
Val-d'Oise □, *France* **18 B5** 49 5N 2 10 E
Val d'Or, *Canada* **70 C4** 48 7N 77 47W
Val Marie, *Canada* **73 D7** 49 15N 107 45W
Valahia, *Romania* **21 B11** 44 35N 25 0 E
Valcheta, *Argentina* **96 E3** 40 40S 66 8W
Valdayskaya Vozvyshennost, *Russia* **24 C5** 57 0N 33 30 E
Valdepeñas, *Spain* **19 C4** 38 43N 3 25W
Valdés, Pen., *Argentina* **96 E4** 42 30S 63 45W
Valdez, *U.S.A.* **68 B5** 61 7N 146 16W
Valdivia, *Chile* **96 D2** 39 50S 73 14W
Valdosta, *U.S.A.* **77 K4** 30 50N 83 17W
Vale, *U.S.A.* **82 E5** 43 59N 117 15W
Valença, *Brazil* **93 F11** 13 20S 39 5W
Valença do Piauí, *Brazil* **93 E10** 6 20S 41 45W
Valence, *France* **18 D6** 44 57N 4 54 E
Valencia, *Spain* **19 C5** 39 27N 0 23W
Valencia, *Venezuela* **92 A5** 10 11N 68 0W
Valencia □, *Spain* **19 C5** 39 20N 0 40W
Valencia, Albufera de, *Spain* **19 C5** 39 20N 0 27W
Valencia, G. de, *Spain* **19 C6** 39 30N 0 20 E
Valencia de Alcántara, *Spain* **19 C2** 39 25N 7 14W
Valenciennes, *France* **18 A5** 50 20N 3 34 E
Valentia Harbour, *Ireland* **13 E1** 51 56N 10 17W
Valentia I., *Ireland* **13 E1** 51 54N 10 22W
Valentim, Sa. do, *Brazil* **93 E10** 6 0S 43 30W
Valentin, *Russia* **30 C7** 43 8N 134 17 E
Valentine, *Nebr., U.S.A.* **80 D4** 42 52N 100 33W
Valentine, *Tex., U.S.A.* **81 K2** 30 35N 104 30W
Valera, *Venezuela* **92 B4** 9 19N 70 37W
Valier, *U.S.A.* **82 B7** 48 18N 112 16W
Valjevo, *Serbia, Yug.* **21 B8** 44 18N 19 53 E
Valkeakoski, *Finland* **9 F18** 61 16N 24 2 E
Valkenswaard, *Neths.* **15 C5** 51 21N 5 29 E
Valladolid, *Mexico* **87 C7** 20 40N 88 11W
Valladolid, *Spain* **19 B3** 41 38N 4 43W
Valldemosa, *Spain* **22 B9** 39 43N 2 37 E
Valle d'Aosta □, *Italy* **20 B2** 45 45N 7 22 E
Valle de la Pascua, *Venezuela* **92 B5** 9 13N 66 0W
Valle de las Palmas, *Mexico* **85 N10** 32 20N 116 43W
Valle de Santiago, *Mexico* **86 C4** 20 25N 101 15W
Valle de Suchil, *Mexico* **86 C4** 23 38N 103 55W
Valle de Zaragoza, *Mexico* **86 B3** 27 28N 105 49W
Valle Fértil, Sierra del, *Argentina* **94 C2** 30 20S 68 0W
Valle Hermoso, *Mexico* **87 B5** 25 35N 97 40W
Vallecas, *Spain* **19 B4** 40 23N 3 41W
Valledupar, *Colombia* **92 A4** 10 29N 73 15W
Vallehermoso, *Canary Is.* **22 F2** 28 10N 17 15W
Vallejo, *U.S.A.* **84 G4** 38 7N 122 14W
Vallenar, *Chile* **94 B1** 28 30S 70 50W
Valletta, *Malta* **23 D2** 35 54N 14 31 E
Valley Center, *U.S.A.* **85 M9** 33 13N 117 2W
Valley City, *U.S.A.* **80 B6** 46 55N 98 0W
Valley Falls, *U.S.A.* **82 E3** 42 29N 120 17W
Valley Springs, *U.S.A.* **84 G6** 38 12N 120 50W
Valley Wells, *U.S.A.* **85 K11** 35 27N 115 46W
Valleyview, *Canada* **72 B5** 55 5N 117 17W
Vallimanca, Arroyo, *Argentina* **94 D4** 35 40S 59 10W
Valls, *Spain* **19 B6** 41 18N 1 15 E
Valognes, *France* **18 B3** 49 30N 1 28W
Valona = Vlóra, *Albania* **21 D8** 40 32N 19 28 E
Valparaíso, *Chile* **94 C1** 33 2S 71 40W
Valparaíso, *Mexico* **86 C4** 22 50N 103 32W
Valparaiso, *U.S.A.* **76 E2** 41 28N 87 4W
Valparaíso □, *Chile* **94 C1** 33 2S 71 40W
Vals →, *S. Africa* **56 D4** 27 23S 26 30 E
Vals, Tanjung, *Indonesia* **37 F9** 8 26S 137 25 E
Valsad, *India* **40 J8** 20 40N 72 58 E
Valverde, *Canary Is.* **22 G2** 27 48N 17 55W
Valverde del Camino, *Spain* **19 D2** 37 35N 6 47W
Vámos, *Greece* **23 D6** 35 24N 24 13 E
Van, *Turkey* **25 G7** 38 30N 43 20 E
Van, L. = Van Gölü, *Turkey* **25 G7** 38 30N 43 0 E
Van Alstyne, *U.S.A.* **81 J6** 33 25N 96 35W
Van Bruyssel, *Canada* **71 C5** 47 56N 72 9W
Van Buren, *Canada* **71 C6** 47 10N 67 55W
Van Buren, *Ark., U.S.A.* **81 H7** 35 26N 94 21W
Van Buren, *Maine, U.S.A.* **77 B11** 47 10N 67 58W
Van Buren, *Mo., U.S.A.* **81 G9** 37 0N 91 1W
Van Canh, *Vietnam* **38 F7** 13 37N 109 0 E
Van Diemen, C., *N. Terr., Australia* **60 B5** 11 9S 130 24 E
Van Diemen, C., *Queens., Australia* **62 B2** 16 30S 139 46 E
Van Diemen G., *Australia* **60 B5** 11 45S 132 0 E
Van Gölü, *Turkey* **25 G7** 38 30N 43 0 E
Van Horn, *U.S.A.* **81 K2** 31 3N 104 50W
Van Ninh, *Vietnam* **38 F7** 12 42N 109 14 E
Van Reenen P., *S. Africa* **57 D4** 28 22S 29 27 E
Van Rees, Pegunungan, *Indonesia* **37 E9** 2 35S 138 15 E
Van Tassell, *U.S.A.* **80 D2** 42 40N 104 5W
Van Wert, *U.S.A.* **76 E3** 40 52N 84 35W
Van Yen, *Vietnam* **38 B5** 21 4N 104 42 E
Vanavara, *Russia* **27 C11** 60 22N 102 16 E
Vancouver, *Canada* **72 D4** 49 15N 123 10W
Vancouver, *U.S.A.* **84 E4** 45 38N 122 40W
Vancouver, C., *Australia* **61 G2** 35 2S 118 11 E
Vancouver I., *Canada* **72 D3** 49 50N 126 0W
Vandalia, *Ill., U.S.A.* **80 F10** 38 58N 89 6W
Vandalia, *Mo., U.S.A.* **80 F9** 39 19N 91 29W
Vandenburg, *U.S.A.* **85 L6** 34 35N 120 33W
Vanderbijlpark, *S. Africa* **57 D4** 26 42S 27 54 E
Vandergrift, *U.S.A.* **78 F5** 40 36N 79 34W
Vanderhoof, *Canada* **72 C4** 54 0N 124 0W
Vanderlin I., *Australia* **62 B2** 15 44S 137 2 E
Vandyke, *Australia* **62 C4** 24 10S 147 51 E
Vänern, *Sweden* **9 G12** 58 47N 13 30 E
Vänersborg, *Sweden* **9 G12** 58 26N 12 19 E
Vang Vieng, *Laos* **38 C4** 18 58N 102 32 E
Vanga, *Kenya* **54 C4** 4 35S 39 12 E
Vangaindrano, *Madag.* **57 C8** 23 21S 47 36 E
Vanguard, *Canada* **73 D7** 49 55N 107 20W
Vanier, *Canada* **70 C4** 45 27N 75 40W
Vankarem, *Russia* **27 C18** 67 51N 175 50W
Vankleek Hill, *Canada* **70 C5** 45 32N 74 40W
Vanna, *Norway* **8 A15** 70 6N 19 50 E
Vännäs, *Sweden* **8 E15** 63 58N 19 48 E
Vannes, *France* **18 C2** 47 40N 2 47W
Vanrhynsdorp, *S. Africa* **56 E2** 31 36S 18 44 E
Vanrook, *Australia* **62 B3** 16 57S 141 57 E
Vansbro, *Sweden* **9 F13** 60 32N 14 15 E
Vansittart B., *Australia* **60 B4** 14 3S 126 17 E
Vanthli, *India* **42 J4** 21 28N 70 25 E
Vanua Levu, *Fiji* **59 C8** 16 33S 179 15 E
Vanua Mbalavu, *Fiji* **59 C9** 17 40S 178 57W
Vanuatu ■, *Pac. Oc.* **64 J8** 15 0S 168 0 E
Vanwyksvlei, *S. Africa* **56 E3** 30 18S 21 49 E
Vanzylsrus, *S. Africa* **56 D3** 26 52S 22 4 E
Var □, *France* **18 E7** 43 27N 6 18 E
Varanasi, *India* **43 G10** 25 22N 83 0 E
Varangerfjorden, *Norway* **8 A20** 70 3N 29 25 E
Varaždin, *Croatia* **20 A7** 46 20N 16 20 E
Varberg, *Sweden* **9 H12** 57 6N 12 20 E
Vardar →, *Macedonia* **21 D10** 41 15N 22 33 E
Varella, Mui, *Vietnam* **38 F7** 12 54N 109 26 E
Varese, *Italy* **20 B3** 45 49N 8 50 E
Varginha, *Brazil* **95 A6** 21 33S 45 25W
Variadero, *U.S.A.* **81 H2** 35 43N 104 17W
Varillas, *Chile* **94 A1** 24 0S 70 10W
Värmlands län □, *Sweden* **9 G12** 60 0N 13 20 E
Varna, *Bulgaria* **21 C12** 43 13N 27 56 E
Värnamo, *Sweden* **9 H13** 57 10N 14 3 E
Vars, *Canada* **79 A9** 45 21N 75 21W
Varzaneh, *Iran* **45 C7** 32 25N 52 40 E
Vasa, *Finland* **8 E16** 63 6N 21 38 E
Vasa Barris →, *Brazil* **93 F11** 11 10S 37 10W
Vascongadas = País Vasco □, *Spain* **19 A4** 42 50N 2 45W
Vasht = Khāsh, *Iran* **40 E2** 28 15N 61 15 E
Vaslui, *Romania* **17 E13** 46 38N 27 42 E
Vassar, *Canada* **73 D9** 49 10N 95 55W
Vassar, *U.S.A.* **76 D4** 43 22N 83 35W
Västerås, *Sweden* **9 G14** 59 37N 16 38 E
Västerbottens län □, *Sweden* **8 D14** 64 58N 18 0 E
Västernorrlands län □, *Sweden* **8 E14** 63 30N 17 30 E
Västervik, *Sweden* **9 H14** 57 43N 16 43 E
Västmanlands län □, *Sweden* **9 G14** 59 45N 16 20 E
Vasto, *Italy* **20 C6** 42 8N 14 40 E
Vatili, *Cyprus* **23 D12** 35 6N 33 40 E
Vatnajökull, *Iceland* **8 D5** 64 30N 16 48W
Vatneyri, *Iceland* **8 D2** 65 35N 24 0W
Vatoa, *Fiji* **59 D9** 19 50S 178 13W
Vatólakkos, *Greece* **23 D5** 35 27N 23 53 E
Vatoloha, *Madag.* **57 B8** 17 52S 47 48 E
Vatomandry, *Madag.* **57 B8** 19 20S 48 59 E
Vatra-Dornei, *Romania* **17 E12** 47 22N 25 22 E
Vättern, *Sweden* **9 G13** 58 25N 14 30 E
Vaucluse □, *France* **18 E6** 43 50N 5 20 E
Vaughn, *Mont., U.S.A.* **82 C8** 47 33N 111 33W
Vaughn, *N. Mex., U.S.A.* **83 J11** 34 36N 105 13W
Vaupés = Uaupés →, *Brazil* **92 C5** 0 2N 67 16W
Vauxhall, *Canada* **72 C6** 50 5N 112 9W
Vava'u, *Tonga* **59 D11** 18 36S 174 0W
Växjö, *Sweden* **9 H13** 56 52N 14 50 E
Vaygach, Ostrov, *Russia* **26 C6** 70 0N 60 0 E
Váyia, Ákra, *Greece* **23 C10** 36 15N 28 11 E
Vechte →, *Neths.* **15 B6** 52 34N 6 6 E
Vedea →, *Romania* **17 G12** 43 53N 25 59 E
Vedia, *Argentina* **94 C3** 34 30S 61 31W
Vedra, I. del, *Spain* **22 C7** 38 52N 1 12 E
Veendam, *Neths.* **15 A6** 53 5N 6 52 E
Veenendaal, *Neths.* **15 B5** 52 2N 5 34 E
Vefsna →, *Norway* **8 D12** 65 48N 13 10 E
Vega, *Norway* **8 D11** 65 40N 11 55 E
Vega, *U.S.A.* **81 H3** 35 15N 102 26W
Vegafjorden, *Norway* **8 D12** 65 37N 12 0 E
Veghel, *Neths.* **15 C5** 51 37N 5 32 E
Vegreville, *Canada* **72 C6** 53 30N 112 5W
Vejer de la Frontera, *Spain* **19 D3** 36 15N 5 59W
Vejle, *Denmark* **9 J10** 55 43N 9 30 E
Velas, C., *Costa Rica* **88 D2** 10 21N 85 52W
Velasco, Sierra de, *Argentina* **94 B2** 29 20S 67 10W
Velay, Mts. du, *France* **18 D5** 45 0N 3 40 E
Velddrif, *S. Africa* **56 E2** 32 42S 18 11 E
Velebit Planina, *Croatia* **20 B6** 44 50N 15 20 E
Vélez, *Colombia* **92 B4** 6 1N 73 41W
Vélez Málaga, *Spain* **19 D3** 36 48N 4 5W
Vélez Rubio, *Spain* **19 D4** 37 41N 2 5W
Velhas →, *Brazil* **93 G10** 17 13S 44 49W
Velikaya →, *Russia* **24 C4** 57 48N 28 10 E
Velikaya Kema, *Russia* **30 B8** 45 30N 137 12 E
Veliki Ustyug, *Russia* **24 B8** 60 47N 46 20 E
Velikiye Luki, *Russia* **24 C5** 56 25N 30 32 E
Velikonda Range, *India* **40 M11** 14 45N 79 10 E
Velletri, *Italy* **20 D5** 41 43N 12 43 E
Vellore, *India* **40 N11** 12 57N 79 10 E
Velsen-Noord, *Neths.* **15 B4** 52 27N 4 40 E
Velsk, *Russia* **24 B7** 61 10N 42 5 E
Velva, *U.S.A.* **80 A4** 48 4N 100 56W
Venado Tuerto, *Argentina* **94 C3** 33 50S 62 0W
Venda □, *S. Africa* **57 C5** 22 40S 30 35 E
Vendée □, *France* **18 C3** 46 50N 1 35W
Véneto □, *Italy* **20 B5** 45 40N 12 0 E
Venézia, *Italy* **20 B5** 45 27N 12 20 E
Venézia, G. di, *Italy* **20 B5** 45 20N 13 0 E
Venezuela ■, *S. Amer.* **92 B5** 8 0N 66 0W
Venezuela, G. de, *Venezuela* **92 A4** 11 30N 71 0W
Vengurla, *India* **40 M8** 15 53N 73 45 E
Venice = Venézia, *Italy* **20 B5** 45 27N 12 20 E
Venkatapuram, *India* **41 K12** 18 20N 80 30 E
Venlo, *Neths.* **15 C6** 51 22N 6 11 E
Venraij, *Neths.* **15 C5** 51 31N 6 0 E
Ventana, Punta de la, *Mexico* **86 C3** 24 4N 109 48W
Ventana, Sa. de la, *Argentina* **94 D3** 38 0S 62 30W
Ventersburg, *S. Africa* **56 D4** 28 7S 27 9 E
Venterstad, *S. Africa* **56 E4** 30 47S 25 48 E
Ventnor, *U.K.* **11 G6** 50 35N 1 12W
Ventspils, *Latvia* **9 H16** 57 25N 21 32 E
Ventuarí →, *Venezuela* **92 C5** 3 58N 67 2W
Ventucopa, *U.S.A.* **85 L7** 34 50N 119 29W
Ventura, *U.S.A.* **85 L7** 34 17N 119 18W
Venus B., *Australia* **63 F4** 38 40S 145 42 E
Vera, *Argentina* **94 B3** 29 30S 60 20W
Vera, *Spain* **19 D5** 37 15N 1 51W
Veracruz, *Mexico* **87 D5** 19 10N 96 10W
Veracruz □, *Mexico* **87 D5** 19 0N 96 15W
Veraval, *India* **42 J4** 20 53N 70 27 E
Vercelli, *Italy* **20 B3** 45 19N 8 25 E
Verdalsøra, *Norway* **8 E11** 63 48N 11 30 E
Verde →, *Argentina* **96 E3** 41 56S 65 5W
Verde →, *Chihuahua, Mexico* **86 B3** 26 29N 107 58W
Verde →, *Oaxaca, Mexico* **87 D5** 15 59N 97 50W
Verde →, *Veracruz, Mexico* **86 C4** 21 10N 102 50W
Verde →, *Paraguay* **94 A4** 23 9S 57 37W
Verde, Cay, *Bahamas* **88 B4** 23 0N 75 5W
Verden, *Germany* **16 B4** 52 58N 9 18 E
Verdi, *U.S.A.* **84 F7** 39 31N 119 59W
Verdigre, *U.S.A.* **80 D5** 42 36N 98 2W
Verdun, *France* **18 B6** 49 9N 5 24 E
Vereeniging, *S. Africa* **57 D4** 26 38S 27 57 E
Vérendrye, Parc Prov. de la, *Canada* **70 C4** 47 20N 76 40W
Verga, C., *Guinea* **50 F2** 10 30N 14 10W
Vergemont, *Australia* **62 C3** 23 33S 143 1 E
Vergemont Cr. →, *Australia* **62 C3** 24 16S 143 16 E
Vergennes, *U.S.A.* **79 B11** 44 10N 73 15W
Verkhnevilyuysk, *Russia* **27 C13** 63 27N 120 18 E
Verkhneye Kalinino, *Russia* **27 D11** 59 54N 108 8 E
Verkhniy Baskunchak, *Russia* **25 E8** 48 14N 46 44 E
Verkhoyansk, *Russia* **27 C14** 67 35N 133 25 E
Verkhoyansk Ra. = Verkhoyanskiy Khrebet, *Russia* **27 C13** 66 0N 129 0 E
Verkhoyanskiy Khrebet, *Russia* **27 C13** 66 0N 129 0 E
Verlo, *Canada* **73 C7** 50 19N 108 35W
Vermilion, *Canada* **73 C6** 53 20N 110 50W
Vermilion →, *Alta., Canada* **73 C6** 53 22N 110 51W
Vermilion →, *Qué., Canada* **70 C5** 47 38N 72 56W
Vermilion, B., *U.S.A.* **81 L9** 29 45N 91 55W
Vermilion Bay, *Canada* **73 D10** 49 51N 93 34W
Vermilion Chutes, *Canada* **72 B6** 58 22N 114 51W
Vermilion L., *U.S.A.* **80 B8** 47 53N 92 26W
Vermillion, *U.S.A.* **80 D6** 42 47N 96 56W
Vermont □, *U.S.A.* **79 C12** 44 0N 73 0W
Vernal, *U.S.A.* **82 F9** 40 27N 109 32W
Vernalis, *U.S.A.* **84 H5** 37 36N 121 17W
Verner, *Canada* **70 C3** 46 25N 80 8W
Verneukpan, *S. Africa* **56 D3** 30 0S 21 0 E
Vernon, *Canada* **72 C5** 50 20N 119 15W
Vernon, *U.S.A.* **81 H5** 34 9N 99 17W
Vernonia, *U.S.A.* **84 E3** 45 52N 123 11W
Vero Beach, *U.S.A.* **77 M5** 27 38N 80 24W
Véroia, *Greece* **21 D10** 40 34N 22 12 E
Verona, *Italy* **20 B4** 45 27N 11 0 E
Veropol, *Russia* **27 C17** 65 15N 168 40 E
Versailles, *France* **18 B5** 48 48N 2 8 E
Vert, C., *Senegal* **50 F1** 14 45N 17 30W
Verulam, *S. Africa* **57 D5** 29 38S 31 2 E
Verviers, *Belgium* **15 D5** 50 37N 5 52 E
Veselovskoye Vdkhr., *Russia* **25 E7** 47 0N 41 0 E
Vesoul, *France* **18 C7** 47 40N 6 11 E
Vest-Agder fylke □, *Norway* **9 G9** 58 30N 7 15 E
Vesterålen, *Norway* **8 B13** 68 45N 15 0 E
Vestfjorden, *Norway* **8 C13** 67 55N 14 0 E
Vestfold fylke □, *Norway* **9 G11** 59 15N 10 0 E
Vestmannaeyjar, *Iceland* **8 E3** 63 27N 20 15W
Vestspitsbergen, *Svalbard* **4 B8** 78 40N 17 0 E
Vestvågøy, *Norway* **8 B12** 68 18N 13 50 E
Vesuvio, *Italy* **20 D6** 40 50N 14 22 E
Vesuvius, Mt. = Vesuvio, *Italy* **20 D6** 40 50N 14 22 E
Veszprém, *Hungary* **17 E8** 47 8N 17 57 E
Vetlanda, *Sweden* **9 H13** 57 24N 15 3 E
Vetlugu →, *Russia* **26 D5** 56 18N 46 24 E
Veurne, *Belgium* **15 C2** 51 5N 2 40 E
Veys, *Iran* **45 D6** 31 30N 49 0 E
Vezhen, *Bulgaria* **21 C11** 42 50N 24 20 E
Vi Thanh, *Vietnam* **39 H5** 9 42N 105 26 E
Viacha, *Bolivia* **92 G5** 16 39S 68 18W
Viamão, *Brazil* **95 C5** 30 5S 51 0W
Viana, *Brazil* **93 D10** 3 13S 44 55W
Viana, *Portugal* **19 C2** 38 20N 8 0W
Viana do Castelo, *Portugal* **19 B1** 41 42N 8 50W
Vianópolis, *Brazil* **93 G9** 16 40S 48 35W
Vibank, *Canada* **73 C8** 50 20N 103 56W
Viborg, *Denmark* **9 H10** 56 27N 9 23 E
Vicenza, *Italy* **20 B4** 45 32N 11 31 E
Vich, *Spain* **19 B7** 41 58N 2 19 E
Vichy, *France* **18 C5** 46 9N 3 26 E
Vicksburg, *Ariz., U.S.A.* **85 M13** 33 45N 113 45W
Vicksburg, *Mich., U.S.A.* **76 D3** 42 7N 85 32W
Vicksburg, *Miss., U.S.A.* **81 J9** 32 21N 90 53W
Viçosa, *Brazil* **93 E11** 9 28S 36 14W
Victor, *India* **42 J4** 21 0N 71 30 E
Victor, *Colo., U.S.A.* **80 F2** 38 43N 105 9W
Victor, *N.Y., U.S.A.* **78 D7** 42 58N 77 24W
Victor Harbor, *Australia* **63 F2** 35 30S 138 37 E
Victoria, *Argentina* **94 C3** 32 40S 60 10W
Victoria, *Canada* **72 D4** 48 30N 123 25W
Victoria, *Chile* **96 D2** 38 13S 72 20W
Victoria, *Guinea* **50 F2** 10 50N 14 32W
Victoria, *Malaysia* **36 C5** 5 20N 115 14 E
Victoria, *Malta* **23 C1** 36 2N 14 14 E
Victoria, *Kans., U.S.A.* **80 F5** 38 52N 99 9W
Victoria, *Tex., U.S.A.* **81 L6** 28 48N 97 0W
Victoria □, *Australia* **63 F3** 37 0S 144 0 E
Victoria →, *Australia* **60 C4** 15 10S 129 40 E
Victoria, Grand L., *Canada* **70 C4** 47 31N 77 30W
Victoria, L., *Africa* **54 C3** 1 0S 33 0 E
Victoria, L., *Australia* **63 E3** 33 57S 141 15 E
Victoria Beach, *Canada* **73 C9** 50 40N 96 35W
Victoria de Durango, *Mexico* **86 C4** 24 3N 104 39W
Victoria de las Tunas, *Cuba* **88 B4** 20 58N 76 59W
Victoria Falls, *Zimbabwe* **55 F2** 17 58S 25 52 E
Victoria Harbour, *Canada* **70 D4** 44 45N 79 45W
Victoria I., *Canada* **68 A8** 71 0N 111 0W

Westall Pt.

Wallowa, *U.S.A.* **82 D5** 45 34N 117 32W
Wallowa Mts., *U.S.A.* **82 D5** 45 20N 117 30W
Wallsend, *Australia* **63 E5** 32 55S 151 40 E
Wallsend, *U.K.* **10 C6** 54 59N 1 30W
Wallula, *U.S.A.* **82 C4** 46 5N 118 54W
Wallumbilla, *Australia* **63 D4** 26 33S 149 9 E
Walmsley, L., *Canada* **73 A7** 63 25N 108 36W
Walney, I. of, *U.K.* **10 C4** 54 5N 3 15W
Walnut Creek, *U.S.A.* **84 H4** 37 54N 122 4W
Walnut Ridge, *U.S.A.* **81 G9** 36 4N 90 57W
Walsall, *U.K.* **11 E6** 52 36N 1 59W
Walsenburg, *U.S.A.* **81 G2** 37 38N 104 47W
Walsh, *U.S.A.* **81 G3** 37 23N 102 17W
Walsh →, *Australia* **62 B3** 16 31S 143 42 E
Walsh P.O., *Australia* **62 B3** 16 40S 144 0 E
Walterboro, *U.S.A.* **77 J5** 32 55N 80 40W
Walters, *U.S.A.* **81 H5** 34 22N 98 19W
Waltham, *U.S.A.* **79 D13** 42 23N 71 14W
Waltham Station, *Canada* **70 C4** 45 57N 76 57W
Waltman, *U.S.A.* **82 E10** 43 4N 107 12W
Walton, *U.S.A.* **79 D9** 42 10N 75 8W
Walvisbaai, *S. Africa* **56 C1** 23 0S 14 28 E
Wamba, *Kenya* **54 B4** 0 58N 37 19 E
Wamba, *Zaïre* **54 B2** 2 10N 27 57 E
Wamego, *U.S.A.* **80 F6** 39 12N 96 18W
Wamena, *Indonesia* **37 E9** 4 4S 138 57 E
Wamsasi, *Indonesia* **37 E7** 3 27S 126 7 E
Wan Xian, *China* **34 E8** 38 47N 115 7 E
Wana, *Pakistan* **42 C3** 32 20N 69 32 E
Wanaaring, *Australia* **63 D3** 29 38S 144 9 E
Wanaka, *N.Z.* **59 L2** 44 42S 169 9 E
Wanaka L., *N.Z.* **59 L2** 44 33S 169 7 E
Wanapiri, *Indonesia* **37 E9** 4 30S 135 59 E
Wanapitei L., *Canada* **70 C3** 46 45N 80 40W
Wanbi, *Australia* **63 E3** 34 46S 140 17 E
Wandarrie, *Australia* **61 E2** 27 50S 117 52 E
Wanderer, *Zimbabwe* **55 F3** 19 36S 30 1 E
Wandoan, *Australia* **63 D4** 26 5S 149 55 E
Wanfu, *China* **35 D12** 40 8N 122 38 E
Wang →, *Thailand* **38 D2** 17 8N 99 2 E
Wang Noi, *Thailand* **38 E3** 14 13N 100 44 E
Wang Saphung, *Thailand* **38 D3** 17 18N 101 46 E
Wang Thong, *Thailand* **38 D3** 16 50N 100 26 E
Wanga, *Zaïre* **54 B2** 2 58N 29 12 E
Wangal, *Indonesia* **37 F8** 6 8S 134 9 E
Wanganella, *Australia* **63 F3** 35 6S 144 49 E
Wanganui, *N.Z.* **59 H5** 39 56S 175 3 E
Wangaratta, *Australia* **63 F4** 36 21S 146 19 E
Wangary, *Australia* **63 E2** 34 35S 135 29 E
Wangdu, *China* **34 E8** 38 40N 115 7 E
Wangerooge, *Germany* **16 B3** 53 47N 7 52 E
Wangi, *Kenya* **54 C5** 1 58S 40 58 E
Wangiwangi, *Indonesia* **37 F6** 5 22S 123 37 E
Wangqing, *China* **35 C15** 43 12N 129 42 E
Wankaner, *India* **42 H4** 22 35N 71 0 E
Wanless, *Canada* **73 C8** 54 11N 101 21W
Wanon Niwat, *Thailand* **38 D4** 17 38N 103 46 E
Wanquan, *China* **34 D8** 40 50N 114 40 E
Wanrong, *China* **34 G6** 35 25N 110 50 E
Wanxian, *China* **33 C5** 30 42N 108 20 E
Wapakoneta, *U.S.A.* **76 E3** 40 34N 84 12W
Wapato, *U.S.A.* **82 C3** 46 27N 120 25W
Wapawekka L., *Canada* **73 C8** 54 55N 104 40W
Wapikopa L., *Canada* **70 B2** 52 56N 87 53W
Wappingers Falls, *U.S.A.* **79 E11** 41 36N 73 55W
Wapsipinicon →, *U.S.A.* **80 E9** 41 44N 90 19W
Warangal, *India* **40 L11** 17 58N 79 35 E
Waratah, *Australia* **62 G4** 41 30S 145 30 E
Waratah B., *Australia* **63 F4** 38 54S 146 5 E
Warburton, *Vic., Australia* **63 F4** 37 47S 145 42 E
Warburton, *W. Austral., Australia* **61 E4** 26 8S 126 35 E
Warburton Ra., *Australia* **61 E4** 25 55S 126 28 E
Ward, *N.Z.* **59 J5** 41 49S 174 11 E
Ward →, *Australia* **63 D4** 26 28S 146 6 E
Ward Cove, *U.S.A.* **72 B2** 55 25N 132 43W
Ward Mt., *U.S.A.* **84 H8** 37 12N 118 54W
Warden, *S. Africa* **57 D4** 27 50S 29 0 E
Wardha, *India* **40 J11** 20 45N 78 39 E
Wardha →, *India* **40 K11** 19 57N 79 11 E
Wardlow, *Canada* **72 C6** 50 56N 111 31W
Ware, *Canada* **72 B3** 57 26N 125 41W
Ware, *U.S.A.* **79 D12** 42 16N 72 14W
Wareham, *U.S.A.* **79 E14** 41 46N 70 43W
Warialda, *Australia* **63 D5** 29 29S 150 33 E
Wariap, *Indonesia* **37 E8** 1 30S 134 5 E
Warin Chamrap, *Thailand* **38 E5** 15 12N 104 53 E
Warkopi, *Indonesia* **37 E8** 1 12S 134 9 E
Warley, *U.K.* **11 E6** 52 30N 1 58W
Warm Springs, *U.S.A.* **83 G5** 38 10N 116 20W
Warman, *Canada* **73 C7** 52 19N 106 30W
Warmbad, *Namibia* **56 D2** 28 25S 18 42 E
Warmbad, *S. Africa* **57 C4** 24 51S 28 19 E
Warnambool Downs, *Australia* **62 C3** 22 48S 142 52 E
Warnemünde, *Germany* **16 A6** 54 9N 12 5 E
Warner, *Canada* **72 D6** 49 17N 112 12W
Warner Mts., *U.S.A.* **82 F3** 41 40N 120 15W
Warner Robins, *U.S.A.* **77 J4** 32 37N 83 36W
Waroona, *Australia* **61 F2** 32 50S 115 58 E
Warracknabeal, *Australia* **63 F3** 36 9S 142 26 E
Warragul, *Australia* **63 F4** 38 10S 145 58 E
Warrawagine, *Australia* **60 D3** 20 51S 120 42 E
Warrego →, *Australia* **63 E4** 30 24S 145 21 E
Warrego Ra., *Australia* **62 C4** 24 58S 146 0 E
Warren, *Australia* **63 E4** 31 42S 147 51 E
Warren, *Ark., U.S.A.* **81 J8** 33 37N 92 4W
Warren, *Mich., U.S.A.* **76 D4** 42 30N 83 0W
Warren, *Minn., U.S.A.* **80 A6** 48 12N 96 46W
Warren, *Ohio, U.S.A.* **78 E4** 41 14N 80 49W
Warren, *Pa., U.S.A.* **78 E5** 41 51N 79 9W
Warrenpoint, *U.K.* **13 B5** 54 7N 6 15W
Warrensburg, *U.S.A.* **80 F8** 38 46N 93 44W
Warrenton, *S. Africa* **56 D3** 28 9S 24 47 E
Warrenton, *U.S.A.* **84 D3** 46 10N 123 56W
Warrenville, *Australia* **63 D4** 25 48S 147 22 E
Warri, *Nigeria* **50 G6** 5 30N 5 41 E
Warrina, *Australia* **63 D2** 28 12S 135 50 E
Warrington, *U.K.* **10 D5** 53 25N 2 38W
Warrington, *U.S.A.* **77 K2** 30 23N 87 17W
Warrnambool, *Australia* **63 F3** 38 25S 142 30 E
Warroad, *U.S.A.* **80 A7** 48 54N 95 19W
Warsa, *Indonesia* **37 E9** 0 47S 135 55 E
Warsaw = Warszawa, *Poland* **17 B10** 52 13N 21 0 E
Warsaw, *Ind., U.S.A.* **76 E3** 41 14N 85 51W
Warsaw, *N.Y., U.S.A.* **78 D6** 42 45N 78 8W
Warsaw, *Ohio, U.S.A.* **78 F2** 40 20N 82 0W
Warszawa, *Poland* **17 B10** 52 13N 21 0 E
Warta →, *Poland* **16 B7** 52 35N 14 39 E
Warthe = Warta →, *Poland* **16 B7** 52 35N 14 39 E
Waru, *Indonesia* **37 E8** 3 30S 130 36 E
Warwick, *Australia* **63 D5** 28 10S 152 1 E
Warwick, *U.K.* **11 E6** 52 17N 1 36W
Warwick, *U.S.A.* **79 E13** 41 42N 71 28W
Warwickshire □, *U.K.* **11 E6** 52 20N 1 30W
Wasaga Beach, *Canada* **78 B4** 44 31N 80 1W
Wasatch Ra., *U.S.A.* **82 F8** 40 30N 111 15W
Wasbank, *S. Africa* **57 D5** 28 15S 30 9 E
Wasco, *Calif., U.S.A.* **85 K7** 35 36N 119 20W
Wasco, *Oreg., U.S.A.* **82 D3** 45 36N 120 42W
Waseca, *U.S.A.* **80 C8** 44 5N 93 30W
Wasekamio L., *Canada* **73 B7** 56 45N 108 45W
Wash, The, *U.K.* **10 E8** 52 58N 0 20 E
Washago, *Canada* **78 B5** 44 45N 79 20W
Washburn, *N. Dak., U.S.A.* **80 B4** 47 17N 101 2W
Washburn, *Wis., U.S.A.* **80 B9** 46 40N 90 54W
Washim, *India* **40 J10** 20 3N 77 0 E
Washington, *D.C., U.S.A.* **76 F7** 38 54N 77 2W
Washington, *Ga., U.S.A.* **77 J4** 33 44N 82 44W
Washington, *Ind., U.S.A.* **76 F2** 38 40N 87 10W
Washington, *Iowa, U.S.A.* **80 E9** 41 18N 91 42W
Washington, *Mo., U.S.A.* **80 F9** 38 33N 91 1W
Washington, *N.C., U.S.A.* **77 H7** 35 33N 77 3W
Washington, *N.J., U.S.A.* **79 F10** 40 46N 74 59W
Washington, *Pa., U.S.A.* **78 F4** 40 10N 80 15W
Washington, *Utah, U.S.A.* **83 H7** 37 8N 113 31W
Washington □, *U.S.A.* **82 C3** 47 30N 120 30W
Washington Mt., *U.S.A.* **79 B13** 44 16N 71 18W
Washington I., *U.S.A.* **76 C2** 45 23N 86 54W
Washougal, *U.S.A.* **84 E4** 45 35N 122 21W
Wasian, *Indonesia* **37 E8** 1 47S 133 19 E
Wasior, *Indonesia* **37 E8** 2 43S 134 30 E
Waskaiowaka, L., *Canada* **73 B9** 56 33N 96 23W
Waskesiu Lake, *Canada* **73 C7** 53 55N 106 5W
Wassenaar, *Neths.* **15 B4** 52 8N 4 24 E
Waswanipi, *Canada* **70 C4** 49 40N 76 29W
Waswanipi, L., *Canada* **70 C4** 49 35N 76 40W
Watangpone, *Indonesia* **37 E6** 4 29S 120 25 E
Water Park Pt., *Australia* **62 C5** 22 56S 150 47 E
Water Valley, *U.S.A.* **81 H10** 34 10N 89 38W
Waterberge, *S. Africa* **57 C4** 24 10S 28 0 E
Waterbury, *Conn., U.S.A.* **79 E11** 41 33N 73 3W
Waterbury, *Vt., U.S.A.* **79 B12** 44 20N 72 46W
Waterbury L., *Canada* **73 B8** 58 10N 104 22W
Waterdown, *Canada* **78 C5** 43 20N 79 53W
Waterford, *Canada* **78 D4** 42 56N 80 17W
Waterford, *Ireland* **13 D4** 52 16N 7 8W
Waterford, *U.S.A.* **84 H6** 37 38N 120 46W
Waterford □, *Ireland* **13 D4** 52 10N 7 40W
Waterford Harbour, *Ireland* **13 D5** 52 10N 6 58W
Waterhen L., *Man., Canada* **73 C9** 52 10N 99 40W
Waterhen L., *Sask., Canada* **73 C7** 54 28N 108 25W
Waterloo, *Belgium* **15 D4** 50 43N 4 25 E
Waterloo, *Ont., Canada* **70 D3** 43 30N 80 32W
Waterloo, *Qué., Canada* **79 A12** 45 22N 72 32W
Waterloo, *S. Leone* **50 G2** 8 26N 13 8W
Waterloo, *Ill., U.S.A.* **80 F9** 38 20N 90 9W
Waterloo, *Iowa, U.S.A.* **80 D8** 42 30N 92 21W
Waterloo, *N.Y., U.S.A.* **78 D8** 42 54N 76 52W
Watersmeet, *U.S.A.* **80 B10** 46 16N 89 11W
Waterton-Glacier International Peace Park, *U.S.A.* **82 B7** 48 45N 115 0W
Watertown, *Conn., U.S.A.* **79 E11** 41 36N 73 7W
Watertown, *N.Y., U.S.A.* **79 C9** 43 59N 75 55W
Watertown, *S. Dak., U.S.A.* **80 C6** 44 54N 97 7W
Watertown, *Wis., U.S.A.* **80 D10** 43 12N 88 43W
Waterval-Boven, *S. Africa* **57 D5** 25 40S 30 18 E
Waterville, *Canada* **79 A13** 45 16N 71 54W
Waterville, *Maine, U.S.A.* **71 D6** 44 33N 69 38W
Waterville, *N.Y., U.S.A.* **79 D9** 42 56N 75 23W
Waterville, *Pa., U.S.A.* **78 E7** 41 19N 77 21W
Waterville, *Wash., U.S.A.* **82 C3** 47 39N 120 4W
Watervliet, *U.S.A.* **79 D11** 42 44N 73 42W
Wates, *Indonesia* **37 G14** 7 51S 110 10 E
Watford, *Canada* **78 D3** 42 57N 81 53W
Watford, *U.K.* **11 F7** 51 38N 0 23W
Watford City, *U.S.A.* **80 B3** 47 48N 103 17W
Wathaman →, *Canada* **73 B8** 57 16N 102 59W
Watheroo, *Australia* **61 F2** 30 15S 116 0 E
Wating, *China* **34 G4** 35 40N 106 38 E
Watkins Glen, *U.S.A.* **78 D8** 42 23N 76 52W
Watling I. = San Salvador, *Bahamas* **89 B5** 24 0N 74 40W
Watonga, *U.S.A.* **81 H5** 35 51N 98 25W
Watrous, *Canada* **73 C7** 51 40N 105 25W
Watrous, *U.S.A.* **81 H2** 35 48N 104 59W
Watsa, *Zaïre* **54 B2** 3 4N 29 30 E
Watseka, *U.S.A.* **76 E2** 40 47N 87 44W
Watson, *Australia* **61 F5** 30 29S 131 31 E
Watson, *Canada* **73 C8** 52 10N 104 30W
Watson Lake, *Canada* **72 A3** 60 6N 128 49W
Watsonville, *U.S.A.* **83 H3** 36 55N 121 45W
Wattiwarriganna Cr. →, *Australia* **63 D2** 28 57S 136 10 E
Watuata = Batuata, *Indonesia* **37 F6** 6 12S 122 42 E
Watubela, Kepulauan, *Indonesia* **37 E8** 4 28S 131 35 E
Watubela Is. = Watubela, Kepulauan, *Indonesia* **37 E8** 4 28S 131 35 E
Waubamik, *Canada* **78 A4** 45 27N 80 1W
Waubay, *U.S.A.* **80 C6** 45 20N 97 18W
Waubra, *Australia* **63 F3** 37 21S 143 39 E
Wauchope, *Australia* **63 E5** 31 28S 152 45 E
Wauchula, *U.S.A.* **77 M5** 27 33N 81 49W
Waugh, *Canada* **73 D9** 49 40N 95 11W
Waukarlycarly, L., *Australia* **60 D3** 21 18S 121 56 E
Waukegan, *U.S.A.* **76 D2** 42 22N 87 50W
Waukesha, *U.S.A.* **76 D1** 43 1N 88 14W
Waukon, *U.S.A.* **80 D9** 43 16N 91 29W
Wauneta, *U.S.A.* **80 E4** 40 25N 101 23W
Waupaca, *U.S.A.* **80 C10** 44 21N 89 5W
Waupun, *U.S.A.* **80 D10** 43 38N 88 44W
Waurika, *U.S.A.* **81 H6** 34 10N 98 0W
Wausau, *U.S.A.* **80 C10** 44 58N 89 38W
Wautoma, *U.S.A.* **80 C10** 44 4N 89 18W
Wauwatosa, *U.S.A.* **76 D2** 43 3N 88 0W
Wave Hill, *Australia* **60 C5** 17 32S 131 0 E
Waveney →, *U.K.* **11 E9** 52 24N 1 20 E
Waverley, *N.Z.* **59 H5** 39 46S 174 37 E
Waverly, *Iowa, U.S.A.* **80 D8** 42 44N 92 29W
Waverly, *N.Y., U.S.A.* **79 D8** 42 1N 76 32W
Wavre, *Belgium* **15 D4** 50 43N 4 38 E
Wâw, *Sudan* **51 G10** 7 45N 28 1 E
Wâw al Kabîr, *Libya* **51 C8** 25 20N 16 43 E
Wawa, *Canada* **70 C3** 47 59N 84 47W
Wawanesa, *Canada* **73 D9** 49 36N 99 40W
Wawona, *U.S.A.* **84 H7** 37 32N 119 39W
Waxahachie, *U.S.A.* **81 J6** 32 24N 96 51W
Way, L., *Australia* **61 E3** 26 45S 120 16 E
Wayabula Rau, *Indonesia* **37 D7** 2 29N 128 17 E
Wayatinah, *Australia* **62 G4** 42 19S 146 27 E
Waycross, *U.S.A.* **77 K4** 31 13N 82 21W
Wayne, *Nebr., U.S.A.* **80 D6** 42 14N 97 1W
Wayne, *W. Va., U.S.A.* **76 F4** 38 13N 82 27W
Waynesboro, *Ga., U.S.A.* **77 J4** 33 6N 82 1W
Waynesboro, *Miss., U.S.A.* **77 K1** 31 40N 88 39W
Waynesboro, *Pa., U.S.A.* **76 F7** 39 45N 77 35W
Waynesboro, *Va., U.S.A.* **76 F6** 38 4N 78 53W
Waynesburg, *U.S.A.* **76 F5** 39 54N 80 11W
Waynesville, *U.S.A.* **77 H4** 35 28N 82 58W
Waynoka, *U.S.A.* **81 G5** 36 35N 98 53W
Wazirabad, *Pakistan* **42 C6** 32 30N 74 8 E
We, *Indonesia* **36 C1** 5 51N 95 18 E
Weald, The, *U.K.* **11 F8** 51 7N 0 29 E
Wear →, *U.K.* **10 C6** 54 55N 1 22W
Weatherford, *Okla., U.S.A.* **81 H5** 35 32N 98 43W
Weatherford, *Tex., U.S.A.* **81 J6** 32 46N 97 48W
Weaverville, *U.S.A.* **82 F2** 40 44N 122 56W
Webb City, *U.S.A.* **81 G7** 37 9N 94 28W
Webster, *Mass., U.S.A.* **79 D13** 42 3N 71 53W
Webster, *N.Y., U.S.A.* **78 C7** 43 13N 77 26W
Webster, *S. Dak., U.S.A.* **80 C6** 45 20N 97 31W
Webster, *Wis., U.S.A.* **80 C8** 45 53N 92 22W
Webster City, *U.S.A.* **80 D8** 42 28N 93 49W
Webster Green, *U.S.A.* **80 F9** 38 38N 90 20W
Webster Springs, *U.S.A.* **76 F5** 38 29N 80 25W
Weda, *Indonesia* **37 D7** 0 21N 127 50 E
Weda, Teluk, *Indonesia* **37 D7** 0 30N 127 50 E
Weddell I., *Falk. Is.* **96 G4** 51 50S 61 0W
Weddell Sea, *Antarctica* **5 D1** 72 30S 40 0W
Wedderburn, *Australia* **63 F3** 36 26S 143 33 E
Wedgeport, *Canada* **71 D6** 43 44N 65 59W
Wedza, *Zimbabwe* **55 F3** 18 40S 31 33 E
Wee Waa, *Australia* **63 E4** 30 11S 149 26 E
Weed, *U.S.A.* **82 F2** 41 25N 122 23W
Weed Heights, *U.S.A.* **84 G7** 38 59N 119 13W
Weedsport, *U.S.A.* **79 C8** 43 3N 76 35W
Weedville, *U.S.A.* **78 E6** 41 17N 78 30W
Weemelah, *Australia* **63 D4** 29 2S 149 15 E
Weenen, *S. Africa* **57 D5** 28 48S 30 7 E
Weert, *Neths.* **15 C5** 51 15N 5 43 E
Wei He →, *Hebei, China* **34 F8** 36 10N 115 45 E
Wei He →, *Shaanxi, China* **34 G6** 34 38N 110 15 E
Weichang, *China* **35 D9** 41 58N 117 49 E
Weichuan, *China* **34 G7** 34 20N 113 59 E
Weifang, *China* **33 C6** 36 47N 119 10 E
Weifang, *Shandong, China* **35 F10** 36 44N 119 7 E
Weihai, *China* **35 F12** 37 30N 122 6 E
Weimar, *Germany* **16 C5** 51 0N 11 20 E
Weinan, *China* **34 G5** 34 31N 109 29 E
Weipa, *Australia* **62 A3** 12 40S 141 50 E
Weir →, *Australia* **63 D4** 28 20S 149 50 E
Weir →, *Canada* **73 B10** 56 54N 93 21W
Weir River, *Canada* **73 B10** 56 49N 94 6W
Weirton, *U.S.A.* **78 F4** 40 24N 80 35W
Weiser, *U.S.A.* **82 D5** 44 10N 117 0W
Weishan, *China* **35 G9** 34 47N 117 5 E
Weiyuan, *China* **34 G3** 35 7N 104 10 E
Wejherowo, *Poland* **17 A9** 54 35N 18 12 E
Wekusko L., *Canada* **73 C9** 54 40N 99 50W
Welbourn Hill, *Australia* **63 D1** 27 21S 134 6 E
Welch, *U.S.A.* **76 G5** 37 26N 81 35W
Welkom, *S. Africa* **56 D4** 28 0S 26 46 E
Welland, *Canada* **70 D4** 43 0N 79 15W
Welland →, *U.K.* **10 E7** 52 43N 0 10W
Wellesley Is., *Australia* **62 B2** 16 42S 139 30 E
Wellin, *Belgium* **15 D5** 50 5N 5 6 E
Wellingborough, *U.K.* **11 E7** 52 18N 0 41W
Wellington, *Australia* **63 E4** 32 35S 148 59 E
Wellington, *Canada* **70 D4** 43 57N 77 20W
Wellington, *N.Z.* **59 J5** 41 19S 174 46 E
Wellington, *S. Africa* **56 E2** 33 38S 19 1 E
Wellington, *Shrops., U.K.* **10 E5** 52 42N 2 31W
Wellington, *Somst., U.K.* **11 G4** 50 58N 3 13W
Wellington, *Colo., U.S.A.* **80 E2** 40 42N 105 0W
Wellington, *Kans., U.S.A.* **81 G6** 37 16N 97 24W
Wellington, *Nev., U.S.A.* **84 G7** 38 45N 119 23W
Wellington, *Ohio, U.S.A.* **78 E2** 41 10N 82 13W
Wellington, *Tex., U.S.A.* **81 H4** 34 51N 100 13W
Wellington, I., *Chile* **96 F1** 49 30S 75 0W
Wellington, L., *Australia* **63 F4** 38 6S 147 20 E
Wells, *Norfolk, U.K.* **10 E8** 52 57N 0 51 E
Wells, *Somst., U.K.* **11 F5** 51 12N 2 39W
Wells, *Maine, U.S.A.* **79 C14** 43 20N 70 35W
Wells, *Minn., U.S.A.* **80 D8** 43 45N 93 44W
Wells, *Nev., U.S.A.* **82 F6** 41 7N 114 58W
Wells, L., *Australia* **61 E3** 26 44S 123 15 E
Wells Gray Prov. Park, *Canada* **72 C4** 52 30N 120 15W
Wells River, *U.S.A.* **79 B12** 44 9N 72 4W
Wellsboro, *U.S.A.* **78 E7** 41 45N 77 18W
Wellsburg, *U.S.A.* **78 F4** 40 16N 80 37W
Wellsville, *Mo., U.S.A.* **80 F9** 39 4N 91 34W
Wellsville, *N.Y., U.S.A.* **78 D7** 42 7N 77 57W
Wellsville, *Ohio, U.S.A.* **78 F4** 40 36N 80 39W
Wellsville, *Utah, U.S.A.* **82 F8** 41 38N 111 56W
Wellton, *U.S.A.* **83 K6** 32 40N 114 8W
Wels, *Austria* **16 D7** 48 9N 14 1 E
Welshpool, *U.K.* **11 E4** 52 40N 3 9W
Wem, *U.K.* **10 E5** 52 52N 2 45W
Wembere →, *Tanzania* **54 C3** 4 10S 34 15 E
Wen Xian, *Gansu, China* **34 H3** 32 43N 104 36 E
Wen Xian, *Henan, China* **34 G7** 34 55N 113 5 E
Wenatchee, *U.S.A.* **82 C3** 47 25N 120 19W
Wenchang, *China* **38 C8** 19 38N 110 42 E
Wenchi, *Ghana* **50 G4** 7 46N 2 8W
Wenchow = Wenzhou, *China* **33 D7** 28 0N 120 38 E
Wendell, *U.S.A.* **82 E6** 42 47N 114 42W
Wenden, *U.S.A.* **85 M13** 33 49N 113 33W
Wendeng, *China* **35 F12** 37 15N 122 5 E
Wendesi, *Indonesia* **37 E8** 2 30S 134 17 E
Wendover, *U.S.A.* **82 F6** 40 44N 114 2W
Wenlock →, *Australia* **62 A3** 12 2S 141 55 E
Wenshan, *China* **32 D5** 23 20N 104 18 E
Wenshang, *China* **34 G9** 35 45N 116 30 E
Wenshui, *China* **34 F7** 37 26N 112 1 E
Wensu, *China* **32 B3** 41 15N 80 10 E
Wentworth, *Australia* **63 E3** 34 2S 141 54 E
Wenut, *Indonesia* **37 E8** 3 11S 133 19 E
Wenxi, *China* **34 G6** 35 20N 111 10 E
Wenzhou, *China* **33 D7** 28 0N 120 38 E
Weott, *U.S.A.* **82 F2** 40 20N 123 55W
Wepener, *S. Africa* **56 D4** 29 42S 27 3 E
Werda, *Botswana* **56 D3** 25 24S 23 15 E
Werder, *Ethiopia* **46 F4** 6 58N 45 1 E
Weri, *Indonesia* **37 E8** 3 10S 132 38 E
Werribee, *Australia* **63 F3** 37 54S 144 40 E
Werrimull, *Australia* **63 E3** 34 25S 141 38 E
Werris Creek, *Australia* **63 E5** 31 18S 150 38 E
Wersar, *Indonesia* **37 E8** 1 30S 131 55 E
Weser →, *Germany* **16 B4** 53 33N 8 30 E
Wesiri, *Indonesia* **37 F7** 7 30S 126 30 E
Wesley Vale, *U.S.A.* **83 J10** 35 3N 106 2W
Wesleyville, *Canada* **71 C9** 49 8N 53 36W
Wesleyville, *U.S.A.* **78 D4** 42 9N 80 0W
Wessel, C., *Australia* **62 A2** 10 59S 136 46 E
Wessel Is., *Australia* **62 A2** 11 10S 136 45 E
Wessington, *U.S.A.* **80 C5** 44 27N 98 42W
Wessington Springs, *U.S.A.* **80 C5** 44 5N 98 34W
West, *U.S.A.* **81 K6** 31 48N 97 6W
West B., *U.S.A.* **81 L10** 29 3N 89 22W
West Baines →, *Australia* **60 C4** 15 38S 129 59 E
West Bend, *U.S.A.* **76 D1** 43 25N 88 11W
West Bengal □, *India* **43 H12** 23 0N 88 0 E
West Beskids = Západné Beskydy, *Europe* **17 D9** 49 30N 19 0 E
West Branch, *U.S.A.* **76 C3** 44 17N 84 14W
West Bromwich, *U.K.* **11 E5** 52 32N 2 1W
West Cape Howe, *Australia* **61 G2** 35 8S 117 36 E
West Chazy, *U.S.A.* **79 B11** 44 49N 73 28W
West Chester, *U.S.A.* **76 F8** 39 58N 75 36W
West Columbia, *U.S.A.* **81 L7** 29 9N 95 39W
West Covina, *U.S.A.* **85 L9** 34 4N 117 54W
West Des Moines, *U.S.A.* **80 E8** 41 35N 93 43W
West End, *Bahamas* **88 A4** 26 41N 78 58W
West Falkland, *Falk. Is.* **96 G4** 51 40S 60 0W
West Fjord = Vestfjorden, *Norway* **8 C13** 67 55N 14 0 E
West Frankfort, *U.S.A.* **80 G10** 37 54N 88 55W
West Glamorgan □, *U.K.* **11 F4** 51 40N 3 55W
West Hartford, *U.S.A.* **79 E12** 41 45N 72 44W
West Haven, *U.S.A.* **79 E12** 41 17N 72 57W
West Helena, *U.S.A.* **81 H9** 34 33N 90 38W
West Ice Shelf, *Antarctica* **5 C7** 67 0S 85 0 E
West Indies, *Cent. Amer.* **89 C7** 15 0N 65 0W
West Lorne, *Canada* **78 D3** 42 36N 81 36W
West Lunga →, *Zambia* **55 E1** 13 6S 24 39 E
West Memphis, *U.S.A.* **81 H9** 35 9N 90 11W
West Midlands □, *U.K.* **11 E6** 52 30N 1 55W
West Mifflin, *U.S.A.* **78 F5** 40 22N 79 52W
West Monroe, *U.S.A.* **81 J8** 32 31N 92 9W
West Newton, *U.S.A.* **78 F5** 40 14N 79 46W
West Nicholson, *Zimbabwe* **55 G2** 21 2S 29 20 E
West Palm Beach, *U.S.A.* **77 M5** 26 43N 80 3W
West Plains, *U.S.A.* **81 G9** 36 44N 91 51W
West Pt. = Ouest, Pte., *Canada* **71 C7** 49 52N 64 40W
West Pt., *Australia* **63 F2** 35 1S 135 56 E
West Point, *Ga., U.S.A.* **77 J3** 32 53N 85 11W
West Point, *Miss., U.S.A.* **77 J1** 33 36N 88 39W
West Point, *Nebr., U.S.A.* **80 E6** 41 51N 96 43W
West Point, *Va., U.S.A.* **76 G7** 37 32N 76 48W
West Pokot □, *Kenya* **54 B4** 1 30N 35 15 E
West Road →, *Canada* **72 C4** 53 18N 122 53W
West Rutland, *U.S.A.* **79 C11** 43 38N 73 5W
West Schelde = Westerschelde →, *Neths.* **15 C3** 51 25N 3 25 E
West Seneca, *U.S.A.* **78 D6** 42 51N 78 48W
West Siberian Plain, *Russia* **28 C11** 62 0N 75 0 E
West Sussex □, *U.K.* **11 G7** 50 55N 0 30W
West-Terschelling, *Neths.* **15 A5** 53 22N 5 13 E
West Virginia □, *U.S.A.* **76 F5** 38 45N 80 30W
West-Vlaanderen □, *Belgium* **15 D3** 51 0N 3 0 E
West Walker →, *U.S.A.* **84 G7** 38 54N 119 9W
West Wyalong, *Australia* **63 E4** 33 56S 147 10 E
West Yellowstone, *U.S.A.* **82 D8** 44 40N 111 6W
West Yorkshire □, *U.K.* **10 D5** 53 45N 1 40W
Westall Pt., *Australia* **63 E1** 32 55S 134 4 E

Yermakovo

Woodridge, Canada 73 D9 49 20N 96 9W
Woodroffe, Mt., Australia 61 E5 26 20S 131 45 E
Woodruff, Ariz., U.S.A. 83 J8 34 51N 110 1W
Woodruff, Utah, U.S.A. 82 F8 41 31N 111 10W
Woods, L., Australia 62 B1 17 50S 133 30 E
Woods, L., Canada 71 B6 54 30N 65 13W
Woods, L. of the, Canada 73 D10 49 15N 94 45W
Woodstock, Queens., Australia 62 B4 19 35S 146 50 E
Woodstock, W. Austral., Australia 60 D2 21 41S 118 57 E
Woodstock, N.B., Canada 71 C6 46 11N 67 37W
Woodstock, Ont., Canada 70 D3 43 10N 80 45W
Woodstock, U.K. 11 F6 51 51N 1 20W
Woodstock, Ill., U.S.A. 80 D10 42 19N 88 27W
Woodstock, Vt., U.S.A. 79 C12 43 37N 72 31W
Woodsville, U.S.A. 79 B13 44 9N 72 2W
Woodville, N.Z. 59 J5 40 20S 175 53 E
Woodville, U.S.A. 81 K7 30 47N 94 25W
Woodward, U.S.A. 81 G5 36 26N 99 24W
Woody, U.S.A. 85 K8 35 42N 118 50W
Woolamai, C., Australia 63 F4 38 30S 145 23 E
Woolgoolga, Australia 63 E5 30 6S 153 11 E
Woombye, Australia 63 D5 26 40S 152 55 E
Woomera, Australia 63 E2 31 5S 136 50 E
Woonsocket, R.I., U.S.A. 79 D13 42 0N 71 31W
Woonsocket, S. Dak., U.S.A. 80 C5 44 3N 98 17W
Wooramel, Australia 61 E1 25 45S 114 17 E
Wooramel →, Australia 61 E1 25 47S 114 10 E
Wooroloo, Australia 61 F2 31 48S 116 18 E
Wooster, U.S.A. 78 F3 40 48N 81 56W
Worcester, S. Africa 56 E2 33 39S 19 27 E
Worcester, U.K. 11 E5 52 12N 2 12W
Worcester, Mass., U.S.A. 79 D13 42 16N 71 48W
Worcester, N.Y., U.S.A. 79 D10 42 36N 74 45W
Workington, U.K. 10 C4 54 39N 3 34W
Worksop, U.K. 10 D6 53 19N 1 9W
Workum, Neths. 15 B5 52 59N 5 26 E
Worland, U.S.A. 82 D10 44 1N 107 57W
Worms, Germany 16 D4 49 37N 8 21 E
Wortham, U.S.A. 81 K6 31 47N 96 28W
Worthing, U.K. 11 G7 50 49N 0 21W
Worthington, U.S.A. 80 D7 43 37N 95 36W
Wosi, Indonesia 37 E7 0 15S 128 0 E
Wou-han = Wuhan, China 33 C6 30 31N 114 18 E
Wour, Chad 51 D8 21 14N 16 0 E
Wousi = Wuxi, China 33 C7 31 33N 120 18 E
Wowoni, Indonesia 37 E6 4 5S 123 5 E
Woy Woy, Australia 63 E5 33 30S 151 19 E
Wrangel I. = Vrangelya, Ostrov, Russia 27 B19 71 0N 180 0 E
Wrangell, U.S.A. 68 C6 56 28N 132 23W
Wrangell I., U.S.A. 72 B2 56 16N 132 12W
Wrangell Mts., U.S.A. 68 B5 61 30N 142 0W
Wrath, C., U.K. 12 C3 58 38N 5 0W
Wray, U.S.A. 80 E3 40 5N 102 13W
Wrekin, The, U.K. 10 E5 52 41N 2 35W
Wrens, U.S.A. 77 J4 33 12N 82 23W
Wrexham, U.K. 10 D4 53 5N 3 0W
Wright, Canada 72 C4 51 52N 121 40W
Wright, Phil. 37 B7 11 42N 125 2 E
Wrightson Mt., U.S.A. 83 L8 31 42N 110 51W
Wrightwood, U.S.A. 85 L9 34 21N 117 38W
Wrigley, Canada 68 B7 63 16N 123 37W
Wrocław, Poland 16 C8 51 5N 17 5 E
Września, Poland 17 B8 52 21N 17 36 E
Wu Jiang →, China 32 C4 29 40N 107 20 E
Wu'an, China 34 F8 36 40N 114 15 E
Wubin, Australia 61 F2 30 6S 116 37 E
Wubu, China 34 F6 37 28N 110 42 E
Wuchang, China 35 B14 44 55N 127 5 E
Wucheng, China 34 F9 37 12N 116 20 E
Wuchuan, China 34 D6 41 5N 111 28 E
Wudi, China 35 F9 37 40N 117 35 E
Wuding He →, China 34 F6 37 2N 110 23 E
Wudu, China 34 H3 33 22N 104 54 E
Wuhan, China 33 C6 30 31N 114 18 E
Wuhe, China 35 H9 33 10N 117 50 E
Wuhsi = Wuxi, China 33 C7 31 33N 120 18 E
Wuhu, China 33 C6 31 22N 118 21 E
Wukari, Nigeria 50 G6 7 51N 9 42 E
Wulajie, China 35 B14 44 6N 126 33 E
Wulanbulang, China 34 D6 41 5N 110 55 E
Wulian, China 35 G10 35 40N 119 12 E
Wuliaru, Indonesia 37 F8 7 27S 131 0 E
Wuluk'omushih Ling, China 32 C3 36 25N 87 25 E
Wulumuchi = Ürümqi, China 26 E9 43 45N 87 45 E
Wum, Cameroon 50 G7 6 24N 10 2 E
Wunnummin L., Canada 70 B2 52 55N 89 10W
Wuntho, Burma 41 H19 23 55N 95 45 E
Wuppertal, Germany 16 C3 51 15N 7 8 E
Wuppertal, S. Africa 56 E2 32 13S 19 12 E
Wuqing, China 35 E9 39 23N 117 4 E
Wurung, Australia 62 B3 19 13S 140 38 E
Würzburg, Germany 16 D4 49 46N 9 55 E
Wushan, China 34 G3 34 43N 104 53 E
Wusuli Jiang = Ussuri →, Asia 30 A7 48 27N 135 0 E
Wutai, China 34 E7 38 40N 113 12 E
Wuting = Huimin, China 35 F9 37 27N 117 28 E
Wutonghaolai, China 35 C11 42 50N 120 5 E
Wutongqiao, China 32 D5 29 22N 103 50 E
Wuwei, China 32 C5 37 57N 102 34 E
Wuxi, China 33 C7 31 33N 120 18 E
Wuxiang, China 34 F7 36 49N 112 50 E
Wuxing, China 33 C7 30 51N 120 8 E
Wuyang, China 34 H7 33 25N 113 35 E
Wuyi, China 34 F8 37 46N 115 56 E
Wuyi Shan, China 33 D6 27 0N 117 0 E
Wuyuan, China 34 D5 41 2N 108 20 E
Wuzhai, China 34 E6 38 54N 111 48 E
Wuzhi Shan, China 38 C7 18 45N 109 45 E
Wuzhong, China 34 E4 38 2N 106 12 E
Wuzhou, China 33 D6 23 30N 111 18 E
Wyaaba Cr. →, Australia 62 B3 16 27S 141 35 E
Wyalkatchem, Australia 61 F2 31 8S 117 22 E
Wyalusing, U.S.A. 79 E8 41 40N 76 16W
Wyandotte, U.S.A. 76 D4 42 12N 83 9W
Wyandra, Australia 63 D4 27 12S 145 56 E
Wyangala Res., Australia 63 E4 33 54S 149 0 E
Wyara, L., Australia 63 D3 28 42S 144 14 E
Wycheproof, Australia 63 F3 36 5S 143 17 E
Wye →, U.K. 11 F5 51 36N 2 40W
Wyemandoo, Australia 61 E2 28 28S 118 29 E
Wymondham, U.K. 11 E7 52 45N 0 42W
Wymore, U.S.A. 80 E6 40 7N 96 40W
Wynbring, Australia 63 E1 30 33S 133 32 E
Wyndham, Australia 60 C4 15 33S 128 3 E
Wyndham, N.Z. 59 M2 46 20S 168 51 E
Wyndmere, U.S.A. 80 B6 46 16N 97 8W
Wynne, U.S.A. 81 H9 35 14N 90 47W
Wynnum, Australia 63 D5 27 27S 153 9 E
Wynyard, Australia 62 G4 41 5S 145 44 E
Wynyard, Canada 73 C8 51 45N 104 10W
Wyola, L., Australia 61 E5 29 8S 130 17 E
Wyoming □, U.S.A. 82 E10 43 0N 107 30W
Wyong, Australia 63 E5 33 14S 151 24 E
Wytheville, U.S.A. 76 G5 36 57N 81 5W

X

Xai-Xai, Mozam. 57 D5 25 6S 33 31 E
Xainza, China 32 C3 30 58N 88 35 E
Xangongo, Angola 56 B2 16 45S 15 5 E
Xánthi, Greece 21 D11 41 10N 24 58 E
Xapuri, Brazil 92 F5 10 35S 68 35W
Xar Moron He →, China 35 C11 43 25N 120 35 E
Xau, L., Botswana 56 C3 21 15S 24 44 E
Xavantina, Brazil 95 A5 21 15S 52 48W
Xenia, U.S.A. 76 F4 39 41N 83 56W
Xeropotamos →, Cyprus 23 E11 34 42N 32 33 E
Xhora, S. Africa 57 E4 31 55S 28 38 E
Xhumo, Botswana 56 C3 21 7S 24 35 E
Xi Jiang →, China 33 D6 22 5N 113 20 E
Xi Xian, China 34 F6 36 41N 110 58 E
Xia Xian, China 34 G6 35 8N 111 12 E
Xiachengzi, China 35 B16 44 40N 130 18 E
Xiaguan, China 32 D5 25 32N 100 16 E
Xiajin, China 34 F8 36 56N 116 0 E
Xiamen, China 33 D6 24 25N 118 4 E
Xi'an, China 34 G5 34 15N 109 0 E
Xian Xian, China 34 E9 38 12N 116 6 E
Xiang Jiang →, China 33 D6 28 55N 112 50 E
Xiangcheng, Henan, China 34 H8 33 29N 114 52 E
Xiangcheng, Henan, China 34 H7 33 50N 113 27 E
Xiangfan, China 33 C6 32 2N 112 8 E
Xianghuang Qi, China 34 C7 42 2N 113 50 E
Xiangning, China 34 G6 35 58N 110 50 E
Xiangquan, China 34 F7 36 30N 113 1 E
Xiangshui, China 35 G10 34 12N 119 33 E
Xiangtan, China 33 D6 27 51N 112 54 E
Xianyang, China 34 G5 34 20N 108 40 E
Xiao Hinggan Ling, China 33 B7 49 0N 127 0 E
Xiao Xian, China 34 G9 34 15N 116 55 E
Xiaoyi, China 34 F6 37 8N 111 48 E
Xiawa, China 35 C11 42 35N 120 38 E
Xiayi, China 34 G9 34 15N 116 10 E
Xichang, China 32 D5 27 51N 102 19 E
Xichuan, China 34 H6 33 0N 111 30 E
Xieng Khouang, Laos 38 C4 19 17N 103 25 E
Xifei He →, China 34 H9 32 45N 116 40 E
Xifeng, China 35 C13 42 42N 124 45 E
Xifengzhen, China 34 G4 35 40N 107 40 E
Xigazê, China 32 D3 29 5N 88 45 E
Xihe, China 34 G3 34 2N 105 20 E
Xihua, China 34 H8 33 45N 114 30 E
Xiliao He →, China 35 C12 43 32N 123 35 E
Xin Xian, China 34 E7 38 22N 112 46 E
Xinavane, Mozam. 57 D5 25 2S 32 47 E
Xinbin, China 35 D13 41 40N 125 2 E
Xing Xian, China 34 E6 38 27N 111 7 E
Xing'an, China 33 D6 25 38N 110 40 E
Xingcheng, China 35 D11 40 40N 120 45 E
Xinghe, China 34 D7 40 55N 113 55 E
Xinghua, China 35 H10 32 58N 119 48 E
Xinglong, China 35 D9 40 25N 117 30 E
Xingping, China 34 G5 34 20N 108 28 E
Xingtai, China 34 F8 37 3N 114 32 E
Xingu →, Brazil 93 D8 1 30S 51 53W
Xingyang, China 34 G7 34 45N 112 52 E
Xinhe, China 34 F8 37 30N 115 15 E
Xining, China 32 C5 36 34N 101 40 E
Xinjiang, China 34 G6 35 34N 111 11 E
Xinjiang Uygur Zizhiqu □, China 32 B3 42 0N 86 0 E
Xinjin, China 35 E11 39 25N 121 58 E
Xinkai He →, China 35 C12 43 32N 123 35 E
Xinle, China 34 E8 38 25N 114 40 E
Xinlitun, China 35 D12 42 0N 122 8 E
Xinmin, China 35 D12 41 59N 122 50 E
Xintai, China 35 G9 35 55N 117 45 E
Xinxiang, China 34 G7 35 18N 113 50 E
Xinzhan, China 35 C14 43 50N 127 18 E
Xinzheng, China 34 G7 34 20N 113 45 E
Xiong Xian, China 34 E9 38 59N 116 8 E
Xiongyuecheng, China 35 D12 40 12N 122 5 E
Xiping, Henan, China 34 H8 33 22N 114 5 E
Xiping, Henan, China 34 H6 33 25N 111 8 E
Xique-Xique, Brazil 93 F10 10 50S 42 40W
Xisha Qundao = Hsisha Chuntao, Pac. Oc. 36 A4 15 50N 112 0 E
Xiuyan, China 35 D12 40 18N 123 11 E
Xixabangma Feng, China 41 E14 28 20N 85 40 E
Xixia, China 34 H6 33 25N 111 29 E
Xixiang, China 34 H4 33 0N 107 44 E
Xiyang, China 34 F7 37 38N 113 38 E
Xizang □, China 32 C3 32 0N 88 0 E
Xlendi, Malta 23 C1 36 1N 14 12 E
Xuan Loc, Vietnam 39 G6 10 56N 107 14 E
Xuanhua, China 34 D8 40 40N 115 2 E
Xuchang, China 34 G7 34 2N 113 48 E
Xun Xian, China 34 G8 35 42N 114 33 E
Xunyang, China 34 H5 32 48N 109 22 E
Xunyi, China 34 G5 35 8N 108 20 E
Xushui, China 34 E8 39 2N 115 40 E
Xuyen Moc, Vietnam 39 G6 10 34N 107 25 E
Xuzhou, China 35 G9 34 18N 117 10 E
Xylophagou, Cyprus 23 E12 34 54N 33 51 E

Y

Ya Xian, China 38 C7 18 14N 109 29 E
Yaamba, Australia 62 C5 23 8S 150 22 E
Yaapeet, Australia 63 F3 35 45S 142 3 E
Yabelo, Ethiopia 51 H12 4 50N 38 8 E
Yablonovy Khrebet, Russia 27 D12 53 0N 114 0 E
Yablonovy Ra. = Yablonovy Khrebet, Russia 27 D12 53 0N 114 0 E
Yabrai Shan, China 34 E2 39 40N 103 0 E
Yabrūd, Syria 47 B5 33 58N 36 39 E
Yacheng, China 33 E5 18 22N 109 6 E
Yacuiba, Bolivia 94 A3 22 0S 63 43W
Yadgir, India 40 L10 16 45N 77 5 E
Yadkin →, U.S.A. 77 H5 35 29N 80 9W
Yagodnoye, Russia 27 C15 62 33N 149 40 E
Yagoua, Cameroon 52 B3 10 20N 15 13 E
Yaha, Thailand 39 J3 6 29N 101 8 E
Yahila, Zaïre 54 B1 0 13N 24 28 E
Yahk, Canada 72 D5 49 6N 116 10W
Yahuma, Zaïre 52 D4 1 0N 23 10 E
Yaita, Japan 31 F9 36 48N 139 56 E
Yaiza, Canary Is. 22 F6 28 57N 13 46W
Yakima, U.S.A. 82 C3 46 36N 120 31W
Yakima →, U.S.A. 82 C3 47 0N 120 30W
Yakovlevka, Russia 30 B6 44 26N 133 28 E
Yaku-Shima, Japan 31 J5 30 20N 130 30 E
Yakut Republic □, Russia 27 C13 62 0N 130 0 E
Yakutat, U.S.A. 68 C6 59 33N 139 44W
Yakutsk, Russia 27 C13 62 5N 129 50 E
Yala, Thailand 39 J3 6 33N 101 18 E
Yalbalgo, Australia 61 E1 25 10S 114 45 E
Yalboroo, Australia 62 C4 20 50S 148 40 E
Yale, U.S.A. 78 C2 43 8N 82 48W
Yalgoo, Australia 61 E2 28 16S 116 39 E
Yalinga, C.A.R. 51 G9 6 33N 23 10 E
Yalkubul, Punta, Mexico 87 C7 21 32N 88 37W
Yalleroi, Australia 62 C4 24 3S 145 42 E
Yalobusha →, U.S.A. 81 J9 33 33N 90 10W
Yalong Jiang →, China 32 D5 26 40N 101 55 E
Yalta, Ukraine 25 F5 44 30N 34 10 E
Yalu Jiang →, China 35 E13 40 0N 124 22 E
Yalutorovsk, Russia 26 D7 56 41N 66 12 E
Yam Ha Melah = Dead Sea, Asia 47 D4 31 30N 35 30 E
Yam Kinneret, Israel 47 C4 32 45N 35 35 E
Yamada, Japan 31 H5 33 33N 130 49 E
Yamagata, Japan 30 E10 38 15N 140 15 E
Yamagata □, Japan 30 E10 38 30N 140 0 E
Yamaguchi, Japan 31 G5 34 10N 131 32 E
Yamaguchi □, Japan 31 G5 34 20N 131 40 E
Yamal, Poluostrov, Russia 26 B8 71 0N 70 0 E
Yamal Pen. = Yamal, Poluostrov, Russia 26 B8 71 0N 70 0 E
Yamanashi □, Japan 31 G9 35 40N 138 40 E
Yamantau, Gora, Russia 24 D10 54 15N 58 6 E
Yamba, N.S.W., Australia 63 D5 29 26S 153 23 E
Yamba, S. Austral., Australia 63 E3 34 10S 140 52 E
Yambah, Australia 62 C1 23 10S 133 50 E
Yambarran Ra., Australia 60 C5 15 10S 130 25 E
Yâmbiô, Sudan 51 H10 4 35N 28 16 E
Yambol, Bulgaria 21 C12 42 30N 26 36 E
Yamdena, Indonesia 37 F8 7 45S 131 20 E
Yame, Japan 31 H5 33 13N 130 35 E
Yamethin, Burma 41 J20 20 29N 96 18 E
Yamma-Yamma, L., Australia 63 D3 26 16S 141 20 E
Yamoussoukro, Ivory C. 50 G3 6 49N 5 17W
Yampa →, U.S.A. 82 F9 40 32N 108 59W
Yampi Sd., Australia 60 C3 16 8S 123 38 E
Yamuna →, India 43 G9 25 30N 81 53 E
Yamzho Yumco, China 32 D4 28 48N 90 35 E
Yana →, Russia 27 B14 71 30N 136 0 E
Yanac, Australia 63 F3 36 8S 141 25 E
Yanagawa, Japan 31 H5 33 10N 130 24 E
Yanai, Japan 31 H6 33 58N 132 7 E
Yan'an, China 34 F5 36 35N 109 26 E
Yanaul, Russia 24 C10 56 25N 55 0 E
Yanbu 'al Baḥr, Si. Arabia 44 F3 24 0N 38 5 E
Yancannia, Australia 63 E3 30 12S 142 35 E
Yanchang, China 34 F6 36 43N 110 1 E
Yancheng, Henan, China 34 H7 33 35N 114 0 E
Yancheng, Jiangsu, China 35 H11 33 23N 120 8 E
Yanchi, China 34 F4 37 48N 107 20 E
Yanchuan, China 34 F6 36 51N 110 10 E
Yanco Cr. →, Australia 63 F4 35 14S 145 35 E
Yandal, Australia 61 E3 27 35S 121 10 E
Yandanooka, Australia 61 E2 29 18S 115 29 E
Yandaran, Australia 62 C5 24 43S 152 6 E
Yandoon, Burma 41 L19 17 0N 95 40 E
Yang Xian, China 34 H4 33 15N 107 30 E
Yangambi, Zaïre 54 B1 0 47N 24 20 E
Yangcheng, China 34 G7 35 28N 112 22 E
Yangch'ü = Taiyuan, China 34 F7 37 52N 112 33 E
Yanggao, China 34 D7 40 21N 113 55 E
Yanggu, China 34 F8 36 8N 115 43 E
Yangi-Yer, Kazakhstan 26 E7 43 50N 68 48 E
Yangliuqing, China 35 E9 39 2N 117 5 E
Yangon = Rangoon, Burma 41 L20 16 45N 96 20 E
Yangpingguan, China 34 H4 32 58N 106 5 E
Yangquan, China 34 F7 37 58N 113 31 E
Yangtze Kiang = Chang Jiang →, China 33 C7 31 48N 121 10 E
Yangyang, S. Korea 35 E15 38 4N 128 38 E
Yangyuan, China 34 D8 40 1N 114 10 E
Yangzhou, China 33 C6 32 21N 119 26 E
Yanji, China 35 C15 42 59N 129 30 E
Yankton, U.S.A. 80 D6 42 53N 97 23W
Yanna, Australia 63 D4 26 58S 146 0 E
Yanonge, Zaïre 54 B1 0 35N 24 38 E
Yanqi, China 32 B3 42 5N 86 35 E
Yanqing, China 34 D8 40 30N 115 58 E
Yanshan, China 35 E9 38 4N 117 22 E
Yanshou, China 35 B15 45 28N 128 22 E
Yantabulla, Australia 63 D4 29 21S 145 0 E
Yantai, China 35 F11 37 34N 121 22 E
Yanzhou, China 34 G9 35 35N 116 49 E
Yao, Chad 51 F8 12 56N 17 33 E
Yao Xian, China 34 G5 34 55N 108 59 E
Yao Yai, Ko, Thailand 39 J2 8 0N 98 35 E
Yaoundé, Cameroon 50 H7 3 50N 11 35 E
Yaowan, China 35 G10 34 15N 118 3 E
Yap I., Pac. Oc. 64 G5 9 30N 138 10 E
Yapen, Indonesia 37 E9 1 50S 136 0 E
Yapen, Selat, Indonesia 37 E9 1 20S 136 10 E
Yappar →, Australia 62 B3 18 22S 141 16 E
Yaqui →, Mexico 86 B2 27 37N 110 39W
Yar-Sale, Russia 26 C8 66 50N 70 50 E
Yaraka, Australia 62 C3 24 53S 144 3 E
Yaransk, Russia 24 C8 57 22N 47 49 E
Yardea P.O., Australia 63 E2 32 23S 135 32 E
Yare →, U.K. 11 E9 52 36N 1 28 E
Yarensk, Russia 24 B8 61 10N 49 8 E
Yarí →, Colombia 92 D4 0 20S 72 20W
Yarkand = Shache, China 32 C2 38 20N 77 10 E
Yarker, Canada 79 B8 44 23N 76 46W
Yarkhun →, Pakistan 43 A5 36 17N 72 30 E
Yarmouth, Canada 71 D6 43 50N 66 7W
Yarmūk →, Syria 47 C4 32 42N 35 40 E
Yaroslavl, Russia 24 C6 57 35N 39 55 E
Yarqa, W. →, Egypt 47 F2 30 0N 33 49 E
Yarra Yarra Lakes, Australia 61 E2 29 40S 115 45 E
Yarraden, Australia 62 A3 14 17S 143 15 E
Yarraloola, Australia 60 D2 21 33S 115 52 E
Yarram, Australia 63 F4 38 29S 146 39 E
Yarraman, Australia 63 D5 26 50S 152 0 E
Yarranvale, Australia 63 D4 26 50S 145 20 E
Yarras, Australia 63 E5 31 25S 152 20 E
Yarrowmere, Australia 62 C4 21 27S 145 53 E
Yartsevo, Russia 27 C10 60 20N 90 0 E
Yasawa Group, Fiji 59 C7 17 0S 177 23 E
Yasin, Pakistan 43 A5 36 24N 73 23 E
Yasinski, L., Canada 70 B4 53 16N 77 35W
Yasothon, Thailand 38 E5 15 50N 104 10 E
Yass, Australia 63 E4 34 49S 148 54 E
Yates Center, U.S.A. 81 G7 37 53N 95 44W
Yathkyed L., Canada 73 A9 62 40N 98 0W
Yatsushiro, Japan 31 H5 32 30N 130 40 E
Yatta Plateau, Kenya 54 C4 2 0S 38 0 E
Yauyos, Peru 92 F3 12 19S 75 50W
Yavari →, Peru 92 D4 4 21S 70 2W
Yavatmal, India 40 J11 20 20N 78 15 E
Yavne, Israel 47 D3 31 52N 34 45 E
Yawatahama, Japan 31 H6 33 27N 132 24 E
Yayama-Rettō, Japan 31 M1 24 30N 123 40 E
Yazd, Iran 45 D7 31 55N 54 27 E
Yazd □, Iran 45 D7 32 0N 55 0 E
Yazoo →, U.S.A. 81 J9 32 22N 90 54W
Yazoo City, U.S.A. 81 J9 32 51N 90 25W
Yding Skovhøj, Denmark 9 J10 55 59N 9 46 E
Ye Xian, Henan, China 34 H7 33 35N 113 25 E
Ye Xian, Shandong, China 35 F10 37 8N 119 57 E
Yealering, Australia 61 F2 32 36S 117 36 E
Yebyu, Burma 41 M21 14 15N 98 13 E
Yechŏn, S. Korea 35 F15 36 39N 128 27 E
Yecla, Spain 19 C5 38 35N 1 5W
Yécora, Mexico 86 B3 28 20N 108 58W
Yeeda, Australia 60 C3 17 31S 123 38 E
Yeelanna, Australia 63 E2 34 9S 135 45 E
Yegros, Paraguay 94 B4 26 20S 56 25W
Yehuda, Midbar, Israel 47 D4 31 35N 35 15 E
Yei, Sudan 51 H11 4 9N 30 40 E
Yekaterinburg, Russia 24 C11 56 50N 60 30 E
Yekaterinodar = Krasnodar, Russia 25 E6 45 5N 39 0 E
Yelanskoye, Russia 27 C13 61 25N 128 0 E
Yelarbon, Australia 63 D5 28 33S 150 38 E
Yelets, Russia 24 D6 52 40N 38 30 E
Yelizavetgrad = Kirovograd, Ukraine 25 E5 48 35N 32 20 E
Yell, U.K. 12 A7 60 35N 1 5W
Yell Sd., U.K. 12 A7 60 33N 1 15W
Yellow Sea, China 35 G12 35 0N 123 0 E
Yellowhead Pass, Canada 72 C5 52 53N 118 25W
Yellowknife, Canada 72 A6 62 27N 114 29W
Yellowknife →, Canada 72 A6 62 31N 114 19W
Yellowstone →, U.S.A. 80 B3 47 59N 103 59W
Yellowstone L., U.S.A. 82 D8 44 27N 110 22W
Yellowstone National Park, U.S.A. 82 D8 44 40N 110 30W
Yellowtail Res., U.S.A. 82 D9 45 6N 108 8W
Yelvertoft, Australia 62 C2 20 13S 138 45 E
Yemen ■, Asia 46 E3 15 0N 44 0 E
Yen Bai, Vietnam 38 B5 21 42N 104 52 E
Yenangyaung, Burma 41 J19 20 30N 95 0 E
Yenbo = Yanbu 'al Baḥr, Si. Arabia 44 F3 24 0N 38 5 E
Yenda, Australia 63 E4 34 13S 146 14 E
Yenisey →, Russia 26 B9 71 50N 82 40 E
Yeniseysk, Russia 27 D10 58 27N 92 13 E
Yeniseyskiy Zaliv, Russia 26 B9 72 20N 81 0 E
Yennádhi, Greece 23 C9 36 2N 27 56 E
Yenyuka, Russia 27 D13 57 57N 121 15 E
Yeo, L., Australia 61 E3 28 0S 124 30 E
Yeola, India 40 J9 20 2N 74 30 E
Yeoryioúpolis, Greece 23 D6 35 20N 24 15 E
Yeovil, U.K. 11 G5 50 57N 2 38W
Yeppoon, Australia 62 C5 23 5S 150 47 E
Yerbent, Turkmenistan 26 F6 39 30N 58 50 E
Yerbogachen, Russia 27 C11 61 16N 108 0 E
Yerevan, Armenia 25 F7 40 10N 44 31 E
Yerilla, Australia 61 E3 29 24S 121 47 E
Yermak, Kazakhstan 26 D8 52 2N 76 55 E
Yermakovo, Russia 27 D13 52 25N 126 20 E

Yermo, U.S.A. 85 L10 34 54N 116 50W
Yerofey Pavlovich, Russia 27 D13 54 0N 122 0 E
Yerólakkos, Cyprus ... 23 D12 35 11N 33 15 E
Yeropótamos →, Greece 23 D6 35 3N 24 50 E
Yeroskipos, Cyprus ... 23 E11 34 46N 32 28 E
Yershov, Russia .... 25 D8 51 22N 48 16 E
Yerushalayim =
  Jerusalem, Israel .... 47 D4 31 47N 35 10 E
Yes Tor, U.K. 11 G4 50 41N 3 59W
Yesan, S. Korea ...... 35 F14 36 41N 126 51 E
Yeso, U.S.A. 81 H2 34 26N 104 37W
Yessey, Russia .... 27 C11 68 29N 102 10 E
Yeu, I. d', France 18 C2 46 42N 2 20W
Yevpatoriya, Ukraine .. 25 E5 45 15N 33 20 E
Yeysk, Russia .... 25 E6 46 40N 38 12 E
Yezd = Yazd, Iran .... 45 D7 31 55N 54 27 E
Yhati, Paraguay 94 B4 25 45S 56 35W
Yhú, Paraguay 95 B4 25 0S 56 0W
Yi →, Uruguay 94 C4 33 7S 57 8W
Yi 'Allaq, G., Egypt .. 47 E2 30 22N 33 32 E
Yi He →, China ...... 35 G10 34 10N 118 8 E
Yi Xian, Hebei, China . 34 E8 39 20N 115 30 E
Yi Xian, Liaoning, China 35 D11 41 30N 121 22 E
Yialiás →, Cyprus .... 23 D12 35 9N 33 44 E
Yialousa, Cyprus ..... 23 D13 35 32N 34 10 E
Yianisádhes, Greece .. 23 D8 35 20N 26 10 E
Yiannitsa, Greece .... 21 D10 40 46N 22 24 E
Yibin, China .... 32 D5 28 45N 104 32 E
Yichang, China .... 33 C6 30 40N 111 20 E
Yicheng, China .... 34 G6 35 42N 111 40 E
Yichuan, China .... 34 G6 36 2N 110 10 E
Yichun, China .... 33 B7 47 44N 128 52 E
Yidu, China .... 35 F10 36 43N 118 28 E
Yijun, China .... 34 G5 35 28N 109 8 E
Yilehuli Shan, China . 33 A7 51 20N 124 20 E
Yimianpo, China ...... 35 B15 45 7N 128 2 E
Yinchuan, China ...... 34 E4 38 30N 106 15 E
Yindarlgooda, L.,
  Australia .... 61 F3 30 40S 121 52 E
Ying He →, China ... 34 H9 32 30N 116 30 E
Ying Xian, China .... 34 E7 39 32N 113 10 E
Yingkou, China ...... 35 D12 40 37N 122 18 E
Yining, China .... 26 E9 43 58N 81 10 E
Yinmabin, Burma .... 41 H19 22 10N 94 55 E
Yinnietharra, Australia 60 D2 24 39S 116 12 E
Yiofiros →, Greece .. 23 D7 35 20N 25 6 E
Yishan, China .... 32 D5 24 28N 108 38 E
Yishui, China .... 35 G10 35 47N 118 30 E
Yithion, Greece ...... 21 F10 36 46N 22 34 E
Yitong, China .... 35 C13 43 13N 125 20 E
Yitiaoshan, China .... 34 F3 37 5N 104 2 E
Yiyang, Henan, China 34 G7 34 27N 112 10 E
Yiyang, Hunan, China 33 D6 28 35N 112 18 E
Ylitornio, Finland .... 8 C17 66 19N 23 39 E
Ylivieska, Finland ... 8 D18 64 4N 24 28 E
Ynykchanskiy, Russia 27 C14 60 15N 137 35 E
Yoakum, U.S.A. 81 L6 29 17N 97 9W
Yog Pt., Phil. .... 37 B6 14 6N 124 12 E
Yogyakarta, Indonesia 37 G14 7 49S 110 22 E
Yoho Nat. Park, Canada 72 C5 51 25N 116 30W
Yojoa, L. de, Honduras 88 D2 14 53N 88 0W
Yöju, S. Korea .... 35 F14 37 20N 127 35 E
Yokadouma, Cameroon 52 D2 3 26N 14 55 E
Yokkaichi, Japan .... 31 G8 34 55N 136 38 E
Yoko, Cameroon ..... 51 G7 5 32N 12 20 E
Yokohama, Japan .... 31 G9 35 27N 139 28 E
Yokosuka, Japan ..... 31 G9 35 20N 139 40 E
Yokote, Japan .... 30 E10 39 20N 140 30 E
Yola, Nigeria .... 51 G7 9 10N 12 29 E
Yolaina, Cordillera de,
  Nic. 88 D3 11 30N 84 0W
Yonago, Japan .... 31 G6 35 25N 133 19 E
Yonaguni-Jima, Japan . 31 M1 24 27N 123 0 E
Yonan, N. Korea ..... 35 F14 37 55N 126 11 E
Yonezawa, Japan .... 30 F10 37 57N 140 4 E
Yong Peng, Malaysia . 39 L4 2 0N 103 3 E
Yong Sata, Thailand . 39 J2 7 8N 99 41 E
Yongampo, N. Korea . 35 E13 39 56N 124 23 E
Yongcheng, China .... 34 H9 33 55N 116 20 E
Yŏngchŏn, S. Korea .. 35 G15 35 58N 128 56 E
Yongdeng, China ..... 34 F2 36 38N 103 25 E
Yŏngdŏk, S. Korea ... 35 F15 36 24N 129 22 E
Yŏngdŭngpo, S. Korea 35 F14 37 31N 126 54 E
Yonghe, China .... 34 F6 36 46N 110 38 E
Yŏnghŭng, N. Korea ` 35 E14 39 31N 127 18 E
Yongji, China .... 34 G6 34 52N 110 28 E
Yŏngju, S. Korea ..... 35 F15 36 50N 128 40 E
Yongnian, China ..... 34 F8 36 47N 114 29 E
Yongning, China ..... 34 E4 38 15N 106 14 E
Yongqing, China ..... 34 E9 39 25N 116 28 E
Yŏngwŏl, S. Korea ... 35 F15 37 11N 128 28 E
Yonibana, S. Leone .. 50 G2 8 30N 12 19W
Yonkers, U.S.A. 79 F11 40 56N 73 54W
Yonne □, France .... 18 C5 47 50N 3 40 E
Yonne →, France ... 18 B5 48 23N 2 58 E
York, Australia ...... 61 F2 31 52S 116 47 E
York, U.K. 10 D6 53 58N 1 7W
York, Ala., U.S.A. ... 77 J1 32 29N 88 18W
York, Nebr., U.S.A. .. 80 E6 40 52N 97 36W
York, Pa., U.S.A. 76 F7 39 58N 76 44W
York, C., Australia .. 62 A3 10 42S 142 31 E
York, Kap, Greenland 4 B4 75 55N 66 25W
York Sd., Australia .. 60 B4 15 0S 125 5 E
Yorke Pen., Australia 63 E2 34 50S 137 40 E
Yorkshire Wolds, U.K. 10 D7 54 0N 0 30W
Yorkton, Canada 73 C8 51 11N 102 28W
Yorktown, U.S.A. ... 81 L6 28 59N 97 30W
Yorkville, U.S.A. 84 G3 38 52N 123 13W
Yornup, Australia ... 61 F2 34 2S 116 10 E
Yoro, Honduras 88 C2 15 9N 87 7W
Yoron-Jima, Japan .. 31 L4 27 2N 128 26 E
Yos Sudarso, Pulau,
  Indonesia .... 37 F9 8 0S 138 30 E
Yosemite National Park,
  U.S.A. 83 H4 37 45N 119 40W
Yosemite Village, U.S.A. 84 H7 37 45N 119 35W
Yoshkar Ola, Russia . 24 C8 56 38N 47 55 E
Yŏsu, S. Korea ...... 35 G14 34 47N 127 45 E
Yotvata, Israel ...... 47 F4 29 55N 35 2 E
Youbou, Canada 72 D4 48 53N 124 13W
Youghal, Ireland 13 E4 51 58N 7 51W
Youghal B., Ireland .. 13 E4 51 55N 7 50W

Young, Australia .... 63 E4 34 19S 148 18 E
Young, Canada 73 C7 51 47N 105 45W
Young, Uruguay 94 C4 32 44S 57 36W
Younghusband, L.,
  Australia .... 63 E2 30 50S 136 5 E
Younghusband Pen.,
  Australia .... 63 F2 36 0S 139 25 E
Youngstown, Canada ... 73 C6 51 35N 111 10W
Youngstown, N.Y., U.S.A. 78 C5 43 15N 79 3W
Youngstown, Ohio,
  U.S.A. 78 E4 41 6N 80 39W
Youngsville, U.S.A. 78 E5 41 51N 79 19W
Youyu, China .... 34 D7 40 10N 112 20 E
Yoweragabbie, Australia 61 E2 28 14S 117 39 E
Yozgat, Turkey .... 25 G5 39 51N 34 47 E
Ypané →, Paraguay .. 94 A4 23 29S 57 19W
Ypres = Ieper, Belgium 15 D2 50 51N 2 53 E
Ypsilanti, U.S.A. 76 D4 42 14N 83 37W
Yreka, U.S.A. 82 F2 41 44N 122 38W
Ysleta, U.S.A. 83 L10 31 45N 106 24W
Ystad, Sweden .... 9 J12 55 26N 13 50 E
Ysyk-Köl = Issyk-Kul,
  Ozero, Kirghizia .... 26 E8 42 25N 77 15 E
Ythan →, U.K. 12 D7 57 19N 2 0W
Ytyk-Kel, Russia ..... 27 C14 62 30N 133 45 E
Yu Jiang →, China .. 33 D6 23 22N 110 3 E
Yu Shan, Taiwan ..... 33 D7 23 30N 120 58 E
Yu Xian, Hebei, China 34 E8 39 50N 114 35 E
Yu Xian, Henan, China 34 G7 34 10N 113 28 E
Yu Xian, Shanxi, China 34 E7 38 5N 113 20 E
Yuan Jiang →, China 33 D6 28 55N 111 50 E
Yuanqu, China .... 34 G6 35 18N 111 40 E
Yuanyang, China ..... 34 G7 35 3N 113 58 E
Yuba →, U.S.A. 84 F5 39 8N 121 36W
Yuba City, U.S.A. 84 F5 39 8N 121 37W
Yūbari, Japan .... 30 C10 43 4N 141 59 E
Yūbetsu, Japan ...... 30 B11 44 13N 143 50 E
Yucatán, Mexico 87 C7 21 30N 86 30W
Yucatán, Canal de,
  Caribbean 88 B2 22 0N 86 30W
Yucatan Str. = Yucatán,
  Canal de, Caribbean . 88 B2 22 0N 86 30W
Yucca, U.S.A. 85 L12 34 52N 114 9W
Yucca Valley, U.S.A. .. 85 L10 34 8N 116 27W
Yucheng, China ...... 34 F9 36 55N 116 32 E
Yuci, China .... 34 F7 37 42N 112 46 E
Yudino, Russia .... 26 D7 55 10N 67 55 E
Yuendumu, Australia . 60 D5 22 16S 131 49 E
Yugoslavia ■, Europe 21 C8 44 0N 20 0 E
Yukon →, U.S.A. 68 B3 62 32N 163 54W
Yukon Territory □,
  Canada 68 B6 63 0N 135 0W
Yukti, Russia .... 27 C11 63 26N 105 42 E
Yukuhashi, Japan .... 31 H5 33 44N 130 59 E
Yule →, Australia ... 60 D2 20 41S 118 17 E
Yulin, China .... 34 E5 38 20N 109 30 E
Yuma, Ariz., U.S.A. .. 85 N12 32 43N 114 37W
Yuma, Colo., U.S.A. .. 80 E3 40 8N 102 43W
Yuma, B. de, Dom. Rep. 89 C6 18 20N 68 35W
Yumbe, Uganda ..... 54 B3 3 28N 31 15 E
Yumbi, Zaïre .... 54 C2 1 12S 26 15 E
Yumen, China .... 32 C4 39 50N 97 30 E
Yun Ho →, China ... 35 E9 39 10N 117 10 E
Yuncheng, Henan, China 34 G8 35 36N 115 57 E
Yuncheng, Shanxi, China 34 G6 35 2N 111 0 E
Yundamindra, Australia 61 E3 29 15S 122 6 E
Yungas, Bolivia 92 G5 17 0S 66 0W
Yungay, Chile 94 D1 37 10S 72 5W
Yunnan □, China .... 32 D5 25 0N 102 0 E
Yunta, Australia ..... 63 E2 32 34S 139 36 E
Yunxi, China .... 34 H6 33 0N 110 22 E
Yupyongdong, N. Korea 35 D15 41 49N 128 53 E
Yur, Russia .... 27 D14 59 52N 137 41 E
Yurgao, Russia ...... 26 D9 55 42N 84 51 E
Yuribei, Russia ...... 26 B8 71 8N 76 58 E
Yurimaguas, Peru ... 92 E3 5 55S 76 7W
Yuscarán, Honduras . 88 D2 13 58N 86 45W
Yushe, China .... 34 F7 37 4N 112 58 E
Yushu, Jilin, China ... 35 B14 44 43N 126 38 E
Yushu, Qinghai, China 32 C4 33 5N 96 55 E
Yutai, China .... 34 G9 35 0N 116 45 E
Yutian, China .... 35 E9 39 53N 117 45 E
Yuxi, China .... 32 D5 24 30N 102 35 E
Yuzawa, Japan ...... 30 E10 39 10N 140 30 E
Yuzhno-Sakhalinsk,
  Russia .... 27 E15 46 58N 142 45 E
Yvelines □, France .. 18 B4 48 40N 1 45 E
Yvetot, France ...... 18 B4 49 37N 0 44 E

Z

Zaandam, Neths. ...... 15 B4 52 26N 4 49 E
Zabaykalskiy, Russia . 27 E12 49 40N 117 25 E
Zabid, Yemen .... 46 E3 14 0N 43 10 E
Zábol, Iran .... 45 D9 31 0N 61 32 E
Zábolī, Iran .... 45 E9 27 10N 61 35 E
Zabrze, Poland ...... 17 C9 50 18N 18 50 E
Zacapa, Guatemala .. 88 D2 14 59N 89 31W
Zacapu, Mexico 86 D4 19 50N 101 43W
Zacatecas, Mexico ... 86 C4 22 49N 102 34W
Zacatecas □, Mexico . 86 C4 23 30N 103 0W
Zacatecoluca, El Salv. 88 D2 13 29N 88 51W
Zacoalco, Mexico 86 C4 20 14N 103 33W
Zacualtipán, Mexico . 87 C5 20 39N 98 36W
Zadar, Croatia ...... 20 B6 44 8N 15 14 E
Zadetkyi Kyun, Burma 39 H2 10 0N 98 25 E
Zafarqand, Iran ..... 45 C7 33 11N 52 29 E
Zafra, Spain 19 C2 38 26N 6 30W
Żagań, Poland ...... 16 C7 51 39N 15 22 E
Zagazig, Egypt ...... 51 B11 30 40N 31 30 E
Zägheh, Iran .... 45 C6 33 30N 48 42 E
Zagorsk = Sergiyev
  Posad, Russia ...... 24 C6 56 20N 38 10 E
Zagreb, Croatia ..... 20 B7 45 50N 16 0 E
Zagros, Kuhhā-ye, Iran 45 C6 33 45N 48 5 E
Zagros Mts. = Zãgros,
  Kuhhā-ye, Iran ..... 45 C6 33 45N 48 5 E
Zähedän, Fārs, Iran .. 45 D7 28 46N 53 52 E

Zãhedãn,
  Sīstãn va Balūchestãn,
  Iran .... 45 D9 29 30N 60 50 E
Zahlah, Lebanon ..... 47 B4 33 52N 35 50 E
Zaïre ■, Africa ..... 52 E4 3 0S 23 0 E
Zaïre →, Africa .... 52 F2 6 4S 12 24 E
Zaječar, Serbia ..... 21 C10 43 53N 22 18 E
Zakamensk, Russia .. 27 D11 50 23N 103 17 E
Zakavkazye, Asia .... 25 F7 42 0N 44 0 E
Zākhū, Iraq .... 44 B4 37 10N 42 50 E
Zákinthos, Greece ... 21 F9 37 47N 20 57 E
Zákros, Greece ..... 23 D8 35 6N 26 10 E
Zalingei, Sudan ..... 51 F9 12 51N 23 29 E
Zambeke, Zaïre ..... 54 B2 2 8N 25 17 E
Zambeze →, Africa . 55 F4 18 35S 36 20 E
Zambezi = Zambeze →,
  Africa .... 55 F4 18 35S 36 20 E
Zambezi, Zambia .... 53 G4 13 30S 23 15 E
Zambezia □, Mozam. 55 F4 16 15S 37 30 E
Zambia ■, Africa ... 55 E2 15 0S 28 0 E
Zamboanga, Phil. ... 37 C6 6 59N 122 3 E
Zamora, Mexico 86 C4 20 0N 102 21W
Zamora, Spain 19 B3 41 30N 5 45W
Zamość, Poland .... 17 C11 50 43N 23 15 E
Zanaga, Congo ..... 52 E2 2 48S 13 48 E
Zandvoort, Neths. .. 15 B4 52 22N 4 32 E
Zanesville, U.S.A. ... 78 G2 39 56N 82 1W
Zangābād, Iran ..... 44 B4 38 26N 46 44 E
Zangue →, Mozam. . 55 F4 17 50S 35 21 E
Zanjan, Iran .... 45 B6 36 40N 48 35 E
Zanjãn □, Iran ...... 45 B6 37 20N 49 30 E
Zante = Zákinthos,
  Greece .... 21 F9 37 47N 20 57 E
Zanthus, Australia .. 61 F3 31 2S 123 34 E
Zanzibar, Tanzania .. 54 D4 6 12S 39 12 E
Zaouiet El-Kala = Bordj
  Omar Driss, Algeria . 50 C6 28 10N 6 40 E
Zaouiet Reggane, Algeria 50 C5 26 32N 0 3 E
Zaozhuang, China ... 35 G9 34 50N 117 35 E
Zapadnaya Dvina, Russia 24 C5 56 15N 32 3 E
Zapadnaya Dvina →,
  Belorussia .... 24 C3 55 35N 28 10 E
Západné Beskydy, Europe 17 D9 49 30N 19 0 E
Zapala, Argentina ... 96 D2 39 0S 70 5W
Zapaleri, Cerro, Bolivia 94 A2 22 49S 67 11W
Zapata, U.S.A. 81 M5 26 55N 99 16W
Zapolyarnyy, Russia . 24 A5 69 26N 30 51 E
Zaporizhzhya =
  Zaporozhye, Ukraine 25 E6 47 50N 35 10 E
Zaporozhye, Ukraine 25 E6 47 50N 35 10 E
Zaragoza, Coahuila,
  Mexico 86 B4 28 30N 101 0W
Zaragoza, Nuevo León,
  Mexico 87 C5 24 0N 99 46W
Zaragoza, Spain 19 B5 41 39N 0 53W
Zaragoza □, Spain .. 19 B5 41 35N 1 0W
Zarand, Kermān, Iran 45 D8 30 46N 56 34 E
Zarand, Markazī, Iran 45 C6 35 18N 50 25 E
Zaranj, Afghan. ..... 40 D2 30 55N 61 55 E
Zarate, Argentina ... 94 C4 34 7S 59 0W
Zãreh, Iran .... 45 C6 35 7N 49 9 E
Zarembo I., U.S.A. .. 72 B2 56 20N 132 50W
Zaria, Nigeria ...... 50 F6 11 0N 7 40 E
Zarneh, Iran .... 44 C5 33 55N 46 10 E
Zarós, Greece ...... 23 D6 35 8N 24 54 E
Zarqā' →, Jordan .. 47 C4 32 10N 35 37 E
Zarrin, Iran .... 45 C7 32 46N 54 37 E
Zaruma, Ecuador ... 92 D3 3 40S 79 38W
Żary, Poland .... 16 C7 51 37N 15 10 E
Zarzis, Tunisia ..... 51 B7 33 31N 11 2 E
Zashiversk, Russia .. 27 C15 67 25N 142 40 E
Zaskar →, India ... 43 B7 34 13N 77 20 E
Zaskar Mts., India .. 43 C7 33 15N 77 30 E
Zastron, S. Africa ... 56 E4 30 18S 27 7 E
Zävareh, Iran ...... 45 C7 33 29N 52 28 E
Zavitinsk, Russia ... 27 D13 50 10N 129 20 E
Zavodovski, I., Antarctica 5 B1 56 0S 27 45W
Zawiercie, Poland .. 17 C9 50 30N 19 24 E
Zãwiyat al Baydã, Libya 51 B9 32 30N 21 40 E
Zãyã, Iraq .... 44 C5 33 33N 35 18 E
Zayarsk, Russia .... 27 D11 56 12N 102 55 E
Zaysan, Kazakhstan . 26 E9 47 28N 84 52 E
Zaysan, Oz., Kazakhstan 26 E9 48 0N 83 0 E
Zayü, China .... 32 D4 28 48N 97 27 E
Zduńska Wola, Poland 17 C9 51 37N 18 59 E
Zeballos, Canada ... 72 D3 49 59N 126 50W
Zebediela, S. Africa . 57 C4 24 20S 29 17 E
Zeebrugge, Belgium . 15 C3 51 19N 3 12 E
Zeehan, Australia ... 62 G4 41 52S 145 25 E
Zeeland □, Neths. .. 15 C3 51 30N 3 50 E
Zeerust, S. Africa ... 56 D4 25 31S 26 4 E
Zefat, Israel .... 47 C4 32 58N 35 29 E
Zeil, Mt., Australia .. 60 D5 23 30S 132 23 E
Zeila, Somali Rep. .. 46 E3 11 21N 43 30 E
Zeist, Neths. .... 15 B5 52 5N 5 15 E
Zeitz, Germany ..... 16 C7 51 3N 12 9 E
Zelenograd, Russia . 24 C6 56 1N 37 12 E
Zelzate, Belgium ... 15 C3 51 13N 3 47 E
Zémio, C.A.R. ..... 54 A2 5 2N 25 5 E
Zemun, Serbia ..... 21 B9 44 51N 20 25 E
Zerbst, Germany ... 16 C7 51 59N 12 8 E
Zeya, Russia .... 27 D13 53 48N 127 14 E
Zeya →, Russia .... 27 D13 51 42N 128 53 E
Zghartã, Lebanon .. 47 A4 34 21N 35 53 E
Zhailma, Kazakhstan 26 D7 51 37N 61 33 E
Zhambyl = Dzhambul,
  Kazakhstan .... 26 E8 42 54N 71 22 E
Zhangbei, China .... 34 D8 41 10N 114 45 E
Zhangguangcai Ling,
  China .... 35 B15 45 0N 129 0 E
Zhangjiakou, China . 34 D8 40 48N 114 55 E
Zhangwu, China .... 35 C12 42 43N 123 52 E
Zhangye, China .... 32 C5 38 50N 100 23 E
Zhangzhou, China .. 33 D6 24 30N 117 35 E
Zhanhua, China .... 35 F10 37 40N 118 8 E
Zhanyi, China ...... 32 D5 25 38N 103 48 E
Zhanyu, China ..... 35 B12 44 30N 122 30 E
Zhao Xian, China ... 34 F8 37 43N 114 45 E
Zhaocheng, China .. 34 F6 36 22N 111 38 E
Zhaotong, China ... 32 D5 27 20N 103 44 E

Zhaoyuan, Heilongjiang,
  China .... 35 B13 45 27N 125 0 E
Zhaoyuan, Shandong,
  China .... 35 F11 37 20N 120 23 E
Zhashui, China ...... 34 H5 33 40N 109 8 E
Zhayyq = Ural →,
  Kazakhstan .... 25 E9 47 0N 51 48 E
Zhdanov = Mariupol,
  Ukraine .... 25 E6 47 5N 37 31 E
Zhecheng, China ... 34 G8 34 7N 115 20 E
Zhejiang □, China .. 33 D7 29 0N 120 0 E
Zheleznodorozhny,
  Russia .... 24 B9 62 35N 50 55 E
Zheleznogorsk-Ilimskiy,
  Russia .... 27 D11 56 34N 104 8 E
Zhen'an, China ..... 34 H5 33 27N 109 9 E
Zhengding, China ... 34 E8 38 8N 114 32 E
Zhengzhou, China .. 34 G7 34 45N 113 34 E
Zhenlai, China ..... 35 B12 45 50N 123 5 E
Zhenping, China .... 34 H7 33 10N 112 16 E
Zhenyuan, China ... 34 G4 35 35N 107 30 E
Zhidan, China ...... 34 F5 36 48N 108 48 E
Zhigansk, Russia ... 27 C13 66 48N 123 27 E
Zhitomir, Ukraine .. 25 D4 50 20N 28 40 E
Zhlobin, Belorussia . 24 D5 52 55N 30 0 E
Zhokhova, Ostrov, Russia 27 B16 76 4N 152 40 E
Zhongdian, China .. 32 D4 27 48N 99 42 E
Zhongning, China .. 34 F3 37 29N 105 40 E
Zhongtiao Shan, China 34 G6 35 0N 111 10 E
Zhongwei, China ... 34 F3 37 30N 105 12 E
Zhongyang, China .. 34 F6 37 20N 111 11 E
Zhoucun, China .... 35 F9 36 47N 117 48 E
Zhouzhi, China ..... 34 G5 34 10N 108 12 E
Zhuanghe, China ... 35 E12 39 40N 123 0 E
Zhucheng, China ... 35 G10 36 0N 119 30 E
Zhugqu, China ..... 34 H3 33 40N 104 30 E
Zhumadian, China .. 34 H8 32 59N 114 2 E
Zhuo Xian, China ... 34 E8 39 28N 115 58 E
Zhuolu, China ...... 34 D8 40 20N 115 12 E
Zhuozi, China ...... 34 D7 41 0N 112 28 E
Zhupanovo, Russia . 27 D16 53 40N 159 52 E
Zhytomyr = Zhitomir,
  Ukraine .... 25 D4 50 20N 28 40 E
Ziārān, Iran .... 45 B6 36 7N 50 32 E
Ziarat, Pakistan .... 42 D2 30 25N 67 49 E
Zibo, China .... 35 F10 36 47N 118 3 E
Zielona Góra, Poland 16 C7 51 57N 15 31 E
Zierikzee, Neths. ... 15 C3 51 40N 3 55 E
Zigey, Chad .... 51 F8 14 43N 15 50 E
Zigong, China ...... 32 D5 29 15N 104 48 E
Ziguinchor, Senegal 50 F1 12 35N 16 20W
Zihuatanejo, Mexico 86 D4 17 38N 101 33W
Żilina, Slovak Rep. . 17 D9 49 12N 18 42 E
Zillah, Libya .... 51 C8 28 30N 17 33 E
Zima, Russia .... 27 D11 54 0N 102 5 E
Zimapán, Mexico ... 87 C5 20 54N 99 20W
Zimba, Zambia ..... 55 F2 17 20S 26 11 E
Zimbabwe, Zimbabwe 55 G3 20 16S 30 54 E
Zimbabwe ■, Africa 55 F2 19 0S 30 0 E
Zinder, Niger ...... 50 F6 13 48N 9 0 E
Zinga, Tanzania .... 55 D4 9 16S 38 49 E
Zion National Park,
  U.S.A. 83 H7 37 15N 113 5W
Zipaquirá, Colombia 92 C4 5 0N 74 0W
Ziros, Greece ...... 23 D8 35 5N 26 8 E
Zitácuaro, Mexico .. 86 D4 19 28N 100 21W
Zitundo, Mozam. ... 57 D5 26 48S 32 47 E
Ziwa, L., Ethiopia .. 51 G12 8 0N 38 50 E
Ziyang, China ...... 34 H5 32 32N 108 31 E
Zlatograd, Bulgaria 21 D11 41 22N 25 7 E
Zlatoust, Russia ... 24 C10 55 10N 59 40 E
Zlin, Czech. .... 17 D8 49 14N 17 40 E
Zlitan, Libya .... 51 B7 32 32N 14 35 E
Zmeinogorsk, Kazakhstan 26 D9 51 10N 82 13 E
Znojmo, Czech. .... 16 D8 48 50N 16 2 E
Zoar, S. Africa ..... 56 E3 33 30S 21 26 E
Zobeyri, Iran ...... 44 C5 34 10N 46 40 E
Zobia, Zaïre .... 54 B2 3 0N 25 59 E
Zomba, Malawi .... 55 F4 15 22S 35 19 E
Zongo, Zaïre ...... 52 D3 4 20N 18 35 E
Zonguldak, Turkey . 25 F5 41 28N 31 50 E
Zonqor Pt., Malta .. 23 D2 35 51N 14 34 E
Zorritos, Peru 92 D2 3 43S 80 40W
Zou Xiang, China .. 34 G9 35 30N 116 58 E
Zouar, Chad .... 51 D8 20 30N 16 32 E
Zouérate, Mauritania 50 D2 22 44N 12 21W
Zoutkamp, Neths. .. 15 A6 53 20N 6 18 E
Zrenjanin, Serbia .. 21 B9 45 22N 20 23 E
Zuetina, Libya ..... 51 B9 30 58N 20 7 E
Zufar, Oman .... 46 D5 17 40N 54 0 E
Zug, Switz. .... 16 E4 47 10N 8 31 E
Zuid-Holland □, Neths. 15 C4 52 0N 4 35 E
Zuidhorn, Neths. .. 15 A6 53 15N 6 23 E
Zula, Eritrea ...... 51 E12 15 17N 39 40 E
Zumbo, Mozam. ... 55 F3 15 35S 30 26 E
Zumpango, Mexico . 87 D5 19 48N 99 6W
Zungeru, Nigeria ... 50 G6 9 48N 6 8 E
Zunhua, China ..... 35 D9 40 18N 117 58 E
Zuni, U.S.A. 83 J9 35 4N 108 51W
Zunyi, China .... 32 D5 27 42N 106 53 E
Zuoquan, China .... 34 F7 37 5N 113 22 E
Zürbatiyah, Iraq ... 44 C5 33 9N 46 3 E
Zürich, Switz. ..... 16 E4 47 22N 8 32 E
Zutphen, Neths. ... 15 B6 52 9N 6 12 E
Zuwārah, Libya .... 51 B7 32 58N 12 1 E
Züzan, Iran .... 45 C8 34 22N 59 53 E
Zverinogolovskoye,
  Russia .... 26 D7 54 23N 64 40 E
Zvishavane, Zimbabwe 55 G3 20 17S 30 2 E
Zvolen, Slovak Rep. 17 D9 48 33N 19 10 E
Zwettl, Austria .... 16 D8 48 35N 15 9 E
Zwickau, Germany . 16 C6 50 43N 12 30 E
Zwolle, Neths. ..... 15 B6 52 31N 6 6 E
Zwolle, U.S.A. 81 K8 31 38N 93 39W
Zymoetz →, Canada 72 C3 54 33N 128 31W
Żyrardów, Poland .. 17 B10 52 3N 20 28 E
Zyryanka, Russia .. 27 C16 65 45N 150 51 E
Zyryanovsk, Kazakhstan 26 E9 49 43N 84 20 E
Zyyi, Cyprus .... 23 E12 34 43N 33 20 E